A Critical And Historical Review Of Fox's Book Of Martyrs, Shewing The Inaccuracies, Falsehoods, And Misrepresentations In That Work Of Deception, Volumes 1-2

A

CRITICAL AND HISTORICAL

REVIEW

OF

𝕱𝖔𝖝'𝖘 𝕭𝖔𝖔𝖐 𝖔𝖋 𝕸𝖆𝖗𝖙𝖞𝖗𝖘,

SHEWING THE

INACCURACIES, FALSEHOODS, AND MISREPRESENTATIONS

IN THAT

WORK OF DECEPTION.

BY

WILLIAM EUSEBIUS ANDREWS.

London:

PRINTED AND PUBLISHED BY W. E. ANDREWS,

3, CHAPTERHOUSE COURT, ST. PAUL's CHURCHYARD,

AND SOLD BY ALL BOOKSELLERS.

1824.

CONTENTS.

CONTENTS.

A REVIEW

OF

𝕱𝖔𝖝'𝖘 𝕭𝖔𝖔𝖐 𝖔𝖋 𝕸𝖆𝖗𝖙𝖞𝖗𝖘,

CRITICAL AND HISTORICAL.

No. 1.   Printed and Published by W. E. ANDREWS, 3, Chapter-house-court, St. Paul's Churchyard, London.   **Price 3d.**

NOVEMBER 5, 1823.

EXPLANATION OF THE ENGRAVING.—*John Fox is seen writing his work, originally called* Acts *and* Monuments, *but now metamorphosed into a* Book of Martyrs. *The devil is looking over his shoulder, prompting him, for under no other influence but that of an evil spirit could he write, since he has been convicted of falsehood by father Parsons, who charges him with telling directly and indirectly not less than ten thousand lies in this work. In the perspective is a printing press chained, to denote that it was shut to the Catholics by the operation of the penal code, as will be seen in the course of the present sheet.*

INTRODUCTORY REMARKS.

IN undertaking to refute and expose the greatest mass of falsehood and calumny ever issued against the social and religious principles of our Catholic fellow-men, we may be condemned for our temerity, but we think we shall stand excused, when the active endeavours of bigotry, to give circulation to what is called *Fox's Book of Martyrs*, are taken into consideration. With some it has been a matter of surprise that such an exposition has not been undertaken before; but when the obstacles which have so long existed to prevent Catholic writers from vindicating their religious doctrines and social maxims are known, and the misfortune is that they are *not* known to the people of this country generally, that surprise will entirely vanish. It is therefore our intention to point out the difficulties which have stood in the way of an appeal to PUBLIC

OPINION by the Catholics in their defence, and the means by which the public mind has been deluded, as a requisite preliminary to the Review of the work before us. To elucidate the subject, however, in as clear a light as possible, it will be necessary that we give a brief outline of the method uniformly pursued by the Catholic church to preserve the truths which have been revealed to her. We are aware that some of our readers may have discarded the necessity of a revealed religion, but we beg of them to be candid in their examination of our pages, before they pass their judgment upon them. It cannot be denied that the greatest part of the civilized world has, in all ages, acknowledged the existence of certain divine truths, emanating from the Deity itself, and surely it must be safer to go with the great bulk of mankind, than to listen to the speculations of certain individuals who prefer fictions to facts, and the fallible opinions of the human mind to an infallible rule of principle established by the Deity. Taking the scripture merely as a work of history, we see much to admire, and in it we find a clear and shining testimony of the immutability of the divine councils. Works on profane history have perished by time, or been destroyed by the hand of barbarism, but the records of religion have been handed down to us with a care unparalleled and striking. Of all the ancient people, the Jews alone preserved the monuments of their religion, and to this very day, they bear testimony to its course and progress, and the miracles and predictions which rendered it immoveable. We see the Messiah appearing at the time predicted by the prophets; we see him foretelling his own death, the progress of the new law, which took place of the old, without violating one single truth, and many other circumstances that have been literally fulfilled. Among other things, he commanded his apostles, twelve humble and unknown men, to go forth to all nations, to teach the truths which he had revealed to them, and promising them that THESE TRUTHS should remain to the end of the world. We see these men, armed only with the spirit of God, go forth to the world, teaching a doctrine opposed to the human passions and the general maxims of the world, yet, in less than one hundred years, and in the midst of the most furious persecutions and the rage of tyrants, they carried and established these truths, not only in the East, where their labours first commenced, that is to say, Palestine, Syria, Egypt, Lesser Asia, and Greece, but also in the West, namely, Italy, the several nations of the Gauls, all the Spanish provinces, Africa, Germany, and Great Britain; likewise into Persia, Armenia, the Indies, Sarmatia, Scythia, and even to the remotest islands. So rapid and extensive a change in public opinion, in favour of a new system of religion, could only be affected by a supernatural power, and the *unity* of that system must strike conviction, we should imagine, in every rational mind, of its emanating from Truth itself.

Having thus given a brief sketch of the establishment of the Christian faith, we will now proceed to shew how its truths have been preserved to this day. It may be proper here to observe, that as this faith was planted in opposition to the wishes of the rulers of the state, that the propagators of it were men of obscure origin and mortified habits, there could be no collusion to *impose* upon mankind, and if there had, why was it not exposed? Why were not the deceivers unmasked, and held up to the contempt of the people? That the Divine Founder of the Christian religion intended that the truths which he commanded the apostles and their successors to teach, should be *openly* taught, and be testified to by PUBLIC OPINION, is clear, not only by his own memorable answer to the high priest, but by the conduct of his ministers in all succeeding ages. When the divine Redeemer was under examination before the rulers of the people, the high priest asked him of his disciples and of his doctrines. "Jesus," says St. Luke, "answered him, I have "*openly* spoke to the world; I have always taught in the temple, whi- "ther all the Jews resort together: and *in secret I have spoken nothing.* "Why askest thou me? Ask them that have heard what I have spoken "unto them: behold *they knew what things I have said.*" Such was the answer given by Christ to the Jewish rulers, and such is the answer which every Catholic is bound to give, when questioned as to his doctrines. After the Jews had crucified Jesus, the apostles began to teach *openly*, and such was the force of their inspired eloquence, for before they were illiterate men, backed by the wonders which they wrought, that the same people, who had but a short time before condemned the Messiah as an *impostor*, now believed in his *divinity*; and the same rulers fearing lest their power should be destroyed, sought to suppress the further propagation of the Christian system.

It is recorded in the acts of the apostles, that Peter and John went up to the temple at the time of prayer, and, after miraculously curing to the astonishment of the multitude, a lame man, in the name of Jesus, Peter addressed THE PEOPLE PUBLICLY, which grieved the priests and magis- trates, and the ancients and scribes, who had the two apostles summoned before them. The constancy of Peter and John surprised the corrupt and infatuated judges; they withdrew to consult privately together, and they said, "What shall we do to these men? for a notorious sign, indeed "hath been done by them to all the inhabitants of Jerusalem: IT IS "MANIFEST, and WE CANNOT DENY IT. But that it no further spread "abroad among the people, *let us threaten them,* that they *speak* no more "in the name (of Jesus) to any man. And calling them, they charged "them that they should not *speak at all,* nor *teach* in the name of Jesus. "But Peter and John answering, said to them, 'If it be just in the sight "of God, to hear you rather than God, judge ye. For we cannot but "*speak the things* which WE HAVE SEEN and HEARD.'" Such was the first attempt by interested rulers to prevent the light of truth from flowing among the people: and we beg the reader to bear this conduct of the priests and scribes and pharisees in mind, as it will be seen that this disposition has been invariably followed by all those who are under the influence of error, and have power in their hands. The Jewish rulers could not *deny* the doctrines taught by the apostles, they could not *deny* the miracle performed by them; they said the people were convinced of the divine mission of these holy men; they dared not to punish the Christian preachers, because of the people, such is the force of public opinion; they therefore *threatened* them, hoping thereby to reduce them to silence, and, by keeping the people in ignor- ance, preserve their tottering situations.

We are aware that the facts we have here stated may be denied by some of our readers; but we wish those who doubt the veracity of scripture to give us some *proof* that the writings of the inspired penmen were *forgeries*, or that they were *altered* in the first ages of Christianity to suit the purposes of faction.. We know that, in latter times, scripture has been mutilated, mistranslated, and perverted, as we shall have occasion to shew by and by ; but Catholics contend, and it has never been *proved* to the contrary, that the writings of the gospel have been handed down by their church to the present day without the least alteration. Those who reject the scripture must do it against the belief of all ages and the voice of all people, speaking generally. Besides, those rejecters of scripture are unable to name *the time* when the supposed alterations were made by the Catholic church ; they cannot allege the motives and manner of the frauds ; nor can they cite the authors of them; therefore it is, we think, an absurdity, and contrary to common sense, to suppose these writings a fallacy without the shadow of a proof, and in opposition too to the general belief of mankind.

To these supposed frauds there must have been one of three parties concerned, namely, the Pagans, the Jews, or the Christians. Upon the first we think there can fall no suspicion, because they had nothing to do with the Christian religion but to persecute it. They tried to eradicate it in vain, and had they wished to make the scripture subservient to their purpose, is it not probable that they would have blotted out the crowd of miracles whereby the Christian religion was established and themselves condemned. But admitting that the Pagans did endeavour to corrupt the sacred writings.—Where were the Christians to allow it unexposed ? Is it possible to think it would be done and no one take the least notice of it ? We think no man of rational understanding will entertain so vain a supposition. For the same reason we cannot charge the Jews as authors of the fraud. Would they not have retrenched those many prodigies whereby they were condemned ? The many censures and rebukes whereby Christ and his apostles attacked the vain tradition of the synagogue, the hypocrisy of the priests, the superstitions of the people, and the vices of the nation ; besides the application of many prophecies relating to Christ and their overthrow. They must therefore be fixed upon the Catholics, who formed the Christian world, previous to the pretended reformation of religion in the sixteenth century. But this is *impossible.* For is it not absurdity itself to suppose that all the Christians unanimously agreed upon the change, and that no one should rise up in defence of TRUTH ? Or is it not equally absurd to suppose that any one single person could do it without being detected ? We find in the writings of Sozomen (*His. Eccle.* c. li.) that great indignation was expressed by Spindion against Triphile for offering to change a single word of no importance ; and we see in the works of St. Augustin (*Epis.* 71 and 81.) the interest that was excited by the like fact in the church of Africa, though it regarded neither faith nor morals.

But allowing the Christians had combined to alter the gospels ; is it likely the Jews would have let such a circumstance pass unnoticed ? Would Porphyrius, a Tyrian philosopher, who was a voluminous writer against the Christians, have passed over such an attempt at deception ? Would Julian the apostate ? Certainly not. Celsus, an Epicurean philosopher, who lived in the reign of the emperor Adrian, and was a bitter enemy to the Christian religion, objected to the Christians that they had falsified the scriptures; but he was answered by Origen, who clearly proved that the heretics had done so, and that the orthodox found as much fault with them for so doing as Celsus himself. We know that heresy existed from the commencement of the Christian church, and this was necessary in order to make the light of truth more brilliant. But how, it may be asked, was the truth preserved in the midst of these contrarieties. We answer, by God himself, the essence of Truth, and *an appeal to the general received conviction of the Christian world.* We read in the acts of the apostles, that when a difference of opinion arose among the first Christians, the apostles did not decide of themselves on the point in dispute, for we see it recorded in *Fleury's Ecclesiastical History,* that there were but five apostles present, the rest being in other parts, preaching the doctrines entrusted to them by their divine master. With these five apostles were present as many priests as could be collected, and St. Peter presided over and opened the council. Each one gave his opinion *freely,* no restraint was allowed; and when the decision was made by a majority of votes, the decree was put into writing, and sent to the particular churches, to be by them received as the word of truth. This was the first council or parliament of the church. The persecutions that existed during the first three hundred years did not allow of the convening any public councils, nevertheless whenever the truths of the Christian religion were attacked by erroneous speculators in theology, there were not wanting learned and able defenders of the apostolic faith, whose writings have been preserved in the church as a testimony of the doctrines received from the apostles. Thus in the first age we have the writings of St. Peter, St. Paul, the four evangelists, St. James the less, the acts of St. Andrew, the apostolic canons and constitutions, &c. &c. In the second age, among other ecclesiastical writers, whose works have been preserved, we have St. Ignatius, St. Polycarp, St. Justin, &c.; and in the third age there were St. Irenæus, bishop of Lyons, Tertullian, St. Clement of Alexandria, Origen, St. Cyprian, &c. and so on in every age down to the present time.

When the conversion of Constantine caused a cessation to the persecuting spirit that had so long raged against the Christian religion, her peace was disturbed by the broaching a new error by one Arius. To settle this division, and make known the truth, a general council was convoked to meet at Nice, the principal city of Bithynia, at which three hundred and eighteen bishops, besides priests and deacons, met, on the 10th day of June, in the year 325. Many of these holy men exhibited marks of the sufferings they had undergone for the true faith, and therefore were competent persons to discuss and decide on the subjects which had convened them together. As we shall have occasion in our Review of the Book of Martyrs to notice the questions which occupied this assembly, we shall content ourself here with observing that the points in dispute underwent a serious and solemn discussion. As in the council of Jerusalem, the utmost freedom of debate was allowed, so in this council every one was at liberty to state his sentiments without fear or affection. To arrive at the truth the council had recourse to scripture and tradition. Every bishop was called upon to declare the doctrine he had received from his predecessors in that particular see, and on this concurring testimony the council decided. Thus it will be seen, that, from first to last, the touchstone of truth in the Catholic church does not consist in the arbitrary will or caprice of *one man*, nor in the decrees of any particular assembly of laymen, but in *the united and unbroken testimony of all ages and nations*, handed down to us by *a continual succession of accredited ministers*, whose duty it is, not to coin *new doctrines*, but to *preserve the genuine apostolic ones*.

Besides this general council of Nice there were others held in the same century, for these councils or ecclesiastical parliaments are of three kinds, namely, ecumenical or general, national, and provincial. They have been held in all ages, and it is only twelvemonths since that a provincial one was held for the kingdom of Hungary. The manner and form of decreeing in these synods or councils we may gather from our own historian, venerable Bede, who thus records the decree of one held in 680 at Hatfield, now called Bishop's Hatfield, at which Theodorus the archbishop of Canterbury presided, and all the bishops of the island were present. The occasion of the convening this assembly was the troubles originated by the heresy of Eutyches. Having the sacred gospel laid before them, they expounded the true Catholic faith, and concluded their discussions in the form following:

" As our Lord Jesus Christ, taking our flesh upon him, did deliver
" unto his disciples, that saw him in person, and heard his speeches,
" and as the symbolum or creed of the holy fathers have delivered unto
" us, and as generally all whole and universal synods, and all the com-
" pany of holy fathers and doctors of the holy Catholic church have
" taught us; so do we, following their steps, both piously and Ca-
" tholicly, according to their doctrine, (inspired to them from hea-
" ven) profess and believe, and constantly confess, according to the
" said holy fathers' belief, that the Father, the Son and the Holy
" Ghost are properly and truly a consubstantial Trinity in Unity, and
" Unity in Trinity, &c. We receive also the holy and universal
" five synods that have been held before our time by the blessed chris-
" tian fathers our ancestors, to wit, those 318 holy bishops in the first
" council of Nice, (anno 325) against Arius and his wicked doctrine,
" and of the 150 other bishops in the first council of Constantinople
" (anno 380) against the heresy of Macedonius, and of the 200 goodly
" bishops of the council of Ephesus (anno 428) against Nestorius and
" his errors, and of the 230 bishops in the council of Chalcedon (anno
" 457) against Eutyches and his doctrine, and of the other 165 fathers
" gathered together in the second general council of Constantinople
" (anno 532) against divers heretics and heresies, &c. We do receive
" all these councils, and we do glorify our Lord Jesus Christ, as they
" glorified him, ADDING NOTHING, NOR TAKING ANY THING
" AWAY."

By this decree the reader may see how the faith of Catholics have been kept pure and uncontaminated, during a series of eighteen centuries; for what the Catholics believe *now* was believed in the *first ages*, nor do they believe *more now* than was believed *then*. Neither can they be justly accused of practising *priestcraft*, nor of being *priestridden*, seeing that every thing relative to faith and morals must be *taught openly*, and therefore liable to detection if erroneous or novel; nor can the pope himself add to, or subtract from, the articles of Catholic faith delivered to us by Christ through his apostles.

The reader having now before him a brief outline of the one undeviating rule by which the Catholic is assured of the divine essence of his religion, it is now time that we shew him how the reformed creed, or rather creeds, was first established in England. We shall confine our remarks principally to this country, because the facts we shall adduce will be easier of detection, should we pervert or misrepresent any part of history. But first we must observe, that in the early ages of Christianity the use of letters was necessarily limited, because the art of printing being then unknown, the copying a work was a tedious process, and rendered it an impossibility to have the copies extensively multiplied. Still, however, there were, as we have shewn before, men in all ages and all nations skilled in the learned languages, and at all times ready to detect any innovation attempted to be made in the rule of faith delivered by the apostles. We must here also observe, that in no age whatever, that we are acquainted with, nor under any sovereign or state, were writers restrained from publishing their sentiments, and discussing theological questions before the reign of our Henry the 8th. In the 15th century the art of printing was invented in Germany, and, according to our earliest writers, was introduced and first practised in England by Wm. Caxton, under the patronage of the abbot of Westminster. Other authorities say, that when printing made some noise in Europe, Thomas Boucher, archbishop of Canterbury, solicited Henry the 6th to use all possible means to procure a printing mould, as it was then called, to be brought into the kingdom. Here then we have the fact, that this new invention, so beneficial to the imparting of useful knowledge, but which has unhappily been employed in the circulation of fraud and falsehood, by which public opinion has been perverted, was encouraged by the Catholic clergy, who are so grossly misrepresented as studious to keep the people in darkness and ignorance. The introduction of this at once useful and hurtful art into England is placed about the year 1464, and as is usual with all infant inventions, its progress was but slow during the first century. This brings us to the period of the reformation, as it is called, but which ought rather to be termed the deformation of religion.

Luther began to rail against the Catholic church about the year 1524; our eighth Harry threw off his spiritual subjection to the Catholic church about ten years after. One of the first ends the evangelical reformers made of the press was, to print an English translation of the new testament, which was followed by another of the old testament, but instead of preserving the original sense of the scripture, which the Catholic church had so carefully done during the long time of 1500 years, the edition by Tindall is stated to have contained no less than TWO THOUSAND corruptions. In the reign of James the 1st, the ministers of Lincoln diocess wrote a book against the Common Prayer, which they delivered to his majesty on the 1st of December, 1606. " In an abridgment of this work," says Ward, in his *England's Reformation*, canto iv. " I find these following observations against it : " First, that the Book of Common Prayer appointed such a translation " of the holy scriptures to be read in the church, *as leaveth but of the*

" *text sundry words and sentences which were given of divine inspiration.*
" pag. 14. It doth *add both words and sentences to the text,* to the *chang-*
" *ing* and *obscuring* of the *meaning of the Holy Ghost.* p. 15. Such a
" translation, as is in many places *absurd,* and such as no *reasonable*
" sense can be made of. p. 16. In many places it *perverteth* the mean-
" ing of the Holy Ghost, *by a false interpretation of the text.* p. 17." Yet,
notwithstanding these charges of *errors, false translations,* and *corrup-*
tions of scripture, the king and his bishops in the book of Canons, made
in their convocation of 1603, and printed in 1704, compel every body
under pain of excommunication to hold the said book of Common Prayer
for *true* and *good. (See Can.* 40.) Now we will here take leave to ask
whether this does not resemble *priestcraft* and being *priestridden* much
more than the rule of principle adopted and practised by the Catholic
church. Such was the use made of the PRESS, by those who pretended
to *reform* religion and correct the supposed *errors* of what they termed
Popery.

 We have shewn that in the Catholic church, when any point was under examination, it was freely discussed and decided by the invariable
rule of scripture and tradition. When Harry the eighth however took
upon him to rule the church of England, he adopted a different plan to
maintain his supremacy. By an act passed in the 25th year of his reign,
it was made treason to call the king a heretic or schismatic. In the
31st and 34th of his reign, he was made independent of parliament,
and, in the last mentioned year, an act was also passed, by which it was
decreed, that " *Nothing* shall be taught or maintained contrary to the
" *king's instructions.* And if any *spiritual* person preach or maintain *any*
" *thing* contrary to the king's instructions or determinations, *made,* or
" TO BE *made,* and shall be thereof convicted, he shall for the first
" offence recant, for the second abjure and bear a fagot, and for his
" third, shall be adjudged a *heretic,* and be *burned,* and lose all his goods
" and chattels." Thus, by an unparalleled stretch of spiritual usurpation, the conscience of every individual in the realm was laid prostrate
at the mercy of an inexorable despot; for had this new English pope,
in the plentitude of his power, ordered the doctrine of the Alcoran to be
preached one week, and that of Judaism the next, all and every one of
his subjects must have submitted to the same, or of course been liable
to the penalties of this conscience-tyrannizing statute. Such was the
change made by those who threw off what was called the yoke of the
pope, who could lay no more upon their shoulders than the laws of the
church permitted him; but here we have a king invested with a degree
of infallibility hitherto unheard of, and the religious opinions and practices of his subjects were to be regulated by his sole will and pleasure.
It was also made *high treason* to PRINT or *publish* any work against the
spiritual supremacy of this monarch. Thus when its free exercise became more necessary to discuss and vindicate the truth, this formidable
instrument to detect error and encroachment was shackled and rendered useless in defence of truth.

 Under Elizabeth the press was more strictly forbidden to the Catholics. It was made high treason for any one to PRINT or publish that the
queen was a heretic, schismatic, tyrant, infidel or usurper. By the
35th, c. 1, entitled, *An Act to retain the queen's subjects in their due obedi-*

ence, amongst other restraints it was enacted, that if any person or persons, above the age of sixteen, " shall at any time after forty days next
" at the end of this session of parliament, by PRINTING, writing, or
" express words or speeches, advisedly or purposely practise, or go
" about to move or persuade any of her majesty's subjects, or any other
" within her highness' realms or dominions, to deny, withstand, or im-
" pugn her majesty's power and authority in cases *ecclesiastical*, united
" and annexed to the imperial crown of this realm, &c. . . . every such
" person so offending, and being thereof lawfully convicted, shall be
" committed to prison, there to remain without bail or mainprise, until
" they shall conform and yield themselves to come to some church,
" chapel, or usual place of common prayer," &c.

Such was the freedom of opinion allowed in matters ecclesiastical
in the *golden days of our good queen Bess*, as they are generally termed
by Protestants! We observe the publishers of the present edition of
Fox's Book of Martyrs have prefaced their work with a pretended representation of the tortures of the inquisition; but they must be reminded that Elizabeth, who settled the reformed religion in this country, did it by means as unconstitutional, as barbarous, and as unjust,
as any act that can be verified against the tribunal of the inquisition; the bare mention of which tribunal makes a Protestant shudder,
while his heart will feel elated at the name of the virgin queen
Bess, of whose remorseless tyranny and despotism he is entirely ignorant, the Catholic press having been shackled, and the Protestant press
finding it more to its interest to keep the real character of Elizabeth
from public view, that its supporters may be at greater liberty to calumniate the Catholics. Be it known then that this queen Elizabeth was
armed by her parliament with the most formidable and inquisitorial
powers. She issued a commission called the high commission court,
authorizing the members thereof to inquire, on the oath of the person
accused, and on the oath of witnesses, of all heretical, erroneous, and
dangerous *opinions*; of *seditious books* and *libels* against the queen, her
magistrates and *ministers*; and to punish the offenders by spiritual censures, by fine, imprisonment, and torture. The jurisdiction of this
court extended over the whole kingdom, and their power was independent of parliament. The punishments they inflicted were *arbitrary*, and
their fines so heavy, as often to bring total ruin on those who had the
misfortune to offend. See Hume, Neale's History of the Puritans, and
other historians. We have heard enough of the Star Chamber exactions under the Stuarts, but scarce a Protestant in the kingdom is acquainted with the cruel and diabolical transactions of Elizabeth and her
ministers. Rymer says, " Whoever will compare the power given to
" this tribunal with those of the inquisition, which Philip II. endeavour-
" ed to establish in the Low Countries, will find that the chief differ-
" ence between the two courts consisted in their names. One was the
" court of *inquisition*, the other of *high commission*. In the first com-
" missions (see one in Strype's Grindal, App. 64.) the power of inter-
" rogating the person upon oath was not expressly inserted; yet the
" judges *always attempted it*, because they were ordered to inquire ' by
" all ways and means they could devise.' " (Rym. xvi. 291. 564.) Let it
not be thought, by the introducing this comparison that we intend to de-

fend the abuses of the inquisition in Catholic countries, we condemn injustice wherever and by whomsoever committed, as a violation of the genuine principles of Christianity; but it is right that the Protestant part of the community should be informed by what means the reformed religion was first established in this country, as well as of the excesses of the inquisition and the imputed cruelties of Catholics.

It was under this system of terror and proscription, when the relater of truth was sure to lose his liberty, if he escaped the loss of limb, that Fox's work, bearing the title of *Acts and Monuments of the Church*, made its appearance in the English tongue, it having been originally compiled in the Latin language. This work was answered by father Parsons, in a work called *The Three Conversions of England*, about the year 1604; but in consequence of the restrictions of the press in this country, and the activity displayed by the pursuivants and informers against Popish books, (for we should have said that all magistrates were at that time empowered to make domiciliary visits at any hour of the day or night in search of printed books in favour of Catholicism, and spies were encouraged to give information,) the work of father Parsons was printed at St. Omers, in Flanders, and could only be brought into this country by stealth, and then not without considerable danger to the owner. Under such peculiar circumstances, truth had no chance in its favour, and an author might write what he pleased without fear of detection. So it was with John Fox; he knew the peril that was suspended over the man who should have the temerity to engage in an exposure of his works; he knew the men whose cause he intended to promote, and he wrote with so little regard to truth, that he actually recorded the deaths of individuals who were living at the very time his *Acts and Monuments* were put into circulation. In proof of this statement, Anthony Wood, the Oxford historian, and a Protestant, recites a remarkable story of one Grimwood being actually present in a church when the clergyman was describing, on the authority of Fox's *Acts and Monuments*, the circumstances of his pretended preternatural death, "his bowels, by the "judgment of God, falling out of his body in consequence." Grimwood in return, brought an action against the clergyman for defamation. (*Athen. Oxon. Hen. Morgan.*)

When the work was first translated into English, it filled three folio volumes, and in the third was inserted a new calendar of Protestant saints, in the room of the one in use amongst Catholics. Although our review will be confined to the examination of this calendar, as published by the present editors, though by the by, in its modern shape, we believe John Fox would hardly be able to recognise the book sent forth in his name, yet we cannot omit quoting the opinion of father Parsons, from his answer to the Protestant martyrologist. In the 2d chapter of the second part of his *Three Conversions*, Parsons writes thus: "He that "will consider the proportion of John Fox's book of *Acts and Monu*-"*ments* in the latter edition, he will find it the greatest perhaps in vo-"lume that ever was put forth in our *English* tongue; and the falsest in "substance, without *perhaps*, that ever was published in any tongue. "The volume consisteth of about a thousand leaves of the largest paper "that lightly hath been seen, and every leaf containeth four great co-"lumns; and yet, if you consider how many leaves of those thousand

"he hath spent in deduction of the whole church, either *his or ours*, and
"the whole ecclesiastical story thereof, for the first thousand years after
"Christ, they are by his own account but three score and four, to wit,
"scarce the thirtieth part of that he bestoweth in the last five hundred
"years." And again, in the *Relation of a Trial before the king of France
between the bishop of Evreux and the lord Plessis Mornay,* p. 58, the same
author writes: "I have had occasion these months past to peruse a great
"part of his last edition of *Acts and Monuments*, printed the fifth time in
"1596, and do find it so stuffed with all kinds of falsehood, and deceit-
"ful manner of telling tales, as I could never, truly, have believed it, if
"I had not found it by my own experience. And I do persuade myself
"fully, notwithstanding all his hypocritical words and protestations,
"which are more and oftener repeated by him, than in all the writers to-
"gether that I have read in my life, that there is scarce *one whole story
"in that large volume,* told by himself, except when he relateth other
"men's words out of records, and thereby is bound to the formality
"thereof, but that *it is falsified* and *perverted* one way or other, either in
"the beginning, middle, or end, by adding, cutting off, concealing, false
"translating, wrong citing, or cunning juggling and falsification, which
"I do not speak for any tooth against the man, that is dead, and whom I
"never knew, but in respect of truth only, and of so many deceived
"souls, as are in danger to perish by his deluding them. Nor when I
"speak of Master Fox's falsehoods, do I make account of any errors or
"oversights, though never so gross that are found in him, as to reckon
"some martyrs that were alive at the making of his book; for this he
"excuseth in his later edition, in that he was deceived by false informa-
"tions: nor do I urge, that others are made calendar martyrs by him,
"whom he cannot gainsay, but that they were malefactors, and some of
"them either mad or denied Christ himself, and placeth he them in his
"calendar for saints. These escaped, I say, are not here to be urged
"by me now, but rather in another place. The points that I for the
"present accuse him of, are *wilful corruptions* and *falsifications that can-
"not be excused;* as many other things, and for example sake, when he
"reciteth any point in controversy of the Catholic's doctrine, he putteth
"it down commonly in plain contrary words and sense, to that which
"he must needs know that they hold and teach; for so much as their
"public books are extant in every man's hands to testify the same."

Parsons, however, does not confine himself to mere assertions, but in
his *Examination of the second part of Fox's Calendar,* he furnishes ample
proofs of the martyrologist's want of veracity. The 19th chapter of
this part is entitled, "*A Note of more than A HUNDRED AND TWENTY LIES
"uttered by John Fox IN LESS THAN THREE LEAVES of his Acts and Monu-
"ments, and this in one kind only of perfidious dealings, in falsifying the
"opinions of Catholics, touching divers chief points of their religion.*" In
the beginning of this chapter, F. Parsons observes, "Albeit there may be
"many sorts of lying and false dealing to be noted in John Fox, yet are
"two most notorious in general, each of them containing sundry mem-
"bers and branches under them. The first may be called *historical,*
"when in his narrations he purposely uttereth falsehood, for when he doth
"it by error, or false information concerning any fact, as when for ex-
"ample in his former edition, he putteth down John Marbeck, single-

" man of Windsor, and some others for martyrs, and describeth the par-
" ticularities of their burnings and yet were never burned; this I ac-
" count for error, and not to be made account of, because his intention
" perhaps, was not to lie.   But when he cannot choose but know, that
" *the thing which he writeth was false,* this I call a *willing* or *wilful lie;* of
" which kind you have had store of examples before,"—that is, in
his Examination of Fox's Calendar.—"The second kind of lying, (con-
" tinues F. P.) may be called *dogmatical,* when not only in fact and ac-
" tions, but of doctrine also, he falsifieth and lyeth of purpose, which is
" so much the more grievous than the former, by how much less he can-
" not pretend ignorance, or misinformation of others; but with his own
" greater reproach, who will reprehend that which he knoweth not,
" and of this kind principally we are to give examples here. . . . And for
" this is a common shift of the heretics of our time, always to set down
" the state of the question guilefully, and never to suffer the reader sin-
" cerely to see how the case standeth between them and us; I have the
" more willingly been induced to lay forth this handful of examples
" in this place, . . . without any large refutation, but only shewing some
" authentical author or place of ours, where we hold the controversy to
" that which he affirmed."

The learned examiner then proceeds to prove his position in a mas-
terly manner on the doctrines of faith and justification, &c. which we
shall pass over, and give his conclusion of the chapter.   " Last of all,"
writes father Parsons, " in the same page 26, n. 25, Fox hath a cer-
" tain definition of a true christian Catholic man, according to the pope's
" religion, *wherein are as many lies as lines,* if not more, as you shall see
" examined more particularly in the next chapter.   Out of which heap
" of lies, I will only now take a dozen to add to the former number,
" though in examination they will arrive, at least, to thrice as many.
" And so by the example of this one chapter, you may consider, in what
" dreadful dreams the more simple sort of Protestants are held, about
" our opinions in matters of controversies, &c.   And if they please to do
" this in their printed books, what will they fear to do in pulpits and
" private speeches, which pass more free from examination and control-
" ment; and the most ignorant are wont to shew the most audacity in
" slandering us and our doctrine, which ordinarily they lay forth so
" sauced and so powdered, as it may seem the most absurd doctrine in
" the world, and themselves jolly fellows in refuting the same.   And
" this shall suffice for a short admonition out of this chapter; the *num-*
" *ber of lies proved against John Fox arising to the number* OF MORE THAN
" SIX SCORE, besides many by me pardoned to him, which the reader
" will easily have observed in reading it over."   Finally, Parsons give
this general character of the work : " From the beginning to the end
" of this whole volume, he commonly setteth down nothing *affirmative*
" or *positive* of his own in matters of religion, nor *any certain rule*
" what to believe; but only carpeth and scoffeth at that which was in
" use before; so as the reader is brought into *unbelief, distrust, and con-*
" *tempt* of that which was accompted piety and religion by his fore-
" fathers, and *nothing certain* taught him in place thereof, but only nega-
" tive or scornful taunts, *the proper means to make* ATHEISTS *and* INFI-
" DELS."

Thus writes the learned antagonist of John Fox. For the information of the reader we will here note, that father Parsons, whose Christian name was Robert, was educated at Oxford university in the Protestant religion, and became not only a fellow of Baliol college there in 1572, but likewise a noted tutor. He however entertained some scruples concerning the reformed religion, and spontaneously resigned his fellowship in 1574, went abroad, and embraced the Catholic faith. He was a man of shining qualities, a great controversial writer, and had a very narrow escape of his life when in England in the exercise of his priestly functions.

As it has been the invariable custom of Protestant writers to represent Catholics as condemning all those who differ from them in matters of faith as *heretics*; and as the words *heresy* and *heretics*, not only occur in these remarks, but will be found in the work we are about to review, we think it necessary, in vindication of the Catholic character, to give a correct definition of these terms. "Those," writes St. Agustin, a great Catholic divine, in one of his epistles, "Those, who do not " defend a false and perverse opinion with violent animosity, especially " if that opinion is not the work of their audacity and presumption, but " the inheritance of parents who were seduced and fell into error them- " selves; those, in short, who freely seek the truth, and are ready to " stand corrected, must *by no means* be reckoned among heretics." By this exposition the reader will perceive that Protestants are *not* indiscriminately accounted to be guilty of heresy; that matter is left to the decision of the all-seeing Judge. Though the Catholic church which is the *pillar* and ground of Truth, condemns every error, as is just and equitable, yet she does not condemn him who *errs*, but prays for him; and this the liberal Protestant reader, we are convinced, will not consider an *uncharitable* act, though he may deem it to be a superstitious one. We beg to observe also, that though we shall have occasion to condemn the conduct of the pretended reformers of past times, and the bigotry of some fanatics of the present day, yet we are far, very far, from imputing the persecuting and intolerant spirit that instigated their deeds, to the liberal and sincere friend to liberty of conscience of whatever religious persuasion he may be. Our desire is, to elucidate TRUTH, the WHOLE TRUTH, and NOTHING BUT THE TRUTH!

THE REVIEW.

THE work begins with a " History of the *first* ten Persecutions of the " primitive church from the year of our Lord 67, till the time of Con- " stantine the great, detailing the lives and actions of the principal " Christian martyrs of both sexes, in Europe and Africa."—Such is stated to be the contents of the *first* book which the publishers have adorned with an engraving purporting to represent the cruelties of the inquisition. Now what analogy this frontispiece bears to the sufferings of the *primitive* Christians, will puzzle, we think, much wiser heads to discover, than the " few plain Christians," who have undertaken to prove that "persecution is inseparable from Popery."—We are presented with three monks, presiding as judges over the sufferers, one of whom is, we suppose, intended for St. Peter, as he is placed on a cross with his head downwards, and this great apostle suffered in that manner. However, the editors of John Fox's *modern* Book of Martyrs must be told that the sufferings of the primitive Christians had long ceased before any order of monks was established, and that the " Christian martyrs of both sexes in " Europe and in Africa," were all firm and stanch ROMAN CATHOLICS. We are aware that this fact was intended to be suppressed; for they cunningly, and not much unlike the animal whose name the martyrologist bears, commence their details thus: " The dreadful martyr " doms which we are now about to describe, arose from the persecutions " of the *Romans* against the Christians, in the primitive ages of the " church, during the space of three hundred years, or till the time of " the godly Constantine."—Thus, by the omission of a word, the uninformed reader is led to conclude that Catholics were the *persecutors* when they were the *persecuted*. It is well known that in this country it is customary with bigoted writers to call the professors of Catholicism *Romans* as well as *Papists*, and thus by the suppression of the term heathens or pagans, an erroneous conclusion is drawn against Catholics. Had John Fox, or his editors, said, from the persecution of the Roman *heathens* against the Roman *Catholics*, no *false* inference could have been drawn; but this would not have suited the intention of the publishers, which they say is, " to excite a hatred and abhorrence of the " crimes of Popery and its professors." However, we shall be able to prove clearly, that neither John Fox nor his admirers have any claim of kindred whatever to these martyrs, nor to the " godly Constantine."

" It is both wonderful and horrible," they say, " to peruse the descrip " tions of the sufferings of these GODLY martyrs, as they are described " by the ancient historians. Their torments were as curious as the inge " nuity of man, tempted by the devil, could devise; and their numbers " were truly incredible." This is true enough; we can remember how much our feelings have been excited in our youth, when reading the extraordinary constancy and fortitude of the primitive martyrs, as well as the *effect* produced by their invincible courage and exemplary piety; and we were convinced that nothing but a divine power could enable them to bear the almost incredible tortures they suffered in the name of Jesus, who had died for them. But, then, these martyrs were not Protestants; they all acknowledged the supremacy of the bishop of Rome, and therefore were Roman Catholics. Now is it not a piece of the strangest absurdity for man to adduce the sufferings of Roman Catholics under Pagan persecutors, to excite in the minds of Protestants, " a hatred and abhor " rence of the crimes of Popery and its professors?"

To come however to facts. " The first martyr," they say " to OUR " *holy religion* was its blessed Founder himself;" and they then go on to give a " brief history of our Saviour." This history is so well known that we need not repeat it here, but go on to what they say of " *The Lives, Sufferings, and Martyrdom of the Apostles, Evangelists,* " *&c.*" St. Stephen is very properly placed first in the catalogue, as he was the protomartyr of the Christian religion. But they make him *a priest*, when according to their own scripture he was only chosen *deacon*. Now there is a great difference between one office and the other: a priest having power to offer *sacrifice*, and the deacon is only authorized to preach and instruct. The concluding part of the account however, is the most curious. After describing the manner of his death, namely, stoning for imputed blasphemy, it says, "On the spot "where he was martyred, Eudocia, the empress of the emperor Theo-"dosius, erected a superb church, and *the memory of him is annually* "*celebrated* on the 26th of December." This statement is correct, but not sufficiently explicit. We have neither authorities nor dates. It is distinctly affirmed in the chronological collections published by Scaliger with Eusebius's chronicle, that the saint suffered on the 26th of December in the same year our Saviour was crucified; but the saint's body was not discovered till the year 415; and it was not till the year 444 that Eudocia built a stately church to God in honour of St. Stephen, about a furlong from the city, *near* the spot where he was stoned. *(See Butler's Saints' Lives.)* And here a few questions may be asked—Of what religious profession was this empress that raised a church to St. Stephen? And who are they that *celebrate* annually his memory? Did John Fox and the evangelical reformers build churches to saints? Do the "plain Christians," who are now circulating his Book of Martyrs, celebrate annually the memory of this saint? Do any other class but the Catholics commemorate the anniversary of the saints and martyrs? These interrogatories must be all answered in the negative, and there-fore it is clear that St. Stephen was not a Protestant, and cannot con-sistently be enrolled in John Fox's list.

St. James the great follows next, and the account of his martyrdom is correctly given. It concludes thus:—" these events took place in "the year of Christ 44; and the 25th of July was fixed by THE "CHURCH for the commemoration of this saint's martyrdom." The church fixed the day of commemoration; but *what* church, "plain "Christians?" Your Protestant religion was not then in existence, nor was there any other church on earth besides the Catholic church.

St. Philip's martyrdom, they say, is commemorated with that of St. James the Less, on the 1st of May; St. Matthew's festival is kept by THE CHURCH on the 21st of September; and St. Mark's death is rightly stated to have "happened on the 25th of April, on which day THE "CHURCH commemorates his martyrdom." St James the Less is next recorded; and here we meet with a remarkable statement, which we did not expect from the present editors of Fox's Martyrs. They say, "He was after the Lord's ascension elected bishop of Jerusalem: "he wrote his general epistles to all Christians and converts whatever, "to suppress a DANGEROUS ERROR then propagating, namely, "'that a faith in Christ was *alone* sufficient for salvation without good "works.'" Here reader we have an avowal that St. James *condemned* the doctrine of faith *alone*, which doctrine was a principal stone in the Babel-like fabric of Protestantism. It is here said to be a "dangerous "error," and that the apostle wrote expressly to all Christians and con-verts "whatever" to suppress this "dangerous error then propagating;" but will it be believed, yet true it is, that this very epistle of St. James was *corrupted* by Martin Luther, the apostle of the *reformed* religion, to agree with his favourite doctrine, and of all the reformers too, that good works were not necessary to salvation. To the text, "We ac-"count a man to be justified by faith," the adverb ONLY was *added;* and when Luther was charged with this corruption, and asked *why* he

did so, the answer he gave was this: "If any papist is displeased at
"this, that I should add to the text the word *only*, tell him from me,
"that a papist and an ass is all one; so I WILL HAVE AS I COMMAND IT;
"MY WILL STANDS FOR REASON AND LAW. We will be no disciples of
"the papists, but rather their masters. Once we will insult and va-
"pour over these asses." Again, "Pry'thee answer these asses no-
"thing else about the word *only*, saving this, LUTHER WILL HAVE IT SO;
"he is the doctor over all papist doctors." *(Epist. ad Amicum de Sola.)*
Such language as this does not display much of the apostolic character
and very little of rationality, nor do we think even "the plain Chris-
"tians" will feel themselves honoured by having such a *father* of their
church, if such it can be called: but the question resolves itself into
this, either St. James or Martin Luther was wrong; Fox, however, by
the admission that the apostle wrote against "a dangerous error," allows him to be right, and sacrifices Luther. The apostle therefore
was a Catholic saint, and as such they honour him to this day. How
short sighted are men when under the influence of error. But there is
another proof of the Catholicism of St. James. This apostle composed
a liturgy or mass, a copy of which was in the university library of Oxford when Dr. Bailey wrote in 1604, and is no doubt there now. This
liturgy contains prayers for the sacrifice of the mass and for the dead,
two doctrines of the Catholic church rejected by the Protestants, and
therefore St. James cannot be a martyr for their faith.

St. Matthias is next mentioned, but in a very brief way. He is followed by St. Andrew, of whom they say, "St. Andrew persisting in the
"propagation of his doctrines, he was ordered to be crucified on a cross,
"two ends of which were transversely fixed in the ground. He boldly
"told his accusers, that he would not have preached the *glory of the*
"*cross*, had he feared to die on it. And again, when they came to
"crucify him, he said, that he *coveted the cross*, and *longed to embrace*
"*it*." Now, this language does not sound much like Protestantism,
because its disciples revile the Catholics for following the example of
St. Andrew in "coveting the cross." Most Protestants reject the use
of the sign of the cross, and those of the church as by law established
retain it only in the ceremony of baptism. How then came these wise
editors to produce the conduct of St. Andrew to confound them? Is it
not a strange piece of absurdity to reproach Catholics for observing
certain ceremonies, and then bring forward an apostle to shew that
he gloried in doing what they are taught to follow? But we can tell
these Foxite editors that St. Andrew gloried in another Catholic rite.
It is stated in the account of his passion, written by the church of
Achaia soon after his death, and cited by Remigius in Psalm xxi;
by archbishop Lanfranc in his book against Berengarius; by St. Bernard in his sermon on St. Andrew, and by many others, that when
the proconsul Ægeas exhorted him to sacrifice to idols, the blessed apostle answered him; "I do sacrifice daily to almighty God
"(that is One and True) not the flesh of bulls or blood of goats,
"but the immaculate Lamb upon the altar, whose flesh, after that
"all the faithful people have eaten the same Lamb that is sacrifi-
"ced, remaineth whole and alive as before." Now this sacrifice offered by St. Andrew daily is that of the mass, now daily offered in the

A REVIEW

OF

Fox's Book of Martyrs,

CRITICAL AND HISTORICAL.

No. 2. Printed and Published by W. E. Andrews, 3, Chapter-house-court, St. Paul's Churchyard, London. Price 3d.

EXPLANATION OF THE ENGRAVING.—*The pillar in the middle is the Monument of London. On the left hand side is seen the ancient city of Rome on fire; and on the right is a representation of the fire of London in 1666. Nero fired the former city, and charged the primitive Christians with doing it, to bring odium upon them; the latter city was struck by the hand of Heaven, and the Protestant Ascendency-men of that day, in the spirit of bigotry and illiberality, not only accused the Catholics as the authors of the calamity, but have endeavoured to perpetuate the calumny to posterity, by causing an inscription to be placed round the base of the pedestal of the above pillar, stating that it was erected in remembrance of the burning of the PROTESTANT city by a POPISH faction, which occasioned Pope to say, in his Ethic Epistles, that this pillar, "like a tall bully lifts its head and LIES."*

CONTINUATION OF THE REVIEW.

Catholic church, which all Protestants in this country, before they can accept civil office, are obliged to swear is damnable and idolatrous. Consequently St. Andrew was no Protestant martyr.

St. Peter is called the "*great* apostle and martyr," and the account given of his life is correct, so far as it goes; but there are many most important omissions. For example; the basis of Protestantism is to allow *individual* interpretation of the scriptures, by which means it is difficult for a man to know what his neighbour's creed is; because what may seem *right* to him to-day he may consider *wrong* to-morrow, and therefore no stability can be placed in this mode of belief, if such it can be called. But the Catholic grounds his faith on the *unerring* word of GOD, as delivered by the apostles and received by the *whole* church; not as *one* man may teach, but what *all* have heard and bear testimony to.   Hence St. Peter, who had hitherto delivered the Christian doctrine by *word of mouth*, finding that certain busy spirits were endeavouring to sow dissension among the converted Jews, wrote two admonitory epistles to them from Rome, in the second of which he tells them, that "*no prophecy of scripture is made by private interpretation*," ch. i. v. 20; and in conclusion he writes, "Even as our beloved brother "Paul also according to the wisdom given unto him hath written unto "you; as also in *all* (his) epistles, speaking in them of these things, "in which are some things *hard to be understood*, which they that are "unlearned and unstable rest, as also *the rest of the scriptures*, unto "THEIR OWN DESTRUCTION. You, therefore, brethren, knowing these "things, take heed lest, led aside by the *error* of the unwise, you fall "away from your own stedfastness." Now here is a very important fact suppressed, which certainly ought to have been noticed, because Catholics are reproached for not allowing private interpretation, following the advice here given to the primitive Christians by St. Peter, by which means they maintain an *unity* in their doctrine, while Protestants are as discordant in their religious notions as the builders of Babel were in their language.   Now, it is as clear as that one and one make two, that there can be but *one* true faith, because Truth is both immutable and indivisible; consequently, among the many creeds in existence, there can be but *one* of them *true*; and *which* that is we should think might be very easily discovered if people would take time to reflect.   In the beginning of Christianity, we find there were teachers of *error*; for example, Simon Magus, Cerinthus, Hymenæus, Ebion, &c. who all differed from each other, but all agreed in condemning the doctrines taught by the apostles; so we see Protestants of endless denominations disputing each other's creed, but all combining to misrepresent and vilify the Catholic faith. Now is this not a singular circumstance?   If the Catholic church taught error, would it not be easy to point out the error, and when it was first introduced?   Yet this never has been done.   And were she *like the rest* of the teachers of the ignorant, as they style themselves, is it likely that she would have to stand against the combined assaults of *all* the various sects any more than either of those which oppose her?   St. Peter, it is clear, by condemning private interpretation, was no Protestant saint, but a Catholic one, and Catholics commemorate his memory to this day.

But to return to the martyrologist.   He says, "His (Peter's) body "being taken down, *embalmed*, and buried in the Vatican, a church was "erected on the spot; but this being destroyed by the emperor Helio- "gabalus, the body was removed till the 20th bishop of Rome, called "Cornelius, conveyed it again to the Vatican: afterwards Constantine "the great erected one of the most stately churches in the universe "over the place."   By this confused account, without dates or authorities, we may form some conclusion on the merit due to Fox's relations. The story of "*embalming*" the body of St. Peter is evidently *false;* because history tells us it was the custom of the Romans to *burn* the dead bodies of their relatives, and the practice of preserving a corpse from putrefaction was probably then unknown to them.   The Egyptians preserved the bodies of their dead, and the Jews buried them in the earth, as we may see by the book of Tobias, and other parts of scripture. From the latter, once the chosen people of God, the primitive Christians, the faithful elect of a crucified Saviour, observed the custom of depositing the remains of the martyrs in the *earth*; so that " embalming" is quite out of the question. And when we consider the state of the Christians at the time; the continual apprehensions they were under, from the cruelty of their oppressors, this story of Fox will appear still more improbable. Then as to the body being buried *in* the Vatican, and a church erected *on* the spot; what can he mean by this statement? The Vatican in the time of the Roman empire was *a hill without* the walls of the city, near the suburb inhabited by the Jews, on which stood two Heathen temples, the one of Apollo, and the other of Idæa, mother of the gods. (*See Bianchini, Praef. in Pontif.* p. 72.) On the spot where these temples stood Constantine the great built a church in honour of the place where St. Peter suffered martyrdom, and where he was in the first instance buried, but afterwards removed to the catacombs. This falling into decay, having stood twelve centuries, pope Leo the 10th projected the present magnificent temple. The means devised by Leo to raise this edifice, may be said to have been one of the causes of Luther's pretended reformation.

Again, is it probable that the Christians could build a church during the persecution, where two temples dedicated to idolatry were already raised? And this church to stand about one hundred years unmolested, till Heliogabalus destroyed it? For observe, Heliogabalus reigned about the year 222, that is about a century and a half after the martyrdom of St. Peter, and upwards of a century before the reign of Constantine the great, when the Christians were first allowed to build public temples to worship the true God. Cornelius, according to the writings of Eusebius, St. Pacianus, St. Cyprian, Tillemont, &c. succeeded St. Fabian, who suffered martyrdom on the 20th of January, 250. Fabian was the 20th bishop of Rome after St. Peter, so that here is a mistake on the part of Fox. At the time of Fabian's death, the violence of the persecution under Decius was so great, that the see of Rome was vacant sixteen months, so that Cornelius did not occupy the episcopal chair of that city until the year 251, thirty years after Heliogabalus. In the life of the holy pope Cornelius, by the Rev. Alban Butler, there is not the least mention made of the circumstance of the removal of St. Peter's body, which would not have been omitted had it really taken place. The fact is, the story of John Fox is mere fiction, and shews how easily those persons who charge the Catholics with being credulous are themselves imposed upon. Cornelius did not fill the chair but sixteen months, himself suffering martyrdom on the 14th of September, 252. Were Protestants to examine history carefully, and look to dates and authorities, they would not be so much deceived by interested writers as they have been.

St. Gregory, who lived much nigher to the primitive ages than John Fox, writes (l. iii. ep. 30.) that the bodies of St. Peter and St. Paul, who suffered on the same day, were buried in the catacombs, two miles out of Rome; and the Rev. Alban Butler says, " The most ancient " Roman calendar published by Bucherius, marks their festival at *the* " *catacombs* on the 29th of June." These catacombs were the ancient cemeteries of the Christians, and therefore the account of St. Gregory is entitled to credit. Mr. A. Butler, in a note to the life of St.

Calixtus, pope and martyr, October 14, writes thus: "The Chris-
"tians never gave into the customs either of preserving the bo-
"dies of their dead, like the Egyptians, or of burning them with the
"Romans, or of casting them to wild beasts with the Persians; but,
"in imitation of the people of God from the beginning of the world,
"buried them with decency and respect in the earth, where, according
"to the sentence pronounced by God, they return to dust, till the ge-
"neral resurrection. At Rome they chose caverns or arenæ for their
"burial places, digging lodges on each hand, in each of which they
"deposited a corpse, and then walled up the entrance of that lodge.
"Boldetti proves the cemetry of St. Agnes to have been enlarged
"after the reign of Constantine; and the same is not doubted as to
"many others. Several inscriptions on sepulchres in the catacombs
"given to the persons there interred the quality of fossores, or diggers
"(of cemeteries). See Aringhi, l. i. c. 13. Boldetti, l. i. c. 15. Botta-
"rius, t. ii. p. 126. The Pagans of Rome burned their dead bodies;
"which is true not only of the rich, but in general; nor is bishop
"Burnet able to produce one contrary instance; though sometimes
"the corpse of a criminal or slave, who had neither friends nor money,
"might be thrown into the Puticuli, upon the heads of the ashes of the
"others, without the ceremony of being burnt. H. Valesius, in his
"notes on Eusebius, p. 186, observes, that it is hard to determine at
"what time the Romans began to leave off the custom of burning their
"dead: but it must have been about the time of Constantine the great,
"probably when he had put an end to the empire of Paganism. The
"Heathens learned of the Christians to bury their dead; and grew at
"once so fond of this custom, that, in the time of Theodosius the
"younger, as Macrobius testifies, (Saturnal. l. vii. c. 7.) there was not
"a body burnt in all the Roman empire." Now, we may here ask,
whether it is likely that the primitive Christians could build *churches*
in honour of the martyrs, when they were obliged to bury them in
caverns privately, and were suffering persecution for conscience sake?
No man of common sense can entertain such an opinion for a moment.
Besides we have it here stated by Mr. Butler, that the Christians rejected the practice of preserving the dead bodies by *embalming*, and
placed them in their mother earth. Hence it is clear Fox was merely
a romance writer, and not a recorder of truth.

"Christians," continues Mr. Butler, "from the beginning, often
"visited *out of devotion* the tombs of the martyrs, and in the times of
"persecution often *concealed* themselves in these catacombs, and as-
"sembled here *to celebrate the divine mysteries*. Whence the persecutors
"forbid them to enter the cemetries, as the judge proconsul declared
"to St. Cyprian, (in actis, p. 11.) and the prefect of Egypt to St. Dio-
"nysius of Alexandria. (ap. Eus. l. vi. c. 11.) See also Eus. l. ix. c. 2.
"Tertullian, (ad Scapul. c. 3.) and several inscriptions importing this
"in Boldetti, (l. i. c. 11.) Mamachi, (t. iii. p. 162.) and chiefly Bot-
"tarius against Burnet. (Roma Sotter. t. i. p. 12.)

"That the catacombs were known to be filled with the tombs of in-
"numerable martyrs, and devoutly visited by the Christians in the early
"ages of Christianity, is incontestible from the testimonies of St. Jerom,
"St. Paulinus and Prudentius. St. Jerom mentions (in c. xl. Ezech.
"t. v. p. 980. ed. Ben.) that 'when he was a boy, and studied at

"Rome, he was accustomed on Sundays to visit in a round the sepul-
"chres of the apostles and martyrs, and frequently to go into the cryp-
"tæ, which are dug in the earth to a great extent, and have in each
"hand bodies of the dead like walls, and with their darkness strike the
"mind with horror,' &c. It is clear he went not thither to play, as
"Basnage answers to this authority, (Hist. de l'Egl. l. xviii. c. 6. n. 8.)
"but to perform an exercise of religion and piety, as all others clearly
"express this practice. St. Paulinus says, that the tombs of the martyrs
"here contained could not be numbered. (Poem. 27, in Nat. 13. S.
"Paulin.)

> " Hic Petrus, hic Paulus proceres ; hic martyres omnes,
> " Quos simul innumeros magnæ tenet ambitus urbis,
> " Quosque per innumerus diffuso limite gentes,
> " Intra Romuleos veneratur ecclesia fines."

Which may be thus translated :—

Here are the chiefs Peter and Paul ; here are all the martyrs, of whom the precincts of the great city contain an immense multitude, and whom the church, spread over innumerable nations within the Roman boundaries, venerates.

We must now notice another fiction John Fox has introduced for the purpose of deception. He says, " Before we quit this article, *it is re-*
"*quisite to observe*, that previous to the death of St. Peter, his wife suf-
"fered martyrdom for the faith of Christ, and was exhorted, when go-
"ing to be put to death, to remember her Saviour." *Why* John thought it requisite to make this observation is not known, we are persuaded, to the great bulk of his readers, and yet the martyrologist had a turn to serve by it. Know then, that a state of continency is enjoined by the Catholic church on her ministers, that they may be the less encumbered to fulfil the duties of their office. Those, however, who undertook to *reform* religion, as they called it, in the sixteenth century, thought other-wise. They had no relish for a life of restraint and mortification, but considered themselves as much entitled to a life of pleasure as the rest of the world. Whoever will look into the new testament, will find that St. Peter and the rest of the apostles, on their being called by their Divine Master, left *all things* to follow him. Father, mother, wife and all. We cannot trace, by any authority whatever, that Peter's wife ever followed him, after he had entered into the apostleship; on the contrary, we have the testimony of St. Jerom and St. Epiphanius, who expressly affirm, that from the time of their calling, the apostles who were married embraced a state of perpetual continency. Martin Lu-ther, John Calvin, and among others, John Fox also, took a different course when they enlisted under the banners of *evangelism*. Fox had taken the vows of celibacy, previous to his being ordained deacon, in 1550, but he afterwards *absolved himself from this oath*, and took to him-self a wife. But as *wiving* was *then* a novel thing among the clergy, John Fox contrived to get Peter's wife to Rome, and insert her in his list of martyrs, as he did others who were never martyred at all, to make the ignorant and credulous believe that she followed him in his labours to preach the gospel, and that therefore the *reformed* clergy had a precedent for sacrificing at the altar of Hymen. Mr. Echard, a Pro-testant divine, in his *Ecclesiastical History*, says, " We are told that
" St. Peter's wife suffered martyrdom before his death by his encourage-
" ment, and that he left behind him a daughter named Petronilla; but
" WE HAVE NO CERTAINTY OF IT." Who after this will believe Fox?

Of the rest of the apostles, namely, SS. Paul, Jude, Bartholomew, Thomas, Simon, and John, and Luke the evangelist, there is nothing said that is materially incorrect or contradictory. It may here be observed, however, that St Jude wrote an epistle to all the churches in the east, and particularly to the Jewish converts, cautioning them against the heresies springing up among the Christians. This epistle Luther called in question, because several ancients doubted it. The *tradition* of the Catholic church however makes it of divine and unquestionable authority, and it is only on *this* testimony that Protestants can receive it as inspired. Of St. Barnabas, Fox writes thus: " He was " a native of Cyprus, but of Jewish parents: the time of his death is " *uncertain*, but it is supposed to be about the year of Christ 73; and " his *festival*, is *kept* on the 11th of June." Now the time of this saint's death is as certain as that of the others which Fox has recorded, but we shall have to speak of this matter by and by. Fox concludes the account of all these saints with stating that " his festival is observed," " the commemoration of this apostle," " the anniversary of his mar- " tyrdom," " his death is commemorated," or " *the church* commemo- " rates," &c. on such a day; but in those which follow, the commemorations, and observances and festivals are omitted. That the church did not stop commemorating the saints and martyrs, with the apostles and evangelists, we think is clearly demonstrated by the extract we have just given from the poem by St. Paulinus who lived about the middle of the fourth century, and was bishop of Nola. This writer affirms, that beside the chiefs Peter and Paul, the church, spread over innumerable nations, venerated an immense multitude of martyrs, then deposited in the catacombs of Rome. Now this church could be no other than the Catholic church, because no other existed that venerated the relics of saints and martyrs. The Catholics of this day are reproached by the editors of John Fox's Book of Martyrs for being superstitious, because they practice what the primitive Christians practised: consequently the primitive Christians were not Protestants, nor were the martyrs of those times Protestant martyrs.

THE FIRST PRIMITIVE PERSECUTION UNDER NERO.

" The first persecution in the primitive ages of THE CHURCH," writes the martyrologist, " was begun by that cruel tyrant Nero Domitius, " the sixth emperor of Rome, and A. D. 67. This monarch reigned for " the space of five years with tolerable credit to himself, but then gave " way to the greatest extravagancy of temper, and to the most atro- " cious barbarities." As an instance of the mildness of his disposition, on first assuming the purple, history records of him, that once when he was about to sign an order for the death of a condemned person, he cried out with compassion, "I wish I could not write." He had for his instructors, Seneca and Burrhus the prefect of the Prætorium, to whose counsels this moderation of temper is chiefly attributed. But both these teachers connived at an adulterous intercourse which Nero had entered into when under their guidance, so defective was the virtue of the best of the heathen philosophers; and to this indulgence of the passions may be laid those infamous debaucheries and that barbarity of heart which stained the succeeding years of Nero. Besides the cruelties he inflicted on the Christians, he caused his mother to be slain in

the year 68, put to death his wife Octavia, and cut off the heads of almost all the illustrious men of the empire. "Among other diabolical
"outrages," says the Book of Martyrs, "he ordered that the city of
"Rome should be set on fire, which was done by his officers, guards,
"and servants. While the city was in flames he went up to the tower
"of Mæcenas, played upon his harp, sung the song of the burning of
"Troy, and declared, 'That he wished the ruin of all things before his
"death.' Among the noble buildings burnt was the circus, or place ap-
"propriated to horse races; it was half a mile in length, of an oval
"form, with rows of seats rising above each other, and capable of re-
"ceiving, with ease, upwards of 100,000 spectators. Many other pa-
"laces and houses were consumed; and several thousands of the peo-
"ple perished in the flames, were smothered, or burned beneath the
"ruins. This dreadful conflagration continued several days; when
"Nero, finding that his conduct was greatly blamed, and a severe
"odium cast upon him, determined to lay the whole upon the Chris-
"tians, at once to excuse himself, and have an opportunity of witness-
"ing new cruelties. The barbarities exercised upon the Christians,
"during the first persecution, were such as even excited the commi-
"seration of the Romans themselves. Nero even refined upon cruelty,
"and contrived all manner of punishments for the Christians. In par-
"ticular he had some sewed up in the skins of wild beasts, and then
"worried by dogs till they expired; and others dressed in shirts made
"stiff by wax, fixed to axle trees, and set on fire in his gardens. This
"persecution was general throughout the whole Roman empire; but
"it rather increased than diminished the spirit of Christianity." The
fire lasted six days together, and of fourteen wards or quarters of the
city, only four escaped. Of the tortures practised on the Christians
Juvenal says,

> "Death was their doom, on stakes impal'd upright,
> "Smear'd o'er with wax, and set on fire to light
> "The streets, and make a dreadful blaze by night."

Now, if the present editors of Fox's Book of Martyrs consider this
conduct of Nero, in charging the primitive Christians with setting fire
to Rome, to cast the odium upon them, as base and infamous; what,
we ask, can they think of the "Protestant ascendency-men," in Charles
the second's reign, who as basely attempted to fix the dreadful fire of
London in 1666 on the *Catholics*, in order to excite the hatred of the ignorant multitude against them? Nay, more than this, these Christian
calumniators raised a monumental pillar to commemorate the dire calamity, and round the pedestal of this column they placed the following
inscription: "THIS PILLAR IS SET UP IN PERPETUAL REMEM-
"BRANCE OF THE BURNING OF THIS PROTESTANT CITY, BY
"THE POPISH FACTION, IN SEPTEMBER, A. D. 1666, FOR
"THE DESTRUCTION OF THE PROTESTANT RELIGION AND
"OF OLD ENGLISH LIBERTY, AND FOR THE INTRODUCTION
"OF POPERY AND SLAVERY."—Thus, without a shadow of a shade
of proof, did these Protestants accuse their Catholic neighbours of set-
ting fire to the city of London, when it was evidently a stroke of the
Divine hand; and they next erect a monument to perpetuate the slan-
der to future ages. Was ever any thing so cruelly unjust, so shamefully

illiberal? We have given a representation of this mark of bigotry and intolerance, which we consider far more disgraceful to Protestant Christians than to Roman heathens. Nero falsely charged the Christians with his own infamous deed, that he might have a pretext for his cruelties; so did the Protestants under Elizabeth and the Stuarts *forge* plots and raise false reports against the Catholics, to give a kind of colour to their clamours for persecuting those whom they named Papists. When James the second came to the throne, he, being a Catholic, had the infamous and lying inscription erased; but such was the fury, such the bigotry of those days, that it was again inscribed on the pillar in the reign of William the third, and remains to this day a striking and incontestible memorial of the intolerant and calumniating spirit of " Protestant-ascendency."

It may here be asked, surely there were *some* grounds for the charge thus publicly and lastingly made against the Catholics? We have said that there was not a shadow of a proof; and that we may not be accused of contenting ourself with bare assertion, we will refer the reader to Rapin's History of England, the author of which being a Calvinist, was a writer by no means favourable to Catholics. Rapin says, " Men failed " not to give a scope to their imagination, and to form conjectures upon " the causes and authors of this fire. The pious and religious ascribed " it to the just vengeance of Heaven, on a city, where vice and immo- " rality reigned so openly and shamefully, and which had not been " sufficiently humbled by the raging pestilence of the foregoing year. " Some again, as I have said, ascribed this misfortune to the malice " of the republicans: others to the Papists. And there were some so " bold, as even to suspect the king and the duke of York. But though " several suspected persons were imprisoned, it was not possible to dis- " cover, or prove that the baker's house, where this dreadful calami- " ty first broke out, was fired on purpose. However, [one Robert " Hubert] a French Hugunot native of Rouen, and a LUNATIC, con- " fessing himself guilty of this fact, was CONDEMNED and EXE- " CUTED. But it appeared *afterwards*, by testimony of the master " of the ship, who brought him from France, that though he was land- " ed at the time, he did not arrive in London till two days after the " fire began. It is pretended likewise, that a Dutch boy, ten years of " age, confessed, that his father and himself had thrown fire-balls " into the baker's house, through a window that stood open. But, be- " sides the objection which may be made to this testimony from the " boy's age, there must have been some circumstance in his narrative " not agreeable to the fact, since it was not thought proper to make " a further inquiry. Perhaps this was only a groundless report."

The continuator of *Baker's Chronicle* makes the following observations on this remarkable visitation of Divine Vengeance: " But a ques- " tion here arises, which having been so much canvassed, it is neces- " sary to make some notice of, which is this; whether this fire were " the sole effect of the will of Heaven, or whether the wickedness of " men was the instrument of Providence to bring on this dismal cala- " mity. To prove the latter, it has been observed, that the extent and " violence of the fire was so great, and it seemed to break out in so " many different places, as makes it hardly credible that it should have

" prevailed so far, and after that manner, against the vigorous opposi-
" tion made to it, had not the mischief been propagated by some other
" cause than its own strength. It is certain besides, that there were
" some persons of the republican party accused of such a design, and
" executed for it not long before, namely John Rathbone, an old army
" colonel, and some others of the same stamp, who were convicted of
" a design to kill the king, and overthrow the government; to effect
" which, they had agreed to set fire to the city of London in several
" places: and had pitched on the third of September for the day.
" There was also one Hubert, a French reputed Papist, who acknow-
" ledged himself guilty of the same, and was HANGED by his own
" confession, *no other* evidence appearing against him. On the other
" side, though the devastation made by the fire was so prodigious, yet
" the causes that propagated it were so numerous and powerful, as to
" seem commensurate enough to the mischief done. The vehemence
" of the wind, the oldness and dryness of the houses, and the narrow-
" ness of the streets, have been above touched on; and it is no great
" wonder that the fire should become very fierce, when it had so great
" helps. And though its breaking out in houses at a great distance from
" those that were on fire, seems to intimate that it was industriously
" carried on; yet it is in truth no more than often happens upon the
" like occasions. When the town of Warwick was burnt about thirty
" years ago, several persons, who thinking themselves safe, went out
" to assist their neighbours, found their houses burnt down in their
" absence; the wind being extremely high, and scattering the flakes
" of fire to such great distances, as could not have been imagined till
" it was found by that fatal experiment. And in a late fire in London
" a like accident happened; a low shed, at the length of a middling
" street from a house that was burning, being set on fire by some flam-
" ing matter carried thither by a high wind, as happened within the
" writer's knowledge. As to Hubert, the man appeared to be not very
" well in his senses; so that what he said cannot be depended on.
" Nor does it seem likely that those of Rathbone's party should venture
" on it, after so many of their accomplices were put out of the way;
" and their scheme no doubt utterly disjointed. For these reasons,
" and because *no solid evidence* appears to prove the contrary, it seems
" most reasonable to incline to the favourable side, and to look upon
" this fire as the act of Providence, intended as a punishment to those
" times and a happiness to our own; the beauty, regularity and health-
" fulness of the new city remaining to ours, and as we may hope, to
" many distant ages; while the loss and calamity of the old one, was
" confined to a very few years after this signal disaster happened."

Dr. Burnet, it is true, in his History of his Own Times, to give
some countenance to the diabolical inscription, for he was a bishop and
a sly courtier, has a vague story of one Grant, a Papist, who procured
himself to be chosen a member of the New River company, that he
might stop the water at the commencement of the fire; but Higgins,
in his Historical Remarks, proves, from dates, that Grant was not a
member at the time of the fire, and that, had he been so, he did not
possess the power in question. And now let the reader compare the
accounts of the above historians with the inscription itself; let him re-

collect that the author of the inscription was a man (Sir Patience Ward) *convicted of perjury*; and then let him candidly say, whether the conduct of " Protestant-ascendency" towards the Catholics, only a century and a half ago, was not more shameful and atrocious than that of Nero towards the primitive Catholics at the birth of Christianity?

Of the martyrs that suffered under Nero, Fox observes, " Besides St. " Paul and St. Peter, many others, whose names have not been trans- " mitted to posterity, and who were some of their converts and fol- " lowers, suffered; the *facts* concerning the principal of whom we " shall proceed to describe." He then mentions Erastus, the chamberlain of Corinth; Aristarchus, the Macedonian; and Trophimus, an Ephesian, as converts of St. Paul, and martyrs for the faith. He also notices Ananias, bishop of Damascus, who, he says, " is celebrated " in the sacred writings for being the person who cured St. Paul of the " blindness with which he was struck by the amazing brightness which " happened at his conversion. He was one of the 70, and was mar- " tyred at the city of Damascus. *After his death a Christian church was* " *built over the place of his burial,* which is *now* converted into a " Turkish mosque." And he records the martyrdom of another saint in these words: "Joseph, commonly called Barsabas, was a primitive dis- " ciple, and is *usually deemed* one of the seventy. He was, in some degree, " related to the Redeemer; and he became a candidate together with " Matthias, to fill the vacant place of Judas Iscariot. The ecclesiasti- " cal writers make *very little other mention of him*; but Papius informs " us, that he was once compelled to drink poison, which did not do him " the least injury, agreeable to the promise of the Lord, to those who " believe in him. He was during his life a zealous preacher of the " gospel; and having received many insults from the Jews, at length " obtained martyrdom, being murdered by the Pagans in Judea."

Such is the account given by John Fox, and we beg the reader's attention to the remarks we shall now offer upon it. In the first place, he gives us no *authority* for his pretended *facts*, nor have we been able to trace any particulars of the martyrdom of the first three personages he has named in the ecclesiastical accounts of Echard, Butler, and others. Of Ananias he speaks with much certainty, though little is known of him, except what is recorded in the acts of the apostles. We cannot find that he is placed in the Roman martyrology, though the Greeks give him a place in their calendar. That no positive records were preserved of him is clear from St. Augustin speaking of him with *doubt*; which would not have been the case had this Ananias been one of the principal sufferers under Nero, as Fox reckons him. " After his death," writes this Protestant martyrologist, " a *Christian* church was built over " the place of his burial, which is now converted into a *Turkish* " mosque." And this account we presume is sufficient to gain credit with a Protestant, though a Catholic, who is repeatedly charged with being credulous and superstitious, would require some *dates* and *authorities* before *he* would believe it. Taking the time of the death of Ananias to be in the last year of the reign of Nero, that is, in the year 68, nearly six hundred years must have transpired before the Turks obtained possession of Damascus. *When* then was this church built? And by *whom?* The gazetteers tell us that there are about 2000 mosques in Damascus, the most stately of which was a Christian church; but to whom it was dedicated they do not mention. That churches were raised to the memory of the martyrs by the primitive Christians in honour of God, we do not doubt, because we know it was the custom with them, as it is with Catholics now, though not so among Protestants; neither do we doubt that the Turks appropriated these churches to their own use, after they had overpowered the Christians, as the Protestants in queen Elizabeth's time took possession of the Catholic churches raised in memory of the saints; but we doubt the accuracy of Fox's statement with regard to Ananias, since he has produced no authority, and we can find no account of him in the most esteemed works by Catholic authors.

We have then only *bare assertion* for this detail, and the credit due to Fox's unverified statements we will now make appear. Joseph, commonly called Barsabas, is "*usually deemed*," he says, one of the seventy. "The ecclesiastical writers," he continues, "make " very little other mention of him," than that he was in some degree related to the Redeemer, and became a candidate with Matthias for the vacant apostleship; yet we are told with great confidence that " he was during his life a zealous preacher of the gospel." Now, reader, this Joseph, commonly called Barsabas, is the SAME PERSON Fox has recorded as a martyr under the name of St. Barnabas, the detail of whose martyrdom we have a little before stated in Fox's words. In the account given by him of St. Barnabas there is not a word of his having been a candidate with St. Matthias to succeed Judas, yet he is placed last with the apostles, and his festival is admitted to be kept on the 11th of June, which the Catholics do to this day. St. Barnabas was not one of the twelve chosen apostles, but is styled so by the primitive fathers, and commemorated as such by the Catholic church; but how came Fox to put him there? He was first called Joses, or Joseph, and was one of the first and chief of the seventy disciples of our Saviour, but after the ascension of Christ, the apostles changed his name to Barnabas. Fox, speaking of this apostle under the name of Barsabas, says the ecclesiastical writers make *very little mention* of him ; yet it will be seen by a reference to the acts of the apostles, that he is frequently spoken of there as the companion of St. Paul in many of his travels, as the latter also testifies in some of his epistles. St. Barnabas is said to have introduced St. Paul to the apostles Peter and James, on his coming to Jerusalem three years after his conversion. He is also mentioned in the acts of the apostles, chapter iv, verse 6, as being the first of the new converts who sold all they had and lived in common. "And Joseph, who was surnamed of the apostles Barnabas, " (which is by interpretation, the Son of Consolation) a Levite, a Cy-" prian born, where he had a piece of land, sold it, and brought the " price, and laid it before the feet of the apostles." So far too were the ecclesiastical writers from making little mention of him, that many authors wrote of him, namely, Sigisbertus, in his book *de Viris illustribus* ; Eusebius in his Ecclesiastical History ; St. Jerom in his work *de Viris illudribus* ; St. Isidore in his book of the Lives of the Fathers ; and venerable Bede, in his *Retractions.* The Rev. Mr. Butler, in his account of this saint's life, says, " Alexander, a monk of Cyprus in the sixth

" age, hath written an account of his death, in which he relates, that
" the faith having made great progress in Cyprus, by the assiduous
" preaching, edifying example, and wonderful miracles of this apostle,
" it happened that certain inveterate Jews, who had persecuted the
" holy man in Syria, came to Salamis, and stirred up many powerful
" men in that city against him. The saint was taken, roughly handled
" and insulted by the mob, and after many torments stoned to death.
" The remains of St. Barnabas were found near the city of Salamis,
" with a copy of the gospel of St. Matthew in Hebrew laid upon his
" breast, written with St. Barnabas's own hand. The book was sent to
" the emperor Zeno in 485, as Theodorus Lector relates." (*Theod.
Lect.* ii. p. 557, *Suidas*, &c.) We can find no account of Fox's story of
this saint being compelled to drink poison; and it appears from the
testimony of this monk of Cyprus, that his death took place in that
island, and not in Judea, as John Fox states. St. Barnabas is represented by St. John Chrysostom and all antiquity as a man of a beautiful and venerable aspect, and of a majestic presence. So much for John
Fox's tale, that ecclesiastical writers make very little account of him.

THE SECOND PRIMITIVE PERSECUTION UNDER DOMITIAN.

The tumults and disorders which occurred in the Roman empire under the emperors Galba, Otho, and Vitellius, and the merciful disposition of Vespasian and Titus, gave peace to the Christians till Domitian
succeeded to the purple, who exceeded in cruelty the first persecutor
of the church, Nero, and was detestable to all men on account of the
brutality and ferociousness of his manners. It is related of him that
in the beginning of his reign he was accustomed to amuse himself in
his closet with catching flies, and sticking them with a sharp bodkin;
Suetonius and Eusebius record, that he debauched his own niece and
impiously took the titles of God and Lord. In the year 95, this tyrant
issued fresh edicts throughout the empire against the Christians, by
which many fell victims to his barbarity, and crowned themselves with
a glorious martyrdom. John Fox tells us that he commanded all " the
" lineage of David to be extirpated;" but, as usual, he gives us no reference to authenticate his story. He then goes on,—" Two Christians
" were brought before him, accused of being of the tribe of Judah, and
" line of David; but from their answers, he *despised them as idiots*, and
" dismissed them according." *Who* these Christians were, we are not
told, nor have we any reason stated why Domitian should have a
greater antipathy to Christians descended from David than from Pontius Pilate or Herod; however we cannot help remarking that this conduct on the part of the Roman emperor forms a striking contrast to
that of " Protestant-ascendency," in Charles the second's reign. We
have it from Rapin and Baker, that a poor fellow, *a lunatic*, a *reputed
Papist*, but a *French Huguenot*, was *condemned* and *executed* upon no other
evidence than his *own* confession,—the confession of a madman—for
setting fire to London—while Fox assures us that the most merciless
of the Roman tyrants had justice enough to despise and dismiss two
Christians because he perceived they were idiots. " *Oh! the times and
" the manners!*" Again, he says, " a law was made, 'That no Christian,
" once brought before the tribunal, should be exempted from punish-

" ment without *renouncing his religion.*" Did John Fox's master, the
protector Somerset, and his mistress the virgin Elizabeth, borrow their
system of legislation from Domitian, when they passed laws *compelling*
Catholics, under *fine* and *imprisonment*, to attend the *new fangled* service of the church as by *law* established, by which they would havere-
nounced their religion? The martyrologist continues,—" During this
" reign there were a variety of tales, composed in order to *injure the*
" *Christians.* Among other *falsehoods* they were accused *of indecent*
" *nightly meetings*, of a *rebellious turbulent spirit: of being inimical to the*
" *Roman empire*, of murdering their children, and of *being cannibals;* and
" at this time, such was the *infatuation of the Pagans*, that if famine,|pes-
" tilence, or earthquakes, afflicted any of the Roman provinces, these
" calamities were said to be the manifestations of the divine wrath oc-
" casioned by their impieties. These persecutions increased the num-
" ber of *informers;* and many, *for the sake of gain, swore away the lives*
" *of the innocent.* When any Christians were brought before the ma-
" gistrates a *test oath* was proposed, when, if they refused to take it,
" *death was pronounced against them;* and if they confessed themselves
" Christians, the sentence was the same."
On reading this statement of Fox, of the situation of the primitive
Catholic Christians under Domitian, we were most forcibly struck with
the condition of the Catholics of this country in the reigns of Elizabeth
and the Stuarts, as bearing a strong parallel to the former. Who has
not heard of the variety of tales composed in order to injure the Catholics, by the unprincipled and self-interested ministers of Elizabeth ? Who has not heard of the falsehoods circulated of indecent intercourses between the secluded inhabitants of the monasteries, in order
to find a plea for destroying them ? What were the new enactments
of treason passed for by the parliaments of Elizabeth and the Stuarts, but
to instil the belief that Catholics were of a rebellious spirit, and their
principles inimical to the British empire ? Are not the Catholics now
daily charged with committing murder through the influence of their
religion ? And the unfortunate misruled and oppressed Irish, with being
cannibals ? And at the time we are alluding to, what was the *infatua-*
tion of the Protestants? Did they not give credit to the most incredible tales ? We shall have occasion, in the course of our review to enter
more at large into this system of invention and infatuation, but we cannot refrain from here asking the reader, what he can think of the state
of men's minds, when they could believe that " an army of Papists were
" training to the use of arms *under ground;*" and that a gunpowder plot
was in progress, for " blowing up the river Thames, and drowning the
" faithful Protestant city of London ?" Yet credibility was given to
such stories as these, as may be seen in the second volume of Grey's
Examination of Neal's History of the Puritans. Search the records of
parliament, and you will find, that in many petitions presented by the
Commons to Charles the first, the Catholics were charged with being
the occasion of all public calamities, and their blood considered a remedy for all public grievances. That of the Commons in 1628 reduces
" all public misery to the increase of idolatry and superstition," which
were the terms given to Catholicism. Then again, as to informers
swearing away the lives of the innocent, can a parallel be found for

tival on the 24th of January, the day on which he was maytyred, so that Timothy was not a Protestant saint and martyr.

We must here mention that, by Domitian's orders, St. John the apostle and evangelist, was put into a cauldron of boiling oil, without the Latin gate at Rome, but came out uninjured. After this miracle he was banished to Patmos, a small barren island of the Sparades, only five miles in circumference, where he wrote the Apocalypse or Book of Revelations. In the early part of Christianity, as at the present day, there were persons who denied the divinity of Jesus Christ. These were Jewish converts, the chief of whom were Ebion, Cerinthus, and Nicholas of Antioch. To confute and silence these heretical declaimers, St. John wrote his gospel, at the request of the bishops of Asia. In this undertaking he did not write that every individual might put what construction he pleased upon his words, but to declare what was the true faith which had already been delivered, and to give a circumstantial account of some facts in the life of our Saviour, which the other evangelists had omitted, thereby to prove that none but God could have performed such extraordinary things. St. John also wrote three epistles, one to all the Catholics in general, the second to a certain lady, whom he styles "the lady elect," and the third to one Gaius. The effect of all these is, to shew the certainty of the Catholic faith, and to exhort them to continue stedfast to the things which they had *heard* taught by him and the other apostles. "That which you have *heard* " from the *beginning* (he says) let it abide in you." (1st epist. ii. 24.) " This is the commandment, that as you have *heard* from the *beginning* " you walk in *the same*, because many *seducers* are gone out into the " world." (2d. epist. 6, 7.) The heathens admired the sublimity of St. John's diction, and a Platonist, speaking of what was written in his gospel of the majesty of the divine Word, that is of Jesus Christ, said it ought to be engraved in letters of gold, and placed in all the churches.

It is also worthy of note, that Josephus the historian, about this period finished his two books against Appion, in which he defends, with much erudition, his *Jewish Antiquities.* He divides this work into 20 tomes, in the 18th of which, chapter 4th, is the following striking testimony of the miracles of Christ: "There was about that time " one Jesus, a wise man; if at least a man he may be called. He was " a great worker of miracles, and teacher of such men, as would " readily embrace the truth, and had many followers, both Jews and " Gentiles. This was the famous Christ, who upon the accusation of " the princes and great men of our nation was crucified by Pontius " Pilate: and yet those that first loved him did not forsake him; for he " appeared to them the third day alive again, as had been foretold by " several prophets, with other wonders that he wrought, and the race " of Christians, who are so called from him, remain to this day."

Josephus was born in the first year of Caius Caligula, and was a great commander for the Jews against Vespasian, to whom he afterwards submitted and became a great favourite.

A REVIEW

OF

Fox's Book of Martyrs,

CRITICAL AND HISTORICAL

No. 3. Printed and Published by W. E. Andrews, 3, Chapter-house-court, St. Paul's Churchyard, London. **Price 3d.**

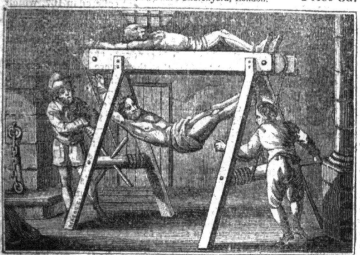

EXPLANATION OF THE ENGRAVING.—*The Roman Rack was a wooden horse; whence its name Equulus. The martyr being laid on two beams joined, with his face turned upwards, and legs across, his arms and legs were bound with cords, called Fidiculæ, which being drawn by pulleys and wheels, or windlasses, distorted and dislocated his body, bruised the feet, and often tore off the nails of the toes. His sides were torn with hooks and scorpions, and burnt with torches. The martyrs often lay several hours in this mangled condition in exquisite torture. By the turning of the cords and pulleys, his body was let fall under the same beams, which opened for that purpose. And whilst he hung by his legs and arms by the cords below the beam, he was interrogated by the judge. This species of torture was exercised with the most wanton barbarity by Protestants in Elizabeth's reign. Edward Campion, a Jesuit, was thrice put to this torture previous to his suffering the punishment of death, and father Robert Owen was racked to death upon it, for no other cause than being Catholic priests.*

THE THIRD PRIMITIVE PERSECUTION UNDER THE ROMAN EMPERORS.

Such is the head given by Fox to his account of the third persecution which the Christian church had to suffer. He says, "Between "the second and the third *Roman* persecution was but ONE YEAR, "Upon Nerva succeeding Domitian, he gave a respite to the Christians; "but reigning only thirteen months, his successor Trajan, in the *tenth* "year of his reign, and in A. D. 108, *began* the third persecution "against them."—Before we proceed any further let us examine this short account here given.—The Christians we are told had only *one year* of peace; and then it is directly stated that the persecution did not begin till the *tenth* year of Trajan, and that he might convey some air of authority, he mentions the year, namely 108. But if the persecution did not *begin* till the *tenth* year of Trajan's reign, and Nerva reigned *thirteen* months, have we not, according to Fox's account, a period of of *eleven years* instead of *one* of peace? However he is not to be relied upon, as we have made clear, and it would have been better for him to have avoided *dates* here, as he did in his account of the two former persecutions; for one of the martyrs he has named, that is, St. Ignatius, was condemned by Trajan himself, and suffered in 107, which is a year *before* the time fixed for the commencement of the persecution by Fox. He then goes on—" Plinius Secundus, *a heathen philoso-* " *pher,* wrote to the emperor, in favour of the Christians, stating that " he found nothing objectionable in their conduct; and that 'the whole " sum of their error consisted in this, that they were wont at certain " times appointed, to meet before day, and to sing certain hymns to " one Christ their God : and to confederate among themselves, to ab- " stain from all theft, murder, and adultery; to keep their faith, and " to defraud no man : which done, then to depart for that time, and " afterwards to resort again to take meat in companies together, both " men and women, one with another, *and yet without any act of evil.*' " To this epistle Trajan returned this indecisive answer : ' That Chris- " tians ought not to be sought after, but when brought before the ma- " gistracy they should be punished.' Provoked by this reply, Tertul- " lian exclaimed, ' O confused sentence ! he would not have them " sought for as innocent men, and yet would have them punished as " guilty.' The emperor's incoherent answer, however, occasioned the " persecution in some measure to abate, as his officers were uncertain, " if they carried it on with severity, how he might choose to wrest his " own meaning.—Trajan, however, soon after wrote to Jerusalem, and " gave orders to exterminate the stock of David; in consequence of " which, all that could be found of that race were put to death. About " *this period* (he adds) the emperor Trajan was succeeded by Adrian; " who continued the persecution with the greatest rigour."

How men, who consider themselves so superior, in point of wisdom and knowledge, to those who believe in the Catholic faith, should be so easily imposed upon by such a random relation as this, is truly a matter of astonishment. And yet this work of John Fox has been, for more than these two centuries, looked upon with nearly the same degree of credit as the gospel itself.—We are told by the martyrologist, that " about *this period* the emperor Trajan was succeeded by Adrian." Now what are we to understand by the two words " this period?"— The only time stated in the passages quoted is the year 108, but Trajan reigned nine years and a half after that date; and Adrian twenty-two years all but one month. The most authentic historians relate that Trajan relented his cruelties before his death, and Adrian did not issue any fresh edicts, nor did the church suffer grievously until the latter emperor had filled the imperial throne eight years.—The occasion of the revival of the persecution by Adrian, is stated by Echard to have been occasioned by the infamous lives of the Gnostics and other heretics, who bearing also the name of Christians, brought odium and scandal on the professors of the true faith. But we must return to the martyrologist's account of Trajan's duplicity. He says, that " while the

"persecution raged Plinius Secundus, *a heathen philosopher*, wrote to
" the emperor in favour of the Christians." Now John Fox must be a
very ignorant or a very impudent writer, for this Plinius Secundus, the
heathen philosopher, was no less a personage than the *governor* of the
Roman provinces of Pontus and Bythinia, Pliny the younger, so called
to distinguish him from his uncle, Pliny the naturalist. Thus we see
Fox confounding the nephew with the uncle, as we proved him, in
our second number, p. 27, making *two* martyrs out of *one* person. In
these provinces, it appears, the Christian religion had spread with astonishing rapidity, and its professors were so eager to lay down their
lives in support of the Divine Truths, that Pliny was at a loss how to
act towards them. He therefore consulted Trajan by letter, and besides the honourable testimony given by this heathen governor to Christian morality, to the progress of Christianity, and the undaunted
courage of its proselytes, he also gives an account of the apostasy of
others, who were base enough to blaspheme the Saviour of the world,
and sacrifice to idols, to escape a little transitory pain.—" While these
" things went on in this manner," writes this governor to Trajan, " the
" error, as is usual, spreading farther, several cases occurred. A li-
" bel was put into my hands with a list of several persons by name ac-
" cused of Christianism; who when they denied, that they either were,
" or had been Christians, and in my presence invoked the gods, and
" offered up wine and incense to your statue, which for that purpose I
" had commanded to be brought with the images of the gods; and
" moreover had cursed Christ, which they say, one can *never force a*
" *good Christian to do*, I dismissed them. Others accused said, they
" had been Christians, but had left off being such, some of them these
" three years, some a great many years ago, and one no less than
" twenty-five years. All these adored your image, the statues of the
" gods, and also cursed Christ." But though these unhappy persons
forsook the truth, through fear or interest, or some other worldly motive, yet Pliny says, they bore witness to the purity of the rites and
ceremonies of the true religion.

Fox and his editors blame the duplicity shewn by Trajan in his
answer above, but his conduct is not more blameable than that pursued by Protestant ascendency-men. Indeed, the situation of the
Catholics under " Protestant ascendency" in this country, forms a
striking similarity to that of the primitive Christians under Pagan
ascendency. In the reign of Elizabeth, such was the terror excited
by the penal laws against Catholics, that many were induced to practice occasional conformity to the *new* church service to save their lives
and estates. When taken up before the magistrates they had only to
forswear their conscience by taking the oath of supremacy, and like
the apostate Christians before Pliny, they were dismissed. Even at
this day let a Catholic, ever so immoral and wicked in his life, but
renounce what are called the errors of Popery, and he instantly becomes
a good Protestant, whilst his apostasy is trumpeted forth in all the public prints as a circumstance worthy of praise. When the Catholics
petition to be placed upon the same *civil* equality as their neighbours,
being now in a state of debasement, exclusively on account of their
religious doctrines; are they not answered by " Protestant ascendency,"

that they have perfect freedom of conscience and perfect toleration, though they are punished with the loss of their *civil* immunities for exercising the freedom of conscience ?   What can we say to this system of duplicity, but in words similar to those used by Tertullian— " O confused and unjust sentence ! you make the crime to punish the " person ; and when he solicits to be relieved from this punishment, " you tell him he is not in a state of infliction !"   Oh ! admirable " Protestant ascendency."

But let us now look to the martyrs recorded by John Fox under this persecution.   The first is thus stated :—" Phocas, bishop of Pontus, " refusing to sacrifice to *Neptune*, was by the *immediate* order of Tra- " jan, cast first into a hot lime-kiln, and being drawn from thence, " was thrown into a scalding bath till he expired."   We might suppose that the hot lime-kiln was sufficient to cause death to the martyr, without the scalding bath, unless indeed he was preserved in the first instance by the hand of Omnipotence.   We have seen that St. John the evangelist was preserved without injury in the cauldron of boiling oil, not that he might immediately undergo death by a different mode, but that he might *live* to bear testimony to the divine Truths he was commissioned by God to teach.   The account is absurd on the face of it, for certainly some reason should have been given for the martyr's escape from the first torture said to have been inflicted.   But what will the reader say, when he is informed that John Fox has fallen into a gross error, and that the person here described as a *bishop* and suffering under Trajan by being *scalded alive*, was *a gardener* of Sinope, in the province of Pontus, who suffered about the year 303, in the *tenth* persecution under Dioclesian, by being *beheaded*. He has, according to his usual custom, confined himself to bare assertion ; we, on the contrary, have examined authorities ; and we find in the Rev. Mr. Butler's *Lives of the Fathers, Martyrs*, &c. an account of St. Phocas, collected from his panegyric, written by St. Asterius, and another written by St. Chrysostom, l. ii, ed. Ben. p. 704, Ruinart. p. 627.   This account says, " St. Phocas dwelt near the gate of Sinope, a city of Pontus, and " lived by cultivating a garden, which yielded him a handsome subsist- " ence, and wherewith plentifully to relieve the indigent....His house " was open to all strangers and travellers who had no lodging in the " place ; and after having for many years most liberally bestowed the " fruit of his labour on the poor, he was found worthy also to give his " life for Christ.   Though his *profession was obscure*, he was well known " over the whole country by the reputation of his charity and virtue." It then goes on to say, that when a cruel persecution was suddenly raised in the church, probably that of Dioclesian in 303, Phocas was immediately impeached as a Christian, and such was the notoriety of his pretended crime, that he was ordered to be put to death without the formality of a trial.   This was executed, by striking off his head, under circumstances wherein his hospitality and courage were peculiarly displayed towards the executioners who were sent to dispatch him. The memory of this martyr, we are assured, was held in the highest veneration by the Catholics in the Euxine, Ægean, and Adriatic seas, and particularly by the sailors, who sung hymns to his honour.   It is related by St. Asterius, bishop of Amasea, about the year 400, in a

discourse which he pronounced on the festival of this martyr, " that a
" certain king of barbarians had sent his royal diadem set with jewels,
" and his rich helmet a present to the church of St. Phocas, praying
" the martyr to offer it to the Lord in thanksgiving for the kingdom
" which his divine Majesty had bestowed upon him." St. Chrysostom
also, in one of two sermons, preached by him on a great festival of this
saint, says, " that the emperors left their palaces to *reverence these relics*
" (of St. Phocas), and strove to share with the rest in the blessings
" which they procure to men." *(See Butler.)* This author further states,
that " the Greeks often style St. Phocas hiero-martyr, or sacred martyr,
" which epithet they often give to eminent martyrs who were *not* bishops,
" as Ruinart demonstrates against Baronius." From this account it is
evidently manifest, that Fox is under *a mistake* in his relation ; and it is
further manifest, that the primitive Christians practised venerating the
relics and invoking the prayers of the saints and martyrs, as Catholics
do at this day, while Protestants believe and swear such practices are
damnable and idolatrous. This point is necessary to be borne in mind,
as without such a retention on the side of the reader it will be impossible
for him to come at the truth, and act the part of an impartial juror be-
between Fox and our Review of him. While, however, we are detect-
ing the lies and errors of John Fox, it is but justice to the public that
we should, to avoid cavil, point out an error in each of our preceding
numbers. In a great part of the impression of the first number the com-
positor put *America* for Armenia (see page 2, line 13 from bottom) ;
and in our second number we have inadvertently, in page 19, named
Leo the 12th for Leo the 10th. These mistakes we have corrected in
the latter impressions.

The next martyr noticed by Fox is the great St. Ignatius, and his account is as follows : "Trajan likewise commanded the martyrdom of
" Ignatius, bishop of Antioch. This holy man was the person whom,
" when an infant, Christ took into his arms and shewed to his disciples,
" as one that would be a pattern of humility and innocence. He receiv-
" ed the gospel afterwards from St. John the evangelist, and was ex-
" ceedingly zealous in his mission. He boldly vindicated the faith of
" Christ before the emperor for which he was cast into prison, and was
" tormented in a cruel manner ; for, after being dreadfully scourged, he
" was compelled to hold fire in his hands, and, at the same time, pa-
" pers dipped in oil were put to his sides, and set alight, His flesh
" was then torn with red hot pincers, and at last he was dispatched by-
" being torn to pieces by wild beasts."

Where Fox obtained his information respecting the infancy of St.
Ignatius, and our Saviour's exhibiting him to his disciples as a future
pattern of humility and innocence, he does not tell us, and we have no
doubt of its being a fiction. Neither have we any substantial evidence
that this martyr suffered the torments which the martyrologist says he
did. Echard writes, that some *reported* that he was subjected to the
most severe and merciless torments ; it is but justice, however, to the
memory of Trajan, by whom St. Ignatius was condemned, to observe,
that not a Catholic writer we have met with describe St. Ignatius as
undergoing any torture but that of suffering death by wild beasts ; two
fierce lions being let out upon him, they instantly devoured him, leav-

ing nothing but his large bones. While, however, we doubt and even deny the accuracy of this part of Fox's statement, we are ready to allow the correctness of his assertion, that this martyr "received the " gospel from St. John the evangelist, and was exceedingly zealous in " his mission." Yes, we have it from the most authentic source, that St. Ignatius was not only a disciple of St. John, but also of SS. Peter and Paul, who united their labours in planting the faith of Christ at Antioch, and that he succeeded St. Peter in that see, after Evodius. Such a character was therefore well able to give an account of the doctrine he was going to suffer for, and such an account he did give, though John Fox thought it best to *suppress* this very important *fact*. St. Ignatius was condemned by Trajan at *Antioch*, and his sentence was, "It is " our will, that Ignatius, who says he carries the crucified man within " him, be bound and conducted to *Rome*, to be there devoured by wild " beasts, for the amusement of the people." Consequently the good bishop had a long journey to undertake, during which it will appear that his zeal in his mission was not in the least abated. On his arrival at Smyrna, he had an interview with the holy bishop of that place, Polycarp, of whom we shall have to speak hereafter. Here also St. Ignatius wrote four epistles to the Christians of four different church-es, namely, the Ephesians, the Magnesians, the Thrallians and Romans. At Troas he wrote three other epistles, one to the church of Philadel-phia, the second to that of Smyrna, and the third to St. Polycarp. It was also his intention to have written to some other churches in Asia, but not being allowed time, he commissioned St. Polycarp to do it for him.

We have observed, in our introductory remarks, that the doctrines of Christ were *openly taught*, both by himself and his apostles; that they were attested by miracles of the most extraordinary kind, and such as could not be wrought but by a divine hand; that by these supernatural occurrences an appeal was made to PUBLIC OPINION, which was so far convincing, that in spite of all the powers of the world, and the work-ings of the human passions, these doctrines, combined with the purest system of morality, made the most rapid progress amongst mankind, and in nations differing in customs and habits, yet preserving the same unity in faith. "The Christian religion," writes the Rev. Mr. Echard, prebendary of Lincoln, in his *General Ecclesiastical History*, "was now " (A. D. 101) spread through the greatest part of Europe, Asia, and " Africa, extending from the British islands to the farthest Indies; and " fixing not only in cities and populous places, but also in towns and " country villages, as Pliny himself testifies. The metropolitan cities " were all under bishops of the greatest eminency and piety; and the " four great cities of the Roman empire, Rome, Alexandria, Antioch, " and Jerusalem, usually styled apostolic churches, were governed by " apostolical men, viz. Evaristus in Rome, Cerdo in Alexandria, Igna-" tius in Antioch, and Simeon in Jerusalem. Besides these, we find " Publius in Athens, Polycarp in Smyrna, Onesimus in Ephesus, Papias " in Hierapolis, with many others of primitive integrity. This was the " state of the church in the beginning of the second century, increasing " and flourishing after a stupendous manner; but grievously afflicted " on one side by the malice of the Jews and Pagans, and the present " persecution under this emperor (Trajan), and no less wounded on the

" other by the heretics, the Simonians, the Gnostics, the Menandrians,
" the Ebonites, the Cerinthians, and the Nicolatians : yet still it stood
" FIRM AS A ROCK against all the powers of hell; *shining and tri-*
" *umphing in the glories of the utmost purity and piety.*"

We also observed, that when the hostile powers of the world prevented the church from assembling her depositaries of this Christian
and immutable faith in general councils or parliaments, to define disputed dogmas, there were always to be fouud learned scholars and able
writers to defend the truth, and enable the people to shun the snares of
error. The first of these, in the second age of the church, was our present martyr, whose death Fox has recorded with much repletion, but
has passed over the most important acts of his life. This it is absolutely necessary to fill up, or the reader will not be able to discover
the truth, which we are desirous he should, for without such knowledge
judgment will be made on *false* premises. At this time, as related by
Echard, there were many teachers of erroneous doctrines, and it was to
caution the true Christians against being *deceived* by these seducers
that St. Ignatius wrote to the different churches founded by the
apostles. In his epistle to the Ephesians he says, " Let no one de-
" ceive himself; if he be not within the inclosure of the altar, he is de-
" prived of the bread of God. There are deceivers who talk much of
" God, but do things unworthy of him : these you must avoid as you
" would the approaches of so many wild beasts ; for they are mad dogs
" who bite unawares : against whom you must guard yourselves, as
" men hardly to be cured. There is but *one* Physician corporeal and
" spiritual, made and *not made*; GOD in man ; true life in death ; first
" passible then impassible ; even Jesus Christ our Lord ... Our GOD
" Jesus Christ... was conceived in the womb of Mary of the seed of
" David, but by the Holy Ghost... Now the virginity of Mary, her
" bringing forth a child, and the death of our Lord were kept secret from
" the prince of the world. *How then became he manifest to the world?*
" A star shone out of the heavens, with a brightness beyond all other
" stars ... to which the sun and moon with all the lesser lights were
" the chorus ... Hence the power of magic grew faint, and every bond
" of wickedness dissolved away." From these words it is incontrovertible that this martyr, who was a disciple of the apostles, believed and taught the *divinity* and *incarnation* of Christ the second
person of the holy Trinity. These mysteries then were part of the
revelations the apostles were commanded to carry throughout the
world, and this *fact* is also worthy of notice, that not a single nation
was converted to Christianity without believing in these mysteries.

In his epistle to the people of Magnesia, he exhorts them to *unity* in
their faith, which is one of the four marks of the true church. He
writes, " Avoiding heterodox opinions, and useless fables—labour to
" be strengthened in the doctrines of the Lord and of the apostles, in
" order that you prosper in all things, in body and spirit, in faith and
" charity—together with your respectable bishop, the united college of
" priests, and holy deacons. Be submissive to the bishop and to one
" another, as Jesus Christ, according to the flesh, was to his Father,
" and the apostles to Christ, and to the Father and the Holy Spirit—

" that your union be in body and spirit." *Ap. ad Magnesios Inter PP. Apost.* t. ii, *p.* 21.   *Ed Amstelædami*, 1724.

This unity is preserved in the Catholic church by all the clergy and laity dispersed throughout the whole universe acknowledging the bishop of Rome to be its head, which Protestants deny.   Many even doubt that St. Peter ever was at Rome, though John Fox admits that he was there put to death, and buried.   Others say, that as St. Peter raised the see of Antioch before he established that of Rome, the bishop of Antioch ought to have the supremacy.   St. Ignatius however, who must have been a better judge of the rights of his church, as he was cotemporary with the apostles, knew different, for in directing his aforesaid epistles he makes a distinction in favour of Rome, *as having a supremacy*.   In saluting the former churches he writes, "To the " blessed church which is at Ephesus : at Magnesia near the Mæander : " at Tralles : at Philadelphia : at Smyrna :" but, in that to the Romans, he changes his style, and addresses his letter : "To the beloved church " which is enlightened (by the will of Him who ordaineth all things " which are according to the charity of Jesus Christ our God), which " *presides* in the country of the Romans," &c. *(See Butler's Saint's Lives, Feb.* 1.)   That St. Ignatius held the doctrine of the real presence in the Eucharist and Mass, or transubstantiation, is also clear from his epistles to the Smyrneans and Romans.   To the first he writes thus of the Gnostic heretics : they "abstain from the Eucharist and from prayer, " because they do not acknowledge the Eucharist to be the flesh of " our Saviour Jesus Christ, which suffered for our sins, and which the " Father by his goodness resuscitated.   Rejecting therefore the gift of " God they die in their disputes." *Ep. ad Smyrn. p.* 36.   *T.* ii. *PP. Apost. Amstelædami*, 1724.   To the latter, "I take no delight in food " that perishes, nor in the pleasures of this life.   What I desire is the " bread of God, the heavenly bread, the bread of life, which is the " flesh of Jesus Christ the son of God, who was born of the seed of " David ; and I desire to drink of God, his blood, which is charity " incorruptible and eternal life." *Ep. ad Rom. p.* 29.   Is it possible to make words more plain and distinct on this article of Christian faith ? yet Protestants not only reject it, but in this country they are compelled to disavow on oath what St. Ignatius had received from the apostles, and are deemed ineligible to civil office until they have made a declaration of its being damnable and idolatrous.   Of course John Fox could have no claim to St. Ignatius as a martyr of his church ; he belongs to the Catholic church, which believes in this doctrine and commemorates his memory to this day, by offering up that sacrifice of the mass to his honour, 'which he himself used to offer to God in honour of the saints and martyrs who preceded him.

Without entering into a doctrinal disquisition, these matters are well worthy the consideration of the reader desirous to find the truth, only as *historical facts;* because they shew what was the belief of the primitive Christians, and will enable him to distinguish between what was *then* and what is *now* taught. These writings of St. Ignatius may be denied, as indeed that proving the *real presence* was denied by John Calvin, but they cannot be *disproved*. Dr. Pearson, the learned Pro-

testant bishop of Chester, most ably refuted the sophism of Calvin, and
"the whole seven epistles, the same which were quoted by St. Irenæus,
"Origen, Eusebius, St. Athanasius, St. Chrysostom, Theodoret, Gildas,
"&c. are published genuine," writes Mr. Butler, "by Usher, Vossius,
"Cotelier, &c. and in English by archbishop Wake in 1710." A copy
of St. Ignatius' works is we believe to be seen in the college at Manchester.

St. Symphorosa and her seven sons are next recorded; but here the
martyrologist commits another *mistake*. He says they "were com-
"manded by *Trajan* to sacrifice to the heathen deities;" whereas according to the most authentic writers the martyrdom of this holy
widow and her sons did not take place till late in the reign of the emperor *Adrian*. Trajan's persecution continued partially during the
first year of the reign of his successor, when Adrian put a stop to it,
being moved, according to conjecture, by the apologies of Quadratus
bishop of Athens, and Aristides, a Christian philosopher of that city,
as well as by a letter written in favour of the Christians by Serenius
Granianus, proconsul of Asia. St. Quadratus, speaking of the prodigies performed in testimony of the divine essence of the Christian religion, says, "But as to the miracles of our Saviour, they always re-
"mained, because they were real and true. The sick cured, and the
"dead by him raised, did not only appear restored, but they remained
"so both whilst Christ was on earth, and long after he was departed,
"so that some of them have come down to our time." Trajan died in
117, and Echard notes the death of Symphorosa and her sons in 125, but
Butler, who takes the account from the genuine acts in Ruinart, places
their martyrdom later. This latter author says, that after some respite
had been granted to the church, it was again subjected to persecution,
in consequence of the Pagans involving the Christians in the disgrace
which the Jews drew upon themselves in their last rebellion, which
gave occasion to the final destruction of Jerusalem in 134. Adrian,
towards the end of his reign, erected a magnificent country palace at
Tibur, now Tivoli, sixteen miles from Rome, which he furnished with
the most curious articles he could collect out of the different provinces.
On completing the building he wished to dedicate it by heathenish ceremonies, and offered sacrifices to induce the idols to deliver their oracles. But, writes Mr. Butler, the demons answered, "The widow
"Symphorosa and her seven sons daily torment us by invoking their
"God; if they sacrifice we promise to be favourable to your vows."—
Adrian, in consequence of this answer, ordered the good widow and
her sons to be brought before him, and when he found that neither
threats nor torments were able to subdue the invincibility of her soul,
he commanded her to be put to death, which was accordingly done by
throwing her into the Tyber. The next day her sons were brought before him, when preserving the constancy of their mother, they were
all put to death by the command of the tyrant, who soon after, namely,
in 138, perished miserably himself.

The paragraph that follows is an admirable specimen of the *confused*
mode John Fox adopts to *enlighten* his readers. "About this time (he
"writes) Alexander, bishop of Rome, after filling that office ten years,
"was martyred, as were his two deacons; and also Quirinus and Hermes,

"with their families; Zenon, a Roman nobleman, and about ten thou-
"sand other Christians." How indefinite is this narrative. What are
we to understand by "*About this time?*" We have just proved the inaccuracy of Fox's calculation with respect to St. Symphorosa's death,
which he says took place in Trajan's reign, and we have proved from
authority must have happened in that of Adrian; so here, if we are to
suppose he alludes to the time of Symphorosa's martyrdom, he has committed another error. St. Alexander succeeded St. Evaristus in 109,
and suffered in 119, consequently he suffered in the second year of Adrian. He is the first bishop of Rome mentioned by Fox after St. Peter
as suffering death for the faith, though his predecessors in the papal
chair, Linus, Cletus, Clement, Anacletus, and Evaristus, all suffered
martyrdom. That Alexander was not a Protestant martyr is clear by
his being named to this day in the canon of the mass, and ranked the
sixth head of the Catholic church from St. Peter. Of the other martyrs named we can trace no account; there is a St. Quirinus in the Roman martyrology, but he suffered in 304, and was a bishop, therefore
he had no family.

THE FOURTH PERSECUTION, UNDER THE ROMAN EMPE-RORS, WHICH COMMENCED A. D. 162.

In this persecution, which finds its place in the reign of Marcus Aurelius, the Christians suffered much, which induced St. Justin, Melito,
Athenagoras and Apollinaris, to write apologies to the emperor, entreating him to clemency. Fox says, " many Christians were martyr-
" ed, particularly in several parts of Asia, and in Franci." This latter assertion is a base falsehood, there being no such country as
France at this period, as we shall shew hereafter. He next repeats the
various modes of torture adopted by the Pagans to shake the constancy
of the Christians, but he does not describe the system of truth they followed, and by which they were distinguished from others laying claim
to the same honourable title. This is a grand omission, because it
leaves the reader in a state of ignorance, and shuts upon him the door
of the temple of truth. We have seen a work purporting to be written *against* the evidence of Christianity, and in *favour* of what is called
Deism. The writer is bold in assertion, very ready in rejecting facts
that bear testimony to the divinity of the Catholic or Universal rule of
faith, equally ready in admitting other facts of an opposite tendency,
though not a bit better authenticated, and confounds every discordant
creed in the term *Christianity.* Here is the source of error; it is the
want of discrimination, the allowing some unerring guide to regulate
our wandering senses, that gives rise to this state of ignorance on
matters so necessary to the happiness of mankind. When we reflect
that religion has existed from the beginning of the world, that
even the rude uncultivated savage has some notion of a supreme being, and some mode of religious worship, we cannot but smile at
the vain folly of the deist, who flatters himself that he shall one
day banish religion from amongst mankind. The unbeliever in revealed religion professes to be a lover of truth; there is nothing so sacred in his eye, as this bright attribute of the Deity; but HOW can
he discover THE TRUTH without admitting SOME RULE OR

GUIDE TO DIRECT HIS MIND? Can he of himself obtain
even the knowledge of sounds, so as to converse with his fellowman,
without an *instructor?* He knows it is impossible. There must be
some general rule, some authority, to cultivate the mind, and if that
rule or authority is departed from, man becomes a bewildered being. To talk then of nature being the god of the deists is, we think,
one of the grossest pieces of absurdity ever uttered. Man to be sure
comes into the world by the law of nature, but he is fitted for society
by the force of example; and it was first by instruction, and next by the
power of example, aided by the demonstration of a divine hand, in performing acts *contrary* to the law of nature, that the Pagan, the Jew, the
Gentile, and the Philosopher, entered the pale of Christianity, and braved
all the terrors of pain and death, to evince their conviction of its divine
origin.   •

The deist contends, that " Whatever is unfolded to the mind of man
" as a *natural* truth, and the *operations* of *nature* as to *that* truth made
" visible to him, he cannot reject, he cannot even doubt it. The im-
" pression is as strongly fixed on his mind, and makes part of his mind,
" as his nose is on his face, and makes part of his face. But such is not the
" case (he says) with the pretended written revelations of the Deity; *every*
" inquirer who has *mental capacity* and *candour* is COMPELLED, from *the*
" *want of evidence*, to reject them, and the *ignorant* and *interested* alone AD-
" HERE TO THEM."—We cannot but smile at the arrogance of these rejecters of divine revelation, who have assumed all the common sense of the
world to themselves, and make the greatest part of mankind no other
than ignorant or interested fools ! ! ! There is certainly a *want* of candour and mental capacity in this assertion, and we think the charge of
ignorance much more applicable to the asserter than to those who are
accused. But *why* the inquirer after divine revelations should be compelled to reject them, from a want of evidence, the deist does not *prove;*
nor can he bring forward a particle of rational evidence in support of
his assertion. The way he attempts to make good his assertion is, by
rejecting evidence as clear to the unprejudiced Christian, as a natural
truth can be to the mind of the deist.—The Christian has *authority* for
his belief, and the deist must have the same for many of his natural
truths. For example, it is a natural truth that the deist had a father
and mother to bring him into the world, and yet this truth he could
not learn of himself, he could only have it from *authority* or *revelation.*
He knows his father and mother he will say.; but *how* can he tell but
by *authority* or *revelation?* He may talk as long as he pleases about a
natural truth being made *visible* to him, but after all he can know
nothing in the *first* instance *without authority* or *revelation.*--Can a human being know a dwelling-house from a barn, without being first
told the difference between the two buildings ?—They may be *visible* to
him, but he could not know the purposes for which they were raised
until he had applied to some authority for information. Hence autho-
-rity or revelation is every thing with mankind, and it should be man's
study to learn the *source* from whence that authority or revelation proceeds : whether it is human or divine. When man was first created,
he did not know from whence he sprung; the information was however *revealed* to him. He knew he did not make himself, that he owed

his existence to a power superior to himself. That power exacted an acknowledgment from man, and man rendered him sacrifice, as a mark of his obedience. Here was the first foundation of RELIGION. This revelation was continued from father to son, by a general tradition, but at length, a written law was given under circumstances clearly contrary to the operations of nature. The Jews then living beheld the scene before them; it was made visible to them, and the impression became as strongly stamped upon their minds as the nose upon their faces. They communicated this fact to their children, and from their children it was handed down to their children's children, who also had the impression fixed upon their minds, and it made a part of their minds as much as any natural truth could on that of the deist. It is believed by them to this day, and they have better authority for believing in the old testament than the deist for disbelieving in it.

At a period foretold by holy men of the Jewish nation, the Messiah or Redeemer, whose appearance in human shape formed an essential part of the divine revelations, was announced; and to the first inquirers after his divine commission, the gospel of St. Matthew says his answer was this : " Go relate to John what you have HEARD and " SEEN. The blind see, the lame walk, the lepers are cleansed, the " deaf hear, the dead rise again, the poor have the gospel preached to " them." (c. xi, 4, 5.) Here then was an appeal to their common sense ; our Saviour did not bid them, rely upon his sole word as man, but he bid them exercise their reasoning faculties ; he referred them to the doctrines they had *heard*, and the prodigies they had *seen*, and then he left them to say whether his *revelations* were or were not entitled to credit, coming as they did from the mouth of one whom the winds and the sea, and even nature itself obeyed. And here, we will take the liberty to ask, if those who heard the sublimity of the precepts laid down for their guidance, and saw these wonders, had not evidence sufficient to convince the most sceptical ? We are aware that 'the deist denies the existence of these miracles ; but we must here retort upon him, and tell him, by this line of conduct he shews his want of candour, by setting up his own single individual notions against the universal belief of the whole Christian world ; and surely it is much more consonant to common sense to *believe* what all the world has believed before us, than to *reject* this belief in the face of such incontrovertible testimony ? It is a common saying, " What every body says must be *true*," and this we consider as strongly applicable to the divine origin of Christianism. After the consummation of the mission of the Redeemer, the men he had chosen to carry his doctrines to all nations began to preach those doctrines in the face of a people hitherto accustomed to a different system of discipline, and before others who were utterly ignorant of divine revelation. Their words were accompanied with the performance of deeds that could not be doubted, and the example of their lives carried conviction of the sincerity of their doctrines. These are facts as well authenticated and as worthy of testimony, as any connected with the history of this country : nay, more so, because there is not a country in the world that has received Christianity but gives credit to these facts, whereas the incidents related as having taken place at certain periods in England, are confined to writers living in the island. Why

then should we doubt what *all* the world believes, yet give credit to what is related of only a small part of it? This is evidently showing a want of mental capacity, and betrays an ignorance of history by no means creditable to the searcher after truth However, considering the use that has been made of THE PRESS in this country, since the pretended reformation of religion, it is not surprising that men should write in this strain of arrogance and ignorance, upbraiding others for wanting that of which they are themselves destitute, as we have shewn by these remarks. We do not wonder that deism has spread so much in this country, when such pains have been taken to disfigure THE TRUTH, through the use of *the press*, of which *Fox's Book of Martyrs* is a striking instance. In the course of his detail of the primitive martyrs we have not a single attempt to elucidate the *doctrines* they preached, but only a recital of their sufferings, and that in a confused manner, frequently accompanied with falsehood. Hence father Parsons, almost prophetically observed, that from the beginning to the end, Fox "com-
"monly setteth down nothing *affirmative* or *positive* of his own in matters
" of religion, nor *any certain rule* what to believe; but only carpeth and
" scoffeth at that which was in use before; so, as the reader is brought
" into *unbelief, distrust, and contempt* of that which was accompted
" piety and religion by his forefathers, and *nothing certain* taught him
" in place thereof, but only negative or scornful taunts, *the proper means*
" *to make* ATHEISTS *and* INFIDELS."
But it is time to leave this digression, and return to the examination of the martyrs. The first recorded under this persecution by Fox is St. Germanicus, whose astonishing constancy when delivered to the wild beasts, he says, caused many Pagans to become Christians, and exasperated others to call for the death of St. Polycarp, bishop of Smyrna. Fox says, the holy bishop, " was the scholar and hearer of John the evan-
" gelist, and was placed by him in Smyrna." This is very true, and so is the account given of his martyrdom; but why not inform the world *what* it was he preached, and *how* he came by the knowledge of his doctrines? *Then*, as is the case *now*, there were constant attempts made to corrupt the TRUTH, which Christ promised should never be contaminated. According to the ecclesiastical history of Eusebius (l. v. c. 20.) we are told that when one Florinus, who had often visited St. Polycarp, had broached certain heresies, St. Irenæus wrote to him in the following terms: " These things were not taught you by the bishops who preced-
" ed us. I could tell you the place where the blessed Polycarp sat to
" preach the word of God. It is yet present to my mind with what
" gravity he every where came in and went out : what was the sanctity
" of his deportment, the majesty of his countenance and of his whole
" exterior, and what were his holy exhortations to the people. I seem
" to hear him now relate how he conversed with John and many others,
" who had seen Jesus Christ; the words he had heard from their
" mouths. I can protest before God, that if this holy bishop had heard
" of any error like yours, he would have immediately stopped his ears,
" and cried out, according to his custom : Good God ! that I should be
" reserved to these times to hear such things ! That very instant he
" would have fled out of the place in which he had heard such doctrine."
St. Polycarp embraced the gospel when young, and was a minister

thereof about 70 years, consequently he was fully competeht to ascertain and teach the truths of Christianity.   That he was a Catholic and
not a Protestant, is proved by a letter from the church of Smyrna to the
faithful of Philomelia, in which is related all that happened to the holy
bishop, and it distinctly says that this illustrious disciple of St. John
" offered up his prayers for the members of the whole Catholic church
" dispersed throughout the world." *Apud Euseb,* l. iv. c. xv.

The next in succession are thus mentioned : "Metrodorus, a minis-
" ter, who preached boldly, and Pionius, who made some excellent
" apologies for the Christian faith, were likewise burnt.   Carpus and
" Papilus, two worthy Christians, and Agathonica, a pious woman, suf-
" fered martyrdom at Pergamopolis, in Asia, about the *same* period."
We have examined the Roman martyrology, and can find no account
at all of the last named martyrs; but of Pionius, we discover John Fox
has made another *mistake* as to his *periods.*   Pionius was a priest of
Smyrna, but, according to the acts of his life, written by eye witnesses, and quoted by Eusebius, l. iv. c. 15, he suffered in 230, under
the persecution of Decius.   There is nothing said in the acts of St.
Pionius of his having made apologies for the Christian faith, but he is
described to have been a truly apostolic man, exceedingly eloquent,
and well grounded in the science of true religion.

Fox next gives an account of the martyrdom of " Felicitatas, an il-
" lustrious Roman lady of a considerable family and great virtues,"
and her seven sons.   He relates that the three younger sons were beheaded, and that " the mother was beheaded with the *same* sword."—
We have here another proof of the little credit due to Fox's veracity.
From their genuine acts in Ruinart and Tillemont, t. ii, the martyrdom of these saints took place under the emperor Antoninus Pius, who
preceded Marcus Aurelius, the fourth general persecutor.—Neither
have we any authority that the *same* sword was used in beheading the
mother which beheaded her three younger sons, for she was not executed till *four months after* her sons suffered.

We now come to notice a martyr of no ordinary degree, namely, St.
Justin, the great philosopher and eloquent apologist for the Christians.
Fox states, " he was a native of Neapolis, in Samaria, and was born
" A. D. 103.   He had the *best education* those times could afford, and
" travelled into Egypt, the country where the polite tour of that age
" was made for improvement.   At Alexandria he was informed of every
" thing relative to the Seventy interpreters of the sacred writings, and
" shewn the rooms, or rather cells, in which their work was perform-
" ed.   Justin was *a great lover of truth* and an *universal scholar*; he in-
" vestigated the Stoic and Peripatetic philosophy, and attempted the
" Phythagorean system; but the behaviour of one of its professors dis-
" gusting him, he applied himself to the Platonic, in which he took
" great delight.   About the year 133, when he was thirty years of age,
" he became a convert to Christianity."---From this account given by
Fox, which is pretty correct, it is clear that St. Justin was not void of
" *mental capacity*;" he was " a great lover of truth," he made every
inquiry possible after it, and instead of being " *compelled*" to reject " the
" pretended written revelations of the Deity," it appears he could not
discover *the truth any where else,* and that he *voluntarily* embraced them,

an age too when the mind was in full vigour. Nay, he did more. After having convinced himself of the mysteries and truths of the Christian religion, he exercised his "*mental capacity*" with zeal and perseverance in defending the system he had adopted after a laborious pursuit, and this with such force and animation, as to set contradiction at defiance. Fox says, "It appears that only seven pieces of the writings "of this celebrated martyr, and great philosopher, are now extant, "viz. the two Apologies ; an Exhortation to the Gentiles ; an Oration "to the Greeks ; a Treatise on Divine Monarchy : a Dialogue with "Trypho the Jew ; and an Epistle to Diagnetus." But why did not the martyrologist give some account of the doctrines defended by "this "celebrated martyr and great philosopher," in proof of the *truth* of the Christian religion ? He could not be ignorant that there were at that time *diversities of creeds*, arising from the perversity of human reason ; therefore he ought, when recording the death of this eloquent apologist, to have given his readers some account of the sentiments of his life. This omission we must supply, as it is absolutely necessary to come at the truth, the whole truth, and we wish to state nothing but the truth.

The first of the apologies was addressed to the emperor Antoninus Pius and his two sons about the year 150. This emperor had published no new edicts against the Christians, yet by virtue of former edicts, they were often persecuted by the governors of provinces, and were every where traduced as an abominable race of wicked and barbarous people, as Catholics are at this present day by the bigots of "Protestant ascendency." The crimes and abominations of the Gnostic and Carpocratian sects, whose practices were too lewd and unnatural to be named by us, were charged to the real Christians ; and these circumstances stirred up the zeal of St. Justin, who thought he could not do a greater service to his fellow Christians than by writing an apology, to which he also affixed his name. Addressing himself to the emperor, he says, "That this discourse may not be looked upon a bold flourish only, we "desire a strict information be made of the crimes laid to the Chris-"tians' charge ; and if upon examination the allegations prove true, "let them be punished, not only according to, but even beyond their "deserts ; but if nothing criminal can be made out against us, reason "dictates, that a harmless people ought not to be injured upon bare "report. You cannot but be sensible that some of your own philoso-"phers teach atheism, and that the poets with a great deal of liberty "play upon Jupiter and his young ones. However the philosophers' "books are not forbid, and the poets if they are but impertinent with "a good grace, their wit shall atone for their boldness, and laurels "crown their heads without fearing a blast from the thunderer, Nay "they are not barely honoured, but rewarded with offices and money "into the bargain. What recompense then do we deserve who make "profession of condemning all sorts of injustice, and abhorring the "impiety of your authors. But you take these things upon trust ; "pardon and punish at random, according as the fury of a brutal pas-"sion, or the instigation of evil demons hurry you on....We of all "mankind are the greatest promoters of public peace, who teach, that "it is impossible for any traitor, villain, or miser, for any one either

" vicious or virtuous to hide himself from God; and that every one is
" stepping to everlasting misery, or endless happiness, according to his
" works; and if all men were once fully possessed with a notion of
" these things, who would make the bold adventure to embrace the
" pleasures of sin for a season, with his eye upon eternal fire at the end
" of the enjoyment? Who would not strive all he could to check him-
" self upon the brink of ruin, and to adorn his mind with such virtues
" as might give him admission to the good things of God, and secure
" him from everlasting vengeance? Now were your offenders....
" fully convinced of the impossibility of concealing any thing from
" God, not only the works of their hands, but even the motion of their
" minds, the direful storm of wrath they see just dropping on their
" heads, would make them haste to a better course of life, as you your-
" self must own; but you seem to be afraid that this notion would force
" every one to be good, and so quite and clean spoil your trade of
" punishing: this executioners perhaps may be afraid of, but surely pious
" princes never can. Our Master Jesus Christ has foretold our suffer-
" ings,... which we see fulfilled according to his prediction; now this
" or nothing is the work of God, to declare a thing shall come to be,
" long before it is in being; and then bring about that thing to pass ac-
" cording to that declaration. This Master, born and crucified under
" Pontius Pilate,.. we know to be the Son of the true God, and there-
" fore honour him in the second place, and the prophetic spirit in the
" third. In obedience to this Master, we who heretofore gave a loose to
" debaucheries, now strictly contain within the bonds of chastity; we
" who devoted ourselves to magic arts; now consecrate ourselves to the
" goodness of God. We who sought after nothing so much as riches,
" now put all our stock in common, and spread it before our indigent
" brethren; we who were pointed with mutual hatred and destruction,
" and would not so much as warm ourselves at the same fire,.. now
" cohabit and diet together, and pray for our enemies; and all our re-
" turns for evils are but the gentle persuasives to convert those that un-
" justly hate us; that by living up to the same virtuous precepts of
" Christ, they may have the same comfortable hopes of obtaining the
" same bliss with us, from that God, who is Lord of all things. The
" inward desires as well as the outward actions, are equally manifest to
" God. And I can produce abundance of both sexes, who have from
" their childhood been discipled unto Christ, and lived in a constant
" course of spotless virginity to 60 or 70 years of age; and I cannot but
" glory in being able to produce so many instances of Christian purity
" out of every nation, and of people of violence and oppression trans-
" formed into quite another nature, perfectly overcome by the passive
" courage of their Christian neighbours. We render unto God only
" the tribute of divine worship, and to you a cheerful obedience in
" all things else; acknowledging you to be emperors and rulers upon
" earth, and offering up our prayers, that you may be found to have
" right reason joined with your sovereign power."

Having thus described, with a strict regard to truth and justice, the
situation and conduct of the Christians, Justin next proceeds to explain
some of their *doctrines.* In consequence of the terror of the times, and
the malice of the enemies of Christianity, its professors were obliged to

A REVIEW

or

Fox's Book of Martyrs,

CRITICAL AND HISTORICAL.

No. 4.   Printed and Published by W. E. Andrews, 3, Chapter-
house-court, St. Paul's Churchyard, London.   Price 3d.

EXPLANATION OF THE ENGRAVING.—*The subject of the present cut is the miraculous deliverance of the Roman army in the year 151, through the prayers of a Christian legion. The army was surrounded by the enemy, and in danger of perishing through famine. The Roman soldiers are represented as fighting and refreshing themselves with the descending rain at the same time; while thunder and lightning are striking terror into the opposing army, and casting both men and horses to the ground. A particular description of this historical fact will be found in this sheet.*

CONTINUATION OF THE REVIEW.

meet in private to celebrate the divine mysteries of the Eucharist and the sacrifice of the Mass; this privacy, forced upon them by circumstances over which they had no control, occasioned a report to be circulated, that the Christians were child-murderers, cannibals, and partakers of human flesh; on which St. Justin describes their faith as well as the ceremonies which take place in these clear and explicit terms: "Our prayers being finished, we embrace one another with the kiss of "peace. Then to him who presides over the brethren, is presented "bread and wine tempered with water; having received which, he "gives glory to the Father of all things in the name of the Son "and the Holy Ghost, and return thanks, in many prayers, that he has "been deemed worthy of these gifts. These offices being duly per- "formed, the whole assembly, in acclamation, answers, *Amen*; when "the ministers, whom we call deacons, distribute to each one pre- "sent a portion of the blessed bread, and the wine and water.

" Some is also taken to the absent. This food we call the Eucharist,
" of which they alone are allowed to partake, who believe the doctrines
" taught by us, and have been regenerated by water for the remission
" of sin, and who live as Christ ordained. Nor do we take these gifts,
" as common bread and common drink; but as Jesus Christ, our Sa-
" viour, made man by the word of God, took flesh and blood for our
" salvation: in the same manner, we have been taught, that the food
" which has been blessed by the prayer of the words which he spoke,
" and by which our blood and flesh, in the change, are nourished, is the
" flesh and blood of that Jesus incarnate. The apostles, in the com-
" mentaries written by them, which are called gospels, have delivered,
" that Jesus so commanded, when taking bread, having given thanks,
" he said: *Do this in remembrance of me: This is my body.* In like man-
" ner, taking the cup, and giving thanks, he said: *This is my blood:*
" and that he distributed both to them only." *Apol.* i. *p.* 95, 96, 97.
Edit. Londini, an. 1772.

In his Dialogue with Tryphon, he proves from the old testament that
Christ was the second person of the blessed Trinity, the Messias, true
God and true Man, the great high priest and sacrifice of the new law.
Speaking the mass, he says, "Inflamed by the word of his calling, as it
" were, by fire, truly we are the sacerdotal offspring of God; as he
" himself attests, saying, that, in every place among the nations, we of-
" fer to him well pleasing and clean victims. These victims he accepts
" from his own priests alone. Wherefore, shewing preference to all
" those, who, through his name, offer the sacrifices, which Christ or-
" dained to be offered, that is, in the Eucharist of bread and the chalice
" which in all places of the earth are celebrated by the Christian people,
" God declares, that they are well-pleasing to him. But the sacrifices
" of you Jews and of your priests he rejects, saying: *I will accept no*
" *offering from your hands; because from the rising of the sun to the*
" *going down of the same, my name is great among the Gentiles: but ye*
" *have profaned it.* Malach. i.—But I myself say, that those prayers
" and thanksgivings are alone perfect, and the victims pleasing to God,
" which are offered by good men. These, Christians alone have learn-
" ed to offer in the commemoration of their dry and liquid food, (bread
" and wine) in which they are reminded of the passion which Christ
" suffered." *Dial. cum Tryphon. Judæo, p.* 386.

Thus then it is manifest that St. Justin, who is described by Fox to
have been " a great lover of truth and an universal scholar," a celebrated
philosopher and a most eloquent and ardent Christian, was not a *Protestant* but a *Catholic* Christian, since the former rejects the doctrine of
the real presence and the mass, which the latter holds in common with
this "godly" martyr. The reader will now see the drift of these suppressions by John Fox, and we shall be glad to learn how the modern
editors of this Book of Martyrs will explain their inconsistency
in allowing men to be "godly" in one age, and damnable and idolatrous in another, though both believed and still believe in the SAME
DOCTRINES? What kind of Christians can *they* call themselves?
The modern editors have openly declared that their object in publishing the work of Fox is, to excite "a hatred and abhorrence of the cor-
" ruptions and crimes of Popery and its professors;" and in their

address "to the *Christian* public," they ask "Who but must shudder "when he reads of the barbarities exercised on those *holy* men, who "*first* dared to preach the religion which *we now* profess? Who but "must be convinced that *that* religion, which could support them in "the midst of the flames, and enable them to seal their belief with "their blood, was from God?" Stop, plain Christians! What do you mean by *that* religion? The religion which *you now* profess is *not* the religion which was *first* preached to the Jews and Gentiles. The holy men you have hitherto described as suffering the most excruciating barbarities for their faith were all *Roman Catholics*, admitting the supremacy of the pope, the real presence, the mass, praying to saints and angels, &c. and therefore the religion *you now* profess, which *rejects* these doctrines, cannot be from God. Admire too your consistency. You bring forward the courageous conduct of Roman Catholics of former ages calling them "holy men," to inspire hatred against Roman Catholics of the present age, and to shew that "persecution is inseparable from Po-"pery." Before, however, we quit St. Justin, let us contrast the situation of the Irish Catholics in this, the nineteenth, century, with those of the Roman empire in the second. St. Justin complained of the false and scandalous reports that were circulated to excite prejudice and clamour against the Catholics in his time, and if we cast our eyes on the Orange press of Ireland, we shall see the same disregard to truth shewn by the worshippers of the "Immortal Memory," as the adorers of Jupiter and the heathen gods and goddesses in the days of Roman Pagan phrensy. At the time we are now writing the Irish papers in the pay of "Protestant Ascendency" are daily sending forth their calumnies and libels couched in the following furious and unchristian language.

"Europe cries out that *Antichrist was come*, that the *Pope was he*, and that all prophe-"sies, relative to the Man of Sin and Perdition, and the great seducer of Mankind were "fulfilled in him....
"At a time like the present, when murder and devastation seem to be the order of the "day, it is the duty of every loyal Protestant and true friend to the Constitution, to be on "the alert, and, with 'an eye of fire,' to watch the movements of those blood-thirsty agents "of Popish intolerance—to observe that Popery is the same in all ages, and in all coun-"tries—that the same ferocious spirit which is predominant in the Ribbonmen of the south, "also appears in those of the north....
"Too true it is that the emissaries of that detestable superstition (Popery) have tra-"versed on 'feet swift to mischief,' the regions of the known world in search of proselytes; "wherever their desolating path has been, '*the plague has gone before, and famine has fol-*"*lowed their arrival.*' It is impossible to mistake the countries they have visited, their "footsteps are too surely tracked in the blood...."

Need we say another word on the spirit evinced in the above passages? Do they not display, in colours too glaring to be misunderstood, a feeling of intolerance and injustice unworthy of the Christian name?

"MIRACULOUS INTERFERENCE OF THE DIVINE BEING."

It is the fashion with many individuals at the present day to decry the idea of supernatural works. Fox and his editors, however, are not, apparently, so sceptical. They have under the above head recorded a miraculous interference of the Deity in favour of the Roman army, when placed in great peril; but in the usual confused and unintelligible manner. This occurrence immediately follows a paragraph concluding the account of the martyrs under the fourth persecution, which begins with the customary indefinite term, "About this time." Fox also commences his relation of this miracle with "At this time," and throughout the whole relation he mentions but *one* authority, that of the emperor, and does not even record a single *name* as evidence in favour of the *fact*. Here then the reader is called upon to give credit to a circumstance contrary to the order of nature—an event wonderful and beyond the power of man's conception, on the bare assertion of the writer: for, as we have just said, he gives us no dates, no names of witnesses, save and except an extract from an epistle of the emperor to the senate, which for ought we know may be as inaccurate as his relation, seeing he has not said from whence it was derived. When details of this kind are given in so slight and indistinct a manner, can we wonder that there are persons ready to doubt them? Can we be surprised that individuals, not conversant with history, and whose minds are not directed to an unerring rule, should refuse assent to a *fact* so extraordinary and so slightly attested? We do not wonder that so much unbelief exists, knowing, as we do, what great pains have been taken for these two centuries past to keep the people of this country from learning the truth. We, however, will adopt a different course. Our object, as we have before said, is, to elucidate the truth, the whole truth, and *nothing but the truth*, and therefore we will give an account of this great instance of the interference of the Deity, at the supplication of Christians, to manifest his power.

The emperor Marcus Aurelius had made many unsuccessful attempts to subdue the Germans. Dissatisfied with his generals, in the thirteenth year of his reign, A. D. 171, he resolved to head a powerful army himself against the enemy. Fox, who is very particular where evidence cannot be had, describes the number of the army to be 975,000 men, but he does not say whether he had the return from the quarter-master-general of the Roman army, or invented it himself. Be this, however, as it may, the emperor had a numerous host under his command, and he had led them beyond the Danube, when the Quadi, a people inhabiting that tract of country now called Moravia, surrounded him in a very disadvantageous situation. There was no possibility of escape, and the men were perishing for want of water. In this extremity, and on the point of being attacked, the twelfth legion, called the Melitine, composed chiefly of Christians, fell upon their knees, and poured forth their supplications to God, who listening to their prayers, the sky on a sudden was darkened with dense clouds, from whence issued a thick and heavy rain, which refreshed the Romans, while, at the same time, a violent wind accompanied with rain and lightning deprived the Germans of their sight, and beat them to the ground. Terrified at this prodigy, the Germans were entirely routed, and the Romans obtained a complete victory. Many thousand prisoners were returned to the Roman camp, and the emperor dictated such conditions of peace as he pleased. This most wonderful event is acknowledged by both heathen and Christian writers of that period. The *fact* is admitted, but the parties differ as to the author of it. It is plainly allowed to be supernatural on both sides; the heathens ascribing it either to magic or their gods; while the Christians recount it as a manifestation of the omnipotent power of Him who made the universe and all things therein, and whom they adored as the only *One* true God, in *three* persons. But why, it may be said by some of our readers, should we believe this account of yours any more than that of John Fox? We answer, because it is verified by eye witnesses, and is as well authenticated as any fact in history. We do not deny the fact stated by Fox, we object only to his account. St. Apollinaris, bishop of Hierapolis, in Phrygia, who wrote a very eloquent apology for the Christians about the year 175, makes mention of the miraculous event; and he adds that the emperor, in testimony of the miracle, gave the legion the name of the *Thundering legion*. The emperor also published an edict on the occasion, in which he confessed himself indebted for his delivery to the shower obtained, perhaps, by the prayers of the Christians; "and more," Mr. Butler justly observes, "he could not say "without danger of exasperating the Pagans." We have demonstrative proof of the accuracy of this observation, in the furious behaviour of the Orange press in Ireland, in consequence of the desire expressed by the present sovereign of these realms, that his Catholic subjects in that country should enjoy the benefit of the laws passed in their favour. Furthermore, the wonderful deliverance of the Roman emperor is represented on the *Columna Antoniniana*, in Rome, by the figure of a Jupiter Pluvius being that of an old man flying in the air, with his arms expanded, and a long beard which seems to waste away in rain. The soldiers are there represented as delivered by a sudden tempest, and in a posture, partly drinking of the rain water, and partly fighting against the enemy; who, on the contrary, are represented as stretched out on the ground with their horses, and upon them only the dreadful part of the storm descending. We forgot to say, that the emperor in the decree, forbad any one under pain of death, to accuse a Christian on account of his religion; but some of the governors paid as little attention to this part of the decree as the Orangemen of Ireland do to the letter in favour of the Catholics from George the fourth. The epistle quoted by Fox is rejected by the best writers as supposititious; but the original letter was extant when Tertullian and St. Jerom wrote, who both make mention of it, as well as of the fact, as do also Eusebius, and St. Gregory of Nyssa. Such an event then we think can no more be doubted by a man of common sense, than that such a person as Julius Cæsar once existed. There are some Protestant Christians who deny the existence of miraculous powers in the church after the death of the apostles, we have here, however, a fact, admitted by John Fox and his editors, inadvertently perhaps on the part of the latter, so plainly authenticated as to render them, we hope, no longer sceptical.

"PERSECUTIONS IN FRANCE."

We come now to one of the most insidious stratagems to deceive the reader that could enter the mind of man. The modern editors of *Fox's Book of Martyrs* have openly professed that their intention is to excite " a hatred and abhorrence of the corruptions and crimes of " Popery," and the way they go to work, to attain this uncharitable end, is to *corrupt* the *truth* of *history* as well as of *religion.* After giving an account of the miraculous deliverance of the Roman army, just noticed, and the effect it had in favour of the Christians, they next proceed to give an account of fresh persecutions, which they infamously state to have happened in *France*, when, in fact, as we have before said, there was no such kingdom in the world. Under a head "PERSECUTIONS IN FRANCE," they say, "Although this manifest " interference of the Almighty in favour of Christians, occasioned the " persecution to subside some time, in those parts immediately un- " der the inspection of the emperor, yet we find that it soon after raged " in *France*, particularly at Lyons, where the tortures to which many " of them were put, almost exceeded the powers of description. All " manner of punishments were adopted, torments, and painful deaths; " such as being banished, plundered, hanged, burnt, &c.; and even " the servants and slaves of opulent Christians were racked and tor- " tured, to make them accuse their masters and employers." Now, reader, mark the scandalous drift of this account. Every body knows that France at this day is a Catholic country. Many persons know that there are Protestants residing at Lyons and the adjacent places; and there are few but remember the outcry raised in this country in the years 1815 and 1816, of "*Persecutions in France*," of which we shall tell a tale when the modern editors disclose their story. But there are few, and very few of the readers of the *Book of Martyrs*, who know, that, at the time of the persecutions under consideration, Lyons was the metropolitan city of the province of *Gaul*, forming part of the *Roman heathen* empire, and the Christians were all Roman Ca- tholics, as we shall shew when we come to relate the martyrdom and works of St. Irenæus, the successor to Ponthinus, bishop of Lyons, who suffered in this persecution. In Brookes' Gazetteer, it is stated that Lyons was founded about the year 42, before the birth of Christ, by the Romans, who made it the centre of the commerce of the Gauls. It was afterwards destroyed by fire, but rebuilt again; and the Gazet- teer says, "many antiquities are still observed that evince its Roman " origin." Clovis was the first Catholic king of France, and his con- version is said to have been wrought by a miraculous victory over the Suevi and Alemanni in Germany, who had passed the Rhine, hoping to dislodge their countrymen the Franks, and obtain for themselves the glorious spoils of the Roman empire in Gaul. This victory was gained in the fifteenth year of his reign, of Christ 496. But the period of persecution said by Fox to have occurred in *France* is three centu- ries anterior to this victory, which caused the sovereign of France to acknowledge the divinity of Christ, and embrace his religion by being baptized in his name. Here then we have another disgraceful instance of the methods resorted to by John Fox and his editors to blind and delude the people, while they hypocritically pretend to be diffusing " among their fellow believers a knowledge and love of the genuine " principles of Christianity."

From the authentic accounts of the sufferers under this persecu- tion in Gaul, it appears that they were chiefly Greeks, who had come from Asia, led by a desire to propagate the kingdom of Christ, and invited by the great intercourse in trade between the ports of Asia and Marseilles. The progress which the gospel made, and the eminent sanctity of the lives of its professors, enraged the wicked and bigotted adherents of Pagan ascendency, who, in a transport of fury, determined to extirpate, as they thought, the very name of Christianity. The conflicts of the martyrs on this occasion were recorded by eye witnesses and companions in suffering, and detailed in a letter to their old friends and brethren, the Christians of Asia and Phrygia. The principal author of this letter is supposed to have been St. Irenæus, who was a priest of Lyons at that time. Though the authors of this letter say that it was impossible to give an exact account of what was endured by the martyrs, we find John Fox detailing an account of the death of two who suffered two years after, with a minuteness that borders on the fabulous. Fox writes, " Valerian " and Marcellus, who were nearly related to each other, were impri- " soned at Lyons, in the year 177, for being Christians. By some " means, however, they made their escape, and travelled different " roads. The latter made several converts in the territories of " Besancon and Chalons; but being apprehended, was carried be- " fore Priscus, the governor of the parts. The magistrate, knowing " Marcellus to be a Christian, ordered him to be fastened to some " branches of a tree, which were drawn for that purpose. When he " was tied to different branches, they were let go, with a design to " tear him to pieces with the suddenness of the jerks. But this inven- " tion failing, he was conducted to Chalons, to be present at some " idolatrous sacrifices, at which, refusing to assist, he was put to the " torture, and afterwards fixed up to the waist in the ground, in which " position he expired, A. D. 179, after remaining three days. Vale- " rian was also apprehended, and, by the order of Priscus, was first " brought to the rack, and then beheaded in the same year as his rela- " tion Marcellus."

Such is the account given by Fox; we have examined Mr. Butler's *Lives of Saints*, which is the most authentic martyrology extant, and we can find no account whatever of the torture by branches of trees, as related by Fox. This learned and accurate martyrologist says, that " Marcellus was apprehended in the country, and after enduring many " torments in that city, was buried alive up to the middle, in which " posture he died on the third day, which was the 4th of September." St. Valerian suffered as described by Fox, but it does not appear from Mr. Butler that they were relations. There is one circumstance, however, connected with the memory of these martyrs, which we cannot refrain from relating, as it will clearly prove that they were not Protestant but Catholic martyrs. The relics of St. Marcellus were honourably kept in the great church which bears his name at Chalons; and another church was built over the tomb of St. Valerian at Tournus, before the time of St. Gregory of Tours. *(See Pet. Fr. Chifflet, Hist. de Tournus, and Abbé Pavillon, Bibliotheque des Auteurs de Bourgogne, 1742.)* In the sixteenth century the Huguenots plundered this church of St. Valerian, and burned part of his relics, but the principal portion of them escaped their search. Thus, then, while Fox extols the conduct of these martyrs ; while he praises the devotion of those who builded churches to their memory, as in the cases of St. Peter at Rome, and Ananias at Damas- cus, we see the Protestant Huguenots of France destroying these

churches, and insulting the remains of the godly martyrs. They cannot
therefore be Protestant sufferers for the faith ; nor can primitive Christianity be Protestant Christianity, or greater respect would be shewn
to the memory of those men who died for true religion. Yet John
Fox and his editors would fain have them pass, as we dare say they
have passed with thousands who knew no better, for Protestant saints.

Fox also describes at some length the martyrdom of SS. Epipodius
and Alexander, whom he describes as celebrated for their great friendship and Christian union. He says, that when the former was before
the governor, he began to tamper with the martyr, and pretended to
pity his condition. "Our deities," observed the governor, according
to Fox, "are worshipped by the greater part of the people in the uni-
" verse, and their rulers; we adore them with feasting and mirth
" while you adore a crucified man; we, to honour them, launch into
" pleasures; you, by your faith, are debarred from all that indulges the
" senses. Our religion enjoins feasting, yours fasting; ours the joys
" of licentious blandishments, yours the barren virtue of chastity.
" Can you expect protection from one who could not secure himself
" from the persecutions of a contemptible people? Then quit a pro-
" fession of *such austerity*, and enjoy those *gratifications which the world*
" *affords*; and which your youthful years demand." Here then we
have the testimony of John Fox, that the primitive Christians practised
fasting, chastity, and the renunciation of sensual gratifications, the same
as Catholics are taught to do at this day, and for doing which they are
reviled and ridiculed by their neighbours as being superstitious. How
many bundles of paper have been wasted in vain to prove that Catholicism was allied to Heathenism; and yet we think that the description given of the state of morals by some of the reformers themselves
of the sixteenth century will go to prove that there was a much greater
degree of affinity between Protestantism and the above delineation of
Paganism. Good works we see are described by the Pagan governor, as
forming part of the doctrine of the primitive Christians; but the primitive apostles of Protestantism abolished this necessary part of the Christian code. Epipodius is made by Fox to reply in these terms to the governor, "Your pretended tenderness is actual cruelty; and the *agreeable*
" *life you describe, is replete with everlasting death.* Christ suffered for us,
" that our pleasures should be immortal, and prepared for his followers
" an eternity of bliss. The frame of man being composed of two parts,
" body and soul, the first, as mean and perishable, should be rendered
" subservient to the latter. Your idolatrous feasts may gratify the mor-
" tal, but they injure the immortal part; they cannot, therefore, be en-
" joying life, which destroys the most valuable moiety of your frame.
" Your pleasures lead to eternal death, and your pains to eternal hap-
" piness." Thus thought and spoke this Catholic martyr; at least so
John Fox testifies; but not so the apostles of the pretended reformation from Catholicism to Protestantism. Luther gave full scope to the
gratification of the senses; "Faith *alone*," he cried, "is necessary for
" our justification; nothing else is either commanded or prohibited."
This doctrine of Luther, so like that preached by the Pagan governor to
Epipodius, and rejected by the godly martyr, was eagerly embraced by
the people of the sixteenth century; and we find Luther, Calvin, and

Bucer, thus lamenting the evil effects of their own *reforming* works. "Formerly," says Luther, "when we were seduced by the pope, *every* *one willingly followed good works*; but *now* people neither say nor know any thing but how to get all to themselves by exaction, pillage, theft, falsehood, usury, &c." *(Luth. in Serm. dom. post. Pent.)* "Of the thou- "sands," says Calvin, "who renounced popery, and seemed eager to "embrace the gospel, how few have amended their lives? Indeed, what "else did the greater part pretend to than by shaking off the yoke of "superstition to give themselves more liberty, and to plunge into eve- "ry kind of licentiousness." *(Calv. l. vi. de Scand.)* "The greater part "of the people," writes Bucer, "seem to have embraced the gospel, "only to live at their pleasure, and enjoy their lusts and lawless appe- "tites without control. Hence they lead a willing ear to the doctrine, "*that we are justified by faith only, and not by good works,* FOR WHICH "THEY HAVE NO RELISH." *(Buc. de Regn. Christ. l. i. c. 4.)* Let the reader compare this account of the effects of Protestant doctrines on the people and the effects of Christianity in the primitive ages on its professors, and say if they can be one and the same.

The next subject worthy of notice is the following paragraph: "About this time succeeded Anicetus, Soter, and Eleutherius, about "the year of our Lord 189. This Eleutherius, at the request of Lucius, "king of Britain, sent to him Damianus and Fugatius, by whom the "king was converted to Christ's faith, and baptized about the year "179." Now, reader, whoever you be, what can you make of this sub- lime piece of intelligence? Did you ever before see such language sub- mitted to the people of England to diffuse among them "a knowledge "and love of the genuine principles of Christianity," as this we have just quoted? "About this time succeeded Anicetus, Soter, and "Eleutherius about the year of our Lord 189." Who are these person- ages, and to what did they succeed? Then again "*this* Eleutherius, "at the request of Lucius, king of Britain, sent to him Damianus and "Fugatius by whom the king was converted to Christ's faith, and bap- "tized about the year 179." Whether the latter date is an error of the press we cannot say, but it is a little extraordinary that the king should be converted and baptized ten years, or more, before he sent for persons to instruct him in the Christian faith. But *who* is Eleu- therius? *Why* not say *where he resided!* Ay, there is the rub. This important fact the modern editors of Fox wished to *conceal*, that they might the better instruct the poor deluded people of this country in the "knowledge and love of the genuine principles of Christianity," by exciting in their minds, "a hatred and abhorrence of the corruptions "and crimes of Popery and its professors." Know then, gentle and candid reader, that "this Eleutherius," was no less a personage than the POPE OF ROME, who deputed two of his missionaries to king Lucius, by whom he was converted, mind, I use the words of the editors of this *Book of Martyrs,*—by these *Roman* missionaries, he "was converted "to CHRIST'S FAITH!" Fox in his original work, the *Acts and Monu- ments of the Church,* found this historical and incontrovertible fact a ter- rible stumbling block to his designs; he therefore made many wind- ings and doublings in his relation of it, which father Parsons most ably traced out. Aware on what fickle ground the supremacy of his master and mistress stood, when it was so clear that even in the second age of Christianity the spiritual supremacy of the bishop of Rome was acknowledged in this island, he endeavoured to make it believed that king Lucius was converted by missionaries from the east, than which a more foul perversion of truth was never attempted. His modern editors probably sensible of this weakness of the martyrologist, thought it better to render the passage totally unintelligible to Protestant readers, who, by the deceptive tricks of the press, know as little of the true history of their country as of the thousand falsehoods told by John Fox. We will therefore endeavour to undeceive them by a short historical detail of authenticated facts, which shall unravel the jargon of the above quoted passage.

Anicetus was the eleventh bishop of Rome after St. Peter, and succeeded Pius the first in the year 157; next to him followed Soter in 168, who had for his successor " this Eleutherius," who was applied to by king Lucius to instruct him and his people in the faith of Christ. Eleutherius was elected to the papal chair in the year 176, and the embassy to Rome from Lucius was sent about 182. The account given by the Rev. Mr. Butler in his life of this holy Christian king, is so very interesting that we here transcribe it for the information of the reader. " We are informed by Bede," writes Mr. Butler, " that in the reign of " Marcus Antonius Verus, and Aurelius Commodus, a British king, " named Lucius, sent a letter to pope Eleutherius, entreating, that by " his direction he might be made a Christian. This must have hap- " pened about the year 182. Lucius must have reigned in some part " of Britain, which was subject to the Romans, as his name indicates. " Tacitus mentions Prasutagus, king of the Iceni, in Norfolk, Suffolk, " Cambridgeshire, and Huntingdonshire, who at his death made the " emperor Nero his heir, hoping by that means his people would be se- " cured from injuries; whereas the contrary fell out; for the country " was plundered by centurians and slaves. The same historian men- " tions, that certain cities were given to Codigunus, ' according to the " ancient and received custom of the Roman people, to make even " kings the instruments of the slavery of nations,' as he observes. " That Lucius was a Christian king in Britain is proved by two medals " mentioned by Usher, and one by Bouterue. Bede tells us, that by " his embassy to Eleutherius he obtained the effect of his pious request; " and that the Britons enjoyed the light of faith till the reign of Dio- " clesian. Lucius therefore was the first Christian king in Europe; it " no where appears in what part of Britain he reigned. The records " of Glastenbury abbey, quoted by Malmesbury, and others, mention- " ed by Usher, tell us, that St. Eleutherius sent over to Britain SS. " Fugatius and Damianus, (rather Dumianus or Duvianus,) who bap- " tized king Lucius, and many others, and were buried at Glasten- " bury. In Somersetshire, in the deanery of Dunstor, there is a parish " church which bears the name of St. Deruvian, as Stow testifies. " This saint is called by the Welch, Duvian or Dwywan, says Usher. " The Christian faith had reached Britain in the times of the apostles. " St. Clement I. pope, affirms, that St. Paul preached to the utmost " bounds of the West. Gildas says, the first dawn of the evangelical " light appeared in this island about the eighth year of Nero. Theodoret

" names the Britons as a nation in which St. Paul sowed the seeds of
" faith ; and in another place says, that this apostle brought salvation
" to the islands that lie in the ocean. Three British bishops assisted
" at the council of Arles, in 314, namely, Eborius of York, Restitu-
" tus of London, and Adelfius who is styled *De civitate Coloniæ Londi-*
" *nensium ;* which bishop Usher takes to have been Colchester ; but
" many more probably understand by it Lincoln, anciently called Lin-
" dum Colonia. Also certain British bishops subscribed to the council
" of Nice against the Arians. The testimonies of St. Justin, St. Irenæus,
" Tertullian, Eusebius, Saint Chrysostom, and Theodoret, demon-
" strate that Christianity had got footing in Britain very soon after
" Christ. We cannot, therefore, wonder that a prince should have
" embraced the faith in this island in the second century: nor do the
" objections which some have raised, deserve notice. Schelstrate, the
" learned prefect of the Vatican library, in his dissertation on the pa-
" triarchal authority, transcribes the following words from an ancient
" manuscript history of the kings of England, kept in the Vatican li-
" brary : ' Lucius sent a letter to pope Eleutherius that he might be made
" a Christian, and he obtained his request.' The same learned author
" copies the following testimony from an ancient catalogue of the popes,
" written in the time of the emperor Justinian, as we are assured by
" the title, found in the library of Christina, queen of Sweden: ' Eleuthe-
" rius received a letter from Lucius, king of Britain, who desired to be
" made a Christian by his command.' " *Butler's Saints Lives,* vol. xii.

Rapin and Echard both record this fact, and the latter, in his *Ecclesiastical History,* states, that this pope Eleutherius degraded from his
priesthood one Florinus, " a disciple of St. Polycarp, who fell into the
" Valentinian heresy, and moreover maintained, that God was the au-
" thor of all kinds of evil." Thus then we have here an established fact,
that Christ's faith, which he solemnly declared should never *change,*
and which has never yet nor ever will change, because TRUTH *must* be
always ONE and the SAME, was sought for by a pagan king of this
island at Rome, and was introduced into this country by missioners in
communion with the church of Rome. This fact, however, it will be
seen, was rendered so obscure by the modern editors of the *Book of
Martyrs,* that the people might have remained ignorant of it till doom's-
day, if we had not thrown some light upon it.

The paragraph that next follows is equally as unintelligible as the
one we have just been commenting on and eliciting. Fox says, " Eu-
" sebius, Vicentius, Potentianus, and Peregrinus, for refusing to wor-
" ship Commodus as Hercules, were likewise martyred." Who these
martyrs were, we have not been able to discover. Butler makes no
mention of them, and Echard says, that " the Christians enjoyed so
" much freedom from persecution, that we find but *one* martyr of note
" in this reign (Commodus), which was Apollonius, an illustrious se-
" nator, eminent for his philosophy and other parts of learning." This
martyr Fox had previously recorded. To the passage just quoted from
Fox, the modern editors have introduced the following paragraph as a
note : " About this time, among other pious teachers whom God raised
" up to confound the persecutors by learning and writing, as the mar-
" tyrs to confirm the truth with their blood, was Seraphion, bishop of

" Antioch; Egesippus, a writer of the ecclesiastical history from Christ's
" passion to his time; Heraclitus, who first began to write annotations
" upon the New Testament and epistles of the apostles; Theophilus,
" bishop of Cesarea; and Dionysius, bishop of Corinth, who wrote
" divers epistles, from whence we learn that it was then the practice of
" the churches, to read the letters and epistles, sent by learned bishops
" and teachers, to the congregations; for, writing to the church of the
" Romans and to Soter, he says, 'This day we celebrate the holy do-
" minical day, in which we have read your epistle, which always we
" will read for our exhortation; like as we do read also the epistle of
" Clement sent to us before,' &c. By him also mention is made of the
" keeping of Sunday holy, of which we find no mention in ancient au-
" thors before his time, except only in Justin the martyr, who in his
" description declares two times most especially used for Christians to
" congregate together: the first, when any convert was to be baptized;
" the second upon the Sunday; because, says he, upon that day God
" made the world, and because Christ upon that day first shewed him-
" self, after his resurrection, to his disciples, &c."
    The introduction of this note is evidently intended to make the un-
thinking and uninformed believe that the primitive Christians were as
great *bible readers*, as the people of this country are now. But this is a
mistake. The bible had not at that period been collected together as
one book, and the portions of scripture were then in the hands chiefly
of the clergy, who certainly did read them to the people assembled, as
was and is the constant practice of the church of Rome, but not that
they should interpret any of the passages according to their own fanciful notions, but that they should learn therefrom the ONE ONLY TRUE
RELIGION OF CHRIST, amidst the many *errors* which even then daily surrounded this undeviating rule of faith. We agree with the writers of
this note, that God raised up pious teachers to confound the ignorant
and perverse by their *writings*, as the martyrs confirmed the truth of
the Christian religion by their invincible courage and disregard of torments and death. We have stated this before in our introductory
remarks, and we have hitherto given, as a proof of the correctness
of our assertion, the doctrines which these learned and pious writers
defended and maintained. And why have not John Fox and his editors
followed the same line of conduct? Because, then the reader would
have gained some knowledge of the TRUTH, which would not have
been to the interests of the party they had to serve, and therefore they
suppressed this essential part of history, that the people might remain
in the dark. Following our own course, we will first see what Serapion says, as he is placed at the head of the list of " pious teachers
" whom God raised up to confound the persecutors by learning and
" writing," according to Fox, " about this time," that is, at the close
of the second century. Serapion succeeded Maximin in the see of
Antioch, in the year 189, or 190, and is said by Echard to have governed that see 21 years. He wrote a treatise against one Domninus,
who in a persecution had fallen into Judaism; and another treatise on
the gospel of St. Peter, to *undeceive* the brethren of the church of
Rossa in Cilicia, in which he has these words : " As for our part we
" *receive* Peter and the other apostles as Jesus Christ himself; but

" those writings which *falsely* bear their name we *reject*, as being well
" apprized, that we never received them from our forefathers." Here
then was an appeal to tradition and public opinion. Here is the rule
adopted by Catholics in all ages to preserve the TRUTH. What we received from our forefathers, who had it from their predecessors, who
received it from the apostles, who had it from their Divine Master, we
believe to be the truth, because truth is always one and the same;
but that which innovators put forth, was never heard of before: it is
therefore *new* and *novel*, and as such must be *rejected*, because it cannot
proceed from truth, and therefore must be erroneous.

Hegessipus was by birth a Jew, but became a Christian. His
death is supposed to have happened about the year 180. In the year
133 he wrote a history of the church, in five books, from the passion
of Christ to his own time, but unfortunately the work is not now extant. Of Heraclitus we find no account in the histories in our possession, and Theophilus of Cesarea is recorded in Echard as presiding
in a council of Palestine on the subject of keeping Easter. In Butler,
however, this learned and illustrious father is stated to have been the
successor of Eros, bishop of Antioch, who died in the year 168.
Theophilus was born of Gentile parents, who trained him up in idolatry, and gave him a liberal education. Grown to man's estate, he
made a diligent search after truth, and found it in the Christian religion; after which, having embraced the faith, he gloried in the name
of Christian, which he calls " dear to God, however despised by igno-
" rant and vicious men." Being fixed in his charge of the see of Antioch, he set himself diligently to promote virtue and true religion; and
draw his flock from error and idolatry. He wrote against the heresies
of Marcion and Hermogenes, and an apology for the Christian religion, in three books, addressed to Autolychus, a pagan philosopher. In
this latter work Theophilus teaches that God the Son, or the Divine
Wisdom, is coeval with the Father. He also gives the name of *Tri-*
nity to the Three Divine Persons in one nature, and is the first writer,
whose works are extant, that employs this word to express this mystery. He tells Autolychus that it is in vain for him to look for the
truth, unless he reforms his heart, and his views are perfectly pure.
" All men have eyes," says he, " yet the sun is veiled from the sight of
" some. It, however, ceases not to emit a flood of day, though those
" whose eyes are blinded, see not its radiant light. But this defect is
" to be laid to their charge, nor can the sun be complained of on ac-
" count of their blindness. Thus, my friend, it is sin that darkens
" your mind, and blunts the edge of your understanding. As the glass
" represents not the image if it be soiled, so the mind receives not the
" impression of God, if it lies immersed in sin. This is a humour
" which greatly obstructs the sight, and prevents the eye from be-
" holding the sun. Thus, my friend, your impiety diffuses a cloud
" over the faculties of your soul, and renders you incapable of receiv-
" ing the glorious light.".... " And as in the sea there are islands
" which are fruitful and furnish good harbours for the shelter of mari-
" ners who fly to them, and are there secured from the tossings of the
" tempests ; so hath God given to the world holy churches, into whose
" safe havens the lovers of truth fly, and all those who desire to be

" saved, and escape the dreadful wrath of God. And there are other
" islands which want water, and are filled with barren rocks, and,
" being uninhabitable, are destructive to sailors, and in which ships
" are dashed to pieces, or are unfortunately detailed: so likewise are
" there erroneous doctrines and heresies which destroy those who are
" seduced and drawn aside by them." The most correct editions of his
books to Autolychus, Mr. Butler says, are, that published by bishop
Fell, at Oxford, in 1604; that given by John Christopher Wolf at
Hamburg, in 1724; and lastly, that of the Benedictins with St. Justin's works.

The next learned father mentioned in the above cited note is Dionysius bishop of Corinth, who is stated to have written several treatises
in defence of the truth. Eusebius mentions in his history several of
the instructive letters of this prelate to other churches cautioning them
not to be led away by *new* and *wild* notions, but to stand stedfast to the
doctrines received from the apostles. He also notices the letter of
thanks to Soter, a passage of which is quoted in the note. But the
editors of Fox do not tell us who Soter was. We are not informed
whether he is a Christian pastor or a heathen philosopher. By consulting however more authentic authors, we find this Soter to be no other
than the twelfth *bishop of Rome* from St. Peter, and one of the three
persons said to have succeeded " about this time" no one knew who,
till we unravelled the mystery. By sending this letter of thanks, and
informing the holy pope, that his epistle should be read for the exhortation of his flock, as also that of St. Clement, a predecessor of St.
Soter in the papal chair, it is clear that the church of Corinth, as did
all the other churches, acknowledged the primacy of the church of
Rome. This is another weighty historical fact, which must be borne
in mind by the reader who wishes to ascertain the truth. The editors
of Fox admit that St. Clement wrote a letter to the Corinthians, following the example of St. Paul, whose epistle to that church makes
part of the new testament. They admit that Dionysius informed St.
Soter that this epistle was *publicly* read to the people; let us now see
why it was sent. St. Clement is the person mentioned by St. Paul in
his epistle to the Philippians, and was the third bishop of Rome after
St. Peter. During his pontificate, some serious divisions arose among
the Christians at Corinth, on which St. Clement wrote them an admonitory and instructive epistle, as head of the Christian church. He
commences thus: " The church of God, which is at Rome, to that of
" Corinth, to those that have been called and sanctified by the will of
" God in our Lord Jesus Christ. May the grace and peace of God,
" the Almighty be increased by Christ Jesus in every one of you."
He then goes on to shew the evil state of anarchy and confusion, and
exhorts them to unity in the following pathetic terms: " Why," asks
the pontiff " Why are there quarrels, why are there divisions among
" you? Have we not all the same God, the same Redeemer, the same
" Spirit, who has sanctified us by our vocation into ONE FAITH in
" Christ Jesus? Why then do we *divide* his members, why do we tear
" our own body into pieces? For surely we can never forget that we
" are all members one of another," &c. This epistle was written about
the year 96, and had the desired effect of healing the divisions lament-

ed. We see also that it is mentioned by Dionysius as being still read in his time, that is nearly a hundred years after it was penned. It may here be observed, that there is a variation between the version given by Fox's editors of the letter written by Dionysius to the church of Rome, and that given by Butler in his life of this saint. The latter gives it thus from Eusebius: "From the beginning it is your cus- " tom to bestow your alms in all places, and to furnish subsistence to " many churches. You send relief to the needy, especially those who " work in the mines; in which you follow the example of your fathers. " Your blessed bishop Soter is so far from degenerating from your an- " cestors in that respect, that he goes beyond them; not to mention " the comfort and advice he, with the bowels of a tender father to- " wards his children, affords all that comes to him. On this day we " celebrated the Lord's Day, (Fox's editors say, the *holy dominical day)* " and read your letter, as we do that which was heretofore written to " us by Clement."

The reader will here see the great and unbounded charity of the primitive Christians, who thought it nothing to divest themselves of every thing to succour their distressed or oppressed neighbours. Before we quit this subject we must direct the attention of the reader to the admission made by these editors, that before the time of Diony- sius, they find no mention made by any writer, except St. Justin, of the transfer of the sabbath-day from the last to the first day of the week. How then was it so universally known and adopted, since it was neither mentioned in Scripture or by writers for near two hundred years after the Christian religion was first established? This is an important question, reader; for on it hangs the rejected doctrine, by Protestants, of tradition. The only answer that can be given is, that it was handed down by word of mouth—it was communicated from fa- ther to son—it was received with the light of truth, and its notoriety carried conviction with it. What absurdity must it then be, to deny the necessity of tradition in one instance when we are obliged to ad- mit it in another.

THE FIFTH GENERAL PERSECUTION UNDER THE ROMAN EMPERORS.

The Christians during the reigns of the emperors Commodus, Perti- nax, and Julianus, Fox tells us, had a respite for several years from persecution. Severus, too, he says, at the beginning of his reign, be- came a great favourer of the Christians, "but the prejudice and fury of " the ignorant multitude again prevailed, and the obsolete laws were " put in execution against the Christians. The pagans were alarmed at " the progress of Christianity, and revived the calumny of placing acci- " dental misfortunes to the account of its professors." Why, yes, this is the usual way with those who are on the wrong side of the post, and especially when they have power in their hands. We are old enough to remember something of "Protestant ascendency" about the year 1778, when a little favour was manifested by Parliament towards the perse- cuted and oppressed Catholics of this country. How the prejudices of the ignorant multitude were then wrought upon by wicked and ill- designing men may be seen by consulting impartial history. The fury of the people was inflamed to such a degree that in the year 1780 it was dangerous for a Catholic to be publicly known as such, and the metropolis of England was threatened with destruction by a lawless and fanatical mob. But let us examine the martyrs set down by Fox, as suffering in this persecution.

The first is thus recorded. "Victor, bishop of Rome, suffered mar-"tyrdom in the first year of the third century, A. D. 201, though the "circumstances are not ascertained."—Four paragraphs further on he adds:—"Victor, the bishop of Rome, wanting to impose a particular "mode of keeping Easter *there*, it occasioned some disorders among "the Christians. In particular, Irenæus wrote him a synodical epistle "in the name of the Gallic churches. This zeal in favour of Chris-"tianity pointed him (Irenæus) out as an object of resentment to the "emperor, and he was accordingly beheaded in A. D. 202." From this account the reader is lead to suppose, by the introduction of the adverb "*there*," that this bishop of Rome meditated an innovation in the practice of the church in his own particular diocess, and that the zeal of St. Irenæus, in resisting this attempt of the holy pope, brought the wrath of the heathen emperor upon him, and was the cause of his martyrdom. But a moment of reflection must shew the absurdity of this story of John Fox. Victor is stated to have been the first sufferer, as he was martyred in 201, and Irenæus was not put to death till the year following. How then could his "zeal in favour of Christianity," in opposing the bishop of Rome, who is also stated to have been a god-ly martyr for Christianity, point him out as an object of resentment to the heathen emperor? Can any one be so besotted as to imagine that this emperor, who was intent upon the destruction of Christianity, cared one jot about the disputes between the head and members of the system? No man of common sense, we are sure, will entertain such an idea. What would it interest "Protestant ascendency" at this day, whether Easter was kept by the Catholics at one time in Ireland and at another in England, and that one of the bishops of that church was more zealous in arguing the question than any of the others? The in-tolerant spirit of "Protestant ascendency" is opposed to the whole sys-tem of Catholicism, not to an individual member or abstract part of it, and so it was with Pagan ascendency in the time of the heathen em-perors. St. Irenæus was an object of resentment, not for disputing with the bishop of Rome, but for his great abilities and influence in con-verting the Pagans from their idolatrous superstitions to the divine truths of the Catholic church.

Mr. Echard, in his Ecclesiastical History, says, "The Christian re-"ligion had now (A. D. 201) diffused itself through all the known-"parts of the world; but more fully and triumphantly in the vast Ro-"man empire, where it was most violently opposed, and met with the "most terrible conflicts. Christians were now in the cities, towns and "villages, in the camp, in the senate, in the palace, and in all places, "besides the pagan temples and theatres; and that in such numbers "and multitudes, that Tertullian assures us, that if they had unani-"mously retired to any other country, the empire would have become "a mere desert and solitude." This astonishing progress of an indivi-sible and undeviating rule of faith among all ranks of people, and of

A REVIEW

OF

Fox's Book of Martyrs,

CRITICAL AND HISTORICAL.

No. 5. Printed and Published by W. E. Andrews, 3, Chapter-house-court, St. Paul's Churchyard, London. **Price 3d.**

EXPLANATION OF THE ENGRAVING.—*The inside of a Roman amphitheatre for enter-taining the people with shews. These edifices contained a great number of seats, made of vast polished stones, one above another, that the spectators might have a perfect view of the whole pit without any hindrance. The arena or pit was strewed with sand, to suck up the blood, and surrounded with iron rails or a balustrade, about a yard from the lowest seats, for a fence, that the wild beasts might not be able to hurt the spectators. Under the walls were dens for the beasts, and dungeons for the condemned prisoners. The two martyrs are SS. Perpetua and Felicitas, attacked by a wild cow.*

CONTINUATION OF THE REVIEW.

all nations, notwithstanding the horrid persecutions of the Pagans, the malice of the Jews, and the treacherous attacks of heretics, must, we think, carry conviction of its divine nature, and be considered a proof of the existence of an omnipotent and all-powerful Being. The holy pope Victor was a very watchful guardian of this divine faith, detect-ing and condemning many heresies that sprung up in his pontificate. He also wished to bring about an uniformity in the time of celebrat-ing Easter, but not to impose a particular mode of keeping it, as the *Book of Martyrs* insinuates. At this time Mr. Butler writes, " the " churches of Lesser Asia kept it with the Jews on the 14th day of " the first moon after the vernal equinox, on whatever day of the week " it fell. The Roman church, and all the rest of the world, kept Eas-" ter always on the *Sunday* immediately following the fourteenth day." This was a matter of *discipline*, and not of *faith*, but still unity was

considered necessary, and Victor was desirous to effect it. Pope Anicetus allowed the Asiatics to follow their own custom even at Rome;
but Soter required that when at Rome they should do as Rome did.
Several councils were held in different parts of the world, and the
decisions were in favour of the Roman custom. Some of the Asiatic
bishops, however, defended their custom as derived from St. Philip,
St. John the evangelist, and St. Polycarp. Victor, seeing them obstinate, thought to bring them round by excommunication, from which
he was dissuaded by St. Irenæus, and died soon after. This is the
correct history of the affair of keeping Easter, so far as Victor was
concerned, which Fox would make us believe was an attempt at imposition on the part of this pope, and the cause of St. Irenæus's martyrdom.

After the death of Victor, Fox places "Leonidas, the father of the
"celebrated Origen, beheaded for being a Christian." Next follows a
confused account of other martyrs, of whose names and sufferings we
can trace no account in the authors before us. Then comes the following paragraph: "Irenæus, bishop of Lyons, was born in Greece,
"and received a Christian education. It is generally supposed that
"the account of the persecutions at Lyons was written by himself.
"He succeeded the martyr Pothinus as bishop of Lyons, and ruled his
"diocese with great propriety: he was a zealous opposer of heresies in
"general, and wrote a celebrated tract against heresy about A. D. 187."

Here then we have it acknowledged by John Fox, that this "godly
"martyr," was not only an orthodox Christian, but likewise "a zea-
"lous opposer of heresies in general, and wrote a celebrated tract
"against heresy." Now, as heresy is defined by Dr. Johnson to be
"An opinion of private men different from that of the Catholic and
"orthodox church," John Fox and his editors, the "few plain Chris-
"tians," who tell the public, in their address, that they "have united
"themselves for the purpose of diffusing among their fellow-*believers*
"a KNOWLEDGE and LOVE of the GENUINE PRINCIPLES OF
"CHRISTIANITY, and CONSEQUENTLY (they add), a *hatred* and
"*abhorrence* of the *crimes* and *corruptions* of POPERY and its professors,"
ought most certainly to have pointed out WHAT THE DOCTRINES
WERE that this "zealous opposer of heresies in general" defended.
For how can their fellow-believers obtain a "*knowledge* of the *genuine*
"principles of Christianity;" unless they are laid down before them
for their information? And how can they "*love*" these principles
while they are ignorant of them? To tell the reader that this martyr
wrote a "celebrated *tract* against heresy," without telling him the
substance of the work, is saying nothing; it is leaving him as much in
the dark as ever. But unfortunately this system of *suppression*, where
information is essentially necessary to obtain a knowledge of truth,
has been invariably followed by the adversaries of Catholicism, until
the people of this country have been cheated out of their faith, and
their understandings bewildered, while they imagine themselves gifted
with a superiority of intellectual wisdom above their fellow-creatures.
Fox says Irenæus wrote a "tract," which means a *small book*, against
heresy in general. Now the fact is, this work was a very elaborate
one, and consisted of *five books*. In the first the learned father and
martyr gives a long list of heresies. In the second he confutes them

from scripture, and from the miracles performed in his day in the Catholic church, which the heretics could never perform. In the third he advances tradition against the heretics. In the fourth he pursues the same subject, and answers the objections of those who denied the incorruptible resurrection of the body. And in the fifth, he explains the mysteries of the church, the fall of man, the consequence of it, the incarnation, the resurrection, &c. These books were written chiefly againt the execrable doctrines of the Gnostics, and of Valentinus, a priest, who fell by pride and jealousy, because another was preferred before him to a bishopric in Egypt. Valentinus had been a Platonic philosopher, and revived the errors of Simon Magus, adding to them many other absurd fictions, as of thirty Æones or ages, a kind of inferior deities, &c. As an author, Irenæus was well versed in the scripture, perfectly understood the Pagan poets, and was thoroughly acquainted with the systems and arguments of the heretics. St. Irenæus was a Greek by birth, and received his instructions in the Christian faith from St. Polycarp, bishop of Smyrna, who was a disciple of St. John the evangelist, and suffered martyrdom in the fourth persecution, as we have mentioned. Consequently, the doctrines held by this orthodox Christian bishop, and "zealous opposer of heresies in "general," must have been received from the apostles, and were therefore genuine. Let us now see then what these doctrines were.

On the contested points regarding the *authority, marks, visibility, apostolicity,* and *infallibility of the Church,* and *primacy of the pope,* which Catholics now and always did maintain, St. Irenæus writes : "Things " being thus made plain (the descent of doctrine from the apostles) it " is not from others that truth is to be sought, which may be readily " learned from the church. For to this church, as into a rich reposi- " tory, the apostles committed whatever is of divine truth, that each " one, if so inclined, might thence draw the dripk of life. This is the " way to life : all other teachers must be shunned as thieves and rob- " bers.—For what? Should there be any dispute on a point of small " moment, must not recourse be had to the most ancient churches, " where the apostles resided, and from them collect the truth?" *Adv.* " *Hæreses, lib.* III. *c.* iv. *p.* 205. *Edit. Oxonii,* 1702.

" It is a duty to obey the priests of the church, who hold their suc- " cession from the apostles, and who, with that succession, received, " agreeably to the will of the Father, the sure pledge of truth. But as " to those who belong not to that leading succession, in whatever place " they may be united, they should be suspected, either as heretics, or " as schismatics, proudly extolling, and pleasing themselves, or as hy- " pocrites actuated by vain glory or the love of lucre. But they who " impugn the truth, and excite others to oppose the church of God, " their fate is with Dathan and Abiron; while schismatics, who violate " the church's unity, experience the punishment which fell on king Je- " roboam." *Ibid. l.* IV. *c.* xliii. *p.* 343, 344.

" The church, extended to the boundaries of the earth, received her " faith from the apostles, and their disciples.—Having received it, she " carefully retains it, as if dwelling in one house, as possessing one soul, " and one heart : the same faith she delivers and teaches, with one ac- " cord, and as if gifted with one tongue : for though in the world there

" be various modes of speech, the tradition of doctrine is one and the
" same.   In the churches of Germany, in those of Spain and Gaul, in
" those of the East, of Egypt, and of Africa, and in the middle regions,
" is the same belief, the same teaching.   For as the world is enlight-
" ened by one sun, so does the preaching of one faith enlighten all
" men, that are willing to come to the knowledge of truth.   Nor, among
" the pastors of the church, does he that is eloquent deliver other doc-
" trine—for no one is above his master—nor he that is weak in speech
" diminish the truth of tradition.   Faith being one, cannot be affected
" by the powers or the want of utterance." *Adversus Hæreses, l.* i. c. ii.
iii. *p.* 45, 46. *Ed. Oxon.* 1702.

" God placed in his church apostles, prophets, doctors; and the
" whole operation of the spirit, of which they do not partake, who are
" not united to the church; but, by their own bad designs and actions,
" they deprive themselves of life.   For where the church is, there is
" the spirit of God; and where this spirit is, there is the church, and
" all grace : the spirit is truth." *Ibid. l.* iii. c. xl. *p.* 266. *Vide l.* iv. c. 62.

" The heretics, of whom I have been speaking, came long after those
" bishops, to whom the apostles committed the care of their churches,
" and they ran into devious paths, foreign from the truth.   But they,
" who adhered to the church, continued to profess, with all nations,
" the doctrine, which the apostles had delivered, with one and the same
" faith, believed in one God, Father, Son, and Holy Ghost; meditating
" on the same precepts; upholding the same ordinances, expecting the
" coming of the Lord, and the salvation of men.   The teaching of the
" church is true and stable, shewing to all men the same one path of
" salvation; for to her has been committed the light and the wisdom
" of God.   As the wise man says : (Prov. c. 1.) *she uttereth her voice in*
" *the streets; she crieth on the highest walls; she speaketh without ceasing*
" *in the city gates.*   Every where the church proclaims the truth; she
" is the candlestick with the seven lamps; (Exod. xxv.) bearing the
" light of Christ." *Adv. Hæreses, l.* v. c. 20. *p.* 430.

" The church, receiving her doctrine from Christ and his apostles,
" and alone preserving it through all regions, delivered it down to her
" children.   Hence it becomes our duty, to afford every assistance
" against the assaults of heretics; to withdraw those that are in error,
" and to strengthen the weak; in order, that they hold fast the faith,
" which they received from that church, which has preserved it invio-
" late." *Adv. Hær. Præf. lib.* v. *p.* 392.

" The apostolic faith, manifested to the whole world, they, who
" would behold truth, may see in every church; and we can enume-
" rate those bishops, who were appointed by the apostles, and their
" successors, down to ourselves, none of whom taught, or even knew,
" the wild opinions of these men (heretics).   Had the apostles really
" possessed any secret doctrines, which the *perfect* only were to hear,
" surely they would have communicated them to those, to whom
" they entrusted their churches.   However, as it would be tedious to
" enumerate the whole list of successions, I shall confine myself to that
" of Rome, the greatest, and most ancient, and most illustrious church,
" founded by the glorious apostles, Peter and Paul; receiving from them
" her doctrine, which was announced to all men, and which, through

" the succession of her bishops, is come down to us. Thus we con-
" found all those, who, through evil designs, or vain-glory, or per-
" verseness, teach what they ought not. For to this church, on account
" of its superior headship, every other must have recourse, that is, the
" faithful of all countries; in which church has been preserved the .
" doctrine delivered by the apostles. They, therefore, having founded
" and instructed this church, committed the administration thereof to
" Linus. Of this Linus, Paul makes mention in his epistle to Timothy.
" To him succeeded Anacletus : then, in the third place, Clement, who
" had himself seen and conversed with those apostles, in whose time
" their preaching yet sounded in his ears. Nor was this alone true of
" him; as many, at that time, were living, whom they had taught.
" To Clement succeeded Evaristus ; to him Alexander ; and then the
" sixth from the apostles, Sixtus, who was followed by Teleophorus,
" Hyginus, Pius, and Anicetus. But Soter having succeeded Anicetus,
" Eleutherius, the twelfth from the apostles, now governs the church.
" By such regular succession, has the doctrine delivered by the apos-
" tles, descended to us : and the proof is most clear, that it is one and
" the same vivifying faith, which coming from the apostles, is at this
" time maintained and taught." *Adv. Hær. l.* III. *c.* iii. *p.* 200, 201,
202, 203.

Against the private interpretation of scripture, now so fashionable
among Protestants, and especially the promoters of Bible societies,
who condemn, one and all, the Catholics for maintaining that THE
CHURCH, and THE CHURCH ONLY, is the expounder of the scriptures, St. Irenæus, the "zealous opposer of heresies in general," as
John Fox justly calls him, teaches thus : " Paul says : God appointed in
" his church apostles, prophets, and doctors. Where therefore are the
" holy gifts of God, there must the truth be learned : with them is the
" succession from the apostles ; and there is the society, whose com-
" munication is sound and irreproveable, unadulterated and pure.
" These preserve the faith of one God, who made all things ; increase
" our love towards his divine Son ; and expound, without danger, the
" scriptures to us, not blaspheming the name of God, nor dishonouring
" the patriarchs, nor contemning the prophets." *Adversus Hær. l.* IV.
c. xlv. *p.* 345.—" To him that believeth, that there is one God, and
" holds to the head, which is Christ—to this man all things will be
" plain, if he read diligently the scriptures with the aid of those who
" are the priests in the church, and in whose hands, as we have shewn,
" rests the doctrine of the apostles." *Ibid. c.* iii. *p.* 355.

" And not only from the evangelical and apostolical writings, which
" they perversely interpret, and wickedly expound, do these, (heretics)
" attempt to prove their assertions ; but also from the law and the pro-
" phets. For as there are in these many parables and allegories, which
" may be forced into various meanings, them they craftily fit to their
" own purpose, and thus draw from the truth those who have not a
" firm faith in one God the Father, and his Son, Jesus Christ." *Adv.*
Hær. l. I. *c.* i. *p.* 19.—" Such being their positions, which the pro-
" phets never preached, nor Christ taught, nor the apostles delivered,
" they boast their own superior knowledge, and attempt to make it
" seem credible ; forming, as it were, a rope of sand, by adducing some

" words from the parables or sayings of the prophets, or of Christ, or
" of the apostles; but so, as to violate the arrangement and order of
" the sacred writings, and, as far as in them lies, dissolve the whole
" connection of truth."—*Ibid. p.* 55. " So varying are their notions
" drawn from the scriptures; and when a discourse has been read,
" shaking their heads with great gravity, they pronounce, that its se-
" cret meaning is above the capacity of all, and that silence is the proof
" of wisdom.—When, therefore, they shall be agreed among them-
" selves on what they draw from the scriptures, it will be our time to
" refute them. Meanwhile, thinking wrongfully, and not agreeing in
" the meaning of the same words, they convict themselves; but we,
" having one true and only God for our master, and making his words
" the rule of truth, always speak alike of the same things; all acknow-
" ledging one God, the creator of the universe, who sent his prophets,
" and in the latter times, manifested his Son, to confound the incredu-
" lous, and draw forth the fruit of justice." *L.* iv. *c.* xix. *p.* 368.

On the contested point of *Tradition,* which Protestants reject and Catholics stoutly hold, and which is neither more nor less than PUBLIC
OPINION, received and delivered down from age to age, this " zea-
" lous opposer of heresies in general," says, " When these heretics are
" convicted from the scriptures, they begin to accuse the scriptures
" themselves, as not being accurate, and void of authority, and so va-
" riously expressed, that from them truth cannot be discovered by those
" who are ignorant of tradition. For that truth came not by writing,
" but by the living voice: wherefore Paul said: (1 Cor. ii. 6.) *How-
" beit we speak wisdom among the perfect; yet not the wisdom of this world.
" *—Now this wisdom each one of them pretends to possess, as he has
" drawn it from himself. For each one in his own perversity, pervert-
" ing the rule of truth, blushes not to vaunt himself. On the other
" hand, when we appeal to that tradition, which, coming from the
" apostles through the succession of ministers, is preserved in the
" churches, they object to it, observing that, being themselves wiser
" than those ministers, and the apostles themselves, they have disco-
" vered the genuine truth.—Thus they assent neither to the scriptures,
" nor to tradition." *Adv. Hæres. l.* iii. *c.* ii. *p.* 199, 200. " And had
" these apostles left us nothing in writing, must not we, in that case,
" have followed the rule of doctrine, which they delivered to those to
" whom they entrusted their churches? To this rule many barbarous
" nations submit, who, deprived of the aid of letters, have the words of
" salvation written on their hearts, and carefully guard the doctrine
" which has been delivered." *Ibid. c.* iv. *p.* 205. " Thus Polycarp
" always taught what he had learnt from the apostles, delivering it to
" the church; and these things alone are true. To them all the
" churches of Asia, and they who, down to this day, have succeeded to
" St. Polycarp, bear testimony. He was a man of much greater au-
" thority, and a witness of truth more faithful, than Valentinus and
" Marcion, and such perverse thinkers. Coming to Rome, in the time
" of Anicetus, he converted many heretics to the church of God, an-
" nouncing the one and only truth, which he had received from the
" apostles, and which he delivered to the church. There is an epistle
" of Polycarp to the Philippians, from which may be collected, what

" was the character of his faith, and the truth which he preached.
" Moreover, the church of Ephesus, which Paul founded, and where
" John resided to the time of Trajan, is itself a witness to the doctrine
" delivered by the apostles." *Adv. Hær. l.* iii. *c.* iii. *p.* 203.

Of the real presence of Christ in the sacrament of the Eucharist, or
Lord's supper, and the sacrifice of the Mass, which Catholics steadfastly
maintain, and even resign their civil rights for the same, as the Protestants of this country have made the rejection of this doctrine a test
of civil capacity, by compelling every person appointed to office to
SWEAR it is DAMNABLE and IDOLATROUS, this " zealous opposer
'· of heresies in general," (observe we quote John Fox) writes thus :—
" It is our duty to make an offering to God, and with a pure heart, a
" sincere faith, a firm hope, and a fervent charity to present the Maker
" of all things the first fruits of his creatures. But this pure oblation
" the church alone makes. The Jews make it not, for their hands are
" stained with blood ; and they receive not the word that is offered to
" God. Nor do the assemblies of heretics make it.—For how can
" these prove, that the bread, over which the words of thanksgiving
" have been pronounced, is the body of their Lord, and the cup his
" blood, while they do not admit, that he is the Son, that is, the Word
" of the Creator of the world? Or how again do they maintain, that
" the flesh turns to corruption, and partakes not of life, which is nou-
" rished with the body and blood of the Lord? Wherefore, let them
" either give up their opinion, or cease from making that offering.
" But our sentiment accords with the nature of the Eucharist, and, the
" Eucharist again confirms our sentiment. The bread that we receive
" is no longer common bread, but the Eucharist, consisting of two
" things, terrestrial and celestial.". *Adv. Hær. lib.* iv. *c.* xxxiv. *p.* 326,
327. " They are truly vain (the heretics), who contemn the whole
" divine system, and denying the salvation and regeneration of the flesh,
" maintain that it is not susceptible of incorruption. According to this
" then, the Lord did not redeem us by his blood ; nor is the cup of the
" Eucharist the participation of his blood, nor the bread, which we
" break, the participation of his body. When therefore the mingled
" chalice and the broken bread receive the word of God, they become
" the Eucharist of the body and blood of Christ, by which the substance
" of our flesh is increased and strengthened : how then can they pre-
" tend, that this flesh is not susceptible of eternal life? And as a sec-
" tion of the vine laid in the earth produces fruit in due season, and in
" like manner the grain of corn is multiplied, by the blessing of God,
" which afterwards are used for the benefit of man, and receiving on
" them the word of God, become the Eucharist, which is the body and
" blood of Christ : so our bodies, nourished by that Eucharist, and then
" laid in the earth, and dissolved in it, shall, in due time, rise again."
Ibid. l. v. *c.* xi. *p.* 395, 397, 399.

" Giving advice to his disciples, to offer their first fruits to God, not
" as if he stood in need of them, but that they might not seem ungrate-
" ful, he took bread into his hands, and giving thanks, said : *This is my*
" *body.* Likewise he declared the cup to be his blood, and taught the
" new oblation of the new Testament, which oblation the church re-
" ceiving from the apostles, offers it to God over all the earth—to him

" who grants us food—the first fruits of his gifts in the new Testament,
" of which the prophet Malachias spoke : *I will not accept offerings from*
" *your hands. For from the rising of the sun to the going down of the*
" *same, my name is great among the Gentiles, and in every place incense is*
" *offered to my name, a clean sacrifice.* Manifestly hereby signifying,
" that the first people (the Jews) will cease to offer to God ; and that
" in every place, a sacrifice, and that clean, will be offered to him, and
" that his name is glorified among the Gentiles." *Adver. Hær. l.* IV.
" *c.* xxxii. *p.* 323, 324. " Therefore the offering of the church, which
" the Lord directed to be made over all the world, was deemed a pure
" sacrifice before God, and received by him ; not that he stands in need
" of a sacrifice from us, but because he that makes the offering, if his
" gift be accepted, is thereby 'rendered worthy of praise. As then
" in simplicity the church offers, her offering is accepted by God as a
" pure sacrifice. *Ibid. c.* xxxix. *p.* 324, 326.

We have been thus prolix in our quotations from this great and learned father of the Catholic church, who is stiled by John Fox himself
" a zealous opposer of heresies in general," because we shall have occasion, in the progress of our review of this mass of falsehoods and calumnies, *the Book of Martyrs,* to contrast the orthodox doctrines of St.
Irenæus, with the notions of John Fox's Protestant saints, in order that
the reader may be able to form his own unbiassed judgment on the
merits of the question between us. We have before noticed the impiety of the test oath put to all persons in this country to qualify for office, from the lord chancellor down to the petty constable, and we now
appeal to the candid reader, whether this qualification, in the face of
these doctrines, so clearly expressed by a martyred "opposer of *heresies*
" in general," is not a disgrace to the country, and therefore ought to
be abolished? For, in the vindication of the orthodoxy of this doctrine
of the Catholic church, and consequently the *heresy* of Protestants,
using the words of John Fox, we have the declaration of the learned
Dr. Grabe, a Protestant divine, who edited an edition of the works of
St. Irenæus. He observes,—"It is *certain* that St. Irenæus, and *all*
" *the fathers*—either contemporary with the apostles, or their immedi-
" ate successors, whose writings are still extant—considered the Eu-
" charist to be the sacrifice of the new law, and offered bread and wine
" on the altar, as sacred oblations to God the Father ; and that it was
" not the *private opinion of* any *particular* church or teacher, but the
" PUBLIC DOCTRINE and PRACTICE of the UNIVERSAL CHURCH,
" which she received from the apostles, as they from Christ, is express-
" ly shewn in this place (alluding to the last extracts above) by Irenæus,
" and before him by Justin M. and Clement of Rome." (See p. 49 of this
Review for St. Justin's words.) What gross impiety and inconsistency
must it then be, for men to swear at this day, that what was the practice of the universal church in former ages, and is proved to have been
received by her from the apostles, is IDOLATROUS and DAMNABLE. What
hypocrisy to raise an outcry against Deism, and persecute those who
are unhappily under its influence, when the persecutors themselves
most impiously protest before the throne of God, that what his Son,
the Redeemer of the world, taught his apostles, is IDOLATRY and SUPER-
STITION, and consequently meriting eternal damnation. We have it

here stated, by John Fox and his editors, that St. Irenæus was "a zeal-
"ous opposer of heresies in general;" we have proved from his works
that the doctrine which he taught is the doctrine now preached by the
Catholic church; yet do these men pretend to be "diffusing among
"their fellow-believers a knowledge and love of the *genuine* principles
"of Christianity," while they scruple not to swear that that is *damnable*
doctrine which St. Irenæus, the "zealous opposer of heresies in gene-
"ral," maintained was ORTHODOX. Reader, is it possible to find a
parallel in any Christian country for impiety and inconsistency like this?

Having thus filled the void made by Fox and his editors in the *doctrines* of the primitive Christians, we will now return to his list of
martyrs under this persecution. From Rome and Gaul, Fox carries
his readers into Africa, where he says, "many were martyred in that
"part of the globe." Of these he mentions in particular, Perpetua
and Felicitas, who suffered with Revocatus, Saturninus, and Secundulus.
Perpetua was a lady of quality, and Felicitas a female slave; the former had a young child at her breast; the latter was in a state of pregnancy, and was delivered of a daughter before she suffered martyrdom. The relation given by Fox is substantially correct, but here he
suppresses an important circumstance or two, the notice of which
would have shewn that neither he nor his church had any claim to these
martyrs. Perpetua is stated to have had a vision, after being condemned
to death, in which she was assured that her youngest brother, who
had been dead some years, had been pardoned some fault committed
by him when living, through her prayers. Thus confirming the doctrine then held as well as now, by the Catholic church, of praying for
the souls in purgatory. When first brought before the people, they
were exposed naked, but the condition of the one and the delicacy of
the other, operated on the judge and the people, and they were allowed
to be covered. A wild cow being let out upon them, it attacked Perpetua first, tossing her up in the air, when falling on her back she
raised herself up in a sitting posture, and adjusted her clothes, which
had been much disordered. She then tied her hair, and getting up,
perceived Felicitas on the ground much hurt by the cow, whom she
helped to rise. They then stood together, expecting another assault,
but the people cried out that it was enough, and they were then led out,
when the sword finished their mortal course, and enabled them to
enter into the joys of heaven. So great was the fame of these two
martyrs, and their feast was celebrated in so solemn a manner in St.
Augustin's time, that persons were annually drawn in great numbers
to visit their relics, which were deposited in the great church of Carthage. Their names are inscribed in the canon of the Mass, as may
be seen by a reference to the missals now in use among Catholics, and
their festival is yearly celebrated by the Catholic church, on the 7th of
March, a convincing proof that these heroic female martyrs were Catholics, and not Protestants. This practice of naming the saints in the
mass, as also of praying for the dead, is coeval with the institution of
the sacrifice itself. Anciently the names of those who were specially
mentioned in the mass, were written on papers or parchments folded
twice, from which they obtained the name of dyptics, and were deposited on the altar. The saints, however, who suffered martyrdom

for the true faith, becoming so numerous as to render it impossible to include them all, they were transferred to the canon, and a few only were inserted, adding thereto the general phrase, "and to all saints." Of the names preserved are those, as we have before stated, of Perpetua and Felicitas.

THE SIXTH AND SEVENTH PERSECUTIONS UNDER THE ROMAN EMPERORS.

The space allotted by Fox to the sixth persecution is so very inconsiderable, that we do not deem it necessary to make a distinct head of it. He describes it as being raised by the emperor Maximus, in the year 235. This emperor raised himself to the purple by the assassination of the emperor Alexander Severus, one of the best of the Roman emperors. Maximus was by birth a barbarian, being the son of a poor herdsman of Thrace, and of gigantic stature, being, it is said, eight feet and a half high. For his cruelty towards all men he is frequently surnamed Busiris, Typhon, and Phalaris, and was a monster of gluttony. Among the martyrs named by Fox in this persecution are two popes, whose deaths are thus recorded. "Pontanius bishop "of Rome, for *preaching against idolatry*, was banished to Sardinia, and "there destroyed. Anteros, a Grecian, who succeeded this bishop in "the see of Rome, gave so much offence to the government by col- "lecting the acts of the martyrs, that, after having held his dignity "only forty days, he suffered martyrdom himself." Now what are we to think of this statement, made by men who swear that Popery is idolatry, and believe the pope to be Antichrist? Here we have it stated that one of these bishops of Rome became a "godly martyr," for "preaching against idolatry," while his successors, since the reformation so called, are represented to be the chiefs of idolaters? The other too is made a "godly martyr," for "collecting" the acts of the "martyrs," which is now-a-days reckoned to be an act of superstition. But, let us here observe, that we think it very improbable that Anteros lost his life through the cause stated by John Fox, because the very short time he filled the pontifical chair did not allow him the opportunity of collecting the acts of the martyrs. Butler, in his account of these two holy popes, makes but slight mention of them; probably from there not being any positive records of the manner of their deaths. Echard says, that Anteros only *designed* the collection of the acts of the martyrs, which Fabian, his successor, carried into execution, the mild reign of the emperor Philip allowing him to accomplish the undertaking.

The account of the seventh persecution is prefaced by Fox and his editors with the following remarks: "In the year 249, Decius being "emperor of Rome, a dreadful persecution was begun against the Chris- "tians. This was occasioned partly by the hatred he bore to his prede- "cessor Philip, who was deemed a Christian, and partly to his jealousy "concerning the amazing increase of Christianity; for the heathen tem- "ples were almost forsaken, and the Christian churches crowded with "proselytes. Decius, provoked at this, attempted, as it were, to extir- "pate the name of Christian; and, unfortunately for the *cause of the gos- 'pel,* many *errors* had about this time crept into *the church:* the Chris-

" tians were *at variance with each other*: and a variety of contentions en-
" sued amongst them. The heathens in general were ambitious to en-
" force the imperial decrees upon this occasion, and looked upon the
" murder of a Christian as a merit to themselves. The martyrs were,
" therefore, innumerable."

Now, reader, if you be a Protestant, we care not of what denomination, so you are unbiased in your mind and desirous to learn the
truth, can you, we ask, make any thing but absurdity out of this statement we have quoted? Fox here talks of " the amazing increase of
" Christianity" as one of the causes of this persecution under Decius,
and then laments the *errors* that had crept into *the church*, at this
time, as a misfortune for the cause of the gospel!!! What contradictory nonsense. Why if Christianity increased with amazing rapidity,
the cause of the gospel must have increased also; or does Fox mean
to insinuate that the cause of Christianity and the cause of the Gospel
are two distinct and separate things? That *errors* abounded, at this
time, as well as in the preceding ages, cannot be denied; but they
had not crept into THE CHURCH, as Fox *falsely* asserts, because
THE CHURCH being the PILLAR and GROUND of TRUTH,
as St. Paul declares, in 1 Tim. iii, 15, on the promise of Christ himself, who assured his apostles that the SPIRIT of TRUTH should
continue with HIS CHURCH to the END of the WORLD, " that
" he might present it to himself *a glorious Church*, not having *spot* or
" *wrinkle*, nor *any such thing*, but that it should be *holy* and *with-*
" *out blemish*," (Ephes. v. 27.) the Church itself COULD NOT ERR;
for, we beg you to observe, had error *once* crept into her foundation,
she could no longer have been the *pillar* and *ground* of *truth*. The
assertion then of Fox, that " many errors had about this time crept
" into the church" is clearly false and blasphemous, as we have shewn
from the works of St. Irenæus, who is accounted by Fox " a zealous
" opposer of heresies in general." Again, he says, a variety of contentions ensued amongst the Christians, and yet a little while before
he says, " the heathen temples were almost forsaken, and the Chris-
" tian churches crowded with proselytes." Now, how are we to reconcile these two statements? These contentions among the Christians,
common sense would lead us to suppose, must have led to the thinning
of the churches; for can any man in his senses imagine that persons
opposed to each other in point of doctrine would cordially assemble
together at one and the same time to crowd the churches, and not
only thus congregate in great masses, but likewise gain proselytes in
the midst of contentions. Let us here take an example. In the sixteenth century the king and parliament of this country thought proper
to change the old established religion; and form a *new* one, of which
the sovereign was constituted the *head* by the power of parliament, and
he was armed with the *civil* sword to control the *consciences* of his subjects. Laws were passed to compel persons to conform to the *new*
mode of worship, and a creed was framed to insure *uniformity*, while
the churches were taken from the old possessors and given to the
ministers of the new religion. Here then we have *a church* protected
by *law*, and every human means adopted to insure its stability. But
it did not long exist before the members of it were at variance with

each other; objections were made to its doctrine and its discipline. Fresh penal statutes were enacted to enforce submission, but still "a "variety of contentions ensued amongst them;" and what was the result? Not the crowding of her churches with proselytes; but the defection of her members to fill conventicles. Each succeeding century has produced additional variations of doctrine, and a greater decrease of attendance at the churches; and at the time we are writing, instead of gaining proselytes to Christianity, the people are daily falling into infidelity and deism, from the confusion and absurdity of so many pretenders to truth. And would not this inevitably have been the case in the third century, had *the church* in that age been infected with *error?* Most undoubtedly it would. Decius would have had no occasion to raise the sword of persecution against Christianity, for in the absence of truth, the pretenders to it would have destroyed themselves, and the Pagans been confirmed in their idolatry; but the church, like a city placed on a mountain, displayed her glorious treasures to the wanderer after truth, and opened her gates to the benighted-traveller. The sublimity of her mysteries, the purity of her morals, the excellency of her precepts, and the unity and indefectibility of her faith, pointed her out as the ONLY GUIDE by which man could direct his steps through the wilderness of this world, and hence the labours of her preachers were crowned with a harvest of glory, in bringing into her fold innumerable proselytes.

Then as to "the heathens in general being ambitious to enforce the im-"perial decrees upon this occasion, and looked upon the murder of a "Christian as a merit to themselves;" was not this cold-blooded conduct imitated by the English Protestants upon the Irish Catholics in the reign of Elizabeth? The late Mr. Wm. Parnell, in his *Historical Apology*, p. 91, says, "When the power and pride of the English be-"came so highly exalted under Elizabeth, the Irish were considered as "a sort of rebel savages, clearly excluded from the contemplation of "the laws of God and man, the violation of whose rights formed no "precedent that could effect civilized nations; and it did not follow "that a man who should *spoil* and MURDER them might not be pos-"sessed of an upright and gentle heart." Nay, do we not read in the public prints of the present day, outrages and murders committed on Irish Catholics by Orange "Protestant-ascendency"-men, as of common occurrence, and the perpetrators escaping punishment through the perjury of their comrades? And from what cause do these last mentioned atrocities arise; but from the same malignant spirit of religious intolerance and jealousy that influenced the Roman pagans to persecute the primitive Christians?

We must now proceed to notice some of the martyrs recorded by Fox as suffering in this persecution. The first is thus related: "Fa-"bian, bishop of Rome, was the first person of eminence who felt the "severity of this persecution. The deceased emperor, Philip, had, on "account of his integrity, committed his treasure to the care of this "good man; but Decius, not finding as much as his avarice made him "expect, determined to wreak his vengeance on the good prelate. "He was accordingly seized; and on the 20th of January, A.D. 250, "suffered martyrdom by decapitation."

Such is the account given by Fox, but is there an individual, whose mind is free from prejudice, who can give credence to so ridiculous a tale? Philip is supposed to have been a Christian in his heart, from the mildness of his disposition, and the lenity he shewed towards them; but granting that he had really embraced the faith of Christ, is any one so stupid and credulous as to believe, merely on the word of John Fox, that this emperor would have dared to make choice of the head of the Christian church for his treasurer, knowing the prejudices of the Roman senate, the nobility, the army, and the people against the Christians? So monstrous an idea could never be entertained for a moment by any man of common sense. None but misguided fanatics, like the adherents of Fox, who wish to excite "a hatred and " abhorrence of the (supposed) corruptions and crimes of Popery and " its professors," could credit such absurdity. We see in history, that the attempt of Charles the first to establish episcopacy and uniformity of worship in Scotland eventually cost him his head. We see that James the second lost his crown through a desire to establish liberty of conscience in the kingdom. And we see the spirit of intolerance pervading "Protestant-ascendency" at this moment, in consequence of the liberal wishes expressed by his present majesty George the fourth that the laws should be equally administered in Ireland. We see the spirit of party heated and inflamed to as high a degree as at any period of Protestant domination; and can we credit that Pagan ascendency would not have taken alarm at the favour and partiality said to have been shewn to pope Fabian? Let the circumcised Jew, or the blind Foxite, believe it; we will not. Echard makes no particular mention of the death of Fabian, and Butler is very concise in his account of the life of this martyr. The latter says he held the Papal see sixteen years, and sent St. Dionysius and other preachers to Gaul, and condemned Privatus, a broacher of a new heresy in Africa, as appears from St. Cyprian. In his life he was a pattern of purity and holiness.

Among other persons recorded as martyrs, Fox sets down "Cyril " bishop of Gortyna;" we have examined Butler's Martyrology, and Echard's Ecclesiastical History, but we can find no such name in either of these authors. In detailing the martyrdom of St. Babylas, bishop of Antioch, and others, Fox falls into another of his gross mistakes. He says, "On Gordian's death, in the reign of Decius, that emperor " came to Antioch, where, having a desire to visit an assembly of Chris- " tians, Babylas opposed him, and refused to let him come in. The " emperor *dissembled* his anger at that time; but soon sending for the " bishop, he sharply *reproved him for his insolence*, and then ordered him " to sacrifice to the Pagan deities as an expiation for his supposed " crimes." Here again we have as improbable a tale as we think can be told. Supposing Decius to have been desirous to see a Christian assembly, is it rational to believe that he, who is represented as one of the most despotic and merciless tyrants that ever breathed, would have submitted to a refusal from Babylas, a Christian bishop, and not only submit to a refusal, but even dissemble his anger? Is it not more likely that the emperor would have ordered Babylas to have been put to death upon the spot, and all the Christians assembled with him, had he met with that opposition to his desires stated by Fox? Is it pro-

bable that an imperious tyrant, unable to brook delay, and unused to
denial, would curb in his rage, and send for the bishop on some future
day, to reprove his insolence and revenge himself for it, by ordering
the prelate to sacrifice to the heathen deities? Such a tale is incredible; yet we see it is told and believed; and believed too by those who
charge their Catholic neighbours with being too credulous and superstitious! The fact is, and it shews the ignorance or impudence of Fox,
it was Philip, the predecessor of Decius, who was refused admittance,
into the temple of God by Babylas.* The account of this transaction is
thus related by Mr. Echard, in his Ecclesiastical History, on the authority of St. John Chrysostom and Eusebius. "Philip, shortly after his
" election, made a dishonourable peace with the Persians, and returned
" to Antioch; where, upon the vigil of Easter, he and his empress at-
" tempted to enter into the Christian church, to partake of the prayers
" of the congregation: but the holy Babylas, bishop of that city, well
" knowing his late crimes, (among others he had ordered the emperor
" Gordian to be assassinated) courageously withstood him, and laying
" his hand upon his heart, pronounced him *unworthy to enter into the*
" *sheepfold of Jesus Christ*, and declared, that he should have no admit-
" tance, unless he made A GENERAL CONFESSION OF HIS SINS,
" *and was placed among the number of the penitents.* To all which, it is
" said, the emperor humbly submitted, and demonstrated in his deeds,
" the sincerity and devoutness of his affections towards the majesty of
" Heaven." From this account we not only see how little Fox is to be
relied on, even in a matter of history, but we also discover that CONFES-
SION OF SINS, now so reprobated by all classes of Protestants, but
practised at this day by Catholics, was a doctrine of the primitive
church. This occurrence is stated to have taken place in the year
244. Babylas suffered in 251.

There is a circumstance connected with the history of this martyr,
related both by Pagan and Christian writers of the earliest ages, so extraordinary and wonderful, that we feel induced to mention it here.
Fox says, St. Babylas was *beheaded*, but the general accounts state that
he consummated his martyrdom by the hardships of his imprisonment,
and that his chains were buried with him. The Christians built a
church it is said over his tomb, where his body rested till the year
351, when Gallus Cæsar translated it to Daphne, five miles from Antioch, to oppose the worship of an idol of Apollo, celebrated for giving
oracles in that place. Gallus erected a church to the memory of St.
Babylas near the heathen temple, and placed the relics of the martyr
in a shrine above the ground. The oracle was struck dumb by the
near approach of the saint's ashes, as is affirmed by St. Chrysostom,
Theodoret, Sozomen, and others, who triumph over the Pagans on
this occasion. In confirmation of the fact, St. Chrysostom gives in his
works the lamentation of Libanius, the celebrated heathen sophist, be-
wailing the silence of Apollo at Daphne. Eleven years after this event,
Julian the apostate, whose hatred of the divine Redeemer has been
imitated by Voltaire, and the present race of deists, came to Antioch,
that is in 362, and by many sacrifices learned of the oracle, that the
cause of its silence arose from the neighbouring places being filled
with dead bones. Julian understood this to allude to the relics of St.

Babylas, and ordered the Christians to remove them, which was done with great solemnity by carrying them back to Antioch. The following evening the temple and idol of Apollo were reduced by lightning to ashes, with all the rich and magnificent ornaments, leaving only the bare walls standing. Upon the news reaching the ears of Julian's uncle, who was governor of the east, he hastened to Daphne, and endeavoured by tortures to compel the idolatrous priests to confess how the accident happened, whether by negligence or through the Christians. It was, however, proved by the testimony of these very priests, and also by some peasants, who saw the fire fall from heaven, that lightning was the cause of the ruin of the temple. Julian was afraid to rebuild the temple, lest vengeance should fall upon his own head, but he breathed the utmost fury against the Christians, when the arm of God overreached him by an untimely death in his expedition against the Persians. We have given this fact upon the testimony of historians living near the period when it occurred, and though some may affect to doubt its reality, we really cannot see on what grounds they can reject it, that would not equally tend to discredit the relations of Hannibal's victories, or any other event in history. Ammianus Marcellinus, a heathen, and Julian's own historian, says, l. ii, p. 225, that he caused all the bones of dead men to be taken away to purify the place, which is a strong corroboration of the above relation.

The next passage worthy of notice is the following:—"The emperor
" Gallus having concluded his wars, a plague broke out in the empire;
" and sacrifices to the pagan deities were ordered by the emperor to ap-
" pease their wrath. On the Christians refusing to comply with these
" rites, they were charged with being the authors of the calamity: and
" thus the persecution spread from the interior to the extreme parts of the
" empire, and many fell martyrs to the impetuosity of the rabble, as well
" as the prejudice of the magistrates. Cornelius, the Christian bishop of
" Rome, was, among others, seized upon this occasion. He was first
" banished to Centum-Cellæ, now called Civita Vecchia; and after hav-
" ing been cruelly scourged, was, on the 14th of September, A. D. 252,
" beheaded, after having been bishop 15 months and ten days. Lucius,
" who succeeded Cornelius as bishop of Rome, was the son of Porphyrius,
" and a Roman by birth. His vigilance, as a pastor, rendered him ob-
" noxious to the foes of Christianity, which occasioned him to be banish-
" ed: but in a short time he was permitted to return. Soon after, how-
" ever, he was apprehended, and beheaded, March the 14th, A. D. 253.
" This bishop was succeeded by Stephanus, a man of fiery temper, who
" held the dignity few years, and might probably have fallen a martyr,
" had not the emperor been murdered by his general Æmilian, when a
" profound peace succeeded through the whole empire, and the persecu-
" tion was suffered to subside."

Here then we have the admission, that of the " godly martyrs" suffering under Gallus, the successor of Decius, those most worthy to be recorded, even by Fox, were two bishops of Rome. We have seen by the works of St. Irenæus, that the bishop of Rome was considered by the primitive Christians to be the supreme head of the church, as he is at this day by the Catholics, and of course these " godly martyrs" could not be Protestant but Catholic bishops. It is not a little curious that

Fox stiles Cornelius "the *Christian* bishop of Rome:" what necessity there could be for this adjunct we cannot perceive, as we do not recollect to have read of any *Pagan* bishops of Rome. It is true, since the reformation so called, it has been familiar with Protestants to call the bishops of Rome by many vile names, which we shall not mention, and style them any thing but "Christians;" however we have it here admitted by Fox, that one of the bishops of Rome at least was a "Chris-"tian," and another a vigilant pastor, which rendered him obnoxious to the foes of Christianity. How Fox came to be so uncivil to pope Stephanus may be a matter of surprise to some of our readers, but it is none to us, nor will it probably be to them, when we inform them that this pope was a resolute opposer of innovations and error, and proceeded to excommunicate some of the most obstinate innovators. Some of the bishops in Spain and Gaul had embraced the novelties of Novatian; others had fallen into the crime of *Libellatici*, that is, had purchased for money licenses of safety, falsely stating they had sacrificed to idols, to save their lives during the persecution. A controversy also arose concerning the rebaptization of heretics, which gave the good pope much trouble. He was traduced as a favourer of heresy, which he bore with much patience, and conducted himself as became a vigilant pastor, as appears by the following account, given of this controversy by the learned Vincent of Lerinus: "When all cried out, "against the novelty, and the priests every where opposed it in pro-"portion to every's one's zeal, then pope Stephen, of blessed memory, "bishop of the apostolic see, stood up, with his other colleagues against "it, but, he in a signal manner above the rest, thinking it fitting, I "believe, that he should go beyond them as much by the ardour of his "faith as he was raised above them by the authority of his see. In his "letter to the church of Africa he thus decrees: 'Let no innovation "be introduced, but let that be observed which is handed down to us "by tradition.' The prudent and holy man understood that the rule "of piety admits nothing new, but all things are to be delivered down "to our posterity with the same fidelity with which they were receiv-"ed; and that it is our duty to follow religion, and not make religion "follow us; for the proper characteristic of a modest and sober Chris-"tian is, not to impose his own conceits upon posterity, but to make "his own imaginations bend to the wisdom of them that went before "him. What then was the issue of this grand affair, but that which is "usual?—antiquity kept possession, and novelty was exploded." Thus it will be seen, that in all difficulties and contentions, *one invariable rule* is followed by the Catholic church, namely, to adhere to PUBLIC OPINION, and exclude whatever savours of novelty.

But what will the reader say of John Fox's veracity, when he is told that this Protestant martyrologist, whose work has been so long held in high estimation, and is now published to "diffuse among *fel-*"*low-believers* a knowledge and love of the genuine principles of Chris-"tianity;" what will the reader say, when we tell him, that this pope Stephanus who, but for his "fiery temper," Fox says, "might probably "have fallen a martyr," is actually recorded by this *same* Mr. Fox as a martyr, in the succeeding persecution under the name of *Stephen*. "In "the same year," Fox writes, that is in the year 257, "Stephen, bishop

A REVIEW

OF

Fox's Book of Martyrs,

CRITICAL AND HISTORICAL.

No. 6. Printed and Published by W. E. Andrews, 3, Chapter-house-court, St. Paul's Churchyard, London. **Price 3d.**

EXPLANATION OF THE ENGRAVING.—*The miraculous appearance of the Cross (by which the Redeemer of Mankind triumphed over the world) to Constantine the great, by which he was assured of victory over the tyrant Maxentius, who had declared war against him. A particular account of this wonderful event will be given in the next number.*

CONTINUATION OF THE REVIEW.

of Rome was beheaded!!!" Well might the editors of the *Encyclopædia Britannica* say, in giving Fox's biography, that "his facts are not always to be depended on," for here we have one of the grossest contradictions ever made by a public writer. That Stephanus and Stephen are one and the same person is evident from the dates used by Fox. Stephanus he says succeeded Lucius, who was martyred in 253, and Stephen was beheaded in 257. Now Stephanus or Stephen was chosen on the 3d of May, in the year mentioned by Fox, and sat four years, two months, and twenty-one days, according to Butler, being beheaded on the 2d of August in the last named year, whilst he was sitting in his pontifical chair. Stephanus is the Latin for the English name Stephen: so much for the accuracy of John Fox's martyrology.

We have now to notice as curious an admission from John Fox and his editors, as ever could be made by inconsistency itself. "Many of " the *errors*," he states, "which crept into the church at this time, " arose from the placing *human reason* in competition with *revelation*; " but the *fallacy of such arguments* being *proved* by the most able

" divines, the *opinions* they had created *vanished before the sublimity of*
" *truth.*" See you this, ye bible-venders and private interpretation-men!
See you this statement from the *Book of Martyrs* of John Fox. And yet
you reproach the Catholics for adhering to revelation and the doctrines
of those able divines, who made " error vanish before the sublimity of
" truth!" You contend for the exercise of human reason in divining the
mystic words of scripture, while Catholics contend for the undeviating
rule of PUBLIC OPINION, received from age to age; and here we have
John Fox telling you that human reason being placed in competition
with the revelations delivered by the apostles, occasioned errors to arise
in the third age of the church. And what was it but human reason, or
rather human depravity, that occasioned the reformation, so called, of
the sixteenth century? What is it but the wanderings of the human
mind, that cause such a multiplicity of incongruous sects as now overspread this once Catholic land? We wish, however, to correct one
assertion made by John Fox. Error did not creep into "the church,"
since she is invulnerable; but it spread among some of her members,
who being detected " by the most able divines," were cast out from her,
agreeably to the words of Christ, as given in the gospel, *He that will
not hear* THE CHURCH, *let him be unto thee as the heathen or publican.*

Of these " most able divines," we have given the sentiments of St.
Irenæus; Fox notices Tertullian, and professes to give an "account
" of Origen;" but such an account as no one can derive any information
as to what doctrines he held and taught. We will therefore supply
the omission of Fox with respect to Tertullian and Origen, as we did
in the case of St. Irenæus. The first two writers held all the same
doctrines as the latter, it will therefore be unnecessary to quote them
on all the heads we have given of the sentiments of St. Irenæus; we will
therefore confine ourselves in this place to the words of Tertullian and
Origen on the mischief arising "from placing human reason in compe-
" tition with revelation." Tertullian was contemporary with St. Irenæus. He wrote several able works, and defended the Christian
cause with zeal and ability. His father was a centurion in the procon-
sular troops of Africa, and he was born at Carthage about the year
160. He confesses that before his conversion to the Christian faith,
he, in his merry fits, pointed his keenest satire against it, had been an
adulterer, and taken a cruel pleasure in the bloody games of the amphitheatre, attained to a distinguished eminency in vice, and was an
accomplished sinner. Notwithstanding these evil propensities, he had
a head well stored with talent, studied the sciences in every branch,
dived into the principles of the different sects, and at length became a
Christian. Having embraced the divine law, he restrained his vicious
passions, but never sufficiently checked the vehemence of his temper.
Formed for controversy, by his lively and comprehensive genius, he
set himself, soon after his conversion, to write in defence of true religion, which was then attacked by Heathens and Jews on the one side,
and on the other by a swarm of corrupted heretics. When the persecution began to rage, he wrote his *Apologetic*, which is considered not
only his master-piece, but one of the best amongst all the works of
Christian antiquity. This piece was addressed to the proconsul and
other magistrates of Africa, and clears, in a most forcible stile, the

Christians from the calumnies of incest and murder thrown upon them. In this apology the author mentions the submission of the Christians to the reigning emperors, their love of their enemies, and their mutual charity, horror of all vice, and constancy in suffering death and all manner of torments for the sake of virtue. The heathens called them in derision Sarmentitians and Semaxians, because they were fastened to trunks of trees, and stuck about with fagots to be set on fire. But Tertullian answers them: "Thus dressed about with fire, "we are in our most illustrious apparel. These are our triumphal robes, "embroidered with palm-branches in token of victory (such the Roman "generals wore in their solemn triumphs,) and mounted upon the "pile we look upon ourselves as in our triumphal chariot. Who "ever looked well into our religion but he came over to it? and who. "ever came over to it but was ready to suffer for it? We thank you "for condemning us, because there is such a blessed discord between "the divine and human judgment, that when you condemn us upon "earth, God absolveth us in heaven."

Among other works, Tertullian wrote a most excellent book entitled *Of Prescription against Heretics*, in which he thus speaks of those who place "human reason in competition with revelation," which Fox says was the cause of error or heresy, but that it "vanished be- "fore the sublimity of truth?"——"We are not allowed to indulge our "own humour, nor to choose what another has *invented*. We have the "apostles of our Lord for founders, who were not themselves the in- "ventors nor authors of what they have left us; but they have faith- "fully taught the world the doctrines which they received from Christ." *De Præscriptione*, c. vi, p. 331. *Edii Pamelii, Rothomagi*, 1662. "Now, "to know what the apostles taught, that is, what Christ revealed to "them, recourse must be had to the churches which they founded, "and which they instructed by word of mouth, and by their epistles. "For it is plain that all doctrine, which is conformable to the faith of "these mother churches, is true, being that which they received from "the apostles; the apostles from Christ; Christ from God; and that "all other opinions must be novel and false." *Ibid.* c. xxi, p. 334.

"What will you gain by recurring to scripture, when one denies "what the other asserts? Learn rather, who it is that possesses the "faith of Christ; to whom the scriptures belong; from whom, by "whom; and when that faith was delivered, by which we are made "Christians. For where shall be found the true faith, there will be "the genuine scriptures; there the true interpretation of them; "and there all Christian traditions. Christ chose his apostles, whom "he sent to preach to all nations. They delivered his doctrine, and "founded churches, from which churches others drew the seeds of "the same doctrine, as new ones daily continue to do. Thus these, as "the offspring of the apostolic churches, are themselves deemed apos- "tolical." *Ibid.* p. 334. "If the truth then be adjudged to us, who "embrace the rule, which the church received from the apostles; the "apostles from Christ; and Christ from God; heretics, it is plain, can- "not be allowed to appeal to the scriptures, in which, we prove, they "have no concern. They are not Christians; and therefore, to them "we may say: who are you! When, and whence came ye? What

" business have you on my estate, you, who are none of mine? Mar-
" cion, by what right do you cut down my wood? Or you Valenti-
" nus, do you turn my streams? Or, Appelles, do you move my boun-
" daries? The possession is mine. What right have any others to
" sow and feed here as they may choose? The possession, I say, is mine;
" has been long mine; mine first : the title deeds are in my hands, de-
" rived from them whose property it was. I am the heir of the apos-
" tles. As they settled it by will, on the conditions they prescribed, I
" hold it. You they disinherited, as aliens and enemies. And why are
" you such but by the diversity of the doctrine which each one of you,
" as he was disposed, produced or received against those apostles?
" Where this diversity of doctrine is, there will the scriptures and the
" expounding of them be adulterated." *Ibid.* c. xxxvii. p. 338.

Origen was contemporary with St. Clement of Alexandria, and succeeded him as catechist or teacher in the celebrated school of that
city. He was a person of great parts, and study made him a most
perfect proficient in every branch of learning, in dialectics, in geo-
metry, in arithmetic, in music, in rhetoric, in the different systems of
philosophy, in the Hebrew language, and in the knowledge of holy
scripture. Such a man was no mean advocate for Christianity, and his
lectures and writings were productive of many proselytes from the
ranks of Paganism. He died about the year 252. On the above occasion of error, that is, as John Fox says, the " placing of human
" reason in competition with revelation," Origen says, " As there are
" many who think they believe what Christ taught, and some of these
" differ from others, it becomes necessary that all should profess that
" doctrine which came down from the apostles, and now continues in the
" church.' That alone is truth, which in nothing differs from what is
" thus delivered." *Præf. Lib.* i. *Periarchon, t.* i. *p.* 47. *Edit. PP. S.*
Mauri, Paris, 1733. " As often as heretics produce the canonical scrip-
" tures, in which every Christian agrees and believes, they seem to
" say, Lo! with us is the word of truth. But to them (the heretics)
" we cannot give credit, nor depart from the first and ecclesiastical
" tradition : we can believe only as the succeeding churches of God
" have delivered." *Tract.* xxix. *in Matt. t.* iii. *p.* 864.

Such were the sentiments of these " able divines" on the fallacy of
" placing human reason in competition with revelation;" a fallacy that
has unhappily produced such an endless variety of contradictory creeds
in this once united land, that it is with much difficulty a person can
find the truth, and is the cause of so many plunging into the gulph of
infidelity.

THE EIGHTH GENERAL PERSECUTION UNDER THE ROMAN EMPERORS.

" After the death of Gallus," Fox writes, " Æmilian, the general,
" having many enemies in the army, was slain, and Valerian elected
" to the empire. This emperor, for the space of four years, governed
" with moderation, and treated the Christians with peculiar lenity
" and respect; but in the year 257, an Egyptian magician, named
" Macrianus, gained a great ascendency over him, and persuaded him
" to persecute them. Edicts were accordingly published, and the per-

"secution, which began in the month of April, continued for three
"years and three months. The martyrs that fell in this persecution
"were innumerable, and their tortures and deaths as various." This
account is substantially correct; some were cut off at one stroke,
others went through the most slow and excruciating tortures: but
though Pagan ascendency and cruelty were exerted to the utmost to
annihilate the name of Christianity, as "Protestant-ascendency" and
penal codes have been put in force to eradicate Catholicism, yet the
efforts of both parties were rendered abortive, for the Christians multiplied under Pagan persecution, and Catholics have increased under
Protestant intolerance.

After giving an account of the martyrdom of SS. Rufina and Secunda,
two accomplished young ladies of Rome, who were beheaded, Fox
writes: "In the same year, Stephen, bishop of Rome, was beheaded,
"and about that time Saturninus, bishop of Thoulouse, was attacked
"and seized by the rabble of that place, for preventing, as they al-
"leged, their oracles from speaking. On refusing to sacrifice to the
"idols, he was treated with many barbarous indignities, and then fas-
"tened by the feet to the tail of a bull. On a certain signal the en-
"raged animal was driven down the steps of the temple, by which the
"martyr's brains were dashed out; and the small number of Christians
"in Thoulouse had not for some time courage sufficient to carry off the
"dead body: at length two women conveyed it away, and deposited it
"in a ditch. This martyr was an orthodox and learned primitive
"Christian, and his doctrines are held in high estimation."

This pope Stephen is the *same* bishop of Rome that Fox said, under
the name of Stephanus, *might have been* a martyr, but for his "fiery
"temper." Of Saturninus Fox says, he was an *orthodox* Christian and
his doctrines *are* held in high estimation. By whom the martyrologist
states not, and we have reason to believe that his modern editors cannot say, except by Catholics. As he was orthodox, the doctrines that
he held were not his *own*, as the language quoted would seem to imply, but those of *the church* of which he was a pastor. We have
looked into Butler's martyrology, the most genuine extant, and we
find him saying, "Fortunatus tells us, that he converted a great num-
"ber of idolaters by his preaching and miracles. This is all the ac-
"count we have of him till the time of his holy martyrdom." Where
Fox got his account he does not mention; that he was an orthodox
Christian there can be no doubt, for if he had not been so, he would
not have been a martyr, nor would the Catholics have raised churches
to his memory, as was done by one of his successors in the see of Toulouse, Silvius, towards the close of the fourth century. This fact will
shew by whom his doctrines were held in high estimation.

Fox next proceeds to detail the martyrdom of another head of the
Catholic church. "Stephen," he says "was succeeded by Sextus as
"bishop of Rome. He is supposed to have been a Greek by birth, or
"extraction, and had for some time served in the capacity of a deacon
"under Stephen. His great fidelity, singular wisdom, and courage,
"distinguished him upon many occasions; and the fortunate conclusion
"of a controversy with some heretics, is generally ascribed to his pru-
"dence. Macrianus, who had the management of the Roman go-

" vernment in the year 258, having procured an order from the em-
" peror Valerian, to put to death all the Christian clergy in Rome, and
" the senate having testified their obedience to this mandate, Sextus
" was one of the first who felt its severity. Cyprian tells us, that he
" was beheaded August 6, A. D. 258; and that six of his deacons suf-
" fered with him."   Here then we have another admission in favour of
the "great fidelity, singular wisdom, and courage," as well as prudence
in suppressing heresy, of the bishops of Rome, who are now looked upon
as the ten-headed monster described in the apocalypse, by the Bible-
zealots and Popery-haters among Protestants.

But the most invidious trick at deception on the part of these modern
editors of Fox remains to be pointed out. The next martyr described
is St. Lawrence, who was so cruelly broiled on a gridiron in this persecution. In the very sheet detailing the martyrdom of Sixtus and
his deacon Lawrence, the modern editors have given a representation of
the latter, and, such is their scrupulous adherence to correctness, that
they have not only made the saint an old man, but they have actually
introduced a figure in the back ground, clothed in the pontifical
habits of a pope, to impress on the minds of the vulgar and unthinking that Lawrence suffered by order of the pope, and therefore became a victim to the cruelties of Popery, when the fact was, the pope
had suffered martyrdom only three days before him, and consequently
could not be present at the execution of his deacon. It is recorded of
St. Lawrence by St. Ambrose (*Amb.* 1. i. *Officior.* c. 41, & 1. ii, c. 28.),
St. Augustin (*Aug. tract.* 27, *in Joan. at Serm. de Sanctus*), and later
authors, that " when Lawrence the deacon saw his bishop Sixtus about to
" be carried away to martyrdom, he began to weep, not for the other's
" sufferings, but for his own remaining behind him ? wherefore he
" cried unto him in these words: whither do you go, O Father, with-
" out your son; and whither do you hasten, O holy priest, without
" you deacon ? You were never wont to offer sacrifice without a
" minister; what then hath displeased you in me, that you leave me
" behind you ? Have you proved me perhaps to be a coward ? Make
" trial, I pray you, whether you have chosen unto yourself a fit minis-
" ter, to whom you have committed the dispensing of our Lord's blood ?
" and then, seeing that you have not denied unto me the fellowship of
" administering sacraments, do not deny me the fellowship of shed-
" ding my blood also with you."

Now this language of St. Lawrence does not savour much of Protestantism, though it does of Catholicism. He here talks plainly of
assisting his bishop at the holy sacrifice of the mass, which Protestants condemn upon oath as idolatrous and superstitious; and when
we take into consideration the speech of the prefect of Rome, before
whom St Lawrence appeared, we shall find the prefect speaking very
like " Protestant-ascendency." According to Prudentius, who was the
glory of the ancient Christian poets, and wrote a famous book *On
the Crown of Martyrs*, somewhere about the close of the fourth century, the prefect addressed Lawrence thus: " You often complain
" that we treat you with cruelty; but no tortures are here thought of;
" I only inquire mildly after what concerns you. I am informed that
" your priests offer in gold, that the sacred blood is received in silver

" cups, and that in your nocturnal sacrifices you have wax tapers fixed
" in gold candlesticks. Bring to light these concealed treasures; the
" prince has need of them for the maintenance of his forces. I am
" told, that according to your doctrine, you must render to Cæsar the
" things that belong to him, I do not think that your God causeth mo-
" ney to be coined; he brought none into the world with him; he only
" brought words. Give us therefore the money, and be rich in words."
Lawrence, however, anticipating that he should soon be called to God,
from what the holy pope Sixtus had told him, had already expended
the treasure he held among the poor widows and orphans, and had
even sold the sacred vessels to increase the sum, laying it all out in
the same manner. He however promised to shew the tyrant the treasures of the church. Accordingly, he gathered together a great number of the decrepid, the blind, the lame, the maimed, the lepers, orphans, widows, and virgins, and then invited the prefect to come and
see them. The prefect was astonished and enraged at what he saw,
and demanded to see the treasures which had been promised. St. Lawrence answered, " What are you displeased at? The gold which you
" so eagerly desire is a vile metal, and serves to incite men to all man-
" ner of crimes. The light of heaven is the true gold which these poor
" objects enjoy. Their bodily weakness and sufferings are the subject
" of their patience, and the highest advantages; vices and passions are
" the real diseases by which the great ones of the world are often most
" truly miserable and despicable. Behold in these poor persons the
" treasures which I promised to shew you; to which I will add pearls
" and precious stones,—those widows and consecrated virgins, which
" are the church's crown, by which it is pleasing to Christ; it hath no
" other riches; make use of them for the advantage of Rome, of the
" emperor, and yourself." This sight before him, and the speech of
the saint, inflamed the prefect with fury, and he ordered Lawrence to
be broiled on a gridiron, under which the coals were partly extinguished, that his sufferings might be the greater. The prefect insulted
the martyr, whilst his body was broiling, but, Lawrence continued in
earnest prayer, imploring the divine mercy, for the conversion of Rome,
for the sake of SS. Peter and Paul, who had there begun to plant the
cross of Christ, and watered it with their blood.

Mr. Butler in his account of St. Lawrence's martyrdom, writes,
" Prudentius doubts not to ascribe to his prayer the entire conversion
" of Rome, and says, God began to grant his request at the very time
" he put it up; for several senators who were present at his death, were
" so powerfully moved by his tender and heroic fortitude and piety,
" that they became Christians upon the spot. These noblemen took
" up the martyr's body on their shoulders, and gave it an honourable
" burial in the Veran field, near the road to Tibur, on the tenth of
" August in 258. His death says Prudentius, was the death of idola-
" try in Rome, which from that time began more sensibly to decline;
" and now, adds the same father, the senate itself venerates the tombs
" of the apostles and martyrs. He describes with what devotion and
" fervour the Romans frequented the church of St. Lawrence, and
" commended themselves in all their necessities to his patronage; and
" the happy success of their prayers proves how great his power is with

" God. The poet implores the mercy of Christ for himself, and begs
" he may obtain by the prayers of the martyrs what his own cannot.
" St. Austin assures us that God wrought in Rome an incredible num-
" ber of miracles through the intercession of St. Lawrence. St. Gre-
" gory of Tours, Fortunatus, and others relate several performed in
" other places. It appears from the sacramentary of pope Gelasius,
" that his feast has been kept with a vigil and an octave at least ever
" since the fifth age. In the reign of Constantine the great, a church
" was built over his tomb, on the road to Tibur, which is called St.
" Lawrence's without the walls; it is one of the five patriarchal
" churches in Rome. Seven other famous churches in that city bear
" the name of this glorious saint."

From these authorities it is an unquestionable fact, that the " godly
" martyr" Lawrence held the Popish doctrines, as they are termed
by Protestants, of the mass and praying to saints, which were consequently the doctrines of the primitive Christians, and therefore ought
to be the doctrines of Protestants, if the latter would believe what
John Fox says are orthodox doctrines. Miracles are also here clearly
established to have been performed since the time of the apostles, and
the veneration of relics and the invocation of saints was also practised in these times. But what can we think of the conduct of the
modern editors of the *Book of Martyrs*, in representing the bishop of
Rome as superintending the execution of his deacon Lawrence, when
they admit, in their relation of this persecution, that the bishop or pope
of Rome was himself a martyr? This proceeding must be considered
by every unbiassed mind a most shameful trick to deceive the super-
ficial and unwary. It is calculated, certainly, " to excite a hatred and
" abhorrence of Popery and its professors," but must be far, very far,
from diffusing a " knowledge and love of the genuine principles of
" Christianity." While we are remarking on this palpable and malicious misrepresentation of an historical fact, we feel called upon to
state, that scarcely one cut that has appeared in this edition of the
Book of Martyrs is correct in its delineation, while others are absolutely
indecent, and deserve the notice of the Vice Suppressing society much
more than some things that have attracted the vigilance of its officers.

After an account of St. Lawrence's death, we have a detail of the
sufferings and conduct of St. Cyprian, bishop of Carthage, but in the
usual confused and unintelligible manner. Fox says, " Fourteen years
" *previous* to *this* period the persecution raged in Africa with great vio-
" lence; and many thousands received the crown of martyrdom, among
" whom the following were the most·distinguished characters." He
then names Cyprian, who, he says, was beheaded in the year 258, and
eight of his disciples, who, according to his words, " were martyred in
" *this* persecution." Now what can we gather from these words, " four-
" teen years *previous to this persecution?*" Does Fox mean that Cyprian
suffered *twice*—that is, some time in the " fourteen years previous," and
again in " this persecution." The previous period must allude to the
seventh general persecution, and Cyprian suffered in the *eighth*. In fact
he was martyred a few weeks after pope Sixtus and his deacon Lawrence, the two latter in the month of August, 258, and the former in
September following. However, we will let this pass, and now look

into the character given by Fox of this great light of the primitive age. "Cyprian, bishop of Carthage," writes Fox, "was an eminent prelate, and a pious ornament of *the church*. HIS DOCTRINES WERE "ORTHODOX AND PURE; his language easy and elegant; and "his manners graceful....Before his baptism he studied the scriptures "with care, and being struck with the beauties of the truths they con- "tained, he determined to practice the virtues they recommended.... "Soon after his baptism he was made a presbyter (that is, a priest); "and being greatly admired for his virtues and his works, on the death "of Donatus, in A. D. 244, he was almost unanimously elected bishop "of Carthage. The care of Cyprian not only extended over Carthage, "but to Numidia and Mauritania. In all his transactions he took "great care to ask the advice of his clergy, knowing that UNANI- "MITY ALONE could be of service to THE CHURCH: this being "one of his maxims, ' That the *bishop* was in *the church*, and *the church* "in the *bishop*; so that unity can only be preserved by a close con- "nexion between the pastor and his flock.'" Very good, John Fox; but before we proceed any further, let us here ask your wise editors, if this language of St. Cyprian be ORTHODOX, and you have admitted that it is so; if the bishop be in the church and the church in the bishop; what become of the numerous sects that have no bishops at all, but reject episcopacy as savouring of Popery and contrary to scripture? The Catholics have ever held this doctrine of St. Cyprian, who learned it from the apostles; and the greater part of the Protestants renounce it, and will have no bishops: consequently they can have no church. For example, the covenanters of Scotland abolished episcopacy, the Swedenborgians, the Wesleyans, the Independents, the Quakers, the Jumpers, the Shakers, and we know not how many other denominations of religionists, contend they can do without them: what then is the natural result? Common sense tells us, that what is orthodox cannot be heterodox; that is, what is sound and pure cannot be unsound and heretical; consequently, those who reject episcopacy stand condemned of heresy by this famous Book of Martyrs, which is published to " diffuse among fellow-*believers* (In what?) a knowledge and " love of the *genuine* principles of Christianity."

Fox goes on, " In the year 250, he (Cyprian) was publicly pro- "scribed by the emperor Decius....The bishop, however, withdrew "from the rage of the populace, and his effects were immediately "confiscated. During his retirement he wrote thirty pious letters to "his flock; but several *schisms* that then crept into the church gave "him great uneasiness. The rigour of the persecution abating, he re- "turned, and *did every thing in his power to expunge erroneous opinions* "*and false doctrines*. A terrible plague now breaking out at Carthage, "it was as usual laid to the charge of the Christians; and the ma- "gistrates began to persecute accordingly, which occasioned an epis- "tle from them to Cyprian, in answer to which he vindicates the cause "of Christianity."——These " erroneous opinions and false doctrines'' should have been pointed out to the " fellow-believers," as well as the orthodox doctrines opposed to them by St. Cyprian; but such a line of procedure did not suit the plan of the modern editors of Fox any more than Fox himself, whose object was to *blind* and not to *enlighten.* Among other errors contested by St. Cyprian, was that of the *Libellatici,* or Lapsed, before mentioned, and the schisms alluded to were raised by Novatus, an infamous priest of Carthage, and one Felicissimus, who had with five priests opposed the election of St. Cyprian to the see of Carthage. These men attempted to sow divisions in the church, and ensnared many to join with them in their impiety, which occasioned the holy bishop to write his work *On the Unity of the Church.* He also defended the doctrines now rejected by Protestants, and admitted by Catholics, as the subjoined extracts will shew, and consequently he was an orthodox Catholic bishop and martyr, and not a Protestant one.

On the Authority and Marks of the Church, that is, of the Catholic church, he writes, " Christ says to his apostles, and through them, to " all ministers, who, by a regular ordination, succeed to them, he that " heareth you, heareth me, and he that despiseth you, despiseth me. " (Luke, x. 16.) And thence have schisms and heresies arisen, when " the bishop, who is one, and who presides over the church, is proudly " despised." *Ep.* lxvi. *p.* 166. *Edit. Oxon.* 1682. The reason why revelation is to be preferred to human reason is thus stated: " Because " they turn not their eyes to the fountain of truth; nor is the head " sought for, nor the doctrine of the heavenly Father upheld. Which " things, would any one seriously ponder, no long inquiry would be " necessary. The proof is easy. Christ addresses Peter: *I say to thee,* " *that thou art Peter, and upon this rock I will build my church, and the* " *gates of hell shall not prevail against it.* ... .He that does not hold this " unity of the church, can he think that he holds the faith? He that " opposes and withstands the church, can he trust that he is in the " church?" *De Unit. Eccl.* p. 105, 106, 108. *Edit. Oxon,* 1682.

On the Unity and Visibility of the Church, he says, " The church is " *one,* widely extended by its fecundity; as there are many rays of " light, but one sun; many branches of a tree, but one root deeply " fixed; many streams of water, but one source. Take a ray from the " sun; the unity of light allows not division: break a branch from the " tree, the branch cannot germinate; cut off the stream from its source, " the stream dries up. So the church—sends forth her rays over the " whole earth: yet is the light one—and its unity is undivided." *Ibid.* p. 108. "God is one, and Christ is *one,* and his church is *one,* and faith " is one, and his people, connected by one solid bond, is *one.* Unity " cannot be severed; nor the one body, by laceration, be divided. " Whatever is separated from the stock, cannot live; cannot breathe " apart; it loses the substance of life." *Ibid.* p. 119. "The church, im " brued with the light of the Lord, sends forth her rays, over the whole " earth; yet is the light one, every where diffused, and its unity un " divided; she extends her branches, by the power of her fecundity, " into all regions, and her streams are as widely spread: yet the head " is one, and the spring is one." *Ibid.* 108.

On the apostolical succession and power of the Church to remit sins, he writes, " Peter, upon whom the church had been built by our " Lord, speaking in the name of all, and with the voice of the church, " answered: *Lord to whom shall we go? Thou hast the words of eternal* " *life.* Signifying and shewing, that they who depart from Christ,

"perish through their own fault: but that the church, which believes
"in Christ, and holds to that which it once learned, never departs
"from him; moreover, that they compose the church, who remain in
"the house of God; and that *the plant is not planted by the Lord.* (Matt.
"xv. 13.) which is not firmly rooted, but is blown about like straw
"by the breath of the enemy." *Ep.* lix. *p.* 131. "The Novatian is not
"in the church! nor can he be deemed a bishop, who, despising evan-
"gelical and apostolical tradition and succeeding to no one, is sprung
"from himself. One not ordained in the church, has no church." *Ep.*
lxix. *p.* 181. "The power of remitting sins was given by Christ to his
"apostles, whom he sent; and to the churches, which they founded;
"and to the bishops who succeeded them in a regular succession."
Inter Cyprian. ep. lxxv. *p.* 225.

On the fallacy of "placing human reason in competition with reve-
"lation," St. Cyprian observes, "Let not some men deceive them-
"selves by an idle interpretation of the words of Christ, when he said:
"*Where there are two or three gathered together in my name, there I am
"with them.* (Matt. xviii. 20.) Corrupting the gospel, and interpret-
"ing falsely, they take the last words, and omit what goes before;
"retaining one part, and craftily suppressing the other. As they are
"cut off from the church, so do they cut off the words of scripture.
"For, recommending to his disciples unanimity and peace, the Lord.
"said to them: *If two of you shall agree upon earth, concerning any
"thing whatsoever they shall ask, it shall be done for them by my father;
"for where there are two or three gathered, &c.* shewing, that much is
"granted, not to the number, but to the unanimity of the supplicants.
"*If two of you,* he says, *shall agree upon earth;* he gives the first place
"to unanimity, to peaceful concord: on this he insists. But how shall
"he agree with another, who has dissented from the body of the
"church and from the whole fraternity? Can two or three be gathered
"together in the name of Christ, who it is plain, are separated from
"him and his gospel? For we did not leave them, but they us.
"Choosing for themselves separate conventicles, they quitted the head
"and the fountain of truth." *De Unit. Eccles.* p. 112.

On the state of celibacy, he published a book *On the Habit of Virgins,* which he addresses to virgins "devoted to God, dedicated to
"Christ," or such "who profess virginity, and a stricter attendance
"than ordinary upon the service of God." Those who thus devote
themselves to prayer and chastity, he says are "the flower of the
"church's flock, the ornament and lustre of spiritual grace, her joyful
"offspring, the very perfection of honour and praise, the image of God
"copied according to the pattern of his holiness, the more illustrious
"portion of the flock of Christ."

St. Cyprian also held the same doctrines on the sacrifice of the mass,
the real presence in the Eucharist, and the primacy of the pope, as
St. Justin, martyr, St. Irenæus, Tertullian, and Origen; and thus we
see that in every age of the church, to the period we are now arrived
at, the faith and doctrines of the Orthodox Christians were ONE and
the SAME; while the heterodox, as at the present day, were rent into
a thousand divisions.

To enumerate the different accounts given by Fox of the sufferings of the "godly martyrs" of the primitive ages, who were all, let it be remembered, Roman Catholics, would tire the reader, and swell our pages to a considerable length; we must therefore confine ourselves to the most prominent statements, where the martyrologist has clearly overstepped the boundaries of truth, or suppressed the most material circumstances of the case. Under this eighth persecution he gives an account of the "martyrdom of 300 Christians" in the following terms: " Perhaps one of the most dreadful events in the history of martyrdom " was that which took place at Utica, where 300 Christians were, by " orders of the proconsul, placed around a burning lime-kiln. A pan " of coals and incense having been prepared, they were commanded " either to sacrifice to Jupiter, or be thrown into the kiln. Unani- " mously refusing, they bravely JUMPED into the pit, and were suf- " focated immediately." Dreadful indeed would have been this event had it occurred as John Fox has related; for had they *jumped* into the pit, instead of being thrown in, they would have been guilty of *suicide*, and could not have been martyrs. We know not from what authority John Fox related this story; we have consulted the martyrology of the Rev. Mr. Butler, and he gives a very different tale. He states that St. Austin reckoned the number to be one hundred and fifty-three, which falls considerably short of three hundred. Then, he says, the victims were offered their choice, either to be thrown into the pit, or to offer sacrifice to the idols. They chose the former, and were *thrown* in, by which they were all consumed together.

Fox next gives a "singular account of a Christian lady," named Eugenia, the daughter of Philippus, governor of Alexandria, who, to avoid the persecution, eloped from her father's house, she having embraced the religion of Christ. "For the purpose of concealment," Fox says, "she " assumed *male* attire, and, calling herself Eugenius, was admitted into " a monastery, or society of Christians, in the suburbs of Alexandria, " of which, at length, by her learning and virtue, she became the head. " Here," he adds, " she performed MANY MIRACLES, and among " others who were cured by her was a certain *matron* of Alexandria, " named Melancia, who, supposing her to be a man, conceived a crimi- " nal passion for her, and so far lost all sense of virtue and decorum, " as to solicit her to gratify her desires. Eugenius exhorted her to " continue in the paths of virtue; but Melancia, enraged at the refusal, " and fearful of exposure, determined to anticipate the accusation, and " therefore immediately charged Eugenius, and other members of the " Christian community, with attempting to debauch her. This matter " being heard before Philippus, and Melancia being esteemed virtuous, " the accusation gained credit, especially as it was brought against the " Christians. Then Eugenius perceiving that she and her fellow-be- " lievers were in imminent danger of death on this infamous charge, " and that it was now no time for dissimulation, desired of the judge " to allow her time and place to make manifest to him the truth; which " being granted, she disclosed to him that she was his daughter, and " that her companions were Protheus and Hiacinthus, two pious " eunuchs; explaining to him and to her brethren, the cause of her " departure from them. By this narration they were convinced of her " innocence, and her malignant accuser was utterly confounded. Phi-

" lippus was afterwards converted to Christianity, made bishop of
" Alexandria, and suffered martyrdom. Eugenia, after the death of
" her father, returning to Rome with Protheus and Hiacinthus, and
" having there converted Basilla (a lady who was to have been mar-
" ried to a Pagan, but now refused in consequence of which she was
" beheaded) was assailed with various kinds of death, from all of
" which she was delivered by the miraculous interference of Heaven;
" first, being tied to a great stone and cast into the Tiber, where
" she was prevented from drowning; then put into the hot baths,
" when the fires were extinguished and she preserved; lastly, being cast
" into a prison to die of hunger, she was fed by a supernatural hand.".

We have given this account at length from Fox, to shew how little
regard he has for the understandings of *his* readers, by detailing such
ridiculous romancing without a single authority to verify his extraordinary narration. That a female Christian should disguise herself in
men's clothes, and should be raised to the head of a body of monks by
her superior learning, is equally as fabulous as the story of Pope Joan,
which Protestant writers have so successfully imposed upon the credulous people of this country. Then again, that an old matron should
fall in love with this young superior! who, in the name of common,
sense, can give credit to such a rodomontade? Of the same piece is
the discovery of her sex, and the conversion of her father, who became himself a martyr, while the young lady is deprived of that
honour by the interposition of a supernatural power in various ways!
We do not deny the existence of miracles; but we are not credulous
enough to believe in such a tale as this, nor any other, unattested by
authorities; for we know that impositions have been practised in
every age; though we also know that the Catholic church was always
careful to guard against these impositions, and caution the people
from being deceived by them. Forgeries and imposture were ever
abominated by the pastors of the church, as her canons sufficiently testify; and pope Adrian I, in an epistle to Charlemagne, says, that no
acts of martyrs are suffered to be read which are not supported by
vouchers. That Fox's " singular account of a Christian lady," as above
cited, is a complete fabrication, we have not a single doubt in our
mind; for, on examining Butler's *Lives of Saints*, we find that learned
and accurate martyrologist gives the following account of this martyr.
Eugenia. "She suffered," he writes, "at Rome, under Valerian,
" about the year 257, and is mentioned by St. Avitus, though we have
" NO AUTHENTIC acts of her sufferings, those recited by Meta-
" phrastes and Surius *deserving no notice*." Thus then it is clear that
Fox's " singular account" is entitled to no credit, and is like many other
fabulous tales in his work, invented to delude the ignorant and credulous. There is one circumstance, however, that must not be overlooked, which is, the admission by Fox, that the Christians, " at this
" period," lived in communities or monasteries, which Protestants now
condemn, and, at the period of the reformation so called, destroyed
with Vandalic barbarity and ruthlessness.

Fox concludes his account of this persecution by giving the fate of
the author of it, the emperor Valerian, which we shall not notice

here, but reserve our remarks till we have got through the remaining
two persecutions.

THE NINTH GENERAL PERSECUTION UNDER THE ROMAN EMPERORS.

This persecution is ushered in with the martyrdom of Felix, bishop
of Rome, who was advanced to the Roman see, Fox says, in 274,
" and was beheaded in the *same* year on the 22d of December." Here
Fox is guilty of a gross mistake. Mr. Echard states that Felix suffered in Rome, " after he held the dignity FIVE YEARS, wanting
" four days," which is a palpable contradiction of John Fox. Mr. Butler corroborates Echard as to the period Felix governed the church,
he having succeeded St. Dionysius in the year 269. Previous to the
pontificate of this holy pope, two councils were held at Antioch, to
inquire into the doctrines advanced by Paul of Samosata, the proud
bishop of that city, *who denied the divinity of Christ*, and taught many
impious errors concerning the mysteries of the Trinity and Incarnation.
In 269 a third council was held at the same place, when Paul was
clearly convicted of heresy and many scandalous crimes. On this
occasion the holy Felix wrote a letter to Maximus, bishop of Alexandria, which is quoted by the council of Ephesus, St. Cyril of Alexandria, and St. Vincent of Lerins, as clearly explaining the Catholic doctrines of the whole mystery of the Incarnation. Neither Butler nor
Echard states the manner of his death, though Fox, on his own authority, says he was *beheaded* on the 22d of December. The Western
martyrologies name him on the 30th of May, on which day he is recorded by Butler.

The next article demanding our notice, is the " massacre of a whole
" legion of Christian soldiers." Fox calls it " a *remarkable* affair," and
states it to have happened in the year 268. In this year Dioclesian associated Maximian with him in the empire, whose disposition was as
cruel, and his hatred to Christianity as malignant, as Dioclesan's. In
the Roman army there was a legion formed of Christians, in number
about 6600, called the Theban legion. The legion was ordered to join
the army of Maximian, who was on the march to Gaul to quell some
disturbances. On their arrival at Octodurum, at that time a considerable city on the Rhine, above the lake of Geneva, now a village called
Martignac or Martigni in the Valais, Maximian issued an order that
the whole army should join in offering sacrifice to the gods for the success of his expedition. Fox adds, that " he commanded that they
" should take oaths of allegiance, and swear, at the same time, to as-
" sist him in the extirpation of Christianity in Gaul." Where Fox
found this part of his tale, we do not know; perhaps he was dreaming
of the oath of allegiance required by Elizabeth from her Catholic subjects, which they could not conscientiously take, and the murderous
attempts made in her reign to extirpate Catholicism in Ireland. Be
this as it may, we have looked into Butler, Echard, &c. and we find
no account whatever of oaths of allegiance and extirmination. The
legion was ordered to sacrifice and refused. On this refusal every
tenth man was put to death, while the rest exhorted them to con-

stancy. A second order was issued, which was followed by another refusal, and a second decimation. " But this second severity," says Fox, " made no more impression than the first; the soldiers preserved " their fortitude, and their principles; but, by the advice of their of- " ficers, drew up a remonstrance to the emperor, in which they told " him, ' that they were his subjects and his soldiers, but could not " at the same time forget the Almighty; that they received their pay " from him, and their existence from God. While your commands " (said they) are not contradictory to those of our common master, " we shall always be ready to obey, as we have been hitherto; but " when the orders of our prince and those of the Almighty differ, we " must always obey the latter. Our arms are devoted to the emperor's " use, and shall be directed against his enemies; but we cannot sub- " mit to stain our hands with effusion of Christian blood; and how, " indeed, could you, O emperor, be sure of our allegiance and fide- " lity, should we violate our obligation to our God, in whose ser- " vice we were solemnly engaged before we entered the army You " command us to search out, and to destroy the Christians; it is not " necessary to look any further for persons of that denomination; we " ourselves are such, and we glory in the name. We saw our com- " panions fall without the least opposition or murmuring, and thought " them happy in dying for the sake of Christ. Nothing shall make us " lift up our hands against our sovereign; we had rather die wrong- " fully, and by that means preserve our innocence, than live under a " load of guilt; whatever you command, we are ready to suffer; we " confess ourselves Christians, and therefore cannot persecute Chris- " tians, nor sacrifice to idols.'

" Such a declaration, it might be presumed, (adds Fox) would have " softened the emperor, but it had a contrary effect; for, enraged at their " perseverance and unanimity, he commanded that the whole legion " should be put to death, which was accordingly executed by the other " troops, who cut them to pieces with their swords." Although Fox and his modern editors may consider this massacre to be " a very re- " markable affair," yet it is not without its parallel under " Protestant- ascendency;" nor is the conduct of Maximian, in rejecting the just re- monstrance of this Christian legion, without an exception. When Elizabeth came to the throne, she formed the plan of subverting the old faith, which her sister Mary had re-established, and of which we shall have occasion to speak hereafter. In place of this ancient faith, a *new* religion was established by the temporal power, and the civil sword was exerted to *compel* the people to conform to it. In Ireland, the Roman Catholic religion, that is, the same religion for which the primitive Christians laid down their lives, was professed by the whole population with scarce an exception. There was not in the whole island at that time one individual in ten thousand that did not profess the Catholic religion, first planted by the preachings and miracles of St. Patrick in the fifth century, and consequently had existed there during an uninterrupted space of ONE THOUSAND YEARS. But Elizabeth, on assuming the popedom of the then new church of Eng- land, adopted a similar mode to that pursued by Maximian towards the Theban legion, to make the Irish renounce their ancient faith, an embrace the novelties of the apostles of the reformation so called. In a work called the *Government of Ireland under Sir John Perrot*, printed in London in the year 1626, it is there stated, that this very merciful and excellent lord deputy under "Protestant-ascendency" drew up a plan of Government for Ireland, in which he recommended to the queen, "That all brehons, caraghes, bardes, and rymers, that infect " the people, friars, monks, Jesuites, pardoners, nunns, and such like, " that openly seeke the maintenence of papacy, a traytorous kinde of " people, the bellowes to blow the coales of all mischiefe and rebel- " lion, and fit spies of Antichrist, whose kingdom they greedily ex- " pect to be restored, *be executed by marshal law, and their favourers and* " *maintainers by due course of law, to be tryed and executed as in cases of* " *treason*." It is also stated by Leland on the authority of the Irish manuscript annals of Elizabeth's reign, that a few years after the trea- cherous assassination of O'Neil, his wife and friends, in 1574, "the " Irish chieftains of the King's and Queen's county were invited to a " treaty of accommodation. But when they arrived at the place of " conference, *they were surrounded by troops, and all butchered on the spot*." Indeed, such were the horrible barbarities practised by "Protestant- ascedency," on the Irish Catholics in the reign of this queen, that Sydney, in his *Letters and Memorials of State*, 1746, vol. i. p. 24, says, " Suche horrible and lamentable spectacles there are to beholde, as " the burninge of villages, the ruyn of churches, the *wastinge of suche* " *as have ben good townes' and castells: yea, the view of the bones and sculles* " *of the dead subjectes, who partelie by murder, partelie by famine, have* " *died in the fieelds, as in troth, hardelie any Christian with drie eyes could* " *beholde*." These enormities are likewise noticed by Holinshed, Cox, Leland, Carew, &c.

Nor must we here forget that mercenary and rancorous spirit of per- secution manifested by the Scottish Puritans of the 17th century, who, in their zeal for reforming religion, looked upon freedom of conscience as the greatest abomination. In the solemn league and covenant first entered into in the year 1643, the subscribers bound themselves " to " EXTIRPATE *Popery, prelacy, superstition, heresy, schism,* and whatso- " ever shall be found to be contrary to sound doctrine and the power of " godliness;" and they further bound themselves to discover (that is, to become INFORMERS) all such as might be guilty of the same, to " receive condign punishment, as the degree of their offences shall re- " quire or deserve." This spirit of intolerance also spread from the north into the south part of the island, for in the journals of the House of Commons it is recorded, that on the 15th of January, 1645-6, a pe- tition was presented from the corporation of London to the House of Lords, praying, " that no toleration of Popery, prelacy, superstition, " heresy, schism, profaneness, or any thing contrary to sound doctrine, " and that all private meetings, contrary to the covenant, may be re- " strained." Such was the mild and Christianlike spirit of Puritan " Protestant-ascendency."

Fox expresses his surprise that the declaration made in the name of this Christian legion should not have softened the Pagan emperor. To be sure, its frankness and sincerity ought to have produced a different effect; but the conduct of Maximian in this affair is not one-half so unjust and in-

A REVIEW

OF

Fox's Book of Martyrs,

CRITICAL AND HISTORICAL.

No. 7. Printed and Published by W. E. ANDREWS, 3, Chapter-house-court, St. Paul's Churchyard, London. **Price 3d.**

EXPLANATION OF THE ENGRAVING.—*The editors of the modern Book of Martyrs have furnished several modes of torture practised on the primitive Christians; but we do not recollect to have seen any so barbarous as the one above represented, enforced by "Protestant-ascendency," on Margaret, the wife of a rich citizen of York, named Clitheroe, for the heinous crime of harbouring a Catholic priest. The place of execution was the tolbooth, six or seven yards from the prison, at York, on the 25th of March, 1586.—An eye witness gives the following account of this cruel and unparalleled scene:—"After she had prayed, Fawcet (one of the sheriffs) commanded them to put off her apparrel, when she, with the four women, requested him on her knees, that, for the honour of womanhood, this might be dispensed with, but they would not grant it. Then she requested that the women might unparrel her, and that they would turn their faces from her during that time. The women took off her clothes and put upon her the long linen habit. Then very quietly she laied her down upon the ground, her face covered with a handkerchief, and most part of her body with the habit. The dore was laied upon her; her hands she joined towards her face. Then the sheriff said, Naie, ye must have your hands bound. Then two sergeants parted her hands, and bound them to two posts, in the same manner as the feet hud previously been fix'd. After this they laied weight upon her, which when she first felt, she said Jesu, Jesu, Jesu, have mercye upon mee, which were the last words she was heard to speake. She was in dying about one quarter of an hower. A sharpe stone, as big as a man's fist, had been put under her back; upon her was laid to the quantitie of seven or eight hundred weight, which breaking her ribs, caused them to burst forth of the skinne,"—Lingard's History of England. Note FF.*

CONTINUATION OF THE REVIEW.

tolerant as that of "Protestant-ascendency" towards the Catholics. The latter have ever been governed by the same sentiments as the Theban legion expressed to their emperor: they profess to be faithful sub-

jects to the state, in all that is not contrary to the law of God; they
have always been ready to shed their blood in the cause of their country; they have always said that were they to violate their duty to God,
there could be no security that they would be faithful to the state; they
have submitted to persecution for justice sake with patience, and seen
their priests executed for no other crime than that of exercising their
sacred functions; they have declared that no power on earth could
make them raise their hands against their sovereign; they confess
themselves to be Catholics, and therefore cannot violate their conscience, by taking oaths contrary to their faith; yet, notwithstanding
these professions, which we think sufficient to satisfy any reasonable
man or party of men, so bloated and mercenary is the spirit of "Protestant-ascendency," that in the face of these professions of the Catholics,
constantly repeated, and invariably confirmed by their conduct, the
bigotted disciples of Protestantism are incessantly calumniating and
vilifying their Catholic neighbours, and calling upon "Ascendency" to
keep them proscribed and chained in slavery, while, through the medium of the press, they are endeavouring, by a series of lies and falsehoods, "to excite a hatred and abhorrence of the (supposed) cor-
"ruptions and crimes of Popery and its professors." Reader, these
facts are undeniable; and we use the words of the editors of this
Book of Martyrs in proof of the unchristian feelings they are trying to
excite among Protestants towards their Catholic neighbours.

We now come to the account given by Fox of " *Alban, the first*
" *British martyr.*" This account we shall give in the words of the
Protestant martyrologist, before we proceed with our comments. He
says, "Alban, from whom St. Alban's, in Hertfordshire, received its
" name, was the first British martyr. He was originally a pagan, and
" being of a very humane disposition, he sheltered a Christian ecclesi-
" astic, named Amphibalus, who was pursued on account of his reli-
" gion. The pious example, and edifying discourses of the refugee,
" made a great impression on the mind of Alban; he longed to become
" a member of a religion which charmed him; the fugitive minister,
" happy in the opportunity, took great pains to instruct him; and be-
" fore his discovery, perfected Alban's conversion. Alban now took a
" firm resolution to preserve the sentiments of a Christian, or to die
" the death of a martyr. The enemies of Amphibalus having intelli-
" gence where he was secreted, came to the house of Alban, in order
" to apprehend him. The noble host, desirous of protecting his guest,
" changed clothes with him in order to facilitate his escape; and when
" the soldiers came, offered himself up as the person for whom they
" were seeking. Being accordingly carried before the governor, the
" deceit was immediately discovered; and Amphibalus being absent,
" that officer determined to wreak his vengeance upon Alban: with this
" view he commanded the prisoner to advance to the altar, and sacri-
" fice to the pagan deities. The brave Alban, however, refused to
" comply with the idolatrous injunction, and boldly professed himself
" to be a Christian. The governor therefore ordered him to be scourg-
" ed, which punishment he bore with great fortitude, seeming to ac-
" quire new resolution from his sufferings: he was then beheaded.
" The venerable Bede states, that, upon this occasion, the executioner

" suddenly became a convert to Christianity, and entreated permission
" either to die for Alban or with him. Obtaining the latter request,
" they were beheaded by a soldier, who voluntarily undertook the task.
" This happened on the 23d of June, A. D. 287, at Verulam, now St.
" Alban's, in Hertfordshire where a magnificent church was erected
" to his memory about the time of Constantine the great. This edifice
" was destroyed in the Saxon wars, but was rebuilt by Offa, king of
" Mercia, and a monastery erected adjoining it, some remains of which
" are still visible."

In this account there are many points to notice, as they will clearly
shew that this protomartyr of England was a Catholic saint, and not
a Protestant one. It is not a little singular besides, that the imputed
offence for which Mrs. Clitheroe suffered under " Protestant-ascendency," a representation of whose death prefaces this number, is the same
as that for which St. Alban was martyred under Pagan ascendency,
namely, having " sheltered a Christian ecclesiastic." And what adds
still more to the singularity of this coincidence is, that as St. Alban was
the *first* martyr in England under Pagan ascendency, so was Mrs. Clitheroe the *first* martyr for the Catholic faith under the remorseless and
unprincipled Elizabeth, on her commencing to persecute that religion
which she swore at her coronation to protect and follow. Thus then,
if Alban be worthy of the rank of a martyr, and John Fox has recorded
him as such, Mrs. Clitheroe is entitled to the same rank, since both
were Catholics; both humanely protected a persecuted fugitive for conscience sake; and both refused to violate their consciences, when called
upon to do so by their judges. Alban was desired to sacrifice to Pagan
deities, which he refused; and Mrs. Clitheroe, when placed at the bar,
refused to plead guilty, because she knew that no sufficient proof could
be brought against her; or not guilty, because she knew such a plea was
equivalent to a falsehood. The only difference between the two cases
is, as we have before said, that Alban was a martyr to the intolerance
of Pagan ascendency; and Mrs. Clitheroe felt the cruel hand of "Protestant-ascendency." The one was a man, whose sufferings were mild
and merciful, compared to the other, a woman, whose death was as
barbarous as it was before unheard of.

We have noticed, page 58, that Christianity was introduced into
this country by Catholic missionaries, regularly sent by pope Eleutherius, at the request of King Lucius, somewhere about the year 182.
The former pagan persecutions, however, seem not to have reached this
island, probably from its isolated situation, and its distance from the
Roman colonies. Fox places the martyrdom of St. Alban in 287, but
most authors say that he suffered in 303, when Dioclesian began his
cruel and general persecution against the Christians. Alban was a native of Verulam, which, for many ages, was one of the strongest and
most populous cities in Britain, till it was reduced to decay by suffering under the sieges of the Saxons. The present town of St. Alban's
rose up close to its ruins. The saint travelled to Rome for improvement, and on his return to Britain he settled at Verulam, where he
appears to have been one of its principal citizens, as the husband of
Mrs. Clitheroe was one of the chief citizens of York. The account
given by Fox as above is nearly correct, as far as it goes, but there are

many circumstances connected with the history of this saint, which
he might have noticed with much greater propriety, because better
authenticated, than many of the stories he has entertained his readers
with, and which we have exposed. For example, he relates, that a
young lady, named Eugenia, performed many *miracles* while she was
playing the *impostor*, by dressing herself up in men's clothes; and this
statement is made upon no authority whatever; nay, in the face of improbability. But the miracles recorded by Gildas, Bede, and others,
as occurring at the martyrdom of this saint, are passed over by Fox.
Indeed, his manner of relation is so confused, that no one can understand what he means. He writes, "The governor therefore ordered
" him (Alban) to be scourged, which punishment he bore with great
" fortitude, seeming to acquire new resolution from his sufferings; he
" was then beheaded. The venerable Bede states that upon *this* oc-
" casion the executioner suddenly became a convert to Christianity, and
" entreated permission either to die for Alban or with him. Obtaining
" the latter request, they were beheaded by a soldier, who voluntarily
" undertook the task."

Now, from this account we are led to suppose that the occasion alluded to by Bede, was the *execution* of the martyr; and yet this could
not be the case, because then the intended executioner could not have
requested "either to die *for* Alban or *with* him. On referring, however, to the authority given, we find venerable Bede relating a strikingly different occasion for the sudden conversion of the executioner
first appointed. Bede says, that the saint being led to the place of
execution, he came to a river, which they had to cross on their way to
the spot selected. Here the bridge was so occupied by the immense
concourse of people crowding from curiosity to see the saint suffer,
that it was found impracticable to pass it that evening. "St. Alban
" therefore," observes the venerable historian, " whose mind was filled
" with an anxious desire to arrive quickly at his martyrdom, approached
" to the stream, and lifting up his eyes to heaven, addressed his prayer
" to the Almighty, when, behold, he saw the water recede, and leave
" the bed of the river dry for them to pass over.' The executioner,
" who was to have beheaded him, amongst the rest, hastened to meet
" him at the place of execution, and, being moved, *by divine inspiration*,
" threw down the sword which he carried, desiring that he might
" rather suffer death with or for the martyr, than be constrained to
" take away the life of so holy a man." This *extraordinary* occurrence, and not the beheading of the martyr, was the occasion then of
the sudden conversion of the executioner. And why was not this fact
stated by Fox, in preference to the pretended miracles wrought by a
female in disguise? Bede mentions also two other miracles that occurred at the execution of St. Alban. After crossing the river, they
had to ascend a hill, which was the spot fixed upon to execute the sentence. " When St. Alban," relates Bede, " had reached the summit of
" this hill, he prayed to God to give him water; and immediately, an
" ever-flowing spring rose at his feet, the course being confined; so
" that every one might perceive that the river had been before obedi-
" ent to the martyr. For it could not be supposed (adds the venera-
" ble writer) that he could ask for water at the top of the hill, who

" had not left it in the river below, *unless he had been convinced that it was*
" *expedient for the* GLORY OF GOD *that he should do so.*" Bede further states, that the real executioner miraculously lost his eyes at the
moment he severed the saint's head from his body.

There are many individuals who deride and disbelieve these relations
of venerable Bede, though, as we have before stated, they are authenticated by other writers of unimpeachable credit. And yet many of
these would-be-thought acute sceptics do not hesitate to believe facts
not so well substantiated, and other relations much more improbable.
Amongst others, Hume has laboured hard to discredit the miraculous
powers of the true church; forgetting that the very same arguments
which he uses against the existence of miracles may likewise be adduced to disprove every tittle that he has written in his History of
England. How much more conformable to common sense is the conduct of Mr. Collier in his *Ecclesiastical History*. This learned Protestant author, speaking of the miracles above related, says, " As for St.
" Alban's miracles, being attested by authors of such credit, I do not
" see why they should be questioned. That miracles were wrought in
" the church at that time of day, is clear from the writings of the an-
" cients. To imagine that God should exert his omnipotence, and ap-
" pear supernaturally for his servants, in no age since the apostles, is
" an unreasonable fancy. For since the world was not all converted by
" the apostles, why should we not believe that God should honour his
" servants with the most undisputed credentials. Why then should St.
" Alban's miracles be disbelieved, the occasion being great enough for
" so extraordinary an interposition."

Before we take leave of this martyr, we must notice another admission made by John Fox. He says, the saint's martyrdom took place
" at Verulam, now St. Alban's, in Hertfordshire, where a magnificent
" church was erected to *his memory* about the time of Constantine the
" great. This edifice was destroyed in the Saxon wars, but was re-
" built by Offa, king of Mercia, and a MONASTERY erected adjoin-
" ing to it, *some remains of which* (he says) *are still visible.*" He should
have added, a sad memorial of the devastating spirit that directed the
pretended evangelical reformers of religion in the sixteenth century.
However, let it not be forgotten that Fox here allows that the memories of the saints and martyrs were honoured by the primitive Christians in Constantine's time, as they are *now* by the Catholics, and the
Catholics *only*, if we except the Greek church. It is also admitted by
him that the Saxon kings, who were the first to receive the Christian
faith, on the second conversion of the island by St. Augustin, erected
monasteries as well as churches to promote the interests of religion;
whereas the reformers of the sixteenth century demolished and destroyed them to put the revenues into their own pockets. Consequently these Christian martyrs and kings, the one suffering for conscience sake, and the other honouring the memories of those who thus
suffered, could not have been Protestants, but must have been Catholics; therefore if they were orthodox, and Fox says they were, the
Catholics of this day must be orthodox too; and then what can we
think of the modern disciples of Fox, whose professed purport is to
excite a " hatred and abhorrence of the (supposed) corruptions and.

' crimes of Popery (that is Catholicism) and its professors?" The monastery of St. Alban's was founded in the year 793, and possessed many privileges; one of which was the seniority of its abbot in parliament over the other twenty-six, and sometimes twenty-eight abbots that held baronies, and sat in the senate till the time of Henry the eighth, when they were suppressed in 1539, a period of more than seven hundred years. · The church is still standing, having been purchased by the townsmen at the dissolution of the monasteries, for four hundred pounds, to be their parochial church. Of the rich shrine of St. Alban nothing is now remaining, as Weever writes, but a marble stone to cover the place where the dust of the remains of the saint lies.

THE TENTH GENERAL PERSECUTION UNDER THE RO-MAN EMPERORS.

We come now to the last general persecution of Christianity under Pagan ascendency. Fox introduces his account of it in the following words :—" Notwithstanding the efforts of the heathens to exterminate " the Christians and abolish their mode of faith, yet they increased so " greatly as to become formidable by their numbers. They, however, " forgot the precepts of their meek prototype, and instead of adopting " his humility, they gave themselves up to vanity, by dressing gaily, " living sumptuously, building stately edifices for churches, &c. which " created a general envy, and particularly excited the hatred of Gale- " rius, the adopted son of Dioclesian, who, stimulated by his mother, a " bigotted Pagan, persuaded the emperor to commence a persecution. " It accordingly began on the 23d of February, A. D. 303, that being " the day on which the Terminalia were celebrated, and on which, as " the Pagans boasted, they hoped to put a termination to Christianity. " The persecution began in Nicodemia; the prefect of that city re- " paired, with a great number of officers and assistants, to the church " of the Christians, where, having forced open the doors, they seized " upon all the sacred books, and committed them to the flames. This " transaction took place in the presence of Dioclesian and Galerius, who " also caused the church to be levelled with the ground. It was fol- " lowed by a severe edict, commanding the destruction of all other " Christian churches and books; and an order soon succeeded, the ob- " ject of which was to render Christians of all denominations outlaws, " and consequently, to make them incapable of holding any place of " trust, profit, or dignity, or of receiving any protection from the legal " institutions of the realm. An immediate martyrdom was the result " of the publication of this edict; for a bold Christian not only tore it " down from the place to which it was affixed, but execrated the name " of the emperor for his injustice and cruelty; he was in consequence " seized, severely tortured, and then burnt alive. The Christian pre- " lates were likewise apprehended and imprisoned; and Galerius pri- " vately ordered the imperial palace to be set on fire, that the Chris- " tians might be charged as the incendaries, and a plausible pretext " given for carrying on the persecution with the greatest severity." Such is the account given by Fox; Mr. Echard, in his History, says, that the officers on breaking into the churches, " sought for the " IMAGE of the God they (the Christians) worshipped: but finding

" none, took the sacred books and other things they found, and threw " them into the fire, filling all places with force and violence." Here then it is avowed by a Protestant writer, that IMAGES were. in use in the primitive ages, as they are by Catholics now, though the practice is condemned by Protestants, evidently on weak and erroneous grounds ; since the Christians of the early ages being allowed to be orthodox, *their* practices could not be *wrong*, for if they were, those who practised them could not be *right ;* and what was right *then* must be right *now*.

We wonder when the modern editors of the *Book of Martyrs* penned this horrible and heart-afflicting account of the sufferings of the Christians under Dioclesian and Galerius, the forlorn and exactly similar situation of the Catholics under the Tudors and Stuarts of this country did not strike them. The only difference that we can see is, that the persecution of Dioclesian lasted ten years, whereas the persecution of the Catholics continued unabated during the reigns of Elizabeth, the Stuarts, and William of " immortal memory," by " Protestant-ascendency ;" a space of more than a century. The persecution of Dioclesian began with the destruction of Christian churches and the burning of books. Consult the annals of Henry VIII. Edward VI. and Elizabeth of England, and you will find the reformation so called commenced with the demolition of churches, chantries, and monasteries, and the entire waste of the most valuable works in literature and sacred history. An order was issued by Dioclesian, " the object of which was " to render Christians of all denominations outlaws, and consequently, " to make them incapable of holding any place of trust, profit or dig- " nity, or of receiving any protection from the legal institutions of the " realm." And what was the object of the penal code of this country and Ireland ? Were not the Catholics rendered outlaws and made incapable of holding any place of trust and profit, or of receiving any protection from the laws ? Search the records of Parliament, and it will be found, that a more persecuting spirit, could not exist against the primitive Christians during the domination of Pagan ascendency, than against the Catholics, especially in Ireland, under the rule of " Protestant-ascendency." Not a Parliament was called by Elizabeth and the Stuarts that did not add to the bloody catalogue of laws framed to prevent the growth of Popery. Were we to cite only the heads of the different statutes passed we should fill a large volume ; but as we do not like to deal in assertion, we select a few passages to prove the truth of what we have advanced.

On the subject of destroying churches, Leland, in his History of Ireland, writes thus : " *Under pretence of obeying the orders of the state, they* " *seized all the most valuable furniture of the churches, which they exposed* " *to sale without decency or reserve.* The Irish annalists pathetically " describe the garrison of Athlone issuing forth with a barbarous " and heathen fury, and pillaging the famous church of Clonmacnoise, " tearing away the most inoffensive ornaments, books, bells, plate, win- " dows, furniture of every kind, so as to leave the shrine of their favour- " ite saint, Kieran, a hideous monument of sacrilege." (*Leland,* ii. 236.)

To render the Catholics odious, the Protestant bishops of Ireland, among whom was the celebrated Usher, in 1627, entered a solemn protest egainst indulging the Catholics with the mere toleration of their religion, in which it was set forth, that "the religion of the Papists is "*superstitious and idolatrous;* their faith and doctrine *enormous and* "*heretical;* their church, in respect to both, *apostatical.* *To give them* "*therefore, a toleration,* or to consent that they may freely exercise their "religion, and profess their faith and doctrine, '*is a grievous sin.*'" (*See Rushworth,* ii. 22.)

In 1642, the Parliament addressed the king, "that such Popish priests "as are already condemned, *may be forthwith executed;* and such as shall "hereafter be condemned, *may likewise be executed according to law.*" (*Parliamentary History,* x. 506.) "It was confidently averred that sir "John Clotworthy, who well knew he designs of the faction that "governed in the house of commons in England, had declared there in a "speech, '*that the conversion of the Papists in Ireland was only to be* "*effected by the bible in one hand and the sword in the other;*' and Mr. "Pym gave out that *they would not leave a priest in Ireland.* To the like "effect sir William Parsons, out of a strange weakness, or a detestable "policy, positively asserted before many witnesses, at a public enter- "tainment in Dublin, that *within a twelvemonth no Catholic should be seen* "*in Ireland.* (*Idem.* xii. 49.) Now what is this but following the foot-steps of Dioclesian and his satellites, "filling all places," as Mr. Echard writes, "with force and violence?"

That Catholics were deprived of the protection of the laws we may gather from Hume, who, in his relation of Oates's infamous plot, says, "*The chief justice gave sanction to all the narrow prejudices and bigoted* "*fury of the populace.* Instead of being counsel for the prisoners, as "his duty required, HE PLEADED THE CAUSE AGAINST THEM; *browbeat* "*their witnesses; and represented their guilt as certain and uncontroverted.* "....When a verdict was given against the prisoner, the spectators "expressed their savage joy, by loud acclamations. The witnesses, on "approaching the court, *were almost torn in pieces* by the rabble. One "in particular, was bruised to such a degree *as to put his life in danger;* "and another, a woman, declared that, unless the court could afford her "protection, she durst not give evidence. But as the judges could "[would more properly] go no further than promise to punish such as "should do her any injury, the prisoner himself had the humanity to "waive her testimony." It was during the ferment of this plot, se disgraceful to the annals of this once great and happy nation, that the declaration against transubstantiation and the invocation of saints was invented, and passed into a law, for the express purpose of excluding from all places of trust, profit or dignity, the professors of the *same faith* that were excluded by Dioclesian, of which the modern editors of Fox complain as an act of injustice, while they as foolishly and wickedly declare that the purport of their labours is to continue this very system of unjust exclusion!!! What barefaced inconsistency.

The cruelties of this tenth persecution, we are told by Fox, were so unendurable that "at last several of the governors of provinces repre- "sented to the imperial court, that 'it was unfit to pollute the cities "with the blood of its inhabitants, or, to defame the government of "the emperors with the death of so many subjects.' Hence many "were respited from execution; but though not put to death, they

" were subjected to every species of indignity." Such was and now is
the case with the Catholics of this country. Under the Stuarts there
were many attempts made to ameliorate the condition of the persecuted,
but these attempts only produced more violent decrees on the part
of " Protestant-ascendency;" and do we not see, with our own eyes,
the fury and intolerance of this faction in opposing the laudable endeavours of the present lord-lieutenant of Ireland, and many liberal
senators, to soften the rigour of those restrictive laws that still disgrace our statute book? Are not the Catholic nobility and gentry at
the present day; ay, and even the commonest of the commonalty of
that body, " though not put to death, ... subjected to every species
" of indignity?" Is not the meanest of the " Protestant-ascendency"
party permitted to lord it over the first peer of the realm, because the
latter chooses to follow the dictates of his conscience by paying adoration to his God in the same form and creed as the primitive Christians
did?

The next subject that demands our attention is the statement of Fox,
that " the Christians refused to bear arms under the Roman emperors."
This is a gross perversion; for the fact is, the Christians, as a general
body, never came to any such determination. However, let us hear
what the martyrologist has to say. " At this time," he writes, " the
" Christians, upon mature consideration, thought it unlawful to bear
" arms under an heathen emperor. Their reasons were :—1. That they
" thereby were frequently under the necessity of profaning the Christian
" sabbath.—2. That they were obliged, with the rest of the army, fre-
" quently to be present at idolatrous sacrifices, before the temples of
" idols.—3. That they were compelled to follow the imperial standards,
" which were dedicated to heathen deities, and bore their representa-
" tions. Such reasons induced many to refuse to enter into the imperial
" army, when called upon so to do; for the Roman constitution obliged
" all young men, of a certain stature, to make several campaigns."—
To these reasons Fox has added a circumstantial account of the martyrdom of Maximilian, " the son of Fabius Victor," who it appears was
himself a Christian soldier in Numidia. How Fox came by his tale, we
are not, as usual, informed. We can trace no account of it in Echard,
and the mention made of this martyr by Butler is very brief. The
latter writer states that the law applied to the sons of soldiers, who were
compelled by it to serve in the army at the age of twenty-one, if found
to be of due stature. Maximilian was found to answer the height prescribed, but refused to receive the mark of enlistment, which was a
print on the hand and a leaden collar about the neck, on which were
engraved the name and motto of the emperor. His plea was, according to Butler, that in the Roman army superstitions, contrary to the
Christian faith, were often practised, with which he could not defile his
soul. For this opinion he was condemned to death, and suffered, according to Ruinart, in 296, seven years previous to the breaking out
of Dioclesian's persecution, yet Fox places the event " at this time;"
that is, in this tenth persecution.

That there were some of the primitive Christians who thought it unlawful to bear arms cannot be doubted; but it did not arise from the
army being under a heathen emperor, for that circumstance could make

no difference. The objection arose from *the laws* being unjust and intolerant, by intrenching on the liberty of conscience, and compelling such Christians to be present at a worship which they knew to be erroneous and sinful. This was the pith of the objection; and this is a hardship to which Catholics are liable at this very day. By the militia laws of England every Catholic is subject to be drawn for that service, and when embodied, he may be *compelled* by the mutiny law to attend at the worship of the established church, though he is conscientiously convinced that the worship there offered is a *false* one, and therefore such an one as he cannot join in without offending God. Here then is a parallel case with the primitive Christians; and be it observed, that when, in 1806, the then administration of this country attempted to secure to the British soldier freedom of conscience under the guarantee of LAW, "Protestant-ascendency" set up the bigotted whoop of " Church in danger," and the ministers were kicked out in disgrace. In Ireland, it is true, because the people are almost wholly Catholic, the liberty of worship is secured to such as may enter the militia in that country while they remain in the island. But the moment they set foot on the shores of Protestant England, that privilege is no longer secured to them, but they may be marched off to the first Protestant church at the will of their commander, or be punished with the lash for disobedience of orders. Now, supposing a Catholic of the present day to be drawn for the militia, and on the ground of conscience, like the young Maximilian, he refuses to join the regiment for which he has been drawn,—what would be the consequence? Fine and imprisonment. And for what offence? Not a dislike to bear arms; not a disinclination to serve his country in the hour of need; no, he is ready to do both: but that country, by its laws, making him liable to become a traitor to his God, by partaking in a false worship, he therefore prefers the laws of God before the edicts of men. Thus then it is not the disloyalty of the Catholic, but the injustice of the law, that occasions the refusal, and the Catholic who may suffer under "Protestant-ascendency" in such a case, is equally entitled to the regard of every hater of persecution as the object of Fox's commiseration.

Fox now enters into a long detail of the different martyrs who suffered in the persecution of Dioclesian, and in order to strike his readers, he has arranged some of them under particular heads, such as " *A Pa-* " *gan father seeks to sacrifice his own son;* "—" *Fortitude and noble conduct* " *of three Christian friends;* "—*Martyrdom of three sisters;* "—" *Numer-* " *ous martyrdoms;* "—" *Martyrdom in Naples;* " &c. &c. Of the martyrs named by Fox, we have no clue to trace the authenticity of their acts, and some of them we have not been able to find any mention whatever by the authorities we have access to. Once more, however, we wish to impress upon the mind of the reader, particularly if he be a Protestant,—that all the martyrs during this period of the Christian church whose acts are authenticated were ROMAN CATHOLICS, professing the SAME faith as is now termed *Popery* by " Protestant-ascendency," and towards the professors of which, the editors of this *Book of Martyrs* say, it is their object to excite the feelings of hatred and abhorrence. Let the reader then remember, we say again, that the " godly martyrs," during these ten persecutions under Pagan ascendency, were ROMAN

CATHOLICS. It is made a subject of special notification that a Pagan father should seek to sacrifice his own son for becoming a Christian; but what is this single case of parental cruelty and bigotry, compared with the laws of "Protestant ascendency," which offered to any unprincipled and unfeeling son the possession of his father's estate, on forsaking the reglion he was brought up in and becoming an apostate. Yes, reader, look into the statute books of England and Ireland and you will there see it enacted by Protestant parliaments, that any undutiful son, on turning Protestant, became, *by law,* the possessor of his Catholic father's property though living, and might thus reduce him to the most abject poverty and distress. How many instances have come to our personal knowledge of Protestant parents disowning their children and turning them out of doors, because they have embraced the doctrines of Catholicism from conviction, the same as this young Christian mentioned by Fox? Nay, we will venture to assert, from the spirit displayed by the modern editors of this Book of Martyrs in their address " to the Chris-" tian public," that were any of their children to become Catholics, they would not hesitate a moment to follow the example of this Pagan father, and sacrifice the child that should dare to exercise this right of every human being, FREEDOM OF CONSCIENCE

" Vitus, a Sicilian of considerable family," writes Fox, "was brought " up a Christian? his virtues increased with his years, his constancy sup-" ported him under all his afflictions, and his faith was superior to " the most dangerous perils and misfortunes. Hylas, his father, who " was a Pagan, finding that he had been instructed in the principles of " Christianity by the nurse who brought him up, used all his endeavours " to bring him back to Paganism; but finding his efforts in vain, he " forgot all the feelings of a parent, and informed against his son to " Valerian, governor of Sicily, who was very active in persecuting the " Christians at that period." So far our martyrologist is correct; and so well convinced was " Protestant ascendency" of the force of early instruction, that she influenced her parliaments to pass laws making it not only penal for a Catholic to become a teacher of youth, even of Catholic parents, but, (so great and inveterate was her hatred of Catholicism) it was also enacted that Catholic parents should not be the guardians and instructors of their own children !!! Such an unnatural law as this is no where to be found, we believe, in any country but England and Ireland; and though the Pagans were cruelly bent upon the destruction of Christianity, yet they did not reach that climax of intolerant legislation to which "Protestant-ascendency" arrived.

Another martyr recorded by Fox we shall here briefly notice; as his authentic acts shew what were, in that age, the doctrines of the Christians. He introduces his account under a head "Conversion and Death " of Cyprian."—He then goes on,—"Cyprian, known by the title of the " magician, to distinguish him from Cyprian, bishop of Carthage, was " a native of Antioch. He received a liberal education in his youth, " and applied himself to astrology; after which he travelled through " India, Egypt, Greece, &c. He afterwards settled near Babylon, and " being skilled in the Chaldean mysteries, he employed his talents in " endeavouring to draw women from chastity and conjugal faith, and " in persecuting the Christians, and ridiculing Christianity. He be-

" came acquainted with Justina, a young lady of Antioch, of high birth,
" beauty, and accomplishments, who had been educated in idolatry,
" but being converted to Christianity, she induced her father and mo-
" ther to embrace the same faith. A Pagan gentleman falling in love
" with her, and not being able to obtain a favourable return to his
" addresses, applied for assistance to Cyprian, who undertook the de-
" sign, but with a treacherous intent; for under pretence of acting for
" his friend, he determined, if possible, to possess the lady himself.
" To effect this he employed all his skill, but his endeavours proving
" ineffectual, he was fully convinced that a superior power protected
" her against his evil intentions. His reflections, on this account,
" caused him to search into the truths of Christianity, and his enquiry
" became so beneficial, that he renounced the errors of Paganism.
" His repentance was truly sincere; he determined to reform his con-
" duct, and to make every amends in his power for the crimes he had
" committed. He therefore burnt his books of astrology and magic,
" received baptism, and became animated with a powerful gift of grace.
" His conversion had a great effect on the lover of Justina, and he also
" in a short time embraced Christianity. During the persecution of
" Dioclesian, Cyprian and Justina were seized upon as Christians, when
" the former was torn with pincers, and the latter chastised; and after
" suffering other torments they were both beheaded."

This event took place in 304, and the empress Eudocia, wife of
Theodosius the younger, wrote the history of these two martyrs in a
beautiful Greek poem, of three books. The original work is lost, but
some extracts have been preserved by Photius. This latter says, quoting from Eudocia, that when Cyprian tried all the magic art he was
possessed of to overcome the resolution of the holy virgin, " she de-
" feated and put to flight the devils by *the sign of the cross.*" St. Cyprian himself, who wrote his Confession, still extant, says, " She armed
" herself with the sign of Christ, and overcame the invocation of the
" demons." St. Gregory Nazianzen adds, " Suppliantly *beseeching the*
" *virgin Mary that she would succour a virgin in danger,* she fortified her-
" self with the antidotes of fasting, tears, and prayers." These quotations shew clearly, that the primitive Christians were in the practice of
making the sign of the cross and invoking the virgin Mary in case of
necessity, as Catholics now do, while Protestants declare the practice
to be damnable and idolatrous. Cyprian it also appears was awfully
struck with reverence, when attending at the divine mystery of the
mass, which he thus describes in his Confession : " I saw the choir of
" heavenly men, or of angels, singing to God, adding at the end of
" every verse in the psalms, the Hebrew word Alleluia, so that they
" seemed not to be men." These testimonies of " godly martyrs," who,
of the most debase of mankind, became the patterns of all virtues and
living witnesses of the grace bestowed by God on those who supplicate
his holy name;—these testimonies, we say, in favour of the doctrines
and practices of the Catholic church ought to make Protestants reflect
and shudder at their daring, when to obtain some office in the state, or
preferment in the church as by *law* established, they present themselves
in the presence of their Maker, and swear by his holy name, that what
the apostles and their successors taught and practised in the primitive

ages, and is now taught and pracised by the greatest body of Christians, is DAMNABLE idolatry and superstition!!! Yet it is urged by "Protestant-ascendency," that those impious tests are the bulwark of Protestantism, as by *law* established!!!!!!

We have now gone through the period of Roman Pagan persecution, and are about to enter a new epoch in the progress of Christianity. During three hundred years this system experienced nothing but opposition from the rulers of the earth and the ambition of sophisters; yet in defiance of this hostility, stained with the blood of innumerable martyrs, and harassed by the deceits of false friends, the ministers of Jesus Christ, inspired by the Holy Ghost, carried his doctrines to the farthest regions, preaching the *same* invariable rule of faith. and uniting every new church under *one* head, namely the pope, or bishop of Rome. The sufferings of the Christians, and the great increase of the Church, had now stamped the divine origin of this system among the people of the Roman empire, but the hearts of their rulers had not yet been touched, and it was reserved for Constantine to receive this special grace from heaven. Hitherto the Roman emperors were men of dissolute habits and brutal passions, with here and there an exception. Constantine, however, a Briton by birth, was endowed with more noble qualities. The character and disposition of Constantine had gained him the hearts of all classes, and with one accord the people and army proclamed him emperor on the death of his father Constantius, which took place at York, about the year 306, Constantine being then about 33 years of age. Being threatened with an attack by the tyrant Maxentius, who ruled over Italy and Rome, the young emperor, like an able general, judged it better to prevent this attack, than to wait the arrival of his enemy. He accordingly penetrated the very heart of Italy, and advanced within two miles of Rome. There he pitched his tent, and resolved to come to a decisive engagement with his proud and sanguinary adversary. In this resolution he was strengthened by the appearance of a wonderful phenomenon, witnessed by his whole army as well as himself. This extraordinary occurrence we shall here give in the words of John Fox, before we proceed to remark upon it

"CONSTANTINE BECOMES THE CHAMPION OF THE CHRISTIANS.

" Constantine the great at length determined to redress the griev-
" auces of the Christians, for which purpose he raised an army of
" 30,000 foot, and 800 horse, with which he marched towards Rome
" against Maxentius, the emperor. But, reflecting on the fatal mis-
" carriages of his predecessors, who had maintained a multiplicity of
" gods, and reposed an entire confidence in their assistance? and con-
" sidering that while his own father adored only one God, he continu-
" ally prospered; Constantine rejected the adoration of idols, and im-
" plored the assistance of the Almighty ; who heard his prayers, and
" answered them in a manner so suprising and miraculous, that Euse-
" bius acknowledges it would not have been credible, had he not re-
" ceived it from the emperor's own mouth, who publicly and solemnly
" ratified the truth upon his oath.

" THE VISION OF CONSTANTINE.

" The army being advanced near Rome. and the emperor employed
" in his devout ejaculations, on the 27th day of October, about three
" o'clock in the afternoon, when the sun was declining, there suddenly
" appeared to him a pillar of light in the heavens, in the form of a
" cross, with this plain inscription on or about it ΤΟΥΤΩ ΝΙΚΑ, 'In this
" overcome.' Constantine was greatly surprised at this strange sight,
" which was visible to the whole army, who equally wondered at it
" with himself. The officers and commanders, prompted by the augurs
" and auspices or soothsayers, looked upon it as an inauspicious omen
" portending an unfortunate expedition; the emperor himself did not
" understand it, till at length our Saviour appeared to him in a vision
" with a cross in his hand, commanding him to make a royal standard
" like that he had seen in the heavens, and cause it to be continually
" carried before his army, as an ensign both of victory and safety.
" Early the next morning, Constantine informed his friends and officers
" of what he had seen in the night, and sending for proper workmen,
" sat down by them and described to them the form of the standard,
" which he then ordered them to make with the greatest art and mag-
" nificence; and accordingly they made it thus: a long spear, plated
" with gold, and a traverse piece at the top, in the form of a cross, to
" which was fastened a four square purple banner, embroidered with
" gold, and beset with precious stones, which reflected an amazing
" lustre; towards the top was depicted the emperor between his two
" sons; on the top of the shaft, above the cross, stood a crown, over-
" laid with gold and jewels, within which was placed the sacred sym-
" bol, namely, the two first letters of Christ in Greek, X and P,
" struck one through the other: this device he afterwards bore not
" only upon his shields, but also upon his coins, many of which are
" still extant."

This account of Fox is substantially correct, but there are some mistakes that require to be corrected. In the first place, Constantine's
father was not a Christian, though Eusebius says, that before his death
he professed the belief of one only God. It is related of Constantius, and
the fact is well worthy the attention of " Protestant ascendency," that
when Dioclesian sent his bloodly edicts to Constantius, who ruled over
the countries on this side of the Alps, namely, Gaul and Britain, he refused to act upon them himself, though some Christians suffered in
Britain through the bigotry and cruelty of the governors, among whom
was St. Alban, whose martyrdom we have related. Constantius, however, soon put a check to their fury; but lest he should be thought to
favour the Christians too much, he suffered the churches to be demolished. Though not a Christian himself, he had many of that
faith among his officers and household. On receiving the edicts
of Dioclesian, he gave them their choice, either to sacrifice or quit
their posts. Many preferred their places to conscience, and offered sacrifice. These apostates Constantius from that time despised and discharged from his service, observing that those who were faithless to
their God would never be faithful to him. But such as refused to sacrifice he kept near his person. (*Eus. Vit. Constant.* 1. i, c, 16.) How

different is the conduct of "Protestant-ascendency" from that of this Pagan emperor. Under the former the apostate from the Catholic faith is rewarded with title and office, while the firm adherent to that faith is stigmatized as a traitor and deprived of his hereditary rights! When will common sense resume its sway amongst our intolerants? In the second place, it does not appear that Constantine raised his army for the purpose of succouring the Christians, as Fox asserts, but to repel the assaults of Maxentius, who, as we before stated, had declared war against Constantine, under pretence of avenging the death of his father Maximinus, whom Constantine had caused to be strangled in 308, having made several attempts on the life of the latter. However, the fact is undeniable, that Constantine began to doubt the efficacy of Pagan sacrifices, and had recourse to the one only true God, whom the Christians adored with such fervour; and it is equally undeniable, that he was favoured with a supernatural appearance of THE CROSS, the banner under which the Christians had fought against the world and the devil, and had carried it victoriously through the ranks of Paganism.

The deist effects to deny supernatural events; but how such a circumstance as the appearance of the cross to Constantine, and his subsequent victory, under that banner, over the tyrant Maxentius, with an inferior army, can be denied, consistently with common sense, we are at a loss to conceive. The phenomenon was not confined to the eye of Constantine; it was visible to the whole army, and a resemblance of it afterwards became the principal standard of the imperial Roman army. Now if this occurrence had been a mere pretension, invented for some sinister purpose, is it possible, we ask, that such an attempt could have met with general credit as it did from all persons living at that time. Lactantius, Eusebius, Artemius the martyr under Julian the apostate, Cyzicenus, Philostorgius, an Arian historian, the Alexadrian, or Paschal Chronicle (published by F. Raderus, and more accurately by Dr. Cange) compiled in 630; Sozomen, Socrates, Glydas, and Eutychius; some of whom wrote from various memoirs, and as vouchers of a fact to which many had been eye witnesses; all agree in stating the actual occurrence of this wonderful spectacle. Lactantius, who was preceptor to Crispus, Cæsar, Constantine's son, in his book *On the Death of the Persecutors*, ascribes the victory of the latter over Maxentius to the miraculous vision he had in his sleep before the battle. This work was written before Eusebius compiled the life of Constantine. The latter writer had the fact from Constantine himself.— According to the Paschal Chronicle, &c. the inscription was formed in bright letters, as it were, of gold, in the perpendicular shaft, or body of the cross from the middle down to the bottom. We shall give a perfect figure of it in our next number. In addition to this body of epistolary evidence, a magnificent triumphal arch was erected in Rome in memory of the victory, in the inscription of which Constantine attributed his success to the miraculous apparition. Besides this public monument at Rome, Eusebius states that he likewise set up in the principal hall of his palace at Constantinople, a great figure of the cross which he had seen in the heavens, and by the power of which he had become victorious. The standard before alluded to was known by the name of the Labarum, and is pretty accurately described as above by Fox. The emperor chose fifty men of the stoutest and most religious among his guards, to carry this banner by turns; it was always borne before the emperor in battle. Constantine also caused banners of the same fashion, but less in size, to be made for every legion, and had the monogram of the name of Christ framed in the form of a Cross, on his helmet, and in the shields of his soldiers. Julian the apostate, on his coming to the purple, changed on his medals this sacred monogram into the old letters S. P. Q. R. But Jovian and the succeeding emperors restored it. In a word, the evidence of these two miracles is so clear and authentic, that we cannot help thinking that every rational and unbiassed mind will exclaim with Baluze, "What history will men believe, if it be allowed to "call in question a fact confirmed by the most unexceptionable wit-"nesses, and by ancient medals and other monuments." (*Not. in* *Lactant.*) We shall give a representation of the Labarum in the next number.

This memorable appearance of the great work of mercy was followed by a complete victory over Maxentius, on the 27th of October, 312, which put Constantine in complete possession of the Western empire. Such signal proofs of divine Providence in his favour we might have supposed sufficient to induce Constantine to declare himself immediately a Christian: but this was not the case. Naturally humane in his disposition, he contented himself at first with proposing to Licinius, his colleague, whom he met at Rome, to stay all persecution on the score of religion, which the latter agreeing to, an edict was published allowing full liberty of conscience, and permitting every one to follow that form of worship he conscientiously deemed right. This act of justice gave offence to Maximin, the tyrant of the east, whose implacable hatred to the Christian name was equal to any of the imperial persecutors who preceded him. He declared war against Constantine and Licinius, was defeated by the latter in battle, and put an end to his life by poison. Thus, by the mysterious dispensation of an all-ruling Power, the tyrants of the earth were all cut off one after the other, and the whole empire was placed under a merciful prince, whose heart, however, was not yet sufficiently touched with divine grace to embrace the heavenly truths which Christ came on earth to reveal.— It was not till he had experienced affliction in his family, and disease in his person, that Constantine began to reflect seriously on the sublime precepts of Christianity, and the necessity of embracing that system which had been watered by the blood of so many glorious and heroic martyrs. This state of uncertainty on the part of the emperor occasioned the augurs or soothsayers to harass and alarm the Christians, who were interrupted by the misguided populace in their religious assemblies, and the pope was constrained to seek his safety by withdrawing himself from Rome to the mountain of Soracte.

While these disorders were going on, Constantine was stricken with a leprosy; and, blinded by the errors of his early education, he consulted the augurs how he could be cured. They told him he must bathe in a bath of infant's blood. This proposition he rejected with horror, and meditated on some past transactions, particularly on the condemnation of death he had passed on his own son Crispus, and his

A REVIEW

OF

Fox's Book of Martyrs,

CRITICAL AND HISTORICAL.

No. 8. Printed and Published by W. E. ANDREWS, 3, Chapter-house-court, St. Paul's Churchyard, London. Price 3d.

EXPLANATION OF THE ENGRAVING.—*The figure on the left hand is a representation of the famous Roman banner, called the Labarum. It was a pole plated with gold, upon which was laid horizontally a cross bar, so as to form the figure of a Cross. The top of the perpendicular shaft was adorned with a crown wrought with gold, and ornamented with sparkling precious stones. In the middle of this crown was a monogram representing the name of Christ by the two initial Greek letters, X, Chi, equivalent to our Ch, and P. Ro, equivalent to our R. This last-mentioned letter was formed in the Chi, and rose a little above it. A purple veil of a square figure hung from the cross bar, spangled with bright jewels, which dazzled the eyes of the beholders. Above the veil were afterward set the images of the emperor and his children.——That on the other hand is a more minute resemblance of the Cross as it appeared to Constantine, see the present sheet, page 115. This heavenly sign extended very wide in the East, the inscription formed as it were in letters of gold in the perpendicular shaft or body of the cross from the middle down to the bottom. On the pedestal of a statue erected in honour of Constantine by the senate of Rome, he caused this inscription to be placed: "By this salutary sign, the true mark of courage, I have delivered your city from the yoke of tyranny, and restored the senate and people of Rome to their ancient glory."*

CONTINUATION OF THE REVIEW.

wife Fausta, the latter having accused the son of attempting her chastity, when she had solicited him to hold incestuous intercourse with her. In this state of perplexity Constantine was visited in his sleep by saints Peter and Paul, who admonished him to seek out the holy pope Silvester, in his place of concealment, and on so doing he would receive a cure through the waters of baptism. The emperor on awaking immediately sought out the good pontiff, who spent some days in instructing Constantine in the necessary points of Christian faith, after which he was baptized with the usual ceremonies in a place adjoining the church of St. John Lateran in the year 324. Immediately, on receiving the waters of baptism, the leprosy left him. This miraculous cure is related by Binius and Baronius, and we see no reason why it should be doubted any more than the wonderful conversion of St. Paul, and his restoration to sight from the hands of Ananias.

We now enter a new era of the Christian church. Hitherto she had experienced the most violent opposition that Jews, Philosophers, Pagans and Heretics could raise against her, for the space of three hundred years; notwithstanding which her doctrines had been gaining ground in every quarter of the globe. She had now received into her bosom the monarch of the world; the imperial ruler of the vast Roman empire; a man who might be said to have attained the summit of earthly grandeur. Hitherto she had experienced persecution from the state; now she had the first civil magistrate in her favour; and what was her conduct in this state of prosperity? Did she, the Catholic church, induce the emperor to exert *force* to spread her doctrines or reclaim error? No; the first step of this Christian emperor was to declare to the world that his change of sentiment arose from a pure conviction of mind, and that it was his resolution to allow every one of his subjects the same freedom of conscience.

The speech Constantine made to the senate, on announcing his baptism, is so clear a definition of the mild and genuine principles of the Catholic religion, in what regards the liberty of conscience, that we here insert it, from *Caussin's Holy Court,* part II, book ii, sec. 9. Having caused a throne to be prepared in the palace of Trajan, and commanded the attendance of the senate, he thus addressed them:—
" Sirs, I doubt not but the change of religion which I have made, will
" appear strange to many, who blame all that which they cannot under-
" stand, and will understand nothing, but what flatters their presump-
" tion. All novelty is odious to those who love the old age of error: yet
" I can tell you, this is no new religion which I have embraced, but
" that which was begun in the purified souls of the golden age, hap-
" pily finished in our days. The first men of the world had verity in
" bloom, we now see the fruit, which we may and shall enjoy, if we
" be not ungrateful to our happiness, and traitorous to our own con-
" science. Believe me, sirs, the world is almost grown out of its non-
" age, for God hath taken pity of the ignorance thereof, and made it
" see, it was not time any longer to place dragons and owls upon altars,
" nor other gods, accounted as monsters, if they would return into the
" life of men. If our ancestors, blinded by mishap, have made to be
" esteemed for divinities so many criminals, for whom our laws do
" now ordain punishments, we are not bound to participate with the
" crimes of the one, nor the errors of the other, under pretext of an-
" tiquity. I must confess, that I from my infancy have had great dis-
" trust upon the follies which I saw in the superstitions of gentiles,
" and that which further confirmed me in this opinion, was, that one
" day I heard the answer of an oracle, which had long time stood
" mute, and being demanded the cause of this silence, answered, the
" just hindered it from speaking, and we found those just were the
" Christians, who then had power to stop the mouths of devils. After-

" wards I began to consider those men, whom I saw so persecuted,
" and that there was not a corner of the earth that was not ruddy with
" their blood, yet were they notwithstanding so patient in their perse-
" cutions, that they had prayers on their lips for those who rent their
" hearts out of their bodies. This then gave me matter of much
" amazement; but when I came to think on their church, which
" flourished among so many storms, and encreased under the
" swords of persecution, this seemed to be more than human; yet
" transported with the torrent of common opinions, I still resisted the
" voice of God which spoke in my heart, when it opened my eyes, and
" made me once lively apprehend the dreadful ends of emperors, who
" had persecuted Christianity, comparing them to the felicity of my
" father Constantius, of most glorious memory, who had preserved his
" hands innocent even to death, free from any stain of Christian blood.
" This was sufficiently potent to move a soul, which would easily yield
" to reason: but God redoubling his inspirations, made me one day
" behold in the heavens a prodigy, which many saw with me, to wit,
" the figure of the cross, composed of most resplendent light, which
" appeared just at that time I was to wage battle against Maxentius. I
" call the living God to witness, that I therein read distinctly these
" words, written as with the rays of the sun, EN TOYTΩ NIKA. And it
" is a wonder that I deferred still to yield myself up, till such time that
" the Saviour of the world admonished me in a vision, to take into my
" standards the sign which I had seen in heaven the day before. I in-
" stantly obeyed, and have seen such prodigious effects succeed in the
" defeat of Maxentius, which you have admired, attributing to man that
" which was a work of the Divinity. I thought then to have disco-
" vered what I was, but considerations of state, which had too much
" force upon my soul, stayed me, and have made me walk along
" hitherto, in a life more licentious than I intended. I now protest
" before the face of heaven and earth, that I am a Christian both in heart
" and professsion; nor shall any motives ever alter that which I have so
" constantly resolved on. Yet for all this I purpose not to force any
" man in his religion, leaving for this time belief as free as the elements:
" yet for the charity I bear towards my good subjects, I cannot but
" wish them as much good as myself. Now all my greatest happiness,
" and which I esteem more than my purple and diadem, is to entertain
" the knowledge of a living God, which has been revealed to us by
" his only son Jesus Christ, the Doctor and Saviour of the world.
" His person is full of miracles, his life of wisdom and goodness, his
" doctrine of purity; and if to conquer our pride, and expiate our de-
" merits, he hath humbled himself to the punishment of the cross, so
" much therefore 'the more it ought to be honourable, since he hath
" done for us all that which an incomparable love can do, and endured
" all that which an invincible patience may suffer. I can do no
" other but love and singularly honour those who are enrolled under
" his standard, as my brothers in religion; and let it not seem strange
" to any, if heretofore shewing myself very liberal to beautify and en-
" rich the temples of Gentilism, I now apply myself to build and adorn
" the churches. I will render what I owe to God and my own con-
" science, nor shall my subjects who are of a religion different from

" mine, be any way interested therein, desiring to preserve them, as
" persons whom I hope one day to have companions in faith, and co-
" heirs in glory, if they add never so little consent to the lights where-
" with the wisdom of God incarnate hath replenished the world. I
" only beseech thee, O great God, on whom all sceptres and crowns
" depend, since you have united the east and west under my hands,
" you will arrange them under the yoke of your law, which is the knot
" of empires, and source of felicity. I offer unto you my person, my
" arms, my sceptre, and all my abilities, humbly begging of you to
" accept my slender service, and to give me the assisting wisdom of
" your throne, to govern in all honour, all justice, all peace and amity,
" the people which you have committed to my charge."

Such were the sentiments of the first royal convert to Christianity,
founded on the genuine principles of the Catholic religion, in which
he had just been instructed by pope Silvester. Our Saviour taught his
apostles to suffer persecution for justice sake, and he reprobated the conduct of Peter, when that apostle drew his sword in defence of his
divine Master. So the Catholic church, from her birth to the present
day, whatever may have been the conduct of some of her children,
and she cannot be blamed for their partial deviation from her principles,
condemns all measures of compulsion in matters of conscience, as contrary to the free will of man. She points out the law to all her children, and while she endeavours to preserve them in the path of Truth,
she can only pray for, and persuade, those who have strayed from her
fold, to retrace their steps. That such were her feelings in the first
ages, we have a testimony in Constantine ; and that she has preserved
this disposition in our own days may be gathered, we think, from this
fact; that while the whole of the Protestant states on the continent
have laws intrenching on the rights of conscience, perfect toleration
in matters of religion has been granted to Protestants by the Catholic states of Germany. To shew farther the feelings of Constantine on
this occasion of his embracing Christianity, the same author says, that
when he had concluded his excellent speech to the senate, acclamations
burst forth from the senators and people in favour of Christianism,
and threats were announced against those who should refuse to abandon
their idols. On these symptoms of popular intolerance appearing, the
Christian emperor commanded silence, and thus addressed the people:
" No," he said, "I intend not any man shall be forced in the matter
" of his religion; the services of the world are oftentimes constrained;
" but those we render to God ought ever to be voluntary. We have
" no greater proof of the Divinity than mercy. God sheweth what
" he is, in so long time, and with such patience, suffering the im-
" pieties and ingratitudes of men. I would have all the world know,
" that I intend not to make Christians by necessity, but by discretion.
" As it is a crime to deny true religion to those who require it, so
" it is an importunity to seek now to impose it by force on such as
" demand it not. They that will not follow my example shall not
" therefore be separated from my friendship. I am the common
" father of all in general, and no man ought to be frustrated of the
" preservation which I owe him."

These words allayed the effervescence of the people, and the declaration of Constantine was followed by the promulgation of salutary laws, which left the Pagans at full liberty to exercise their superstitions, on condition that they forbore to speak against the honour of our Saviour, or molest the Christians. In a word, he would not allow that any degree of force should be used to convert a Pagan, nor were the Pagans allowed to exercise any control over their servants or children, to prevent them from embracing Christianity, on being convinced of its truths.

In concluding this first book of Fox's work, the editors have made some " *Remarks on the Vengeance of God towards the Persecutors of the* " *Christians.*" Many of these are so pertinent and apposite, while others require a little elucidation, that we feel it a duty to lay them before our readers, accompanying them with a few observations which we trust will throw some further light upon the subject. " We cannot " close our account of the ten persecutions under the Roman emperors," write the editors, "without calling the attention of the Christian " reader to the manifestations of the great displeasure of the Almighty " against the persecutors. History evidently proves, that no nation or " individual can ultimately prosper, by whom Christ Jesus, the Son of " God, is contemned. During the persecutions of the holy martyrs " which we have related above, the Roman people were the victims of " the cruelty and tyranny of their rulers, and the empire was perpe- " tually torn and distracted by civil wars. In the reign of Tiberius, " five thousand persons were crushed to death by the fall of a theatre, " and on many other occasions the divine wrath was evinced against " that cruel and merciless nation.

" Neither did the emperors themselves escape their just reward.— " Tiberius was murdered, as were his three immediate successors. " Galba, after a reign of only seven months, was put to death by Otho, " who being vanquished by Vitellius, killed himself. Vitellius, shortly " after, was tortured, and his body thrown into the Tiber. Titus is " said to have been poisoned by his brother Domitian, who was after- " wards slain by his wife. Commodus was strangled. Pertinax and " Didius were put to death ; Severus killed himself ; Caracalla slew " his brother Geta, and was in his turn slain by Marcinus, who, with " his son, was afterwards killed by his own soldiers. Heliogabalus " was put to death by the people. Alexander Severus, a virtuous em- " peror, was murdered by Maximinus, who was afterwards slain by his " own army. Pupienus and Balbinus were murdered by the prætorian " guards. Gordian and Philip were slain. Decius was drowned, and " his son killed in battle. Gallus and Volusianus were murdered " by Æmilianus, who within three months afterwards was himself " slain. Valerian was taken prisoner by the Persians, and at length " flayed alive, and his son Gallienus was assassinated. Aurelian was " murdered ; as were Tacitus, Florianus, and Probus. Galerius died " in a miserable manner, as did Maximinus of a horrible loathsome dis- " ease. Maxentius, being conquered by Constantine, was drowned in " his attempt to escape ; and Licinius was deposed, and slain by his " soldiers.

" The Jews, also, for their obstinacy and wickedness in rejecting the " gospel so graciously offered to them by Jesus Christ, were signally

" punished. Forty years had scarcely elapsed from their crucifixion of
" our Saviour, when Jerusalem was levelled with the ground, and more
" than a million of the Jews killed; innumerable multitudes sold for
" slaves, and many thousands torn to pieces by wild beasts, or other-
" wise cruelly slain. Indeed, the nation may be said to have been an-
" nihilated—its political existence was terminated, and the descendants
" of that people, which was once peculiarly favoured of God, are now
" scattered over the face of the earth—a by-word and a reproach among
" the nations.

" Thus (add the editors) it is evident that wickedness and infidelity
" are certainly, though sometimes slowly, punished, by Him who is
" just, although merciful; and *if he has hitherto graciously refrained*
" *from visiting the sins of this nation with the punishment which they de-*
" *serve,* let us not be vain of that exemption; let us not attribute it to
" any merit of our own; but rather let it afford an additional motive
" to our gratitude and praise; let us unfeignedly thank him for his ten-
" der mercies daily vouchsafed to us; and, while we bow before him
" in humble adoration, let us earnestly endeavour *to preserve our wor-*
" *ship of him free from that ungodliness and superstition of which it has*
" *been happily purged and cleansed by the blood of the holy martyrs.* So
" shall we not only secure our happiness in this world, but, in the end,
" attain everlasting joy and felicity, through the merits of our blessed
" Lord and Saviour Jesus Christ, who gave up himself as a precious
" sacrifice for our transgressions.

" If we (continue the editors) be negligent in *the defence of the pure*
" *religion* which he has vouchsafed to impart unto us; if we allow *that*
" *glorious fabric,* which cost so much blood to raise, to *be overturned* by
" the open attack of *the Infidel,* or the more dangerous sap and mine of
" *the Catholic Emancipator;* we alone are justly blameable for the con-
" sequences that will infallibly ensue, and on our heads will rest the
" dreadful responsibility of having surrendered the citadel of our secu-
" rity to those who await, in anxious expectation, the moment when
" the weakness of some, and the indifference of others, shall allow the
" power to pass from their hands, under the delusive hope of seeing
" it exercised with moderation."

We cordially agree with the "few plain Christians," who have undertaken the publication of the present edition of the *Book of Martyrs*
of John Fox, " that wickedness and infidelity are *certainly,* though
" sometimes *slowly,* punished by Him who is just although merciful;"
and had they turned their eyes to the real history of their own country,
and looked more closely into the transactions that have passed upon
the continent, since the breaking out of what is called the reformation of
the sixteenth century, they would have found that the vengeance of God
has been as awfully manifested towards the promoters of that event and
the persecutors of Catholics, as against the persecutors of the primitive
Christians. These "few plain Christian" tell us, that they " have
" united themselves for the purpose of diffusing among their fellow-
" believers a *knowledge* and *love* of the *genuine principles of Christianity,*
" and CONSEQUENTLY, (they add) a hatred and abhorrence of the cor-
" ruptions and crimes of Popery and its professors." Now, we will
tell these " few plain Christians" in return, that they know not, or at

least they practise not, the " *genuine principles of Christianity*," by endeavouring to excite a " hatred and abhorrence" of their fellow-men, since one of the principles of Christianity is, to love our neighbours as ourselves. The Christianity professed by these " few plain Christians" is as widely different from the Christianity of Constantine and the Catholic church, as the North is separate from the South pole. Constantine, when he forsook the superstitions of Gentilism for the sublime principles of Christianism, did not foster a resentment against the persons of such as could not see as he did, though he detested the errors to which they still adhered; so the Catholic church, as we have before stated, though she condemns the erroneous opinions opposed to her divine truths, yet she labours to bring back the strayed sheep, not by compulsion, but by prayer and mental conviction. The " few plain Christians" talk of " the defence of pure religion;" of the " glorious " fabric that cost so much blood to raise;" and insinuate that this " glorious fabric" is in danger of being " *overturned* by the open attack " of the Infidel, or the more dangerous sap and mine of the Catholic " emancipator." Here for the first time we have the word " CATHOLIC" mentioned in John Fox's Book of Martyrs, notwithstanding the " glorious fabric" of " pure religion," fertilized by the blood of so many " godly martyrs," was the HOLY CATHOLIC CHURCH, so designated by the apostles themselves in the creed or symbol of belief which they drew up as a mark of the unity of their faith, previous to their separating to carry the doctrines of their crucified Master to the utmost bounds of the earth. We have shewn that the most eminent and learned of these martyrs maintained the *same* doctrines as the Catholics profess now; and we have, at the same time, complained of the suppression of these doctrines by John Fox and his editors, for the purpose of keeping their readers in a state of ignorance and delusion; we most therefore be allowed to smile at the silly conceit of these wise men of Gotham, who expect that the Catholic church is to be overturned by the liberal emancipator of Catholics from civil slavery. We are aware that these " few plain Christians" may retort upon us and say that the " pure religion" and " glorious fabric" they allude to is the system of Protestantism. To this we rejoin, that Protestantism is *no* system; for the term system means a commixture of many things united in order; but there is neither order nor unity in Protestantism, nor can there be such, since its fundamental basis is, that every man has a right to propound a religion for himself, and so many has been propounded, that the same confusion exists among them as among the builders of the tower of Babel, after God had struck them for their pride and conceit. But in the Catholic church there is a system of divine faith which preserves its unity and perfection throughout all the nations that have embraced it, thus forming a " glorious fabric" of pure and undefiled religion, not the work of human hands, but the production of an all-wise God, whose finger is extended to protect it from all danger.

As to this " glorious fabric" being overturned, have the " few plain Christians" never read the scripture? Or have they read the word of God only to pervert it? Have they not seen the promise of Christ recorded therein, that this " glorious fabric," this seat of " pure religion "which he has vouchsafed to impart to us," is founded on a rock, imperishable, and impenetrable by error, for neither earth nor hell, he assures us, has any power to injure it. We have seen it brave the storm of ten persecutions in three hundred years, emitting during that period the light of faith to nations long enveloped in Pagan blindness; and even now it exists in as perfect purity as in former days. The "plain Christians," with more impiety than wisdom, speak of the necessity of endeavouring " to preserve their worship of Him free from *that un-* " *godliness* and *superstition* of which it has been happily *purged* and " *cleansed* by the blood of the holy martyrs." If they would endeavour to tell truth and shame the devil, they would be much better employed. What ungodliness! what superstition! has yet contaminated the pure religion imparted to the world? How can such a thing occur, unless the divine Founder of that religion has falsified his promise? And where is the Christian that dares openly to charge the God of Truth with being a Liar? Yet do these " few plain Christians" dare insinuate, that a pure religion, which was never to be sullied, according to the solemn declaration of God himself, has been " *purged* and *cleansed* by " the blood of the holy martyrs!!!" That it was fertilized by their sacred blood, and produced abundant fruit by their sufferings, we readily admit; but a religion once contaminated can never recover its purity, and it was the conviction of the invulnerability of the Catholic church that caused so many martyrs to prefer dying in it, than to live in the mazes of error and infidelity.

The " plain Christians" further insinuate, that God " has hitherto " graciously refrained from visiting the sins of this nation with the " punishment which they deserve;" this may, and we believe is the case, for much does it still deserve at the hands of divine Vengeance. But let it not be supposed that it has been *exempt* from punishment, for if we look back, and take a cursory view of the events that have taken place since the dawn of the reformation so called, we shall see as strong " manifestations of the great displeasure of the Almighty against " persecutors," as any detailed by the editors of John Fox, before quoted. It is a fact that cannot be disputed, that the introduction of the Catholic religion, in the time of the Saxon heptarchy, was followed by the establishment of the most just and salutary laws; laws calculated to secure the liberty of the subject and render a nation happy. Under the great Alfred, many wise institutions were formed, particularly the trial by jury, and so moral were the people at that time, that it is stated by historians a purse of gold could be left on the highway for successive days without being touched. Edward the confessor, a saint of the Catholic church, added to the immunities and comforts of the nation; and the great lord chancellor Fortescue, who died about the year 1471, says, that the people of this country, in his days, had plenty of every necessary of life, and wanted for nothing. These are periods of Catholic ascendency, we will now then take a few examples under " Protestant-ascendency."

It is well known to all, that Henry the eighth was the first monarch that renounced the spiritual supremacy of the bishop of Rome, which was acknowledged by Constantine the great, on embracing Christianity; and also by every Christian sovereign of this realm, from the time of the conversion of Ethelbert, by St. Augustin, at the close of the sixth century, to the twenty-fifth year of the reign of Henry, embracing the space of nearly ONE THOUSAND YEARS. Harry, it is true, could not be said to be himself a Protestant, but the germe of Protestantism took root through this monarch's disposition, injustice, and oppression. The first measure we shall notice was the suppression of forty monasteries at the instigation, and to gratify the ambition, of cardinal Wolsey. This proud churchman also first put into the king's head the scruples respecting his marriage with Catharine, his rightful queen, which led to the king's claiming the spiritual authority of the church of England. Wolsey soon after fell under the displeasure of Henry, was stripped of his possessions, and died a beggar of a broken heart.— Catharine was divorced, but maintained her honour and character with dignified courage and fortitude, whilst Anne Boleyn was raised to her place. This latter lady was looked upon by Cranmer, who was promoted to the primate's chair of England, as the prop of the Protestant interest. She was an adulteress, being with child by the king before a divorce ensued between him and Catharine, and was actually married to her privately, previous to the public separation being announced between Harry and his lawful wife. But a short time elapsed however before this prop of the Protestant cause, this Anne Boleyn, was accused of adultery and incest, and her days were shortened by the axe; the last of which was the bridal day of her royal master to another bed-fellow. The memory of this Protestant lady is still stained with dishonour, her innocence not being clearly established. Here let us note, that before the marriage of Anne, and while the king was dallying with her, a sweating sickness appeared among her female attendants, and spread among the gentlemen of the king's privy chamber. So great was the progress of the disease, that public business was suspended, and numbers were carried of by it in all parts of the kingdom.——Another measure acted upon by this monarch was the further suppression of monasteries for his own use. Cromwell, a blacksmith's son, was chosen to be the instrument to carry this act of pillage and injustice into effect. He was made secretary of state and *vicar general*, a new office never before known in the kingdom. Cromwell executed his office with remorseless cruelty and oppression, and he soon met a violent death, being condemned without a trial and beheaded. Another of Harry's Protestant queens was ripped open to give birth to a son, who afterwards succeeded his father to the throne. A fourth was divorced—his fifth was executed for adultery—and the sixth had nearly experienced the same fate, but had the good luck to escape. When Henry came to the throne, his exchequer was well filled; the destruction of the monasteries yielded him more money than all his predecessors for five centuries had received; yet at the latter end of his reign he was compelled to issue a base coinage, not only of tin and copper, but even of leather. In short, to accomplish his views he corrupted parliament, the members of which in return passed bloody laws and created new treasons, thus placing the lives of the people at the sole disposal of the king; he beheaded and burned without distinction those who opposed his will; his life after assuming the spiritual supremacy was one of disquietude and vexation, his death without the consolation of religion, and his name is never mentioned without his crimes, which excite universal execration.

Edward VI, who was ripped from his mother's womb, succeeded his father at the age of nine years, and was proclaimed head of the Church of England. His uncle Somerset was declared protector of the realm; the principal measures of whose administration were the destruction of church property and innovation in religion, to the enriching of himself and his favourites. He caused the death of his own brother, and was afterwards executed himself. The young king was compelled by Cranmer and Latimer to sign the death warrants of Boucher and Von Paris, who were burned for heresy, and in two years after the king was carried off by death, not without suspicion of being poisoned. During his sway general discontent pervaded the kingdom; a law was passed in the first year of his reign by which two justices of the peace might order the letter V to be burnt on the breast of every poor man, who should be found loitering about three days for want of employ, and adjudge him to become the slave of the informer, who might fix an iron ring round his neck, arm, or leg, and make him "labour at any work, however vile it might be, by beating, chaining, "or otherwise." If the poor fellow absented himself a fortnight from his occupation, the letter S was to be burnt on his cheek or forehead, and he became *a slave for life.* (*See* Stat. 1 Ed. VI. 3.) This infamous law under "Protestant-ascendency" was in force two years, when it was repealed. Insurrections broke out in Oxfordshire, Devonshire, and Norfolk, in consequence of the extension of inclosures and a new mode of letting rack rents, and the want of that relief formerly distributed at the gates of the monasteries. "In his fifth year;" says Baker, in his *Chronicle,* " a sweating sickness infested first Shrewsbury, and then "the north parts, and afterwards grew most extreme in London, so as "in the first week there died eight hundred persons; and was so vio- "lent that it took men away in four and twenty hours, sometimes in "twelve, and sometimes in less. Amongst others of account that died "of this sickness, were the two sons of Charles Brandon, duke of Suf- "folk, who died within an hour after one another, in such order that "both of them died dukes. This disease was proper to the English na- "tion, for it followed the English wheresoever they were in foreign "parts, but seized upon none of any other country." As to the national morals, if we may judge from the portraits drawn by the reformed preachers themselves, they were at the lowest ebb. Strype has collected several passages from the old preachers on this point. "They "assert," writes Dr. Lingard, "that the sufferings of the indigent were "viewed with indifference by the hard heartedness of the rich, that in "the pursuit of gain the most barefaced frauds were avowed and jus- "tified; that robbers and murderers escaped punishment by the partiality "of juries, and the corruption of judges; that church livings were given "to laymen, or converted to the use of the patrons; that marriages were "repeatedly dissolved by private authority; and that the haunts of pros- "titution were multiplied beyond measure."

Mary, the eldest daughter of Henry, succeeded her brother, after a feeble attempt to supplant her on the throne on the part of "Protestant-ascendency." She promised liberty of conscience on assuming the sceptre, being a Roman Catholic, and during the first two years of her reign not an individual suffered for religious opinions. This is a fact, that deserves particular notice, and we shall take occasion to establish it beyond contradiction, when we come to expose the lies of John Fox in this queen's reign. During the above space, however, Mary was disturbed by insurrections, conspiracies and seditions, and her council at length determined to try the force of persecution. In her fourth year, Baker says, the people were afflicted with hot-burning agues, and other strange diseases, of which no less than seven aldermen of London died. Calais was taken by the French, and after a short reign of five years Mary died of a broken heart.

Her half sister Elizabeth next mounted the throne, and she in her turn persecuted the Catholics with the most relentless fury. Her reign, which is usually represented by interested writers as glorious to the nation, was one of blood, rapine, and proscription. Her court was the most lewd and licentious ever seen before in England. Her deeds were marked by despotism, and her ministers the most profligate and mercenary that ever cursed a people. She beheaded a female sovereign, the beautiful Mary Stuart, and cut off the head of her own paramour Essex. She established domiciliary researches, made new treasons, encouraged informers, and created the star chamber. The courts of justice were corrupted by her connivance, imprisonment exercised at her pleasure, and loans raised by force and exaction. Torture was used to extort confession, and her whole reign in short was one of arbitrariness and cruelty. Such a succession of unchristian proceedings could not go unpunished; Baker in his Chronicle relates that in her third year the spire of St. Paul's cathedral was destroyed by lightning. Many strange births also happened. In her sixth year the pestilence was brought into England, of which there died in London 21,500 persons in one year. In her thirteenth year a prodigious earthquake occurred in the east parts of Herefordshire. In her sixteenth year there was a great dearth. In the year following, the river Thames ebbed and flowed twice within the hour, and in the month of November the heavens seemed to be all on fire. "On the 24th of February," in the succeeding year, the same Chronicler writes, "being a great frost, after a great "flood, there came down the river Severn such a swarm of flies and "beetles, that they were judged to be above a hundred quarters; the "mills thereabouts were dammed up by them for the space of four days, "and were then cleaned by digging them out with shovels." In her nineteenth year, it is related by Mr. Anthony Wood, the Protestant historian of Oxford, that on the 4th of July, Mr. Roland Jinks, a Catholic bookseller in Oxford, for having in his shop the pope's bulls and Catholic papers, was cast into prison, and most unjustly condemned to lose all his property, and to have both his ears nailed to the pillory, and to deliver himself by cutting them off with his own hands; but no sooner was the sentence passed, than a most dreadful disease burst forth in the midst of the court, and seized upon all there present. Great numbers dropped down dead on the spot; others rushed out of the court half suffocated, and died a few hours afterwards. In the space of two days, nearly all the witnesses died; and in the first night about 600 lost their lives, and the next day it seized upon 100 in the nearest streets,

The disease was a kind of fury; for the sick leaped out of bed, and beat with their sticks all those who came to assist them; some ran through the courts and streets like madmen; and others threw themselves down headlong into deep waters. Every hall, every college, every house had their dead; and what is more remarkable, all the grand jury, except one or two, died as soon as they had left Oxford. *Hist. Anti. Univ. Oxon.* l. p. 294.) " In her two and twentieth year," writes Baker, " a " strange apparition appeared in Somersetshire, threescore personages " all clothed in black, a furlong in distance from those that beheld " them; after their appearing, and a little while tarrying, they va- " nished away, but immediately another strange company in like man- " ner, colour, and number, appeared in the same place; and they en- " countered one another, and so vanished away : and a third time ap- " peared that number again, all in bright armour, and encountered one " another and so vanished away: This was examined before sir George " Norton, and sworn by four honest men that saw it to be true. In her " three and twentieth year, in the beginning of April, about six o'clock " after noon, happened an earthquake not far from York, which in some " places struck the very stones out of buildings, and made the bells in " churches to jangle. The night following the earth trembled once or " twice in Kent, and again the first day of May." In her twenty-sixth year, (A. D. 1588,) a similar earthquake happened in Dorsetshire as had taken place in Herefordshire in 1571. In her thirty-fifth year there was such a drought that the springs were dried up and cattle died for want of water: the Thames was so low that a man on horseback might ride over it at London bridge. The year following there was a great plague in London and the suburbs, of which there died, besides the Lord Mayor and three aldermen, 17,890 persons. In her thirty-eighth year, lord Hundsdon, being sick to death, saw six of his companions, already dead, come to him one after another. The first was Dudley, earl of Leicester, all in fire; the second was secretary Walsingham, also in fire and flame; the third, Pickering, so cold and frozen, that touching Hundsdon's hand, he thought he should die of cold; the fourth, Hatton, lord chancellor; the fifth, Henneage; and the sixth, Knolles. These three last were also on fire: they told him that sir William Cecil, one of their companions yet living, was to prepare himself to come shortly to them. All this was affirmed upon oath by the said lord Hundsdon, who a few days after died suddenly. This is recorded by Fr. Costerus, in *Compendio veteris Orthodoxæ Fidei*; and also by Philip D'Oultreman, in his book entitled *Pedegogue Chretienne*, p. 166. It is stated by F. Parsons in his *Discussion of Barlow's Answer*, printed in 1612, p. 218, that queen Elizabeth, in the beginning of her last sickness, told two of her ladies that she saw one night, as she lay in bed, her own body exceeding lean and fearful, in a light of fire. Camden, the panegyrist of this queen, and the writer of her history, gives this account of her last sickness. " In the beginning of her sickness, the almonds of her " throat swelled, but soon abated again; then her appetite failed her " by degrees; and withal she gave herself over to melancholy, and " seemed to be much troubled with a peculiar grief, for some reason " or other; whether it were through the violence of her disease, or for " want of Essex, &c. She looked upon herself as a *miserable forlorn wo-*

" *man*, and her grief and indignation extorted from her such speeches
" as these : *They have yoked my neck. I have none whom I can trust. My*
" *condition is strangely turned upside down.*" (*See Cambd. Hist.* lib. v,
pp. 659, 660.) F. Parsons in his *Discussion* before mentioned, says that
" she sat two days and three nights upon her stool ready dressed, and
" could never be brought by any of her council to go to bed, or to eat
" or drink, only the lord admiral persuaded her to take a little broth :
" she told him if he knew what she had seen in her bed, he would not
" persuade her as he did. Shaking her head, she said with a pitiful
" voice, *My lord, I am tied with a chain of iron about my neck; I am tied,*
" *and the case is altered with me.*"

Dr. Lingard, in his recently published *History of England*, thus relates
her conduct during her illness.—" Sir John Harrington, her godson,
" who visited the court about seven months after the death of Essex,
" has described in a private letter, the state he found the queen. She
" was altered in her features and reduced to a skeleton. Her food was
" nothing but manchet bread and succory pottage. Her taste for dress
" was gone : she had not changed her clothes for many days. Nothing
" could please her : she was the torment of the ladies who waited upon
" her person. She stamped with her feet and swore violently at the
" objects of her anger. For her protection she had ordered a sword to
" be placed by her table, which she often took in her hand, and thrust
" with violence into the tapestry of her chamber. About a year later he
" returned to the palace, and was admitted to her presence. ' I found
" her,' he says, ' in a most pitiable state. She bad the archbishop ask
" me, if I had seen Tyrone. I replied, with reverence, that I had seen
" him with the lord deputy. She looked up with much choler and grief
" in her countenance, and said, ' O now it mindeth me, that you was
" one who saw this man elsewhere ;' and hereat she dropped a tear,
" and smote her bosom. She held in her hand a golden cup, which she
" often put to her lips : but, in truth, her heart seemed too full to need
" more filling. In January she was troubled with a cold, and about
" the end of the month removed, on a wet stormy day, from Westmin-
" ster to Richmond. Her indisposition increased : but, with her cha-
" racteristic obstinacy, she refused the advice of her physicians. Loss
" of appetite was accompanied with lowness of spirits, and to add to
" her distress, it chanced that her intimate friend, the countess of Not-
" tingham, died. Elizabeth now spent her days and nights in sighs
" and tears : or, if she condescended to speak, she always chose some
" unpleasant and irritating subject : the treason and execution of Essex,
" or the pretensions of Arabella Stuart, or the war in Ireland, and the
" pardon of Tyrone. At last she fell into a state of stupor, and for some
" hours lay as dead. As soon as she recovered, she ordered cushions
" to be brought and spread on the floor. On these she seated herself,
" under a strange notion, that if she were once to lie down in bed, she
" should never rise again. No prayers of the secretary, or the arch-
" bishop, or the physicians, could induce her to remove, or to take any
" medicine. For ten days she sat on the cushions, generally with her
" finger in her mouth, and her eyes wide open, and fixed on the ground.
" Her strength rapidly decayed : it was evident she had but a short
" time to live." (Vol. v. pp. 610, 611, 4*to. edit.*)

Her death was that of one in despair, and after her decease her body burst the coffin which contained it with so great a violence, attended with such a dreadful noise, that it split the wood, lead, and tore the velvet, to the horror and astonishment of the six ladies who were watching it. So states F. Parsons in the aforesaid work. The demise of this queen took place in the year 1602, and the 45th of her reign.——We have been thus prolix from the length of her sway over these realms, and her being the foundress and she-pope of the Church as by law established. How different was the conduct of this monarch in forming a *new* religion to that of Constantine on embracing Christianity, and how dissimilar their ends. The Christian emperor submitted with resignation to the decrees of heaven with the utmost piety and humility, after a reign of thirty-one years; while the Protestant queen fell into a state of melancholy and despair at her approaching dissolution.

James the first of England, and sixth of Scotland, next ascended the throne. He was the son of Mary queen of Scotland, so unjustly put to death by Elizabeth, and was baptized and confirmed in the Catholic church. His reign was a continued scene of confusion and struggling between him and his parliaments. The flame of irreligious fanaticism ignited, and while the Puritans were contending against the members of the establishment, both cordially agreed in persecuting the Catholics. In the first year of his reign the plague in London was so great that there died of it no fewer than 38,244 persons. In his fourth year, two great inundations occurred, the one in Somersetshire and Gloucestershire—the other at Coventry. Stratford upon Avon was burnt down, and 160 houses in Bury St. Edmund's shared the same fate in his sixth year. His eldest son, prince Henry, was carried off by a premature death, and the king himself was suspected of being poisoned.

The reign of his son and successor, Charles I. was marked by the most deep-rooted hatred to Catholicism, and the most disastrous civil wars, which ended in the public execution of the king, and the overthrow of the church. After an interregnum or commonwealth, Charles II. was restored to his throne, and perjury of the most horrible nature was resorted to, for the purpose of exciting "a hatred and abhorrence of " the (pretended) corruptions and crimes of Popery and its professors." The lives of innocent Catholics were sworn away without the least remorse, and the city of London experienced a most dreadful visitation by fire, which continued burning three days and three nights, laying waste 600 streets, 89 churches, St. Paul's cathedral, and more than 30,000 houses. The year previous the plague carried off 109,000 inhabitants of that city. In 1675 the town of Northampton was almost totally consumed by fire; and in the year succeeding, no fewer than 600 houses were burned in the borough of Southwark. Several comets were also seen in this reign.

James II. succeeded his brother Charles, but, being a Roman Catholic, was soon driven from his throne to make way for a Dutchman, who had married his daughter. In the reign of William III, the nation was continually involved in continental wars, and the foundation of the present enormous debt was laid. The death of this king was occasioned by a fall from his horse. Anne, the daughter of James II, succeeded him. A great part of her reign too was occupied in fighting battles and raising taxes. In the second year of her reign there happened one of the most dreadful storms of wind ever known. Baker says it would fill a large work to relate distinctly the particulars of the mischief done throughout England by its violence. Distracted by the intrigues of the factious statesmen who ruled in her days, this queen died of a broken heart. George the first now ascended the throne, and the most remarkable circumstance in his reign was a rebellion in Scotland, and the blowing up of the South sea bubble. This latter transaction caused great discontent; and Goldsmith says, "the corruption, venality, and "avarice of the times, had encreased with the riches and luxury of the "nation. Commerce introduced fraud, and wealth introduced prodi- "gality." The death of this king was sudden. His son George II. succeeded to the sceptre, and the nation was still scourged with war and taxes. In 1745 a second rebellion broke out in Scotland, in which many lives were lost on both sides. This prince also died suddenly in his palace at Kensington.

He was succeeded by his grandson George III, under whom the Catholics experienced a little breathing, but not till the nation had felt the heavy hand of calamity. To record all the striking events of this most eventful reign would require more space than we can spare; we must therefore be content with recounting a few of them. The innate disposition of his late majesty would not allow of persecution; but the spirit of "Protestant-ascendency," which predominated in his councils, was frequently manifested by its acts. The reign of George the third was ushered in by war, and though the longest of any sovereign that ever wielded the British sceptre, the intervals of peace were of short duration. The seven years war was scarcely concluded when a commotion took place in the North American colonies, which broke out into an open rupture, and after a prodigal waste of blood and treasure, finally ended in the separation of the colonies from the mother country, and their erection into an independent state. Just before the close of this war, and while consternation reigned for the safety of the kingdom, a slight amelioration of the penal laws was granted to the Catholics, and further lenity towards them was meditated, in consequence of their unimpeachable loyalty. This roused the bigotry of "Protestant-ascendency," and associations were entered into to perpetuate the system of intolerance and persecution. A fanatic of noble extraction, lord George Gordon, was placed at the head of these combined intolerants, and the flame of irreligious fury soon burst forth, committing the most wanton outrages on the Catholics. Chapels were destroyed in England and Scotland, calumnies were circulated in abundance, the lives of individuals were threatened, and even the safety of the city of London was endangered, before the effervescence of popular prejudice could be restrained. These disgraceful proceedings took place in 1780. Lord George Gordon was tried for high treason, and acquitted; he was afterwards convicted of a libel, and sentenced to be imprisoned. Previous to his conviction, however, this champion of "Protestant-ascendency" renounced the Christian religion and embraced Judaism, ending his days in prison, unpitied and unnoticed. Shortly after this manifestation of the persecuting spirit of "Protestant-ascendency," the kingdom was thrown into considerable agitation by the state of the king's health, which rendered him incapable of exercising the royal authority. The monarch was happily restored to his health, but the nation had hardly recovered from the shock, when it was again thrown into disorder by the breaking out of the French revolution, which once more involved the country in war, from the effects of which the next generation probably will not recover. The heavy expenses incurred by a protracted contest of twenty-five years duration, have reduced the country to a state of indigence and poverty.' A debt of more than eight hundred millions of pounds sterling has placed her in a state of insolvency, and pauperized her people. The nominal capital of the debt is principally in the possession of the Jews, into whose hands the estates of the nobility are silently passing, some of them obtained from the church at the beginning of the reformation, while the poor in some parts of the kingdom are reduced almost to the same state as in the reign of Edward VI. For want of regular employment they are compelled to labour on the roads, drawing gravel in carts like beasts of burden, for a shilling a day, and in some places the magistrates have fixed the sum for subsisting a man, his wife, and three children, at ten pence a day. The only buildings of note now are prisons and penitentiaries; in days of yore, they were churches and castles. It has been stated in the house of commons that perjury is now become a system of pecuniary emolument; the prisons are filled with offenders of every description; the crime of self-murder is encreasing in a frightful degree; and whole parishes in Ireland have been in a dying state from starvation. While bible societies have been established and multiplied to circulate the scriptures, infidelity and deism have been rapidly increasing among the ranks of Protestantism; the established churches are nearly deserted, or made places of assignation; while dissenting meeting-houses are hourly raising in the kingdom; yet this is the time when the "few plain Christians," in the face of these undeniable facts, would persuade their readers, that this nation has been exempt from calamity and had not felt the hand of divine vengeance!!! What infatuation are some men blinded with, when pride and self-conceit take the place of truth and common sense.

The period of the primitive persecutions by the Roman emperors embraced three centuries; the space from the commencement of the reformation to the present day, during which the Catholics have been the objects of persecution, is of the same duration. We have confined our remarks to occurrences in this country, which are more easily to be detected if misstated, and we appeal to the unbiassed reader whether our observations are not astonishingly analogous to the " *Remarks on* " *the vengeance of God towards the Persecutors of the Christians*," made by the modern editors of the modern *Book of Martyrs* ?

Before we take leave of the subject, however, we will here slightly notice the awful end of some of the principal reformers on the continent. Luther, by his own confession, held intercourse with the devil, and was found dead in his bed. Zuinglius was killed in battle, fighting sword in hand for his new doctrine. Œcolampadius, soon after Zuinglius's tragical end, was found dead in his bed, strangled, as Luther would have it, by the devil. Cranmer, after pampering to the vices and passions of Henry the eighth, conniving at the spoliation

A REVIEW

OF

Fox's Book of Martyrs,

CRITICAL AND HISTORICAL.

No. 9. Printed and Published by W.E. ANDREWS, 3, Chapter-house-court, St. Paul's Churchyard, London. **Price 3d.**

EXPLANATION OF THE ENGRAVING.—*The virgin queen Elizabeth, whose notorious amours with her court favourites are acknowledged by both historians and novelists; and whose cruelties towards the Catholics were not excelled by Nero or Domitian, is seen, after a reign of forty-two years, lying in bed and viewing the appearance of her own person, lean and fretful, in a flame of fire.—See preceding number, page 124.*

CONTINUATION OF THE REVIEW.

of church property by Edward's courtiers, and burning others for heresy, was himself sentenced to the stake, after having engaged in a treasonable conspiracy to rob his master's daughter of her legal rights. Ridley, Latimer, and others, who were apostates from their faith, and violaters of their clerical vows, as well as partakers in the treason of Cranmer, also shared his fate. But enough: we shall have to enter more fully into the lives of these three last-named characters, when we come to the reign of Mary, under whom they suffered, and for which they have been raised by Fox to the rank of Protestant saints.

BOOK II.

"AN ACCOUNT OF THE PERSECUTIONS OF THE CHRISTIANS IN PERSIA BY "SAPORES; IN EGYPT, &c. BY THE ARIAN HERETICS; BY JULIAN THE "APOSTATE; BY THE GOTHS, VANDALS, &c. &c."

Book is the head chosen by John Fox for the second book of his work; and it is worthy of notice, that not a word of Popery is yet introduced by him, nor are the Catholics charged yet as being persecutors. The natural inference therefore to be drawn is, that the Catholics were the persecuted, and that this was the fact we shall be able to prove by the most unquestionable testimony. The first section of this book commences with the "Persecutions of the Christians in Persia." The editors say, that "in consequence of the gospel hav- "ing spread itself into Persia, the Pagan priests became greatly alarm- "ed, dreading the loss of their influence over the minds of the peo- "ple. They therefore complained to the emperor, that the Christians "were enemies to the state, and held a treasonable correspondence with "the Romans, the great enemies of Persia. The emperor, being him- "self averse to Christianity, gave credit to their accusations, and issued "orders for the persecution of the Christians throughout the empire." If the reader will take the trouble to look into any of the numerous writings that have been published by the adherents of "Protestant ascendency," he will observe that the charges brought against the Catholics of this day are the same that were brought by the Persians against the Christians in the fourth century; and what is not less worthy of observation, that they take their rise from the same feeling. Catholicism, cries "Protestant-ascendency," is rapidly increasing in this country, we must therefore sound the alarm, lest our churchmen lose "their influence over the minds of the people." The press instantly groans with charges ten thousand times repeated, and as often refuted, and the ears of the people are stunned with the sounds of "No-popery,"—"The Church in danger," &c. The people are told that the Catholics are disloyal because they hold "correspondence with the "Romans, the great enemies of England;" and that the emancipation they are striving for "in reality means the power of overthrowing all those "sacred institutions to establish which our ancestors bled on the scaf- "fold, and expired at the stake." But if these same people would lay aside their idle prejudices, and look steadily at the situation of the country, while they turn their eyes over the page of history and see what their country was when their ancestors were Catholics, they would soon learn that the "sacred institutions," which raised England so high in the scale of nations, were established in Catholic times, and that they are now little more than nominal under "Protestant-ascendency."

Of the martyrs noticed by Fox who suffered under this persecution we shall say but little, and that little is, *they were unquestionably Roman Catholics*, and held the divinity of Jesus Christ. The first martyr on Fox's list under Persian persecution is St. Simeon, archbishop of Cte- siphon and Seleucia, and primate of Persia, who, on being taken before king Sapor, boldly avowed, "We Christians have no Lord but Christ "who was crucified." This then was the belief of the Christians in Persia at the beginning of the fourth century; and for *this* belief, ob- serve reader, they underwent the most cruel tortures, and submitted to death rather than disavow it. It may here be remarked, that the Rev. Alban Butler, in his martyrology, assures us, that this king, in order to abolish the Christian religion, decreed, "that whoever should "embrace it should be made a slave, and he oppressed the Christians "with double taxes." So were the Catholics of England and Ireland oppressed by "Protestant-ascendency" with a double land tax, and their situation rendered worse than slavery by a penal code professedly enacted to annihilate the Popish (as Catholicism is termed) religion. But the Christian religion was not abolished in Persia, nor is what is called Popery eradicated in these islands.

The second section is headed "*Persecutions* by the Arian HERE-TICS," and is a most important part of the work. The acknowledg-ments here made, together with the studied omissions in the relation, demand our most serious attention, and we beg the reader will give the subject all the reflection he is master of. Fox commences with stating, that "the sect denominated the Arian HERETICS, had its "origin from Arius, a native of Lybia, and priest of Alexandria, who, "in A. D. 318, began to publish his ERRORS. He was *condemned* by "a council of Lybian and Egyptian bishops, and the sentence was con-"*firmed* by the *council of Nice*, A. D. 325. After the death of Constan-"tine the great, the Arians found means to ingratiate themselves into "the favour of Constantius, his son and successor in the East; and "hence a *persecution* was raised against the ORTHODOX bishops and "clergy. The celebrated Athanasius, and other bishops, were banish-"ed at this period, and their sees filled with Arians." To this para-graph the modern editors have added the following remarks in two notes: "Arius, the founder of this *sect* of *heretics* and the *first cause* of "the persecutions which are related in this section, died miserably at "Constantinople, just as he was about to enter the church in triumph." "...How humiliating is it to perceive that the Christians had scarcely "escaped from the persecutions of their general enemy, ere they be-"gan to persecute *each other* with the most unrelenting fury! How "could these men dare to arrogate to themselves the exclusive title of "*Christians*, when every part of their conduct was at direct variance "with the precepts and practice of the Divine Founder of the religion "which they professed? How absurd is the expectation of *enforcing* "belief; and how *criminal to attempt to effect conviction by the sword.*"

Here then we have a grand specimen of the system pursued by "Protestant-ascendency" to instruct and enlighten the people. "The "sect denominated the Arian heretics," we are told, had its origin from Arius. So far it is true, but *what* was the *heresy* this Arius taught? Not a word is said to throw the least light upon this most important part of the subject. He was *condemned*, they further say, by a council of bishops; but for *what* was he condemned? Why did they not state the *offence* he had committed, as well as the fact of his condemnation? Suppose, for example, one of the clergy of the church of England as by law established took it into his head openly to impugn the doctrine of the thirty-nine articles, and for this act was condemned by the bishops, as guilty of broaching error; what should we say of that writer who professed to give a statement of the occurrence, yet studiously omit-ted to mention the most essential part of the fact, namely, the doc-trine he attempted to establish in opposition to that which he attacked, and which constituted the offence. There are several persons now in prison for denying Christianity and attacking its principles; but would it not be thought a complete piece of delusion were a future historian, in recording the fact, merely to say, these persons were the founders of a sect, for which they were condemned?. The reader would naturally expect the WHY and WHEREFORE, or how could he form a just conclusion on the case? This, however, was not the object of Fox and his editors; they did not wish the TRUTH should be *known*, and therefore they took special care not to relate the whole of it. We will however take upon ourself to supply the omission.

But before we enter on this task we must here make a remark on the second note introduced by the modern editors. They observe, " How " humiliating is it to perceive that the Christians had scarcely escaped " from the persecutions of their general enemy, ere they began to per- " secute *each other* with the most unrelenting fury !" This is a gross misrepresentation, for the Orthodox or Catholic Christians never persecuted the Arians, but contented themselves with defending their cause by the force of reason and public opinion, as we shall speedily prove. We agree with the modern editors that it is absurd to expect to *enforce* belief in any creed, and criminal to effect conviction by the civil sword, nor did the Catholic church ever attempt so unchristian a compulsion; though let it be remarked, this is invariably the case with *those* who are in *error*. They know that there is no *other* way to establish their false notions and doctrines generally than by the effect of the civil sword, and they of course are doubly guilty ; that is, of falsehood, by teaching that which is erroneous; and of injustice, by using coercive means to make hypocrites, for it is nonsense to call it *conviction*. It is clear, that the divine Founder of Christianity never intended that his system of heavenly truths and mysteries was to depend on earthly power, or he would never have chosen unarmed and defenceless men to carry it through the world. Men would never have become convinced of its divine origin, if they had not seen as well as heard the powerful voice of God through these unsuccoured agents, as far as worldly interests were concerned. For three centuries these truths had been thus spread and maintained, in defiance of the powers of earth and hell; and having subdued the first monarch of the world to the obedience of faith, it is not to be supposed that a change or revolution would take place in that system which it was promised should last for ever. But it is time to return to our martyrologist, and supply the omissions he has made in the history of Arianism.

That the sect of Arians had their origin from Arius, and that he was a native of Lybia is quite correct. That he was a broacher of HERE- SY, is also true; and his heresy consisted in his DENYING THE DI- VINITY OF JESUS CHRIST, which is the case with the Antitrinita- rians, the Unitarians, the Socinians, and the Deists; therefore, as the Arian doctrine is HERESY, according to John Fox's statement, so must the doctrine of the sects just named be *heresy* also, and we should not wonder if many of the professors of these doctrines have been active in thus publishing their own shame, in order, as they say, " to ex- " cite a hatred and abhorrence of Popery and its professors." By the rule of common sense, those who *now* deny the divinity of our Saviour, stand convicted by this *Book of Martyrs* of HERESY, which, accord- ing to Johnson, is, " an *opinion* of *private men*, different from that of " the CATHOLIC or ORTHODOX church," if those who denied this divine essence in the fourth century were heretics. And that the doc- trine of Arius WAS heresy, we shall now proceed to prove.

We have shewn in the preceding pages that the belief of the divinity of the Son of God was an essential point of Christianity, and held by all the martyrs recorded by John Fox, who laid down their lives for this faith. Arius, however, having been censured by his bishop for joining in a schism to disturb the church of Alexandria, and disappointed in not being elected to the patriarchal chair of that city, through envy and malice, conceived the project of gratifying his evil passions by thwarting the new patriarch St. Alexander, in the instructions which the latter gave to his clergy. St. Alexander, like his predecessors, maintained the mystery of the Trinity, and the Incarnation of the Son of God, as the revealed doctrine of Christ himself to his apostles, and by them delivered to their successors in the different churches that had been raised by them. Arius, on the contrary, contended that the Son was a creature made out of nothing; that there was a time when he did not exist; and that he was capable of sin, besides other impieties. Being a man of grave deportment and of pleasing conversation, he not only succeeded in seducing two Lybian bishops with some priests and deacons, but he publicly avowed his doctrines, and was drawing many ignorant people, led away by novelty, into his errors. In this state of things the patriarch had recourse to the usual custom of the church, which is, not to rely on individual opinion, but on the united and concurrent testimony of competent judges. Accordingly he assembled a council or ecclesiastical parliament at Alexandria of one hundred bishops of the provinces of Egypt and Lybia, who discussed the propositions of Arius, and *condemned them as erroneous, and contrary to the revealed truths derived from Truth itself.* Arius persisting in his falsely conceived notions, was excommunicated and expelled the church. Here then we see the sure foundation on which the Catholics rest their faith, and the sandy ground on which those who differ from them raise their rickety edifice of a church. The Catholic church, founded on a solid rock, stands immoveable amidst the storms of persecution and heresy that assail her, while the sects that spring from the perversion of reason and common sense, make a stand for a while, commit havock around the building, but are dispersed like a rope of sand by one breath of the divine Vengeance. Well here we see one hundred individuals, renowned for their learning and irreproachable conduct, deciding, upon the strongest ground imaginable, that is, by the concurrent testimony of their predecessors to the very time of the apostles, in favour of the divinity of Jesus Christ; and is it not more reasonable to suppose that these men, chosen to be the instructors of others in the way of truth, must be better judges of what was revealed to the apostles, than one man who could not produce a single witness to testify in favour of his notions, but relied for success on the subtilties of his mind and the web of sophistry? The reader must answer this question in the affirmative; and yet such is the conduct of those who follow the notions of this or that sectarian, instead of clinging steadfast to the undeviating Spirit of Truth, to be found only in the Catholic church.

Arius thus foiled in his impious attempts to rob the Redeemer of Mankind of his Divinity by public discussion, had recourse to private intrigue and artifice. He succeeded in gaining over Eusebius, bishop of Nicomedia, to his cause, who, having great influence in the court of Constantine, through the favour of Constantia, the emperor's sister, and wife of Licinius, contrived to introduce Arius to his patroness, who gained her over, by hypocrisy and flattery, to espouse his cause. Here then we see the progress of error. Defeated by the force of reason and tradition, but unwilling to confess the truth, its next resource is stratagem and dissimulation, and finally brute force is pressed to its service. Arius now attempted to poison the mind of Constantine, through the influence of Constantia, but the emperor was too well impressed with the truths he had learned to be carried away by the arts laid to ensnare him. In the mean while several bishops were persuaded to join the factious heresiarch, and they thought to carry all before them by assembling a mock council of their party, in which they decreed that the doctrine of Arius was orthodox, and that the patriarch Alexander should receive it or be declared a heretic. Thus then the church, which had but lately been rescued from the persecutions of the Roman pagans under the miraculous banner of the cross, now found herself troubled with the divisions of her own children, and the peace of the empire was threatened by the tumults and seditions created by the factious opposition of Arius and his adherents to the decisions of the church, exercising that power given to her by her divine Founder: *He that heareth you, heareth me.*

In this state of confusion and disorder, Constantine had recourse to pope St. Sylvester, who had instructed him in the principles of Christianity, and advised with him as to the best means to restore peace and harmony to the church and the empire. The measure proposed and agreed on was such as every rational man must approve, and the most congenial to common sense that could be devised. It was to call a convocation of bishops from every part of the empire, who were to discuss and decide theologically the question that had created such contention and disturbance. Various provincial assemblies of the kind had been held during the time of persecution, when disputes on doctrine had arisen, but this was the first general council or spiritual parliament convened by the church, and as such, is deserving our particular notice. The emperor Constantine was then residing at Nicomedia, and it was resolved that the council should be held at Nice, the principal city of Bithynia, to which place the bishops were invited to repair. Accordingly, three hundred and eighteen bishops, besides priests and deacons, resorted to the place of assemblage, and on the 19th day of June, 325, the council was opened in a spacious hall suitable to that purpose. In this solemn parliament of Christendom were to be found the greatest and most famous men in the world, both for their extraordinary learning, the remarkable holiness of their lives, and the honourable marks which they carried with them of having suffered for their faith. The great Hosius, bishop of Cordova in Spain, presided as the representative of the pope, assisted by the priests Vitus and Vincentius. Then there were the three celebrated patriarchs, namely, Alexander of Alexandria; Eustathius of Antioch; and Macarius of Jerusalem; all rendered famous for their deep knowledge of the scripture. The church of Africa was represented by the renowned Cecilian, primate of that country, who had lately triumphed over the Donatists. [Men who contended that the true church had absolutely fallen, except in those places where Donatism was professed; and complimented the Catholic church with the appellation of the whore of Balon, from whom we presume our "few plain Christians" have taken the example.]   Besides these great personages came those courageous defenders of the faith, Hypatius of Gangra, who was afterwards martyred; Eupsychius of Tynæ,Longinus of Neocæsarea, Protogenes of Sardica, Eutychius of Amasea, whom the illustrious martyr Basileus caused to be chosen in his stead; Alexander of Byzantium, (now Constantinople) Arestanes of the greater Armenia, the famous Leontius of Cæsarea in Cappadocia, and the celebrated Nicolas, archbishop of Myra, the capital of Lyra, a large ancient province of Asia.   This last named holy man was so famed for the miracles he wrought through the divine power of Jesus Christ, that altars and churches were everywhere raised to his memory.   To add to the sanctity of the assembly, many of its members were maimed in defence of the divinity of Jesus Christ, and had come to the council to defend by their suffrages that doctrine they had confessed by their sufferings.   Of these there were the venerable Potamo of Heraclea in Egypt, one of whose eyes had been plucked out in the persecution of Maximin.   Paphnutius, bishop of higher Thebais, who, during the fury of that persecution, had his right eye put out, and his left arm cut off, and was buried alive as it were in the mines.   Paul, bishop of Neocæsarea upon the Euphrates, who in the time of Licinius, had both his hands burned with hot irons; James, bishop of Nisibis in Mesopotamia, who displayed invincible resolution while suffering the most cruel torments under Maximin; and the holy Spiridion, bishop of Tremithus in Cyprus, who likewise lost a leg and and an eye in the persecutions of Maximian Galerius.   These facts are stated in the writings of Socrates, Sozomen, Theodoret, and other ancient writers.   On the other hand, there were Eusebius of Cæsarea, Maris of Chalcedon, and Theognis of Nice, who had denied our Saviour in the persecution, to save themselves from torments, besides several Pagan philosophers, who challenged the council to dispute upon religion, which the members accepted.   In the midst of the hall was laid on a magnificent throne the book of the holy gospels, to take the place, as it were, of Christ himself.

Matters being thus settled, the fathers came to the council, and held their sittings every day, the speakers having the most perfect freedom of debate, in order to come to a right conclusion.   Arius was heard in his own defence, as were also those who took part with him. The different points of dispute were examined and sifted with much minuteness; an exact inquiry was made into all the texts of scripture that bore upon the questions; and the arguments advanced on both sides were canvassed with nice discrimination.   The proceedings of the provincial council of Alexandria were read, as were also some letters written by Eusebius the friend of Arius, and the decision was, that three hundred bishops declared that the Son of God was consubstantial with his Father, and entirely equal to him in all his divine perfections. On this decision of the council being declared, the doctrine of Arius was reduced to several propositions and anathematized as new, erroneous and blasphemous.   Eusebius of Nicomedia with seventeen of the bishops stood out, and rejected the term *consubstantial,* but on further reflection, fourteen of these afterwards subscribed to the decision of the council, so that there were only two left in favour of Arius and his friend Eusebius.

It may here be necessary to remark, that this council was not called to decree *new* articles of faith, but to decide between that which was *original* and that which was *counterfeit*. The doctrine promulgated by Arius was evidently a *novelty*, or the people would not have been so shocked and affected on hearing it. Being *new*, it could not have been that which the apostles had received from God, and therefore could not be of divine origin, but must have been of human invention. How then could it have been supposed that the inventor would have the power to make the world believe, by the means of persuasion, that he alone was *right* and all the rest were *wrong*? Such a thing was impossible. He might, however, by *deceit* and *hypocrisy*, impose upon some, and by *threats* and *torments* compel others to join his standard. The guardians of truth, on the other side, proceeded upon an infallible ground. They referred to the *gospels* and the *tradition of the fathers*, which they found to be invariably decisive on the subject of Christ's DIVINITY, as a revealed truth derived by the apostles from God himself, and as such indispensable to be believed. They had not to form a *new* belief, as we before observed, but to give testimony to the *old* one; and when we find three hundred bishops from all parts of the world, many of whom had never seen each other before, yet all coincided in the *exact same* opinion, as did also the people over whom they were placed, should we not act contrary to common sense to reject that doctrine which is thus miraculously shewn to be divine, (for nothing but a divine power could cause such an unity in belief) and embrace the vain notions of a proud hypocrite as the oracle of divine wisdom? Who can answer us in the negative? Thus then the reader is in possession of the rule by which Catholics are guided in their religious belief. They do not take this upstart, nor that pretender, for their guide; but they rely on the divine promises of the Founder of their church, and when any difference of sentiment is started, they look to the general opinion of the whole body, and not to an isolated branch of the church, or two or three factious members of it, as the only rational rule by which to decide with certainty.

Let us, by way of illustration, suppose a case to happen in this country. We all know that the privilege of trial by jury is one of the grand palladiums of British freedom. It is a fundamental principle of the English civil constitution, the same as the divinity of the Son of God is the fundamental principle of Christianity; for if you take away the divine essence of the Founder of the church of God, you make it stand on human strength; so if you take away the right of trial by jury, you take away the essence of civil liberty, and become subject to be condemned by individual caprice. Well, a man takes it into his head to dispute the efficacy of this fundamental principle of civil liberty. He contends that though the trial by jury has existed for a long, very long period of years, yet it is of no benefit to the security of the people, and therefore ought to be abolished. That such a man would find disciples there can be no doubt; for, in fact, the trial by jury was disregarded by the parliaments of Harry and Elizabeth, on their assuming the right to govern the consciences of the people of England, as head of the church; the former being made absolute in his will, and the latter establishing the star chamber. But could he get the sound part of the nation to concide with him? No, that would be impossible. By craft and cunning he might gain a party over to him, and that party or faction would create confusion and disorder in the realm. To allay this heat and restore quiet among the people, we will suppose the reigning monarch to be animated with a spirit of truth and justice; and, acting under the influence of this spirit, he sends out a proclamation summoning the most learned and celebrated men in the kingdom to meet him in parliament; there, after hearing what arguments can be advanced in favour of the new doctrine and what in defence of the old practice, to pronounce their judgment on the case, according to the strength of the evidence laid before them. Accordingly they meet, and the theory of the new plan is laid down by the inventor of it, and those of his disciples who are disposed to defend it are likewise allowed to speak their sentiments with freedom and control. To these theories are opposed a regular gradation of historical facts, tracing the institution up to the time of Alfred the great, and displaying an uninterrupted exercise of the privilege for a series of nine hundred years, during which space innumerable instances of its utility are produced from the records of our best historians. With such a body of evidence before them, the assembly, with the exception of the broacher of the doctrine and a few adherents, all declare by acclamation in favour of the old practice, and this decision is ratified by the monarch, who officially announces to the people the result of the important deliberations, as a guide for their own conduct. Now, under such circumstances as these, and with a full knowledge of the facts, what would be the general opinion of the people of England? Would they not approve and applaud the wisdom of the parliament? Would they not consider the decision as the oracle of Truth; for where so many agreed and so few dissented, what stronger or more rational ground could there be to command conviction. There might be some infatuated men allured by the plausible and specious conduct of the innovator and his disciples; but such individuals could only excite the pity of those who felt the conviction of truth, and be considered as warped in their senses. So it was with the council of Nice, in the fourth century of the Christian era. The fathers decided by the general testimony of the witnesses of each preceding age, and the universal assent of the people of whole Christendom confirmed the accuracy of their decision.

Another circumstance connected with this council must be here recorded, as it conveys, in our opinion, a most striking proof of the invulnerability and duration of the Catholic Faith. Before the council separated, the fathers drew up a formula of faith, which is called the Nicene Creed, and stands to this day, in the Catholic church, the touchstone of orthodox belief in the divinity of Jesus Christ. It is also one of the creeds admitted by the church of England as by law established, the eighth of her thirty-nine articles stating " the three creeds, " Nicene creed, Athanasius's creed, and that which is commonly cal- " led the Apostles' creed, ought thoroughly to be received and believed; " for they may be proved by the most certain warrants of holy scrip-

"ture."   The author of this second named creed, was a deacon of the church of Alexandria, and attended the council of Nice, where, by his eloquence and learning, he contributed much to elucidate the truth of the divine mysteries of the Trinity and Incarnation. He was afterwards chosen patriarch of Alexandria, and is mentioned by Fox as having encountered much persecution and suffering through the violence and tyranny of the Arian party, when they succeeded in gaining the temporal power over to their interest. The creed bearing the name of St. Athanasius commences thus: "Whosoever will be saved: be-"fore all things it is necessary that he hold the CATHOLIC faith. "Which faith except every one do keep whole and undefiled: without "doubt he shall perish everlastingly. And the CATHOLIC faith is "this: That we worship one God in Trinity, and Trinity in Unity: "neither confounding the Persons nor dividing the Substance." It then goes on to explain the nature of the three persons in God, after which it states the belief of the Incarnation in these words: "Furthermore, "it is necessary to everlasting salvation: that he also believe the In-"carnation of our Lord Jesus Christ. For the RIGHT FAITH IS, "that we believe and confess: that our Lord Jesus Christ, the Son of "God, is GOD and man; God of the Substance of the Father begot-"ten before the world: and man of the substance of his mother, born "in the world; perfect God and perfect Man: of a reasonable soul and "human flesh subsisting; equal to the Father as touching his god-"head: and inferior to the Father as touching his manhood," &c. Such then was the doctrine of the primitive Christians; such was the faith of every nation in the world that forsook the superstitions and idolatry of Paganism for the sublime truths of Christianism. And mark, reader, not one country in the whole world was ever converted to the Catholic or Christian faith, that did not believe and confess the divinity of the Son of God. This one simple fact, a fact incontrovertible and undeniable, we think sufficient to startle the Unitarian, the Socinian, and the Deist, without entering into a theological discussion on different points of doctrine. This important fact must carry conviction to the unprejudiced mind, and assure him that that system of faith only which had its ORIGIN FROM GOD can be of divine institution, and, consequently, that all others of later date, are of man's invention, and come within the definition of heresy.

The above quotations from the Athanasian creed are taken out of the common prayer book of the church of England, the ministers of which church are commanded to read or sing the same at morning prayer on thirteen specified festivals in the year, instead of the Apostles' creed, as a confession of Christian faith. In these times, however, of mock liberality, this creed is looked upon by many as of such an intolerant nature, that it ought to be expunged from the service of the Protestant church of England. Nay, we have seen it stated in the public prints, as a proof of the benevolent disposition of his late majesty, George the third, that when he was assisting at the solemn ser-.vice of the church of which he was the head, whenever the creed of St. Athanasius was read, he was remarked to omit answering the officiating minister, when he read the damnatory clauses, as they are called, of that formulary. Now this sort of liberality we consider inconsistent, and tending to religious indifferency and infidelity; for what does the creed say more than the scripture? Christ himself says, "he that believeth not shall be condemned." Mark, xvi. 16. He that heareth not the church, let him be as the heathen or publican. And what does the creed of St. Athanasius say more? Common sense tells us, that Truth cannot contradict itself; and therefore if the primitive Christians were right, Arius, and those who think as he did, must be wrong. To say that *both* were right, is a gross absurdity; and it cannot be supposed that God can approve of so many different religious creeds, when he came on earth to establish ONE, and ONE ONLY, which was to last for ever. The gospel says, in as plain words as it is possible to dictate, that "there shall be *one* fold and *one* pastor," John, x. 16; to say, then, that *all* religions are *right*, is to oppose *reason*. Religion is an institution established by God himself, whereby he makes known to man how he is to worship Him, his creator, and what he is to believe to obtain salvation. Nothing can be more reasonable. He made us, we are his creatures; he holds the thread of life in his hands, and surely he has a right to exact the terms on which he would accept the homage due to him from the work of his hands. We have then before us the terms he has imposed; we see these terms embraced by thousands and thousands of the most learned and highly endowed men of all nations and in all ages; we see other systems spring up and are immediately opposed, their errors pointed out, and condemned by public opinion, that is, the voice of *all* nations professing the *one* faith; and surely it cannot be illiberality, it cannot be unchristian to say, that error *is* error, and that man must believe that which God has revealed and commanded. The anti-christian spirit appears when men seek to *force* the consciences of their fellow-men by pains and penalties, and not by the power of reason and truth. This was the case with the Pagans when they had the civil sword in their hands; this was the case with the Arians when they got the ascendency; and this was the case with the reformers when they established "Protestant-ascendency" in these realms; and it will be shewn to have been the case in every instance where men have deviated from the truth.

While Constantine lived, the Arian faction were obliged to be circumspect in their conduct. They therefore dissembled, and put forth all the arts of secret intrigue and chicanery to support their baffled cause. By calumny and misrepresentation they succeeded in prejudicing the mind of Constantine against many of the most zealous defenders of the Catholic faith; but, on the other hand, to preserve the peace of the empire, he had banished Arius, and the most factious of his party to distant provinces. In the mean time the sister of the emperor Constantine, whom we have before mentioned as having been infected with the heretical doctrine, fell sick, and was attended by an Arian priest. The reader will here observe, and we beg to impress it strongly on the mind of the Protestant of whatever denomination he may be, that these Arian heretics believed all the articles of faith, and practised all the rites and ceremonies, now believed in and practised by the church of Rome, with the exception of the fundamental truth of Christ's divinity. They held confession, the real presence, the sacrifice of the mass, prayers for the dead, the invocation of saints, and, in fact, all those points of doctrine that have been rejected by the reformation, so called, of the sixteenth century. Had they followed the plan of our modern reformers, and stripped religion of every thing consoling to the mind and stimulating to devotion, the people would easily have discovered their impious attempts; they therefore craftily maintained those doctrines and ceremonies which hinged on the fundamental divinity of the Son of God, while by speculative theory and subtle quibblings they attempted to rob their Redeemer of his godhead! Well, the Arian priest used his influence with Constantia to prevail on her imperial brother, who really loved her, to recall the heresiarch Arius and his adherents from banishment, and she unhappily for the peace of the church and mankind succeeded with the emperor, but not without exacting that these heretics should subscribe to the decision of the council. This Arius consented to, and by an equivocal and counterfeit submission he deceived Constantine and was recalled from exile.

Thus far successful, the Arians set about spreading their heresy through all the east, and the better to insure success, they corrupted the second son of Constantine, whereby they might the better triumph over their inflexible opponents, who stoutly defended the cause of truth, by the spiritual weapons allowed to the church, prayer and persuasion, without having recourse to the civil sword. Although Constantine was a zealous Catholic, and of course a firm believer in the divinity of his Saviour, yet, following the precepts of his Redeemer, he strictly adhered to the professions he made in his speech to the senate, on the occasion of his baptism, which we have recorded in our preceding pages; for no one, that we can find in history, was ever persecuted by him for holding erroneous opinions in religion only; nor can we discover, through the same source, one single instance of an application to him from a Catholic to punish an Arian believer. That the "*orthodox* bishops and clergy," as Fox styles them, were Catholics, is incontrovertible, from the title given to the Christian church by the apostles in their creed, "I believe in the holy CATHOLIC "church;" which title was also adopted by the Nicene fathers in their creed, to distinguish the orthodox from the heterodox: "And in one holy CATHOLIC and apostolic church;" therefore, as we have repeatedly remarked, the Catholics have hitherto been the persecuted, and not the persecutors. It is also obvious that the suppression of the word Catholic by Fox, and the substitution of the term "orthodox," is purposely made to impose upon the unthinking and illiterate reader, whose mind would be startled, and his prejudices somewhat shaken, if not completely removed, were he but to know that the professors of the *same* creed are represented in these days as cruel and wicked by modern editors, while they are extolled for their piety and forbearance in the primitive ages.

Before, however, we enter into a brief detail of the Arian persecutions, as noticed by Fox, we must here be allowed to put upon record another historical fact, entirely overlooked by Protestant writers, but carrying the most powerful evidence in favour of the divinity of Jesus Christ, now so universally impugned by the disciples of Protestantism.

It was the invariable custom of the Jews to make a great hole near where the body of a criminal was buried, and throw into it, as detestable objects, such things as belonged to his execution. From this custom the cross on which Christ suffered had lain hidden during the Roman persecutions, and from the care which the Pagans had used to conceal the place where Christ was crucified, there was no mark or tradition to discover the identical spot where our Saviour was buried, and the instruments of his death deposited. The heathens too out of an aversion to Christianity, had done all they could to conceal the spot of our Saviour's burial place; for besides heaping upon it a great quantity of stones and rubbish, and building a temple to Venus, they erected a statute to Jupiter, according to St. Jerom, where Christ rose from the dead, which figure continued there from the time of the emperor Adrian to Constantine. Arianism observe began to bud about the year 318. Till that time the church had to contend with open enemies, now she was attacked by treacherous foes. Heathenism was subdued under the standard of the CROSS, and Arianism was now about to sustain a signal discomfiture by the same instrument. St. Helena, Constantine's mother, though eighty years of age, undertook a journey to Palestine in 326. On her arrival at Jerusalem she felt a strong desire to discover the identical cross on which Christ had suffered. With this view she consulted the most intelligent people in Jerusalem, and was informed by them that if she could find out the sepulchre, she would be sure to find also the instruments of punishment. The pious empress accordingly ordered the profane temples to be erased, the statutes to be destroyed, and the rubbish to be removed from the place where it was supposed the crucified Saviour had been interred. After digging some depth, they came to the holy sepulchre, and near it they found three crosses, together with the nails that had pierced Christ's hands and feet, and the label which had been fixed to his cross. But, as the title was separated from the cross, a difficulty arose to distinguish which was the identical cross on which the Redeemer had suffered. In this perplexity, according to the testimony of Sozomen, Theodoret, and Rufinus, the holy bishop Macarius of Jerusalem suggested to the empress to have the crosses carried to a person then sick unto death, not doubting but God, on such an occasion, would manifest the true one. The suggestion was adopted, and the crosses being severally applied, the patient was perfectly recovered by the touch of the third, the other two having been applied without effect. Sceptics may sneer at this extraordinary event, and attempt to deny it; but they might as well attempt to deny the existence of such a character as Constantine himself, as to invalidate this fact. A church was erected on the spot by St. Helena, where part of the cross was lodged and held in great veneration. Another church was built by Constantine at Constantinople, where a second part of the cross was deposited. A third church was built at Rome by order of the said empress, to which she conveyed the remainder of the cross, which church still remains, and is called *Of the Holy Cross of Jerusalem*. Besides, the very same pope that baptized Constantine, who, as before related, was converted through the appearance of the cross, instituted a festival in the church on the 3d of May, in honour of this discovery, which festival has been observed ever since, in every Catholic country to this day, as it is also in the Greek church. Such a weight of evidence we think too ponderous for unbelievers to remove, and it was considered by the Catholics of the fourth century, as it is by those of the present day, a most signal and triumphant victory over the enemies of Christianity.

Constantine at his death left three sons, namely, Constantine, Constantius, and Constans, in favour of whom he divided the empire into three parts. Constantine and Constans were Catholics, but Constantius was infected with Arianism. While the elder brother was alive Constantius was held in fear by him, and dared not to enter into the views meditated by the Arians. But the former being cut off by death, the heretics soon threw off the mask and exhibited the most vindictive fury against the Catholics. Fox states that thirty bishops were martyred in Egypt and Lybia, and many other *Christians* cruelly tormented. By distinguishing these sufferers as *Christians*, it is inferred that Fox deemed the persecutors anti-Christians, which is perfectly correct, as they certainly could not be Christians since they wanted to rob Christ of his divine nature, the groundwork of Christianity, and evinced a spirit of vindictiveness and cruelty the very reverse of Christ's precepts. Fox further says, that "George, the Arian bishop of "Alexandria, under the authority of the emperor, began a persecution "in that city, and its environs, which was continued with the utmost "severity," equalling, if the martyrologist is to be credited, and he may be believed here, in fierceness and barbarity any of the ten Pagan persecutions that preceded it. George, after rioting in the blood of the Catholics, was himself slain by the Pagan people of the city for his cruelties and oppressions. Arius, too, as Fox admits, met with a miserable death, but the nature of his end is not stated by him. It was as follows. The emperor Constantine, some short time before his death, had been persuaded by Arius that his profession of faith was orthodox, and through the influence of Eusebius of Nicomedia, was weak enough to issue an order to St. Alexander, the last bishop of Byzantium and the first of Constantinople, to admit Arius into the communion of the Catholic church. This order was an usurpation of authority Constantine had no right to assume, and the holy bishop refused to conform to it. Eusebius, however, was resolved to enforce it, and a day was fixed for its execution. A Sunday was chosen that the act might be the more notorious. The holy bishop Alexander, who had assisted at the council of Nice, had nothing to oppose to this violence but prayers, which he offered up to God with great fervency. Arius and his friends, relying on the power of the civil magistrate, went to the church in great pomp and insolence. In their way, the heresiarch felt a sudden attack of nature; he stepped aside to a place of convenience, while the procession halted to await his return. Some time having elapsed the party grew impatient, and some of them were sent to see what was become of him. They entered the place, and there found him dead, his bowels voided out upon the ground. Thus perished the impious impugner of his Redeemer's divinity. This signal stroke of the divine judgment was immediately proclaimed by the public voice, and for a time the Arians were struck dumb.

The remainder of the section is occupied with the "*Persecution of*

"*Paul*," the holy bishop of Constantinople. The venerable and learned prelate was a continual sufferer, from the malice and fury of the
Arian party. The practice of these heretics was to flatter and gratify
the passions of the reigning prince, whereby they succeeded in glutting their vengeance on those who boldly and effectually detected and
exposed their errors. When by violence and injustice they exasperated
the public voice against them, they basely represented to the emperor,
that the advocates of truth were the aggressors, and the causers of the
seditions and tumults occasioned by their own malpractices; and the
affection which the people entertained for a good pastor was made a matter of complaint. So it is now with "Protestant ascendency." The attachment shewn by the Irish Catholics to their truly exemplary and
indefatigable clergy is, in these days of professed illumination, described as a mark of their superstition and proneness to priestcraft.
Fox says, that Paul "being very much concerned at what the orthodox
"bishops suffered from the power and malice of the Arian faction, he
"joined Athanasius who was then in Italy, in soliciting a *general* coun-
"cil. This council was held at Sardica in Illyrium, in the year 347,
"at which were present one hundred bishops of the western, and se-
"venty-three of the eastern empire. But disagreeing in many points,
"the Arian bishops of the east retired to Philippopolis, in Thrace; and
"forming a *meeting* there, they *termed* it the council of Sardica, from
"which place they *pretended* to issue an excommunication against Ju-
"lius bishop of Rome; Paul bishop of Constantinople; Athanasius bi-
"shop of Alexandria; and several other prelates." So, then, the bishop of *Rome* is here acknowledged an orthodox bishop, and the attempt to excommunicate him a *pretension*. The assembly at Sardica is
admitted to be a general council of the church, and the club formed
by the seceders is called *a meeting*. Very good, most sapient editors
of the *Book of Martyrs*; but why not be more explicit in this affair?
Why not tell us the cause of the Arian bishops running away, and the
points on which they disagreed? How can any man come at the knowledge of the transactions of this council and meeting, so as to form a
judgment upon them, from the bungling and confused relation you
have made? Is it not evident that your object is the suppression, not
the illustration, of truth? Be it then our province to clear it up.

The council of Sardica was convened at the instance of Julius bishop
of Rome, through the intervention of the emperor Constans, who wrote
to his brother Constantius on the subject, being desirous to settle the
unhappy disputes that afflicted the church. Having communicated his
sentiments to this effect, Constantius was at length prevailed upon to
consent to his brother's proposition. Constans, it should be observed,
reigned over the western part of the empire, and Constantius governed
in the east. Sardica was chosen as being on the boundaries of the two
empires, and affording equal facility to those who came from the east
or the west. Above three hundred bishops composed the assembly,
according to the best historians, selected from upwards of thirty-five
provinces, among whom were some who had attended the council of
Nice twenty-two years before. Hosius, bishop of Cordova in Spain,
presided in this council as the representative of the pope, as he had
done in that of Nice. The famous confessor Paphnutius, who had suf-

fered so much for his divine Master under the Roman persecutions, and had vindicated his cause at Nice, repaired also to Sardica, even in the extremity of old age to fight again his battles. The Arians mustered about eighty of their party, who, on finding that every thing was to be conducted according to the laws and customs of the church, and that there were neither courtiers nor soldiers to prevent the most perfect freedom of discussion, refused to attend the meetings, and kept themselves shut up in the place where they had taken lodgings. The majority of the fathers finding this faction deaf to all entreaties and obstinate in their secession, proceeded to open the council, and examine into the causes of contention that existed. They restored several orthodox or Catholic bishops, who had been unjustly deprived of their sees, and passed many canons of discipline, with a view to prevent irregularities from again taking place. As to matters that concerned faith, they confined themselves to confirming that which had been declared at Nice. Of the twenty-one canons agreed to, the first provided against bishops being transferred from lesser dioceses to greater, without the consent of the church; a practice which the Arians had introduced, and was considered an abuse by the Catholics. The chief of these canons, however, was that which related to the supremacy of the church of Rome. The Arians, to carry on their innovating purposes, had recourse frequently to councils composed of their own creatures, in which they passed decrees of deposition against such of the Catholic prelates as were most obnoxious to them. To guard against this abuse the council of Sardica decreed, that if a bishop thinks himself unjustly condemned in a synod, he may have recourse to the bishop of Rome as his lawful Judge. Another canon forbids a successor to be elected till the bishop of Rome had passed sentence in the cause. Here then it is clear that the supremacy of the pope was held by the primitive Christians in the fifth century, as it is now by the Catholics of the present day, and for which they are calumniated and abused by "Protestant ascendency."

The council having concluded its proceedings, and communicated the same to the pope, Julius, the emperors were also addressed and entreated to allow the church a full and entire liberty to govern the faithful by its own laws. In the mean while the factious bishops had withdrawn to Philippopolis, situated in the territories of Constantius, where they continued their cabals, and as Fox states *pretended* to excommunicate pope Julius, &c.; and, to add to their inconsistencies, they called this meeting at Philippopolis the council of Sardica. They next proceeded to prepossess Constantius in their favour, and having gained the Arian emperor over to their cause, they set no bounds to their fury and implacability towards the Catholics. Paul, the holy bishop of Constantinople, was strangled, after being thrown into a dungeon and left there six days without any kind of sustenance. In short, the outrages committed by these heretics, as Fox properly calls them, were of so horrible a nature, that we cannot better describe them than in the words of the martyrologist himself: "Arming them-
" selves with swords, clubs, &c." he says, " they broke into one of the
" principal churches of Alexandria, where great numbers of orthodox
" Christians were assembled at their devotions; and falling upon them in

A REVIEW

Fox's Book of Martyrs,

CRITICAL AND HISTORICAL.

Printed and Published by W.E. ANDREWS, 3, Chapter-house-court, St. Paul's Churchyard, London.

EXPLANATION OF THE ENGRAVING.—*This cut represents the miraculous defeat of the attempt of the Jews, at the instigation of Julian the apostate, to rebuild the temple of Jerusalem; a full account of which is given in this number, page 154.*

CONTINUATION OF THE REVIEW.

"a most barbarous manner, without the least respect to sex or age,
" butchered the greater number. Potamo, a venerable bishop of Hera-
" clea, who had formerly lost one of his eyes in Diocletian's persecution,
" fell a martyr upon this occasion; being so cruelly scourged and beaten
" that he died of his wounds. The Arians also broke into many places,
" public and private, under a pretext of searching for Athanasius, and
" committed innumerable barbarities: robbing orphans, plundering the
" houses of widows, dragging virgins to private places to be sacrifices
" of desire, imprisoning the clergy, burning churches and dwelling
" houses belonging to the orthodox Christians; besides other enormous
" cruelties." Such is the account given by Fox of the persecutions
commenced by the Arian heretics against the Catholic Christians.

The third section of this book is headed, " *Persecutions under Julian*
" *the apostate*," and commences with the following account of this renegado monarch. "Julian the apostate was the son of Cholorus Con-
" stantius, and the nephew of Constantine the great. He studied the
" rudiments of grammar under the inspection of Mardonius, an eunuch
" and a heathen. His father sent him afterwards to Nicomedia, to be

" instructed in the Christian religion, by Eusebius his kinsman; but
" his principles were corrupted by the pernicious doctrines of Maxi-
" mus the magician, and Ecebolius the professor of rhetoric. Con-
" stantius died in the year 361, when Julian succeeded him; but he
" had no sooner attained the imperial dignity, than he renounced
" Christianity and embraced Paganism. He again restored idolatrous
" worship, by opening the several temples that had been shut up, re-
" building such as were destroyed, and ordering the magistrates and
" people to follow his example; but he did not issue any edicts against
" Christianity. He recalled all banished Pagans, allowed the free ex-
" ercise of religion to every sect, but deprived the Christians of all
" offices, civil and military, and the clergy of the privileges granted
" to them by Constantine the great. He was chaste, temperate, vigi-
" lant, laborious, and apparently pious; so that by his hypocrisy and
" pretended virtues, he for a time did more mischief to Christianity
" than the most profligate of his predecessors. Accordingly, this per-
" secution was more dangerous than any of the former, as Julian, un-
" der the mask of clemency, practised the greatest cruelty, in seeking
" to delude the true believers; and the Christian faith was now in
" more danger of being subverted than it ever had been, by means
" of a monarch, at once witty and wicked, learned and hypocritical;
" who, at first, made his attempts by flattering gifts and favours; be-
" stowing offices and dignities; and then, by prohibiting Christian
" schools, he compelled the children either to become idolaters, or to
" remain illiterate. Julian ordered that Christians might be treated
" coldly upon all occasions, and in all parts of the empire, and em-
" ployed witty persons to turn them and their principles into ridicule.
" Many were likewise martyred in his reign; for though he did not
" publicly persecute them himself, he connived at their being murder-
" ed by his governors and officers; and though he affected never to re-
" ward them for those cruelties, neither did he ever punish them. We
" shall recount the names, sufferings, and martyrdoms of such as
" have been transmitted to posterity."

Such is the testimony of John Fox as to the conduct of this renoun-
cer of Christianity, and in the whole it may be taken as correct. We
here see that the same system was pursued by the Pagan emperors and
by the Arians, as in later times by "Protestant-ascendency," in the
two islands of Great Britain and Ireland, to annihilate the professors of Catholicism, but without effect. When Elizabeth assumed the
throne, she renounced Catholicism, which she had professed during her
sister Mary's reign, and embraced Protestantism. That is, she rejected that spiritual authority admitted by all nations previous to the
reformation so called, and set herself up as the director and governor
of the consciences of all her liege subjects. She destroyed churches,
and opened others with her new-fangled mode of worship. In the first
part of her reign she did not issue any public edicts against the Catholics, but her ministers covertly poisoned the minds of the people
against them, by hatching up pretended plots and conspiracies, in order the better to put in execution the mercenary laws contemplated
to ruin them. They were assailed on one side with bribery; on the
other they were threatened with tortures and death, and confiscation

of their property, if they did not abandon the religion of their forefathers. They were deprived of offices, civil and military, and the clergy were thrust out of their livings, and deprived of the privileges they enjoyed under Magna Charta, to make way for a set of unprincipled hypocrites and illiterate pretenders to clerical functions. Elizabeth was represented as being of chaste manners, the same as Fox has pourtrayed Julian, though it is notorious that she indulged in her amours with shameless indecency; and when it suited her purpose she could be as base a dissembler as Julian is stated to have been. Elizabeth raised a persecution against the Catholics, in which cruelty was practised under the mask of clemency; and the better to eradicate the seeds of Catholicism, the children of Catholics were compelled to become Protestants, or to remain illiterate. In these days, the people of Ireland, who are almost all Catholics, are charged by "Protestant-ascendency" with being ignorant and uneducated, though this ignorance has been occasioned by the cruel and unjust code of laws that mark the blood-stained annals of this ascendency. Under "Protestant-ascendency" it was made transportation and death for a Catholic to teach an unlettered Catholic, or instruct him in those principles of Christianity which led so many persons in the primitive ages to suffer martyrdom, rather than violate the least of them. John Fox says that many Christians were martyred in Julian's reign, though he did not publicly persecute them himself. So in the reign of Elizabeth, the founder of "Protestant-ascendency," Catholics were put to death for conscience sake, but, to give a colour to these proceedings, it was made high treason to practise the religion of the primitive Christians. Thus, by a species of Machiavelism unparalleled, Catholics were put to death for being Catholic Christians, while the ignorant multitude were made to believe they suffered as traitors. Fox further says, that though Julian affected never to reward those who practised cruelties on the Christians, neither did he ever punish them. Similar was the conduct of Elizabeth towards many of her officers, who manifested a zeal for "Protestant-ascendency," by oppressing and murdering the Catholics. Witness her behaviour towards sir Amias Paulet, the keeper of the unfortunate Mary queen of Scots, and the earl of Essex, the cruel and mercenary governor of Ireland under her. Even though the ill-fated queen of Scots suffered by the official consent of Elizabeth, yet did this dissembler profess to be ignorant of the proceedings, and rated the ministers for using her authority.

As Fox has given a character of this apostate Julian, we will here insert the character of the hypocrite Elizabeth, by the pen of Dr. Lingard. "An intelligent foreigner (he writes) had described Elizabeth, " while she was yet a subject, as haughty and overbearing: on the throne " she was careful to display that notion of her own importance, that " contempt for all beneath her, and that courage in the time of dan- " ger, which were characteristic of the Tudors. She seemed to have " forgotten that she ever had a mother: but was proud to remind both " herself and others that she was the daughter of a powerful monarch, " Henry VIII. On occasions of ceremony she appeared in all her " splendour, accompanied by all the officers of state, and with a nu- " merous retinue of lords and ladies dressed in their most gorgeous

" apparel. · In reading the accounts of her court, we may sometimes
" fancy ourselves transported into the palace of an eastern princess.
" When Hentzner saw her, she was proceeding on a Sunday from her
" own apartment to the chapel. First appeared a number of gentle-
" men, barons, earls, and knights of the garter; then came the chan-
" cellor with the seals, between two lords carrying the sceptre and the
" sword. Elizabeth followed: ·and wherever she cast her eyes, the
" spectators instantly fell on their knees. She was then in her sixty-
" fifth year.   She wore false hair of a red colour, surmounted with a
" crown of gold, The wrinkles of age were imprinted on her face;
" her eyes were small, her teeth black, her nose prominent. The col-
" lar of the garter hung from her neck; and her bosom was uncovered,
" as became an unmarried queen. Behind her followed a long train of
" young ladies dressed in white; and on each side stood a line of gen-
" tlemen pensioners, with their gilt battle-axes and splendid uniforms.
   " The traveller next proceeded to the dining room. Two gentle-
" men entered to lay the cloth, two to bring the queen's plate, salt,
" and bread. All, before they approached the table, and when they
" retired from it, made three genuflections. Then came a single and
" married lady, performing the same ceremonies. The first rubbed
" the plate with bread and salt; the second gave a morsel of meat to
" each of the yeomen of the guard, who brought in the. different
" courses: and at the same time the hall echoed to the sound of twelve
" trumpets, and two kettle drums. But the queen dined that day in
" private: and, after a short pause, her maids of honour entered in
" procession, ·and with much reverence and solemnity took the dishes
" from the table, and carried them into an inner appartment." ....
   " Of her vanity the reader will have noticed several instances in the
" preceding pages: there remains one of a more extraordinary·descrip-
" tion. It is seldom that females have the boldness to become the
" heralds of their own charms: but Elizabeth by proclamation an-
" nounced to her people, that none of the portaits, which had hitherto
" been taken of her person, did justice to the original: that at the re-
" quest of her council she had resolved to procure an exact likeness
" from the pen of some able artist: that it should soon be published
" for the gratification of her loving subjects; and that on this account
" she strictly forbad all persons whomsoever, to paint or engrave any
" new portraits of her features without licence, or to shew or publish
" any of the old portraits, till they had been reformed according to the
" copy to be set forth by authority.
   " The courtiers soon discovered how greedy their sovereign was of
" flattery. If they sought to please, they were careful to admire: and
" adulation, the most fulsome and extravagant, was accepted by the
" queen with gratitude, and rewarded with bounty. Neither was her
" appetite for praise cloyed, it seemed rather to become more craving,
" by enjoyment.   After she had passed her grand climacteric, she ex-
" acted the same homage to her faded charms, as had been paid to her
" youth; and all who addressed her, were still careful to express their
" admiration of her beauty, in the language of oriental hyperbole.
   " But however highly the queen might think of her person, she did
" not despise the aid of external ornament. At her death, two, some

" say three, thousand dresses were found in her wardrobe, with a nu-
" merous collection of jewellery, for the most part presents, which
" she had received from petitioners, from her courtiers on her saint's
" day and at the beginning of each year, and from the noblemen and
" gentlemen, whose houses she had honoured with her presence. To
" the austere notions of the bishop of London, this love of finery ap-
" peared unbecoming her age, and in his sermon he endeavoured to
" raise her thoughts from the ornaments of dress to the riches of
" heaven : but she told her ladies, that if he touched upon that subject
" again, she would fit *him* for heaven. He should walk there without
" a staff, and leave his mantle behind him.

" In her temper Elizabeth seemed to have inherited the irritability
" of her father. The least inattention, the slightest provocation, would
" throw her into a passion. At all times her discourse was sprinkled
" with oaths; in the sallies of her anger it abounded with imprecations
" and abuse. Nor did she content herself with words: not only the
" ladies about her person, but her courtiers and the highest officers in
" the state felt the weight of her hands. She collared Hatton, she
" gave a blow on the ear to the earl marshal, and she spat on sir Mat-
" thew ——, with the foppery of whose dress she was offended.

" To her first parliament she had expressed a wish that on her tomb
" might be inscribed the title of ' the virgin queen.' But the woman
" who despises the safeguards, must be content to forfeit the reputa-
" tion of chastity. It was not long before her familiarity with Dudley
" provoked dishonourable reports. At first they gave her pain : but
" her feelings were soon blunted by passion : in the face of the whole
" court she consigned to her supposed paramour an apartment conti-
" guous to her own bed-chamber ? and by this indecent act proved that
" she was become regardless of her character, and callous to every
" sense of shame. But Dudley, though the most favoured, was not
" considered as her only lover: among his rivals were numbered Hat-
" ton and Raleigh, and Oxford and Blount, and Simier and Anjou; and
" it was afterwards believed that her licentious habits had survived,
" even when the fires of wantonness had been quenched by the chill of
" age. The court imitated the manners of the sovereign. It was a
" place in which, according to Faunt, ' all enormities reigned in the
" highest degree,' or according to Harrington, ' where there was no
" love, but that of the lusty god of gallantry, Asmodeus.'

" Elizabeth firmly believed, and zealously upheld the principles of
" government established by her father, the exercise of absolute au-
" thority by the sovereign, and the duty of passive obedience in the
" subject. The doctrine, with which the lord keeper Bacon opened
" the first parliament, was indefatigably inculcated by all his succes-
" sors during her reign, that, if the queen consulted the two houses,
" it was through choice, not through necessity, to the end that her
" laws might be more satisfactory to her people, not that they might
" derive any force from their assent. She possessed by her prero-
" gative whatever was requisite for the government of the realm. She
" could, at her pleasure, suspend the operation of existing statutes, or
" issue proclamations which should have the force of law. In her opi-
" nion the chief use of parliaments was to vote money, to regulate the

" minutiæ of trade, and to legislate for individual and local interests.
"To the lower house she granted, indeed, freedom of debate; but it
" was to be a decent freedom, the liberty of 'saying aye or no;' and
" those who transgressed that decency were liable, as we have repeat-
" edly seen, to feel the weight of the royal displeasure.

"A foreigner, who had been ambassador in England, informs us,
" that under Elizabeth the administration of justice was more corrupt
" than under her predecessors. We have not the means of instituting
" the comparison. But we know that in her first year the policy of
" Cecil substituted men of inferior rank in the place of former magis-
" trates; that numerous complaints were heard of their tyranny, pecu-
" lation and rapacity; and that a justice of the peace was defined in
" parliament to be 'an animal, who, for half a dozen chickens would
" dispense with a dozen laws:' nor shall we form a very exalted no-
" tion of the integrity of the higher courts, if we recollect the judges
" were removable at the royal pleasure, and that the queen herself
" was in the habit of receiving, and permitting her favourites and la-
" dies to receive, bribes as the prices of her or their interference in the
" suits of private individuals.

"Besides the judicial tribunals, which remain to the present day,
" there were in the age of Elizabeth, several other courts, the arbi-
" trary constitution of which were incompatible with the liberties of
" the subject; the court of high commission, for the cognizance of re-
" ligious offences; the court of star-chamber, which inflicted the se-
" verest punishments for that comprehensive and undefinable trans-
" gression, contempt of the royal authority; and the courts martial,
" for which the queen, from her hasty and imperious temper, mani-
" fested a strong predilection. Whatever could be supposed to have
" the remotest tendency to sedition, was held to subject the offender to
" martial law; the murder of a naval or military officer, the importa-
" tion of disloyal or traitorous books, or the resort to one place of se-
" veral persons who possessed not the visible means of subsistence.
" Thus in 1595, under the pretence that the vagabonds of London were
" not to be restrained by the usual punishments, she ordered sir Tho-
" mas Wyllford to receive from the magistrates the most notorious
" and incorrigible of these offenders, and 'to execute them upon the
" gallows according to the justice of martial law.'

"Another and intolerable grievance was the discretionary power
" assumed by the queen, of gratifying her caprice or resentment by
" the restraint or imprisonment of those who had given her offence.
" Such persons were ordered daily to present themselves before the
" council till they should receive further notice, or to confine them-
" selves within their own doors, or were given in custody to some
" other person, or were thrown into a public prison, In this state they
" remained, according to the royal pleasure, for weeks, or months, or
" years, till they could obtain their liberty by their submission, or
" through the intercession of their friends, or with the payment of a
" valuable composition.

"The queen was not sparing of the blood of her subjects. The
" statutes inflicting death for religious opinions have been already no-
" ticed. In addition, many new felonies and new treasons were created

"during her reign; and the ingenuity of the judges gave to these en-
"actments the most extensive application. In 1595 some apprentices
"in London conspired to release their companions, who had been con-
"demned by the star-chamber to suffer punishment for a riot; in 1597
"a number of peasants in Oxfordshire assembled to break down inclo-
"sures, and restore tillage; each of these offences, as it opposed the
"execution of the law, was pronounced treason by the judges; and
"both the apprentices in London, and the men of Oxfordshire, suffer-
"ed the barbarous death of traitors.

"We are told that her parsimony was a blessing to the subject, and
"that the pecuniary aids voted to her by parliament were few and in-
"considerable, in proportion to the length of her reign. They
"amounted to twenty subsidies, thirty tenths, and forty fifteenths. I
"know not how we are to arrive at the exact value of these grants:
"but they certainly exceed the average of the preceding reigns: and
"to them must be added the fines of recusants, the profits of monopo-
"lies, and the monies raised by forced loans: of which it is observed
"by Naunton, that 'she left more debts unpaid, taken upon credit of
"her privy seals, than her progenitors did take, or could have taken
"up, that were a hundred years before her.' "

Such is the description of the public and private qualities of the founder
of "Protestant ascendency," by one of the first writers of the day: need
we then wonder that the situation of the Catholics during her reign, was
equally as horrible as that of the Christians under Julian the apostate?
Let the reader judge, now he has the character of these two monarchs
before him. But to return to Fox. He begins his account of the sufferers under Julian with the "*Martyrdom of Basil*," who, he says, made himself famous by his opposition to Arianism and Paganism. That after
being put to the rack and otherwise tortured without making the least
impression on his constancy, he was reserved for an examination before Julian himself. The Rev. Alban Butler has given us the following
interesting account of this examination in his life of this saint. "When
"Julian," writes Mr. B. "arrived at Ancyra, St. Basil was presented
"before him, and the crafty emperor, putting on an air of compassion,
"said to him: 'I myself am well skilled in your mysteries; and I can
"inform you, that Christ in whom you place your trust, died under
"Pilate, and remains among the dead.' The martyr answered: 'You
"are deceived, who have renounced Christ, at a time when he confer-
"red on you the empire. But he will deprive you of it, together with
"your life. As you have thrown down his altars, so will he overturn
"your throne; and as you have violated his holy law, which you had
"so often announced to the people (when reader in the church) and
"have trodden it under your feet, your body shall be cast forth with-
"out the honour of a burial, and shall be trampled on by men.'" For
this answer Julian sentenced the saint to have his skin torn off every
day in seven different places, until there was none left. Before he
died he was laid on his belly and pierced with red hot spikes, under
which torture he expired on the 29th of June in 362. As this holy
martyr suffered for the Catholic religion under Pagan and Arian ascendency, so did father Campion under "Protestant ascendency," in the
reign of Elizabeth. Father Campion was a Catholic priest who com-

batted the errors of the reformation with more than ordinary zeal.
He proposed to dispute on religion before the queen, the council and
the two universities, and declared himself ready to suffer every kind
of torment, and shed his blood, if necessary, for the propagation of the
Catholic faith. This bold challenge to defend the truth was answered
by an arrest, after having eluded the vigilance of his enemies for more
than twelve months. He had scarcely been lodged in the Tower when
he was put to the rack, which torture was repeated three times, and
with such unrelenting cruelty, that on the third repetition it was thought
he had expired. After suffering thus, Campion was brought before
Elizabeth herself, by her own order, and questioned as to his allegiance; he was then arraigned with twelve other priests and one layman, condemned to death, and was hanged, bowelled, and quartered.
(See Lingard's Hist. of Eng.)

Fox also tells us, that "when Julian intended an expedition against
"the Persians, he imposed a large fine upon every one who refused to
"sacrifice to the idols, and by that means got a great sum from the
"Christians towards defraying his expenses. Many of the officers, in
"collecting these fines, exacted more than their due, and some of
"them tortured the Christians to make them pay what they demanded,
"at the same time telling them in derision, ' that when they were in-
"jured, they ought to take it patiently, for so their God had com-
"manded them.'" So have the Catholics been treated by "Protestant-ascendency." In Elizabeth's reign it is confessed by her eulogist Camden, that "emissaries were dispersed everywhere abroad,
"to collect rumours and catch unguarded expressions," in order to
seize upon the persons of Catholics and confiscate their property. False
informers and apostates from their faith too, we are told by the same historian, were encouraged to accuse the Catholics At this day, the Catholics are deprived of their civil rights, through the means of an infamous oath, and when they complain of the injustice done them, they
are told in derision, that they have no right to complain, as their refusal to take the oath is a proof of their half-allegiance, though no
class of the community can be more attached to the constitution of the
country than Catholics. So that what has been advanced by Fox against
Julian for his treachery and barbarity, is equally applicable to the virgin queen Elizabeth and her ministers. The martyrs under Julian
were Catholics, and the objects of Elizabeth's vengeance were Catholics too. In Julian's reign the Catholics were termed Galileans; so
in Elizabeth's, to brand them with odium, they were termed Papists;
which appellation is still applied to them by bigots and intolerants.

But the most important fact that took place in Julian's reign has
been omitted by Fox. He allows him to have abandoned Christianity
and returned to Paganism; he allows him to have persecuted the Christians, and heaped oppressions upon them; but he does not tell us of
the vain and blasphemous attempt he made to falsify the prediction of
Christ, regarding the temple of Jerusalem. In various parts of scripture are to be found the denunciations of Jesus Christ against the city
of Jerusalem and its temple, where the Jewish sacrifices were offered
according to the old law, but were to give way to that unbloody sacrifice of the new law established by Christ himself. In St. Matthew's

gospel, chapter 23, it is stated, that, a little before his passion, Christ foretold the Jews the miseries they should suffer for their ingratitude. "Behold," he says, "I send unto you prophets, and wise men, and "scribes, and some of them ye shall kill and crucify, and some of them "ye shall scourge in the synagogues, and persecute them from city to "city: that upon you may come all the righteous blood shed upon the "earth, from the blood of righteous Abel, unto the blood of Zacharias, "son of Barachias, whom ye slew between the temple and the altar: "Verily I say unto you, all these things shall come upon this genera- "tion. O Jerusalem, Jerusalem, thou that killest the prophets, and "stonest them that are sent unto thee, how often would I have ga- "thered thy children together, even as a hen gathereth her chickens "under her wings, and ye would not? behold, your house is left unto "you desolate."—St. Luke says in his gospel, chapter 19, that when our Saviour entered Jerusalem, some days before his crucifixion, he wept over the city, and said, "Ah! if thou hadst known, even thou, at least "in this thy day, the things which belong unto thy peace! but now "they are hid from thine eyes. For the days shall come upon thee, "that thine enemies shall cast a trench about thee, and compass thee "round, and keep thee in on every side, and shall lay thee even with "the ground, and thy children within thee; and they shall not leave "in thee one stone upon another, because thou knowest not the time "of my visitation." St Mark also records, chapter 13, that when one of his disciples spoke of the temple and its costly materials, Jesus an- swered, "Verily I say unto you, there shall not be left here one stone "upon another, that shall not be destroyed." These predictions testi- fied to by three of the evangelists, who all wrote at different times and at different places, we see verified in the reign of the Roman emperor Titus, in the year of our Lord 72, that is near forty years after they were foretold. The horrors of the siege of this city are stated by Josephus, to whom we refer the reader. Suffice it to say, the prophecy of Christ was fulfilled to a tittle, and conveyed another irrefragable proof of his divine wisdom and power.

Well, Julian after declaring war against Christ and his disciples, thought himself strong enough to make void his predictions, and prove the divine Founder of Christianity to be, what our poor infatuated deists, ignorantly we hope, call him—an impostor. To complete his designs upon the Christians, Julian took into his special protection the Jews, then, as now, the refuse of the world. He excited them to build again their temple, and the more to encourage them in the undertaking, he gave them large sums of money, and assisted them with all the force of the empire. The Jews were elated with the designs of Julian, and flocked from all parts of the empire to Jerusalem, behaving with great insolence to the Christians. Contributions came in from all hands, and the women stripped themselves of their most costly ornaments to swell the funds necessary for the building. The most able workmen were drawn from all quarters, and persons of high rank appointed as overseers, having at their head Julian's intimate friend Alypius, who had formerly been pro-prefect of Britain. All things were now in rea- diness. The necessary materials were collected, and the Jews of both sexes animated to share in the labour of the building. But behold the

power of Christ, and the puny attempts of man to set aside his
never-failing prophecies. The very means intended to render false the
words of God, were designed by him to have his predictions fulfilled.
Till this time some of the foundations and part of the walls of the temple were standing; and these ruins were demolished by the Jews themselves to clear a foundation for the new projected building. Thus then
they concurred in accomplishing our Saviour's prediction, that not one
stone should be left upon another, of that building so highly prized by
themselves. Having thus cleared the way, they began to prepare the
foundation, in which many thousand workmen were employed. But to
the great surprise of those engaged in the work, what they had cast up
in the day was thrown back by earthquakes in the succeeding nights.
Nothing daunted, they proceed with hardened obstinacy in the work,
but are met with still more terrible supernatural impediments. Ammianus Marcellinus, a Pagan writer, and a zealous defender of Julian,
relates these wonders in the following words: "And when Alypius the
"next day earnestly pressed on the work with the assistance of the
"governor of the province, there issued (he says) such horrible balls
"of fire out of the earth, near the foundations, which rendered the
"place, from time to time, inaccessible to the scorched and blasted
"workmen. And the victorious element continuing in this manner
"obstinately and resolutely bent, as it were, to drive them to a distance,
"Alypius thought proper to give over the enterprize." Several Christian authors likewise record the fact, and mention other extraordinary
circumstances and appearances attending this triumphant victory of
Christianism over its implacable enemies. As infidelity and deism is
rapidly spreading in this once Christian country, and as this historical
fact is but little known among the readers of the present age, we will
here subjoin the Rev. Mr. Butler's account of it, from his life of St.
Cyril, archbishop of Jerusalem.

"This judgment of the Almighty," says the learned writer, "was
"ushered in by storms and whirlwinds, by which prodigious heaps
"of lime and sand and other loose materials were carried away. (Theod.
"Hist. l. iii. c. 20.) After these followed lightnings, the usual conse-
"quence of collision in clouds and tempests. Its effects were, first the
"destroying the more solid materials, and melting down the iron in-
"struments; (Soc. lib. iii. c. 20.) and, secondly, the impressing shining
"crosses on the bodies and garments of the assistants without distinc-
"tion, in which there was something that in art and elegance exceeded
"all painting or embroidery; which when the infidels perceived, they
"endeavoured, but in vain, to wash them out. (St. Greg. Naz. Or. 4. adv.
"Julian.) In the third place came the earthquake, which cast out the
"stones of the old foundations, and shook the earth into the trench or
"cavity dug for the new; besides overthrowing the adjoining build-
"ings and porticos wherein were lodged great numbers of Jews design-
"ed for this work, who were all either crushed to death, or at least
"maimed or wounded. The number of the killed or hurt was increas-
"ed by the fiery eruption in the fourth place, attended both with storms
"and tempests above, and with an earthquake below. (St. Greg. Naz.
"Or. 9.) From this eruption, many fled to a neighbouring church for
"shelter, but could not obtain entrance; whether on account of its be-

" ing closed by a secret invisible hand, as the fathers state the case,
" or at least by a special providence, through the entrance into the ora-
" tory being choked up by a frightful crowd, all pressing to be fore-
" most. 'This, however,' says Gregory Nazianzen, (Or. 4. adv. Julian.)
" 'is invariably affirmed and believed by all, that as they strove to force
" their way in by violence, the *Fire*, which burst from the foundations
" of the temple, met and stopt them, and one part it burnt and de-
" stroyed, and another it desperately maimed, leaving them a living
" monument of God's commination and wrath against sinners.' This
" eruption was frequently renewed till it overcame the rashness of the
" most obdurate, to use the words of Socrates; for it continued to be
" repeated as often as the projectors ventured to renew their attempt,
" till it had fairly tired them out. Lastly, on the same evening, there
" appeared over Jerusalem a lucid cross, shining very bright, as large
" as that in the reign of Constantine, encompassed with a circle of
" light. 'And what could be so proper to close this tremendous scene
" or to celebrate this decisive victory, as the *Cross* triumphant, encir-
" cled with the *heroic* symbol of conquest?'

" "This miraculous event, with all its circumstances, is related by
" the writers of that age; by St. Gregory Nazianzen in the year imme-
" diately following it; by St. Chrysostom, in several parts of his works,
" who says that it happened not twenty years before, appeals to eye-
" witnesses still living and young, and to the present condition of those
" foundations, 'of which,' says he, 'we are all witnesses;' by St. Am-
" brose in his fortieth epistle, written in 388; Rufinus, who had long
" lived upon the spot; Theodoret, who lived in the neighbourhood in
" Syria; Philostorgius the Arian; Sozomen, who says many were alive
" when he wrote who had it from eye witnesses, and mentions the vi-
" sible marks still subsisting; Socrates, &c. The testimony of the
" heathens corroborate this evidence; as that of Ammianus Marcellinus
" above quoted, a nobleman of the first rank, who then lived in the
" court of Julian at Antioch and in an office of distinction, and who
" probably wrote his account from the letter of Alypius to his master,
" at the time when the miracle happened. Libanius, another pagan
" friend and admirer of Julian, both in the History of his own life,
" and in his Funeral oration on Julian's death, mentions these earth-
" quakes in Palestine, but with a shyness which discovers the disgrace
" of his hero and superstition. Julian himself speaks of this event in
" the same covert manner. Socrates testifies, that at the sight of the
" miracles, the Jews cried out at first that Christ is God; yet returned
" home as hardened as ever. St. Gregory Nazianzen says, that many
" Gentiles were converted upon it, and went over to the church. The-
" odoret and Sozomen say many were converted; but as to the Jews,
" they evidently mean a sudden flash of conviction, not a real and last-
" ing conversion. The incredulous blinded themselves by various pre-
" tences: but the evidence of the miracle leaves no room for the least
" cavil or suspicion. The Christian writers of that age are unanimous
in relating it with its complicated circumstances, yet with a diversity
" which shews their agreement, though perfect, could not have been
" concerted. The same is confirmed by the testimony of the most ob-
" stinate adversaries. They, who, when the temple at Daphne was con-

" sumed about the same time, by lightning, (See Review, p. 78) pretended
" it was set on fire by Christians, were not able to suspect any possibility
" of contrivance in this case: nor could the event have been natural.
" Every such suspicion is removed by the conformity of the event with the
" prophecies; the importance of the occasion, the extreme eagerness
" of Jews and Gentiles in the enterprise, the attention of the whole
" empire fixed on it, and the circumstances of the fact. The eruption,
" contrary to its usual nature, was confined to one small spot; it obsti-
" nately broke out by fits, and ceased with the project, and this in such
" a manner, that Ammianus himself ascribes it to an intelligent cause.
" The phænomena of the cross in the air, and on the garments, were
" admirably fitted, as moral emblems, to proclaim the triumph of
" Christ over Julian, who had taken the cross out of the military en-
" signs, which Constantine had put there to be a memorial of that cross
" which he had seen in the air that presaged his victories. The same
" was again erected in the heavens to confound the vanity of its impo-
" tent persecutor. The earthquake was undoubtedly miraculous; and
" though its effects were mostly such as might naturally follow, they
" were directed by a special supernatural providence, as the burning
" of Sodom by fire from heaven. Whence Mr. Warburton concludes
" his dissertation on this subject with the following corollary. 'New
" light continually springing up from each circumstance, as it passes
" in review, by such time as the whole event is considered, this illus-
" trious miracle comes out in one full blaze of evidence.' Even Jew-
" ish rabbins, who do not copy from Christian writers, relate this event
" in the same manner with the fathers from their own traditions and
" records. This great event happened in the beginning of the year 363."

The florid but infidel Gibbon, in his Roman History, is obliged to admit this most miraculous event, but then he attempts to weaken the
testimony adduced by base and groundless insinuations. Quoting the
confession of Ammianus Marcellinus, which we have before given,
Gibbon says, " Such authority should satisfy a believing, and must asto-
" nish an incredulous, mind. Yet a philosopher may still require the
" original evidence of impartial and intelligent spectators. At this im-
" portant crisis, any singular accident of nature would assume the ap-
" pearance, and produce the effects of a real prodigy. This glorious
" deliverance would be speedily improved and magnified by the pious
" art of the clergy at Jerusalem, and the active credulity of the Christian
" world; and at the distance of twenty years, a Roman historian, care-
" less of theological disputes, might adorn his work with the specious
" and splendid miracle." What miserable and contemptible sophistry
have we here! and yet this Mr. Gibbon is looked upon by the present
race of Protestant Englishmen as one of the greatest ornaments of literature. But what can the man of unprejudiced mind think of such a
writer? and particularly when he is the panegyrist of an apostate from
the Christian faith; when he calls one of the most subtle and mercenary tyrants that ever stained human nature " a devout monarch, labour-
" ing to restore and propagate the religion of his ancestors!!!" But let
us look a little into the philosophy of Mr. Gibbon. He allows the testimony of Ammianus Marcellinus to be unexceptionable, and such as
" should satisfy a believing and must astonish a credulous, mind;" but

the *philosopher*, he says, "*may* still require the *original evidence* of *im-* "*partial* and *intelligent spectators!*" Now, is not this language a little too barefaced to lay before a reader of common understanding? Why who could be more impartial and intelligent than the *Pagan* writer named? He could have *no* interest whatever in lending his aid to favour the "pious arts of the clergy of Jerusalem," nor in strengthening " the credulity of the *Christian* world;" on the contrary, it is clear that his prejudices would have led him to disown the fact, if it had been possible for him to do so. For observe, he was not speaking of a theological question, but of a public occurrence, never disputed till it was thought necessary by modern reformers to rob the Christian world of some of its brightest attributes. Besides, was not St. Gregory Nazianzen a competent witness, as he wrote his account of it a year after the event took place. St. Chrysostom appeals to *eye-witnesses* for the truth of his statement, and is not contradicted. Sozomen wrote from eye-witnesses, and appeals to marks still visible, without contradiction. What stronger or more original evidence would an impartial man require than what is here offered to substantiate an historical fact? The historian, though he can doubt himself, would have us believe, that, at that time, "*any* singular accident of *nature* would assume the appear- "ance, and produce the effects of a *real* prodigy." But was it an *acci-dent* of *nature* for balls of fire to come out of the bowels of the earth, and drive the workmen away, scorched and blasted? Did Gibbon ever hear of a similar "accident of nature" occurring, before or since the event related by Ammianus and other writers? Must it not then have been a real and singular prodigy? Mr. Gibbon states that St. Gregory of Nazianzen boldly says " that this preternatural event was not disputed by the infidels;" he should have added of St. Gregory's days, for it seems that Gibbon was infidel enough to doubt it when he wrote. Now what more convincing proof can we require, to satisfy our credibility, than this circumstance,—that the fact was not disputed by the spectators, the living witnesses of all classes, both Christians, Jews, and Pagans? Of what temper then must that *philosopher* be, who may still require " the *original* evidence of impartial and intelligent spectators?" Such philosophers as these would strike at the root of ALL testimony; for how are we to come at the *original* evidence of occurrences that have taken place centuries ago? How can we tell that the veil of the temple was rent when our Saviour expired? How do we know that Christ was ever crucified? What *original* evidence have we or can we have of these facts? And yet they are believed by all mankind, with the exception of a few vain but ignorant mortals; and so is the glorious miracle above detailed, by every mind not tainted with the folly of scepticism; for surely never was there an event more extraordinary nor better verified. In a word, how do we know that the history written by Gibbon himself is not all fiction; for we have no " *original* evidence of impartial and intelligent spectators" to vouch for *his* statements. That much of it is false may be safely concluded from the example we have selected on this subject of the miraculous destruction of Jerusalem; but that we may not be charged with confining ourselves to one single case, we will here give Mr. Gibbon's account

of the last words of this cruel and impious tyrant, and then contrast
it with the statements of other writers.

Julian, it is confessed by all historians, met with an untimely death,
foretold, according to the *Book of Martyrs*, with a prophetic spirit by
St. Basil, when examined by the emperor himself.   Engaged in a war
with Persia, the Roman army was placed in a situation of danger and
distress, when Julian found it necessary to engage the Persians under
all disadvantages.   In the midst of the battle, Julian received a wound
from a javelin, which transpierced his ribs and fixed in his liver.
From what hand the javelin was thrown was never positively discovered; some historians say the wound was inflicted by an invisible hand:
others that he fell by the hand of one of his own soldiers. Be it as it may,
he received a mortal wound, and was carried to his tent, where, if we
may believe Gibbon, he finished his course more like a saint and a
hero, than a bloody and superstitious tyrant as he lived.   Our infidel
writer says, "the philosophers who had accompanied him in this fatal
"expedition, compared the tent of Julian with the prison of Socrates;
"and the spectators, whom *duty*, or *friendsihp*, or *curiosity* had as-
"sembled round his couch, listened with *respectful* grief to the funeral
"oration of the dying emperor. 'Friends and fellow soldiers, the sea-
"sonable period of my departure has now arrived, and I discharge,
"with the *cheerfulness* of a *ready debtor*, the demands of nature. I
"have learned from philosophy, how much the soul is more excellent
"than the body; and that the separation of the nobler substance should
"be the subject of joy, rather than affliction. I have learned from
"*religion*, that an early death has often been the reward of *piety*; and
"I accept as a favour of the gods, the mortal stroke that secures me
"from the danger of *disgracing a character*, which has hitherto been
"supported by *virtue and fortitude*. I die without *remorse*, as I have
"lived without *guilt*. I am pleased to *reflect* on the *innocence* of my
"*private* life; and I can affirm with confidence, that the supreme au-
"thority, that emanation of Divine Power, has been preserved in *my*
"hands *pure* and *immaculate*. Detesting the corrupt and destructive
"maxims of despotism, I have considered the happiness of the people
"as the end of government. Submitting my actions to the laws of
"prudence, of justice, and of moderation, I have trusted the event to
"the care of Providence. Peace was the object of my councils, as
"long as peace was consistent with the public welfare; but when the
"imperious voice of my country summoned me to arms, I exposed my
"person to the dangers of war, with the clear foreknowledge (which
"I had acquired from the art of divination) that I was destined to fall
"by the sword. I now offer my *tribute of gratitude to the Eternal*
"*Being*, who has not suffered me to perish by the cruelty of a tyrant,
"by the cruel dagger of conspiracy, or by the slow tortures of linger-
"ing disease. He has given me in the midst of *an honourable career*,
"a *splendid* and *glorious departure from the world*; and I hold it equally
"absurd, equally base, to solicit, or to decline, the stroke of fate.
"Thus much I have attempted to say; but my strength fails me, and
"I feel the approach of death.—I shall cautiously refrain from any
"word that may tend to influence your suffrages in the election of an

"emperor. My choice might be imprudent or injudicious; and if it
"should not be ratified by the consent of the army, it might be fatal
"to the person whom I should recommend. I shall only, as a good
"citizen, express my hopes, that the Romans may be blessed with the
"government of a virtuous sovereign.'" Such is the discourse attributed to Julian by Ammianus, and to which, it seems, Mr. Gibbon
would have his readers give implicit credit, though he finds fault with
this Pagan writer for believing and recording the miraculous prevention
of the attempt to rebuild the temple of Jerusalem. In a note, Gibbon says, "The whole relation of the death of Julian is given by Am-
"mianus, (xxv. 3.) an intelligent spectator. Libanius, who turns
"with horror from the scene, has supplied some circumstances. (Orat.
"Parental. c. 136-140, p. 359-362.) The calumnies of Gregory, and
"the legends of more *ancient* saints, (he adds) may now be *silently*
"despised." But *why* so, Mr. Gibbon? *Why* should we despise the
testimony of men, who, you say, wrote nearer the time of the event,
and who of course must have better means of information? Are we
to reject their testimony because they were *saints:* that is, holy and
virtuous men? By this kind of logic we are then to reject the evidence of men of probity, and give credit only to the interested and unprincipled. This method of belief may suit the infidel and the fanatic, but it will not satisfy the Catholic, nor, we will add, the honest Protestant, desirous of learning the truth.

Historians agree that Julian was a vain babbler, and truly such a
piece of silly conceit and bombast as Gibbon has treated us with, we
do not recollect to have seen attributed to a dying man, though he is
ranked by our historian as a hero, fascinated with the love of virtue
and of fame. This panegyric by Julian on his own supposed good
deeds, reminds us, to be sure, of the fulsome eulogies bestowed by
hireling and ignorant writers on the pretended blessings derived from
Elizabeth's reign, but a slight examination of the statements on either
side, accompanied with the actual result of their measures, will soon
remove the gloss of these tinselled fables. The speech attributed to Julian is a medley of falsehood and vanity, contradicted even by the historian himself, while he calls for implicit credit from his reader. For
example: Julian is made to say that he dies without *remorse*, as he has
lived without *guilt;* yet the historian tells us a few pages before, that
previous to the battle in which he received his mortal wound, "when-
"ever he closed his eyes in short and interrupted slumbers, his mind
"was agitated with painful anxiety;" somewhat, we suppose, like our
Richard the third. Now, would the man with a guiltless conscience
be thus disturbed in his slumbers? Again, he talks of having "learn-
"ed from religion that an early death has often been the reward of
"piety." Piety indeed, to forswear that religion, and embrace Pagan
idolatry. He then accepts the *favour* of death from *the gods,* and offers
his "tribute of gratitude to *the Eternal Being,*" that is, *one God,* for
preserving him from some dangers he apprehended. This jumble of
the one Supreme Being with a plurality of gods, reminds us of the
consistency of our "few plain Christians," who allow every discordant
creed to be right but Catholicism, where truth only is to be found.
Then Julian detests despotism, and always considered the happiness of

the people as the end of government. But how came Gibbon to tell
us that this very Julian treated the Christian part of the people with
contempt and hatred? a feeling the "plain Christians" are attempting
to excite against the Catholics. Fox says, the persecution of the
Christians under Julian raged at times with more than usual violence,
and the tortures inflicted were of the most horrible kind. This does
not look like detesting despotism. Fox, among his recorded martyrs,
mentions "Maxentius and Juventius, two Christian officers, put to
"death for reproving the emperor on account of his idolatries." These
two individuals are stated by Theodoret, l. iii, c. 15, to have suffered
from another cause. Julian, to ensnare and perplex his Christian subjects, while residing at Antioch, ordered the wells and meat in the
market place to be polluted with the oblations offered to the heathen
deities; these gross profanations excited the indignation of the above-
named officers, who belonged to the emperor's guard, and while they
were at an entertainment they, among other things, let fall these words
of the three children: "thou hast delivered us into the hands of the
"most hateful forsakers of God; and to an unjust king, and the most
"wicked of all the world." This opinion of his officers seems to have
been quite at variance with Julian's opinion of himself, and Mr. Gibbon's opinion of him too. Well the sentiments of Maxentius and Juventius were carried to Julian, who ordered them before him and questioned them on the subject, when they gave him this answer:—"We
"have been so happy, sir, as to be educated in the true religion; we
"have been used with pleasure to pay an entire obedience to those ex-
"cellent laws and constitutions which your predecessors, Constantine
"and his sons established; and therefore with so much the more sor-
"row and anguish of mind, we behold your majesty dispensing diaboli-
"cal admonitions everywhere, and scattering them even upon our
"victuals and drink." This was enough for Mr. Gibbon's immaculate
detester of despotism, and as he governed for the happiness of the people, he ordered the two officers to suffer the most cruel deaths.

Gibbon would fain persuade us that the testimonies of St. Gregory
Nazianzen "and the legends of more ancient saints," should be *silently*
passed over as "calumnies:" this we are not surprised at, since their relations give a very different colour to the character of our historian's
favourite emperor. St. Gregory is said to have predicted the evils
the empire would suffer under his reign, and Socrates describes his
death as attended with far different circumstances than those detailed
by Gibbon on the authority of Ammianus. The latter allows that Julian had a foreknowledge of his death through the mystery of *divination;* Fox says he was told the fatality of his end by St. Basil, who was
martyred by him. Socrates states that when the apostate tyrant was
wounded, he fell into a rage, and casting some of his blood towards
heaven, exclaimed "O Gallilean, thou hast conquered." This statement
is corroborated by Theodoret and Sozomen, writers of the most unblemished reputation and nearly cotemporary with the event. Much more
might be said on the flippancy and inconsistency of this popular historian, but enough has been given to shew why he thought it best that
"the legends of the more ancient saints should be *silently* despised."
The fact is, that while he was charging the clergy of Jerusalem of the

A REVIEW

OF

Fox's Book of Martyrs,

CRITICAL AND HISTORICAL.

No. 11.   Printed and Published by W. E. ANDREWS, 3, Chapter-house-court, St. Paul's Churchyard, London.   **Price 3d.**

Christ is God

EXPLANATION OF THE ENGRAVING.—This cut represents Hunnericus, the Vandal Arian king, ordering the tongue of the deacon Reparatus to be cut out, for maintaining the divinity of our Saviour, and the young deacon, after suffering the loss of his tongue, miraculously proclaiming with an audible voice, that "Christ is God."—See page 174 of this sheet.

CONTINUATION OF THE REVIEW.

fourth century with practising the pious art of delusion, he himself was writing under the base influence of pelf, well knowing that the people of England, in his days, were like the Jews in the days of Isaiah, and would pay him better for writing smooth things, that is for telling them lies, than they would for telling the truth.

We must be allowed to make one more observation before we dismiss Mr. Gibbon.—Julian, it will be seen, declined naming his successor, and the choice of the army fell upon Jovian, who happened to be a soldier and a man of talent, as well as a Christian. This circumstance is lamented by the historian in these words: "The *triumph of* "*Christianity*, and the *calamities of the empire*, may, in some measure, " be ascribed to Julian himself, who had neglected to *secure the future* " *execution of his designs*, by the timely and judicious nomination of an " associate and successor."—So, then, the "*triumph* of Christianity" is a matter of *regret* with this writer, and the stopping of persecution a calamity to the empire! What an outrage to humanity! And yet this man's work is to be found in the libraries of most Protestants who can afford to purchase it. Need we wonder that infidelity is spreading so rapidly among the higher classes of this country? That the "future " designs of Julian" were the extirpation of Christianity cannot be doubted; but He who supports it by the might of his power, laughed the blasphemer to scorn, and shewed that the designs of an apostate were as impotent as the malice of the heathen. That the divine Justice was more immediately concerned in the circumstance of Julian's death, may fairly be inferred from the series of public calamities and judgments that befel the empire on the occasion, such as terrible earthquakes, a season of excessive heat and drought, with the necessary consequence, famine and pestilence. So the ancient historians testify.

The fourth section of this second book is headed, " *Persecutions of the Christians by the Goths, &c.*"—Fox informs his readers, that, "during " the reign of Constantine the great, several Scythian Goths embraced " Christianity, the light of the gospel having spread considerably in " Scythia, though the two kings of that country, and the majority of " the people continued Pagans." Hence then it is manifest, that there was something more than human in the system of Christianity, or how could the truths of the gospel overcome the force and stratagems of the world, and effect such extraordinary changes in the character of those who embraced this system ?—The martyrologist then goes on: " Fritigern, king of the Western Goths, was an ally of the Romans; " but Athanaric, king of the Eastern Goths, was at war with them. The " Christians, in the dominions of the former, lived unmolested; but " the latter having been defeated by the Romans, wreaked his ven- " geance on his Christian subjects. Sabas, a Christian, was the *first* who " felt the enraged king's resentment. Sabas was humble and modest, " yet fervent and zealous for the advancement of the church. Indeed " the sanctity of his life, and the purity of his manners, gave the " greatest force to his doctrines. In the year 370, Athanaric gave " orders, that all persons in his dominions should sacrifice to the Pagan " deities, and eat the meat which had been offered to the idols, or be " put to death for disobedience. Some humane Pagans, who had " Christian relations, endeavoured to save them by offering them meat " which had not received the idolatrous consecration, while the magi- " strates were made to believe that all had been done according to their " direction. But Sabas too well knew St. Paul's principles to imagine, " that the sin lay in eating; he knew that giving the enemies of the " faith an advantage over the weak was all that made that action cri- " minal in Christians. He therefore not only refused to comply with " what was proposed to him, but publicly declared, that those who " sheltered themselves under that artifice, were not true Christians." Fox goes on with a few other minor circumstances of this saint's martyrdom, and says, that he suffered by drowning on the 12th of April, A. D. 372.

Before we enter on a criticism of this account, it will not be uninteresting to the reader to give a brief detail of these Gothic kingdoms, and shew how the light of Catholicism was first spread among them. The Goths were a barbarous people inhabiting the province of Gothland in Sweden, from whence they passed into Pomerania, according

to Tacitus, and thence extended themselves along the Danube and
into Thrace and Greece.   By their furious incursions into the Roman
empire, they proved themselves troublesome neighbours, and finally
overthrew the Western part of it, erecting on its ruins the kingdom of
the Ostrogoths, or Eastern Goths, in Italy, and of the Visigoths or
Western Goths, in the northern parts of France and Spain.—These
people began to receive the light of the Catholic faith about the reign
of Valerian, who wore the purple from 260 to 268, from certain priests
whom they had made captives and carried away, in their inroads, from
Galatia and Cappadocia.   These pious ecclesiastics, by healing their
sick, and preaching the gospel, converted several among them, according to Sozomen and Philostorgius.   In the great council of Nice, the
subscription of Theophilus, bishop of Gothia, is to be found; and consequently he was a Catholic bishop, as were the converted Goths at that
time.   In the year 374, St. Basil, a father of the Catholic church, commended the faith of the Goths; but Ulphilas, the successor to Theophilus, being sent on some occasion to Constantinople in 376, he was
gained over by the Arian heretics, and on his return perverted the faith
of his countrymen.   Athanaric, king of the Thervingian Goths who
bordered on the empire, raised, as Fox says, a bloody persecution against
the Christians in 370.   Fritigernes, the king of the Western Goths,
was at war with Athanaric, and being in danger from the superiority of
his adversary, he sought the alliance of the emperor Valens, and, in
order to induce the latter to succour him, he embraced Christianity
and the Arian heresy at the same time, the emperor himself being an
Arian.   Thus was Arianism introduced among the Goths from worldly
interest, while the Catholic faith obtained its footing by the sublimity
and purity of its heavenly principles.—The reader will here observe,
that as the persecution noticed by Fox commenced in 370, and as
Arianism was not introduced till six years after, the martyrs suffering
under it were all Catholics, of which fact we shall soon offer a convincing proof.

It is now time to examine Fox's account of St. Sabas.—He says, that
this martyr "was the *first* who felt the enraged king's resentment;"
and yet it appears, by his own statement, that the persecution raged
two years before Sabas suffered!   Now are we to suppose that there
was not a Christian martyred during two long years of persecution, and
that persecution too represented to be a bloody one?   Besides, Fox
says, "Sabas was soon after apprehended and carried before a magis-
"trate, who inquired into his fortune and circumstances, when finding
"that he was a person of obscure station, he was *dismissed as unworthy*
"*of notice.*"   Now how are we to reconcile these contradictory statements?   In one place the martyr is made the *first* to feel the *king's ven-*
geance; and immediately after he is dismissed by *a magistrate* as *un-*
worthy of notice.   We point out this discrepancy in the martyrologist's
language, to shew the little reliance that can be placed in his accounts,
and the almost total disregard to truth that appears throughout his
work.   From the authentic acts of this martyr's life, which may be
found in the Rev. Alban Butler's *Saints' Lives*, the Greeks commemorate fifty-one martyrs who suffered, the two most illustrious of which
were SS. Nicetas and Sabas.   In the account of the former saint's

death, Mr. Butler states that the usual method of the persecutors was to burn the Christians with the children in their houses, or in the churches where they were assembled together: sometimes, he says, they were stabbed at the foot of the altar; consequently there were many, very many, that suffered during these two years, and therefore St. Sabas could not be the first, as John Fox asserts and afterwards contradicts.—The records of this martyr's death are contained in a letter from the church of Gothia to that of Cappadocia, which concludes thus: "Wherefore offering up the *holy sacrifice* on the day whereon " the martyr was crowned, impart this to our brethren, that the Lord " may be praised throughout the Catholic and Apostolic church for " thus glorifying his servants." Here then we have a convincing testimony that this martyr and the church to which he belonged were Catholic; for the holy sacrifice mentioned is the *mass*, which Protestants swear is *idolatrous;* and it was offered in honour of the saint's glorious martyrdom, which Protestants say is idolatry also. This fact is further stated to be imparted, that it may become publicly known throughout the Catholic and Apostolic church, which clearly shews that this doctrine, rejected by Protestants, was the doctrine of the primitive Christians and martyrs, derived from the apostles. This doctrine is still that of the Catholics throughout the world, and therefore the Catholics, and the Catholics only, can lay claim to the faith once, and for all, delivered to the saints.

Previous to quitting this account of Fox, we will take leave to draw the notice of the reader to the snares which he says the Gothic persecutors laid to entrap the Christians. Our martyrologist speaks indignantly of these artifices, but he forgets that the same or similar practices were put in force by the first evangelical reformers to Protestantism, and are now in full use by the disciples of "Protestant-ascendency." In Elizabeth's reign, an act was passed to *compel* all persons to attend to her *new* form of worship, under corporal pains and penalties, and many Catholics, through weakness, made occasional conformity to secure their liberty and property. This act of hypocrisy was condemned by the Catholic church in Elizabeth's days as it was by St. Sabas, who is applauded for so doing by Fox; and Catholics in these days, by refusing to take the impious test oaths, by which they are deprived of the exercise of their civil rights, act on the same principle laid down by St. Paul, and which caused St. Sabas to declare himself *openly* a Christian. But what difference is there, we ask, between the conduct of these Gothic persecutors of the Christians, in commanding the latter to eat forbidden meats, to save their lives, and the conduct of "Protestant-ascendency," in forcing Catholic children into schools where a forbidden book is used to proselyte them, to obtain a false education, or remain ignorant of letters? For our part we can see no difference, except that the Goths put the Christians to death in case of refusal, and "Protestant-ascendency" contents itself with keeping the Catholics in ignorance, and then taunt them with being so!!! The one sends the Christians to heaven by a temporary suffering, the other keeps the Catholics on earth in continual slavery, and revile them for persisting in their religious belief.

Catholics know that the sin does not lay in *reading* the book, any more than the mere *eating* of the forbidden meats was condemned by Sabas; the crime consists in "giving the enemies of the faith an ad- "vantage over the weak," and thereby hazarding their salvation by falling into the snares of error. The basis of Protestantism is the spirit of self-interpretation, which leads to endless contradictions and diver- sity of creeds. The basis of Catholicism is submission to divine *autho- rity*, by which Truth and Unity are preserved in the church, though that church is spread through the whole world, and embraces all nations. Were then the Catholics to conform to this rule of reading the scripture without note or comment, they would act in contradiction to the prin- ciples of their church, and become hypocrites, like the Christians in the persecution of the Goths, who appeared to conform to the decrees of the king by eating meats, which though not actually profaned by heathen sacrifices, were nevertheless supposed to be so by their persecutors, and thus they belied their faith though they did not partake of the polluted offerings. The fact is, the Catholic church has invariably condemned the immoral doctrine of equivocation and mental reservation, and as constantly inculcated that simplicity and godly sincerity are truly Chris- tian virtues, necessary to the conservation of justice, truth, and the se- curity of the rights of society. We do not attempt to deny that many of her members, both kings and ministers, and prelates and magistrates, and people, have been guilty of duplicity, as we see in the case of this persecution of Athanaric; but the church, as a body, is not to be blamed for the defalcation of individual members, any more than the principles of the British constitution are to be condemned, because some bad men may and do violate them. Now if Sabas was right in publicly declar- ing "that those who sheltered themselves under that artifice were not "*true* Christians;" must not the Catholic clergy be right also, and de- serving of the same praise as Fox bestows upon St. Sabas, in declaring, that those who shelter themselves under the artifices of Bible-school promoters to obtain education, are not *true* Catholics? We are sure the unprejudiced reader will decide in the affirmative.

The next article is the "*opposition of Eusebius to the Arian heresy*." Fox tells us, that "Eusebius, bishop of Samosata, made a distinguish- "ed figure in ecclesiastical history, and was one of the most eminent "champions of Christ against the Arian heresy;" and he gives a pretty fair account of the dispute between him and the emperor Constantius, concerning the deposition of Meletius, patriarch of Antioch, who was also a stout opposer of this impious heresy, and a firm defender of the faith of the Nicene council. But the most important statement made by Fox, and to which we call the particular attention of the Protestant reader, is this: "About this time," he writes, "the see of Cæsarea "having become vacant, Eusebius was instrumental in promoting Ba- "sil to it, on which occasion Gregory the younger calls him, The PILLAR "of TRUTH, the light of the world, the FORTRESS of the CHURCH, the "RULE of FAITH, the support of the faithful, and an instrument in the "hands of God for bestowing favours on his people." Thus then it is admitted by Fox, and, of course by his modern editors, "the few plain Christians," that "about this time," namely, the middle of the fourth century, there was a pillar of truth, a rule of faith, and a church of God, of which church the fathers and bishops were the fortresses un-

der whose fire, or by whose writings and preachings, the faithful found
support against the wiles of heresy and the attacks of heretics. But
why, we ask, as we did in the case of St. Ignatius, *(see our Review,*
p. 39) of St. Polycarp *(Ibid.* 45*),* St. Justin the martyr (p. 47), St. Irenæus
(p. 66.), and Tertullian (p. 83.); WHY, did not John Fox inform his
readers WHAT DOCTRINES this pillar of truth, Eusebius, and his
fellow-prelates Basil and Gregory the younger, taught? Why did he
leave them in a state of darkness as to the sum and substance of their
belief, contenting himself with the bare statement that Eusebius " was
" one of the most eminent champions of Christ against the Arian here-
" sy," and that " Gregory the younger calls him, the pillar of truth,"
&c.? Such a statement conveys no light to the reader, who may form
to himself any thing or nothing. And this, as we have before observed,
was the intention of John Fox, as it is also that of his modern editors.
Neither of them desire that the *truth* should be told; but as we have
pledged ourself that our intention is *to give the truth, the whole truth, and
nothing but the truth,* we will here fill up the chasm made by John Fox,
in his account of the persecution of the Christians by the Arians.

Eusebius was, as Fox records, an eminent champion of Christ against
the Arians, and spent the greater part of his episcopal life in travelling
through Syria, Phœnicia, and Palestine, to strengthen the Catholics in
their faith by his preachings, until he fell a victim to Arian malice, at
Dolicha, a small city forty-one miles from Samosata, in 380. His death
was occasioned by a tile thrown from the top of a house by an Arian
woman, as he was passing in the street. It does not appear that he
left any writings behind him, but the two prelates named with him as
his associates, have left us their sentiments in writing, which have been
preserved to this day. St. Basil, we are rightly told by Fox, was
promoted to the archiepiscopal see of Cæsarea, by the aid of Eusebius,
and he was praised for this act by " Gregory the younger," that is St.
Gregory Nazianzum, who was bishop of Constantinople, which see he
afterwards vacated, and retired to Nazianzum, near which city he was
born, and from which he took the name, to distinguish himself from
a younger brother called Gregory of Cesarius. It is allowed by Fox
that these great lights of the church opposed the heresy of the Arians,
which was a denial of the divinity of Jesus Christ. St. Gregory, in
his orations, and St. Basil in his book against Eunomius, maintains the
divine essence of the Son of God, as did all the fathers that preceded
them. They also maintained all the doctrines now held by Catholics
and condemned by Protestants as idolatrous and superstitious, as will
be seen by the following quotations, which, on comparison with those
referred to above, will be found to be perfectly uniform and consistent; a convincing proof that the never-failing promises of Christ,
that the Spirit of Truth should abide with his church, and teach her
all truth to the end of the world, was given to the Catholic church,
and to that church alone.

We will begin with St. Basil, as he died in 379, ten years before St.
Gregory Nazianzum. On the Authority and Marks of the Church, St.
Basil writes: "The order and government of the church, is it not ma-
" nifestly, and beyond contradiction, the work of the Holy Ghost?
" *For he gave to his church* (1 Cor. xii. 28.) *first apostles; secondly pro-*

"*phets; thirdly teachers, &c.*" *L. de Spiritu. S. c.* 16. *t.* iii. *p.* 34. *Edit.*
PP. S. Mauri, Paris. 1721, 1722, 1730.—"We indeed ourselves are of
" little value; but, by the grace of God, we remain ever the same,
" unaffected by the common changes of things. Our belief is not one
" at Seleucia, and another at Constantinople; one at Lampsacus, and
" another at Rome; and so different from what it was in former times,
" but always one and the same." *Ep.* 251. *ad. Evæsinos. t.* iii. *p.* 386. *Edit.*
Bened. Parisiis, 1721.—" As many as hope in Christ, are one people,
" and they, who are of Christ, form one church, though it be named
" in many places." *Ep.* 161. *ad Amphil. t.* iii. *p.* 252.—" It is more just
" to judge of our concerns, not from this or that man, who walk not
" in truth; but from the number of bishops, who, in all regions, are
" united to us. Let the cities of Asia, the sound part of Egypt and of
" Syria, be interrogated. These by letter communicate with us, and
" we with them. From these you may learn, that we are all unani-
" mous; all think the same thing. Wherefore, he, who declines our
" communion, may be considered by you, as separated from the uni-
" versal church. It is better we should lose our lives, and that the
" churches should remain unanimous, than that, on account of our
" childish feuds, the faithful should be so much injured." *Ep.* 204.
ad Neocæs. t. iii. *p.* 307.——St. Gregory Nazianzum says, " *To one, in-*
" *deed, is given the sword of wisdom; to another the sword of knowledge,*
" 1 Cor. xii. 8. My brethren, let us respect, and guard, and main-
" tain this order. Let some hear, others speak, and others act."
Orat. xxvi. *t.* l. *p.* 450. *Edit. Coloniæ,* 1690.

On the Succession of the Pastors of the Church, from the apostles,
St. Basil writes,—" If we depart from the life-living root, the faith in
" Christ; like withered branches, we are cast out and committed to
" the flames. For if we do not rest on the foundation of the apostles,
" being unsupported, we are lost." *Com. in Esaiam. t.* 1. *p.* 391.——On
the name of Catholic, St. Gregory signs himself in the document called his *Will*, " Gregory, bishop of the *Catholic* church of Constantino-
" ple."

On the disputed point of *Private Interpretation*, now so warmly and
pertinaciously contested by Protestants, St. Basil thus addresses a
heretic:—" What is it you say? Shall we not allow more to antiquity?
" Does not the multitude of Christians claim respect, who now are,
" as well as those who went before us? These abounded in every grace,
" and must we disregard them against whom you have lately brought
" out your impious discoveries? Must we shut our eyes, and, sup-
" pressing all recollection of every holy man, submit our understand-
" ings to your deceits, and idle sophistries? Truly, your influence
" must be great, if, what the devil could not effect by his wiles, we
" should concede to your dictations; that is, persuaded by you,
" we should prefer your inventions to that tradition of belief, which,
" in all former times, prevailed under the direction of so many holy
" men." *L.* 1. *Adv. Eunom. t.* 1. *p.* 210.——St. Gregory Nazianzum says,
" *To one indeed, is given the word of wisdom: to another the word of*
" *knowledge*; (1 Cor. xii. 8.) My brethren, let us respect, and guard,
" and maintain this order. Let some hear, others speak, and others
" act. We must not all exercise the office of the tongue, which is

" the most prompt and ready member; for all are not apostles; nor
" prophets, nor expounders. To teach is great and eminent; but to
" learn is void of danger. · You that are a sheep, why do you arrogate
" the function of the shepherd ? . Being the foot, why will you be the
" head?   Why do you pursue the great, but uncertain and perilous,
" gains of the ocean; when you may till the earth in safety?" *Orat.*
xxvi. *t.* 1. *p.* 450. " Truly, there should have been a law among us,
" whereby—as among the Jews young men were not allowed to read
" certain books of scripture—not all men, and at all times, but
" certain persons only, and on certain occasions should be permitted
" to discuss the points of faith." *Ibid.* p. 462. " If these heretics
" may freely teach and promulgate their opinions, who does not see
" that the doctrine of the church will be condemned, as if truth were on
" their side?   But two opposite doctrines, on the same point, can-
" not possibly be true." *Orat.* xlvi. *p.* 722.——Rufinus, a priest of Aquileia, who flourished from the years·372 to about 410, relates of these
two saints, that " during the thirteen years they spent at Athens, lay-
" ing aside all profane words, they applied solely to the sacred writ-
" ings, explaining them, not from their own presumption, but by the
" authority of those ancient fathers, who, it was plain, had received
" the rule of interpretation, from apostolical succession." *Hist. Eccles.*
l. 11. *c.* 9. *p.* 256.   *Edit. Basil.* 1562.

On apostolical Tradition,* which Protestants reject, St. Basil writes,

* In our first number, p. 4, we spoke of the utter impossibility that *error* should be introduced into the doctrines of the church of Christ without detection from some one, and
we gave two instances, from the writings of Sozomen and the works of St. Augustin, as
proofs of the care observed by the guardians of faith in the Catholic church, lest a *word*
should be improperly applied in defining her doctrines. (*Ibid.*) We have now the opportunity of furnishing a third instance in our own case, and as we lay no claim to infallibility, and have no other desire than that of stating to our readers the truth, and nothing
but the truth, we feel more pleasure than reluctance in acknowledging a mistake we have
inadvertently committed. In giving the sentiments of St. Irenæus on the doctrine of
TRADITION, p. 70, we observed, that this " is neither *more* nor *less* than PUBLIC OPI-
" NION, received and delivered down from age to age." This observation has drawn
from a very learned and most excellent divine the following remarks. " What! Tradition,
" which is the *word of God*, unwritten indeed, but delivered by Christ to his apostles; the
" unerring word of God, revealed by God to man—Tradition, which has been made known
" to us and decided upon by the inspired councils, assisted by the Holy Ghost, the pro-
" mised Paraclete—Tradition, which conveys to us the truths of Heaven with certainty
" equal to the inspired writings, and which, in fact, gives authenticity, meaning and ef-
" fect to the sacred books themselves—Tradition is here said to be no *more* (say nothing
" of less), no more than the *opinion* of Men ! Opinion ! nothing more than opinion ! of
" which some one says ' opinion varies, because it is opinion ; but faith is ever unchange-
" able, because it is *faith* and cometh from God.' Faith, and what is divinely taught, is the
" object of tradition, and therefore is not matter of opinion, which may change according
" to circumstances ; and therefore the *voice of Tradition* is not to be worked on by human
" efforts such as you have recommended; it is the *voice of God* and not of man ; the express
" testimony of the God of truth, and not the mere opinion of men. By calling it *public*
" opinion you do not clear up the difficulty, for as long at it is *opinion*, it is subject to er-
" ror. You talk of appealing to *opinion*, but it is *Tradition* that is to govern and direct
" opinion and belief. I have said enough I think to make you see the immense difference
" between this *opinion*, which is the result of human reasoning, and *Tradition*, which is re-
" vealed Truth, the *unwritten* word ; and I might say that this is no more *opinion*, or de-
" pendent upon opinion, than is the *written* word of God in the scriptures the result of hu-
" man study, or to be explained by human opinion, wit, or fancy." We thank our inestimable friend for his clear and luminous definition of this doctrine, in which we perfectly
agree with him. In making our objectionable statement, we did not allude to the *doctrines*
and *ceremonies* taught and practised by the apostles and their successors, we only intended,
by the expression, to convey to the Protestant reader, that when any *new* or *novel* doctrine was attempted to be foisted on the people, by pretenders to inspiration, that Catho-

" Among the points of belief and practice in the church, some were deli-
" vered in writing, while others were received by apostolical tradition in
" mystery, that is, in a hidden manner; but both have equal authority, nor
" are they opposed by any one, who is but slightly versed in ecclesias-
" tical rites. For if we attempt to reject, as matters of little moment, such
" points as were not written, we shall, by our imprudence, offer a signal
" injury to the gospel, confining the whole preaching of faith to a mere
" name." He then alludes to many practices in use among the Eas-
" tern churches at that day, and inquires in what part of scripture they
" are to be found. "But," he observes, "by TRADITION they
" would be brought down to us; and the day would not suffice me,
" were I to enumerate all those points which have been *thus* delivered."
De Spir. Sancto, c. 37. *t.* iii. *p.* 54. " If nothing else that is unwritten
" be received, then this may not. But if the greater part of our sa-
" cred rites is unwritten, together with many others, let us receive
" this. In my opinion, it is apostolical to adhere to unwritten tradi-
" tions." *Ibid. c.* 29, *p.* 60. " Separate not the Holy Spirit from the
" Father and the Son; let tradition deter you. For so the Lord taught,
" the apostles preached, the fathers maintained, the martyrs confirm-
" ed. Be satisfied to speak, as, you were instructed." *Serm,* vi. *adv.*
Sabel. t. ii. *p.* 194. " Some turn to Judaism on account of the (ap-
" parent) confusion of the divine persons, and others to Paganism from
" other motives: so that neither the divinely inspired scripture has any
" effect on them; nor can the apostolical traditions compose their dif-
" ferences." *De Spirit. Sanct. c.* xxx. *t.* iii. *p.* 66. " Let us now con-
" sider, what are our notions concerning the Divine Spirit, as well
" those which we have drawn from the scriptures, as what we
" have received from the unwritten tradition of the fathers." *Ibid.*
c. ix. *p.* 19. " It is the common aim of all the enemies of sound
" doctrine, to shake the solidity of our faith in Christ, by annulling
" apostolical tradition." He adds: " They dismiss the unwritten
" testimony of the fathers as a thing of no value." *Ibid. c.* x. *p.* 21.
From these latter extracts we may learn the sentiments of this great
defender of the true faith on the mystery of the holy Trinity.——St.
Gregory Nazianzum says, on the doctrine of Tradition, "I wish,
" to the last breath of life, that deposit should be confessed of those
" holy fathers, who lived nearest to Christ, and to the origin of our
" faith, and that profession maintained, which we imbibed with our
" milk, which we uttered with our first speech." *Orat.* vi. *t.* 1. *p.* 141.
" My sheep hear my voice, that voice which was instructed by the sacred
" oracles, and the writings of the holy fathers. What I have learnt
" from them, I shall always teach, not varying in a single point as the
" times may vary. In that profession I was born; in that I will die."
Orat. xxv. *p.* 440.
On the Supremacy of St. Peter and his successors in the see of Rome,

lics did not ground their faith on the word of this or that man, but on the universal tradition or testimony of the Church, from the time of the apostles to the present moment.
Opinion, we are now convinced, is too vague and incorrect a term, and therefore we have
no hesitation in renouncing it. We cannot however, quit the subject without calling the
attention of the Protestant reader to the strong hold which Catholics are thus demonstrated
to have of the inerrability of their faith.

St. Basil writes,—" Peter, from being a fisherman, was called to the
" apostleship; and from the eminence of his faith, received on him-
" self the building of the church." *Adv. Eunom. l.* 11. *t.* 1. *p.* 240.
St. Gregory Nazianzum says,—" You see, how Peter, among the disci-
" ples of Christ, all great and all worthy of choice, is called a rock,
" and receives on the profession of his faith the foundations of the
" church; while John is particularly beloved, and rests on the breast
" of Christ; and the other disciples bear this preference without re-
" pining.", *Orat.* xxvi. *t.* 1. *p.* 453.   In his seventh oration he stiles
Peter, " the pillar of the church." *Ibid. p.* 142.

On the doctrine of the Real Presence of Christ in the holy Eucharist,
or Lord's Supper, which Protestants deny, and those of the church of
England as by law established, make the denial of it on oath a qualification for civil and ecclesiastical office, St. Basil writes,—" About the
" things, that God has spoken, there should be no hesitation, nor
" doubt, but a firm persuasion, that all is true and possible, though
" nature be against it.   Herein lies the struggle of faith.   *The Jews*
" *therefore strove among themselves, saying: How can this man give us his*
" *flesh to eat?   Then Jesus said to them: Amen, amen I say unto you:*
" *except you eat the flesh of the Son of man, and drink his blood, you shall*
" *not have life in you.*" (Jo. vi. 53, 54.)   *Regula* vii. *Moral. t.* ii. *p.* 240.
" With what fear, with what conviction, with what affection of mind,
" should we partake of the body and blood of Christ?   The apostle
" teaches us to fear, when he says: *He that eateth and drinketh unwor-*
" *thily, eateth and drinketh judgment to himself* (1 Cor. xi. 29.); while
" the words of the Lord: *This is my body, which shall be delivered for*
" *you* (ibid. 24), create a firm conviction." *Ibid. in Reg. brev. quæst.*
clxxii. *p.* 472.   " The Christian must be without spot or stain—and
" thus prepared to eat the body of Christ, and drink his blood." *Ibid.*
in Moral. reg. lxxx. 22. *p.* 318.——St. Gregory Nazianzum says, speaking of his sister, who laboured under a grievous disorder, " Despair-
" ing of all other help, she has recourse to the universal physician—
" she falls down in faith before the altar, and calls upon him who is
" there adored." *Orat.* 11. *t.* 1. *p.* 186.   " Without doubting, eat the
" body and drink the blood, if thou desirest to live." *Ibid. Orat.* xlii.
p. 690.

On the sacrifice of the Mass, which Luther abolished in his system
of pretended reform, at the instigation of the devil, if we may believe
his own words, and Protestants of the church of England as by law
established swear to be idolatrous, St. Gregory Nazianzum writes,
" And where, and by whom could God be worshipped in those mystic
" and elevating sacred rites, than which nothing among us is greater
" nor more excellent, if there were no priesthood, or sacrifice?
" Knowing this, and knowing besides that no one was worthy of this
" great God, this sacrifice, and this priesthood, who had not first of-
" fered himself a victim to the Lord—how should I dare to offer to
" him that external sacrifice, that antitype of great mysteries, or to
" take up the name and habit of a priest?"   *Orat.* 1. *t.* 1. *p.* 3, 38.
" Julian, in impure and wicked blood, washes away his baptismal rite,
" opposing initiation to initiation—he defiles his hands, in order to pu-
" rify them from that unbloody sacrifice, through which we commu-

" nicate with Christ, with his divine nature, and his sufferings." *Orat.*
iii. in Julian. t. 1. *p.* 70.

On the doctrine of Confession, rejected and reviled by Protestants,
but now practised by Catholics, St. Basil writes, " In the confession of
" sins, the same method must be observed, as in laying open the in-
" firmities of the body. For as these are not rashly communicated to
" every one, but to those only who understand by what method they
" may be cured; so the confession of sins must be made to such per-
" sons as know how to apply a remedy." *In Quæst. Brev. Reg.* 229.
t. ii. *p.* 492. He afterwards states who those persons are: " Necessarily,
" our sins must be confessed to those, to whom has been committed
" the dispensation of the mysteries of God." *Ibid. Reg.* 288. *p.* 516.
St. Gregory Nazianzum says, alluding to the works of penance then
appointed by the church to be performed, and the danger lest the sinner be surprised by death before they are completed,—" But, perhaps,
" supplicantly thou wilt pray to the Lord, that he will yet spare the
" vine, and not cut it down, accused as it is of sterility, but permit thee
" to manure round it: that is, to employ tears, and groans, and prayers,
" and watchings, and the maceration of soul and body, and in fine that
" correction which consists in the confession of sins, and the lowly
" humiliation of life." *Orat.* xl. *t.* 1. *p.* 642. "Think it not hard to
" confess thy sin, reflecting on the baptism of John, in order that, by
" present shame, thou mayest escape the shame of the next life. Thus
" will it be made manifest, that thou really hatest sin, having deemed
" it deserving of contumely, and having triumphed over it." *Ibid. p.*
657.

On the doctrine of Purgatory, so much contemned and derided by
Protestants, but steadily maintained by Catholics, St. Basil writes,
" The words of Isaiah, *Through the wrath of the Lord is the land burn-*
" *ed,* (ix. 19,) declare, that things that are earthly shall be made the
" food of a punishing fire; to the end that the soul may receive favour
" and be benefitted. *And the people shall be as the fuel of the fire* (Ibid.):
" This is not a threat of extermination; but it denotes expurgation,
" according to the expression of the apostle: *If any man's works burn,*
" *he shall suffer loss; but he himself shall be saved, yet so as by fire.* (1
" Cor. iii. 15.)" *Com. in c.* ix. Isai. *t.* 1. *p.* 554. "*And the light of Israel*
" *shall be for a fire.* (Isai. x. 17.) The operative powers of fire are
" chiefly two; it enlightens, and it burns. The first is cheerful and
" pleasant; the second bitter and afflicting. The prophet adds: *And*
" *he shall sanctify him in a holy fire, and consume the glory of his forest as*
" *grass.* He here shews the nature of fire. It enlightens and purifies.
" But how does this fire purify, if it consumes? Truly, since our God
" is called a *consuming fire,* he will consume the wood, and what vices
" arise from matter, which adhere to the soul, in the flesh, not in the
" spirit. And when the fire shall have consumed all the wood of sin,
" as it does grass, then that matter being destroyed which was fuel to
" the chastising fire, the prophet says: *The burnt mountains shall repose,*
" *and the hills, and the thick forests, and the consuming fire shall cease,*
" *that feed upon them.*" Ibid. *p.* 563.

On Religious Ceremonies, and particularly on making the sign of
the cross, whereby Catholics attest their belief in the blessed Trinity,

and the Incarnation and Death of our Saviour, St. Basil writes,—" If we
" attempt to reject those practices, as things of little moment, which
" rest on no written authority, we shall, by our imprudence, materi-
" ally injure the gospel itself; even we shall reduce the very preach-
" ing of our faith to a mere name. Such (to mention that in the first
" place which is most common) is the practice of making the sign of
" the cross, by those who put their hope in Christ. In what writing
" has this been taught?" *Lib. de Spiritu. S. c.* xxvii. *t.* iii. *p.* 54.

On the doctrine of Fasting, and more particularly on the fast
of Lent, which Catholics observe at this day, as a primitive institution
of their church, derived by tradition from the apostles, and Protestants
deride as superstitious, St. Basil writes, " To them, who willingly un-
" dertake it, fasting is at all times, profitable—but chiefly now, when
" a solemn fast is everywhere published. There is no island, no con-
" tinent, no city, no nation, no corner of the earth, where it is not
" heard. Let no one then exclude himself from the number of fasters;
" in which number every age, all ranks take their place." *Homil.* ii. *de
Jajun. t.* ii. *p.* 11.

On the honour and respect due to the Relics of Saints, which Catholics now practise and Protestants declare to be superstitious and idolatrous, St. Basil writes, "Affection to our departed brethren is refer-
" red to the Lord, whom they served; and he who honours them that
" died for the faith, shews that he is inspired by the same ardour; so
" that one and the same action is a proof of many virtues." *Ad.
Ambros. Mediol. Ep.* cxcvii. *t.* iii. *p.* 287. " If any one suffer for the
" name of Christ, his remains are deemed precious. And if any one
" touch the bones of a martyr, he becomes partaker, in some degree,
" of his holiness, on account of the grace residing in them. *Where-
" fore, precious in the sight of God is the death of his saints.*" *Serm. in hæc
verba Psal.* cxv. *t.* i. *p.* 375. " I am greatly pleased, that you have
" raised an edifice to the name of Christ. And I am desirous, should
" I be able to procure some relics of martyrs, to join you in your soli-
" citude and labour." *Ep.* ccccviii. *Arcadio. Episc. t.* iii. *p.* 142.

So on the invocation of Angels and Saints, the rejection of which on
oath is made a qualification to office in this country, St. Basil and St.
Gregory are very explicit. The former, in celebrating the feast of the
forty martyrs of Sebaste, in the Lesser Armenia, who suffered under
the emperor Licinius, in 320, and whose memory is commemorated to
this day by the Catholic church on the 10th of March, thus addresses
his hearers, " These are they, who, having taken possession of our
" country, stand as towers against the incursions of the enemy. Here
" is a ready aid to Christians. Often have you endeavoured, often have
" you toiled, to gain one intercessor. You have now forty, all emit-
" ting one common prayer. Who is oppressed by care, flies to their
" aid, as does he that prospers: the first to seek deliverance; the se-
" cond that his good fortune may continue. The pious mother is found
" praying for her children; and the wife for the return and the health
" of her husband. O ye guardians of the human race! O ye power-
" ful messengers before God! let us join our prayers with yours."
Homil. xx *in.* xl. *Martyr. t.* ii. *p.* 155, 156. The latter, in his funeral
oration on this very saint Basil, his particular friend, says, " and now

" he, indeed, is in heaven; there, if I mistake not, offering up sacrifices
" for us, pouring out prayers for the people: for he has not left us so,
" as to have deserted us. And do thou, sacred and holy spirit, look
" down, I beseech thee, on us: arrest by thy prayers that sting of the
" flesh which was given to us for our correction, or teach us how to
" bear it with fortitude: guide all our ways to that which is best: and,
" when we shall depart hence, receive us then into thy society; that
" with thee, beholding more clearly that blessed and adorable Trinity,
" which now we see in a dark manner, we may put a final close to all
" our wishes, and receive the reward of the labours which we have
borne," *Orat. xx. de Laud. S. Basil,* t. i. p. 272, 373. In the same language he addresses St. Athanasius, and adds,—" He, in a good old age,
" dying after many conflicts, now regards, I doubt not, our concerns,
" and being himself freed from the bonds of the flesh, stretches out his
" hand to us." *Orat.* xxiv. p. 425.

By these quotations from the writings of two great and eminently
gifted prelates of the primitive church, it is plain what was *then* believed by the members of that church. From a comparison too with the
extracts we have given from the fathers of the first and second century,
it will be seen that the doctrines of ALL of them were ONE AND THE
SAME. There is not the slightest deviation to be found, and these same
doctrines are still taught by the ministers of the Catholic church, and
by them *only,* at this present day. Now, if Eusebius of Samosata,
who opposed the Arian heresy, and who was instrumental in promoting
Basil, the teacher of the foregoing doctrines, to the see of Cæsarea, and
for which conduct he was called by " Gregory the *younger*" as Fox
styles him, though he happened to be the *elder* brother, " The pillar of
" truth, the light of the world," &c. was deserving of this distinguished
character, and it appears that Fox allows him to be so entitled, it necessarily follows that the aforesaid doctrines ARE ORTHODOX TRUTHS;
and then what are we to think of those who *reject* them? Ay, and not
only reject them, but absolutely *swear* that some of them are IDOLA-
TROUS and DAMNABLE!!! We must leave the modern editors of
John Fox's *Book of Martyrs* to explain this manifest piece of inconsistency and impiety.

Before we take leave of the persecutions carried on by the Arians,
we must be allowed to record a fact, which, though of the most astonishing nature, is nevertheless so clearly authenticated that none but a
sceptic can reject it. About the year 484, Hunnericus, king of the
Goths, persecuted the Catholics with the most barbarous and unrelenting fury, The tortures inflicted upon these bold confessors of the
divinity of Christ exceeded, if possible, those exercised upon the Christians by the Pagan emperors. All Africa abounded with martyrs, and
wooden horses, iron hooks, fire, flaming blades, wild beasts, and other
instruments of cruelty, were put in requisition to shake the constancy
of the Catholics. Cyrola, a notary and the false patriarch of the Arians,
having invaded the bishopric of Typasus in Mauritania, the inhabitants
of that city refused to submit to his jurisdiction, and many of them
quitted the country to avoid him. By art and persuasion, however, he
induced some of them to stay, and endeavoured by prayers and threatenings to induce them to embrace Arianism; but he found them all

steadfast, which threw him into the highest rage. The impious in-
·truder made his complaints to Hunnericus, charging the Catholics with
meeting to celebrate the holy mysteries, and sing openly the praises of
Jesus Christ, consubstantial with his Father. This representation highly
·incensed the tyrant, and he immediately sent his officers to Typasus,
with orders to cut out the tongues even to the root of all those who
would not become Arians. This bloody order was executed with more
than ordinary barbarity on persons of all distinctions, who nevertheless
continued to proclaim aloud that Jesus Christ was true God. Nor was
this the impulse of the moment, for it is recorded that these wonderful
confessors of Christ's godhead continued to speak, during the rest of
·their lives on all subjects, as before their tongues were plucked out,
with the exception of two,·who falling into the sin of incontinency,
were deprived of this grace, and became utterly dumb.

Such an illustrious miracle as this we are aware is not generally
known, even among Catholics, and is sufficient to stagger the credibility of many of our readers. Some of them will probably exclaim,
Such a tale as this might do for the dark ages, but in these *enlightened*
·days who will believe it? We do not give it as an article of faith, but
we ·state it as a recorded fact, attested by living witnesses, and therefore though wonderful and incomprehensible, yet not to be discredited
·by a rational mind, for in this case there can be no rule for giving credence to any circumstance recorded in history. We have now before
·us *Maimbourg's History of Arianism*, translated into English by Wm.
Webster, A. M. Curate of St. Dunstan's in the West, from which we
take the following extract.—Speaking of the forementioned miracle,
the author says,—"Now this is not one of those imaginary wonders, or
" fables, nor any of those deceits, or subtle illusions which your too cre-
" dulous people are apt to take for miracles. For there are so many unde-
" niable witnesses who assure it, not only upon the credit of those that
" saw it, as hath done St. Gregory the great, *(Dialog.* 1. 2, c. 32,) but upon
" having seen it themselves, and inquired into the matter with all the
·" strictness imaginable at Constantinople, where several of those saints
" had retired, that it is impossible to disown it without purposely and
" impudently belying those men whose veracity is incontestible. Vic-
·" tor of Utica, who was then on the place, wrote some time after con-
" cerning it, wherein he says, that if any one cannot easily believe it,
" he desires him to take a journey to Constantinople in order to be con-
·" firmed in it by his own eyes, because he may there see the deacon
" Reparatus, who speaks perfectly well, without his tongue,·and is for
" that reason in great honour at the court of Zeno, and particularly es-
" teemed by the empress Ariadne, *(Constitut de Offic. P. Præt. Afric. Ni-*
ceph. l. 17. c. 11.) who even pays him a kind of religious veneration.
" The emperor Justinian, who was then at court, declares that he him-
·" self saw those venerable men, who gave a plain account of their mar-
·" trydom without any tongue. Procopius, the historian, *(Lib.* 1. *de bell.*
" *Vand.* c. 8.) who was a man of undeniable honour, and who served in
" that emperor's army with great reputation, says, that in his time he saw
" several of them at Constantinople, who could talk with a great deal
" of freedom. Æneas of Gaza, a Platonic philosopher, *(Tom.* 5, *Bibl.*
P. P.) who has given us an excellent dialogue upon the immortality

" of the soul, and who flourished in those days, says, in this work which
" was written under the name of Axitheus, that being invited thither
" by the report of so wonderful a thing, he was resolved to see with
" his own eyes, and examine these miraculous men, and having caused
" them to open their mouths, he found that their tongues were cut out
" to the root, and that nevertheless they talked freely and distinctly,
" and gave him a perfect account of the whole affair. So many great
" men all agreeing in the same thing, and giving testimony of it in
" their public writings, undoubtedly would have been convicted of fal-
" sity by a prodigious number of the inhabitants of Constantinople, had
" they been so impudent as to aver publicly that they had seen a thing
" in that city which had never happened. Now after this I cannot
" well conceive that any man of common sense would say that he did
" not give credit to it."

We cannot take leave of this extraordinary supernatural event, without laying before our readers the reasoning of a living author, whose
arguments we consider completely decisive on the subject. A work
has lately been published in the united states of America, where the
greatest freedom prevails on religious matters, in defence of the divinity of Jesus Christ. The author is the Rev. A. Kohlman, superior of
the Catholic seminary of Washington city, and the work is entitled,
" *Unitarianism Philosophically and Theologically Examined, in a series of*
" *periodical numbers; comprising a Complete Refutation of the Leading*
" *Principles of the Unitarian System.*" Speaking of this astonishing miracle at Typasus in confirmation of the divinity of Christ, and arguing
very strongly in its favour, the author observes,—" It may still be ob-
" jected, that it is an undeniable fact, that church history is replete
" with false legends, and spurious miracles, and that from the impos-
" sibility of discerning true and genuine miracles from such as are false,
" it would be wise to reject them all indiscriminately. To this ob-
" jection I thus reply, and ask, will sound logic sanction this strange
" way of reasoning: there is a false and spurious coin, therefore
" there is no genuine coin: there are errors among men, therefore
" there is no truth: the testimony of the senses and the testimony
" of men, have at times deceived men, therefore they always de-
" ceive men. Philosophy frowns at such conclusions, and directs us
" to argue with an ancient keen philosopher, (Tertullian,) in a quite
" contrary way: there exists a spurious coin, therefore there exists a
" genuine one, because the spurious is but an imitation of the genuine
" one. There exists error among men, therefore there exists likewise
" truth: for error, being nothing but a mimic imitation of truth, neces-
" sarily presupposes truth. At times, our senses and men deceive us;
" therefore they always do so; if this conclusion be true, then it will be
" absolutely impossible to be sure of any thing that surrounds us, or
" that has come to pass before us, and it will be very easy for any one to
" prove to you, that Alexander and Cæsar are nothing but empty names
" of imaginary beings that never existed, and that this universe itself
" is nothing more than an empty dream. Such reasoning, therefore, is
" not philosophical. How, therefore, shall we arrive at the certain
" knowledge of both historical and physical truths? By listening to the
" immutable principles imprinted in our souls by the hand of our Creator,

"which dictate to us to keep equally aloof from opposite extremes,
"and to admit as unquestionable, no testimony, either of our senses,
"or of men, but such as is accompanied with all the characteristics of
"truth and veracity. In conformity with this principle, we shall re-
"ject, or at least look with suspicion, upon any fact that is not suffi-
"ciently attested, either by our senses, or by men; and we shall, on
"the contrary, admit as indubitable, any public, solemn, and inter-
"esting fact, that comes recommended to us by a constant and uniform
"evidence of our senses, when sound and duly applied, or of men, es-
"pecially of most unquestionable probity and veracity. A fact thus
"attested, is so absolutely certain, that we feel our mind irresistibly
"impelled to give it, in spite of us, our assent. Now, any one ac-
"quainted with church history, must acknowledge, that a considerable
"portion of the wonders which, for the space of these eighteen hun-
"dred years, occur in the annals of Christianity, are of this character,
"and are attested to the highest degree of moral certitude. They were
"sensible facts, perfectly within the reach of our senses; they were
"public facts, wrought in the midst of the most populous cities, they
"were interesting facts, as relating to the great concerns of salvation,
"than which Christians have nothing dearer in this world: they were
"facts recorded at the time they happened, and when those on whose
"persons they were wrought, were still living; they were facts attested
"by friends and enemies, when these would have had the greatest in-
"terest to deny them, if it had been in their power to do so. Of this
"description, were numbers of miracles related in the annals of the
"church; of this character was the very miraculous fact of men speaking
"without tongues, which has been quoted above. This fact, therefore,
"has been unanswerably proved, and of course, it alone, at once de-
"cides the famous controversy between Christians and Unitarians: for
"it undeniably proves, that the consubstantiality of the Son with the
"Father, which the primitive Christians defended, is a divine doctrine,
"and Arianism was, and still is, an impiety. For it is manifest, that
"God in no way can sanction a religion or doctrine more solemnly,
"than by stamping upon it, in a most authentic manner, the seal of his
"supreme authority and approbation, that is to say, by working an un-
"questionable miracle in its confirmation. Do you, in fine, deny the
"the existence of miracles, because church history relates none, and
"keeps a deep silence on this subject? But can you possibly open any
"monument of antiquity, where your eyes will not meet with some
"prodigy, wrought on the most important and public occasions, and
"may we not here well apply the well known passage of the Roman
"orator, ' Plenæ sunt omnes sapientum voces, pleni sapientum libri, plena
"exem rorum vetustas;' expunge from the annals of the church the stu-
"pendeous wonders, with which the Lord has been pleased to illustrate
"his holy church, and to recommend her as his own work to all nations,
"and you will strip the monuments of venerable antiquity of at least
"one-third of their contents, of one-third, too, the most interesting of
"all that they contain in the scriptures."

In closing the account of the horrible excesses of the Arian persecutors, we will briefly detail the progress and duration of this heresy,
in order to shew the mutability and diversity of error, contrasted with

A REVIEW

OF

Fox's Book of Martyrs,

CRITICAL AND HISTORICAL.

No. 12.   Printed and Published by W. E. ANDREWS, 3, Chapter-house-court, St. Paul's Churchyard, London.   Price 3d.

EXPLANATION OF THE ENGRAVING.—*The holy pope Martin is seen returning from an examination by the Sacellarius, in the presence of the senate, stripped of all his clothes except a tunic, the executioner dragging him along through the city of Constantinople by a chain fixed to his neck. A few of the people are crying Anathema, but the rest are overwhelmed with grief at the cruel treatment of their spiritual father for resisting the innovations of error.*

CONTINUATION OF THE REVIEW.

the unchangeableness and indivisibility of truth. The birth of Arianism took place about the year 306, and its ascendancy to power may be dated from the death of Constantine the great, in 337, when his son Constantius, who succeeded his father in the government of the east, embraced the heresy, and took its abettors into protection. In the field of argument the Arians, like our present sectarians, were powerless; they therefore grounded their success on fraud and violence. Relying on the protection of the civil authority, they deposed the orthodox prelates at their pleasure, and filled their places with Arians, the same as the Catholic bishops of England were displaced by Elizabeth, and creatures of the Reformation, so called, substituted in their sees. In the year 325 a council of bishops was assembled at Nice to the number of 348, who decided against the doctrine of Arius. In 357 another council of 250 bishops was held at Sardica in Illyricum, of whom there were 80 of the Arian party. The Arians seeing that they could not carry their measures, seceded; the rest of the prelates proceeded canonically, and confirmed the decision of the Nicene fathers. In 359 a third council was held at Arminium in Italy of above 400 bishops, of whom 80 were Arians. Here the latter had recourse to fraud, and by using ambiguous expressions, imposed upon many of the fathers assembled a formulary of faith which they took to be orthodox. But truth is always to be found when sought for; and the trick was no sooner discovered than those who had signed the fictitious formulary immediately withdrew their signatures, and professed their adherence to the true faith. We have related how this heresy was introduced among the Goths, and enough has been said of the horrible cruelties and outrages committed by its adherents. Before the end of the century, (the fourth) the Arians, as is the case with all who depart from the truth, began to differ among themselves concerning their own tenets and divided into various sects, as we see Protestantism now sundered; these divisions weakened their strenth, and the hand of God soon became visible upon them. The Ostrogoths were converted by degrees to the Catholic faith, and their kingdom extinguished in 552 by the death of their king Totila, who was defeated and slain by the emperor Justinian's troops. The Visigoths in Spain were brought over, with their king Reccard, to the Catholic faith, about the year 587, by St. Hermenegild. The Seuvi, a German people, were converted from Arianism a few years before. In 535 the emperor Justinian sent Belisarius into Africa, who defeated the Arian Vandals and put an end to their kingdom and power. In 572 the Lombards conquered part of Italy and established a kingdom and with it Arianism; but Charlemagne vanquished them in 774, and extinguished their dominion. Hunneric, one of the most cruel of the Arian persecutors, died a miserable death, being eaten up by worms. Ancient Rome too, in 546, was totally destroyed by fire and famine, a striking example of the vengeance of God, on those who persecute his saints and contemn his laws.

The next article worthy of notice in the *Book of Martyrs* is headed " BISHOP MARTIN," and professes to give an account of the chief actions of the life of this prelate. We are now got into the seventh century, and the account given is so very extraordinary for a Protestant martyrologist, that we here give it at length :—"Martin, bishop of " Rome, was born at Lodi, in Italy. He was naturally virtuous, and " his parents bestowed on him an excellent education. He took or- " ders, and on the death of Theodore, bishop of Rome, was advanced to " that IMPORTANT SEE, by an unanimous election, in which all par- " ties gave him the fullest praise, and admitted, that he well merited a " trust of such importance. The first vexation he received in his epis- " copal capacity, was from a set of HERETICS, called MONOTHE- " LITES ; who not daring, after the *express decisions of the council of* " *Chalcedon*, to maintain the unity of nature in Christ, asserted *art-* " *fully*, that he had but one will and operation of mind. This sect " was patronized by the emperor Heraclius ; and the first who at- " tempted to stop the progress of these errors, was Sophronius, bishop " of Jerusalem. Martin, who on this occasion coincided in sentiments " with the bishop of Jerusalem, *called a council*, which consisted of 105 " bishops, and they *unanimously condemned the errors in question*. But " the emperor, provoked at these proceedings, ordered Olympius, his

" lieutenant in Italy, to repair to Rome, and seize the bishop. The
" lieutenant performed the journey; but on his arrival at Rome, he
" found the prelate too much beloved to induce him to attempt any
" open violence; he therefore suborned a ruffian to assassinate him at
" the altar; but the fellow, after promising to execute the deed, was
" seized with such horror of conscience, that he had not the power to
" perform his undertaking. Olympius thus finding it would be very
" difficult to destroy Martin, put himself at the head of his troops, and
" marched against the Saracens, who had made some inroads into Italy,
" but during this expedition he died. His successor was Calliopas,
" who received express orders to seize Martin, which, with the assist-
" ance of a considerable body of soldiers, he performed; shewing the
" clergy the imperial mandate, which commanded him to dispossess
" Martin of his bishopric, and carry him a prisoner to Constantinople.
" Having endured various hardships, during a tedious voyage, he
" reached the imperial city of Constantinople, and was thrown into
" prison. While in confinement, he wrote two epistles to the emperor
" to refute the calumnies forged against him with respect to his faith
" and loyalty; for a proof of the soundness of the former, he appeals
" to the testimony of the whole clergy, and his own solemn protesta-
" tion to defend the truth as long as he lived; and in answer to the
" objections made against the latter, he declares he never sent either
" money, letters, or advice to the Saracens, but only remitted a sum
" for the relief of poor Christians among those people : he concludes
" with saying, that *nothing could be more false than what the heretics had
" alleged against him concerning the blessed Virgin*, WHOM HE FIRM-
" LY BELIEVED TO BE THE MOTHER OF GOD, AND WOR-
" THY OF ALL HONOUR AFTER HER DIVINE SON. In his se-
" cond letter he gives a particular account of his being seized at Rome,
" and his indisposition and ill usage since he was dragged from that
" city; and ends with wishing and hoping his persecutors would re-
" pent of their conduct, when the object of their hatred should be re-
" moved from this world. The fatigues that Martin had undergone,
" and his infirmities, were so great, that on the day appointed for his
" trial, he was brought out of prison in a chair, being unable to walk.
" When he was before the court, the judge ordered him to stand,
" which not being able to do, two men were ordered to hold him up.
" Twenty witnesses were produced against him, who swore as they
" were directed, and charged him with pretended crimes. Martin be-
" gan his defence, but as soon as he entered upon an investigation of
" the errors which he had combatted, one of the senators stopped him,
" and said, that he was only examined respecting civil affairs, and
" consequently that ecclesiastical matters had nothing to do in his de-
" fence. The judge then prevented him from going on. Martin was
" then ordered to be exposed in the most public places of the town,
" and to be divested of all marks of distinction; but all these rigours
" he bore with Christian patience. After lying some months in prison,
" he was sent to an island at some distance; and there cut to pieces.
" A. D. 655."

Here are some very important facts to attract the attention of the
reader. In the first place it must be observed, that Mahometanism

had began its career, and was making great progress in the east, while the Christian emperors, it appears, were giving encouragement to *heresy* in their dominions. We have before noticed the destruction of the ancient city of Rome and the fall of the empire, yet here we see it acknowledged by John Fox, that the "*important see*" of that city still survived, and that the bishop was exercising his high jurisdiction over the church. Can we have a greater proof, or a plainer confession, of the supremacy of the pope, than this statement of the *Book of Martyrs*, which the "few plain Christians" are now publishing with a view, as they profess, to diffuse "among their fellow-believers a knowledge and "love of the *genuine principles* of Christianity?" The pope is here praised for his opposition to the *heresy* of the Monothelites, as the former popes and martyrs have been praised for their opposition to Arianism and other heresies. Now, if the popes were right in opposing heresy in the seventh and preceding centuries, and who can doubt it, since John Fox says so? they must be also right in opposing it in the sixteenth or nineteenth centuries; for error must be resisted and truth maintained in all cases and in all ages. By the relation of Fox it would seem that the emperor Heraclius was the persecutor of this holy pope, whereas it was this emperor's son Constans, who, three years after the martyrdom of the saint, fell himself by the hand of an assassin. Indeed the whole relation of Fox, though true in substance, is a jumble of circumstances without order, and erroneous in detail. The martyrologist says, the *first* vexation pope Martin "received in his episcopal " capacity was from a sect of heretics called Monothelites; who not " daring, after the express decisions of the council of Chalcedon, to " maintain the unity of nature in Christ, asserted artfully, that he had " but one will and operation of mind."—Again, he says, " the *first* who " attempted to stop the progress of these errors was Sophronius, bishop " of Jerusalem. Martin, who *on this occasion* coincided in sentiment " with the bishop of Jerusalem, called a council, which consisted of " 105 bishops, and they unanimously condemned the errors in ques- " tion." Now by this account the reader is led to suppose, in the first place, that the Monothelites sprung up in the time of Martin's popedom, and in the next place that he called the council of 105 bishops in conjunction with Sophronius, the bishop of Jerusalem. But this is quite erroneous. This heresy, which was no other than the old one, broached by Eutyches, in a new shape, started up about the year 633; it was patronized by the emperor Heraclius, who published an edict in its favour, called Ecthesis, or the Exposition, which declared there was only one will in Christ, namely, that of the Divine Word, and denounced heavy penalties against those who should assert the contrary. Thus we see the civil power was resorted to, as in the case of the Arians, to enforce a belief that was contrary to the true doctrine received from the apostles. St. Sophronius was appointed to the patriarchate of Jerusalem in 634, and he was no sooner established in his see, than he called a council of all the bishops in his patriarchate, to examine the Monothelite heresy. The prelates accordingly met, and not only condemned the heresy, but composed a synodical letter to explain and prove the Catholic faith. The council of Chalcedon, alluded to by Fox, was held in 451, nearly two hundred years prior to the time of

Sophronius; but this letter was confirmed in the sixth general council held subsequently in 680. This proceeding on the part of St. Sophronius most certainly induced the abettors of Monothelism to practise craft and delusion, the same as the abettors of Protestantism are compelled to do to keep their dupes in the dark; and it was in consequence of these practices that the holy pope Martin called a council of bishops in the Lateran church at Rome in 649; not, however, in conjunction with St. Sophronius, for that holy prelate died in 639, according to some writers, or, as Papebroke thinks, in 644. Martin, observe, was elected to the "important see" of Rome in 649, and it was this proceeding in support of the true faith that led to the vexations and sufferings he afterwards experienced from the tyranny of the temporal power. We noticed the edict issued by Heraclius; his son Constans published another called the Typus, which imposed silence on both parties. The Lateran fathers censured both documents; the one for favouring heresy, the other for enjoining silence when truth was in danger. "The "Lord," said the fathers, "hath commanded us to shun evil, and do "good; but not to reject the good with the evil. We are not to deny "at the same time both truth and error." The condemnation of the latter edict occasioned the persecution of the pope by Constans.

Of the various hardships endured by this holy pope, in the discharge of his divine functions, there is nothing very contradictory except the account of his death. Fox says he was cut to pieces, but Mr. Alban Butler makes no mention of this circumstance, and seems to infer that he died in prison, worn out with the cruel treatment he had undergone. It is not a little singular, however, that the charge brought by the heretics against this holy martyr should be similar to those alleged against the Catholics by " Protestant-ascendency," and particularly by the infamous plotters of that foul conspiracy which had Titus Oates for its chief instrument. Martin, it seems, was charged with disloyalty, with aiding the enemies of government, with sending money to the Saracens; and witnesses were procured who could perjure themselves for profit, but could not establish what they swore. So it has been since the reign of Protestantism. Plots have been invented and charged upon the Catholics, from the time of Elizabeth to the end of the Stuart rule; and even to this day in Ireland allegations of this kind are made by the Orange partisans and papers. The creatures of " Ascendency" are ever ringing the changes on the pretended disloyalty of Catholics, because they hold the spiritual supremacy of the pope over the Christian church, though this supremacy was held by all the martyrs that Fox has hitherto recorded. Unable to encounter this stubborn fact; unable to wipe out of the annals of history that the pope was the supreme ecclesiastical head of the Christian world before the reformation, so called, of the sixteenth century, the founders of " Protestant-ascendency" made the belief of the pope's supremacy a *civil* offence, and when a Catholic was put upon his trial, for adhering to this article of his creed, he was condemned to suffer the death of a traitor to his temporal sovereign, and not anathematized as the broacher or favourer of error. He was examined, as one of the senators is said to have observed to pope Martin, " respecting civil affairs, and consequently that ecclesiastical matters " had nothing to do in his defence."

But what are we to think of the defence made by this holy pope; at least that which Fox and his editors have imputed to him? Is it possible that Martin could be a Protestant martyr, after the doctrine he is stated to have defended in his epistle to the emperor? It is true we do not find the Rev. Alban Butler, in the life of this saint, mentioning any thing about these epistles, nor are we aware that there was any circumstance in the times that called for the pope's declaration of doctrine; but Fox has said it, and we beg the reader's particular attention to it. In the first epistle Fox says, this "godly martyr" declared, "that nothing could be more *false* than what the *heretics* had " alleged against him concerning the blessed Virgin, whom he *firmly* " *believed* to be the *mother of God*, and *worthy of all honour after her* " *divine Son*." See you this, gentle reader; see you this declaration put to the account of a bishop of Rome—one of John Fox's "godly martyrs,"—for the purpose of "diffusing . . . a knowledge and love of " the genuine principles of Christianity," and by men too who *swear*, that to honour the blessed Virgin is downright idolatry!!! What the *heretics* of those days had alleged against pope Martin we do not know, but Fox says the pope declared the charges to be false, and that he firmly believed the blessed Virgin ought to be honoured as the mother of God. So do the Catholics believe at this day; and they are not only stigmatized by "Protestant-ascendency" as idolatrous, but are excluded from civil office by means of an infamous test brought forward under the most infamous circumstances, when the lives of Catholics were sworn away by a set of the most infamous wretches that ever disgraced the human form, who were paid by the parliament for this infamous work out of the people's money: we allude to the horrid conspiracy of Shaftesbury and Titus Oates.

Now, reader, if the doctrine of pope Martin was *genuine* in the seventh century, it must also be genuine in the nineteenth; for *truth* is always *one* and the *same*. If it were rank heresy to deny honour to the blessed Virgin *then*, it must consequently be so *now?* HERESY, you will please to observe, is defined by Dr Johnson to be, "An "*opinion of private men*, different from that of the *Catholic* and " *orthodox* church;" and here we have John Fox telling us that the head of that church in the seventh century, in opposition to certain heretics, that is certain private men, declared in writing that the blessed Virgin is worthy of all honour next to her divine Son. So say the Catholic and orthodox church *now*, and so she always did and always will. What then are we to think of those who deny her this honour upon oath, and who are, compared in numbers with the Catholic church, but a body of private men? The Protestant reader will do well to reflect on this discrepancy between the genuine doctrines of pope Martin, and the modern doctrines of "Protestant-ascendency." We would also have him bear in mind the different modes pursued by the Catholic church and "Protestant-ascendency" when a point of doctrine is disputed. We see by John Fox's statement, that pope Martin did not decide on his own individual judgment in the case of Monothelism, which was "an opinion of private men different from the " Catholic and orthodox church;" but he assembled a council of 107 bishops, all learned and competent men, who were also governed by a rule the most safe and certain that could be devised. This rule was to examine the written and unwritten word of God; that is, to compare the gospels with the apostolical traditions, and decide that what had *always* been taught by the church, and had been received by the apostles, must be of divine institution and faith; and consequently what could not be proved to have such an origin must be *human invention*. Such a mode of proceeding as this is consistent with sound reason, and forms a chain of evidence incontestable and unbroken. On the other hand, Protestantism has nothing of this kind to rely upon. Luther, Calvin, Harry the eighth, Elizabeth, and in fact the whole clan of evangelical reformers were innovators, by imposing their own "*pri-*" *vate opinions*" upon the ignorant and credulous for divine truths. Some by the power of the sword, and others by the cant of hypocrisy. When Henry established his ecclesiastical supremacy, it was under the terror of pains and penalties; and by the same means did Elizabeth assume the popeship of the church of England. Protestantism was not raised by the supernatural hand of God, but by the operation of human power and deception. In England, for example, when the thirty-nine articles and book of common prayer were framed for the uniformity of belief and worship, the universal church was not consulted as to their orthodoxy and antiquity, but their merits were submitted to a lay-parliament; to a body, in comparison with the church of Christ, of private men, deputed by the people of England to manage their temporal concerns, but who assumed the right to manage their spiritual affairs, heretofore regulated by the councils of bishops from all parts of the world. Thus then the "genuine principles of Christianity" became subjected to the whim of lay-legislators, and articles of faith were made to vary according to the taste of the times or the schemes of plotting statesmen. Hence the endless diversity of creeds that now distract the minds of those who still retain some spark of religious sentiments, and the great increase of infidelity among others, who, witnessing the gross contradictions of the contending sects, and the abuses that arise from a state clergy, conclude that religion is only a political instrument to further the interests of the ambitious. But it is not so with the Catholic, who can see in the history of his church the mark of a divine hand, and an undeviating guide to the haven of salvation. Abuses may creep in, with regard to some of her ministers, who are subject to the same frailties as other human beings, but in her faith and morals she is always ONE, always HOLY, always CATHO-LIC and APOSTOLICAL. This fact has been acknowledged by John Fox to the seventh century, as we see in his account of "*Bishop Martin*," and we shall be able to prove, in the course of our review of his Book of Martyrs, that it is still the same.

Constans, the murderer of the holy pope Martin, as we have before stated, was murdered in his turn by an assassin. He was succeeded by his son Constantine Pogonatus, a virtuous and orthodox prince. Under his reign the sixth general council of the church was called at Constantinople, being the third which was held in that city, with a view of healing the divisions that had so long disturbed the Christian world. Two hundred and sixty bishops from all parts of the east assembled on the 7th day of November, in the year 680. Each bishop sat in order according to the dignity of the see he represented, and in the middle of the assembly, according to ancient custom, was placed the book of the holy gospels. The pope's legate presided and opened the council. The question for discussion was this,—Whether in our Lord Jesus Christ there were two natural wills or only one—two operations or only one, as the Monothelite party had asserted. The leaders of the party were present, and were called upon to state the grounds of their opinion. They did so, and were heard with attention, The council next proceeded to examine what had been written for and against the doctrine, what the gospels said, what the fathers testified, what preceding councils had defined, and what apostolical tradition had handed down. This examination occupied eighteen sessions, so that it is clear the members of this council did not decide hastily. The decision of the council was, that the doctrine was *new* and *false*, being contrary to that taught by the apostles. They therefore decreed as follows, " We de-" fine, that in Jesus Christ there are two natural wills, and two natural " operations, and we forbid the contrary to be taught." This decree was properly authenticated, the council dissolved, after sitting ten months, and Monothelism shortly afterwards expired.

We have alluded to the rise of Mahometanism; it is now necessary to give a brief outline of its progress. It will be seen that heresy had been most fruitful in the eastern churches. Arianism, which denied the divinity of Christ, had its birth in Alexandria; Macedonianism, which denied the divinity of the Holy Ghost, took its rise in Constantinople; Donatism commenced in Africa; Pelagianism took root in Carthage; Nestorianism began at Constantinople, as did also Eutychianism; all which errors were more or less encouraged and countenanced by the temporal rulers of that part of Christendom. Such opposition to the divine commands, not to mention the violent acts of injustice committed against the liberty of conscience, by the persecutions of the faithful believers, could not be expected to remain long unpunished. If the Pagan emperors experienced the vengeance of Heaven for their enormities against the primitive Christians, we must look for heavier judgments against the apostates from Christianism and the oppressors of the orthodox. Accordingly we see the sword of Mahometanism raised to chastise the rebellious monarchs of the east, and carry destruction to those places that favoured the impious heresies we have named. Arabia was soon overrun by the barbarian followers of this pretended prophet, who was an Unitarian, and taught his partisans to take up arms for religion, promising them a paradise of all the sensual pleasures, if they died fighting in the cause. In 634, Omar, the second caliph after Mahomet, invaded Syria, where he defeated the brother of the emperor Heraclius, and soon became master of Damascus. He then divided his army, one part of which he sent against Egypt. In 636, Jerusalem, after a siege of two years, surrendered to his arms. Antioch soon followed, and in the course of ten years this chieftain made himself master of all Syria, Palestine and Egypt. Alexandria stood a siege of fourteen months. The library of this city was destroyed by express order of the caliph, and the number of volumes was so great, that, it is said, they sufficed to light the fires of four thousand baths for six months. The next enterprise of these ruthless wartiors was against the kingdom of Persia, which had persecuted the Christians, and now felt the hand of Mahometanism, being subjected to its dominion. In 662 they invaded other parts of the eastern Roman empire, and in 712 they passed from Africa into Spain, where they spread terror all over the country by their horrid cruelties. The amazing growth of this strange power now received a shock by the desertion of some of its chiefs, who renounced subjection to the Arabian caliph and proclaimed themselves independent. These disputes for power gave rise to civil wars, which for a time stayed their further irruptions into the remaining provinces of the Greek or Constantinopolitan empire. While these events were passing on the borders of the empire, her internal state was again agitated and thrown into disunion by the schism commenced by one Photius, who had been nominated, though but a layman, by the emperor, to the patriarchal chair of Constantinople, in the year 858. This schism led to many disorders, and several attempts were made to heal the breach, but in the end they proved fruitless. The Greeks remained obstinate, and for their contumacy to the divine authority, the Almighty abandoned them to the mercy of the Mahometans. After years of wasteful warfare, in 1453 Mahomet the second laid siege to the city of Constantinople, which after a brave resistance was carried by storm, and an end put to the empire of the Greeks. The fate of Constantinople was truly deplorable. Forty thousand Greeks perished in the slaughter, and 60,000 were afterwards sold for slaves. The churches were profaned, meat was served up in the sacred chalices, and for three days the barbarians rioted with such licentiousness, that they committed the most enormous and horrible crimes it was possible to perpetrate.

While these disorders were going on in the east, the true faith was making great progress in the Pagan nations in the north and west. In 532 St. Eleutherius converted the people about Tournay. In 536 St. Vedast converted the people in Artois. In 537 St. Paternus carried the light of the gospel to the people of Constance; and Spain received the faith from Rome. In 596 our own country renounced idolatry for Catholicism, on the preaching of St. Augustin; and the year following the people of Little Britany embraced the gospel from the hands of St. Paul de Leon. In the seventh century the South Saxons were converted by St. Wilfrid; the West Saxons by St. Birinus; the East Angles by St. Felix; and the Mercians by St. Ceadda. St. Swibert preached the faith in Germany, St. Willibrord in Friesland; St. Kilian in Franconia, St. Columba among the Swedes, and St. Eligius among the Flemish. In the eighth century Germany received the light of faith, which was first carried there by one of our own countrymen, of whom Fox has taken some considerable notice in his *Book of Martyrs*. And here we beg the reader to keep in remembrance, that this propagation of truth was invariably effected by the preaching of holy and unarmed men, fortified only with the divine Spirit, the precepts and morality of the gospel, and the gift of performing miracles, to flash conviction of their heavenly authority. In no instance was Catholicism planted among heathen or apostate nations but by the power of persuasion and the strength of truth; nor can a case, we believe, be pointed out, where the Catholic faith was ever totally annihilated, after having once taken root. Though the countries of the east have been, from the destruction of Constantinople in 1453, under the dominion of Mahometanism, yet the Catholic religion still exists in that capital, and in almost every part of the Turkish empire. Neither could the violence nor craft of the reformers of the sixteenth century destroy the seed of truth, though in many places they nearly choaked it with the weeds of error. Though Protestantism, like Arianism, &c. was supported in almost every country, where it reared its head, by the influence and power of the civil magistrate, and corporal pains and inflictions were exercised on those who adhered to the ancient and true faith, yet there is not a place in the world, where Protestantism is professed, nor any other error arising from apostasy, but there are also believers in the Catholic and orthodox faith. This we must consider a striking fact of the universality and genuineness of that creed which the "few plain Christians" abuse, calumniate, and wish to excite a hatred against.

The second section of the second book of Fox is headed "PERSECU-"TIONS FROM THE EIGHTH TO THE TENTH CENTURY," and commences with an "ACCOUNT OF BONIFACE." This Boniface is the great saint of that name, who, by his extraordinary missionary labours, was the illustrious instrument of bringing the people of Germany to the knowledge of the faith of Christ. Fox, in his account, admits that our saint, who was an Englishman, and a native of Devonshire, was gifted with most eminent talents and was a profound scholar; that he was indebted to the care and skill of the abbot of Nutscelle for his knowledge in the divine law, and that he could explain "the holy scriptures in the literal, moral, and "mystical senses." That the abbot "seeing him *qualified* for the priest-"hood, *conferred* upon him that *holy order*, when he was about thirty "years of age. From that time (Fox continues) he began to labour "for the *salvation of his fellow creatures*; in the progress of which he "gave the first proofs of that apostolical zeal, which afterwards made "such glorious conquests in a most savage and barbarous part of the "world." The martyrologist then goes on to state, that Boniface was induced "to forsake his country, relations and friends, in order to be of "service to THE FAITH, and extend CHRISTIANITY on the conti-"nent;" that the abbot would have dissuaded him from the attempt, but finding him resolute, he sent two of the monks to assist him. That on arriving on the continent, he found the time of conversion was not yet come, and therefore returned to the monastery: that the abbot dying, he was chosen to fill his place, but that "he either never accepted of "that post, or quitted it very soon; for he obtained letters from Daniel, "bishop of Winchester, his diocesan, which recommended him to THE "POPE, and *all* the *bishops, abbots*, and *princes*, he should find on his "way to ROME, where he arrived in the beginning of the year 719. "He was received (Fox states) by Gregory the second with great "friendship, and after several conferences with him, finding him full "of zeal, he dismissed him with A COMMISSION AT LARGE TO "PREACH THE GOSPEL to the Pagans, wherever he found them." Fox then goes on, "Having passed through Lombardy and Bavaria, he "(Boniface) came to Thuringia, which country had before received "the light of the gospel; but at the time that Boniface arrived there, "it had made little progress. His first exertions, therefore, were to

" bring the corrupted Christians back TO THE PURITY OF THE
" GOSPEL; and having completed this pious work with great assi-
" duity, and hearing that Radbord, whom he formerly in vain attempted
" to convert, was dead, he repaired to Utrecht, to assist Willebrod, the
" first bishop of that city. During the space of three years, these wor-
" thy pastors laboured, in conjunction, in EXTIRPATING IDOLA-
" TRY and PROPAGATING THE FAITH; and so far succeeded,
" that most of the people received baptism, and many of the Pagan
" temples were converted into Christian churches." After stating
some further successes of the saint, Fox says, he was called to Rome
by pope Gregory, who conferred upon him the episcopal character,
that he might pursue his labours " with more authority and to greater
advantage." He then goes on: " Being thus qualified for forming his
" new church, he left Rome, having with him six letters from the pope;
" one to Charles Martel; a second to all bishops, priests, counts, &c.; a
" third to the clergy and people under his more immediate direction;
" a fourth to the five princes of Thuringia, and their Christian subjects;
" a fifth to the Pagans in their dominions; and a sixth to the whole
" body of Saxons. The purport of all these was, to recommend him to
" the protection of the Christian powers, and exhort the Pagans to hear
" him, and quit their errors and superstition." Though the statement
of Fox on the whole is pretty accurate, we cannot help thinking he has
outstretched the truth here, or else he has made the influence of the pope
much greater than even Catholics suppose him possessed of. That the
holy father should recommend the zealous missionary to the care and
protection of the *Christian* powers is very natural, but that he should
address the Pagan people by letter, and volunteer his exhortations
where he was neither known nor cared for, and where it was uncertain
whether Boniface would obtain a hearing, is a very improbable tale;
but our martyrologist likes to deal more than a little in the marvellous,
when he thinks it will suit his purpose.

Fox next proceeds to enumerate the transactions of this apostle of
the Germanic church, in the erection of monasteries and bishoprics,
which we here give in his own words:—" In the year 731, Gregory
" the third succeeded to the papal chair, upon whose accession Boni-
" face sent persons to Rome, to acquaint him with the success of his
" labours, testifying *his obedience*, and desiring assistance in some diffi-
" culties which occurred in his mission. The pope not only answered
" the message by assuring him of *the communion and friendship of the
" see of Rome*, but, as a mark of respect, sent him the pallium, grant-
" ed him the title of archbishop, or metropolitan of all Germany, and
" empowered him to erect new bishoprics. Boniface, in consequence,
" not only erected new bishoprics, but built several monasteries. He
" then made a third journey to Rome, in 738, when Gregory, who had
" much affection for him, detained him there the greatest part of the
" year. At length having left Rome, he set out for Bavaria, upon the
" invitation of Odillo, duke of that country, *to reform some abuses in-
" troduced by persons who had never received holy orders.* At this time
" Bavaria had only one bishop; he therefore, pursuant to his commis-
" sion from Rome, erected three new bishoprics, one at Saltzburg, a
" second at Freisigen, a third at Ratisbon, and thus all Bavaria was

" divided into four dioceses. This regulation was soon after *confirmed*
" *by the pope.* He next established four other bishoprics; viz. at Er-
" furt, Barabourg, Wurtzbourg, and Achstat. In the year 741, Gre-
" gory the third was succeeded in the popedom by Zachary, who con-
" *firmed* Boniface in his power, and approved of all he had done in Ger-
" many, making him at the same time archbishop of Mentz, and me-
" tropolitan over thirteen bishoprics. He did not, however, lose his
" simplicity, or forget his innocence in his ecclesiastical dignity. Dur-
" ing the ministry of this prelate, Pepin was declared king of France;
" and it being that prince's ambition to be crowned by the most holy
" prelate he could find, Boniface was solicited to perform that cere-
" mony, which he did at Soissons in 752." Fox concludes his account
with the martyrdom of the saint who was killed with fifty-two of his
disciples, by a body of Pagans, on the 5th of June, 755.

  In concluding, Fox observes, " thus fell the great father of the Ger-
" manic church, the honour of England, and the glory of his barba-
" rous age." To this observation, his modern editors have added the
following remarks by way of note. " Having given the fair side of the
" character of Boniface, the archbishop, it behoves us to say, that he
" was *a great abettor* of *all* the *absurdities* and BLASPHEMIES of Po-
" pery: though for *this* he is *not so much to be blamed;* because in *his*
" *time* the *candle of the true gospel was not lighted.* By his authority
" Childeric, king of France, was *deposed*, and Pepin, the *betrayer* of
" his master, was recognised as king. From Boniface *proceeded that*
" *detestable doctrine* which now stands registered in the pope's decrees,
" *(dis. 40. cap. si papa;)* which states, that in case the pope were of
" most filthy living, and forgetful or negligent of himself, and of Chris-
" tianity, in such a degree, that he led innumerable souls with him to
" hell; yet ought no man to rebuke him for so doing, ' for he hath,'
" says he, ' power to judge all men, and ought of no man to be judged
" again.' "

  Here then we have the ".few plain Christians" at variance with their
favourite author, and making assertions that are flatly contradicted by
the work they are editing " to excite a hatred and abhorrence of the
" corruptions and crimes of Popery and its professors." They give
" the fair side of the character of Boniface, the archbishop," from the
book of John Fox, but then it behoves them to SAY,—yes, yes, reader, to SAY, but not to *prove*—" that he was a great abettor of *all* the
" *absurdities* and BLASPHEMIES of *Popery;*" but although he was an
abettor of *blasphemy*, yet *he* was not *even blameable* in the eyes of these
pious exciters of hatred against the present professors of Catholicism,
because, because, good souls, they have got it into their heads that
" in *his* time the *candle* of the *true gospel was not lighted.*" These wise
editors talk of the absurdity and blasphemy of Popery; but we ask the
man of common understanding whether their *own* absurdity and blasphemy do not exceed that imputed by them to Popery; though, by the
by, we are not told in what the latter consist. Enough has been said
however to convict the former of both. We are now got into the *eighth*
century of the Christian church, we have had innumerable " godly
martyrs" recorded as suffering for the faith of Christ, among whom
are many of the bishops of Rome, and behold we are told by the " few

plain Christians" that "the *candle* of the gospel was not yet light-
"ed" !!! What! did Christ leave his apostles and their successors, and
all the victims of Pagan and Arian vengeance, in the shade of darkness; though he himself stated that he came to enlighten and to redeem the world? Did he permit the Pagan nations to be converted to
Christianity, working miracles to confirm the authority of the missiona-
aries, and allow them to teach blasphemy in his name? What horrible
impiety! What barefaced absurdity is this! Such matchless impudence and falsehood was never before submitted to a people laying claim
to rationality. And will you, Protestants of England, suffer yourselves
to be any longer deluded and imposed upon by such groundless assertions as these? Compare the statement of Fox with the assertion of
his modern editors, and say if they are not the most unblushing liars
that ever stained paper.

To make their want of veracity plain to the meanest capacity, we
will enter a little further into the merits of this case. Fox bears the
clearest testimony to the true faith being taught by the church of
Rome at this period, and the zealous labours of our countrymen to
carry that faith to those nations that were under the shade of darkness;
consequently the candle *was* burning in our own island, and the light
of the true gospel was spread by the efforts of Englishmen, holding
their commission from the pope. St. Austin was sent to England in
596, by pope Gregory the great, where he imparted the light of faith,
and it was carefully treasured in those establishments of learning and
piety, the monasteries, which were so ruthlessly destroyed by the tyrant Harry and his successor. That Rome was then, as she now is,
the mother of the Christian world, is unequivocally admitted by Fox,
as he states that Boniface received his commission from one pope, and
that his commission was *confirmed* by two successive pontiffs filling the
see of Rome. Again, it appears from Fox's account that some parts of
the continent had received the light of the gospel, and its professors
by some means or other became *corrupted*; but that Boniface set himself to reform them, and *completely succeeded* in bringing them back to
the purity of the gospel. Now how could he do this, if we are to believe the modern editors of this Book of Martyrs? They say, " the
" candle of the true gospel was not lighted" in the time of Boniface—
while Fox says, he brought back corrupted Christians to the purity
of the gospel, and propagated the faith among Pagan idolaters. Here
is a contradiction which the wise editors probably did not expect to see
exposed. They thought they had only to impute absurdity and blasphemy to Popery, and all would be well. Truth was not their object,
though they pretended to be influenced by a desire " of diffusing among
" their fellow-believers a knowledge and love of the genuine principles
" of Christianity." Where these " genuine principles" are to be found
they have not yet shewn their " fellow-believers;" and we suppose
the tallow-chandler is not yet born that is to make *their* candle of the
gospel.

That Boniface was a Catholic missionary, there can be no doubt; and
that he possessed the pure faith, we have the evidence of John Fox,
whose testimony being confirmed by the most authentic historians,
will go much further with the man of unbiassed mind, than the unsup-

ported and irreligious assertions of the "few plain Christians." The Rev. Alban Butler, in his life of this great man, says, "A collection "of St. Boniface's letters was published by Serrarius, in 1605.... "By his epistles it appears, that, in all his designs and actions, he had "nothing in view but piety and the service of God..... In the fourth, "speaking of the necessity of confession, he says: 'If we should "conceal our sins, God will discover them publicly in spite of us. "And it is better to discover them to one man than to be publicly ex- "posed and covered with confusion for them in the sight of all the in- "habitants of heaven, earth, and hell.' (Hom. iv. p. 195.)....The "style of this saint's writing (Mr. B. observes) is clear, grave, and "simple. He everywhere in them breathes an *apostolical* spirit, and "his thoughts are just and solid." The same author states, that "St. "Boniface wrote a circular to all the bishops, priests, deacons, ca- "nons, monks, nuns, and all the people of England, conjuring them "earnestly to join in holy prayer, to beg of God, who desires that all "may be saved, that he would vouchsafe, in his infinite mercy, to "shower down his blessings upon the labours of all those who are "employed in endeavouring to bring souls to his saving knowledge and "holy love." These sentiments, we think, do not savour much of absurdity and blasphemy, while they exhibit a heart influenced with true charity, and inspired with the light of divine faith. In a letter to Cuthbert, archbishop of Canterbury, the saint gives us a true pic- ture of the zealous pastor, and shews how ardently he desired to labour to plant the light of faith among infidels. "Let us fight," he says, "for the Lord in these days of bitterness and affliction. If this "be the will of God, let us die for the laws of our fathers, that we "may arrive with them at the eternal inheritance. Let us not be dumb "dogs, sleeping centinels, hirelings that fly at the sight of the wolf: "but watchful and diligent pastors, preaching to the great and small, "to the rich and poor, to every age and condition, being instant in "season and out of season." Such is the man whom these "few plain Christians" have charged with being "a great abettor of all the ab- "surdities and blasphemies of Popery;" and yet, oh! absurdity sublime! was himself *blameless*, because the true gospel was then *unknown!!!* Would it not be better for society, if these exciters of hatred against Popery and its professors were imbued with similar Christian senti- ments as this imputed abettor of absurdity and blasphemy?

Fox informs us that Boniface was invited into Bavaria for the pur- pose of reforming "some abuses introduced by persons *who had never* "*received holy orders;*" and, as usual, he omits to tell us *what* those abuses were. But what shall we say of those preachers "who have never "received holy orders?" It is clear that John Fox considered *orders* necessary for the exercise of the ecclesiastical functions, or he would not have noticed this circumstance in his account of Boniface. And what then shall we say of those men who lay claim to the *call* of preach- ing by *inspiration?* Of being sent, not by the regular line of succession from the apostles, but by their own conceit and fanciful ideas? Such as these, we think, must stand condemned as well in these days as in the time of Boniface. But let us see what the abuses were that our saint had to reform. Fox gives Odillo the credit of sending for St. Boniface;

Mr. A. Butler however says that the merit is due to Carloman, the son of Charles Martel, mayor of the palace and prince of Lorrain, and brother to Pepin, who afterwards changed the mayoralty into a kingdom. This prince subdued Odilo, the duke of Bavaria, and made him tributary; while his chief aim, we are told, was to consult by peace the happiness of his people, to protect religion, and to cultivate the useful arts. "He bent his whole authority," writes Mr. Butler, "to second " the zeal of our saint in all his undertakings. Two impostors were " stirred up by the devil, to disturb the infant church of Germany. " The one, Adalbert, a Frenchman, pretended to know the secrets of " hearts, gave his own hair and the parings of his nails as relics, and " wrote his own life, filled with absurd pretended miracles, enthusiasm, " and pride. The other, called Clement, a Scotsman, rejected the ca- " nons or ecclesiastical laws, taught that Christ in his descent into hell " delivered all the souls of the damned; he also held heterodox opi- " nions concerning predestination. St. Boniface, in a council in Ger- " many, condemned them both in 742....and the sentence of the saint " and his council was afterwards confirmed by the pope in a synod at " Rome in 745." (Conc. t. vi. p. 14, 15, and St. Bonif. ep. 138.) Here we see again the carefulness of the pastors of the church to guard against every degree of imposition, and their diffidence in not presuming to act on their own individual authority, but by the common consent and advice of their confreres in solemn convocation.

But, the "few plain Christians" will exclaim, you have not noticed our charge against him, of deposing, by his authority, the king of France, and broaching that detestable doctrine, that no man ought to rebuke the pope, let him be ever so wicked and scandalous in his life. As to the latter charge, if there be an individual of common understanding capable of giving credit to so foul an accusation, we really pity him. It is of so stupid and gross a nature, it is so improbable and disgusting, that we should be trespassing upon common sense to undertake its refutation: but it is not so with the former allegation. This has been a fruitful source of calumny and misrepresentation, which neither the seat of justice nor the walls of parliament have been able to withstand. The *deposing power* has been a bugbear of long standing, and was invented by the reformers of the sixteenth century, as a cloak to cover their own deformity; but, we think, by this time it is become threadbare. However, as the charge involves an historical fact of an interesting nature, we will go somewhat at large into the question, for the information of the reader. The "plain Christians" say, that "by his " (Boniface's) authority, Childeric, king of France, was *deposed*, and " Pepin, the betrayer of his master, was *recognised* as king." Now this assertion is as palpable a falsehood, as that of the candle of the true gospel *not* being lighted in Boniface's time. The saint had no more to do with the deposition of Childeric than we had. It is true he crowned Pepin *after* he was *chosen* king by the unanimous voice of the nation, and we cannot see any great crime in that action. William the third was crowned king of England by the then archbishop of Canterbury, after James the second, his father-in-law, had been driven from the throne; therefore we trust it is not absurdity and blasphemy in a Catholic prelate to crown a king chosen by a Catholic people; and consistency and piety, when a Protestant bishop does the same for a monarch elected by a Protestant people! As well might the modern editors of John Fox charge the death of Louis XVI. in 1793 to the account of Boniface, as the deposition of Childeric, because pope Pius VII. some years afterwards crowned Napoleon Bonaparte emperor of France. These events in temporal affairs are the inscrutable designs of Divine Providence to chastise indolent kings as well as depraved people, in which religious faith has as little share as the " few plain Christians" partake of common sense. This act of the meek and lowly Pius has given rise to much animadversion on the part of many stanch and good Catholics, which is a flat contradiction to the pretended doctrine imputed to Boniface, that the conduct of a pope is not to be censured, be his life ever so wicked or scandalous.

The affair of deposing Childeric is thus stated by Alban Butler, in a note to the life of St. Boniface :—" The Merovingian race, so called " from king Meroveus, in whom the French crown was first made he- " reditary, filled the throne three hundred and thirty-five years, under " twenty-two successive reigns of kings in Paris. The Carlovingian " line, so called from Charles Martel, possessed the crown during four- " teen reigns, and terminated in Lewis V. in 987, who died without " issue. The nobility passing by his uncle Charles duke of Lorrain, " chose Hugh Capet, son of Hugh the great, the powerful count of " Paris, who defeated Charles, and imprisoned him for life. The Ca- " petian race of French kings reigns to this day, but was subdivided " into two younger branches ; the Valesian, which begun in Philip VI. " of Valois in 1328 ; and that of Bourbon, which was called to the " throne in Henry IV. in 1587, and was descended from Robert, fourth " son of St. Lewis count of Clermont, who marrying Beatrix of Bour- " bon, his posterity took that title. The kings of France of the first " race, from Clovis II. son of Dagobert I. in 643, to Childeric III. in " 752, during ten reigns successively through a whole century, had " given themselves up to an inactive life, and were sunk in indolence, " never concerning themselves with the state, in which the supreme " authority was entrusted to the mayor of the palace : and this magis- " tracy was often the cause of wars, and became at length hereditary. " Thus, the kings were merely titular. This form of government was " a source of continual factions, and other disorders, very prejudicial " to the public weal. The crown, in all the barbarous nations which " came from the north, was originally elective, as Robertson shews in " his learned preliminary discourse to his history of Scotland; but " among the French and most others it soon became hereditary. The " constitution of the French government being become inconsistent " with itself, on this occasion, it was judged necessary to restore the " original form, and for this purpose to transfer the crown upon him " whom the laws of the state had already vested with the whole regal " power and authority. Childeric III. surnamed the Stupid, having " been titular king nine years, was shaved a monk at Sithiu or St. " Bertin's in 752, and died there in 755....How difficult soever (the " writer adds) it may be to excuse Pepin from taking ambitious steps " to prepare the way for this revolution, the case is very different as " to the persons who only acquiesced in an unanimous resolution taken

A REVIEW

OF

Fox's Book of Martyrs,

CRITICAL AND HISTORICAL.

No. 13. Printed and Published by W. E. ANDREWS, 3, Chapter-house-court, St. Paul's Churchyard, London.   Price 3d.

EXPLANATION OF THE ENGRAVING.—*This cut represents the actual blowing up of king Henry Darnley, husband of the unfortunate Mary Queen of Scots, with all his servants and attendants, as he lay sick at his house of Kirk-a-field. The contrivers and perpetrators of this act of villany, were the Protestant earls of Murray, Morton, Bothwell, Lethington, &c. the principal leaders, with Knox, in the reformation of Scotland.*

CONTINUATION OF THE REVIEW.

" by those who were best acquainted with right and law in a succes-
" sion, which till then seemed only hereditary, under certain restric-
" tions, as frequent examples in the French, English, and other new
" kingdoms, of the same original, from the northern transmigrations,
" shew....The circumstances of the dethroning of Childeric, and of
" Pepin's election, are related so differently, and the true history is so
" obscure, that it is easy for every writer to give it his own gloss.....
" That the election of Pepin was *unanimous*, and a transaction of the
" *whole nation*, and of all the powers that could be consulted in it, is
" proved in note 43 on Serrarius Rerum Mogunticar, by Georgius
" Christianus Joannis. Francoi. 1723, p. 332."

   From this authentic statement the reader will be able to pronounce
the infamy due to the assertions of the modern editors of Fox, to defame the character of a " godly martyr," who is acknowledged by the
martyrologist himself to have been an honour to his country. Boniface *deposing* a king by his *own* authority! Was ever so idle a calumny

before invented? What authority could Boniface possess of himself, when it is clearly and repeatedly stated by Fox, that the martyr held himself in obedience to the pope, and that he received his commission or authority from the see of Rome. Deposing power indeed! Who ever exercised the deposing power so effectually as the heroes of the Reformation, so called, of the sixteenth century? Much clamour we know has been raised against the supposed deposing power of the popes, and Catholics are obliged at this day to renounce on oath this power, which never was an article of their faith, while Protestants claim the right of exercising it under certain conditions. Not an instance can be produced of a sovereign being actually deposed by a pope, though many were deprived of their dominions by "Protestant-ascendency." The reformers of Scotland deposed Mary, the unfortunate queen of that country, after blowing up her husband with gunpowder. Christina, queen of Sweden, was obliged to resign her sceptre by her reforming subjects. The Protestants tried hard to depose Charles the fifth of Germany; and many attempts were made by the Huguenots of France to depose their sovereigns. Did not "Protestant-ascendency" endeavour to shut Mary out of the throne of England, and were not Charles I. and his son James II. deposed by Protestants? Is it not a part of the statute law of the kingdom, at this moment, that should the sovereign become a Catholic, or marry a Catholic princess, he is instantly deposed? Is it not a principle with Orangemen to swear allegiance to the king *conditionally?* And are Catholics still to be taunted with the *deposing power* attributed by bigots to the popes, but never allowed them by the church! We are not sorry that the charge has been made, because it has given us the opportunity of rebutting it with facts that are incontestible and overwhelming. When the Catholic religion was introduced among Pagan nations, no alteration was made in the civil privileges or customs of the country, where they were not contrary to faith and morals. The system of Catholicism is purely spiritual and not of this world, therefore it is adapted to every form of civil government, nor has it any divine commission to interfere in the concerns of kingdoms and states.

The martyrologist proceeds to give an account of " *Massacres by the " Saracens,*" and the death of " *Winceslaus, duke of Bohemia,*" which we shall pass over, as containing nothing worthy of remark. His next subject is " *Adalbert, bishop of Prague,*" on which we must be allowed to say something. After stating the great virtues and endowments of Adalbert, he says, that " soon after the decease of Dithmar (the arch-" bishop), an assembly was held for the choice of a successor, which " consisted of the clergy of Prague and the nobility of Bohemia. Adal-" bert's character determined them to raise him to the vacant see, " which they did on the 19th of February, 983, and immediately dis-" patched messengers to Verona, *to desire Otho II. would confirm the " election.* The emperor granted the request, ordered Adalbert to re-" pair *to court for investiture,* gave him the *ring* and *crosier,* and then " sent him to the archbishop of Mentz for consecration. That cere-" mony was performed on the 29th of June the same year; and he " was received at Prague with great demonstrations of public joy." From whence Fox takes this account we are not told; all is assertion;

not a single authority is quoted: and we have reason to conclude that it is wholly groundless. Hitherto, as in the case of St. Boniface, Fox has acknowledged the supremacy of the pope, or bishop of Rome, but now he makes an attempt to shift the supremacy to the emperor Otho.

The *emperor* was requested to confirm Adalbert's election, he says, on which the monarch sent for the prelate-elect to court for investiture, and there giving him the ring and crosier, ordered him off to the archbishop of Mentz to be consecrated. This tale is very plausible, but not quite correct, if we are to believe the Rev. A. Butler, in his life of this saint; and as the latter martyrologist has given us authorities for what he has related, it is more reasonable, we think, to give credit to a writer who brings forward evidence in support of his relation than a man who does not. Mr. Butler says, Adalbert was chosen by an assembly held a few days after the death of his predecessor, that he endeavoured to prevent his election, but ineffectually, and was consecrated in 983 by the archbishop of Mentz. Not a word about going to court, and receiving the ring and crosier from the emperor; and it would seem, from Mr. B.'s account, that the emperor did not see Adalbert until some years after he was made bishop. The claim of investiture had not then, we believe, been raised by the temporal sovereigns; and if it had, the emperor could not have issued orders for consecration to the archbishop, for that being a purely spiritual act, no temporal authority could be exercised to enforce it. The pope and the pope only could grant spiritual jurisdiction, and it is he, by virtue of the authority given by Christ to Peter and his successors, that confirms the election of all bishops. In the *eleventh* century, it is true, the kings of Germany, of France and England, laid claim to the privilege of investiture, which is a term used to express the right and the act of investing persons with certain powers, both ecclesiastical and civil. The ceremony as regarded bishops and abbots was the delivery of the ring and crosier, but as it bore the appearance of simony, the act was condemned by the supreme pontiffs, and resisted by those prelates who were remarkable for the sanctity of their lives and the uprightness of their conduct. Of these St. Anselm, archbishop of Canterbury, in the time of William Rufus, was a brilliant example.

Fox next states, that Adalbert " divided the revenue of his see into " four parts, *according to the directions of the canons extant in the fifth* " *century*. The first was employed in the building and ornaments of " the church; the second went to the maintenance of the clergy; the " third was laid out for the relief of the poor; and the fourth reserved " for the support of himself and family, which was always made to in- " clude twelve indigent persons, to whom he allowed daily subsist- " ence." Mr. Butler adds, that these twelve poor men were kept in honour of the apostles, and that the holy prelate employed the whole of his own patrimony in alms. " He had in his chamber a good bed," writes Mr. B. " but on which he never lay; taking his short rest on a " sackcloth, or on the bare floor. His fasts were frequent, and his " life most austere." Hence, then, it is clear, that this martyr, honoured by Fox, was a Catholic and not a Protestant bishop. The latter prelates are so little inclined to relinquish the comfort of a good bed,

that they add to the enjoyment by taking bed-fellows besides, and
bed-fellows too that would not share lodgings with them if they slept
on *sackcloth*, like the holy Adalbert.   But we wish particularly to impress upon the mind of the reader, especially if he be a Protestant, the
admission here made, by Fox and his modern editors, that by the canons
extant in the *fifth* century, the revenues given to the church were divided into four parts, namely, one to raise and repair places of worship,
a second to maintain the clergy, a third to relieve the poor, and the
fourth to support the bishop.   We wish him also to bear in mind, that
while this kingdom was Catholic, the church revenues were thus invariably appropriated, and oftentimes made to contribute largely to the
exigencies of the state.   But is this the case now?   Has the nation bettered itself by the change introduced at the reformation, so called, of
the sixteenth century?   Who is the individual, not interested in the
question, that will answer us in the affirmative?   In the time of Adalbert, and in all Catholic countries at this period, the clergy are enjoined
celibacy, so that their wants are few, and their cares for a family less.
When this country was Catholic, no rates were raised beyond the tithe
to build and repair churches; none to support the poor, nor were taxes
levied to relieve the indigent clergy and their families.   The most beautiful fabrics were raised to become temples of worship for the living
God; alms-houses and hospitals were erected for the poor and infirm,
and all this without a tax, except the tithe levied for the civil establishment of the clergy.   But when the state began to meddle with religion;
when it was thought necessary to reform that system of divine revelation which was never to be altered or stand in need of alteration, what a
change has this intermeddling made in the situation of the country.
The revenues heretofore destined to works of charity and hospitality,
were given to hungry and corrupt courtiers; and, as the practice of good
works and self-denial were laid aside, as superstitious customs, the
clergy were allowed to marry.   Till this period a married clergyman
was a nonentity, and by the laws of the country, the offspring of an
ecclesiastic, if such were unfortunately born, were rendered incapable
of inheritance, so strong was public feeling against the abuse of a discipline derived from the apostles, and held sacred by the Catholic
church.

The adversaries of this church, however, as we before observed, had
no taste for restraints of the flesh, but they gave an unbridled license
to the passions, and secured, as far as they could, the means of gratifying them.   Laws were passed to allow the *reformed* clergy to marry
and legitimate their issue; while, for the support of their families, the
whole of the tithes were given to them, leaving the churches and the
poor wholly unprovided for.   The impolicy of this system soon made
its appearance, by the disturbances and discontents of the indigent, and
new laws were passed to levy rates on land and trade to maintain the
poor and keep the churches in repair.   At first these measures bore
lightly on the people, and the delusive dread of Popery, which the interested were continually instilling into the public mind, prevented the
bulk of the nation from discovering the woful change that had been
made from an unmarried to a married clergy.   The present posture of
affairs has, however, contributed greatly to open the eyes of the peo-

ple, and nothing but the most stupid folly could induce the modern editors of *Fox's Book of Martyrs* to notice so creditable an instance of disinterestedness and self-devotion on the part of Adalbert, a Catholic bishop in the tenth century, when the conduct of the reformed clergy in the nineteenth is the subject of censure and reproach for their selfishness and want of attention to the instruction of their flocks. These exciters of "hatred and abhorrence of the (supposed) corruptions and "crimes of Popery and its professors," should have recollected that those who live in glass houses ought not to be the first to throw stones : and when they undertook the publication of this mass of falsehood and fact, compounded together for deception, but professedly given to diffuse "among their fellow believers *a knowledge* and *love* of the *genuine* "*principles of Christianity,*" they should have cast a view over the present situation of "Protestant-ascendency," and have ascertained whether the corruptions and crimes of her followers are not more enormous and censurable than those they impute to Popery. While they are extolling Adalbert for dividing the revenues of his see into four portions for religious purposes, the public press is daily teeming with instances of avariciousness and extortion on the part of "Protestant-ascendency." It is a fact undeniable, that the clergy of the establishment are paid better than any other clergy in the whole world, and less worked. In Ireland alone, where the mass of the people are Catholic, the clergy of the establishment are computed to receive more than the clergy, Catholic and Protestant, of the rest of the civilized world. And yet, while bishops are dying worth 300,000*l.* property and upwards, the people are saddled with taxes to maintain the sons and daughters of clergymen in the shape of pensioners and half-pay officers; to keep the poorer clergy from going to the workhouse; and to raise churches, when dissenting places of worship are erecting by the side of them!! But this is not all. In Catholic times, hospitals and charitable foundations were established by donations given through motives of piety; now the people are called upon, besides paying their poor and church rates, to contribute towards national schools, bible schools, societies for promoting Christian knowledge, missionary societies and numerous other establishments, ostensibly formed for charitable purposes, but principally applied to support idle hangers-on, too lazy to work and too proud to beg.

While we are now writing, a bill is pending in parliament to empower the inhabitants of a parish in Ireland to repair the cathedral, in consequence of the neglect of the bishop and clergy to do so. This fact forms so striking a contrast to that related by Fox of the holy Adalbert, that we feel impelled to record it, as we find it given in the public papers.—"A bill," says the *Dublin Evening Post,* "a private "bill, is at present before parliament to enable the inhabitants of the "parish of Templemore, in which the cathedral of Derry stands, to "raise a sum of money for its repair, and to create an economy fund "for its future maintenance: we shall, probably, never hear a word "about the business, for it is a private bill, and, like other matters of "that kind, managed in the snuggest manner by the honourable house; "but we happen to have heard something about this matter, and a "more objectionable job, a more barefaced manœuvre of certain digni-

" taries of the church to shove a burden from their own to the shoulders
" of the inhabitants of the parish of Templemore, we have never heard
" of.—Who will believe it?   The cathedral of Derry is in ruins.—The
" cathedral upon whose roof the cannon were planted against king
" James's army, is in ruins.   The bishop who gets *only* 20,000*l.* a-year
" from this poor diocese has not been within its walls for many a-year.
" The dean, who, poor fellow, has only 4,000*l.* a-year, has not per-
" formed service in it for two years.   Bishop, dean, and prebendaries,
" have all forsaken it, and the only memorial of its former splendour,
" save, indeed, its dilapidated walls, is a snuff box in possession of the
" club of Derry apprentices, formed out of the oak-beam upon which
" the aforesaid cannon was placed.   Oh, Derry, Derry, *fuit Ilion*.   But
" now for the job.   Some good natured citizens, a few years ago, who
" were proud of their cathedral, subscribed to the amount of 2,000*l.* for
" its repair; with becoming deference they left the money in the hands
" of the bishop, and he, after building up and pulling down, with about
" as much taste as he has shown in the building of his own many-
" headed monster at Fahan, determined at last to put up four wooden
" pinnacles upon the tower, dashed over with sand and gravel to imi-
" tate stone; but the winds had no more respect for his pinnacles
" than his lordship had for the cathedral, and down they came one
" stormy night.   The citizens were indignant; the bishop was grand
" and mighty; and when they demanded an account, he abruptly left
" his palace in his chaise and four, and vowed that he would never
" again patronize the ungrateful citizens of Derry.   He kept his word;
" for many years he never slept in Derry, because his palace stood op-
" posite the cathedral, and for years never put his foot within its walls.
" But still the cathedral became worse and worse, and at last the con-
" gregation, dean, chapter, and all, were obliged to leave it, and to beg
" permission to repeat their prayers in the Presbyterian meeting house.
" Such has been the condition of the cathedral of Derry for the last
" two years; the cathedral of a diocese, whose lands are to be num-
" bered in *no less than forty-nine parishes*, whose rental, if set at full
" value, would be at least 120,000*l.* a-year, which gives a net income
" of 20,000*l.* to its bishop, and contains the greatest patronage of any
" diocese in the empire.   Loud, frequent, but vain were the applica-
" tions made to the bishop and dean; they were wise in their genera-
" tion, and having consulted the statute book, they found that no law
" could compel them to spend one shilling—as for respect for the church,
" had not the bishop sufficiently shown his zeal for it, by giving all the
" best livings in his diocese to his sons and nephews—what more could
" be expected from him?   If the citizens of Derry wanted a place of
" worship, they were to pay for it; as all solicitation was in vain, the
" citizens did not think it necessary to exert themselves, and they ac-
" cordingly agreed to assess themselves in an annual sum for ever for
" the repair of the church.   The corporation did the same—a second
" subscription was raised, but all would not do.   Sir G. Hill was there-
" fore instructed to bring a bill into parliament to enable the parish to
" raise a sum of money upon the faith of the annual assessment of the
" parish, and the subscription of the corporation; and, after a great
" deal of difficulty, he persuaded the dean, with the concurrence of the

" bishop, to saddle *his successor* in the deanery with an annual contri-
" bution of five hundred pounds for the future repairs of the cathedral.
" Now this is a rank job—it is felt to be a job by the citizens of Derry,
" and it will, when known, be stigmatized as a job by every honour-
" able mind, by every well-wisher of the church." Now, reader, taking leave of these wooden pinnacles, turn your eyes to those beautiful
and grand specimens of taste and architecture, still standing as monuments of the skill and devotion of our ancestors, and then look at the
paltry erections now going on under the name of churches. In the one
you see sublimity and grandeur of design; in the other a parsimony of
execution that flashes conviction of the superiority of the *dark ages* over
these *enlightened days,* at least in the science of ecclesiastical architecture; and when we take into consideration that the churches raised by
the Catholics were done without a single act of parliament or the least
compulsory tax upon the people, save and except the tithe, while nothing can be done in these days without the force of parliament and the
aid of the tax-gatherer, it must be acknowledged the position of the
two periods will not bear a contrast.

But we must return from this digression to the martyrologist. Adalbert is represented as the most amiable of characters, and the people
over whom he was placed the most depraved. Unable to recover them
from their state of impiety, " he determined," we are told by Fox, " to
" CONSULT THE POPE, and made a journey to *Rome*" for that purpose. Hence it is incontestible that Adalbert was what our modern
editors call a Papist, and John Fox, " a godly martyr," and that the
pope was at this time the head of the church; for we are further told
by John Fox, that the pope advised Adalbert to give up his bishopric,
that the archbishop of Mentz applied to the pope to send him back to
it, that he was sent back by the pope with *leave* to retire again if he
found the people still incorrigible, that finding them as bad as ever, he
left his bishopric and directed his attention to the conversion of the
Poles, that the archbishop of Mentz applied to the pope a second time,
and Adalbert was *commanded* to return. The people were obstinately
bent on opposing his admonitions, and going to preach the faith at
Dantzic, he met with death on the 23d of April 997, being stabbed
with lances. With this acknowledgment of the supremacy of the pope
in the tenth century, Fox closes his third book. The next introduces
us to most important subjects; we therefore give it a distinct head.

BOOK IV.

" PERSECUTIONS IN VARIOUS COUNTRIES, FROM THE ELEVENTH TO THE
" SIXTEENTH CENTURY."

The first section of this book is distinguished by a sub-head, entitled,
" *Persecutions in the eleventh century,*" and commences with an " *account*
" *of archbishop Alphage,*" who filled the see of Canterbury from 1006
to 1012. This prelate, according to Fox's account, was a stanch Catholic and *a monk.* He was also a man of the most exemplary piety
and abstemious habits. " The see of Winchester," writes Fox, " being
" vacant by the death of Ethelwold, a dispute arose respecting a suc-
" cessor to that bishopric. The clergy had been driven out of the ca-

" thedral for their scandalous lives, but were admitted again by king
" Ethelred, upon certain terms of reformation. The monks, who had
" been introduced upon their expulsion, looked upon themselves as the
" chapter of that church; and hence arose a violent contest between
" them and the clergy who had been re-admitted, about the election of
" a bishop; while both parties were vigorously determined upon sup-
" porting their own man. This dispute at last ran so high, that Dun-
" stan, archbishop of Canterbury, as primate of all England, was ob-
" liged to interpose, and he consecrated Alphage to the vacant bi-
" shopric, to the general satisfaction of all concerned in the elec-
" tion. The behaviour of Alphage was a proof of his being equal to
" the dignity of his vocation. Piety flourished in his diocese; unity
" was established among his clergy and people; and the conduct of
" the church of Winchester made the bishop the admiration of the
" whole kingdom. Dunstan had an extraordinary veneration for Al-
" phage, and when at the point of death, made it his ardent request to
" God, that he might succeed him in the see of Canterbury; which ac-
" cordingly happened, though not till about eighteen years after Dun-
" stan's death. In the course of that period, the metropolitan church
" was governed by three successive prelates; the last of whom was
" Alfric; upon whose decease in 1006, Alphage was raised to the see of,
" Canterbury. The people belonging to the diocese of Winchester
" were too sensible of the loss they sustained by his translation, not to
" regret his removal to Canterbury. Soon after he was made archbi-
" shop, he went to Rome and received the pall from pope John XVIII."
    That this prelate was a Catholic, or, as the modern editors of Fox
would say, " a Papist," admits of no doubt, since he went to *Rome*
to receive the pall from pope John XVIII. We have no account here
of his being sent to court for investiture, and receiving the ring and
crosier from the *king*, but on his appointment to the primacy of the
English church, Elphege, as he is named by Catholic writers, goes to
Rome and receives his commission from the *pope*, consequently this
" godly martyr" admitted the supremacy of the chair of St. Peter, as
did also the whole nation. Fox amuses his readers with a supposed dispute about a successor to the see of Winchester, on the death of Ethelwold; we have consulted the Rev. A. Butler's martyrology, and that
very learned work, Dr. Milner's *History of Winchester*, in neither of
which do we find the least mention of such a contest; it is therefore
to be placed among the many fables to be found in this work of delusion and falsehood. That there were scandals existing at this period
among the clergy, cannot be denied, and among other offences, some
of the secular priests had taken to themselves wives in violation of
the canons, for which they were expelled the churches by St. Dunstan, and St. Ethelwold, the predecessor of Elphege, following the
example of the holy primate, ejected the secular canons from his cathedral at Winchester, and placed monks in their stead. As the attempts on the part of good prelates to restore discipline and preserve
morals have become the subject of virulence and abuse with many of
our Protestant historians, and particularly of that popular writer, Mr.
Hume, it may not be amiss to enter briefly into the subject, as occasion may offer in the course of our review, to make references to this

period. That the discipline of the primitive ages enjoined continency to the clergy is proved to demonstration by the numerous canons, in those ages of pure Christianity, against the marriage of bishops, priests, and deacons. St. Jerom, an unimpeachable witness in the fourth age, testifies that in the three great patriarchates of Rome, Alexandria, and Antioch, no individuals were admitted into the ecclesiastical state but such as voluntarily embraced a life of celibacy, or were mutually and freely separated from their wives. So when this country received the faith of the gospel in the time of pope Gregory the great, the same discipline was introduced by St. Augustin, by whose apostolical exertions the light of truth was enkindled in this island. The constant inroads made by the Danes upon our ancestors occasioned great disorders, and the excesses of the lower orders of the clergy were a source of scandal to the nation. The bishops exhorted and reproved in vain, and strong measures were absolutely necessary to reduce men to a sense of their duty, who were grown callous through the force of bad habits. Accordingly, in the year 944, a synod of bishops, abbots, and nobles was convened, in which, by the joint concurrence of the civil powers, it was decreed, "That all clergymen in higher orders " shall lead a chaste life, conformable to the character they bear, un-" der the penalty of forfeiting their temporalities, and being deprived " of Christian burial, if they die impenitent." By many writers this decree has been looked upon as an act of tyranny, and there are many persons now, though they exclaim against the burden of paying tithes, that think it hard the clergy should not be allowed to marry. The experience of eighteen hundred years on the part of the Catholic church, and that of three centuries on the side of the reformists, will suffice, we think, to convince any reasonable mind of the vast advantages obtained by the former over the latter. And what degree of harshness or oppression can be substantiated in the above decree? No person is compelled to enter into ecclesiastical orders, and on doing so they do it with a full knowledge of the engagements they enter into; the act therefore being voluntary on their part, there can be neither injustice nor tyranny on the part of the church for maintaining that state of discipline which is necessary to make her ministers respected and their morals unblemished. The Saxon king Edgar, on occasion of these disorders, thus addressed an assembly of prelates convened to remedy the scandal. "These sacred foundations," says he, " we now " see sacrilegiously wasted by dissolute churchmen upon their dogs, " their birds, and their concubines. In vain have you expostulated, " exhorted, rebuked. The houses of the clergy are become the seats " of riot and intemperance, the resort of libertines, of singers, and buf-" foons. The people murmur, all good men are scandalized. The " evil increases, efficacious remedies must be applied. The sword of " St. Peter is in your hands, I wield that of Constantine. The spiri-" tual power is yours, the civil mine. The joint exertions of both is " necessary to suppress the present insults offered to religion, to ba-" nish vice, and to purify the polluted altar of God. Unclean intru-" ders have taken possession of the sanctuary; it is time they should " be compelled to quit their concubines or their livings. Too long " have they bid defiance to the laws and all lawful authority. But

" still let justice be tempered with humanity; let us give encourage-
" ment to repentance; we offer them the choice either to submit to the
" chaste and ancient discipline of the church, or to relinquish their
" ecclesiastical possessions." These sentiments, worthy a Christian
king, were delivered about the year 969, and we find the effect produced by them in the statement of John Fox, who says, that through
the exertions and behaviour of Elphege, "piety flourished in his dio-
" cess, unity was established among his clergy and people, and the
" conduct of the church of Winchester made the bishop the admira-
" tion of the whole kingdom." Such reforms as these, governed by
the spirit of true religion and justice, are sure to lead to the same results, namely, the happiness and improvement of the people of every
rank and condition; but the measures pursued by those who called
themselves reformers in the sixteenth century, originated in the worst
passions of human nature, and have consequently been attended with
the greatest evils that can possibly afflict mankind, as we shall have
occasion to shew in the progress of our labours.

Fox next proceeds to detail the events which led to the martyrdom
of Elphege by the Danes, in which the holy prelate shewed the greatest
devotion to the interests of his people, and the utmost disregard for his
own fate. After being translated to the see of Canterbury, having
filled the episcopal chair of Winchester twenty-two years, the Danes
laid siege to the former city, and took possession of it. Fox, in his
narrative, says, these barbarians took the place by storm, and destroyed all that came in their way; that the monks endeavoured to detain
the bishop in the church, but he broke from them, and ran into the
midst of the danger; that the Danes seized him, and obliged him to
remain till the church was burned and the monks massacred; and then,
he continues, they "decimated all the inhabitants, both ecclesiastics
" and laymen, leaving only every tenth person alive : so that they put
" 7286 persons to death, and left only *four* monks and 800 laymen alive."
We notice this statement to shew what little reliance can be placed
upon the details of this martyrologist, and the contempt he has for the
understandings of his readers. How could he come with such exactness at the population of this city in the eleventh century, as to know
the precise number to a single individual that suffered in this decimation, especially as it took place, according to his own account, *after*
an indiscriminate slaughter of the people, and a total massacre of the
monks? Will any man of common sense believe it possible for Fox to
become acquainted with such particulars at such a distant period?
Does it not carry every appearance of fiction, and prove how careful
the reader ought to be in crediting the statements made by him, when
given with such pretended minuteness? Were any man to attempt at
this day to enumerate to a single life, the loss of killed and wounded in
storming a besieged town, would he be believed? Would he not be
taken for an impudent asserter, and laughed at or kicked for his impudence? We think such would be his fate with every rational man, and
such should be the treatment towards the author and editors of the
Book of Martyrs.

To afford our readers the opportunity of contrasting the account of
this martyr's death, as given by Catholic writers, with that related by

Fox, we here extract a passage from Butler's *Saints' Lives*, relative to this event. "During the siege," Mr. B. writes, "he often sent out to "the enemies to desire them to spare his innocent sheep, whom he en-"deavoured to animate against the worst that could happen. And "having prepared them, by his zealous exhortations, rather to suffer "the utmost than renounce their faith, he gave them the blessed eu-"charist, and recommended them to the divine protection. Whilst he "was thus employed in assisting and encouraging his people, Canter-"bury was taken by storm. The infidels, on entering the city, made "a dreadful slaughter of all that came in their way, without distinc-"tion of sex or age. The holy prelate was no sooner apprised of the "barbarity of the enemy, but breaking from the monks, who would "have detained him in the church, where they thought he might be "safe, he pressed through the Danish troops, and made his way to "the place of slaughter." Dr. Milner, in his *History of Winchester*, says, "He was seen to rush between the murderers and their helpless "victims, crying out to the former: 'If you are men, spare at least "the innocent and the unresisting; or, if you want a victim, turn your "swords upon me; it is I who have so often reproached you with "your crimes, who have supported and redeemed the prisoners whom "you have made, and have deprived you of many of your soldiers, by "converting them to Christianity.' The person and the merit of St. "Elphege were well known to the Danes; having been sent upon dif-"ferent embassies to them, and rendered them many charitable offices. "Hence they did not dare to strike him, but satisfied themselves with "seizing upon him, and committing him to close custody, intending "to extort an enormous sum for his ransom. During his confinement "of seven months, these Pagans, being alarmed at an epidemical dis-"temper which afflicted them, were upon the point of releasing him, "without any ransom. At length, however, their avarice prevailing, "they sent for him to Greenwich, where their fleet then lay, and put "the question finally to him, whether he was prepared to pay the 3000 "marks of gold, which they had imposed as his fine. His answer "was, that all the money which he could command, had been spent "upon the poor, and that if he had more, it would be their property; "in a word, that he had no gold to bestow upon those, in whose pre-"sence he stood, except that of true wisdom, which consisted in the "knowledge of the living God. Being provoked at this answer, they "beat him to the ground, and began to overwhelm him with stones, "and the horns of slaughtered oxen; whilst he, raising up his eyes to "heaven, thus addressed himself to his divine Master: *O good Shep-"herd, do thou watch over the children of thy church, whom, with my last "breath, I recommend to thee.* Our saint having pronounced this prayer, "and continuing to suffer, a Dane, by name Thrun, whom he had the "day before baptized, moved by a cruel kind of pity, struck him on "the head, with his battle axe, and completed his martyrdom." Here we see these two Catholic writers confining themselves to general facts, which do not admit of dispute, and such should be the rule of every author who is desirous to narrate the truth and nothing but the truth.

The last martyr recorded by Fox, in this book, to whom Catholicism

can lay claim, is Stanislaus, bishop of Cracow. The character given
of this holy prelate by the martyrologist is of the most glowing description. He was a prodigy in learning, amiable in his disposition,
austere in his devotions, and fixed in embracing the ecclesiastical state.
On being admitted to holy orders, the then bishop of Cracow made
him a canon of his cathedral. "In this capacity," says Fox, "he lived
" in a most exemplary manner, and performed his duties with unre-
" mitting assiduity." His virtues charmed the bishop, and he would fain
have resigned his bishopric in favour of Stanislaus, on account of his great
age, but the latter refused to accept of it on account of his want of
years. The bishop however died in 1071, and all concerned selected
Stanislaus for his successor, but he still refused, for the reason before
stated. "At length," continues Fox, "the king, clergy, and nobility
" unanimously joined in writing to pope Alexander II. who, at their
" entreaty, sent an express order that Stanislaus should accept the bi-
" shopric. He then obeyed, and exerted himself to the utmost in im-
" proving his flock. He was equally careful with respect both to
" clergy and laity, kept a list of all the poor in his diocese, and by
" feeding the hungry, clothing the naked, and administering remedies
" to the sick, he proved himself not only the godly pastor, but the phy-
" sician and benefactor of the people." Here then it is clear that this
" godly pastor," this "physician and benefactor of the people," was
" a Papist," as the modern editors of Fox would call him, that is, a Catholic, according to the right sense of his creed. He is explicitly stated
as yielding to the commands of the pope, therefore he must have allowed the authority and supremacy of the pope, and so must the king
and clergy and nobility of Poland, by making their application to Alexander II. to enforce their election. Thus it is manifest the supremacy
of the pope was received with the light of Christianity, which would
not have been the case had there not been divine authority for it. Fox
next proceeds to detail the martyrdom of the saint, which arose from
his courageous opposition to the unbridled lust and brutish extravagan-
cies of the then king of Poland, Boleslas II. This monarch, it appears
was an archetype of our Henry VIII. who murdered the pious bishop
Fisher, for adhering to the same spiritual supremacy that Stanislaus
acknowledged, and who refused to sanction Henry's enormities as Stanislaus reprobated the cruelties of Boleslas. Why Fox should make a
distinction between such characters, either in the case of the monarchs
or the prelates is irreconcileable to common sense; yet so it is, and
the modern editors of his book are busily employed in circulating this
mass of delusion and inconsistency, in order, they say, to diffuse
" among their fellow-believers a knowledge and love of the genuine
" principles of Christianity!!" Precious principles of Christianity
must they be that require falsehood and deceit for their support. But
to return to Stanislaus. After several unsuccessful attempts to bring
the king to a sense of his duty to himself and to his people, Stanislaus
excommunicated the monarch, and forbad him to be received into the
church during divine service. Boleslas in his rage dispatched some of
his servants to get rid of the bishop, but they were awed by his venerable aspect, on which the king plunged his dagger into the saint's
heart at the foot of the altar, where the martyr was at his devotions.

This happened in 1079. We cannot quit this account without calling the attention of the reader to the amiable self-devotion and charity exhibited in the conduct of these two Catholic bishops, and the general course of life of the *reformed* (as they are called) bishops and ministers under "Protestant-ascendency."

PERSECUTIONS OF THE WALDENSES IN FRANCE.

We are now arrived at a very important period of our review, and we beg the reader's most earnest attention to the subjects that may come before him. Hitherto the martyrs recorded by Fox have been Catholics, renowned for their exemplary devotion and sincere piety; practising every act of charity, and believing in *one* system of faith, derived from the apostles, and carried by their successors into all nations. The whole of Europe had at this time received the Catholic faith, and in every country a regular hierarchy had been established, over each of which the pope held the spiritual supremacy, as head of the whole, by divine appointment. In the preceding pages, we have seen how *heresy* rose up in the churches of Asia and Africa, and as every error became known, was condemned by the pastors of the church, in which condemnation Fox has joined most cordially; we have seen that the broachers and adherents of the erroneous doctrines invariably had recourse to the civil sword, when foiled in argument, and now it was that the eastern countries were nearly subdued by the sword of Mahometanism for their impiety and presumption. With the exception of the note introduced by the modern editors of Fox to the life of St. Boniface, we have no intimation whatever of any *error* having crept into the church of Christ, nor could such be the case, since Christ had promised that HIS church should NEVER ERR, but that the Spirit of Truth should abide with her even to the end of the world. Now, unless we could rely upon this promise of Christ, and who shall we believe before God himself? would it not be more consistent to renounce Christianity at once, than to be so beset with folly as to give credit to the notions of this pretender to inspiration, then to that railer against what is called Popery, without examining what claim they have to be believed in preference to the whole church of Christ? Without some rule for our guide, it is impossible we can go right, and we have before us the rule which was followed by the successors of the apostles, and by every church after the seal of truth was imparted to the people. But, in contradiction of this rule, in the very face of history, and without a single tittle of evidence, we are now assured by Fox, that the system of faith which had civilized the Pagan world, was become infected with error and superstition. Here are his words, sensible reader, and we beg your particular attention to them. "Before " this time (he writes) the church of Christ was tainted with *many* of " the *errors of popery*, and superstition began to predominate; but *a* " *few*, who perceived the pernicious tendency of such errors, deter-" mined to shew *the light of the gospel in its real purity*, and to disperse " those clouds which *artful priests* had raised about it, in order *to delude* " *the people*. The *principal of these worthies* was Berengarius, who, " about the year 1000, boldly preached *gospel truths* according to their "*primitive purity*. Many, from conviction, went over to his doctrine,

" and were, on that account, called Berengarians. Berengarius was
" succeeded by Peter Bruis, who preached at Toulouse, *under the pro-*
" *tection of an earl*, named Hildephonsus; and the *whole tenets of the*
" *reformers*, with the *reasons* of their *separation from the church of Rome*,
" were published in a book written by Bruis under the title of Anti-
" Christ. In the year 1140, the number of *the reformed* was very *great*,
" and the probability of their *increasing* alarmed the pope, who wrote to
" several princes to *banish* them their dominions, and employed many
" learned men *to write* against them. In 1147, Henry of Toulouse,
" being deemed their most eminent preacher, *they* were called Henri-
" cians, and *as they would not admit* of *any proofs relative to religion but*
" *what could be deduced from the scriptures themselves*, the popish party
" gave them the name of Apostolics. Peter Waldo, or Valdo, a native
" of Lyons, at this time became *a strenuous opposer of popery*; and from
" him the reformed received the appellation of Waldoy, or Waldenses.
" Waldo was a man eminent for his learning and benevolence; and his
" doctrines were adopted by multitudes. The bishop of Lyons, taking
" umbrage at the freedom with which he treated the pope and Romish
" clergy, sent to admonish him to refrain in future from such discourses;
" but Waldo answered, 'That he could not be silent in a cause of such
" importance as the salvation of men's souls; wherein he must obey
" God rather than man.' "

Such is the introduction made by Fox, on *changing* his tone respecting the subject of religion; let us now examine his statements by the
test of history. We have shewn the impossibility of the smallest degree of error in points of faith creeping into the church of Christ,
though Fox blasphemously asserts that it was tainted with many corruptions; but we do not mean to deny that there were artful priests,
who sought to delude and lead others into error. Among these we
have seen Arius and his abettors, both bishops and priests, condemned
by Fox himself, Novatus, Eutyches, Nestorius, and a swarm of heretics,
who were immediately detected and denounced by the guardians of the
true faith as soon as their novelties began to be made public. The
same was the case with Berengarius, who is named by John Fox as the
principal among " the worthies," who, about the year 1000 " preached
" gospel truths according to their primitive purity." This " worthy,"
this gospel preacher, was honoured with the Catholic priesthood,
and nominated archdeacon of Angers, in France, by Hubert of Vendome, bishop of the see, about the year 1039. He first broached errors against marriage and infant baptism, about the year 1047, but soon
corrected himself. He next began to teach his novelty respecting the
real presence of our Saviour in the blessed eucharist, about fifty years
after the period stated by Fox, and as soon as he had declared himself,
his own schoolfellow, Adelman, bishop of Brescia, warned him that he
stood in opposition to the sense of the *whole* Catholic church. Here
then we have a man placing his own individual *opinion* against the
general *conviction* of the whole Christian world; and is there a being simple enough to believe that Berengarius knew better than the
whole of mankind put together, and that he *only* was in possession of
the truth? To entertain such an idea would be madness, and yet here
are a set of men putting forth such folly, in order to diffuse, they say,

among " their fellow-believers (Must not those who believe with them
" be fellow-fanatics?) a knowledge and love of the genuine principles
" of Christianity." A very rational idea of Christianity truly!

Bossuet, in his learned and acute *History of the Variations of the Protestant Churches*, says, that Berengarius was not only reproached by
Adelman, but that *all* the authors of that age upbraided him with im-
pugning the faith of the *whole universe*, and consequently the notions
he taught must be as downright heresy as the notions of Arius, and
others, stigmatized as such in this *Book of Martyrs*. For we wish the
reader to bear in mind, that heresy, as defined by Dr. Johnson, is, " an
" opinion of *private* men *different* from that of the Catholic and orthodox
" church;" and a heretic, according to the same authority, is, " one
" who propagates his *private opinions* in opposition to the Catholic
" church." By these definitions it is evident that Berengarius was *a
heretic*, and his notions *heresy*, because he was but a *private* individual
opposing the *Catholic church*, and his opinions were embraced only by
a few private men. Fox, in his account of the persecutions of the
Catholics by the Arians, and of the martyrdom of pope Martin, allows the right and authority of councils to define matters of faith;
now, if the popes and bishops possessed rightly that power in time
of persecution, they could not be divested of it in time of peace;
the power vested in the guardians of faith in the fourth and seventh,
must also be vested in them in the eleventh and nineteenth centuries;
and we see them exercising this right with the same forbearance and
clemency towards Berengarius, though the civil authorities were then
Catholic, as when the temporal power was in the hands of heretics,
and Catholics were the objects of persecution. This is a fact which
cannot be too often repeated, since it is little known to the Protestant
community, it having been the object of the writers of that party to
suppress and misrepresent every circumstance that might tend to elicit
the *truth* of history, and bear in favour of that faith which is immutable
and can never change. The proceedings against Berengarius we find
so clearly detailed by the Rev. Alban Butler, in a note to his life of St.
Leo IX, and the authorities he has produced so numerous and conclusive, that we should be guilty of a dereliction of our duty to the public were we not to lay before them the account of this judicious and
accurate writer.

" The news of this heresy," says Mr. B. " no sooner reached Rome,
" but St. Leo IX. condemned it in a council which he held in that city
" after Easter in 1050. But as Berengarius could not be heard in per-
" son, the pope ordered another council to meet at Vercelli three months
" after, at which the heresiarch was summoned to appear. He was
" soon informed of the condemnation of his error at Rome, and imme-
" diately repaired into Normandy to the young duke William the bas-
" tard. In a conference before that prince at Brione, he and a cleric,
" who was his scholar, and on whom he much relied in disputation,
" were reduced to silence by the Catholic theologians, and revoked
" their errors. But Berengarius insolently renewed them at Char-
" tres, whither he withdrew, as we are informed by Durand, abbot of
" Troarn, (l. de Corpore Domini, p. 437. (See also Mabillon,) Acta
" Bened. n. 16. et Anal. l. 59. n. 74.) St. Leo IX. opened the council

" at Vercelli in September, at which Berengarius did not appear, but
" only two ecclesiastics in his name, who were silenced in the disputa-
" tion: the doctrine which they maintained was condemned, and the
" book of John Scotus Erigena [from which he took his errors] thrown
" into the flames. In October the same year, 1050, a council at Paris,
" in presence of king Henry, unanimously condemned Berengarius and
" his accomplices, and the king deprived him of the revenue of his be-
" nefice. In 1054, Victor II. having succeeded the holy pope Leo IX.
" held immediately a council at Florence, in which he confirmed all
" the decrees of his predecessor. He caused another to be assembled:
" the same year at Tours by his legates, Hildebrand and cardinal
" Gerard, in which Berengarius made his appearance according to sum-
" mons.) He at first began to vindicate his error, but at length so-
" lemnly retracted it, and bound himself by oath to maintain with the
" Catholic church, the faith of the real presence in the blessed eu-
" charist.' This retractation he signed with his own hand, and
" thereupon was received by the legates to the communion of the
" church. (Lanfranc. p. 234. Anonym, de multiplic, condemn. Be-
" reng. p. 361. Guitm. l. 3. t. 18. Bibl. Patr. p. 462. Mabillon, &c.)
" Yet the perfidious wretch, soon after he was come from the council,
" made a jest of his oath, and continued secretly to teach his heresy.
" To shut every door against it, Maurillus, archbishop of Rouen, made
" an excellent confession of the Catholic faith, which he obliged all to
" subscribe: in which many other prelates imitated him. (See Mabil-
" lon, Act, t. 9. p. 226, et Annal, t. 2. p. 460, &c.) Eusebius Bruno,
" bishop of Angers, in his letter to Berengarius, mentions a second)
" council held at Tours against him. After the death of pope Stephen,
" who had succeeded Victor, Nicholas II. assembled at Rome in 1059,
" a council of one hundred and thirteen bishops, at which Berenga-
" rius was present, signed the Catholic confession of faith on this
" mystery presented him by the council, and having kindled himself
" a fire in the midst of the assembly, threw into it the books which
" contained his heresy. The pope sent copies of his recantation to all
" places where his errors had raised a disturbance, and admitted him
" to communion. Nevertheless, the author being returned into France,
" relapsed into his error, and spoke injuriously of the see of Rome, and
" the holy pope Leo IX. Alexander II. wrote him a tender letter, ex-
" horting him to enter into himself, and no longer scandalize the church.
" Eusebius Bruno, bishop of Angers, formerly his scholar, and after-
" wards his friend and protector, did the same. In 1076, Gerard, car-
" dinal bishop of Ostia, presided in a council at Poitiers against his
" errors. Maurillus, archbishop of Rouen, had condemned them in a
" council at Rouen, in 1063. (Mabillon, Analect. p. 224, 227, and
" 514.). Hildebrand having succeeded Alexander II. under the name
" of Gregory VII. called Berengarius to Rome in 1078, and in a coun-
" cil there obliged him to give in a Catholic confession of faith. The
" bishops of Pisa and Padua thinking afterward that he had not suffi-
" ciently expressed the mystery of transubstantiation and his former
" relapses having given reason to suspect his sincerity, the pope de-
" tained him a year at Rome, till another council should be held. This
" met in February, 1079, and was composed of two hundred and fifty

A REVIEW

OF

Fox's Book of Martyrs,

CRITICAL AND HISTORICAL.

No. 14.   Printed and Published by W. E. Andrews, 3, Chapter-house-court, St. Paul's Churchyard, London.   Price 3d.

EXPLANATION OF THE ENGRAVING.—*The subject of this cut is the assassination of Peter of Castelnau or Chateauneuf, the pope's legate, on the 15th of January, 1208, by a servant of the count of Toulouse, the protector of the Albigenses, and another ruffian. This outrage, and other violences, such as plundering churches, massacreing the priests, and pillaging towns, occasioned the crusade raised against these misguided and desperate wretches.*

CONTINUATION OF THE REVIEW.

" bishops. In it Berengarius declared his firm faith that the bread and
" wine are substantially changed into the body and blood of Christ, and
" prostrating himself, confessed that he had till then erred on the mys-
" tery of the eucharist. (See Martenne, Anecdot. t. i. p. 109.) After
" so solemn a declaration of his repentance he returned to the vomit
" when he arrived in France. Then it was that Lanfranc, who had been
" nine years bishop of Canterbury, in 1079, wrote his excellent confu-
" tation of this heresy, in which he mentions the pontificate of Gregory
" VII. and the last council at Rome, in 1079. From which, and other
" circumstances, dom Clemencez demonstrates that he could not have
" published this work whilst he was abbot at Caen, as Mabillon and
" Fleury imagined. About the same time Guitmund, afterward bishop
" of Aversa, near Naples, a scholar of Lanfranc, published also a learned
" book on the body of Christ, against Berengarius. Alger, a priest and
" scholastic at Liege, afterwards a monk of Cluni, who died in 1130,
" wrote also an incomparable book on the same subject, by the reading

" of which Erasmus says his faith of the truth of that great mystery,
" of which he never doubted, was much confirmed, and he strongly
" recommends to all modern Sacramentarians the perusal of these three
" treatises, preferably to all the polemic writers of his age. Durand,
" monk of Fecam, afterward abbot of Troarn, about the year 1060,
" likewise wrote on the body of our Lord, against Berengarius, which
" book is published by D'Archery in an appendix to the works of Lan-
" franc.

 " These treatises of Lanfranc and Guitmund doubtless contributed to
" open the eyes of Berengarius, who never pretended to make any re-
" ply to either of them, and whose sincere repentance for the eight last
" years of his life is attested by irrefragable authorities of the same
" age, as by Clarius the monk, who died ten years after him, and almost
" in his neighbourhood. (Spicileg. t. ii. p. 747.) Richard of Poictiers,
" a monk of Cluni, (Ap. Martenne, Ampl. Collect. t. v. p. 1168.) the
" Chronicle of Tours, (Ap. Martenne, Anecd. t. iii.) and others. These
" eight years he spent in prayer, alms-deeds, and manual labour, in the
" isle of St. Cosmas, below the city, then belonging to the abbey of
" Marmoutier, where he died in 1088. William of Malmsbury writes,
" that he died trembling, after making the following declaration: 'This
" day will my Lord Jesus Christ appear to me either to glory, by his
" mercy, through my repentance; or, as I fear, on the account of others,
" to my punishment.' Oudin, the apostate, betrays a blind passion in
" favour of the heresy, which he had embraced, when he pretends to
" call in question his repentance. (De Script. Eccles. t. ii. p. 635.)
" Cave carries his prejudices yet farther, by exaggerating beyond all
" bounds, the number of his followers. If it amounted to three hun-
" dred, this might seem considerable to Malmesbury and others, who
" complain that he seduced many. Not a single person of note is men-
" tioned among them. Cave says, his adversaries were only the monks.
" But Hugh, bishop of Langres, Theoduin of Liege, Eusebius Bruno of
" Angers, the two scholastics of Liege, Gossechin and Adelman, many
" of the bishops who condemned him, and others who confuted his
" error, where not of the monastic order. Never was any heresy more
" universally condemned over the whole church. The unhappy author
" is convicted from his writings of notorious falsifications (Martenne,
" loc. cit. p. 111. &c.) and of perfidy from his three solemn retracta-
" tions falsified by him, viz. in the Roman council of pope Nicholas II.
" (Conc. t. ix. p. 1101.) and in those of St. Gregory VII. in 1078 and
" 1079; not to mention that which he made before William the bastard,
" duke of Normandy. From the fragments and letters of this here-
" siarch which have reached us, it appears that his style was dry,
" harsh, full of obscure laconisms, no ways equal to the reputation which
" he bore of an able grammarian, or to that of the good writers of the
" same age, Lanfranc, Adelman, St. Anselm, &c. His manner of writ-
" ing is altogether sophistical, very opposite to the simplicity with
" which the Christian religion was preached by the apostles. We have
" extant the excellent writings of many, who entered the lists against
" him; Hugh, bishop of Langres, Theoduin, bishop of Liege, Eusebius
" Bruno, bishop of Angers, (who had been some time his protector),
" Lanfranc, Adelman, scholastic of Liege, afterward bishop of Brescia,

" Guitmund, monk of the cross of St. Leufroi, afterward bishop of
" Aversa, B. Maurillus, archbishop of Rouen, Bruno, afterward bishop
" of Segni, Durand, abbot of Troarn in Normandy, B. Wholphelm,
" abbot of Brunvilliers, near Cologn. Ruthard, monk of Corwei, after-
" ward abbot of Hersfield; Geoffery of Vendome, whose first writing
" was a treatise on the body of our Lord; St. Anastasius, monk of St.
" Michael, afterward of Cluni, Jotsald, monk of Cluni, Albert, monk of
" mount Cassino, Ascelin monk of Bec, Gosechin, scholastic of Liege,
" an anonymous author published by Chifflet, &c. See the History of
" Berengarius, wrote by Francis le Roye, professor in laws at Angers,
" in 4to. 1656: and by Mabillon in his Anacleta, t. ii. p. 477. and again
" in his Acta Bened. t. ix. Fleury, Histor. Eccles. and Ceillier, t. xx.
" p. 280. have followed this latter in their accounts of this famous he-
" resiarch. But his history is most accurately given by FF. Clemences
" and Ursin Durand, in their continuation of the Historie Literaire de
" la France, t. viii. p. 197, who have pointed out and demonstrated seve-
" ral gross mistakes and misrepresentations of Oudin and Cave, the
" former in his Bibl. Scriptor. Eccles. t. ii. the latter in his Hist. Liter."
    From this statement, it is plain that Berengarius could not be a
preacher of " gospel truths, according to their primitive purity," as
Fox asserts; nor did the popes, by whom his doctrine was condemned,
do more than Fox allowed the popes had a right to do, in his account
of the martyrdom of pope Martin in the seventh century. By a
reference to page 178 of our Review, it will be seen that Fox stated
that Martin called a council of bishops, on the heresy of the Monothelites, by whom the heresy was condemned; and by the account quoted
from Mr. Butler, it appears that Leo XI. and his successors did no
more towards Berengarius. His opinion was new and novel, like the
opinions of the Monothelites; and as such, it was condemned by the
ministers of Christ's church, appointed to guard the faith delivered to
them, that no novelty or error may creep therein. The only difference
that we can discover in the two cases is, that in the case of the Monothelites the civil powers were against the pope; whereas, in that of
Berengarius, the temporal monarchs were in unity with the head of
the church. In the case of pope Martin, he exhibited, in the persecutions he suffered for defending " gospel truths according to their pri-
" mitive purity," a mind impressed with the truths he preached, and a
courage unshaken at the torments he endured; whereas Berengarius
displayed baseness and treachery in his conduct; violating his solemn
oath, and at last repenting his misdeeds, and declaring his doctrine,
which Fox calls pure gospel-truths, to be no other than FALSEHOOD.
Had Berengarius been inspired with the Spirit of Truth, as the apostles,
and Catholic fathers, and bishops were, why did he not preach his
doctrines with the same undeviating firmness as they did, sealing their
conviction with their blood, and in every instance defying tortures
and death to the renunciation of those truths which had been imparted
to them? We see council after council called to consider and decide
upon the new opinions of this heresiarch; we see all these synods
agree in deciding against him, and yet we are told that he " preached
" gospel-truths according to their primitive purity." A very pretty
worthy must he be, that could retract and return to his vomit time

after time, and at last die condemning and renouncing the gospel-truths he preached ! ! !

But, we are told by Fox, this " principal" of " the worthies" was succeeded by " Peter Bruis, who preached at Toulouse, under the " *protection* of an *earl:* and the *whole tenets* of the reformers, with the " *reasons* of their *separation* from the church of Rome, were *published* " in *a book* written by Bruis, under the title of ANTICHRIST ;" a valuable composition, we have no doubt, and not to be excelled, for fable and falsehood, the *Book of Martyrs of John Fox* excepted. But what necessity could there be for Peter to preach *under the protection of an earl,* if he were commissioned, like the apostles of Christ, to teach all nations? The apostles and the primitive fathers did not preach under the protection of men of this world, but against the passions by which men of this world are generally influenced. We could have wished that John Fox had given us some quotations from this famous work of Peter Bruis, *published* some hundred years before printing was invented !! Why did not John give an extract or two from this book, that his readers might have learned *what* the tenets of the earl-protected Peter were? Fox has hitherto been sadly defective here ; and we have frequently had to supply his omissions, as we shall do in the case of his friend Peter. Know then, reader, that this Peter de Bruis was a native of Dauphine in France, and began to dogmatize when but young, some time about the middle of the twelfth century. By an hypocritical demeanour, he gained reputation among the populace, and particularly women : while the writers of that time charge him with committing the most wicked actions, and being the most corrupt in morals. Mr. Butler tells us, in a note to his life of St. Dominic, that Peter the venerable, abbot of Cluni, wrote against the errors of Peter de Bruis, and reduced them to five, viz. " That he denied the validity " of infant baptism : condemned the use of churches and altars ; and, " *wherever his rabble was strong enough, beat them down:* rejected the " mass : denied that alms and prayers avail the dead, and forbade the " singing of the divine praises in churches : rejected the veneration of " crosses, broke them down, and made bonfires of the wood, on which " he boiled great pots of broth and meat, for a banquet, to which he " invited the poor." This disposition *is* not much allied to the demeanour of the apostles and the primitive fathers, who neither stirred up sedition nor broke the peace of the country in which they preached. But if the doctrines of Peter de Bruis be " gospel-truths, according to " their primitive purity," why do not the " few plain Christians," who have edited this account, for the purpose of diffusing " among their " fellow-believers (or fellow-fanatics) a knowledge and love of the " genuine principles of Christianity," follow the *same* gospel-truths ? We know that they have, like Peter de Bruis, rejected the mass and prayers for the dead, and the veneration of crosses ; but why not deny the validity of infant baptism also? Why not knock down the churches, as well as destroy the altars ? Why not forbid singing in the churches? To be consistent, if these were " gospel-truths" in the *twelfth* century, they must be " gospel-truths" in the *nineteenth.* The truths for which the martyrs, heretofore recorded by Fox, laid down their lives, were divine revelations committed by Christ to his apostles, and by them to their successors, *all* of which, and no more, have been held by the Catholic church from her first foundation to the present day; while it appears, from the account of John Fox, that the *reformers*, or dogmatizers against that church, could never agree on their "gospel-truths." The primitive Christians, too, be it observed, raised up churches and altars to offer up the august sacrifice of the mass, and assembled therein to sing praises to the most High; but Peter de Bruis, we see, beat them down, and rejected the mass. Now, if Peter preached "gospel-truths according to their primitive purity," the martyrs of the primitive ages could not be "godly martyrs," though John Fox styles them so, because they were opposed to these "gospel-truths;" and truth, we all know, must be *one* and the *same*. It cannot be *this* to-day, and *that* to-morrow; but the *same* yesterday, and to-day, and for ever. Leaving the "few plain Christians" to get out of this dilemma, we will proceed a little further in our remarks.

Fox goes on, "In the year 1140, the number of the reformed was "very great; and the *probability* of their increasing *alarmed the pope*, "who wrote to several princes to *banish* them their dominions, and "employed many learned men to write against them." This latter admission is something in favour of Popery, since it is allowed that there were "learned men," who could WRITE against these pretended reformers, and we will add, with accuracy too. Many of their works are still extant, and are referred to as evidence of the impiety and inconsistency of John Fox's new allies. But what shall we say to the pope's writing to "several princes" to "banish" the reformers from their dominions? *Who* were the princes, and to *what* part of the world were the reformers to be sent? The only place in Europe at this time infected with error was the south of France, all the rest of this division of the globe was Catholic; therefore, to banish the reformers from their own country would only be to spread the error wider, and this we can hardly conceive the pope would consent to. Besides, to what country, as we before asked, could they be banished? Where were the vessels to convey them to foreign parts? It is manifest that Fox is here speaking at random, and with no regard to truth or the understanding of his readers; and had he not written before that period, we should have been led to suppose that he borrowed his idea from the report spread in the time of Oates's plot, which, though ridiculous in itself, was almost universally believed: namely, that the Jesuits intended to convert this kingdom to Popery, by cutting the throats of *all* the Protestants in it. A grand plan of proselytism. The fact, however, is, that besides the learned men employed to *write* against these pretended reformers, other zealous men were engaged to *preach* to them, amongst whom were St. Dominic and St. Bernard, who converted a great many of them back to the Catholic faith by the force of reason and the aid of miracles, which they worked in evidence of their divine commission, if we are to credit the most respectable writers of that age.

Fox next says, "In 1147, Henry of Toulouse, being deemed their "most eminent preacher, they were called Henricians; and as they "would not admit of any proofs *relative to religion*, but what could be "deduced from *the scriptures themselves*, the Popish party gave them

" the name of *Apostolics*." Why the disciples of this Henry should be called *Apostolics*, rather than *Scripturists*, which we think would have been a more appropriate term, if their notions were such as Fox describes them to be, we have not been able to learn. Indeed, we have every reason to believe that this term is an invention of Fox's brain, as we cannot trace it in any of the Catholic writers we are acquainted with. But what credit will the reader be henceforth inclined to give John Fox, when he is informed that the Apostolics or Henricians, so far from deducing *scripture* proofs for their religious, or rather irreligious, opinions, actually *rejected* the old testament, and admitted only a part of the new. Following the customary rule of the church, as allowed by Fox in the case of the Monothelite heresy, a council was held in the year 1176, at Lombez, near Alby, where the errors were examined, proved, and condemned. Bousset says, the acts of this council are recited at length in Roger de Hoveden's Annals of England, who begins his account thus: " There were heretics in the pro-
" vince of Toulouse, who would have themselves be called good men,
" and were maintained by the soldiers of Lombez. Those said, they
" neither received the law of Moses, nor the prophets, nor the psalms,
" nor the old testament, nor the doctors of the new, except the gospels,
" St. Paul's epistles, the seven canonical epistles, the acts, and the
" revelations." A very neat way of deducing proofs from scripture, and a very respectable set of " worthies," to preach " gospel-truths
" according to their primitive purity." To shew the *true* character of the *new allies* of John Fox and his modern editors, to traduce the Christian faith now spread over the world, we here subjoin the Rev. Mr. Butler's description of this " most eminent preacher," as Fox styles him, Henry of Toulouse. " His (Peter Bruis) disciple Henry, a pre-
" tended hermit, an eloquent but illiterate man, propagated his errors.
" Hildebert, the zealous and pious bishop of Mans, famous for his
" elegant letters, sermons, and other works, tells us, that while he
" went to Rome to procure the pope's leave to retire to Cluni (which
" he did not obtain), that hypocrite, who went barefoot even in the
" middle of winter, and ate and slept on some hill in the open air, ob-
" tained surreptitiously leave to preach penance in his diocess. When
" he had gained crowds of innumerable followers, by railing against
" their superiors and the clergy, then he openly discovered his heresies.
" Regardless of the censures which the clergy fulminated against him,
" he continued his seditious discourses, though the clergy convicted
" him of having committed adultery on Whitsunday, &c. Fanaticism
" often extinguishes all sense of modesty and decency. Henry, attach-
" ing lewd women to his party, persuaded them that they obtained the
" pardon of all past sins by public immodesties in the church, and
" made innumerable marriages among the people, all which he caused
" to be contracted with the like shameful ceremonies, as is related
" in the history of the bishop of Mans, Acta Episc. Cenoman. Hilde-
" bert, upon his return, was surprised to see the havoc which the wolf
" had made in his flock, but in a short time regained their confidence,
" convicted Henry publicly of ignorance and imposture, and obliged him
" to leave his diocess, and return to his own country. Hist. de l'Egl. de
" Fr. l. 22. t. viii. p. 191. Now, we will here ask the reader what he thinks

of the " few plain Christians," who have put out this *Book of Martyrs* with the view, as they say, of diffusing among their " fellow-believers " a knowledge and love of the *genuine* principles of Christianity?" Could such a fellow as this Henry be a teacher of Christianity ? And yet this book tells us, upon no authority whatever but the bare assertion of its author, that he was one of the " most eminent preachers" of the reformed; one of the " worthies," who had determined to shew *the light of the gospel in its real purity*; while the most unquestionable authorities represent him as a lewd and corrupt hypocrite, an instigator of sedition, and a violator of the laws of morality. What precious auxiliaries have these " few plain Christians" colleagued themselves with, in order to create " a hatred and abhorrence of the (supposed) corruptions and crimes of Popery and its professors !"

The next of these " worthies" is the chief of the sect called *Waldenses*, of whom Fox thus speaks : " Peter Waldo, or Valdo, a native " of Lyons, at *this time* became a strenuous opposer of Popery; and " from him the *reformed* received the appellation of Waldoys, or Wal- " denses. Waldo was a man eminent for his learning and benevolence; " and his doctrines were adopted by multitudes. The bishop of Lyons " taking umbrage at the freedom with which he treated the pope and " the Romish clergy, sent to *admonish* him to refrain in future from " such discourses; but Waldo answered, ' That he could not be silent " in a cause of such importance as the salvation of men's souls, wherein " he must obey God rather than men.' " Such is the introduction given by Fox to the transactions narrated concerning these deluded and unhappy sectarians; for, that they did not follow the " genuine principles of Christianity" must be taken as certain, since their notions never obtained general circulation like the revealed mysteries of the Catholic church, and were of themselves variable. Peter Waldo, by Fox's account, laid claim to the care of men's souls; but who gave him authority to do so? He could produce no other title to preach " gospel- " truths according to their primitive purity," than his own individual assertion, unaccompanied by any testimony of a divine charge; and was it likely that the whole Christian world would listen to such a fanatic? As well might the " few plain Christians" have linked themselves with the mad prophet Brothers, or the cunning mother of the expected Shiloh, Johanna Southcott, to diffuse the " genuine principles of Chris- " tianity" among their fellow-believers, as to ally themselves with Peter Waldo, the infatuated merchant of Lyons, He certainly succeeded in deluding the unwary in his days, as Brothers and Johanna have in our own; but happily their notions never became general, and therefore could not be genuine. By this statement, too, it is clear that persecution was not then an inseparable ingredient in Popery, as the " few plain Christians" assert; for it appears that Waldo was only *admonished*, not punished, for his abuse of the clergy. But we must now see what Waldo had to say against Popery, and what doctrines he taught, which Fox has placed under special titles, and we copy them literally.

" ACCUSATIONS OF PETER WALDO AGAINST POPERY.

" His principal accusations against the Roman Catholics were, that " they affirm the church of Rome to be the only infallible church of

" Christ upon earth; and that the pope is its head, and the vicar of
" Christ; that they hold the absurd doctrine of transubstantiation, in-
" sisting that the bread and wine given in the sacrament is the very
" identical body and blood of Christ which was nailed to the cross;
" that they believe there is a place called purgatory, where the souls of
" persons, after this life, are purged from the sins of mortality, and
" that the pains and penalties here inflicted may be abated according
" to the masses said by and the money paid to the priests; that they
" teach, the communion of one kind, or the receiving the wafer only,
" is sufficient for the lay people, though the clergy must be indulged
" with both bread and wine; that they pray to the Virgin Mary and
" saints, though their prayers ought to be immediately to God; that
" they pray for souls departed, though God decides their fate imme-
" diately on the decease of the person; that they will not perform the
" service of the church in a language understood by the people in
" general; that they place their devotion in the number of prayers,
" and not in the intent of the heart; that they forbid marriage to the
" clergy, though God allowed it; and that they use many things in
" baptism, though Christ used only water. When pope Alexander the
" third was informed of these transactions, he excommunicated Waldo
" and his adherents, and commanded the bishop of Lyons to extermi-
" nate them: thus began the papal persecutions against the Wal-
" denses."

" TENETS OF THE WALDENSES.

" 1. That holy oil is not to be mingled in baptism.

" 2. That prayers used over things inanimate are superstitious.

" 3. Flesh may be eaten in Lent; the clergy may marry; and auri-
" cular confession is unnecessary.

" 4. Confirmation is no sacrament; we are not bound to pay obe-
" dience to the pope; ministers should live upon tithes; no dignity
" sets one clergyman above another, for their superiority can only be
" drawn from real worth.

" 5. Images in churches are absurd; image-worship is idolatry; the
" pope's indulgences ridiculous; and the miracles pretended to be
" done by the church of Rome are false.

" 6. Fornication and public stews ought not to be allowed; purga-
" tory is a fiction; and deceased persons, called saints, ought not to
" be prayed to.

" 7. Extreme unction is not a sacrament; and masses, indulgences,
" and prayers, are of no service to the dead.

" 8. The Lord's prayer ought to be the rule of all other prayers."

Well, here we have the accusations of Peter Waldo, and the tenets
he attempted to establish. For the first time, we have something in
the shape of doctrine in the *Book of Martyrs;* and let us now compare
these accusations and doctrines with the truths taught and believed by
the primitive Christians. Hitherto Fox's " godly martyrs" have been
all of them Catholics; but now, all at once, the reformers have become
possessed of the " gospel truths preached according to their primitive
" purity." The first of his principal accusations against the Roman
Catholics, we are told, is, " that they affirm the church of Rome to be
" the only infallible church of Christ upon earth; and that the pope is

" its head, and the vicar of Christ." To be sure, the Catholics do insist upon this article; and would they not be fools to put their trust in a church which they believed to be *fallible?* What reliance could they have on the correctness of the tenets they believed, if they were not sure they had them from unerring authority? Would they not rest on *human* assurance, if the church they followed was liable to error? Would they not be more consistent by rejecting their church at once, if they thought her fallible? As to the church of Rome being the *only* infallible church, there can be but *one* true church, which must be infallible; and there is no other but the Catholic church that can lay claim to infallibility, because she, and she only, can trace her doctrines up to the apostolic ages. For example, by referring to page 39 of our Review, it will be seen that St. Ignatius, who is ranked by Fox a " godly martyr," and was cotemporary with the apostles, succeeding St. Peter in the see of Antioch, held the infallibility of the church of Rome, and the supremacy of the bishop of that see over the whole church; consequently, Peter Waldo was opposed to this " godly martyr." St. Irenæus, bishop of Lyons, who is termed by Fox " a zealous op-" poser of *heresies* in general," maintained in his writings, and sealed with his blood, the *same* doctrines held by St. Ignatius, see page 67. Tertullian also defended the infallibility of the church, see page 83. St. Cyprian, who lived in the third age, and whose " doctrines were orthodox and pure," according to the testimony of Fox himself, bore witness to the infallibility of the church, disputed by Waldo, as may be seen in page 90. St. Basil, admitted by Fox to have been a " pillar of truth," and St. Gregory Nazienzum, cotemporary with St. Basil, both living in the fourth century, preached the doctrines of infallibility and supremacy, see pp. 166, 167, 169, 170. So much for the first accusation.

The second charge is, " that they (the Catholics) hold the *absurd* " doctrine of transubstantiation, insisting that the bread and wine given " in the sacrament is the identical body and blood of Christ which was " nailed to the cross." Well, and in believing this doctrine, they believe no more than what the apostles taught, and the primitive Christians believed. See our preceding pages; namely, 40, for the sentiments of St. Ignatius on this point; p. 49 and 50, for those of St. Justin, a Christian philosopher, who suffered at Rome about the year 166; p. 71, for those of St. Cyprian; and pp. 169 and 170, for the belief of St. Basil and St. Gregory.

The third charge is, " that they believe there is a place called pur-" gatory." So did St. Basil and St. Gregory Nazienzum, see our Review, p. 171, as a doctrine received from the apostles. Tertullian, in his work *De Cor. Milit.* p. 289, mentions " oblations for the dead on " the anniversary day." And, in his treatise on single marriages, he advises the widow " to pray for the soul of her departed husband, " entreating repose to him, and participation in the first resurrection, " and making oblations for him on the anniversary days of his death; " which, if she neglected, it may be truly said of her, that, as far as in " her lies, she has repudiated her husband."—*De Monogamia,* c. x. p. 955. St. Cyprian says, on this point, " Our *predecessors* prudently " advised, that no brother departing this life should nominate any

" churchman his executor; and should he do it, that no *oblation* should
" be made for him, nor *sacrifice* offered for his repose."—Ep. 1, p. 2.
Numberless other witnesses could be adduced in favour of this doctrine; but we think those we have produced, and who are admitted by
Fox to have been supporters of orthodox doctrines and opposers of
heresies, will be deemed sufficient by the reader.

The next charge is rather premature, and does not belong to
Peter Waldo: it is, " that they teach the communion of one
" kind, or the receiving the wafer only, is sufficient for the lay
" people, though the clergy must be indulged with both bread
" and wine." The receiving under one kind is not an article of faith,
but a matter of discipline; and in Peter Waldo's time, it appears that
the laity as well as the clergy received under both kinds. It was not
till John Huss began to dogmatize, that it was finally ruled by the
council of Constance, that communion should be administered to the
laity under one kind only. Thus, then, John Fox is at his old trade of
lying, and nothing more need be said about it here.

Catholics are next accused of praying " to the Virgin Mary and
" saints, though their prayers ought to be immediately to God." On
this point, we shall refer the reader to St. Basil and St. Gregory, both
competent judges, by Fox's admission, whose sentiments will be found
p. 172. Pope Martin, too, (see p. 179,) maintained the doctrine of
honouring the Virgin Mary next to God; and surely, as he was a
" godly martyr," he could not be a heretic, and a preacher of Popish
doctrines.

The rest of the accusations are not worthy of notice here, and would
take more space than we can spare to refute them; we will therefore
content ourself with observing, that as we have proved, by the evidence
of unimpeachable witnesses, that the leading charges here made in
Peter Waldo's name, against the church of Rome, apply with equal
force against all the " godly martyrs" hitherto recorded by John Fox,
the modern editors of his *Book of Martyrs* must either expunge them
from this book, or put Peter Waldo among the list of heretics admitted
by Fox to be such in his records of the acts of his godly Catholic martyrs. Of the tenets imputed by Fox to the Waldenses we must say a
few words, because, like his other statements, they are fabulous and
absurd. Of the first and second nothing need be said, they are rites
instituted by the church, and not revealed articles of faith. So we may
say of the third, with the exception of confession, which is of apostolic
institution, and flesh meat *is* eaten by Catholics in Lent; but what will the
reader say, when we shall prove that the Waldenses rejected marriage
altogether, and held that confession was valid if made to laymen. Of
the fourth, confirmation was not a subject of dispute with them; they
held obedience to the pope until he condemned their errors; and instead of allowing ministers tithes, they were to hold *nothing*, but live
upon alms. How would the established and dissenting clergy like
such a tenet should be taught by any of their flocks ? And then as to
the *equality* of dignity, is not this a thorough *levelling* system ? Will
the " plain Christians" say that this tenet is one of the " genuine prin-
" ciples of Christianity." Of the fifth, there is not the least appearance
in history that Waldo ever troubled his head about it; and of the sixth so

far was he from disallowing fornication and stews, that he, as we before said, abrogated matrimony as unlawful, and encouraged the promiscous intercourse of the sexes. The rest we have already shewn to be contrary to the belief of the primitive Christians, and therefore could not be *orthodox*. Of the seventh, extreme unction was not a contested point, and masses were not wholly abolished, as one was allowed to be celebrated every year. In this denial we are borne out by Bossuet, in his *Variations of the Protestant Churches*, who in his 11th book, vol. IV, after giving an account of a conference held between the Catholics and Waldenses, says, No. 80, "Without examining here which side "was right or wrong in this debate, it is plain what was the ground of "it, and which were the points contested; and it is more clear than "day, that in these beginnings, far from bringing the real presence, "transubstantiation or the sacraments into question, they did not as "yet so much as mention praying to saints, nor relicks, nor images."

As Fox has favoured us with his version of the tenets of the Waldenses, we will here give them as stated by his first antagonist father Parsons, on the authority of all the writers that exerted themselves to controvert the erroneous notions of these infatuated people, and lived contemporary with them.

" 1. That all carnal concupiscence and conjunction is lawful when " lust doth burn us.

" 2. That all oaths are unlawful unto Christians for any cause what- " soever in this world, because it is written, *nolite jurare*, Do not swear, " *Matt.* v. *Jac.* v.

" 3. That no judgment of life and death is permitted to Christians " in this life, for that it is written, *nolite judicare*, Matt. 7. Luc. 6.

" 4. That the creed of the apostles is to be contemned, and no ac- " count at all to be made of it."

" 5. That no other prayer is to be used by Christians but only the " *Pater noster* set down in scripture.

" 6. That the power of consecrating the body of Christ, and of hear- " ing confessions, was left by Christ not only to priests, but also to lay- " men if they be just.

" 7. That no priests must have any livings at all; but must live on " alms, and that no bishops or other dignitaries are to be admitted in " the clergy, but that all must be equal.

" 8. That mass is to be said once only every year, to wit, upon " *Maunday Thursday*, when the sacrament was instituted and the apos- " tles made priests: for that Christ said, *do this in my remembrance* to " wit (say they) that which he did at that time.

" 9. *Item*, That the words of consecration must be no other, but " only the *Pater noster*, seven times said over the bread, &c."

These and other articles, to the number of thirty-three, were condemned by the church in council, as in the case of Arius, Donatus, and the Monothelites, mentioned by Fox; and we think it but just that the author of the *Book of Martyrs* and his modern editors, the "few plain Christians," should shew *when* and *how* the pope and prelates of the church *lost* the right of condemning *error* in doctrine. Besides, to what a wretched situation must the "plain Christians" be reduced, when they find it necessary to associate themselves with sectarians of

an immoral character, and who differed from them too in many points
of doctrine as widely as Protestants do from Catholics, for the purpose
of diffusing, they say, " among their fellow believers a love and know-
" ledge of the genuine principles of Christianity," and " a hatred and
" abhorrence of the corruptions and crimes of popery and its *professors.*"
But we must now leave the reader to form his own unbiassed conclusions on the tenets of the Waldenses, which are represented by Fox
and his editors to be " gospel truths according to their primitive pu-
" rity," and enter into the *historical* transactions related by the martyrologist.

Fox writes, " Waldo remained three years undiscovered in Lyons,
" though the utmost diligence was used to apprehend him; but at
" length he found an opportunity of escaping from the place of his
" concealment to the mountains of Dauphiny. He soon after found
" means to propagate his doctrines in Dauphiny and Picardy, which
" so exasperated Philip, king of France, that he put the latter pro-
" vince, which contained most of the sectaries, under military execu-
" tion; destroying above 300 gentlemen's seats, erasing some walled
" towns, burning many of the reformed, and driving others into Flan-
" ders and Germany.

" Notwithstanding these persecutions (Fox continues), the reformed
" religion seemed to flourish; and the Waldenses, in various parts,
" became more numerous than ever. At length the pope accused them
" of heresy, and the monks of immorality. These slanders they, how-
" ever, refuted; but the pope, incensed at their increase, used all
" means for their extirpation; such as excommunications, anathemas,
" canons, constitutions, decrees, &c. by which they were rendered in-
" capable of holding places of trust, honour, or profit; their lands
" were seized, their goods confiscated, and they were not permitted to
" be buried in consecrated ground. Some of the Waldenses having
" taken refuge in Spain, Aldephonsus, king of Arragon, at the instiga-
" tion of the pope, published an edict, strictly ordering all Roman
" Catholics to persecute them wherever they could be found; and
" decreeing that all who gave them the least assistance should be
" deemed traitors. The year after this edict, Aldephonsus was severely
" punished by the hand of Providence; for his son was defeated in a
" great battle, and 50,000 of his men slain, by which a considerable
" portion of his kingdom fell into the hands of the Moors. The re-
" formed ministers continued to preach boldly against the Romish
" church; and Peter Waldo, in particular, wherever he went, asserted,
" that the pope was antichrist, that mass was an abomination, that the
" host was an idol, and that purgatory was a fable."

Now, through the whole of this account we have not one single authority quoted to substantiate the accuracy of it, but, as usual, all is
assertion, bare assertion. However, with the man of sense and penetration, the statement carries with it its own refutation. But unhappily there are too many hurried away by their own prejudices and passions to discover the specious mode of the narration, and therefore it is
our duty to lay bare the falsity of this account. Of the pope, the mass,
and purgatory, enough has been said to shew that Waldo's notions were contrary to the belief of the " godly martyrs" of John Fox,

from the first to the eleventh century, therefore they could not be
" gospel truths according to their primitive purity," but were "opi-
" nions of private men, different from that of the Catholic and orthodox
" church," which Dr. Johnson defines to be HERESY.—But to the narrative of Fox. Waldo, he says, was secreted at Lyons three years, notwithstanding all the diligence used to apprehend him, and at last escaping to the mountains of Dauphiny, he soon after found means to propagate his doctrines in that province and Picardy. This put the king
of France in a passion, and " he put the latter province, which con-
" tained most of the SECTARIES," we quote Fox's own words, "un-
" der military execution; destroying above 300 *gentlemen's* seats, eras-
" ing some walled towns, burning many of the reformed, and driving
" others into Flanders and Germany." First let us observe, that let
the tenets of Peter Waldo be what they might, they could not be the
doctrines of the Christian church, because Fox says that those who held
them were "*sectaries*," and Dr. Johnson tells us, *a sectary is* "one who
" divides from public establishments, and joins with those distinguish-
" ed by some particular WHIM ;" not it appears by "gospel truths
" according to their primitive purity," but some foolish WHIM of the
human brain, and therefore worse than stupid must those be, who, in
these enlightened days, entertain the idea that Waldo's tenets were
right, and the doctrines of the church of Rome were wrong, when
the latter had been in existence nearly twelve hundred years, and could
be traced to the apostles themselves. Then we are told that the king
was exasperated merely at the preaching of Waldo, and caused military execution to be enforced, towns to be erased, and a great number
of gentlemen's seats to be destroyed. Now the fact is, Fox has jum-
bled the history of the Albigenses with that of the Waldenses, though
he afterwards makes a section of the persecutions of the former. Let
us come to dates and we shall soon see what reliance is to be placed on
Fox's assertions. Peter Waldo began to turn *reformer*, as these dogmatizers are unaptly termed, about the year 1160, in consequence of the
sudden death of one of his fellow merchants, while conversing with
others on business. Fox says he was sought for but remained undiscovered *three* years in Lyons ; Bousset, however, in his *Variations*, gives
quite a different tale. The latter writer proves, from dates and authorities, that Waldo preached about *twenty* years, before any official notice was taken of his conduct, when pope Lucius III. condemned their
errors in 1181. The same writer states, that about the year 1194 a
statute of Alphonsus or Ildephonsus, king of Arragon, reckons the
Waldenses amongst heretics anathematized by the church. "After
" this pope's death," writes Bousset, " when in spite of his decree these
" heretics spread themselves far and near, and Bernard, archbishop of
" Narbonne, who condemned them after a great inquest, could not stem
" the current of their progress, many pious persons, ecclesiastics and
" others, procured *a conference* in order to reclaim them in an *amicable*
" manner. *Both sides* agreed to choose for umpire in the conference, a
" holy priest called Raimond of Daventry, a man illustrious for birth,
" but much more so for the holiness of his life. The assembly was
" very solemn, and the dispute held long. Such passages of scripture,
" as each party grounded itself on, were produced on both sides. The

" Vandois (or Waldenses) were condemned and declared heretics. It
" thereby appears (continues Bousset,) that the Vandois, though con-
" demned, had not as yet broken all measures with the church of Rome,
" in that they had agreed to the umpirage of a Catholic and a priest."
It also appears that the Waldenses were not then objects of *persecution*
seeing that the church, acting on the principle of charity and moderation, sought to convince these mislead men of their errors by persuasion, and to bring about a reconciliation in an amicable manner. That
the erasing walled towns and destroying gentlemen's seats are fictions
we have not the least doubt, as is also that of driving the reformers
into *Flanders* and *Germany*; for if the reader will only take a glance at
the geographical situation of the respective countries, he will find the
two last mentioned places on the north side of France, while the Waldenses infested the southern provinces. Had Fox said they were driven
into Spain and Italy he would have been less liable to objection.
     Having carried destruction among the ranks of the Waldenses, which
only made them, he says, fructify, Fox next assures us, that " the
" pope at length accused them of heresy, and the monks of immorality.
" These slanders (he asserts) they, however, refuted; but the pope,
" incensed at their increase, used all means for their extirpation; such
" as excommunications, anathemas, canons, constitutions, decrees, &c.
" by which they were rendered incapable of holding places of trust,
" honour, or profit," &c.   Let us here ask the sensible reader if such
an account as this carries with it the semblance of truth?   From what
Fox here states, the persecution was commenced by *military* execution,
and ended by *spiritual* censures.   And why did not the defender of the
Waldenses give us a specimen or two of their refutation of the charge
of immorality brought against them by the monks?   To say that these
slanders, as Fox calls them, were refuted, is saying just nothing. Any
one may deny a fact; but to *deny* a fact and to *prove* it *false*, are very
different things. Any of the unfortunate women that prowl the streets
of the metropolis for hire may assert that she is a virtuous woman; but
if she can be *proved* to have been guilty of incontinence by unimpeachable witnesses and her own declaration, what becomes of her
assertion of innocence?   So it was with the Waldenses; they stood
condemned by their own tenets and conduct, and it is for those who
call truth slander to *prove* the injustice of the charge. But this Fox
has not done, nor can he or his modern editors do so, because the evidence of real history is against him.   From the manner in which Fox
speaks of excommunications, &c. and the deprivation of places, &c. we
might be led to suppose, that the pope was all powerful and the state
of the Waldenses very pitiful; but observe, reader, there were very
few places in those days of profit, office being then considered more of
honour than of gain; (would to heaven such feelings prevailed now-
a-days in this Protestant country,) and the Waldenses renounced all
such things, for which they were also called *The Poor Men of Lyons.*
Of the edict of Aldephonsus, of which we have before spoken, it does
not appear to have been one of persecution, since measures of concilia-
tion were resorted to after its promulgation.
     We come now to Fox's account of the " *origin of the inquisition,*"
which he gives in these words : " *These* proceedings of Waldo, and

" his reformed companions, occasioned the origin of inquisitors; for
" pope Innocent III. authorized certain monks inquisitors, to *find* and,
" deliver over the reformed to the secular power. The monks upon
" the *least surmise* or *information*, gave up the reformed to the magis-
" trate, who delivered them to the executioner; for the process *was*
" *short, as accusation* supplied the place of *evidence*, and *a fair trial*
" was NEVER GRANTED to the *accused*."—If this account be true,
though we are inclined to believe that there is not a man of sense capable of giving credit to it, the Catholics in those days must have been
the most inhuman of all oppressors, and influenced by the most diabolical spirit. But, reader, is not this account over-coloured? Can you
believe that a country but lately rescued from a state of barbarism by
the benign influence of the Catholic religion; for, take notice, France
was converted to Christianity by Catholic missionaries acting in obedience to the pope; can you believe, we ask, that the ministers of that
religion which had civilized barbarians, and taught them the principles
of charity and justice, would all at once become so corrupt and lost to
every sense of tenderness and compassion, as they are here described
to have been? We cannot think it. We feel convinced that you will
put this account to the credit of bigotry and shameless assertion, and
not to a plain statement of facts.—"Accusation supplied the place of
" evidence; and a fair trial was NEVER granted to the accused!"—
God of heaven! that men calling themselves Christians, and professing
to be influenced with a desire of diffusing " a love and knowledge of the
" genuine principles of Christianity," should, in these enlightened days,
put forth so palpable a falsehood. But let us try this account by the
test of dates and history.—Waldo, as we have before stated, began to
dogmatize about the year 1160; Innocent succeeded to the popedom
in 1198, which makes a space of thirty-eight years between the appearance of the one as a preacher of " gospel-truths according to their pri-
" mitive purity," to use John Fox's words, and of the other as the
establisher of the inquisition. Now the inquisition was not established
till two years after Innocent had been elected to the papal chair, and
then not in consequence of the " proceedings of Waldo and his reformed companions," but in consequence of the immoralities and outrages
of another sect of heretics, called Albigenses, whose proceedings threatened destruction to civilized society, and called upon every well-wisher
to decency and rectitude of conduct to oppose the pernicious designs of
those disturbers of the public peace. We are not the defender of the
inquisition, because as an Englishman and a Catholic we have nothing
to do with it. It never was an establishment in this country, when the
king and people and parliament were Catholic, though tribunals similar, if not worse and more oppressive, such as high commission courts
and star-chambers, were instituted as soon as the nation became, as it
was called, *reformed*, in the reigns of Henry the 8th, Edward 6th, Elizabeth, and the Stuarts. Nay, at the very moment we are writing; at
the very time when the " few plain Christians" are circulating this mass
of calumny and lies to "excite hatred and abhorrence of the pretended
" corruptions and crimes of Popery and its professors;" a body of
people in Scotland called *Freethinkers* are petitioning the legislature of
this Protestant country against proceedings not unlike those laid to the

charge of the monk inquisitors of the twelfth century. As we do not deal in assertion and fiction, like John Fox and his modern editors, we here annex the petition as a document of singular interest, after all the bales of paper that have been wasted to inculcate the notion that "per-" "secution is inseparable from Popery," and that liberty of conscience was obtained by the reformation, so called.—The public journals report that Mr. Hume, on presenting the petition to the house of Commons on the evening of the 18th of May, 1824, said, the petitioners "complained" "of the interference of the magistracy and police with their discussions. "Their room had been forcibly entered, and the whole of their books" "taken from them by the public officers. Were men in the p——" "enlightened times to be subject to this kind of inquisition? The——" "lately appeared in the papers a decree, signed by Ferdinand, wi—" "whom we seemed to be running a race, in putting an end to all——" "quiry. Ferdinand, however, only took 'forbidden books' fr——" "who possessed them. We were not content with that, but we p——" "ed the persons of the possessors! Was it to be endured, that b——" "a man differed in opinion from the authorities in Scotland, ——" "on that account be at once imprisoned. He trusted some answ——" "be given to the case of the petitioners. The Lord Advocate ——" "that the honourable member for Aberdeen was very ill-informe——" "respect to the circumstances of the case which he had descri——" "which however he (the Lord Advocate) would not go.—M——" "remarked, that as the learned lord would not make answer,——" "Hume) should set it down that there was an inquisition in S——" "and that the learned lord was the grand inquisitor." The fo—— is the petition, which was ordered by the honourable house ——printed.

"Unto the Honourable the Commons of the United Kingdom of Great Britain and Ire- land, in Parliament assembled ; the Petition of the undersigned Individuals, who were Members of the Edinburgh Free-thinkers' Zetetic Society ; humbly sheweth,

"That your petitioners are of opinion, that severe laws, made to suppress free discussion, and punish those who question the truth and divine origin of religion, are extremely per- nicious to society, as they are often employed to support error and suppress truth; and thus fettering the human mind in its progress of knowledge and improvement, they make men ignorant bigots or pretending hypocrites. Such laws are seeming proofs of the weak- ness of religion, and make inquiring men suspect it is imperfect, and unable to support itself. That if the Christian Religion is a divine revelation, no discussion can injure it, nor any human efforts overturn it ; if it is founded on truth, free discussion will exhibit that truth, and consequently strengthen every rational mind in the belief of it ; but if it is founded on errors, severe laws may harrass individuals who criticise it, and may prop it up for a time, but cannot permanently support it against truth and reason.

"That the laws of Scotland, made for the support of the Church, and the punishment of what is called blasphemy, were so severe and oppressive, that they suppressed all inquiry into the foundation of Christianity, or the truth of its doctrines, and compelled every one to submit to the established opinion, whether right or wrong. That though two of the statutes which awarded the punishment of death for what is called blasphemy were re- pealed by the Unitarian Act, passed in 1813, yet as free discussion on religious subjects is still considered by every one to be very dangerous, your petitioners apprehend that there are other laws yet in force for the protection of established religion, which are far too severe for the enlightened and inquiring spirit of the present time.

"That your petitioners, though peaceable members of society, and strongly attached to their country, regard these laws as still allowed to exist for their oppression ; and even if these laws should be considered in disuetude (which is doubtful), the uncertainty of that matter, and the apprehension lest they should be prosecuted for the open expression of their opinion, keeps their minds in a state of great uneasiness, and creates a dislike to the laws of their country, instead of a respect for them.

"That your petitioners conscientiously differ in opinion from the established religion of their country, but have no wish whatever to disturb it : they conceive that Deists and

· A REVIEW

OF

Fox's Book of Martyrs,

CRITICAL AND HISTORICAL.

No. 15. Printed and Published by W. E. ANDREWS, 3, Chapter-house-court, St. Paul's Churchyard, London. **Price 3d.**

EXPLANATION OF THE ENGRAVING.—*At a conference between St. Dominic and some of the Albigensian chiefs, the former drew up in writing a short exposition of the Catholic faith, with proofs of each article from the new testament. This writing he gave to the heretics to examine. Their ministers and chiefs, after much altercation about it, agreed to throw it into the fire, saying, that if it burned, they would regard the doctrine it contained as false. Being cast into the flames it was not damaged in the least. This extraordinary circumstance occasioned the conversion of numbers of the Albigenses, and is recorded by Jordan, and by the ancient writers of St. Dominic's life, Theodoric of Afolda, Bernard Guidonis, and F. Humbert make mention of it.*

CONTINUATION OF THE REVIEW.

Christians, if they act according to their professions, and are not knaves and hypocrites, may carry on their discussions with temper and moderation, and live together in peace, vying with each other in good works, and not striving for each other's destruction.

"That your petitioners are not anxious to engage in theological controversy; but as they are weekly consigned to eternal perdition from the pulpit, and daily by many of the people, they have surely the strongest reasons to examine the truth of these doctrines, and the merit of these books, from which they are threatened with such unrelenting severity. That your petitioners being consigned to eternal misery in a life to come, and also unfairly dealt with in this, they are not allowed by the law to answer the arguments and examine the doctrines of those Christians who attack their opinion, abuse their character and motives, and use every exertion to make them detested by their fellow men.

"That, as your petitioners are compelled to pay their full proportion of the established clergymen's stipends, they consider that these reverend gentlemen would act more consistent with their professions, if they were to visit those whom they think have gone astray, and endeavour to instruct them, rather than so rashly to pronounce their condemnation. That, by the prosecutions instituted against all those who are known to print or sell their books, your petitioners are prevented from obtaining those books which defend or advocate their own opinions, and are thus deprived of the benefit of the press, and excluded from the same privileges which are enjoyed by every other sect, however extravagant.

"That your petitioners being liable to be punished if they meet together for public discussions or instruction, are convinced that it is through the forbearance of the civil authorities, and not under protection of the laws, that they can meet for that purpose; consequently, in their present state, they have as little interest in the stability of the laws and institutions of their country, as Jews or Aliens.

"That your petitioners, in publishing their opinions concerning revealed religion, and in defending their opinions, conceive that they are no more guilty of blasphemy than the Jews, who openly dispute and ridicule the doctrines of Christianity, and even reproach the character of its founder, yet are protected by law.

"That your petitioners have no motive but the love of truth in questioning the divine origin of Christianity, and can have no interest in following error when it is so dangerous; they have as deep an interest in discovering and supporting true religion as any other men: they question the divine origin of Christianity from the sincere conviction of their minds, which their inquiries into its origin have produced, and not from any wish to disturb the peace of society or the happiness of individuals.

"That your petitioners do not conceive that their public discussions or the circulation of their books are dangerous to religion; as it is only reflecting men who engage in such inquiries, their principles are never likely to be generally embraced; besides, divines inculcate that the church is founded on a rock, and cannot be overthrown; and many who have studied the human character, are convinced that the principle of devotion is so deeply planted in the human heart, and so much influenced by surrounding circumstances, that it will never be destroyed by any arguments, however rational or strong. That the unrestrained circulation of books, and free discussion of all religious subjects, would be of great benefit in clearing away error and superstition, and displaying the merits of true religion, and also in directing and assisting the human mind in acquiring knowledge, and thus promoting the improvement and happiness of mankind."

Let it be here noticed, that these complaints of persecution are not made against Popish tyranny in the " dark ages," but against " Protestant-ascendency" in our own enlightened days. Not against the ministers and authorities of the Catholic church, but against laws enacted by men who had thrown off the yoke, as they termed it, of Popish supremacy, and raised up what was called the standard of evangelical liberty. Here let us revert to the case of Berengarius, and compare the conduct of the Catholic divines in that age to the steps taken against these complaining " Freethinkers" of Scotland. When the errors of Berengarius became known, the pen and tongue were employed to convince him and those who espoused his notions that they were in the wrong. Council after council was called; he was allowed to defend his ideas without restraint; he did defend them, but the strength of Truth was too powerful for him to withstand it; he was forced by reason and facts, not by pains and torments, to give way, and his opinions soon became buried in oblivion. And why is not the same course pursued towards these Freethinking petitioners. The answer is obvious. The chain of divine authority was broken by the pretended evangelical reformers of the sixteenth century; all was left to human fallibility, and conviction lost its hold in an unerring guide. To carry their point, therefore, they had recourse to the civil sword; and the temporal magistrate was called in to restrain the mind, and put in force human laws passed to establish an " Ascendency," wherever the reformers obtained the upper hand, raised by human interests and human power. But, it may be asked, did not the Catholics call in the civil sword and human laws to coerce conscience and punish those who differ from them in opinion? When this difference was confined to opinion, and not extended to actions, threatening the safety of the community, we believe NEVER. Not a single instance of such an infringement on the liberty of conscience on the part of the Catholic church can be produced, because she is not invested with human but divine authority, and if there have been any such violation in particular Catholic countries, from *local* circumstances, the *church* itself is no more involved in the outrage, than Protestants of the present day can be charged with the villanous perjuries of Titus Oates, and the fanatic gullibility of the parliament of that day in believing his absurd and palpable lies. It does not appear that the Waldenses experienced any *persecution,* while they confined themselves within the bounds of peace, nor has Fox been able to make the founder of this sect a martyr, which no doubt he would have done had Peter Waldo met with a violent death. Mr. Alban Butler says, they subsisted in certain vallies in Piedmont till 1530, when Œcolampadius and the Sacramentarians of Switzerland entered into a treaty with them, which, however, was unsuccessful. " Six years after this," continues the same writer, " Farel and other Calvinistic ministers, by shewing " them that their temporal safety made it necessary, effected a union, " but obliged them to reject several errors which they maintained, and " to acknowledge that a Christian might sometimes lawfully swear be- " fore a magistrate, and punish malefactors with death; also that the " ministers of the altar might possess temporal estates, and that wicked " ministers validly confer the sacraments. They likewise engaged " them to maintain that the body of Christ is not in the eucharist, and " that there is no necessity of confessing one's sins : which points were " contrary to their former doctrine. Notwithstanding this union, most " of the Vaudois adhered to their own principles till, in 1630, they " were compelled for protection to receive Calvinistic ministers." *(Note to Life of St. Dominic.)* From this statement it is clear that the Waldenses were not in possession of the religious truths imparted to the apostles, and it is equally certain that *self-interest* influenced them to yield to the dogmatical spirit of the Calvinistic ministers, who could not *convince* the former of their error though they could *terrify* them into submission through fear of their personal safety. An examination into the history of this country, of Ireland, and in fact of all Protestant countries, since the era of the reformation, so called, will shew that Catholics were not to be so cajoled or alarmed out of their faith, which they know to be of divine origin, and therefore must not be bartered away for temporal interests.

As this is the question on which the principal and most odious of the charges brought against the Catholics rests, namely *Religious Persecution,* it may not be amiss, before we enter further into Fox's statements, to give a few authorities on the subject. We have stated that *persecution* is no tenet of the Catholic *church,* and we solemnly declare that were such a tenet to form part of her system, we would instantly leave her communion, and turn our pen against such an unhallowed violation of the right of conscience. Up to this period history furnishes not a single case of penal proscription, other than spiritual censures and excommunications, which the church was authorized by her divine Founder to exercise, as we find in the words of scripture, *He that will not hear the church, let him be unto thee as the heathen or publican.* Accordingly, in the case of the Arians, the Monothelites, &c. who are recognised as heretics by Fox, we see the church declaring the doctrine received from the apostles, and anathematizing those who obstinately oppugned the truth. But nothing further. No physical force was exercised to compel submission on the part of the Catholics; but, on the contrary, whenever the Arians gained the *civil* "ascendency," the former became victims of persecution. When Arianism was subdued by the triumph of truth, and Catholicism became the general belief of the Christian world, no other means were applied than the decision of councils and spiritual powers of the church, to caution believers against the specious notions of Berengarius. It is true, an attempt was made at the latter end of the fourth century, by a Spanish bishop named Ithacius, to raise a persecution against Priscillian and his followers who were guilty of heresy, but his conduct was reprobated and opposed by St. Ambrose, bishop of Milan, and St. Martin, bishop of Tours, two of the greatest ornaments of the Catholic church, who are held in the highest veneration to this day by Catholics. The Rev. A. Butler thus speaks of this affair in his life of St. Martin. " Neither St. Ambrose nor St. Martin, " would communicate with Ithacius or those bishops who held com- " munion with him, because they sought to put heretics to death. We " cannot wonder at the offence these saints took at their prosecuting " Priscillian in such a manner, when we consider how much the church " abhorred the shedding of blood even of criminals, and never suffered " any of her clergy to have any share in such causes. St. Martin con- " tinually reproved Ithacius for his conduct, and pressed him to desist " from his accusation. He also besought Maximus not to spill the " blood of the guilty; saying, it was sufficient that they had been de- ". clared heretics, and excommunicated by the bishops, and that there " was no precedent of an ecclesiastical cause being brought before a " secular judge." From these sentiments which are the genuine senti- ments of the church, nothing can be clearer than that persecution forms no part of her system. Whatever of blood that has been shed under pretence of religion is not to be laid at her door, but has been occa- sioned by the circumstances arising out of the erroneous doctrines dis- seminated, which have universally been productive of tumults and se- ditions, endangering the public peace, and threatening the destruction of property and civil society. When disorders such as these arise out of the preaching of fanatical empirics in religion, it becomes the duty of every friend to social order and justice to do his best in stemming the torrent of irregularity and error thus commenced, and preserve by the enforcement of just laws that order which is essential to the safety of the community or nation to which he belongs.

In support of this axiom we need not look for authorities in the " dark ages," as they are called by the upholders of " Protestant-as- cendency," since we have been furnished with the decisions of men in high official situations under this very ascendency, and in these en- lightened days. At the Lent assizes for Cornwall, held at Launceston, on the 1st of April, in the year we are writing, (1824) a young woman was tried for the murder of her younger brother, which it appeared she committed under the influence of religious frenzy, imbibed by her con- nexion with a sect of Methodists called *Revivers*. The learned judge (Burrough) before whom the unhappy creature was tried, in stating the case to the jury, said,—" The Almighty had expressly declared " that murder and suicide were two of the highest crimes that called

" for his vengeance; but such was the delusion this young woman had
" laboured under, that she first murdered her brother, and then con-
" templated self-destruction, conceiving that by committing these high
" offences she should be securing a way to heaven. It appeared that
" this young female had been in the habit of attending *religious* meet-
" ings, as they were *called*, where the wildest and most extravagant
" excitements were used that could possibly operate on the minds of
" the weak, and *lead them from a just sense* of the importance and duties
" of religion. He knew nothing of the particular sect of persons that
" had been spoken of to-day, and God forbid that he should be con-
" ceived as wishing to restrain any person from following those re-
" ligious customs which were most conformable to the conscience;
" that he did conceive *that the general benefit of society should be attended*
" *to*, and therefore he could not but consider, that *the doctrine and mode*
" *of worship, which inculcated the pernicious principles* this young woman
" had acted upon, *were injurious to society*, and OUGHT TO BE SUP-
" PRESSED. He therefore guarded the pastors of those congregations
" against continuing those practices, as being *derogatory to true religion,*
" and *dangerous to the safety of the community*." Such is the decision of
an English Protestant judge, and will the " few plain Christians " who
have published a cheap edition of the *Book of Martyrs*, to diffuse " a
" knowledge and love of the *genuine* principles of Christianity," and
excite " a hatred and abhorrence of the (pretended) corruptions and
" crimes of Popery and its professors;" will they, we ask, dare to contravene these excellent sentiments from the seat of justice ? We
doubt if they have effrontery sufficient, and yet they must do it, or give
up the new allies and martyrs of John Fox.

About the same time the above bewildered young creature was committing murder in this Protestant country, through the delusion of
religious fanaticism, a still more horrid scene was going on in the
Protestant canton of Zurich, in Switzerland, the particulars of which
were communicated through the public papers, and are these: A young
woman, who had lived for some time a very irregular life, persuaded
herself, all at once, that God demanded her life, to obtain at the price
of her blood the salvation of sinners. She succeeded in making her
family adopt this idea. One of her sisters under her tuition devoted
herself also to death. They armed the hands of their parents and
friends, and expired slowly under their blows. According to their
express commands they were fixed to crucifixes, and their executioners
waited patiently for three days, in expectation of their resurrection,
agreeably to the assurances of the young prophetess. The murderers
and their accomplices, to the number of eleven, having among them
the father, brother, sisters, and four of the principals, have been condemned to imprisonment and hard labour for life, or for a period of
years in proportion as they took a more or less active part in the horrid scene of carnage. The house where this deed was perpetrated has
been demolished, and it has been forbidden to build another on the
spot.—Here then we have the doctrine of the English judge acted upon
by the authorities of this Protestant canton, and will the " few plain
Christians," make it out that these fanatical murderers were *martyrs*
for religion, and the punishment inflicted on them is *religious persecu-*

tion? They must do so, we can tell them, or they must give up their dear auxiliaries in opposing Popery, the Albigenses, who were a set of wretches infinitely worse than the poor misled creatures we have just noticed.

To these authorities we have to add another, whose character and that of the assembly before which the opinions were delivered and applauded, must have considerable weight with the reader, especially if he be a Protestant. At the anniversary meeting of the "*Protestant Society for the Protection of Religious Liberty*," held on the 15th of May, 1824, lord Holland, who acted as chairman, said, " With *opinions* the " legislature had nothing to do ; it was for them only to look at *acts*— " the *fruits of opinions* ; and as long as those acts in no way interfered " with the *tranquillity* or *prosperity* of the country, he should always " look upon any interference as a needless and unadvised proceeding." This declaration, we are told by the papers, was very warmly cheered by the meeting, and we think very justly. Folly it most certainly is, to attempt to control or suppress *opinions* by legislative measures, because while man is endowed with free will no human force can prevent him from exercising his thoughts or stating his mind, unless he is deprived of the use of speech and pen—but when these *opinions* are converted into *acts*, and when these *acts* interfere with the *tranquillity* and *prosperity* of the country, then indeed legislative interference becomes necessary, according to the authorities quoted, not to *persecute* for *opinions*, but to secure the tranquillity of society from outrage and disorder. The petitioning Freethinkers of the nineteenth century do not appear to have committed one breach of the peace ; they call for the instruction of the established clergy, to bring them into the path of truth, if they shall find that they have strayed therefrom ; and yet while a nest of bigots calling themselves "plain Christians," are circulating a work abounding with falsehood, calumny, and misrepresentation, with a view to instil a deadly prejudice against the Catholics, as being persecutors from principle, Freethinking Protestants are complaining against the persecutions of ascendency Protestants ; and persecution for *opinion* too, and not for any violation of the civil rights of society. These "plain Christians" *assert* that " persecution is inseparable from Popery ;" we have already shewn, by historical facts, that persecution never was practised by the Catholic church to the period of the Waldenses, and we shall now proceed to shew that the crusade entered into against the Albigenses was not a persecution for religious opinions, but an opposition of force against force ; a defensive resistance of diabolical acts that menaced the whole of Christendom with blood and immorality.

THE ALBIGENSES.

Of these wretched people Fox gives the following account. " The " Albigenses," he says, "were people of the *reformed* religion, who " inhabited the country of Albi. They were condemned *on account of* " *religion*, in the *council of Lateran*, by order of pope Alexander III. ; " but they increased *so prodigiously*, that many cities were inhabited by " persons *only of their persuasion*, and several *eminent noblemen* embraced " their doctrines. Among the latter were Raymond, earl of Toulouse, " Raymond, earl of Foix, the earl of Beziers, &c. The pope, at length,

" *pretended* that he wished to draw them to the Romish faith by *sound*
" *argument* and *clear reasoning*, and for this end ordered *a general dis-*
"*putation;* in which, however, the popish doctors were *entirely over-*
" *come* by the *arguments* of Arnold, a *reformed* clergyman, whose rea-
" sonings were *so strong*, that they were *compelled to confess their force.*"
Such is the account given by Fox, which we think carries with it its
own refutation. For the reasonable man would naturally observe, if
the Popish doctors were entirely overcome; if the reasonings of Arnold
were so strong as to compel his antagonists to confess their force; how,
did it happen that he could not carry his truths, as they are represented to be by Fox, through the world, as the apostles and their
Popish successors did the revelation of Christ? If the Albigenses possessed the true faith, how was it they did not propagate it by preaching,
instead of causing sedition, rebellion, and carnage? Why did they not
imitate the apostles and primitive Christians, by suffering martyrdom
for their faith, without having recourse to physical force as other heretics had done before them?—Fox says they were condemned on account
of *religion:* no such thing; they were condemned on account of their
irreligion, as we shall hereafter shew.—They were condemned, he
says, in the council of Lateran, by order of Pope Alexander III. There
are *four* councils of Lateran, in the second of which Arnold's errors
appear to have been condemned. This council was held in 1139,
under pope Innocent II. and consisted of nearly a thousand bishops;
now are we to believe that Arnold's powers of eloquence were so
forcible as to be able to vanquish such a host of learning and wisdom
as was here congregated together?—Arnold too, it appears from the
most authentic historians, was not a leader of the Albigenses, for the
Rev. Alban Butler says, " The followers of this heresiarch were called
" Publicans or Poplicans."—Thus they were a sect, having no claim to
the unerring system of the universal church, and as such dwindled into
nothing. The third general council of Lateran, held by Alexander III.
do not seem to have noticed this heresy, being called for another purpose. A council was held at Tours in 1163, during the same pontificate, at which St. Thomas à Becket, archbishop of Canterbury, assisted,
where the heresy was examined and condemned. The fourth Lateran
council was held in 1215, under Innocent III. and was composed of
upwards of four hundred bishops, and eight hundred abbots and friars,
summoned from all parts of Christendom, and as the different sovereigns
were represented in it by their ambassadors, it may with perfect propriety be called the parliament of Christendom. This assembly did
most certainly take into consideration the innovations and impious
novelties of the Albigenses, and in so doing they adhered strictly to the
established customs of the church, as practised in the time of the Arians
and Monothelites, when Fox had so much regard to councils as to allow those to be heretics who were condemned by these ecclesiastical
parliaments. In the first place, the fathers examined the propositions
advanced by the Albigenses, and compared them with the constant
belief of the Catholic church, as handed down from the apostles, and
confirmed by preceding councils. They found the propositions to be
erroneous and contrary to the revealed truths of God, and opposed to
the morality of the gospel, and consequently they were condemned by

the Lateran fathers, as the council of Nice condemned the errors of Arius, and Fox acknowledges him and his followers to be heretics. After defining the faith, the council next proceeded to make regulations for the reformation of manners, and in passing these rules of public discipline, the council had the sanction of the civil power, so that there was the unanimous consent of the two powers, and of the Christian people against these pretended *reformers* of religion. From this brief statement, and a reference to the dates we have given, but which Fox has studiously avoided, some estimate may be formed of the confused manner in which the martyrologist gives his relations.

It is now time to give the reader some idea of these auxiliaries of John Fox and his modern editors. The Albigenses were a desperate sect sprung from the Waldenses, and embracing all the worst part of the Manichean heresy. Among other immoralities, they declared marriage to be unlawful, professed to abhor the sex, and practised that most horrible of crimes, which shall be nameless, the perpetration of which now-a-days excites so just a horror in the mind of the people. —Bousset, in his *Variations*, notices the sermons of St. Bernard, who was very instrumental in bringing a number of these deluded souls to the path of truth and unity and the bosom of the Catholic church. " But what he (St. Bernard) most insists on," writes Bousset, " is the " *hypocrisy,* not only in the deceitful appearance of their austere and " penitential life, but also in the custom they constantly observed of " receiving the sacraments with us (Catholics) and *professing* our doc- " trine *publicly,* which they inveighed against in *secret.* St. Bernard " shews, their piety was all dissimulation. In appearance they blamed " commerce with women, and nevertheless were all seen to pass days " and nights apart with them. The profession they made of abhorring " the sex, seemed to warrant their not abusing it. They believed all " oaths forbidden, yet, examined concerning their faith, did not stick " at perjury: such oddness and inconstancy is there in extravagant " minds ! . . . . St. Austin (writes the same author) informs us that " these people [the Manicheans, from whom the Albigenses sprung], " who debarred themselves of marriage, allowed liberty for every thing " else. What, according to their principles, they properly had in ab- " horrence, (I am ashamed to be forced to repeat it), was conception, " whereby it appears, what an inlet was opened to the abominations " whereof the old and new Manicheans stand convicted." This learned prelate enters into the history of the rise and errors of these heretics in a very elaborate manner, and produces a host of writers, who encountered their false doctrines, and exposed their wild and impious notions.—Alanus, a Cistercian monk, surnamed the universal doctor, wrote two books against the Albigenses and Waldenses about the year 1212. Peter of Vaux-Sernay wrote a history of the Albigenses, and describes their errors. Luke, bishop of Tuy, in Spain, we are informed by the Rev. Alban Butler, wrote three books against the Albigenses, about the year 1270. In the first he establishes the intercession of saints, purgatory, and prayers for the dead ; in the second, the sacraments, sacrifice, and benedictions of the church, and the veneration of crosses and images ; and in the third, he detects their fallacies, lies, dissembling of their sentiments, setting up false miracles, and *corrupt-*

ing the writings of Catholic doctors. Rainerius Sacho, who from a chief of the Waldenses became a Catholic and a friar, in 1250, and consequently was a perfect master of the mysteries of the sect, wrote a book soon after his conversion, which he entitled, *De Hæreticis*, that is, *Of Heresies*, wherein he lays open the abominable vices of this most pernicious heresy.—Having quoted these and many authors in support of his exposure of the enormities of these "people of the *reformed* religion," as John Fox calls them, [How much nigher to the truth would he have been had he said *deformed?*] Bousset observes, "Such were " the Albigenses by the testimony of all their cotemporary authors, " not one excepted. The Protestants blush for them, and all they can " answer is, that these excesses, these errors, and all these disorders of " the Albigenses, are the calumnies of their enemies. But have they " so much as one proof for what they advance, or even one author of " those times, and for more than four hundred years after, to back " them in it? For our parts, we produce as many witnesses as have " been authors in the whole universe who have treated of this sect. " Those that were educated in their principles have revealed to us their " abominable secrets after their conversion. We trace up the damn- " able sect even to its source : we shew whence it came, which way it " steered its course, all its characteristics, and its whole pedigree " branching from the Manichean root."

But, it may be observed, you have given us authorities only on one side ; you have not stated any writer but who was a Catholic, and therefore must be considered with some degree of suspicion. Well, then, to remove this objection, we will quote the testimony of a Protestant historian, whose evidence we imagine will not be suspected. Mosheim, in his Ecclesiastical History, speaking of the Albigenses, and other heretics of the 13th century, says, "Certain writers, who have accustomed " themselves to entertain a high idea of the sanctity of all those who, " in the middle ages, separated themselves from the church of Rome, " suspect the inquisitors of having attributed falsely impious doctrines " to the Brethren of the Free Spirit. [By which name some of the Al- " bigenses designated themselves.] But this suspicion is *entirely* " *groundless* .... Their shocking *violation of decency* was *a consequence* " of their *pernicious system.* They looked upon *decency* and *modesty as* " *marks of inward corruption.* .... Certain enthusiasts amongst them " maintained that the believer could not sin, let his conduct be ever so " horrible or atrocious." Vol. iii. p. 284, Maclaine's Translation.—After this description of John Fox's "people of the *reformed* religion," may we not justly say with Bousset, "How comes it then to pass that the " Protestants undertake the defence of these villains? The reason (he " answers) is but too evident. It is the earnest desire they have of find- " ing out predecessors. They meet with none but such as these that " stood out against venerating the cross, praying to saints, making ob- " lations for the dead. They are concerned to find no where the foot- " steps of their reformation but amongst the *Manicheans.* Because they " inveigh against the pope and church, the reformation is inclined to " favour them." See here what worthy associates the "few plain Christians" have chosen as models of example to "diffuse among their " fellow-believers a knowledge and love of the genuine principles of

"Christianity;" and to excite "a hatred and abhorrence of the (pre-
"tended) corruptions and crimes of Popery and its professors."

Having now given a correct sketch of the *opinions* of the Albigenses,
it follows that we furnish some account of their actions—the *fruits* of
their opinions. But first of all we must give John Fox's account of the
"PERSECUTION OF THE EARL OF TOULOUSE," which he details in these
words, to which we beg the particular attention of the reader.—"A
"friar, named Peter, having been murdered in the dominions of the earl
"of Toulouse, *the pope* made the murder *a pretence to persecute* that
"nobleman and *his subjects.* He sent persons throughout all Europe,
"in order to raise forces to act coercively against the Albigenses, and
"promised Paradise to all who would assist in this war, (which he
"termed holy), and bear arms for *forty* days. The same indulgences
"were held out to all who entered for this purpose, as to such as en-
"gaged in crusades to the holy land. The pope likewise sent orders
"to *all archbishops, bishops,* &c. to excommunicate the earl of Toulouse
"*every Sabbath and festival;* at the same time absolving all his subjects
"from their oaths of allegiance to him, and commanding them *to pur-*
"*sue his person, possess his lands, destroy his property,* and *murder such*
"of his subjects as continued *faithful to him.* The earl of Toulouse,
"hearing of these mighty preparations against him, wrote to the pope
"in a very *candid* manner, desiring not to be *condemned unheard,* and
"assuring him that he had not the least hand in Peter's death: for that
"friar was killed by *a gentleman,* who, immediately after the murder,
"fled out of his territories. But the pope, *being determined on his de-*
"*struction, was resolved not to hear his defence:* and a formidable army,
"with several *noblemen* and *prelates* at the *head of it,* began its march
"against the Albigenses. The earl had only the alternative to oppose
"force by force, or submit: and as he despaired of success in attempt-
"ing the former, he determined on the latter. The pope's legate being
"at Valence, the earl repaired thither, and said, 'He was surprised
"that such a number of armed men should be sent against him, before
"*the least proof of his guilt had been deduced.* He therefore came volun-
"tarily to surrender himself, armed only with the testimony of *a good*
"*conscience,* and hoped that the troops would be prevented from *plun-*
"*dering his innocent subjects,* as he thought himself a sufficient pledge
"for any vengeance they chose to take on account of the death of the
"friar.' The legate replied, that he was very glad the earl had volun-
"tarily surrendered; but, with respect to the proposal, he could not
"pretend to countermand the orders to the troops, unless he would
"consent to deliver up *seven* of his best fortified castles as securities for
"his future behaviour. At this demand the earl perceived his error
"in submitting, but it was too late; he knew himself to be a pri-
"soner, and therefore sent an order for the delivery of the castles. The
"pope's legate had no sooner garrisoned these places, than he ordered
"the respective governors to appear before him. When they came, he
"said, 'That the earl of Toulouse having delivered up his castles to the
"pope, they must consider that they were now the *pope's subjects,* and
"not the earl's; and that they must therefore act conformably to their
"*new* allegiance.' The governors were greatly astonished to see *their*
"*lord thus in chains,* and themselves *compelled* to act in a manner so

"contrary to their *inclinations* and *consciences*. But the subsequent
"treatment of the earl afflicted them still more; for *he was stripped*
"*nearly naked*, led *nine times round the grave of friar Peter*, and severely
"scourged before all the people. Not contented with this, the legate
"obliged him to *swear* that he would be *obedient to the pope* during the
"remainder of his life, *conform to the church of Rome*, and make *irrecon-*
"*cilable* war against the Albigenses; and even ordered him, by the
"oaths he had newly taken, to join the troops, and inspect the siege of
"Bezieres. But thinking this too hard an injunction, he took an op-
"portunity privately to quit the army, and determined *to go to the pope*,
"*and relate the ill usage he had received.*"

Before we make any comment on this relation, we will here ask the
reader if he ever read a more delectable piece of improbabilities and
contradictions? What are we to think of the rationality of those people who can take such a tale for fact, when there is not a date nor an
authority for one single circumstance detailed? Here is injustice,
murder, cruelty, robbery, nay every crime in the black catalogue of
human depravity imputed to the pope and his legate, while the poor
earl is represented as a precious jewel of the first water, and his subjects as pure as the martyred innocents under Herod. Out upon such
barefaced misrepresentations and falsehoods! Shame on such credulity as this book has met with. By this account the archbishops and
bishops are converted into lieutenants and major generals, and the
pope's legate is made commander in chief, while the pope himself is
one of the best recruiting sergeants we recollect to have met with in
our course of reading, seeing he could raise a formidable army at his
beck, headed by noblemen and prelates. The pope first orders *all the*
archbishops, bishops, &c. to excommunicate the poor luckless earl
every sabbath and festival; then the bishops, or the earl's subjects, or
both, for we cannot say which is named by the pronoun "them," are
commanded to pursue this persecuted earl, to possess his lands, to destroy his property, to murder his faithful subjects, and yet he not only
escapes from all these terrible evils, but he writes a candid, very candid
letter, to the pope, desiring not to be condemned unheard, and assuring
the holy father that it was a GENTLEMAN, yes, reader, a GENTLE-
MAN who killed the friar Peter, and then ran away!!! Believe this,
ye readers of Fox, if you will, but pray do not charge the Catholics in
future with credulity. Take it in for gospel if you like, good "plain
Christians," but let us hear no more of the absurdities of Popery.
Well, finding all the fulminations of the bishops and archbishops ineffectually, though so frequently repeated, for how *long* a time Fox does
not say; finding the pursuit of his person, the possession of his lands,
the destruction of his property—for all this we are told was commanded
before the earl complained—it does not appear that a hair of his head
was touched, and the pope, who is bent upon his destruction, orders a
formidable army, with noblemen and prelates at the head of it, to march
forthwith, but not against the *earl*; no, the papal wrath is all at once directed against the Albigenses. Then again we have the earl upon the
boards. The Albigenses are nothing and the earl is every thing. He finds
it necessary to submit because he cannot overcome by force, and submit
he does with *a good conscience*, to save his *innocent subjects*. What a para-

gon of a ruler? What an immaculate patriarch of the "*reformed peo-ple!*" But do you really believe this tale, reader?" Do you really think the one party so grossly unjust, and the other so *conscientiously* innocent? But to the narrative. One would suppose that this sub-mission would have been sufficient to have gratified the most obdurate heart; but no, John Fox knew the capability of his reader's mind, and his modern editors seems to have as high an opinion of the capa-city of their reader's credulity, or they would not have ventured to impose these absurdities upon them. The legate, however, who is here commander in chief and civil governor too, is not satisfied; he must have *seven* of the strongest castles as securities for the earl's good behaviour, though he had been long before dispossessed of his property, unless indeed the bishops' excommunications and commands were dis-regarded by the people, and then what becomes of the power of the pope? The eyes of the earl, we are told, were now opened, and he saw his error, but it was too late, and away went his castles. Well, the le-gate, like a cautious general, and he seems to have understood military tactics better than ecclesiastical discipline, by a happy stroke of leger-demain, instantly transforms the earl's subjects into subjects of the pope, and the governors of the castles are *astonished*, yes "greatly asto-nished," to find "themselves *compelled* to *act* in a manner so *contrary* "to their *inclinations* and *consciences.*" Bless us! what pretty con-*sciences* the "*reformed* people" had in those days. The primitive mar-tyrs could not be compelled to violate their consciences. Dungeons, tortures, and death, had no effect on them; they suffered all with in-vincible constancy, in which example they were followed by the Ca-tholics when persecuted by "Protestant-ascendency;" but here, it is said, the pope's legate could make these lords and governors of the "*reformed* people" act against their consciences, without any resistance on their part. Those who will believe this account will believe any thing. In conclusion, the poor earl is *whipped* round the *grave* of the friar, made to swear obedience to the pope, to conform to the church of Rome, to make interminable war against his *innocent* subjects, the Albigenses, and moreover, installed *by compulsion* inspector general of the siege of a fortified town in which the Albigenses had taken refuge!!!! Now, reader, what is your opinion of John Fox? Do you not think him a complete master of the art of falsification? But what must we think of the mental faculties of those who have so long looked upon his *Book of Martyrs* as a specimen of historical veracity? What but prejudice the most clouded, and bigotry the most bloated, could induce any one to credit such a mass of palpable absurdity and impro-bability as we have here dissected?

But it is time we should lay before the reader a more faithful and authenticated account of the origin of these unhappy transactions. The Rev. Alban Butler writes thus:—"Charles the bald, king of France, in "855, made Raymund, son of the governor of Toulouse, hereditary go-"vernor and count, reserving only a homage to be paid to himself and "successors. Raymund V. the tenth sovereign count of Toulouse, duke "of Narbonne, and marquis of Provence, died a zealous Catholic, in 1194, "His son Raymund VI. openly protected these impious heretics, who "in armed troops expelled the bishops, priests, and monks, demolished

" monasteries, and plundered churches. They were also countenanced
" in their seditions and violences by the earls of Foix and Comminge,
" the viscount of Bearn, and other princes in those parts. Pope Inno-
" cent III. ordered Arnold, abbot of Citeaux, to employ his monks in
" preaching against these heretics in Languedoc. Accordingly twelve
" abbots of that order were charged with that commission. But the
" princes opposed their endeavours, and Peter of Chateau-nuef, a Cis-
" tercian monk, the pope's legate in Languedoc, who exerted his au-
" thority against the heretics, was assassinated on the banks of the
" Rhone, near the town of St. Giles's, where he and some other mis-
" sionaries were coming out from a conference with the count of Tou-
" louse, in 1208. The pope excommunicated the murderers, and espe-
" cially the count of Toulouse, who was looked upon as the principal
" author; and exhorted Philip Augustus, king of France, and the lords
" of that kingdom, to raise a crusade against the Albigenses and the
" said count." By this statement, which is gathered by Mr. Butler
from the most ancient and authentic historians, a different colour is
given to the conduct of the conscientious earl of Toulouse and his dear
innocent subjects. It is here stated that the Albigenses were the originators of the disorders which produced such scenes of carnage and
blood as stain the annals of that period. One of the opinions held out
by these people was, that the clergy had no right to temporalities; the
fruits of which opinions we see, were the demolition of monasteries
and the plundering of churches. In these outrages the people were
encouraged by the earl of Toulouse, a feudatory lord to the king of
France, who, no doubt, thought it a fine opportunity to add to his fortune at the expense of the church, as our reformers of the sixteenth
century did. Thus it was not the murder of the legate *only*, as Fox
represents, but the previous seditions and violences of a lawless horde
of impious desperadoes, that occasioned the crusade entered into to put
them down. And even *force* was not attempted until the power of
persuasion was found to be unavailing. Again it is here stated that the
king of France was *exhorted* by the pope to raise an army to restore the
seditious to obedience; but Fox makes the pope and his legate not only
the raisers but the directors of the army. Of course this was done to
" excite a hatred and abhorrence of the (pretended) crimes and corrup-
" tions of Popery and its professors;" and to accomplish this act of
Christian charity, an adherence to truth was not at all necessary on the
part of John Fox, and his modern editors. Not a word does Fox mention of the sending preachers to reclaim the misguided people from
their errors, which was the province of the head of the church and father of the faithful; not a syllable of the excesses committed by the
seduced multitude before the force of arms was applied to subdue
them; no, this was not his object, because then it would have been
clearly seen that the measures taken to repress the outrages were only
measures of defence and security, whereas John Fox wanted to make
them measures of persecution. In this account by Mr. Butler there is
every appearance of truth. He gives us names and dates, and his language has none of that high-colouring which distinguishes Fox's relation. It is clear that the Albigenses were the occasion of the crusade
by the excesses they committed. These excesses they were not con-

tent to perpetrate in their own country, but they overran several other provinces·in bodies of from four and five to eight thousand men, laying towns in waste, pillaging the country, and furthering the priests; some of whom they flayed alive. Father Parsons, in his reply to Fox, says, that they were guilty of the most beastly and filthy actions in the churches, committing fornication therein and other acts of immorality. Now, we will here ask the "few plain Christians" if any set of men were to be guilty·of the like offences in this country and in these days, whether all parties would not unite in reducing them by force of arms to subjection, and punish the ringleaders with death? Whether the military would not be instantly sent against them to prevent their further progress and outrages? And whether any man would be be-sotted enough to call such a mode of preventing robbery, sacrilege and murder, a religious persecution? Had the Albigenses confined them-selves to *opinions*, and not violated the bounds of decency and disturbed the peace of society, they would not have been the objects of military vengeance, but would have·been reclaimed by the usual arguments of the church, persuasion and truth; but as the fruits of their opinions shewed themselves in acts of violence and injustice, and as they refused to listen to the voice of reason, the civil authorities found themselves necessitated to repel force by force, and this is the persecution which bigotry is ever and anon bellowing in the ears of the ignorant and cre-dulous, to inspire "a hatred and abhorrence·of the (pretended) corrup-"tions and crimes of Popery and its professors;" or, in other words, to excite a hatred and abhorrence against that church in which the real truths of religion are to be found.

Fox next gives an account of the "Siege of Bezieres," and in such exaggerated terms that we lay it before our readers, as another speci-men of the little regard paid by this historian to the rational faculties of his readers. He writes, "The army, however, proceeded to besiege "Bezieres; and the earl of Bezieres, who was governor of that city, "thinking it impossible to defend the place, came out, and presenting "himself before the legate, implored mercy for the inhabitants; inti-"mating, that there were as many Roman Catholics as Albigenses in "the city. The legate replied, that all excuses were useless; the place "must be delivered up at discretion, or the most dreadful consequen-"ces would ensue. The earl of Bezieres returning into the city, told "the inhabitants he could obtain no mercy, unless the Albigenses would "abjure their religion, and conform to the worship of the·church of "Rome. The Roman Catholics pressed the Albigenses to comply with "this request; but the Albigenses nobly answered, that they would "not forsake their religion for the base price of their frail life: that "God was able, if he pleased, to defend them; but if he would be glo-"rified by the confession·of their faith, it would be a great honour to "them to die for his sake. They added, that they had rather displease "the pope, who could but kill their bodies, than God, who could cast "both body and soul into hell. On this the Popish party, finding their "importunities ineffectual, sent their bishop to the legate, beseeching "him not to include them in the chastisement of the Albigenses; and "representing, that the best means to win the latter over to the Roman "Catholic persuasion, was by gentleness, and not by rigour. The le-

" gate 'upon hearing this,' flew into a violent passion with the bishop,
" and declared that, ' If all the city did not acknowledge their fault,
" they should taste of one curse without distinction of religion, sex,
" or age.' "

Here the legate is again represented as the most bloodthirsty and
cruel of monsters. He is still commander-in-chief and director of all
the military operations. Inexorable alike to the Catholics and Albigenses, nothing can move him to mercy, nothing satisfy him but slaughter and destruction. The Catholics and Albigenses are equally balanced, just as many of the one as the other, and then how kind to
each other. The Catholics pressing the Albigenses to abjure their *re-*
ligion ; pretty religion truly that taught them to destroy churches and
murder priests. Then the Albigenses nobly refuse to "*forsake* their
" *religion* for the *base price of their frail life* : that God was able, if he
" pleased, to defend them ; but if he would be glorified by the confes-
" sion of their faith, it would be a great honour to them to die for his
" sake." What cant and hypocrisy is this ! Pretty confessors of the
faith, truly, to teach that marriage was unlawful, and practice the most
indecent acts. But if they wished to be glorified by the confession of
their faith, why did they not follow the example of the primitive martyrs, who were glorified by the confession of Christ's faith ? These
holy men did not resort to fire and sword to propagate and defend the
faith they had received from the apostles, though they continued stoutly
to maintain the truths revealed to them by word of mouth and writing,
but no further. They inculcated the necessity of practising every
moral virtue, and submitting to lawful authority; whereas we have
shewn that John Fox's new confessors of the faith preached and prac-
ticed the most abominable vices. Well, but the Catholics finding the
Albigensian confessors obstinate, sent their *bishop* to the legate, " be-
" seeching him not to include them in the chastisement of the Albi-
" genses ;" and they moreover took the liberty to represent to the
legate, through the bishop, " that the best means to win the latter
" over to the Roman Catholic *persuasion*, was by *gentleness*, and not by
" *rigour*." This sensible hint, we are told, put the legate into a violent
passion with the bishop, and he declared that " if *all* the city did not
" acknowledge their fault, they should taste of *one curse* without dis-
" tinction of *religion*, sex, or age."—Now if this character of the legate
were true ; if these barbarous and unjustifiable proceedings were occasioned by the principles of the Catholic religion, as the bigots of
ascendency insinuate; if the Albigenses were such innocent and good
men, as John Fox represents them to be; is it not, gentle reader, a
subject of astonishment with you, as it is with us, that the Catholics
did not become disgusted with a religion that could instigate the representative of the head of their church to become such a monster of
cruelty, and instantly renounce so horrible a system ? yet we do not
find that this was the case, but on the contrary, while the crusaders
were contending against the Albigenses in the south of France, Pomerania, Finland, Sweden, and the northern nations were receiving the
Christian faith from Catholic missionaries.

It is but too true that cruel excesses were committed by the crusaders on taking the town of Bezieres, but not by the direction of the

legate. The earl of Toulouse had then made his peace with the powers assembled, and the army having nothing to do, siege was laid to Bezieres, where the Albigenses had fortified themselves, which being taken by assault, the inhabitants were barbarously put to the sword.—Fox says, 60,000 persons were murdered; the Rev. Alban Butler reduces the number to one-fourth. This latter writer, speaking of this and other transactions of the crusaders, says, "The inhumanity of "which action is not to be palliated, though the inhabitants of that "town were robbers and murderers, and guilty of all manner of crimes, "as Peter of Vaux-Sernay (c. 16.) and, from him, Fleury observe; "and though the innocent perished by their own fault by refusing to "separate themselves from the guilty, when required so to do.... "Crimes and seditions (Mr. B. continues,) are not to be punished or "revenged by other crimes. Avarice, ambition, or revenge in many, "only covered themselves under a cloak of zeal for religion."—These just sentiments are those of every Catholic writer, and are conformable to the genuine principles of the Catholic church. How unjust and disgraceful then must that conduct be, which charges the Catholic religion with the crimes and excesses arising from the worst passions of human nature, and which that religion was established by God himself to curb and conquer.

To enter into an exposure of the whole of the misrepresentations and exaggerations, fictions and falsehoods, of Fox, in his account of the Waldenses and Albigenses would require a bulky volume, we must therefore be content with a few of the most prominent instances of his utter disregard of veracity as an historian. The following account is given under the head, "CRUELTIES OF THE POPE, AND ARTIFICES OF DOMINIC.—"When the pope (writes Fox) found that these cruel means "had not the desired effect, he determined to try others of a milder na- "ture; he therefore sent several learned monks to preach among the "Waldenses, and induce them to change their opinions. Among these "monks was one Dominic, who appeared extremely zealous in the "cause of popery. He instituted an order, which, from him, was called "the order of Dominican friars; and the members of this order have "ever since been the principal inquisitors in every country into which "that horrid tribunal (the inquisition) has been introduced. Their "power was unlimited; they proceeded against whom they pleased, "without any consideration of age, sex, or rank. However infamous "the accusers, the accusation was deemed valid; and even anonymous "informations were thought sufficient evidence. The dearest friends "or kindred could not, without danger, serve any one who was im- "prisoned on account of religion; to convey to those who were con- "fined a little straw, or give them a cup of water, was called favouring "the heretics; no lawyer dared to plead even for his own brother, or "notary register any thing in favour of the reformed. The malice of "the papists indeed, went beyond the grave, and the bones of many "Waldenses, who had been long dead, were dug up and burnt. If a "man on his death-bed were accused of being a follower of Waldo, his "estates were confiscated, and the heir defrauded of his inheritance: "and some were even obliged to make pilgrimages to the Holy Land, "while the Dominicans took possession of their houses and property, "which they refused to surrender to the owners upon their return."

A REVIEW

OF

Fox's Book of Martyrs,

CRITICAL AND HISTORICAL.

No. 16.   Printed and Published by W. E. Andrews, 3, Chapter-
house-court, St. Paul's Churchyard, London.   Price 3d.

EXPLANATION OF THE ENGRAVING.—*The subject of this cut speaks for itself. The piety of our ancestors was conspicuously displayed in the beautiful architecture and embellishments of their religious temples; the vandalic fury of the deformers of religion in the nineteenth century destroyed most of those monuments of taste, skill, and devotion, and little now is left to bear testimony of the superiority of the eleventh and twelfth centuries, commonly called the "dark ages," over the eighteenth and nineteenth, in the erection of churches for the worship of the living God.*

CONTINUATION OF THE REVIEW.

Not a date, nor an authority, is here given as a voucher for the correctness of this story, but all, as usual, is bare assertion.; yet overcharged and false, as it evidently is, how many are there that have credited these atrocious calumnies? We have shewn by dates in our last number, that Waldo began his preaching forty years before the origin of the inquisition, and St. Dominic, according to the Rev. A. Butler, was not born till ten years after Waldo turned *deformer*, namely, in the year 1170, at Calarauga, in Old Castile. St. Dominic was of noble parents, but renounced worldly grandeur to become a servant of God. He was famed for his proficiency in learning and knowledge of the holy scriptures, and his life, as given by the ancient and best writers of it, that is, F. Theodoric, of Arolda, Constantine, bishop of Orvieto, Bartholomew, bishop of Trent, F. Humbert, and Nicholas Trevet, is represented as one of charity and self-denial, and that he had no more to do with

·the origin of the inquisition than John Fox had.—But mark the accuracy of Fox's account. He says, that "when the pope found that these
" cruel means (the proceedings of the inquisition) had not the desired
" effect, he determined to try others of a milder nature : he therefore
" sent several learned monks to preach among the Waldenses, and in-
" duce them to change their opinions. Among these was one Dominic,
" who appeared extremely zealous in the cause of Popery." That St.
Dominic was zealous in the cause of true religion cannot be denied ;
but Fox has here transformed the Albigenses into the Waldenses, for it
was against the former heretics that St. Dominic preached, and not
against the latter, as we have shewn by a comparison of dates. Neither
could the pope have tried the cruel means stated by Fox *before* he sent
the learned monks to preach, for St. Dominic died on the 6th of August, 1221, and the project of the first court of inquisition was formed
in 1229. It is true that some authors make the legate Peter of Castelnau, the first inquisitor, in 1204 ; this is the legate that was murdered
" by *a gentleman*," and the Bollandists, in a long dissertation, endeavour
to shew that St. Dominic was the first inquisitor ; but, writes the Rev.
A. Butler, in a note to the life of this saint, "Touron observes, (ch. 13,
" p. 88.) that the Albigenses in Languedoc neither were, nor could be
" the object of such a court as an inquisition while St. Dominic preached
" there ; far from being occult, they were armed, preached publicly,
" and had the princes in their interest. He, secondly, takes notice that
" St. Dominic is never mentioned by the original authors of his life to
" have employed against the heretics any other arms than those of in-
" struction and prayer, in which they descend to a very particular de-
" tail."—William of Pay-Laurens, chaplain to Raymund VII. count of
Toulouse, in his Chronicle, (c. 43.) and Bernard Guidonis, relate that
pope Gregory IX. in 1233, that is, *twelve years after the death of St. Dominic*, nominated two Dominican friars in Languedoc the *first* inquisitors. That St. Dominic was the founder of the monastic order of Dominicans is undoubted, and that monks of this order were employed in
the inquisition is not to be denied ; that some of them may have been
guilty of excesses and cruelties we do not pretend to dispute ; but that
the crimes and offences of individuals are to be charged to the whole
body, is neither just nor liberal ; and as well might Catholics charge
the Protestants of this day with the horrid atrocities committed by the
Huguenots and "Protestant-ascendency" in the sixteenth century, as
the "few plain Christians" attempt to fix the excesses which took
place in the south of France in the thirteenth century on the Catholics
of the nineteenth or their religion.

As Fox has given us a pretended account of the artifices and cruelties of St. Dominic, and represented his order as blood-thirsty inquisitors, it is no more than justice that the public should be informed that
if they are stated in the *Book of Martyrs* to have been mercenary and
unprincipled tormentors of heretics, other writers shew they were also
the civilizers and instructors of the savage race of barbarians.—Mr.
Butler says, " St. Dominic made frequent missionary excursions ; and
" founded convents at Bergamo, Brescia, Faenza, and Viterbo, and vi-
" sited those he had already founded. He sent some of his religious
" into Morocco, Portugal, Sweden, Norway, and Ireland ; and brother

" Gilbert with twelve others into England, who established monasteries
" of this order in Canterbury, London, and Oxford. The holy patriarch
" in his second general chapter, held at Bologna in 1221, divided his
" order into eight provinces, and sent some of his religious into Hun-
" gary, Greece, Palestine, and other countries. Among these missiona-
" ries F. Paul of Hungary founded in Lower Hungary the monasteries
" of Gever and Vesprim, converted great numbers of idolaters in Croa-
" tia, Sclavonia, Transylvania, Valachia, Moldavia, Bosnia, and Servia;
" and leaving the churches which he had there founded under the care
" of other labourers, preached with like success in Cumania, the inha-
" bitants of which country were most savage and barbarous. He bap-
" tized among them a duke called Brut, with his vassals, and one of
" the chief princes of the country name Bernborch, Andrew the king
" of Hungary and father of St. Elizabeth, standing godfather. This
" zealous apostle of so many nations suffered a glorious martyrdom
" with ninety religious friars of his order, dispersed in those parts;
" some being beheaded, others shot with arrows, stabbed with lances,
" or burnt by the Tartars in 1242, in their great irruption in those
" countries. Bishop Sadoc, with forty nine religious of this order,
" were butchered for the faith by these barbarians in a second irruption
" in 1260, at Sendomir in Poland, and are honoured on the second of
" June."

. , The truth of this statement can be verified by the histories of the
countries named, and we think it forms a complete contrast to the random tales of Fox. While he is charging the pope and the Dominicans
with being the authors of all the cruelties, real or imaginary, practised
upon the Albigenses, we see the brightest members of this same order,
with the holy founder at their head, engaged in converting infidels to
the faith of Christ, with no other means than the force of persuasion
and the holiness of their lives, and, like the primitive Christians, suffering martyrdom for their faith with meekness and fidelity. How unlike is this conduct to that pursued by John Fox's " reformed people ;"
the one converting ruthless savages into pious Christians by the mild
and persuasive truths of the Catholic faith ; the other brutalizing the
ignorant multitude by their impious notions, and exciting commotion
in every society by the practice of the most indecent and outrageous
actions.

After giving many other incredible tales, unaccompanied with the
least authority, he concludes his account of the surrender of the earl of
Toulouse, with stating some conditions which the earl was compelled,
he says, to enter into. He then adds, " After these cruel conditions,
" (spurious ones) a severe persecution took place against the Albigen-
" ses, many of whom suffered for the faith ; and express orders were
" issued that the laity should not be permitted to read the sacred writings!"
Though this statement is given as coming from Fox, we have no doubt
that it is an invention of his modern editors, intended to suit the taste
of the present bible-reading age. But, reader, if you only look to the
period when this supposed order was made, it will at once strike you,
that there could be no necessity for making it, because at that day
scarcely any of the people could read, and as printing was not then invented, copies of the sacred writings were scarce, and chiefly in the

hands of the clergy, the only persons *capable of reading* them, who regularly expounded the most important parts to the people.

The editors then go on,—" From this period we find no further account of the Albigenses till the commencement of the *seventeenth* century; but although they are not *distinctly mentioned*, they suffered in *common* with their *Protestant* brethren, at various times; and in " 1620, a cruel persecution was commenced against them." And this statement is sufficient to gain credit with the *enlightened* people of this country ! At least so think the " few plain Christians," or, we take it for granted, they would not have made it. We, however, have a better opinion of our countrymen, though they have long been the victims of delusion and hypocrisy. The first period alluded to by the editors must be the *thirteenth* century, and if history make no mention of them till the *seventeenth*, where have they been stowed during the intervening four hundred years ? Is it not strange that history should all at once become silent on these pretended interesting victims of persecution? Then again, they are not *distinctly* mentioned even in the seventeenth century, and yet it is boldly averred that they suffered in common with Protestants. Then the Albigenses were *not* Protestants, though they are stated to be *brethren*. Now is not this likewise somewhat strange? If the Albigenses were *right* the Protestants must have been *wrong*; for two varying creeds could not both be true. It is an unerring principle of the Catholic faith, that it is *always one* and *the same*. Never changing or dividing, but indivisible, and therefore true. Here, however, we have two distinct appellations of religionists, both represented as suffering indiscriminately for their faith, and ranked of course as martyrs, though the one must have condemned the other as holding erroneous opinions, since both could not be right. Such is the inconsistency of man when he deviates from the true path, and seeks his road in the wilderness of error.

Before we quit this part of the *Book of Martyrs*, we must offer a few words on what is laid to the charge of St. Dominic and the Papists.— Fox says, that " if a man on his *death-bed* was accused of being *a follower of Waldo*, his estates were confiscated, and the *heir defrauded of his inheritance*." Supposing this statement, for the sake of argument, to be true, what is this compared to the cruelties of the penal code invented by " Protestant-ascendency" against the followers of the ancient faith ? not, observe, new and vague and impious notions, but the old Catholic faith derived from the apostles. We have only to refer to the statute book, since the reign of the young *pope* Edward VI. and we shall find that laws have been passed twenty times more unjust than any here laid to the charge of the Dominicans. In the time of Elizabeth neither age nor sex was spared ; forged letters were introduced into the houses and on the persons of Catholics, in order to form a plea for seizing their persons and property. Informers the most infamous were employed to swear away the lives of the most innocent ; and a son, by turning Protestant, was legally empowered to rob his Catholic father of his estate, and his brothers and sisters of their inheritance, without waiting till he or they were on their death-bed. And are the Catholics of England and Ireland, while such horrible and unjust decrees continue to disgrace the statute-book of this Protestant country, to be reproached with abuses that may, and we will say have, crept into the jurisprudence of foreign countries, because the people of those countries happen to profess the same faith? Were indeed those abuses to be sanctioned by the principles of their church, then they would deserve censure and execration; but as this is *not* the case, the conduct of those who endeavour to mislead and deceive the ignorant for the purpose of exciting hatred and abhorrence of their fellow subjects, richly merits the loathing and detestation of every friend to justice and good faith.

To shew the gullibility of some persons, when Catholicism or Popery, as the "plain Christians" call it, is the theme of declamation and slander, we will here insert an account given under a head entitled "CRUELTY OF THE BISHOP OF AIX." Fox, or his modern editors, says, "The "bishop of Aix being at Avignon, with some priests, they were one "day walking along the streets with some courtesans, and seeing a man "who sold obscene pictures, they purchased several, and presented "them to the women. A bookseller, who had a great number of bibles "in the French language for sale, lived at hand. The bishop stepping "up to him said, 'How darest thou be so bold as to sell French mer- "chandize in this town?' The bookseller replied with a kind of sneer, "'My lord, do you not think that bibles are as good as those pictures "which you have bought for the ladies?' Enraged at the sarcasm, the "bishop exclaimed, 'I'll renounce my place in paradise if this fellow "is not one of the Waldenses. Take him away, take him away to pri- "son.' These expressions occasioned him to be terribly used by the "rabble; and the next day he was brought before the judge, who, at "the instigation of the bishop, condemned him to the flames. He was "accordingly burnt, with two bibles hanging from his neck, the one "before and the other behind."

Such is the first part of the story, and we beg the reader particularly to remark, that this bishop is not specially named but generally; neither is there a single date by which we can trace the truth or falsehood of the statement. But will any one believe that in those days, or in these, the clergy would be so callous to decency as openly to walk the streets with courtesans and purchase obscene prints? Then as to the French bibles, and the boldness of the bookseller, is it probable, if the bishops and priests were such characters, that the bookseller would thus accost them? Besides, in the time of the Waldenses printing was unknown, and bookseller's shops were of course not in existence. It is therefore clear that the man was not burnt with his *two* bibles, and we dare be bound that the reader will think with us, that this part of the story is a bungling attempt at lying.

The tale goes on, "The principal persecutor of the Merindolians was "this bishop of Aix, who persuaded the president and counsellors of "the court of parliament to send a great army through all Provence, "in order to destroy those who professed the reformed religion. These "poor people, on seeing the army, recommended themselves to God, "and prepared for death. While they were in this grievous distress, "mourning and lamenting together, news was brought that the army "was retired, and no man knew at that time *how*, or by *what means*; "but it was afterwards known that the lord of Alenc, a wise and good "man, declared to the president of Cassanée, that he ought not to pro-

" ceed against the inhabitants of Merindol by force of arms, without
" judgment or condemnation; and used many arguments to this effect.
" The president was at length persuaded to recall the commission
" which he had given out, and cause the army to retire. The Merin-
" dolians understanding that the army was retired, gave thanks to God,
" comforting one another with admonition and exhortation always to
" have the fear of God before their eyes."—Now reader, what can you
make of this account? Here we have a bishop of Aix, but of what
name, and when living, we are not informed, persuading the court of
parliament to incur the expense of raising and marching an army to
extirpate such of the people of Provence called Merindolians as professed the *reformed* religion; we have the people patiently waiting their
destruction, when, all on a sudden, the terrible army disappears, without rhyme or reason, in the midst of the mourning and lamentation of
the people. It however soon after turns out, that this lucky flight was
occasioned by the declaration of a *wise* and *good* man, called the lord of
Alenc, to the president of Cassanée, that *he* ought not to proceed to extremities without listening to justice and mercy. This had the intended
effect, and the Merindolians, whoever they are, began to comfort and
exhort one another, " always to have the fear of God before their eyes."
This disgusting cant may do for some folk, but we think the days of
hypocrisy and delusion are wearing fast away.—We have no dates to
govern us, therefore we cannot learn the period of this wonderful transaction. Indeed we have no hesitation to pronounce the whole a *fiction*,
clumsily manufactured; but at the time it was coined, the author was
well aware that the more marvellous the story, so it aspersed the Catholics, the more readily it would gain credit among the bewildered
Protestants. However, one thing may be drawn from this part of the
tale, and that is, by Fox's own shewing the Catholics are not invariably
a persecuting sect, since they could in this instance listen to the voice
of justice, and leave the reformed unmolested. The court and parliament were Catholics as well as the pretended persecuting bishop; the
army was of course Catholic, and there is every reason to suppose the
wise and good lord of Alenc was a Catholic, if not, the greater the merit and forbearance of the Catholic president of Cassanée in acting on
the advice of *a reformed* lord. Thus then it is made manifest, by Fox's
own confession, that persecution is separable from Popery, and consequently the " few plain Christians" are no less than a few plain liars,
by stating that " persecution is inseparable from Popery."
     But the best part of the story yet remains to be told; it is as fol-
lows :—" Shortly after, the bishop of Cavaillon came to Merindol, and
" calling before him the *children*, gave them *money*, and commanded
" them to learn the paternoster and the creed in *Latin*. Most of them
" answered that they *knew* the paternoster and the creed already in *La-
" tin*, but they could *not understand what they spake, except in the vulgar
" tongue.* The bishop answered that it was *not necessary they should*;
" it being sufficient that they knew it in Latin; and that it was not re-
" quisite for their salvation *to understand or expound the articles of their
" faith*; for there were many bishops and *doctors of divinity* whom it
" would *trouble to expound* the paternoster and the creed. The bailiff
" of Merindol, named Andrew Maynard, asked what *purpose* it would

"serve to say the paternoster and the creed, and *not to understand the*
"*same :* for in so doing they should but mock and deride God. Then
"said the bishop, ' Do *you* understand what is signified by these
"words, 'I believe in God?' The bailiff answered, ' I should think
"myself very miserable if I did not understand it :' and he began to
"*give an account of his faith.* Then said the bishop, ' I did not think
"there had been such great doctors in Merindol.' The bailiff answered
"' The least of the inhabitants of Merindol can do it more readily than
"I : but I pray you question one or two of these *young children,* that
"you may understand whether they be well taught or no.' But the
"bishop either *knew not how* to question them, or *would not.* On this
"a person named Pieron Roy said, ' Sir, one of these children may
"question with another, if you think fit ;' and the bishop consented.
"Then one of the *children* began to question with his fellows, with *as*
"*much grace and gravity* as if he had been *a schoolmaster;* and the chil-
"dren, one after another, answered so to the purpose, that it was *won-*
"*derful to hear them.* When the bishop saw he could not *thus* prevail,
"he tried another way, and went about by *flattering words* to effect his
"purpose. Wherefore he said, that he now perceived they were *not*
"*so bad* as many *thought them to be;* notwithstanding, to satisfy their
"*persecutors,* it was necessary that they should make some *small* ab-
"juration, which *only the bailiff,* with *two officers,* might make in *his*
"*presence,* in the *name of all the rest,* without any notary to record the
"same in writing ; and by *so doing* they would obtain *the favour* even
"of those who *now persecuted* them : and that this proceeding might
"*not be misrepresented,* it should be reported *only to the pope,* and to the
"*high court of parliament* of Provence. The CHILDREN, however,
"*unanimously refused,* and said that *they conceived* the way in which they
"had been instructed was *the pure faith of Jesus Christ,* and that in *ab-*
"*juring it,* they would be *denying their Redeemer.*"

This is as delectable a dish of the marvellous as we ever recollect
seeing served up to satiate the palates of the most barbarously ignorant and credulous of the Protestant race. It has long been fashionable
to charge Catholics with being too easy of belief and giving credit to
the most absurd tales of the priesthood, but we defy the most determined opposer of the Catholic faith to produce a pretended fact from a
Catholic writer that shall equal in absurdity and improbability the story
we have just quoted. Who the bishop of Cavaillon is no one can tell,
but admitting him to have been a *real* character, is it probable that he
would have conducted himself as he is represented to have done. He
is pourtrayed as a dunce and a hypocrite, while the children of the
Merindolians are diamonds of the first water. Now, if we understand
John Fox, the Merindolians were of the *reformed* religion, but of *what*
creed he doth not say. They are however opposed to the Catholic doctrine, and is it likely that a Catholic bishop should go amongst such a
people, and not only *command* their children to say their prayers in a
language they did not understand, but openly acknowledge that many
of his dignified brethren were *ignoramuses.* John Fox, you may have
been as cunning as the animal whose name you bear, but this story will
not do in these days. It is here intended to cast an insinuation against
the service of the Catholic church being said in Latin, and therefore

the bishop is made to say that it was not requisite for their salvation that they (the children) should *understand* or *expound* the articles of their faith. Certainly not to *expound* them, because it is not to be expected that children are able to teach when they stand in need of being taught. It was always a principle however of the Catholic church, that the people should *understand* the articles of their faith, and for this purpose Christ the divine Founder of this church appointed pastors and teachers, to whom he promised the Spirit of Truth, which should lead them into all truth, and he commanded them to teach and instruct the people all that he had revealed to them. And the better to accomplish this, he gave them the gift of tongues, so that they spoke in the vernacular language of the people they preached to. To say that it is not necessary to understand the articles of faith is an insult to common sense, and could only be made by those who are void of that quality. In no instance whatever can the Catholic church be proved to have prevented the people from praying in their mother tongue, and the clergy were alway assiduous in *expounding* the scriptures to them in the same language. In fact, this is one of the ends for which they were appointed; and not, as is the case with Protestant preachers, to dupe the people out of their money and appropriate it to their own support, while they tell them to expound the faith for themselves.

Then as to the learned bailiff of Merindol, Mr. Andrew Maynard; he is made to say that unless he understood what was signified in the words "I believe in God," he should be very miserable; and forthwith he gives the bishop an account of *his faith*, to the great surprise of the prelate. Now what kind of a faith master Andrew held we are not told; whether it agreed with the Waldenses, or the Albigenses, or was peculiar to the Merindolians, or any other *reformed* creed. This dealing in generals is very convenient to avoid detection, and therefore we must be content to leave the very knowing Mr. Andrew Maynard, bailiff of Merindol, in the year *nothing*, to enjoy his theological wisdom, while we look a little further into Fox's statement. Wise as the bishop found Andrew the bailiff, the latter had the very great modesty to underrate himself, and give the preference to the *children* of his town. A wonderful generation of religionists these Merindolians must have been, when the infant race were more wise than the experience of mature age. Well might the poor bishop exclaim, he "did not think there "had been such great doctors in Merindol." He, poor man, though a bishop, was an ignorant fellow compared to Andrew the bailiff; but how insignificant must he have appeared when the little Solomons began to question one another. The bishop was so confounded, it appears, with Andrew's astonishing lore, that he did not, or would not know how to question the young wiseacres, so one Pierron Roy is conjured up to propose that the infant theologians should question each other, to which the bishop consented. Now comes the grand trial; one more wise than all the rest, we presume, jumped up as the questioner, and he performed his part with so much grace and gravity, that it was charming to behold him, as well as wonderful to hear the pert answers that were given. Oh! astonishing race! but what a pity that so much learning and wisdom should not have descended to future generations. Well, the bishop was astounded, and well he might be, at witnessing such a set of young doctors in divinity; still he was not to be diverted from his purpose, and he now tried to cajole them by a species of flattery. They were not so bad now as he thought they were; but perfect as they appeared to be, something must be done to appease their persecutors. Who these persecutors were we are left to conjecture; hitherto the pope and the bishops have been described as the most relentless tormentors of the human race, but now a bishop is made the mediator. Well something must be done; some trifling concession must be made; and a small abjuration on the part of the bailiff and two officers in the presence of the bishop, would suffice. Furthermore, that this proceeding might *not* be *misrepresented*, it was *not* to be stated *in writing*, the only way we should have thought to *prevent* its being misrepresented, and it was only to be reported to the pope and the parliament, who we suppose were to be satisfied with this piece of hypocrisy, and the Merindolians were to save their bacon. But mark, reader; whether the bailiff and grown up people were inclined to fall into the scheme of the bishop is not stated, but we are told that the CHILDREN, yes, the CHILDREN UNANIMOUSLY REFUSED to accede to the plan, declaring " that they 'CONCEIVED," Oh! how ripe were their understandings; that " they 'CONCEIVED the way in which *they* had been " instructed was the *pure faith* of Jesus, and that in *abjuring it*, they " would be *denying* their Redeemer." Let Munchausen beat that, and I will consent to become a believer in John Fox's *Book of Martyrs*. Not a word is said of the pure faith this race of Solomons had been instructed in; not a syllable of its doctrine. All is bare assertion; all is left to conjecture. After this specimen of the manner adopted by Fox to describe the persecutions of the Waldenses and Albigenses, we need enter no further in our remarks on that part of the book.

The next section is devoted to the relation of " PERSECUTIONS IN " FRANCE PREVIOUS TO AND DURING THE CIVIL WARS OF THAT NATION." —The first story told is the following :—" In the year 1524, at a town " in France called Melden, one John Clark affixed a bill on the church " door, in which he called the pope antichrist : for this offence he was " repeatedly whipped, and then branded in the forehead. His mother, " who saw the chastisement, cried with a loud voice, ' Blessed be " Christ, and welcome these marks for his sake.' He went afterwards " to Metz, in Lorraine, and demolished some images, for which he had " his right hand and nose cut off, and his arms and breasts torn by pin- " cers ; while suffering these cruelties, he sang the 115th psalm, which " expressly forbids superstition. On concluding the psalm, he was " thrown into the fire and burnt to ashes."—Admitting this tale to be true, though we much doubt it in the whole, we will take leave here to ask, if this Protestant martyr did not give the first provocation ? We are not going to justify the treatment he experienced, nor shall we applaud the zeal of his mother, who imagined he was suffering for Christ's sake, because he was punished for a breach of the peace and abusing the head of the Catholic church. Now, we should be glad to know if a Catholic were to fix up a bill against the door of St. Saviour's church, in the borough of Southwark, in which parish, we believe, the " few plain Christians" reside ; if, we say, a Catholic were to fix up a bill against the said church door, reflecting on the character of his present

majesty as head of the church, and calling him by vile names, would
he not be taken before a magistrate and punished for the offence? And
would not these "plain Christians," who condemn the punishers of John
Clark, be the first to approve of the sentence on the Catholic offender?
We have not a doubt but they would, and not think it persecution
either. And were he to have a mother encourage him under chastisement, as John Clark had, they would look upon her as a fanatic old
woman. Then as to his demolishing of images; under what authority
did he so act? Who gave him commission to begin the work of destruction? He might *think* these images were put to superstitious
purposes, and while he confined his opinions to himself no one could
reach him; but when he began to manifest the fruits of his opinions,
he clearly became a violator of the law—a breaker of the peace—and
therefore subjected himself to the penalty of the law.—As we before
said, we are not the defender of persecution, nor are we the justifier of
cruel and unnecessary punishments; but we contend that John Clark
did that for which he would be punished in this Protestant country, and
therefore he is not entitled to the honour of being a martyr for religion.
Suppose a Deist were to take it into his head to pull down and destroy
the crosses which adorn the new Protestant churches just erected in
this country; would he not feel the severity of the law for so doing?
And would the "few plain Christians" place him among John Fox's
martyrs in their next edition of the work? This John Clark was a
carder of wool by trade, in the town of Meaux, according to father Daniel's history, not Melden, as Fox states erroneously. He is recorded
by Theodore Beza as the first founder of the Calvinist churches of
Meaux and Metz, as well as a martyr of that sect. Luther, it is here
to be observed, began to dogmatize in 1517, six years before the period of Clark's execution; the pretended reformation had, of course,
made some progress in Germany and France, and the outrageous conduct of Clark is considered the forerunner of those evils that afterwards afflicted the latter country. Clark was no doubt a disciple of
Zuinglius, who began to preach against indulgences at Zurich in
Switzerland, in the year 1519, two years after Luther had begun at
Wittemberg. In the year 1522, he, in conjunction with some other
priests that had embraced his party, presented a request to the civil
magistrates of Switzerland, to be allowed to have wives, declaring
that he and his had not the gift of continence, and that the deeds of
the flesh had rendered them *infamous*, to the great scandal of the faithful. (See *Zuinglius's works*, t. i. p. 115.) Dr. Heylin, in his *History of
the Presbyterians*, says, "The Zuinglian reformation was begun in de-
"facing images, (*see the cut to this number*) decrying the established
"fasts and appointed festivals, abolishing set forms of worship, deny-
"ing the old Catholic doctrine of a real presence, and consequently all
"external reverence in the participation of the blessed sacrament;
"which Luther seriously laboured to preserve in the same estate in
"which he found them at present. They differed also in the doctrine
"of predestination, which Luther taught according to the current of
"the ancient fathers, who lived and flourished before the writings of
"St. Augustine; so that the Romanists had not any thing to except
"against in that particular, when it was canvassed by the schoolmen

" In the council of Trent." Thus it is indisputably clear, that this pretended martyr was a violator of the peace, and suffered for invading the security of society, not for his *religious opinions.*

The next tale we shall notice is the following :—" Shortly after the " coronation of Henry the second, a tailor was apprehended for *working* " *on a saint's day* ; being asked why he gave such an offence to reli- " gion, his reply was, ' I am a poor man, and have nothing but my " labour to depend upon ; necessity requires that I should be indus- " trious, and my conscience tells me there is no day but the sabbath " which I ought to keep sacred from labour.' Having expressed him- " self thus, he was committed to prison, and the affair being soon after " rumoured at court, some of the nobles persuaded the king to be pre- " sent at the trial. On the day appointed, the monarch appeared in a " superb chair of state, and the bishop of Mascon was ordered to in- " terrogate the prisoner. The tailor, on perceiving the king, paid his " obedience to him in the most respectful manner. The king was " much affected with his arguments, and seemed to muse ; on which " the bishop exclaimed, ' He is an obstinate and impudent heretic ; " let him be taken back to prison, and burnt to death.' The prisoner " was accordingly conveyed to prison ; and the bishop artfully insinu- " ated, that the heretics, as he called the reformed, had many spe- " cious arguments, which, at first hearing, appeared conclusive ; but " on examination, they were found to be false. He then endeavoured " to persuade the king to be present at the execution, who at length " consented, and repaired to a balcony which overlooked the place. " On seeing the king, the tailor fixed his eyes steadfastly upon him, " and even while the flames were consuming him, kept gazing in such " a manner, as threw the monarch into visible confusion, and obliged " him to retire before the martyr was dead. He was so much shocked, " that he could not recover his spirits for some time ; and what added " to his disquiet was, his continually dreaming, for many nights, that " he saw the tailor with his eyes fixed upon him, in the same manner " as during the execution."—Whether this tale was invented as a coun- ter-part of Henry the eighth's examination of Nicholson *alias* Lambert, for denying the real presence, we know not ; but we cannot help thinking the poor tailor was highly honoured by the French king's re- ceiving him in a superb chair of state. Monarchs now-a-days are not so condescending. But will any one, in his sober senses, believe that a king would trouble himself so much about a man's working on a saint's day ? We think not ; and when it is taken into consideration that there was not that system of taxation that now grinds the people to the earth ; that there was not so much poverty, and consequently not so much necessity to work as in these days, we may put this story down as another fiction, invented to excite the ignorant to hatred against Catholicism. The relater would make us believe the tailor could make an impression upon the *king* though he could not on the *bishop* ; and to get him burned, he is compelled to make the *bishop* a *king*, and the *king* a *cypher.* The bishop orders the poor tailor to prison and to be executed, and this too upon his bare command. Then the bishop per- suades the king to be present, though he had before witnessed his merciful disposition towards the tailor. The king consents, and the tailor fixes his eyes so steadfastly on the monarch, that not even the tortures of the fire could make him change his countenance, and the king was at length obliged to retire. But even here the tailor would not leave him, for his image continued to haunt his majesty for many nights, but *how many* Fox is not able, or was not willing, to declare. Really such stories as these, and so long and repeatedly told, and we lament to say, implicitly credited, reflect no great degree of sagacity on the part of the people of England. We have not seen its equal except in this same *Book of Martyrs*, where three men are represented hanging on a gibbet for eating *roast goose* on a *Friday*.

One more tale, and we will turn to another subject : " Peter Serre," writes Fox, " was *originally* a priest, but reflecting on the errors of " Popery, he, at length, embraced the *reformed* religion, and learned " the trade of *a shoe-maker*. Having a brother at Toulouse, who was a " *bigoted* Roman Catholic, Serre, out of fraternal love, made a journey " to that city, in order to dissuade him from his superstitions: the bro- " ther's wife not approving of his design, lodged a complaint against " him, on which he was apprehended, and made a full declaration of " his faith. The judge asked him concerning his occupation, to which " he replied, ' I have of late practised the trade of a shoemaker.' ' Of " late !' said the judge, ' and what did you practise formerly ?'—' That " I am almost ashamed to tell you,' exclaimed Serre, ' because it was " the *vilest* and most *wicked occupation imaginable*.' The judge, and all " who were present, from these words, supposed he had been a mur- " derer or thief, and that what he spoke was through contrition. He " was, however, ordered to explain precisely what he meant; when, " with *tears in his eyes*, he exclaimed, ' O; I was formerly a Popish " priest !' This reply so much exasperated the judge, that he con- " demned Serre to be *first degraded*, then to have his tongue cut, and " afterwards to be burnt." Had we been Peter's judge we certainly should not have condemned him to the stake, but would have confined him to the lapstone till he had enough of it. Vile and wicked as the occupation of a Popish priest is represented to be, we think Peter Ser- re's case is almost a solitary one, for there have not been many priests, we believe, that have exchanged their breviary for a last, though many a cobbler has forsaken his last to become what is called a minister of the gospel, since the days of evangelical liberty, or rather self-inter- preting licentiousness. Peter the cobbler, however, must have been better off than the poor tailor whose case we just noticed. Snip could not allow himself to be idle on a saint's day, but Snob could leave his work to convert his brother from Popery; and by a singular coinci- dence, both Snip and Snob were burned for their pains, if we are to believe John Fox. When the reformed religion got the ascendency in this country, and the Catholic priests were made to quit their livings, that cobblers, tinkers, and weavers, might occupy them, [at least such is the statement of Dr. Heylin, a Protestant writer] the Catholic priests were so little inclined to leave their vile and wicked occupation, that our Protestant legislature absolutely found it necessary to offer them a *bribe*, and accordingly an act of parliament was passed allowing all apostate priests from the church of Rome an annuity of twenty pounds a year; but even this could not induce them to betray their trust; on the contrary, they preferred death, dungeons, tortures, banishment, and every degree of persecution from " Protestant-ascendency," to the renouncement of their sacred profession. This is an incontestible fact, and can that be a vile and wicked occupation, when men who follow it, renowned for the superexcellent qualities of the mind, and spotless purity of character, cannot be induced to forsake it under circumstances of either terror or temptation? This is a question we would recommend the "few plain Christians" to ponder over well. They may get a few ignorant creatures to believe their tale about Peter Serre, but the sensible part of the people will think with us, that there is neither authenticity nor probability in the relations of John Fox; in a word, that they are too high coloured to be true.

BOOK V.

" HISTORICAL ACCOUNT OF THE INQUISITION IN SPAIN, PORTUGAL,
ITALY, &c."

Such is the head of the fifth book of this *Book of Martyrs*, and a more fruitful theme to alarm the sensitive feelings of English Protestants was never invented. From our infancy we have been accustomed to hear of the terrible cruelties of the Popish inquisition, and we can well recollect listening to an itinerant vender of trash, who constantly attended Norwich market some forty years ago, holding forth in a canting, whining tone, on the blood-thirsty principles of the Catholic religion, to induce the gaping multitude to purchase his lies, which they did with avidity, and, no doubt, put them down as gospel facts. Young as we were then, the abominable lies we heard told for truths made an impression on our mind never to be erased; and we could not then help feeling indignant at that system of pretended religion, which had recourse to falsehood, calumny, misrepresentation, ay, every species of defamation and injustice, to excite prejudice and ill-will against the professors of truth. What we then heard stated as the principles of Catholics we knew to be palpable and barefaced lies, because we were then under a course of instruction by our venerable pastor, which inculcated and enforced the very opposite doctrines. The purest spirit of charity, we were told, was the corner-stone of the Catholic religion, and never have we known any other spirit to influence those who follow and practice the precepts of that religion. If men, professing to be Catholics, give way to their passions or suffer themselves to be governed by temporary policy, or unjust and cruel motives, religion itself is not to be condemned because such men make a mockery of or insult its divine mandates. Abuses we know have been committed, in the name of religion, by Catholics as well as Protestants, and this will always be the case while human nature remains what it is; but religion itself, that is pure and undefiled religion, being of divine origin, can never vary nor be any other than worthy of its divine Founder, who while on earth, went about doing good to all men, suffering evils from others, but offering none in return.

The first section commences with the " ORIGIN, PROGRESS, AND " CRUELTIES OF THE INQUISITION," in the following words :—" When " the *reformed* religion began to diffuse the *pure light* of the gospel

" throughout Europe, the bigoted Roman Catholics, fearing the expo-
" sure of the *frauds* and *abuses* of their church, determined to leave no-
" thing unattempted to crush the *reformation* in its infancy; pope In-
" nocent III. therefore instituted a number of *inquisitors*, or persons
" who were to make inquiry after, apprehend, and punish the profes-
" sors of the reformed faith. At the head of these inquisitors was one
" Dominic, who was canonized by the pope, in order to render his au-
" thority the more respectable. *He* and *the other inquisitors* visited the
" various *Roman Catholic* countries, and treated the *Protestants* with
" the utmost severity: but at length the pope, not finding them so
" useful as he expected, resolved upon the establishment of fixed and
" regular courts of inquisition; the first office of which was established
" in the city of Toulouse, and Dominic became the first inquisitor.
" Courts of inquisition were also erected in several other countries;
" but the Spanish inquisition became the most powerful, and the most
" dreadful of any. Even the *kings* of Spain themselves, though arbi-
" trary in all other respects, were *taught to dread its power;* and the
" horrid cruelties exercised by the inquisition, compelled *multitudes*
" who differed in opinion from the Catholics, *carefully to conceal their*
" *sentiments.* The Dominicans and Franciscans were the most zealous
" of all the monks: these, therefore, the *pope* invested with an *exclu-*
" *sive right* of presiding over, and managing the different courts of in-
" quisition. The friars of those two orders were always selected from
" the *very dregs of the people,* and therefore were *not* much troubled
" with *scruples of conscience;* they were obliged, by the rules of their
" respective orders, to live very austere lives, which rendered their
" manners unsocial, and better qualified for their barbarous employ-
" ment. The pope gave the inquisitors the *most unlimited powers,* as
" judges delegated by *him,* and immediately representing *his* person: they
" were permitted to excommunicate, or sentence to death, whom they
" *thought proper,* upon the *slightest information of heresy;* were allowed
" to publish crusades against all whom they deemed heretics, and en-
" ter into leagues with *sovereign princes,* to *join* those crusades with
" *their forces.* About the year 1244, their power was further increased
" by the emperor Frederick the second, who declared himself the *pro-*
" *tector* and *friend* of all inquisitors, and published two cruel edicts,
" viz. that all heretics, who continued obstinate, should be burnt; and
" that those who repented, should be *imprisoned for life,* This zeal in
" the emperor for the inquisitors, and the Roman Catholic persuasion,
" arose from a report which had been propagated throughout Europe,
" that he intended to turn *Mahometan;* the emperor therefore *judiciously*
" determined, by the *height of bigotry and cruelty* to shew his attach-
" ment to *Popery.*"

This is Fox's account of the origin and progress of the inquisition;
but such an account as can only be believed by the most besotted
mind. In the first place, Innocent III. had been dead *three hundred*
years previous to the reformed religion, or what is so called, making its
appearance in Europe. Secondly, St. Dominic was not canonized till
thirteen years *after his death,* that is, in 1234, by Gregory IX, therefore it is a DIRECT FALSEHOOD to say he was thus honoured to
make his imputed office of inquisitor the more respectable. Thirdly,

we have shewn, in our preceding pages, that St. Dominic was sent to preach against the Albigenses, and that the members of his order were employed to gain over Pagan countries to Catholicism; and how, we should be glad to learn, could St. Dominic treat Protestants with severity, when there was not a Protestant in Europe till some hundred years after this first pretended inquisitor had paid the debt of nature? Fourthly, he says, the kings of Spain were taught to dread the power of the inquisition, and yet it was by the power of the king that this tribunal was established. Fifthly, multitudes who differed in opinion from the Catholics were, he says, compelled carefully to conceal their opinions. An odd sort of a reformed religion this must be, that its professors were careful to conceal it. This was not the case with the primitive Christians; with John Fox's first martyrs; they made open profession of their faith, as Catholics always did, in spite of knives, halters, or gibbets. Sixthly, the pope, he says, invested the Dominicans and Franciscans with an exclusive right of presiding in this tribunal, because these friars were always selected from the very dregs of the people, and therefore not much troubled with scruples of conscience; and yet he admits they were obliged to lead very austere lives! This is no very great compliment on the part of John Fox towards the people; however history tells us, that among the Dominicans and Franciscans, there were a number of the most learned men and exemplary characters. Seventhly, he says, the pope gave the inquisitors *unlimited* powers, and afterwards these powers were *increased* by the emperor Frederic II. Now if the pope could grant them unlimited power, how could the emperor add to that power? Then, he says, these inquisitors were *allowed* by the pope to enter into leagues with *sovereign princes*, and to join them with their *forces*. Surely, if this be true, these inquisitors, sprung from the dregs of the people, must be wonderful fellows to raise forces without holding territories, and colleaguing with sovereigns though having no scruples of conscience. Eighthly, how fortunate was it for the Roman Catholics, that a report should be raised that the emperor was about to become a Mahometan. But for this lucky circumstance, we suppose, the Catholic church would not have had a stone to rest upon, so *judiciously* for her did the emperor determine to shew his attachment to Popery by the heighth of bigotry and cruelty. Ah! how many of our enlightened Protestants have been duped by this miserably told tale; this compound of falsehood and nonsense.

But before we proceed any further in our remarks we will here give some extracts from the *Encyclopedia Methodique*, respecting this tribunal. The articles in that work, relating to religious subjects were furnished by the abbè Bergier, a canon of Paris, and director to the present king of France. This divine is in high estimation among Catholics, and as it will be seen that he animadverts very freely on the institution, it must necessarily follow that this tribunal is totally unconnected with the religion of Catholics.

" INQUISITION.—An ecclesiastical tribunal, erected by the sovereign
" pontiffs in Italy, Spain, Portugal, and the Indies, with a view to the
" extirpation of the Jews, Moors, Infidels, and Heretics. It is not by
" any means our object to eulogise this tribunal or its manner of pro-

" ceeding, but, as it has been to heretics and infidels a fruitful subject
" of calumnies and imposture, one naturally seeks to ascertain what is
" true and what is false in the reports relating to it. The date of its
" institution is about the year 1200. It was erected by pope Innocent
" the third, against the Albigenses, a set of perfidious heretics, who
" were guilty of profaning the sacraments, a belief in which they ex-
" cluded from their creed. But the council of Verona, held in 1184,
" had, before this time, directed the bishops of Lombardy to make
" strict search after heretics, and if, when apprehended, they remained
" obstinate, to deliver them over for corporal punishment to the civil
" magistrate. (Fleury's Hist. Eccl. l. 73, n. 54.) The count of Tou-
" louse adopted this tribunal in 1229; and in 1233 pope Gregory the
" ninth confined the management of it to the Dominicans. Innocent
" IV. established it in every part of Italy excepting Naples. It was
" established in Spain in 1448, in the reign of Ferdinand and Isabel,
" and in Portugal, under John the third, in the year 1557. In these
" two kingdoms it was subject to the same regulations. In the year
" 1545, Paul the third had formed the congregation of the Inquisition
" under the name of the Holy Office, which was confirmed by Sixtus the
" fifth in the year 1588. When the Spaniards established themselves
" in America, they introduced the inquisition also there, and it was
" introduced into the Portuguese dominions in the East Indies as soon
" as it had been sanctioned at Lisbon.

" From this detail, and from what we shall afterwards take occasion
" to observe, it will satisfactorily appear, that in NO kingdom in Chris-
" tendom was the tribunal of the inquisition erected *without the consent
" (in some instances indeed it was at the request) of the sovereign.*
" This is a fact of essential consequence; a fact, however, studiously
" omitted in declamations against this court. The authors of these de-
" clamations would insinuate that it has always owed its erection to
" the mere authority of the pope; and that too in violation of the rights
" of the sovereign; whereas it is demonstrable, that *in no single instance
" has the inquisitorial court exercised its jurisdiction unless supported by
" the supreme authority.*

" In 1255, Alexander the third, with the consent of St. Louis, estab-
" lished the Inquisition in France. The grand inquisitors were the
" superior of the Cordeliers of Paris, and the provincial of the Domi-
" nicans. The papal bull directed the inquisitors to consult the bi-
" shops, to whose advice, however, they were not obliged to submit.
" This novel species of jurisdiction gave umbrage equally to the eccle-
" siastical and the civil authorities, and the opposition which it met
" with shortly reduced the dignity of these monks to a mere name.
" Had the bishops in other states exhibited the same firmness, their
" authority might have continued undiminished.

" The inquisition had been established at Venice in 1289, but, instead
" of being dependant on the pope, as in other states, it was entirely sub-
" ject to the senate; and in the 16th century it was decreed that the as-
" sistance of three senators should be necessary for every judicial pro-
" cess. This decree made it easy to elude the authority of the court of the
" inquisition, which authority was in consequence annihilated in this
" state."

A REVIEW

OF

Fox's Book of Martyrs,

CRITICAL AND HISTORICAL.

No. 17. Printed and Published by W. E. Andrews, 3, Chapter-house-court, St. Paul's Churchyard, London. Price 3d.

EXPLANATION OF THE ENGRAVING.—*In the year 1799, the Rev. P. O'Neil, an Irish Catholic priest, was taken up by the inquisitors of "Protestant-ascendency," and after being thrown into a loathsome place in the barracks of Youghal, called the black hole, was from thence conducted to the Ball-ally, where he received two hundred and seventy-five lashes inflicted by six right and left handed men; after which a wire-cat was introduced, armed with scraps of tin or lead, with which he was flogged to make him shake the triangle. This horrible torture was used for the purpose of extorting from him the secrets of the confessional, but without effect.—A recital of the sufferings of this innocent victim of the Orange system, or "Protestant-ascendency," will be found in this sheet.*

CONTINUATION OF THE REVIEW.

"The sovereigns of Naples and Sicily claimed a right, from papal
" concessions, to the exercise of ecclesiastical jurisdiction. This claim
" gave rise to disputes between the pope and the king about the right
" of appointing the inquisitors—the consequence was, that none were
" appointed. And if the inquisition was at length established in Sicily,
" (A.D. 1478) as it had been in Spain, it was still more than in Spain
" a privilege of the crown.

"Torquemada, a Dominican, who was made cardinal and grand-in-
" quisitor, gave to that tribunal in Spain the juridical form which it
" still retains. It is said that in the space of fourteen years he insti-
" tuted more than 80,000 juridical processes, and that not less than
" five or six thousand people suffered. But this account is evidently
" exaggerated.

" One word as to the mode of proceeding. The accused is not con-
" fronted with his accuser, and every informer is attended to, though
" a child, a courtezan, or a criminal stigmatized by the hand of jus-
" tice. A son deposes against his father, a wife against her husband,
" a brother against his brother. In fine, the accused is obliged to be-
" come his own accuser, and to divine and confess the crime that is im-
" puted to him, and of which he has no knowledge.

" This unheard-of mode of proceeding is calculated, no doubt, to
" keep all Spain in a state of alarm, but it must not be imagined that it
" is adopted to the letter. It is not every accusation, though it may ex-
" cite suspicion in the inquisitors, that authorizes them to arrest or pu-
" nish the accused. *In Spain a man, whether native or foreigner, may*
" *live as securely, and with as much liberty as elsewhere, provided a dog-*
" *matizing spirit does not incite him to disturb the public peace.*

" The declaimers against the inquisition have drawn in the blackest
" colours the punishment inflicted by this tribunal, which they style
" *auto da fé,* acts of faith. A priest, say they, in a surplice, or a monk,
" whose profession is that of mildness and charity, is the person who, in
" a vast and dreary dungeon, directs the torture of a fellow creature;
" the unhappy victim follows a procession of monks to the pile prepared
" for his execution, and the king, whose presence dispenses mercy to
" criminals, assists, on a seat lower than the inquisitor's, as witness to
" the death of his own subjects expiring in the flames.

" All this is undoubtedly very pathetic. But it should be qualified
" by the following observations. 1st. It bespeaks a want of candour
" to insinuate, that the fire is the portion of all whom the inquisition
" condemns. It is the punishment inflicted only for crimes, which are
" visited in the same manner among those nations in which the inqui-
" sition is not known. Such as sacrilege, profanation, apostasy, magic.
" Other crimes are punished with perpetual imprisonment, confinement
" in a monastery, the discipline and other species of penance, 2dly.
" It is a custom in all Christian nations, that criminals should be as-
" sisted at their execution by the priest, who exhorts them to patience.
" He is often accompanied by members of the confraternity of the cross,
" who offer up their prayers for the criminal, and bestow the right of
" sepulture on his body. Query. Is this a mark of cruelty? 3dly.
" Capital punishments are very rare both in Spain and Portugal, and
" no single instance can be produced of its having been inflicted at
" Rome. At Rome the inquisition was always less severe than any
" where else, and the form given to it by Torquemada has never been
" received at Rome. The suppression of these matters is a reflection
" on the candour and sincerity of our declaimers.

" Again, it is somewhat absurd to denominate these executions hu-
" man sacrifices. To all punishments inflicted for crimes against reli-
" gion, this appellation might with equal justice be applied. These
" profound gentlemen will have some difficulty to persuade the Chris-
" tian world that no offences of this nature ought to be punished with
" death.

" Reproach a Spaniard with the horrors of the inquisition—he will
" answer, that wars on account of religion, in the kingdom of France
" alone, have caused more blood to be shed than has been spilt by the

" tribunals of the inquisition over the whole world : and he will add,
" that by means of the inquisition, Spain has been preserved from any
" infection of the infidelity which at this day overspreads the rest of Eu-
" rope. . Tell him that wars are of a temporary nature, and must soon
" subside ; but that the inquisition it would seem, once established, be-
" comes a permanent institution—he will reply by an appeal to facts—
" France, Germany, the states of Venice, have suppressed, after having
" admitted it ; and the king of Portugal has very much disarmed it of
" its terrors in his dominions. He has ordained that the procurator-
" general, who is the prosecutor, shall communicate to the accused the
" articles of impeachment and the name of the witnesses. 2dly, That
" the accused shall have the power of choosing an advocate with
" whom he may also confer ; and 3dly, That no sentence of the inqui-
" sition shall be put into execution until it has been confirmed by his
" council.

" The person who has declaimed with the greatest virulence against
" this tribunal, acknowledges, however, that excesses have frequently
" been imputed to it, of which it has not been guilty. In his opinion
" it betrays a want of judgment to ground an invective on uncertain-
" ties, and still more so on falsehoods. It were well had he acted on
" this principle, and discovered a little more candour in his relations.

" We cordially congratulate France and Germany that they are free
" from the influence of this tribunal. Yet we have no hesitation in
" declaring our firm conviction, that were our infidel philosophers to
" become masters, they would establish an inquisition much more se-
" vere than that of Spain."

We have here given Fox's statement of the origin and progress of
the inquisition, and a counter statement of a more modern date, from
the pen of a Catholic. The reader has therefore before him two sides
of the question, and consequently is better able to make his conclusions. We have shewn that the first statement is palpably false ; the
second bears the stamp of authenticity, and the institution not being
approved of by the writer, corroborates what we have before asserted,
and again repeat, that the tribunal of the inquisition has no more to
do with the revealed truths of the Catholic religion, than Christianity
had in the establishment in these countries of the high commission
courts, the star-chamber, and the penal statutes enacted against Catholicism.—Taking the origin of the inquisition at its earliest date, the
Catholic faith had existed 1200 years without it ; in many parts, England, for example, it never had existence in Catholic times, and of
course it was not a component part of the Catholic church.—Fox says
it was established by the authority of the pope ; the abbé Bergier, on
the contrary, asserts, that in no single kingdom in Christendom was
this tribunal erected without the consent of the civil power. Hence it
was clearly a *civil* tribunal, having ecclesiastical officers to assist and
guide its process in matters of doctrine. No country previous to the
reformation, so called, was more devoted to the Catholic faith than
England, and yet, as we have before observed, this tribunal of the inquisition was never dreamed of. Had the pope the power of establishing it at his own will and pleasure, as Fox represents him to have had,
would he not have erected this powerful institution in every country

where his influence extended; that is, in every part of Christendom? for, with the exception of Turkey and Russia, the Catholic religion was established in every quarter of the globe, when the reformers of the sixteenth century began to preach evangelical liberty, or rather self-interpreting licentiousness. From the account given by Fox, the reader is led to conclude that none but diabolical monsters could have any concern in the inquisition, and that none but a diabolical religion could sanction such proceedings. Could the principles of Catholicism be fairly proved as leading to persecution and the horrible proceedings imputed to the inquisition, we would instantly renounce our church, though we should certainly be at a loss *where* to find another that has the marks of being *a true one.* But we know they cannot; we know that she will remain pure and undefiled, protected by the promises of her divine Founder, though many of her children may violate her precepts and cause scandals to arise among the ignorant and prejudiced.

But why are the Catholics of England and Ireland to be so unsparingly and unremittingly taunted with the excesses and abuses of the Spanish and Portuguese inquisitions, when cruelties more horrible and barbarous have been committed by the enlightened disciples of Protestantism in their own countries? In this *Book of Martyrs* we have accounts of *auto da fés,* of the mode of torturing, of the barbarities of the inquisition, its treachery, its enormities, and we know not what abuses, all imputed to the spirit of Popery, but we do not see a word of the cruelties, the cold-blooded enactments, the perjuries, the proscriptions, the rackings, the half-hangings, the burnings, the whippings, the deportations, and the whole-hangings that have been put in execution in England and Ireland on Catholics, and, in fact, in every country where Protestantism gained the ascendency, from the sixteenth century to our own times. It is an incontrovertible fact, recorded in the page of history, and not disputed by the enemies of Catholicism, that the Catholic religion was introduced into all countries in opposition to Pagan persecution, and that it was the ascendant religion for centuries before any decrees of corporal punishment were passed against persons infected with heretical opinions. And *why* were these decrees passed? *Why* were penal inflictions resorted to at last? The answer is obvious and irrefutable. Because with theoretical opinions physical proceedings, the fruits of these opinions, were combined, which threatened the security of property and peace of society; therefore the lawful authorities were *compelled* by duty, and a just regard for the safety of the state, to repel force by force, when the influence of persuasion had failed. Had not the Albigenses been imbued with the most horrible fanaticism, and had they not sought to propagate their beastly doctrines by sedition and rebellion, massacre and plunder, the inquisition would probably never had existence; and what can add greater weight to this opinion than the fact that this tribunal was only partially established in the Catholic states of Europe? But let us look to the effects produced by the dissemination of Protestantism, and we shall see that it had scarcely begun to breathe before persecution and proscriptions appeared in its train. So true is the concluding observation of the abbé Bergier, in his account of the inquisition, "that were our infidel " philosophers to become masters, they would establish an inquisition

" much more severe than that of Spain." Look to the reign of our eighth Henry, and the successive sovereigns that have filled the throne of this empire. Look to the laws that were passed by "Protestant ascendency," and the executions that were repeatedly enforced on Catholics, and only for being Catholics. Passing over for the present the long and bloody civil wars engendered by the pernicious doctrines of the evangelical reformers in France, Germany, and England, a mere glance at the executions which took place, by the power of "Protestant ascendency," will suffice to shew that persecution is, in fact, an ingredient of error, whereas truth will triumph better by the force of reason than of the civil sword.

Harry was no sooner invested by his servile parliament with the title of supreme head of the church of England, than he contrived to have a law passed, by which power was given to him to punish such of his subjects as would not conform to his whims and caprices in matters of religious doctrine. That is, who would not believe this thing to-day, and that to-morrow, according as the supreme head should dictate and command. How numerous were the executions in this tyrant's reign, both of Catholics and Protestants. In his successor's short rule, Cranmer, the apostle of Protestantism in England, obliged the young king, Edward to sign the death warrants of Van Parre and Joan Bucher, in, which he was joined by Ridley, the Protestant bishop of Gloucester.— Besides the almost innumerable Catholic missionary priests who suffered in Elizabeth's reign, after undergoing the tortures of the rack, the scavenger's daughter, the little ease, and other instruments of cruelty, which we shall notice hereafter, the unfortunate Mary queen of Scotland was beheaded, after suffering eighteen years imprisonment for her religious belief.

During James the first's reign, the parliament was unceasingly employed in petitioning the king for severe laws being enforced against the Papists. In Charles the first's reign, a solemn league and covenant was entered into to exterminate Popery and Prelacy, and an archbishop of the established church was murdered by a band of Puritans heated by religious frenzy. This Puritan faction afterwards obtaining the ascendency, the king himself was brought to the block, and is now honoured by the established church as a royal martyr. So clear it is, that when *error* gains the ascendency, *persecution* is a constant attendant in its train. Did not Calvin burn Servetus for opposing him in his mad and blasphemous doctrines? Did not the Huguenots persecute the Catholics with fire and sword, and cruelties unspeakable, wherever they got the ascendency? We shall furnish instances of this when the time arrives, that will make even the few "plain Christians" blush, if they have a spark of shame left. Fox lays great stress upon the Dominicans and Franciscans being appointed inquisitors; but do we not see it stated daily in the public journals of this country, that clergymen of the established church are in the commission of the peace and made visiting magistrates of prisons, where the severest restrictions are imposed on the convicted offenders, and in many cases on the unfortunate debtors immured therein? *Why* then, we once more repeat, should the Catholics of England and Ireland be reproached because Spanish and Portuguese ecclesiastics are employed in a civil tribunal erected in their own country, when Protestant clergymen are similarly employed in England and Ireland.

A considerable space of this *Book of Martyrs* is occupied in detailing the supposed sufferings of individuals whose *names* are given, but neither date nor authority is mentioned to furnish a clue whereby inquiry may be instituted to learn the accuracy of the statements made. We have a description of an *auto da fé* at Madrid in the year 1682, nearly a century and a half ago, but on whose authority not a word is said.—This story, however, must not be placed to Fox's account, since he had been dead some hundred years before the affair is said to have happened; it is nevertheless as highly-coloured as many of his improbabilities, and therefore entitled to just the same degree of credit. We will here give the concluding part of this tale, and the reader will then be able to say whether we have done injustice to its author. "Next followed " the burning of *twenty-one* men and women, whose *intrepidity* in suf- " fering that horrid death was *truly astonishing :* some thrust their hands " and feet into the flames with the *most dauntless fortitude ;* and all of " them yielded to their fate with *such resolution,* that many of the " *amazed spectators* lamented that such heroic souls *had not been more* " *enlightened!* The situation of the king was so near to the criminals, " that their *dying groans* were very *audible to him :* he could not, how- " ever, be absent from this dreadful scene, as it is esteemed a *religious* " one; and his *coronation oath obliges him to give a sanction by his pre-* " *sence to all the acts of the tribunal."* The least reflection will shew the gross absurdity of this relation. The astonishing intrepidity and dauntless fortitude of these victims are stated to be such as to excite the amazement of the spectators, while their dying groans are represented as having a contrary effect upon the king. But why should not the sovereign be equally as much amazed at the fortitude of the sufferers as the people? And why did not these reputed martyrs evince the same fortitude to the last as they are represented to have shewn at first? In the case of the primitive martyrs we find nothing of dying groans, but all is borne with chearful fortitude and invincible courage; the most excruciating tortures producing nothing but praises and adoration of the glorious name of Jesus Christ, the second person of the blessed Trinity, whom they acknowledged to be GOD, by whose power and grace they were enabled to suffer for his sake? Why then did not these victims of the inquisition follow so glorious an example? This question the few "plain Christians" will find some difficulty in solving; for it is much easier to make a lie than it is to turn falsehood into truth. But the most barefaced part of this relation is the conclusion, which states that the king is bound by his *coronation* oath "to " give a sanction by his *presence* to *all* the *acts* of the tribunal." No such clause we positively assert is to be found in the Spanish coronation oath, for if it were, would not those who objected to the abolition of this tribunal by the cortes in 1814 have urged this very clause in support of their opposition? We know very well that when Mr. Pitt, in 1801, contemplated relieving the Catholics of this kingdom from the effects of the penal laws, far more grinding than the proceedings of the Spanish inquisition, the advocates for bigotry and proscription raised a scruple in the royal mind respecting the obligations of his coronation oath, which had the effect of keeping one-third of his subjects in a state of civil slavery, and exalting a faction to tyrannize over them with mercenary ascendency and cold-blooded cruelty, as we shall hereafter prove beyond contradiction. In this remark we wish not to convey the slightest censure upon the memory of George the third, because we consider him to have been sincere in his scruples, and therefore entitled to the regard of every honest man; our remarks are directed to those who took advantage of the king's veneration of his oath to construe the clause into a meaning not contemplated by the framers of it, for the purpose of withholding justice from their fellow subjects.

One more tale, and we shall arrive, we think, at the climax of impudence and lying, even in this *Book of Martyrs*. " A *Protestant* tailor " of *Spain*, named John Leon," say the editors, "travelled to *Germany* " and from thence to *Geneva*, where hearing that a great number of " *English* Protestants were returning to their *native country*, he, and " some more Spaniards, determined to go with them. The *Spanish* " inquisitors being apprized of their intentions, sent a number of fami- " liars *in pursuit* of them, who overtook them at a seaport in *Zealand*. " The prisoners were heavily fettered, handcuffed, gagged, had their " heads and necks covered with a kind of iron net-work, and in this " miserable condition they were conveyed *to Spain*, thrown into a dun- " geon, almost famished, barbarously tortured, and then burnt." p. 130. We think the father of lies himself cannot beat this precious *morceau*, dished up to tickle the palates of English Protestants.—Surely these Spanish inquisitors must be gifted with omnipotence to perform all that they are here said to have done. Why, if these fellows could send their familiars to seize renegado tailors in independent states; if a Spaniard was not free from the fangs of the inquisition, though under the protection of a foreign independent power; what security could there have been in England from the gripe of these familiars? We wonder when puritan bigotry invented the tale that the Jesuits had laid a train of gunpowder to blow up the Thames and drown poor Protestant London, they did not also add, that the familiars of the Spanish inquisition were to fly away with the people, to have them all burned in Spain or turned into Papists. Let any one take a gazetteer in his hand, and lay a map of Europe before him; let him then read this statement in the *Book of Martyrs*, and after he has cast his eye over the geographical situation of Spain, Germany, Geneva, and Zealand, let him say, whether it be possible, without the aid of a supernatural power, for even Spanish inquisitors to make a seizure such as is described by Fox's editors. Whether the Zealand here named is intended for Denmark, or one of the united provinces of Holland, we are not told, nor have we any date when the affair took place; but let whichever of the two be selected by the few "plain Christians," we beg the reader to notice that both are *Protestant* states, and is it therefore likely that the familiars of the inquisitors could take the *whole* of the travellers, at one fell sweep, and convey them over to Spain. For observe, the narrator is not content with having the poor Spanish tailor seized by the familiars, but the English Protestants and some more Spaniards were all snared by these sagacious and far-scented tracers of heretic tailors, and so forth. What next will the "plain Christians" assert to alarm the prejudices of the ignorant and credulous in this enlightened age? Enough we think has been shewn on our part to make common sense blush for the credulity of our countrymen, and yet we fear there are some who require to be still farther convinced before they will relinquish the long-rooted prejudices imbibed from their infancy.

The third section of this book is specially devoted to the "Trial "and Sufferings of Mr. Isaac Martin," whose case, we are told, "was "published by the desire of secretary Craggs, the archbishops of Can-"terbury and York, the bishops of London, Winchester, Ely, Norwich, "Sarum, Chichester, St. Asaph, Lincoln, Bristol, Peterborough, Bangor, "&c." Mr. Martin, it is stated, went to Malaga, in the Lent of 1714, with his wife and four children. His baggage being examined, *a bible* and other books were discovered and seized. But notwithstanding the bible would bespeak him a Christian, the Spaniards took him for a *Jew* at first, because his own name was *Isaac* and one of his sons was named *Abraham.* After some other round-about improbabilities and ridiculous descriptions, the narrative goes on, "He was then remand-"ed to his dungeon; was shaved on Whitsun-eve, (*shaving* being al-"lowed only *three* times in *the year*); and the next day one of the "gaolers gave him some *frankincense* to be put into the fire, as he was "to receive a visit from the lords of the inquisition. Two of them "accordingly came, asked many trivial questions, concluding them, as "usual, with, 'We will do you all the service we can.' Mr. Martin "complained greatly of their having promised him a lawyer to plead "his cause; 'when, instead of a proper person,' said he, 'there was "a man whom you called a lawyer, but he *never spoke* to me, nor *I to* "*him:* if all your lawyers are so quiet in this country, they are the "quietest in the world, for he hardly *said* any thing but *yes* and *no*, to "what your lordship said.' To which one of the inquisitors gravely "replied, 'Lawyers are not allowed to speak here.' At this the gaoler "and secretary *went out* of the dungeon *to laugh*, and Mr. Martin could "scarce refrain from *smiling in their faces*, to think that his cause was to "be defended by a man who scarce dared to open his lips." p. 134. Let those who are credulous enough believet his relation; we have too high an opinion of our countrymen, however, to think it will be generally credited now. The inquisitors are not such fools as to make a mockery where none is required, and what shall we say to the extreme delicacy of the gaoler and secretary, who went out of the dungeon to give vent to their mirth at the witty replies of the inquisitor, while the prisoner himself had much to do to prevent his laughing in their faces. But is it not better to have dumb lawyers, than to stop them in their defence if they say that which is not pleasing to the judges before whom the prisoner is tried? What is the difference to the prisoner between an advocate being silenced in his defence, and an advocate who makes no defence at all? The result of Isaac Martin's trial is next given in these words: "About a month afterwards, he had a rope put round his neck, "and was led by it to the altar of the great church. Here his sentence "was pronounced, which was, that for the crimes of which he stood "convicted, the lords of the holy office had ordered him to be *banished* "out of the dominions of Spain, upon the penalty of two hundred lashes, "and being sent five years to the galleys; and that he should at pre-

" sent receive two hundred lashes through the streets of the city of
" Grenada. Mr. Martin was sent again to his dungeon that night, and
" the next morning the executioner came, stripped him, tied his hands
" together, put a rope about his neck, and led him out of the prison. He
" was then mounted on an ass, and received his two hundred lashes,
" amidst the shouts and peltings of the people. He remained a fort-
" night after this in gaol, and at length was sent to Malaga, Here he
" was put in gaol for some days, till he could be sent on board an Eng-
" lish ship : which had no sooner happened, than news was brought of
" a rupture between England and Spain, and that ship, with many
" others, was stopped. Mr. Martin not being considered as a prisoner
" of war, was put on board of a Hamburgh trader, and his wife and
" children soon came to him; but he was obliged to put up with the
" loss of his effects, which had been embezzled by the inquisition."—
The singularity of this sentence, and the lucky rumour of a rupture
with England, are rather improbable stories. It is needless to impose
a penalty of two hundred lashes upon a man after he is sent out of your
reach, and you have given him a specimen of the lash, by executing
the sentence before hand; and we might be led to suppose that Mr.
Martin would be less likely to escape from the hands of the Spaniards
in the event of a war, than in the time of profound peace. But probably the bishops, at whose desire the case of Isaac Martin was published, were of opinion with Shaftesbury, the promoter of Oates's infamous plot, that the greater the lies the more likelihood was there of
the credulous people of England swallowing them for facts. So true
is the observation of Mr. Cobbett, that of all nations of the earth for lying, Protestant England is the greatest.

Hitherto we have seen only one side of the question, excepting our
criticisms on the language used by Fox and his editors; it is therefore
time to lay open another perspective, that the reader may perceive the
accuracy of our statement, that persecution is concomitant with error.
Fox says, in his account of the origin, progress, and cruelties of the inquisition, that " when the reformed religion began to diffuse the pure
" light of the gospel throughout Europe, the bigoted Roman Catholics,
" fearing the exposure of the frauds and abuses of their church, deter-
" mined to leave nothing unattempted to crush the reformation in its
" infancy; pope Innocent III. therefore instituted a number of inquisi-
" tors, or persons who were to make inquiry after, apprehend, and pu-
" nish the professors of the reformed faith." We have shewn that Innocent III. was dead long before the reformation, so called, had existence; and if we only look across St. George's channel, we shall find that
the pure light of the reformation-gospel was attempted to be forced on
the benighted Irish, under the influence of terror and death, and that
as pretty a race of inquisitors were produced there by queen Bess, which
race has continued to this day, as any that have disgraced the most
bigoted Catholic country in the world. The greatest captain of the
age, as the duke of Wellington is styled, who owes most of his military exploits to Irish talent and courage, and who in return dooms the
people of Ireland, by his votes in parliament, to perpetual slavery, has
avowed that the Protestant religion was attempted, but ineffectually,
to be thrust down the Irish by the mouth of the cannon and the point

of the bayonet. We have in our Review, pages 96 and 103, detailed some of the enormities practised upon that ill-fated people; it now becomes us to shew, by the most indubitable testimony, that, while the bawlers against Popish cruelty have been ringing the changes, without intermission, on the pretended horrors of the inquisition, Catholic Ireland has been suffering the most grinding acts of injustice, the most sanguinary and cold-blooded cruelties, under the inquisitors of "Protestant-ascendency," that the most merciless of human-kind could inflict on his weaker fellow-mortal. Elizabeth came to the crown in the year 1558, and her "first concern (says Mr. Plowden in his History " of Ireland,) was to promote the *reformed* religion through Ireland, " as successfully as she had through England, not only as to the spi- " ritual supremacy, which alone her father had attempted, but as to " several dogmatical points of faith. Conscious that this innovation " would be strongly opposed even by a parliament of the pale, she gave " special instructions to her lieutenant to predispose the members to " forward her views, and ordered writs to be issued to the representa- " tives of ten counties instead of six, as had heretofore been usual. " Being tolerably secure of a majority in both houses, a parliament was " convened in the second year of her reign; by which it was enacted, " that the spiritual jurisdiction should be restored to the crown; that " all the acts of her sister Mary, by which the civil establishment of " the Roman Catholic religion had been renewed, should be repealed; " that the queen should be enabled to appoint commissioners to exer- " cise ecclesiastical jurisdiction; that all officers and ministers, eccle- " siastical or lay, should on pain of forfeiture and total incapacity take " the oath of supremacy; that every person, as well as his aider, abet- " tor, or counsellor, who should in any way maintain the spiritual " supremacy of the bishop of Rome, should forfeit for the first offence " all his estates real and personal (or be imprisoned for one year if not " worth 20*l.*); incur a *præmunire* for the second offence, and become " guilty of high treason for the third; that the use of the common " prayer should be enforced as in England; that every person should " resort to the established church, and attend the new service under " pain of ecclesiastical censures, and of the forfeitures of twelve-pence " for every offence, to be levied by the churchwardens by distress of " the lands or chattels of the defaulter; that the first-fruits and twen- " tieths of all church revenues should be restored to the crown; and " the old writ and form of *congé d'elire* superseded by the king's letters " patent, by which in future all collations to vacant sees were to be " made. These ordinances were followed by an act of recognition of " the queen's title to the crown; and it was made a case of *præmunire* " to speak, and *treason to write* against it." Such were some of the means adopted to spread the pure light of the gospel, in the infancy of the reformation, among the Catholics of Ireland, by that dear and immortalized (by Protestant bigots) she pope of England, the *virgin* queen Elizabeth.

It must here be observed, that the Irish had been professors of the Catholic religion for about one thousand years when her *holiness* Elizabeth and her ministers took it into their heads to compel them to relinquish that faith which had existed so long by the power

of conviction, and which it was vainly conceived was now to give way to the power of acts of parliament. Had there been *frauds* and *abuses* in the *church* of Rome, why were they not exposed to the Irish by the new reformers? An exposition of this kind would have had a much greater effect upon the acute minds of the Irish than the smell of gunpowder and the sight of naked steel. The detection of a single piece of priestcraft would have done more good than the burning of twenty cottages and hanging of fifty peasants for constructed treason, that is, merely because they would not become traitors to their God. The case here is quite different to that of the Albigenses, over whom Fox has made such doleful lamentations. The Albigenses wanted to introduce *new* theories, many of which were productive of immorality and endangered the peace of society. The Irish were in possession of a religion which had stood the test of fifteen hundred years, and in possession of property and privileges too to which they had an inalienable right. This property was wrested from them, their privileges were invaded, and they were persecuted to death to make them forswear their faith. An odious oligarchy called "Protestant-ascendency" was established, with all the ramifications of inquisitors, courts of inquiry, torturing to extort confessions on suspicion of being Catholics, and every species of cruelty and injustice were put in practice by the propagators of the reformed religion. Dr. Curry writes, says Mr. Lawless in his History of Ireland, that "unheard of cruelties were com-
" mitted on the provincials of Munster by the English. Great compa-
" nies of those provincials, men, women and children, were often forced
" into castles and other houses, which were then set on fire; and if any
" of them attempted to escape from the flames, they were shot or
" stabbed by the soldiers who guarded them. It was a diversion to
" these monsters of men to take up infants on the points of their spears,
" and whirl them about in their agony, apologizing for their cruelty by
" saying, ' that if they suffered them to live to grow up, *they would have*
" *become Popish rebels.*' Many of the women were found hanging on
" trees, with their children at their breasts, strangled with their mo-
" ther's hair." We name not these unparalleled enormities, committed by the propagators of the "pure light of the gospel," in the infancy of the reformation, so called, with an intention to excite hatred or revenge against the present professors of Protestantism, but with the view of calling down the indignation of every honest man on the publishers of Fox's *Book of Martyrs*, who have given circulation to a mass of improbable fiction, for the avowed purpose of exciting "a hatred
" and abhorrence of the (imputed) crimes and corruptions of Po-
" pery and its professors," while the page of history is so black with the deeds of "Protestant-ascendency." In the succeeding reigns, the same scenes of blood and proscription were acted over and over again, and would be too tedious to the reader were we to recount them; we will therefore, for brevity sake, come down to our own times, in order to shew that the spirit of "Protestant-ascendency" is ever the same, that is, vindictive and mercenary towards the Catholics. It has ever been a favourite tactic with the ascendency faction to create false alarms, and work upon the fears and prejudices of the people. Hence has originated the greatest part of the palpable lies in the *Book of Martyrs*, and the details of imaginary massacres laid to the

charge of the Catholics. Hence too the reports of outrages and risings, and conspiracies in Ireland, to be found in the Orange and ascendency papers of both countries.

Although Ireland had ever been the theatre of religious animosity, from the period of the reformation, yet in the year 1778, the managers began to manifest their bigotry and power in a more than usually prominent manner. This disposition first began to shew itself in the county of Armagh, the most Protestant county in all Ireland, and continued fomenting till the year 1794, when it broke out into open violence. Of these acts of violence, which we shall not here particularize, the late Mr. Curran this spoke in his place in the senate: He could speak, he said, "as an eye witness, declaring them to be " scenes of more atrocity and horror than he had ever seen in a court " of justice. It was what the Catholics might have expected, when " they found their avowed enemies continued in authority, and the ma- " lice of an implacable government left to indemnify itself by vengeance " what it had lost by law." This gentleman, we must here observe, was a Protestant. On the 1st of July, 1795, a reverend divine of the established church preached a sermon in commemoration of the battle of the Boyne at Portadown. In his discourse the Protestant divine worked so well upon the minds of his hearers, that in going home they attacked the houses and persons of their Catholic neighbours, and murdered two unoffending peasants. This may be considered the first grand exploit and commencement of the Orange system. Of the spirit and progress of this pillar of "Protestant-ascendency," Mr. Plowden writes thus in his valuable History of Ireland, from the Union to 1810. "Elated with " their success at the Diamond, the Orangemen advanced boldly in " their work of extermination. They confided in the protection, and " boasted of the support, of the magistrates, before several of whom " that battle was fought. Not only the profession of the Catholic re- " ligion, but connexion with a Catholic by marriage, or dependence " upon a Catholic by servitude, exposed the individual to the brutal fe-, " rocity of these exterminators. Some magistrates directly promoted, " others countenanced and encouraged, and most of them allowed these " outrages to be committed with impunity. At that time commenced " that dreadful system, which Mr. Grattan described, as 'a persecution " conceived in the bitterness of bigotry, carried on with the most fero- " cious barbarity by a banditti, who, being of the religion of the state, " had committed with greater audacity and confidence the most horrid " murders, and had proceeded from robbery and massacre to extermi- " nation.' 'Those insurgents,' said he, 'call themselves Orangemen or " Protestant Boys; that is, a banditti of murderers, committing mas- " sacre in the name of God, and exercising despotic power in the name " of liberty.' "

At a meeting of the magistrates of Armagh, convened on the 28th of December, 1795, to concert measures most likely to stop the progress of these disgraceful enormities, lord Gosford thus addressed the meeting: "It is," said his lordship, "no secret, that a persecution, " accompanied with all the circumstances of ferocious cruelty, " which have in all ages distinguished that calamity, is now raging " in this county. Neither age nor sex, nor even acknowledged inno- " cence, as to any guilt in the late disturbances, is sufficient to excite

" mercy or afford protection. The only crime which the wretched
" objects of this ruthless persecution are charged with, is a crime in-
" deed of easy proof: *It is simply a profession of the Roman Catholic faith,*
" or an intimate connexion with a person professing that faith. A law-
" less banditti have constituted themselves judges of this new species
" of delinquency, and the sentence they have denounced is equally con-
" cise and terrible! It is nothing less than a confiscation of all pro-
" perty, and an immediate banishment. It would be extremely painful,
" and surely unnecessary, to detail the horrors that attend the execution
" of so rude and tremendous a proscription. A proscription, that certain-
" ly exceeds, in the comparative number of those it consigns to ruin
" and misery, every example that modern and ancient history can sup-
" ply: for where have we heard, or in what story of human cruelties have
" we read, of more than half the inhabitants of a populous country de-
" prived at one blow of the means, as well as of the fruits, of their in-
" dustry, and driven, in the midst of an inclement season, to seek a
" shelter for themselves and their helpless families where chance may
" guide them. This is no exaggerated picture of the horrid scenes
" now acting in this county. Yet surely it is sufficient to awaken sen-
" timents of indignation and compassion in the coldest bosoms. These
" horrors are now acting with impunity. The spirit of impartial jus-
" tice (without which law is nothing better than an instrument of
" tyranny) has for a time disappeared in the county, and the supineness
" of the magistracy of Armagh is become a common topic of conver-
" sation in every corner of the kingdom."

In a debate in the Irish House of Commons on the 20th of February,
1796, Mr. Grattan thus describes the horrible practices of the Orangemen:—" These insurgents have organized their rebellion, and formed
" themselves into a committee, who sit and try the Catholic weavers
" and inhabitants, when apprehended falsely and illegally, as deserters.
" That rebellious committee they call the committee of Elders, who,
" when the unfortunate Catholic is torn from his family and loom,
" and brought before them in judgment; if he give them liquor or
" money, they sometimes discharge him, otherwise they send him to
" a recruiting officer as a deserter. They generally give the Catholics
" notice to quit their farms and dwellings, which notice they plaister on
" their houses conceived in these short but plain words: *Go to hell,*
" *Connaught won't receive you. Fire and faggot, Wm. Thresham, and*
" *John Thrustout.* They followed these notices with faithful and punc-
" tual execution of the horrid threat. In many instances they threw
" down the houses of the tenantry, or what they called racked the
" house, so that the family must fly or be buried in the grave of their
" own cabin. The extent of the murders that had been committed by
" that atrocious and rebellious banditti he had heard, but not so ascer-
" tained, as to state them to the house; but from all the inquiries he
" could make, he collected, that the Catholic inhabitants of Armagh
" were actually put out of the protection of the law; that the ma-
" gistrates had been supine and partial, and that the horrid banditti had
" met with complete success, and from the magistracy with very little
" disencouragement."

Among the suffererers from these atrocities was Mr. Bernard Coile,

then an eminent muslin and cambric manufacturer in the town of Lurgan. This gentleman was a Catholic, and had exerted his influence to preserve the peace of his neighbourhood, and keep his Catholic countrymen within the bounds of the law. The consequence was, he became a marked victim of "Protestant-ascendency." A principal part of his property, then in the hands of weavers, was destroyed. He applied to a magistrate, named Greer, for redress, who refused to take examinations or grant warrants. Mr. Coile prosecuted this corrupt magistrate and cast him. He was sentenced to six months imprisonment and fined 200*l.* As a matter of course he was committed to Newgate and his name erased from the list of magistrates. But Mr. Greer was a stanch supporter of "Protestant-ascendency," his fine was therefore reduced to *sixpence,* and lord Clare restored him to the commission of the peace. So much for the offender: now mark what fell to the injured Catholic. A conspiracy was entered into against Mr. Coile to take away his life upon a false charge of high treason, and he was committed to prison, says Mr. Plowden, in his aforesaid History, "upon the following ex-
" travagantly false charge, of being a reputed Papist, distributing a
" large quantity of ball cartridges amongst a number of Papists, for
" the purpose of destroying the Protestants, and also at the same time
" swearing a person to be one of his soldiers, to assist in overthrowing
" the king, government, and all magistrates. The Rev. Mr. Mansell,
" the evangelizer of Portadown, before whom the examinations of
" the conspirators were sworn, induced such of them as were or had
" been Catholics, to read their recantation before they were examined.
" Mr. Coile was confined above eight months in prison, vainly entreat-
" ing and urging to be put upon his trial. Four of the conspirators
" against his life, touched with remorse, deposed, in the mean time,
" before different magistrates, that they had been suborned to swear
" falsely against him. Some of them added, that they had been com-
" pelled by twelve men, whom they named in their affidavits, to swear
" false oaths against him and others, that they had been rewarded for
" having done so with clothes and money. Mr. Coile was enlarged
" without trial, after an imprisonment of eight months. Wishing to
" prosecute the rest of the conspirators, he was prevented from doing
" it by the judge, because his own trial was still hanging over him,
" whenever it might be expedient for the crown to bring it forward.
" This management of justice bespeaks the spirit of those by whom it
" was administered." Nor was this all. Finding his life in danger, he went to Dublin, where persecution still followed him. He was not only refused the use of the Linen-hall to vend his goods like other merchants, but, on purchasing a house for that purpose, he had no sooner taken possession of it, when forty-eight women and children and four troopers were billeted upon him for ten weeks and four days. Nor did his sufferings here cease; for in 1803 he was arrested under a false charge and committed to Newgate in Dublin, from whence he was removed to Kilmainham, in which two gaols he suffered three years and a half imprisonment, a considerable time in solitary confinement and loaded with 56lbs. weight of irons. These are facts that can be verified on oath, as the gentleman is still living, without a shade of guilt being proved against him, other than his being

a sound and inflexible Catholic, and he has declared his readiness to prove the truth of what is here stated, and more than we have stated, at the bar of the senate.

We have another tale to relate still more horrifying and unjust, which is the case of the Rev. Mr. O'Neil.—The few "plain Christians" may storm about the unlimited powers granted by the pope to the inquisitors, while it is stated by a more creditable witness that this unlimited power was clipped by the king of Portugal, if it were ever granted; but we defy them to produce an instance of religious persecution duly authenticated, equal in ferocity to the treatment experienced, under "Protestant-ascendency," by father O'Neil, the present parish priest of Ballymacoda. This Catholic pastor was taken up in 1799, by Orange inquisitors, on *suspicion*, only on *suspicion*, observe reader, of having sanctioned some murders in the year preceding. One of the accusations against the inquisition is, that the accused is never confronted with the accuser, and that every informer is attended to: well let us now see father O'Neil's account of what he had to undergo from the hands of the "Protestant-ascendency" inquisition in Ireland. The extracts we have here given are taken from the humble remonstrance of Mr. O'Neil, dated October 23, 1803, and addressed to the nobility and gentry of the county of Cork, in which his parish is situated. The remonstrance was occasioned by his being charged by a "Protestant-ascendency" law lord, in that same year, with having been "*proved* to have been guilty of sanctioning the murders of 1798, trans- "ported to Botany bay, and since pardoned by the mercy of govern- "ment." After denying in the most solemn manner that he was guilty of the smallest offence charged against him, and challenging his persecutors to produce the slightest proof of criminality, the Rev. Mr. O'Neil thus proceeds :—" It was my peculiar misfortune that the " charges then made against me, were not only withheld from myself, " but even my friends had no intimation of them, except by common " report, which then was busily employed in disseminating the various " atrocities, supposed to have been committed by me: but nothing " specifically authenticated had transpired: the very committal was " so vague, as to have excited the astonishment of a professional friend " of mine in Dublin, and to have eventually led to my discharge. I " shall now proceed to the particulars of my case. Immediately upon " my arrest, I was brought into Youghal, where, without any previous " trial, I was confined in a loathsome *receptacle of the barrack*, called " the black-hole; rendered still more offensive by the stench of the " common necessary adjoining it. In that dungeon I remained from " Friday until Monday, when I was conducted to the Ball-ally to re- " ceive my punishment. No trial had yet intervened, nor ever after. " I was stript and tied up; six soldiers stood forth for this operation; " some of them right-handed, some of them left-handed men, two at " a time (as I judge from the quickness of the lashes) and relieved at " intervals, until I had received two hundred and seventy-five lashes, " so vigorously and so deeply inflicted, that my back and the points of " my shoulders were quite bared of the flesh. At that moment a letter " was handed to the officer presiding, written, I understand, in my fa- " vour by the late Hon. Capt. O'Brien, of Rostellan. It happily inter-

" rupted my punishment. But I had not hitherto shaken the triangle;
" a display of feeling which it seems was eagerly expected from me.
" To accelerate that spectacle, a *wire-cat* was introduced, armed with
" scraps of tin or lead. (I judge from the effect and from the descrip-
" tion given me.) Whatever were its appendages, I cannot easily for-
" get the power of it. In defiance of shame my waistband was cut for
" the finishing strokes of this lacerating instrument. The very first
" lash, as it renewed all my pangs, and shot convulsive agony through
" my entire frame, made me shake the triangle indeed. A second in-
" fliction of it penetrated my loins, and tore them excruciatingly; the
" third maintained the tremulous exhibition long enough—the specta-
" tors were satisfied.

" I should spare you, my lords and gentlemen, the disgusting mi-
" nuteness of this last detail, but it will be found materially connected
" with a most dreadful charge which appears upon the minutes of a
" court of inquiry, held to investigate my case the year following in
" Youghal, under gen. Graham, by order of the marquis Cornwallis.
" Before this court I was not brought; nor any friend of mine sum-
" moned thither to speak for me. It was even a subject of sarcastic
" remark in the prison-ship, that while I stood there among the sailors,
" my trial, as they termed it, was going on in Youghal. With the pro-
" ceedings of that court I am to this day unacquainted. It was ordered
" I know, in consequence of a memorial upon my situation, handed to
" a distinguished nobleman, and by him presented at the castle. I was
" not consulted with regard to its contents. Unfortunately for me, it
" was penned with more zeal than accuracy; setting forth among
" other hardships, that after my punishment, I had been left without
" medical assistance (on the report, I presume of a sister-in-law, who
" visited me in the interval between the whipping and apothecary's ar-
" rival); it further stated that I had been *whipt and thrown into a dun-*
" *geon;* instead of stating, as it ought to have done, that I had been
" *thrown into a dungeon and whipt.* This inversion was fatal to me. For
" the evidence of Mr. Green, apothecary, most plausibly contradicted
" these allegations of the memorial; and that circumstance, when
" coupled with the subsequent horrid charges audaciously *forged and*
" *foisted into* the minutes of the inquiry, excited an almost invincible
" prejudice in the mind of the merciful lord Cornwallis against me.
" For when, after a considerable lapse of time, my professional friend
" in Dublin, renewed his efforts to serve me, at the risk of being deemed
" importunate and troublesome, he was still graciously honoured with
" an audience, wherein to preclude all future interference, as quite in-
" effectual and hopeless, his excellency directed colonel Littlehales to
" read these minutes to my patron. They reported that I had freely
" avowed to Mr. Benjamin Green, apothecary, while he was dressing
" my wounds, at the time I was about to be sent on board the prison-
" ship, that I deserved all I had suffered and more; for I was privy to
" the murders, &c. &c. committed in my parish: that I could account
" for my conduct in no other way, than by attributing it to the instiga-
" tion of the devil: and that I deserved to be shot. The cruel edge of
" this *forged evidence*, was still further whetted by subjoining to it, that
" this Mr. Green was a *Roman Catholic.* My respectable intercessor,

A REVIEW

of

Fox's Book of Martyrs,

CRITICAL AND HISTORICAL.

No. 18. Printed and Published by W. E. Andrews, 3, Chapter-house-court, St. Paul's Churchyard, London. Price 3d.

EXPLANATION OF THE ENGRAVING.—*This cut represents a poor Catholic peasant in the hands of the inquisitors and familiars of the Orange ascendency in Ireland, who, to amuse themselves, when any of these unfortunate creatures were taken upon suspicion, and placed in their hands, would cut the hair of a prisoner's head very closely, in form of the cross, and after rubbing gunpowder through the remaining hair, set it on fire. This shocking process was frequently repeated, until every atom of hair that remained could be easily pulled up by the roots, and the head left totally and miserably blistered.—See Mr. Hay's Insurrection of Wexford, in 1798.*

CONTINUATION OF THE REVIEW.

" being quite unprepared to meet such an accusation, hung down his
" head and withdrew. But he lost no time in communicating this re-
" verse to my ordinary, doctor Coppinger, who was equally astonished
" at these assertions; but who seized the opportunity, until a refutation
" of all could be procured, to point in the interim, to the designing and
" notorious falsehood of Mr. Green's *Catholicity*. In a very few days
" Mr. Green himself spontaneously furnished my bishop with a pe-
" remptory denial of the above particulars, under his own hand: de-
" claring moreover in a written acknowledgment, that no conversa-
" tion had passed between him and the prisoner, but as between a
" *medical man and his patient*. This same gentleman also ingenuously
" presented himself at the parish chapel of Ballymacoda, offering to
" make oath that he had not given the evidence here attributed to him.

" Another respectable gentleman is represented in these minutes to
" have said, that immediately after my punishment, I acknowledged to
" him that I was privy to the murder of two soldiers; that I knew of
" a gun kept in my parish for the purpose of murder, and remarkable
" for the certainty of its aim: he is there beside stated to have said,
" that I made this declaration, not under any apprehension of punish-
" ment, but I seemed rather to speak, *as one clergyman would to another*
" *in a moment of contrition:* such at least is the substance of this gentle-
" man's words, as far as my friend in Dublin, to whom the evidence
" was read, could recollect it. Now from the nature of the commu-
" nication, which it is here asserted I made, it will be naturally sup-
" posed, that the gentleman had a private interview with me after my
" punishment: but he himself is thoroughly persuaded that he had
" not. I never laid my eyes on him since I saw him at that time, in
" the public Ball-alley. During my flagellation he stood opposite me,
" close to the triangle, with a paper and a pencil in his hand, noting
" down whatever then occurred to him. He asked, *did you not know*
" *that fire-arms were taken from my house?* My answer was rather too
" short, *Sir, I heard you say so;* but I felt at the moment, by heavier
" strokes, the consequence of my impoliteness. I really considered that
" gentleman, on account of his apparent insensibility at the time, as
" the very reverse of a friend; and while I now positively deny my
" having made the acknowledgment above reported, I shall take the
" liberty to ask; first, whether it be consistent with likelihood, that
" when such a severe punishment and *so* witnessed by *him*, was over,
" I had selected that very gentleman in order to criminate myself to
" such a confident, without any possible advantage? I beg leave to
" ask in the second place, if I had made this acknowledgment at the
" Ball-alley, why a certain subaltern, declaring that he had power to act
" as he pleased by me, should take me (naked and bleeding as I was)
" into a small room in the corner of the Ball-alley, and sternly tell me that
" if I would not now make an avowal of guilt, I should be brought out
" to receive a repetition of my punishment; and afterwards to be shot.
" And why he should repeat that menace the same evening in the gaol
" and still more forcibly the day following. The circumstances of his
" exertions on that occasion are too striking to be omitted. After I
" had answered him in the corner of the Ball-alley, that I would suffer
" any death rather than acknowledge a crime whereof I was not
" guilty, he told me I should be set at liberty if I would agree to a cer-
" tain proposal which he then made me; but justice and truth com-
" manded me to reject it. When conducted to gaol, after a lapse of
" three hours, I was presented with a refreshment: it appeared to be
" wine and water, but must have had some other powerful ingredient;
" for it speedily brought on a stupor. The same officer soon roused me
" from my lethargy, with a renewed effort to extort this avowal from
" me: he drew his sword; he declared he would never part with me
" until it were given in writing; he threatened that I should be forth-
" with led out again; flogged as before; shot; hanged; my head cut
" off to be exposed upon the gaol-top, and my body thrown into
" the river: that he would allow me but two minutes to determine.
" Then going to the door, he called for a scrip of paper, while the sen-

"timel swore terribly at the same time, that he would blow my brains
"out if I persisted longer in my refusal. Under this impression I
"scribbled a note to my brother, which they instantly cried out, was
"what they wanted; the precise expressions of it, I do not at this mo-
"ment recollect; it purported a wish that my brother might no longer
"indulge uneasiness upon my account, for I deserved what I got.
"The officer withdrew; my sister-in-law then got admittance: she told
"me, she had just heard the sentinel say, that during my entire punish-
"ment, nothing was against me: however that the paper I had just
"written would assuredly hang me. I exclaimed that their dreadful
"threats had compelled me to write it; which exclamation being car-
"ried to the officer, he returned the next day: he called me to the
"gaol window commanding a view of the gallows, whereon two men
"were hanging: their bodies so bloody that I imagined they wore red
"jackets. A third halter remained yet unoccupied, which he declared
"was intended for me, should I persist in disclaiming the aforesaid note.
"Look, said he, at these men; look at that rope; your treatment shall
"be worse than theirs, if you disown what you wrote yesterday: adding
"that it was still in my power to get free. I imagined from this that
"he wanted money from me; or a favourite mare which I had occa-
"sionally lent him. My answer was, if you liberate me you shall
"always find me thankful; there is nothing in my power that I will
"not do. Do not then attempt, said he, to exculpate yourself, and so
"retired. I now procured paper, whereon I wrote a formal protest
"against what he had extorted from me as above; that, should I be ex-
"ecuted, this protest might appear after my death. I wrote a second,
"with the same design; but I left them both after me in the gaol; ap-
"prehensive, that should they be found in my possession, they might
"cause me to be treated with additional severity. Neither did I after-
"wards while in gaol, openly assert my innocence for that very reason.
"Now, so little credit seems to have been attached to this paper, in
"any subsequent proceeding, that it was never after, to my knowledge,
"produced against me. Indeed there is reason to imagine that what this
"gentleman is reported to have advanced in the above minutes, was
"never said by him; because the same audacity which *forged* a decla-
"ration for Mr. Green, might be daring enough to *forge* a similar de-
"claration for this gentleman."

Such is father O'Neil's account of the system of torturing under
"Protestant-ascendency," only twenty-five years ago, and we challenge
the "few plain Christians" to produce an authenticated parallel instance
of cruelty practised by any of the inquisitors in Catholic foreign countries, from the time of the Albigenses to the present day. We do not
see that Fox has any where laid *forgery* to the charge of the inquisition,
but here, in the case of father O'Neil, we find a direct charge made on
the "Protestant-ascendency" inquisitors of *forging* evidence against
the unfortunate prisoner, and in his absence too, for the purpose of
having him further punished. The modes of process adopted by the
inquisition, according to the account of this *Book of Martyrs*, are,
"1st, To proceed by imputation, or prosecute on common report; 2,
"by the information of any indifferent person who chooses to impeach
"another; 3, on the information of spies who are retained by the in-

" quisition; and, 4, on the confession of the prisoner himself." Very well, admitting this statement to be correct, has not " Protestant-ascendency" acted upon the self-same modes, from her very birth to the present period? In 1584, Elizabeth issued an ecclesiastical commission, empowering twenty-four members, half clerics and half laics, or any three of them, to visit and reform all errors, heresies and schisms; to regulate all opinions, and to punish every breach of uniformity in the public worship. The jurisdiction of these commissioners extended over the whole kingdom, and their power was despotic, being under no control. They had directions to proceed in which ever way they thought proper, either by the rack, by other species of torture, by fine, or by imprisonment. Suspicion was sufficient to create guilt, and suspected persons were frequently tortured to implicate their relatives. Spies and informers were encouraged and paid to hunt out and impeach the Catholic for following the dictates of his conscience, and the Catholic priest for exercising his ministerial functions. In short, a system of espry was established by the first reformers under " Protestant-ascendency," which has continued ever since, a disgrace to its founders and to the country which tolerates it. We make not this statement upon bare assertion, but refer the reader to Neale's History of the Puritans and Hume's History of England, where a corroboration of our statement will be found. The " few plain Christians" may say what they please of the tyranny of the pope, and the power of his supremacy, but a reference to the statute-book of England, when England was Catholic and since she has been Protestantized, will demonstratively prove, that the supremacy of Rome was perfect mildness to the ascendency of Protestantism.

On the charge of *forgery*, which the Rev. Mr. Whitaker, in his Vindication of Mary Queen of Scots, says, is peculiar to Protestantism, we will here notice a case in the *Book of Martyrs*. More than six pages of this precious mass of lies are occupied with the pretended sufferings of a William Lithgow in Spain, who, it is stated, was a man of a good family and a great traveller. No date is given in the account, but we have now before us a work, published in 1692, and purporting to be the *tenth* edition of " Lithgow's Nineteen Years Travels through the " most eminent places in the World, &c. also an Account of the Tor- " ture he suffered under the Spanish Inquisition, by racking, and other " inhuman usages, for his owning the Protestant Religion. Together " with his *miraculous* deliverances from the Cruelties of the Papists, " which far exceeded any of the Heathen countries herein largely de- " scribed." Now by the author's own account, he appears to have visited every Catholic country in Italy, without meeting the least molestation, and his arrest at Malaga was on suspicion of his being *a spy*, not on account of his religion. But the period of his travels (if he ever did travel, which we much doubt, and think the work a compilation from other works, written for the purpose of alarming the credulous puritans of that day against Popery) took place when prejudice ran high against the Catholic faith, and there can be no doubt but it was written to gratify the credulity and prejudices of the English people. It is a beastly composition, abounding with obscenity and falsehood, which "the few plain Christians" have very properly suppressed. They have also taken care to give a *new version* of Mr. Lithgow's own words, and if they can take such a freedom in one instance, who can doubt but they will do so in other cases?

LITHGOW'S ACCOUNT.	FOX'S ACCOUNT.
William Lithgow, in 1692, says as follows:—	The Book of Martyrs, in 1824, detailing Lithgow's tale, puts the following words into the mouth of the inquisitor :—
"Then the inquisitor arising, expressed himself thus, 'Behold the powerful majesty of God's mother, commander of her Son, equal to the Father, wife to the Holy Ghost, queen of heaven, protector of angels, and sole *gubernatrix* of the earth, &c. How thou being first taken as a spy, accused for treachery, and innocently tortured, (as we acknowledge we were better informed lately from Madrile of the English intention) yet it was her power, her divine power, which brought these judgments upon thee ; in that thou hast wrote calumniously against her blessed miracles of Loretta, and against his holiness, the great agent, and Christ's vicar on earth. Therefore thou hast justly fallen into our hands, by her special appointment : thy books and papers are miraculously translated by her special providence with thy own countrymen ; wherefore thou mayest clearly see the impenetrable mysteries of our glorious lady in punishing her offenders ; and for a humble satisfaction, repent thee of thy wickedness, and be converted to the holy mother church.'" p. 441,	"After some time, the inquisitor addressed Mr. Lithgow in the following words ; ' You have been taken up as a spy, accused of treachery, and tortured, as we acknowledge, innocently ; (which appears by the account lately received from Madrid of the intentions of the English) yet it was the divine power that brought those judgments upon you, for presumptuously treating the blessed miracle of Loretto with ridicule, and expressing yourself in your writings irreverently of his holiness, Christ's vicar upon earth ; therefore you are justly fallen into our hands by their special appointment : your books and papers are miraculously translated by the assistance of Providence influencing your own countrymen.'" p. 144.

Here we see that Lithgow accuses the inquisitor with giving *divine power* to the blessed Virgin Mary, which in his day was most implicitly believed ; for the press being then shut against the Catholics, no opportunity was afforded them to remove so gross and calumnious a falsehood, and therefore the people of England, not seeing the accusation contradicted, very naturally gave credit to it. But now, since the press has been opened to the Catholics, and the public mind is in a great measure disabused of this most preposterous idea, that the greatest proportion of the Christian world gave divine honours to the Mother of God, and allowed her to be *equal* to God the Father ; now that Catholic writers can vindicate the principles of their faith, and throw the falsehood in the teeth of the falsifier, a little more caution is deemed necessary in deceiving the people, and words less liable to objection, and of different meaning from those used by the author, are substituted by the modern editors of this *Book of Martyrs*. This simple but irrefutable fact we think will be sufficient to enable the reader how to appreciate the veracity of the work, we are reviewing, in detailing the tortures said to have been practised on Lithgow and others by the inquisition.

We have already given one instance of modern torture practised by the inquisitors of "Protestant-ascendency," we shall now state a few more cases executed on individuals, and under the same modes of process said to be adopted by foreign inquisitors. In Mr. Hay's History of the Insurrection of Wexford in 1798, speaking of the transactions which took place *before* the rising of the people, that is, prior to any

overt acts of riot or breach of the peace, and when the poor Catholic peasantry were merely *suspected* by the Orange or "Protestant ascendency," of being united Irishmen, that gentleman writes thus:—
"The orange system made no public appearance in the county of Wexford, until the beginning of April, on the arrival there of the north
"Cork militia, commanded by lord Kingsborough. In this regiment
"there were a great number of orangemen, who were zealous in making proselytes, and displaying their devices; having medals and
"orange ribbons triumphantly pendant from their bosoms. It is believed, that previous to this period, there were but few actual orange-
"men in the county; but soon after, those whose principles inclined
"that way, finding themselves supported by the military, joined the
"association, and publicly avowed themselves, by assuming the devices of the fraternity.

"It is said, that the north Cork regiment were also the inventors—
"but they certainly were the introducers of pitch-cap torture into the
"county of Wexford. Any person having their hair cut short, (and
"therefore called a croppy, by which appellation the soldiery designated an united Irishman,) on being pointed out by some loyal neighbour, was immediately seized and brought into a guard-house, where
"caps either of coarse linen or strong brown paper, besmeared inside
"with pitch, were always kept ready for service. The unfortunate
"victim had one of these well heated compressed on his head, and
"when judged of a proper degree of coolness, so that it could not be
"easily pulled off, the sufferer was turned out amidst the horrid acclamations of the merciless torturers; and to the view of vast numbers
"of people, who generally crowded about the guard-house door, attracted by the afflicted cries of the tormented. Many of these persecuted in this manner, experienced additional anguish from the
"melted pitch trickling into their eyes. This afforded a rare addition
"of enjoyment to these keen sportsmen, who reiterated their horrid
"yells of exultation, on the repetition of the several accidents to which
"their game was liable upon being turned out; for in the confusion
"and hurry of escaping from the ferocious hands of these more than
"savage barbarians, the blinded victims frequently fell or inadvertently
"dashed their heads against the walls in their way. The pain of disengaging this pitched cap from the head must be next to intolerable.
"The hair was often torn out by the roots, and not unfrequently parts
"of the skin were so scalded or blistered as to adhere and come off
"along with it. The terror and dismay that these outrages occasioned
"are inconceivable. A serjeant of the north Cork, nicknamed *Tom the*
"*Devil*, was most ingenious in inventing new modes of torture. Moistened gunpowder was frequently rubbed into the hair cut close and
"then set on fire; some, while shearing for this purpose, had the tips
"of their ears snipt off; sometimes an entire ear, and often both ears
"were completely cut off; and many lost part of their noses during the
"like preparation. But, strange to tell, these atrocities were publicly
"practised without the least reserve in open day, and no magistrate or
"officer ever interfered; but shamefully connived at this extraordinary
"mode of quieting the people."

Mr. Alexander, a Protestant gentleman, who wrote on the same event, and was master of an academy at Ross, relates the following instances of torture:—" I now heard of many punishments of suspected persons" both by flogging and strangulation, being put into execution in the "barrack-yard, (in Ross) to extort confession of guilt. There were "two of these victims brought from the barrack to the court-house to "undergo a repetition of former punishments. One of them of the "name of Driscol, was found in Camlin-wood, near Ross, where he "said, he generally wandered as a hermit. Upon him were found two "Roman Catholic prayer-books, with which it was supposed he ad-"ministered oaths of disloyalty. He had been strangled three times, "and flogged four times during confinement, but to no purpose! his "fellow-sufferer was one Fitzpatrick of Dunganstown, near Sutton's "parish. This man had been a Newfoundland sailor, but long utterly "disqualified to follow that occupation, by reason of an inveterate "scurvy in his legs. He therefore commenced abecedarian, near Sut-"ton's parish. It happened that a magistrate who was a yeoman, and "others of his corps, passed by his noisy mansion, which was no other "than a little thatched stable, that like a bee-hive, proclaimed the in-"dustry of its inhabitants. The magistrate entered, followed by the "other yeomen. 'Here is a man,' says the magistrate, speaking of the "master, as I shall call him, though his authority was now for some "time to have an end; and a severe vacation it was, 'Here is a man "who, I presume, can have no objection to take the oath of allegiance. "—What do you say, Mr. Teacher?'—'O dar a leoursa,' (i. e. by this "book) 'I will take it, sir, and thank you for bringing it to me.' So "saying, he took the book, which the magistrate held forth, and not "only took the oath with the most cordial emphasis, but added another "expressive of his loyalty at all times. Upon this, the magistrate re-"garded his companions with a look of dry humour, and observed, that "*this must be a loyal man indeed.* 'Well then, my loyal friend, I sup-"pose you will readily swear to all the pikes, and to the owners and "possessors of them, of which you have any knowledge?' The man "swore he had no certain knowledge of the kind; and that he never "saw a rebel's pike in his life, or a pike of any kind since the rebellion. "' Then,' says the magistrate, 'you shall swear that you will, to the "utmost of your future knowledge, or information this way, give in the "best manner you can, all such information to a lawful magistrate, or "other officer in his majesty's service.' 'No, sir,' answered Fitzpatrick, "' I will not swear that: I will bring no man's blood on my head, and "if I do inform, who will support and protect me, when I have lost all "my scholars, and my neighbours turn upon me?' Upon this he was "immediately apprehended and escorted to Ross: he was not strangled "however, but flogged with great severity; and it was not with dry "eyes that I saw the punishment inflicted on this humble pioneer of "literature."

To these horrible inflictions are to be added the daily transportations of unfortunate victims, who were sent off in cart-loads from twelve to fifteen at a time, without trial by jury. In Enniscorthy, Ross, and Gorey, several persons were not only put to the torture in the usual way, but a great number of houses were burnt, and measures of barbarous cruelty practised. " At Carew things were carried to still greater

" lengths; for independently of burning, whipping, and torture in all
" shapes, on Friday the 25th of May, twenty-eight prisoners were
" brought out of the place of confinement, and deliberately shot in a
" ball-alley by the yeomen, and a party of the Antrim militia; the in-
" fernal deed being sanctioned by the presence of their officers!—Many
" of the men thus inhumanly butchered, had been confined on mere
" suspicion!!!" *Hay's Wexford*, p. 76.—But, it may be said, these men
were punished for *disloyalty* and not for *heresy*. Be it so; and so said
the punishers of the *Albigenses*. There is one great difference, however, in the two cases; which is, the Albigenses were opposed because
their notions led to immorality and disorder, and outrages had been
committed by them before they were coerced; while the Catholics of
Ireland were tortured on *suspicion* only, and professed a religion that
had been established in the country fourteen hundred years. It matters not to the sufferer for why he is tortured, whether for heresy or suspected disloyalty; we cannot see any difference in the scale of humanity; but there is a wide distance in the parties charged, the one
accusing the other with what he is guilty of himself; while the other
remains quiet and say nothing. What can we think of men who are
making the most strenuous exertions to inculcate the belief that
" Popery is inseparable from persecution," by the detail of transactions
said to have taken place some centuries back, while in the neighbouring country of Ireland, under the rule of their own beloved " Protestant-ascendency," the most horrible tortures have been practised on
Catholics within the last twenty-five years? " Change but the name,
" the tale is told of you."

In reading the abuses imputed by Fox to the inquisitions of Catholic
countries, we are most forcibly struck with the analogy they bear to
the conduct of " Protestant-ascendency" in that ill-fated country, Catholic Ireland.—For example; the *Book of Martyrs* says, " Most of the
" inquisitor's cruelties are owing to their rapacity: they destroy life to
" possess the property; and under pretence of zeal, plunder individuals
" of their rights." How far this charge is correct, with regard to the
Spanish and Portuguese inquisitors, we know not; nor have we any
means of ascertaining from the account Fox has given us, the whole of
it as usual resting upon assertion. Were what he states to be true, we
must suppose these fellows of the inquisition, who, by-the-by, according to Fox, are friars selected from the dregs of the people, to be the
richest dogs in the world. And yet we do not hear any thing of their
immense wealth through any authentic source, nor can we divine what
they could do with it, seeing they were not allowed to have wives and
families to expend their riches upon. It is true we have read of Protestant bishops and clergymen dying worth hundreds of thousands,
wrung out of the labour of poor Catholic peasants, but then they had
sons and daughters looking to them for fortunes, and that of course
alters the case. But the cruelties of the inquisitors, it is alleged, were
owing to their rapacity, and life was wantonly sacrificed to possess
property. We have before stated that the reformed religion was attempted to be enforced in Ireland by the bayonet and sword; we have
now to add, that the murders committed by these reformed inquisitors
could only be outdone by their insatiable rapacity. So voracious was

the appetite of these spreaders of the *pure light of the gospel*, that nothing less than the total extirpation of the natives and the seizure of all the lands would satisfy them. We have it on record, that in the reign of James the first, and at the restoration of his grandson Charles the second, the natives of Ireland were despoiled of no less than 10,636,837 acres, and when the revolution under William the Dutchman was completed, 1,060,792 acres more were added to this plunder. Here then we have rapacity in good earnest; here we have Catholics robbed of their property to satisfy Protestant invaders; here we have the rights of Catholics trampled upon and violated under pretence of zeal for the pure light of the gospel. It makes us smile to see the "few plain Christians" exclaiming against the rapacity of Catholic inquisitors, when the voracious appetite of "Protestant-ascendency" is grinding the poor Catholics of Ireland to the lowest state of poverty by her parish-vestries, church-rates, and tithes. It appears from the parliamentary debates, that in the year 1807, there were no less than 1286 actions on cases connected with tithes in five counties in Ireland. At the October quarter sessions at Gort, in 1822, one tithe-proctor processed eleven hundred persons for tithes. They were all, or most of the lower order of farmers or peasants:—the expense of each process about eight shillings. A Mr. Collis, at one of the late tithe-meetings in Ireland, is stated to have addressed the auditors thus:—" In 1816, " they could not but recollect, that one half of the crop was completely " destroyed by the heavy rains which fell incessantly during the har- " vest-season, and the other half so materially damaged, as really to " injure life while it seemed to sustain it. At that unexampled period " of public calamity, when their fellow-creatures were perishing every " where around them with hunger and disease, did the tithe-owners " from humanity at least, if not from justice, reduce their impositions, " in proportion to the injury of the crop. No—far from abating one " jot of either the rate or the rigour, they levied their usual charges " with their usual severity." Another instance is thus related by Mr. Grattan, in one of his speeches:—" I have two decrees in my hand from " the vicarial court of Cloyne; the first excommunicating one man, the " second excommunicating four men illegally, most arbitrarily, for re- " fusing to pay tithe for *turf*." In a pamphlet entitled, " A Report of " the Committee of the Parish of Blackrath, in the County of Kilken- " ny," we find the following specimen of the expenses to which a poor man is put by a citation to the bishop's court, a species of inquisition far more intolerable to the Catholic peasant in Ireland, than the inquisition in Spain is to a Protestant. " The whole sum in dispute is 6s.; " the fee to counsel is a guinea. The very first step, therefore, that " the poor man takes for his defence, he has to pay nearly four times " the amount of the demand he contests. He has next to pay two cita- " tions for his two witnesses, 13s. 6d.—that is to say, 12s. 6d. for the " first, and 1s. for the second.' The trial generally ends in a decree " against the unfortunate peasant, which is followed up by a monition " —and the costs of both are stated to add near 2l. 16s. 8d. to his losses. " He is then handed over to the secular arm; ' The parson processes " his wretched parishioner to the civil-bill court: there he is decreed, " as a matter of course, without being even allowed (strange to say!)

" to enter into the merits of his case. And what costs follow? The
" costs of the decree are 1s. 11d.; the costs of the warrant 1s. 1d.;
" the fees of the bailiff who executes the warrants are 2s. 4d.; the fees
" of the two keepers who watch the distress for four days and nights
" amount (at 2s. 6d. a day for each) to 1l.; and lastly, the auctioneer's
" fees come to 6s. 3d. making altogether the sum of 6l. 12s. 2d., so that
" the clergyman sells the whole crop to satisfy the tithes, and turns
" the miserable wretch, his wife and children, to the road, to beg or
" to steal, or to starve. High-spirited as the poor Irishman may be,
" he will never have the courage to renew the contest against such
" powerful odds." Here is "Protestant-ascendency" rapacity with a
vengeance! Let the "few plain Christians" beat this specimen of
spoliation and extortion in any Catholic country whatever, and we will
be silent.

Fox further tells us, "Upon all occasions the inquisitors carry on
" their processes with the utmost severity. They seldom shew mercy
" to a Protestant; and a Jew, who turns Christian, is far from being
" secure; for if he is known to keep company with another new-con-
" verted Jew, a suspicion arises that they privately practice together
" some Jewish ceremonies; if he keep company with a person who
" was lately a Protestant, but now professes Popery, they are accused
" of plotting together; but if he associate with a Roman Catholic, an
" accusation is often laid against him for only pretending to be a Papist,
" and the consequence is a confiscation of his effects, and the loss of
" his life if he complain." Here again the martyrologist must have
drawn his picture from the inquisitors of "Protestant-ascendency" in
Ireland. The abbé Bergier says, that a man may reside as securely in
Spain as in any other country, provided he does not use a dogmatizing
spirit to disturb the peace of society; but this is not the case with the
Catholic in Ireland even at this day. The Orange or "Protestant-ascendency" inquisitors have no feeling of mercy for a Catholic, and
scarce a year passes over without some murder being committed by
Orangemen on Catholics. If a Protestant turns Catholic, he instantly
becomes an object of persecution and ridicule among his bigotted acquaintance; and if a Catholic priest were to marry a Catholic and Protestant, he incurs the penalty of transportation, and thus an association of the most tender kind is forbidden by "Protestant-ascendency"
between a Catholic and Protestant. Nay to such a pitch was this system of separation carried, that the Protestant coal-porters petitioned
the house of Commons to prevent Catholics in the same employment
from associating and working with them, and the respectable body of
Protestant hackney coachmen did the same very liberal act. Then as
to the security of personal liberty; for years have the Catholics in some
parts of Ireland been liable to be transported, without trial by jury,
merely for being found out of his house between sun-set and sun-rise;
and hundreds have been actually torn from their wives and children,
and suddenly sent off to Botany bay for no other offence. Let not then
the few "plain Christians" talk any more of insecurity or plotting, or
associating, in Spain, while such transactions as I have just described
are going on in Ireland.

Again Fox says, "This dreadful engine of tyranny may at any time be

" introduced into a country where the *Catholics have the upper hand*,
" and hence how *careful ought we to be*, who are *not cursed* with such an
" *arbitrary court*, to prevent *its introduction!* In treating of this sub-
" ject, an elegant author pathetically says, ' How horrid a scene of
" perfidy and inhumanity! What kind of community must that be,
" whence gratitude, love, and mutual forbearance with regard to hu-
" man frailties are banished! What must that tribunal be, which
" obliges parents not only to erase from their minds the remembrance,
" of their own children, to extinguish all those keen sensations of ten-
" derness and affection wherewith nature inspires them, but even to
" extend their inhumanity so far as to force them to commence their
" accusers, and consequently to become the cause of the cruelties in-
" flicted upon them! What ideas ought we to form to ourselves of a
" tribunal which obliges children not only to stifle every soft impulse of
" gratitude, love, and respect, due to those who gave them birth, but
" even forces them, and that under the most rigorous penalties, to be
" spies over their parents, and to discover to a set of merciless inqui-
" sitors the crimes, the errors, and even the little lapses to which they
" are exposed by human frailty! In a word, a tribunal which will not
" permit relations, when imprisoned in its horrid dungeons, to give
" each other the succours, or perform the duties which religion enjoins,
" must be of an infernal nature. What disorder and confusion must
" such conduct give rise to in a tenderly affectionate family! An ex-
" pression, innocent in itself, and, perhaps, but too true, shall, from an
" indiscreet zeal, or a panic of fear, give infinite uneasiness to a family;
" shall ruin its peace entirely, and perhaps cause one or more of its
" members to be the unhappy victims of the most barbarous of all tri-
" bunals. What distractions must necessarily break forth in a house
" where a husband and wife are at variance, or the children loose and
" wicked! Will such children scruple to sacrifice a father, who en-
" deavours to restrain them by his exhortations, by reproofs, or paternal
" corrections? Will they not rather, after plundering his house to sup-
" port their extravagance and riot, readily deliver up their unhappy pa-
" rent to all the horrors of a tribunal founded on the blackest injustice?
" A riotous husband, or a loose wife, has an easy opportunity, assisted
" by means of the persecution in question, to rid themselves of one who
" is a check to their vices, by delivering him, or her, up to the rigors
" of the inquisition."

Now all this is very pathetic and sublime, but there is one requisite
necessary to render it credible, and that is, its want of truth. One
would suppose, from this relation, that Protestants were extremely plentiful in Spain, and that the most unnatural consequences resulted to families by this pretended mode of proceeding by the inquisition; but this
never was the case. Scarcely a Spanish Protestant, nay we believe not
one, was to be found in the whole kingdom at the period spoken of;
those who were of that persuasion being foreigners engaged in commercial pursuits, and who were as safe in the enjoyment of their natural rights and endearments as the Catholics themselves. But let us
look a little nearer home, and we shall see, that as great restraints and
as inquisitorial procedures were practised in England and Ireland,
though under a different name, as what Fox has here brought forward

against the inquisition in Spain. For example, when the modern editors of this *Book of Martyrs* spoke of the tribunal which "obliges parents not "only to erase from their minds the remembrance of their own children," &c. did not the *Protestant Charter* and *Foundling Schools* in Ireland occur to them? These establishments were founded in the year 1733, for the purpose of proselyting the children of Catholic parents; and so eager were the managers of them to obliterate from parents the remembrance of their children, and from children the knowledge of their parents, that those who were *bought* or kidnapped in the south were sent to the schools in the north of Ireland, and, *vice versa*, those obtained in the north were sent to the southern schools, where their names were *changed*, and their parents never suffered to see them. Now what are we to think of such a system as this, encouraged too by large grants of the public money by "Protestant-ascendency." We defy the few "plain Christians" to produce institutions of a similar unnatural nature in any civilized or even barbarous country in the world. Then again as to the refusal of relatives to visit unhappy prisoners in their dungeons, we need only to look into the regulations now lately adopted by the visiting magistrates of our gaols at home to find something of a parallel to the complaints of John Fox and his editors. And as to the children plundering the house of their father and rioting on his property; was not every encouragement given by "Protestant-ascendency" to the undutiful and profligate child to rob his Catholic father of his property and reduce him to beggary, by only declaring himself *a Protestant?* In an address presented by the Catholics of Ireland to the father of his present majesty, in 1775, this most unnatural law, this horrible act of injustice, this specimen of Protestant legislation, is thus described:—" By the laws now in force in this kingdom, a son, how- " ever undutiful or profligate, shall not merely by the merit of con- " forming to the established religion deprive the Roman Catholic father " of that free and full possession of his estate, that power to mortgage " or any other way dispose of it, as the exigencies of his affairs may " require, but shall himself have full liberty immediately to mortgage " or otherwise alienate the reversion of that estate from his family for " ever;—a regulation by which a father, contrary to the order of na- " ture, is put under the power of his son, and through which an early " dissoluteness is not only suffered but encouraged, by giving a per- " nicious privilege, the frequent use of which has broken the hearts of " many deserving parents, and entailed poverty and despair on some of " the most ancient and opulent families in this kingdom." Oh! shame, where is thy blush? Ought not, candid reader, these "few plain Christians" to hide their heads until they can erase this most infamous law from the page of history.

To enter into a minute refutation and comparison of the gross charges brought by the "plain Christians" against the Spanish inquisition, would fill a large volume; we shall therefore content ourselves with noticing one more as connected with the liberty of the press; a privilege much prized, but scarcely enjoyed, by the people of this country. The *Book of Martyrs* states as follows:—1. "The inquisition also " takes cognizance of all new books; and tolerates or condemns with the same *justice* and *impartiality* by which all its proceedings are dis-

" tinguished. When a book is published, it is carefully read by some
" of the familiars ; who, too ignorant and bigotted to distinguish the
" truth, and too malicious to relish beauties, search not for the merits,.
" but for the defects of an author, and pursue the slips of his pen with .
" unremitting diligence. They read with prejudice, judge with par-
" tiality, pursue errors with avidity, and strain that which is innocent
" into an offensive meaning. They misapply, confound, and pervert
" the sense ; and when they have gratified the malignity of their dis-
" position, charge their blunders upon the author, that a prosecution
" may be founded upon their false conceptions, and designed misrepre-
" sentations.

2. " Any trivial charge causes the censure of a book ; but it is to be
" observed, that the censure is of a three-fold nature, viz. 1. When
" the book is wholly condemned. 2. When it is partly condemned,
" that is, when certain passages are pointed out as exceptionable;
" and ordered to be expunged. 3. When it is deemed incorrect ; the
" meaning of which is, that a few words or expressions displease the
" inquisitors. These, therefore, are ordered to be altered, and such
" alterations go under the name of corrections.

3. " There is a catalogue of condemned books annually published
" under the three different heads of censures, already mentioned, which
" being printed on a large sheet of paper, is hung up in the most con-
" spicuous places. After which, people are obliged to destroy all such
" books as come under the first censure, and to keep none belonging
" to the other two censures, unless the exceptionable passages have
" been expunged, as in either case disobedience would be of the most
" fatal consequence ; for the possessing or reading the proscribed books
" are deemed very atrocious crimes. The publisher of such book is
" usually ruined in his circumstances, and sometimes obliged to pass
" the remainder of his life in the inquisition.

4. " Where such an absurd and detestable system exercises its deadly
" influence over the literature of a nation, can we be surprised that the
" grossest ignorance and the most bigotted superstition prevail ? How
" can that people become enlightened, among whom the finest produc-
" tions of genius are prohibited, all discussion prevented, the most in-
" nocent inquiries liable to misconstruction and punishment, the mate-
" rials for thinking proscribed, and even *thought* itself chained down,
" and checked by the fear of its escaping into expression, and thus
" bringing certain and cruel punishment on him who has dared to ex-
" ercise his reason, the noblest gift of his Almighty Creator. Surely
" every well wisher to the human race, must rejoice in the downfal of
" this most barbarous and infernal of all tribunals ; and must view with
" indignation and abhorrence the iniquitous attempts now making to
" re-establish it in those unhappy countries which so long groaned
" under its sway."

Now with regard to paragraph 1, the people of England are too ready
to condemn foreign institutions without looking into the state of their
own country. The inquisition takes cognizance of all new books, and
is it not the office of the attorney-general here to do the same ? Is he
not empowered to file *ex officio* informations against any author or
publisher who may write or publish what he may deem a libel ? Is

not the person so informed against put to considerable expense and inconvenience to defend himself, and, if found guilty in the opinion of the jury, consigned to prison at the discretion of his judges? As to the *justice* and *impartiality* by which all the proceedings of the inquisition are distinguished, do we not see the partisans of those in power here allowed to do that which an opponent of the ministry dare not do? Pray what can we think of the fact that while Mr. Hone was thrice acquitted by London juries for writing and publishing a political parody on the liturgy of the established church, a publisher of the same work in the country was found guilty by another jury, and sent to prison for the offence. If the familiars of the inquisition are too ignorant and bigotted to distinguish truth, we can say the same of the "few plain Christians;" if the former read with prejudice, &c.; if they misapply, confound, and pervert the sense of the author, &c. is not this the case in England! Can any one be so unacquainted with the proceedings here in libel cases as not to discover this similarity? Are not counsel engaged and paid, the one to misapply, confound and pervert, the other to defend, elucidate and justify the author. Are not authors sometimes (to be sure it is rarely) acquitted of libel cases in England, and is not the prosecution of course founded upon "false conceptions " and designed misrepresentations?"

We come now to paragraphs 2 and 3, which relate to the censure of books. We will not here enter into the propriety of a censorship, though we scruple not to say, that that society must be more happy and free where falsehood is suppressed and truth preserved, than where falsehood and immorality is allowed with impunity, and truth, if told too plainly, frequently punished. By the shewing of the "few plain Christians," there is at least some appearance of justice and consistency in the rules of the censorship. Works are not wholly suppressed it seems, unless they are wholly objectionable; but by erasing the objectionable passages, or altering them, the work may be published. This regulation, we take it for granted, regards works in manuscript, therefore if the author is obstinate and persists in publishing the matter objected to, he does it at his peril *knowingly*; whereas in England he has no means of knowing what is right and what is wrong, until the whole expense of printing is incurred, and should he feel the weight of the attorney-general's displeasure, and a jury is called to give their opinion, for it is opinion, and not *fact*, (except that of selling or writing) that determines a libel in England, away he goes to prison, and the printer probably loses his bill. Thus the jury here are called upon to penetrate into the heart of the defendant, to decide upon his *motives*, (which is the attribute of God and not of man) and to say whether he was actuated by *malice*. As the catalogue of prohibited books are made public, there can be no plea of ignorance; and if the publisher of prohibited books will set himself up in face of the authority of the country, why he must take the consequences that follow this act of disobedience. But this is not the case in England; let a book be ever so obscene and immoral, it may be printed, and how many are there of this nature in general circulation in this kingdom? There is here no law or rule laid down by which an author may be able to guide his remarks, but all is licentiousness, unless some familiar gets offended, and then a spy is sent to purchase a copy, an indictment or information follows, the publisher is fined and imprisoned, and sometimes ruined in his circumstances, and obliged to pass the remainder of his life in prison or in poverty.

In paragraph 4 we have a lamentation over the ignorance and superstition of the people living under the inquisition; but we again say to the "plain Christians," look at home.—We are ready to allow that there is much useful knowledge to be found in England now among the middling ranks of life; but if we look back only a century past, we shall find that as much, nay more, ignorance and superstition prevailed in England as ever could exist in Spain and Portugal. The modern editors talk of *thinking* being proscribed, "and *thought* itself chain-" ed down, and choaked by the fear of its escaping into expression, and " thus bringing certain and cruel punishment on him who has dared to " exercise his reason, the noblest gift of his Almighty Creator."—Surely we must live under a blessed state of freedom, when such inexpressible grief is raised at the state of Spain. And yet, reader, let it not be forgotten, that while these men are vomiting their execrations against the Spanish inquisitors for chaining down thought, should any man *think* meanly of the government and legislature of this country, he dare not let his thoughts escape into writing, or he is sure of " bringing " certain and cruel punishment on him who has dared thus to exercise " his reason, the noblest gift of his Almighty Creator;" there being a law that subjects a man to imprisonment and transportation should he write any thing that may *tend* to bring the government and parliament into contempt. Are the " few plain Christians" aware that Mr. Cobbett was shut up two years in Newgate, and paid a fine of one thousand pounds, besides entering into heavy recognizances, for expressing his thoughts; for daring " to exercise his reason, the noblest gift of God." —Have they forgot that Mr. L. Hunt, and his brother Mr. John Hunt, have both suffered fine and imprisonment in Coldbath-fields prison for expressing their thoughts? A number of other instances could be produced where Englishmen have been punished for daring " to exercise " their reason, the noblest gift of the Almighty Creator."—We should rejoice, with every well-wisher to the human race, in the downfall of all barbarous and infernal tribunals; and if the attempts made to establish them in Spain are iniquitous, we detest and abhor them. However, we cannot help reminding the " few plain Christians" that we are not disposed to take their account of the conduct of the inquisition for our guide, and we think they would be as charitably employed in endeavouring to ameliorate the condition of their own countrymen and the people of Ireland, instead of spending their hypocritical benevolence on those who neither ask them for it nor stand in need of it.

It is a failing peculiar to the English, since the people have been Protestantized, to mind every body's business and neglect their own. Thus, every opportunity is taken to relate the horrors of the inquisition in foreign countries, but scarce any attention is given to the internal state of their own. Noise enough is made of the number of persons said to be burnt by the inquisition, and the more marvellous the statement the more readily it is believed. It is represented that the Dominican Torquemada instituted more than 80,000 juridical processes in the space of fourteen years. This the abbé Bergier says is evidently an exaggeration. We think so too. It was stated in *The Times* daily paper, of March 31, 1820, under the head Spanish intelligence, that from the year 1621 to 1665, a space of 44 years, 2,816 persons were burnt alive by the inquisition, making an average of 64 in a year. From 1665 to 1700, a space of thirty-five years, 1,728, averaging little more than 49 in a year. From 1700 to 1746, a space of forty-six years, 1,564, being an average of thirty-four annually. From 1746 to 1754, a period of eight years, only 10 were burnt. From 1759 to 1788, a space of twenty-nine years, no more than four suffered. From 1788 to 1808, a period of 20 years, not ONE individual was burnt. Such is the statement in *The Times* paper, and it is alleged to be given to shew the diminution of its violence with the increase of knowledge. Since then this tribunal is grown so harmless and inoffensive, that not ONE single person has been burned by it within the last thirty-six years, and only four within the last fifty-nine years, is it not infamy in the extreme to endeavour to excite a hatred and abhorrence in the minds of Protestants against their Catholic neighbours, by means of exaggerated and false representations respecting this tribunal.

We will now, by way of contrast, change the scene, and take a view of the situation of Protestant England. Let us here observe, that the inquisition takes cognizance of other offences besides that of heresy; such as sacrilege, profanation, &c. and that the people may not be ignorant, they are frequently reminded from the pulpit of the laws in force; a manifest proof that there exists in Spain and Portugal a desire to prevent an increase of crime. We have seen too that as knowledge has increased, the executions under the inquisition have decreased. But is this the case with Protestant England? We have now before us an official return of "the number of persons charged with criminal offences, who were committed to the different gaols in England and Wales for trial, from the year 1805 to 1818," a space of fourteen years, from which we make the following selection. Of persons committed there were 98,483, of which number 37,282 were discharged, no proof of guilt being established against them. Of the 61,201 convicted, 8,440 were condemned to death, and of these 1,035 were executed, making an average of better than seventy-four persons in a year, which exceeds the number laid to the charge of the inquisition two hundred years ago. The sufferers under the inquisition at the distant period alluded to, amounted to 2,816 in forty-four years, while the executions in England, in the enlightened days of scriptural knowledge, as they are called, and in one-third of the time, amounted to 1,035, being nearly two-fifths of those in Spain, where Bible societies, and Bartlett's-building Societies for promoting Christian Knowledge by slander and lies, are not known. When the "few plain Christians" again expatiate on the enormities of the inquisition, we would recommend them to place before their eyes this official account of the state of the English criminal courts, and we think the balance will be in favour of the Catholic countries. Only think, Christian reader, while the papers were admitting that from the year 1788 to the present day, not one criminal was executed by the inquisition, in only FOURTEEN years of that period ONE THOUSAND AND THIRTY-FIVE of our unfortunate fellow-creatures were hanged for different crimes in this enlightened

A REVIEW

OF

Fox's Book of Martyrs,

CRITICAL AND HISTORICAL.

No. 19. Printed and Published by W. E. ANDREWS, 3, Chapter-house-court, St. Paul's Churchyard, London. Price 3d.

EXPLANATION OF THE ENGRAVING.—This cut represents the baron d'Adrets sig-nalizing his barbarity by forcing his Catholic prisoners to jump from the towers upon the pikes of his soldiers. This inhuman leader of the gospel reformers obliged his children to wash their hands in the blood of Catholics.

CONTINUATION OF THE REVIEW.

Protestant country of England and Wales, where thought is allowed to exercise itself in abusing Catholics and their religion with impunity, but where truth is seldom encouraged and sometimes punished. In this space of time, too, that is from 1805 to 1818, no less than ELEVEN THOUSAND, NINE HUNDRED AND FORTY-THREE persons were sentenced to banishment in England and Wales. It must here be remarked, that as the labours of the Bible societies increased, and their calumnies against the Catholic clergy were multiplied, the num-ber of convictions and executions augmented in a frightful degree. In 1813, no less than 7,164 commitments took place, of which number 1,731 were females—120 were hanged, and 767 transported. In 1815, the number of commitments was 7,818, executions 57, transportations 958. In 1817, committed 13,932, of these 2,174 females—executed 115, transported 1,734. In the year following, 13,567 were sent to prison, of whom 2,932 were females—1,254 were sentenced to death, 97 hanged, and 2,052 transported.

Was ever such a picture as this exhibited in any Christian country? yet do we find the prostituted press of this country incessantly boasting of the wisdom and superiority of its people over other nations. Could we give credit to the vain-boasting assertions of the hirelings of the press, this country,—while exhibiting the most deplorable scene of immorality and crime; of misery and wretchedness on one hand, and luxury and debauchery on the other,—would appear to have reached the very *acmé* of bliss and perfection. What can we think of the illiberality and hypocrisy of the "few plain Christians," who have congregated to diffuse the most abominable lies and misrepresentations among the people of England, for the avowed purpose of exciting hatred and abhorrence against one-third of the population of the united empire, merely for being Catholic, while such scenes of dishonesty and crime as we have just described, are going on under "Protestant-ascendency?" They may talk of the deadening influence of the inquisition over literature; of prohibiting the finest productions of genius; of the ignorance and superstition of the people; but let them tell us where the press is more abused than in England? Where crime is more frequent? Where punishments are more numerous? When they have done this, then let them rant, and whine, and lie about the inquisition as much as they please, we will not oppose them. But until they can do this, we do hope the good people of this country will not permit the foul tales of this *Book of Martyrs* to have any influence over them, but that they will keep a steady eye to the situation of their own country, before they trouble themselves with what their neighbours are doing.

We have frequently referred the reader to the statute-book for proof of the inquisitorial and mercenary spirit of "Protestant-ascendency" towards the professors of Catholicism. As the greater part of our readers may not have access to this book, we will here give an abstract of *some* of the laws passed regarding education, marriage, property, and the clergy, which will be sufficient to convey a just idea of the feelings which pervaded those who could enact and pass such decrees to harrass and punish men, women, and children, for no other cause than their professing that faith which was first planted by the apostles, and was the faith of England nine hundred years before a brutal and lascivious monarch thought proper to deform it.

EDUCATION.

7 W. 3. s. 1, c. 4. Sending a child abroad to be educated in the Popish religion, either in a public seminary or a private family, or sending any thing for its maintenance, was punished with disability to sue or prosecute in law or equity for any wrong or any demand, or to be guardian or executor, to take any thing by legacy, deed, or gift, or to bear any office, with forfeiture of goods and chattels, land, tenements, hereditaments, annuities, offices, and estates of freehold during life. And a single justice upon suspicion might summon and examine the persons suspected, to have evidence against themselves, and summon witnesses to answer upon oath; and if the offence seemed probable, bind the suspected party to the sessions, and there he was bound to answer *instantly*; and should the offence upon trial appear *probable*, then the offender is bound to prove where the child was, for what the money was sent, and the fact is to be presumed unlawful, till the suspected party prove *the negative*; and being entered on record shall be a conviction, not only of the supposed sender of the child, but of the absent child; and the infant convict shall incur the like disabilities: and of these forfeitures the booty is to be divided between the king and the pious informer.

There is indeed a proviso that the infant upon his return or twelve months after coming of age, may by prayer or motion in open court, obtain a trial; but upon that trial he must prove negatively that he was not sent contrary to the act, or it shall be taken for granted against him as if it had been fully proved. And if he should do so, still he shall loose his goods and chattles, and all the profits of his lands prior to his conviction, and the rest be restored only upon condition of swearing certain constrained oaths, and making formed metaphysical declarations of belief in open court.

N. B. To avoid future repetitions, it may be here briefly stated, that the oaths, and declarations generally intended throughout, are those of allegiance, abhorrence, abjuration, and against transubstantiation.

2 Ann. s. 1. c. 6. Sending or suffering to be sent a child under 21, except sailors, ship boys, merchants' apprentices, or factors, without special license of the queen or chief governor and four privy counsellors, like penalties.

A judge or two justices suspecting any child to be sent, may convene father, mother, relation or guardian, require them to produce the child within two months, and unless they prove it to be in England or Scotland, it is to be convicted as one educated in foreign parts, and suffer accordingly.

8 Ann. s. 3. Protestants converted from Popery must educate their children under fourteen in the established religion, or forfeit all offices of trust or profit, and be disabled from sitting in either house of parliament, or being barrister or attorney, and be for ever disqualified.

2 Ann. s. 1. c. 6. Where either father or mother is a Protestant, the chancellor is to make an order for educating the child a Protestant till eighteen, appointing where it shall be educated and how, and also by whom; the father to pay all the charges directed by the court: and the child may be taken away from the Popish parent.

7 W. 3. s. 1. c. 4. Papists are forbid to instruct youth in any public school, and even in private houses, unless those of the family, under pain of fine and imprisonment.

8 Ann. c. 3. s. 16. A Papist teaching publicly or privately, or entertained as an usher to a Protestant schoolmaster, to be esteemed a *Popish regular clergyman convict*, and suffer all the pains inflicted upon such, that is, 1st, to be imprisoned in the common gaol; 2d, to be transported; 3d, if he returns to his friends and native land, to suffer as a traitor. Any person entertaining such teachers to forfeit 10l. to be distributed in equal shares between the king and the informer. Any person *discovering* such teacher, to have 10l. levied like money for robberies, all upon the Papists. All persons of sixteen years of age may be summoned and forced to become informers upon oath, touching the being and residence of such teachers, on pain of 20l. or twelve months imprisonment. A Protestant permitting a child under fourteen to be educated a Papist, to suffer as a Papist.

MARRIAGE.

9 W. 3. c. 29. If a Protestant maid, being heir apparent, or having interest in lands, or a personal estate of 500l. marry any man without a certificate from a minister, bishop, and justice, attested by two creditable witnesses, that he is *a known Protestant*, the estate shall go to the next of kin, and all Popish intervening heirs deemed dead and *intestate*, and the Protestant maid to be *dead in law*: and husband and wife to be for ever disabled from being guardian, executor, &c.; and the person who married them to be imprisoned a year and forfeit 10l. half to the king, and half to the informer, who will sue by bill or suit, and no essoign shall be allowed.

6 Ann. c. 16. If a woman persuade an heir apparent to marry her, by secret delusions, insinuations or menaces, she loses thirds dower, and all real and personal estate; and all accessaries before the fact, to suffer three years imprisonment.

Ib. s. 2. If any Protestant shall marry any maiden or woman without such certificate, he is for ever disabled from being heir, executor, administrator, guardian, &c. or to sit in parliament, or bear any employments, civil or military, unless he procures her to be converted in one year, and a certificate thereof under hand and seal of the archbishop, bishop, or chancellor, to be enrolled in chancery.

2 Ann. s. 1. c. 6. Any person having real or personal estate in the kingdom who mar-

ries a Papist abroad—like disabilities and penalties as if he married within the kingdom.

9 W. 3. c. 28. Whoever marries a soldier to any uncertified wife, to be imprisoned till he pay 20l. half of which is to reward the informer.

6 Ann. c. 16. § 1. 3. 6. If any person above the age of fourteen, by fraud, flattery, or fair promises, shall allure any maid or widow, having substance, to marry him without consent of parents or guardian, and the person who celebrate the marriage be a Popish priest; or if a Popish priest celebrate any marriage knowing one party to be a Protestant, he shall be deemed, and suffer all the pains of a Popish regular—be imprisoned, transported, and, on returning, be drawn, hanged, quartered, beheaded, embowelled, entrails burned alive, head and quarters given to the queen, and attainted and blood-corrupted.

8 Ann. c. 3. The knowledge of the fact is to be presumed against the priest, and he to be convicted, unless he produce a certificate from the Protestant parish minister that neither were Protestants.

12 Geo. 1. c. 3. s. 1. A Popish or reputed Popish priest, celebrating marriage between a Protestant or reputed Protestant and a Papist, or between two Protestants or reputed Protestants—death, as a felon, without benefit of clergy. N. B. 19 Geo. 2. c. 13. annuls such marriages without process, judgment, or sentence.

23 Geo. 2. c. 10. s. 3. makes it felony in the priest, notwithstanding the marriage be annulled.

§. 1. And any two justices may summon all persons suspected to have been so married, or to have been present, and examine them on oath, where, by whom, with what form and ceremony such marriage was celebrated, and who were present; and upon neglect to appear or refusal to become informers against their friends, commit them to prison for three years without bail or mainprize, unless they will enter into recognizance to prosecute all the offenders.

7. G. 2. s. 6. A converted justice acting while his wife is a Papist, or his children educated as such, to be imprisoned one year, pay 100l. half to the king, half to the informer, and he for ever disabled to be executor or guardian.

7 G. 2. c. 5. s. 12. Barristers, six clerks, and attorneys disabled, unless they convert their wife in a year, and enrol a certificate thereof in chancery.

8 Ann. c. 3. A wife conforming in the life-time of her husband, may file a bill against him, and have all appointments or execution of powers as he might make in her favour, if he were willing, decreed, whether he will or not, and notwithstanding any disposition of his to the contrary, have one third of his chattels real and personal.

RELIGION—CLERGY.

7, 9 W. 3. S. 1. c. 26. s. 1. All Popish archbishops, bishops, vicars general, deans, regular Popish clergy, exercising any ecclesiastical jurisdiction, to leave the kingdom in three months, or be transported, wherever the chief governor shall think fit. And if he return, be dragged and hanged, quartered and beheaded, blood-corrupted and attainted, entrails burned alive, and head and quarters at the king's disposal, to be piked or gibbeted, as was most for his royal pleasure and the honour of God, and forfeit all as in case of high treason.

§. 1. No such shall come into the kingdom, under pain of twelve months imprisonment, transportation, and in case of return, the same pains of high treason, hanging, dragging embowelling, &c.

2 Ann. c. 3. s. 1. Extends these pains to every clergyman of the Popish religion, secular as well as regular; and for their easier conviction, gives a trial in any county at the option of the queen.

Ib. s. 4. Concealing any person so ordered to leave the kingdom, or forbid to enter it, to forfeit for the first offence 20l. for the second, 40l. and for the third, lands and goods, half of the goods to the king, and half to the informer, provided, that the informer's share shall not exceed 100l. however more the king's may be, the surplusage shall remain to the king; and shall be recoverable in any of his courts of record.

Ib. s. 3. The fines of 10l. and 40l. to be levied by a single justice, who has power to summon parties and witnesses, and to convict and commit to prison in default of payment.

Ib. s. 8, 9, 10.. Justices are commanded to issue their warrants *from time to time*, for apprehending and committing archbishops, bishops, &c. remaining in the kingdom, and give an account in writing of their proceedings on pain of 100*l.* to the king and the informer.

8 Ann. c. 3. s. 21. Two justices may summon any Popish person of sixteen years or upwards, to give testimony on oath where he last heard mass, who celebrated it, what persons were present, and also touching the being and residence of any Popish clergyman or secular priest resident in the country, and upon neglect or refusal to become informer, commit him for twelve months, unless he pay 20*l.*

8 Ann. c. 3. s. 16. & 20. Any person discovering against the clergy so as they may be prosecuted to conviction, to have for discovering an archbishop or vicar-general, 50*l.* for a regular or secular not registered 20*l.* and for a schoolmaster 10*l.*

1 Geo. 1. c. 9. Every justice may tender the oath of abjuration to every suspected person.

2 Ann. c. 7. s. 2. Priests converted to have a maintenance till otherwise provided for, and to read the liturgy in the English or Irish language. This statute gives 20*l.* by subsequent ones it is increased to 40*l.* yearly.

2 Ann. c. 6. s. 1. Persuading any person to be reconciled to the see of Rome, the reconciler and the party reconciled both subject to the pains of premunrie.

BURIAL OF THE DEAD.

7 & 9 W. 3. st. 1. c. 26. None to bury any dead in a suppressed monastery, abbey, or convent, if it be not used for divine service according to the liturgy of the established church, upon pain of 10*l.* upon all that shall be present, one half to the informer, to be levied summarily by a single justice.

PARENTS AND CHILDREN.

2 Ann. s. 1. c. 6. s. 7. A child of a Popish parent professing a desire to become a Protestant, may institute a chancery suit against his parent, and be decreed a present maintenance, and a portion after the parent's descease.

8 Ann. c. 3. A child on conforming may also oblige his father to discover upon oath the full value of all his real or personal estate, and have a new bill, *toties quoties.*

N. B. Though the parent should abandon all his property, yet if he afterwards acquired any thing, he might be vexed with a new bill as often as an undutiful child might think fit, to the end of his life.

2 Ann. st. 1. c. 6. 3. The eldest son by conforming, may, by filing a bill against his father, divest him of his fee, rendering him bare tenant for life, and take the reversion, subject only to maintenance and portions for younger children, not exceeding one-third of the value.

Ib. s. 5. No Papist to have the guardianship of an orphan child, and if there be no Protestant relation, the child to be committed to a stranger, who shall be bound to use his utmost endeavours to make the child a Protestant; and any Papist who takes upon himself such guardianship, to forfeit 500*l.* to the blue coat hospital.

6 Geo. 1. c. 6. Children of Popish parents bred Protestants from the age of twelve years, and receiving the sacrament of the established church, to be reputed Protestants, and enjoy their rights; but if, after eighteen, they are present either at matins or vespers, to suffer the penalties of converted Papists relapsing into Popery.

2 Ann. s. 1. c. 6. Disables priests from purchasing lands in their own name or in trust, or even any rents or profits issuing out of lands, or to take a lease for more than 31 years, and not that, unless two-thirds of the yearly value be reserved—all other estates to be void.

Ib. s. 7. 8. & 9. No Papist who will not renounce his religion to take any estate, in fee simple, or in tail, by descent or purchase, but the next Protestant to take as if he were dead. The children of Papists to be taken as Papists, a Papist conforming may be heir to a Papist disabled; wife, *if a Protestant*, to have dower.

2 Ann. c. 6. s. 12. If the heir at law of a Papist be a Protestant, he must enrol a certificate of that matter in chancery; if a Papist, he has a year, within which, if he renounce his religion, he may have his land.

English Stat. 1. Ann, S. 1. c. 32. s. 7. enacts, that the lands theretofore forfeited and vested in trustees, should be sold to Protestants only, and if any title in the same shall accrue to any Papist, he must renounce his religion, or as it was commonly expressed, the errors of the church of Rome, in order to enjoy the estate; and if any make or assign a lease to a Papist, both grantor and grantee, to forfeit treble the yearly value; with the exception of a cottage or cabin with two acres of land to a day labourer; and any Protestant might file a bill of discovery against any person supposed privy to any trust, to which neither plea nor demurrer was allowed, and on trial of any issue, none to be jurors but Protestants.

TRADE.

8 Ann. c. 3. s. 37. No Papist *who is or shall be permitted* to follow any trade, craft, or mystery (except hemp or flaxen manufactory) to have two apprentices, nor any for a less time than 7 years, on pain of 100*l.*

25 Geo. 3. c. 42. s. 11 and 12. The 4000*l.* granted by this act, to be expended in apprentices fees, for apprentices taken from charter schools or hospitals, to *Protestant tradesmen only.*

No persons making locks or barrels for fire-arms, or swords, skeins, knives, or other weapons, shall instruct an apprentice of the Popish religion on pain of 20*l.* one moiety to the king, and one to the informer, and the indentures of apprenticeship shall be void, and such apprentice exercising, to suffer the like penalty, and refusing to take the oaths shall amount to a conviction.

The modern editors of the *Book of Martyrs* tell us that the foreign inquisitors "seldom shew mercy to a Protestant;" but what mercy, we should be glad to know, was shewn by these penal statutes to the Catholics, who formed the bulk of Ireland, while in Spain and Portugal scarce a Protestant was to be found? They also talk of scenes of perfidy and treachery—of distractions between husband and wife—of disobedient and wicked children—but could laws be invented better calculated to produce these horrible evils in society than those which have been just described? Observe too, these laws were not passed by Spanish inquisitors, but by a PROTESTANT LEGISLATURE, to prevent the further growth of Popery—by men who pretended to be enlightened by the spirit of the gospel, and influenced by the light of pure religion. What a perversion of the sublime principles of charity and justice! Under pretence of promoting the pure light of the gospel, every principle of law was reversed and religion insulted; parental affection, private friendship, filial duty, and conjugal love violated; family dissension promoted; education prevented; spies and informers encouraged; and industry proscribed; in short, nothing left unattempted that the evil spirit could devise to torment and drive the Catholic from his faith; and all this while the credulous people of England were made to believe that Catholics, and Catholics only, were the most barbarous and brutalized of mankind. Surely it is time that our liberal Protestant fellow-countrymen should begin to open their eyes, and see through the base stratagems which have been practised to mislead and blind them.

We have before said that the tribunal of the inquisition forms no part of the system of the Catholic religion; it is a civil tribunal, which may or may not be established in any country, either Catholic or Protestant, that consents to adopt it. In England it never existed while she remained Catholic, therefore it is baseness in the extreme to attempt to affix the abuses which may have existed in this tribunal in foreign Catholic countries on the Catholics of England and Ireland. Were the

Catholics here to get the upper hand, there could be no danger of the inquisition being introduced, as it never did exist here, and is incompatible with the principles of the British constitution, founded by our Catholic ancestors. With these remarks we may take leave of this part of the *Book of Martyrs*, having, we flatter ourself, sufficiently shewn the falsehoods and misrepresentations of the editors on this head, and made it clearly appear, that their attention had better be directed to the excesses and cruelties committed by the minions of " Protestant-ascendency" nearer home than the pretended enormities of the Spanish inquisition.

BOOK VI.

" FARTHER HISTORICAL ACCOUNT OF THE PERSECUTIONS, SUFFERINGS,
" AND CRUEL DEATHS OF PROTESTANT MARTYRS IN FOREIGN COUNTRIES,
" DURING THE SIXTEENTH AND SEVENTEENTH CENTURIES.

" SECTION I.

" BRIEF RELATION OF THE HORRIBLE MASSACRE IN FRANCE, ANNO 1572.

Such are the titles chosen to adorn the sixth book and first section of the work we are engaged to review.—They are well calculated to strike the sensitive mind with horror, and excite abhorrence of the deeds perpetrated; but we must beg the reflecting reader to suspend his judgment until he has seen what we have to advance in palliation of the transactions which occupy this first section of the sixth division of *John Fox's Book of Martyrs.* Before however we commence our remarks, we will here give the martyrologist's brief relation of the massacre of 1572.—"After a long series of troubles in France, the Papists seeing no-
" thing could be done against the Protestants by open force, began to
" devise how they could entrap them by subtlety, and that by two
" ways: first by pretending that an army was to be sent into the lower
" country, under the command of the admiral, prince of Navarre and
" Condé; not that the king had any intention of so doing, but only
" with a view to ascertain what force the admiral had under him, who
" they were, and what were their names. The second was, a marriage
" suborned between a prince of Navarre and the sister of the king of
" France; to which were to be invited all the chief Protestants. Ac-
" cordingly they first began with the queen of Navarre; she consented
" to come to Paris, where she was at length won over to the king's
" mind. Shortly after she fell sick, and died within five days, not
" without suspicion of poison; but her body being opened, no sign
" thereof appeared. A certain apothecary, however, made his boast,
" that he had killed the queen by venomous odours and smells, pre-
" pared by himself.

" Notwithstanding this, the marriage still proceeded. The admiral,
" prince of Navarre and Condé, with divers other chief states of the
" Protestants, induced by the king's letters and many fair promises,
" came to Paris, and were received with great solemnity. The mar-
" riage at length took place on the 18th of August, 1572, and was so-
" lemnized by the cardinal of Bourbon, upon an high stage set up on
" purpose without the church walls: the prince of Navarre and Condé
" came down, waiting for the king's sister, who was then at mass. This

" done, the company all went to the bishop's palace to dinner. In the
" evening they were conducted to the king's palace to supper. Four
" days after this, the admiral coming from the council table, on his way
" was shot at with a pistol, charged with three bullets, and wounded
" in both his arms. Notwithstanding which, he still remained in
" Paris, although the vidam advised him to flee.

" Soldiers were appointed in various parts of the city to be ready at
" a watch-word, upon which they rushed out to the slaughter of the
" Protestants, beginning with the admiral, who being dreadfully
" wounded, was cast out of the window into the street, where his head
" being struck off, was embalmed with spices to be sent to the pope.
" The savage people then cut off his arms and privy members, and
" drew him in that state through the streets of Paris, after which, they
" took him to the place of execution, out of the city, and there hanged
" him up by the heels, exposing his mutilated body to the scorn of the
" populace.

" The martyrdom of this virtuous man had no sooner taken place
" than the armed soldiers ran about slaying all the Protestants they
" could find within the city. This continued many days, but the
" greatest slaughter was in the three first days, in which were said to
" be murdered above 10,000 men and women, old and young, of all
" sorts and conditions. The bodies of the dead were carried in carts
" and thrown into the river, which was all stained therewith; also
" whole streams in various parts of the city ran with the blood of the
" slain. In the number that were slain of the more learned sort, were
" Petrus Ramus, Lambinus, Plateanus, Lomenius, Chapesius, and others.

" These brutal deeds were not confined within the walls of Paris,
" but extended into other cities and quarters of the realm, especially
" by Lyons, Orleans, Toulouse, and Rouen, where the cruelties were
" unparalleled. Within the space of one month, 30,000 Protestants, at
" least, are said to have been slain, as is credibly reported by them who
" testify of the matter.

" When intelligence of the massacre was received at Rome, the
" greatest rejoicings were made. The pope and cardinals went in so-
" lemn procession to the church of St. Mark to give thanks to God. A
" jubilee was also published, and the ordnance fired from the castle of
" St. Angelo. To the person who brought the news, the cardinal of
" Lorraine gave 1,000 crowns. Like rejoicings were also made all
" over France for this imagined overthrow of the faithful."

Before we enter into the historical transactions here detailed, we
must be allowed to lay down the causes of those long series of troubles
in France, which Fox admits preceded the horrible event of 1572.
This is a most essential point to our coming to the truth, and unless
we have a perfect knowledge of the whole case, how is it possible we
can come to a just conclusion? The "*pure light of the gospel*," as it is
called by this *Book of Martyrs*, began to be taught by Martin Luther
about the year 1517, and among other doctrines preached by this pretended reformer of religion, though religion itself, if we are to believe
the words of God, was *never* to be in want of reform, but was always to
remain pure and inviolate, were the following:—" If," says Luther, in
his book against Sylvester Prieras, " we dispatch thieves by the gallows,

" highwaymen by the sword, heretics by fire; why do we not rather
" attack with all kinds of arms these masters of perdition, these car-
" dinals, these popes, and all this sink of the Romish Sodom, which
" corrupts without ceasing the church of God, and wash our hands in
" their blood." Again, he says in a book which he composed to oppose
the ecclesiastical hierarchy :—" All those who will venture their lives,
" their estates, their honour and their blood, in so Christian a work,
" as to root out all bishoprics and bishops, who are the ministers of
" satan, and to pluck up by the roots all their authority and jurisdic-
" tion in the world: these persons are the true children of God, and
" obey his commandments."—*Contra statum Ecclesia*, &c. Nor did he
confine these declamations to the clergy, for he shortly after proceeded
to attack the temporal authorities both in his writings and preachings.
" You must know," said he, " that from the beginning of the world to
" this day, it has ever been a rare thing to find a wise prince; but
" more rare to find one that was honest: for commonly they are the
" greatest fools and knaves in the world."—*De Sæculari Potest*. Again:
" You must know, my good lords," said he, " that God will have it so,
" that your subjects neither can, nor will, nor ought any longer to en-
" dure your tyrannical governments."—*Contra Rusticus*. " If it is law-
" ful for me," he again says, to his patron, the elector of Saxony,
" for the sake of Christian liberty; not only to neglect, but to trample
" under my feet the pope's decrees, the canons of councils, the laws
" and mandates of the emperor himself, and of all princes; think you
" I shall value your orders so much, as to take them for laws?"—*Contra Ambr. Catharin*. Calvin was equally as seditious in his religious
dogmas as Martin Luther. He writes—" They are beside their wits,
" quite void of sense and understanding, who desire to live under ab-
" solute monarchies; for it cannot be, but that order and policy must
" decay, where one man holds such an extent of government."—*Comment. in Dan*. c. ii. v. 39. " These kings," he goes on, " are in a man-
" ner all of them a set of blockheads and brutish men."—*Ibid*. c. vi.
v. 3. Again, " Princes forfeit their power when they oppose God in
" opposing the reformation; and it is better in such cases to spit in
" their faces than to obey."—*Ibid*. v. 22. Theodore Beza, a disciple
of Calvin, supported the same doctrine as his master, as may be seen
in his preface to his translation of the New Testament; and again in
his book *Vindiciæ contra Tyrannos*. " We must obey kings for God's
" sake, when they obey God," he writes, but otherwise " as the vassal
" loses his fief or tenure, if he commit felony, so does the king lose his
" right and realm also." This doctrine is similar to the allegiance of
the Orangemen at this day, which is given only so long as the king remains a Protestant. Muncer, one of the leaders of the new sect of
Anabaptists, pretended that he had received from God " the sword of
Gedeon," in order to depose and kill all idolatrous (Catholic) magistrates, and *compel* the people to acknowledge the fanatical notions of a
distempered brain, which they called the new kingdom of Jesus Christ.
We could multiply these impious and seditious doctrines, till we swelled
out this number, but enough has been here said to shew how dangerous these doctrines were to the peace and security of society; and we
will now proceed to shew what the consequences were that followed

their promulgation. In doing this we beg the reader to pay particular attention to dates.

The propagation of the doctrines above quoted were soon followed by a general rising of the peasantry in Germany, (where the reformation, as it is called) had taken root, who carried devastation through the provinces of Suabia, Franconia, and Alsatia. In their progress, these fanatic insurgents plundered and burned churches, monasteries, and castles, and killed the priests, monks, and noblemen. Alarmed at the desolating progress of these propagators of " *the pure light of the gos-*" *pel*," the Catholic sovereigns and people very naturally confederated together to preserve their own rights and creed, against a band of lawless disturbers of the peace, dubbed by John Fox and " Protestant-ascendency," evangelical reformers and holy martyrs. Precious reformers of the gospel and sufferers for true religion ! Well, in the year 1525, just eight years *after* Luther began to preach his *new* doctrines, and forty-seven *before* the massacre we have to notice, a battle took place at Frankhusen, between the favourers of the new creed, and the defenders of Catholicism, when the former were defeated, and Muncer and Phiffer, the chiefs of the fanatics, were taken prisoners and soon after executed. This defeat, however, did not suppress the tumults, and for a long series of years the whole empire of Germany was distracted and convulsed with murder, sacrilege, and rapine, under the cloak of religion. Similar scenes were also acted in Switzerland. The cantons that had embraced the fantasies of Zuinglius, were not content with pleasing themselves, but they were determined that their Catholic neighbours should do as they had done, whether they liked it or no. This occasioned a war to ensue, and Zuinglius, the reforming apostle, was slain while directing a battle fought in the year 1531. As our remarks must be confined to the massacre of 1572 in France, we shall leave Germany with these few facts, which are necessary to be known, as they shew how differently the reformation, as it is called, of the sixteenth century was ushered into the world, to what the Catholic religion always was, wherever it was planted, whether from the beginning of its foundation by the apostles, or it resuscitation at this present moment in France, after having suffered years of persecution by the infidel philosophers in that country. Catholic missionaries are armed only with the authority of God, the purity and zeal of a religious mind, a cross, and a breviary. They follow the doctrines of their Divine Master, and they treasure up his words: " Behold, I send you as sheep in the midst " of wolves."—They act by the precepts of the two great apostles, SS. Peter and Paul, " Be ye subject," says the former, " to every human " creature for God's sake," &c. 1 Ep. c. ii. v. 13. And the latter, " Let " every soul be subject to higher powers ; for there is no power but " from God; and those that are, are ordained of God."- *Rom.* xii. 1.— Consistent with these precepts, St. Justin the martyr, in his *Apology* to the emperor, writes, " Our hopes are not fixed on the present world, " and therefore we make no resistance to the executioner that comes " to strike us. . . . We adore only God, but in all other things we cheer-" fully obey you." So writes Tertullian in his *Apology.*—" We Chris-" tians pray to God, that he may grant to the emperors a long life, a " peaceable reign, safety at home, victorious arms, a faithful senate,

" virtuous subjects, universal peace, and every thing that a man and
" emperor can desire."—How different was the spirit of Christianity in
the first ages, as evinced by these apostles and primitive writers, and
the spirit of the chief reformers of the sixteenth century. The former
practised and preached a system of submission to authority, self-denial
and pure morality; the latter inculcated resistance to all authority but
their own, let loose the worst passions of human nature, and deluged
the world with blood, rapacity and wickedness. Compare again, we
say, the means by which truth was propagated by Catholic missionaries
throughout the world, and the means resorted to by those who espoused
the cause of error, and it will soon be seen whether the creatures of the
reformation are worthy the distinguished character of *martyrs for religion or conscience-sake*, which the people of England have been so long
taught, by the falsification of historical facts, and the misrepresentations
of designing men, to consider them. Have we not seen the Arians attempting to force their errors by persecution and not by reason? Have
we not seen that the Albigenses were guilty of outrage and rebellion,
the fruit of their impious notions? And here, in the sixteenth century,
we see the physical force of infuriated men employed to circulate those
abominable doctrines (which reason could not accomplish when opposed by
truth) where the constituted authorities were against them; and the
same weapons are used by the temporal rulers against the people, where
the former are infected with error, and instigated by avarice and pillage.
From the detail given by Fox, the reader is led to suppose that the
sufferers in this massacre of 1572 were the most inoffensive and injured
of all human beings. Let it not be understood that we are going to
justify the bloody deed, because we are taught, by the principles of our
religion, to consider the act to be unjustifiable; yet there may be some
truths and circumstances attending and preceding the deed, which may
throw a different shade upon the matter, and rescue religion from having any share in it, though Fox and his editors have endeavoured to fix
all the odium upon the Catholic church. We have shewn that the doctrines of Calvin as well as Luther were calculated to produce turbulence
and disaffection, and in fact they did produce rebellion and civil war in
France, some years before the event we are now treating of took place.
Dr. Heylin, in his History of the Presbyterians, devotes one whole
book in describing " the manifold seditions, conspiracies, and insur-
" rections in the realm of France, their (the reformers) libelling against
" the state, and the wars there raised by *their procurement*, from the
" year 1559 to 1585." As this historian was a Protestant, and by no
means friendly to the Catholics, he may be looked upon as an unexceptionable witness in this cause. The same historian in another work
called *Cosmography*, speaking of these new sectarians, the Presbyterians,
says, " Rather than their discipline should not be admitted, and *the
" episcopal government destroyed in all the churches of Christ*, they were
" resolved *to depose kings, ruin kingdoms*, and SUBVERT THE FUN-
" DAMENTAL CONSTITUTIONS OF ALL CIVIL STATES." Such
being the disposition of these religionists, if such they ought to be
called, need we wonder that those who were in possession of power,
should exercise their force and authority to awe and intimidate these
turbulent and revolutionary spirits into subjection? We think not.

But, we will here ask, what sort of Christianity must that be, which can employ rebellion, fire, pillage, murder and sacrilege in its train? Can peace, charity, and security to society be the fruits of such a disposition as that which Dr. Heylin says influenced the disciples of Calvin at the period we are treating of? Most undoubtedly not; and therefore the "long series of troubles in France," which Fox admits preceded this massacre, were occasioned, not by the intolerant or cruel spirit of the Catholics, who were then in possession of that kingdom, but by the treacherous and perfidious principles disseminated by the preachers of the pretended reformation.

The object of the Calvinists or Hugonots, as the adherents of the faction were called, from their going through St. Hugo's gate in the city of Tours to attend their secret meetings, as we have before said was to overthow the Catholic religion in France by *force of arms*, and plant Calvinism on its ruins. It was natural, therefore, that the Catholics should be prepared to resist *this* plan, and preserve that religion which they and their forefathers had professed for ages, as well as the form of civil government which had existed for many centuries also. Thus, then, faction was introduced by the birth of the pretended reformation, and to the spirit of faction we must attribute all the evils that have visited every state in Christendom since Luther first began to dogmatize. The premature death of Henry II. of France in 1559, weakened the government of that kingdom, and gave the greatest advantage to the Calvinist party. This monarch left three sons, the eldest but fifteen years of age, who all succeeded him in the throne. The first, Francis II, who married the unfortunate queen of Scotland, reigned only one year, consequently the sovereigns were for some time minors, while the kingdom was distracted by the ambition of certain powerful families. The house of Guise, related to the royal family, headed the Catholic party, though the mother of the sovereign, Catherine de Medicis, acted as regent, and the prince Condé headed the confederacy of the Hugonots. Having contrived to raise a powerful force, it was agreed upon by the Hugonot chiefs, says Dr. Heylin, that " a certain number " of them should repair to the king at Bloise, and tender a petition to " him in all humble manner for the free exercise of the religion which " they then professed, and for professing which they had been perse- " cuted in the days of his father. But these petitioners were to be " backed with multitudes of armed men, gathered together from all " parts on the day appointed; who, on the king's denial of so just a " suit, should violently break into the court, seize on the person of the " king, surprize the queen, and put the Guises to the sword: and, " that being done, liberty was to be proclaimed, free exercise of reli- " gion granted by public edict, the managery of affairs committed to " the prince of Condé, and all the rest of the confederates gratified with " rewards and honours." This scheme, however, was frustrated, and the armed bands were completely routed, while such was the clemency of the monarch and the moderation of the duke of Guise, that a general pardon was proclaimed on the 18th of March, 1560, to all those who had entered into the conspiracy, provided they laid down their arms and retired peaceably to their homes. This lenient dispositon, however, had no effect on the chiefs of the Hugonots, for they caused great tumults to be raised in Poictiers, Languedoc, and Provence. To which places, writes Dr. Heylin, "the preachers of Geneva were forthwith called, " and they came as willingly; their followers being much increased " both in courage and numbers, as well by their vehemency in the pul- " pit, as their private practices. In Daupheny, and some parts of Pro- " vence, they proceeded further, seized upon divers of the churches for " the exercise of their religion, as if all matters had succeeded answer- " able to their expectation. But on the first coming of some forces " from the duke of Guise they shrunk in again, and left the country in " the same condition wherein they found it." Still proceeding on the side of clemency, a proclamation was issued to convene an assembly of the most eminent persons in the kingdom, where all parties were to be at liberty to propound their grievances and advise on some expe- dient for redress thereof. These salutary measures towards a rational reform of abuses were imputed by the Hugonots to consternation in the government, and they resolved to seize on such towns and places of strength as might enable them to defend their party against all oppo- nents, and, thus fortified, to demand of the assembly of the states to *depose the queen regent*, remove the Guises from the goverment, declare the king to be in a minority till he came to twenty-two years of age, and appoint the king of Navarre and the prince of Condé, the chiefs of the Hugonot party, to be his tutors and governors. This plot, like the former one, failed, and after many incidents not necessary to mention here, an edict was published by the French government, on the 28th of January, 1561, decreeing "that the magistrates should be ordered to " release all prisoners committed for matters of religion, and to stop " any manner of inquisition appointed for that purpose against any person " whatsoever; that they should not suffer any disputation in matters of " faith, nor permit particular persons to revile one another with the " names of *Heretic* aud *Papist*; but that all should live together in peace, " abstaining from unlawful assemblies, or to raise scandals or sedition."

Could any thing be more tolerant and just than the above document, which breathed the spirit of "peace and good will unto all men;" yet such was the turbulence of the Hugonots, that they were not content with its provisions, and resolved to have further concessions. For, writes the same historian, "thinking the queen-regent not to be in a condition to " deny them any thing, much less to call them into question for their " future actings, they presently fell upon the open exercise of their " own religion, and every where exceedingly increased both in power " and numbers. In confidence whereof, by public assemblies, insolent " speeches, and other acts the like unpleasing, they incurred the hatred " and disdain of the Catholic party; which put all places into tumult, " and filled all the provinces of the kingdom with seditious rumours: " so that contrary to the intention of those that governed, and contrary " to the common opinion, the remedy applied to maintain the state and " preserve peace and concord in the king's minority, fell out to be dan- " gerous and destructive, and upon the matter occasioned all those dis- " sensions which they hoped by so much care to have prevented. For " as the cardinal informed the council, the Hugonots were grown by " this connivance to so great a height, that the priests were not suf- " fered to celebrate their daily sacrifices, or to make use of their own

" pulpits; that the magistrates were no longer obeyed in their juris-
" dictions; and that all places raged with discords, burnings and
" slaughters, through the peevishness and presumption of those, who
" assumed to themselves a liberty of teaching and believing whatsoever
" they listed." This outrageous conduct of the Hugonots, caused a
parliament to be assembled on the 13th of July, at Paris, where it was
debated and decreed, in consequence of the numerous insurrections
stirred up by the Hugonots, that the ministers of that faction should
be expelled the kingdom, and none but the Catholic religion tolerated.

The admiral Coligini, who had now become an active leader of the
Hugonot party, and the prince of Condé finding themselves thwarted
by this latter decree, proposed a disputation between the Calvinistic
ministers and Catholic doctors, which proposition was agreed to, and
a conference appointed to be held at Poissy on the 10th of August, 1561.
The result of the disputation, however, was not attended with any good
effect, but rather increased the evil, since both parties separated without coming to a final conclusion, and each claimed the victory, if we
are to credit Dr. Heylin. The conduct of the Hugonots was, as usual,
every thing but orderly and peaceable. "The king of Navarre," this
historian writes, " appeared much unsatisfied by noting the differences
" of the ministers amongst themselves, some of them adhering to the
" Augustinian and others to the Helvetian confession, in some points of
" doctrine; which made him afterwards more cordial to the interests
" of the church of Rome, notwithstanding all the arguments and insi-
" nuations used by his wife, a most zealous Hugonot, to withdraw him
" from it. But the Hugonots gave out on the other side, that they had
" made good their doctrines, convinced the Catholic doctors, con-
" founded the cardinal of Lorrain, and gotten license from the king to
" preach; which gave such courage to the rest of that faction, that
" they began of their own authority to assemble themselves in such
" places as they thought most convenient, and their ministers to preach in
" public, and their preachings followed and frequented by such multi-
" tudes, as well of the nobility as the common people, that it was
" thought impossible to suppress, and dangerous to disturb their meet-
" ings. For so it was, that if either the magistrates molested them in
" their congregations, or the Catholics attempted to drive them out of
" their temples, without respect to any authority, they put themselves
" into arms, and in the middle of a full peace, was made a shew of a
" most terrible and destructive war."

Here it will be seen that nothing but resistance would satisfy these
new-modelled Christians. That meekness of spirit and self-denial
which marked the lives of the primitive Christians and martyrs; their
readiness to die for the faith of Christ, and submission to the stroke of
the executioner, formed no part of these new gospellers; but turbulence,
blood, and pillage, marked their footsteps wherever they found footing.
Now, we ask once more, if men imbued with such a spirit can lay claim
to the title of martyrs for conscience-sake? Can other men be blamed
for endeavouring to quell and reduce to silence such disturbers of the
public peace? And yet here we have John Fox and his editors representing the violators of all law and justice, these pretenders to evangelical wisdom, as sufferers for religion, while they were making re-

ligion *a cloak* for their injustice and perfidy. The queen regent finding these disturbances were in part occasioned by the edict of the 13th
of July, and having raised a strong party against her by the decree of
the 28th of January, now began to exercise a different kind of policy,
by playing into the hands of both parties. The king of Navarre and
the duke of Guise entered into a combination to defend the Catholic
religion, while the admiral Coligni and the prince of Condé were confederated to support the Calvinistic doctrine, and Catharine the queen-
regent now shewed favour to this party, now to that. This sort of state
policy only increased the heat of faction, and tended greatly to aid the
admiral and prince in their intrigue, for Condé at length grew into such
confidence, that he assumed to himself, Dr. Heylin says, the management
of all great affairs. An incident occurred about this time, which shews the
disposition of the Hugonot party, and how ready they are to take advantage of the least trifling matter to excite the flame of religious prejudice.
This affair with its consequences we will give in Dr. Heylin's own
words. " The duke (of Guise) was then at Joinville in the province
" of Champaigne, and happened in his way upon a village called Vas-
" sey, where the Hugonots were assembled in great numbers to hear a
" sermon. A scuffle unhappily is begun between some of the duke's
" footmen, and not a few of the more unadvised and adventurous Hugo-
" nots : which the duke coming to part, was hit with a blow of a stone
" upon one of his cheeks, which forced him with the loss of some blood
" to retire again. Provoked with which indignity, his followers, being
" two companies of lances, charge in upon them with their fire-locks,
" kill sixty of them in the place, and force the rest for preservation of
" their lives into several houses This accident is by the Hugonots
" given out to be a matter of design; the execution done upon those
" sixty persons, must be called a massacre; and in revenge thereof the
" kingdom shall be filled with blood and rapine, altars and images de-
" faced, monasteries ruined and pulled down, and churches brutishly
" polluted." Can any one, after reading this statement of Dr. Heylin,
avoid being struck with the great similarity between the conduct of
the Hugonots in 1561 and bawlers against Popery in 1815. It must be
in the recollection of the reader, what outcries were raised in the
latter year about religious persecution and the intolerance of Catholics,
in consequence of an affray at Nismes of far less import than what
took place in the village of Vassey. What pamphlets were published
in this country, and an address even carried to the throne by the corporation of London, calling upon the government to interfere in the
internal concerns of an independent state, merely because one of the
parties professed what is called Protestantism. Why, admitting that
these modern sufferers were punished for *religion's* sake, why make
such an outcry? Who made such a noise when the primitive Christians were persecuted? Who felt for the unfortunate Catholics of Ireland and England, groaning under a code of laws more inhuman than
the laws of Draco, for upwards of three hundred years? But we are
promised by the modern editors a full detail of these pretended persecutions in the south of France, and therefore we must reserve our
remarks till we see what they have to offer.

Nor was resistance to authority the only evil which France suffered

by the proceedings of the Hugonots; for wherever they obtained the possession of towns and places, devastation and oppression was sure to follow their steps. Dr. Heylin observes, that having made themselves masters of the city of Orleans, they "handselled their new go-
"vernment with the spoil of all the churches and religious houses,
" which either they defaced or laid waste and desolate. Amongst which
" none was used more coarsely than the church of St. Crosse, being the
" cathedral of that city; not so much out of a dislike to all cathedrals
" (though that had been sufficient to expose it unto spoil and rapine)
" as out of hatred to the name. Upon which furious piece of zeal they
" afterwards destroyed all the little crosses which they found in the
" way between Mont Martyr and St. Denis, first raised in memory of
" Denis the first bishop of Paris, and one that passeth in account for
" the chief apostle of the Gallic nations."

France was thus rendered a scene of contention and desolation by the doctrines and practices of these reforming gospellers, which before had been a kingdom of internal tranquillity and wealth, under the influence of Catholicism. After various successes, the Hugonots made themselves masters of several of the strongest towns and cities, and nothing would content them now but the banishment of the constable of France, the cardinal of Lorrain, and the duke of Guise; free liberty of religion and churches to be taken from the Catholics for their use; the pope's legate to be sent out of the kingdom, all honours and offices to be opened to them; and the emperor, the queen of England, and other potentates to become guarantees that the first mentioned three personages should not return to France, till the king had arrived at the age of twenty-two. These measures were of course opposed by the opposite party, and this opposition led to a circumstance which we are surprised has never been noticed by Catholic writers to our knowledge, but which ought to have been made as public as possible, since it proves that the doctrine imputed to Catholics, of *not keeping faith with heretics*, which has been so formally and solemnly denied by them, was absolutely taught, and it appears practised by the Hugonots in France. We give the affair at full length, as related by Dr. Heylin in his History aforesaid.

" These violent demands so incensed all those which had the go-
" vernment of the state, that the prince and his adherents were pro-
" claimed traitors, and as such to be prosecuted in a course of law, if
" they laid not down their arms by a day appointed. Which did so
" little benefit them, as the proposals of the prince had pleased the
" others. For thereupon the Hugonots united themselves more strictly
" into a confederacy to deliver the king, the queen, the kingdom, from
" the violence of their opposers, to stand to one another in the defence
" of the edicts, and altogether to submit to the authority of the prince
" of Condé, as the head of their union: publishing a tedious declara-
" tion with their wonted confidence, touching the motives which in-
" duced them to this combination. This more estranged the queen
" from them than she was at first; and now she is resolved to break
" them by some means or other, but rather to attempt it by wit than
" by force of arms. And to this end she deals so dexterously with the
" constable and the duke of Guise, that she prevailed with them to

A REVIEW

OF

𝕱𝖔𝖝'𝖘 𝕭𝖔𝖔𝖐 𝖔𝖋 𝕸𝖆𝖗𝖙𝖞𝖗𝖘,

CRITICAL AND HISTORICAL.

No. 20. Printed and Published by W. E. Andrews, 3, Chapter-house-court, St. Paul's Churchyard, London. Price 3d.

EXPLANATION OF THE ENGRAVING.—*In the year 1562, the city of Orleans was be-sieged by the duke of Guise, who was shot by one Poltrot, at the instigation of Beza, the apostle of the Hugonot party, and other divines of the Calvinist school.* See p. 367.

CONTINUATION OF THE REVIEW.

" leave the court, and to prefer the common safety of their country
" before their own particular and personal greatness: which being
" signified by letters to the prince of Condé, he frankly offered under
" his hand, that whensoever these great adversaries of his were retired
" from the court (which he conceived a matter of impossibility to per-
" suade them to) he would not only lay down arms, but quit the king-
" dom. But understanding that the constable and the duke had really
" withdrawn themselves to their country houses, divested of all power
" both in court and council, he stood confounded at the unadvisedness
" and precipitation of so rash a promise as he had made unto the queen.
" For it appeared dishonourable to him not to keep his word; more
" dangerous to relinquish his command in the army; but most destruc-
" tive to himself and his party to dissolve their forces, and put himself
" into a voluntary exile, not knowing whither to retreat. At which
" dead lift he is refreshed by some of his Calvinian preachers with a
" cordial comfort. By which learned casuists it was resolved for good
" divinity, that the prince having undertaken the maintenance of those

"who had embraced the purity of religion, and made himself by oath
"protector of the word of God, no following obligation could be of
"force to make him violate the first. In which determining of the
"case, they seemed to have been guided by that note in the English
"bibles, translated and printed at Geneva, where in the margin to the
"second chapter of saint Matthew's gospel, it is thus advertised: viz.
"*That promise ought not to be kept, when God's honour and the preaching
"of the truth is hindered; or else it ought not to be broken.* They added,
"to make sure work of it, (at the least they thought so) that the
"queen had broken a former promise to the prince, in not bringing the
"king over to his party, as she once assured him; and therefore that
"he was not bound to keep faith with her, who had broke her own.
"But this divinity did not seem sufficient to preserve his honour; an-
"other temperament was found by some wiser heads, by which he
"might both keep his promise, and not leave his army. By whose
"advice it was resolved, that he should put himself into the power of
"the queen, who was come within six miles of him with a small re-
"tinue, only of purpose to receive him; that having done his duty to
"her, he should express his readiness to forsake the kingdom, as soon
"as some accord was settled; and that the admiral, d'Andelot, and
"some other of the principal leaders, should on the sudden shew them-
"selves, forcibly mount him on his horse, and bring him back into
"the army. Which lay device, whether it had more cunning or less
"honesty than that of the cabal of divines, it is hard to say: but sure
"it is, that it was put in execution accordingly; the queen thereby
"deluded, and all the hopes of peace and accommodation made void
"and frustrate."

From this testimony of Dr. Heylin, it is clear that the pretended gospel-reformers were the parties who broached the doctrine of not keeping faith with those who differed from them in religious opinions, and
that their divines blasphemously perverted the sense of scripture to
forward their purposes, while they at the same time charged the Catholics with holding the infamous doctrine taught by themselves, that
the odium might attach to the professors of Catholicism. Perfidy and
treachery too we also see were pressed into the ranks of the Hugonots
to further their views, and yet these are the men that are held up by
the editors of this *Book of Martyrs* as the *innocent* victims of religious
persecution. Having preached the violation of good faith to secure
success to the propagation of their erroneous notions, the Calvinistic
divines now went a step further, and held it for sound doctrine, that
subjects might lawfully call in a foreign force against their lawful
sovereign, when the interests of *true* religion and freedom of conscience
were at stake; and on the grounds of this doctrine, the Hugonots actually entered into an agreement with Elizabeth of England to surrender
some of the strong places in Normandy to a British force, and were
supplied with money and arms by this Protestant princess to carry war
and destruction into the heart of their own country. They also admitted German auxiliaries into the country, and allowed them to spoil
and plunder wherever they got possession. Of these traiterous doings
Dr. Heylin thus speaks:—"It was on the 17th July, 1563, that New-
"haven was yielded to the French, that being the last day of the first

" war which was raised by the Hugonots, and raised by them on no
" other ground, but for *extorting* the free exercise of their religion *by*
" *force of arms*, according to the doctrine and example of the mother-
" city. In the pursuit whereof they did not only with their own hands
" ruinate and deface the beauty of their native country, but gave it
" over for a prey to the lust of strangers. The calling in of the Eng-
" lish to support their faction, whom they knew well to be the ancient
" enemies of the crown of France, and putting into their hands the
" chief strength of Normandy, of whose pretensions to that dukedom
" they should not be ignorant, were two such actions of a disloyal im-
" polite nature, as no pretence of zeal to that which they called the
" gospel, could either qualify or excuse. Nor was the bringing in of
" so many thousand German soldiers of much better condition, who
" though they could pretend no title to the crown of France, nor to
" any particular province in it, were otherwise more destructive to the
" inside of that country, and created far more mischief to the people of
" it, than all the forces of the English; for being to be maintained on
" the pay of the Hugonots, and the Hugonots not being able to satisfy
" their exorbitant arrears, they were suffered to waste the country in
" all parts where they came, and to expose the whole kingdom, from
" the very borders of it toward Germany to the English channel, unto
" spoil and rapine; so that between the Hugonots themselves on the
" one side, and these German soldiers on the other, there was nothing
" to be seen in most parts of the kingdom, *but the destruction of churches,*
" *the profanation of altars, the defacing of images, the demolishing of mo-*
" *nasteries, the burning of religious houses, and even the digging up of the*
" *bones of the dead,* despitefully thrown about the fields and unhallowed
" places."

Nor were these traiterous designs and horrible outrages the only unjustifiable measures resorted to by the Hugonots to gain their ends;
for the same author relates, that when the French royalists laid siege
to the town of Orleans, under the command of the duke of Guise, one
Poltrot, a man of good family, who had lived many years in Spain, but
afterwards embraced the Calvinian doctrines, was stirred up by Beza,
the leader of that sect, and the rest of the Hugonot ministers, as well
as by the admiral Coligni, under the hope of great rewards both here
and hereafter, to murder the Catholic commander, which he at length
perpetrated, under the most perfidious circumstances, by shooting him
with a musquet loaded with three bullets. The people of England
have been repeatedly told of the assassination of Henry IV. of France
by one Raviallac, but who ever before heard of this base murder committed by a Calvinist at the instigation of his *religious* teachers, as they
are called? We question if there be one Protestant in five thousand,
at this day, that is at all acquainted with the above circumstance, though
few are ignorant of the nature of the death of Henry. The murderer of
the king of France was a professed Catholic, and though the crime was
committed in direct violation of the principles and doctrines of that
church, yet have the people of this besotted country been led to believe,
by means of the press, that the act was perpetrated in consequence of
the pernicious tenets of the church of Rome. Nay, to this very day,
are Catholics obliged, before they can be legally secured from the ef-

fects of the penal laws, to go into an open court of justice, and there
take a solemn oath that their religion do not teach them to depose
and murder princes! Thus this gross imputation on the character of
the ancient and only true church is still upheld by legislative enactments, and the Catholic is compelled to go through the humiliating
act of proclaiming that he is not by religious profession a murderer!!
But the time, we trust, is near at hand, when every uncharitable insinuation will be consigned to oblivion, and the people of England will
form their conclusions, not from what this or that party may represent,
but from historical and well-authenticated FACTS. It has been the
misfortune of Protestants, that they have hitherto seen history only on
one side of the question. It has been the study of most, we might say
all, writers on the side of Protestantism to bespatter the Catholics with
every degree of moral turpitude possible, while the professors of the
reformed, or rather deformed creeds, (for innumerable have been and
are the professions of faith, if such they can be called, since the days
of Luther, Calvin, Beza, &c.) are represented as the very emblems of
purity and perfection, though real history depicts them the most immoral of men, the most outrageous disturbers of the public peace,
and, in power, the most sanguinary of all rulers. This is done by the
suppression of some facts, and the misrepresentation of others, while
the operation of the penal code, preventing the Catholics from exposing the falsehoods and tricks of these mercenary writers, their works,
by remaining so long uncontradicted, have been considered irrefutable,
and thus the most implicit credit has been given to them. We flatter
ourself, however, that we shall be able to throw some light on this
state of blindness in which our countrymen have been so long kept, and
draw aside the veil of obscurity that has for so many years prevented
the light of truth from shedding its rays among them.

But we must return again to the proceedings of the French Hugonots previous to the massacre of St. Bartholomew, as it is termed,
which took place in 1572. What we have already related, we wish
the reader to bear in mind is anterior to that date, and we have now to
record other instances of the diabolical spirit by which these propagators of the *pure light of the gospel*, as John Fox's modern editors call
them, were instigated. We have seen the disorders and miseries
brought upon France in 1563, from the introduction of foreign mercenaries into that country by the French gospel-reformers, it is now time
to shew the reader what followed these lamentable proceedings through
the fanaticism and cruelty of the native Hugonots. A peace had been
concluded between the contending parties, by which the Hugonots were
secured in the free exercise of their religion in such towns as should be
allotted them, and other privileges were granted them, but the restless
spirit of innovation would not permit them to be quiet, and the kingdom became the theatre of fears, jealousies and discord. In the year
1566, writes Dr. Heylin, "the Hugonots had some thoughts of sur-
" prising Lyons, but the plot miscarried; they practised also upon
" Narbonne, a chief city of Languedoc, and openly attempted the
" pope's town of Avignon; but were prevented in the one and sup-
" pressed in the other. A greater diffidence was raised against them
" by the unreasonable zeal of the queen of Navarre, who, not content

" with settling the reformed religion in the country of Berne when she
" was absolute and supreme, suffered the Catholics to be infested in her
" own provinces which she held immediately of the crown; insomuch
" that at Pamiers, the chief city of the earldom of Foix, the Hugonots,
" taking offence at a solemn procession held upon Corpus Christi day,
" betook themselves presently to arms, and falling upon those whom
" they found unarmed, not only made a great slaughter amongst the
" churchmen, but in the heat of the same fury burnt down their houses.
" Which outrage being suffered to pass unpunished, gave both encourage-
" ment and example to some furious zealots to commit the like in other
" places, as namely at Montauban, Cœlion, Lodez, Preieux, Valence, &c.
" being all situate in those provinces in which the Hugonots were pre-
" dominant in power and number. But that which most alarmed the
" court, was a seditious pamphlet, published by a native of Orleans, in
" which it was maintained (according to the Calvinian doctrines) that
" the people of France were absolved from their allegiance to the king
" then reigning, because he was turned an idolater. In which reason
" it is lawful also to kill him, as opportunity should be offered. Which
" doctrine being very agreeable unto some, designs which were then
" every where in agitation amongst the Hugonots, was afterwards
" made use of for the justifying the following wars, when the opinion
" grew more general and more openly maintained both from press and
" pulpit." Here then we have the fact, that where the Hugonots were
predominant they made no scruple to murder indiscriminately such
Catholics as fell into their power, and destroy their houses. We have
it stated also, that the press and PULPIT were employed to propagate
the doctrine, that it was lawful to absolve subjects from their allegiance, and to kill their king for being an *idolater*, as Catholics were
then, and now are, miscalled. These heinous charges have been constantly imputed to Catholics, and it was not till Mr. Pitt, the late
heaven-born minister of this country, consulted the divines of six Catholic universities on them, who one and all denied that the Catholic
church ever taught such horrible doctrines, that the sanguinary code of
laws, passed to grind the professors of Catholicism in this country and
Ireland, was mitigated; and then, as we have before remarked, not
until the Catholic goes into an open court of justice, and denies upon
oath the infamous imputations. Yet here we see it recorded in the work
of a Protestant writer, that Protestant reforming divines did absolutely
teach those impious doctrines which were falsely laid to the Catholics!
Acting upon these doctrines, we are told, by the same author, that in
the year following (1567), the Hugonots entered into a conspiracy to
seize upon the king and royal family, who were to be put to death, in
the event of falling into the hands of the conspirators, in order to set
aside the succession, and place the crown on the head of the prince of
Condé. In this design they were, however, frustrated, and they then
attempted to gain possession of Paris, to which city they laid siege,
but were driven from it by the king's forces. In the year succeeding
they prevailed upon the elector Palatine to furnish them with a band of
mercenaries, and they obtained supplies from England to keep their
country in a state of civil warfare and confusion. This rebellious spirit of
the Hugonots determined the king to forbid them the exercise of their

religion, and ordered their ministers and preachers to be banished out of the kingdom, the reasons for which conduct the king stated to be, the ill requital the Hugonots had made of his indulgence, the many rebellions and conspiracies they had raised against him, their bringing foreign forces into the kingdom, their contempt of his authority, and the continual disturbance and destruction of his subjects made by them under the pretence of zeal for religion. This edict was followed by a solemn covenant on the part of the Hugonots, who bound themselves by oath to persevere till death in defence of what they called religion. How far the doctrines they preached and practised were consonant to the true practice of Christianity, let the reader judge when he has compared the conduct of these Hugonot gospellers with the behaviour of the primitive martyrs, which Fox has recorded, and we have noticed in our preceding pages. In the latter we perceive the spirit of meekness and charity—a forbearance towards their persecutors, and an inflexible courage to meet the most excruciating tortures rather than violate the principle of their faith, or sully the purity of their motives in the choice of that faith. But in the gospel reformers of the sixteenth century we see nothing but turbulence, violence, and sedition. We see them, in the absence of reason and truth, acting with force and treachery to accomplish their ends. We see them involving their country in all the horrors of civil war, introducing foreign mercenaries to pillage and oppress the people, murder the clergy, and destroy the churches. And can such men be the propagators of the pure light of the gospel, as the editors of the *Book of Martyrs* insinuate they were? Were they not, on the contrary, the greatest enemies to public peace, the destroyers of their country's happiness, and the plunderers of their neighbours' property. Admitting that there were abuses existing in the church of Rome that needed reforming, could the existence of these abuses justify such outrageous proceedings on the part of the evangelical reformers as we have cited from the page of history, where it is fixed in characters too indelible to be removed? They may be partially suppressed; they may be glossed over, as the editors of Fox have glossed them over; yet they will stand a monument of the impiety and outrage which marked the progress of what is called THE REFORMATION, but which should be termed the *Deformation of Religion, and the Violation of every principle of Charity and Justice.*

But we have not yet enumerated all the outrages committed by these much-injured and innocent gospellers, as the modern editors of Fox would persuade us the French Calvinists or Hugonots were. The pious admiral Coligni, who, according to the *Book of Martyrs*, believed himself to be beloved of God, finding himself to be reduced to great straits by the forces of the king, shut himself up with his confederates in the strong town of Rochelle, a seaport in the bay of Biscay, and then advised the inhabitants to go forth in their ships to spoil and pillage such vessels as they might meet with, in order to provide him with the necessary means to maintain the war. Thus piracy was added to the many other acts of injustice and violence committed by these pretended reformers of religion! These proceedings took place about 1568-9, and were followed by another rebellion, in which foreign auxiliaries were again called in, and the treasures of the church were to be seized, wherever the Hugonots got the ascendency, to support the combined forces of the rebels and mercenaries. The result of this rebellion was the death of the prince of Condé in battle, the condemnation of the admiral, the confiscation of his lands, the plunder of his houses, and the execution of his effigy. "The loss of the famous battle of Mont-Con-"taur by the Hugonot party anno 1569," says Dr. Heylin, "forced "them to abandon all their strong holds, except Rochelle, Angouleme, "and St. Jean d'Angely, and finally to shut themselves up within Ro-"chelle only; after which followed such a dissembled reconciliation "between the parties, as proved more bloody than the war." It was in this state of feeling then that the transaction we have now to notice took place. We do not mean to vindicate the parties implicated in it, but we shall endeavour to place it in its true colours, and rescue the religion we profess from having any share in it. The editors of Fox say, "the Papists seeing nothing could be done against the Protestants by "open force, began to devise how they could entrap them by subtlety." This we grant; but it must be observed, that the determination was formed without consulting either the ministers of the church, the precepts of religion, or the workings of conscience. No, the royalist party (for the Papists or Catholics, as a body, had no more to do with the event than John Fox or his editors) merely followed the example so often set them by the Hugonots, and endeavoured to subdue their adversaries by the same unchristian weapons which had been used against themselves, namely, perfidy and stratagem. We have shewn that the Hugonots could massacre unoffending priests and people, in the exercise of their religious ceremonies; that they could preach against keeping faith with Catholics; that they could bring foreign troops to plunder and destroy the people; and are these the men to complain when deceit and treachery is practised upon them? We again repeat that we do not intend to justify the horrible deed, but we do contend that men who are guilty of the most perfidious conduct cannot fairly complain if they should happen to fall into the same or similar snares which they have laid for their opponents. What would be thought of a man who should prosecute another in a court of justice for robbing him, when it should turn out that the prosecutor had been the instructor of the offender in his dishonest practices? The culprit must of course be considered guilty, but his situation would excite the compassion of the audience, while the prosecutor would be entitled to and receive their just indignation. So it must be with every rational mind regarding the massacre of St. Bartholomew, as it is called. The Catholic party were exasperated at the treacherous and restless conduct of the Hugonots; they were desirous of peace and good order; they had seen the country a prey to disorder and devastation through the perfidy of the pretended reformers; and they resolved, contrary to religion and justice, to get rid of the enemies of their peace, by the same means as their peace had been disturbed. Had, indeed, the Hugonots confined themselves to the exercise of their intellectual powers, and not had recourse to physical force; had they conformed strictly to the laws, instead of violating them; then might the editors of the Book of Martyrs have justly sent forth their execrations against the French Catholics; but while the page of history bears testimony to the violent and perfidious transactions of the Hugonots, previous to the deed in question, we are convinced the sensible reader will agree with us, that the less the bigotted opposers of Catholicism say about the matter, the better it will be for their characters. This massacre, of which so much is said, was occasioned by a struggle between two parties for political ascendency; the one having had the ascendency for some centuries, and the other wishing to obtain it by force or fraud. Religion itself, as we have before said, having no concern in the business, no further than the two parties making it a cloak for their proceedings, and thus scandalizing that sacred name which they pretended to hallow. That neither hatred to the religion of the Hugonots, nor affection to the creed of the church of Rome influenced the king, or rather the queen regent, in this transaction, may be gathered from the proclamation issued out on the very day of the massacre, in which the king declared, that " all had been done " by his express orders; and that he had been prompted to it, not by " any hatred of their religion, but to obviate the wicked conjurations " of Cologni (the admiral) and his friends." *Thuan.* 1. 52. That the king had received great provocation cannot be denied, for in addition to the facts we have related at some length on the authority of Dr. Heylin, Maimbourg asserts, that the Hugonots actually threatened the king with the indiguities of whipping and binding him apprentice to a trade. What would be said were the Catholics of Ireland, who have groaned under a system of persecution for three hundred years, to offer such indignity to the monarch of these realms? Why " ascendency" would never be tired in ringing the changes upon such audacity; and yet for the purpose of slandering the Catholics, and making them the fautors of the crimes produced by the pretended reformation, facts are suppressed on the one side, and falsified on the other, to hoodwink and delude the public.

The admiral is stiled by the editors of Fox a " virtuous man;" but could that man be virtuous who recommended and practised perfidious and treasonable acts? Could he be a man of virtue, when he was guilty of violating his most solemn promise by a stratagem as base as it was dishonourable? The relation of this fatal day by the editors of the *Book of Martyrs* is evidently high-coloured, and, of course, not correct. It is a picture overdone, and consequently must rather disgust than convince the rational mind. Who can credit, for example, the statement that the admiral's head, in the midst of the massacre, was carefully prepared, in order to be embalmed with spices and sent to the pope. The holy father, we will venture to say, cared as little for the head of the traitor Coligni as he did for the archpatriarch of the disgraceful commotions produced by the pretended reformation, Martin Luther. To be sure we are told by these editors that " when intelli- " gence of the massacre was received at Rome, the greatest rejoicings " were made. The pope and cardinals went in solemn procession to " the church of St. Mark to give thanks to God. A jubilee was also " published, and the ordnance fired from the castle of St. Angelo. To " the person who brought the news, the cardinal gave 1000 crowns. " Like rejoicings were also made all over France for this imagined " overthrow of the faithful." Faithful victims truly! But on what authority is this statement made? Where are the records of the jubilee, and the procession, and the rejoicings? Not one single authority is there produced to substantiate the assertion, and will the people of England be so credulous as to take all for granted, however improbable, that the editors of this work may think fit to put forth? But allowing that the pope and cardinal did go in procession to return thanks, it does not follow that Catholics are answerable for such conduct. Every act of a pope is not binding on Catholics, any more than the lies of John Fox are to be believed by every Protestant. Catholics are not responsible for the acts of individuals, and were the pope to order a jubilee for the restoration of Ferdinand and the inquisition in Spain, the Catholics of England and Ireland would not be bound to join in it. But have not the editors of this *Book of Martyrs* heard of a *Protestant* country where a massacre took place in this same month of August, about five years ago, when many persons were killed and hundreds wounded without any redress being made to the latter, or punishment inflicted on the perpetrators. Nay, the managers of the slaughter were publicly thanked in the name of the king of the country, who was also head of the church established there by law. It is therefore clear that massacres are not peculiar to Catholic countries. We have seen that the Hugonots could murder unoffending Catholics previous to the slaughter of these sectarians at Paris; and we have likewise seen that Protestants can, in these enlightened days, have recourse to the sword when they think the possession of the good things of this world is in danger. It was not a question of *religion*, but of *property* and *security*, that prompted the king of France to the deed of darkness; and so it was that led to the late massacre above hinted at. There was, however, a considerable difference in the two cases. In that which occurred in 1552 there was the greatest provocation given on the part of the sufferers; whereas in that which took place in 1819, the law had not been violated by those who were the victims; yet the act was justified on the ground of alarm being excited in the minds of the partisans of those who were in power.

The account of the massacre at Paris is followed by the detail of several others at various places in France, but as we have no authorities stated to give currency to the relation, we shall pass them over with one observation. While these editors are publishing stale and authenticated accounts of massacres said to have taken place in France two hundred and fifty years ago, scenes of a similar nature, though on a smaller scale, are yearly occurring in Ireland in these days, where the Orange disciples of "Protestant-ascendency," infuriated with religious bigotry and prejudice, seize every opportunity to glut their vengeance on the Catholics, and oftentimes escape the hands of justice through the perjury of juries composed of the same faction. Now, we will here ask the reader, if the editors of Fox had not better remove this real stigma from "Protestant-ascendency" before they again attempt to fix cruelty and persecution on the Catholic religion? To shew the accuracy observed by these editors in stating historical facts, we will here notice their account of the death of one of their martyrs. They say, "The prince of Condé, being taken *prisoner*, and *his life pro-* "*mised him*, was shot in the neck by Montisquius, captain of the duke " of Anjou's guard." Now Dr. Heylin states that this prince lost his life in the battle of Jarnac. But it was necessary to give a colouring to the fact, in order to make the credulous people believe that Condé lost his life by treachery, and that Catholics were faithless to their promises.

We now quote a passage from this *Book of Martyrs* by which the reader will be able to judge of the spirit which animated the propagators of the pure light of the gospel in those days, and the loyalty of the doctrine which the adherents of "Protestant-ascendency" are holding up in these times. "The *enemies of the truth*, now glutted with "slaughter, began every where to triumph in the fallacious opinion, "that they were the sole lords of men's conscience; and, truly, it might "appear *to human reason*, that by the destruction of *his people*, God "had abandoned the earth to the ravages of his enemy. But he had "otherwise decreed, and thousands yet, who had not *bowed the knee to* "*Baal*, were called forth to *glory and virtue*. The inhabitants of Ro-"chelle, hearing of the cruelties committed on their brethren, resolved "to defend themselves against *the power of the king*; and their example "was followed by *various* other towns, with which they entered into "*a confederacy*, exhorting and inspiriting one another in the common "cause. To crush this, the king shortly after summoned *the whole power* "*of France*, and *the greatest of his nobility*, among whom were *his royal* "*brothers*; he then invested Rochelle by sea and land, and commenced "a furious siege, which, but *for the immediate hand of God*, must have "ended in its destruction. Seven assaults were made against the "town, none of which succeeded. At one time a breach was made by "the tremendous cannonade; but through the undaunted valour of the "citizens, assisted even by their wives and daughters, the soldiers were "driven back with great slaughter. The siege lasted seven months, "when the duke of Anjou being proclaimed king of Poland, he, in "concert with the king of France, entered into a treaty with the people "of Rochelle, which ended in a peace: conditions, containing 25 articles, "having been drawn up by the latter, embracing many immunities both "for themselves and other Protestants in France, were confirmed by the "king, and proclaimed with great rejoicings at Rochelle and other "cities. The year following died Charles IX. of France, *the tyrant* "*who had been so instrumental* in the calamities above recorded. He "was only in the 25th year of his age, and his death was remarkable "and dreadful. When lying on his bed, the blood gushed from various "parts of his body, and, after lingering in horrible torments during "many months, he at length expired." pp. 150, 151.

Such is the account given by the modern editors of Fox of the siege of Rochelle, and the conduct of the Hugonots. But how unlike the example set them by the primitive Christians. We have it stated here that these gospel-reformers entered into a confederacy to oppose the government of their lawful sovereign, which, we cannot help thinking, is a somewhat singular way of disseminating religious truths. Neither the apostles of Christ, nor their successors, stirred up rebellion, or opposed the government of the states and kingdoms, into which they carried the tidings of Christianity; but while they preached the revelations of God, and established a kingdom which was not to be of this world, they inculcated obedience to the laws, and a submission to the authorities, whether monarchical or democratical, according as the people were governed. Here, however, we see the gospel-reformers waging war against their rulers, and imputing to their sovereign the calamities which their own turbulence and restlessness had brought upon their country. The Catholics are here stiled " the enemies of truth," and represented as being " glutted with slaughter." Well, then, why did not the Hugonots remain quiet. Oh ! dear no ; the Catholics began to imagine " they were the sole lords of men's conscience," and therefore the thousands " who had not yet *bowed the knee to Baal*," were called upon to share in the " *glory and virtue*" of rebellion and slaughter. Admirable system of Christianity? Precious mode of reforming religion ! Excellent propagators of the pure light of the gospel ! But here we have a number of facts clumsily mixed together, which shews that the editors are a set of men the most stupidly ignorant or the most impudently false, that ever exercised the press. The confederacy is stated to have been entered into subsequent to the massacre, whereas Dr. Heylin says, that the confederates were reduced to the greatest extremities before the slaughter took place. That after that event the whole kingdom of France was reduced to obedience, except *three* cities, namely Nismes, Montauban, and Rochelle ; therefore " the summoning of the whole power of France, and the greatest " of his nobility, among whom were his royal *brothers*," is all fabulous, as a proof of which the king had only *one* brother, and consequently could not summon his *brothers*. We will say nothing of the romancing account of the siege, and the valour of the wives and daughters of the pious gospellers, but come to the terms granted to the Rochellers, and the general conduct of these meek sufferers, for conscience sake, as we find them in Dr. Heylin's History. The treaty was signed on the 11th of July, 1573, just eleven months after the affair of Paris, and consequently the royalists must have been very expeditious in bringing the whole power of France into action, as well as the rebel Hugonots in maturing their confederacy, had all the work been performed *after* the slaughter of the Protestants, especially as we are told the siege of Rochelle occupied seven months out of the eleven. The editors are as cunning as Fox, for they carefully suppress dates where they are necessary, and omit giving the particulars of documents that are easy to be scrutinized.—The terms of this treaty, according to Dr. Heylin, were,—" that all offences should be pardon- " ed to the said three cities, on their submission to the king ; and " that it should be lawful for them to retain the free exercise of " their religion, the people meeting in the same unarmed, and but " few in number ; that all the inhabitants of the said three cities " should be obliged to observe, in all outward matters (except bap- " tism and matrimony) the rights and holidays of the church ; " that the use of the Catholic religion should be restored in the " said cities and all other places, leaving unto the clergy and reli- " gious persons their houses, profits, and revenues ; that Rochelle " should receive a governor of the king's appointment, (but without " garrison) renounce all correspondences and confederacies with fo- " reign princes, and not take part with any of the same religion against " the king ; and finally, that the said three towns should deliver hos-

" tages for the performance of the articles of the present agreement,
" to be changed at the end of every three months, if the king so pleased:
" it was also condescended to in favour of particular persons, that all
" lords of free manors throughout the kingdom might in their own
" houses lawfully celebrate marriage and baptism, after their own
" manner, provided that the assembly exceeded not the number of ten;
" and that there should be no inquisition upon men's consciences, li-
" berty being given to such as had no mind to abide in the kingdom,
" that they might sell their lands and goods, and live where they
" pleased.'

How far the editors are correct in attributing the evils that afflicted
France to the tyranny of Charles IX, let the reader judge, when he has
read the following summary of the conduct of the Hugonots, extracted
from the historian aforesaid.—" Such," he writes, " were the actings
" of the French Calvinians, as well by *secret practices* as *open arms*, dur-
" ing the troublesome reign of Francis the second and Charles the
" ninth, and such their variable fortunes according to the interchanges
" and successes of those broken times, in which for fifteen years toge-
" ther there was nothing to be heard but wars and rumours of wars;
" short intervals of peace, but such as generally were so full of fears
" and jealousies, that they were altogether as unsafe as the wars them-
" selves. So that the greatest calm of peace seemed but a preparation
" to a war ensuing; to which each party was so bent, that of a poison
" it became their most constant food. In which distraction of affairs
" died king Charles the ninth, in the five and twentieth year of his age,
" and fourteenth of his reign, leaving this life at Paris on the 30th of
" May, 1574."—After stating the succession of Henry, the brother of
Charles, to the throne of France, and the policy he acted upon to manage the two parties, the doctor goes on, " About this time (1574),
" when all men stood amazed at these proceedings of the court, the
" state began to swarm with libels and seditious pamphlets, published
" by those of the Hugonot faction, full of reproach, and fraught with
" horrible invectives, not only against the present government, but
" more particularly against the persons of the queen and all her chil-
" dren. Against the authors whereof, when some of the council pur-
" posed to proceed with all severity, the queen-mother interposed her
" power, and moderated by her prudence the intended rigours; affirm-
" ing, as most true it was, that such severity would only gain the greater
" credit to those scurrilous pamphlets, which would otherwise vanish
" of themselves or be soon forgotten. Amongst which pamphlets
" there was none more pestilent than that which was composed in the
" way of a dialogue, pretending one Eusebius Philadelphus for the au-
" thor of it. Buchanan building first upon Calvin's principles, had pub-
" lished his seditious pamphlet *De jure Regni apud Scotos*, together
" with that scurrilous and infamous libel which he called The Detec-
" tion, replete with nothing but reproaches of his lawful sovereign.
" But this Eusebius Philadelphus, or whosoever he was that masked
" himself under that disguise, resolved to go beyond his pattern in all
" the acts of malice, slandering, and sedition; but be outgone by none
" that should follow after him in those ways of wickedness. ... He first
" defames the king and queen in a most scandalous manner, exposes

" next that flourishing kingdom for a prey to strangers; and finally
" lays down such seditious maxims, as plainly tend to the destruction
" of monarchical government. He tells us of the king himself, that he
" was trained up by his tutors in no other qualities than drinking,
" whoring, swearing, and forswearing, frauds, and falsehoods, and what-
" soever else might argue a contempt both of God and godliness; that
" as the court by the example of the king, so by the example of the
" court all the rest of the kingdom was brought into a reprobate sense,
" even to manifest atheism; and that as some of their former kings were
" honoured with the attributes of *fair, wise, debonnaire, well-beloved*, &c.
" so should this king be known by no other name than *Charles the trea-*
" cherous. The duke of Anjou he sets forth in more ugly colours than
" he doth the king, by adding this to all the rest of his brother's vices,
" that he lived in a constant course of incest with his sister the princess
" Margaret, as well before as after her espousal to the king of Navarre.
" For the queen-mother he can find no better names than those of *Frede-*
" gond, Brunechild, Jezabel, and *Messalina;* of which the two first are as
" infamous in the stories of France, as the two latter in the Roman and
" sacred histories. And to expose them all together, he can give the
" queen-mother and her children, (though his natural princes) no more
" cleanly title than that of a *bitch-wolf and her whelps;* affirming, that in
" luxury, cruelty, and perfidiousness, they had exceeded all the tyrants
" of preceding times; which comes up close to those irreverent and
" lewd expressions which frequently occur in Calvin, Beza, Knox, &c.
" in reference to the two Marys, queens of England and Scotland, and
" other princes of that age, which have been formerly recited in their
" proper places. The royal family being thus wretchedly exposed to
" the public hatred; he next applies himself to stir up all the world
" against them both at home and abroad. And first he laboureth to ex-
" cite some desperate zealot to commit the like assassination on the
" king then reigning, as one Bodillus is reported in some French his-
" tories to have committed on the person of Chilprick, one of the last
" kings of the Merovignians, which he commemorates for a noble and
" heroic action, and sets it out for an example and encouragement to
" some gallant Frenchman for the delivery of his country from the ty-
" ranny of the house of Valois, the ruin whereof he mainly drives at in
" his whole design." What can the sensible reader say to this conduct?
Is this the spirit of Christianity? Is this the way to insure the peace of
society, and the security of property? Are these the maxims of the
gospel? Is this the pure light which the reformers had undertaken to
disseminate? If so, can we wonder that the Catholics fled to arms in
defence of their religion and civil rights? Can we be surprised that
outrages were committed, and prejudices excited, when such scenes
were daily exhibited before them, and the happiness of the realm threatened by such outrageous fanatics?

Before we proceed in our review of this book, we will take leave to
observe, that had such been the conduct of the Catholics of England
and Ireland, how many would have been the volumes written to transmit it down to posterity? That they have been represented as such
characters, and from principle too, we have great reason to complain,
but never was the charge fairly fixed upon them; and we can safely

say it never will be. At this moment the Catholics are engaged in a struggle to gain their civil rights and religious freedom, secured to the Irish by a solemn treaty, which was violated almost as soon as signed by "Protestant-ascendency." But in this struggle we see none of those despicable arts and open violences which mark the behaviour of the Hugonots towards their sovereign and country in the sixteenth century. The Catholics certainly pursue their cause with manliness and activity, but it is by peaceable and constitutional means; by reason and argument—by the quill and the tongue and the press—and not by broils, massacres, and perfidiously selling their country to a foreign power. Were the Catholics to resort to such illegal and unjustifiable means, we would be the first to renounce their advocacy; and it is on the same principle that we expose the disgraceful proceedings of Fox's pretended martyrs, who were clearly rebels to their king, and destroyers of their countrymen, and therefore more to be execrated than held up as examples of Christian suffering for the sake of conscience. Conscience, truly! why what conscience could those men have, who could issue forth such slanderous imputations and foul falsehoods as are related by Dr. Heylin in the foregoing passage from his history?

" THE MASSACRE AT VASSY, IN CHAMPAIGNE."

Under this head, the editors of Fox have given us such a delectable specimen of romancing—of a total contempt for the understandings of their readers, and of gullibility in those who give credit to their tales,—that though it is of considerable length, we cannot forbear inserting the whole account, that our readers may have on record one proof at least, of the capacity of "Protestant-ascendency" at lying:—" The duke of " Guise, on his arrival at Joinville, asked, whether the people of Vassy " used to have sermons preached constantly by their minister? It was " answered, they had, and that they increased daily. At the hearing of " which report, he fell into a violent passion; and upon Saturday, the " last day of February, 1562, that he might the more covertly execute " his conceived wrath against the Protestants of Vassy, he departed " from Joinville, accompanied with the cardinal of Guise, his brother, " and those of their train, and lodged in the village of Dammartin, " distant about two miles and a half. The next day, after he had heard " mass very early in the morning, he left Dammartin, with about two " hundred armed men, passing along to Vassy. As he went by the " village of Bronzeval, which is distant from Vassy a quarter of a mile, " the bell (after the usual manner) rang for sermon. The duke hear- " ing it, asked those he met, why the bell rang so loud. A person " named La Montague told him, it was for the assembling of the Hu- " gonots; adding, that there were many in the said Bronzeval who fre- " quented the sermons preached at Vassy; therefore, that the duke " would do well to begin there, and offer them violence. But the duke " answered, ' March on, march on, we shall take them amongst the " rest of the assembly.'

" Now, there were certain soldiers and archers accompanying the " duke, who compassed about Vassy; most of them being lodged in " the houses of Papists. The Saturday before the slaughter, they were " seen to make ready their weapons, arquebuses, and pistols; but *the*

" *faithful* not dreaming of such a conspiracy, thought the duke would
" offer them no violence, being the king's subjects ; also, that not
" above two months before, the duke and his brethren passing by the
" said Vassy, gave no sign of their displeasure.

" The duke of Guise being arrived at Vassy, with all his troops, they
" went directly towards the common-hall or market-house, and then
" entered into the monastery ; where, having called to him one Des-
" sales, the prior of Vassy, and another whose name was Claude le Sain,
" provost of Vassy, he talked a while with them, and issued hastily out
" of the monastery, attended by many of his followers. Then command
" was given to the Papists to retire into the monastery, and not to be
" seen in the streets, unless they would venture the loss of their lives.
" The duke perceiving others of his retinue to be walking to and fro
" under the town hall, and about the church yard, commanded them
" to march on towards the place where the sermon was, being in a
" barn, about an hundred paces distant from the monastery. This com-
" mand was put in execution by such of the company as went on foot.
" He that marched foremost of this rabble, was La Brosse, and on the
" side of these marched the horsemen, after whom followed the duke
" with another company of his own followers, likewise those of the car-
" dinal of Guise, his brother. By this time, Mr. Leonard Morel, the
" minister, after the first prayer, had begun his sermon before his au-
" ditors, who might amount to about twelve hundred men, women, and
" children. The horsemen first approaching to the barn within about
" twenty-five paces, shot off two arquebuses right upon those who were
" placed in the galleries joining to the windows. The people within
" perceiving this, endeavoured to shut the door, but were prevented by
" the ruffians rushing in upon them, who drawing their swords, furiously
" cried out, ' Death of God, kill, kill these Hugonots.'

" Three persons were slain at the door ; and the duke of Guise, with
" his company, rushed in among the congregation, striking the poor
" people down with their swords, daggers and cutlasses, not sparing
" any age or sex : besides, they within were so astonished, that they
" knew not which way to turn them, but running hither and thither,
" fell one upon another, flying as poor sheep before a company of ra-
" vening wolves entering in among the flock. Some of the murderers
" shot off their pieces against them that were in the galleries ; others
" cut in pieces such as they lighted upon ; some had their heads cleft
" in twain, their arms and hands cut off ; so that many of them gave
" up the ghost even in the place. The walls and galleries of the place
" were dyed with the blood of those who were every where murdered :
" yea, so great was the fury of the murderers, that part of the people
" within were forced to break open the roof of the house, in hopes to
" save themselves upon the top thereof. Being got thither, and then
" fearing to fall again into the hands of these cruel tigers, some of them
" leaped over the walls of the city, which were very high, flying into
" the woods and amongst the vines, which with most expedition they
" could soonest attain unto ; some hurt in their arms, others in their
" heads, and other parts of their bodies. The duke presented himself
" in the house with his sword drawn in his hand, charging his men to
" kill especially the young men. Only, in the end, women with child

" were spared. And pursuing those that went upon the house tops,
" they cried, ' Come down, ye dogs, come down !' using many cruel
" threatening speeches to them. The cause why the women with
" child escaped, was, as the report went, for the duchess's sake, his
" wife, who, passing along by the walls of the city, and hearing so
" hideous outcries amongst these poor creatures, with the noise of the
" pieces and pistols continually discharging, sent in all haste to the
" duke, her husband, with much entreaties to cease his persecution, for
" frighting women with child.

" During this slaughter, the cardinal of Guise remained before the
" church of Vassy, leaning upon the walls of the church-yard, looking
" towards the place were his followers were busied in killing and slay-
" ing all they could. Many of this assembly being thus hotly pursued,
" did in the first brunt save themselves upon the roof of the house, not
" being discerned by those who stood without : but at length some of
" this bloody crew espying where they lay hid, shot at them with long
" pieces, wherewith many of them were hurt and slain. The house-
" hold servants of Dessalles, prior of Vassy, shooting at the people on
" the roof, one of that wretched company was not ashamed to boast,
" after the massacre was ended, that he for his part had caused six at
" least to tumble down in that pitiful plight, saying, that if others had
" done the like, not many of them could possibly have escaped.

" The minister, in the beginning of the massacre, ceased not to
" preach, till one discharged his piece against the pulpit where he stood,
" after which, falling down upon his knees, he entreated the Lord not
" only to have mercy upon himself, but also upon his poor persecuted
" flock. Having ended his prayer, he left his gown behind him, think-
" ing thereby to keep himself unknown : but whilst he approached to-
" wards the door, in his fear he stumbled upon a dead body, where he
" received a blow with a sword upon his right shoulder. Getting up
" again, and then thinking to get forth, he was immediately laid hold
" of, and grievously hurt on the head with a sword, whereupon being
" felled to the ground, and thinking himself mortally wounded, he
" cried, ' Lord, into thy hands I commend my spirit, for thou hast re-
" deemed me, thou God of truth.' While he thus prayed, one of this
" bloody crew ran upon him, with an intent to have ham-stringed him ;
" but it pleased God his sword broke in the hilt. Two gentlemen know-
" ing him, said, ' He is the minister, let him be conveyed to my lord
" duke.' These leading him away by both the arms, they brought him
" before the gate of the monastery, from whence the duke, and the
" cardinal his brother, coming forth, said, ' Come hither ;' and asked
" him, saying, ' Art thou the minister of this place ? Who made thee
" so bold to seduce this people thus ?' ' Sir,' said the minister, ' I am
" no seducer, for I have preached to them the gospel of Jesus Christ.'
" The duke perceiving that this answer condemned his cruel outrages,
" began to curse and swear, saying, ' Death of God, doth the gospel
" preach sedition ? Provost, go and let a gibbet be set up, and hang this
" fellow.' At which words the minister was delivered into the hands
" of two pages, who misused him vilely. The women of the city, be-
" ing ignorant Papists, caught up dirt to throw in his face, and with
" great outcries, said, ' Kill him, kill this varlet, who hath been

A REVIEW

OF

Fox's Book of Martyrs,

CRITICAL AND HISTORICAL.

No. 21. Printed and Published by W. E. Andrews, 3, Chapter-house-court, St. Paul's Churchyard, London.   Price 3d.

EXPLANATION OF THE ENGRAVING.—*This cut represents the boarding of a Portuguese vessel, having forty Jesuits on board, bound for South America, to preach to the Indians, by James Sorius, who, for his cruelty to the Catholics, was called the Admiral of Navarre, having received his authority for pirating from Jane d'Albert, the Hugonot queen thereof. On boarding the vessel, the sanguinary commander slew several of the unfortunate Jesuits, and ordered the others to be maimed and cast into the sea. This barbarous mandate was executed with such cruelty, that some of the fathers had their arms cut from their bodies, and some their bowels torn open, before they were thrown into the ocean, and surrendered up their souls to God.*

CONTINUATION OF THE REVIEW.

" the cause of the death of so many.' In the mean time, the duke
" went into the barn, to whom they presented *a great bible*, which they
" used for the service of God. The duke taking it into his hands, call-
" ing his brother the cardinal, said, ' Lo, here is one of the Hugonot
" books.' The cardinal viewing it, said, ' There is nothing but good
" in this book, for it is the bible, to wit, the holy scriptures.' The
" duke being offended, that his brother suited not to his humour, grew
" into a greater rage than before, saying, ' Blood of God, how now?
" What! the holy scripture? It is one thousand five hundred years
" ago since Jesus Christ suffered his death and passion, and it is but a
" year since these books were printed, how then say you that this is the
" gospel? You say you know not what.' This unbridled fury of the
" duke displeased the cardinal, so that he was heard secretly to mut-

" ter, ' An unworthy brother!' This massacre continued a full hour,
" the duke's trumpeters sounding the while two several times. When
" any of these desired to have mercy shewed them for the love of Jesus
" Christ, the murderers in scorn would say unto them, ' You use the
" name of Christ, but where is your Christ now?'

" There died in this massacre, within a few days, threescore persons:
" besides these, there were about two hundred and fifty, as well men
" as women, that were wounded, whereof many died. The poor's box,
" which was fastened to the door of the church with two iron hooks,
" containing twelve pounds, was wrested thence, and never restored.
" The minister was closely confined and frequently threatened to be
" sewed up in a sack and drowned. He was, however, on the 8th of
" May, 1563, liberated at the earnest suit of the prince of Portien."

There reader, now you have gone through this most minute description, tell us if you do not think many of the circumstances related
more than improbable? It is certainly well calculated to excite the
blood of the ignorant fanatic, nor need we wonder that so much prejudice has existed against the Catholics and their religion, when such
tales have remained so long uncontradicted. But let us look a little
closely into this pretended massacre, and examine the circumstances
related by the editors. The account sets out with the duke of Guise
making inquiry whether the minister of the Hugonots preached to his
flock, and being told that he did, and that his flock increased, the duke
falls into a great passion.—Now what occasion had the duke to ask so
silly a question as this, unless indeed this minister was like some of
the ministers of a church we could name established by law. But
though in a passion at the news he heard, he still dissembled his wrath,
that he might the more covertly execute his vengeance on the poor
Protestants of Vassy, and he goes off with his brother, a cardinal, to
some further distance. It does not however appear from authentic sources
that the cardinal was travelling with the duke in this expedition, but it
was necessary to answer the end proposed, to have an ecclesiastic in
the business, and who so proper as a cardinal? As a lie must be told,
the greater it is the better it will go down with some folk. On the
journey some further information is conveyed to the duke about the
preachments of the gospel-diviners, but the duke takes no notice of it.
Now come some archers and soldiers on the stage, who, though they
lodged with Papists, are seen by the Hugonots, or as Fox calls them,
" the faithful," busily occupied in preparing their weapons, and yet,
poor souls, they never dreamed of the use they were about to be put.
Next the duke returns back to Vassy with all his troops, who are made
to pass the common-hall, and are then crammed into a monastery:
very minute indeed. After some conference with the prior, the duke
hastily quits the monastery with many of his followers, and orders all
the Papists into the place he had just quitted, if they wished to save
their lives. We should like to know the size of this monastery, and
the number of Papists that entered it; for we cannot help thinking the
monastery must have been a pretty large place to contain all the Papists of Vassy, as well as some of the duke's retinue. Well, matters
being thus arranged with the Papists, and having got " the faithful,"
who all along suspected nothing amiss, safely housed and at prayers,

the work of mischief commences, and the description is so truly pathetic and pointed, that we know not which to admire most, the hypocrisy or the impudence of the relater. The Hugonots were assembled in *a barn*, to the number of twelve hundred men, women and children; they were first attacked by a body of horse, who advanced within about twenty-five paces, and then fired off *two* arquebuses right upon the people, who were placed in galleries joining to the windows.—*Windows and galleries* in *a barn!!!* mind that reader. A barn fitted up with galleries and windows by the Hugonots! What will come next? Well, whether these *two* shots did any mischief, we are not told; but the people ran to shut *the door*, lest any more shots should come in at the windows. In this, however, they were disappointed, for the ruffians anticipated them, and rushing in, cried, "Death of God, kill these Hu-"gonots." "Death of God!" what is the meaning of these words? There is something so outlandish in the term, that we wish the sapient editors had thought it worth their while to define it. Now then begins the work of slaughter. *Three* persons are slain at the door, and in rushes the duke himself with his company of murderers—they cut away right and left—swords, daggers, and cutlasses are put in requisition—neither age nor sex is spared—the *galleries* are again attacked—some have their heads cut in twain, some their arms and hands cut off—the fury of the murderers is without bounds—the walls are died with blood —the poor creatures are induced to break through the roof of the *house*, (by what means they could do this we are not informed, and it is difficult to conjecture)—they accomplish their ends, but are still so frightened that they JUMP OVER THE WALLS OF THE CITY, though very high, and fly into the woods amongst the vines, which they no sooner reach than they are maimed in their heads and other parts of their bodies, but we do not learn whether any of them are killed. Next the duke is introduced into *the house*, where he employs himself in "charging his men to kill especially the young men. Only *in the end* "women with child were spared." From this we may presume they were *not* spared in the *beginning*. This act of mercy is attributed to the duchess, who sent to the duke in great haste to know what he meant by frightening women with child. The story however is not yet complete. The cardinal now appears upon the boards, and his followers are occupied in shooting such of the poor fellows as fled *to the tops of the houses for safety*, and were afraid, we presume, to jump over the high walls, for fear of breaking their necks. Next the *household servants* of the *prior* are brought forward, one of whom was so clever as to tumble six of them down from the house top. Now comes the minister upon the carpet. He, good man, went on with his prayers, which having completed, he doffs off his gown, thinking thereby to escape with a whole skin. In this, however, he is mistaken, for he is wounded on the shoulder and on the head; and escaped being hamstringed through the miraculous interposition of two gentlemen, and the sword of the assailant snapping asunder. These gentlemen take the minister, faint and bleeding, by both arms, and lead him to the duke, who is now got to the monastery along with the cardinal his brother. Here he is questioned at the gate of the monastery, after receiving a sword wound on the head and shoulder, which he apprehended to be mortal, by one of the party, but whether the duke or the cardinal we cannot discover. Being called a seducer, he denies the insinuation, and declares himself to be a preacher of the gospel of Jesus Christ. So do many a tinker and cobbler at this day, and like them this minister does not tell us what doctrines he preached, but contents himself with saying he is a preacher. This answer makes the duke ashamed of himself, the story tells us, and in a passion he charges the minister with preaching sedition, and orders him to be hanged. This done, two pages get hold of the minister, and the women, Papist women, pelt him with dirt. While this is going on, the duke is conveyed into *the barn*, though we might have supposed that what with the killing and slaying, and with the destruction of the roof to escape, the barn must have been choked up with rubbish and dead bodies. However, the duke goes into the barn, and there, reader, he is presented with A BIBLE, used for the service of God. How this bible came to escape the fury of the Papists is more than wonderful, and what is still more wonderful, the two brothers, the duke and cardinal, though stanch Papists, quarrel about this book; the cardinal saying there is nothing but good in it, and the duke flying into a rage to hear his brother say so. The rage of the duke displeases the cardinal, and the latter is heard to mutter, " An unworthy brother ! ! !" Was ever such nonsense dressed up in any other country but England to tickle the prejudices of the poor ignorant people ?

Well, reader, you have now seen how much has been done by these unbridled bloody Papists. They assault the barn, they detroy the people in it, and make them break through the roof of the barn; they cause the people to jump over high walls, hunt them out of the vineyards, amuse themselves by shooting at the Hugonots on the house tops, and how long do you suppose this dreadful massacre lasted ? Why the relater says, just ONE HOUR—only sixty minutes, by his watch, " the duke's trumpeters sounding the while *two* several times." Then again look at the number of the slain, notwithstanding the desperate fury said to have been displayed by the Papists, there were just threescore died *within a few days*, so that there were scarcely any slain outright, though such terrible havock is stated to have been made among the Hugonots. Then there were two hundred and fifty *wounded* whereof *many died*; so that here is a *double* return of killed and wounded for a single massacre; and to make the measure of iniquity more full, these rascally Papist murderers run away with the *poor box* of their own *church*; notwithstanding it was fastened with *two iron* hooks; and though it was never restored, John Fox or his modern editors received information that there were exactly *twelve pounds* in cash therein, though the French reckon their sums by francs. Who will hereafter give credit to this tale ? Is there an individual that will believe this random story now we have dissected it ? Why Tom Thumb and Jack the Giant-killer carry more probability in the incidents related of these heroes than the tale of the massacre of Vassy by John Fox.

But, reader, what will you say to the impudence, the shameless effrontery, to the barefaced deception of the relaters of this pretended massacre, which is placed in this *Book of Martyrs* as arising out of the massacre of Paris—as subsequent to the latter deed; what, we say, will you think of these " few plain Christians," who have published this book for the pretended purpose of enlightening their readers;—what will you think of their pretensions to honesty and veracity, when we tell you that the event thus related by Fox or his editors with such flourishing imagery, is no other than the affair mentioned by us in page 308, originating in a scuffle between the duke of Guise's servants and some hot-headed Hugonots, and taking place some ten years previous to the Paris slaughter. This very circumstance, too, which is here made a matter of cruelty and bloodthirstiness against the Catholics, is stated by Dr. Heylin to have been purely accidental, and was made a pretence by the Hugonots to fill the kingdom of France with blood and rapine, the pollution of churches, defacing of altars and images, and the destruction of monasteries. So dexterous are the calumniators of Catholics in turning their own cruelties and outrages on their adversaries. Similarly fictitious and absurd are the rest of the tales related under this section; and one in particular, detailing the pretended martyrdom of a woman, the wife of a jeweller, named Philip le Doux, of what town or city no one knoweth, is so shockingly indecent and improbable, that we cannot soil our pages with the recital. This woman is represented as on the point of child-birth; the midwife is in attendance, a knocking is heard at the door, and entrance demanded in the king's name; the wife of the jeweller, not the midwife, reader, goes to open the door; " the furies," as the story terms them, enter, stab the husband, and prepare to serve the wife the same, but the midwife entreats them to stay till the child is born. In spite of the midwife's entreaties, they thurst a dagger into the wife's body up to the hilt, and in this state, finding she is *mortally wounded*; who would not suppose her to have been killed outright?—in this state she runs into *a hay-loft* to give birth to the infant, followed by " the furies," who again stab her in the belly, and throw her out of the window into the street, the fall from which gives birth to the child, " to the great astonishment and confusion of " the Papists"!!! Astonishment and confusion, indeed! Not, reader, at the deed detailed, because it is palpably forged and fictitious; but at the impudence of those who could attempt to palm such a lie upon the people of England, and the stupidity of that people in giving credit to such a barefaced improbable falsehood.

Another instance of falsehood dressed to please the taste of credulity and diabolical bigotry is thus related: " Not many months after, " when these tragedies were ended, the pope sent cardinal Ursin, as " legate to the king, who was received with great solemnity at Ly- " ons. On his return from St. John's church, where he had been to " hear mass, a great number of persons presented themselves before " him, at the door, and kneeled down for his absolution. But the le- " gate not knowing the reason of it, one of the leaders told him, they " were those who had been the actors in the massacre. On which " the cardinal immediately absolved them all." The subject of absolution has been a fertile source of slander and misrepresentation on the part of bigotry to malign the Catholic religion, and we wonder that Fox and the " few plain Christians" have not availed themselves more frequently on this point. Absolution is an essential part of the sacrament of penance, and is of divine institution. The reformation, as it is called, abrogated penitential works, and made the road to heaven as smooth and as easy as the most voluptuous epicurean could wish; while the Catholic church, ever guided by the Holy Spirit and unalterable in her doctrine, continued, and still continues, to hold fast what she has received from her Divine Founder through the apostles. The church of England as by law established, rejected the sacrament of penance, but she retains the form of absolution in her ritual, and acknowledges that Christ has " left power to his church to " absolve all sinners who truly repent and believe in him." So believes the Catholic. He admits the power of the church to absolve from sin, but the church enacts certain conditions before she consents to confer this grace. These conditions are, a hearty and sincere sorrow for the offence committed, a firm resolution of amendment of life, and a pledge to perform such religious acts as the absolver shall require. On these conditions absolution is given, and without this necessary disposition every Catholic knows the absolution would be null and void. But here, in this relation, the people are represented as kneeling down for absolution as a matter of course, and to a person too who is ignorant of what is craved. Then one of the leaders whispers into the ears of the cardinal that the humble petitioners were no other characters than the murderers of the Hugonots, and immediately the boon is granted without any further formality. There is one thing, however, in this statement, which Fox and his editors have overlooked. We have contended, that persecution never was a principle of Catholic faith, and that it is not, we think, is clearly shewn in this relation of the *Book of Martyrs.* Were it a principle of Catholic doctrine to persecute and murder heretics or Hugonots or Protestants, or any that differ from the church in faith, such deeds must be considered meritorious, and therefore not requiring absolution, which is only given to sinners; consequently, these "actors in the massacre" must have been conscious that they had not only transgressed the laws of God, but had placed themselves under the bans of the church, or why require an acquital or discharge for the offence from a minister of the church? Had indeed the editors said they asked the cardinal for his *blessing* instead of *absolution*, the statement might have passed off without detection, though we can never be brought to believe that such a sanction would ever be given by a minister of the Catholic church to murder in any shape, much so by wholesale; but by enlarging too much, the " plain Christians" have clearly convicted themselves of falsehood; they have placed themselves in a dilemma out of which they will find it difficult to get extricated.

Of the sufferers stated to have been put to death in this pretended persecution, we do not find that many of them made a profession of their faith, and therefore it is difficult to know what they believed. It is true, some of them are charged with absenting themselves from mass, and others for singing psalms, but in general the charges are so vague and confused, as to render it extremely difficult to learn, as we just observed, whether they belonged to any church or no church. To us, supposing them to be real characters, they appear to be a set of ignorant fanatics and extravagant enthusiasts, incapable of defining what they professed, and professing the wildest notions that ever dis-

turbed the brain of man. We find, however, that the whole of them
are represented by the *Book of Martyrs* to have been *deeply learned in
the scriptures*, which must have been by inspiration, as the editions of
the scriptures at that time, in the vulgar tongue, were all incorrect, and
it is a matter of great doubt whether many of these gospel martyrs
could read at all. To shew the skill of these reformers in biblical
lore, we will here cite a passage from the relation of the burning of
" Robert Oguier, his wife, and two sons," at Lisle, in the year 1556.—
The provost of Lisle, with his sergeants, we are told, armed themselves on the 6th of March, in that year, at *ten* o'clock at night, (see
how exact our martyrologists can be to time) to make a search after
Protestants, but none were assembled at their *houses*. They came,
however, to the *house* of Robert Oguier, which *house* we are further
informed " was a LITTLE CHURCH, where both *rich* and *poor* were
" *familiarly* INSTRUCTED in the *scriptures*." From this statement
we may infer that *self*-interpretation had not then been discovered, since
it is here avowed that the rich and poor were equally and freely instructed, that is, *taught* to understand the scriptures. Now whether
Robert Oguier was the teacher of the rich and poor, as well as the
owner of the house-church, or church-house, which you like, we are not
told; but we do hope that the " few plain Christians," and their fellow-
labourers in the work of deception, the bible-distributors, will no
longer be angry with, and abuse the Catholic clergy for familiarly instructing the rich and poor of their church in the scriptures. If the
gospel-reformers were at liberty to *instruct* the rich and poor of their
sect, in 1556, surely the priests of the Catholic church ought to
have the same freedom of action *now* as they had before the period
named, notwithstanding the parsons of another church established by
law, and the preachers of divers sects established by *folly*, have got it
into their heads that the people ought to interpret the bible themselves, and pay them at the same time to do it. But to proceed.—
When the provost and his sergeants entered Oguier's house, they found
certain books which they carried away, but the principal person they
wanted, that is Robert Oguier's son, was not in the way, he being
" gone abroad to commune and talk of the work of God with some of
" his brethren." Yet, strange to tell, he came home just in the nick
of time to be caught, and so foolish was this wiseacre in scripture
divination, that though his brother Martin (not Luther, reader) watched
his return to warn him of his fate, he was bent on destruction, and
got it into his head that his brother mistook him for some one else.
So in he went, and fell into the hands of the sergeants. Thus obtaining
the principal object of their search, they laid hold of the whole of the
family in the emperor's name; however they left " the two daughters
to look to the house," which was very kind of them; the rest were
taken to prison. What was afterwards done we must give in the martyrologist's own words. " A few days after, the prisoners were
" brought before the magistrates, and examined concerning their
" course of life. They first charged Robert Oguier with not only
" absenting himself from the celebration of mass, but with dissuading
" others from attending it, and 'maintaining conventicles' in his
" house. He confessed the first charge, and justified his conduct *by*

" *proving from the scriptures* that the saying of *mass was contrary to.*
" *the ordinances of Jesus Christ, and a mere human institution;* and he.
" defended the religious meetings in his house by showing that they.
" were authorized and commanded by our blessed Saviour himself."
Thus then it appears the gospel-reformers of those days, like the bible-
distributors in our own, objected to the sacrifice of the mass, as an
human institution, and they shewed, it is said, from *scripture* that they
were *authorized* and *commanded* by our Saviour himself to hold religious
meetings in their houses. What wonderful scripturists the pretended
reformation has produced. They are so deeply versed in the art of
interpretation, that they can shew us what is not to be seen, and make
that of human origin which was instituted by God himself.

Well here we have something in the shape of doctrine. The mass
is proved from scripture by these reformers and martyrs to be contrary to the ordinances of Jesus Christ. But how then came the primitive martyrs to believe and prove from scripture that the mass *was*
an ordinance of Christ, and enforced by his apostles. By referring to
page 40 of our Review, it will be seen that St. Ignatius, recorded by
Fox as a holy martyr, held the doctrine of the mass as of divine institution. St. Justin, martyr, did the same, see pages 49, 50. St. Irenæus, described by Fox as a " zealous opposer of heresies in general"
maintained the same faith regarding the mass as Catholics did in the
sixteenth century and now do in the eighteenth, see page 71, and gave
proofs from scripture for the same. Now we must suppose that a saint
so learned as St. Irenæus was, ought to know the sense of scripture
as well as Robert Oguier and his sons, and as the former was a " zea-
" lous opposer of heresies in general," and held the doctrine of the
mass, master Oguier must have been in *error*, for it is effrontery in the.
extreme to say that two opposite doctrines are to be proved from
scripture at two distant periods. What was the word of God in the
time of St. Irenæus was the word of God in the time of Robert Oguier,
because God is Truth itself and is unchangeable. Therefore since
Fox says that St. Irenœus was a " zealous opposer of heresies in ge-
" neral," and it is proved from his writings that he was a strenuous advocate for the divine institution of the mass, the doctrine of the modern editors of Fox, that the mass is of human institution is FALSE
and HERETICAL, and poor Robert Oguier and his sons were false
teachers. It is very easy for John Fox or his modern editors
to assert that Robert Oguier, in the year 1556, proved from scripture that the " mass was contrary to the ordinances of Jesus Christ
" and a mere *human* institution;" but the man of common sense will
very aptly inquire, If this be the case,—how came the primitive Christians to believe this ceremony of the mass to be of *divine* institution,
received from the apostles? How came it about that every nation, on
embracing Christianity, embraced the doctrine of the mass at the same
time, as an ordinancee of Christ? And if the mass be of mere human
invention, why not tell us by whom it was first invented, in what age,
and in what country? These questions the " few plain Christians"
will find very difficult to answer; but answer them they must, before
they can overthrow the Catholic doctrine of the mass.

Besides the testimonies before referred to, there are many others who stand high in the estimation of John Fox, and, of course, his modern editors likewise. Of this number we must rank St. Cyprian, bishop of Carthage, in the third century. This great divine is one of Fox's martyrs, and recounted by him " an eminent prelate, and a pious ornament " of the church. His doctrines were ORTHODOX and PURE," Fox says; " his language easy and elegant; and his manners graceful." Well then, surely such an ornament of the church must be better qualified to expound the scripture, and understand its right sense, than Robert Oguier's son, or Robert Oguier himself, and as St. Cyprian's doctrines were *orthodox* and *pure*, neither Fox nor his modern editors can dispute them. Let us then see what St. Cyprian says of the mass. " Although I am sensible," he writes, " that most bishops, set over the " churches of God, hold to the maxims of evangelical truth and divine " tradition, and depart not, by any human and innovating discovery, " from that which Christ our master taught and did; yet as some, " through ignorance or simplicity, in the sanctification of the cup of " the Lord, and in delivering it to the people, do not that, which Jesus " Christ, our Lord and God, *the teacher and founder of this sacrifice,* " himself did and taught; therefore, I judge it necessary to write to " you, in order that, if there be any one still in that error, when he " sees the light of truth, he may return to the root and fountain of " Christian tradition." Then proceeding to the point, he says : " Be " then advised, that, in offering the cup, the rule, *ordained by Christ,* " be followed, that is, that the cup, which is offered in commemoration " of him, be wine mixed with water. For as he said : *I am the true* " *vine;* not water; but wine, is the blood of Christ. And what is in " the chalice cannot be thought the blood, by which we obtained re-" demption and life, if wine be wanting, whereby that blood is shewn, " which, as all the scriptures attest, was shed." *Ep.* lxiii. p. 148, " In " the priest Melchisedech we see prefigured the sacrament of the " Christian sacrifice, the holy scriptures declaring : *Melchisedec king of* " *Salem brought forth bread and wine; and he was the priest of the most* " *high God, and he blessed Abraham.* (Gen. xiv.) And that he bore the " resemblance of Christ, the Psalmist announces : *Thou art a priest for* " *ever according to the order of Melchisedec.* (Ps. cix.) This order thus " comes and descends from that sacrifice; that Melchisedec was the " priest of the Most High; that he offered bread and wine; and that " he blessed Abraham. And who was so much a priest of the most " high God, as our Lord Jesus Christ? He offered sacrifice to God the " Father; he offered the same as did Melchisedec, that is, bread and " wine, his own body and blood: and the blessing given to Abraham, " now applies to our people." " But, in the book of Genesis, that the " blessing given to Abraham might be properly celebrated, the repre-" sentation of the sacrifice of Christ, appointed in bread and wine, pre-" cedes it; which our Lord perfecting and fulfilling it, himself offered " in bread and wine; and thus he who is the plenitude, fulfilled the " truth of the prefigured image." Ibid. p. 149.—He afterwards adds : " If Jesus Christ, our Lord and God, be himself the high priest of his " Father; and if he first offered himself a sacrifice to him, and com-" manded the same to be done in remembrance of him; then that priest " truly stands in the place of Christ, who imitates that which Christ

" did, and then offers in the church a true and complete sacrifice
" to God the Father, doing what he ordained. For the whole disci-
" pline of religion and of truth is subverted, if that which was
" commanded be not faithfully complied with.'" Ibid. p. 155.—
Here then we find this *orthodox* martyr of the third century declaring
that Jesus Christ, our Lord and GOD, was *the teacher* and *founder of
this sacrifice*, and consequently the mass *was* of *divine* institution, and an
ordinance of our blessed Saviour. What then becomes of Robert
Oguier's doctrine? Could he be right and St. Cyprian too? Is there
not a great inconsistency between these two expounders of scripture?
Who then are we to believe? Common sense will tell us, he who had
the testimony of the apostles and their successors received in all ages
and all nations, and not the fanciful reveries of a no one knows who.

BOOK VII.

" FARTHER ACCOUNT OF THE PERSECUTIONS IN FOREIGN COUNTRIES."

SECTION I.

" PERSECUTIONS IN BOHEMIA AND GERMANY."

We are now going back to the fourteenth century, for "the few
plain Christians" seem to pay as little regard to *order* as they do to
truth. The preceding book treated on the real and pretended enormities of the sixteenth century in France; the present takes us into
Bohemia and Germany two centuries prior to the reformation so called,
when printing too was not invented and the records of passing events
very circumscribed. Nevertheless the statements are made with as
much precision, but with as little regard to truth as in the former case.
Before we proceed with our remarks we will here give the opening account of the *Book of Martyrs* of this part of church history. "The se-
" verity exercised by the Roman Catholics over the reformed Bohe-
" mians, induced the latter to send two ministers and four laymen to
" Rome, in the year 977, to seek redress from the pope. After some
" delay their request was granted, and their grievances redressed.
" Two things in particular were permitted to them, viz. to have divine
" service in their own language, and to give the cup in the sacrament
" to the laity. The disputes, however, soon broke out again, the suc-
" ceeding popes exerting all their power to resume their tyranny over
" the minds of the Bohemians; and the latter, with great spirit, aiming
" to preserve their religious liberties.
" Some zealous friends of the gospel applied to Charles, king of
" Bohemia, A. D. 1375, to call a council for an inquiry into the abuses
" that had crept into the church, and to make a thorough reformation.
" Charles, at a loss how to proceed, sent to the pope for advice; the
" latter, incensed at the affair, only replied, ' Punish severely those
" presumptuous and profane heretics.' The king, accordingly, ba-
" nished every one who had been concerned in the application; and to
" show his zeal for the pope, laid many additional restraints upon the
" reformed Christians of the country.
" The martyrdom of John Huss and Jerome of Prague, greatly in-
" creased the indignation of the believers, and gave animation to their

" cause. These two great and pious men were condemned by order
" of the council of Constance, when fifty-eight of the principal Bohe-
" mian nobility interposed in their favour. Nevertheless they were
" burnt; and the pope, in conjunction with the council of Constance,
" ordered the Romish clergy, every where, to excommunicate all who
" adopted their opinions, or murmured at their fate. In consequence
" of these orders, great contentions arose between the Papists and
" reformed Bohemians, which produced a violent persecution against
" the latter. At Prague it was extremely severe, till, at length, the
" reformed, driven to desperation, armed themselves, attacked the
" senate-house, and cast twelve of its members, with the speaker,
" out of the windows. The pope, hearing of this, went to Florence,
" and publicly excommunicated the reformed Bohemians, excit-
" ing the emperor of Germany and all other kings, princes, dukes,
" &c. to take up arms, in order to extirpate the whole race; promising,
" by way of encouragement, full remission of all sins to the most
" wicked person who should kill one Bohemian Protestant. The re-
" sult of this was a bloody war; for several Popish princes undertook
" the extirpation, or at least expulsion, of the proscribed people:
" while the Bohemians, arming themselves, prepared to repel them in
" the most vigorous manner. The Popish army prevailing against
" the Protestant forces at the battle of Cuttenburgh, they conveyed
" their prisoners to three deep mines near that town, and threw seve-
" ral hundreds into each, where they perished in a miserable manner."

We have here as gross and confused a misrepresentation of history
as we ever recollect to have met with, even in our research through
this mass of lies and slander. The reader is here told by Fox, that the
reformed Bohemians were induced, as early as the year 977, to send a
deputation to Rome to obtain redress from the pope against the severities exercised on them by the Roman Catholics. But how came
the *reformed* Bohemians to think of seeking redress from the pope?
Did they acknowledge his supremacy? If so, were they not Roman
Catholics as well as those who persecuted them? The grievances
complained of and redressed, Fox says, were, " to have divine servicein
" their own language, and to give the cup in the sacrament to the
" laity." Now it does not appear, from the authorities within our
reach, that the receiving of the cup was a matter of dispute at the
period named, and Fox has wholly mistaken the time regarding the
liturgy. The Bohemians were converted to the Catholic faith somewhere about the latter end of the ninth century, by SS. Cyril and Methodius, who, says the Rev. Alban Butler, in his account of the lives of
these two saints, " translated the liturgy into the Sclavonian tongue,
" and instituted mass to be said in the same. The archbishop of Saltz-
" burg, and the archbishop of Mentz, jointly with their suffragans,
" wrote two letters, still extant, to pope John VIII. to complain of this
" novelty introduced by the archbishop Methodius. Hereupon the
" pope, in 878, by two letters, one addressed to Tuvantarus, count of
" Moravia, and the other to Methodius, whom he styles archbishop
" of Pannonia, cited the latter to come to Rome, forbidding him in the
" mean time to say mass in a barbarous tongue. Methodius obeyed,
" and repairing to Rome, gave ample satisfaction to the pope, who

" confirmed to him the privileges of the archiepiscopal see of the Mo-
" ravians, declared him exempt from all dependence on the archbishop
" of Saltzburg, and approved for the Sclavonians the use of the liturgy
" and breviary in their own tongue, as he testifies in his letter to count
" Sfendopulk, still extant.   It is clear from the letters of pope John,
" and from the two lives of this saint, that this affair had never been
" discussed either by pope Nicholas or pope Adrian, as Bona and some
" others have mistaken.   The Sclavonian tongue is to this day used in
" the liturgy in that church.   The Sclavonian missal was revised by an
" order of Urban VIII. in 1631, and his brief and approbation are pre-
" fixed to this missal printed at Rome in 1745, at the expense of the
" congregation De Propagandâ Fide.   By the same congregation, in
" 1688, was printed at Rome, by order of Innocent XI. the Sclavonian
" breviary, with the brief of Innocent X. prefixed, by which it is ap-
" proved and enjoined.   The Sclavonians celebrate the liturgy in this
" tongue at Leghorn, Aquileia, and in other parts of Italy."

As this is a very interesting subject, and little known to the generality of readers, we will here give a few further extracts from Mr. A.
Butler's work, by which it will be seen how careful the church has
ever been to preserve the purity and consistency of her liturgy in all
ages.   " The Sclavonian tongue," writes Mr. B. in a note to SS. Cyril,
&c. " is used in the liturgy by the churches of Dalmatia and Illyricum
" who follow the Latin rite ; and by those of the Russians, Muscovites,
" and Bulgarians, who follow the Greek rite.   And by this the Russian
" and Sclavonian rites are distinguished.   The use of the Sclavonian
" language in the liturgy and office of the church is approved in the
" synod of Zamosci in 1720, under Clement XI. confirmed by Innocent
" XIII. and by Benedict XIV.   Inter Plures Const. 98, datâ an. 1744 in
" his Bullary, (t. i. p. 376.)   The sacred use of that tongue both in
" those Sclavonian churches which follow the Greek, and in those
" which follow the Latin rite was approved by John VIII. Urban VIII.
" Innocent X. and by Benedict XIV.   Const. 66.   Esti dubitare non
" possumus. an. 1742, in his Bullar, t. i. p. 217.   Whence in Moravia,
" Dalmatia, and Illyricum, in some places mass and the divine offices
" are celebrated in the Sclavonian tongue ; in others in Latin, but in
" several of these, after the gospel has been read in Latin, it is again
" read to the people in a Sclavonian translation.   (See Jos. Assemani
" Præf. in t. iv. comm. in Kalendaria Univ. t. iv. par. 2, c. 4. p. 4416.)
" Pope Benedict XIV. confirms this approbation of the Sclavonian li-
" turgy.   Const. Ex pastorali munere. anno 1754.   As he had before
" confirmed the use of the Greek tongue in the liturgy and divine of-
" fices to the Italian Greeks, and Greek Melchites.   Const. 57. Et si
" Pastoralis, and Const. 87. Demandatum cœlitus, in his Bullary, (t. i.
" p. 167 and 290.)   A synod held at Spalatro, under John the archbi-
" shop of Salona, (which see was soon after translated to Spalatro) and
" Maynard, the pope's legate, about the year 1070, forbid the use of
" the Sclavonian tongue in the divine office, which decree was con-
" firmed by Alexander II. but this must be restrained to the churches
" lying toward Poland and Moravia, or it was never carried into execu-
" tion.   Even in the diocess of Spalatro itself ten chapters and colle-
" giate churches, besides thirty parishes, celebrate mass and the divine

" office in the Sclavonian tongue, as we are assured by Orbinus, (n. 32.)
" quoted by Caraman, the learned archbishop of Jadra, Diss. De Lin-
" guâ Sclavicâ literali indivinis celebrandis, (n. 32.) The same is tes-
" tified by Robert Sala, (Observations ad card. Bona Rer. Liturg. l. i.
" c. 9. § 4. p. 152.) who adds, that in the aforesaid diocess only eight
" parishes use the Latin tongue in the church. Pope Gregory VII.
" forbid the use of the Sclavonian tongue in the mass, but to the Bo-
" hemians, (l. 7. ep. 2. ad Uratislaum Bohemiæ Ducem.) The grant
" of John VIII. for the sacred use of this tongue was obtained by St.
" Methodius after the death of his brother Cyril, and was never ex-
" tended to Poland and Bohemia. Whence it was prohibited when
" some began to introduce it there, probably Moravian priests, whose
" kingdom was extinguished by the Turks, that is, Hungarians in the
" tenth age, as Constantine Porphyrogenetta relates.

" Cardinal Bona, among other mistakes on this head, calls this Scla-
" vonian the Illyrican tongue. (Liturg. l. 1. c. 9. § 4.) Whereas this
" name can only be given to the modern dialect of the Sclavonian now
" in use in that country. The Sclavonian which is allowed in the
" liturgy, is the ancient Sclavonian, mother of the modern dialects, and
" called the Sclavonian language of the schools or of the learned. 'Idio-
" mate, quod nunc Sclavum literale appellant.' says Benedict XIV.
" which Urban VIII. and Innocent X. &c. also express. Caraman, af-
" terwards archbishop of Jadra, revised the breviary and missal of this
" rite, printed at Rome in 1741, according to the rules of the ancient Scla-
" vonian tongue, of which a dictionary is extant for the use of their cler-
" gy, called *Azbuquidarium*, that is, Abecedarium. There is also a gram-
" mar of the same, composed by Smotriski, a Russian Basilian monk,
" printed at Vilna in 1619, and at Moscow in 1721, &c. How much the
" ancient Sclavonian, or that of the Litterati, differs from all the modern
" dialects derived from it, appears from specimens of them exhibited
" from the different translations of the bible given by Le Long, (Bibl.
" Sacra. t. 1. art. 6. sect. i. ii. iii. iv. v. p. 435, &c.) and of the Lord's
" prayer given in thirteen dialects of the Sclavonian tongue, (ibid.) and
" in Reland, (ad calcem partis iii. diss. Miscell.)

" The learned cardinal Stanislas Hosius, bishop of Warmia in Poland,
" (Dial. De Sacro. Vernacule Legendo) observes, that though the Bo-
" hemians, Moravians, Poles, Muscovites, Russians, Bosnians, Servi-
" ans, Croatians, Bulgarians, and some other nations use the Sclavo-
" nian tongue, (which is extended through one quarter of Europe,) yet
" these dialects differ so much, that a Pole understands no more of the
" language of a Dalmatian than a high German, or a native of Switzer-
" land, understands the low Dutch. This author thinks the Sclavonian
" the most extensive of all languages; but the Arabic reaches much
" farther, being used not only by the Christians who inhabit Arabia,
" Syria and Egypt, but also by the Mahometans in Asia, Africa, and a
" considerable part of Europe. The church, to prevent the frequent
" changes to which the modern languages are subject, allows in her
" office only the Chaldaic or modern Hebrew, which is the ancient sa-
" cred language; the Greek, the language of the philosophers and all
" the Oriental schools; Latin, the language of the learned in the West,
" and the Sclavonian. Herbinius (de Religiosis Kioviensibus Chryp-

"tis) contends that it is a primitive language, being the mother of the
" Russian, Muscovite, Polish, Vandallic, Bohemian, Croatian, Dalma-
" tian, Valachian, and Bulgarian. It is esteemed that it holds a mid-
" dle place between the Hebrew and other Oriental languages, and
" those used in the West; and it suits all climates. Some add, that it
" seems most adapted of all others to be made a universal language.
" Some have attributed the Sclavonian alphabet and translation of the
" bible to St. Jerom, but erroneously. For the Latin was in his time
" the language of that country; and this St. Jerom calls his transla-
" tion into his own tongue, as Banduri (Animadv. in Constant. Porphy-
" rog. de administ. imper. p. 117.) takes notice. The Sclavonian let-
" ters have no affinity with the Gothic; but were invented by St. Cyril
" and Methodius, who derived them from the large Greek alphabet.
" The Sclavonians have another alphabet of smaller characters for com-
" mon use, particularly in esteem in Dalmatia, Carniola, and Istria;
" also a third alphabet almost wholly different, which they seem to have
" borrowed from the Croatians and Servians. This last is falsely as-
" cribed to St. Jerom. (See Cohlij Introductio in Historiam Sclavorum;
" Jos. Assemani, l. 4.) Of all the Sclavonian dialects the Polish has
" been most cultivated. The Lithuanians are of a very different ex-
" traction, as their language, which is a dialect of the Sarmatian, de-
" monstrates.'

So much for the liturgy in their own tongue; now as to the tyranny
of the popes over the Bohemians. When Fox made, this charge why
did he not state some of the acts of oppression committed by the popes,
instead of contenting himself with generalities? Surely he could have
furnished us with some specific case to enable us to judge how far the
popes were deserving of censure, and how far the people merited praise.
It might have so happened that the people of Bohemia were deluded
by false teachers and false prophets, as the people of England have
been long duped, and by none more so than by this *Book of Martyrs*;
and this we are convinced, would be found to have been the case in
Bohemia, if we could come at the facts alluded to by Fox. It is not
every struggle of the people that leads to liberty, either civil or religious; for what were the struggles during the unhappy reign of our
Charles the first, but the struggles of one party to oppress the other,
and not to establish a system of freedom, which their ancestors enjoyed
in full plenitude, before the pretended reformation was begun by the
cruel and lascivious Henry the eighth. It too often happens that the
people lend themselves to designing men, who raise the cry of liberty
to gratify their own passions, which was the case with John Huss,
Jerome of Prague, Luther, Calvin, and other pretended reformers, and
the people *lost* their liberty instead of preserving it. From the year 977
Fox makes a skip to the year 1375, when a few " zealous friends of the
gospel," are introduced as applying to Charles, king of Bohemia, to
call a council to make an inquiry into abuses, and effect a reformation
in the church. This request, we are told, embarrasses Charles, who
not knowing what to do, applies to the pope for advice, and is instantly
recommended to " punish severely those profane and presumptuous
" heretics." Accordingly, it is said, the king banished all those who
had been concerned in making the application to him, and laid addi-

tional restraints upon the *reformed* Christians of the country. Now, we must here ask, *who* were these " zealous friends of the gospel ?" Had they not a name ? Why not give us the names and places of abode, the rank they held in society, and other particulars necessary to come at the truth ? The fact is, at the time stated by Fox, there were no reformed Christians in Bohemia, but all were Roman Catholics. It was not till fifty years after, when John Huss and Jerome of Prague began to dogmatize, that Bohemia became disturbed with religious fanaticism and fury. Fox tells us that the martyrdom of these two men increased the indignation of the believers, and gave animation to their cause. Indeed! But why not submit with resignation and true courage, like the primitive Christians ? Why not bear patiently the strokes of the executioner for conscience sake ? Oh, no! such a disposition, which distinguished the primitive martyrs, and excited so much admiration in the Pagans, that many of them became Christians, never influenced the *reformers* of the gospel. They flew to the sword, and according to the predictions of Christ, they have perished by the sword.

Fox states, that in consequence of the condemnation of Huss and Jerome by the council of Constance, and the excommunication of their followers, "contentions arose between the Papists and the reformed "Bohemians, which produced a violent persecution against the latter;" and he proceeds to give a detail of some of the consequences. Now the fact is, the doctrines of Jerome and Huss, like those of Wickliff in England, of which we shall have occasion to say something hereafter, aimed destruction against society under the cloak of religion. Had Jerome or Huss preached this doctrine to the Americans at the present day, they would have been sentenced most probably to death, but certainly to banishment or imprisonment. The opposition made to, and punishment of the dogmatizers could not, consistently with truth, be called *persecution*, because the resistance was merely self-defence, self-security against innovators, that threatened to destroy the peace of society, and spread disorder and confusion among mankind. It is admitted by Fox, that the reformed cast twelve of the senators out of the windows, and committed other outrages. That a bloody war ensued, the *reformed* Bohemians arming themselves, to repel force by force. As to the pope going to Florence to excommunicate the Bohemians, and promising " full remission of all sins to the most wicked person " who should kill one Bohemian *Protestant*," there is just as much truth in this statement as in many others we have detected. Surely the pope could have excommunicated the reformed Bohemians as well at Rome as at Florence, for the latter place was not in his possesion, while the former was his chief seat and episcopal see. Neither were the refractory Bohemians Protestants, for be it observed, they held the doctrine of the mass, the seven sacraments, and many other points of faith which Catholics believe and Protestants reject. So that a Bohemian *Protestant* was unknown in those days, and consequently the pope would hardly be so foolish, if he had it in his power, to grant a remission of sins for killing what did not exist.

That a bloody war ensued is but too true, and many were the

cruelties practised by both parties ; but it is neither just nor generous to make the Catholics all sanguinary and the revolting Bohemians all merciful. The pope sought other means than the sword to bring the infatuated disciples of Huss and Jerome to their senses. He employed the proper weapons of the church to bring them to a sense of duty and truth. He sent preachers among them, armed with eloquence and persuasion, one of whom, St. John Capistran, is stated by Mr. Alban Butler to have converted, in Moravia alone, four thousand of these deluded creatures. While these pious missionaries were occupied in wielding the arm of reason among the disciples of Huss, the leaders of his sect were engaged in spreading blood and carnage over the country. " To revenge the death of John Huss," writes Mr. Butler, " Zisca (whose true name was John of Trocznou) a veteran general, " assembled an army of his followers, and plundered the whole country " with unheard-of barbarity. After the death of king Wenceslas, in " 1417, he opposed the election of Sigismund, who was emperor of " Germany, defeated his armies eight times, built the strong fortress " which he called Thabor, amidst waters and mountains, and died in " 1424. Sigismund had made peace with him before his death, and at " the council of Basil promised the archbishopric of Prague to John " Rockysana, a clergyman, who had been deputed by the Hussites to the " council of Basil, but who abjured that heresy, upon condition that the " laity in Bohemia might be allowed to communicate in both kinds. " The deputies of the council of Basil, and the catholic assembly at " Iglaw, in the diocess of Olmutz, in 1436, acquiesced ; but required " this condition, that in case of such a concession, the priest should de- " clare before giving the communion in both kinds, that it is an error " to believe that Christ's body or blood is alone under either kind. This " Rockysana boggled at : nor would the pope ever grant him his bulls. " His partisans, however, styled him archbishop, and he appeared at " their head till his death, which happened a little before that of " George Pogebrac, in 1471, who had been king of Bohemia from the " year 1458 ; though secretly a Hussite, he demolished the fortress of " Thabor, that it might not serve for a retreat to rebels."

Thus it appears that religion was made a cloak for sedition and rebellion, which has been the case in almost every instance with the innovators of truth. The *reform*, as it is called, meditated by John Huss and Jerome of Prague, was a system of the most pernicious licentiousness, and would no more be tolerated in the united states of America at this day, than it was in Bohemia in the fifteenth century. The doctrines preached by these dogmatizers struck at the foundation of all order and authority, and in the course of time must have rendered society a chaos of confusion and outrage. For example:—One of their tenets was, that the clergy ought to have no temporal possessions; now what would the clergy of the church of England, and the preachers of the sectarians in this same country, who are unanimous in their opposition to Catholicism, say, were a person to start up and maintain such a doctrine as this? Would they not call for a prosecution; or at least would they not oppose him with all the force they possessed? There cannot be a doubt but they would. And yet the resistance to such a doctrine in the fifteenth century by the fathers and professors of the

A REVIEW

OF

Fox's Book of Martyrs,

CRITICAL AND HISTORICAL.

No. 22. Printed and Published by W. E. Andrews, 3, Chapter-house-court, St. Paul's Churchyard, London. **Price 3d.**

EXPLANATION OF THE ENGRAVING.—*This cut represents the martyrdom of brother Michael Grellett, superior of a monastery of the Franciscan order, in France, who was hanged on a tree in the presence of the Hugonot admiral Gaspar de Coligni, and other chiefs of that party, notwithstanding the most solemn oaths had been given to the inhabitants of the town in which the monastery stood, that the Catholics, both clergy and laity, should remain secure and undisturbed. After the martyr was strangled and his body thrown from the tree, the cruel and impious band vociferated three times,* Live the Gospel !!! *A pretty sort of gospel these reforming miscreants followed.*

CONTINUATION OF THE REVIEW.

Catholic faith, is made a charge of persecution, by men too who are at the same time combined to continue the persecuting laws against the Catholics, imposed for conscience sake.

Another of the tenets was, that persons in authority forfeited all claim to jurisdiction and power, while in a state of sin. Thus, then, supposing the president of the united states of America to be in the habit of tippling to excess, he would, according to John Huss's notions, be divested of his power. But were a citizen of America to disseminate such a doctrine at this day, and were he to get some people to believe him, would he be allowed to propagate his error under the cloak of religion, in these states, where perfect religious freedom is established? We are convinced there is not a reader endowed with a rational mind that would answer us in the affirmative: why then should the Catholics of the fifteenth and present centuries be reproached for doing that which Protestants would do for their own personal security at the time we are writing? What would a by-stander say, if a criminal, on being taken

before a police magistrate to answer some charge preferred against
him, were to deny the power of the justice to take cognizance of the
offence, because he, the magistrate, had committed some breach of the
commandments of God, and therefore had forfeited all power vested in
him by the state? Would he not be struck with dread and astonishment that such an idea should be entertained, and immediately perceive
that, were it to become general, society would be disorganized? Most
assuredly he would, and applaud the man who should endeavour to remove such pernicious prejudices from the mind of the offender.

The editors conclude this section " with an account of a pretended
" Persecution by the Emperor Ferdinand."—Such is the head or
title they have selected, and they usher in their account with the following statement :—" The emperor Ferdinand, whose hatred to the
" Protestants was unlimited, not thinking he had sufficiently oppressed
" them, instituted a high court of reformers, upon the plan of the in-
" quisition, with this difference, that the reformers were to remove
" from place to place. The greater part of this court consisted of Je-
" suits, and from its decisions there was no appeal. Attended by a
" body of troops, it made the tour of Bohemia, and seldom examined
" a prisoner; but suffered the soldiers to murder the Protestants as they
" pleased, and then to make report of the matter afterwards." Such
is the introductory account of this persecution, which no doubt has obtained innumerable believers. But it must be observed, that there were
three emperors bearing the name of Ferdinand; the first reigned in the
sixteenth century, and the other two in the seventeenth; how then are
we to trace the accuracy of this account, when there is no clue left us
for that purpose? Not a date, not an authority, and no specification
in which of the three reigns this affair occurred. Is this the way an
honest historian would go to work to obtain credit We think not.
None but those well acquainted with the gullibility of Protestant prejudice would dare to send forth such a tale. The institution of a high
court of *reformers*, upon the plan of the inquisition,, to *reform* the *reformers* of religion, is a clever idea to work upon the imagination; and
the composing this court of *reformers* with Jesuits completes the climax. Then the summary mode of proceeding is calculated to excite
the compassion of the reader: only think of this court of reforming Jesuits making the tour of Bohemia, and leaving the work of slaughter
to the soldiers. A tour of pleasure to the court and a journey of labour to the soldiers. The Protestants murdered in the first instance
and reported afterwards : something like the Irish chairmen knocking
a passer-by down, and begging his leave to pass when the course is
clear. There being no time specified, we are at a loss to know whether
the sufferers were Hussites or Protestants; the editors say the latter, but
we have our doubts on the subject. After some further improbable
relations, a list is given of twenty prisoners who are said to have been
executed in regular order, among whom are five lords, one earl, one
knight, one doctor of physic, four gentlemen, a cripple, and seven without rank. All of them are described as making use of some common-
place talk, very suitable to delude the enthusiast, but, as we have so
frequently had occasion to remark, not a date nor a voucher is produced,
but all is mere assertion. It would therefore be a waste of time to

enter into any criticism on such unauthenticated relations, and we shall proceed to the next section.

" SECTION II

" LIFE, SUFFERINGS, AND MARTYRDOM OF JOHN HUSS."

As the life and. conduct of this man have been an almost endless source of vilification of Catholic principles, and wishing to put the question at rest in future, we shall go at some length into the affair, and then leave the reader to form his own conclusions. Fox has devoted this section wholly to John Huss, and we cannot better illustrate the propensity which Fox has to lying than to give his own account as it appears, in this modern edition, and compare it with an account before us from another Protestant martyrologist. Fox writes thus :—

"John Huss was born in the village of Hussenitz, in Bohemia, about the year 1380. His parents gave him the best education they could bestow, and having acquired a tolerable knowledge of the classics, at a private school, he was sent to the university of Prague, where the powers of his mind, and his diligence in study, soon rendered him conspicuous.

"In 1408, he commenced bachelor of divinity, and was successively chosen pastor of the church of Bethlehem, in Prague, and dean and rector of the university. The duties of these stations he discharged with great fidelity, and became at length so conspicuous for the boldness and truth of his preaching, that he attracted the notice, and raised the malignity of the pope and his creatures.

"His influence in the university was very great, not only on account of his learning, eloquence, and exemplary life, but also on account of some valuable privileges he had obtained from the king in behalf of that seminary.

"The English reformer, Wickliffe, had so kindled the light of reformation, that it began to illumine the darkest corners of Popery and ignorance. His doctrines were received in Bohemia with avidity and zeal, by great numbers of people, but by none so particularly as John Huss, and his friend and fellow-martyr, Jerome of Prague.

"The reformists daily increasing, the archbishop of Prague issued a decree to prevent the farther spreading of Wickliffe's writings. This, however, had an effect quite the reverse to what he expected, for it stimulated the converts to greater zeal, and, at length, almost the whole university united in promoting them.

"Strongly attached to the doctrines of Wickliffe, Huss strenuously opposed the decree of the archbishop, who, notwithstanding, obtained a bull from the pope, authorizing him to prevent the publishing of Wickliffe's writings in his province. By virtue of this bull, he proceeded against four doctors, who had not delivered up some copies, and prohibited them to preach. Against these proceedings, Huss, with some other members of the university, protested, and entered an appeal from the sentences of the archbishop. The pope no sooner heard of this, than he granted a commission to cardinal Colonna, to cite John Huss to appear at the court of Rome, to answer accusations laid against him, of preaching heresies. From this appearance, Huss desired to be excused, and so greatly was he favoured in Bohemia, that king Winceslaus, the queen, the nobility, and the university, desired the pope to dispense with such an appearance; as also that he would not suffer the kingdom of Bohemia to lie under the accusation of heresy, but permit them to preach the gospel with freedom in their places of worship.

"Three proctors appeared for Huss before cardinal Colonna. They made an excuse for his absence, and said, they were ready to answer in his behalf. But the cardinal declared him contumacious, and accordingly excommunicated him. On this the proctors appealed to the pope, who appointed four cardinals to examine the process: these commissioners confirmed the sentence of the cardinal, and extended the excommunication not only to Huss, but to all his friends and followers. Huss then appealed from this unjust sentence to a future council, but without success; and, notwithstanding so severe a decree, and an expulsion from his church in Prague, he retired to Hussenitz, his native place, where he continued to promulgate the truth, both from the pulpit and with the pen.

"He here compiled a treatise, in which he maintained, that reading the books of Protestants could not be absolutely forbidden. He wrote in defence of Wickliffe's book on the Trinity: and boldly declared against the vices of the pope, the cardinals, and the clergy of those corrupt times. Besides these, he wrote many other books, all of which were penned with such strength of argument, as greatly facilitated the spreading of his doctrines.

" In England, the persecutions against the Protestants had been carried on for some time with relentless cruelty. They now extended to Germany and Bohemia, where Huss and Jerome of Prague were particularly singled out to suffer in the cause of religion.

" In the month of November, 1414, a general council was assembled at Constance, in Germany, for the purpose of determining a dispute then existing between three persons who contended for the papal throne.

" John Huss was summoned to appear at this council; and to dispel any apprehensions of danger, the emperor sent him a safe-conduct, giving him permission freely to come to, and return from the council. On receiving this information, he told the persons who delivered it, ' That he desired nothing more than to purge himself publicly of the imputation of heresy; and that he esteemed himself happy in having so fair an opportunity of it, as at the council to which he was summoned to attend.'

" In the latter end of November, he set out to Constance, accompanied by two Bohemian noblemen, who were among the most eminent of his disciples, and who followed him merely through respect and affection. He caused some placards to be fixed upon the gates of the churches of Prague, in which he declared, that he went to the council to answer all allegations that might be made against him. He also declared, in all the cities through which he passed, that he was going to vindicate himself at Constance, and invited all his adversaries to be present.

" On his way he met with every mark of affection and reverence, from people of all descriptions. The streets, and even the roads, were thronged with people, whom respect, rather than curiosity, had brought together. He was ushered into the towns with great acclamations; and he passed through Germany in a kind of triumph. ' I thought,' said he, ' I had been an outcast. I now see my worst friends are in Bohemia.'

" On his arrival at Constance, he immediately took lodgings in a remote part of the city. Soon after, came one Stephen Paletz, who was engaged by the clergy at Prague to manage the intended prosecution against him. Paletz was afterwards joined by Michael de Cassis, on the part of the court of Rome. These two declared themselves his accusers, and drew up articles against him, which they presented to the pope, and the prelates of the council.

" Notwithstanding the promise of the emperor, to give him a safe-conduct to and from Constance, he regarded not his word; but, according to the maxim of the council, that ' Faith is not to be kept with heretics,' when it was known he was in the city, he was immediately arrested, and committed prisoner to a chamber in the palace. This breach was particularly noticed by one of Huss's friends, who urged the imperial safe-conduct; but the pope replied, *he* never granted any such thing, nor was he bound by that of the *emperor.*

" While Huss was under confinement, the council acted the part of inquisitors. They condemned the doctrines of Wickliffe, and, in their impotent malice, ordered his remains to be dug up, and burnt to ashes; which orders were obeyed.

" In the mean time the nobility of Bohemia and Poland used all their interest for Huss; and so far prevailed as to prevent his being condemned unheard, which had been resolved on by the commissioners appointed to try him.

" Before his trial took place, his enemies employed a Franciscan friar, who might entangle him in his words, and then appear against him. This man, of great ingenuity and subtlety, came to him in the character of an idiot, and with seeming sincerity and zeal, requested to be taught his doctrines. But Huss soon discovered him, and told him that his manners wore a great semblance of simplicity; but that his questions discovered a depth and design beyond the reach of an idiot. He afterwards found this pretended fool to be Didace, one of the deepest logicians in Lombardy.

" At length, he was brought before the council, when the articles exhibited against him were read: they were upwards of forty in number, and chiefly extracted from his writings.

" On his examination being finished, he was taken from the court, and a resolution was formed by the council, to burn him as an heretic, unless he retracted. He was then committed to a filthy prison, where, in the day-time, he was so laden with fetters on his legs, that he could hardly move; and every night he was fastened by his hands to a ring against the walls of the prison.

" He continued some days in this situation, in which time many noblemen of Bohemia interceded in his behalf. They drew up a petition for his release, which was presented to the council by several of the most illustrious nobles of Bohemia; notwithstanding which, so many enemies had Huss in that court, that no attention was paid to it, and the persecuted reformer was compelled to bear with the punishment inflicted on him by that merciless tribunal.

" Shortly after the petition was presented, four bishops and two lords were sent by the emperor to the prison, in order to prevail on Huss to make a recantation. But he called God to witness, that he was not conscious of having preached, or written, any thing against his truth, or the faith of his orthodox church. The deputies then represented the great wisdom and authority of the council: to which Huss replied, 'Let them send the meanest person of that council, who can convince me by argument from the word of God, and I will submit my judgment to him.' This pious answer had no effect, because he would not take the authority of the council upon trust, without the least shadow of an argument offered. The deputies, therefore, finding they could make no impression on him, departed, greatly astonished at the strength of his resolution.

" On the 4th of July he was, for the last time, brought before the council. After a long examination he was desired to abjure, which he refused, without the least hesitation. The bishop of Lodi then preached a sermon, the text of which was, ' Let the body of sin be destroyed,' (concerning the destruction of heretics) the prologue to his intended punishment. After the close of the sermon his fate was determined, his vindication rejected, and judgment pronounced. The council censured him for being obstinate and incorrigible, and ordained, ' That he should be degraded from the priesthood, his books publicly burnt, and himself delivered to the secular power.'

" He received the sentence without the least emotion; and at the close of it he kneeled down with his eyes lifted towards heaven, and, with all the magnanimity of a primitive martyr, thus exclaimed: ' May thy infinite mercy, O my God! pardon this injustice of mine enemies. Thou knowest the injustice of my accusations: how deformed with crimes I have been represented; how I have been oppressed with worthless witnesses, and a false condemnation; yet, O my God! let that mercy of thine, which no tongue can express, prevail with thee not to avenge my wrongs.' These excellent sentences were received as so many expressions of heresy, and only tended to inflame his adversaries. Accordingly, the bishops appointed by the council stripped him of his priestly garments, degraded him, and put a paper mitre on his head, on which were painted devils, with this inscription: ' A ringleader of heretics.'

" This mockery was received by the heroic martyr with an air of unconcern, which appeared to give him dignity rather than disgrace. A serenity appeared in his looks, which indicated that his soul had cut off many stages of a tedious journey in her way to the realms of everlasting happiness.

" The ceremony of degradation being over, the bishops delivered him to the emperor who committed him to the care of the duke of Bavaria. His books were burnt at the gates of the church; and on the 6th of July he was led to the suburbs of Constance, to be burn alive.

" When he had reached the place of execution, he fell on his knees, sung several portions of the psalms, looked steadfastly towards heaven, and repeated, ' Into thy hands, O Lord! do I commit my spirit: thou hast redeemed me, O most good and faithful God.'

" As soon as the chain was put about him at the stake, he said, with a smiling countenance, ' My Lord Jesus Christ was bound with a harder chain than this, for my sake, why then should I be ashamed of this old rusty one?'

" When the faggots were piled around him, the duke of Bavaria desired him to abjure " No,' said he, 'I never preached any doctrine of an evil tendency; and what I taught with my lips I now seal with my blood.' He then said to the executioner, ' You are now going to burn a goose, (Huss signifies goose in the Bohemian language) but in a century you will have a swan whom you can neither roast nor boil.' If this were spoken in prophecy, he must have meant Martin Luther, who flourished about a century after, and who had a swan for his arms.

. " As soon as the faggots were lighted, the heroic martyr sung a hymn, with so loud and
cheerful a voice, that he was heard through all the cracklings of the combustibles, and the
noise of the multitude.   At length his voice was interrupted by the flames, which soon put
a period to his life."

This is the account given in the *Book of Martyrs*, and by it we
might be led to suppose that John Huss was as immaculate a character as the apostles who founded the church of God, under the guidance
of the Holy Spirit.   Shackled as the Catholic press has been since the
first dawn of what is called the *Reformation*, the writers in favour of
that event have turned history into romance, and represented persons
of the most wicked and notorious lives, as angels of light, without fear
of contradiction.   It has been well observed, that "the real dignity of
" history does not consist in set speeches made by the author at plea-
" sure, to shew his ability in that way, nor in other rhetorical orna-
" ments; but in SOLID TRUTH and HONESTY, which alone can
" render it worthy of that denomination.   He who takes pains to
" transmit a rebel to posterity under such disguise as may render his
" character doubtful, is to be looked upon as a slanderer, not an his-
" torian, and, as such, deserves to be severely punished for depriving
" an ill man of the reproach due to him, as he that should go about to
" defame a good man."   These just sentiments we have extracted
from the preface to a book, now before us, called " *The History of
" King-killers; or, The Fanatic Martyrology*," published in London, in
the year 1720.   In this work we find a life of John Huss somewhat
different to that related by John Fox, and stated to be gathered from
another work, entitled, " *The pretended Reformers; or, The History of
" John Wickliffe, John Huss, and Jerome of Prague, made English from
" the French original, by* MATTHIAS EARBERY, *Presbyter of the Church of
" England.   London*, 1717. *Octavo*."   This translator, being a member
of the church as by law established, his testimony must have greater
weight with the generality of the people of England, being Protestant,
than the word of a Catholic, who would be looked upon as an interested evidence.   But it may be said, the original being in the
French language, there cannot be a doubt that the author of the history
was a Catholic.   Well, be it so; still it must be allowed, that, as the
translator was a Protestant, and of course opposed to the Catholic
church, he was convinced of the accuracy of his account, or he would
not have taken the trouble to translate, nor incurred the expense of
printing and publishing, what he suspected or knew to be false.   Here
then we have an unexceptionable witness, of whose evidence we shall
avail ourself, to contravene the lies and misrepresentations of John
Fox.

Fox commences with saying, that the *parents* of Huss gave him the
best education they could bestow; but Mr. Earbery tells us that the
extraction of Huss was so base that he did not know his father, and
was compelled to take the sirname of the town in which he was born.
We do not notice this fact as any disgrace to Huss, because we are
well aware that one of the brightest ornaments in English history,
namely William of Wykeham was as meanly born, but only to shew
the want of integrity in Fox, and how little *he* is entitled to credit.
That Huss was a man of good natural parts is not denied ; but it is not,

reader the possession of talents, but the right use of them that constitutes the learned and great man. Fox next says, he discharged the duties of his office, as rector of the university, " with great fidelity, and " became at length so conspicuous for the boldness and *truth* of his " preaching, that he attracted the notice, and raised the malignity " of the pope and his creatures." Mr. Earbery, on the contrary, assures us he was opposed to the truth, and became a fomenter of discord. Instigated by revenge, on being refused a doctor's degree, he set about dividing the university of Prague, and expelling such of the professors as were native Germans from their seats. To effect this, Huss and his party referred the dispute to the civil magistrate, though the cognizance belonged to the archbishop. The Germans refused to appear before the magistrates, and the question was decided by them in favour of Huss. This made his party so insolent and outrageous, that the Germans were obliged to fly for safety into Thuringia. Being thus far successful in securing the ignorant and licentious in his favour, he began *openly* to teach the doctrines of Wickliff, and translated into the Bohemian language the most pernicious of Wickliff's works. In this labour he was assisted by Jerome of Prague and one Jacobel, of whom we shall have to speak hereafter, and the latter, in order to increase the murmurs of the people, railed at their being denied the sacrament in both kinds. The whole city being thus placed in a state of confusion and tumult, the magistrates perceived the error; but, like too many who are invested with power, thinking to strike the people with awe by a little coercion, they seized three of the most forward in exciting disorder, and executed them as traitors. The Hussites did not oppose the execution, but they took down the quarters of the traitors, carried them in triumph to the church of Bethlehem, of which, Fox says, Huss was the pastor, and there worshipped them as relics. This last act, we think, is sufficient to prove that the Hussites were not Protestants, because the latter deem the worshipping of relics to be idolatry, and therefore we are at a loss to reconcile this ranging of Huss as a good Protestant martyr. Besides, Huss was a priest, and said mass, and believed in transubstantiation; whereas, Fox says, that one of the Hugonot martyrs, old Oguier, proved from scripture that the saying of mass was contrary to the ordinances of Jesus Christ. In this case one or other of these martyrs must be wrong, for they could not both be right, yet are they here represented as preachers of *truth*, though teaching and preaching contrary doctrines. But to return to John Huss. He was suspected, Mr. Earbery informs us, of being deeply implicated in the above affair, for which reason a warrant was issued out against him, and he fled to the village from which he took his name, where he put himself under the protection of the lord of the castle. It was here that the Hussite party was completely formed. This was in the year 1409, that is, in the year after Fox says Huss took bachelor's degrees. Thus it appears, by Mr. Earbery's account, which is corroborated by all authentic writers, that Huss was the aggressor, that he was a disturber of the peace, a preacher of sedition, and an evil disposed person.

Fox says, " The English reformer Wickliff had so kindled the light " of reformation, that it began to illumine the darkest corners of

" Popery and ignorance. His doctrines (he goes on) were received
" in Bohemia with avidity and zeal, by great numbers of people, but by
" none so particularly as by John Huss and his friend and fellow mar-
" tyr, Jerome of Prague." In another place Fox writes, "In England,
" the *persecutions* against the *Protestants* had been carried on for some
" time with *relentless cruelty*. They *now* extended to Germany and
" Bohemia, where Huss and Jerome of Prague were *particularly singled
" out* to suffer in the *cause of religion*." By such false and impudent
statements have the people of England been deluded and led astray
from the real state of the case. That Huss and Jerome of Prague were
" particularly singled out" cannot be denied, nor would justice have
been done, if they had not been so selected. They were the ringleaders,
the fomenters of the disorders which ensued, in consequence of the
promulgation of their *seditious* doctrines, cloathed with religious hypocrisy, and therefore to have punished the deluded instead of the de-
luders would have been an act of extreme injustice. Fox insinuates
that they were " singled out to suffer in the *cause of religion*;" this we
deny; for it was not in the cause of religion that they were engaged,
but in the cause of irreligion. Their doctrines tended to the *corruption
of morals*, to sow strife and crime, and therefore religion was not honoured by their preachings, but scandalized and disgraced. It is very
easy to *assert* that Wickliff was a reformer, and that Huss and Jerome
of Prague were martyrs; but as the goodness of the tree is only to be
known by its fruits, so should the seeker of truth look to the fruits
produced by these pretended reformers before he concludes that they
suffered in the cause of religion. By so doing he will find that the
name of religion was never more grossly perverted than by Fox and
his modern editors and adherents. As we have often observed, there
can be but *one true* religion, because Truth being always the same,
never varying nor changing, so religion, which was founded by God,
who is Truth itself, can never change or be reformed, because the
very idea of altering implies the *existence* of error and the *want* of *truth*,
which is an utter impossibility.

We have in our preceding pages shewn how the Catholic church
proceeds to preserve inviolate the true faith, and that Fox has admitted, in his account of the primitive martyrs, the right of the pope to
call and preside in councils for the purpose of examining and detecting
heresy, and pronouncing against erroneous doctrines. This was the
case with the arch-heretic Arius, in the fourth century, with the heresy
of the Eutychians and Monothelites, in the tenth century, and in all
other cases that call for solemn deliberation. In every age the faith of
the Catholic church has been preserved and continued under the guidance of the Holy Spirit, by the writings and preachings of learned doctors, the deliberations and decisions of councils selected from all parts
of the world, or confined to a province or kingdom, but approved by
the head and received by the members of the whole church. By this
rule Catholics have a guarantee which those who differ from their
church cannot claim; and no sooner is an attempt made to introduce
error or innovation into the unerring creed of Catholicism, than the
innovator is denounced, and the Catholic is put upon his guard to avoid
the evil snares laid to entrap him. Thus it was with John Huss and

Jerome of Prague. When the former began to preach his erroneous and seditious doctrines openly, the archbishop of Prague denounced him as a teacher of error and an innovator, which it was his duty to do as a conservator of truth, and a guardian over the morals of the people committed to his care. Fox says this proceeding had a contrary effect, " for it stimulated the converts to greater zeal." That the ignorant multitude were unhappily deceived by these-innovators is but too true, nevertheless it does not make the case more in favour of Huss, for if his doctrines were true, why did they not spread over the world and eradicate Popery, as Catholicism is called? Why were their doctrines confined to a local spot, and supported by rebellion, murder, and sacrilege? These outrages are carefully concealed by the author of the *Book of Martyrs,* but they are detailed at some length by the author of the *Fanatic Martyrology.* We have given Fox's account, and have thus dealt fairly by him; our next duty is to act with the same degree of fairness towards our readers, by letting them see the *other side* of the question. Mr. Earbery, the author of *The Fanatic Martyrology,* states that " John Huss, the more to incense his followers against pope " John XXIII, who had condemned him, FALSELY persuaded them " that the church of Rome held as an article of faith the necessity of " believing in the pope, as well as that of believing in God; and *to re-* " *tain on his side all men of wicked lives,* he taught that those sinners " who were punished in this world, would not be punished in the next." Amiable conduct truly! An excellent mode to serve the *cause of religion;* and well worthy the *modern* martyrs of John Fox! Here we see it stated, that to incite his followers to vengeance against the pope, he preached FALSEHOOD; and to oppose those good men who defended *truth,* he enlisted wicked men into his ranks, by deceiving them and hazarding their souls to eternal perdition. And this is the gentleman who is represented by Fox as the *promulgator of truth.* That his doctrines were received with avidity and zeal by those who led abandoned lives there cannot exist a doubt; but what are we to think of the morals of those writers who can hold such a character in estimation merely from his being opposed to Popery, as it is called?

Fox further says; that Huss was so greatly favoured in Bohemia, " that king Winceslaus, the queen, the nobility, and the university, " desired the pope to dispense with such an appearance [namely, be- " fore the court of Rome, to which he had been cited]; as also that " he would not suffer the kingdom to lie under the accusation of " *heresy,* but permit them to preach the gospel with freedom in their " places of worship." On consulting Mr. Earbery, we find tha the gives quite a different version of this fact. From his statement it appears that Wenceslaus had the rank of emperor, and was a character as infamous as Huss himself, wholly addicted to pleasures and averse to business. That on the death of the then archbishop of Prague, he appointed " one Arbile to succeed him, a debauched wretch, and as " vile in all respects (observes Mr. Earbery) as the emperor who ad- " vanced him. Winceslaus (continues Mr. E.) being so brutal, was " deposed by the Germans, and his brother Sigismund succeeded him, " who, being a prince zealous for religion, with indefatigable industry " prevailed to have a council assembled, as it accordingly was, after

" many difficulties, in the city of Constance." Thus then it appears that this Winceslaus, who was fond of Huss, according to Fox, was one of those wicked men whom that hieresiarch had retained on his side by his false doctrines. A worthy ruler to solicit the pope to let Huss preach the gospel with freedom. But what was there to prevent Huss from preaching the truth, if his doctrines were correct, when he had the king, and queen, and nobility, and university on his side? How was the pope to prevent him when he was thus backed? The apostles preached the gospel, they published the revealed truths of religion fearlessly and openly, without being supported by kings, or queens, or noblemen, nay, in direct opposition to the temporal power, and the counsels of princes; and they and their successors fulfilled the words of their divine Master in every respect. Why, then, if Huss was a preacher of truth, did he not succeed? Why did he retract, and recant, and retract again; and his followers divide, as is the case with all who are in error, into various sects, all differing from each other, but all claiming to be right, and condemning each other for being wrong? Fox and his editors may endeavour to gloss over these facts, and try to conceal these contradictions, but, it is our duty to bring them to the light, and leave the reader to decide on the merit of the case.

The account given by Fox of the proceedings entered into against Huss by his ecclesiastical judges, is of a piece with his other falsehoods and misrepresentations; therefore, to enable the reader to draw his own conclusions of the bungling and romancing method adopted in this *Book of Martyrs* to hoodwink and delude the ignorant and credulous, we will here insert the account given by Mr. Earbery of the acts of the council of prelates, and of the general council of Constance, and request a careful comparison between the two relations in order to come at the truth :—

A council of prelates and learned men being assembled by order of the aforesaid pope John at Prague, John Huss appeared before them, behaved himself very modestly, declared his submission to the church, and publicly disowned all or most of the heresies he had so publicly preached and taught; whereupon that council restored him to the communion of the church, only suspending him for a short time from the exercise of the priestly function. He, as soon as the council was broke up, taught more insolently than ever the same propositions he had abjured, and to fulfil the measure of his impudence, endeavoured to depreciate amongst men the authority of the fathers of the church. Having thus insulted the authority of the church, and at the same time worked the whole kingdom into a rebellion, for all his open insolences could be called by no other name, at length, the general council met at Constance, and John Huss having obtained a pass from the emperor Sigismund, and another from that city, repaired thither, attended by some gentlemen of Bohemia. He visited pope John XXIII. and all the other prelates, and caused it to be affixed at all the church doors in that place, whilst his friends spoke the same throughout all Germany, that he had presented himself before the council to give an account of his faith, and that he invited all those who doubted of his religion, or who held him in suspicion, to bring in their actions against him before that most august tribunal in Christendom. By this those fathers made out that he had recognized them and sued to them to be his judges, whereupon pope John aforesaid gave leave to John the patriarch of Constantinople, the bishop of Suree, and Bernard, bishop of Cita de Castello, to draw a breviate of the case of John Huss, and to make their report thereof to the council; which done, he was acquainted that the witnesses had appeared against him, and that he was not to depart Constance till judgment had been pronounced against him, which struck a mighty terror upon him, and he began to question his safety. The witnesses were so numerous that they could not possibly be corrupted; and their agreement so perfect, that they could not be rejected. No legal exception could be made against them, and their large and circumstantial depositions clearly proved, that John Huss had been the cause of all the disturbances, which for six years before had happened in Bohemia upon the account of religion, and that to him were principally owing the sacrilegious acts that had been there committed, the profaneness which had been there authorised, and that through him vows of chastity had been violated, and ecclesiastical revenues pillaged. To all these crimes proved upon him, be added another, which was exercising of his priestly function, after having been in Bohemia suspended by the archbishop of Prague, and again at Constance prohibited doing the same by the bishop of that place. John Huss began now not to think himself safe in Constance, and his friends advised him to fly. Accordingly, he disguised himself like a peasant, and buried himself in a cart laden with forage, but Henry de Salsembroc, who was his chief assistant in managing this affair, was at the same time the principal spy upon him, and discovered all the management, so that as soon as he was without the gate, the cart was stopped and he taken out. At first he pretended that he was not the person they looked for, and when that would not serve him, he pleaded the emperor's pass. In fine, he was conducted back, and shut up in a room after a stricter manner than he had been before. Jerome of Prague, the most considerable of his disciples, was also confined, and the 5th of April appointed for them to give an account of their doctrine. Then the council proceeded to condemn the forty-five articles of Wickliffe, and censured his memory, declaring him unworthy of Christian burial, which last was supposed to be done to intimidate John Huss and Jerome of Prague by so severe an example, by showing them what they must expect, unless they did retract their tenets; and the cardinals of Florence and Cambray made this severe act the foundation of their exhorting the two prisoners to make a surrender of themselves. This they consented to, and demanded of the council, that they would be pleased to present to them a form of abjuration. They persisted in this resolution a second time, and the emperor was desired to allow each of them a stipend capable of subsisting six persons to live on about the frontiers of Sweden, and never more to return into Bohemia. John Huss and Jerome of Prague made no scruple at the retractation and banishment; but the necessity of disavowing their doctrine in the language of their own country, shocked them more than fire and faggot. At length, to hinder the fathers from proceeding farther in the condemnation, John Huss presented to them a writing, urging, that he could not resolve to retract all the articles in general wherewith he was charged, for that his conscience did not reproach him with having taught them; yet offering, after many more evasions, to retract whatsoever should be found contrary to religion in his books. The commissioners appointed for the affair of John Huss answered, that truth following the expression of holy writ was established in the mouth of two or three witnesses, that they had twenty against him; all of them without exception, and the most part of them doctors, who had deposed nothing but what they had seen or heard, and that their evidence did so agree together, that it was impossible to find therein the least contradiction, &c. Next Huss excepted against two of the commissioners, but his exceptions against them were found empty and frivolous. In the beginning of July, the cardinal of Cambray charitably pressed him to make his retractation in the form the council had appointed; but he after some formal submissions being urged to sign, pretended that it was the fear of lying that hindered him. He was twice again exhorted by the emperor himself to make his retractation, but in vain, and the 6th of July appointed to terminate this affair; before which four bishops and as many gentlemen of his own country were sent to persuade him, who brought back nothing but ambiguous reasons. When the day was come, he was brought forth into the cathedral church, where the council sat, and was required to pronounce an anathema against the errors of Wickliffe, from which he excused himself by a long discourse, which turned upon these two heads: the one, that it was against his conscience so to do; the other, that he did not hold as absolutely false all that Wickliffe had taught, and that he thought himself bound at least to except three propositions. The first of which was, that Constantine had offended God in granting to the church civil powers; the second, that a priest who had fallen into deadly sin was not a valid administrator of the sacraments; and the third was, that tithes were but mere alms; whereof he was then accused and convicted. Then was the sentence pronounced against John Huss by the bishop of Concord, in terms, whereof the sense was, that he had been duly attainted and convicted of the crime of heresy; that his appeal was scandalous, injurious, and ridiculous, as calling in doubt the supreme jurisdiction of an ecclesiastical tribunal; that he had seduced by his sermons and books the Christian people of Bohemia, and that he was not willing to remedy those evils of which he had been the author by an authentic disavowal of them. Wherefore the holy council decreed, that he should be degraded from the order of priesthood, of which he was unworthy, and gave it in charge to the bishops of Milan, Montefalco, Ast, Alexandria, Prague and Venice, to see the sentence of degradation executed upon him in the form prescribed in the canon law, and that the criminal should be delivered over to the secular arms. John Huss heard the sentence pronounced against him without ever attempting to interrupt the person that pronounced it; for that he imagined it would have been permitted him afterwards to harangue the whole assembly in such manner as he had proposed to himself, in order to move their compassion; but he was enjoined silence the very moment he began to speak: he was by force taken down from the place where he had got up, and they hastened to put upon him the sacerdotal vestments, that they might with shame strip them off again. The ceremony was concluded with putting upon his head a bonnet of paper with this inscription: *Lo this is the Heresiarch*. Then the duke of Bavaria, on the 6th of July, 1415, delivered him into the hands of the magistrate, who caused him to be led, after he had been shaven all over, as sorcerers are used in Germany, to the market place, where was prepared a pile of wood about a stake. Before he was fastened to the stake, it was demanded of him whether or no he would retract; but this he refused to do with greater resolution than when he was before the council."

This account differs materially from that given by John Fox, and, as the reader will have observed, is devoid of the high-colouring and romancing style which marks the statement in the *Book of Martyrs*.— By answering the summons of the council, Huss admitted the right of the assembly to interrogate him, and judge of his doctrines. The story of the safe-conduct is a stale one, so often refuted, that it is not necessary to notice it here, and beside it is incorrectly stated by Fox. As to the maxim of the council, that "Faith is not to be kept with heretics," the account of the proceedings of that council towards Huss, as given by Mr. Earbery, shews that the assembly acted with the most scrupulous nicety and justice. Notwithstanding Huss had repeatedly broken his faith with the council, the fathers proceeded according to the regular form, and produced witnesses so perfect in their evidence, and so many in number, that they could not be disputed nor corrupted. Hence it is clear that truth and justice was on the side of the council, and as Huss was determined to remain obstinate, he drew the consequences upon his own head. How unfair is it then to cast blame or reproach on the council for doing their duty, and extol the conduct of a man who acted in defiance of both law and justice. It was clearly proved, Mr. Earbery states, that John Huss had been " the cause of all the disturbances, which, " for six years before, had happened in Bohemia on account of religion, " and that to him were principally owing all the sacrilegious acts that " had been there committed, the profaneness which had been there au- " thorized, and that through him vows of chastity had been violated, " and ecclesiastical revenues pillaged." And is a man so loaded with crimes, unanswerably proved upon him, to be looked upon as a martyr to religion because he received the punishment imposed by the laws of his country for such crimes? What strange perversion is this! Huss could not be ignorant of the punishment that awaited him in the event of his being found guilty, and unable to escape from the hand of justice. That he was sensible of his situation is shewn by his attempt to elude his keepers, and we cannot help here remarking, how singular are the designs of Providence, that he who had acted treacherously towards his judges was betrayed by the chief of his associates. That the coun-cil did not wish to act harshly towards Huss is clearly manifested by their soliciting the emperor to allow him a stipend on his making a retractation, and consenting to banish himself from Bohemia. But such is the force of prejudice, and such the bane of a corrupted mind, that an act of pure justice is perverted into tyranny, and a measure of self-defence converted into persecution. Another circumstance related by Fox will shew the accuracy of these observations. He says, " As soon " as the faggots were lighted, the *heroic martyr* sung a hymn, with so " *loud* and *cheerful* a voice, that he was heard *through all the cracklings* " *of the combustibles,* and *noise of the multitude.* At length his voice " *was interrupted by the flames,* which soon put an end to his life." Well said, John Fox, and if Baron Munchausen beats this tale, he cer-tainly may be crowned the emperor of liars. Huss must have had an ex-cellent pipe to have made himself heard in spite of the cracklings and bel-lowings. Believe it who can :—but credulous must he be who can take this for granted. The fact is, according to Mr. Earbery, who is cor-roborated by Mr. Reeve, in his History of the Christian Church, Huss was suffocated by the smoke as soon as the pile was fired, and never spoke a word after.

Before we quit Huss, we must be allowed to say another word in de-fence of the council of Constance, which has been charged with hold-ing the maxim, " Faith is not to be kept with heretics". This unjust charge is not confined to the *Book of Martyrs,* but the historian Hume, and other infidel and reformed writers, represent the fathers of Con-stance as guilty of this doctrine, and having acted upon it towards Huss. Hume says, the act of executing Huss " proves this melancholy truth, " that toleration is none of the virtues of priests in any form of ecclesi-" astical government." This is a sweeping condemnation it must be allowed, and is evidently made without reflection, though the writer knew it would go down in this country, where the people are so little given to reflection and so much to credulity when the Catholic religion is concerned. Now the fact is, the council had as little to do with the execution of John Huss, as it had with the death of Wat Tyler. The council had authority to decide on the merits of the doctrines taught by Huss, and, on mature deliberation, it did decree that what he taught was *erroneous,* and ordered him to be stripped of his priestly dignity ; but having fulfilled this duty, it resolved as follows : " This sacred " synod of Constance, considering that the *church of Christ* has nothing " farther that it can do, decrees to *leave* John Huss to the *judgment* of " the STATE." Thus it is plain, and beyond contradiction, that Huss was not put to death for conscience sake, but for the many crimes he had committed against the authority of the temporal power, and the peace of society. He suffered, in fact, for *offences* committed, and not for *opinions* held. Huss had *free liberty* to urge whatever he pleased in defence of his cause, which it appears, from the public jour-nals, has not been allowed in this Protestant country to offenders charged with vending Deistical works and professing Deism. He was not stopped in his defence by the fathers of the council, as judges are reported to have stopped the advocates of Deism on their trials ; there-fore a greater toleration was granted to Huss in the fifteenth century, by a Catholic council than is allowed to infidel pleaders in the present age by Protestant criminal courts of justice. This being the fact, we think the writers against Catholicism might be a little more moderate with their insinuations against the intolerance of the church of Rome.

With regard to the maxim, that "Faith is not to be kept with here-" tics," the council of Constance condemned the doctrine instead of enforcing it. About the latter end of the thirteenth century a sect sprung up, to which the name of *Flagellants* were given. Among other errors taught by this sect was the following :—"That *all* oaths, after " what manner so ever taken, were *prohibited*, yet it was better the " Flagellants should be sworn and *fore-sworn* before the inquisition, " than that they should betray themselves and their brethren, seeing " that *perjury might be expiated by flagellation*." This error accords with that charged to the account of Huss by Mr. Earbery, namely, that those who suffered punishment for their crimes in this life would not suffer in the next; a doctrine that evidently struck at the system of morality; for if a man imagined he could expiate perjury by merely flogging his body, or believed his salvation sure if he were deprived of his pleasures here, what reliance could be placed on his words or actions? Who would believe him? Who could trust him? To stem this evil a bull was published by the authority of the council of Constance, and sent to all the countries infested with this heresy, which document is to be found in the acts of this council, published at Haguenian, in the year 1500, and bears this title: "The errors of Wickliff of England', " and of John Huss of Bohemia, condemned in the general council of " Constance." Among the questions put to suspected persons, under this bull are these : "Whether he believes it is not lawful to swear in " any case? Whether he does not think that *all* wilful perjury com-" mitted upon *any* occasion whatsoever for the preservation of one's " life, or another man's, or *even for the sake of faith*, is a mortal sin?" From these queries it is evident that the *Flagellant* heretics were the teachers of that impious doctrine, that "faith is not to be kept" with Catholics; and that the Catholic council of Constance condemned the doctrine as erroneous and mischievous, and made it a test of Catholic communion that men *must not perjure themselves even for the sake of religion*. What stronger evidence can be produced to shew the falsity of the charge made by Fox, that the council of Constance taught that " faith is not to be kept with heretics."

We have mentioned an accomplice of Huss, named Jacobel, and as this man was a chief of the Hussite party, we will here state some of his proceedings after the death of Huss, in order that the reader may see the effects produced by the doctrines of Wickliffe and Huss, which are so much extolled by John Fox, that in his original work, he dates the visibility of his church from the time of Wickliffe. We shall have occasion to speak of the disorders which took place in this country, in consequence of the licentiousness of Wickliffe's notions at a future period; we therefore request the reader's serious perusal of the following extract from the life of Jacobel, in Mr. Earbery's *Fanatic Martyrology* :—" Jacobel had remained at Prague," writes Mr. E. " when " John Huss and Jerome of Prague went to the council at Constance, " and understanding that Huss had been there burnt for his heresies

" and prevarications, he apprehended that the same would be his lot,
" if he did not secure himself against the punishment due to his past
" crimes by committing greater. Hereupon, conspiring with others
" who were under the same circumstances, it was agreed, that the only
" way to provide for their own safety was to raise a rebellion. Accord-
" ingly they lost no time, but assembling the Hussites together the
" same night in the most considerable place of the city of Prague, after
" having invoked their prophet Huss, whom they looked upon as a
" martyr, they divided themselves into several troops, to revenge his
" death upon those of the clergy, whom they suspected to have pro-
" cured it. They surrounded the houses of those persons and broke
" them open. It was to no effect to offer them money, or to expose the
" most valuable goods to their discretion, they said they were come
" neither for money nor goods. The most secret places were searched
" for those whom they had doomed to die, till they had found them
" and glutted their rage upon them, by depriving them of life, and dis-
" figuring their bodies after a thousand extravagant manners. Then
" they dragged them into the river Molde, and plunged them into
" those places where the course of the water was most rapid, under
" pretence of preventing their being made relics. But their principal
" effort was against the house of the archbishop, about which the great-
" est number of the Hussites was got together. The obstinate resist-
" ance of that prelate's domestics could not prevent the breaking open
" of the house, and only served to give their master the opportunity of
" escaping through a back-door. The magistrates finding themselves
" unable to quell this tumult, waited till it should calm itself; and the
" Hussites convinced of their power by that connivance, grew more in-
" solent. Hence ensued all the desolation of the kingdom of Bohemia;
" but what farther part this Jacobel had in it I have not yet found."

Is this the spirit of religion? or rather is it not the spirit of diabo-
lism? To say that these men were the friends of *religion*; that they
were the reformers of Popery: why could Popery, were it as bad as
it is represented to be by " Protestant-ascendency," produce greater
evils, more horrid outrages, or savage barbarities, than are here stated
to have been committed by the dear friends and auxiliaries of the " few
" plain Christians," the disciples of Huss? Besides this Jacobel, another ringleader of the name of Zisca, was equally conspicuous for the
ferocity of his temper and the atrociousness of his cruelties. He
sought to establish the errors of Huss by force of arms: and commenced an unprovoked rebellion against his lawful sovereign. To
instigate his followers to pursue the same unlawful course of sedition,
and robbery, and murder, he directed in his will, that after his death
his skin should be converted into parchment, of which a drum should
be made to rouse the Bohemian boors to arms against the Catholic
princes. Thus we see in every instance where error is obstinately pursued, and truth is disregarded, those under the former impression have
recourse to *force* to propagate their opinion and extend their power.
But what can we think of men, who, at this period, pretend to be the
most *enlightened* of human beings; what, we say, can we think of men
who profess to teach the ignorant the path of knowledge, yet are
here convicted of falsifying the plainest historical fact, and represent-

ing the most diabolical wretches as sufferers in the cause of religion. Alas! how depraved; how blind; how infatuated; how bloated in error, and how averse to truth are the modern editors of John Fox's *Book of Martyrs*, alias of freebooters, murderers, and rebels.

"SECTION III.

"LIFE, SUFFERINGS, AND MARTYRDOMS OF JEROME OF PRAGUE."

Another section is devoted to the account of this ringleader of error and disorder in Bohemia. As we intend to deal fairly with John Fox, we shall here give his relation in his own words, as we did in the case with John Huss:—

"THIS hero in the cause of truth, was born at Prague, and educated in its university, where he soon became distinguished for his learning and eloquence. Having completed his studies, he travelled over great part of Europe, and visited many of the seats of learning, particularly the universities of Paris, Heidelburgh, Cologne, and Oxford. At the latter he became acquainted with the works of Wickliffe, and translated many of them into his own language.

"On his return to Prague he openly professed the doctrines of Wickliffe, and finding that they had made a considerable progress in Bohemia, from the industry and zeal of Huss, he became an assistant to him in the great work of reformation.

"On the 4th of April, 1415, Jerome went to Constance. This was about three months before the death of Huss. He entered the town privately and consulting with some of the leaders of his party, was easily convinced that he could render his friend no service.

"Finding that his arrival at Constance was publicly known, and that the council intended to seize him, he retired, and went to Iberling, an imperial town, a short distance from Constance. While here, he wrote to the emperor, and declared his readiness to appear before the council, if a safe-conduct were granted to him; this, however, was refused.

"After this, he caused papers to be put up in all the public places in Constance, particularly on the doors of the cardinals' houses. In these he professed his willingness to appear at Constance in the defence of his character and doctrine, both which, he said, had been greatly falsified. He farther declared, that if any error should be proved against him, he would retract it; desiring only that the faith of the council might be given for his security.

"Receiving no answer to these papers, he set out on his return to Bohemia, taking the precaution to carry with him a certificate, signed by several of the Bohemian nobility then at Constance, testifying that he had used every prudent means in his power to procure an audience.

"He was, however, notwithstanding this, seized on his way without any authority at Hirsaw, by an officer belonging to the duke of Sultzback, who hoped thereby to receive commendations from the council for so acceptable a service.

"The duke of Sultzback immediately wrote to the council, informing them what he had done, and asking directions how to proceed with Jerome. The council, after expressing their obligations to the duke, desired him to send the prisoner immediately to Constance. He was, accordingly, conveyed thither in irons, and on his way was met by the elector palatine, who caused a long chain to be fastened to him, by which he was dragged, like a wild beast, to the cloister, whence, after an examination, he was conveyed to a tower and fastened to a block, with his legs in stocks. In this manner he remained eleven days and nights, till becoming dangerously ill in consequence, his persecutors, in order to gratify their malice still farther, relieved him from that painful state.

"He remained confined till the martyrdom of his friend Huss; after which he was brought forth and threatened with immediate torments and death if he remained obstinate. Terrified at the preparations which he beheld, he, in a moment of weakness, forgot his resolution, abjured his doctrines, and confessed that Huss merited his fate, and that both he and Wickliffe were heretics. In consequence of this his chains were taken off, and he was treated more kindly; he was, however, still confined, but in hopes of liberation. But his enemies suspecting his sincerity, proposed another form of recantation to be drawn up and

A REVIEW

OF

Fox's Book of Martyrs,

CRITICAL AND HISTORICAL.

No. 23. Printed and Published by W. E. Andrews, 3. Chapter-house-court, St. Paul's Churchyard, London.   Price 3d.

EXPLANATION OF THE ENGRAVING.—*A Priest, named Octavian Ronier, having fallen into the hands of the savage Hugonots, the sanguinary monsters, after applying to him various kinds of torture, fastened horse shoes to his feet with nails, and finally dragged him to a tree, to which they bound him with cords, and shot him dead.* Vide Theatrum Crudelitatum Hæreticorum, Antwerp, 1592.

CONTINUATION OF THE REVIEW.

proposed to him. To this, however, he refused to answer, except in public, and was, accordingly, brought before the council, when, to the astonishment of his auditors, and to the glory of truth, he renounced his recantation, and requested permission to plead his own cause, which was refused ; and the charges against him were read, in which he was accused of being a derider of the papal dignity, an opposer of the pope. an enemy to the cardinals, a persecutor of the prelates, and a hater of the Christian religion

" To these charges Jerome answered with an amusing force of elocution, and strength of argument. After which he was remanded to his prison.

" The third day from this, his trial was brought on, and witnesses were examined. He was prepared for his defence, although he had been nearly a year shut up in loathsome prisons, deprived of the light of day, and almost starved for want of common necessaries. But his spirit soared above these disadvantages.

" The most bigotted of the assembly were unwilling he should be heard, dreading the effects of eloquence in the cause of truth, on the minds of the most prejudiced. At length however, it was carried by the majority, that he should have liberty to proceed in his defence ; which he began in such an exalted strain, and continued in such a torrent of elocution, that the most obdurate Heart was melted, and the mind of superstition seemed to admit a ray of conviction,

" Bigotry however prevailed, and his trial being ended, he received the same sentence as had been passed upon his martyred countryman, and was, in the usual style of Popish duplicity, delivered over to the civil power; but, being a layman, he had not to undergo the ceremony of degradation.

" Two days his execution was delayed, in hopes that he would recant; in which time the cardinal of Florence used his utmost endeavours to bring him over. But they all proved ineffectual: Jerome was resolved to seal his doctrine with his blood.

" On his way to the place of execution he sung several hymns; and on arriving there, he knelt down and prayed fervently. He embraced the stake with great cheerfulness and resolution; and when the executioner went behind him to set fire to the faggots, he said, 'Come here, and kindle it before my eyes; for had I been afraid of it, I had not come here, having had so many opportunities to escape.'

" When the flames enveloped him, he sung an hymn; and the last words he was heard to say were, ' This soul in flames I offer, Christ, to thee !'

We might suppose, from this account, that the members of the council were immersed in brutal ignorance, and monsters in human shape, callous to every sentiment of mercy, and delighting in acts of oppression; but we have a witness to bring forward, whose relation of Jerome's conduct will give a different colouring to the life of this martyr of Fox's coining. It will be found that " this hero in the cause of truth," was a convicted propagator of falsehood, a dissembler and perjurer—very amiable qualities for a Protestant martyr. The cruelties stated to have been practised on Jerome will be seen to be mere fiction, fabricated to excite compassion in his favour, and abhorrence of his persecutors. It will be seen that this heresiarch was treated by the council with lenity and tenderness, which he returned with treachery and deceit; and that it was in consequence of his own bad conduct that he was executed. It is admitted even by John Fox, that he condemned the doctrines of John Huss and Wickliff, under the hope of being liberated, but when he found himself mistaken, he then retracted his solemn declaration; thus shewing himself a prevaricator for self-interest. The charges produced against him, it will be seen, were not those given in the *Book of Martyrs*, but others more impious and irreligious. He was, it appears, a *prosecutor himself*, and *even a murderer*. From Fox's description of his eloquence, we might be led to imagine that he was gifted with tongues as the holy apostles were, and his reasoning overwhelming. It does not, however, appear that he was so highly gifted a man, though certainly possessed of great abilities. We should have been better pleased with Fox, if he had given us some of Jerome's fine arguments, that we might have compared them with the sentiments of the primitive fathers. To tell us that he was ready " to appear at Constance in defence of his character and doc- " trine, both which, *he said*, had been greatly falsified," is telling us nothing. To believe it is to pin our faith upon the sleeve of a CON- VICTED LIAR, and surely there is no Protestant, laying claim to common sense, will take a statement, *unauthorized*, for fact, because John Fox *asserts* it is so and so. Catholics are accused of being led blind- folded by their priests, but what can we say of those Protestants who are led to give credit to tales that carry with them the air of improba- bility, and have no clue of authority to verify them? If Jerome's doc- trines were falsified, why not lay before us the way in which they were perverted? If true, why not point out in what his adversaries erred? He was an " hero in the cause of truth," Fox says; what then were the truths he taught in opposition to the supposed errors in existence.—

Christ had promised that his church should never err, be it observed. This is plainly and explicitly recorded in the gospels of the new Testament. His church was never to swerve from the Truth, and consequently the Truth was always to be found, and to be found only in his church. Where then was the Truth, of which Jerome of Prague was the hero? When was it obscured, and how did Jerome bring it to light? These are questions which every person desirous of coming at the truth should ask. At the time of the council of Constance the Christian world was divided into two classes, the church of Rome and what is called the Greek church, the latter suffering dreadfully from the attacks of the Mahometans, in punishment of their swerving from the Truth. The church of Rome was then acknowledged to be the most ancient church; the period could be named when the Greeks seceded from her authority, but retained all her doctrines, all her sacraments, all her ceremonies; for the only difference between the Latin or Catholic church and the Greeks is, the latter deny the supremacy of the pope, and differ in the article regarding the procession of the Holy Ghost from the Father and the Son. Jerome of Prague acknowledged the supremacy of the pope, and the authority of general councils, by consenting to appear before the synod of Constance; but he differed in some points of doctrine from all the fathers and doctors of the two churches, and consequently from all the Christian world.— Now is it likely that a man, living fourteen hundred years after the Truth was promulgated, should be the only individual in possession of this attribute of God? The idea is monstrous; and yet this is the notion inculcated by Fox, at different periods, when he places the most notorious and violent propagators of error as godly martyrs for the cause of truth. For example, Wickliffe had no supporters in the first instance: the doctrines he broached were the production of his own brain. Huss and Jerome of Prague had each their own visionary fancies: the doctrines they taught differed from each other, and their disciples divided into various sects, namely, the Orebites, Adamites, Drecentians, Gallacians, Rochezanites, Jacobites, Thaborites, and so on. Luther, when he commenced dogmatizer, stood *alone*; his doctrines were *new*, and like all other errors, there was no stability in them. He modelled and re-modelled his opinions at pleasure; his disciples did the same; an innumerable spawn of religion-makers followed, each claiming to be the *true one*, but none of them capable of sustaining their claim.

How different, however, is the foundation of the Catholic church. She had only *One* Architect, who raised his fabric on twelve pillars, and appointed divers Shepherds to guard and protect the sheep which he might gather into the fold of Truth, from the ravages of those who came as wolves in the clothing of sheep to infect them with the contagious breath of error. There was one main pillar to which all the others turned, but that head pillar was supported by the rest, and the fabric was formed of imperishable materials. Now this Architect was God himself, and mark, reader, though he selected *one* of the twelve apostles to be a pivot of unity and subordination, yet he commissioned the whole twelve to teach the *same* doctrines which he had revealed to them all. Though he constituted *one* to be the *head* of all the rest, and the pope is now, and always has been, the head of the Catholic church, yet he did not commission that one, namely, St. Peter, to teach his brother apostles, but he taught them himself, and commissioned them to teach others. This they did according to the command of their divine Master; but in matters of dispute, arising from the frailty of the human mind, and in points of spiritual jurisdiction, they applied to St. Peter, as their successors do at this day to his successor the pope. Thus it will be seen that the Catholic church was not originally erected by one human individual, but by God himself, who being Truth itself, no doctrine can be true or lasting but what emanates from him. He, when clothed in human shape, revealed his doctrines to *twelve* persons, and commanded them to communicate the same to others. They did so, and those to whom the truths were made known imparted them to their successors; and thus they were handed down from father to son, and from age to age, to the time of Jerome of Prague, without the *least deviation* from their original form and meaning. What a gross perversion of common sense must it then be, to suppose that all the Christian world was steeped in error, and only *one* man in the possession of truth; and that man too *contradicting himself!!!* Why this is absurdity without a parallel; and yet the "few plain Christians" have had the folly and impudence to publish it in these days of approaching reason, that their motive in circulating the Book of Martyrs, is to diffuse among their fellow-*believers*, " a *knowledge* and love of the *genuine prin-* " *ciples* of Christianity." Well, reader, let us then see of what materials the Christianity of Jerome of Prague consisted, as stated in *The Fanatic Martyrology*, from which we have before quoted, and the facts in which we are convinced are drawn from the best authorities.

The author, after reciting what passed between the council and Huss and Jerome, as given in our criticism of the life of the former, proceeds to say that both of these heretics agreed to make a retractation of their errors, and requested that a form of abjuration might be sent to them to sign. Upon consultation it was decided that Huss and Jerome should make a retractation and be banished to certain towns in the bounds of Sweden, and that they should subscribe and sign the abjuration of their errors in the Bohemian language, which was afterwards to be sent and published throughout all the churches of that realm, to inform their followers how they had been deluded. The author then goes on,—

" John Huss and Jerome of Prague, made no scruple at the retraction and banishment; but the necessity of disavowing their doctrine in the language of their own country, shocked them more than fire and faggot. John Huss then offered several exceptions against the proceeding, but all availed him not, (as we shall see when we come to treat of him, on the 6th of July 1415, the day on which he was executed.) When that ringleader was dispatched, the council took into consideration the verbal process which the archbishop of Vienna had issued out against Jerome of Prague. As his affair was common with John Huss, so the fathers were resolved to put an end to it, all the difficulties which could possibly attend it being removed, although the matter was prolonged and delayed till the year following, by an egregious court.

" The cardinal of Cambray, the chief commissioner appointed to examine Jerome of Prague, thought himself obliged to begin with a serious exhortation; which he pressed so close, that he thought he had surmounted the obstinacy of the criminal. And indeed Jerome of Prague did not only appear to have changed his sentiments, but likewise to pay a blind deference to the judgment of the council; and that it was but to prescribe what was necessary, and befitting his conversion, to be convinced by experience that it was sincere. The Cardinal made his report to the council, and took it upon himself to draw up in good form an abjuration of the errors of Wickliffe and John Huss. As soon as this was prepared, Jerome of Prague was sent for by the council, who commanded him to stand upon an high seat, from whence he might easily be heard by the whole assembly. He began his discourse by an exposition of what had obliged him to appear before so august a body, and he went on speaking very meanly of himself, and comparing himself to those Jews, who gave nought but trifles towards the building of the Tabernacle, whereas others brought silver and gold, and precious stones. Then he read the abjuration, which had been drawn up, with a very intelligible voice, and added three things, which were important. The first was, that he had been deceived by the appearance of virtue, which was conspicuous in the person of John Huss. The second, that he would live in a perfect and entire submission to the council. And the third was, that in case he should happen to maintain, in any manner, any one of those articles which he abjured, he would renounce all privileges, and would consent that they should proceed against him, by all the ways canonical and civil, which had been appointed against Heresiarchs. He had expected by a declaration so formal and so general, that they would have given him his full liberty, and that they would have permitted him to return to Bohemia, where he imagined that he should succeed to the whole authority of John Huss. But his example had prevailed with the council to proceed with more circumspection, in regard to the prisoner that remained, and not to release him till he had given sufficient proofs and assurances of his conduct for the future. They suffered him, nevertheless, to see all manner of persons, and to entertain himself familiarly, and without inspection, with all whosoever should have the curiosity to visit; that is, they gave him an opportunity to ruin himself, without thinking of it. For instead of using discreetly, the indulgence granted him, until the dissolution of the council, he discovered himself too soon, and ceased not to boast of his having dissembled with the council until such time only as the Hussites sent a delegate to the council, to expostulate with them the death of their prophet and to demand reparation for it. That step, which was followed by a like proceeding from Poland, the Hussites in that country, having given the like commission to the archbishop of Gnesna, and the archdeacon of Posnania, suggested so much presumption to Jerome of Prague, that he believed he might safely speak his thoughts before his countrymen, without regarding whether or no they were favourers of him. And indeed so it was, that they declared themselves against him, and accused him of a relapse into heresy.

"The council, provoked at the inconstancy of that Proteus, who made no scruple, either of lying or perjury, provided that he could thereby accommodate his sentiments to his fortune, obliged him to appear before them the 27th day of April, 1516; and witnesses, against whom no exception could be made, deposed, that he had attempted to instil into their minds the errors of Wickliffe, since that he himself had condemned them. A trespass so sudden and so manifest having opened the scene to all accusations of error, whether old or new, Henry of Prague, prolocutor to the council, objected to him, that he had endeavoured to pervert Germany, Hungary, Poland, and Bohemia; that he had fled out of prison at Vienna, contrary to the promises he had made of tarrying there, until he had cleared himself of certain scandalous propositions, which he was said to have taught there. He added, that in his experimental essays, the same Jerome of Prague had broke out into detestable and impudent actions; that he had writ very severe satires against the dukes of Austria and Bavaria, the clergy of Prague and the holy see; that in the year 1412, upon the feast of St. Vences, the patron of his country, he had stirred up the Hussites, to penetrate with their main body into a monastery of fanatic friars, where they had profaned the altars, and trod under foot the relics of the saints; that he had caused a preacher to be imprisoned, only for having declaimed against Wickliffe; and that the said clergyman had not been released, till he had suffered all the indignities which barbarians usually inflict upon their worst enemies; that he had publicly struck a Franciscan with his fist; that he had been seen in the habit of a priest, though holy orders had never been conferred upon him ; that he had maintained 'in the town of Heidelberg, the capital city of the palatinate, that there was a quaternity in the Godhead ; and that he had endeavoured to unite the Hussites with the schismatics in Poland.

"Jerome of Prague defended himself from one part of these crimes, by assuring the fathers that he had no share in them; and from the other, by ascribing them to such causes, as were not black enough to take away his life. But there was a second charge against him, which was better proved and more perplexing. This began with a supposal, that, if he should be sent back into Bohemia without sufficient proof of his conversion, he would cause much greater disorders in the church than had been at other times fomented by the Arians; for that his doctrine concerning the flesh and blood of Christ, would be sooner and more universally embraced than that of the nature of the work, which was purely spiritual, and had no manner of relation to the senses. That in all the parishes where the said Jerome had preached up his errors, he had met with so much success, that the number of his disciples was greater than that of the remaining Catholics; that he had in a tumultuary manner driven away the pastors, and introduced into their cares such of the clergy as he had already perverted, and had commanded them to take upon themselves the whole pastoral care, without another commission than what they had received from him; that he made a journey into England, upon no other design, than to transcribe a correct copy of the works of Wickliffe; and that he had persuaded the youth to read them, by telling them, that there they would find true and solid divinity; but that in other books they would find little else than deceit; that after the execution of Huss, he had revered him as a saint, and had caused him to be painted with a circle of boys around his head, and in the same posture as the Catholic church represents the saints which had died in the fiery pile; that he had caused a priest, named Fabri, to be scourged in an outrageous manner, insomuch that he died under the lash; that he had freed himself from a Franciscan priest, who had pressed him too close in the heat of dispute, by ordering his disciples to cast him into the river Molde, which they accordingly did; that he had taught that the eucharist was no more than a sign, that the doctrine of Wickliffe was the only and true Gospel; that he had promised an eternal reward to those who should die in defence of it; that he had translated in rhyme the words of consecration, and the principal articles of his creed, to draw away disciples after him; that he had attempted to overthrow the government of the church, in persuading the laity, that they might consecrate the body and blood of Jesus Christ; that he had taught them to despise ecclesiastical censures; that he had endeavoured to render indulgences ridiculous; that he had not contented himself in saying, that the ministry of the word of God was inseparably annexed to baptism, and by consequence common to all Christians (in the acts of the 20th session) but had also himself preached, though a mere layman, and had given a commission to preach to the most adventurous of his sect; that he had defended with an invincible obstinacy all the heresies contained in the forty-five articles of Wickliffe; that he caused to be tied to the breasts of lewd women, and to be burnt publicly in the market-place of New Prague, dispensations granted by the holy see; that he had renewed the heresy of the Iconoclasts; and that within two years before, being in a church belonging to the Franciscans, he had caused a crucifix to be covered over with ordure, under pretence that it was idolatry to suffer images to be there; and that the Hussites had been principally animated by such like discourses to prophane the churches, and to dip their hands in the blood of their countrymen, who had opposed them.

"The prolocutor of the council explained himself more largely in the addition of informations, which began with important advice to the fathers, not to suffer themselves to be imposed upon by the eloquence and vain promises of the criminal, who had already so oft abused the indulgence and credulity of his judges, lest that after he had escaped out of prison, he should become a greater and more pernicious enemy to religion, than he had been before; for that when he was a student at Paris, having been accused of believing and maintaining in his discourses, that God could not annihilate any of his creatures, the members of that university pressed him to make a public recantation thereof; which having promised to do, the night before the day appointed for this recantation, he betook himself to flight, and not daring to continue in France, he took his journey to the town of Heidelberg, where he presently made himself known by certain theses filled with new doctrines, almost wholly heretical, which he had the assurance to present to the syndic of that university; but that doctor, who had exactly performed the duties of his office, having communicated them to the other doctors, and taken measures with them how to arrest Jerome of Prague, he was informed thereof, and by a sudden retreat prevented the imprisonment they had prepared for him. He chose for the third place of his residence, the university of Cracow, where the professors were not more favourable to him, since that they had issued out a warrant against him, which compelled him to change the air, and go to Vienna, where the officers of the archbishop seized upon his person, though he soon let them see by experience, how skilful faithful he was in opening the prison doors. Besides the plentiful entertainments he required in prison, and the pleasure he took in eating and drinking more than was necessary and decent, marked well that his repentance was not sincere, from whence the prolocutor concluded, that he ought to be reduced to bread and water, and if he did not retract in another manner, be put to the torture.

"The council shewed no regard to his conclusions, either because they looked upon them as too severe, or that they thought indulgence was to be used, they only ordained, that Jerome of Prague should appear before a great assembly on the last day of April, 1416, to be there convicted. Accordingly he was brought before them, and the witnesses having face to face persisted in their accusation, the patriarch of Constantinople pressed him sincerely to clear himself of heresy.

"It is impossible to know whether a conjuncture of such importance, the criminal being ashamed again to retract his opinions, or his fear of being condemned, even though he should make a disavowal thereof, cast him into despair, and threw him into obduracy and impenitence; but sure it is, that he made a public profession of the articles of Wickliffe, instead of condemning them; that he satirically reproached the cardinals with their luxury and effeminacy; that he accused the bishops and doctors of Germany with arrogance; that he endeavoured to revive the natural antipathy which was betwixt them and those of Bohemia, to the end that he might set them at variance one against another; that he boasted of being the principal instrument of the revolution which happened in the university of Prague; that the dread of the flames had before prevailed with him to retract, and that now he was overjoyed to expiate by the same punishment the fault he had fallen into. In fine, he spoke as one transported with rage and passion, except that he declared to persevere in the common faith as to the eucharist.

"The next thing therefore was to deliver him over to the secular power; yet the council deferred that till the opening of the twenty-fifth session, upon the 30th of May, at which time the bishop of Lody made a long reprimand to the criminal, for that he had resolved more obstinately than ever to maintain the errors of Wickliffe and Huss, those only excepted which respected the holy sacrament, and indulgences for which reasons he was condemned and delivered over to the punishment of the magistrate, who conducted him to the pile, where he expired repeating the apostles' creed, with a very intelligible voice. There are some authors who relate that he prophesied that out of his ashes would arise, an hundred years after his death, a man who should revive his doctrine, and who should not be so imprudent as to throw himself into the hands of his enemies. This the same authors have interpreted of Luther, from the number of years and conformity of his sentiments. But as the accounts of his death which are given us, both by the council and the gentlemen of Bohemia, who were his friends, are wholly silent in this matter, we cannot but look upon it as falsehood and fable."

From this account, which carries with it the mark of verity, and is founded on the authority of the best writers of that age, it is clear that Jerome of Prague was a restless and daring aspirant, impelled by human ambition and careless of truth. A despot when in possession of power, he paid no regard to justice or the sufferings of others; and when in custody, he made no scruple to lie and forswear himself to obtain his liberty. As he himself and his followers had set the example of persecuting the Catholic clergy, by driving them from their churches and scourging them, it was not to be supposed that he was to come off scot free when the civil magistrates, who were Catholics, got hold of his person. We are not going to justify the execution of Jerome of Prague; all we shall say on his execution is, that the civil authorities considered him a dangerous character, a violater of the public peace, a preacher of sedition, and a fomenter of tumults, and therefore they had as much right to put the laws in force on Jerome, as the English ministry have to make it death to pass forged notes, and execute individuals who trespass against the law. In conclusion, we beg the reader to compare the two accounts we have given of Jerome's life and character; to weigh well the charges made and proved against him by the council, and then say whether this unprincipled man is deserving of the title of a martyr for religion, which Fox has given him, when his whole conduct was a disgrace and scandal to that sacred name. In Fox's account Jerome is represented to have been nearly starved to death, but the counter statements represent him to have been a glutton, and for his intemperance he was put on bread and water, which is the prison diet of this Protestant land, we believe. It is also stated by Fox, that Jerome, in his defence, spoke " in such an exalted strain, and continued " in such a torrent of elocution, that the most obdurate heart was melted." Mr. Earbery however says, that " he spoke as one *transported* " *with rage and passion;*" a feeling very unfit for " *a godly martyr.*" With these remarks we leave the character of these two notorious violaters of the public peace to the judgment of the reader, and proceed to another era of imputed persecution.

SECTION IV.

" GENERAL PERSECUTIONS IN GERMANY."

This is the title selected for the fourth section of this book, and the period is a most interesting one. Fox ushers in his pretended persecutions with the following prefatory remarks :—" Martin Luther, by " unmasking Popery, and by the vigour with which he prosecuted his " doctrines, caused the papal throne to shake to its foundation. So ter- " rified was the pope at his rapid success, that he determined, in orde " to stop his career, to engage the emperor, Charles V. in his scheme " *of utterly extirpating all who had embraced the reformation.* To accom- " plish which, he gave the emperor 200,000 crowns; promised to " maintain 12,000 foot, and 5,000 horse, for six months, or during a " campaign; allowed the emperor to receive one half of the revenues " of the clergy in Germany during the war; and permitted him to " pledge the abbey-lands for 500,000 crowns, to assist in carrying on " hostilities. Thus *prompted* and *supported*, the emperor, with a heart " *eager*, both from *interest* and *prejudice*, for the cause, undertook *the* " *extirpation of the Protestants:* and, for this purpose, raised a formida- " ble army in Germany, Spain, and Italy. The Protestant princes, in " the mean time, were not idle; but formed a powerful confederacy, " in order to repel the impending blow. A great army was raised, and " the command given to the elector of Saxony, and the landgrave of " Hesse. The imperial forces were commanded by the emperor in per- " son, and all Europe waited in anxious suspense the event of the war. " At length the armies met, and a desperate engagement ensued, in " which the Protestants were defeated, and the elector of Saxony and " landgrave of Hesse both taken prisoners. This calamitous stroke was " succeeded by a persecution, in which the most horrible cruelties " were inflicted on the Protestants, and suffered by them with a forti- " tude which only religion can impart." The editors then proceed to enumerate some supposed cruelties, said to have been practised by count Tilly, who is represented to be a sanguinary monster, because he happened to be a Catholic commander, while the Protestants are, gentle creatures, stated to have acted only on the *defensive*. There are, however, two ways in telling a tale, though there can be only one that is right and true. The reader has seen that told by Fox, it will now be, our duty to give a brief but correct description of the transactions arising out of this reformation, so called. As to Luther's unmasking Popery, by which term Catholicism is called by the "few plain Christians," it had never been concealed or obscured, and therefore could not stand in need of being unmasked. That Luther prosecuted his doctrines with vigour, and that these doctrines threatened destruction to religion and morality, we readily admit, for certainly Luther and his associates were the cause of the most horrible outrages and most bloody struggles that stain the annals of Christian states. The pope had no occasion to engage Charles the fifth in a scheme of utter extirpation of the reformers, for Charles found himself under the necessity of assuming a warlike attitude to prevent the Catholics and himself from being utterly extirpated; for we shall make it clear that these innocent reformers, (as Fox would make them appear) meditated and were bent upon the extinction of every thing that savoured of Catholicism.

We have detailed some of the outrages committed by the Hugonots of France, under pretence of serving religion; the same conduct and ferocious disposition marked the progress of the reformation so called every where. We refer the reader to page 297 of this Review for a specimen of some of the doctrines taught by Luther and Calvin, which doctrines could not fail to be productive of the evils which ensued. By an attention to dates, it will be found that the Protestants had entered into confederacies against Charles before that monarch had recourse to arms against them. It must also be mentioned that the empire was threatened at this time with irruptions from the Turks, so that; in fact, Charles had other occupation for his arms than contending against his own rebellious subjects. We must here also observe, that the name first assumed by the reformers of these days was that of *Evangelists* or *Gospellers*; till the year 1529, when they took the name of *Protestants*. Luther threw off his monastic habit in 1524, after having created a tumult in Germany, which made it necessary for him to flee to a place of safety. In consequence he retreated to a castle belonging to the duke of Saxony, who became his protector. His next step was to marry a nun, who, like himself, was bound by solemn vows to lead a life of chastity and virtue. This step put Luther's friends into some confusion, but he knew too well what the influence of love and pleasure would have upon the human frame, when not guarded by the evangelical virtues of self-denial, prayer, fasting, temperance, continence and sobriety, and he soon gained an ascendency over the corrupt and vicious part of mankind. To gain the civil power on his side, he proposed to the princes of the empire to take into their possession the rich abbeys, bishoprics, and church lands. The proposition was no sooner made than it was acceded to by several of the chief magistrates and princes of Germany. Dr. Heylin a Protestant divine, in his Cosmography, p. 106, edit. London, 1612, says, that Frederick I, having deposed his nephew Christiern II, seized on the throne of Denmark; and introduced the Lutheran doctrines into that kingdom. This change he effected by removing all the old bishops, not one of whom could he persuade to the introduction of a new faith, and substituting others in their places, shorn of a great part of their revenues, and deprived of a great part of their power. In the year following Gustavus Ericus expelled Christiern from the throne of Sweden, and began his reign over that kingdom by the introduction of Lutheranism, to which he was chiefly moved "by a desire to appropriate to himself *the goods of the* " *church.* And this appears to have had some strong influence on him " in it, that he presently seized upon what he pleased, and made a law " that bishops should enjoy no more than the king thought fit." *Cosmog.* p. 120. In the kingdom of Poland similar scenes were carried on, with this difference only, that in the two former kingdoms the spoliations were committed by the magistrates, but here the change and outrages originated with a fanatic rabble. "Dantzick," writes Heylin, " was the first town in the kingdom of Poland, which gave entrance to " the doctrines of Luther, anno 1525, but in so tumultuous a manner, " that they that favoured his opinions, deposed the old common-coun-" cil men, and created new ones of their own, profaned the churches, " robbed them of their ornaments, and shamefully abused the priests " and religious persons, abolished the mass, and altered all things at " their pleasure. But by the coming of the king they grew somewhat " quieter, leaving one convent of black friars, and two of nuns, who " still enjoy the exercise of their religion."—*Ibid.* p. 148.

Other towns were soon initiated in this work of desolation and insubordination. The same historian says, "That in the year 1528, re-" ligion being altered, in a tumult of the people, in the canton of " Bern, near adjoining to Geneva, Viret and Farellus, two Zuinglian " preachers, did endeavour it in Geneva also. But, finding that the " bishop and clergy did not like their doings, they screwed themselves " into the people, and, by their aid in a popular tumult, compelled the " bishop and his clergy to abandon the town. Nor did they only in " that tumult alter the doctrine and orders of the church before esta-" blished, but changed the government of the state also, disclaiming all " allegiance both to duke and bishop, and standing on their own " liberty as a free commonwealth. And though all this was done by " Viret and Farellus, before Calvin's coming to that city, which was " not till 1536; yet being come, no man was forwarder than he to " approve the action."—*Ibid.* p. 136.

Speaking of the means adopted by Calvin and his disciples to propagate their errors and discipline, Dr. Heylin tells us, "That rather " than their discipline should not be admitted, and the episcopal " government destroyed in all the churches of Christ, they were re-" solved to depose kings, ruin kingdoms, and to subvert the funda-" mental constitutions of all civil states. And hereunto their own am-" bition gave them spur enough, affecting the supremacy in their seve-" ral parishes; that they themselves might lord it over God's in-" heritance, under the pretence of setting Christ upon his throne. " Upon which love to the pre-eminence they did not only prate against " the bishops with malicious words, &c. but not therewith content, " neither would they themselves receive them, nor permit them that " would, casting them out of the church with reproach and infamy.— " Which proud ambition in the ordinary parochial minister was cun-

" singly fomented by some great persons, and many lay-patrons in all
" places, who underhand aimed at a further end; the one to raise
" themselves great fortunes out of bishops' lands; the other to keep
" those tithes themselves, to which by the law they only were to
" nominate some deserving person. Such were the helps by which this
" new device of Calvin was dispersed and propagated."—*Ibid.* p. 137.

Though Luther stood *alone* in the beginning of his work of deformation, he was not long without helpmates; but as their master built
his notions on the false pride of the human heart, so those who became
enamoured with his doctrines, soon differed from their leader, and
commenced for themselves. Among these was one Nicholas Stork, who,
in 1524, conceived that infants could not be justified by baptism, and
that rebaptism was necessary to salvation. From him sprung the sect
of Anabaptists. This Stork pretended familiarity with God by an angel promising him a kingdom if he would reform the church and destroy
the princes that should injure him. Carlostadius, Muncer, and others
adopted the notions of Stork, and the Anabaptists became a powerful
sect, even in Wirtemberg itself, where Luther had fixed his seat.
The grand apostle took the alarm, he thundered from the pulpit against
Muncer, Stork, and Carlostadius, but finding he could not make them
come into his views, he caused them to be banished from Wirtemberg.
Thus Luther became a persecutor of the reformers, as they called themselves, before a Catholic prince raised the sword against them. The
events of this period are so strikingly awful and interesting, that we
feel ourselves impelled to enter somewhat fully into the details, in order
that the reader may be the more able to form a correct conclusion on
the transactions of those days, and the spirit which influenced them.
Being compelled to quit Wirtemberg, Carlostadius retired to Switzerland, where he became the founder of a new sect, called the Sacramentarians; while Stork and Muncer dogmatised in Suabia, Thuringia,
and Franconia, preaching alike against Luther and the pope.

" Stork and Muncer," writes the Rev. Mr. Bell, in his *Wanderings of
the Human Intellect, &c.* "now conceived the design of forming in the
" heart of Germany a new and independent monarchy; while some of
" their brethren, of more pacific dispositions, thought it criminal to
" stand upon their own defence even against the most wanton and un-
" provoked attacks of their enemies. The people of Mulhausen re-
" spected Muncer as a prophet, divinely commissioned to free them
" from oppression. They expelled their magistrates, declared all pro-
" perty to be common stock, and proclaimed Muncer judge of Israel.
" This new Samuel wrote to the sovereigns and various states of Eu-
" rope, to notify to them that the time was now come when a final pe-
" riod should be put to the oppression of the people and the tyranny of
" kings; and that God had commanded him to exterminate the whole
" race of tyrants, and to establish over the people men of virtue and
" real merit. The flame of sedition quickly spread over the greatest
" part of Germany; and Muncer soon found himself at the head of a
" formidable army; whole districts suddenly rising in rebellion and
" flying to his standard. The disorders committed by this religious
" banditti, alarmed the princes of the neighbouring states, and forced
" them to take the field. At their head was the landgrave of Hesse,

" who fell upon Muncer before he could be joined by the several bo-
" dies of insurgents on their march to reinforce him. Muncer was
" discomfited; and more than seven thousand Anabaptists perished on
" this occasion. Their fanatic leader was himself taken, and a short
" time after executed. (See Catrou, Hist. des Anab. Sleidam, l. 10,
" Seckendorf Comment. Hist. &c.) The defeat and death of Muncer
" did not extinguish Anabaptism in Germany: the party, indeed, was
" no longer formidable; although it seemed even to increase in num-
" bers. Its sectaries, odious alike to Catholics, to Protestants, and Sa-
" cramentarians, were persecuted and defamed through the German
" territories. In Switzerland, the Low Countries, and in Holland, they
" were treated with still greater rigour; numbers were put to death,
" and the prisons were crowded with these poor deluded people. Their
" enthusiasm, however, could not be subdued by terror; and they still
" continued to increase. From time to time, there appeared among
" them impostors who promised them more happy times. Matthew-
" son, a baker at Haarlem, sent ten apostles into Friesland, to Munster
" and other places. At Munster there were already some Anabaptist
" proselytes, who received the new apostles as emissaries from hea-
" ven. They all assembled together in a body at night; and Matthew-
" son's vice-deputy conferred upon them the apostolic spirit which
" they were eagerly waiting to receive. They appeared not much in
" public, till their numbers were greatly augmented; when they sud-
" denly ran up and down the country exclaiming: *Repent ye, and do pe-*
" *nance and be baptized, that the wrath of God may not fall upon you.*
" The spirit of fanaticism was quickly diffused; and when the magis-
" trates set forth an ordinance against them, the Anabaptists flew to
" arms, and seized upon the market place: the townsmen took their
" post in another quarter of the city. Thus they guarded each other
" during three days; till they at length agreed to lay down their arms,
" and that both parties should mutually tolerate each other, notwith-
" standing their difference of sentiments in matters of religion.

" Meanwhile the Anabaptists dispatched secret messages to different
" parts, informing by letter their adherents, that a prophet inspired by
" the Holy Spirit was come to Munster; that he predicted marvel-
" lous events, and instructed men in the true method of saving their
" souls. In consequence of this intelligence, a prodigious number of
" Anabaptists repaired to Munster; upon which several of the party
" ran up and down the streets, crying out with all their might: *Re-*
" *tire all ye wicked from this place, if you wish to escape entire destruc-*
" *tion: all those who refuse to be rebaptized will be knocked on the head.*
" The clergy and the natives then abandoned the town; and the Ana-
" baptists pillaged the churches and forsaken houses; and committed
" to the flames all books indiscriminately, except the bible. Soon after
" the town was besieged; and Matthewson, sallying out upon the as-
" sailants, was himself numbered among the slain. His death was a
" thunderbolt to the party; till John Becold revived their drooping
" spirits by running naked through the streets, and crying out: *the*
" *king of Sion is at hand.* After this extraordinary frolic, he retired to
" his lodgings, and dressed himself as ordinary; but stirred not out of
" doors. The next morning the people attended in crowds to learn the

" cause of so mysterious a proceeding. John Becold answered not a
" word; but signified in writing, that God had enjoined him silence for
" three days. The term of his mutism was expected with impatience;
" and then with a prophetic tone he declared to the people, that God
" had commanded him to establish twelve judges over Israel. He
" named them, and introduced in the government of Munster whatever
" alterations he thought fit. When the impostor deemed himself suf-
" ficiently secure of the good opinion of the multitude, a certain gold-
" smith presented himself before the judges, and said to them : ' Hear
" what the Lord God eternal saith. As heretofore I established Saul
" king of Israel, and after him David, although he was but a simple
" shepherd; so I this day establish my prophet Becold, king in Sion.'
" Another prophet stepped forth and presented him with a sword, say-
" ing : ' God establish thee king, not of Sion only, but of all the earth.'
" The credulous people, in transports of joy, proclaimed the new king
" of Sion, and caused a crown of gold to be made for the occasion, and
" money to be coined in his name.

" Without loss of time, Becold dispatched twenty-six apostles to their
" various destinations, with commission every where to propagate his
" empire. Confusion and disorder marked the progress of these new
" missionaries, particularly in Holland, where John of Leyden pre-
" tended that God had made him a present of Amsterdam, and of se-
" veral other cities. Here the Anabaptists, after exciting much tumult
" and sedition, were many of them punished with death. The king of
" Sion learnt with extreme concern the deplorable mischances of his
" apostles. All was now despondency in Munster; the town was taken,
" and king Becold himself was put to an ignominious and cruel death.
" Thus terminated the reign of Anabaptism at Munster, in the year
" 1536." So far Mr. Bell.

The *Fanatic Martyrology* is more explicit on the freaks of this king
of Sion, and as we are threatened, not altogether with as violent outrages, but with equally as fanatical prophets and preachers, we feel it
our duty to shew the extremes to which the human mind will go,
when unrestrained by divine authority, and acting upon that unstable
guide, *called* REASON. Within these few days, a shoemaker, named
Hale, after realizing an independent property by his trade in the Strand
took it into his head to be inspired with scriptural wisdom, and discovered that war was against the sacred text, and therefore every soldier
who fought in defence of his country would be damned. Not willing
to confine this opinion to himself, he caused his notion to be printed in
the form of a pamphlet, and set about converting the soldiers in the
barracks to his way of thinking, Had he succeeded, we should have
had very little security for our property or our lives; the civil authorities,
however, held him to bail for his good behaviour, which he, fired with
enthusiasm, refusing to give, the result has been a commitment to prison to take his trial for the offence. Had this business happened in a
Catholic country, instead of Protestant England, there is no doubt but
the " few plain Christians" would have made the treatment of Mr.
Hale a subject of *religious persecution*. At the time we are now writing (Oct. 8, 1824) the papers are filled with a detail of fanaticism
scarcely surpassed in the frensied days of the pretended Reformation

of the sixteenth century, on which we are treating. A set of self-in-terpreting bible-readers, after following an old woman, the late Johanna Southcot, as a prophetess, have taken it into their heads to adopt the ceremonial of the old law, circumcision, and, in some instances, of long beards, to appear like the patriarchs of old. In performing the rite of circumcision on a child of 14 days old, however, from the unskilfulness of the high priest, death ensued; the priest has been found guilty of manslaughter, and committed to Lancaster gaol. Being in a Protestant country, we do not hear of any outcry against the proceeding, but we have not a doubt, had the affair taken place in Spain, and the circum-ciser been put into the inquisition, that the "few plain Christians" would have made him *a confessor of the faith* in their next edition of this Book of Martyrs.

From the statement given by Fox, the reader is induced to believe that every thing was perfectly quiet and regular on the part of the reformers, until Charles declared war against them. We wish the reader not only to examine dates, but to be made acquainted with some of the *diabolical doctrines* propagated by these pretended reformers of religion, the dear and beloved friends of the "few plain Christians," who have united to "diffuse among their fellow-believers a knowledge " and love of *the genuine principles of Christianity*." Well, then, reader, among other notions imbibed by these scripture-readers, it was held by them, that all those who were not re-baptized MUST BE IMME-DIATELY SLAIN! A very moderate mode of propagating the truth, and by no means partaking of the spirit of persecution. They also believed all books but the Bible useless, and accordingly they burned all they could meet with, to shew their great love for learning and the sciences. *The Fanatic Martyrology* tells us that John of Leyden de-clared, " that a man should not be tied to one wife, but might marry " as many as he pleased. Some scrupling to approve of this doctrine, " he summoned them to appear before the twelve governors, where " he swore upon the evangelists, that this doctrine had been revealed to " him from Heaven, and to testify the evidence of the spirit, he com-" manded some of the opposers to be beheaded. Immediately his " preachers confirmed this doctrine; but the greatest confirmation " was the prophet's practice, who presently married three wives, and " never gave over till he had made them up fifteen. Many followed " his example, and it was looked upon as honourable to have many " wives, nay so eager were those holy brothers, that as soon as the " revelation was made public, they all ran after the handsomest women, " lying with them beforehand, without any matrimonial contract, for " fear of being disappointed."

. Of the horrid freaks carried on by this mock king, and submitted to by the infatuated victims of delusion, the reader may form some idea from the last mentioned work :—" This upstart king, being originally " taylor, soon converted the rich copes and vestments he had stolen " from the churches, into robes to adorn his vile person, and appeared " glittering in gold and silver ; and even his horses had all their fur-" niture suitable, their saddles, hoosings ,&c. being embroidered. The " taylor king rode abroad daily in much state, attended by his officers. " Next before him went two young men, the one carrying a bible

" and the other a sword. About his neck he wore a great chain, in
" the nature of the collar of some order of knighthood, with this
" motto, *rex justitiæ hujus mundi*, the king of righteousness of this
" world. He was followed by 50 persons well clad. Thrice a week
" he gave public audience, and sat in judgment on an high throne.—
" Under him sat Knipperdoling, his governor of the city, and some-
" what lower his four great councellors of state. In this court he de-
" cided all controversies, which were principally about divorces ; for
" by the new erected scheme of libertinism, every man that was weary
" of his wife, might put her away, and take another. The tyrant pre-
" tended king to shew his authority, being offended at one of his wives,
" brought her forth into the market-place, and struck off her head, caus-
" ing all his other wives to dance about her, and give thanks to their
" heavenly Father, after which he began to dance himself, and com-
" manded all the people to do the like.

" Another time, when he was sitting on the throne, in great ma-
" jesty, his prophet Thuscocurer came to him and said, king John, the
" gospel was renewed by thee, thus said the Lord God. Go and say to
" the king of *Sion*, that he prepare my supper in the church-yard of
" the great church ; and that he send forth preachers of my word unto
" the four quarters of the world, to teach all nations the way of
" righteousness, and to bring them, by the spirit of their mouths, unto
" my sheepfold.

" Accordingly a public communion was celebrated being a full meal,
" a solemn feast, for the number of persons and plenty of meat ; the
" communicants, as they called them, being about 4000, and the com-
" munion three courses of meat ; between the which courses there was
" a bloody inter-mess, for John of Leyden, during the entertainment,
" accused a man of treason, and cut off his head, and returning with
" his hands reeking with the blood, took upon him to administer the
" communion, assisted by his queen, performing the office of a deacon,
" and the like was done by the principal officers of state."

The scenes here described demonstratively prove that the reformation so called was ushered in by very different means to those pursued by the apostles of Christ and their successors. The maxims
laid down by the latter and enforced by example carried conviction to
the Jews and Gentiles, and softened the barbarian nations into civilized Christians. The notions, however, instilled by the reformers of
the sixteenth century brutalized their followers and made them ignorant and cruel. The fruit of Catholicism was the raising of noble edifices to the worship of God, and public institutions for the support of
the indigent and infirm ; the fruit of Protestantism was the demolition
of these sacred temples, and the confiscation of the patrimony of the
poor. But even in the midst of these disorders, the arm of force was
not raised until the power of persuasion was shewn to be unavailable,
At the instigation of the pope, Leo X. and the princes of the empire,
the emperor Charles assembled a diet at Worms in 1521, to discuss and
deliberate on the most effectual means to put a stop to the disorders
that troubled their states. Luther was summoned and attended,
but eloquence and truth were lost on this ambitious and immoral man.
He would not retract ; an imperial edict was therefore passed, con-

demning his books, and placing him under the ban of the empire.—
Luther thought fit to secure his safety by flight, and the emperor
being called suddenly into Spain, the edict was not acted upon. In
1524 another diet met at Nuremburg, and two others at Spire in 1526
and 1529, but to no purpose. In the year 1530 the Lutheran doctors
published a profession of faith in twenty-one articles, called the Confession of Augsburg, and in the year following the famous league of Smalkald was entered into, by which the confederate princes of the new
confession bound themselves to support each other against the emperor,
and protested against all compulsive measures he might think fit to
adopt to bring them to a sense of duty. From this Smalkald protest,
the reformers acquired the appellation of Protestants. Notwithstanding this warlike disposition on the part of the Protestants, Charles did
not assume a similar attitude. He recommended plans of pacification,
such as the calling of a general council, and a committee of divines on
each side to compose a formulary of faith that should be agreeable to
all parties. To this mode of proceeding there could be no objection,
provided TRUTH was the object of each; but as the Catholics could
make no change in the doctrines they had received from God, and as
the Lutherans were not disposed to give up the indulgent system they
had adopted, the recommendation was fruitless and nugatory.

As we have before shewn, when error has been carried to an extreme
height, and the exertions of the provincial guardians of the faith are
been ineffectual in suppressing it, recourse has usually been had to general councils, for preserving and pointing out the Truth. This conduct was pursued by the church against the Arians in 325; the Mace-
donians in 381; the Nestorians in 430; the Eutychians in 451; the Monothelites in 680; the Iconoclasts in 757; the Photians in 869; the Manicheans and Albigenses in 1139; the Wickliffites, Hussites, &c. in
1414; and the Lutherans, in 1545. The motive of these councils is
not to encourage or sanction persecution, but to remove the current of
abuses, by adopting salutary measures of reform; and to silence error
by a solemn declaration of the truths received from the apostles and
handed down from the primitive ages to the period in which these sacred synods or ecclesiastical parliaments were held. Thus on the 13th
day of December, in the year 1545, a considerable number of prelates
and divines assembled from all parts of Christendom, in the cathedral
of Trent, a free city of the Germanic empire, under the authority of a
bull issued by pope Paul III. Besides Italian, French, and Spanish
bishops, there were some from Portugal, Greece, Poland, Germany,
Hungary, Illyrica, Moravia, Croatia, Flanders, Ireland, and one from
England. Thus it may be very justly said, the Catholic church was
fairly represented from all parts of the world, and the deputed fathers
could testify as to the belief held in their respective countries. The
Irish bishops were Thomas O'Herlihy, bishop of Ross, in Munster, who
died in 1597, Donat Mac-Congail, bishop of Raphoe, in Ulster, who died
in 1589; and Eugene O'Hart, a Dominican bishop of Achonry, in Connaught, who died in 1603, at the age of one hundred years. The English
prelate was Thomas Goldwell, bishop of St. Asaph's. Besides the prelates
above, a hundred and fifty theologians, some of the ablest of all Catholic nations attended, and discussed every point in the conference —

A REVIEW

OF

Fox's Book of Martyrs,

CRITICAL AND HISTORICAL.

No. 24. Printed and Published by W. E. Andrews, 3, Chapter-house-court, St. Paul's Churchyard, London. Price 3d.

EXPLANATION OF THE ENGRAVING.—On the left side, are the abbé William of Bre-cailes and another priest, who were captured by the inhuman Hugonots and suspended like meat in the shambles. To lengthen their torments, food was given them, until one died, and then the other was beheaded. On the right side is the abbé Simon Sciot, a Sexagenarian, who being taken prisoner, he effected his ransom with a sum of money, when on returning home as he thought restored to liberty, some of the emissaries of the Hugonot faction fol-lowed him, and after putting out his eyes, they drew out his tongue from beneath his chin.

CONTINUATION OF THE REVIEW.

There were also many superiors of religious orders, and a great num-ber of eminent canonists. Of such men was this last general council composed; and a more learned body could not be assembled to deli-berate on subjects which regarded the eternal happiness of mankind. The order in which the council was conducted we shall give in the Rev. Alban Butler's own words; it shews the sincere desire enter-tained by those who composed the synod to come at the truth, and their readiness to listen to every objection that might be started. In a word, free discussion was exercised by every one, and in this council, as in all others canonically called, arguments and facts were opposed to sophistry and error.

"Matters were discussed," writes Mr. Butler, "in particular con-" gregations; and, lastly, defined in the sessions. After some debates, " it was agreed that points of faith and matters of discipline should be " jointly considered, and the condemnation of errors, and the decrees

" for the reformation of manners carried on together; there being
" abuses in practice relative to most points of doctrine. The doctrine
" of faith is first explained in chapters; then the contrary errors are
" anathematized, and the articles of faith defined in canons. This faith
" is in no point new, but the same which the apostles delivered, and
" which the church in all ages believed and taught. When F. Barnard
" Lami, the Oratorian, had advanced that the chapters or exposition of
" doctrine in this council are not of equal authority with the canons,
" Bossuet, in a few words, charitably convinced him of his mistake,
" which the other readily corrected and recalled, as archbishop Lan-
" guet relates. The decrees for the reformation of manners, and eccle-
" siastical discipline, particularly in the clergy, follow the chapters and
" canons of doctrine in the several sessions. Points relating to the
" holy scriptures, original sin, free-will, justification, the sacraments in
" general, and those of baptism and confirmation in particular, are ex-
" amined in the seven first sessions held under Paul III. On account
" of an epidemical distemper at Trent, he had consented that the pre-
" lates might remove the council to Bologna; this was decreed in the
" eighth session, and the ninth and tenth were held at Bologna, but no
" business done; the emperor and some of the prelates being displeased
" at the translation, so that the pope suspended the council on the
" fifteenth of September, and died November the tenth, 1549. His
" legates a latere in the council were cardinal Del Monte, bishop of
" Palestrino, cardinal Marcellus Cervinus, and cardinal Reginald Pole.
" The first of these was chosen pope, after the death of Paul III. took
" the name of Julius III. and re-assembled the council of Trent in 1551.
" His legates there were cardinal Marcellus Crescenti, legate a latere,
" and Sebastian Pictini, archbishop of Manfredonia, and Aloysius Lip-
" pomannus, bishop of Verona. The eleventh and twelfth sessions
" were preparatory: in the thirteenth and fourteenth the eucharist,
" penance, and extreme-unction were explained: in the fifteenth the
" Protestants were invited under a safe conduct; and in the sixteenth
" the council was suspended on account of the wars in Germany.
" Julius III. died March the twenty-third, 1555, and cardinal Marcellus
" Cervinus, an excellent, courageous, and pious man, was chosen pope,
" and took the name of Marcellus II. but died within twelve days.
" Cardinal Caraffa was chosen pope, May the twenty-third, 1555, and
" called Paul IV. The surrender of the empire by Charles V. a war
" between France and Spain, and some difficulties which arose between
" the emperor Ferdinand and Paul IV. protracted the suspension of
" the council, and this pope died the eighteenth of August, 1559.
" Pius IV. who succeeded, obtained the concurrence of the emperor and
" Catholic kings to restore the council, and published a bull for the
" indiction of the same, November the twenty-fifth, 1560. At the
" head of five papal legates at Trent was the cardinal of Mantua, Her-
" culus Conzaga, and after his death cardinal Morone. In the seven-
" teenth session, held on the eighteenth of January, 1562, the council
" was opened. In the following, the prohibition of books was treated
" of, and letters of safe-conduct sent to the Protestants. In the twen-
" ty-first, the question about communion in both kinds; in the twenty-
" second, the holy mass; and, in the twenty-third and twenty-fourth,

" the latter sacraments were treated of; in the twenty-fifth and last,
" held on the fourteenth of December, 1563, the doctrine of purgatory,
" images, invocation of saints, and indulgences was handled, and the
" council concluded with the usual acclamations and subscriptions.
" After the fathers had subscribed, the ambassadors of Catholic kings
" subscribed as witnesses in a different schedule."

How different is this line of conduct from that pursued by the impugners of truth. We here see the utmost pains taken by the pastors
of the church, to elicit the doctrines taught by and received from the
apostles of Christ. Here was no precipitation used; no hasty conclusions; no rejection of testimony unimpeachable; no reliance on private
opinion; no display of empty learning; but the most careful research
was made into the constant practice of the primitive ages, and of the
different nations in the world on their first receiving the light of the Christian faith. Not so, however, the pretended reformers of religion at this
time, whose demeanour was a scandal to that sacred name, and a display of irreligious blasphemy and insolence outraging common sense
and decency. Luther is stiled by Fox the unmasker of Popery, and is
ranked the father of the pretended reformation. Let us now see the
disposition which prepared him for this work, so much extolled by
those who hate the Catholic religion for their own temporal interest.
In the preface to the first tome of his works, printed at Wirtemberg in
1582, Luther says, " I was mighty desirous to understand Paul in his
" Epistle to the Romans : but was hitherto deterred, not by any faint-
" heartedness, but by one single expression in the first chapter, viz.
" *therein is the righteousness of God revealed.* For I *hated* that word,
" *the righteousness of God;* because I had been taught to understand it
" of that *formal and active righteousness,* by which God is righteous and
" punishes sinners, and the unrighteous. Now knowing myself, though
" I lived a monk of an irreproachable life, to be in the sight of God a
" sinner, and of a *most unquiet conscience,* nor having any hopes to ap-
" pease him with my own satisfaction, *I did not love,* nay, *I hated this*
" *righteous God,* who punishes sinners ; and with *heavy muttering,* if not
" *with silent blasphemy, I was angry with God,* and said, as if it were not
" enough for miserable sinners, who are lost to all eternity by original
" sin, to suffer all manner of calamity by the law of the Decalogue,
" unless God by the gospel adds sorrow to sorrow, and even by the
" gospel threatens us with his righteousness and anger. *Thus did I*
" *rage with a fretted and disordered conscience.*" These, reader, are
Luther's OWN WORDS, and must be not have been a most extraordinary instrument to work a reformation in the church of God, supposing him to have been actually commissioned to perform such a
work? A man, by his own confession, raging " with a fretted and dis-
" ordered conscience,"—" angry with God,"—murmuring against him
—hating him—and silently blaspheming his justice. Precious dispositions for a reformer of religion ! Yet this is the man who is held up
by the editors of Fox's Book of Martyrs as an object of veneration!
But let us see what he says of the ancient fathers :—" To what purpose
" should any man rely on the ancient fathers, whose authority *was revered*
" *for so many ages?* For were not they too all blind? And even neg-
" lected Paul's clearest and most obvious words?—Brag now of the

" authority of the ancients, and depend on what they say: when, as
" you see, every man of them neglected Paul, the brightest and most
" intelligible doctor; and were so deeply plunged into carnal sense,
" as kept them in a manner designedly at a distance from this morn-
" ing star, or rather from this sun."—*Lib. de Serv. Arb. tom.* 2. *fol.*
480. 2.   " Had Austin in plain terms asserted, that there is a power
" in the church to make laws, what is Austin?   Who shall oblige us
" to believe him?   If then so great an error, and such a sacrilege
" prevailed against the word of God for so long a time, with the con-
" sent, or submission, or approbation of *all mankind*—let them consider
" if there be not good reason, why God would have no creature to be
" credited."—*Cont. Reg. Ang. tom.* 2. *fol.* 345. 1.   "Neither do I con-
" cern myself what Ambrose, Austin, the Councils, or practice of ages
." say.   Nor do I want king Harry to be my master in this point.   I
" know their opinions so well, *that I have declared against them*"—*Ibid.*
fol. 347. 1.

    Enough we think has been said to shew that while Catholics rely
upon the promises of Christ, and refer to the testimony of all ages,
Protestants have no other grounds for their faith than the visionary
productions of self-conceit, and oftentimes arrogance.   This boundless
license was the occasion of those struggles and wars of desolation that
fill the blood-stained pages of the annals of those times.   The superiority
of the Catholic mode of ascertaining truth over any other, cannot be
better shewn than by relating an anecdote to be found in Butler's *Saints'*
Lives, on the authority of the archbishop of Braga, in Portugal, one of
the deputies of the council of Trent.   Two of the prelates present at
that synod, from their attachment to Lutheranism, acted as spies to
condemn its decrees.   By assisting, however, at the conferences and
deliberations, in which all points were discussed before the decisions,
they were edified and confirmed in the Catholic faith, by observing the
extreme difference of the method which the reformers pursued, who,
in their deliberations about faith, consulted only their own private
opinions, caprice, and fancy, as we have seen above in Luther, and that
followed by the Catholics, who weighed every thing in the balance of
the sanctuary, and by the most careful search into the undeviating and
primitive tradition, and the faith of all nations, as we before observed,
set the true doctrine of the church of Christ in a clear and perspicuous
light.   One of them afterwards distinguished himself by his advocacy
of truth, and his successful efforts in refuting and converting the Calvinists and other sectaries.   It is the practice with the adversaries of
Catholicism, to represent its professors as blindly led by the priesthood,
and it is said, that when a Catholic begins to *inquire,* he ceases to be a
member of that church.   The ignorance and falsity of such an assertion
must be manifest to all who have read the preceding observations;
because we have clearly proved that it is *by inquiry,* by searching into
the records of past ages, and comparing them with the generally received opinions of the present, that Catholics become more and more
confirmed in the truth of their faith.   When Catholics see, on inquiry,
the reformers of the sixteenth century bearing testimony to the evils
produced by their own doctrines, and compare these evils with the
good works resulting from a correct observance of the laws of God,

and the precepts of the Catholic church, how can they do otherwise, as men of common sense, than adhere to *that* system which is *the best*? Dare not inquire, truly! Oh, yes; they *dare* and *do* inquire, and in their researches they find the apostles of the pretended reformation complaining in these terms :—

"Men," says Luther, "are now more revengeful, covetous, and li-"centious, than they were ever in the Papacy."—*Postil. super Evang. Dom.* 1. *Adv.* And *Dom.* 26. *Post. Trinit.* "Heretofore," says he, "when we were seduced by the pope, every man did willingly follow "good works : and now no man neither sayeth or knoweth any thing, "but how to get all to himself by exactions, pillage, theft, lying, "usury, &c."

Calvin, *L. de Scandalis.* "Of so many thousands, who renouncing "Popery, seemed eagerly to embrace the gospel, how few have amended "their lives? Nay, what else did the greater part pretend to, but by "shaking off the yoke of superstition, to give themselves more liberty "to follow all kinds of lasciviousness."

Melancthon, on Matthew vi. says, "It is plain, that in these coun-"tries, (he speaks of those countries which first embraced Luther's "reformation) men's whole concern almost is about banquetting, "drunkenness, and carousing ; and so strangely barbarous are the "people, that most men are persuaded, that if they do but fast one day, "they must die the following night."

Paulus Eberus, a learned Lutheran divine, in his preface to *Melanc-thon's Commentaries on the first Epistle to the Corinthians*, speaking of Protestants in general, writes thus : "Our whole evangelical congre-"gation abounds with so many divisions and scandals, that it is nothing "less than what it pretends to be. If you look upon the evangelical "teachers themselves, you will see that some of them are spurred on "with vain-glory, and an invidious zeal, &c. some of them raise un-"reasonable debates, and then maintain them with unadvised heat. "There are many of them who pull down, by their wicked lives, what "they had built up by the truth of their doctrine. Which evils, as "every one sees with his own eyes, so has he great reason to doubt "whether your evangelical congregation be the true church, in which "so many and such enormous vices are discovered."

Andrew Dudith, in his epistle to Beza, (*Beza's Theological Epistles,* *ep.* 1.) writes as follows : "What sort of people are our Protestants, "straggling to and fro, and carried about with every wind of doctrine, "sometimes to this side, and sometimes to that? You may perhaps "know what their sentiments in matters of religion are to-day ; but "you can never certainly tell what they will be to-morrow. In what "article of religion do those churches agree among themselves, who "have cast off the bishop of Rome? Examine all from top to bottom, "you shall scarce find one thing affirmed by one, which is not imme-"diately condemned by another for wicked doctrine."

Jacobus Andreas, on Luke, xxi. "The other part of the Germans, "(viz. the Protestants) give due place to the preaching of the word of "God ; but no amendment of manners is found among them ; on the "contrary, we see them lead an abominable, voluptuous, beastly life ; "instead of fasts, they spend whole nights and days in revellings and "drunkenness."

Wolfingus Musculus, in his *Common Pieces, cap. de Decalogo.* "Our
"gospellers have grown so unlike themselves, that whereas under
"Popery they were religious in their errors and superstition; now in
"the light of the known truth, they are more profane, light, vain and
"temerarious, than the very children of this world."—*Explanat.* 3.
Præcepti, p. 85. *edit.* 1560.

The Catholic by inquiry discover no signs of amendment at the
present period. He sees in this Protestant country the prisons filled
with criminals, the gaol deliveries exhibiting scenes of immorality and
vice unknown in Catholic countries, where religion is duly practised;
he sees hundreds rushing into the presence of their God in horrible
fits of despair, with their hands imbrued with their own blood; and
with such scenes before him, with a knowledge of the consolations
derived from the sacraments of the Catholic church, whether in plenty
or misery, can it be a subject of wonder that no good Catholic thinks
of turning Protestant, while the thinking Protestants are daily coming
over to the Catholic faith? Fox has noticed the miserable end of the
Roman emperors who persecuted the primitive Christians, but he does
not tell us of the untimely fate of the principal reformers of the sixteenth century. The death of Christ's apostles and their successors in
fence of the faith they taught is to this day looked upon as a glorious
mark of their divine commission, for nothing but the grace of God
could enable men to withstand such tortures as they endured, or maintain such invincible courage in support of the divinity of Jesus Christ.
How unlike was the conduct and end of the sham apostles of Protestantism. Luther, after a life of intemperance and lust, was suddenly
taken ill after supper, and died in the night, in the year 1546.—
Zuinglius was killed in battle, fighting against the Catholic cantons
in Switzerland, in 1530. Œcolampadius was not long after found dead
in his bed, killed, as Luther writes in one of his works, by the devil.
L. de Missa Privita et Unct. Sacerd. t. vii. fol. 230. Calvin died in the
year 1504 of a dreadful complication of distempers, which his friend
Beza says he bore with Christian fortitude, but the Catholics and some
Protestants say, he died in despair, blaspheming God, and invoking
devils. This is related by Bolseck in his *Life of Calvin*; Schlussel-
berg, a learned Lutheran, in *Theolog. Calv.* printed in 1594; and He-
rennius a Calvinist preacher, who states he was himself aneye-wit-
ness of Calvin's tragical end; and that he died in despair of a most
filthy stinking disease. See *Libello de vita Calvini.*

The reader will now be able to estimate the manner pursued by the
reformers to unmask Popery, as Catholicism is termed, and the vigour
with which they prosecuted their doctrines. We have disclosed the
outrages committed by the mad fanatics, in the name of religion; and
we have shewn the mode followed by the Catholic divines to reclaim
them from their error and draw them back to the path of truth. We
have shewn that deliberation was attempted in the diet at Worms in
1521; at Nuremberg in 1524; at Spire in 1526 and 1529, but to no
effect; that a Protestant profession of faith was announced in 1530;
and a Protestant league the year following; that the council of Trent
assembled in 1545; and it now remains for us to state, that it was
not till the year 1546 that Charles declared war against the confederate princes, not however as Protestants or heretics, but as rebels

and enemies to the empire. Thus was civil war enkindled in the very heart of Germany, which continued nearly six years, when both parties agreed to sheath the sword, and restore peace to the country. Whatever violences may have taken place, we think it is clear that they cannot be fairly classed as religious persecutions, and we have made it as clear as the sun at noon day, that the reformed or Protestant party were the aggressors; that the Catholics acted on their own defence; and, therefore, whatever disasters might befall the Protestanty party, they arose out of their own misconduct.

"SECTION V.

"Persecutions in the Netherlands."

This section is prefaced with the following passage :—" The glo-" rious light of the gospel spreading over every part of the continent, " and chasing thence the dark night of ignorance, increased the alarm " of the pope, who urged the emperor to commence a persecution " against the Protestants; when many thousands fell martyrs to super-" stitious malice and barbarous bigotry."—Fox then proceeds to de-tail the pretended martyrdoms of " a pious widow, named Wendeli-" nuta," two Protestant clergymen, a minister of the reformed church, and many others, for offences so trivial as to be utterly unworthy of credit. He then goes on, " In Flanders, about 1543 and 1544, the per-" secution raged with great violence. Many were doomed to perpetual " imprisonment, others to perpetual banishment; but the greater num-" ber were put to death either by hanging, drowning, burning, the " rack, or burying alive," and concludes the section with an account of the assassination of the prince of Orange. As usual we have no au-thorities, nor are we told which prince of Orange was assassinated, nor when, nor where. Such is the method adopted by the " few plain " Christians" to diffuse among their " fellow believers, a knowledge " and love of the genuine principles of Christianity." *They* do not, we imagine, expect their fellow-*believers* to enter into an *inquiry*, for if they did they would at least have made some greater shew of authority for their assertions. We hope however that these fellow-believers *will* in-quire, and to assist them in the course of their research, we will here furnish them with an extract or two from Dr. Heylin's *History of the Presbyterians*, treating of the period chosen by the " few plain Chris-tians" for the time of persecution. The time selected by Fox or his editors is between 1543 and 1544, when, he says, " the persecution " raged with great violence." We are at a loss to know what he means by the term persecution, for the doctrines preached by the reformers did not inculcate submission to authority, and the bearing of injuries for conscience sake, but encouraged sedition, pillage and murder, as we shall see presently. The resistance therefore made to the turbulent and illegal proceedings of these sham *reformers* of religion could by no means be called a persecution, but a measure of self-defence to pre-serve the already established authorities, ecclesiastical and civil, both of which the then New Lights meditated the destruction. It does not appear from Dr. Heylin that a persecution was commenced at that time by the Catholics, but, he states that measures were taken, as we before observed, to restrain the "rascal rabble," as he calls them, from violating the laws, to which they were instigated by the Calvinistic preachers. This was done by the introduction of the Spanish inquisition, but the edict for erecting this tribunal in the Netherlands bears date the 20th of April, 1548, which is four years after the latest date named by the Book of Martyrs. The erection of this inquisition furnished an opportunity to the leaders of the reformers to declaim against the authority of the pope, and raise a false cry about liberty. The Calvinists sent two preachers at the same time to two of the chief cities in French Flanders, namely, Valenciennes and Hainault, in the first of which the preacher collected after his sermon, a mob of one hundred people, and in the latter, the missioner had no fewer than six hundred, who paraded the streets singing David's psalms, according to the custom of the Hugonots of France. To suppress these proceedings, the governor seized the two preachers and put them into prison; on this the people threatened the judges if any harm was done to them. At the end of seven months, however, they were tried and sentenced to be burned; but when they were brought out for execution, "there presently arose a "tumult so fierce and violent," writes Dr. Heylin, "that the officers "were compelled to take back their prisoners, and to provide for their "own safety, for fear of being stoned to death by the furious multi-"tude. But the people having once begun, would not so give over; "for being inflamed by one of their company, whom they had set up "in the midst of the market-place to preach an extemporary sermon, "two thousand of them ran tumultuously to the common goal, force "open the doors, knock off the shackles of the prisoners, restore them "to their former liberty, and so disperse themselves to their several "dwellings. The news of which sedition being brought to Brussels, the "governess despatcheth several companies of foot, and some troops of "horse, with orders to the marquis of Bergen to appease the disorders "in the town. But they found all things there so quiet, that there was "little need of any other sword than the sword of justice; by which "some of the chief ring-leaders of the tumult, and one of their preachers "(who had unhappily fallen into their hands) were sentenced to that "punishment which *they had deserved.*"

This riotous conduct was followed by tumult after tumult, which induced the king to give orders to his sister (the governess of the province) to see his father's edicts severely executed. This order was resisted by some of the lords of the council, who, in the end, entered into a covenant similar to the famous Scotch covenant, which engaged to extirpate Popery, Prelacy, and so forth, with fire and the sword, under the hypocritical and blasphemous pretence of promoting true religion and God's glory. This league was ratified and sworn to at a drunken carousal by, the historian writes, a set of "men of dissolute lives and broken fortunes, or in plain English, *rogues* and *beggars.*" By such missioners was "the glorious light of the gospel" spread over every part of the continent. Things being thus prepared, the next proceeding was to spread *false reports*, and issue *counterfeit papers* against the old religion and the government. Having thus excited the feelings of the people, and brought matters to a considerable height, the next object in view was to embroil the country in a civil war. To accomplish

this end, Dr. Heylin writes, " With these French preachers and Calvi-
" nian minister, there entered several emissaries sent from the admiral
" Colligni, the prince of Conde, and others of the heads of the Hugo-
" not faction, whose interest it was to embroil the Netherlands, that
" they themselves might fear no such danger on that side, as formerly
" they had received. And these men played their parts so well, that a
" confused rabble of the common people, furnished with staves, hatchets,
" hammers and ropes, and armed with some few swords and muskets,
" upon the eve of the Assumption of the Blessed Virgin, fell violently
" into the towns and villages about St. Omers, one of the chief cities of
" Artois, forced open all the doors of churches and religious houses, if
" they found them shut; demolished all the altars, and defaced the
" shrines, and broke the images in pieces, not sparing any thing which
" in the piety of their ancestors was accounted sacred. Encouraged by
" which good success, they drive on to Ipres, a town of Flanders, where
" they were sure to find a party prepared for them, by which the gates
" of the city were set open to give them entrance: no sooner were they
" entered, but they went directly to the cathedral, (their multitudes
" being much increased all the way they came) where presently they
" fell to work; some beating down the images with staves and ham-
" mers, some pulling down the statues of our Saviour with ropes and
" ladders; others defacing pulpits, altars and sacred ornaments, burn-
" ing the books, and stealing the consecrated plate. With the same fury
" they proceeded to the burning of the bishop's library, and the destroy-
" ing of all churches and religious houses within that city; in which
" they found as little opposition from the hands of that magistrate, as
" if they had been hired and employed in that service by the common
" counsel. About the same time, that is to say, on the morrow after the
" Assumption, another party being of the same affections, and taking
" both example and encouragement from this impunity, fall into Menim,
" Commines, Vervich, and other towns upon the Lys: in all which
" they committed the like impious outrages, carrying away with them
" plate and vestments, and all other consecrated things which were
" easily portable; but burning or destroying what they could not
" carry. The like they would have done also at the town of Seclin,
" but that the people rose in arms, assaulted them, and drove them
" back, not without great slaughter of that mutinous and seditious
" rabble, and some loss of themselves."

Here is a specimen of the means by which " the glorious light of the
" gospel" was spread " over every part of the continent," that ought to
make the " few plain Christians," who have united to " diffuse among
" their fellow-believers a knowledge and love of the genuine principles
" of Christianity," redden with shame, if they have any in them. The
same scenes were exhibited at Antwerp. After a sermon preached to
them in a field, the rabble reformers brought their preacher into the
city in triumph on horseback, attended by a guard both of horse and
foot. To quell these tumultuous proceedings, the governess sent the
count of Megan and afterwards the prince of Orange, who treacherously
betrayed their trust, and sided with the reformers. Encouraged secretly by these traitors, they followed a procession of the clergy in honour of the blessed Virgin on the anniversary of her Assumption into

the cathedral, " where," Dr. Heylin says, " they first fall to words, and
" from words to blows, and from blows to wounds ; to the great scan-
" dal of religion, and the unpardonable profanation of that holy place."
This historian then goes on, " But this was only an essay of the fol-
" lowing mischief : for on the same day se'nnight, being not only more
" numerous, but better armed, they flocked to the same church at the
" evening service; which being ended, they compel the people to for-
" sake the place, and possess themselves of it.   Having made fast the
" doors for fear that some disturbance might break in upon them, one
" of them begins to sing a psalm in Marot's metre, wherein he is fol-
" lowed by the rest; that such a holy exercise as they were resolved
" on, might not be undertook without some preparation : which fit of
" devotion being over, they first pulled down a massy image of the
" Virgin, afterwards the image of Christ, and such other saints as they
" found advanced there, on their several pedestals ; some of them tread-
" ing them under foot, some thrusting swords into their sides, and
" others haggling off their heads with bills and axes : in which work as
" many were employed in most parts of the church, so others got upon
" the altars, cast down the sacred plate, defaced the pictures, and disfi-
" gured the paintings on the walls, whilst some with ladders climbed
" the organs, which they broke in pieces ; and others, with like horri-
" ble violence, destroyed the images in the windows, or rather broke
" the windows in despight of the images.   The consecrated Host they
" took out of the pixes, and trampled under their feet ; carouse such
" wine as they brought with them in the sacred chalices, and greased
" their shoes with that chrysome, or anointing oil, which was prepared
" for some ceremonies to be used at baptism, and in the visiting of the
" sick.   And this they did with such despatch, that one of the fairest
" churches in Europe, richly adorned with statues and massy images of
" brass and marble, and having in it no fewer than seventy altars, was
" in the space of four hours defaced so miserably, that there was nothing
" to be seen in it of the former beauties.   Proud of which fortunate
" success, they broke into all other churches of that city, where they
" acted over the same spoils and outrageous insolencies ; and after-
" wards forcing open the doors of monasteries and religious houses,
" they carried away all their consecrated furniture, entered their store-
" houses, seized on their meat, and drank off their wine ; and took from
" them all their money, plate, and wardrobes, both sacred and civil, not
" sparing any public library wheresoever they came ; a ruin not to be
" repaired but with infinite sums : the havoc which they made in the
" great church only, being valued at four hundred thousand ducats by
" indifferent rates.   The like outrages they committed at the same time
" in Gaunt and Oudenard, and all the villages about them ; the seve-
" ralties whereof would make up a volume : let it suffice, that in the
" province of Flanders only, no fewer than four hundred consecrated
" places were in the space of ten days thus defaced, and some of them
" burnt down to the very ground."
    When the news of these intolerable outrages reached the seat of
government at Brussels, orders were given, as a matter of course, to
repress them ; but the meek and pious spreaders of " the glorious light
" of the gospel" intimated, that if any of the rebels were molested or

punished on account of their *religion*, (What a perversion of terms!)
the government would immediately see all the churches in Brussels
fired, the priests murdered, and the governors imprisoned. Nor were
they backward in fulfilling, in some measure, their threats; for, in a
short time after, the reformed party seized some churches in Mechlin,
Antwerp, Tournay, and Utrecht; and to complete their insolencies and
violations, a tumult was raised at Amsterdam, "where some of the re-
"formed rabble" Dr. Heylin writes, "broke into a monastery of the
"Franciscans, defaced all consecrated things, beat and stoned out the
"religious persons, and wounded some of the principal senators who
"opposed their doings." Provoked at these indignities and sacrileges, the government resolved at last to bring the reformers to obedience by force of arms; the covenanters prepared to resist, and hence
arose a long and bloody civil war, in which excesses were committed
by both parties disgraceful to the character of Christians. The modern
editors of Fox may falsely represent these proceedings as persecutions,
but the unprejudiced man will always regard them as the contentions
of human ambition for temporal power and interest. The unbiassed
man will not fail to see the baseness of bloated bigotry, in perverting
historical facts to lead the unthinking into error, and excite hatred and
animosity under the pretence of diffusing "a knowledge and love of the
"genuine principles of Christianity." For example; Dr. Heylin states,
that when the Prince of Orange, of whom we shall have something to say
soon, took Dendermond and Oudenard by storm, the soldiers there and
in all places "made spoil of churches, and, in some places, tyrannized
"over the dead, whose monuments they robbed and pillaged. But
"none (he adds) fared worse than the poor priests, whom, out of hate
"to their religion, they did not only put to death, but put to death
"with tortures; and, in some places which fell under the power of the
"Baron of Lume, hanged up their mangled limbs or quarters, as but-
"chers do their small meats in common shambles; which spoils and
"cruelties so alienated the affections of all the people, that his power
"in those parts was not like to continue long."

Here the reader will further see by what means "the glorious light of
"the gospel" was spread over the Netherlands by Protestant pretended
reformers. The *Book of Martyrs* talk of the many thousands that fell
"martyrs to superstitious malice and barbarous bigotry," but we hear
not a word of the cruel barbarities and sacrilegious injustices practised
by these pretended martyrs wherever they got the ascendancy over the
Catholics. We have here, however, torn the mask aside, and displayed
the origin of the reformation, so called, in all its terrific deformity.
Nor was the conduct of their leaders less base than cruel, for the same
historian relates, that when Amsterdam was constrained to yield to the
rebel reformers, after an almost miraculous resistance on the part of
the people in favour of their old religion, they yielded on condition of
enjoying the free exercise of their ancient faith, and of having the town
garrisoned by native citizens. "But (writes Dr. Heylin) when they
"had yielded up the town, they were not only forced to admit a garri-
"son, but to behold their churches spoiled, their priests ejected,
"and such new teachers thrust upon them as they most abominated.
"But liberty of religion being first admitted, a confused liberty of

" opinions followed shortly after, till, in the end, that town became the
" common sink of all sects and sectaries which hitherto have disturbed
" the church, and proved the greatest scandal and dishonour of the
" reformation." What a scene of perfidy, villany, and impiety is here
disclosed; and this is what the " few plain Christians" call spreading
" the glorious light of the gospel!!!"—Oh! shame, where is thy blush!

We will quote another passage from this Protestant historian and
divine, who wrote when the circumstances he recorded were fresh upon
the mind of every intelligent person, to shew the irreligious and blasphemous pretensions of those religion-menders, and the stupid credulity of the people in listening to and following the depraved and fanatical impostors that were daily starting up to spread " the glorious
" light of the gospel," and chase from the continent " the dark night of
" ignorance." " Holland had lately," continues Dr. Heylin, " been too
" fruitful of this viperous brood, but never more unfortunate than in pro-
" ducing David George of Delft, and Henry Nicholas of Leyden, the
" two great monsters of that age: but the impieties of the first were
" too gross and horrid to find any followers; the latter was so smoothed
" over as to gain on many, whom the impostor had seduced. The
" Anabaptists out of Westphalia had found shelter here in the beginning
" of the tumults; and possibly might contribute both their hearts and
" hands to the committing of those spoils and outrages before remem-
" bered. In imitation of whose counterfeit piety and pretended single-
" ness of heart, there started up another sect as dangerous and destruc-
" tive to human society as the former were; for, by insinuating them-
" selves into the heart of the ignorant multitude, under a shew of
" singular sanctity and integrity, they did afterwards infect their minds
" with damnable heresies, openly repugnant to the Christian faith. In
" ordinary speech they used new and monstrous kinds of expressions, to
" which the ears of men brought up in the Christian church had not
" been accustomed, and all men rather wondered at than understood.
" To difference themselves from the rest of mankind, they called their
" sect by the name of the *Family of Love*, and laboured to persuade
" their hearers, that those only were elected unto life eternal which
" were by them adopted children of that Holy Family; and that all
" others were but reprobates and damned persons. One of their para-
" doxes was (and a safe one too) that it was lawful for them to deny
" upon oath whatsoever they pleased, before any magistrate, or any other
" whomsoever that was not of the same family or society with them.
" Some books they had, in which their dotages were contained and
" propagated; first writ in Dutch, and afterwards translated into other
" languages as tended most to their advantage; that is to say, *The Gos-.*
" *pel of the Kingdom; The Lord's Sentences; The Prophesy of the Spirit*
" *of the Lord; The Publication of Peace upon Earth*, by the author H. N.
" But who this H. N. was, those of the Family could by no fair means
" be induced or inforced by threatenings to reveal. But after it was
" found to be this Henry Nicholas of Leyden, whom before we spake of,
" who, being emulous of the glories of king John of Leyden, that most
" infamous botcher, had most blasphemously preached unto all his
" followers, that *he was partaker of the divinity of God, as God was of his*
" *human nature.*"

Here we shall close our remarks on the method taken to spread "the light of the gospel" in the Netherlands, and the impious fruits this pretended light produced; before however we quit this section we shall take leave to expose a gross perversion of history for the purpose of delusion. The account of the assassination of the prince of Orange is thus stated :—" Balthazar Gerard, a native of Franche Comté, a " bigotted and furious Roman Catholic, thinking to advance his own for- " tune and the popish cause by one desperate act, resolved upon the as- " sassination of the prince of Orange. Having provided himself with " fire-arms, he watched the prince as he passed through the great hall " of his palace to dinner, and demanded a passport. The princess of " Orange, observing in his tone of voice and manner something con- " fused and singular, asked who he was, saying she did not like his " countenance. The prince answered, it was one that demanded a " passport, which he should have presently. Nothing farther trans- " pired until after dinner, when on the return of the prince and princess " through the same hall, the assassin, from behind one of the pillars, " fired at the prince ; the balls entering at the left side, and passing " through the right, wounded in their passage the stomach and vital " parts. The prince had only power to say, ' Lord have mercy upon " my soul, and upon this poor people,' and immediately expired.

" The death of this virtuous prince, who was considered as the " father of his people, spread universal sorrow throughout the United " Provinces. The assassin was immediately taken, and received sen- " tence to be put to death in the most exemplary manner ; yet such " was his enthusiasm and blindness for his crime, that while suffering " for it, he coolly said, ' Were I at liberty I would repeat the same.' "

This is the statement in the *Book of Martyrs*, and we might suppose by it that this "virtuous prince," this looked-upon "father of his " people," was the paragon of governors and the most faithful of Christians. Other writers, however, give a different colour of his cha- racter, and represent him as a dissembler, a cheat, and an oppressor; and differ from Fox as to the manner of his assassination. Dr. Heylin writes, in his history aforesaid, that as there was no hopes of reducing Holland and Zealand to the king of Spain's subjection, while the prince of Orange remained at the head of the insurgents, and as there was no chance of overcoming the prince by open force, it was resolved to take his life by treachery. This was an unjustifiable determination, and it is evident that religion had no more to do with it, than it had with the horrible massacre of Gleneowe by the prince of Orange of England. However the decision was made and acted upon. The first who made the attempt was a young fellow, who discharged a pistol in his face when he was attending on the duke of Anjou at Ant- werp, but without effect. " Being recovered of that blow," says Dr. Heylin, " he was not long after shot with three poisoned bullets, by " one Balthasar Gerard, a Burgundian born, *whom he had lately taken* " *into his service :* which murder was committed at Delph, in Holland, " on the 10th of June, 1584, when he had lived but fifty years and " some months over." Here then we have a different relation of this transaction. Heylin says the assassin was a servant of the prince, and being such, we may suppose he was *not* a Catholic, his master being;

like the "few plain Christians," a Catholic-hater. The assassin, we are told by Fox, "was put to death in the most *exemplary* manner," but what kind of death he suffered we are not informed, though we are told it was worthy of imitation. Fox represents this leader of armed spreaders of "the light of the gospel," to be a "virtuous " prince; but Dr. Heylin gives a different account of him. The doctor says, "For compassing his designs he made use of that religion which " best served his turn : being bred a Lutheran by his father, he professed " himself a Romanist under Charles the fifth; and after finding the " Calvinians the more likely men to advance his purposes, he declared " himself chiefly in their favour, though he permitted other sects and " sectaries to grow up with them; in which respect he openly op-" posed all treaties, overtures, and propositions, looking towards a " peace, which might not come accompanied with such a liberty of " conscience, both in doctrine and worship, as he knew well could " never be admitted by the ministers of the Catholic king."

That the prince has occasion to exclaim "Lord have mercy upon " my soul, and upon this *poor people*," we verily believe; for, in the first place he was the cause of much blood being shed, and, in the second, he took care to fleece the "poor people" pretty closely to carry on his ambitious designs. In concluding his account of "their " (the Presbyterians) positions and proceedings in the higher Ger-" many; their *dangerous doctrines* and *seditions*; their *innovations* in " the *Church*, and *alteration* of the *civil* government of the Belgic " provinces from the year 1559 to the year 1585," Dr. Heylin records the successful artifice practised to cheat the clergy of the tithes, and transfer them to the coffers of this " virtuous prince."——This trick is so curious that we shall give it in the doctor's words, to shew how easily a bewildered and fanatic people can be cheated out of their faith and property. "They," (the Calvinist declaimers) he writes, "had " besides, so often preached down tithes as a Jewish maintenance im-" proper and unfit for ministers of the holy gospel, when they were " paid unto the clergy of the church of Rome, that at the last the peo-" ple took them at their word, believe them to be so indeed, and are " spurred on the faster to a change of religion, in which they saw some " glimmering of a present profit. Of these mistakes the prince of " Orange was too wise not to make advantage; giving assurance to " the land-holders and country villagers, that if they stood to him in " the wars against the Spaniard, they should from thenceforth pay no " tithes unto their ministers, as before they did. The tithes in the " mean time to be brought into the common treasury toward the charges " of the war, the ministers to be maintained by contributions at an easy " rate. But when the war was come to so fair an issue, that they " thought to be exempted from the payment of tithes, answer was made " that they should pay none to the ministers, as they had done for-" merly, whereby their ministers in effect were become their masters; " but that the tithes were so considerable a revenue to the common-" wealth, that the state could not possibly subsist without them; that " therefore they must be content to pay them to the state's commis-" sioners, as they had done hitherto; and that the state would take " due care to maintain a ministry. By means whereof they do not only

" pay the tithes as in former times ; but seeing how much the public al-
" lowance of the state doth come short of a competency (though by
" that name they please to call it) they are constrained, as it were,
" out of common charity, if not compelled thereto by order, to con-
" tribute over and above with the rest of the people, for the improve-
" ment and increase of the ministers' maintenance. But as they bake,
" (observes the doctor) so let them brew, to make good the proverb."
So say we, and here we may safely leave the persecutions in the
Netherlands to the judgment of the reader.

" SECTION VI.

" Persecutions in Lithuania."

The country here selected is a large portion of Europe now forming part of the kingdom of Poland, with the title of a grand duchy.
The following is the account given by the *Book of Martyrs* of the pretended persecutions in this country :—" The persecutions in Lithuania
" began in 1648, and were carried on with great severity by the Cos-
" sacks and Tartars. The cruelty of the former was such, that even
" the Tartars, at last, revolted from it, and rescued some of the in-
" tended victims from their hands.

" The Russians perceiving the devastations which had been made in
" the country, and its incapability of defence, entered it with a consi-
" derable army, and carried ruin wherever they went. Every thing
" they met with was devoted to destruction. The ministers of the
" gospel were peculiarly singled out as the objects of their hatred,
" while every Christian was liable to their barbarity.

" Lithuania no sooner recovered itself from one persecution, than
" succeeding enemies again reduced it. The Swedes, the Prussians,
" and the Courlanders, carried fire and sword through it, and continual
" calamities, for some years, attended that unhappy district. It was
" afterwards attacked by the prince of Transylvania, at the head of an
" army of barbarians, who wasted the country, destroyed the churches,
" burnt the houses, plundered the inhabitants, murdered the infirm,
" and enslaved the healthy.

" In no part of the world have the followers of Christ been exempt
" from the rage and bitterness of their enimies; and well have they
" experienced the force of those scripture truths, that they who live
" godly in Christ, shall suffer persecution, and those who are born af-
" ter the flesh have always been enemies to such as are born after
" the spirit: accordingly the Protestants of Poland suffered in a dread-
" ful manner. The ministers in particular were treated with the most
" unexampled barbarity ; some having their tongues cut out, because
" they had preached the gospel truths ; others being deprived of their
" sight on account of having read the bible ; and great numbers were
" cut to pieces for not recanting. Several private persons were put to
" death by the most cruel means. Women were murdered without the
" least regard to their sex; and the persecutors even went so far as to
" cut off the heads of sucking babes, and fasten them to the breasts of
" their unfortunate mothers !

" Even the silent habitations of the dead escaped not the malice of

" these savages; for they dug up the bodies of many eminent persons,
" and either cut them to pieces and exposed them to be devoured by
" birds and beasts, or hung them up in the most conspicuous places.
" The city of Lesna, in this persecution, particularly suffered; for be-
" ing taken the inhabitants were totally extirpated."

We have here the date when the persecutions are said to have commenced, but the rest is all assertion, and, we will add, in a great measure fiction. In the first place we must observe, that the beginners of
the persecution being stated to be Cossacks, and Tartars, the Catholics
cannot surely be blameable for their deeds, as they were infidels or Mahometans, and the victims most probably, we believe really, were Catholics. Then the Russians carried on what was begun by the Cossacks and Tartars. Well, the Russians were not Catholics, they had
seceded from the church of Rome, and therefore the professors of that
church cannot consequently be made responsible for the actions of the
seceders. Then the Swedes and Prussians, and the Courlanders carried
fire and sword through it; here again the persecutors are not Catholics. These people were Protestants, reader; they were the children of
the reformation, so called; is it right that poor Popery should be bur-
thened with the sins of others? Next comes the prince of Transylvania
and his army of barbarians, who wasted the country, destroyed the
churches, and carried total destruction before him. This prince and his
barbarians were Mahometans, and by the demolition of churches we
may suppose the victims were Catholics, for they were the builders of
the churches. We agree with Fox, that "in no part of the world have
" the followers of Christ been exempt from the rage and bitterness of
" their enemies;" this was foretold by Christ, and the page of history
bears testimony to the accuracy of the prophecy. The primitive Catholic Christians suffered persecution from the Pagans; they suffered
from the Arians, they suffered under Mahometanism, and they felt the
persecuting hand of Protestantism, whenever the latter gained the ascendency. At this very day this intolerant spirit is shewing itself in
Ireland, where the unoffending Christian, who forsakes the path of error to embrace the glorious light of truth, is sure to be marked out as
the victim of persecution by the Orange faction.

But to return to the *Book of Martyrs*. The Protestants of Poland are
said to have suffered in a dreadful manner, and a brief account is given
to harrow up the feelings of the reader;—but if they did suffer, they
have themselves to blame, for they were the basest traitors to their
country that ever a country was cursed with. From motives of revenge
they introduced foreign mercenaries into their native country, created a
civil war, and finally occasioned it to fall into the hands of the neighbouring powers. Poland had long been a prey to faction, from the formation
of her civil constitution, and when the seeds of the reformation were sown
in that country, and began to fructify, to civil faction was united religious
regard on one side, and fanaticism on the other. We have now before us
De la Croix's Review of the Constitutions of the principal States of Europe,
from whose account of the Constitution of Poland we here make some extracts. We know not what religion this author professed, but it is clear
he was not a Catholic, and therefore he could have no predilection for
that faith. He writes, "The Protestant doctrines which were spread all

A REVIEW

OF

Fox's Book of Martyrs,

CRITICAL AND HISTORICAL.

No. 25. Printed and Published by W. E. ANDREWS, 3, Chapter-house-court, St. Paul's Churchyard, London.   Price 3d.

EXPLANATION OF THE ENGRAVING.—*The Hugonots forced a priest, on whom they laid their hands, to celebrate mass, for no other cause than that they might make a jest of it. While celebrating the divine mysteries, the barbarous miscreants wounded the martyr in several parts of his body with their poignards,—they then fastened him to a cross in the church by his hands and feet, and in that posture they shot at him till he was dead.*

CONTINUATION OF THE REVIEW.

" over Germany, had penetrated Poland, and were there opposed by
" persecutions. Novelties, which would die away, if treated with in-
" difference, increase and multiply under intolerance. This new faith
" had already made such a progress, that Sigismund-Augustus, instead
" of persecuting his Protestant subjects, as his father had done, took
" the wiser part of granting them full liberty of exercising their reli-
" gion; and admitted them, as well as those of the Greek church, and
" other sectaries, to a right of suffrage in the diets; and of all the ho-
" nours and privileges which the Catholics were desirous of enjoying
" exclusively. But this prince, worthy of the name of Augustus, dif-
" fused his own spirit of moderation and impartiality with such effect
" through the whole nation, that the people consented that no differ-
" ence of opinion in religious matters should produce any in civil or

which is sufficient to denote that they followed the Catholic religion, as Protestantism had not then gained a footing in Italy. Next the controversy is referred "to the pope, and the society for the *propagation* of the CHRISTIAN FAITH." Observe ye this. We have it here acknowledged that the missionaries who first attempted to plant Christianity in China were in communion with, and under subjection to, the see of Rome, and that in this very city of Rome, the seat of the supreme head of the Catholic church, there was, as there now is, a society for the propagation of the CHRISTIAN faith. Remember too, reader, at the very time this society for the propagation of the Christian faith was consulted by the planters of Christianity in China, the pretended reformers were condemning the Catholic religion as being anti-Christian. Now, how will you, consistent with common sense, reconcile this gross inconsistency of conduct?" What are we to think of the intellectual faculties of the "few plain Christians," who have put out this book to diffuse, they say, "a knowledge and love of the genuine principles of "Christianity?" Can a system of religion be Christian and anti-Christian at the same time? Can a system of religion that teaches its followers to submit to persecution for conscience sake, be the teacher of persecuting principles? It is impossible. Fox may as well assert that black is white, or that the sun shines upon the earth when that luminary is obscured by a dark thunder cloud.

He goes on to say that this society for the propagation of the Christian faith pronounced that the ceremonies objected to *were idolatrous* and intolerable, which sentence was confirmed by the pope. Here then, we have the pope *condemning idolatry* upon the authority of John Fox and his modern editors, and these very same editors charging the pope and Catholics with being damnable idolaters. Is not this another piece of barefaced inconsistency? For how can Catholics be idolaters when the Church condemns idolatry? The wise editors were not aware of the admission they were here making. But the pope, it is said, acted with precipitation; he passed sentence upon a wrong statement, and the decision was treated with contempt by the Chinese. A true statement was afterwards sent him, and he found the customs objected to were entirely free from idolatry, and merely political. This is represented as placing the holy father in difficulty; but how so? If the pope had been deceived he could not help that; nor can we see how his decision could be affected. He condemned certain ceremonies to be idolatrous, supposing them to have been followed; but it afterwards turned out that these ceremonies were fictitious, and that others quite harmless and purely political were allowed. Well then the decree could not affect the innocent and political customs, it only went to condemn those which were wrong and sinful. The decree did not require to be revoked, because the customs supposed must still remain condemned, and the Chinese Christians would be thereby warned against falling into them, should such ever be proposed to them. To get out of this difficulty Fox causes the holy father to have recourse to the inquisition, a civil tribunal, emanating from the pope himself as temporal sovereign of Rome. This is as silly a device as any Fox or his editors ever had recourse to for the purpose of deception. If the inquisition reversed the sentence, it must have had the sanction of the pope as head of the church, or chief magistrate of the state, and surely it would have been quite as easy for the society for the propagation of the Christian faith, to have revoked their own decree as the inquisition. The society alluded to is a congregation or tribunal perfectly independent of the inquisition, and entirely occupied with matters of religion. It is totally unconnected with political affairs, and does not suffer, we believe, the inquisition to interfere in the least with its decrees and regulations. To set the reader right, and allow him the opportunity of seeing both sides of the case, we here insert a very interesting account of the progress of Christianity in China, and the means by which it was introduced by the Jesuits, from the Rev. Alban Butler's Lives of the Saints, vol. ii. p. 65.

"St. Francis Xavier had made the conversion of China the object of his zealous wishes; but died, like another Moses, in sight of it. His religious brethren long attempted in vain to gain admittance into that country; but the jealousy of the inhabitants refused entrance to all strangers. However, God was pleased, at the repeated prayers of his servants, to crown them with success. The Portuguese made a settlement at Macao, an island within sight of China, and obtained leave to go thither twice a year for to trade at the fairs of Canton. F. Matthew Ricci, a Roman Jesuit, a good mathematician, and a disciple of Clavius, being settled a missionary at Macao, went over with them several times into China, and in 1583, obtained leave of the governor to reside there with two other Jesuits. A little catechism which he published, and a map of the world, in which he placed the first meridian in China, to make it the middle of the world, according to the Chinese notion, gained him many friends and admirers. In 1595, he established a second residence of Jesuits, at Nanquin; and made himself admired there by teaching the true figure of the earth, the causes of lunar eclipses, &c. He also built an observatory, and converted many to the faith. In 1600, he went to Pekin, and carried with him a clock, a watch, and many other presents to the emperor, who granted him a residence in that capital. He converted many, and among these several officers of the court, one of whom was Paul Siu, afterwards prime minister, under whose protection a flourishing church was established in his country, Xankai, (in the province of Nanquin) in which were forty thousand Christians when the late persecution began. Francis Martinez, a Chinese Jesuit, having converted a famous doctor, was beaten several times, and at length expired under the torment. Ricci died in 1617, having lived in favour with the Emperor Vanlie.

"F. Adam Schall, a Jesuit from Cologn, by his mathematics, became known to the emperor Zonchi; but in 1636, that prince laid violent hands upon himself, that he might not fall into the hands of two rebels who had taken Pekin. The Chinese called in Xunte, king of a frontier nation of the Tartars, to their assistance, who recovered Pekin, but demanded the empire for the prize of his victory: and his son Chunchi obtained quiet possession of it in 1650. From that time the Tartars have been emperors of China, but they govern it by its own religion and laws. They frequently visit their original territories, but rather treat them as the conquered country. Chunchi esteemed F. Schall, called him father, and was favourable to the Christians. After his death the four regents put to death five mandarins for their faith, and condemned F. Schall, but granted him a reprieve; during which he died. The young emperor Camhi coming of age, put a stop to the persecution, and employed F. Verbiest, a Jesuit, to publish the yearly Chinese calendar, declared him president of the mathematics in his palace, and consequently a mandarin. The first year he opened the Christian churches, which was in 1671, above twenty thousand souls were baptized; and in the year following an uncle of the emperor, one of the eight perpetual generals of the Tartar troops, and several other persons of distinction. The succeeding emperors were no less favourable to the Christians, and permitted them to build a most sumptuous church within the enclosure of their own palace, which in many respects surpassed all the other buildings of the empire. It was finished in 1702. The Dominican friars, according to Touron, (Hommes illustr. t. 6.) entered China in 1556, converted many to the faith, and, in 1631, laid the foundation of the most numerous church of Fokien, great part of which province they converted to the faith. Four priests of this order received the crown of martyrdom in 1647, and a fifth, named Francis de Capillas, from the

and seditious delinquents, the violaters of law and justice, was perversely represented to be a religious persecution. While these transactions were going on between the Catholic and Lutheran party, a new religious order was established by a Spaniard of a noble and ancient family named Ignatius of Loyola. He had, in the early part of his life followed the military service, but serious reflection induced him to change his habits, and devote himself to the service of God and religion. Far different from Martin Luther, who, on claiming an evangelical mission, threw off his monastic habits and restraints, to follow a life of voluptuousness and intemperance, Ignatius laid aside that disorderly conduct almost inseparable to a military life, and became a pattern of abstemiousness and piety. Beholding the dreadful havock which heresy and schism were making in the Catholic church, he cast his eyes on the immense countries in America and Asia, and glowed with the desire of carrying the true light of the gospel into those infidel and distant regions. Nor did he neglect the state of religion in Europe; but the plans he had in contemplation were too extended to be carried into effect by one man. He therefore communicated his ideas to a few others, and in the year 1534, Ignatius and nine of his disciples consecrated themselves to the cause of God, and the salvation of souls. In 1537 they repaired to Rome, and made an offer of service to the pope, Paul III, who made a trial of their virtue in the hospitals of the capitol, before he formally accepted their tender. In the year 1540, however, his holiness felt himself so satisfied of the utility of these disinterested men, that he erected them into a religious order under the title of the Society of Jesus. The end of this society was not confined to the sanctification of its own members, by following the evangelical counsels, but they bound themselves, each in his respective sphere, to preach the word of God, to combat vice in all its hideous forms, and to teach the principles and practices of true religion. This was the origin of the Jesuits, who are known only in this country, among the generality of Protestants, as a body of men influenced by the most artful cunning and chicanery, and devoid of all moral rectitude. The progress this society of men made on the continent, by the force of their eloquence and the unspotted purity of their lives, alarmed the blind followers of error; the establishment of a college abroad for the English students to become missionaries here, struck terror into the adherents of the new church, and it was made high treason for any Englishman to become a Jesuit. To make a cloak for so cruel an enactment, plots were hatched to keep the people in alarm, and the Jesuits were made the framers, the directors and the actors in them. By such means were the people instigated to look upon the new order as a set of monsters; and whenever a member of the body appeared in this island, the yell of Jesuitism was instantly raised; he was hunted like a wolf night and day; his pursuers never relaxed from the chase, until he fled the kingdom, or expiated by an ignominious death the crime of having sought to reconcile his repentant countrymen to the faith of the primitive Christians and martyrs. Nay, at this very day; when a man is guilty of acting treacherously or playing a double part, his conduct is called Jesuitical, from the supposition that the system of the Jesuits is one of deceit and perfidy, than which nothing is more false. We have thought it necessary to make these prefatory observations to enable the reader better to understand the duplicity and cunning of Fox and his modern editors. We will now proceed to give his account word for word.

"PERSECUTIONS IN CHINA.

" At the commencement of the 16th century, three Italian missionaries, namely, Roger the Neapolitan, Pasis of Bologna, and Matthew Ricci of Mazerata, entered China with a view of establishing Christianity there. In order to succeed in this important commission, they had previously made the Chinese language their constant study.

" The zeal displayed by these missionaries in the discharge of their duty was very great; but Roger and Pasis in a few years returning to Europe, the whole labour devolved upon Ricci. The perseverance of Ricci was proportioned to the arduous task he had undertaken. Though disposed to indulge his converts as far as possible, he disliked many of their ceremonies, which seemed idolatrous. At length, after eighteen years labour and reflection, he thought it most advisable to tolerate all those customs which were ordained by the laws of the empire, but strictly enjoined his converts to omit the rest; and thus, by not resisting too much the external ceremonies of the country, he succeeded in bringing over many to the truth. In 1630, however, this tranquillity was disturbed by the arrival of some new missionaries; who, being unacquainted with the Chinese customs, manners, and language, and with the principles of Ricci's toleration, were astonished when they saw Christian converts fall prostrate before Confucius, and the tables of their ancestors, and loudly censured the proceeding as idolatrous. They occasioned a warm controversy; and not coming to any agreement, the new missionaries wrote an account of the affair to the pope, and the society for the propagation of the Christian faith. The society soon pronounced, that the ceremonies were idolatrous and intolerable, which sentence was confirmed by the pope. In this they were excusable, the matter having been misrepresented to them; for the enemies of Ricci had declared the halls, in which the ceremonies were performed, to be temples, and the ceremonies themselves the sacrifices to idols.

" The sentence was sent over to China, where it was received with great contempt, and matters remained in the same state for some time. At length, a true representation was sent over, explaining that the Chinese customs and ceremonies alluded to, were entirely free from idolatry, but merely political, and tending only to the peace and welfare of the empire. The pope, finding that he had not weighed the affair with due consideration, sought to extricate himself from the difficulty in which he had been so precipitately entangled, and therefore referred the representation to the inquisition, which reversed the sentence immediately.

" The Christian church, notwithstanding these divisions, flourished in China till the death of the first Tartan emperor, whose successor, Cang-hi, was a minor. During his minority, the regents and nobles conspired to crush the Christian religion. The execution of this design was accordingly began with expedition, and carried on with severity, so that every Christian teacher in China, as well as those who professed the faith, was surprised at the suddenness of the event. John Adam Schall, a German ecclesiastic, and one of the principals of the missions, was thrown into a dungeon, and narrowly escaped with his life, being then in the 74th year of his age.

" In 1695, the ensuing year, the ministers of state published the following decree: 1. That the Christian doctrines were false. 2. That they were dangerous to the interests of the empire. 3. That they should not be practised under pain of death.

" The result of this was a most furious persecution, in which some were put to death, many ruined, and all in some measure oppressed. Previous to this, the Christians had suffered partially; but the decree being general, the persecution now spread its ravages over the whole empire, wherever its objects were scattered.

" Four years after, the young emperor was declared of age; and one of the first acts of his reign was to stop this persecution."

We have before remarked that Fox was particularly cautious to keep the creed of these missionaries from view, yet with all his caution he has let enough out to prove they were Catholics, and acknowledged the supremacy of the pope. The missionaries are described to be Italians,

"political rights : in consequence of which, one of the articles inserted
" in the *pacta conventa*, which the successors of Sigismund have been
" obliged to subscribe, imports that the subscriber *shall maintain peace*
" *among the dissenters :* by this word *dissenters* is understood all who
" differ in religious opinions." Here it is stated that the Protestant religion was opposed by persecution, but he does not say how it came to
be so opposed; we must therefore leave that part of the question, and
come to their subsequent conduct. After the death of Sigismund,
Henry of Valois wished to avoid subscribing to this article of toleration, and was threatened with the loss of his crown : the result was,
he consented to sign it. Soon after a persecution is said to have been
entered into against the Arians, of which sect there were many in that
kingdom; which persecution was not confined to the Catholics, but
Protestants and Greeks took a part in it. In 1733, the Catholics gained
an ascendency, and excluded the Protestants from the diet or parliament. This exclusion, which the Catholics of this country have borne
for upwards of two hundred years, with exemplary patience, was re-
sented by the Protestants of Poland with the deepest rancour. They
formed confederacies with foreign powers, and particularly with Russia, which in the end, as we have before stated, laid the independence
of their country prostrate. This base abandonment of duty is thus recorded by the author of the above-named Review : " The Catholics of
" Poland were the original aggressors. One of their fundamental laws
" directed that, *without paying regard to religious opinions, every citizen,*
" *duly qualified to enter into the diets, should be admitted there, and parti-*
" *cipate the honours and dignities of the republic :* and this law ought to
" have remained inviolable. But the dissenters were guilty of a still
" greater wrong, by calling foreign troops to their aid, and drawing
" the fury of civil war upon their country, because they were excluded
" from those situations and honours in which they had a right to share.
" In the year 1764, when the Protestants made their last demand, there
" were only two hundred churches in Poland : but they were every
" where permitted the free exercise of the Protestant religion in their
" houses; their property was respected; and they held, in common
" with the Catholics, not only the *starosties,* but all military appoint-
" ments. What more was necessary for them, if they had confined
" their views to the single object of rendering, to the Supreme Being,
" the adoration which they believed most worthy of him ? Could they
" not have made the sacrifice of some vain honours to the Power whom
" they worshipped ? If they had not set a higher value on these ho-
" nours than on their religion, they would have resigned them, rather
" than shed the blood of their unjust brethren, or do an injury to pub-
" lic liberty, and subject their country to foreign despotism."

Fox, in the former part of his book, takes notice of the miserable
end of the Roman emperors, who were persecutors of the Christians.
It is not a little remarkable that the Protestants of Poland, who were
so instrumental in selling their country, because they were excluded,
against the fundamental laws of the kingdom, from their seats in the
diet, did not gain their wishes. On the dismemberment of their country, they were left unprotected by the power to whom they sold them-

selves. " The court of Russia," says M. De la Croix, " appeared satis-
" fied that they were granted the use of their churches, though on con-
" dition of their not using bells to assemble the congregations: that
" they were permitted to perform their religious duties, and have se-
" minaries: and that they might sit in the inferior courts of justice.
" They were also allowed to claim the admission of three dissenters, as
" jurors in the tribunals before which any cause respecting religion
" should be brought by appeal. Such were the fruits which the dissenters
" reaped from the troubles *excited by them* in Poland. Nor will it be for-
" gotten that they enjoyed, before these troubles, the free exercise of
" their religion: that the grand object of their desires was to be admitted
" to the diets: and that thus, after having brought foreign troops into the
" kingdom; after having involved their country in all the horrors of civil
" war; after having proved the occasion of part of their fellow-citizens
" being subjected to the dominion of their three powerful enemies, they
" were themselves disappointed of the advantage they expected to de-
" rive from their measures. What a lesson does this afford to the peo-
" ple, among whom are found some individuals, so affected by the loss
" of certain privileges, as to demand the assistance of foreigners for
" reclaiming them!" A lesson, indeed! And here we may leave the
events represented to be a religious persecution, but which is evidently
the struggle of political faction under the guise of religion. Had Fox,
instead of telling his readers that " Lithuania no sooner recovered it-
" self from one *persecution* than succeeding enemies again reduced it,"
stated that Poland no sooner recovered from one faction, than another
succeeded in embroiling her again in trouble, till the *Protestant faction*
willed her to be erased from the list of nations, he would have come
much nearer the truth. That however is not the end he purposed in
penning his *Book of Martyrs*, nor the " few plain Christians" in repub-
lishing it.

" SECTION VII.

" PERSECUTIONS IN CHINA AND JAPAN."

From Lithuania we are carried by Fox into China and Japan, and it is
not a little singular that the pretended persecutors in Europe and the
really persecuted in China and Japan, professed the very *same* faith, that
is, Catholicism. Fox carefully abstains from telling his readers what
kind of Christianity was established in these Pagan countries; he contents himself with using a general term, leaving the uninformed and prejudiced reader to suppose that the Christianity alluded to must be that
system, if such it can be called, falsely represented as " the light of the
gospel" spread by a specious set of reformers of religion, who ought
rather to be called *deformers* of Christianity. The time of this attempt
on the part of the Catholic missionaries is said to be the commencement
of the 16th century, that is soon after Martin Luther commenced his dogmatizing. After the doctrines of Martin and of the other spoilers of
the Christian system had made some progress in the different states of
Europe and produced rebellions and civil wars, the Catholic sovereigns,
as we have before proved, found it necessary to arm themselves in defence of public security, and the punishment inflicted on the rebellious

convent of Valladolid, the apostle of the town of Fogan, was cruelly beaten, and soon after beheaded on the fifteenth of January, 1648, ' because, as his sentence imported, he contemned the spirits and gods of the country.' Relations hereof were transmitted to the congregation de propagandâ fide, under pope Urban VIII.

" Upwards of a hundred thousand souls zealously professed the faith, and they had above two hundred churches. But a debate arose whether certain honours paid by the Chinese to Confucius and their deceased ancestors, with certain oblations made either solemnly by the mandarins and doctors at the equinoxes, and at the new and full moons, or privately in their own houses or temples, were superstitious and idolatrous. Pope Clement XI. in 1704, condemned those rites as superstitious, *utpote superstitione imbutas*, the execution of which decree he committed to the patriarch of Antioch, afterward cardinal Tournon, whom he sent as his commissary into that kingdom. Benedict XIV. confirmed the same more amply and severely by his constitution, *ex quo singulari*, in 1742, in which he declares, that the faithful ought to express God in the Chinese language by the name Thien Chu, i. e. the Lord of Heaven: and that the words Tien, the heaven, and Xang Ti, the Supreme Ruler, are not to be used, because they signify the supreme god of the idolaters, a kind of fifth essence, or intelligent nature in the heaven itself: that the inscription, king Tien, worship thou the heaven, cannot be allowed. The obedience of those who had formerly defended these rites to be merely political and civil honours, not sacred, was such, that from that time they have taken every occasion of testifying it to the world. By a like submission and victory over himself, Fenelon was truly greater than by all his other illustrious virtues and actions.

" The emperor Kang-hi protected the Christian religion in the most favourable manner. Whereas his successor, Yongtching, banished the missionaries out of the chief cities, but kept those religious in his palace who were employed by him in painting, mathematics, and other liberal arts, and who continued mandarins of the court. Kien-long, the next emperor, carried the persecution to the greatest rigours of cruelty. The tragedy was begun by the viceroy of Fokieu, who stirred up the emperor himself. A great number of Christians of all ages and sexes were banished, beaten, and tortured divers ways, especially by being buffeted on the face with a terrible kind of armed ferula, one blow of which would knock the teeth out, and make the head swell exceedingly. All which torments even the young converts bore with incredible constancy, rather than discover where the priest lay hid, or deliver up the crosses, relics, or sacred books, or do any thing contrary to the law of God. Many priests and others died of their torments or of the hardships of their dungeons. One bishop and six priests received the crown of martyrdom. Peter Martyr Sans, a Spanish Dominican friar, arrived in China in 1715, where he had laboured fifteen years when he was named by the congregation bishop of Mauricastre, and ordained by the bishop of Nanquin, assisted by the bishops of Pekin and Macao, and appointed Apostolic Vicar for the province of Fokieu. In 1732, the emperor by an edict banished all the missionaries. Peter Sans retired to Macao, but returned to Fokieu, in 1738, and founded several new churches for his numerous converts, and received the vows of several virgins who consecrated themselves to God. The viceroy provoked at this, caused him to be apprehended amidst the tears of his dear flock, with four Dominican friars, his fellow labourers. They were beaten with clubs, buffeted on the face with gauntlets made of several pieces of leather, and at length condemned to lose their heads. The bishop was beheaded on the same day, the twenty-sixth day of May, 1747. The Chinese superstitiously imagine, that the soul of one that is put to death seizes the first person it meets, and therefore all the spectators ran away as soon as they see the stroke of death given; but none of them did so at the death of this blessed martyr. On the contrary, admiring the joy with which he died, and esteeming his holy soul happy, they thought it a blessing to come the nearest to him, and to touch his blood; which they did as respectfully as Christians could have done for whom a pagan gathered their blood, because they durst not appear. The other four Dominican friars, who were also Spaniards, suffered much during twenty-eight months cruel imprisonment, and were strangled privately in their dungeons on the twenty-eighth of October, 1748. Pope Benedict XIV. made a discourse to the cardinals on the precious death of this holy bishop, September 16, 1748. See Touron, t. 6. p. 729.

, " These four fellow-martyrs of the order of St. Dominic were, Francis Serranus, fifty-two years old, who had laboured nineteen years in the Chinese mission, and during his last imprisonment was nominated by pope Benedict XIV. bishop of Tipasa; Joachim Rolo, fifty-six years old, who had preached in that empire thirty-three years; John Alcober, forty-two years old, who had spent eighteen years in that mission; and Francis Diaz, thirty-three years old, of which he had employed nine in the same vineyard. During their imprisonment a report that their lives would be spared filled them not with joy, but with grief, to the great admiration of the infidels, as pope Benedict XIV. mentions in his discourse to the consistory of cardinals, on their death, delivered in 1752: in which he qualifies them crowned, but not declared martyrs: *martyres consummatos, nondum martyres vindicatos.* In the same persecution two Jesuits, F. Joseph of Atemis, an Italian, and F. Antony Joseph Henriquez, a Portuguese, were apprehended in December, 1747; and tortured several times to compel them to renounce their religion. They were at length condemned to death by the mandarins, and the sentence, according to custom, being sent to the emperor, was confirmed by him, and the two priests were strangled in prison on the 12th of September, 1748. On these martyrs see F. Touron, Hommes Illustres de l'Ordre de S. Domin. t. 6. and the letters of the Jesuit missionaries. On the history of China, F. Du Halde's Description of China, in four vols. fol. Mullerus de Chataiâ, Navarette, Tratados Historicos de la China, an. 1676, Lettres Edificantes et curieuses des Missionaires, vol. 27, 28. Jackson's Chronology, &c.

In Tonquin, a kingdom south-west of China, in which the king and mandarins follow the Chinese religion, though various sects of idolatry and superstition reign among the people, a persecution was raised against the Christians in 1713. In this storm one hundred and fifty churches were demolished, many converts were beaten with a hammer on their knees, and tortured various other ways, and two Spanish missionary priests of the order of St. Dominic, suffered martyrdom for the faith, F. Francis Gil de Federich, and F. Matthew Alfonso Leziniana. F. Gil arrived there in 1735, and found above twenty thousand Christians in the west of the kingdom, who had been baptized by priests of his order. This vineyard he began assiduously to cultivate; but was apprehended by a neighbouring bonze, in 1737, and condemned to die the year following. The Tonquinese usually execute condemned persons only in the last moon of the year, and a rejoicing or other accidents often cause much longer delays. The confessor was often allowed the liberty of saying mass in the prison; and was pressed to save his life, by saying that he came into Tonquin as a merchant: but this would have been a lie, and he would not suffer any other to give in such an answer for him. Father Matthew, a priest of the same order, after having preached ten years in Tonquin, was seized while he was saying mass; and because he refused to trample on a crucifix, was condemned to die in 1743: and in May 1744, was brought into the same prison with F. Gil. The idolaters were so astonished to see their ardour to die, and the sorrow of the latter upon an offer of his life, that they cried out: 'Others desire to live, but these men to die.' They were both beheaded together on the twenty-second of January, 1744. See Touron, t. 6. and Lettres Edif. and Curieuses des Missionaires.

"Many other vast countries, both in the eastern and western parts of the world, received the light of the gospel in the sixteenth century: in which great work several apostolic men were raised by God, and some were honoured with the crown of martyrdom. Among the zealous missionaries who converted to the faith the savage inhabitants of Brazil in America, of which the Portuguese took possession in 1500, under king John II. F. Joseph Anchieta, is highly celebrated. He was a native of the Canary islands, but took the Jesuits habits at Coimbra; died in Brazil, on the ninth of June, 1597, of his age sixty-four; having laboured in cultivating that vineyard forty-seven years. He was a man of apostolic humility, patience, meekness, prayer, zeal, and charity. The fruit of his labours was not less wonderful than the example of his virtues. See his life by F. Peter Roterigius, and F. Sebastian Beretarius. The sanctity of the venerable F. Peter Claver, who laboured in the same vineyard, was so heroic, that a process has been commenced for his canonization.

"F. Peter Claver was nobly born in Catalonia, and entered himself in the society at Tarragon, in 1602, when about twenty years old. From his infancy he looked upon nothing small in which the service of God was concerned; for the least action or circumstance which is referred to his honour is great and precious, and requires our utmost application: in this spirit of fervour he considered God in every neighbour and superior; and upon motives of religion was humble and meek towards all, and ever ready to obey and serve every one. From the time of his religious profession, he applied himself with the

Christianity? Here we are at a stand again; for how is it possible, we again ask, to know what this lord Bexley, or any other lord, means by the doctrines of Christianity, when there are hundreds of discordant sects in this country laying exclusive claim to the doctrines of Christianity? But the society has been in existence TEN YEARS, during which period, or at least till within a short time, for nothing is stated definitively, the effects produced were scarcely visible. This we believe to be verily true; save and except the visible effects of collecting money from silly people to be appropriated to the benefit of the missioners and the managers of the society. Now, Christian reader, is this the way the world was brought to know the light of the gospel? Did the apostles go forth under the auspices of a Missionary society? Did the saintly converters of the nations of the world (always excepting the nameless nation in the South seas) take their credentials from a heterogeneous club of sectarians of the most discordant creeds? To be sure not. They one and all received their commission from the supreme head of the Catholic church on earth, and the nations that received the light of faith rendered obedience in spirituals to that head. Neither did they go armed with bibles which the people could neither read nor understand. They went under a divine commission received from God, and they preached his holy word, which is always one and the same. To shew the effects produced by those missionaries duly authorized to preach the light of the gospel, and those who go commissioned by self-intruders in the work of the vineyard, we shall here give an account of the progress of Catholicism in Japan, from Mr. Butler's Saints' Lives, to which we shall add a few more particulars by way of contrast with the effects of the modern Missionary Society established by Bible Saints:—

" The divine seed sown by St. Francis Xavier in Japan increased so much, that when the persecution was raised, there were reckoned in that empire four hundred thousand Christians. Paul, the first fruits, or rather the father of this church, died happily, and in great sentiments of piety and holy spiritual joy in 1557. The prince of Omura was baptized in 1562. That prince and the two kings of Bungo and Arima, who had received baptism, sent ambassadors of obedience, who were their own near relations, to pope Gregory XIII. in 1582. They were conducted in their voyage by F. Valegnani, a Jesuit, and received with great honour in the principal cities of Portugal, Spain, and Italy, through which they passed, and especially at Rome. The faith flourished daily more and more in Japan, and in 1596, there were in that empire two hundred and fifty churches, three seminaries, a noviciate of the Jesuits, and several Franciscans. The Cubo or emperor Nabunanga, at least out of hatred to the Bonzas, was very favourable to the missionaries, and his prime minister, Vatadona, viceroy of Meaco, was the declared protector of the Christian religion. When the conversion of all Japan was looked upon as at hand, this undertaking was entirely overturned. Nabunanga was cut off by a violent death, and Taikosama usurped first the regency for the son of Nabunanga, and afterward the empire, by contriving to have their heir put to death. Partly by policy and partly by force, he subdued all Japan, and extinguished the Jocatas or petty kings. For some time he was favourable to the Christians, till, by various accidents, he was excited to jealousy at their numbers and progress. In 1586, he, by an edict, forbad any Japanese to embrace the faith, and shortly after caused many Christians to be crucified: in the year 1590, no fewer than twenty thousand were put to death for the faith. In 1597, the twenty-six martyrs suffered, whom Urban VIII. thirty years after, declared such. On their death and miracles see Charlevoix, L. x. c. 4. p. 330, and this work on Febr. 5. Taikosama died in 1598; and Ijedas (to whom he left the regency and care of his young son Fidejori, a prince fond of the Christians) having murdered the heir, his pupil, and usurped the throne, continued the persecution; and in

1615 banished all the missionaries, forbidding entrance for the time to town under pain of death. The year following Fide-Tadda, his son, succeeded him in the throne, and put great numbers of Christians to barbarous deaths. Xogan or Toxogunsama, to whom he resigned the crown, or at least the regency, in 1622, carried his cruelty against the Christians to the last excess, and put incredible numbers to the most barbarous deaths. In 1630 the Dutch accused to this emperor, Moro and other Japanese Christians of a conspiracy with the Portuguese against the state, which Kaempfer (b. 4, c. 5,) pretends to have been real: but Charlevoix endeavours to prove counterfeit, (t. 2, p. 406.) This charge exceedingly enraged the persecutors. The Christians in numberless crowds had suffered martyrdom with the most heroic patience and constancy: but many of those who remained, in the kingdom of Arima, by an unjustifiable conduct, very opposite to that of the primitive Christians, broke into rebellion, and with an army of forty thousand men took some strong places: but being at length forced, all died fighting desperately in the field, in 1638. After this, Toxogunsama continued the persecution with such fury, that at his death, in 1650, very few had escaped his fury; and his successor, Jietznako, who pursued the same course, seems to have discovered very few to put to death. The researches have been so rigorous that in some provinces all the inhabitants have been sometimes compelled to trample on a crucifix. Only the Dutch are allowed to trade there under the most severe restrictions, but their factory is confined to the isle of Desima, i. e. isle of De, which is one long street, before the harbour, and joined by a bridge to the city of Nangasaki, on the western coast of the island Ximo. This city was subject to Sumitanda, prince of Omura, one of the first sovereigns in Japan who embraced the faith, which he established alone throughout all his dominions, situate in the kingdom of Arima. That king was himself baptized with a considerable part of his subjects. After several Christian kings, king John, otherwise Protasius, suffered martyrdom: his son Michael apostatised to preserve the crown, and became a persecutor. The rebellion of 1638 totally extinguished the faith in this kingdom and in the rest of Japan. Nangasaki in the time of the Portuguese was all Christians, and counted sixty thousand inhabitants: now about eight thousand only, and these Japanese idolaters. It is the only town in Japan which any strangers are now allowed to approach: and are here watched as if prisoners. By an inviolable edict of the emperor, all other nations except the Dutch are forbid these dominions, and all their natives are commanded to remain in their own country. The missionaries who have attempted to find admittance, seem never to have succeeded. The last that is known, was M. Sidotti, a Sicilian priest who, in 1709, found means to land in Japan: but what became of him after this was never known in Europe. See Charlevoix, Dr. Kaempfer, and Hist. Moderne, t. 2. des Japanois. Also Hist. Provincia Philippine, Dominica. et Jac. Lefenas, Annal Dominican. et F. Sardimo, Jesuit. Catalogus Regularium et Sæcularium qui in Japania et sub quatuor Tyrannis sublato sunt. Also the history of the Martyrs who in Japan suffered cruel and intolerable torments and death for the Roman Catholic religion, in Dutch, by Rier Guyesberts, (who was an eye-witness to several living at Nangasaki, in 1692.) printed at the end of Caron's Description of Japan. See also relations of this persecution, published by several Jesuits, Dominicans, &c." &c. Vol. xii, p. 41.

This account by Mr. Butler differs materially from that given by John Fox, and is much more clear and intelligible. Fox says the faith was first introduced in 1552, by some Portuguese missionaries, but this is contradicted by the former martyrologist, who shews that the seed of faith was sown by St. Francis Xavier, who had for his companion a Japanese, whom he had converted and baptized by the name of Paul, in Malacca. St. Francis landed in Japan in 1549. To prove the efficacy of Catholic preaching over Bible distribution, we have only to observe that the success of St. Francis Xavier, who, by the by, was a Jesuit, in the countries he visited for the purpose of carrying among the people the light of the gospel, was widely different from the success the missionaries of the Missionary Society are stated to have met with. St. Francis landed at Goa, the capital town of the Portuguese settlement of that name, in the year 1542, and the first of his missionary labours

" among their fellow-believers a knowledge and love of the genuine
" principles, of Christianity." What barefaced effrontery! But we
must return to their precious mass of lies and fabrications. The next
head is,

" PERSECUTIONS IN JAPAN."

Under this title we have the following account which it is our intention to contrast with a more authentic one, and we therefore give it
in Fox's own words :—

" The first introduction of Christianity into the empire of Japan, took place in 1552, when
some Portuguese missionaries commenced their endeavours to make converts to the light
of the gospel, and met with such success as amply compensated their labours. They continued to augment the number of their converts till 1616, when being accused of having
meddled in politics, and formed a plan to subvert the government, and dethrone the emperor, great jealousies arose, and subsisted till 1622, when the court commenced a dreadful persecution against foreign and native Christians. Such was the case of this persecution,
that during the first four years, 20,570 Christians were massacred. Death was the consequence of a public avowal of their faith, and their churches were shut up by order of government. Many, on a discovery of their religion by spies and informers, suffered martyrdom with great heroism. The persecution continued many years, when the remnant of the
innumerable Christians with which Japan abounded, to the number of 37,000 souls, retired to the town and castle of Siniabara, in the island of Ximo, where they determined
to make a stand, to continue in their faith, and to defend themselves to the very last extremity. To this place the Japanese army followed them, and laid siege to the place. The
Christians defended themselves with great bravery, and held out against the besiegers three
months, but were at length compelled to surrender, when men, women, and children,
were indiscriminately murdered; and Christianity from that time ceased in Japan.

" This event took place on the 12th of April, 1638, since which time no Christians but the
Dutch have been allowed to land in the empire, and even they are obliged to conduct
themselves with the greatest precaution, to submit to the most rigorous treatment, and to
carry on their commerce with the utmost circumspection."

The introduction of Christianity into Japan is here granted to the
Portuguese : now the Portuguese being well known to be Catholics,
the Christianity introduced by them must have been Catholicism; that
is the very system which the evangelical reformers in Europe were condemning as idolatrous and superstitious. That very system which the
" few plain Christians" themselves now represent in their prospectus as
inseparable from persecution. That the Christianity introduced into
Japan is the *same* that the Catholics of this day profess is undeniable,
because there has been no deviation in Popery, as it is called, from the
time it was *introduced* into Japan, and attempted to be *overthrown* by
Martin Luther and his fellow-labourers in the work of error and iniquity
in Europe. This work of opposition to Catholicism is still going on in
this land of Bibles and delusion; for it is only while we are writing
(Nov. 5th, 1824, the anniversary of the publication of the first number
of this Review) a newspaper has been put into our hands containing a
report of the proceedings of the London Auxiliary Bible Society, held
on the day preceding at the Mansion-house, by permission of the Lord
Mayor, who presided at the meeting. At this meeting the days of Catholicism were termed by several of the sapient speakers the days of
darkness, of bigotry, superstition, and persecution; while the very
Book of Martyrs testify that Portuguese Catholic missionaries in the
latter days of *darkness* made numerous converts " to the *light* of the gos-

pel" among the superstitious Pagans of Japan!!! Was ever a people so
duped and gulled as the people of England have been, since the period
of the pretended Reformation, and are at the present day? We have
before said that the Catholic church was the only church that has produced missionaries to convert Pagan nations to the true light of the
gospel; but we now find, in the just named report, that the London
Missionary Society lays claim to the conversion of *one* whole nation
to *Christianity*; but what kind of Christianity is not defined. As this
statement is somewhat connected with the subject under discussion,
we will here give the words of the report, as we find them in *The Morning Chronicle*. Lord Bexley (who a short time ago was Mr. Nicholas
Vansittart, and Chancellor of the Exchequer,) represented himself at
this meeting as the representative of his Majesty's government, and is
stated to have said, that " the Bible existed in the language of almost
" every nation and tribe in the world; this he granted was only *a pre-
" parative;* but he had *no doubt* that *good fruits would speedily arise from
" it,* although *the seed might appear to have been lost.* An instance of
" this might be seen in the London Missionary Society—a Society es-
" tablished for *the purpose of converting* the inhabitants of the islands
" of the South Seas. This society *for many years met with no success.*
" Some of its Missionaries *died* in the prosecution of their labours—
" others *returned,* having *relinquished their task as hopeless,* conceiving
" that there was no hope, where nothing but brutality and sensuality
" were triumphant; but *perseverance* at length accomplished the *mighty
" task.* The savages acknowledged the true God, and now *almost for
" the first time since the days of the apostles,* may be seen *a whole nation
" removing their idols, and adopting the only *faith* that could *lead them
" to salvation.*" Well said, my lord; you are a very modest gentleman.
But why did you not give us the *name* of this people who have thus
been so *suddenly* blessed with the light of the " *only faith*" that could
lead them to salvation, through the means of the London Missionary
society? Besides, my lord Bexley, how long have this lucky Missionary
society been in the exclusive possession of the " *only faith*" that leads
to salvation? If they really have this peculiar grace, why did they
go so far away to teach it? Why not impart it to their countrymen
at home? As there is, according to the words imputed to you, but
one faith, is not this something like the doctrine of *exclusive* salvation, against which so much has been said and written to make the
Catholic church intolerant? But what are we to think of your charity,
when you here consign nearly the whole world, from the time of the
apostles to the present day, to perdition,—this single whole nation
being the only *one,* you say, adopting the only faith that could lead them
to salvation! We wish you had been more explicit; but that is not
the forte of Bible-meeting speechifyers, whether lay or clerical, who
love to deal in mystification rather than in plain language.
The report in *The New Times* tells us you informed the meeting that
this Missionary Society was established ten years back; that for a long
time the efforts arising from it were *scarcely visible;* but the illumination broke forth at *once,* and in their own time they had before them
the example of a whole nation embracing the doctrines of *Christianity.*
This is something like the language of John Fox. The doctrines of

greatest ardour to seek nothing in this world, but what Jesus Christ in his mortal life, that is, the kingdom of his grace: for the only aim of this servant of God was, the sanctification of his own soul, and the salvation of others. He was thoroughly instructed that a man's spiritual progress depends very much upon the fervour of his beginning; and he omitted nothing both to lay a solid foundation, and continually to raise upon it the structure of all virtues; and he sought and found God in all things. The progress which he made was very great, because he set out by the most perfect exterior and interior renunciation of the world and himself. Being sent to Majorca to study philosophy and divinity, he contracted a particular friendship with a lay brother, Alphonsus Rodriguez, then porter of the college, an eminent contemplative, and perfect servant of God: nor is it to be expressed how much the fervent disciple improved himself in the school of this humble master, in the maxims of Christian perfection. His first lessons were, to speak little with men, and much with God; to direct every action in the beginning with great fervour to the most perfect glory of God, in union with the holy actions of Christ; to have God always present in his heart; and to pray continually for the grace never to offend God: never to speak of any thing that belongs to clothing, lodging, and such conveniencies, especially eating or drinking; to meditate often on the sufferings of Christ, and on the virtues of his calling.

"F. Claver, in 1610, was, at his earnest request, sent with other missionaries to preach the faith to the infidels at Carthagena, and the neighbouring country in America. At the first sight of the poor negro slaves, he was moved with the strongest sentiments of compassion, tenderness, and zeal, which never forsook him; and it was his constant study to afford them all the temporal comfort and assistance in his power. In the first place he was indefatigable in instructing and baptizing them, and in giving them every spiritual succour: the title in which he gloried was that of the slave of the slaves, or of the Negroes; and incredible were the fatigues which he underwent night and day with them, and the many heroic acts of all virtues which he exercised in serving them. The Mahometans, the Pagans, and the very Catholics, whose scandalous lives were a reproach to their holy religion, the hospitals and the prisons were other theatres where he exercised his zeal. The history of his life furnishes us with most edifying instances, and gives an account of two persons being raised to life by him, and of other miracles; though his assiduous prayer, and his extraordinary humility, mortification of his senses, and perfect self-denial, might be called the greatest of his miracles. In the same rank we may place the wonderful conversions of many obstinate sinners, and the heroic sanctity of many great servants of God, who were by him formed to perfect virtue. Among his maxims of humility he used especially to inculcate, that he who is sincerely humble desires to be contemned, he seeks not to appear humble, but worthy to be humbled, is subject to all in his heart and ready to obey the whole world. By the holy hatred of ourselves, we must secretly rejoice in our hearts when we meet with contempt and affronts; but must take care, said this holy man, that no one think that we rejoice at them, but rather believe we are confounded and grieved at the ill treatment we receive. F. Claver died on the eighth of September, 1654, being about seventy-two years old; having spent in the society fifty-five years, in the same uniform crucified life, and in the constant round of the same uninterrupted labours, which perhaps requires a courage more heroic than martyrdom."

Having compared the two accounts together, the reader will now be able to conclude which is the most deserving of credit. In that given by Fox, we have no authorities, according to his usual custom; it rests solely on his bare assertion, and is related in his usual loose and unintelligible stile. Mr. Butler, on the contrary, gives us names, dates, and vouchers, and his narrative is at once clear and convincing. That the persecuted in China were CATHOLICS is undeniable; that the missionaries who spread the light of Christianity among these Pagans were CATHOLIC PRIESTS is equally incontestible. Thus, then, while the pretended reformers were saturating their respective countries with the blood of their fellow countrymen, and destroying churches and monasteries, the seats of learning, with Vandalic fury and barbarity, we have it on record, and it is admitted by Fox, though in a covertly way, that Catholic missionaries were planting the cross of Christ in the vast empire of China, and watering it with their blood. That this *Book of Martyrs* was written with the express intention of misleading the reader is demonstratively clear, from the ambiguity of its language. Amidst the various sects which the reformation, so called, has produced, all laying claim to Christianity, how is it possible that the uninformed should be able to gather what system of Christianity it was that the three Italian missionaries planted in China? To a Catholic enough is said to afford him a clue for discovery; but a Protestant who knows nothing of "the society for the propagation of the *Christian* faith" must remain in a state of darkness, unless by accident he meets with a correct history of the transactions, to throw a flood of light on the gross and obscure perversions we have here exposed. The term "Christian" is studiously used for the proper name Catholic, which is the only system of Christianity, the only Church that has produced missionaries to convert nations to the light of the gospel, by the aid of reason, example, and the gift of miracles. Looking at the account of Mr. Butler, one is struck with the heroic fortitude, the divine charity, and the extraordinary knowledge and abilities possessed by the Jesuit missionaries; a class of men so scandalously and unjustly reviled by the infidels of France and the bigots of England.— Where among the canting hypocritical Missionary societies, now existing in this deluded country, shall we find such self-devotion, such ardent zeal, such immense labours, and so successful a harvest, as the Jesuits displayed and obtained, during their cultivation in this part of the vineyard of their divine Master? With equal ardour, fidelity, and fortitude did the other religious orders of the Catholic church co-operate in carrying the knowledge of the Christian faith among benighted nations, and with the like success. How different too was the mode which they pursued. We here see that skill, meekness, prayer, and preaching were the means used in China in the sixteenth century, to inspire confidence and gain attention to the divine truths the missionaries were commanded to impart. This was the uniform practice of Catholic apostles in every age and every clime. Having gained converts to the faith, their next object was the raising temples for the worship of the living God. Alas! how different were the ways of the pretended reformers. Pride, ambition, revenge, lust, and brutal violence, marked their progress in every country where they could get a footing.—Not a single place can be found, where the reformers of the sixteenth century had any influence, that did not suffer, more or less, dilapidation and pillage. Churches were defaced, monasteries destroyed, libraries ransacked and burned, and priests and religious murdered and persecuted. Nor was this all: crimes were laid to the charge of the innocent to excite the ignorant and unthinking to fury, and falsehood was resorted to for the purpose of deceiving the multitude and blackening the character of those who held steadfast to truth. We have here an instance in this Book of Martyrs, in every page of which misrepresentation, perversion, and want of veracity are to be found. And this is the work which a set of men calling themselves "plain Christians," have undertaken to circulate, for the pretended purpose of "diffusing

was to reform the manners of the Portuguese settlers who were only
Christians in name. This act of charity performed to men already bearing the Christian name, his next efforts were directed to those who
were ignorant of the name of Christ. From Goa the holy missionary
bent his steps towards the coast of the peninsula which stretches to the
south and ends in a point called Cape Comorin. He was but little
skilled in the Malabar language, but he had the address to make himself understood, and many of the people in the numerous villages that
covered the country believed in his doctrines and were baptized. He
pursued his course to the populous kingdom of Travancore, and here
the harvest was so great, that in the space of one month he baptized
with his own hands ten thousand souls. In a short time the whole kingdom became Catholic. From thence he crossed to the eastern shore of
the peninsula, and went as far as Meliapor, where the Portuguese had
erected a town and named it St. Thomas, from a tradition that St.
Thomas the apostle suffered martyrdom there. From this place the
saint went on board a vessel and sailed across the gulf of Bengal to Malacca, and from thence to the islands of Molucca, preaching the faith of
Christ wherever he went. At Malacca he met with the native of Japan
before-mentioned, and accompanied by him he sailed to Japan and
landed at Cangoxima, the capital of the kingdom of Saxuma, and the
birth-place of Paul. Before St. Francis Xavier had been a year in this
island, he made innumerable converts to the Catholic faith, and a persecution was raised, in which many of the converts sealed their faith
with their blood.

The missionaries to the islands of the South Seas carried with them
wives and bibles, and some of them died, we are told, while others returned, without any *visible* effects from their labours. Query. How
much money did these missionaries receive from the London Society,
collected by fools' pence? St. Francis did not carry a bible with him,
but like the apostles of Christ, he carried on his back all the necessary
utensils for the sacrifice of the mass, and when he made converts he
had copies of the Apostles' creed and a Life of Christ translated into
the Japonese language, and distributed them amongst his converts.
We question whether the Japonese Christians ever saw a bible, any
more than the primitive Christians. Such a thing was impossible in
the latter instance, because the bible was not then collated into one
book; and in the former case it is more than improbable, as it was too
laborious and difficult a task to translate and print so ponderous a volume into the Japonese tongue. We even doubt whether the Bible
Societies have yet a copy of the bible in the Japonese character, though
they boast of having the sacred volume in one hundred and fifty different languages.—From Cangoxima the holy missionary went to Firando,
where he baptized more in twenty days than in the former place during a year. In these labours St. Francis was joined by other Jesuit
missionaries, some of them natives, and at each place he left one or
more in care of the souls converted, while he went in search of fresh
harvests.

In the extract we have given from Mr. Butler there are dates, and
names, and authorities, but in Fox there are none, nor has my lord
Bexley been so good as to tell us which of the islands in the South

seas has had the happiness to embrace the *only* Christian faith that could lead them to salvation. There was a farce to be sure got up in London a few weeks ago, by these Bible and Missionary Saints, who introduced a king and queen of the Sandwich islands into the metropolis, and much notice was taken of them by a part of his Majesty's government. It was said that their Sandwich majesties were to have been introduced to his Britannic majesty had they not been prevented by another majesty, the grim king of terrors. We do not recollect the name of this Sandwich sovereign and his royal consort, but that is no great matter. He came over to England, and was represented as a convert to Christianity, made by the English missionaries. The conversion, therefore, of this petty monarch is, we presume, the conversion of the whole nation to the only Christian faith that could lead to eternal salvation. Well, be it so; but mark, reader, the conclusion. Their sable majesties had not been long in town before that fatal malady the small pox laid hold of them, and his majesty took it so to heart that he died, and was shortly after followed by his spouse. The public papers told us that he was *a Christian*, and they further informed us that though a Christian, yet he had *several wives* in his own country: thereby shewing that his kind of Christianity was a very easy one, seeing that it would allow him to have more wives than one. In every case where Pagan nations were converted by Catholic missionaries, both kings and people were compelled to relinquish their sensual passions and keep themselves continent. Only one lawful wife was permitted, though Pagan custom might have allowed an unlimited plurality, and not an instance can be named where a sovereign was admitted to the sacraments of the church that did not consent to renounce polygamy. Our modern missionaries, however, do not seem to be so rigid in their discipline; and if such be the Christian faith which is to lead the Sandwichers to salvation, we shall, for our part, prefer the old road, which was taught by the apostles and their successors, and has been followed by every nation that held to the Catholic church.

Before we quit this part of the globe, we cannot help contrasting the success of the Chinese and Japan missionaries, and that of the modern gentlemen sent to the South seas by the London Missionary society. The latter, we are told, laboured hard, till some died and others returned without producing any fruit, though they ploughed with the bible. It was not till the lapse of ten years that a blossom appeared upon the tree, and whether it be real or fictitious is very doubtful, as we have no authentic clue on which to ground the fact, and certain we are that, allowing the nameless nation to have embraced the doctrines of these missionaries, the creed they have received is not the creed taught by the apostles. Let us now look to the empires of China and Japan. In the former we see it related, on authority, that hundreds of thousands of souls embraced the Catholic faith on the preaching of a few poor Jesuits, and two hundred churches were raised by the converts. We see a persecution created to prevent the increase of the Catholic faith; we see the new converts laying down their lives for this faith, and fresh ones springing up in their stead, animated with the heroic constancy and fortitude displayed by these Catholic Christian martyrs. In Japan we see thousands of Pagans renouncing their errors and embracing the rigid system of Catholicism by the preaching of *one* missionary, divinely commissioned, St. Francis Xavier. We see these fruits raised almost instantaneously by the fructifying word of God, orally delivered, not bound up in a book ; and we see the same effects as were produced in China. Princes and persons of rank became the disciples of a crucified God, as well as the meanest of the people; submission was rendered in spirituals to the see of Rome; churches were raised for the public worship of that God, whose doctrines they believed in; and persecutions followed to sift the chaff from the wheat. But where are the persecutions to try the faith of the Sandwichers? Where are the churches raised in honour of the God of Truth? When we have seen these highly-favoured Christians, who are stated to have adopted the *only* faith that could lead them to *salvation*, laying down their lives for this faith, as Catholics in every age and every country have done;—when we see them erect splendid temples and offer up the divine sacrifice as the first apostles and the primitive Christians did;—then, indeed, we will allow the truth of my lord Bexley's statement;—but till then we must consider the newly made peer as labouring under a great mistake, led away, probably, by artful misrepresentations.

Mr. Butler agrees with Fox as to the fact of the opposition made in Japan to the persecutors by some of the Christians, but he speaks of their conduct in very different terms. The language used by Fox implies approbation of this resistance, whereas Mr. Butler plainly states it was *unjustifiable*, and very opposite to that of the primitive Christians. Rebellion, or resistance to lawful authority, cannot be justified on the plea of *religion*, because religion being an emanation from God, it cannot be made a cloak for any worldly policy on any account whatever without a heinous offence against the Divine Majesty. To such a martyrologist as Fox, whose labours have been devoted to make martyrs of men whose deeds have been of the most rebellious kind, the conduct of these Japanese Christians may appear meritorious, it does not seem to have been so, however, in the eye of God, and it was probably to mark his divine displeasure that the Christian religion no longer flourished in a country where its followers, forgetful of the promises of its Divine Founder, that all the powers of hell should not prevail against it, irreligiously attempted to defend it by force of arms. There is another subject connected with this rebellion worthy of observation, which Fox has very slyly passed over. He says, " The persecution continued many " years, when the *remnant* of the innumerable Christians with which " Japan abounded, to the number of 37,000 souls, retired to the town " and castle of Siniabara," &c. Mr. Butler on the contrary says, the Christians broke into rebellion and took the field with 40,000 men; that they took several strong places, but being at length forced, they died desperately fighting in *the field*, in 1638; and that a persecution reigned after this affair. But mark, reader, the preface of this rebellion. The Christians who were Catholics were accused to the emperor by the Dutch, who were Protestants, of being in *a conspiracy* with the Portuguese, who were also Catholics, which enraged the persecutors against the Catholic Japanese, and irritated the latter to make physical resistance to the sanguinary oppressions they experienced. Hence it appears

seas has had the happiness to embrace the *only* Christian faith that could lead them to salvation. There was a farce to be sure got up in London a few weeks ago, by these Bible and Missionary Saints, who introduced a king and queen of the Sandwich islands into the metropolis, and much notice was taken of them by a part of his Majesty's government. It was said that their Sandwich majesties were to have been introduced to his Britannic majesty had they not been prevented by another majesty, the grim king of terrors. We do not recollect the name of this Sandwich sovereign and his royal consort, but that is no great matter. He came over to England, and was represented as a convert to Christianity, made by the English missionaries. The conversion, therefore, of this petty monarch is, we presume, the conversion of the whole nation to the only Christian faith that could lead to eternal salvation. Well, be it so; but mark, reader, the conclusion. Their sable majesties had not been long in town before that fatal malady the small pox laid hold of them, and his majesty took it so to heart that he died, and was shortly after followed by his spouse. The public papers told us that he was *a Christian*, and they further informed us that though a Christian, yet he had *several wives* in his own country: thereby shewing that his kind of Christianity was a very easy one, seeing that it would allow him to have more wives than one. In every case where Pagan nations were converted by Catholic missionaries, both kings and people were compelled to relinquish their sensual passions and keep themselves continent. Only one lawful wife was permitted, though Pagan custom might have allowed an unlimited plurality, and not an instance can be named where a sovereign was admitted to the sacraments of the church that did not consent to renounce polygamy. Our modern missionaries, however, do not seem to be so rigid in their discipline; and if such be the Christian faith which is to lead the Sandwichers to salvation, we shall, for our part, prefer the old road, which was taught by the apostles and their successors, and has been followed by every nation that held to the Catholic church.

Before we quit this part of the globe, we cannot help contrasting the success of the Chinese and Japan missionaries, and that of the modern gentlemen sent to the South seas by the London Missionary society. The latter, we are told, laboured hard, till some died and others returned without producing any fruit, though they ploughed with the bible. It was not till the lapse of ten years that a blossom appeared upon the tree, and whether it be real or fictitious is very doubtful, as we have no authentic clue on which to ground the fact, and certain we are that, allowing the nameless nation to have embraced the doctrines of these missionaries, the creed they have received is not the creed taught by the apostles. Let us now look to the empires of China and Japan. In the former we see it related, on authority, that hundreds of thousands of souls embraced the Catholic faith on the preaching of a few poor Jesuits, and two hundred churches were raised by the converts. We see a persecution created to prevent the increase of the Catholic faith; we see the new converts laying down their lives for this faith, and fresh ones springing up in their stead, animated with the heroic constancy and fortitude displayed by these Catholic Christian martyrs. In Japan we see thousands of Pagans renouncing their errors and embracing the rigid system of Catholicism by the preaching of *one* missionary, divinely commissioned, St. Francis Xavier. We see these fruits raised almost instantaneously by the fructifying word of God, orally delivered, not bound up in a book ; and we see the same effects as were produced in China. Princes and persons of rank became the disciples of a crucified God, as well as the meanest of the people ; submission was rendered in spirituals to the see of Rome ; churches were raised for the public worship of that God, whose doctrines they believed in ; and persecutions followed to sift the chaff from the wheat. But where are the persecutions to try the faith of the Sandwichers? Where are the churches raised in honour of the God of Truth? When we have seen these highly-favoured Christians, who are stated to have adopted the *only* faith that could lead them to *salvation*, laying down their lives for this faith, as Catholics in every age and every country have done ;—when we see them erect splendid temples and offer up the divine sacrifice as the first apostles and the primitive Christians did ;—then, indeed, we will allow the truth of my lord Bexley's statement ;—but till then we must consider the newly made peer as labouring under a great mistake, led away, probably, by artful misrepresentations.

Mr. Butler agrees with Fox as to the fact of the opposition made in Japan to the persecutors by some of the Christians, but he speaks of their conduct in very different terms. The language used by Fox implies approbation of this resistance, whereas Mr. Butler plainly states it was *unjustifiable*, and very opposite to that of the primitive Christians. Rebellion, or resistance to lawful authority, cannot be justified on the plea of *religion*, because religion being an emanation from God, it cannot be made a cloak for any worldly policy on any account whatever without a heinous offence against the Divine Majesty. To such a martyrologist as Fox, whose labours have been devoted to make martyrs of men whose deeds have been of the most rebellious kind, the conduct of these Japanese Christians may appear meritorious, it does not seem to have been so, however, in the eye of God, and it was probably to mark his divine displeasure that the Christian religion no longer flourished in a country where its followers, forgetful of the promises of its Divine Founder, that all the powers of hell should not prevail against it, irreligiously attempted to defend it by force of arms. There is another subject connected with this rebellion worthy of observation, which Fox has very slyly passed over. He says, " The persecution continued many " years, when the *remnant* of the innumerable Christians with which " Japan abounded, to the number of 37,000 souls, retired to the town " and castle of Siniabara," &c. Mr. Butler on the contrary says, the Christians broke into rebellion and took the field with 40,000 men ; that they took several strong places, but being at length forced, they died desperately fighting in *the field*, in 1638 ; and that a persecution reigned after this affair. But mark, reader, the preface of this rebellion. The Christians who were Catholics were accused to the emperor by the Dutch, who were Protestants, of being in *a conspiracy* with the Portuguese, who were also Catholics, which enraged the persecutors against the Catholic Japanese, and irritated the latter to make physical resistance to the sanguinary oppressions they experienced. Hence it appears that to Protestant reformers the Japanese Catholics were indebted for some of the cruelties inflicted upon them by their Pagan rulers, and it is a fact not less worthy of notice, but carefully suppressed by Fox, that the reason why the Protestant Dutch were the only Christians allowed to trade with Japan, was because they were the only people pretending to Christianity, that, for the sake of merchandize, would impiously trample on the image of their crucified Saviour.

In concluding our review of this account given by Fox of the persecutions in China and Japan, we will just observe that there have been many editions published of his *Book of Martyrs*, from the folio size down to a duodecimo. In one of the former, now before us, edited by the Rev. Henry Southwell, LL. D. Rector of Asterby, in Lincolnshire, and late of Magdalen college, Cambridge ; and *author* of *The Universal Family Bible*, we find the following character drawn of the Christian religion first introduced into Japan. "They," (the Japanese) writes this reverend editor, " soon perceived, on the comparison, that their own " religion was calculated to make them cruel, uncharitable, perfidious, " unnatural, unsocial, unhuman ; and that the Christian faith, on the " contrary, would render them kind, benevolent, sincere, humane, " social, tender. The contrast (he adds) was too striking for the " balance not to turn in favour of the Christian truth.—Happy then (he " elsewhere observes) must the people be to receive a faith which " pointed out every virtue, divine and human, and taught the practice " of whatever could lead to happiness here and hereafter." Now this system of pure religion we have *proved* to be the Catholic faith, introduced by Catholic missionaries, and at a time when the evangelical reformers were reviling it, as blasphemous and idolatrous. What then are we to think of these editiors of Fox's *Book of Martyrs ?* We here find one representing the Catholic faith introduced into Japah to be a system of the purest benevolence, humanity, and happiness, while the " few plain Christians" assert that it is a system inseparable from cruelty and persecution, Can these men be worthy of credit after such contradictory statements ?

" BOOK VIII.

" Persecutions of the Protestants in various Countries not before described."

This book is divided into ten sections, but as it would be tedious to enter into all the misrepresentations and falsehoods contained in . them, and as it is time we should bring the first volume of our labours to a close, we shall content ourselves with noticing the most prominent perversions of historical facts, convinced that what we shall point out to the reader will be deemed satisfactory that the rest is unworthy of credit. The first head is " Persecutions in Abyssinia," which are thus related by Fox. " About the end of the fifteenth century, some Portu" guese missionaries made a voyage to Abyssinia, and began to propa" gate the Roman Catholic doctrines among the Abyssinians, who pro" fessed Christianity before the arrival of the missionaries. The " priests gained such an influence at court, that the emperor consented " to abolish the established rites of the Ethiopian church, and to admit " those of Rome ; and, soon after, consented to receive a patriarch

" from the pope, and to acknowledge the supremacy of the latter. This
" innovation, however, did not take place without great opposition.—
" Several of the most powerful lords, and a majority of the people, who
" professed the primitive Christianity established in Abyssinia, took up
" arms, in their defence, against the emperor. Thus, by the artifices of
" the court of Rome and its emissaries, the whole empire was thrown
" into commotion, and a war commenced, which was carried on through
" the reigns of many emperors, and which ceased not for above a cen-
" tury. All this time the Roman Catholics were strengthened by the
" power of the court, by means of which conjunction the primitive
" Christians of Abyssinia were severely persecuted, and multitudes
" perished by the hands of their inhuman enemies."

We have just quoted an editor of this famous, or rather most infamous, *Book of Martyrs*, who says the Japanese were induced to embrace Christianity, by comparing the beauties of that system to the deformity of Paganism. We beg the reader will follow the example and
compare the account given by the " few plain Christians" in their edition of this book of the introduction of Christianity into China and Japan, and the propagation of the Roman Catholic doctrines in Abyssinia. The time selected is much about the same; the introduction of
Christianity into China being stated at the *commencement* of the *sixteenth* century by Italian missionaries; that of Japan about the middle of
the *same* century, by Portuguese missionaries; and of the Roman Catholic
doctrines about the *end* of the *fifteenth* century, by Portuguese missionaries. The Portuguese, as we have before stated, were all Catholics,
and can it be supposed then that the doctrines which the Portuguese
missionaries carried into Japan and the doctrines which other Portuguese missionaries carried into Abyssinia a few years previous were not
one and the same. How then came the doctrines in Abyssinia to lead to
such bad consequences, and the doctrines in Japan to be so fertile in
good works? This is a strange contradiction which the short-sighted
" plain Christians" in their hurry to diffuse this work among their " fellow-believers," overlooked, and which they will find difficult to explain.
We will, however, endeavour to set the reader right, and leave him then
to form his own conclusions of Fox and the " plain Christians."

It is admitted by Fox that the missionaries gained an ascendency
over the Christianity of the Abyssinians and that the emperor consented
to abolish the *established* rites of the Ethiopian church and admit those
of Rome; that this innovation, as he calls it, did not take place without
great opposition, and that a majority of the people who professed the
primitive Christianity established in Abyssinia TOOK UP ARMS IN
THEIR DEFENCE AGAINST THE EMPEROR. Observe ye this,
reader. Men taking up arms against their sovereign, because he thought
fit to embrace the Catholic faith. What were these pretended primitive Christians Orangemen, like the bigotted and half-loyal Orangemen of Ireland, who swear allegiance to the king of England so long
as he shall continue a Protestant, and no longer? But why did these
Abyssinian primitive Orange Christians—bless their Christianity!—
why did they take up arms? Could they not reason and convince
their adversaries, without having recourse to force? No, reader
they were in *error*, as we shall presently prove; and error, you know

can never stand a fair contest with truth. It is clear from Fox's account that the Catholic missionaries had not recourse to *force*; that the mock primitive Christians did take to arms, and rebelled against their sovereigns; and that the empire was thrown into confusion and civil war by this rebellion. But then he attributes this state of things to the *artifices* of the court of Rome and its emissaries, who were strengthened, he says, " by the power of the court, and by means of this junction " the primitive Christians were *persecuted*." What *artifices* the court of Rome could practice in such a distant empire we are at a loss to conjecture, nor can we perceive what advantage the pope could derive from them. But it is time the reader should see another side of the question, and we beg his earnest attention to it.

The Abyssinians or Ethiopians received the first light of Christianity, according to the testimony of Eusebius, from the eunuch of their queen, who was baptized by St. Philip the deacon, as we read in the Acts of the Apostles, chapter viii, verse 7. They were not grounded in their faith, nor wholly converted, however, till the fourth century, when St. Frumentius gained them over to the Catholic faith by his preachings and miracles. Subsequently to this, that is, in the fifth century, the Abyssinians engaged in the Eutychian heresy, which heresy was condemned by the council of Chalcedon as contrary to the doctrines of the apostles.— Eutychianism acknowledged only one nature in Jesus Christ, whereas the Catholic doctrine declares there are two, the divine and the human. Thus then it turns out that the primitive Christianity of the Abyssinians was a heresy, afterwards called Demi-Eutychianism or Monothelism, and was justly condemned by pope Martin, according to Fox's account of the martyrdom of that holy bishop. (*See our Review*, p. 178.) Here is another contradiction on the part of John Fox. In his relation of the death of pope Martin in the seventh century, he praises the head of the Catholic church for condemning the Monothelites, who were, he said, heretics; and now, in the sixteenth century he is representing this same condemned heresy as pure primitive Christianity. The Abyssinians still adhere to this heresy, for which they took up arms in 1604, and slew their emperor Zadenghel in battle. But no persecution did they suffer, on the contrary, these Eutychians banished the missionaries and persecuted the converts to Catholicism till they eradicated that primitive faith. Still the reader must understand that the Abyssinians, though they deny more than one nature in Christ, yet they hold many of the doctrines of the Catholic church which Protestants deny.

The next head is " PERSECUTIONS IN TURKEY," which commences with an account of Mahomet, and ends with a victory of the Christians over the sultan Solyman, who besieged the city of Vienna in the year 1529. In the detail of this victory we have not a single name besides that of Solyman, any more than we have in his account of the siege of Vienna. Who the generals were not a word is said to throw the least light upon the circumstance, and the whole is a jumble of facts from which nothing accurate can be drawn. Were it not for his mentioning the name of Solyman, we should not have been able to distinguish which siege of Vienna Fox alluded to, as that city sustained two desperate attacks from the Turks, and by the bravery of the besieged saved Christendom from being overrun by the barbarian hordes of Mahometans. In these times Protestantism was unknown. There were only two classes of Christians, namely, the Catholics who adhered to the faith of the apostles and acknowledged the bishop of Rome as the supreme head of the church; and the Greeks, who differed in the article of the procession of the Holy Ghost from the Father and the Son, and refused obedience to the pope as head of the church. Several attempts were made to reconcile the Greeks to the centre of unity without effect. The eastern empire had long suffered from the ravages of the Mahometan power. Province after province was wrested from it, and Constantinople, the seat of the empire, had been several times attacked. During these misfortunes the Greeks were several times warned of the impending vengeance of the Divine arm, for their obstinate resistance to the truth, without effect. At length, in 1453, Mahomet II. laid siege to the city of Constantinople with an army of 300,000 men, and above 100 gallies, with 130 smaller vessels. After sustaining a siege of some continuance with much bravery, on the 29th of May the Ottoman commander made dispositions for a general assault both by sea and land. The Turks advanced with great bravery and were met by the Greeks with an equal resistance, but the fate of the latter was sealed. They had too long set the commands of God at nought, and he withdrew his protection from them, leaving them to the mercy of their enemies. Notwithstanding the desperation of the Greeks, the victory was obtained by the Turks, the city was given up to slaughter and pillage, and it is reckoned that there perished in this sacking of Constantinople, forty thousand Greeks, and sixty thousand were sold for slaves. By this annihilation of the Greek empire in 1453, it is clear that the opponents of the Mahometans in 1529 were Catholics. The persecutions therefore of the Turks were levelled against the professors of the Catholic faith, as we have shewn the persecutions in every age and nation to have been invariably inflicted on that class of Christians.

We are now led into Georgia and Mingrelia, where the persecutors are the Turks and Persians, and then we are carried to the states of Barbary of which nothing need be said here, the conduct of these barbarians being familiar to every one, and every body knows they are not Catholics. From Barbary we are taken to Calabria, to which country, we are told, a great many Waldenses of Pragela and Dauphiny emigrated, having received permission to settle in some waste lands, which they soon, it is asserted, converted into " regions of beauty and fertility." Then follows an account of pope Pius the fourth meditating the destruction of these Waldenses, and sending a cardinal Alexandrino, a man of violent temper and a furious bigot, to act as inquisitor, and put the pope's determination into effect. The detail then goes on in the usual way, with the refusal of the Waldenses to comply with the request of the inquisitors, and the soldiers being sent to massacre them, and hunt them down like wild beasts. This account occupies more than two pages, and throughout the whole there is not a single date or authority. The Waldenses are said to have emigrated about the *fourteenth* century, and Pius the fourth did not fill the papal chair till the middle of the sixteenth century. The Waldenses are said to have built the town of St. Xist, but we should like to know how they came to name it after a *saint* who must have been a Roman Catholic, for we have no saints of any other religion. Besides a glance of the map will show that Calabria is the furthermost point of Italy, and forms part of the kingdom of Naples, the inhabitants of which, we believe, were all Catholics. One of the merits of the Waldenses, be it observed, was that of *fighting* for their faith, not of *suffering* for it, as the primitive Christians did, and the Catholics now do, for conscience sake. From Calabria we come back to Piedmont, which occupies six pages, but of such ridiculous rodomontade as we think unnecessary to notice. We are next carried to Venice, where we are told a great many Protestants fixed their residence, before the terrors of the inquisition were known in that city, and many converts were made "by the *purity* of their *doctrines* and the *inoffensiveness* of " their *conversation*. The pope, (it is added,) no sooner learned the great " increase of Protestantism, than *he*, in the year 1542, sent inquisitors " to Venice to apprehend *such* as they might *deem obnoxious.*" Here then was not to be a total extermination; only the obnoxious few were to be selected. The pope is also made paramount here, but it is to be remarked that Venice was an independent republic, governed by its own laws, and the authorities, though Catholics, were extremely jealous of his holiness. It is therefore more than improbable that they permitted him to interfere with their jurisdiction. Be it observed too, that here *is* a date, namely 1542, at which time Protestantism may be said to have been in its cradle. Next we have, " *Martyrdoms in various parts of Italy*, in the same loose and unauthenticated style. Pope Pius the fourth is represented as commencing a general persecution of the Protestants throughout the Italian states, sparing neither age nor sex.— Now it so happens that this pope was the opposite of a persecutor, and the modern editors seem so convinced of this, that they have declined giving a single fact relating to this pretended persecution, but have contented themselves with inserting an anonymous letter, evidently fabricated, purporting to come from a learned and humane *Roman Catholic* to a nobleman. A small space is apportioned to " *Persecutions in the marquisate of Saluces*," of which neither ends nor sides can be made, and then we have eleven pages filled with " *Persecutions in Piedmont, in the seventeenth century.*" Under this head we will select one tale, which we think will suffice as a sample of the rest. " Some of the " Irish troops having taken eleven men of Garcigliana prisoners, they " heated a furnace red hot, and forced them to push each other in till " they came to the last man, whom they themselves pushed in." No doubt, supposing the tale to be true, the man could not push himself in, but we think the "few plain Christians," when their hand was in, might have made these Irish troopers raise the devil to do their persecuting work. The next persecutions are those of Michael de Molinos, and the Quietists. Michael was a Spanish priest, and had a mind to be thought clever. He broached some *new* doctrines, and as a matter of course they were condemned by the pope, not for being *true*, but for being *new*, such as were not heard of before, and therefore could not be those God had revealed to his apostles. Michael was obstinate and got into the inquisition, and no more was heard of the Molinists. As for the Quietists, no one would have known about this sect, had not Fox brought the professors from their graves, where they were *quiet* enough. The " plain Christians" say, the Quietists were so terrified by

the sufferings of their leader, that the greater part of them abjured his
mode, and remained *quiet*; while the assiduity of the Jesuits totally extirpated *Quietism.* From this admission it is clear that *Quietism* was
not true Christianism, because Christ said the latter should last till the
end of the world, whereas the former evaporated like a cloud of smoke.
The tenth section closes the book, and contains the pretended martyrdom of a John Calas of Thoulouse, which, like the rest of the tales, is
unauthenticated and exaggerated. We pass it over, therefore, to notice more particularly the ninth section, which purports to give the

"PERSECUTIONS OF THE PROTESTANTS IN FRANCE DURING THE SIX-
"TEENTH AND SEVENTEENTH CENTURIES."

The account admits that Henry III. of France favoured the Protestants, though it is insinuated that it was more from policy than religion.
Henry IV. succeeded. He was a Protestant,' but afterwards became a
Catholic from conviction. This was a sad blow to the Protestants;
our editors lament the fact, but still they are compelled to admit that
in all other respects he was entitled to the appellation of *Great.* Henry,
it is stated, applied himself to the cultivation of the arts of peace, and by
an edict issued in 1598, called the Edict of Nantes, he granted to his
Protestant subjects a full toleration and protection of the exercise of
their religious opinions. All this was as it should be. He did what
every Catholic king should do, and what every Catholic king would do,
when his subjects deserved such toleration by their peaceable behaviour.
Henry was also a great favourer of the Jesuits, which the modern editors should have noticed, as they allow him to be worthy the title of
Great. Thus, then, Henry IV. was the protector and friend of the
Jesuits and the Protestants, and we applaud him for it. This king was
the first of the Bourbon family that now fills the throne of France,
and gives protection to the Protestants of that kingdom, while the Catholics of England and Ireland are still excluded from their civil rights.
In consequence of this edict, the modern editors say, "the *true* church
" of Christ abode in peace during many years, and flourished exceed-
" ingly." We cannot refrain from smiling at this statement, as the
" few plain Christians," would make us believe that the Hugonots of
France, who had deluged their country with blood and pillage; who
had, as far they were able, sold her to foreign mercenaries, to revenge
themselves of their religious adversaries, were the sons of the true
Church of Christ, though the Divine Founder had more than once, or
twice, or thrice, assured his disciples that this true Church should embrace all the nations of the world, and in fact has been spread in every
nation in the globe by Catholic missionaries, receiving their commission
from the supreme head, the pope of Rome.

This state of peace was however soon broken, for, we are told,
" Henry was at length assassinated in 1610, by Ravaillac, a Jesuit,
" filled with that frantic bigotry which the Roman Catholic religion
" has so peculiar a tendency to inspire and cherish." That Henry was
assassinated by Ravaillae is but too true; and notwithstanding the
" frantic bigotry" which our modern editors say " the Roman Catholic
" religion has a peculiar tendency to inspire and cherish," there is not
a Roman Catholic that does not lament the fate of this great and good

king. This monarch's life was twice attempted, the first time in 1593 by Barriere, and it was then asserted that the Jesuits were the instigators of the attempt. The king, however, bore testimony to the falsity of this assertion, for he plainly told the president de Harlay, that it was from a Jesuit he had information of the plot against him, and that a Jesuit had used all the influence he possessed to persuade the assassin from his purpose, assuring him that he would be damned if he took it in hand. The wretch himself declared, both on the rack and on the scaffold, that he had no accomplice. Besides, taking the circumstances in which the Jesuits then stood in France, nothing but the blindest bigotry and prejudice could induce any one to think of charging the Jesuits with the murder of Henry IV. That religious order of men had been banished the kingdom by the parliaments, for some imputed offence, and Henry had just recalled them in opposition to the parliament: now, does it stand to reason, that men would lift up their hands and embrue them with the blood of their best friend and protector? The story may do for the ignorant and bloated bigot, but the man of common sense will never give credit to it. The English Puritans, however, took the advantage of the then state of the press and the public mind to represent the assassination as having been committed through the instigation of the Jesuits, and a proclamation was issued by our James the first, banishing every one of that religious order and all Catholic priests out of this kingdom.

The death of Henry IV. made way for Louis XIII. his son, who being a minor, the kingdom, we are told, " was *nominally* governed by " the queen mother, but *really* by her *minion*, cardinal Richelieu, a man " of great abilities, which were unhappily perverted to the worst pur- " poses. He was cruel, bigotted, tyrannical, rapacious, and sensual ; " he trampled on the civil and religious liberties of France; and hesi- " tated not to accomplish his intentions by the most barbarous and in- " famous methods." Here is a character for poor cardinal Richelieu! but we do not wonder at the picture, as we are subsequently informed that when the mild and meek Hugonots resolved to take up ARMS and FIGHT like warriors, not preach like apostles, for their new-fangled theories, this cardinal-minister defeated all their enterprizes, and caused the walls and fortifications of their chief town, Rochelle, to be destroyed. This success on his part was quite sufficient to earn him so good a name from the advocates of these *fighting* religionists. The narrator next says :—

" During the fifty years which succeeded the reduction of Rochelle, the Protestants suffered every indignity, injustice, and cruelty, which their barbarous persecutors could devise. They were at the mercy of every petty despot, who, ' drest in a little brief authority,' wished to gratify their malice, or signalise the season of his power, punishing the heretics, and evincing his attachment to the *infallible church*. The consequences of this may easily be imagined ; every petty vexation which can render private life miserable, every species of plunder and extortion, and every wanton exertion of arbitrary power, were employed to harrass and molest the Protestants of all ranks, sexes, and ages. At length, in 1684, the impious and blasphemous tyrant Louis XIV. who, in imitation of the worst Roman emperors, wished to receive divine honours, and was flattered by his abject courtiers into the belief that he was more than human, determined to establish his claim to the title of *le grand*, which their fulsome adulation had bestowed on him, by the extirpation of the *heretics* from his dominions. Pretending, however, to wish for their conversion to the *true faith*, he gave them the alternative of voluntarily becoming papists, or being *compelled to it.* On their refusal to apostatize, they were *dragooned*; that is, the dragoons, the most ruffianly and barbarous of his *Christian* majesty's troops, were quartered upon them, with orders *to live at discretion.* Their ideas of *discretion* may easily be conceived, and accordingly the unhappy Protestants were exposed to every species of suffering, which lust, avarice, cruelty, bigotry, and brutality, can engender in the breasts of an ignorant, depraved, and infuriated soldiery, absolved from all restraint, and left to the diabolical promptings of their worst passions, whose flames were fanned by the assurances of the bishops, priests, and friars, that they were ;fulfilling a sacred duty, by punishing the enemies of God and religion !"

He then goes on to state that more than *five hundred thousand* persons escaped or were banished ; that those who either were purposely detained, or were unable to escape, were condemned to the gallies, and chained, and imprisoned, and marched from one end of the kingdom to the other ; till at length " the Lord (Oh ! bless the cant) of his infinite mercy," raised up a deliverer in the person of queen Anne of England, who interfered in their favour, and Lewis in a fright released the captives from their sufferings.

We have not space to enter into a minute refutation of the barefaced falsehoods contained in this narration ; nor is it necessary, as the whole is evidently a piece of exaggeration carrying its own refutation. We shall therefore content ourselves with giving a testimony on the other side of the question, and leave the decision with the public. Fox endeavours to make the revocation of the edict to arise from *religious* motives, whereas it was occasioned by the *rebellious* proceedings and disposition of the Hugonots. That the French government were desirous they should be converted from the restless doctrines of Calvinism there can be no doubt, but the mode adopted, and the revocation of the edict of Nantes, is very differently related by Proyart, in his *Life of the Dauphin*, father to Louis XV. and son to the revoker of the edict. 'This author gives a letter from the Dauphin on this very subject, in which the prince says : —

" I shall not detail that chain of enormities, which have been consigned, in so many authentic records, those secret assemblies, those oaths of confederation, those leagues with foreign powers, those refusals to pay the public taxes, those seditious threats, those open conjurations, those sackings and burnings of towns, those massacres in cold blood, those assaults upon the kings' persons, those multifarious and unheard of sacrileges. It is sufficient to say, that, from Francis I. down to our days, that is, under seven consecutive reigns, all those evils have desolated the kingdom, with more or less fury. This is,the historical fact, which may be loaded with a variety of incidents, but the substance of which cannot be denied, or called in question. Now, if the prince has not the right of commanding the conscience, he has that at least of providing for the safety of the state, and of chaining down fanaticism, which threatens to introduce anarchy and confusion. Although the king knew well enough, that the Hugonots had nothing for the primordial titles of their privileges, but injustice and violence; although their late infractions of the edicts appeared to him a sufficient reason to deprive them of the legal existence, which they had invaded in arms, yet his majesty wished to take counsel. Among other things, it was objected, that the Hugonots, depending upon the assistance of the princes of their religion, might possibly take up arms, &c. The king answered, he was prepared for the worst ; that nothing would be more painful to him, than being forced to shed a single drop of the blood of his subjects ; but that he had armies, and good generals, and would employ them in case of necessity against rebels, who wished to bring destruction upon their own heads. The suppression of the edict was agreed upon unanimously. The king, who always wished to treat his most disaffected subjects, as a pastor, and a father, neglected no measures that could win their hearts, and, at the same time, remove their ignorance. He granted pensions, distributed alms, established missions, caused books to be circulated, both for the use of the illiterate and the learned. Success attended the wisdom of his measures. And though it should seem, if credit were given to the infuriated declamations of some of the Hugunot ministers, that the king had armed one half of his subjects, to slaughter the other half; yet the truth is, that every thing passed to the great satisfaction of the king, *without effusion of blood*, and without disturbance. The most seditious, stunned by this vigorous blow, shewed thrmselves the most tractable of all. As to those who were more tenacious of their erroneous tenets, they left the kingdom, and took away with them the seeds of all our civil wars.' The prince adds, that 'although the number of the Hugunots, who went out of France, at this time' should amount, according to the most exaggerated accounts, to 67,732 persons, including all ages and sexes,—their retreat did not cost the state so many useful members as would have been snatched away by one single year of civil war.' "

The whole account of this imputed persecution is false and garbled. The excesses which were committed on the Hugonots some time after the revocation of the edict had been executed, were occasioned by the turbulent conduct of the Hugonots themselves. The "plain Christians" extol queen Anne "for her Christian interference in their favour;" but they forget that this queen was one of the most cruel persecutors of her own Catholic subjects that ever filled the throne of England. The revocation of the edict of Nantes is a favourite theme with the partisans of Protestantism and intolerance, but they carefully conceal the perfidious and disgraceful violation of the treaty of Limerick by William III. and his ministers, before the ink was dry on the parchment which contained the contract. This treaty was made with the Catholics of Ireland under the walls of Limerick, by which the Catholics surrendered up the country to the new monarch, who pledged himself that the Catholics should have perfect liberty of conscience, and the exercise of their civil rights in common with their Protestant brethren. The treaty received the sanction of the great seal of England; yet two months had not elapsed before it was infringed by the Protestant contractors in the face of the whole world; while the Catholics rigidly adhered to its stipulations. Nay, the very pulpits were made instrumental to justify the violation of the treaty, and a Bishop of Meath was not ashamed to preach that faith was not to be kept with Catholics. This breach of a solemn engagement was followed up by the enactment of the most cruel and oppressive laws the ingenuity of man could invent to harrass and persecute his fellow man. An act was passed to prevent Catholics from being educated. Another was passed to disarm them. A third to banish the clergy out of the kingdom. By a fourth Protestants were prevented from intermarrying with Catholics; and others still more severe followed upon the unhappy sufferers under "Protestant-ascendency."

When Anne came to the crown new crimes and new sufferings were prepared for the Catholics. They were deprived of their paternal inheritances, and prevented from aequiring an inch of land in the kingdom. The late Mr. Edmund Burke, in his Letter to Sir Hercules Langrishe, alluding to the cruelty of the penal code under which the Catholics groaned, says, "You abhorred it, as I did, for its *vicious perfection*. " For I must do it justice. It was a complete system, full of coherence " and consistency; well digested and well composed in all its parts. It " was a machine of wise and elaborate contrivance, and as well fitted " for the OPPRESSION, IMPOVERISHMENT, and DEGRADATION " of a people, and the *debasement in them of human nature itself*, as ever

" proceeded from the perverted ingenuity of man." In short, during this queen's reign, who is lauded by the " few plain Christians," for her merciful interference in favour of the rebellious Hugonots, the legislature was chiefly occupied in devising persecuting statutes to extirpate Popery, as Catholicism was called, and encouraging magistrates and informers to put these cold-blooded laws into force. On the 17th of March, 1704, the Irish Parliament resolved unanimously that all magistrates and other persons whatsoever, who neglected or omitted to put the laws against Catholics in due execution, were betrayers of the liberties of the kingdom. And they moreover resolved that the PERSECUTING and INFORMING against Papists, was an HONOURABLE service to Government. The better, too, to encourage the trade, 50l. was the price offered for a bishop or archbishop's head; 20l. for that of a priest; and 10l. for that of a Catholic school-master, usher, or private tutor. " Charity," says the proverb, " begins at home," and we think it would be well if the " few plain Christians" were to set about verifying it. They have shewn a wonderful degree of sympathy for the people of every nation and clime, but those of their own country, who differ from them in religious opinions, and prefer the old faith to new theories. For the fanatics who carried fire and sword into the heart of their native land, they can spare all the milk of human kindness, but not a drop can be spared for the Catholics of England and Ireland.— Though groaning under laws the most barbarous and brutal; though placed worse in their native land, than the black slaves in the West Indies, no sympathetic sigh is offered for their suffering condition, but they have to bear insult, reproach, invective and calumny, as well as the most cruel privation of civilized rights. The supposed persecution of Protestants has been the constant theme of Englishmen; every stratagem has been devised to excite hatred against the Catholics as persecutors from principle, while the statute books of England and Ireland exhibit a continued catalogue of the most remorseless and barbarous laws invented and passed to persecute and oppress the Catholics, for no other cause than their adhering from conscientious motives to the faith taught by the apostles and primitive fathers. What hypocrisy and inconsistency.

We now close the first volume of our labours, having noticed the most prominent historical facts touched upon by Fox as regards foreign countries, and proved them, in almost every case, to have been misstated, falsified, or corrupted. Our next volume will be devoted to an examination of Fox's account of the Reformation in England, and the Persecutions which, he says, preceded it. This is a point of history peculiarly interesting to the reader, and we shall endeavour to illustrate it to the best of our ability.

END OF VOLUME THE FIRST.

A

CRITICAL AND HISTORICAL,

REVIEW

OF

Fox's Book of Martyrs,

SHEWING THE

INACCURACIES, FALSEHOODS, AND MISREPRESENTATIONS

IN THAT

WORK OF DECEPTION,

BY

WILLIAM EUSEBIUS ANDREWS.

VOLUME II.

London:

PRINTED AND PUBLISHED BY W. E. ANDREWS,

3, CHAPTERHOUSE COURT, ST. PAUL'S CHURCHYARD.

1826.

CONTENTS.

CONTENTS.

A REVIEW

OF

Fox's Book of Martyrs,

CRITICAL AND HISTORICAL.

No. 27. Printed and Published by W. E. ANDREWS, 3, Chapter-house-court, St. Paul's Churchyard, London. Price 3d.

VOLUME SECOND.

INTRODUCTORY REMARKS.

WE are now arrived at a very interesting period of our Review, in-asmuch as it relates to the history of our own country, about which so much has been written to no purpose, a great deal to delude and keep the people in ignorance, and but a small portion to instruct and inform the searcher after truth. As we, at the commencement of the first vo-lume of this work, shewed *how* the Christian or Catholic religion was first established and propagated by the apostles of Christ in the east, and *how* it was *preserved* when it had spread to other parts of the globe, so we purpose here, by way of preface to this volume, to shew *how* this *same* system of Christianity was *introduced* and *preserved* in England, till the era of what is called the Reformation. Fox begins his eighth book, or the "few plain Christian" editors for him, in *their* edition, with "*a brief history of the Reformation, and the remarkable circumstances* "*which preceded it, from the time of Wickliffe to the reign of queen Mary,*" so that the reader is left in total darkness concerning the events which occurred previous to the heresy of Wickliffe. It is true, we have some

" particulars relative to the great ascendency of the popes throughout
" Christendom, in the *middle* ages;" but these particulars are given, as
usual, in so confused and unauthorized a manner, that it requires considerable ingenuity to unravel them, and no little space to refute them with
that accuracy which is essential to carry conviction to the prejudiced
reader of our pages.

The precise period when Christianity was first announced in Britain
is not accurately known; some contend that St. Peter brought the glad
tidings of " peace on earth to men of good will," while others give the
honour to Joseph of Arimathea. This much however is certain, and it
is admitted by both Fox and his modern editors, that king Lucius, a
British prince, sent to pope Eleutherius to solicit the aid of Christian
missionaries, and that the holy pope sent to him two zealous prelates,
St. Fugatius and Damianus, by whom he was instructed in the Catholic faith, and who preached to and converted many of his people. This
event happened about the year 182, and we refer the reader to page 58
of the first volume, where he will see an account of it taken from authentic writers. Lucius on receiving the light of Christianity, immediately began to provide for its support and duration, by the erection of
churches, and appointing revenues for the maintenance of the priesthood. Gildas, Nennius, and Bede, say that he founded churches in each
of the cities in his dominions. It may here be remarked, that our
island, though governed by native sovereigns, was tributary to the Roman empire, and with Lucius ended the dynasty of British princes.
The emperors, on his death, governed the island by their own officers,
having reduced it into four provinces; but in the course of time, the
most powerful of these governors assumed the title of emperor. The
first of these, we are informed, was Clodus Albinus, who proclaimed
himself emperor in 193. This state of things continued during a century, and as a proof that Christianity still existed in the island, we have
the testimony of Fox and his editors, who have recorded the martyrdom
of St. Alban, who suffered in the persecution of Dioclesian, and was a
Catholic martyr, as we have proved in our first volume, page 99.

This persecution did not last above two years in Britain, but the
Christians did not dare to hold their religious assemblies or raise temples to the worship of God, until they were authorized so to do by the
edict of Constantine the great, in 312. On the appearance of this decree, the British Catholics began to vie with each other in the beauty
and magnificence of the churches they raised, which they accomplished
by voluntary contributions, there being no British sovereign to assist
them in the pious work. That these Christians were Catholics, and acknowledged the supremacy of the pope is clear from their prelates
joining in the general councils and synods on all public occasions. Some
of them were present at the first council of Arles in 313, when the wrong
celebration of Easter was condemned; and at the general council of
Sardica in 347, in which the liberty of appeals to the bishop of Rome
was confirmed. On the decay of the Roman power, the western provinces of that vast empire experienced various revolutions, but none
was so complete as that of our island. Several of the provinces fell
under the sway of different rulers, until a sense of danger induced the
people to choose a chief magistrate or king, in order to resist the

daring attempts of barbarous invaders, who were incessantly making inroads on the island. The choice fell on Vortigern, and a more unlucky selection could not have been made. He was slothful and sensual, and when threatened with invasion by the Picts or Caledonians, he had the baseness to propose, and the address to persuade the council of the Britons to accept with open arms, the assistance of a foreign nation, to repel their warlike neighbours. Accordingly in the year 449, the Saxon leaders Hengist and Horsa, two brothers, with a formidable body of that nation, landed in the isle of Thanet, and soon after they gave signal proofs of their valour by defeating and totally routing the army of the Picts and Scots in the vicinity of Stamford in Lincolnshire. By the fresh arrival of Saxons, Hengist found himself strong, and throwing off the yoke of obedience, he founded the first Saxon kingdom of Kent in the year 457. For upwards of a century continual struggles were entered into between the native British and the Saxon invaders, which ended in the erection of six more Saxon kingdoms, the last of which, Mercia, was founded in 585, by which extraordinary revolution one race of men was totally rooted out, and another planted on the same soil. With the extirpation of the British race religion also fell, a signal punishment of a degenerate and sinful nation, and Pagan idolatry was again established in the island of Great Britain.

The darkness of Paganism, however, had scarcely covered the island, when a ray of light beamed in the horizon which shortly extended its rays over the whole country. We have before noticed the conversion of the ancient Britons by two holy prelates, sent from Rome by pope Eleutherius, it is now our duty to shew the reader *how* our Saxon ancestors became acquainted with the blessings of Christianity. The first mover of this work of piety and charity was St. Gregory the great, who filled the chair of St. Peter, that is, was bishop of Rome, and head of the Catholic church, from the year 590 to 604. Previous to his elevation to the papal throne, Gregory had raised himself in public estimation by his great prudence, sanctity, and writings. Walking one day through the market place of Rome, Gregory noticed several youths of fine features and complexion that were exposed for sale, and inquired what country they came from. He was answered that they came from Britain. He then asked if they were Christians or heathens; and was told the latter. On this he fetched a deep sigh, and lamented that so fine an outside should have so little of the grace of God within. Bede relates, that on being answered that the natives of Britain were called Angli or Angles, Gregory replied, "Right, for they have angelical "faces, and it becomes such to be companions with the angels in "heaven. What is the name (he continued) of the province from which "they are brought?" It was replied, that it was called Deiri, "Truly, "Deiri," said he, "because mercy withdrawn from wrath, and called "to the mercy of Christ," alluding to the Latin, *De irâ Dei eruti*. He asked further, "How is the king of that province called?" He was told his name was Alle; on which Gregory, in allusion to the word, said, "Alleluia, the praise of God the Creator, must be sung in those parts."

Fired with these holy ideas, Gregory applied to pope Benedict I. to have some persons sent to preach Christianity in Britain. Not finding ny one disposed to undertake the mission, he solicited the pope's consent and obtained his approbation to apply his own labours in the conversion of the island. Accordingly he set forward with some of his fellow monks on the journey, but he was stopped by the people, who complained to the holy father, and requested him not to suffer Gregory to depart from Rome. On this pressing occasion, Gregory was ordered to return, which he did with much reluctance, and after some time had elapsed, in which he distinguished himself by his great qualities, Gregory was called to the papal chair himself, by the unanimous voice of the clergy, the senate, and the people. Placed in the apostolical chair, the holy pope did not forget the impression made upon him in favour of Britain, and he selected St. Augustin, then prior of the monastery to which Gregory belonged, to be superior of the mission, in which he was assisted by several of the monks. Having received their commission, the missionaries set out with zeal and joy, and on their way through France, an attempt was made to turn their intention aside, by representing the English people as ferocious and cruel, but no obstacles could deter these holy men from their purpose. Taking some Frenchmen along with them for interpreters, they landed in the isle of Thanet, in the year 597, being in all about forty persons.

It is not a little singular that this isle was the spot on which the Saxon hordes first placed their feet, by whom Christianity was rooted out of the island; and now about 150 years after, the ambassadors of Christ appeared to regain the people from the power of Satan, and bend them to a yoke that is both sweet and light. From this place Augustin sent a message to Ethelbert, king of Kent, announcing his mission, and assuring him of the divine promise of a kingdom that never was to end. Ethelbert was not a stranger to the Christian faith, as his queen was a daughter of Caribert, king of Paris, and had with her a bishop for her director and almoner. After some days, the king went in person to the isle, and ordered Augustin to his presence in the open air.— The religious men came to him in procession, with joy and devotion, carrying for their banner a silver cross, and an image of our Saviour painted on a board, singing, as they walked the litany, and praying for the souls they came to save. Being admitted into the presence of the king, who was seated under a tree (see the cut), they announced to him the word of life. The king listened with attention, seemed pleased with the interesting truths he heard, and promised to take them into his serious consideration. It may not be unworthy of remark here, that these proclaimers of God's truths did not go forth with a large stock of bibles, which in those days were useless, as but few could read, but they were armed with the Spirit of Truth, and they carried with them the *image* of the crucified GOD they came to announce, which is the practice of the Catholic missionaries at this day; and for which they are reprobated by the advocates for Bible-reading. That the Bible never was intended by God or by the writers of it for indiscriminate reading is most certain, from the fact that no nation whatever has been converted through the means of the bible, though many have been perverted from the truth by having recourse to their own fanciful theories, instead of guiding their reason by the unerring rule of truth. It was by *preaching* the word which God commanded them to announce to all nations that the world was Catholicized, and the adherents of the bible-system may be assured, that all their efforts to un-Catholicize them, by forcing the bible upon the people, will prove futile. The king was pleased with the holy lives of these missionaries, so much is example above precept in captivating the human mind; he gave them permission to preach to the people, and he even received the waters of regeneration himself. On receiving the grace of baptism, Ethelbert became a new man; he permitted the holy missionaries to build and repair churches every where, and he afforded them every assistance in this pious work his kingly prerogative allowed him. Having thus far succeeded, St. Augustin went to Arles, where he was consecrated bishop, and on his return to Britain he dispatched two of his fellow-labourers to Rome, to solicit a further supply of workmen to cultivate the vineyard he had thus planted. The good pope Gregory sent him over several of his own disciples, among whom were Mellitus, the first bishop of Rochester; Paulinus, the first archbishop of York; and Rufemanus, the third abbot of Augustin's. "With this colony of new mis-"sionaries," writes our countrymen, venerable Bede, "the holy pope "sent all things in general for the divine worship and the service of the "church, viz, sacred vessels, altar-cloths, ornaments for churches, and "vestments for priests and clerks; relics of the holy apostles and mar-"tyrs, and many books."

We have thus shewn *how* the Christian religion was introduced amongst our Saxon ancestors; it now remains to prove *what* that system of religion was. This is a point which Fox and his modern editors gloss over, though it is the most essential of any, to come at the knowledge of truth. Gildas and Bede testify, that the faith which was planted by St. Augustin was the same that was held at Rome, and that our ancestors, like the primitive Christians, were ever watchful to preserve it pure and untainted. Thus, when Arianism shot its baneful sprouts, it was immediately detected and extirpated. Pelagianism had no sooner infected the church, than recourse was had to the proper authorities, who checked the growing evil, and eventually eradicated it. Now this faith, thus carefully preserved, is the same as that preached by the apostles of Christ, and followed by the Catholics of this day. The Saxons on embracing Christianity, admitted infant baptism, for which there is no warranty of scripture, and therefore must be followed from tradition. They believed in *seven* sacraments, though the church of England now admits of only two. They held confession, absolution, transubstantiation, purgatory, the invocation of saints and angels, prayers for the dead, the mass, celibacy, and, in short, every article of faith, and discipline of the church, rejected at the so much vaunted event called the *Reformatiom*. Let the reader now refer back to the beginning of our first volume, and it will there be seen, that all these points of doctrine were held and taught by the fathers of the Catholic church in every age, from the apostles to the period of the conversion of our island by St. Augustin, and we shall shew in the course of our work that they were maintained with undeviating accuracy till Luther began his work of infamy and delusion. Since which they have remained unaltered the creed of Catholics, and will remain to the end of time, a testimony of the promise of Christ, that his words should not fail.

The " few plain Christians" have represented the Catholic religion, or Popery, as they call it, as inseparable from persecution—a blood thirsty system of cruelty and intolerance; it will not be, therefore, irrelevant to our purpose if we lay before the reader a short outline of the character of our Saxon ancestors when under the influence of Paganism, and the change which took place in their manners after they submitted to the benign precepts of the Catholic faith. This outline we will not trust to our own pen, but give it in the words of an elegant and classical writer of the present day, who has made the ancient history of this country his peculiar study. The Rev. Dr. Lingard, in his *Antiquities of the Saxon Church,* writes thus :—" By the ancient writers, " the Saxons are unanimously classed with the most barbarous of the " nations, which invaded and dismembered the Roman empire. Their " valour was disgraced by its brutality. To the services they generally " preferred the blood of their captives; and the man, whose life they " condescended to spare, was taught to consider perpetual servitude " as a gratuitous favour. Among themselves, a rude and imperfect " system of legislation intrusted to private revenge the punishment of " private injuries ; and the ferocity of their passions continually multi- " plied these deadly and hereditary feuds. Avarice and the lust of sen- " sual enjoyment had extinguished in their breasts some of the first " feelings of nature. The savages of Africa may traffic with Europeans " for the negroes whom they have seized by treachery, or captured in " open war : but the more savage conquerors of the Britons sold with- " out scruple to the merchants of the continent, their countrymen, and " even their own children. Their religion was accommodated to their " manners, and their manners were perpetuated by their religion. In " their theology they acknowledged no sin but cowardice ; and revered " no virtue but courage. Their gods they appeased with the blood of " human victims. Of a future life their notions were faint and waver- " ing : and if the soul were fated to survive the body, to quaff ale out " of the skulls of their enemies was to be the great reward of the vir- " tuous : to lead a life of hunger and inactivity the endless punishment " of the wicked.

" Such were the Pagan Saxons. But their ferocity soon yielded to " the exertions of the missionaries, and the harsher features of their " origin were insensibly softened under the mild influence of the gospel. " In the rage of victory they learned to respect the rights of humanity. " Death or slavery was no longer the fate of the conquered Britons : " by their submission they were incorporated with the victors; and " their lives and property were protected by the equity of their Chris- " tian conquerors. The acquisition of religious knowledge introduced " a new spirit of legislation : the presence of the bishops and superior " clergy improved the wisdom of the national councils ; and laws were " framed to punish the more flagrant violations of morality, and prevent " the daily broils which harrassed the peace of society. The humane " idea, that by baptism all men become brethren, contributed to me- " liorate the condition of slavery, and scattered the seeds of that libe- " rality, which gradually undermined, and at length abolished so odious " an institution. By the provision of the legislature the freedom of the " child was secured from the avarice of an unnatural parent ; and the

"heaviest punishment was denounced against the man, who presumed
"to sell to a foreign master one of his countrymen, though he were
"a slave or a malefactor. But by nothing were the converts more distin-
"guished than by their piety. The conviction of a future and endless
"existence beyond the grave elevated their minds, and expanded their
"ideas. To prepare their souls for this new state of being, was to many the
"first object of their solicitude : they eagerly sought every source of in-
"struction, and with scrupulous fidelity practised every duty which they
"had learnt. Of the zeal of the more opulent among the laity, the nu-
"merous churches, hospitals, and monasteries which they founded,
"are a sufficient proof: and the clergy could boast with equal truth of
"the piety displayed by the more eminent of their order, and of the na-
"tions instructed in the Christian faith, by the labours of St. Boniface
"and his associates. In the clerical and monastic establishments, the
"most sublime of the gospel virtues were carefully practised: even
"kings descended from their thrones, and exchanged the sceptre for
"the cowl. Their conduct was applauded by their contemporaries:
"and the modern, whose supercilious wisdom affects to censure it, must
"at least esteem the motives which inspired, and admire the resolution
"which completed the sacrifice. The progress of civilization kept equal
"pace with the progress of religion; not only the useful but the agree-
"able arts were introduced; every species of knowledge, which could
"be attained, was eagerly studied; and during the gloom of ignorance,
"which overspread the rest of Europe, learning found, for a certain pe-
"riod, an asylum among the Saxons of Britain. To this picture an
"ingenious adversary may indeed oppose a very different description.—
"He may collect the vices which have been stigmatized by the zeal of
"their preachers, and point to the crimes which disgraced the charac-
"ters of some of their monarchs. But the impartial observer will ac-
"knowledge the impossibility of eradicating at once the fiercer passions
"of a whole nation; nor be surprised, if he behold several of them re-
"lapse into their former manners, and on some occasions unite the ac-
"tions of savages with the profession of Christians. To judge of the
"advantage which the Saxons derived from their conversion, he will
"fix his eyes on their virtues. They were the offsprings of the gospel;
"their vices were the relics of paganism."

To give an instance of the power and efficacy of the Catholic religion
to reclaim sinners from their evil ways to the paths of rectitude and
virtue, of whatsover rank and condition they may be, we will here quote
a fact related by the above learned author, in his valuable *History of
England*,—"Ethelbert (writes the historian) died in 616. The crown
"devolved upon his son Eadbald, the violence of whose passions had
"nearly replunged the nation into that idolatry from which it had just
"emerged. The youth and beauty of his stepmother, the relict of
"Ethelbert, induced him to take her to his bed; and when the mis-
"sionaries admonished him to break the unnatural connexion, he aban-
"doned a religion, which forbade the gratification of his appetites. At
"the same time the three sons of Saberet, (their father was dead) re-
"stored the altars of the gods, and banished from their territory the
"bishop Mellitus. With Justus of Rochester he retired into Gaul :
"and Laurentius, the successor of Augustin in the see of Canterbury,

" had determined to follow their footsteps. On the morning of his in-
" tended departure, he made a last attempt on the mind of Eadbald,
" His representations were successful. The king dismissed his step-
" mother and recalled the fugitive prelates. The sincerity of his con-
" version was proved by his subsequent conduct : and Christianity, sup-
" ported by his influence, assumed an ascendancy which it ever after-
" wards preserved."—Here then we have a striking effect of the influence of religion on the mind, when supported by the voice of spotless
ministers. How different was the conduct of this Christian and Catholic
bishop to that of a modern prelate of London, who on a memorable occasion asserted in his place in parliament that a king of England could
do no wrong.

The Catholic religion being thus established in our island, a regular
hierarchy was founded for the regulation of ecclesiastical affairs, and the
preservation of true doctrine. Thus, when any dispute occurred, or any
grievance was complained of, recourse was had to the regular authority ;
from the suffragan bishop the matter was carried to the metropolitan,
either of Canterbury or York, who, if need required, summoned a provincial synod to discuss the point, and the decision was submitted to the
pope as the supreme head of the universal church. By these means
the Catholic religion was preserved entire for the space of nine hundred
years, until Henry the eighth severed the branch from the parent stock,
and made himself head of a separate church, which had no other claim
to jurisdiction than what the lay power of the state granted to it.
During the period of Catholicism, the spiritual authority of the Church
was quite distinct from the authority of the state. The king and nobles
were obliged to submit to the same discipline as the peasant and the
beggar, because the Church being a kingdom of another world, knows
no distinction in her system of morality between the monarch and the
vassal.—With these remarks we shall proceed in our Review of the work
before us.

" BOOK VIII.

" CONTAINING A BRIEF HISTORY OF THE REFORMATION, AND THE REMARK-
" ABLE CIRCUMSTANCES WHICH PRECEDED IT, FROM THE TIME OF
" WICKLIFFE TO THE REIGN OF QUEEN MARY. "

" SECTION I.

" PARTICULARS RELATIVE TO THE GREAT ASCENDANCY OF THE POPES
" THROUGHOUT CHRISTENDOM, IN THE MIDDLE AGES.

Fox commences this section with the following string of assertions :—
" In the introduction will be found an account of the rise and pro-
" gress of popery, from the commencement of its usurpations to the
" tenth century. From this period, till the reformation was attempted
" by Wickliffe, the abominations of these arch and unchristian heretics
" increased with rapid strides, till at length all the sovereigns of Europe
" were compelled to do them the most servile homage. It was in the
" reign of Edgar, king of England, that monks were first made spiritual
" ministers, though contrary to the decrees and custom of the church ;

"and in the time of this sovereign they were allowed to marry, there
" being no law forbidding it, before the papacy of Gregory VII.

" To relate the tyrannical innovations upon the religion of Christ
" during the space of more than three hundred years, would be the
" province of a writer on church history, and is quite incompatible with
" our limits. Suffice it to say, that scarcely a foreign war or civil broil
" convulsed Europe during that period, which did not originate in the in-
" fernal artifices of popes, monks, and friars. They frequently fell vic-
" tims to their own machinations; for, from the year 1004, many popes
" died violent deaths : several were poisoned ; Sylvester was cut to pieces
" by his own people ; and the reigns of his successors were but short.
" Benedict, who succeeded John XXI. thought proper to resist the em-
" peror Henry III. and place in his room Peter, king of Hungary ; but
" afterwards being alarmed by the success of Henry, he *sold* his seat to
" Gratianus, called Gregory VI. At this time there were three popes in
" Rome, all striving against each other for the supreme power; viz. Bene-
" dict IX. Sylvester III. and Gregory VI. But the emperor, Henry, com-
" ing to Rome, displaced these three monsters at once, and appointed
" Clement the Second, enacting that henceforth no bishop of Rome
" should be chosen but by the consent of the emperor. Though this
" law was necessary for public tranquillity, yet it interfered too much
" with the ambitious views of the cardinals, who accordingly exerted
" themselves to get it repealed ; and failing in this, on the departure of
" the emperor for Germany, they poisoned Clement, and at once vio-
" lated the law by choosing another pope, without the imperial sanction.

" This was Damasus II. who being also poisoned, within a few days
" from his appointment, much contention took place. Whereupon the
" Romans sent to the emperor, desiring him to give them a bishop ;
" upon which he selected Bruno, a German, called Leo IX. This pope
" was poisoned, in the first year of his popedom.

" After his death Theophylactus made an effort to be pope, but Hil-
" debrand, to defeat him, went to the emperor, and persuaded him to
" assign another bishop, a German, who ascended the papal chair under
" the title of Victor II. The second year of his papacy, this pope also
" followed his predecessors, like them being poisoned.

" On the death of Victor, the cardinals elected Stephen IX. for pope,
" contrary to their oath, and the emperor's assignment. From this
" period, indeed, their ascendancy was so great, that the most power-
" ful sovereigns of Europe were obliged to do them homage ; and
" Nicholas, who succeeded Stephen, established the Council of the
" Lateran. In this council first was promulgated the terrible sentence
" of excommunication against all such as ' do creep into the seat of
" Peter by money or favour, without the full consent of the cardinals ;'
" cursing them and their children with the anger of Almighty God ;
" and giving authority and power to cardinals, with the clergy and
" laity, to depose all such persons and call a council-general, where-
" soever they will, against them. Pope Nicholas only reigned three
" years and a half, and then, like his predecessors, was poisoned."—
pp. 121, 122.

In what part of the introduction the rise and progress of Popery are
to be found we have not been able to discover. There is no precise

period stated, nor any particular dates, whereby we can trace the accuracy of the assertions here made. When did Popery commence? This question never has been correctly answered. Some have fixed it at one period, some at another, but none agree on the same point. Now Catholics can tell the exact time when every heresy of note was broached, from the days of Simon Magus to those of Martin Luther and downwards. The theories put forth by the heresiarchs are always distinguished by the names of the inventors; as Arianism, from Arius the heretic; Donatism, from Donatus the broacher of that error; Pelagianism, from Pelagius who taught it; Lutheranism, from Luther, the apostle of the Reformation, so called; Calvinism, from Calvin, a branch spreader of the Reformation; and so on of the three or four hundred different sects into which this land of bibles is now divided. But the same cannot be said of that system which Protestant writers term Popery. The word is derived from the title of Pope given to the bishop of Rome, who is by divine right supreme head of the Catholic or universal church. Of these bishops there were more than one hundred in the first nine centuries of the Christian church, but not one of them can be selected by *name* as the institutor of Popery, or the inventor of heresy, though Fox is pleased to stile them in the gross " arch and unchristian heretics." It must not be forgotten that in the seventh century Fox allows the Catholic church to have been ORTHODOX, for he ranks the holy pope Martin amongst *his* martyrs, and says he was an opposer of the heresy of Monothelism. That he called a council of 105 bishops, who unanimously condemned the errors of that sect. This pope was martyred in 655; in the next century we find Fox admitting another martyr into his calendar, who received his commission from Rome to *preach the gospel* to the Pagans and extirpate heresy. This martyr is St. Boniface, the apostle of Germany, who suffered in 755. This was the middle of the eighth century, so that we have brought the time into a small compass, and yet not a *date* nor a *name* can be given for the origin of Popery unless, indeed, we go back to the apostles themselves, from whom the church is stiled Apostolic as well as Catholic.

It is stated by Fox, that " from this period (the tenth century) till " the *reformation* was *attempted* by Wickliffe, the abominations of these " arch and unchristian heretics (the popes) increased with rapid strides, " till at length all the sovereigns of Europe were *compelled* to do them " the most *servile* homage." These popes were strange fellows, truly! and how did they go to work to *compel* all the *sovereigns* of Europe, every one of them, to render their holinesses the most *servile* homage? There must have been something supernatural in "these arch and unchristian heretics," which no other heretics possessed, to perform such feats as these. To *compel* kings and emperors, whether tyrants or fathers of their people, to render them the most *servile* homage, is no less than a miracle, and heretics were never able to claim one of these gifts of the Divine Being. That the sovereigns of Europe rendered homage to the popes at this time cannot be denied; but it was not a servile homage; it was only that spiritual obedience which is now given to the head of the Catholic church by sovereigns in her communion, and it was in consequence of their receiving the light of faith from missionaries sent by their authority. The "abominations" which increased with "such rapid strides," were the *blessings* imparted by the conversion of the nations of Europe to the Catholic faith, an account of which advantages, both spiritual and temporal, we have given in our relation of the conversion of this island to Catholicism.

Fox goes on to say, that monks were first made spiritual ministers in the reign of our Edgar, contrary to the decrees and customs of the church; and that in this monarch's time they were allowed to marry, there being no law forbidding it till the papacy of Gregory VII.—We thank the martyrologist for this statement, because we have something that is tangible, and can prove. it *false* by the test of authentic history.—In Rapin's History of England, there is a long speech of Edgar's to the council he had assembled for the reformation of abuses and the correction of manners. In this speech the monarch inveighs in strong terms against the incontinent lives of the clergy, which he said was a scandal to the people, and a public complaint.—This author, commenting on the dissolute lives of the clergy in this age, says, " it must be observed, " the popes had FOR SOME TIME *prohibited the clergy from marrying,* " and were very severe to all who refused to comply with their de- " crees."—This is the testimony of a Calvinist writer, who cannot be charged with any partiality towards Catholics.—The assertion then made by Fox, that there was no law forbidding the marriage of the clergy before the popedom of Gregory VII, is proved to be FALSE by Protestant evidence. We will now introduce a witness of another character, whose work has received the approbation of the most learned and eminent personages of the present day. Speaking of Edgar's days, Dr. Lingard says, in his History, " The tranquillity of Edgar's reign, " his undisputed superiority over the neighbouring princes, and his at- " tention to the welfare of his people, have contributed to throw a lustre " around his memory : the reformation of the church, undertaken by the " prelates, and effected with the aid of his authority, though it was re- " ceived with gratitude by his contemporaries, has been marked with " unmerited censure by modern writers. The Danish invasion had both " relaxed the sinews of ecclesiastical discipline, and dissolved the greater " number of the monastic and clerical establishments. The most opu- " lent monasteries had been laid in ruins by the rapacity of the barba- " rians : and their lands, without an owner, had been seized by the " crown, or had been divided among the nearest and most powerful " thanes. Under former kings, efforts had been made to restore the mo- " nastic order, but they had proved ineffectual. The prejudices against " it were nourished by the great proprietors now in possession of its an- " cient revenues ; even the monastery of Ethelingey, which Alfred had " peopled with foreign monks, had been gradually deserted : and the " two abbeys of Glastonbury and Abingdon, the fruits of the zeal of " Dunstan, had been dissolved by the resentment of Edwy. The cle- " rical order was more fortunate. Though shattered and disfigured, it " had survived the tempest. But the friends of religious severity, " when they compared the clergy of their day with the clergy of an- " cient times, saw much in their conduct to lament and correct. For- " merly they had lived in communities under particular regulations : " and their seclusion from temporal pursuits insured the faithful dis- " charge of their spiritual functions. But during the Danish wars they

" had been dispersed amidst their relatives, had divided among them-
" selves the revenues of their respective churches, and, substituting
" others for the performance of the service, indulged in the pleasures
" and dissipation of the laity.   But that which gave particular offence
" to the more devout was their marriages.   It is most certain, that
" during the two first centuries of the Saxon church the profession of
" celibacy was required from every clergyman advanced to the orders
" of priest, or deacon, or sub-deacon: but amid the horrors of succes-
" sive invasions the injunctions of the canons had been overlooked or
" contemned: and, on many occasions, necessity compelled the prelates
" to ordain, for the clerical functions, persons who had already engaged
" in the state of matrimony.   Similar causes had produced similar ef-
" fects in the maritime provinces of Gaul ; and Dunstan had witnessed,
" during his exile, the successful efforts of the abbot Gerard to restore
" the ancient discipline in the churches of Flanders.   Animated by his
" example, the metropolitan made a first essay to raise the monastic
" establishments from their ruins: and his labours were zealously se-
" conded by two active co-operators, the bishops Oswald and Ethel-
" wold.   The former governed the church of Worcester: the latter,
" his favourite disciple, had been placed at his request in the see of
" Winchester.   To them Edgar was induced to sell, or grant, the lands
" of the monasteries, which had fallen to the crown: and of those
" which remained in the hands of individuals, a portion was recovered
" by purchase, and still more by the voluntary resignation of the pos-
" sessors.   Persons were soon found ready to embrace an institute re-
" commended by the prelates and sanctioned by the king : as fast as
" buildings could be erected, they were filled with colonies of monks
" and their novices: and within a few years the great abbeys of Ely,
" Peterborough, Thorney, and Malmsbury, rose from their ashes, and
" recovered the opulence and the splendour which they had formerly
" enjoyed.   The next object of the metropolitan was the reformation
" of the more dissolute among the clergy, principally in the two dio-
" ceses of Winchester and Worcester.   For this purpose a commission
" was obtained from Rome, and a law was enacted, that every priest,
" deacon, and subdeacon should live chastely, or be ejected from his
" benefice."
        From this passage it will be seen that the monks *did* exercise spi-
ritual functions before Edgar's reign, and that the celibacy of the clergy
was a discipline of the church in the first period of the Saxon church.
In fact the rule was coeval with Christianity, though in the early ages
marriage was permitted in some cases.   On this subject we will give
another authority, who has treated the matter very elaborately, and
who stands unimpeached as a controversialist and historian.   The
Right Rev. Dr. Milner, in his excellent History of Winchester, says,
" It would be too tedious a task to cite all the canons, made in the pri-
" mitive church, against the marriage of bishops, priest and deacons.
" Let it suffice to refer to Concil. Elib. can. xxxiii. 2 Concil. Cathag.
" can. ii. 1 Concil. Œcum. Nicen. can. iii. 2 Concil. Arelat. can. ii.—
" St. Jerom, in the fourth age, testifies that, in the three great patriar-
" chates of Rome, Alexandria, and Antioch, no persons were received
" amongst the clergy, but such as were either single men, or entirely

" separated from their wives. *Liber adversus Vigilant.* The testimony
" of the learned bishop St. Epiphanius, is to the same effect. *Heres.* 59.
" —Not to multiply quotations, the centuriators of Magdeburg allow,
" that, about the time of the conversion of our ancestors, a synod was
" held by St. Gregory the Great, in which an anathema was pro-
" nounced against bishops, priests, or deacons, who should presume to
" marry. Cent. x. f. 642.—The discipline of the Greek church, in
" subsequent times, became less strict, in this point, than that of the
" Latin church. Its bishops did not refuse to ordain married persons,
" to serve amongst the inferior clergy, (for no prelate, even amongst
" them, was ever allowed to have a wife) ; hence even their schisma-
" tical council, called Quinisext, or In Trullo, after their separation
" from the Latin church, utterly condemned the contracting of mar-
" riage, when a person was once initiated into holy orders, and such
" their discipline has remained down to the present day.—With respect
" to our ancient English church, if the truth must be told, we are
" bound to say, that its discipline was strictly conformable to that of
" the Latin church in general, of which it formed a part, and of course,
" that it was *never* lawful for any clergyman in holy orders, whe-
" ther secular or regular, to enter into the married state ; nor could
" any married man, unless he was first separated from his wife by
" mutual consent, ever be ordained to the higher orders. This we may
" gather, in the first place, from the above quoted passage of Venerable
" Bede, according to which, only those who were *not in holy orders*
" were allowed, in any case whatever, to marry or live in the married
" state. The same is still more clear from another passage of that
" primitive author, whom Camden calls the friend of truth. In his
" exposition of the first chapter of St. Luke, having observed that the
" priests of the old law were obliged to be continent only during the
" stated times of their ministry ; he goes on : ' but now an injunction is
" laid upon priests to observe chastity continually, and ever to abstain
" from the use of marriage, to the end they may always assist at the
" altar.' It does not appear that any of the clergy ever attempted to
" infringe this law, until after the confusion, which followed the Danish
" devastations, in 860. Soon after this we find Pulco, archbishop of
" Rheims, congratulating king Alfred on the firm and zealous conduct
" of his primate Plegmund, in extirpating what he calls the error of
" those who held it lawful for the clergy to marry. Flodoard. Hist.
" Rhemens. l. iii.—In the reign of king Edmund, viz. in 944, we meet
" with the particulars of a great synod, as it was called, held at London,
" by the two archbishops and a great number of prelates, and other
" considerable personages ; in the very first ordinance of which it is
" enjoined " that all, initiated in sacred offices, shall be careful, as their
" state requires, to lead their lives chastely, whether they be men or
" women, which, if they fail to do, let them be punished as the canon
" enjoins.' Spelman, De Concil.—The same learned writer proves,
" from the Penitential, which he publishes, that bishops, priests, and
" deacons, no less than monks, were conceived, in those times, to be
" guilty of a great crime, if they ever returned to the state of marriage,
" which they had renounced at their ordination. This brief disser-
" tation may serve to rectify the mistaken notions which modern readers

" may have hastily taken up on this point of ecclesiastical history,
" from Parker, Godwin, Tanner, H. Wharton, Carte, Hume, the late
" historian of Winchester, and other ignorant or interested writers.
" Amongst others comes forward, at the present day, a writer, who has
" miserably waded beyond his depth, wherever he has ventured to
" treat of ecclesiastical antiquities. Speaking of the revolution in the
" church of Worcester, which took place at the same time with that
" mentioned above in our cathedral, he says, ' the popes had found it their
" interest to exact celibacy from the clergy, they incited the monks to
" raise an outcry against those who, instead of devoting their whole
" time to spiritual employments, gave a part of it to the company of
" their wives, &c.   Priests that were members of the cathedral col-
" leges had not as yet been restrained from marrying.'   Valentine
" Green's History of Worcester, p. 26.—From this passage it appears
" that the writer had never met with a single canon, or ecclesiastical
" authority, enforcing clerical celibacy, anterior to the tenth century,
" and that he ascribes the measures then taken by king Edgar and St.
" Dunstan, St. Oswald, and St. Ethelwold, to certain negociations
" between them and the popes, and to some new laws which the latter
" had just then enacted on this subject for their own interest. It was
" incumbent on him to have pointed out the negociations and laws in
" question. Unfortunately, however, too many of the popes in that
" age were abandoned to licentiousness themselves, instead of watching
" over the morals of the other clergy. The true policy of this original
" law of clerical celibacy, after all the sagacity of modern writers, will
" be found in 1 Cor. chap. vii. v. 32, 33.

Such clear documentary evidence as we have here produced must,
we imagine, put the question to rest; at least it is sufficient to satisfy
every reasonable mind, and we know not what can be adduced to convince those who are determined to remain in their error. On the subject of celibacy in the clergy much might be offered in a political point
of view, and we cannot help considering those who advocate the married life of men, whose sole duties should be to labour in the Lord's
vineyard, very ill-advised as far as regards their own interest, and the
country's welfare. In the time of Catholicism, the provision made for
the clergy did not go solely to fill their own coffers, nor to maintain
their own families. They voluntarily embraced a single life, and they
engaged to perform duties which it would be unjustifiable to call upon
a married man to execute. For instance, in the time of pestilence, or
of an individual infected with a contagious disease, the consolations of
religion are not to be denied to the afflicted. But who is to convey
these consolations to the dying under such circumstances? It cannot
be expected that a married clergyman would rush into danger which
might affect his own life, and thus leave his wife and family destitute;
or, by carrying home the infectious effluvia, might cause the pestilence
to spread in his family, and though he might escape, yet he might sip
the cup of affliction in the loss of his wife and children. We have
learned at the time we are writing of a young Catholic priest, eminent
for his talents and abilities, falling a sacrifice to this act of godlike
charity, in Dublin; and the same disregard of life to impart the cheer-
ing and soothing comforts of religion to the infected poor of his flock,

has deprived the Catholics of Manchester of a faithful servant of God in the very prime of his life. Many are the instances where Catholic priests thus fall victims to their zeal and total disregard of life in the exercise of their sacred duties; but how few, if any, can he produced of Protestant clergymen thus offering themselves in sacrifice. Nor is it to be expected, when they are clogged with the cares of a family, and have the temporal happiness of others depending on their own existence. The Catholic priest, on the other hand, is unencumbered with these ties; he has voluntarily embraced a single life, that he may become a father to the flock over whom he is placed, and when grim death meets him in the discharge of his pastoral duties, he cheerfully resigns his life to render an account of his stewardship to his heavenly Lord and Master.

Besides, how inconsiderate must it be in a people to provide not only for the clergy, but for the families of the clergymen. In this country, for example, since the Reformation, as it is called, the provisions for the Church establishment, except that portion which fell into lay hands, go entirely to support the clergy, and is not found to be sufficient for that purpose, as many hundreds of thousands of pounds sterling have been lately voted away by parliament, to relieve the poorer part of the clergy. Whereas, when the church establishment was in the hands of the Catholic clergy, they had the poor, and sick, and aged to maintain; the churches to build and repair, and the rights of hospitality to fulfil, out of their income. To which we must add, that they contributed too, out of their revenues, to carry on the wars in which the sovereigns were engaged, either to secure the safety, or to preserve the honour, of the country; by which means the people were eased of taxes, and a national debt was unknown. But now, alas! the case is altered quite. Taxes are raised to support the poor; taxes are raised to repair and build churches; taxes are raised to relieve the poor clergy and their families; and taxes are raised to pension off many of the sons of the clergy in the shape of half-pay officers and clerks in government offices. And is it wise, is it prudent, when the country is in such a situation, to rail at the economical and judicious regulations of the Catholic church and our Catholic ancestors respecting the celibacy and provisions of the clergy. Of all the cavils raised against the doctrines and discipline of the Catholic church, this we cannot help deeming the most stupid and besotted. Even granting the practice was not introduced till the time of the seventh Gregory, so wise a regulation ought to immortalize his name at least with the patriot and the statesman.

Having disposed of this disputed point we come now to the next charge made by Fox. He says, "to relate the *tyrannical innovations* "upon the *religion of Christ* during the space of *more* than three hun-"dred years, would be the province of a writer on church history, and "is quite incompatible with our limits. Suffice it to say, that scarcely a "foreign war or civil broil convulsed Europe during *that* period, which "did not originate in the *infernal artifices* of popes, monks and friars." If we are to believe this account, the world must have been in a very comfortable state, and true religion must have been banished from the earth. We commend the modern editors, however, for declining to be church historians, as they must have convicted themselves in that case.

But what are we to make of the "more than three hundred years"? They tell us that all the evils which arose during "THAT PERIOD" originated with popes, monks and friars. What are we to gather from "*that* period"? We have no *specified* time stated; how then are we to ascertain what foreign wars or civil broils are alluded to? This is all froth and fury. Tell us the innovations, who made them, and when they were introduced. It would not take up much space to *name* ONE of them, nor can it be incompatible with truth to give us a plain fact. The most authentic writers on church history give a very different account of the conduct of these popes, and represent them as the healers of division, and the arbiters of justice between the sovereigns of Europe, and frequently between rulers and the people." We are ready to admit, that in the tenth century, when the continent of Europe was subjected to intestine wars, entered into by rival chieftains, there were many popes whose lives were a scandal to the high and sacred office they filled. But these were personal vices, and by no means affected the truth and purity of that church of which they were the head, any more than the tyrannical or lewd conduct of a king of England could sully the excellent maxims of the British constitution. The faith of the church could not be affected by the personal crimes of her chief pastors, because her existence does not rest on the individual merit of any man, but on the power and promises of a Crucified God, her Divine Founder, who declared that she should remain pure and unsullied, both in faith and morals, till the end of the world, and we have seen her stand unmoveable and unspotted for more than eighteen hundred years. As a proof of our assertion, history records that while Rome was the seat of scandal as well as of religion, the northern nations of Europe were receiving the light of the gospel, and becoming civilized and good Catholics. Hungary, Prussia, Poland, Germany, Denmark, and Sweden, were converted to Christianity in the tenth century. A glance too at the annals of our own country will shew, that in this age lived an Alfred, an Edgar, and an Edward, to whom we are indebted for the best of our political institutions, and whose memory reflects honour on the country, and the religion by which they were influenced to confer such benefits on mankind.

We have next a confused account of a pretended resistance of pope Benedict to the emperor Henry III; of this pope *selling* his seat to Gregory VI; of there being three popes at one time; of the emperor going to Rome, displacing "these monsters," and ordering that henceforth no bishop of Rome should be chosen without the consent of the emperor; of the discontent of the cardinals at this law, and their poisoning two other popes. Many of these circumstances we are unable to trace in history, and therefore it cannot be expected that we should go into the whole detail of them. We cannot find the least appearance of a breach between Henry and Benedict, and the former is represented by the authors in our possession as a good and pious prince. There were certainly antipopes, but nobody troubled their heads about them. If we can prove but *one* brazen falsehood against Fox, in this long list of assertions the rest must loose their credit. To come then to the point. The period we are treating of is the eleventh century: Fox says the order of Henry did not suit the ambitious views of the *cardinals,* and

A REVIEW

OF

Fox's Book of Martyrs,

CRITICAL AND HISTORICAL.

No. 28. Printed and Published by W. E. Andrews, 3, Chapter-house-court, St. Paul's Churchyard, London. Price 3d.

EXPLANATION OF THE ENGRAVING.—*This cut represents St. Cuthbert, Bishop of Lindisfarne, appearing to king Alfred in a vision, while sojourning in the bogs of Somerset-shire, after his various disasters with the Danes. The saint told the unfortunate monarch that God had sent him as a messenger of comfort, and that, in respect of the former virtues of the English, although he had permitted them to be chastised by their enemies, they should henceforth prosper, and that he, Alfred, should raise the kingdom to the highest pitch of fame and glory. The sequel shews the accuracy of the prophecy.*

CONTINUATION OF THE REVIEW.

that they violated his commands by poisoning one pope and choosing another. Now the cardinals had not the privilege of electing a pope till 1160, if we can credit a little work before us, called *The Tablet of Memory*, and this fact is confirmed by the Rev. Alban Butler, who, in his life of St. Leo IX. says, " after the death of pope Damasus II.
" in 1048, in a diet of prelates and noblemen, with legates and deputies
" of the church of Rome, held at Worms, and honoured with the pre-
" sence of the pious emperor Henry III. surnamed the Black, Bruno,
" who had then governed the see of Toul twenty-two years, was pitched
" upon as the most worthy person to be exalted to the papacy. He
" being present, used all his endeavours to avert the storm falling on his
" head ; and begged three days to deliberate upon the matter. This
" term he spent in tears and prayers, and in so rigorous a fast that he
" neither eat or drank during all that time. The term being expired,
" he returned to the assembly, and (hoping to convince his electors of

" his unworthiness,) made public a general confession before them of
" the sins of his whole life, with abundance of tears, which drew also
" tears from all that were present; yet no man changed his opinion.
" He yielded at last only on condition that the whole clergy and
" people of Rome should agree to his promotion." They did agree,
and *thus* was Leo elected. Fox says, he was poisoned in the first year
of his popedom ; now, unfortunately for Fox's veracity, Leo filled the
see of Rome FIVE YEARS AND TWO MONTHS, and died a natural and holy death. This pope condemned the error of Berengarius in
a council held at Rome, in 1050, the year after he was chosen pope,
and died on the 10th of April, 1054, in the fiftieth year of his age. So
much for Fox's pope-poisoning and cardinal-electing.

Another mistake made by Fox, is the succession of Stephen IX. after
Victor II., and his election by cardinals. Stephen IX. succeeded Leo
VII. in 939 ; it was Stephen X. that followed Victor II. and his election being in 1057, the cardinals could not have elected him contrary to
their oath, because they were not, as we have before shewn, empowered
at that time to choose the sovereign pontiffs. Nicholas, who succeeded
Stephen, is said to have established the " council of the Lateran."—
This is gross falsehood. The first council of Lateran was held in the
year 1123, and Nicholas, who was the second of that name, died in
1061 : the " terrible sentence of excommunication" alluded to by Fox,
thus turns out to be a fable, invented to alarm the tremulous, as are
also his stories about these different popes being poisoned.

We now come to another tale, which he has placed under a special
head, and entitled, " SUBMISSION OF THE EMPEROR HENRY IV. TO THE
POPE." As we like fair play, we shall give the story in the martyrologist's own words :—" To such a height had papal insolence now at-
" tained, that, on the emperor Henry IV. refusing to submit to some
" decrees of pope Gregory VII. the latter excommunicated him, and
" absolved all his subjects from their oath of allegiance to him : on this
" he was deserted by his nobility, and dreading the consequences,
" though a brave man; he found it necessary to make his submission.
" He accordingly repaired to the city of Canusium, where the pope then
" was, and went barefooted with his wife and child to the gate ; where
" he remained from morning to night, fasting, humbly desiring absolu-
" tion, and craving to be let in. But no ingress being given him, he
" continued thus three days together : at length, answer came, that his
" holiness had yet no leisure to talk with him. The emperor patiently
" waited without the walls, although in the depth of winter. At length
" his request was granted, through the entreaties of Matilda, the pope's
" paramour. On the fourth day, being let in, for a token of his true
" repentance, he yielded to the pope's hands his crown, and confessed
" himself unworthy of the empire, if he ever again offended against the
" pope, desiring for that time to be absolved and forgiven. The pope
" answered he would neither forgive him, nor release the bond of his
" excommunication, but upon condition, that he would abide by his ar-
" bitrement in the council and undergo such penance as he should enjoin
" him; that he should answer to all objections and accusations laid
" against him, and that he should never seek revenge ; that it should be
" at the pope's pleasure, whether his kingdom should be restored, or

" not. Finally, that before the trial of his cause, he should neither use
" his kingly ornaments, nor usurp the authority to govern, nor to exact
" any oath of allegiance from his subjects, &c. These things being
" promised to the pope by an oath, the emperor was only released from
" excommunication."

Where Fox found this pretty relation he does not tell us, as, according
to his usual custom, there is neither date nor authority, to vouch for his
facts. We should be glad to have seen such a tyrant, (for such was
Henry IV. in a superlative degree) thus reduced to a sense of humility;
but this was not the case with this emperor Henry. Father Parsons
gives us a very different account of this affair, in his reply to Fox, and
names many writers at the time, who represent Gregory VII. as a
learned, wise, and courageous man; while the emperor is described as
an immoral and depraved character. Platina Sabellicus, and others,
record the election of this pope in these terms:—" We have chosen this
" day, the 21st of May, 1072, for true vicar of Christ, a man of much
" learning, great piety, prudence, justice, constancy, and religion," &c.
Lambert of Aschafnaburg, also saith, " The signs and miracles which
" oftentimes were done by the prayers of pope Gregory VII. and his
" most fervent zeal for the honour of God and defence of ecclesiastical
" laws, did sufficiently defend him against the venomous tongues of de-
" tractors."—This is the character given by authentic writers of this
pope, which we could multiply, were it necessary, but enough has been
said to shew he was not the person Fox makes him. Let us now look
at the description of Henry IV. for whom Fox has so much pity and
compassion. We will here give the account from father Parsons.

" But what do the same authors, yea Germans themselves, write of
" their emperor, his enemy, Henry IV.? Surely it is shameful to re-
" port his adulteries, symoniacal selling of benefices, robberies, and
" spoiling of poor particular men, thrusting in wicked men into places
" of prelates, and the like : ' He did request the princes of the empire
" (saith Lambert) that they would suffer him to put away his wife, tell-
" ing them what the pope by his legate had opposed to the contrary.'
" Which being heard by them, they were of the pope's opinion: the
" princes affirmed, that the bishop of Rome had reason to determine as
" he did, and so the king (rather forced than changed in mind) ab-
" stained from his purposed divorce.

" Lo here the first beginning of falling out betwixt the emperor and
" the pope; which was increased, for that two years after (as the same
" author saith) the pope deprived one Charles for simony and theft, to
" whom the emperor had sold for money the bishopric of Constance.
" And this he did by a council of prelates and princes held in Germany
" itself, the emperor being present : ' Bishop Charles (saith Lambert) was
" deposed, notwithstanding that the king was present in that judgment,
" and defended him and his cause as much as he could.' (Lamb. Schaf.
" A. D. 1071.) And this was an increase of the falling out between
" them : but the constancy (saith the same author) and invincible mind
" of Hildebrand against covetousness, did exclude all arguments of hu-
" man deceits and subtilties. (Ibid.)

" Urspergensis in like manner, who lived in the same time, reckoneth
" up many particulars of the emperor's wicked behaviour in these

" words: ' He began to despise the princes, oppress the nobles and no-
" bility, and give himself to incontinency.' *(Ursp. A. D.* 1068.) Which
" Aventinus (an author not misliked by the Protestants) uttereth more
" particularly in these words : ' The very friends of Henry the emperor
" do not deny that he was infamous for his wicked life and lechery,
" fornication, and adultery.' *(Lib.* 4. *Annalium Boiorum.)*

 " And finally, not to name any one, Marianus Scotus (that lived in
" those days) writeth thus of the whole controversy between them :—
" Gregory VII. (saith he) being stirred up by the just clamours of Ca-
" tholic men, and hearing the immanity of Henry the emperor's wicked-
" ness, cryed out against by them, did excommunicate him for the same,
" but especially for the sin of simony, in buying and selling bishoprics ;
" which fact of the pope did like very well all good Catholic men, but
" displeased such as would buy and sell benefices, and were favourers
" of the said emperor." *(Mar. Scot. Inchron. A. D.* 1075.)

 Thus wrote the learned father Parsons, more than two hundred years
ago, who was well acquainted with the authorities he has quoted,
and who, it appears, lived cotemporary with Gregory and Henry, and
must therefore have been in perfect possession of the facts they stated.
The Rev. Alban Butler, who compiled the life of this holy pope from
some of the ablest and most authentic writers of that and succeeding
ages, enters more deeply into the transactions between Gregory and
Henry. He confirms the testimony of father Parsons as to the character of this prince, who fell, when young, into the hands of ambitious
and unprincipled men, by whom his passions were inflamed and indulged,
that they might carry on their own vicious designs. Hence by his
tyranny and injustices he provoked his own subjects, and caused the
princes and nobility of the empire to appeal to the pope. It must here
be observed, that the lives of some of the higher orders of the clergy
were scandalous in the extreme, and that many of them had been
guilty of simony, having *purchased* their bishoprics of Henry. Gregory, who was exalted to the papacy by compulsion, and with the consent
of Henry, was no sooner seated in the chair of Peter, than, like a good
and pious pontiff, he meditated a reform in the morals of the clergy,
as the best and surest means of producing a general change for the better. Accordingly, he called a council at Rome, and after due deliberation, a decree was passed, by which all persons guilty of simony were
declared incapable of receiving any ecclesiastical jurisdiction, and disqualified for holding any benefice whatever. This mandate was of
course not pleasing to those bishops who had purchased their benefices
from the emperor, and who were not willing to part with them ; they
therefore made complaint to Henry, who espoused their cause. This
monarch, like all other tyrants and oppressors, could dissemble when it
served his ends, and accordingly he wrote a letter to Gregory on his exal-
tation to the papal see, condemning himself for having sold the benefices of
the church, and promising amendment. The pope answered him in
terms of the greatest charity and apostolic zeal. But when Henry
found Gregory inflexible in the pursuit of a reformation in the conduct
of the clergy, he shewed that his former professions of repentance were
dictated by hypocrisy, and he resolved to continue the patronizer of
corruption and exaction. Pursuing this determination, on the 23d of

January, 1076, he assembled at Worms a conventicle of simoniacal bishops, who presumed to depose Gregory from the pontificate on the most shallow pretences. Henry sent this mock sentence to Rome, together with a contumelious letter. On the receipt of this sentence and letter, Gregory called a council at Rome, and declared the emperor and his schismatical adherents excommunicated; and he further took upon him to pronounce that Henry, for his tyranny and oppressions, had forfeited his right to the crown.

That Gregory had a right to excommunicate Henry and his adherents cannot be doubted, since the affair for which he was condemned was one of *spirituals*. With the affairs of the church the temporal power has no jurisdiction. Henry therefore could not depose the pope without creating a schism, and for this he was liable to exclusion from the benefit of the sacraments. By the sentence of excommunication he was cut off from receiving any part of the treasures of the church; but the decree of deposition was quite a different thing. Christ had left no power in his church to depose sovereigns, nor would he admit the power of sovereigns to interfere with his kingdom; the general opinion of those times, however, had constituted the reigning pope, from the nature of their high office, a kind of arbiter or judge in the disputes which arose between contending sovereigns, or the discontents which might occur between a sovereign and the nobles and people. In this case the pope acted not by divine right, but by general consent; and if both kings, and princes, and people, are content to refer their temporal concerns to the head of the church, that head cannot be blamed for using his best endeavours to see justice done to each party, by the removal of public abuses and the establishment of just laws. This was the aim of Gregory VII. and for this most praiseworthy and honourable intention, he is the subject of invective and calumny.

The reader will now perceive the *cause* of the decree issued by Gregory, and the motives which induced Henry to refuse submission. We must now notice Fox's pathetic tale of the *barefooted* pilgrimage of Henry, his wife, and child, and the three days sojournment before the walls of the pope's palace, into which he is said to have gained admission at last through the entreaties of a lady named Matilda, and said to be the pope's paramour. By the name of the pretended paramour we are inclined to believe that this lady is no other than the countess of Tuscany, who was the daughter of Beatrice, sister to the emperor Henry III. by her husband Boniface lord of Lucca, and was therefore cousin to the emperor Henry IV. She was a woman of great virtue and heroism, and the wife of Guelpho the younger duke of Bavaria. Her mother Beatrice and herself were great admirers and protectresses of Gregory, and were directed by his counsels in the paths of perfection; it is not therefore likely, but is evidently a gross calumny, that Matilda was a paramour of the pope, who was too serious in his design to bring the clergy to a state of continency to violate it himself.

The sentence of Gregory against Henry, added to his own oppressions and misconduct, caused the princes of the empire to assemble in diet to take into consideration the state of the empire, and decide whether Henry should be any longer their emperor. This state of things, and the repentance of many of his adherents alarmed Henry, and he set off to Rome to obtain a reconciliation with the pope as the surest way to preserve his crown. The monarch put on the garb of penitence, and begged an audience, but Gregory knowing his former insincerity, kept him in suspense till the fourth day, when they were reconciled on certain conditions, the emperor promising to make all the satisfaction in his power for the injuries he had committed. The conditions of this reconciliation as related by Fox are fabulous, as the subsequent conduct of the monarch will clearly shew. This part of the history Fox has *suppressed*, but it is necessary to be known, in order to clear up the mist thus thrown around it. Gregory, with the sincerity of an upright man, sent off a messenger instantly to the princes of Germany, informing them of the important reconciliation, and requesting them to suspend their deliberations until he and Henry should appear amongst them. Henry, on the contrary, like all dissemblers, made excuses, and tried to prolong his appearance and that of the pope in the assembly. The council or diet of the princes was held at Foreheim in Franconia, the members of which growing weary of delay, and expecting no good from a faithless sovereign, proceeded to the election, and on the 15th of March, 1077, chose Rodolph, duke of Suabia, for their emperor.

Henry finding his enemies resolute, and not being disposed to part with his crown without a struggle, the seeds of civil war were sown, and a contest was carried on with various success for three years. The death of Rodolph, who fell in battle, left Henry sole master of the empire, and elated with his victory he renewed his violences against the church, summoned a crowd of simoniacal prelates to depose the pope, and published again the mock deposition. Gregory, in consequence of this arbitrary and insulting conduct, renewed his former censures against Henry, who, full of revenge, marched an army into Italy, set up an anti-pope, and laid siege to the city of Rome. The pope shut himself up in the castle of St. Angelo, where he remained secure till Robert Guischard, the heroic duke of Calabria, relieved the city and caused Henry to retreat into Lombardy. Though again master of Rome, the spirit of party ran so high that Gregory deemed it most prudent to retire, which he did first to Monte Cassino, and then to Salerno, where he fell sick, and ended his days on the 25th of March, 1085. Thus then this pope, who is reprobated for his insolence, which we are told had attained, at this time, a formidable height, died a proscribed exile, through the villanies and intrigues of a man who is held out to the people of England as an object of pity. The last words of Gregory were, " I " have loved justice and have hated iniquity, therefore I die in a strange " land." Gifted as this pontiff was with the most heroic qualities and amiable virtues, it would have been a wonder if his character had not been assailed by some writers, and more especially by those who are interested in keeping up similar abuses which Gregory opposed, and who hate that system of religion of which he was the head. His own writings, however, will bear testimony against these slanders, and when we add the evidence of a writer by no means partial to any pope, we may consider the character of Gregory as rescued from the foul blots which unjust authors have attempted to cast upon it. Dupin, a French author, says, " It must be acknowledged that pope Gregory VII. was " an extraordinary genius, capable of great things; constant and un-

" daunted in the execution; well versed in the constitution of his pre-
" decessors; zealous for the interests of the Holy See; an enemy to
" simony and libertinism (vices which he vigorously opposed); full,
" of Christian thoughts and of zeal for the reformation of the manners
" of the clergy; and there is not the least colour to think that he was;
" not unblemished in his own morals. This is the judgment which we
" suppose every one will pass upon him who shall read over his letters
" with a disinterested and unprejudiced mind. They are penned with
" a great deal of eloquence, full of good matter, and embellished with
" noble and pious thoughts; and we boldly say that no pope since,
" Gregory I. wrote such fine and strong letters as this Gregory did."—
Du Pin, Cent. 11, ch. 1, pp. 67, 68.

As to the emperor Henry IV. after carrying on the contest with three
of Gregory's successors, his own sons rebelled against him, and joined
the malcontents. In these contests he suffered the severest checks of
fortune, and died at Liege in the year 1106 and 46th of his age, leaving
behind him a name odious for his execrable lust, refined hypocrisy, and
barbarous cruelties. Yet such a character as this has Fox enlisted
among his auxiliaries to traduce and defame the religion of the primitive Christians and the successors of the apostles.

The next story is headed,—" KING JOHN SURRENDERS HIS CROWN TO
" THE POPE;" which occurrence he gives in these words:—" The
" ascendency of the popes was never more fully evinced than by a re-
" markable fact in the history of our own country. King John, having
" incurred the hatred of his barons and people by his cruel and tyran-
" nical measures, they took arms against him, and offered the crown to
" Louis, son of the French king. By seizing the possessions of the
" clergy, John had also fallen under the displeasure of the pope, who
" accordingly laid the kingdom under an interdict, and absolved his
" subjects from their allegiance. Alarmed at this, the tyrant earnestly
" sued for peace with his holiness, hoping, by his mediation, to obtain
" favourable terms from the barons, or, by his thunders, to terrify them
" into submission. He made the most abject supplications, and the
" pope, ever willing to increase the power of the church, sent cardinal
" Pandulf as legate to the king at Canterbury; to whom John resigned
" his crown and dominions; and the cardinal, after retaining the crown
" five days, in token of possession, returned it to the king, on condition
" of his making a yearly payment of 1000 marks to the court of Rome,
" and holding the dominions of England and Ireland *in farm* from the
" pope. But if John expected any benefit from this most disgraceful
" transaction, he was disappointed; and instead of enjoying the crown
" which he had so basely surrendered and received again, the short re-
" mainder of his life was disturbed by continual insurrections, and he
" at last died either of grief, or by poison administered to him by a
" monk of the convent of Swineshead in Lincolnshire. The latter cause
" is assigned by many historians, and we are told that the king, sus-
" pecting some fruit which was presented to him at the above convent
" to be poisoned, ordered the monk who brought it to eat of it, which
" he did, and died in a few hours after."

As this subject is most obscurely given in this passage, and as the
transactions in this king's reign are of great interest, even at this mo-

ment, and, as well as the days of Alfred, will require to be referred to in our examination of Fox's account of the Reformation, we will here enter somewhat copiously into the principal facts of the reigns of Alfred and John, as regard the religious and political institutions of those times, and the influence which religion had on these two monarchs in wielding the sceptre. We have shewn, in the preceding number, how the Catholic religion was introduced into this kingdom, under the Saxon heptarchy, in the sixth century, and the beneficial effects it produced on the manners and dispositions of our converted ancestors. By the advice of the prelates, who are the guardians of faith and morals, laws founded on the true principles of justice were established under the best and wisest of their kings, and when the ravages of war and the turpitude of sovereigns had debased the morals of the people, the clergy were the foremost to sieze the opportunity, whenever one was offered, to bring the nation back to a state of virtue and happiness. In this pursuit they always found the best and most efficient aid in a religious and active monarch. Such was the renowned Alfred, whose deeds as a Christian, a soldier, and a statesman, reflect a lustre on that religion by which they were influenced. This great monarch was the fourth and youngest son of Ethelwolph, the pious king of the West Saxons, and the second sovereign of all England. He was born at Wantage in Berkshire, in 849, and at an early age was sent to Rome. Leo IV. who then filled the chair of St. Peter, adopted him as his son, and the foundation of those virtues which afterwards shone with such brilliancy in his actions, was no doubt laid in his heart by the instructions he received at the papal court. How then can that religion be inseparable from persecution which leads the mightiest monarchs to establish the most equitable laws? And how can the men be monsters, as Fox and his editors represent the popes to have been, that planted such noble feelings in the mind of our Alfred and those other British sovereigns whose names glitter in the page of history, and throw a dark shade on the vices of those monarchs who rejected and violated the principles of their religion.

Alfred came to the crown in the 22nd year of his age, when the Danes were pouring their hordes into the kingdom and sweeping every thing before them. Various were the vicissitudes he experienced in his endeavours to recover the kingdom from the invaders, and at last he was driven to the extremity of seeking safety in some woody and boggy parts of the county of Somerset. Here he lay hid for six months, employing himself in prayer and meditation, and listening to the instructions of his spiritual director. In this state of exile, several of our best historians relate, that falling into a slumber, he received an assurance from St. Cuthbert that God would shortly restore him to his kingdom. Encouraged by this vision, Alfred renewed active operations, and succeeded in reconquering the kingdom, making the Danes surrender to his prowess, and acknowledge him victor. The first use he made of his triumph was to grant liberty of conscience to the Danish prisoners, by allowing those who did not choose to become Christians to return to their own country; those who embraced the faith were settled in the kingdom of the East Angles. He next turned his attention to maritime affairs, and founded that navy which has raised British glory so high among the nations of the world. The arts, sciences, and literature, then occupied his notice, and he also employed himself in erecting castles, fortresses, churches and monasteries, which had been overthrown by the devastation of the Danes. But that which raised Alfred's name above the rest of our monarchs, was the indefatigable assiduity and superior wisdom he manifested in bringing about a reformation of abuses, and laying the foundation of British freedom.

"Nothing," writes the Rev. Alban Butler, in a note to the Life of St. Neot, a near relative of Alfred's, "is more famous in the reign of "this king than his care and prudence in settling the public tranquillity "of the state, by an exact administration of justice. In the preceding "times of war and confusion, especially whilst the king and his fol-"lowers lurked at Athelney, or up and down and in cottages, the Eng-"lish themselves became lawless, and in many places revolted and "plundered their own country. Alfred, by settling a most prudent "polity, and by a rigorous execution of the laws, restored so great a "tranquillity throughout the whole kingdom, that, according to the "common assertion of our historians, if a traveller had lost a purse of "money on the highway, he would find it untouched the next day. "We are told in Brompton's Chronicle, that gold bracelets were hung "up at the parting of several highways, which no man durst presume "touch.

"Alfred compiled a body of laws from those of Ina, Offa, and Ethelbert, "to which he added several new ones, which all tended to maintain the "public peace and safety, to enforce the observance of the divine pre-"cepts, and to preserve the respect which is due to the church and its "pastors. For crimes they inflict fines or mulcts proportioned to the "quality and fortune of the delinquent; as, for withholding the Peter-"pence, for buying, selling, or working on the Lord's day or holiday, a "Dane's fine was twelve ores or ounces, an Englishman's thirty shil-"lings: a slave was to forfeit his hide, that is, to be whipped. The "mulct of a Dane was called Lash-lite, that of an Englishman Weare-"wite, or gentleman's mulct. Were or Weregild was the mulct or "satisfaction for a crime: it was double for a crime committed on a "Sunday or holiday, or in Lent. By these laws it appears that slaves "in England enjoyed a property, and could earn for themselves, when "they worked at times in which they were not obliged to work for "their masters; in which they differed from strict slaves of whom the "Roman laws treat. Alfred's laws were mild, scarce any crimes except "murder being punished with death; but only with fines, or if these "could not be paid, with the loss of a hand or foot. But the severity "with which these laws were executed maintained the public peace. "Alfred first instituted trials to be determined by juries of twelve unex-"ceptionable men, of equal condition, who were to pass judgment upon "oath as to the evidence of the fact or crime; which is to this day one "of the most valuable privileges of an English subject. To extirpate "robberies which, by the confusion occasioned by Danish devastations, "were then very common, this king divided the kingdom into shires, "(though there were some shires before his time) and the shires into "hundreds, and the hundreds into tythings or tenths, or in some places "into wapentakes, and every district was made responsible for all rob-

" beries committed within its precincts. All vagabonds were restrained
" by every one being obliged to be enrolled in some district. The
" capital point in Alfred's administration was, that all bribes or presents
" were most rigorously forbid the judges, their conduct was narrowly
" inspected into, and their least faults most severely punished. Upon
" any information being lodged against a judge or magistrate, he was
" tried by a council established for that purpose by the king, who him-
" self presided in it; he is said to have condemned in one year forty-
" five judges to be hanged for crimes committed by them in their
" office. By this severity he struck a terror into all his magistrates;
" and such was the effect of his perspicuity and watchfulness in this
" respect, that, as Milton says, in his days justice seemed not to flourish
" only, but to triumph.

" This prince who was born for every thing that is great, was a lover
" and zealous patron of learning and learned men. He considered that
" arts and sciences cultivate and perfect those faculties in men in which
" the excellency of their nature consists, and bestow the empire of the
" mind, much more noble, pleasant, and useful than that of riches;
" they exceedingly enhance all the comforts and blessings of life, and
" extend the reputation and influence of a nation beyond any conquests.
" By this encouragement of learning have so many great geniuses been
" formed, to which the world stands most indebted; and to this the
" greatest nations owe their elegance, taste, and splendour, by which
" certain reigns have been distinguished. By what else did the golden
" elegant ages of Rome and Athens differ from the unknown brutal
" times of savage nations? Certainly nothing so much exalts the glory
" of any reign, or so much improves the industry and understanding,
" and promotes the happiness of a people, as the culture of leading
" geniuses by well-regulated studies. As Plato says, (l. 6. de leg.)
" man without culture and education is the most savage of all creatures
" which the earth nourishes. But sciences are still of infinitely greater
" importance with regard to religion; and this consideration above all
" others recommended the patronage of learning to this pious king.
" The ancient public schools being either destroyed or almost fallen to
" decay with the monasteries during the wars, Alfred founded the uni-
" versity of Oxford, Alfred, canon of Beverly, in 1120, writes in his ma-
" nuscript history, that king Alfred stirred up all gentlemen to breed their
" sons to the study of literature, or if they had no sons, some servants or
" vassals whom they should make free. He obliged every free man who
" was possessed of two hides of land to keep their sons at school till
" they were fifteen years of age for, said the king, a man born free,
" who is unlettered, is to be regarded no otherwise than a beast, or a
" man void of understanding. It is a point of importance, that persons of
" birth, whose conduct in life must necessarily have a strong and exten-
" sive influence over their fellow creatures, and who are designed by
" Providence to be charged with the direction of many others, be formed
" from their infancy to fill this superior rank which they hold with dig-
" nity, and to the general advantage of their species. In order to be
" qualified for this purpose, their tender hearts must be deeply impressed
" with the strongest and most generous sentiments of sincere piety and
" religion, and of true honours: by being inured to reason in their

" youth they must acquire a habit of reasoning well and readily, and of
" forming right judgments and conclusions. Their faculties must be
" raised and improved by study, and when, by passing through the
" circle of the sciences, their genius has been explored, their studies
" and employs ought to be directed into the channel, which, by their
" rational inclinations, talents, particular duties, and circumstances of
" life, the great Author of nature and Master of the world shall point
" out to each individual. King Alfred also exhorted the noblemen
" to choose, among their country vassals or villains, some youths
" who should appear by their parts and ardent inclinations to piety,
" particularly promising to be trained up to the liberal arts. As for
" the rest, it was not then the custom to give the poorer sort too much
" of a school education, which might abate their industry and patience
" at manual labour. But this prince was solicitous that care should be
" taken for the education and civilizing of all by religious instructions
" and principles. Agriculture, in the first place, and all the useful and
" mechanical arts never had a greater patron or protector."

Who can have the hardihood, after this account of the transactions of
Alfred, to charge the Catholic church with a desire to keep her children
in ignorance? Nothing but the most barefaced impudence and
bigotted prejudice could induce a man to utter so groundless a falsehood. Do we not here see in the ninth century the strenuous exertions
of a Catholic king, seconded by the Catholic clergy, in founding seminaries of education, and imparting the advantages of learning to those
who seek them. These schools and colleges were preserved and others
added to them out of the revenues of the church and through the piety
of the clergy, till the rapacious Henry the Eighth came to the crown,
when taking it into his head to become a religious tinker, he and his
successor seized upon most of these seats of knowledge, and destroyed
the learned labours of their inhabitants. Camden, the panegyrist of
Elizabeth, in his introduction to the Annals of that queen, says, "Eng-
" land sate weeping to see her wealth exhausted, her coin debased, and
" her abbeys demolished, which were the monuments of ancient piety;"
while another writer, Sir John Denham speaking of this scene of
desolation, exclaims,—

Who sees these dismal heaps but will demand,
What barbarous invader sack'd the land !
But when he hears no Goth, no Turk, did bring
This desolation but a Christian King ;
When nothing but the name of zeal appears,
'Twixt our best actions, and the worst of theirs,
What does he think our sacrilege would spare,
Since these th' effects of our devotion are.—*Cooper's Hill.*

Of Alfred, on the contrary, Sir Henry Spelman (*Conc. Brit.*) speaks
thus in strains of rapture : "O, Alfred, the wonder and astonishment of
all ages ! If we reflect on his piety and religion, it would seem that
he had always lived in a cloister : if on his warlike exploits, that he
had never been out of camps ; if on his learning and writings, that he
had spent his whole life in a college ; if on his wholesome laws, and
wise administration, that these had been his whole study and employment[a]." Such is the character given of Alfred, who, we wish the reader

to bear in mind, was a Catholic king, governed by the divine precepts of the Catholic church, while the " few plain Christians" tell us that the Catholic religion is inseparable from persecution, and its professors bloodthirsty and superstitious.

We must now return to the martyrologist. Fox says " the ascen-" dency of the popes was never more fully evinced than by a remarkable " fact in the history of our own country ;" which fact turns out to be the surrender which John made of the crown of England to Innocent III. This fact he has taken care to envelope in much darkness, and when placed in its true light, the ascendency of the popes in those days will appear to be not half so pernicious as the ascendency of an Orange faction in our own. It is confessed by Fox that John was hated by the barons and people for his cruel and tyrannical measures, and that they offered the crown to Louis, son of the French king. It is true they did so ; and it is also true that this offer was made subsequent to the surrender of the crown by John to Innocent, so great was the ascendency of the popes in those days ! Fox places this circumstance *before* the affair between the king and the supreme pontiff, whereas, as we have just said, it should have been put *after* the mighty resignation. The case was this : John was a faithless and perfidious character; he divorced his wife, and murdered his nephew; which latter crime drew upon him the indignation of his subjects, and the Bretons, in particular, swore to be revenged on the murderer. His foreign dominions in Normandy were attacked, and John was compelled to retire to England, where he raised forces, and applied to the pope to compel his antagonist, the French king, by ecclesiastical censures, to observe his engagements.

. It must here be noticed, that at the period we are treating of, the principle upon which our ancestors were governed was the feudal system; and it was no uncommon thing to see the king of England doing homage as *the vassal* of the king of France; and the king of Scotland swearing fealty to the king of England ; the one for territories held in Normandy ; the other for lands held under the English crown. Hence in many of their disputes, when the fate of arms was doubtful, or had turned out disastrous, the soverign pontiffs were appealed to as the common father of Christendom, to use their spiritual influence, which was almost invariably exercised on the side of justice. In the case with John, the pope entered warmly into the affair, and endeavoured to bring about a reconciliation. The matter, however, turned out disastrous to the English monarch's interests, and he soon found himself involved in a dispute with Innocent himself.

In those times the choice of a bishop was not as now, a mere matter of course, at the will of a minister, but a canonical election was deemed necessary, and the church being independent of the state, in point of *spirituals*, a rigid adherence to forms was the consequence. It happened that the see of Canterbury became vacant, and John wanted to put one of his own creatures into the primate's chair ; the monks, who had the right of election, differed from the king, and elected another candidate, but fearing John's displeasure, they disregarded the first choice, and made a selection of John de Grey, bishop of Norwich, according to the recommendation of the king. As this was an affair that regarded the spiritual jurisdiction of the church, recourse was had to the pope, who pronounced both elections void, and ordered a canonical one to be entered into, when Stephen Langton, an Englishman of great eminence and learning, who had been honoured by Innocent with the purple, was chosen, and his election confirmed by the pope. The bishop of Norwich not being willing to lose the object of his ambition, insinuated bad advice into the ear of his royal master, who refused to acknowledge the election of Langton, and in the fury of disappointment, he turned his rage upon the monks, seized on their revenues, and banished them from the kingdom. Innocent tried by persuasive means to bring the king to a state of reason and justice, but he was inexorable; three bishops, by order of the pope, beseeched him in the most moving terms, to accept the new bishop; but he only answered them with oaths and insults. The king was then laid under an interdict, and was subsequently excommunicated, in the hope of bringing him over to justice. John continued to deride these measures till he found the barons were not to be relied upon, so great was their detestation of his conduct and injustices, and his crown was threatened by his rival the French king. He was then panic-struck, and in a fit of guilty cowardice, he resigned the crown into the hands of the pope's legate, and swore fealty to the Roman see. Fox insinuates, that this transaction originated in the willingness of the popes to increase the power of the church; but if this were the case, Innocent must have felt himself much disappointed, as his power did not receive the least augmentation by the transaction, as we shall find in the sequel.

The king being reconciled, the new archbishop Langton, was allowed to take possession of his see and the revenues thereof. The first act of the archbishop, on revoking the sentence of excommunication, was, we are told by Dr. Lingard, to make the king swear, " that he would abo- " lish all illegal customs, and revive the laws of the good king Edward." John took the oath, but he did not mean to keep it, so perfidious was his disposition. Some of the barons having fallen under the king's displeasure, he resolved to punish their disobedience by military execution. In this resolution the monarch found himself opposed by the noble-minded and honest archbishop, who reminded him that it was the right of the accused to be tried by his peers. John disregarded his admonitions, on which the archbishop told the king, says the last named author, that if he " persisted to refuse them the justice of a trial, he " should deem it his duty to excommunicate every person, with the ex- " ception of the king himself, who should engage in so impious a war- " fare. John yielded with reluctance, and for the sake of form, sum- " moned the accused to appear on a certain day before him or his jus- " tices." This conduct of the archbishop, may be thought by some as insolent and disrespectful to the sovereign; but to those who admit that a monarch holds his crown for the benefit of the people, it will appear an act of the purest patriotism, and shew how beneficial it is that churchmen should not owe their situations to the crown, but be independent of ministerial influence for their elevation.

The continued treachery and vexations of John, induced the cardinal archbishop to seek other measures to ensure the safety of persons and property from the lawless rapacity of the king. Accordingly, at a meeting of the barons at St. Paul's, he called them aside, read to them the chapter of liberties confirmed by Henry I. and commented upon its provisions. The barons swore upon oath to conquer or die in defence of their liberties. The reader will observe that during these proceedings, John held his crown in fealty to the pope, and was courting his support against the barons, as well as against the king of France, with whom he was at war. The contest with France proved unsuccessful, and John having concluded a truce of five years, returned to England to receive further mortification. On the 20th of November 1214, the barons met at the Abbey of St. Edmundsbury, where they took a solemn oath before the high altar, to demand in a body of the king, a redress of their grievances and a restoration of their civil liberties. This was done accordingly, and the king demurring, both parties appealed to the pope, who took the part of his vassal, John. In a letter to Langton he condemned the conduct of the barons as unjust, accused the archbishop of being the fomenter of the dispute, and commanded him to exert all his authority to restore harmony between the king and his subjects. The question was not one of *spirituals*, but a political struggle for temporal claims, and Langton knew how to distinguish between the two authorities. While he bowed submission to Innocent as head of the church, he declined to obey his mandate as lord paramount of the state, when the command was contrary to the rights and interests of the nation. Thus, when the cardinal primate was urged by the legate and the bishop of Exeter to excommunicate the barons, Langton refused to listen to their propositions, and told them that unless John dismissed the foreign troops he had introduced into the kingdom, he should think it his duty to oppose them with all his power. The barons thus fortified by this courageous dignitary of the church, again pressed their demands on the king, who wished to refer the question to the pope, but the barons refused to let the matter be sent to Rome, and at length obtained on the plains of Runnymead the signature of the king to that charter of liberties, which is referred to at the present day as one of the fundamental pillars of British freedom, and is called the Great Charter.

Thus it is clear, that whatever might be the ascendency of the popes, and however disgraceful the conduct of John might be in surrendering the crown to Innocent, a Catholic cardinal and bishop, and Catholic barons and knights knew how to treat this ascendency, when it stood in the way of their rights and grievances. The idea of the dominions of England and Ireland being held in *farm* from the pope may suit some prejudiced minds, but the page of history will prove that none were more attached to the *see* of Rome, on subjects of spiritual jurisdiction, nor more opposed to the *court* of Rome, when the rights and independence of the country were interfered with, than our Catholic ancestors. They knew, as we have before observed, how to distinguish between the two authorities, and if they occasionally appealed to the pope to heal any differences between crowned heads, or between the rulers and the people, when any stretch of power was exerted on the part of the pontiffs, there were always professors of the canon and civil law to point out the act of encroachment, and all parties were at liberty to abide by it or reject it. So much for this mighty bugbear, which was conjured up to alarm the haters of Popery out of their senses, as well as out of those liberties which our Catholic forefathers were so tenacious in preserving.

After John had signed the charter of liberties, he used every endeavour to render the privileges granted by it nugatory, and sought to wreak vengeance on the heads of those who were instrumental in forcing him to sign that important document. His cruelties were unparalleled, and his rapacity insatiable; which induced the barons to offer the crown to Louis the son of the king of France. Louis accepted the offer, and an unsuccessful attempt was made by the pope's legate to prevent both father and son from invading a kingdom, which, he said, was a fief of the holy see. Here we have another proof how little the pretended ascendency of the popes was regarded, when it stood in the way of kingly ambition. The fact is, as we have frequently repeated, and it ought not to be forgotten, the ascendency of the popes, arose from the high situation they held, and the general opinion entertained of their virtues and learning, and love of justice. Innocent III. like Gregory VIII. was a divine renowned for his great knowledge and stern integrity. Of Innocent, who governed the church eighteen years. Blondus, amongst other authors, writes thus, "The fame and odour of this pope's " gravity, holiness of life, and greatness of actions, was most sweet, " throughout all France," &c. (*Blond. decad.* 2. 1. vii, p. 297.) The Rev. Alban Butler says, that Innocent III. was "famous for his great " actions, and for several learned and pious books which he composed." There are writers to be sure who have endeavoured to blacken the fame of this eminent pontiff, but their slanders are evidently the effect of malicious or prejudiced minds, and therefore, wholly unworthy of credit. Innocent convened the fourth general council of Lateran, and condemned the Albigenses; it is therefore, no wonder that he should be abused by Fox and his modern editors, the "few plain Christians," who claim so near a kindred in religion with that impious and diabolical sect.

Let us now see what the character of John was from the best historians. Dr. Lingard thus describes it :—" When Geraldus delineated the cha- " racters of the four sons of Henry, John had aleady debased his facul- " ties by excess and voluptuousness. The courtly eye of the preceptor " could indeed discover the germ of future excellence in his pupil : " but history has recorded only his vices : his virtues, if such a mon- " ster could possess virtues, were unseen, or forgotten. He stands be- " fore us polluted with meanness, cruelty, perjury, and murder; uniting " with an ambition, which rushed through every crime to the attain- " ment of its object, a pusillanimity which often, at the sole appearance " of opposition, sank into despondency. Arrogant in prosperity, abject " in adversity, he neither conciliated affection in the one, nor excited " esteem in the other. His dissimulation was so well known, that it " seldom deceived : his suspicion served only to multiply his enemies : " and the knowledge of his vindictive temper, contributed to keep open " the breach between him and those who had incurred his displeasure. " Seldom perhaps was there a prince with a heart more callous to the " suggestions of pity. Of his captives many never returned from their " dungeons. If they survived their tortures, they were left to perish " by famine. He could even affect to be witty at the expense of his " victims. When Geoffry, archdeacon of Norwich, a faithful servant, " had retired from his seat at the exchequer on account of the interdict,

" the king ordered him to be arrested, and sent him a cope of lead to
" keep him warm in his prison. The cope was a large mantle, cover-
" ing the body from the shoulders to the feet, and worn by clergymen
" during the service. Wrapt in this ponderous habit, with his head
" only at liberty, the unhappy man remained without food or assistance
" till he expired. On another occasion he demanded a present of ten
" thousand marks from an opulent Jew at Bristol, and ordered one of
" his teeth to be drawn every morning till he should produce the
" money. The Jew was obstinate. The executioners began with his
" double teeth. He suffered the loss of seven : but on the eighth day
" solicited a respite, and gave security for the payment.

" John was not less reprehensible as a husband, than he was as a
" monarch. While Louis took from him his provinces on the conti-
" nent, he had consoled himself for the loss in the company of his beau-
" tiful bride : but he soon abandoned her to revert to his former
" habits. The licentiousness of his amours is reckoned by every ancient
" writer among the principal causes of the alienation of his barons,
" many of whom had to lament and revenge the disgrace of a wife, or
" daughter, or sister."

We have here given a faithful account of the circumstances which
occured between Henry IV. of Germany and Gregory VII. and John of
England and Innocent III. together with a true character of these respective personages from the best authorities. It will here be seen that
the auxiliaries pressed by Fox into his cause are of the most worthless
and irreligious cast, whose crimes bring discredit on human nature, and
whose deeds are a blot in the history of nations. On the other hand,
the " infernal artifices," attributed by him to the " popes, monks, and
" friars," we find have led to the most beneficial consequences, and
have been the means of exalting the human mind ; extending the arts
and sciences through every country where Catholicism was planted,
and in none more so than in our own beloved island, as the remains of
our ancient buildings and the stately cathedrals that now adorn the
kingdom bear testimony. The foreign wars and civil broils that convulsed Europe are also imputed to these " infernal" artificers ; with how
much truth let the admirable laws and regulations of those days, in our
country, the work of the most pious kings and learned divines, bear witness. We have shewn *how* the Catholic religion was planted by the
care of popes in this country, and how the purest maxims of justice and
civil government were established under its benign influence ; another
picture now remains to be unfolded, in which the depravity of error
will appear in that light which Fox and his modern editors have endeavoured to cast upon the ministers and disciples of the Catholic church.

Before we enter on this comparison, we must be allowed to lay before our readers another detectable tale by the martyrologist, which he
has headed thus : "An Emperor trodden on by the Pope."—Oh horrible!! Who could ever have supposed such a thing! The popes must
be "monsters" indeed, to tread upon emperors! But let us see what
Fox himself says upon his extraordinary deed. "The papal *usur-*
"*pations*," he writes, "were extended to every part of Europe. In
" Germany, the emperor Frederic was compelled to submit to be trod-
" den under the feet of pope Alexander, and dared not make any resist-

A REVIEW

OF

Fox's Book of Martyrs,

CRITICAL AND HISTORICAL.

No. 29. Printed and Published by W. E. Andrews, 3, Chapter-house-court, St. Paul's Churchyard, London. **Price 3d.**

EXPLANATION OF THE ENGRAVING.—*This cut represents Sir John Oldcastle, at the place of execution, he having been condemned to death for treason and heresy, in the reign of Henry V. addressing the people, and telling them that he should rise again on the third day. The non-accomplishment of this prophecy somewhat staggered the faith of his followers.*

CONTINUATION OF THE REVIEW.

" ance. In England, however, a spirit of resentment broke out in va-
" rious reigns, in consequence of the oppressions and horrible conduct
" of those anti-christian blasphemers, which continued with more or
" less violence till the time of the great Wickliffe, of whom we shall
" speak more fully in the following pages."—P. 223.

Can any one refrain from smiling at this account by Fox? These
German emperors, according to his account, must have been shockingly
base dastards, to have submitted to such humiliation. But they " *dared*
" not," he says, " make any resistance!" No, indeed ; *who* was to
prevent them? Tell us by *what* power, and under *what* authority, the
popes were so exalted and the emperors so humbled. Let us have
chapter and verse, and do not let this tale rest on bare assertion. We
have shewn that Henry II. attacked the pope with arms in his very
capital, and is it likely that an emperor, we cannot say whether a *predecessor* or *successor* of this Henry, for we cannot tell by the relation of
Fox which of the popes named Alexander, there having been *seven* of
that name, nor which emperor called Frederick, of whom there have
been *four* ; is it likely, we say, that an emperor would submit to such

an indignity, or a pope, whose interest it must have been to live in
peace and amity with a powerful sovereign, require such an act of submission from a monarch? No man of unclouded mind can ever believe
it; nor could such a story ever have gained credit in this country, had
not the people been previously hoodwinked and begulled out of their
wits.

. But though the German emperors were such cowards, our ancestors,
it seems, were not to be humbled and trodden upon by "those *anti-christian*
"*blasphemers*," as Fox and his editors call the popes. A "spirit of re-
"sentment," it is said, "broke out in various reigns." Well, and why
not *specify distinctly* the reigns in which this spirit made its appearance,
and the *cause* of its appearing? There is history to refer to, and by
making this reference a disposition would have been manifested to court
inquiry into the truth of the fact. That some opposition was made to
the *temporal* encroachments of some of the popes is what no Catholic
will deny; nay, our best Catholic writers frequently mention the stand
made by our ancestors in terms of praise, and cite these instances as a
proof of the spirit of *independence*, not of resentment, that animated the
Catholics of those days, denominated by silly ignorant bigots the "days
of darkness." However, as Fox says he shall speak more fully of these
days in his account of Wickliffe, we shall do the same, and follow him
inch by inch in his catalogue of lies.

"SECTION II.

"ACCOUNT OF WICKLIFFE, AND OF THE MARTYRS WHO SUFFERED IN DEFENCE OF HIS DOCTRINES."

This is a most important period in the history of our country, and
deserves much attention. According to his custom, Fox introduces his
account with a mixture of truth and falsehood, of facts and fictions,
well calculated to work on the generous credulity of Englishmen, who
are proverbial for their dislike to every thing oppressive, and their
attachment to justice; but who are unfortunately so misled by the
misrepresentations and falsehoods of interested writers, that they mistake error for truth, despotism for freedom, and wrong for justice.
The following are the introductory remarks made by Fox regarding the
errors of John Wickliffe.—"The first attempts made in England to-
"wards the reformation of the church, took place in the reign of Ed-
"ward III. about A. D. 1350, when John Wickliffe appeared. This
"early star of the English church was public reader of divinity in the
"university of Oxford, and, by the learned of his day, was accounted
"deeply versed in theology, and all kinds of philosophy. This even his
"adversaries allowed, as Walden, his bitterest enemy, writing to pope
"Martin, says, that he was wonderfully astonished at his strong argu-
"ments, with the places of authority which he had gathered, with the
"vehemence and force of his reasons, &c. At the time of his appear-
"ance, the greatest darkness pervaded the church. Scarcely any
"thing but the name of Christ remained; his true doctrine being as far
"unknown to the most part, as his name was common to all. As to
"faith, consolation, the end and use of the law, the office of Christ, our
"impotency and weakness, the greatness and strength of sin, of true

" works, grace, and free justification by faith, wherein Christianity con-
" sists, they were either unknown or disregarded. Scripture learning
" and divinity were known but to a few, and that in the schools
" only, where they were turned and converted into sophistry. Instead
" of Peter and Paul, men occupied their time in studying Aquinas and
" Scotus : and, forsaking the lively power of God's spiritual word and
" doctrine, were altogether led and blinded with outward ceremonies
" and human traditions, insomuch that scarcely any other thing was
" seen in the churches, taught or spoken of in sermons or intended or
' " sought after in their whole lives, but the heaping up of ceremo-
" nies upon ceremonies; and the people were taught to worship no
" other thing but that which they saw, and almost all they saw they
" worshipped. But Wickliffe was inspired with a purer sense of reli-
" gion; and knowing it to be his duty to impart the gracious blessing
" to others, he published his belief with regard to the several articles
" of religion, in which he differed from the common doctrine. Pope
" Gregory XI. hearing this, condemned some of his tenets, and com-
" manded the archbishop of Canterbury, and the bishop of London, to
" oblige him to subscribe the condemnation of them ; and, in case of re-
" fusal, to summon him to Rome. This commission could not easily be
" executed, Wickliffe having powerful friends, the chief of whom was
" John of Gaunt, duke of Lancaster, son of Edward III. The archbishop
" holding a synod at St. Paul's, Wickliffe appeared, accompanied by the
" duke of Lancaster and lord Percy, marshal of England, when a dispute
" arising whether Wickliffe should answer sitting or standing, the duke
" of Lancaster proceeded to threats, and treated the bishop with very
" little ceremony. The people present thinking the bishop in danger,
" sided with him, so that the duke and the earl marshal thought it pru-
" dent to retire, and to take Wickliffe with them. After this an insurrec-
" tion ensued, the clergy and their emissaries spreading a report that the
" duke of Lancaster had persuaded the king to take away the privileges
" of the city of London, &c. which fired the people to such a degree
" that they broke open the Marshalsea, and freed all the prisoners : and
" not contented with this, a vast number of them went to the duke's
" palace in the Savoy, when missing his person, they plundered his
" house. For this outrage the duke of Lancaster caused the lord mayor
" and aldermen to be removed from their offices, imagining that they
" had not used their authority to quell the mutineers. After this, the
" bishops meeting a second time, Wickliffe explained to them his sen-
" timents with regard to the sacrament of the eucharist, in opposition
" to the belief of the papists; for which the bishops only enjoined him
" silence, not daring at that time to proceed to greater extremities
" against him."—Pp. 224, 225.

The martyrologist is not correct, even in his setting out; the attempt of Wickliffe and his followers were not to *reform,* which means
to change from worse to better, but to *deform,* that is, to disfigure, to dishonour the church, and convulse the state. In the first case, however,
he was frustrated, as we shall presently shew, by the watchful eye of her
Divine Founder, and the vigilance of her lawful pastors ; in the latter
he was unfortunately more successful. The greatest *darkness,* we are
told, pervaded the *church* at the time of Wickliffe's appearance, and the

true doctrine of Christ, it is said, was *unknown* to the most part of the
world. " *Scripture learning* and divinity, were known but to a few,
" and that in the schools only, where they were turned and converted
" into sophistry. Instead of Peter and Paul, men occupied their time
" in studying Aquinas and Scotus—and the people were taught to wor-
" ship no other thing but that which they saw, and almost all they saw
" they worshipped."—These are bold assertions, but a little reflection,
and a slight glance at sacred and profane history will soon shew how
groundless they are. Christ has said, that his words should not fail;
that his church should be guided by the Spirit of Truth; that the
gates of hell should not prevail against her; that she should continue one
and the same to the end of the world; and, that she should never be
obscured by the mist of darkness, but should be like a city placed on
the top of a mountain, a light and guide to all men. These are plain
and unequivocal texts from scripture, which every one may read and *understand* too, unless reason is perverted, and the brain is disordered
with chimerical notions. Now, then, how could the church be pervaded
with darkness, unless the promises of Christ became void? And, is
there a man laying claim to the name of a Christian, that has the hardihood openly to avow that Christ has failed in his promise? Fox calls
the popes " anti-christian blasphemers," but, is he not here a blasphemer himself, in asserting that the church was at one time in darkness, in opposition to the promises made by GOD, that the church
never should be in darkness?

But it was not *wholly* in darkness, it may be said; a spark of the
gospel was still treasured up, to burst forth upon the world, and chase
away the abominations of Popery. This is a fine flight of imagination,
and much used by the adversaries of the Catholic church, to lull the
credulous into belief. However, let us look to the history of the
world, and see how this light shone forth, and how the darkness, as it
is called, enveloped it. We have, in our first volume, displayed the
progress of Christianity in the early ages of the church, and shewn
how the errors of dogmatizers were detected and condemned.—That
the greatest care was taken by the pastors of the Catholic church,
either by general councils, or provincial synods, or written epistles, or
word of mouth, to condemn every species of novelty, and caution the
people to beware of the deceits of designing men, whose object was to
involve them in confusion, and ensnare them in the meshes of error.
We have shewn that Fox himself, so late as the seventh century, admitted the right of the pope to assemble synods, and condemn heretics. He has classed the holy pope Martin amongst his "godly martyrs," and praised him for condemning the errors of the Monothelites;
nor has he, in one single instance, shewn any authority by which the
popes were deprived of that right which he has allowed them, and
which they have exercised from the first foundation of the church to
the present day, and will continue to exercise it, in spite of the world
and the devil, to the end of time. At the commencement of this volume we have shewn how the Catholic faith was introduced into this
island by missionaries sent from Rome, and the same faith was propagated by missionaries sent by the popes in all the different countries of
the world which did not receive it personally from the apostles. Wick-

liffe began his career about the year 1371, so that England had been
in the possession of the Catholic faith near EIGHT HUNDRED
YEARS, had acknowledged the spiritual supremacy of Rome during
that time, and was governed in spiritual matters by a regular and unbroken hierarchy. A consecutive list of archbishops and bishops of
all and every diocess in the kingdom can be produced from their first
foundation to the time when they were displaced by the ruthless hand of
Elizabeth, and intruders thrust into the vacant sees, in which they
were secured by act of parliament. The kings of England, the emperors of both the eastern and western empires (with the exception of
some of the former who held schismatical opinions, but agreed in
point of faith, and were for their disobedience consigned by the vengeance of God to the infidel Mahometans) with the kings of France and
the other monarchs of Europe, were all of one faith and one religion
with the other. There were in every age a number of the most eminent doctors and professors of divinity, and for some hundred years
the monks and friars of England had raised high the character of the
country, in point of science, literature, and theology. If they studied
Aquinas and Scotus, they also studied Peter and Paul, for Aquinas believed and taught the same doctrines as those blessed apostles received
and preached by the command of their Divine Master. During this period, as in former ages, several synods and councils were held in divers
countries, for the suppression of error and sectarianism, which occasionally started up, such as the Bogomilians, Petrobusians, Waldenses,
Albigenses, Flagellantes, Begardians, and others, some of which we
have noticed in our first volume.

We are told that Wickliffe was *inspired* with a purer " sense of reli-
" gion; knowing it to be his duty to impart the gracious blessing to
" others, he published his belief with regard to the several articles of reli-
" gion, in which he *differed* from the *common doctrine*." This is very true;
he *did* differ from the common doctrine, and it was for differing from the
truth, that is from the common faith of the whole world, that he was
condemned as a *false* teacher. But he was an inspired man! This assertion may suit the fanatic who deals in private inspiration; the sensible man however will require some test to prove his inspiration. From
whom did he receive his credentials? Who commissioned him to preach
a doctrine, differing from those taught by the apostles, and believed in
common by all the world? The fact is, if Wickliffe were inspired, it
was by the spirit of revenge for a disappointment he experienced in
losing the wardenship of Canterbury-hall, in Oxford, into which place
he had contrived to hedge himself. Wickliffe made his appeal to the
pope, who decided against him, which inspired him with fresh resentment, and was the principal cause of his opposition to the pope. He
had previously been engaged in a dispute with the friars, and finding
himself not likely to obtain the promotion he sought for, he determined
to rail against benefices and temporalties generally, to have his revenge on the whole body of the clergy, his own creatures excepted.—
Such doctrines could not fail to meet with admirers among hungry ambitious courtiers, and as he declaimed also against tithes, the people,
who were oppressed at that time, owing to the expensive wars of
Edward the third, were ready to catch at his doctrine. The novelty

and danger of Wickliffe's tenets, and the conduct of his " poor priests," as the fanatics who enlisted under his banners were called, soon became matter of astonishment and complaint. He was summoned by the archbishop of Canterbury and the bishop of London to appear before them. He did so, as Fox relates, accompanied by John of Gaunt, duke of Lancaster, and Percy the lord marshal. An altercation ensued between these haughty and irreligious peers and the prelates, and the people present certainly sided with the latter, in consequence of the outrageous and insolent behaviour of the peers, whose object was to intimidate their opponents. It is equally true that an insurrection ensued; not, however, from the insinuations of the clergy and their emissaries, as Fox falsely asserts, but through the influence of Wickliffe's doctrines, which heightened the discontent of the people, whose minds were already soured by taxation and disappointment. To add to the discontent, a new tax was levied of so much a head on every person, according to his rank and estate. As this tax accelerated the rebellion of Wat Tyler, of which so much has been written, and so little is clearly known, and as the scale of taxation is very curious, we well here subjoin an abridgment of it, from Dr. Lingard's History of England.

	l.	s.	d.
1. The dukes of Lancaster and Bretagne were rated at	6	13	4
2. The justices of the king's bench and common pleas, and the chief baron of the exchequer	5	0	0
3. An earl, earl's widow, and the mayor of London	4	0	0
4. A baron, banneret, knight equal in estate to a banneret, their widows, the aldermen of London, mayors of great towns, serjeants at law, and great apprentices of the law	2	0	0
5. A knight, esquire who ought to be a knight, their widows, apprentices who followed the law, jurats of great towns, and great merchants	1	0	0
6. Sufficient merchants	0	13	4
7. Esquires, their widows, the widows of sufficient merchants, attornies at law	0	6	8
8. Others of less estate in proportion	0	3	4
or	0	2	0
or	0	1	0
9. Each married labourer for himself and wife	0	0	4
10. Single men and women not mendicants	0	0	4

Rot. Parl. iii. 57, 58.

The clergy, who possessed the right of taxing themselves, adopted a similar rate.

	l.	s.	d.
Archbishops paid	6	13	4
Bishops and other spiritual peers	4	0	0
All having benefices above the yearly value of 200l.	2	0	0
From 100l. to 200l.	1	10	0
From 66l. 13s. 4d. to 100l.	1	0	0
From 40l. to 66l. 13s. 4d.	0	13	4
From 20l. to 40l.	0	10	0
From 10l. to 20l.	0	5	0
All other clergymen	0	2	0

Monks and nuns paid per head, according to the value of the houses so which they belonged, 40d. or 20d. or 12d. or 4d. Wilk. Con. iii. 141, 142.

From this scale it will be seen that the clergy in those days contributed their fair quota to the exigencies of the state, even of the lowest degree, besides maintaining the poor; but in these days, the days of the blessed Reformation and bible-reading, the people are taxed to maintain the poor clergy as well as the poor laity. Such is the difference between a married and unmarried clergy, We should add, that the above capitation tax falling short of the estimated sum, a further grant was voted by parliament, and the clergy in a convocation granted a tax of 6s. 8d. from all prelates, priests, (both regular and secular) and nuns, and of one shilling from all deacons and inferior clerks. (Conc. iii. 150.) But to return to Wickliffe and his doctrines.—At this period there was a great ferment among the mass of the people of all nations, and those of England were encouraged to resist the authorities by the diffusion of the doctrines of Wickliffe, among which he maintained that the right of property was founded in grace, and that no man, who was by sin a traitor to his God, could be entitled to the services of others. Thus a man had only to conceive himself to be in a state of grace, and his neighbour to get drunk, when the latter forfeits his right to property, and the former becomes entitled to it. Such notions as these could not be long entertained without disjointing the scale of society, and we find their propagation by itinerant preachers, who took care likewise to inculcate the natural equality of mankind, and the tyranny of artificial distinctions, soon wound the people up to a pitch of madness, and caused them to commit the greatest violences.

To enter into every particular here would occupy too much space, but to shew the effects of these doctrines, we will give the words of Stowe, an authority of great repute and much referred to by historians :—" The fame of these doings (that is the murder of the collector " by Wat Tyler, and the subsequent rising of the Kentish-men) spread " into Sussex, Hertford, Essex, Cambridgeshire, Norfolk, Suffolk, &c. " and when such assembling of the common people daily increased, " and that their number was now made almost infinite, so that they " feared no man to resist them, they began to shew some such acts as " they had considered in their minds, and took in hand to behead all " men in law, as well apprentices as utter barristers and old justices, " with all the jurors of the country, whom they might get into their " hands; they spared none whom they thought to be learned, especially " if they found any to have pen and ink, they pulled off his hood, and " all with one voice crying out, ' Hale him out, and cut off his head!' " They also determined to burn all court rolls and old monuments, " that the memory of antiquities being taken away, their lords should " not be able to challenge any right on them from that time forth. " These commons had to their chaplain or preacher a wicked priest, " called Sir John Ball, who counselled them *to destroy all the nobility* "*and clergy*, so that there should be *no bishop* in England, but one " archbishop, which should be himself." This Sir John Ball, the same historian informs us, had employed himself for some years in preaching at " divers places those things which he knew to be liking to the com- " mon people, slandering as well ecclesiastical persons as secular lords, " seeking thereby rather the benevolence of the common people, than " merit towards God: he taught that tithes were not to be given to " churchmen, except the party who should give the same should be " richer than the vicar or the parson that should receive it. Also, that " tithes and oblations were to be withdrawn from curates, if the pa- " rishioners or parishoner were of better life than the curate. Also,

" that no man was meet for the kingdom of God, that was not born in
" matrimony." These and many other things, Stowe says he taught,
for which he was prohibited by the bishops in whose dioceses he had
attempted to spread them; and as they prevented him from preaching
in churches, he went forth into the streets, and highways, and fields,
where there wanted not common people to hear him, whom he ever
sought to allure to his sermons, by detracting of the prelates. For
these seditious practices he was committed to prison, from which he
was released by the mob, and, after being thus delivered, he followed
them, for the purpose of instigating them to do evil. "That his
" doctrines," writes Stow, "might infect the more numbers of people,
" at Blackheath, where there were many thousands of the commons
" assembled, he began his sermon in this manner:—

"When Adam delve and Eve span,
' Who was then a gentleman?

" And, continuing his begun sermon, he sought by the word of that
" proverb, which he took for his theme, to introduce and prove, that
" from the beginning all were made alike by nature, and that bondage
" or servitude was brought in by unjust oppression of naughty men
" against the will of God; for if it had pleased God to have made bond-
" men, he would have appointed them from the beginning of the
" world, who should have been slave and who lord. They ought to
" consider, therefore, that now there was a time given them by God,
" in the which, laying aside the yoke of continual bondage, they might,
" if they would, enjoy their long wished-for liberty. Wherefore he
" admonished them, that they should be wise, and after the manner of
" a good husbandman that tilled his ground, and did cut away all noi-
" some weeds that were accustomed to grow and oppress the fruit,
" that they should make haste to do now at this present the like.
" First, the archbishops and great men of the kingdom were to be
" slain; after lawyers, justiciars, and questmongers; lastly, whomsoever
" they knew likely hereafter to be hurtful to the commons, they should
" dispatch out of the land, for so might they purchase safety to them-
" selves hereafter, if the great men being once taken away, there were
" among them equal liberty, all one nobility, and like dignity, one sem-
" blable authority or power. These (adds the writer) and many such
" mad devices he preached, which made the common people to esteem
" of him in such manner, as they cried out, he should be archhishop of
" Canterbury and chancellor of the realm, for he only deserved the
" honour."

At Canterbury several citizens were slain by the insurgents, and in
every place they demolished the houses and pillaged the manors of the
lords, burnt the court rolls, and cut off the heads of every justice, lawyer,
and juror, who fell into their hands. In Southwark they demolished
the houses belonging to the Marshalsea and the King's Bench, forced
their way into the palace of the archbishop of Canterbury at Lambeth,
and burnt the furniture with the records belonging to the chancery.
In the city they demolished Newgate and set the prisoners free, plundered and destroyed the magnificent palace of the Savoy, and burnt the
Temple with the books and records. The next objects of their vengeance were the natives of Flanders, sixty of whom they seized in va-

rious parts of the city, and struck off their heads with shouts of savage triumph. They next rushed into the Tower, and laying hands on the archbishop of Canterbury, who was also lord chancellor, Sir Robert Hales, William Apuldore the king's confessor, Legge the farmer of the obnoxious tax, and three of his associates, they were instantly led to execution. Walsingham relates the death of the archbishop with much minuteness. His head was carried through the streets on the point of a spear in triumph, and fixed on London bridge; and that it might be better known, the hat or bonnet worn by him was nailed to the skull:

The reader will now be able to judge of the credit due to Fox, who has endeavoured to skreen the pernicious and revolutionary tendency of Wickliffe's preachings, by insinuating that the clergy were the instigators of the insurrection, when it is clear, from the testimony of the most authentic writers, that they were the victims and not the fautors of the seditious and lawless spirit of those times. As to the duke of Lancaster displacing the lord mayor and aldermen for their remissness, it is one of the many fabrications which abound in this work, for Rapin tells us that the duke was in the north during the rising, and being himself suspected, he retired into Scotland till the storm was appeased, by which time the lord mayor went out of office by regular order. We are then told that " *after this*, the bishops had a meeting a " second time, when Wickliffe explained to them his sentiments with " regard to the sacrament of the eucharist, in opposition to the belief " of the Papists ;" that is, of the whole kingdom, and of all Christendom, in fact, as there was then no division or contradiction in belief on the real presence either in the Greek or Latin church. For being so kind as to *explain*, the bishops, he says, " only enjoined him to silence, " not *daring*, at that time, to proceed to greater extremities." We know not whether we ought to smile or feel indignant at the subterfuges practised by the anti-Popery writers, who will never give to the Catholic church her just due. The bishops in enjoining silence to Wickliffe, only acted according to the mild precepts of their church, and proved by their conduct that persecution was not an ingredient of their creed. By this false and base writer it is imputed to fear. But what cause had the bishops to fear? They had the king and people on their side, by Fox's own shewing. Nay, according to his account, they (the people) had even gone so far as to commit outrages at the instigation of the clergy; and now in the same breath we are assured that they dare not punish Wickliffe for fear of the people or something else. What contradiction have we here, and to diffuse, as it is pretended, " a " knowledge and love of the genuine principles of Christianity," among their fellow-believers. The truth is, the bishops were the appointed guardians of " the faith once delivered to the saints " they were bound to preserve the truths which they received from their predecessors, who received them from St. Augustin, who had them from the Roman bishop, and this bishop from his predecessors in the see up to the apostles. They did not act on their own *private* opinion, as Wickliffe did, and as all other heresiarchs do, who depart from the truth, and promulgate error, but they followed the example set them by the apostles in the council of Jerusalem, and by the fathers of the preceding ages of the church in the various councils held to examine into the pre-

tensions of impostors, and explain the revealed truths of the Catholic
faith. The bishops assembled in synod to listen to Wickliffe, to deliberate, and to decide. They had to pronounce judgment before the whole
kingdom, and if that judgment had been erroneous, is it to be believed
that some one of talent, learning and respectability, would not have
taken up the cause of Wickliffe, and denounced the conspiracy of the
bishops to lead the people into error, and impugn the truths of the
gospel? And yet it is a fact, that not one individual of rank in the
school of letters came forward to assist this heresiarch. He could find
no followers but those of the most ignorant and depraved cast, and the
two peers named patronized him merely to gratify their ambitious intentions and glut a revenge they had long entertained. This we shall
see as we proceed in our review of the martyrology.

The next event noticed by Fox is the "great schism in the church of
" Rome," which we shall treat of hereafter, as it interferes with the
subject under discussion. He then proceeds to give an account of
Wickliffe, under the head, "WICKLIFFE TRANSLATES THE BIBLE," which
we shall transcribe for the amusement of the reader.—" Wickliffe," he
says, "paying less regard to the injunctions of the bishops than to his
" duty to God, continued to promulgate his doctrines, and gradually to
" unveil the truth to the eyes of men. He wrote several books, which,
" as may be supposed, gave great alarm and offence to the clergy. But
" God raising him up a protector in the duke of Lancaster, he was secure
" from their malice. He translated the bible into English, which, amidst
" the ignorance of the times, may be compared to the sun breaking forth
" in a dark night. To this bible he prefixed a bold preface, wherein he
" reflected on the immoralities of the clergy, and condemned the worship
" of saints, images, and the corporal presence of Christ in the sacrament :
" but what gave the greatest offence to the priests, was, his exhorting
" all people to read the scriptures, in which the testimonies against all
" those corruptions appeared so strongly. About the same time the
" common people, goaded to desperation by the oppressions of the no-
" bility and clergy, rose in arms, and committed great devastations ;
" and, among other persons of distinction, they put to death Simon of
" Sudbury, archbishop of Canterbury. He was succeeded by William
" Courtney, who was no less diligent than his predecessor had been, in
" attempting to root out heretics. Notwithstanding all opposition,
" however, Wickliffe's sect increased, and daily grew to greater force,
" until the time that William Barton, vice-chancellor of Oxford, who
" had the whole rule of that university, assisted by some monastic
" doctors, issued an edict, prohibiting all persons, under a heavy pe-
" nalty, from associating themselves with any of Wickliffe's favourers ;
" and threatening Wickliffe himself with excommunication and impri-
" sonment, unless he, after three days canonical admonition or warn-
" ing, did repent and amend. Upon this, Wickliffe wished to appeal
" to the king : but the duke of Lancaster forbade him ; whereupon he
" was forced again to make confession of his doctrine ; in which con-
" fession, by qualifying his assertions, he mitigated the rigour of his
" enemies. Still his followers greatly mutiplied. Many of them, in-
" deed, were not men of learning ; but being wrought upon by the
" conviction of plain reason, they were the more steadfast in their per-

" suasion. In a short time his doctrines made a great progress, being
" not only espoused by vast numbers of the students of Oxford, but
" also by many of the nobility, particularly by the duke of Lancaster
" and lord Percy, earl marshal, as before mentioned. Wickliffe may
" thus be considered as the great founder of the reformation in this king-
" dom. He was of Merton College in Oxford, where he took his doc-
" tor's degree, and became so eminent for his fine genius and great
" learning, that Simon Islip, archbishop of Canterbury, having founded
" Canterbury College, now Christ Church, in Oxford, appointed him
" rector; which employment he filled with universal approbation, till
" the death of the archbishop. Langholm, successor to Islip, being de-
" sirous of favouring the monks, and introducing them into the college,
" attempted to remove Wickliffe, and put Woodhall, a monk, in his
" place. But the fellows of the college being attached to Wickliffe,
" would not consent to this. Nevertheless, the affair being carried to
" Rome, Wickliffe was deprived in favour of Woodhall. This did not
" at all lessen the reputation of the former, every one perceiving it was
" a general affair, and that the monks did not so much strike at Wick-
" liffe's person, as at all the secular priests who were members of the
" college. And, indeed, they were all turned out, to make room for the
" monks. Shortly after, Wickliffe was presented to the living of Lut-
" terworth, in the county of Leicester, where he remained unmolested
" till his death, which happened December 31, 1385. But, after the
" body of this good man had lain in the grave forty-one years, his
" bones were taken up by the decree of the synod of Constance, pub-
" licly burnt, and his ashes thrown into a river. The condemnation of
" his doctrine did not prevent its spreading all over the kingdom, and
" with such success, that, according to Spelman, ' two men could not
" be found together, and one not a Lollard, or Wickliffite.' "

This plausible story have had its day, and too long a day for the cause
of truth, and the happiness of the country. It is one of those fashionable themes which have caused hundreds in the present age to part with
their money and their wits, to encourage a knot of pretenders not a jot
better than Wickliffe himself. He is commended for translating the
bible into English; but his greatest offence, we are told, was, " his ex-
" horting all people to *read* the scriptures, in which the testimo-
" nies against all those corruptions appeared so strongly." What those
testimonies and what those corruptions *were* are not pointed out to the
reader, so that he is as completely left in the dark concerning them, as
the adversaries of Catholicism charge the Catholic priesthood with keeping the people in ignorance respecting the scriptures. At that time
the copies of the sacred writings were few, and confined chiefly to the
libraries of the monasteries and universities. The great mass of the
people, including many of the nobility and gentry, could not read, from
the want of facility in teaching and the paucity of books, the art of printing not being then discovered, so that the exhortation of the heresiarch
to *all* the people to *read* the scripture is a mere fiction, invented to conceal the deception of intriguers and knaves. It is true that Wickliffe
translated the scriptures, and that he multiplied the copies as much as
he could with the aid of transcribers, and by the aid of his disciples, who
were the off-scum of the clergy, and called "poor priests," he dissemi-

nated those texts among the illiterate which favoured his doctrines, by word of mouth, and he inculcated the now favourite and delusive notion of private interpretation, by which he undermined the authority of the Church, and set the people and their pastors at variance. Of the novelties preached by Wickliffe, two of them are said to be the condemnation of the worship of saints and the corporal presence of Christ in the sacrament. We could have wished for more explicitness. Why did not Fox give us the precise grounds on which Wickliffe rested his condemnation ? We have shewn in our first volume, by quotations from the fathers, that the *invocation* of saints was practised and taught in all times by the apostles and doctors of the Church ; that the opposite doctrine had been condemned as false and erroneous ; therefore that which was false before the time of Wickliffe could not be rendered truth by him, let him be ever so deeply inspired. That Wickliffe was not a Protestant is beyond contradiction, since he inculcated the doctrine of purgatory, and strenuously maintained the efficacy of the mass, both of which Protestants deny upon oath. He also admitted the seven sacraments of the Catholic church, while the Protestants of the Church as by law established hold only two, and many deny them altogether.— Consequently, if Wickliffe was *right*, Protestants must be *wrong*, and if the latter are *right*, why then the former must be *wrong*, and what becomes then of his being inspired ? It could not be by the Spirit of Truth, but must have been by the Father of Lies. :

Fox admits that the common people rose in arms, and put several persons of distinction to death: among others Simon Islip, the archbishop of Canterbury, who gave Wickliffe the wardenship of Canterbury college. But then he endeavours to throw the blame upon the clergy as well as the nobility. We have shewn that the clergy were *not* the oppressors and drainers of the people, but that they contributed to relieve them of a considerable share of taxation, by heavy impositions on every rank of the ecclesiastical order. And if William of Courtney was diligent in rooting out heretics, he only followed the example of pope Martin, who, as we have before observed, and which should not be forgotten, is extolled by Fox for his vigilance in preserving truth and condemning heresy, and is placed among his " godly martyrs." The term " to root out *heretics*," is here improperly used, because at this period there was no law to inflict corporal punishment on those who had became infected with heresy. It was the *error*, the *heresy*, not the individual contaminated with it, that the clergy were diligent to root out, as it became their duty so to do. The story of Barton, the vice-chancellor of Oxford, issuing an edict of prohibition to *all* persons not to associate with Wickliffe or his followers is another fiction, for Barton had not the authority to issue so general an edict. His jurisdiction extended only to the university of Oxford, of which Wickliffe was not then a member.

. But what shall we say to the admission of Fox, that Wickliffe " was " *forced* again to make confession of his doctrine; in which confession, by " QUALIFYING his assertions, he mitigated the rigour of his enemies." Here is a pretty apostle " to unveil the truth to the eyes of men !" He is *compelled* to make a confession of his faith, and in making this confession he *qualifies* his expressions, he softens, that is, he plays the *deceiver*, to molify his judges, and save his bacon. What an admission!

Who could rely on such a juggling scoundrel? And yet this is a man who is held forth as the precursor of that "blessed" work of robbery, and pillage, and corruption, both in faith and morals, called the *Reformation*. To be sure he was a fit person to precede so irreligious a work, and, as we have shewn, his doctrines were productive of similar disorders, only the wisdom and firmness of the king and his councillors, in those days of darkness, nipped the evil in the bud. How different is this conduct of Wickliffe to the example set by the primitive martyrs? How different to the illustrious and innumerable confessors of the Catholic faith in all ages. They did not want to be *compelled* to make a confession of their faith; they gloried in it, and openly professed it in the face of their judges and executioners. They never practised the art of dissimulation, as, we are assured by Fox, John Wickliffe did; but they declared, in plain and unequivocal language, the tenets of their creed, and braved the malice and rigour of their enemies. Wickliffe, however, was not made of such materials: he did not aspire to be a martyr, and therefore when he appeared before his lawful judges, to render an account of his doctrines, he read a confession of faith with some reluctance, in their presence, which being considered satisfactory, he was allowed to remain in peace, at his rectory at Lutterworth, where he died two years afterwards, whilst assisting at the mass of his curate. That Fox gave a true character of Wickliffe, when he represented him as a *qualifier* of doctrine, is confirmed by Dr. Lingard, who thus describes his manner of managing disputation.—"On many points of doctrine," writes the doctor, "it is not easy to ascertain the *real* sentiments of "this reformer. In common with other religious innovators, he claimed "the two-fold privilege of *changing his opinion at will*, and of being *infal-* "*lible in every change*: and when he found it *expedient to dissemble*, could "so *qualify* his doctrines with *conditions*, or *explain them away* by *dis-* "*tinctions*, as to give an *appearance of innocence* to tenets of the most "*mischievous tendency*." Here then the historian and Fox are agreed, and it cannot now be doubted or disputed that John Wickliffe, the precursor of the Reformation, an inspired reformer of religion, appointed by God, according to Fox, "gradually to unveil the truth to the eyes of "men," was a PREVARICATOR and DISSEMBLER!!! He must have been an admirable teacher of Truth.

Fox next gives us the "TENETS OF WICKLIFFE;" that is, those which were condemned as heretical. They are as follows:—

1. "The substance of material bread and wine doth remain in the sacrament of the altar after the consecration.

2. "The accidents do not remain without the subject in the same sacrament, after the consecration.

3. "That Christ is not in the sacrament of the altar truly and really, in his proper and corporal person.

4. "That if a bishop or a priest be in deadly sin, he doth not order, consecrate, nor baptize.

5. "That if a man be duly and truly contrite and penitent, all exterior and outer confession is but superfluous and unprofitable unto him.

6. "That it is not found or established by the gospel, that Christ did make or ordain mass.

7. If the pope be a reprobate and evil man, and consequently a mem-

ber of the devil, he hath no power by any manner of means given unto him over faithful Christians.

8. "That since the time of Urban the sixth, there is none to be received for pope, but every man is to live after the manner of the Greeks, under his own law.

9. "That it is against the scriptures, that ecclesiastical ministers should have any temporal possessions.

10. "That no prelate ought to excommunicate any man except he knew him first to be excommunicate of God.

11. "That he who doth so excommunicate any man, is thereby himself either an heretic or excommunicated.

12. "That all such which do leave off preaching or hearing the word of God, or preaching of the gospel for fear of excommunication, they are already excommunicated, and in the day of judgment shall be counted as traitors unto God.

18. "That it is lawful for any man, either deacon or priest, to preach the word of God, without authority or license of the apostolical see or any other of his Catholics.

14. "That so long as a man is in deadly sin, he is neither bishop nor prelate in the church of God."

Speaking of the 4th article, father Parsons, in his reply, observes, "Will Fox yield to this article, think you? For, if he do, we may "call in doubt whether ever he were well baptized, and consequently "whether he were a Christian; seeing it may be doubted whether the "priest that baptized him were in mortal sin or no when he did it."— Of the ninth, the same learned writer remarks, "This article, if Fox "will grant, yet his fellow ministers, and his lords the bishops, I pre- "sume, will hardly yield thereunto, but will pretend scriptures to the "contrary against Wickliffe." With regard to the first three articles, we refer the readers to the primitive fathers we have quoted in the first volume, who contended for the opposite doctrine, and vouched for the real presence as of divine institution, derived from Christ to the apostles.—As to the sixth, which rejects the mass, Wickliffe attended at this sacrifice to the day and hour of his death, as we have before stated. But, what will the modern editors of Fox say to the two following tenets, which they have prudently suppressed in these ticklish times about tithes.

16. "That temporal lords may, according to their own wills and "discretion, take away the temporal goods from any churchmen, when- "soever they offend.

17. "That tithes are mere alms, and may be detained by the pa- "rishioners, and bestowed where they will at their pleasure."

These are some of the *truths* which Wickliffe thought proper "gra- "dually to unveil to the eyes of men," and we will here ask the reader, if another Wickliffe were to rise up now and preach the same doctrines, whether the clergy of the church as by law established would not one and all contend for his being punished and silenced. There cannot be a doubt but they would, and the impostor severely feel the weight of the law. He might try to persuade the clergy and the people that he was an inspired man; that they were all in the dark, and he alone was commissioned to shed light upon them; but not one of the clergy would he get to believe him, unless it was some poor half starved curate, who could lose nothing by the experiment. So it was with Wickliffe; he found greedy ignorant clerks to imbibe his notions in hopes of benefiting from the credulity of the people, and the duke of Lancaster was not averse to the improving his estate by the possessions of the church, which, however he was not allowed to do; such robbery being reserved for the beastly Henry and his rapacious courtiers. The effect of Wickliffe's doctrines, nevertheless, were too apparent in the disturbances they created, and the treasons they gave rise to, nor were the evil consequences ever entirely removed.

To give another specimen of the daring attempts of the disciples of Wickliffe, who, Fox says, felt himself called upon "gradually to unveil "the truth to the eyes of men," Dr. Lingard relates, that while Richard II. was "establishing his power in Ireland, he was suddenly "recalled to his English dominions. The disciples of Wickliffe, under "the denomination of Lollards, had seized the opportunity of his absence "to commence a fierce attack upon the revenues and the discipline of "the church. Not content with affixing libels against the clergy in "the most public places in the capital, they had prepared an inflamma-"tory petition, which was to be presented to the House of Commons. "This instrument is a strange compound of fanaticism and folly. It "complains, that ever since the church had been endowed with worldly "possessions, faith, hope, and charity have been banished from Eng-"land: that the English priesthood is a false priesthood; because sin-"ners can neither impart nor receive the Holy Spirit : that the clergy "profess a life of celibacy, but pamper themselves too much to observe "it; that by accepting places under the government, they become "hermaphrodites, obliging themselves to serve both God and mammon: "that they teach transubstantiation, which leads to idolatry; enjoin "confession, which makes them supercilious; authorize war and cri-"minal executions, which are contrary to the law of Christ, a law of "mercy and love; and permit men to exercise the trades of the gold-"smith and sword-cutler, which are unnecessary and pernicious under "the dispensation of the gospel. The prelates, alarmed at the boldness "of these fanatics, solicited the protection of the king; who at their "prayer returned to London, and reprimanded the patrons of the Lol-"lards with so much severity, that they did not venture to move the "subject in parliament." By this extract the reader must be now convinced that there was neither truth nor justice on the part of these disturbers of the public peace, but only faction and a lawless desire of abolishing the constituted authorities of the realm.

BURNING OF THE WICKLIFFITES.

As this subject is one of the utmost importance, and but little understood by the great mass of the people of England, we have distinguished it by a head line, and intend to elucidate it with as much perspicuity as we are master of. But, first we will see what Fox has got to say. He writes, "In the council of the Lateran, a decree was made with re-"gard to heretics, which required all magistrates to extirpate them "upon pain of forfeiture and deposition. The canons of this council "being received in England, the prosecution of heretics became a part

" of the common law; and a writ (stiled *de heretico comburendo*) was
" issued under king Henry IV. for burning them upon their conviction;
" and it was enacted, that all who presumed to preach without the li-
" cence of the bishops, should be imprisoned, and be brought to trial
" within three months. If, upon conviction, they offer to abjure, and
" were not relapses, they were to be imprisoned and fined at pleasure;
" but if they refused to abjure, or were relapses, they were to be de-
" livered up to the secular arm; and the magistrates were to burn
" them in some public place. About this time William Sautre, parish
" priest of St. Osith, in London, being condemned as a relapse, and de-
" graded by Arundel, archbishop of Canterbury, a writ was issued,
" wherein burning is called the common punishment, and referring to
" the customs of other nations. This was the first example of that sort
" sort in England. The clergy, alarmed lest the doctrines of Wickliffe
" should ultimately become established, used every exertion in their
" power to check them. In the reign of Richard II. the bishops had
" obtained a general licence to imprison heretics, without being obliged
" to procure a special order from court, which, however, the house of
" commons caused to be revoked. But as the fear of imprisonment
" could not check the pretended evil dreaded by the bishops, Henry IV.
" whose particular object was to secure the affection of the clergy,
" earnestly recommended to the parliament the concerns of the church.
" How reluctant soever the house of commons might be to prosecute
" the Lollards, the credit of the court, and the cabals of the clergy, at
" last obtained a most detestable act, for the burning of obstinate here-
" tics; which bloody statute was not repealed till the year 1677. It
" was immediately after the passing of this statute that the ecclesiasti-
" cal court condemned William Sautre above-mentioned."

We always have contended, and still contend, that PERSECUTION is
not a part and parcel of the system of Catholicism. The precepts and
maxims of the Catholic church are founded on the purest principles of
Charity; nay, it is Charity itself, which is an emanation from the Deity,
and by the Deity was the Catholic church founded. We have here the
acknowledgment of Fox, that the execution of the priest Sautre, " was
" the FIRST example of the sort in England." Now the Catholic
church had been established in this island, reckoning from the landing
of St. Austin, in 596, to the execution of Sautre, in 1399, *eight hundred
and three years*, without one single instance of corporal coercion for
matter of opinion, though difference of opinion had occasionally arisen,
and in the case of Wickliffe we find to some height. That this man was
treated with the utmost lenity is confessed by Fox, and we find him remaining unmolested in his rectory till the day of his death. From what
cause then could spring this writ, stiled *de heretico comburendo*, of which
so much as been said to bring odium on the Catholic religion, and so
little understood by the Protestants of England? Fox alludes to the
council of Lateran, a decree of which, he says, required all magistrates
to extirpate heretics upon pain of forfeiture and deposition. This decree, admitting that there was such a one passed, was not of faith, and
therefore binding on none without the consent of the temporal power,
and at this council, which may be consistently called the parliament of
Christendom, there were present, either in person or by their ambassa-

A REVIEW

OF

Fox's Book of Martyrs,

CRITICAL AND HISTORICAL.

No. 30. Printed and Published by W. E. Andrews, 3, Chapter-house-court, St. Paul's Churchyard, London. **Price 3d.**

EXPLANATION OF THE ENGRAVING.—*The mock divorce of Henry the Eighth from his lawful and virtuous queen, Catherine of Arragon, after having lived twenty years in wedlock, and had three children by her. Of this divorce, a full account will be given in the succeeding numbers.*

CONTINUATION OF THE REVIEW.

dors all the sovereigns of Europe, to give their consent to such decrees of discipline as might be deemed conducive to the morals of society and the tranquillity of their states. The real version of the decree, according to Dr. Lingard, was this, that persons convicted of heresy "should be left to the *secular* power to be dealt with according to the "due form of law." Now what could be more correct than this?— Every state has an undoubted right to provide for its own internal as well as external security, and should an individual imbibe a notion that he is commissioned by God to preach novelties tending to disturb the peace, and raise tumults and rebellions, why, in the name of common sense, are not laws to be passed to prevent such lawless doings, no matter whether committed under the garb of a *religious* or *political reformer?* Who will have the hardihood to answer us in the negative? The same was the conduct of the Wickliffites; they sought, under the cloak of religion, to revolutionize all ranks and property; and when they had thus declared their intentions, and made them manifest by

their actions, then, and not till then, and with a view of self-preserva-
tion, not of personal cruelty and ambition, did the authorities take upon
them to protect themselves and the people, by this statute *de heretico
comburendo.* So long as the heresy of Wickliffe was confined to mere
matter of opinion, the spiritual weapons only of the church were exerted
to counteract the poison, and convince the ignorant of their error; but
when the infected proceeded to lawless outrages and murders, surely it
was time to use the arm of the civil sword to restrain them within due
bounds. Nor can the measures thought necessary at that time to be
adopted be justly termed persecution, seeing they were enforced on
none but the most obdurate miscreants of the day.

When such a disposition reigned among the ignorant and illiterate
people, it is no wonder that the clergy should become alarmed and use
every means in their power to check the progress of the pernicious
doctrines; nor were the laity less anxious to subdue the spirit of depredation that influenced the Lollards. Fox would fain have us believe
that the house of commons reluctantly passed the act; Dr. Lingard,
however, tells us a different sort of story. This able and accurate
writer states, that the commons were more zealous at that time in opposing the Lollards, than the nobility and the clergy. On this interesting point we shall give the learned historian's own words. "Encou-
" raged by the royal invitation, and the disposition of the commons,
" the clergy presented a petition to the king in parliament; and an act
" was passed for the protection of the church, and the suppression of
" the new sect. The preamble sets forth, that divers unauthorized
" preachers go about teaching new doctrines and heretical opinions,
" making conventicles and confederacies, holding schools, writing
" books, misinforming the people, and daily committing enormities too
" horrible to be heard: and that the bishops are unable to repress these
" offences, because the offenders despise ecclesiastical censures, and
" when they are cited before their ordinaries, depart into another dio-
" cese: the statute therefore provides, as a remedy for these evils, that
" the bishop shall have power to arrest and confine persons defamed or
" vehemently suspected of such offences, till they make their canonical
" purgation; and, if they be convicted, to punish them with imprison-
" ment, and a fine to the king. It then enacts that if any person so con-
" victed shall refuse to abjure such preachings, doctrines, opinions,
" schools, and informations, or after abjuration shall be proved to have
" relapsed, then the sheriff of the county, or the mayor and bailiffs of
" the nearest borough shall, on requisition, be present at the pronuncia-
" tion of the sentence, shall receive the person so condemned into cus-
" tody, and shall cause him to be burnt on a high place before the peo-
" ple, that such punishment may strike terror into the minds of others.
" (*Rot. Parl.* iii. 466. *Wilk. Conc.* iii. 252.)

" During this very parliament (whether before or after the passing
" of the act is uncertain) a petition was presented to the lords and com-
" mons by William Sawtre, begging that he might be permitted to dis-
" pute before them on the subject of religion. Such a request excited
" considerable surprise: but the enthusiast aspired to the crown of
" martyrdom; and had the satisfaction to fall a victim to his own folly.
" He had been rector of Lynn in Norfolk: but about two years before

" had been convicted of heresy, and deprived of his living. On his re-
" cantation he had been lately admitted a chaplain in St. Osith's, in Lon-
" don. The character of Sawtre, and the nature of his request, induced
" the convocation to summon him before them : and six days were al-
" lowed him to prepare his answer. The articles objected to him were
" those of which he had been accused before the bishop of Norwich.
" With unparalleled effrontery he denied his former conviction and re-
" cantation; explained the other articles in an orthodox sense; but
" refused to give any satisfaction on the subject of the eucharist. The
" trial was adjourned from day to day : and the archbishop, notwith-
" standing the contempt and insolence of his answers, made a last effort
" to save him, by asking if he were content to stand on that question
" by the determination of the church. He answered that he was, pro-
" vided the determination were agreeable to the will of God : an eva-
" sion which of course was rejected. The record of his former convic-
" tion and recantation were now produced from the registry of the
" bishop of Norwich ; and on the eleventh day from his arraignment
" he was pronounced by the primate a relapsed heretic, was degraded
" from his orders, and delivered into the custody of the constable and
" mareschal of England. (Con. iii. 255-260.) About a week after-
" wards, Henry consulted the temporal lords sitting in parliament;
" and by their advice issued a precept to the mayor and sheriffs to exe-
" cute the sentence of the law upon Sawtre. The unhappy man, instead
" of being shut up in an asylum for lunatics, was burnt to death as a
" malefactor, in the presence of an immense multitude : and the com-
" mons by their speaker returned thanks to the king that, whereas 'by
" bad doctrine the faith of holy church was on the point of being over-
" turned, to the destruction of the king and kingdom, he had made and
" ordained a just remedy to the destruction of such doctrine and the
" pursuers thereof.'
" This severity did not, however, subdue the boldness of the preach-
" ers. They declaimed with redoubled animosity against the tempo-
" ralties of the clergy, till the lay proprietors became alarmed for the
" security of their own possessions, In 1407 the subject attracted the
" notice of the house of lords : a petition was sent by them to the com-
" mons for their concurrence ; and it was afterwards presented by the
" speaker to the king. It stated that the preachers excited the people
" to take away the possessions of the church, of which the clergy were
" as assuredly endowed as the temporal lords were of their inheritances;
" and that unless these evil purposes were speedily resisted, it was pro-
" bable that in process of time they would also move the people to take
" away the possessions and inheritances of the temporal lords, and
" make them common, to the open commotion of the people, and the
" utter subversion of the realm. In consequence it was enacted that
" such persons, together with those who maintained that king Richard
" was still alive, and others who published false prophecies to delude
" the people, should be arrested and brought before the next parliament
" to receive such judgment as the king and peers in their judicial au-
" thority should pronounce."
From this authentic relation, nothing can be plainer that persecution
is no part or parcel of the Catholic church. No act of violence was

offered nor could be offered by the clergy as clergymen; they petitioned the king in parliament, as members of the state, not as ministers of the church, in consequence of their temporalties being endangered by lawless and erroneous pretensions. The power was granted to them by the civil supreme authorities of the land, and it will not, we apprehend, be disputed, that the representatives of the people, that is, the *real* representatives of the people, for such was then the case, had the right to grant and delegate the power of preserving the peace of the kingdom to whomsoever they pleased. How far it was consistent with sound policy and a due regard of religion is mere matter of opinion; the then parliament thought it wise, and in this they were probably right, for as some part of the crime was an error in judgment, and as the clergy were then the most learned class of men in the country, and the most able to decide on the case, none could be so proper to act as they in matters requiring discriminate nicety. That they acted with every degree of forbearance, charity and mildness, is conspicuous in their conduct towards the unfortunate Sawtre. This unhappy ecclesiastic was a bold impudent enthusiast; a recanter, a prevaricator, and frontless liar. When rector of Lynn, he was convicted of heresy, and retracted. The infection of heresy necessarily deprived him of his living; for it would have been inconsistency itself to have continued a man as the instructor of others, who was himself under the influence of error. On renouncing that error, we find him appointed to another situation, which does not display a vindictive or persecuting spirit on the part of the clergy; nor do their conduct in putting off his condemnation from time to time evince a sanguinary feeling towards him. Finding him obstinate, they had nothing left to do but to pronounce what he evidently was, a relapsed heretic, that is, a man wilfully attached to erroneous opinions—opinions which he must know, and which he had acknowledged, to be heretical. Having done this, they delivered him over to the officers of the civil power to do with him as the laws of the *state*, not of the church, authorized them. We agree with Dr. Lingard that it would perhaps have been better had Sawtre been confined in a madhouse instead of being burnt; but the king and the commons thought otherwise; they thought it best that the wretched man should be made a sacrifice to deter others from the like offence, and he suffered accordingly. Why such an outcry should be raised by the admirers of Fox's lies against this single statute by Henry IV. while so many bloody laws were passed against Catholics by Elizabeth and her successors, for no other cause than their adherence to truth and rejection of error, is somewhat incomprehensible. It must arise from the most stupid ignorance or the basest impudence, and when they have made their choice, there is plenty of cause to make them blush. During the whole space when Catholicism was in power, from the time of passing the act to the assumption of the spiritual supremacy by Henry 8th, embracing a period of more than 130 years, fewer persons suffered under the writ *de heretico comburendo* than in the last fifteen years of the first *spiritual* temporal head of the church of England. But it is time to see what kind of martyrs Fox has selected to grace his martyrologist and stamp credit on Wickliffe's doctrines.

MARTYRDOM OF THOMAS BADBY.

The first after Sawtree, named by the modern editors, is an inspired *tailor* of the above name, and is distinguished by the above title line. Fox writes,—" Thomas Badby was a layman, and by trade a tailor. He
" was arraigned in the year 1409 before the bishop of Worcester, and con-
" victed of heresy. On his examination he said, that it was impossible
" any priest could make the body of Christ sacramentally, nor would he
" believe it, unless he saw, manifestly, the corporal body of the Lord to
" be handled by the priest at the altar; that it was ridiculous to imagine
" that at the supper Christ held in his own hand his own body, and
" divided it among his disciples, and yet remained whole. . 'I believe,'
" said he, 'the omnipotent God in trinity; but if every consecrated host
" at the altars be Christ's body, there must then be in England no less
" than 20,000 gods.' After this he was brought before the archbishop
" of Canterbury at St. Paul's church, and again examined in presence
" of a great number of bishops, the duke of York, and several of the
" first nobility. Great pains were used to make him recant; but he
" courageously answered, that he would still abide by his former
" opinions, which no power should force him to forego. On this the
" archbishop of Canterbury ratified the sentence given by the bishop of
" Worcester. When the king had signed the warrant for his death, he
" was brought to Smithfield, and there being put in an empty tub, was
" bound with iron chains fastened to a stake, and had dry wood piled
" around him. And as he was thus standing in the tub, it happened
" the prince of Wales, the king's eldest son, was there present; who
" being moved with compassion, endeavoured to save the life of him
" whom the hypocritical Levites and Pharisees sought to put to death.
" He admonished and counselled him, that having respect unto himself,
" he should speedily withdraw himself out of these dangerous labyrinths
" of opinions, adding oftentimes threatenings, which might have daunted
" any man not supported by the true faith. Also Courtney, at that time
" chancellor of Oxford, preached unto him, and informed him of the
" faith of holy church. In the mean time, the prior of St. Bartholo-
" mew's, in Smithfield, brought with all solemnity the sacrament of
" God's body, with twelve torches borne before, and shewed the sacra-
" ment to the poor man at the stake. And then they demanded of him
" how he believed in it, he answered that he knew well it was hallowed
" bread, and not God's body. And then was the tun put over him, and
" fire put unto him. And when he felt the fire he cried. ' Mercy!' (call-
" ing upon the Lord), when the prince immediately commanded to take
" away the tun, and quench the fire. He then asked him if he would
" forsake heresy, and take the faith of holy church, which if he would
" do, he should have goods enough, promising him also a yearly pension
" out of the king's treasury. But this valiant champion of Christ,
" neglecting the prince's fair words, as also contemning all men's de-
" vices, refused the offer of worldly promises, being more inflamed by
" the spirit of God, than by any earthly desire. Wherefore, as he con-
" tinued immovable in his former mind, the prince commanded him
" straight to be put again into the tun, and that he should not after-
" wards look for any grace or favour. But as he could be allured by
" no rewards, he was not at all abashed at their torments, but, as a

" valiant soldier of Christ, persevered invincibly till his body was re-
" duced to ashes, and his soul rose triumphant unto him who gave it."

To this rodomontade account the modern editors have added the following note: " It will not be uninteresting to our town readers, to be
" informed, that that part of Smithfield where the large board contain-
" ing the laws and regulations of the market formerly stood, is the
" very spot on which their forefathers suffered for the cause of Christ.
" There many an English martyr's body mingled with dust; from
" thence ascended many a soul to inherit everlasting glory." So far
as the Wickliffites were concerned, we shall shew that the cause for
which they suffered was not that of Christ nor of Christianity, and the
reader must be informed that Catholic martyrs suffered in Smithfield
under the beastly Henry, who was the founder of that devastating thing
called the Reformation, in greater numbers than the fanatical disciples
of the Reformation so called. We agree with the author of the note
that many an English martyr's body there mingled with the dust, and
that many a soul ascended from thence to everlasting glory; but then
they were martyrs to the cause of truth, and not the enthusiast victims
of visionary theories.

But what shall we say to this learned tailor of the fifteenth century,
whose knowledge of divinity is here stated to have been so great as to
bear down all the clergy with the king and the duke of York to boot.
Why this reverend knight of the thimble must have excelled the famous tailor of Leyden, who, though he assumed the title of king of
Sion, does not appear to have been a cool disputant with divines, whose
lives had been spent in studying the fathers and exploring sacred history. But where did Fox, or his editors, find this narrative of the life,
behaviour, and death of this " valiant champion of Christ," Tom Badby, layman and tailor? We have looked into Stowe, Baker, Rapin,
Echard, and Lingard, but we can find no trace in their pages of any
such transaction. Nay, we have by us an edition of Fox, by a Rev.
Henry Southwell, LL. D. who does not mention our learned tailor. It
is true there is a History of England, by one Russell, a work scarcely
heard of, in which it is stated, that in the year 1410, " One Bodby a
" taylor took upon him to exclaim violently against the absurdity of
" the real presence in the sacrament. This person, therefore, was
" singled out by the clergy for exemplary punishment. He was ac-
" cordingly tried and condemned to the stake; and the prince of Wales
" had the curiosity to be a spectator of the execution. When the
" flames first reached the body of the criminal he cried out in so horrid
" a manner, that the prince ordered the fire to be removed, and offered
" the man his life, together with a pension out of his private purse, as
" the flames had disabled him from following his business, on condition
" he would renounce his opinions. Bodby, however shocked when he
" first felt the flames, he refused the offered pardon; he loved his opin-
" ions better than his life; and he was accordingly committed again
" to the fire, and there resigned his breath as a forfeit to his faith."—
For this account there is not the least voucher, and we may therefore
conclude, that as the most authentic writers are silent on the subject,
the story is a ficitious one.

That some of the circumstances connected with the tale, are spurious and self-made, we think, probable. Can it be supposed, for one moment, by any rational mind, that so much interest should be shewn towards an individual in so humble a station of life, by the king and the principal nobility, as well as the dignified clergy, as to honour him with a public examination in St. Paul's church? Then again, why is the *duke of York* introduced? Who was the duke of York of that day? Not a son of the King. reader, but one among the rest of the nobles, of no great eminence for talent or ability, that we read of. The whole story, the more it is examined, the more improbable it appears. The tailor is first arraigned before the bishop of Worcester, and convicted of heresy; then he is brought before the archbishop of Canterbury, and examined in the presence of the king and nobility, in St. Paul's church, when the sentence is ratified by the primate, and the warrant for his death signed by the king. Truly the tailor is a most important personage, that the ordinary process of the law was not sufficent to convict him, but the most extraordinary proceedings must be entered into to overcome his novelties and vagaries. Firm as the tailor was before the prelates and the monarch, when the fire began to warm him, we are told, his heart failed him and he cried out for mercy! A precious witness for the truth of the gospel to be sure! How different from the conduct of the primitive martyrs, and the Catholic sufferers under Protestant ascendency. These latter braved their torments, and scorned to cry for mercy from their persecutors. They gave testimony of the truth, by the invincible fortitude of their behaviour, nor did they rest their faith on their own fanciful reason, but learned it from the apostles and their successors.

The tailor, it is said, denied that any priest could make the body of Christ sacramentally, and "that it was ridiculous to imagine that at " the supper, Christ held in his own hand his own body, and divided it " among his disciples, and yet remained whole." Ridiculous as Tom Badby might suppose such doctrine to be, the learned fathers of the Catholic church, who derived their faith from the apostles themselves, who were present at this very supper, believed differently from John Fox's tailor. Their sentiments may be seen in the first volume of this work, pp. 40, 50, 91, 170, and we beg the reader will refer to them before he proceeds any further, and compare them with the ridiculous nonsense put into Badby's mouth. The mode of execution, as described by Fox, is ludicrous in the extreme, invented probably to please the taste of ignorant people, who delight in the marvellous, or borrowed from the tub-preachers of some sectarians.—At that time it was usual, we believe, to hang first and burn afterwards. At least such was the way in which Sir John Oldcastle suffered.

One word more, and we close with the tailor. From what is stated to have passed between the prince and Badby, it cannot be said that he was persecuted. Every mode of persuasion, it seems, was used to overcome the fellow's obstinacy. He was promised goods and a pension by the prince if he would but believe as all the world then believed, but as soon as he lost the pain of the fire, he became *inspired*, and renounced the " offer of worldly promises, being more inflamed by the " spirit of God than by any earthly desires." What cant and hypocrisy, to insinuate that a tailor, who must of necessity have been ignorant in the extreme, so far as literary knowledge was concerned, the use of letters being then chiefly confined to the clergy, and printing not invented; what hypocrisy, we say, what cant to represent this man as *inspired* of God, and the holder of the true faith, in opposition to the belief of the whole nation for upwards of eight hundred years. Really such rant is truly disgusting, and fit only for bedlamites.

The modern editors of Fox have been rather concise respecting the persecutions, as they are called, of the Wickliffites or Lollards, as they have confined themselves to two cases only, namely, this tailor Badby and Sir John Oldcastle, of whom we shall speak hereafter. Other editors of this martyrology, as well as Fox himself, however, have been more prolix, and the historians of England, with a single exception or so, have grossly misrepresented the conduct of the clergy and the then constituted authorities, in their proceedings to stem the torrent of sedition and rebellion rushing through the kingdom, and threatening destruction to civil society from the pernicious tendency of Wickliffe's doctrines.— These writers have studiously represented the question as one of religion, and the only opposition shewn as raised against the supposed encroachments and corruptions of the church of Rome. This, however, was not the case, as we shall proceed to shew, by a few instances it is our intention to cite from a work issued by Protestant hands, and therefore the less exceptionable to the generality of the people. In doing this we are influenced by a desire to disabuse the public mind, which has been so long led astray by interested writers, and is so little informed on those points of history which it is so important they should know, to be able to distinguish the truth. On no subject are the people of England less informed than on that of sacred history, and of profane too, where the interests of the Catholic church are concerned. The measures judged prudent and precautionary by our ministers and legislature in these days of Protestant enlightendeness to preserve order and regularity in the state are represented as sanguinary and persecuting, the offspring of a bloodthirsty religion and the invention of cruel churchmen in the days of Catholic darkness, though precisely of the same nature, and adopted for the same ends. The law of *de heretico comburendo*, though directed against heresy, was occasioned by the SEDITIOUS and TRAITOROUS tendency of those who imbibed the erroneous opinions, and though those who suffered might have been convicted of heresy, yet it must also be observed that they were guilty of TREASON and SEDITION, and suffered hanging for the latter crimes. This we shall proceed to prove by the following examples, which we have selected from a work we have before quoted, namely, *The History of King-killers; or, The Fanatic Martyrology*, published in the year 1720. The facts recorded therein are authenticated, and are stated to have been derived from another work written by a Church of England divine, the Rev. Mr. Earbery, and entitled, *The pretended Reformers; or The History of John Wickliffe*, &c. We beg the reader's serious attention to the statements made, and likewise to the remarks which the author makes on Fox, for introducing such desperate villains and barefaced hypocrites into his famous, or rather infamous, Book of Martyrs.

WILLIAM CLAYDON.

"This fellow was a currier by trade, but running mad with an enthusiastic spirit communicated to him by the followers of that known rebel sir John Oldcastle, he quitted his lawful profession to bear arms against his sovereign, king Henry V. in the year 1413. In relation to this man, the best account we find is in Walsingham, who speaking of Oldcastle, says thus, 'In the mean time, their leader and chief, sir John Oldcastle, 'coming abroad, sent a messenger to the lord Abergavenny, that he 'would be revenged of him for the injuries received; but he wisely 'preventing him, and departing from his castle at midnight, got so 'many men about him that sir John was obliged to fly again to his re-'treat; however, the lord Abergavenny took a priest of his, who con-'fessed where his arms, banners, &c. lay; and soon after was taken an 'old Lollard of the same gang, called William Claydon, who depending 'on the notions of his sect was become so mad, that being himself a 'layman, he pretended to confer holy orders on his son, and to make 'him a priest, and to celebrate mass in his house on the day of his mo-'ther's rising from childbed, for which he being apprehended, examined, 'and legally convicted, he was burnt in London. The reader is here to 'observe, that though this wretch was burnt as a heretic, he was taken 'in open rebellion, and must have died for the same if the crime of 'heresy, being a rebellion against God, had not taken place.' It is true Fox sets him down as a martyr, and on the same day, which does not in the least exempt him from this calendar, because nothing is more plain than that he was a rebel, and indeed Fox has been very free in canonizing any such if they came in his way, as is visible by a very considerable number of his martyrs, whom all historians acknowledge to have been traitors. As for the wild notions of this fanatic, more of them may be seen where we treat of others of his gang, and I believe any member of the church of England will be convinced of the brutality of this fellow, when he finds him taken in open rebellion, and practising an episcopal power, being himself an illiterate, graceless, and base currier."

WILLIAM MURLE.

"Thomas Walsingham, the author above quoted in the life of William Claydon, gives us the following short account of this William Murle, who was one of the same wicked gang with Claydon, last spoken of. 'This Murle, more closely following the opinions of John Old-'castle, had perfidiously been more vexatious to many of the orthodox 'than any other of his sect. And this fellow having been in St. Giles's 'Fields, and understanding that the king was coming thither, he with-'drew into the country for fear, and hid himself there. He had before 'made preparations for receiving the order of knighthood at the hands 'of sir John Oldcastle, to which purpose he had brought with him two 'fine horses, with rich furniture, adorned with gold, and a pair of gilt 'spurs in his bosom, for the same effect the which were found upon 'him when taken, soon after his flight from the field. Being dragged 'from his lurking place he was drawn, hanged, and burnt; an end 'which he well deserved. Among other things there was found upon 'him a list of the names of monks, which he had taken from the chan-

' ter of St. Alban's, and those monks he intended to have destroyed, in
' order to obtain, by the gift and donation of the aforesaid John Old-
' castle, the place and possessions of the monks of St. Alban's. Many
' others, as well priests as laymen, were taken, convicted, and con-
' demned for this conspiracy, and had like ends; most of whom died
' impenitent.' Thus Walsingham.

"This Murle was a maltster, of Dunstable, and having by that trade
acquired wealth, the same turned his brain, so as to entertain thoughts
of being a knight, and enjoying all the large possessions of the abbey of
St. Alban's, and all this by joining in rebellion with sir John Oldcastle.
The devil had blinded him, and being purse-proud, there was nothing
so heinous but what he could attempt to raise himself above his mean
state, and accordingly he was advanced to the gallows, the fittest preferment for such scoundrels. His life and death was at the same time
with William Claydon, the next above him."

SIR ROGER ACTON.

"The heresy of Wickliffe, for such Mr. Earbery has sufficiently
proved it to be, having spread itself in England, under the protection of
the duke of Lancaster, who favoured the same in order to exclude his
elder brother's son from the succession to the crown, and to usurp the
same himself, it occasioned, as the same author informs us, many seditions, murders, and rebellions, which we have not here room to mention. The same spirit, says Mr. Earbery, which began Wickliffe's reformation, animated his followers after his death, to rebel under sir John
Oldcastle in England, &c. Sir Roger Acton was one deeply engaged
in that rebellion.

"In the reign of king Henry V. and in the year 1413, the Wickliffian
heretics posted it up in writing on the church doors in London, that
there were an hundred thousand of them ready to rise up in arms against
such as opposed their sect. One sir John Oldcastle, called lord Cobham, for having married a kinswoman of that nobleman, was their chief,
having been before convicted of heresy, and made his escape out of
custody. This sir Roger Acton of whom we here speak, was engaged
with Oldcastle, and next to him in post. Their design was to murder
the king and his brothers, and to destroy all the religious houses in
London. The king having sufficient information of these practices, and
that the rendezvous of the rebels was appointed to be in the wood at St.
Giles's, came privately away from Eltham, where he had kept Christmas, to Westminster, on the day after the feast of the Epiphany, and
having ordered the lord mayor to keep the city gates shut, that the rebels in the city might not join those in the wood, went himself to the
said wood after midnight with a considerable body of men, where he
took above 80 men of that gang in armour, who being thus surprized
and not knowing by whom, all owned that they came to the lord Cobham. He and the rest, being thus disappointed, fled; but in the pursuit several of his men were killed or taken, of the latter, 69 were convicted as TRAITORS at Westminster, of which number, 37 were on
the 13th of January, drawn from the Tower of London to Newgate, and
so to St. Giles's, and there all hanged in a place called Ficket's field;
seven of them were also burnt with the gallows on which they hung.—

Some time after sir Roger Acton having skulked about and lain concealed among his party, was discovered and taken, and the fact being so notorious, that there was no difficulty to convict him; so that on the 10th of February he was drawn and hanged, and buried under the gallows. Though Fox in his Martyrology has given these and many others for martyrs, having found them no other than rebels, by the universal consent of all our historians, there is no reason why they should not have their due place here among the fanatic martyrs and king-killers, for to murder the king was their intention, and to involve the nation in blood and rapine under a false pretext of religion, the cloak for all rebellions. Walsingham and other ancient historians do inform us, that this sir Roger Acton was a very lewd fellow, reduced to beggary by his riotousness, and thus sought to recover himself by the spoil of his country."

WILLIAM MANDEVILLE AND RICHARD RUSSEL.

" The heresy of Wickliffe having spread abroad in several parts of England, and disposing the people to libertinism and rebellion, there were many executed at several times for the same. William Murle is one instance hereof on the fourth of February, and we shall hereafter speak of others in their proper places. The two saints we here treat of were of that gang, rank enthusiasts, and infatuated with the poison of those abominable doctrines. Being both obscure fellows, and their reign in villainy but short, we have only the following brief account of them in Stow. Soon after Easter, in the year 1414, being the 10th of king Henry the VIth, who was still in his minority, the lord protector was warned of an assembly of certain lewd persons, under pretence of religious minded men, to be assembled at Abington, wherefore he sent thither certain persons, and also rode thither himself, and there arrested the baily of the town, named William Mandeville, a weaver, the which was appointed for a captain, who had named himself Jack Sharp of Wigmer's Land in Wales, who being examined, confessed that he meant to have done many mischiefs, especially against priests, so that he would have made their heads as cheap as sheep's heads, that is to say, three or four a penny, or as some write, ten for a penny. Many of his accomplices were taken and sent to divers prisons. Their captain Mandeville was drawn, hanged and beheaded at Abington, and his head was sent to London, and set on the bridge; his other fautors were executed in divers places, and countries, to the terror of others.

" I here join to this scoundrel another like him, though he belongs to another day, because he is too inconsiderable to deserve a place to himself. Stow in the same place above quoted, goes on thus. Also the 13th of July, Richard Russel, woolman, was drawn, hanged and quartered, for that he would have made dukes and earls at his pleasure. Here we see the nature of wicked sectaries, who are wholly bent upon cruelty; Mandeville was for murdering of all clergy, which was the meaning of making their heads so cheap, and Russel could design no less than the destruction of the ancient nobility, to make room for his rabble of dukes and earls, and both could aim at no less than the slaughter of their sovereign, usurping such barbarous authority themselves."

ELEANOR COBHAM, DUCHESS OF GLOUCESTER.

" She was the daughter of Reginald Cobham, lord of Stirbrough, and
wife to Humphrey, duke of Gloucester. Having been infected with
the fanatic notions of John Wickliffe, she abandoned herself to all sorts
of wickedness, and associated with infamous persons. Among these
were Roger Bolinbroke, an astrologer, and Thomas Southwell, canon
of St. Stephen's chapel at Westminster, both of them reputed necro-
mancers; as also Margery Gurdemaine, commonly called the witch of
Eye, by whose sorceries it was then thought that the lady Eleanor, had
induced the duke of Glocester to love and marry her : all these persons
conspired to destroy king Henry VI. by sorcery or witchcraft, and
Roger Bolingbroke and Thomas Southwell being apprehended and examined, both of them confessed their guilt, and declared that what
they had done, had been at the instigation of the said duchess. For
this, Roger Bolingbroke did public penance on a scaffold, in St. Paul's
churchyard. On the Tuesday following, the duchess knowing herself
guilty, fled by night into the sanctuary at Westminster. Being cited,
upon the information of the parties aforesaid, to appear before Henry
Chicheley archbishop of Canterbury, Henry Beaufort bishop of Winchester, and cardinal John Kemp archbishop of York, and cardinal William
Aiscoth bishop of Salisbury, &c. in St. Stephen's chapel at Westminster,
to answer to twenty-eight articles of necromancy, witchcraft, sorcery,
heresy, and treason, she appeared accordingly, and Roger Bolingbroke
charging her with having employed him in those mischiefs, she was on
the 11th of August committed to the custody of sir John Steward, sir
William Rolfe, John Stanley, esq. and others, to be conveyed to the
castle of Leeds, there to remain till three weeks after Michaelmas.
Not long after she was indicted of high treason, in Guildhall in London, before the earls of Huntingdon, Stafford, Suffolk and Northumberland, the treasurer sir Ralph Cromwell, John Cornwall, lord Fanhope,
sir Walter Hungerford, and some judges of both benches. On the 21st
of October, she appeared in the chapel of St. Stephen at Westminster,
again, before Robert Gilbert, bishop of London, William Alnewick of
Lincoln, and Thomas Brown of Norwich, where Adam Molins, clerk of
the king's council, read the articles of sorcery and witchcraft laid to
her charge, whereof some she denied, and others she confessed. On
the 23d of October, she appeared again, and the witnesses against her
being examined, she was fully convicted. Being then asked, whether
she had any thing to object against the witnesses, she answered in the
negative, and submitted herself. On the 27th of October, she abjured
the articles, and was ordered to appear again on the 9th of November,
which she accordingly did, before the archbishop and others, and was
enjoined penance, which she performed as follows.

" On Monday the 13th of November, she went from Westminster
by water, and landed at the Temple bridge, whence she proceeded
through Fleet-street, with a wax candle of two pounds in her hand,
without an hood, but with a kerchief, to St. Paul's, where she offered
her taper at the high altar. On the Wednesday following, she landed
at the Swan in Thames-street, and went through Bridge-street, Grace-
church-street, &c. straight to Leaden-hall, and so to Christchurch by
Aldgate. On Friday she landed at Queen-hithe, and proceeded to Cheap-

side, to St. Michael's in Cornhill, in the same manner as aforesaid. At all these times the mayor, sheriffs, and tradesmen of London met and accompanied her. After all this she was committed to the custody of sir Thomas Stanley, so to remain during her life in the castle of Chester, having 100 marks a year allowed for her maintenance; but in the 22d year of king Henry the VI. she was removed to Kenilworth. Her pride, coveteousness, and lust, were the cause of her confusion.

"This is one as well as some others before mentioned, whom Fox has thought fit to canonize as a saint in his Book of Martyrs, and indeed we have here shown, that she was a king-killer in intention, though she could not compass her design, and being a practitioner in sorcery and witchcraft, she may well have a place among fanatic saints, such as many are of those transmitted to us by that latitudinarian writer. It is true, there are many at this time, who altogether explode all notions of sorcery or witchcraft, it is not our business to enter upon this controversy, but all the persons here mentioned having confessed their guilt in that crime, it must be supposed that they best knew what they had done, and whether they had really any compact with the devil or not, their confession sufficiently evinces, that they practised such things as they looked upon as charms, and that the end of the same was to destroy the king, which is enough to prove they were intentional regicides, and so far answers our purpose."

"MARTYRDOM OF SIR JOHN OLDCASTLE.

We come to another of John Fox's martyrs, of whom more has been said by historians than of the Tom Badby, and we shall therefore be better able to detect the falsehoods and misrepresentations of the martyrologist. But first let us have his account of the affair. "The persecu- "tions of the Lollards," he says, "in the reign of Henry V. were "owing to the cruel instigations of the clergy, who thought the most "effectual way to check the progress of Wickliffe's doctrine, would be "to attack the then chief protector of it, viz. Sir John Oldcastle, baron "of Cobham; and to persuade the king that the Lollards were en- "gaged in conspiracies to overturn the state. It was even reported, "that they intended to murder the king, together with the princes, his "brothers, and most of the lords spiritual and temporal, in hopes that "the confusion which must necessarily arise in the kingdom, after such "a massacre, would prove favourable to their religion. Upon this a "false rumour was spread, that sir John Oldcastle had got together "20,000 men in St. Giles's in the Fields, a place then overgrown with "bushes. The king himself went thither at midnight, and finding no "more than fourscore or a hundred persons, who were privately met "upon a religious account, he fell upon them and killed many. Some "of them being afterwards examined, were prevailed upon, by pro- "mises or threats, to confess whatever their enemies desired; and "these accused sir John Oldcastle.

"The king hereupon thought him guilty; and in that belief set a "thousand marks upon his head, with a promise of perpetual exemption "from taxes to any town which should secure him. Sir John was appre- "hended and imprisoned in the Tower; but escaping from thence, he "fled into Wales, where he long concealed himself. But being after-

"wards seized in Powis land, in North Wales, by Lord Powis, he was
"brought to London, to the great joy of the clergy, who were highly
"incensed against him, and resolved to sacrifice him, to strike a terror
"into the rest of the Lollards.—Sir John was of a very good family,
"had been sheriff of Hertfordshire under Henry IV. and summoned to
"parliament among the barons of the realm in that reign. He had
"been sent beyond the sea, with the earl of Arundel, to assist the duke
"of Burgundy against the French.   In a word, he was a man of extra-
"ordinary merit, notwithstanding which he was condemned to be
"hanged up by the waist, with a chain, and burned alive. This most
"barbarous sentence was executed, amidst the curses and imprecations
"of the priests and monks, who used their utmost endeavours to pre-
"vent the people from praying for him. Such was the tragical end of
"sir John Oldcastle, who left the world with a resolution and con-
"stancy, that answered perfectly to the brave spirit with which he had
"ever maintained the cause of truth and of his God.

"Not satisfied with his single death, the clergy induced the parlia-
"ment to make fresh statutes against the Lollards. It was enacted,
"among other things, that whosoever read the scriptures in English,
"should forfeit land, chattels, goods, and life; and be condemned as
"heretics to God, enemies to the crown, and traitors to the kingdom;
"that they should not have the benefit of any sanctuary; and that, if
"they continued obstinate, or relapsed after being pardoned, they
"should first be hanged for treason against the king, and then burned
"for heresy against God. This act was no sooner passed, but a violent
"persecution was raised against the Lollards; several of them were
"burnt alive, some fled the kingdom, and others were weak enough to
"abjure their religion, to escape the torments prepared for them."

Such is the account given by Fox or his modern editors; the reader,
by a comparison with the foregoing accounts of some of Oldcastle's
comrades, will be able to appreciate the credit due to the relation of
the martyrologist. As usual all is bare assertion; not a voucher has
he produced to prove the authenticity of the incidents he mentions, but
we are called upon to take for granted whatever he has thought proper
to advance. The time however is come, when facts must be produced
to obtain credit, and it would have been well for the people of England
had they always demanded unquestionable authority for the statements
of historians. With Catholic writers it has been the invariable rule to
lay down the source from whence any extraordinary circumstance has
been derived, in order that the suspecting party might satisfy themselves by a reference to the authority cited; while, on the other hand,
the oppugners of truth always shun plain and open dealing, and have recourse to trick and deception to make up what may be wanted of
common honesty. Such is the case with Fox in his account of the death
of sir John Oldcastle. He commences his tale by attributing the persecutions of the Lollards in Henry Vth's time, "to the cruel instigations
"of the clergy," who he says, "thought that the most effectual way
"to *check* the progress of Wickliffe's doctrines, would be to attack the
"then *chief protector* of them," this sir John Oldcastle, and "to *persuade*
"the king that the Lollards were engaged in conspiracies to overturn
"the state." We trust the people of England will no longer be *per-

suaded by Fox and "the few plain Christians," his modern editors, to take these gross perversions of history for genuine fact. Let us refer to dates, which are the best guides to come at disputed facts. Wickliffe's doctrines had been broached about fifty years, when sir John Oldcastle was apprehended. Several rebellions had been occasioned by their dissemination, during the reign of Henry's father, and his predecessor, Richard II. so that there could be no occasion for the clergy to *persuade* the king that conspiracies were *intended*, when he had himself the perfect knowledge that such had *actually* been entered into to dethrone his father, and were in progress to wrest the sceptre from himself. To charge the clergy, therefore, with being the instruments of *persecuting* a nest of traitors and plunderers, because these treason-hatchers had the adroitness to screen their lawless and wicked designs under a pretence of reforming *religion*, and purifying the morals of the clergy, is brazen impudence and mendacity in the extreme.

Henry, when prince of Wales, had joined the lords and commons in petitioning his father to arrest the progress of the preachers and punish them, as may be seen by searching the records of parliament. This fact is an indisputable proof of the lying qualities of Fox. Sir John Oldcastle had been one of the intimate companions of Henry in the follies of his youth, and on the reformation of the monarch on his coming to the crown, he was dismissed his presence, in consequence of the opinions he held and the immorality of his conduct. Henry therefore did not require the instigation of the clergy. Fuller (p. 168) tells that sir John Oldcastle was, among our more ancient dramatists, the debauched but facetious knight who now treads the stage under the name of sir John Falstaff. Thus we have the same personage pourtrayed by Fox as a "godly martyr," and by Shakspeare as a "beastly "debauchee." What an edifying saint to grace the martyrology of John Fox. To return, however, to the narrative. Fox says, the persons who were assembled in St. Giles's and surprised by the king, "were pri- "*vately* met upon a RELIGIOUS account," and that "he fell upon 'them and killed many." In contradiction to this gross falsehood, we refer the reader to the account of the death of Sir Roger Acton above, page 58, which is copied from Stow. Of the extraordinary merit of this notorious traitor we have before given an account; his death, which is represented to have been most tragical, was no other than what many others less deserving have undergone, without exciting the notice or pity of John Fox. The execution of this base villain took place when the king was engaged with his army in France, and is thus related by Dr. Lingard:—"But while the king was thus occupied with "the conquest in Normandy, a feeble attempt had been made to deprive "him of England. In consequence of a secret understanding between "the Scottish cabinet and the chiefs of the Lollards, the duke of Albany "and the earl Douglass suddenly crossed the borders, and laid siege, "the former to the castle of Berwick, the latter to that of Roxburgh. "It proved, however, a 'foul raid.' They had persuaded themselves "that the kingdom had been left without a competent force for its "protection: but when they learned that the dukes of Bedford and "Exeter were approaching at the head of one hundred thousand men, "they decamped with precipitation, and disbanded their armies. At

"the same time sir John Oldcastle emerged from his concealment,
"and arrived in the neighbourhood of London. The retreat of the
"Scots defeated all his projects. At St. Alban's he eluded by a preci-
"pitate flight the pursuit of his enemies: in the marches of Wales he
"was taken after an obstinate resistance by sir Edward Charlton, a
"retainer of the lord Powis. At the petition of the commons (the par-
"liament was then sitting) he was arraigned before the peers : the
"indictment on which he had been formerly outlawed, was read ; and
"he was asked in the usual form by the duke of Bedford, why he
"should not receive sentence of death. Instead of replying directly to
"the question, he preached a long sermon on one of the favourite doc-
"trines of his sect, that it is the duty of man to forgive, and to leave
"the punishment of offences in the hands of the Almighty. Being
"interrupted, and required to return a direct answer, he said that he
"would never acknowledge the authority of that court, as long as his
"liege lord, king Richard II. was alive in Scotland. Judgment was
"instantly pronounced; that he should be hanged as a traitor, and
"burnt as a heretic. St. Giles's fields, which had been the theatre of
"his rebellion, witnessed also his punishment. By his partisans he
"would have been revered as a martyr, had not their faith been stag-
"gered and scandalized by a non-accomplishment of a prophecy, which
"he was said to have uttered at the gallows, that he should rise again
"from the grave on the third day."

Looking at this account by Dr. Lingard, and that given by Fox, the
shameless mendacity of the latter is most conspicuous, and must make
the unprejudiced Protestant blush at the depravity of the mind that
could deliberately and purposely invent such brazen lies to vilify the
clergy of former times, who were the fathers of the people and the protectors of the poor. Alas! how have the people of England been deceived and beguiled, since the pretended Reformation, by the means of
the press. From the moment the spiritual supremacy was connected
with the state, the press became the instrument of forgery, falsehood,
misrepresentation, calumny, and fanaticism. By a long career of near
three hundred years in this wholesale system of iniquity, the people of
this country have been plunged into the densest mists of error and imposition. Thus the most palpable lies have been swallowed as indisputable facts ; the most depraved villains have been taken for the most
pious saints ; and the most humane and self-devoted order of religious
men for the most sanguinary and malignant miscreants. The time,
however, is rapidly approaching, when the rays of Truth will dispel
this dark gloom, and exhibit the hypocrites and falsifiers in all their
horrid deformity. In this relation of the death of sir John Oldcastle,
Fox, with his usual malice and want of veracity, has represented the
Catholic priests and monks as the bitterest enemies of the hoary traiter,
though it is clearly proved by Dr. Lingard and other authorities, that
he was arraigned at the petition of the representatives of the people,
and that he confessed himself a traitor to the reigning king. Fox also
states that he was hung "by the *waist* with a chain, and *burnt alive.*"
This statement, made for the purpose of exciting horror and indignation against the supposed cruelty and barbarity of our Catholic ancestors, is positively contradicted by Stow, who had better means of ascer-

A REVIEW

OF

𝕱𝖔𝖝'𝖘 𝕭𝖔𝖔𝖐 𝖔𝖋 𝕸𝖆𝖗𝖙𝖞𝖗𝖘,

CRITICAL AND HISTORICAL.

No. 31. Printed and Published by W. E. ANDREWS, 3, Chapter-house-court, St. Paul's Churchyard, London. Price 3d.

EXPLANATION OF THE ENGRAVING.—*This cut represents the mock marriage of Henry to Anne Boleyn by Dr. Lee, in the presence of Cranmer, before Catharine was divorced, of which we shall have occasion to remark hereafter.*

CONTINUATION OF THE REVIEW.

taining the fact than Fox. The former says, "he (sir John Oldcastle) " was hanged by the *neck* in a chain of iron, and AFTER consumed with " fire." Who, after this palpable detection, can believe the statements in this *Book of Martyrs?* Fox talks of Oldcastle's " resolution and con- " stancy," and his " *brave* spirit," but he does not note his *fanatical* spirit, which led him to predict his resurrection from death after the third day, which is recorded by Stow, and as Dr. Lingard observes, staggered not a few of his deluded disciples on finding his prophecy not fulfilled.

Fox next asserts that " not satisfied with his (Oldcastle's) *single* death, " the *clergy* induced the parliament to make fresh statutes against the " Lollards." In *whose* reign, and in *what* year, were these *fresh* statutes made? It was surely an easy task to have given chapter and verse by a reference to history and the statute book. He talks here of the *single* death of Oldcastle, after having recorded the martyrdoms, as he calls the death of Sawtre and Badby, and recounted the killings of many of Oldcastle's followers, as persecutions by the clergy. We have, from authentic testimony, named several traitors that suffered death for their crimes, and were classed as martyrs by Fox; how then can he here speak of only *one* single death, namely Oldcastle's? The insinuation is base and groundless, and like the rest of the assertions made by this lying martyrologist. For instance, he says, "it was enacted, among " other things, that whosoever *read* the scriptures in English, should " forfeit land, chattels, goods, and life; and be condemned as *heretics* " *to God, enemies to the crown,* and *traitors to the kingdom.*" Was ever such improbabilities before put forth for facts? People in general, at that time, were not able to read; but why not punish the *translators* and *copyists,* as well as the *readers?* If it was made *heresy* and *treason* merely to *read,* what ought to have been the crime and punishment of those who were the instigators of this heresy and treason? But who ever heard of the mere *readers* of the scriptures becoming heretics, and heretics to God too? What nonsense, sheer stupid nonsense. is this.— HERESY, as defined by Johnson, is " an opinion of private men differ- " ent from that of the Catholic and Orthodox church;" and a HERETIC, " one who *propagates* his *private* opinions in opposition to the Catholic " church." Now a man might *read* the scripture, as hundreds and thousands have read the sacred volume, and yet remain Catholics—sound orthodox Catholics; therefore to make it heresy and treason merely to read the bible is preposterous folly, and such as our Catholic ancestors, though they are said to have lived in the dark ages, would never have been guilty of. No, no; it was not the *reading* then, nor is it the *reading* now, of the scriptures, that the Catholic church objects to; it is the *misinterpretation* of the sacred text that she condemns; and it was the corruption of the meaning to traitorous purposes that caused our ancestors to pass the law *de heretico comburendo,* as we have shewn by indisputable facts, accompanied by the clearest testimony.

This account of the death of Oldcastle is self-contradictory in the extreme. Fox says that Oldcastle was burned alive, and in the same column he says the punishment of the Lollards was, to be hung *first* for treason against the king, and *then* burned for heresy against God.— Again, he says, there were *fresh statutes* made against the Lollards, and immediately after he speaks of only *one.* " *This act*" he writes, was " no sooner passed, but a violent persecution was raised against the " Lollards; several of them were burnt *alive,*" &c. Yet this very law, by his own statement, enacted that they should be hung in the first instance, and burned afterwards. Verily those who believe such a narrator as Fox, will believe any thing, however incredible and monstrous.

CONFESSION OF SIR JOHN OLDCASTLE.

Fox next proceeds to give an account of the religious creed of this infamous and debauched knight, Oldcastle. He says, " The following " is the confession of this *virtuous* and *true* Christian, which, from its " *clearness* and *simplicity,* is well worthy of remembrance. He com- " mences with the Apostles' creed thus:

" I believe in God the Father Almighty, maker of heaven and earth; " and in Jesus Christ his only Son our Lord, *which* was conceived by " the Holy Ghost, born of the Virgin Mary, suffered under Pontius Pi- " late, crucified, dead, and buried, went down to hell, the third day

" rose again from death, ascended up to heaven, sitteth on the right
" hand of God the Father Almighty; and from thence shall come again
' to judge the quick and the dead. I believe in the Holy Ghost, the
" *universal* holy church, the communion of saints, the forgiveness of
" sins, the uprising of the flesh, and everlasting life, amen.

" And for a more large declaration of this my faith in the *catholic*
" church, I steadfastly believe, that there is but one God Almighty, in
" and of whose godhead are these three persons, the Father, the Son,
" and the Holy Ghost, and that those three persons are the self-same
" God Almighty. I believe also, that the second person in this most
" blessed Trinity, in most convenient time appointed thereunto before,
" took flesh and blood of the most blessed Virgin Mary, for the safe-
" guard and redemption of the universal kind of man, which was before
" lost in Adam's offence.

" Moreover I believe, that the same Jesus Christ our Lord, thus
" being both God and man, is the only head of the whole Christian
" church, and that all those that have been or shall be saved, be mem-
" bers of this most holy church.

" Whereof the first sort be now in heaven, and they are the saints
" from hence departed.. These as they were here conversant, conformed
" always their lives to the most holy laws and pure examples of Christ,
" renouncing Satan, the world, and the flesh, with all their concupis-
" cence and evils.

" The other sort are here upon earth, and called the church militant.
" For day and night they contend against crafty assaults of the devil,
" the flattering *prosperities* of this world, and the rebellious filthiness
" of the flesh."

Such is the confession which the *modern* editors of Fox have put into
the mouth of sir John Oldcastle, traitor, heretic, and martyr, which they
are pleased to describe as " well worthy of remembrance," from " its
clearness and simplicity." But, reader, though sir John *might* make
this confession, it was not the creed he always held, and he made other
acknowledgments, which it did not suit the convenience of the " few
plain Christians" to make public. These modern editors set forth that
their purpose in publishing this *Book of Martyrs*, was to " diffuse a
" knowledge and love of the genuine principles of Christianity;" but
they have taken special care to SUPPRESS in this edition, many other
things which Fox admitted in his original work, and other editors have
inserted in their editions of the Martyrology. Before we notice these
suppressions, we will here ask the modern editors, by *whose* authority
did they change the word *Catholic* for " *universal*" in the apostles'
creed ? Sir John Oldcastle, we are sure, never made use of the term
" universal," nor could there be any occasion for it in their edition, as
they allow that he professed the CATHOLIC faith in his confession. Now
the Catholic faith *then* was the *same* as the Catholic faith *now*, and consequently cannot be the Protestant faith, if the endless diversities of sects
into which Protestantism is divided can be called *faith*. But what will
the reader say of John Fox, and John Oldcastle, and Fox's modern editors, when we inform him that this valiant martyr, this *virtuous* and
true Christian, professed his belief in the *real presence* of the sacrament
of the Eucharist, and also many other tenets of the Catholic church,

which Protestants deny? One of the editors of Fox, in his edition, remarking on the confession of faith made by Oldcastle, says, "the " *sincere* Lollards had rather *confused notions* of the gospel; and it " appears from some remarks of lord Hale's, that they were not *all* of ʺ the *same* sentiments." Men of common sense, what do you think of this! The *sincere* Lollards had *confused notions*. Well, then, what were they but men tossed to and fro with every wind of doctrine, and not the disciples of that church built upon a rock, that was to remain unchangeable to the end of time. They were not *all* of the *same* sentiments; then they had none of the marks of TRUTH with them, which is always the same, and ever will be the same, as long as time endureth. To declare that men *disagreed* in their sentiments, that they had *confused notions*, and yet followed TRUTH, is an outrage to common sense, and deserves universal reprobation.

We have had occasion to speak of the reply of father Parsons to this lying compilation of Fox, who wrote while John was living. On this subject of the Wickliffian heresy and Oldcastle's confession, the learned father is so plain and argumentative, that we should not do justice to his memory and great talents were we not to record his remarks. By so doing too, we furnish a clear proof of the consistency of the defenders of the Catholic faith, who in every age and of every nation, followed the *same* rule, and consequently wrote, with the *same* spirit, namely, that of Truth. Examine the works of the Catholic controvertists from the time of the apostles and evangelists to the present day, and you will find sincerity in their language, without any confusion of notions or diversity of sentiments, on whatever concern the revealed truths of religion. This test of unity no class of sectarians can boast, and therefore they can have no more claim to the truths of the gospel than the heathen or publican.

We have given a picture of some of the most prominent martyrs, as Fox calls them, of the Wickliffian faction, from which the reader has learned that they were traitors to their king, and disturbers of the country's peace; this picture is not only confirmed by father Parsons, but he goes further into the conduct of Sir John Oldcastle, and proves that he was not only a traitor, but a self-convicted heretic. Parsons writes :—ʺ But there is yet another point worse than this; which is, that " he (Fox) doth not only allow of the religion of these men, but defendeth " also and justifieth their life and actions in what case soever; and though " never so orderly and lawfully condemned by the church or state of " those days, yea, though they were convinced to have conspired the " king's murder, and ruin to the state, or had broken forth into open " war and hostility against the same. As did sir John Oldcastle (by ⸰" his wife called lord Cobham) sir Roger Acton and many other their " followers, in the first year of king Henry V. which story you may " read in John Stow truly related out of Thomas Walsingham, and " other ancient writers.

" He setteth down also without blushing (I mean Fox) as well the " records of the Chancery, as the act of parliament itself, whereby they " were condemned of open treason, and confessed rebellion; for which " sixty-nine were condemned in one day by public sentence; and yet " doth the mad fellow take upon him to excuse and defend them all

" by a long discourse of many leaves together, scoffing and jesting as
" well at their arraignment and sentence given, as also at the act of
" parliament holden at Leicester, *anno* 2, *Hen*; 5, *cap*. 7. and in the year
" of Christ 1415. And after all he setteth forth, in contempt of this
" public judgment, a great painted pageant or picture of those that
" were hanged for that open fact of rebellion in St. Giles's Field in
" London, as of true saints and martyrs; namely, of sir Roger Acton
" and others, *p*. 540. And some leaves after that again, he setteth out
" another particular pageant of the several execution of sir John Old-
" castle, with this title: 'The Description of the cruel Martyrdom of
" Sir John Oldcastle, Lord Cobham.' And more than this, he appointeth
" unto them their several festival days in red letters, (which were the
" days of their hanging) as unto solemn martyrs. The first upon the
" sixth of January, with this title; 'Sir Roger Acton, Knight, Martyr:'
" and the other upon the fifth of February, with this inscription in his
" Calendar; 'Sir John Oldcastle, Lord Cobham, Martyr.' Whereby
" we may see that these men do not measure things as they are in
" themselves, but as they serve to maintain their faction.

" And it is further to be noted, that albeit these two rebellious
" knights (Acton and Oldcastle) besides all other their convicted crimes
" did make public profession of a far different faith from John Fox (as
" may be seen by the confessions and protestations set down by Fox him-
" self) yea, and the latter of them also did openly recant all the errors
" and heresies that he had held before; yet notwithstanding will not
" Fox so let them go, but perforce will have them to be of his church,
" whether they will or no. It would be over long to rehearse many
" examples; some few shall you have for a taste.

" Page 512. Fox setteth down the protestation of sir John Old-
" castle with this title; 'The Christian belief of the Lord Cobham.'
" By which title you may see that he liketh well of his belief, and
" holdeth it for truly Christian. Well, mark what followeth! When,
" after other articles about the Blessed Trinity, and Christ's Deity, sir
" John Oldcastle cometh to treat of the sacrament of the altar, he pro-
" testeth thus: 'And forasmuch as I am falsely accused of a misbelief
" in the sacrament of the altar, I signify here to all men that this is my
" faith concerning that: I believe in that sacrament to be contained
" very Christ's body and blood, under the similitudes of wine and bread,
" yea, the same body that was conceived of the Holy Ghost, born of the
" Virgin Mary, hung on the cross, died and was buried, arose the third
" day from the dead, and now is glorified in heaven. This was his
" confession, and is related here by Fox: and will Fox agree to this,
" think you? It may be he will, for that he saith nothing against it at
" all in this place.

" But some leaves after, repeating another testimonial of the said
" Oldcastle's belief, witnessed by his own friends, concerning this
" article, he writeth thus: 'Furthermore he believeth that the blessed
" sacrament of the altar is verily and truly Christ's body in the form of
" bread. Upon which words Fox maketh this commentary in the
" margin: 'In form of bread, but not without bread, he meaneth.'
" Yea, John, is that his meaning? How than standeth this with his
" former words, 'Under the similitudes of bread and wine?' Is the

" similitude of bread true bread? Who seeth not this silly shift of
" a poor baited Fox, that cannot tell whither to turn his head? But
" mark yet a far worse shift!

" Sir John Oldcastle shewing his belief about three sorts of men, the
" one of saints now in heaven, the second in purgatory, the third here
" militant upon earth, saith thus: 'The holy church I believe to be
" divided into three sorts or companies; whereof the first are now in
" heaven, &c. the second sort are in purgatory, abiding the mercy of God,
" and a full deliverance of pain; the third upon earth, &c. To this speech
" of purgatory, Fox thought best (lest it might disgrace his new mar-
" tyr) to add this parenthesis of his own, ' (if any such place be in the
" scriptures, &c.)' And by this you may perceive how he proceedeth
" in all the rest, to wit, most perfidiously, like a Fox in all.

" Furthermore, he setteth down at length a very ample and earnest
" recantation of the said sir John Oldcastle, taken out of the records,
" as authentically made as can be devised. Wherein he thus protested:
" ' In nomine Dei. Amen. I John Oldcastle, denounced, detected and
" convicted of and upon divers articles favouring heresy and error, &c.
" I, being evil seduced by divers seditious preachers, have grievously
" erred, heretically persisted, blasphemously answered, and obstinately
" rebelled, &c.' And having recounted at length all his former con-
" demned and heretical opinions, he endeth thus: 'Over and besides all
" this, I John Oldcastle, utterly forsaking and renouncing all the afore-
" said errors and heresies, and all other like unto them, lay my hand
" here upon this book and evangel of God, and swear, that I shall never
" more from henceforth hold these aforesaid heresies, nor yet any other
" like unto them wittingly, &c.' All which recantation and abjuration
" being related by John Fox, he saith nothing at all against it, but
" only that it was devised by the bishops without his consent; alleging
" no one author, witness, writing, record, reason, or probable conjec-
" ture for proof thereof, but followeth the fond shift before touched by
" me against the Magdeburgenses of him that being accused of heinous
" crimes, bringeth in first the best witnesses of all the city to prove
" the same against himself, and then answereth all with only saying,
" ' that they are liars, and know not what they say.' "

In conclusion, we beg the reader to refer to the confession put into
the mouth of sir John Oldcastle by the modern editors of Fox, (see p.
67) and the declaration quoted by father Parsons from the original
work of Fox above. It will be seen by the latter, that sir John, this
"virtuous and true Christian," held that the church was divided into
three sorts or companies, the second sort being in a _middle_ state or purgatory; but this article of his belief is studiously left out in the latter,
and he is made to name expressly but _two_ sorts. This palpable contradiction; this barefaced suppression of a material fact in the original
work, by the modern editors is sufficient to stamp their character for
veracity, and consign them to the too numerous company of _falsifiers_
produced by the pretended Reformation. It is clear from the words of
father Parsons, that when Wickliffe began to dogmatize, the belief of
whole Christendom was, that of the Catholic faith, and that he and his
disciples were _not_ Protestants, because they held doctrines which Protestants deny.—The real presence, the invocation of saints, purgatory,

and the seven sacraments, were then, as now, articles of Catholic faith, though rejected by Protestants. Tithes, surplice fees, benefices, oblations, and every emolument pertaining to temporal aggrandizement are now maintained by Protestants of the church as by law established, though these were disputed by Wickliffe and the Lollards; yet are they ranked by Fox and his editors as virtuous and true Christians, and godly martyrs, while authentic history represents them as the most depraved and perfidious traitors. If to disturb the peace of society, by the propagation of seditious doctrines; if to rebel against the lawful authorities of the state, from motives of faction; if to set father against son; brother against brother; if to involve the country in murder and strife, and violate all the principles of charity, be the essence of Christianity, why then Wickliffe and his disciples were true and virtuous Christians. But that flame could not be the light of the gospel which only blazed like a meteor, and was heard of no more; nor is its appearance known now but only by the evils produced by its exhalations. To sum up the true causes of Wickliffe's doctrine, so highly extolled by Fox, they were, 1st. A desire of revenge against the bishops and the clergy, on the part of Wickliffe, in consequence of his being deprived of a benefice in Oxford, which he had possessed unjustly. 2dly. He was moved with envy against monks, together with a desire of gaining over the duke of Lancaster, who had an eye to the crown, and his followers, by teaching them that it was lawful to invade church livings at their pleasure; and 3dly. The duke and his adherents were stirred up by the same motives of ambition, covetousness, and emulation against the bishops and clergy. These causes we gather out of Stow and Walsingham, and they are confirmed by the general voice of all the world. The opinions of Wickliffe were condemned by the whole universal church as heretical; and the parliaments of Richard II. and Henry IV. who best knew their lives, condemned his followers by their public acts, for " hypocrites, seditious, and pernicious people in manners." Here then we close our remarks on the Wickliffites, having, we flatter ourselves, satisfactorily established the real character of this class of Fox's Martyrs.

GREAT SCHISM IN THE CHURCH OF ROME.

During the heresy of Wickliffe, the Christian church was afflicted with schism, originating from the ambition of some of the cardinals, and the loose conduct of others, which pope Urban VI. was desirous of reforming. The schism was noticed by Fox, in his account of the proceedings against Wickliffe, but we passed it over, rather than interrupt the order of the subject.—Fox imputes this event to the providence of God, in favour of the progress of truth, and lest it might be thought that there was some failure of the promises of Christ in the church of Rome, we have deemed it right to place the martyrologist's account upon record, and a counter-relation of the affair after it, that the reader may be allowed to judge for himself, how far Fox is entitled to credit. He writes under the above head. "A circumstance occurred at this period, " by the providence of God, which greatly tended to facilitate the progress " of truth. This was a great schism in the church of Rome, which origi- " nated as follows : After the death of Gregory XI. who expired in the

" midst of his anxiety to crush Wickliffe and his doctrines, Urban VI. suc-
" ceeded to the papal chair. This pope was so proud and insolent,
" and so intent on the advancement of his nephews and kindred, which
" he frequently accomplished by injuring other princes, that the great-
" est number of his cardinals and courtiers deserted him, and set up
" another pope against him, named Clement, who reigned eleven years.
" After him Benedict the Thirteenth, who reigned twenty-six years.
" Again, on the contrary side, after Urban the Sixth, succeeded Boni-
" face the Ninth, Innocent the Eighth, Gregory the Twelfth, Alexander
" the Fifth, and John the Thirteenth. To relate all the particulars of
" this miserable schism, would require volumes ; we shall merely take
" notice of a few of the principal occurrences from which the reader
" may form an idea of the bloodshed and misery brought on the Chris-
" tian world by the ambition and wickedness of these pretended repre-
" sentatives of our blessed Saviour ; and may judge how widely they
" departed from his blessed maxims of peace and goodwill to all men.
" Otho, duke of Brunswick and prince of Tarentum, was taken and
" murdered. Joan, his wife, queen of Jerusalem and Sicily, who had
" sent to pope Urban, beside other gifts, 40,000 ducats in gold, was
" afterwards, by his order, committed to prison, and there strangled.
" Many cardinals were racked, and tortured to death ; battles were
" fought between the rival popes, in which great multitudes were slain.
" Five cardinals were beheaded together, after long torments. The
" bishop of Aquilonensis, being suspected by pope Urban, for not riding
" faster when in his company, was slain on the spot by the pope's order.
" Thus did these demons in human form torment each other for the
" space of thirty-nine years, until the council of Constance."

Fox here insinuates that it would require volumes " to relate all the
" particulars of this miserable schism," and he goes on to tell us that
cardinals were racked and put to death, battles were fought, and murders committed by " these demons in human form," namely, the popes
or anti-popes, for we are left to conjecture, as it cannot be supposed
that all these horrible crimes are to rest upon Urban's shoulders, though
he is the only pope accused by name. We cannot tell from whence
Fox borrowed his testimony, as he has given us no reference, according to custom, but we have no hesitation in pronouncing the statement
to be a tissue of falsehoods, excepting that a schism *did* exist. We
have looked into the authorities within our reach, but we cannot find
any allusion to the horrible transactions related by Fox, and we think it
very improbable, that had five cardinals been *beheaded* together, such
a circumstance would have escaped their notice. Fox represents
Urban as a monster of cruelty and injustice ; other authors, who are
more entitled to credit, give a different version of his character.—The
Rev. Mr. Reeve, in his *History of the Christian Church*, says of Urban,
that he was " famed for his knowledge of the canon law, devout, humble, and disinterested ; an enemy to simony, zealous for justice and
purity of morals ; virtuous and learned himself, he encouraged virtue
and learning in others.—The abuses committed by the agents and
officers of the court of Rome, long had been the subject of complaint.
A laudable zeal for effecting a reform, carried the religious pontiff to a
degree of severity which was thought imprudent. In his exhortations

and reprimands, he spared not the cardinals themselves. They felt the justness of his animadversions, but rather than curtail their luxuries of life, they chose to throw the whole church into confusion." Thus then, it appears that this schism did not arise from the injustices of Urban, but from his desire, his too anxious wish, to have those abuses removed, which had crept into the court over which he presided. The cardinals fled from him, not for his cruelty, but for his honesty. He was a reformer of real abuses, and therefore it was not to be wondered that he should meet with opposition from those who stood in need of reform; nor can we be surprised that his meritorious intentions are misrepresented by those who delight in calumny and falsehood.—As to the murders of dukes and cardinals and queens, the falsity of these charges are too glaring to need refutation. That there was a schism in the church at this period is not denied, but a schism is not a failure of orthodoxy. Though there might be a doubt as to the canonical head of the church, there was not the slightest disagreement as to the articles of faith propounded. The fact is, there was a dispute among the clergy respecting who was the rightful head of the church, and some nations adhered to one claimant, and some to the other; but during the space of this contention about the headship, there was not a division on doctrine, save and except the heresy of Wickliffe, which was not of that nature to require the convening of a general council, the guardians of the church in England, that is, the ecclesiastical hierarchy of the kingdom, being deemed sufficient. Subsequently, the errors spreading on the continent, and the schism continuing, the council of Constance assembled to put an end to one, and give judgment on the other.

This council met on the 5th day of November, in the year 1414, and like the other general councils of the Catholic church, was composed of the most eminent prelates and divines from Italy, Germany, France, Spain, and England. Here then we have a tangible proof of the existence of *a church*, that should be a judge and a guide to those who were unruly and in error. Our blessed Saviour told his disciples, as the gospel of St. Matthew informs us, that when any dissension took place, as was natural among human beings, an appeal was to be made to THE CHURCH, and, when the church had decided, those who refused to hear her were to be considered as heathens or publicans; that is, cut off from her communion, and deprived of the spiritual blessings her Divine Founder had commissioned her to dispense. Now if there had been no authority to decide on this schism, it would have lasted till this day, and in all probability exhibited the same features we now behold in Protestantism—an endless division of sectarians, and an innumerable number of unbelievers. But here, as we before observed, we have a proof of the Divine hand, in the protection of his church. She was threatened with a division of the seamless garment, but her guardians assembled, under the protection of the Holy Spirit, in the city of Constance, overtures were made to settle the matter amicably, the parties would not consent, they were deposed, a new pope was elected, the whole universe acknowledged the choice, and a termination was put to the jarrings that had too long distracted the peace of the church, but had never shook her faith. Thus then, by the Providence of God, to use the words of Fox, that event which the enemies of Truth had anticipated would prove the downfall of the Church, was the means of establishing her solidity in the eyes of the world, and from that day to this moment schism never infected the centre of supremacy.

THE CHURCH.

Upon this Rock I will build my Church; and the gates of Hell shall not prevail against it.—Matt. xvi. 18.

THE REFORMATION.

WE now enter upon the most important epoch of English, we may say general, History that can interest the mind, and shall have to detail a series of events, some highly expressive of the divine nature of the Catholic church, and others declaratory of the evils attending an unbridled sway of the human heart. We are aware that one of the most extraordinary and able writers of the age has preceded us in this portion of our labours, but as he does not intend to enter into the *doctrinal* part of the subject; as the line he has drawn out for himself is to be confined to the *political* evils and the *earthly* miseries brought on the people of England by this great revolution in the religion and constitution of the country, we shall not interfere much with each other's pursuits, as it will be our duty to detect the manœuvres practised by the interested slaves of faction and irreligion to draw the unsuspecting from the road to Heaven, while our highly gifted cotemporary will point out the means adopted to fleece them on earth. But let it not be understood that we purpose to exclude from our history the great political changes that took place in the progress of the creeds, which have, in part, supplanted the ancient faith. Such is not our intention. We have undertaken to examine and criticise the most material facts recorded of the Reformation in the late edition of *Fox's Book of Martyrs*, and it will be our duty to follow the author, step by step, as we have hitherto done by his preceding statements, through this eventful period. In the performance of this task we shall meet with many facts so interwoven with divinity and politics, that it will be impossible to separate them without making the history incomplete. We shall therefore endeavour to elicit the TRUTH in the best manner we can, and rely upon the candour and good sense of the reader for our reward.

PROGRESS OF THE REFORMATION UNDER HENRY VIII.

Under this head or title Fox ushers in his narrative of king Henry's reign. He commences with these words;—"The reader will, doubt-" less, attend to the transactions recorded in his reign, with peculiar in-" terest. It was in this period that God, through the instrumentality " of the king, *liberated* this country from the *Papal yoke*, when Eng-" land became as it were, a RELIGIOUS WORLD dependant on itself." He then goes on to notice the termination of the civil wars between the two houses of York and Lancaster, by the accession of Henry the Seventh, who married the princess Elizabeth, heiress of the house of York, by whom he had Henry the Eighth, "the instrument under God," Fox says but he should have said the great enemy of mankind, by which this country was separated from the universal Church of Christ. Fox then mentions the popular actions of the latter Henry on coming to the throne, his disgracing and punishing Empson and Dudley, the ministers of his father's avarice, and his great acquirements in literature and the sciences. Amidst these many good qualities, Fox tells us he was open to flattery, and with his usual malice towards the clergy of that day, he charges them with administering this subtle poison in copious draughts. He also records Henry's entering the list of controversy with Luther, by writing a work on the seven sacraments of the Catholic church, for which the pope bestowed upon him the title of *Defender of the Faith*, still retained by the sovereigns of these realms, though the modern editors say in a note "absurdly enough." This work of Henry's is still in circulation, and is held in repute. Luther wrote an answer, but with such coarse language and invective, as gave scandal to his friends and joy to his enemies. Ass, blasphemer, liar, were some of the epithets bestowed upon the royal author. Henry complained to the German reformer's patron, and the princes of that country considering Luther's work an insult to crowned heads, he was induced to write an apology, and offered to write a book in the king's praise. The apology, however, did not please the king, because Luther hinted that Henry was not the author of the Defence of the Seven Sacraments, and that he was beginning to favour the new doctrine. He accordingly wrote an answer to Luther, and avowed himself the author of the work which bore his name. This exasperated Luther, and in a boiling rage he publicly announced his regret that he had stooped to apologize to Henry. Such was the result of the dispute between Henry and Luther. Fox next gives us a " character " of cardinal Wolsey," and " the manner of promotion to bishoprics and " abbeys;". the latter having but little relation to the main subject we shall pass over. Wolsey may certainly be ranked the first instrument of the reformation, as it is called, he being the principal instigator of that coldness which ensued between Henry and his virtuous queen Catharine, after nineteen years affectionate cohabitation. The cardinal was proud, aspiring, ambitious, witty, revengeful, and malicious. Catharine, who was a woman of irreproachable conduct, devout without ostentation, and endowed with skill and penetration, could not endure the cardinal; and her nephew Charles V. refusing to grant this ambitious churchman the archbishopric of Toledo, to which he aspired as well as to the popedom, Wolsey determined to be revenged of the nephew, who was out of his reach, by seeking the ruin of the aunt. He therefore, Camden says, " caused a scruple to be put in the king's head that his present marriage with queen Catharine, who before had been his brother's wife, was forbidden by the law of God.

It was Wolsey too who first set the work of dissolution on foot, by obtaining several grants from the king and the pope to suppress about forty monasteries, and appropriate their revenues to the erecting and supporting two noble colleges he had projected at Ipswich and Oxford. Although there was a sensible difference in the motives of this measure and the general destruction of the religious houses, which afterwards followed, yet if we may be allowed to hazard an opinion on the dispensations of Providence, the proceedings of Wolsey were offensive to the throne of Heaven.

Stow says, the monasteries suppressed by the cardinal were of "good fame and bountiful hospitality," and he relates the following disastrous consequences which befell the principal actors in this work of suppression. "In the executing of this business, five persons were his chief "instruments, who on a time made a demand to the priory and convent "of the monastery of Daventry, for occupying of certain of their grounds, "but the monks refusing to satisfy their requests, straightway they "picked a quarrel against the house, and gave information to the "cardinal against them, who taking a small occasion, commanded the "house to be dissolved, and to be converted to his new college, but of "this irreligious robbery done of no conscience, but to patch up pride, "which private wealth could not furnish, what punishment hath since "ensued at God's hands (says mine author) partly ourselves have seen, "for of these five persons, two fell at discord between themselves, and the "one slew the other, for the which, the survivor was hanged : the "third drowned himself in a well : the fourth being well known, "and valued worth two hundred pounds, became in three years so "poor, that he begged till his dying day : and the fifth, called doctor "Allan, being chief executor of these doings, was cruelly maimed in "Ireland, even at such time as he was a bishop : the cardinal falling "after into the king's grievous displeasure, was deposed, and died "miserably : the colleges which he meant to have made so glorious a "building, came never to good effect : the one at Ipswich clean pulled "down, and the other in Oxford unfinished : and pope Clement himself, "by whose authority these houses were thrown down to the ground, "was after inclosed in a dangerous seige within the castle of St. Angelo "in Rome by the imperials, the city of Rome was pitifully sacked, "and himself narrowly escaped with his life." Such was the beginning of the work of reformation, as it is called, but which is more properly stiled the deeds of devastation, and such was the end of the performers in this first scene of the drama.

The next subject we find in Fox is the imprisonment of Hun for heresy, and his *murder*, as he terms it. This circumstance is not connected with the reformation, still we must notice it, as it shews the glaring disregard of truth in this instance as in numerous others which we have detected. Fox says,—"Not long after this (alluding to "a pretended contest concerning ecclesiastical immunity"), an event "occurred, that was productive of great consequence. Richard Hun, "a merchant in London, was sued by his parish-priest for a mor- "tuary in the legate's court ; on this, his friends advised him to sue the "priest in the temporal court for a præmunire for bringing the king's "subjects before a foreign and illegal court. This incensed the clergy "so much that they contrived his destruction. Accordingly, hearing "that he had Wickliffe's bible in his house, he was upon that put in the "bishop's prison for heresy ; but being examined upon sundry articles, "he confessed some things, and submitted himself to mercy ; upon "which they ought, according to the law, to have enjoined him "penance, and discharged him, this being his first crime ; but he could "not be prevailed on by the terror of this to let his suit fall in the tem-

" poral court; so one night his neck was broken with an iron chain,
" and he was wounded in other parts of his body, and then knit up in his
" own girdle; and it was given out that he had hanged himself; but the
" coroner's inquest, by examining the body, and by several other evi-
" dences, particularly by the confession of the sumner, gave their ver-
" dict, that he was murdered by the bishop's chancellor, Dr. Horsey,
" and the bell-ringer. The spiritual court proceeded against the dead
" body, and charged Hun with all the heresy in Wickliffe's preface to
" the bible, because that was found in his possession; so he was con-
" demned as an heretic, and his body was burnt. The indignation of
" the people was raised to the highest pitch against this action, in which
" they implicated the whole body of the clergy, whom they esteemed
" no more their pastors, but barbarous murderers. The rage went so
" high that the bishop of London complained, that he was not safe in
" his own house. The bishops, chancellor, and sumner were indicted
" as principals in the murder. In parliament an act passed, restoring
" Hun's children; but the commons sent up a bill concerning his mur-
" der, which was laid aside by the peers, where the spiritual lords had
" the majority."
    This account, we find is not from Fox, reader, though it is fastened
upon him by the modern editors; but is extracted from " The Abridg-
" ment of the History of the Reformation of the Church of England, by
" GILBERT BURNET, D.D." an author of equal veracity as Fox, and
as great a liar and romancer. The event is here said to have been productive of *great* consequences, yet so little was the death of Hun thought
of by our most popular historians, that Rapin, who was a Calvinist, and
has enlarged a great deal on the supposed persecutions of the Catholic
clergy, takes no notice of the circumstance at all; neither does Mr.
Echard, who was a divine of the established church, make mention of
Hun's death; and Dr. Lingard in his recent admirable history notices it
but slightly, as a legend unauthenticated. Stow says nothing of the barbarous circumstances narrated by Burnet, nor of the trial of the bishop,
&c. He merely says,—" Richard Hun, a merchant tailor, of London,
" dwelling in the parish of St. Margaret, in Bridge-street, who (for deny-
" ing to give a mortuary, such as was demanded by the parson for his
" child being buried) had been put in the Lollards tower, about the end
" of October last, was now the 6th of December, found hanged with his
" own girdle of silk in the said tower, and after he was burned in Smithfield." This was in the year 1514, and the 6th of Henry's reign. We are
not going to justify the treatment of this man, because the circumstances
are not clearly before us, and the authority of *Burnet*, who, by the by,
was a bishop of William the Dutchman's making, we believe, and the
originator of that huge debt which now presses the country to the
ground, and steeps the people in misery and poverty, is no authority at
all, seeing he neither gives *dates* nor *names*. Is it to be supposed that
a murder so circumstantially related by Burnet, and attended with
such horrid cruelties, would not have been more minutely detailed by
Stow, if the circumstances had been true? There cannot be a doubt
but he would have noticed it more fully, especially if the indignation
of the people had been so great as to implicate the WHOLE BODY
of the clergy. The story is evidently a tissue of falsehoods, interwoven

with a simple fact, and fabricated for the express purpose of inflaming the people against the ancient religion of the country. That our conjecture is true there is every reason to suppose, and we are sure the reader will agree with us when he has read the following article from this *Book of Martyrs*.

"PERSECUTION OF THE LOLLARDS.

"In the beginning of this reign, several persons were brought into "the bishops' courts for heresy, or Lollardism. Forty-eight were ac- "cused: but of these, forty-three abjured, twenty-seven men and six- "teen women, most of them being of Tenterden; and five of them, "four men and one women, were condemned; some as obstinate he- "retics, and others as relapses: and, against the common laws of na- "ture, the woman's husband, and her two sons, were brought as wit- "nesses against her. Upon their conviction, a certificate was made "by the archbishop to the chancery: upon which, since there is no "pardon upon record, the writs for burning them must have been is- "sued in course, and the execution of them is little to be doubted. The "articles objected to them were, that they believed that in the eucha- "rist there was nothing but material bread; that the sacraments of "baptism, confirmation, confession, matrimony, and extreme unction, "were neither necessary nor profitable; that priests had no more "power than laymen; that pilgrimages were not meritorious, and that "the money and labour spent in them were spent in vain; that images "ought not to be worshipped, and that they were only stocks and "stones; that prayers ought not to be made to saints, but only to God; "that there was no virtue in holy water, or holy-bread. By this it will "appear, that many in this nation were prepared to receive those doc- "trines which were afterwards preached by the reformers, even before "Luther began first to oppose indulgences."

This is as pretty a piece of trickery as we have met with in the course of our review of this *Book of Martyrs*, and proves the shifts to which our modern editors are reduced to make out their charge of persecu- tion. This extract we find in *Burnet's Abridgment*, almost verbatim, with the following passage, however, suppressed. "Those who ab- "jured, did swear to discover all that held those errors, or were sus- "pected of them; and they were enjoined to carry a fagot in proces- "sion, and to wear on their clothes the representation of one in flames, "as a public confession that they had deserved to be burnt. There were "also four in London that abjured almost the same opinions; and FOX "SAYS, that six were burnt in Smithfield, who MIGHT be PERHAPS "those whom Warham had condemned; *for there is no mention of any* "*that were condemned in the registers of London.*" This passage should come in between the words "holy bread." and "By this," in the 4th line of the extract above from the bottom. So, then, here are charges made of proceedings "against the common laws of nature," and burn- ings taking place, upon *mere conjecture*. There are no registers in the regular courts, and yet they "MIGHT be PERHAPS" burned, because Fox *says* there were six that suffered in Smithfield.—Dr. Lingard writes, "In Henry's *third* and *thirteenth* years the teachers of Lollardism had "awakened by *their intemperance* the zeal of the bishops; and the

" king by proclamation, charged the *civil* magistrates to lend their aid to
" the spiritual authorities.   Of the numbers brought before the primate
" and the bishops of London and Lincoln, *almost all* were induced to *ab-*
" *jure;* a few of the more obstinate, forfeited their lives."   And the
authorities the doctor relies upon are *Fox* and *Burnet,* as we judge by
a reference, so that, on the whole, we may conclude, for want of better
evidence, that the number of sufferers, while the bishops continued
faithful to their creed, were trifling indeed.   Here let it be understood
that we are not justifying the act of burning for heresy, but only detecting the extravagant and unfounded tales, so basely coined by Fox
and his followers, to delude the credulous, and excite hatred against
truth.   What can we think of the veracity of the writer, and the gullibility of his readers, when such narratives as we have just recorded,
are published and believed, and believed too by a people hitherto
priding themselves as the most enlightened in the world !   Here, as we
have frequently remarked, are neither dates nor names, whereby the
accuracy of the circumstances can be ascertained or detailed; it is even
confessed by the original writer, though that fact is *suppressed* by the
modern editors, " a few *plain Christians,*" that there is no mention of
any persons being condemned in the registers of London; it is stated,
that there is *no record of pardon,* and yet it is brazenly insinuated, that
because there is *no pardon* there *must have been executions ! ! !*   But
we trust the time is now come, when the people of England *will* think
for themselves, and not take every shallow and inconsistent narrative
that dwells upon the supposed cruelties of ancient Catholic times for
gospel truths.   Is it not more probable, that since there were no registers of executions, and no record of pardon in the chancery, and the
authors and editors were unable to give a name to the sufferers, that
these martyrs are only victims of straw—phantoms of the imagination,
conjured up for the basest of purposes, and reflecting indelible disgrace
on those who have been so besotted as to give credit to such villanous
fabrications?

With regard to the doctrinal articles which are here objected to, we
have proved beyond dispute, in our first volume of this work, from the
testimony of the fathers of the first five ages of the church, when she is
allowed by Protestants to have been pure, that they were taught and believed by that church, as derived from the apostles ; they were received
by the Saxons, when Catholicism was first planted in the island, by St.
Augustin ; they continued to be believed by the people from that time
to Henry's reign ; and is it consistent with common sense, that a few
ignorant men, unversed in history, uninformed of the real sense of
scripture, and unacquainted with the sentiments of the fathers and
doctors of the church, whose writings were then confined to the
libraries of the colleges and bishops? Is it consistent, we say, with common sense, that these illiterate people should set up their silly and vain
notions in opposition to the general voice of the kingdom ? Is it consistent with common sense to believe that they only were right and all
the rest of the world were wrong ? But what shall we think of such
men as Fox and Burnet, who both held benefices in the Church of England, applauding fanatics who held, among other opinions, " that priests
" had no more power than laymen ?" If this were true, why did Fox

A REVIEW

OF

Fox's Book of Martyrs,

CRITICAL AND HISTORICAL.

No. 32. Printed and Published by W. E. Andrews, 3, Chapter-house-court, St. Paul's Churchyard, London. Price 3d.

EXPLANATION OF THE ENGRAVING.—*This cut represents the martyrdom of the learned and virtuous John Fisher, Bishop of Rochester, for refusing to acknowledge the lustful Henry the Eighth supreme head of the Church of England,*

CONTINUATION OF THE REVIEW.

and Burnet officiate as clergymen? We will not say as priests, because they were not entitled to that sacred character, as both disavowed the great Christian sacrifice of the Mass, which was celebrated by the apostles, by the command of their Divine Master, and has been celebrated by the priests of the Catholic church from that time to this. These two worthies would, no doubt, have sent Master John Wickliffe to the stake with very little ceremony, had he been alive in their time and endeavoured to oust them of their livings; but as he was opposed to the then order of things, that is, to a Catholic establishment and some doctrines of the Catholic church, though he held the chief of what Fox and Burnet deny, these rogues in grain seized the opportunity of making him an instrument to blind the people of England by misrepresenting facts, and making him the apostle of truth, when he was the preacher of error. For example; the Lollards are represented as objecting to the sacrament of baptism, as being neither profitable nor necessary. Now Fox and Burnet's church by law established expressly says in her Catechism, that baptism IS necessary to salvation. Could

then these Lollards preach a true doctrine, and the church of England
be right at the same time? But enough has been said to shew the palpable discrepancies amongst these reformers, or rather deformers, of religion, and pretended martyrs to truth.

PROGRESS OF LUTHER'S DOCTRINE.

We must here remind the reader that we are not Reviewing the work
of John Fox, but of the right reverend father in God, GILBERT BURNETT,
bishop of Sarum, who wrote a History of his own Time, which work
for lying and misrepresentation was a counterpart of John Fox's notorious *Acts and Monuments of the Church*, commonly called the *Book of
Martyrs*. This History by Burnett being too bulky and expensive for
general circulation, he made an *abridgment* of it, and it is from this
abridgment the "few plain Christians" have extracted the account of
the "progress of the Reformation," as coming from Fox's pen. These
things premised, let us now see what this famous, or rather infamous,
writer and church of England bishop had to say on Luther's preaching.
" The rise and progress of the doctrines of Luther," he says, " are well
" known; the scandalous sale of indulgences gave the first occasion to
" all that followed between him and the church of Rome; in which,
" had not the corruptions and cruelties of the clergy been so visible
" and scandalous, so small a cause could never have produced so great
" a revolution. The bishops were grossly ignorant; they seldom re-
" sided in their dioceses, except on great festivals; and all the effect
" their residence at such times could have, was to corrupt others by
" their ill example. They attached themselves to princes, and aspired
" to the greatest offices. The abbots and monks were wholly given up
" to luxury and idleness; and their unmarried state gave infinite scan-
" dal to the world : for it appeared, that the restraining them from
" having wives of their own, made them conclude that they had a right
" to all other men's. The inferior clergy were no better : and not
" having places of retreat to conceal their vices in, as the monks had,
" they became more public. In short, all ranks of churchmen were so
" universally despised and hated, that the world was very easily pos-
" sessed with prejudice against the doctrines of men whom they knew
" to be capable of every vice; and the worship of God was so defiled
" with gross superstition, that all men were easily convinced, that the
" church stood in great need of a reformation. This was much increased
" when the books of the fathers began to be read, in which the differ-
" ence between the former and latter ages of the church, did very evi-
" dently appear. It was found that a blind superstition came first in
" the room of true piety; and when by its means the wealth and in-
" terest of the clergy were highly advanced, the popes had upon that
" established their tyranny; under which all classes of people had long
" groaned. All these things concurred to make way for the advance-
" ment of the reformation; and, the books of the German reformers
" being brought into England, and translated, many were prevailed on
" by them. Upon this, a furious persecution was set on foot, to such a
" degree, that six men and women were burnt in Coventry in passion-
" week, only for teaching their children the creed, the Lord's prayer,
" and the ten commandments in English. Great numbers were every

"where brought into the bishops' courts; of whom some were burnt,
"but the greater part abjured." He then mentions Henry's book
against Luther, and continues,—"Tindal's translation of the New
"Testament, with notes, drew a severe condemnation from the clergy,
"there being nothing in which they were more concerned, than to keep
"the people unacquainted with that book. Thus much may serve to
"shew the condition of affairs in England both in church and state,
"when the process of the king's divorce was first set on foot."

So much for the affairs of England, both in church and state, when
the divorce was set on foot, according to Burnett's story; we shall,
however, be able to place them in a very different light, and upon the
testimony of unimpeachable witnesses, which Burnet scorns to produce,
but contents himself with his own bare assertions. In the first place,
it was not the sale of indulgences that first set Luther to oppose the
church, but a supposed neglect of the pope, in appointing the Dominican order of the church to preach these indulgences, instead of the
Augustinian order, of which latter Martin Luther was then a prominent
member. Martin conceived his pride to be wounded, and from this
spirit of pride and jealousy arose the disputes which afterwards followed
between him and the church of Rome. That there was a laxity of discipline among some of the clergy cannot be denied, but the doctrine
was unimpaired, and continued the same as it ever had been, and ever
will be. That there was gross ignorance in the higher order of the
clergy, or lasciviousness among the monks, is a base insinuation, as we
shall shew by and by; that *reports* of such a nature were industriously
circulated to screen the designs of Henry and his courtiers in their invasion of church property is true enough, but they were mere reports,
not a single charge of the kind was ever substantiated, while humerous
instances occurred where learned and pious men laid down their lives
rather than sacrifice their conscience. That the unmarried state of the
clergy gave infinite scandal to the world is clearly contradicted by the
English act of parliament passed in the reign of Edward the sixth,
which allowed the new order of parsons to marry, yet nevertheless declared that it would be more edifying to the people, if they remained
single. That all ranks of churchmen were universally despised and
hated, is contradicted by the fact that the people rose in many parts of
England in defence of the clergy and monasteries, which may be seen
by consulting the historians of the country. Of superstition and the
tyranny of the popes we shall say nothing—the supposed tyranny of the
pope was changed for an absolute despotism in the monarch, and England's liberties were bartered when a base parliament gave spiritual
supremacy to Harry. The furious persecution set on foot, in consequence of the translation of German books into English never existed,
except in the brain of Fox or Burnet; and the execution of the six men
and women for teaching their children the creed, the Lord's prayer,
and the commandments in English, is one of the most brazen lies ever
told. The people of all countries were, from the commencement of
Christianity, *all* taught to repeat the Lord's prayer, and instructed in
the commandments and creed in their vernacular tongue, and parts of
Scripture were explained to them by the clergy in the same familiar
way. To represent, therefore, that men and women were burned for

performing a duty to their children enjoined them by the Catholic church, for such was the case; the clergy taught both parents and children, and the parents were exhorted to aid the clergy by reminding them of their duty; to represent, we say, men and women as being burned for such an act, is one of the most frontless, most malignant, and most diabolical lies, ever invented to blacken and defame the oldest class of Christians in the world.

We must now say a word on the morals of the world, when Luther began to preach *his* doctrines, and the state they were in *after* his doctrines had taken root. Burnet states the bishops were grossly ignorant, the regular clergy absorbed in luxury and debauchery, the inferior clergy public scandalizers by their unblushing immorality, and the people groaning under a system of despotism and blind superstition. We have admitted that there was a laxity of morals among both clergy and people, but certainly not to that extent here described. Had there not been a debasement of conduct among the clergy, we should not have had such a crew of beastly reformers as sprung up after the example set them by Luther. What the effects of their pretended reforms in religion produced let them bear testimony themselves, and in so doing we shall see them contradicting the description given by Burnet of the state of Catholicism at that period. " Heretofore," says Luther, that is, in the days of Catholicism, " Heretofore, when we were *seduced* " by the pope, every man willingly *performed good works,* but NOW no " man says or knows any thing else but how to get all to himself by " exactions, pillage, theft, lying, usury, &c." *Postil. super Evang. Dom. 26. post Trin.* Here then we have the acknowledgment of Luther himself, that before he began to preach, every man was occupied in performing *good works,* and surely the exercise of good deeds could not be productive of ignorance and immorality. He may call it being seduced by the pope, but who is the man, who is the Christian, that would not be seduced to perform the works of Charity, rather than be charmed by some evil spirit to delight in the ways of the devil, as Luther confesses was the case with those who embraced his doctrines. A great outcry has been raised against the sale of indulgences in the Church of Rome; now that no ill effects were derived from *this* traffic, allowing for the sake of argument that such a mart was established, is proved by the testimony of Luther, who says that men then delighted in the performance of good works, an indulgence certainly very commendable, and highly conducive to the happiness of a people. But the moment Luther began to preach against the sale of indulgences, he gave such a gratuitous license to his followers to indulge in all the base passions of human nature, that shortly after, he tells us, every kind of good doings was totally obliterated from their minds, and the sole study of every individual was " how to get all to himself by *exactions,* pillage, " theft, lying, usury, &c." And he further states, that men were then " more revengeful, covetous, and licentious than they ever were in the " papacy." But need we wonder that such should be the result of the progress of Luther's doctrines when the preacher himself was a prey to his own lust and intemperance. We have it from his own pen that he had conferences with the devil, and in the preface to the first tome of his works he thus describes the state of his own mind, and his dis-

position towards God, previous to his commencing reformer. "I was
" mighty desirous," he says, " to understand Paul in his Epistle to the
" Romans: but was hitherto deterred, not by any faintheartedness, but by
" one single expression, in the first chapter, viz. *therein is the righteous-*
" *ness of God revealed.* For I hated that word, *the righteousness of God*:
" because I had been taught to understand it of that *formal and active*
" *righteousness*, by which God is righteous and punishes sinners, and
" the unrighteous. Now knowing myself, though I lived a monk of an;
" irreproachable life, to be in the sight of God a sinner, and of a *most*
" *unquiet conscience*, nor having any hopes to appease him with my own
" satisfaction, *I did not love*, nay *I hated this righteous God*, who punishes
" sinners, and with *heavy muttering*, if not *with silent blasphemy, I was*
" *angry with God*, and said, as if it were not enough for miserable sin-
" ners, who are lost to all eternity by original sin, to suffer all manner
" of calamity by the law of the Decalogue, unless God by the gospel
" adds sorrow to sorrow, and even by the gospel threatens us with his
" righteousness and anger. *Thus did I rage with a fretted and disordered*
" *conscience.*" What a fit apostle to reform religion! What precious
marks of a divine commission! What charming fruit must such a tree
produce! Here we have a man declaring that he hated a righteous
God; that he raged and fretted with a disordered conscience; that he
muttered against the will of Heaven, and silently blasphemed his justice
—and yet this man, this impious wretched blasphemer, is held up as the
pattern of excellence, and the reformer of that system which its Divine
Founder said should never be reformed. This libidinous monk taught
that adultery was lawful, notwithstanding one of the commandments of
God is so positive against that crime; he said that "a person that
" is baptized could not, though he would, lose his salvation by any sins
" how grievous soever, unless he refused to believe. For no sin could
" damn a man but unbelief alone." *Capt. Bab.* tom. ii. fol. 74, 1.—
Where is the wonder that men should be guilty of lying, theft, usury,
exaction, and the like, when they had such a blessed counsellor in this
reformer of religion? Again, he says, "The Papists teach that faith in
" Christ justifies indeed, but that God's commandments are likewise to
" be kept. Now this is directly to deny Christ and abolish faith." *In
Ep. ad Gal.* tom. v. fol. 311. 2. An excellent mode of reasoning, if such
it can be called. If the commandments are not to be kept why were
they enjoined? Before we take leave of Luther we will just mention
his golden rule for the interpretation of scripture, which can be considered in no other light than a general indulgence to commit every degree of enormity that a man's inclinations may lead him to. "Let
this," he says, "be your rule; where the scripture commands the
" doing a good work, understand it in this sense, *that it forbids thee to*
" *do a good work*, because thou canst not do it." Tom. iii. fol. 171. 2,
   What the "few plain Christians" will say to this rule of interpreting
scripture we cannot divine, the effects of it however, have been dreadful,
as we gather from the page of history, and the writings of the reformers
themselves.—Calvin wrote in similar strains to Luther, on the increase
of iniquity among the disciples of the reformation so called. " Of the
" many thousands," he said, " who, renouncing Popery, seemed eagerly
" to embrace the gospel, how *few* have amended their lives, Nay, what

" else did the greater part pretend to, but by shaking off the yoke of
" superstition, give themselves more liberty to follow all kiuds of
" licentiousness."—*Lib. de scandalis.*—Erasmus who was no advocate
for the Catholics, lamented the degeneracy of morals brought on by the
change of religion. " Take a view," says he, " of this evangelical people," the Protestants—" Perhaps 'tis my misfortune; but I never yet
met with one, who does not appear changed for the worse." *Epist. ad
Vultur. Neoc.* And again : " Some persons," says he, " whom I knew
" formerly innocent, harmless and without deceit, no sooner have I seen
" joined to that sect, (the Protestants,) but they begun to talk of
" wenches, to play at dice, to leave off prayers, being grown extremely
" worldly, most impatient, revengeful, vain, like vipers tearing one
" another.—I speak by experience." *Ep. ad Fratres infer. Germaniæ.*—
" The greater part of the people," adds Bucer, " seem to have embraced
" the gospel, only to live at their pleasure, and enjoy their lusts and
" lawless appetites without control. Hence they lend a willing ear to
" the doctrine, *that we are justified by faith only, and not by good works,*
" for which they have no relish." *(Burde Regn. Christ. b. 1. c. 4.)*
There is one more witness we shall produce, because his testimony goes
to shew that lying, and perjury, and forgery, were the instruments by
which the reformers maintained their ground, and cheated the people
out of their senses.—" I am indignant," says the Protestant professor
Zanchius, " when I consider the manner in which most of us defend
" our cause. The true state of the question we often, on set purpose,
" involve in darkness that it may not be understood; we have the im-
" pudence to deny things the most evident : we assert what is visibly
" false : the most impious doctrines we force on the people as the first
" principles of faith, and orthodox opinions we condemn as heretical :
" we torture the scriptures till they agree with our own fancies; and
" boast of being the disciples of the fathers, while we refuse to follow
" their doctrine : to deceive, to calumniate, to abuse, is our familiar
" practice : nor do we care for any thing, provided we can defend our
" cause, good or bad, right or wrong. O what times ! what manners !"
—*(Zanchius ad Stormium,* tom. viii. col. 828.)

We have advanced enough to shew " the rise and progress of Luther's
" doctrines" in a different light than what Burnet has pourtrayed
them. He has, with the same dexterity as Fox and other reformed
writers, followed the course complained of by Zanchius. The true
question is studiously involved in darkness, that it may not be clearly
seen; facts the most evident are denied or suppressed; the most impious doctrines are imposed upon the people as divine truths; and the
scriptures are tortured and twisted to suit the notions of every cobbler
or coalheaver that fancies himself inspired. How different are the
ways of the Catholic church. Regulated by one system of divine
jurisprudence, and governed by the Spirit of Truth, she, in cases of
difficulty, assemble the guardians of faith from the different quarters of
the world, to pronounce on the novelties that may arise, and declare
what is, has been, and always was, the faith of the church received by
her from Christ, through the apostles. This done, canons or laws
were devised for the repressing of abuse and the correction of morals,
and thus her unity, holiness, apostolicity, and Catholicity have been

made manifest to the world. The last of these general councils was held at Trent during the progress of the reformation, and in the seventh session the fathers of that assembly decreed as follows :—To " those " *who persevere in good works to the end*, and trust in God, eternal " life is to be proposed, both as a grace mercifully promised to the " sons of God, *through* Jesus Christ, and as a reward which accord- " ing to the promise of God will be faithfully rendered to their good " works and merits." Let the reader compare this doctrine with the irreligious preachings of the lustful reformers, and say whether the superstition of the former, as it is called, is not to be preferred to the libertinism of the latter.

HISTORY OF HENRY'S MARRIAGE WITH CATHARINE.

The "few plain Christians" usher in this marriage with the following observations : " As this incident is so replete with consequences, a par- " ticular relation of its cause will not, it is presumed, be unacceptable " to the reader;" and they then proceed with extracts from Burnet's *Abridgement* under the name of Fox. Burnet states the marriage of Catherine with prince Arthur, and their being bedded together. He also insinuates that the marriage was consummated, though it is well known that Arthur was a sickly prince, and died soon after the mar- riage, and that Catharine always declared that she was a virgin when she came to Henry's bed. He further says, that the second match be- tween Henry and Catharine originated from the avarice of Henry's father ; that Warham, archbishop of Canterbury, objected to the second marriage, and Fox, bishop of Winchester was for it ; that "the " pope's authority was *then* so well established that it was *thought* a " dispensation was sufficient to remove all objections." and accordingly one was obtained. The two paragraphs following we quote verbatim from the *Book of Martyrs*, and we beg the reader's particular attention to the words we have put in italic characters :—

" The pope was then at war with Lewis the Twelfth of France, and " so would refuse nothing to the king of England, being perhaps not un- " willing that princes should contract such marriages, by which the le- " gitimation of their issue depending on the pope's dispensation, they " would be thereby obliged in interest to support that authority. Upon " this *a marriage followed, the prince yet being under age ; but the same* " *day* in which *he came to be of age,* he did *by his father's orders* make *a* " *protestation that he retracted and annulled his marriage.*

" Henry the Seventh on *his deathbed* charged his son to *break it off* " *entirely,* being perhaps apprehensive of such a return of confusion " upon a controverted succession to the crown, as had been during the " wars of the houses of York and Lancaster ; but *after* his father's " death, Henry the Eighth *being then eighteen years of age, married her :* " she bore him two sons, who died soon after they were born ; and a " daughter, Mary, afterwards queen of England. After this the queen " *contracted some diseases that made her unacceptable to the king ;* who at " the *same time beginning to have some scruples of conscience* with regard " to the *lawfulness of his marriage,* determined to have the affair *inves-* " *tigated ! !* "

Did the world ever before see such a specimen of barefaced lying as this bishop of the Church-of-England, this Gilbert Burnet, D. D.

has here furnished. In the first paragraph he says a marriage followed the dispensation, while the prince was under age, but as soon as he came of age, obeying his fathers orders like a dutiful child, he made a *protestation* that he *retracted*, and *annulled his marriage*. Now what are we to understand by this protestation, and the order of Henry's father?— If his father ordered him to annul the marriage when he came of age, how came he to permit the marriage to be contracted: And if it were in the power of Henry, on coming of age, to retract and annul the marriage, why was a dispensation required to allow him to contract the marriage, and why did he seek, twenty years after, for a dispensation from the same authority, but another person, to have the marriage annulled? But mark, reader; having married Henry under age, and made him when of age, according to his father's orders, protest, retract, and annul the marriage, he next marries Henry at eighteen years of age, after his father's death, and in *opposition* to his *father's dying request*, lest civil war and confusion should ensue, and he continues to live with this same wife, in connubial happiness we suppose, till disease renders her unacceptable, and *then*, the moral Henry begins to have *some scruples of conscience!* So we may suppose that had Catharine remained buxom and gay, instead of waxing old and infirm, Harry would never have had any scruples of conscience about his brother's wife, nor called for an investigation. Really when we see such gross imposture as this permitted to be circulated, and that too for a long series of time, without contradiction, and believed by a people claiming to themselves a superiority of intellect over other nations, we fell abashed and vexed for the honour of our country. Another insinuation to notice is, that of the readiness of the pope to grant the dispensation to Henry's father, because he was at war with the king of France, and could refuse Henry the seventh nothing. Now is not this pliant disposition contradicted by the conduct of this pope's successor, who, when applied to by Henry the eighth to annul the contract entered into under this dispensation, would not comply with Henry's wishes, though he (the pope) was then shut up in the castle of St. Angelo, in Rome, by the emperor Charles Vth, the nephew of Catharine, and Henry was able to assist his holiness in his difficulties?

THE KING'S SCRUPLES CONCERNING HIS MARRIAGE.

Burnet says, " He (the king) seemed to lay the greatest weight on " the prohibition, in the levitical law, of marrying the brother's wife, " and being conversant in Thomas Aquinas's writings, he found, that " he and the other schoolmen looked upon these laws as moral, and for " ever binding; and consequently the pope's dispensation was of no " force, since his authority went so far as to dispense with the laws of " God. All the bishops of England, Fisher of Rochester only excepted, " declared under their hands and seals, that they judged the marriage " unlawful. The ill consequences of wars that might follow upon a " doubtful title to the crown, were also much considered. It is not " probable that Henry's affection for any other lady was the origin of " these proceedings; but rather, that, conceiving himself upon the point of being freed from his former marriage, he gave free scope to his affections, which settled on Anne Boleyn.' Harry was certainly conversant with the writings of Thomas Aquinas, as he is said to have been intended for the church by his father, previous to the death of his brother Arthur, and was educated accordingly. This will account for his eagerness and ability in taking the lists against Luther. We will also admit that the pope had no authority to dispense with the laws of God, and consequently that a papal dispensation to that effect was of no force. Yet we doubt much that Harry ever laid any great weight upon the prohibition of the levitical law, since the levitical law was super- oeded by the Christian law, and the levitical law enjoined the marriage of a brother to a brother's wife if he died without issue. But if Harry had been so fond of the levitical law, why did he not turn Jew that he might, without scruple of conscience, have followed this law to the very letter, without all that mass of hypocrisy and dissimulation which co- vered his cruel and detestable actions. Burnet further says, that " all " the bishops of England, Fisher of Rochester only excepted, declared " under their hands and seals, that they judged the marriage unlawful." This is another mistake, since it is declared by Dr. Bailey, in his Life of Bishop Fisher, that the seals and signatures of many of the bishops were affixed to the instrument of dissent *without their privity*, though they had not the courage to make that declaration as Fisher did.

Burnet also insinuates that it is not probable that Harry's affections for any " other lady, was the *origin* of these proceedings ; but rather " that, conceiving himself upon the point of being freed of his former " marriage, he gave *free* scope to his affections, which settled on Anne " Boleyn."—It may be that Harry's lust for young Anne, was hot the original cause of his seeking a divorce from his virtuous queen, but it is a somewhat singular way of pleading an excuse for a lecherous monarch, though well suited to a Protestant bishop, to talk of his giving *scope* to his *affections*, (read passions) which at length fixed on Anne Boleyn.—The plain fact is, Harry gave way to voluptuousness and debauchery, after Wolsey had gained such an ascendency over him.— Before this he attended to the royal duties, now he left business to his favourite, and courted the embraces of loose women. When he married Catherine, he was only eighteen years of age, she was twenty-six. At that time she was beautiful and lovely, as well as adorned with every amiable quality. Twenty years, attended with delicate health, had made ravages in her person, though her mind was as pure and exalted as in her youth.—The infirmities of age weaned the affections of Harry, but could not eradicate his regard for her, so powerful were the graces of her soul.—While he was attached to Catherine, he preserved decency in his amours, but he was not without his mistresses !—Of these Dr. Lingard enumerates as the first, Elizabeth, the daughter of Sir John Blount, and relict of Sir Gilbert Talbois, by whom he had a son. To her succeeded Mary Boleyn, daughter of Sir Thomas Boleyn, and SISTER to the famous miss Nancy, afterwards queen of England.—So that Burnet was not much out when he said that Harry gave " free scope to his affections" (passions,) even *before* he considered himself on the *point* of being freed from his marriage with Catherine. The origin of the divorce, we have said, may be laid to Wolsey's account. who put the scruple into Harry's head, with a view to strengthen his interest with the French court, by engaging the king to marry a sister of the king of France, and thus revenge himself of the emperor Charles and his aunt Catherine; but the devil put it into Harry's head to take a liking to Anne Boleyn, that the ambitious minister might be thwarted. Anne was more cunning then her sister Mary, and would not consent to the king's wishes without she became his wife. She took care to throw out her allurements in the king's presence so artfully, that she enkindled a raging fire in Harry's breast, who resolved to have her cost what it would.

Here let us examine a little closer into the scruples of this very scrupulous monarch, the first head of the Church as by law established.— Burnet says he laid great stress upon the levitical law, and that he felt great repugnance at living with his brother's wife. But if Harry was so conscientious in this affair after having lived with Catharine twenty years, why was he not equally scrupulous in cohabiting with Anne Boleyn, her own sister having been his mistress. The stress of the divorce with Catharine laid upon prince Arthur having carnal knowledge of her, which she most solemnly denied; but it cannot be denied that Henry had carnal knowledge of Anne's sister, yet he scrupled not to make Anne in appearance his wife. The relationship between brother and brother could not be nearer than sister and sister, it is therefore evident that Harry's scruples were a mockery and cloak for his lustful passions. Another fact too, we may notice here, to show what Harry himself thought of his scruples, when threatened with the danger of mortality. In the year 1528, when the king was deep in love with Miss Boleyn, the court was affected with a sweating sickness, which first made its appearance among Anne's attendants. By the king's orders she was immediately packed off to her father's seat in Kent, where she was attacked with the disease but recovered. Henry, finding the contagion spreading among the gentlemen of his privy chamber, took the alarm, and, forgetting all his scruples of conscience, fled to his virtuous queen, whom he joined in her devotional exercises, confessing himself every day, and communicating every Sunday and festival. These particulars, Dr. Lingard tells us, may be found in the Letters of the Bishop of Bayonne. Here then we find the king laying aside his "scruples," when under the fear of death, and joining the society of that woman whose marriage with whom he is represented to have considered incestuous. Nay, what is still more corroborative of the hypocrisy of these scruples, when cardinal Campegio, who was sent as joint legate with Wolsey by the pope, arrived in London, Harry sent the lady Anne, away for decency sake, and again joined the company of his queen. He lived with her, writes Dr. Lingard, "apparently on the same terms as " if there had been no controversy between them. They continued to " eat at the same table, and to sleep in the same bed. Catharine care- " fully concealed her feelings, and appeared in public with that air of " cheerfulness which she used to display in the days of her greatest " prosperity. The arrival of Campegio had added to the popularity " of her cause, and though Wolsey had taken every precaution to pre- " vent disturbance, he could not silence the common voice of the peo- " ple, who publicly declared, that, let the king marry whom he pleased, " the husband of the princess Mary should be his successor on the " throne." We mention this last circumstance with feelings of pleasure, as it reflects the highest credit on the character of the people of England, who on all occasions have been found on the side of virtue, and have taken part with the persecuted and oppressed. We say on all occasions, because in those days of frenzy and lawless outrage, when the perjuries of Oates led innocent victims to the scaffold, and the ravings of lord George Gordon threatened destruction to the metropolis, the people were misled by interested villains, and taught to look upon the Catholics as dangerous and perfidious men. Had the people been rightly informed; had they known the real character of those who were deluding them, we have no doubt but their vengeance would have been turned upon the base conspirators against truth and justice, and the same feeling have been manifested for the oppressed Catholics as was shewn in favour of the unfortunate but magnanimous Catharine.

To enter into all the details concerning the king's marriage with Catharine, and his divorce from her, as detailed by Burnet, and re-edited by the "few plain Christians," under the *Book of Martyrs*, would swell our Review to an enormous bulk, and tire the patience of the reader; we shall therefore pass over many of the subtleties of Burnet, and supply a few of the omissions he has made of most material facts to give a false colour to his relations. But first we must notice his insinuations against the election of popes. Speaking of the illness of pope Clement, who filled the papal chair during the agitation of the divorce, Burnet says, " About this time, the pope was taken suddenly ill, upon which the Im-" perialists began to prepare for a conclave; but Farnese, and the car-" dinal of Mantua, opposed them, and seemed to favour Wolsey: " whom as his correspondents wrote to him, 'they reverenced as a " Deity.' Upon this he dispatched a courier to Gardiner, then on his way " to Rome, with large directions how to manage the election; it was " reckoned, that on the king of France joining heartily with Henry, of " which he seemed confident, there were only six cardinals wanting to " make the election sure, and besides sums of money, and other re-" wards, that were to be distributed among them, he was to give them " assurance, that the cardinal's preferments should be divided among " them. These were the secret methods of attaining that chair: and " indeed it would puzzle a man of an ordinary degree of credulity, to " think that one chosen by such means could presume to be Christ's " vicar, and the infallible judge of controversies. The recovery, how-" ever, of the pope, put an end to these intrigues."

When Burnet was casting his slanders against the conclave, he should have reflected on the way he obtained his prelacy, for it would puzzle a man of more than ordinary credulity to think that men chosen as he was were filled with the Holy Ghost, though they swear it to be so with might and main.—To prevent ambitious men from intriguing is impossible, while human nature remains as it is; to guard therefore against these intrigues, every precaution has been devised in the regulation of the conclave, and no pope is elected until two-thirds of the votes are given in favour of the cardinal elected.—To obtain this number of votes is frequently a work of time, and as there is no communication whatever with the electors after the conclave is once closed, there is no election, we feel convinced, so pure and free from suspicion as that of the head of the Catholic church.—We do not wonder that Burnet should sneer at the belief held by all Catholics, that the pope is Christ's vicar on earth; but it is to be observed, that this belief has been held by all the world at one time, and is now by the greatest part of Christendom, including many monarchs and eminent statesmen, and we cannot help feeling, that there is more of presumption in those who reject this title of the pope, so long and so universally credited, than there is of credulity in those who maintain it.—As to the secret method of attaining the papal chair, we have said before, that ambitious men, like Wolsey, cannot be prevented from *aspiring* to, and *intriguing* for, so high a dignity; but history tells us, that those who resorted to such unjustifiable practices, like Wolsey, invariably met with a defeat.

In October, Burnet says, Campegio " arrived in England, and advised " the king to relinquish the prosecution of his suit; and then counselled " the queen, in the pope's name, to enter into a religious community; " but both were in vain; and he, by affecting an impartiality, almost " lost both sides." And why was Campegio's advice unavailing with the queen? This Mr. Burnet has not thought proper to inform his readers, lest they should see too much into this scene of iniquity and injustice, which led to the deformation of religion, and paved the way for his promotion; which would never have been the case had the old faith not been subverted. Catharine, we are told by Dr. Lingard, listened to the legate with modesty and firmness, and then gave him for answer, " that it was not for herself that she was concerned, but " for one whose interests were more dear to her than her own; that " the presumptive heir to the crown was her daughter Mary, whose " right should never be prejudiced by the voluntary act of her mother; " that she thought it strange to be thus interrogated without previous " notice on so delicate and important a subject; that she was a weak ' illiterate woman, a stranger without friends or advisers, while her " opponents were men learned in the law, and anxious to deserve the ' favour of their sovereign; and that she therefore demanded as a right " the aid of counsel of *her own choice*, selected from the subjects of her " nephew." Thus spoke this noble-minded and persecuted woman to the legate of the pope, and this dignified conduct she pursued throughout the whole of her cruel and unmanly case. Her request was partially granted. In addition to nine English counsellors, composed of prelates and canonists, the queen was permitted to choose two foreign advocates, provided they were natives of Flanders, and not of Spain. The two counsel came from Flanders, but left England before the trial began.

These proceeding against so virtuous and unprotected a woman, occasioned loud murmurs and discontents among the people. " Of the " coming of this legate," Stow writes, " the people, especially the wo- " men, talked largely, and said, that the king would for his own plea- " sure have another wife, and had sent for this legate to be divorced " from his queen with many foolish words, insomuch, that whoever " spoke against the marriage was of the common people abhorred and " reproved, which common rumour was related to the king." Such an ebullition of popular feeling was by no means agreeable to a monarch of Harry's temperament, so he caused all the nobility, judges, counsellors, the lord mayor, aldermen, and principal citizens, to come to his palace

of Bridewell, on Sunday the 8th of November, 1528, before whom he
entered into an explanation of his conduct, and the reasons which induced him to have his marriage with Catharine examined into. The
speech of the king is given at length in Stow, and is so full of hypocrisy
that we give the conclusion, to shew how Harry could dissemble as well
as play the tyrant. After noticing the civil wars between the houses
of York and Lancaster about the succession of the crown, and the necessity of guarding against such calamities for the future, he touched
on the rumours which were afloat doubting the legitimacy of the princess
Mary his daughter, in consequence of her mother having been his brother's wife, which, he said, was directly against God's law and his precept.
He then goes on,—" Think you, my lords, that these words touch not my
" body and soul; think you that these doings do not daily and hourly
" trouble my conscience and vex my spirits : yes, we doubt not but
" if it were your own cause, every man would seek remedy, when the
" peril of your soul and the loss of your inheritance is openly laid to
" you. For this only cause I protest before God, and in the word
" of a prince, I have asked counsel of the greatest clerks in Christen-
" dom, and for this cause I have sent for this legate, as a man indiffer-
" ent, only to know the truth, and to settle my conscience, and for none
" other cause, as God can judge. And as touching the queen, if it be
" judged by the law of God that she is my lawful wife, there was never
" thing more acceptable to me in my life, both for the discharge of my
" conscience, and also for the good qualities and conditions which I
" know to be in her: for I assure you all, that beside her noble parent-
" age of the which she is descended, (as all you know) she is a woman
" of most gentleness, of most humility, and buxomness, yea, and of all
" good qualities appertaining to nobility, she is without comparison, as
" I these twenty years almost have had the true experiment, so that if
" I were to marry again, if the marriage might be good, I would surely
" choose her above all other women: but if it be determined by judg-
" ment, that our marriage was against God's law and clearly void, then
" I shall not only sorrow the departing from so good a lady and loving
" companion, but much more lament and bewail my unfortunate chance,
" that I have so long lived in adultery, to God's great displeasure, and
" have no true heir of my body to inherit this realm. These be the
" sores that vex my mind, these be the pangs that trouble my conscience,
" and for these griefs I seek a remedy : therefore I require of you all,
" as our trust and confidence is in you, to declare to our subjects our
" intent, according to our true meaning, and desire them to pray with
" us that the truth may be known, for the discharge of our conscience,
" and saving of our soul : and for declaration hereof I have assembled
" you together, and now you may depart." This speech shewed the
king to be as consummate a hypocrite, when he thought he could carry
his cause with a plausible share of religion, as he proved a despot and
cold-blooded murderer, when he found himself disappointed in these
views. What can we think of the man who here made such a parade
about conscience, and his scruples at living with a virtuous woman,
because she had been married to his brother, but remained a virgin,
when he was meditating to be married to a wanton, whose sister he
had kept as a mistress ? Out upon such a conscience as this. We learn,

however, this fact, from the king and his nobles, that it was *then*, as it long had been, the belief of the whole kingdom, that the pope was the *only* legitimate authority to decide on *spiritual* questions, which was the case between Henry and Catharine. The king and the people knew that the pope held this authority by divine right, for nothing but a divine commission could have preserved it so long, or extended it so universally as it then was, every monarch and nation in Christendom voluntarily yielding obedience to it.

On recomparing Burnet's abridgment with the account given by the "few plain Christians," we find that the latter have been suppressing many facts related by the former. Now this suppression upon suppression is a very likely way to instruct the people in the "knowledge and "love of the genuine principles of Christianity." It may tend to excite "a hatred of the (supposed) crimes and corruptions of popery," but it cannot convey to the reader the least perception of truth. The account of the "Progress of the Reformation" is a garbled and unfair extraction from a partial historian, and consequently carries with it the design of misleading instead of instructing the people on the important matters under consideration. For example, we have a title of the coming of Campegio into England; but from this circumstance, and the illness of the pope, which we have before noticed, the "few plain Christians" pass over to the "queen's appeal to the pope," leaving out the commencement of the process of divorce, which occasioned the ill-fated Catharine to appeal to the common father of Christendom. By the by, we should have noticed, that the king and his prime minister, Wolsey, left no means untried to obtain the consent of the pope, who as firmly resisted every sinister measure to seduce him from his line of duty. Involved in a dispute with the emperor, money and troops were proffered him, but Clement regarded them not. Threats were then applied with as little success. Even his sick bed was no security to him from the importunities of the emissaries of Henry, who went so far as to accuse the pontiff of ingratitude to his best friend, and of indifference to the prosperity of the church. "To all their remonstrances," writes Dr. Lingard, "he returned the same answer, that he could not refuse to "Catharine what the ordinary forms of justice required; that he was "devoted to the king, and eager to gratify him in any manner con- "formably with honour and equity; but that he ought not to require "from him what was evidently unjust, or they would find that when "his conscience was concerned, he was equally insensible to consider- "ations of interest or danger." Burnet and the "few plain Christians" may attempt to throw a stigma on the election of popes, but the words and resolution of this head of the church reflect no disgrace upon either the church or himself.

The "few plain Christians," quoting from Burnet, say, "At length "the legates began the process, when the queen protested against "them as incompetent judges. They, however, proceeded according "to the forms of law, although the queen had appealed from them to "the pope, and objected both to the place, to the judges, and her law- "yers: yet they pronounced her contumacious, and went on to examine "witnesses, chiefly as to the consummation of her marriage with prince "Arthur." This part of the affair is so very interesting, the conduct of the oppressed queen so truly heroic, and her appeal so pathetically touching, that we should be doing injustice to the cause of virtue and religion, and leave our readers in the dark, did we not give her defence in full. The same arts practised upon the pontiff were tried upon the queen. Burnet says, (but this passage the "few plain Christians" have omitted) "Endeavours were used to terrify her into some compliance; " it was given out that some had intended to kill the king or the car- " dinal, and that she had some hand in it, that she carried herself very " disobligingly to the king, and used many indecent arts to be popular; " that the king was in danger of his life by her means, and so could no " more keep her company neither in bed nor at board: but (continues " Burnet) she was a woman of so resolute a mind that no threatenings " could daunt her." While these intrigues and menaces were carrying on against the queen, Anne Boleyn was gaining a complete ascendency at court, and at length obtained the supreme control of the ministry. Harry allowed her a princely establishment, ordered his courtiers to attend her daily levees, the same as they had done those of the queen, who was now banished to Greenwich.

Seven months had now elapsed since the arrival of Campegio, which time had been spent in fruitless negociations with Rome, when it was deemed necessary that some public proceeding should take place, to bring the question to an issue. Accordingly, a court was held at the Blackfriars, the first session of which, began on the 31st of May, 1529. Wolsey and Campegio, sat as judges, being joint legates of the pope; the chief managers on the part of the king were, Dr. Sampson, Dr. Hall, Dr. Petre, and Dr. Tregonel; those that pleaded for the queen were, Dr. Fisher bishop of Rochester, Dr. Standish bishop of Asaph, and Dr. Ridley, a very learned civilian.—Before this court, the king and queen appeared, but previous to their being called, the bishop of Rochester presented the legates with a book, which he had composed, in defence of the marriage; making therewith a grave and learned speech, in which he cautioned them as to what they did in so important an affair, calling to their minds the many dangers and inconveniences that might ensue, not only to the realm, but to the whole of Christen- dom, by their decision.—The bishop having concluded, the king was called by name, who answered, Here; and repeated in substance, what he had said before the assembly of the nobility.—Then the queen was called, who made no answer, but rising from her chair, she kneeled be- fore the king, and in sight of the legates and the whole court, thus ad- dressed him—" Sir, I beseech you do me justice and right, and take " some pity upon me! for I am a simple woman, and a stranger born " out of your dominions, and have no friend but you, who now being " become my adversary, alas! what friendship or assurance of indiffer- " ency in my council can I hope to find amongst your subjects? What " have I done? Wherein have I offended you? How have I given you " any occasion of displeasure? Why will you put me from you in this " sort? I take God to be my judge, I have been a true, humble, and " faithful wife unto you; always conformable to your will and pleasure: " Wherein did I ever contradict or gainsay whatever you said? When " was I discontented at the thing that pleased you? Whom did I love " but those whom you loved, whether I had cause or not? I have been

" your wife these twenty years; you have had divers children by me:
" when you took me first unto your bed, I take God to be my witness, I was
" a virgin; and, whether that be true or not, I put it to your conscience.
" Now, if there be any just cause that you can allege against me, either
" of dishonesty or the like, I am contented to depart the realm, and
" you, with shame and infamy; but, if there be no such cause, then I
" pray you let me have justice at your hands. The king your father
" was in his time of such an excellent wit, as that for his wisdom he
" was accounted a second Solomon; and Ferdinand my father was
" reckoned to be one of the wisest princes that reigned in Spain for many
" years before his days. These being both so wise princes, it is not to
" be doubted but they had gathered unto them as wise counsellors of
" both realms, as they in their wisdoms thought most meet; and, as I
" take it, there were, in those days, as wise and learned men in both
" kingdoms, as there are now to be found in these our times, who thought
" the marriage between you and me to be good and lawful; but for this I
" may thank you, my lord cardinal of York, who have sought to make this
" dissension between my lord the king and me, because I have so often
" found fault with your pompous vanity and aspiring mind. Yet I do not
" think that this your malice proceeds from you merely in respect of myself;
" but your chief displeasure is against my nephew the emperor, because
" you could not at his hands attain unto the bishopric of Toledo, which
" you greedily desired; and after that was by his means put by the chief
" and high bishopric of Rome, whereunto you most ambitiously aspired;
" whereat being sore offended, and yet not able to revenge your quarrel
" upon him, the heavy burthen of your indignation must fall upon a fe-
" male weakness, for no other reason but because she is his aunt. And
" these are the manly ways you take to ease your mind; but God for-
" give you! Wherefore, sir, (applying herself to the king) it seems to
" me to be no justice that I should stand to the order of this court, see-
" ing one of my judges to be so partial; and, if I should agree to stand
" to the judgment of this court, what counsellors have I but such as
" are your own subjects, taken from your own council, to which they
" are privy, and perhaps dare not go against it? wherefore I refuse to
" stand to their advice or plea, or any judgment that is here, and do
" appeal unto the see apostolic, before our holy father the pope; hum-
" bly beseeching you, by the way of charity, to spare me, till I may know
" what further course my friends in Spain will advise me to: and, if
" this may not be granted, then your pleasure be fulfilled."

Having concluded this tender and moving remonstrance, she rose, and
making her obeisance to the king, she left the court, the members of
which were extremely affected, many of them shedding tears. After it
was discovered that she had taken her entire departure, for it was
imagined that she would have returned to her place after a time, the
king commanded that she should be called back again; but she resolutely
refused to appear, saying to her attendants,—" This is no place for me
" to expect equity; for they are all agreed what they will do, and the
" king is resolved what shall be done." The king finding that she
would not return, and that her address had made a strong impression
on the court, delivered himself as follows.—" Forasmuch as the queen
" is now gone, I will declare in her absence, before you all, that she

A REVIEW

OF

𝕱𝖔𝖝'𝖘 𝕭𝖔𝖔𝖐 𝖔𝖋 𝕸𝖆𝖗𝖙𝖞𝖗𝖘,

CRITICAL AND HISTORICAL.

No. 33. Printed and Published by W. E. Andrews, 3, Chapter-house-court, St. Paul's Churchyard, London. **Price 3d.**

EXPLANATION OF THE ENGRAVING.—*The execution of Dr. John Forest, a friar observant, for objecting to Harry's spiritual supremacy. The celebrated Hugh Latimer, then bishop of Worcester, preached a sermon against the friar, who told Latimer that if an angel should come down from heaven and teach any other doctrine than that which he had received, and believed from his youth, he would not now believe him. And that if his body was cut joint after joint, he would not turn from his old profession. So, says Stow, he was hanged and burned, as is shewed, and a huge great image, named Darvell Gathern, having been brought out of Wales to the gallows in Smithfield, was there burned with the said friar Forest.*

CONTINUATION OF THE REVIEW.

" hath ever been to me, as true, obedient, and conformable a wife as I
" could wish, or any man desire to have, as having all the virtuous
" qualities that ought to be in a woman of her dignity: she is high
" born, (as the quality of her conditions do declare,) yet of so meek a
" spirit, as if her humility had not been acquainted with her birth, so
" that if I sought all Europe over, I should never find a better wife;
" and therefore how willingly I would, if it were lawful, continue her
" to be my wife till death make the separation, ye may all guess; but
" conscience, conscience is such a thing,—who can endure the sting
" and prick of conscience, always stinging and pricking within his
" breast? Wherefore, my lords, this woman, this good woman I may
" say, sometime being my brother's wife, as ye all know, or have heard,
" hath bred such a scruple within the secrets of my breast, as daily

" doth torment, cumber, and disquiet my mind, fearing and mistrusting
" that I am in great danger of God's indignation; and the rather, be-
" cause he hath sent me no issue-male, but such as died incontinently
" after they were born. Thus my conscience being tossed to and fro
" upon these unquiet waves, (almost in despair of having any other
" issue by her) it behoveth me, I think, to look a little farther, and to
" consider now the welfare of this realm, and the great danger that it
" standeth in for lack of a prince to succeed me in this office; and
" therefore I thought good, in respect of the discharging of my con-
" science, and for the quiet state of this noble realm, to attempt the law
" herein, that is, to know by your good and learned counsel, whether I
" might lawfully take another wife, by whom God may send me issue-
" male, in case this my first marriage should appear not warrantable;
" and this is the only cause for which I have sought thus far unto you,
" and not for any displeasure or disliking of the queen's person or age,
" with whom I could be as well contented to live, and continue (if our
" marriage may stand with the laws of God) as with any woman living:
" and in this point consisteth all the doubt, wherein I would be satisfied
" by the sound learning, wisdom, and judgments of you, my lords, the
" prelates and pastors of this realm, now here assembled for that pur-
" pose; and according to whose determination herein, I am contented
" to submit myself with all obedience; and that I meant not to wade
" in so weighty a matter (of myself) without the opinion and judgment
" of my lords spiritual, it may well appear in this, that, shortly after the
" coming of this scruple into my conscience, I moved it to you my lord
" of Lincoln, my ghostly father: and forasmuch as you yourself, my
" lord, were then in some doubt, you advised me to ask the counsel of
" the rest of the bishops; whereupon I moved you, my lord of Canter-
" bury, first, to have your license (inasmuch as you were the metro-
" politan) to put this matter in question, as I did to all the rest; the
" which you have all granted under your seals, which I have here to
" shew."

Here we have the king again appealing to conscience, as if he were
the most scrupulous man in his kingdom; and we have him solemnly
protesting his regard and affection for his amiable queen, whose virtues
he could but extol, and whose conduct towards him had been irreproachable. We have him also protesting his obedience to spiritual
authority in this case as one of conscience, and acknowledging that authority against which he afterwards protested, when he found he could
not gain his ends. Let us now then proceed farther into the proceedings of the divorce, and see if the protestations of Harry were sincere.
The king had won the archbishop of Canterbury to his design, and the
archbishop had got as many of the bishops as he could to consent to
the divorce under their hands and seals, and of those he could not prevail upon to give their formal consent, he took the liberty of consenting
for them, and added their signatures to an instrument which had been
drawn up for the purpose. Bishop Fisher, however, undauntedly denied
before the king that he had ever consented to have his hand and seal to
the deed; nor could the archbishop disprove his denial. The king,
who was all submission before, now proceeded to try another line of
conduct. He browbeat Fisher, and threatened him, to make the bishop

come into his views. What now became of Harry's conscience?—Finding Fisher resolute, and the other bishops, who had been trepanned, silent from fear, the king consoled himself with these remarkable words :—" Well, well, my lord of Rochester, it makes no great matter; " we will not stand with you in argument : you are but one man amongst " the rest, if the worst fall out." So we see it was not the force of truth and reason that Harry wanted, but numbers to blind the ignorant and unthinking.

The court, though thus thrown into confusion by the disappearance of the queen, was not dissolved, and upon the next meeting there was much matter propounded. Witnesses were heard touching the consummation of the marriage, and when their depositions had been taken, bishop Fisher, who, it will be remembered, was one of the queen's counsel, spoke as follows :—" All that has been said is no more than what hath " formerly been deposed, examined, thoroughly debated, and scanned " by the best and most learned divines and lawyers that could possibly " be got; which time I do very well remember, and am not ignorant of " the manner of their proceedings, when and where all the allegations " (in respect of what was then produced to the contrary) were then " adjudged vain and frivolous; whereupon the marriage was con- " cluded : which marriage was afterwards approved, and ratified by the " see apostolic, and that in such large and ample manner, as that I " think it a very hard matter now again to call the same question be- " fore another judge."

After him stood up another of her majesty's counsel, Dr. Ridley, who is described as a little man, but of great spirit and profound learning. He said—" My lords, the cardinals, we have heard how the queen her- " self, here in the face of the whole court, and in the presence and hear- " ing of the king himself, called the great God of heaven and earth to " witness, that she was a pure virgin when she first came into the " king's bed, and how she put it to his conscience, speaking unto him " face to face : and, if it were otherwise, we cannot imagine that either " the queen durst so appeal unto him; or the king, so spoke unto, (if " unworthily) would not have contradicted her. Besides, we have here " the testimony of a most reverend father, who hath deposed upon his " oath how the queen had often, *sub testimonio conscientiæ suæ*, said unto " him, how that she never had any carnal knowledge of prince Arthur. " Now, my lords, that such a frolic, or a jest (as that about a cup of " ale, which, together with all the rest that hath been said, are but " mere conjectures and presumptions) should stand in competition with " so great a testimony as a sovereign princess's solemn attestation of " her cause upon the king's conscience, and that conscience clearing " her from such presumption by its own silence, should cause us to lay " aside all reverence which we owe to former power and authority, as " that all the determinations, consultations, approbations, confirmations " of all former powers, even of the see apostolic itself, should become " void, by your calling this matter again into question, is a thing, in my " conceit, most detestable to be rehearsed, and a great shame to this " honourable court to hear such stuff ripped up to no other purpose but " in contempt of former power, and calling the wisdom of our ancestors " and predecessors, together with our own, into question and derision."

This defence somewhat nettled one of the judges, Wolsey, who was supposed to be the originator of the scruples, while Campegio was intent on doing justice.   He desired that Dr. Tonstal, bishop of London, should be called.   This was a man of profound judgment and great erudition, and had written an excellent treatise in defence of the queen's marriage, which was intended to have been read in court, but Harry, the conscientious Harry, though professing to rely on the sound learning of the prelates, took care to have this able advocate of justice out of the way, by sending him on an embassy into Scotland.   The general opinion entertained was, that if the queen had not appealed to Rome, the marriage would have been confirmed in this session of the court; but the appeal being carried to a higher tribunal, on the motion of the bishop of Ely, another of the queen's counsel, the legates determined to hear no further pleadings.

The king, who thought all was going right, found himself thus disappointed, upon which he intrigued, good conscientious man, with the cardinal of York, to get the queen to consent to the judgment of the court, but she was not to be persuaded from her first determination.—The king was now growing impatient, and to bring the matter to an issue, he directed that another session should be held, at which be attended in person and urged a final sentence.   The proceedings of the court having been read, the king's counsel called for judgment; on which Campegio replied in these words:—" Not so; I will give no " sentence before I have made a relation of the whole transactions of " these affairs unto the pope, whereunto I am obliged by virtue of the " queen's appeal, considering whose commissioners we are, and by " whose authority we here sit. I come not hither for favour or dread- " sake, to pleasure any person living, be he king or subject; neither " for any such respect-sake will I offend my conscience, or displease " my God. I am now an old man, both weak and sickly; and should I " now put my soul in danger of God's displeasure and everlasting dam- " nation, for fear or favour of any prince in this world, it is not all the " princes in this world can give me comfort. I come hither to do jus- " tice, according to my conscience; I have heard the allegations, the " party hath appealed from our sentence, as supposing us to be unfit " judges in her cause, being subjects (under so high authority, and in " his own realm) that dare not do her justice, fearing the king's dis- " pleasure; wherefore I will not do an act which I cannot answer to " God, nor my superior; and therefore I adjourn the court for this time." Thus the court was dissolved.

To illustrate the question we will digress from the present proceedings, and notice a precedent in the history of France, in which the pope's authority was more successful than in the case of Catharine.   Harry's divorce is not the only instance in the annals of our own country of royal separations, as John was divorced from his wife Avisa, by some unprincipled churchman, in order that he might marry Isabella of Angouleme, with whose beauty he was captivated.   But as the repudiated wife did not seek the restoration of her conjugal rights by an appeal to Rome, the holy see did not take cognizance of the matter.   It was not so however with the cause of Ingelburga, queen of France, about the same period.   Philip, the French king, on his return from Palestine, found himself a widower, by the death of his queen Isabella, and not liking a state of single blessedness he wished to marry again. Accordingly he deputed the bishop of Noyon to the king of Denmark with proposals to marry his sister Ingelburga. The Danish monarch assented, the princess was sent off with a suitable train of attendants, she arrived in France, and was married to Philip by the archbishop of Amiens. On the next day she was solemnly crowned queen of France, but by some unaccountable cause, during the ceremony Philip conceived an utter aversion for the person of his queen, and at the end of three months measures were concerted to obtain a divorce. No reason was assigned for this strange change in the king's mind; Ingelburga was lovely and virtuous; but a monarch's taste must be indulged.

The doctrine of the Catholic church is, that when a marriage is lawfully contracted, no power on earth can dissolve it. Even adultery is not a sufficient ground for a divorce, though it may be for a separation. Since the reformation so called, however, it has been discovered, in this country at least, that parliament can dispense with that ordinance of our Maker,—" What God hath joined together let no man put asunder." It has been found, since Harry the eighth established the precedent, that adultery is a sufficient cause to dissolve the marriage contract, so that a married couple, rich enough to pay for an act of parliament, if tired of each other's company, have only to commit an offence, which God ordered the Israelites to punish with death, and they can have a parliamentary indulgence to engage in a second marriage, during each other's lives.

Such a license to commit sin is not legally known in the Catholic church. There have been, and there always will be, men ready to barter the sacred functions of their office, to gratify the ambition, or feed the lustful appetite, of monarchs; but the abandonment of individual duty cannot be fixed on the church collectively, unless indeed it can be proved, that she has sanctioned by her laws and councils any such unholy doings. Thus in the case of Philip and Ingelburga, the archbishop of Rheims, who was uncle to the king, and had married him to the unfortunate queen, was weak enough to become the tool of Philip, and declared the marriage null, on the ground of consanguinity. For observe, in this case a plea was set up, to shew that the marriage was not originally lawful, and therefore could not be binding.—The proceedings were communicated to Ingelburga, who had all along been kept ignorant of the king's intentions, and was confined in a convent. Though ignorant of the French language, she was not ignorant of her religion. With the spiritual instructions she had received, she was taught to look upon the pope as the common father of all Christendom, and therefore as soon as she had recovered from the shock given her by the intimation, bursting into tears, she intimated that she appealed to Rome, from the unjust sentence that was pronounced against her marriage.—Her brother Canute, when he was informed of the treatment she had received, seconded her appeal, and sent agents to Rome, with ample proofs to invalidate the plea on which the archbishop had grounded his sentence of divorce.—Proceedings of this kind move slowly at Rome, and Philip, impatient of delay, publicly married Agnes, the daughter of Bertold, duke of Bohemia.—This last act Canute deemed an insult added to injury, and a defiance of justice and decorum. Instead, however, of appealing to arms, as is now the case, and shedding the blood of his subjects, he deputed other deputies to Rome, and pressed for a sentence.—At this time Innocent III. filled the papal chair. Alive to every act of oppression, he warmly espoused the cause of Ingelburga, and proceeded to examine the documents.—While this examination was pending, he admonished Philip to remove the adulteress, but the king was obdurate. The kingdom was laid under an interdict. Philip in revenge, seized the temporalties of the clergy, and tried to gain them over to his ends.—They, however, remained firm, refused his bribes, and told him he must submit.—The king at last complied ; he dismissed Agnes, and the cause of Ingelburga was to undergo another discussion.—A council met at Soissons ; Philip appeared on one hand, attended with the prelates and nobles of the land ; on the other was the queen, with some bishops and a retinue of friends, sent from Denmark by her brother Canute. The king demanded to be separated from Ingelburga, to whom, he said, he was related within the prohibited degree. The Danish minister appealed to the marriage treaty, and proved that the allegation of kindred was altogether unfounded. They saw, however, in the legate's countenance, who presided, a determined partiality in favour of the king, and they therefore said, we appeal from that judge to the pope. A few days after, in consequence of this objection, another legate, a man of unshaken integrity, was appointed, and the discussion was resumed. But the Danes, not imagining such haste, had left the place, and Ingelburga was without an advocate.—The king's counsel pleaded, and called for a reply. At first no answer was given ; but after a short pause, an unknown ecclesiastic stepped forth, meanly habited and of an humble aspect, and requested to be heard. Permission was granted ; he repelled the objections, and demonstrated the law, with such force and eloquence, that he carried conviction to the judges. The king was told that judgment would be pronounced against him ; on which he told the legate he was satisfied, and taking Ingelburga, she was acknowledged as queen, but in return for his dismissal of Agnes, the unfortunate Ingelburga was shut up in the royal castle of Etampes, where she was secluded, not only from the king's society, but from all intercourse with the world. Innocent frequently corresponded with her, and unceasingly urged Philip to be reconciled to her. At length, after a barbarous confinement of twelve years, he took her to his bed and treated her with kindness.

We may here see, by this occurrence, the utility and benefit of having a supreme judge in matters which regard conscience, and are of that nature that justice could not be obtained without such an appeal. Although Philip had not the appointment of bishops in his kingdom, as is now the case with all Protestant states, yet there was always a sort of influence attached to the power of a monarch over the temporalties of the clergy that warped the judgment and conduct of many dignified ecclesiastics, as we see in history, and none more strikingly so than the reign of our eighth Henry. Against this partiality and abandonment of justice the appeal to Rome was always a barrier, and the innocent invariably found justice at the hands of the pope. Thus it was in the case of Ingelburga, and thus it will be found to be with Catherine.

There is another case, likewise, of a royal divorce, and of recent date, which we think will interest our readers, and is not irrelevant to the illustration of the question we are discussing. We allude to the divorce of Napoleon and Josephine, after the former became emperor of France. This couple were originally united under the civil code of the revolutionary reign. When, however, Napoleon took it into his head to be crowned by the late pope Pius VII. whom he dragged across the Alps in the depth of winter, and at an advanced age, to perform the ceremony, the holy father refused to place the crown on Josephine's head, or appear in the ceremony, unless they were married according to the rites of the Catholic church. In consequence of this objection Napoleon consented, and they were married by the pope himself on the eve of the coronation-day. Some time after, the emperor took it into his head that he must form a new dynasty, and as his present empress was too old to lead him to hope for issue, he persuaded her to consent to a divorce, that he might take to himself a youthful bride. Josephine yielded to his wish, and Napoleon found a ready ecclesiastic in the person of cardinal Maury, to whom he had promised the archbishopric of Paris, to give this divorce the mockery of a *religious* sanction. This done, Napoleon woos the eldest daughter of the emperor of Austria, a Catholic sovereign, who, for state purposes, basely consents to give her up, having found prelates to reconcile his conscience to the proceeding. This marriage, like the divorce, had the sanction of a religious ceremony from the same pander as pronounced the separation of the first lawful marriage. But mark; though Josephine did not appeal to the pope, the holy father never would acknowledge the second marriage, nor has it ever been acknowledged by the Church. Thus maintaining the incontrovertible force of the Divine injunction, which forbids man to put asunder what God has joined. The issue by this second marriage was a son; but soon after his birth the father was compelled to resign his throne, from which he was conveyed to a dreary rock, where he lingered a solitary exile till death set him free; his second empress became a widowed wife, to be pitied but unheeded, and the boy is now an orphan under the care of his grandfather. Such is the fate of those who set the precepts of God at nought, and it too often happens that the innocent are involved in the punishment brought on by the guilty. Having thus shewn how careful the Catholic church has ever been to preserve unsullied the divine commands, and how beneficial the supreme authority of the pope is to prevent injustice and check corruption, we shall now proceed in our review of the compilation of lies and misstatements of Fox and Burnet.

The next subject introduced by the *Book of Martyrs* is an " ACCOUNT OF CRANMER," and is given in these words :—" At this period, Dr. Cran-
" mer, a Fellow of Jesus College in Cambridge, meeting accidentally
" with Gardiner and Fox at Waltham, and entering into discourse upon
" the royal marriage, suggested, that the king should engage the chief
" universities and divines of Europe, to examine the lawfulness of his
" marriage ; and if they gave their resolutions against it, then it being
" certain that the pope's dispensation could not derogate from the law
" of God, the marriage must be declared null. This *novel* and *reason-*
" *able* scheme they proposed to the king, who was much pleased with

" it, as he saw this way was better in itself, and would mortify the
" pope. Cranmer was accordingly sent for, and on conversing with
" him, the king conceived a high opinion both of his learning and pru-
" dence, as well as of his probity and sincerity, which took such root in
" his mind, that no artifices, nor calumnies, were ever able to remove
" it." Of the probity and sincerity of this *saint* of the reformation, we
shall have occasion to speak much hereafter, and produce facts that will
shew how well he possessed these excellent qualities. At present we
must confine ourselves to his conduct before he entered on the service of
the king, as an advocate for the divorce of the marriage between Catharine and Henry. Cranmer was admitted into Jesus College, Cambridge, but was deprived of his fellowship for entering into a matrimonial engagement. How he contrived to maintain his wife, we do not
find related in history, but it is stated that after his wife died, he betook himself again to an academical life, entered into holy orders,
and became the tutor to two young gentlemen at Cambridge, sons of
Mr. Cressy at Waltham, to which latter place he retired with his pupils
during the time that university was infected with the plague. It was
here Cranmer fell in with Fox, the king's almoner, and in the course of
conversation on the marriage, Cranmer is said by Fuller, in his Church
History, to have observed, that " if it could be proved that marrying a
" brother's wife is contrary to the law of God, a dispensation would be
" out of the pope's power." This remark being communicated to
Harry, it agreed so well with his *conscientious* scruples, that he determined to ground his case upon it. Cranmer was now made chaplain to
the earl of Wiltshire, Miss Nancy's father, and was recommended by
him to the king, who employed him both in Italy, Germany, and France,
to forward the cause of his divorce in the universities of those countries.
Such was the man selected to manage the foreign universities, by a
" novel and reasonable scheme," as the modern editors call his proposition. By the outset of his life, he appears to have been a fit instrument to conduct the nefarious business, and his subsequent demeanour
will prove him to have been one of the most diabolical villains that
ever stained human form.

THE UNIVERSITIES DECLARE AGAINST THE KING'S MARRIAGE.

After devoting a small space to the disgrace of Wolsey, we are favoured with an account of the decisions of the universities in the following words :—" The king now intending to proceed in the method pro-
" posed by Cranmer, sent to Oxford and Cambridge, to procure their
" conclusions. At Oxford, it was referred by the major part of the con-
" vocation to thirty-three doctors and bachelors of divinity, whom that
" faculty was to name : they were empowered to determine the ques-
" tion, and put the seal of the univerity to their conclusion. And they
" gave their opinions, that the marriage of the brother's wife was con-
" trary both to the laws of God and nature. At Cambridge, the convo-
" cation referred the question to twenty-nine; of which number, two-
" thirds agreeing, they were empowered to put the seal of the univer-
" sity to their determination. These agreed in opinion with those of
" Oxford. The jealousy of Dr. Cranmer's favouring Lutheranism,
" caused the fierce Popish party to oppose every thing in which he was

"engaged. They were also afraid of Ann Boleyn's advancement, who
" was believed to be tinctured with these opinions. Crook, a learned
" man, was employed in Italy, to procure the resolution of divines there;
" in which he was so successful, that besides the great discoveries he
" made in searching the manuscripts of the Greek fathers concerning
" their opinions in this point, he engaged several persons to write for
" the king's cause: and also got the Jews to give their opinions of the
" laws in Leviticus, that they were moral and obligatory; yet, when a
" brother died without issue, his brother might marry his widow within
" Judea, for preserving their families and succession; but they thought
" that might not be done out of Judea. The state of Venice would not
" declare themselves, but said they would be neutral, and it was not
" easy to persuade the divines of the republic to give their opinions, till
" a brief was obtained of the pope, permitting all divines and canonists
" to deliver their opinions according to their consciences. The pope
" abhorred this way of proceeding, though he could not decently oppose
" it: but he said, in great scorn, that no friar should set limits to his
" power. Crook was ordered to give no money, nor make promises to
" any, till they had freely delivered their opinion; which he is said to
" have faithfully observed. He sent over to England an hundred se-
" veral books, and papers, with many subscriptions; all condemning
" the king's marriage as unlawful in itself. At Paris, the Sorbonne
" made their determination with great solemnity; after mass, all the
" doctors took an oath to study the question, and to give their judg-
" ment according to their consciences; and after three weeks study,
" the greater part agreed on this: ' that the king's marriage was un-
" lawful, and that the pope could not dispense with it.' At Orleans,
" Angiers, and Toulouse, they determined to the same purpose."

The sensible reader must smile at this account which is given by
Burnet, a man who ranked as a Christian bishop, yet would persuade
his readers that the Christian advocates of a Christian (so he thought
himself) king, required the opinions of the *Jews*, whether his marriage
contracted under a Christian dispensation, was lawful. Well, they appear to decide against him, for, they say, when a brother died without
issue, his brother might marry his widow; but to get out of this dilemma, they limit the operation of the law to Judea for the preservation of
the succession of families, and make it nugatory out of that country.
What pitiful sophistry is this! Why if the Jews were allowed to take
the brother's widow in Judea to preserve the succession, why not a king
in England, especially after the church of which he was a member had
given a sanction to the contract? Then the Oxford divines gave their
opinion, that " the marriage of the brother's wife was contrary both to
" the laws of God and nature." Prodigious wise! But on what ground
did they form this judgment? On the levitical law? This could not
be, since God had commanded the Jews to marry the brother's wife in
certain cases. On the canons of the Christian or Catholic church? The
church had already decided that the marriage *was* lawful, and had
granted a dispensation by her supreme head to prevent future cavil.
The grounds of this decision was the non-consummation of the marriage,
and the death of one party, which made the former contract completely
void; for as Catharine was a virgin, after the death of the king's bro-

ther, she could hardly be said to have been a wife. The fact is, the decisions given by the universities were founded on false premises, for the essential circumstance of the virginity of the queen, after the death of her first husband, was studiously and partially kept back by the propounders of the question. The Cambridge doctors disputed the case, and those who were against the divorce were not influenced by the injustice attempted on the queen, but from a fierce jealousy of the immaculate Dr. Cranmer, forsooth, who was suspected of favouring Lutheranism; and a fear of Miss Boleyn's advancement. Burnet, we presume, in imputing these unworthy motives to men who had nothing to gain, but every thing to lose by the cause they espoused, measured his neighbour's corn by his own bushel, as he was no unwilling pander to corruption and falsehood. Then, again, we have a learned Dr. Crook fishing up manuscripts from the Greek fathers in Italy condemning the marriage, as if these fathers anticipated the dispute, and left their opinions as a legacy to Harry, to indulge in his adulterous courses under their sanction. This Mr. Crook it seems had another commission entrusted to him, and that was, to influence the cause with the charm of money. Oh! bless the conscience of Harry. Before his nobles and people he could profess the most pious and dutiful submission to the decision of his spiritual guides and judges, and his love of his queen's virtue and person, and that if it were lawful, and he had his choice again, he would select Catharine of all women for his wife. Yet all this while the arch-hypocrite was dying for love of Anne Boleyn, and causing search to be made for the most artful and unprincipled villians that could be found, to cheat the universities of Europe out of a decision against his virtuous and faithful partner, that he might shelter himself under the cloak of religion. But the ways of God are just, and the hoary lecher was compelled to appear in his proper garb.

So determined was the religious Harry to settle his conscience, that it seems he was not content to have the opinions of the *Jews*, but he must also have the sentiments of the *reformers*, the leader of whom he had openly attacked as a heretic and false apostle. The account given of the opinions of these gentlemen are not less ludicrous than those of the universities. " Calvin," we are told, " thought the marriage null, " and all agreed that the pope's dispensation was of no force. Osian-" der was employed to engage the Lutheran divines, but they were " afraid of giving the emperor new grounds of displeasure. Melanc-" thon thought the law in Leviticus was dispensable, and that the " marriage might be lawful; and that, in those matters, states and " princes might make what laws they pleased; and though the divines " of Leipsic, after much disputing about it, did agree, that those laws " were moral, yet they could never be brought to justify the divorce, " with the subsequent marriage; but the pope was more compliant, " for he offered to Cassali, to grant the king dispensation for having " another wife, with which the imperialists seemed not dissatisfied."— From this statement there appears to have been as much difference of opinion among the *reformers* on the question of divorce, as there was on their articles of faith. The offer of the pope to grant Harry a couple of wives we conjecture was introduced by Burnet to cover the disgrace of the patriarchs of the reformation, who, by a written document, under their signatures, granted the Landgrave of Hesse permission to have two wives at once. This gentleman was a disciple of the reformation, and, like Henry, he gave way to the lusts of the flesh, on embracing the *new* doctrines. The cause of this disorder he imputes to his wife, whom he says, he never loved, and whose bed he left a few weeks after mariage to wallow in adultery. As a remedy, therefore, to this course of life, and without which, he avows, he will never change it, he proposes to the reforming divines to allow him to have *another* wife, on the ground " that Luther and Melancthon, to his own knowledge, " advised the king of England not to break off the marriage with the " queen his wife, but, besides her, also to marry another." So then this idea of two wives did not originate with the pope, as Burnet falsely insinuates, but with master Martin Luther and his coadjutors in reform and iniquity. The gospel-loving and pious Landgrave was touched with scruples as well as our Henry, and like him, too, he had the tenderest regard for the character of the woman on whom he might fix his choice, as well as the greatest dread of giving scandal, unless the shield of religion was thrown over their deeds. Here are the Landgrave's words, well worthy of being recorded with the proceedings of the first head of the new church of England :—" But if they apprehend such a certificate " may turn to scandal at this time, and prejudice the gospel-cause, " should it be printed, I desire at least, they will give me a declara- " tion in writing that God would not be offended, should I marry in pri- " vate; and that they will seek for means to make this marriage public " in due time; to the end, that the woman I shall wed may not pass for " a dishonest person; otherwise, in process of time, the *church* would " be scandalized." Then he assures them, that " they need not fear, " lest this second marriage should make him injure his first wife, or " even separate himself from her, since, on the contrary, he is deter- " mined in this occasion to carry his cross, and leave his dominions to " their common children. Let them, therefore, grant me," continues this prince, " in the name of God, what I request of them; to the " end I may both live and die more cheerfully for the gospel-cause, " and more willingly undertake the defence of it; and on my side, I " will do whatsoever they shall in reason ask of me, whether they de- " mand THE REVENUES OF MONASTERIES, or other things of the like na- " ture." Rather than lose such a precious disciple in the " gospel-cause," and to avoid having their *new* church scandalized, these evangelical doctors of the reformation did grant an indulgence under their hands and seals to the petitioner to marry another wife, his present one being still living, thus establishing polygamy as a doctrine of the reformation. This document may be seen at length in Bosuet's Variations.

To place the subject of the divorce in as clear a light as possible, as on this point, we may say, hinged the change of religion in England, and to shew the means resorted to by the adversaries of the queen to gain the semblance of a spiritual confirmation of the king's pretended scruples, we will here insert the account given by Dr. Lingard of these transactions, from his History of England. But first we must observe, that though Crook is represented to have had orders not to make " pro- " mises to any till they had freely delivered their opinions," the same delicacy was not preserved towards the nephew of Catharine, as Henry,

by his ambassadors, promised the emperor Charles, " the sum of three
" hundred thousand crowns, the restoration of the marriage portion paid
" with Catharine, and security for a maintenance suitable to her birth,"
if he would consent to the divorce.   But Charles was inflexible, and told
the worthy representatives of Henry, " he was not a merchant to sell
" the honour of his aunt.   The cause was now before the proper tri-
" bunal.   If the pope should decide against her, he would be silent;
" if in her favour, he would support her cause with all the means which
" God had placed at his disposal."   This fact is related by Dr. Lingard,
and is extracted from Letters written from Bologna by the bishop of
Tarbes, the French ambassador to the English court.   Failing in this
quarter, he rested his hopes on the decisions of the universities, the success of which plan is thus detailed by Dr. Lingard.

    " The new ministers," says that able writer, " condescended to pro-
" fit by the advice of the man whom they had supplanted; and sought,
" in conformity with his recommendation, to obtain in favour of the di-
" vorce, the opinions of the most learned divines, and most celebrated
" universities in Europe.   Henry pursued the scheme with his charac-
" teristic ardour : but, if he was before convinced of the justice of his
" cause, that conviction must have been shaken by the obstinacy of the
" opposition which he every where experienced.   In England it might
" have been expected that the influence of the crown would silence the
" partisans of Catharine : yet even in England it was found necessary
" to employ commands, and promises, and threats, sometimes secret
" intrigue, and sometimes open violence, before a favourable answer
" could be extorted from either of the universities.

    " In Italy the king's agents were active and numerous : their success
" and their failures were perhaps nearly balanced : but the former was
" emblazoned to catch the eye of the public, while the latter were dis-
" creetly concealed.   From the pontiff they had procured a breve, ex-
" horting every man to speak his sentiments without fear or favour;
" and taking their respective stations in the principal cities from Venice
" to Rome, they distributed according to their discretion the monies
" which had been remitted to them from England.   They drew an in-
" genious, but in this case not very intelligible, distinction between a
" fee and a bribe : and contended that when they rewarded the sub-
" scriber for his trouble, they paid him nothing as the price of his sub-
" scription.   The result of their exertions were the real or pretended
" answers of the universities of Bologna, Padua, and Ferrara, and the
" subscriptions of some hundreds of individuals.

    " In the Germanic states Henry was less successful.   Not one public
" body could be induced to espouse his cause : even the reformed di-
" vines, with a few exceptions, loudly condemned the divorce; and
" Luther himself wrote to Barnes the royal agent, that he would rather
" allow the king to have two wives at the same time, than to separate
" from Catharine for the purpose of marrying another woman.

    " It was therefore from France and her fourteen universities that the
" most valuable aid was expected.   The bishop of Bayonne had been
" for some months employed in soliciting the votes of the leading mem-
" bers of the different faculties : and Henry had written to the king to
" employ the royal authority in his favour.   But Francis artfully pre-

" tended that he dared not risk the offence of Charles, as long as his
" two sons were detained prisoners in Spain: nor could they be libe-
" rated according to the treaty, till he had paid two millions of crowns
" to the emperor, five hundred thousand to the king of England, and
" had redeemed, in favour of Charles, the lily of diamonds, which Phi-
" lip of Burgundy had formerly pawned to Henry VII. for the sum of
" fifty thousand crowns. The impatience of the king swallowed the
" bait: he was content to make every sacrifice, that he might obtain
" the subscriptions which he sought: he forgave the debt, made a pre-
" sent of the pledge, and added to it a loan of four hundred thousand
" crowns.

" Still the business languished till the earl of Wiltshire was returned
" from Bologna. The university of Paris had long possessed the first
" place among the learned societies of Europe: and it was deemed of
" the greatest importance to obtain from it a favourable decision. Henry
" wrote to the dean with his own hand: Francis commanded the faculty
" of divinity to deliberate on the subject: Montmorency, his prime
" minister, canvassed for votes from house to house: and every absent
" member in the interest of the court was summoned to Paris. Yet
" the majority was decidedly hostile to the pretensions of the king of
" England. From the beginning of June to the middle of August they
" continued to meet and adjourn: and in one instance only, on the se-
" cond of July, was a plurality of voices obtained, by dexterous ma-
" nagement, in favour of Henry. By the order of the court the bishop
" of Senlis carried away the register, that the entry might not be ef-
" faced or rescinded in any subsequent meeting, and an attested copy
" was forwarded to England, and published by the king as the real de-
" cision of the university of Paris. From Orleans and Toulouse, from
" the theologians of Bourges, and the civilians of Angers, similar opi-
" nions were received: but the theologians of the last city pronounced
" in favour of the existing marriage. The other universities were not
" consulted, or their answers were suppressed.

" It had been originally intended to lay before the pontiff this mass
" of opinions and subscriptions, as the united voice of the Christian
" world pronouncing in favour of the divorce. But Clement knew (and
" Henry was aware that he knew) the arts by which they had been
" purchased or extorted: and both were sensible, that, independently
" of other considerations, they did not reach the real merits of the ques-
" tion: for all of them were founded on the supposition that the mar-
" riage between Arthur and Catharine had actually been consummated,
" a disputed point which the king was unable to prove, and which the
" queen most solemnly denied. In the place of these opinions it was
" deemed more prudent to substitute a letter to the pontiff, subscribed
" by the lords spiritual and temporal, and by a certain number of com-
" moners, in the name of the whole nation. This instrument complains
" in forcible terms of Clement's partiality and tergiversation. What
" crime had the king of England committed that he could not obtain
" what the most learned men, and the most celebrated universities de-
" clared to be his right? The kingdom was threatened with the cala-
" mities of a disputed succession, which could be avoided only by a
" lawful marriage; and yet the celebration of that marriage was pre-

" vented by the affected delays and unjust partiality of the pontiff, No-
" thing remained, but to apply the remedy without his interference. It
" might be an evil : but it would prove a less evil, than the precarious
" and perilous situation in which England was now placed.

" To this uncourteous and menacing remonstrance, Clement replied
" with temper and firmness : that the charge of partiality would have
" come with more truth and a better grace from the opposite party :
" that he had pushed his indulgence for the king beyond the bounds of
" law and equity, and had refused to act on the queen's appeal, till the
" whole college of cardinals unanimously charged him with injustice :
" that, if he had not since proceeded with the cause, it was because
" Henry had appointed no attorney to plead for him, and because his
" ambassadors at Bologna had asked for additional time : that the opinions
" which they mentioned, had never been officially communicated to
" the holy see, nor did he know of any, which were fortified with rea-
" sons and authorities to inform his judgment : that if England were
" really threatened with a disputed succession, the danger would not
" be removed, but augmented, by proceedings contrary to right and
" justice : and if lawless remedies were employed, those with whom
" they originated must answer for the result : that, in short, he was
" ready to proceed with the cause immediately, and to shew to the king
" every indulgence and favour compatible with justice : one thing
" only he begged in return, that they would not require of him,
" through gratitude to man, to violate the immutable commandments
" of God."

This account differs very widely from that given by Burnet, and is
more entitled to credit, not only from its carrying the air of probability
and sincerity, but because the historian has given the sources from
whence the facts stated are derived: Thus then we see that the king's
agents were encouraged to employ every species of art and chicanery
to settle the scruples of the conscientious Henry, while, on the other
hand, the holy father was solely intent on doing justice where justice
was due, and preventing the injured party, as far as he could, from
being oppressed. The sovereign pontiff had a conscience to satisfy,
without being disturbed by the violence of criminal passions like Harry,
and therefore his mind was influenced with a desire to see the commandments of God fulfilled and not violated. When Harry found his
case so hopeless, he himself felt a desire to submit to the difficulties
which he found opposed to him ; but this disposition was no sooner
discovered, than Anne Boleyn and her friends took the alarm, and she
was instructed to play off all her arts to win the king from this inclination to become just. The ruin of the ministry, all Anne's creatures,
was predicted, when Cromwell, who had been raised into some note by
the means of Wolsey, stepped forward and rescued them from the danger
by which they were threatened. Of this man we shall have to say more
hereafter, when we come to the dissolution of the monasteries ; we
shall therefore dismiss him for the present, that we may not break in
upon the narrative of the divorce.

During the whole of these discussions, Catharine remained steady to
her resolution of leaving the question in the pope's hands ; every artifice was used to persuade her to consent to a separation, but to no

purpose. "Several lords," writes Dr. Lingard, "were deputed to wait
"on the queen, and to request that for the king's conscience, she would
"refer the matter to the decision of four temporal and four spiritual
"peers. 'God grant him a quiet conscience,' she replied, 'but this
"shall be your answer: I am his wife lawfully married to him by order
"of holy church; and so I will abide until the court of Rome, which
"was privy to the beginning, shall have made an end thereof.' A
"second deputation was sent with an order, for her to leave the palace
"at Windsor. 'Go where I may,' she answered, 'I shall still be his
"lawful wife.' From that day (July 15, 1531) they never more saw
"each other. She repaired to the Moor, thence to Easthamstead,
"and at last fixed her residence at Ampthill." Though Harry had
banished the queen from his presence, he still craved the authority of the
pope to dissolve the contract, and the cause was urged at Rome by the
king's agents with much assiduity. In the mean time, Catharine wrote to
the holy father announcing her formal expulsion from the king's presence,
and praying justice at his hands. Clement could no longer refuse the
prayer of an injured and defenceless woman: he wrote to Henry a
moving letter, in which he painted the infamy of his proceedings; that
having married a most virtuous princess, with whom he had lived in
conjugal happiness for twenty years, he now drove her from his court,
to cohabit with another woman. He therefore exhorted the king to
recall his injured queen, and dismiss the wanton who had supplanted
her. But Harry's conscience, we suppose, was now seared, for instead
of listening to the admonitions of the holy father, he began to shew
symptoms of disobedience to that authority which he had hitherto professed to acknowledge as lawful. The clergy had already been placed
in a præmunire, and now they were forbidden to make constitutions,
although such had been their imprescriptible right, in faith and morals,
from the first foundation of the church. These things being reported
at Rome, Clement pronounced against the claim, and issued a breve
complaining that the king, in defiance of public decency, continued to
cohabit with his mistress. We must here leave the unfortunate Catharine to bring before the reader her supplanter.

THE KING MARRIES ANNE BOLEYN.

We now return to the *Book of Martyrs*, where we find the following
account detailed under the above head:—" Soon after this, the king
"married Anne Boleyn; Rowland Lee (afterwards bishop of Coventry
"and Lichfield) officiated, none being present but the duke of Norfolk,
"and her father, mother, brother, and Cranmer. It was *thought* that the
"former marriage being *null*, the king *might proceed to another*; and per-
"haps, they *hoped*, that as the *pope* had formerly *proposed this method*, so
"he would *now approve* of it. But though the pope had joined himself to
"France, yet he was still so much in *fear* of the emperor, that he dared
"not provoke him. A new citation was therefore issued out, for the
"king to answer to the queen's complaints; but Henry's agents pro-
"tested, that their master was a sovereign prince, and England a *free
"church*, over which *the pope had no authority*; and that the king could
"expect no justice at Rome, where the emperor's power was so great."
This is Burnet's story, and the excuse he makes for the actors in the

scene is, that they *thought* and *hoped*, that the pope would be found as kind as Luther and Co. and grant the scrupulous Harry leave to have *two wives* at once. From this account it is clear the marriage with Anne could not be *lawful*, because no one had pronounced formally against the marriage with Catharine, which, for decency sake, we think should have been done.—The day on which Anne was married to the king, was the 25th of January, 1533, five years after the scruples of Harry's conscience began to work, three of which he scrupulously spent in adultery with Anne; nor is it likely he would have married her so soon, had she not proved to be in a condition to give him hopes of an heir.—In the September preceding he had created her marchioness of Pembroke, and settled upon her a yearly pension of one thousand pounds, out of the ecclesiastical revenue of the bishopric of Durham; so that this lady, who is looked upon as a prime Protestant *saint*, commenced her career by robbing a virtuous woman of the affections of her husband, and the church of her property.—Well, the pious couple were tacked together by Dr. Lee, but not till the king had told him a lie; for when Lee discovered the object of the king, he demurred, having his scruples as well as the royal bridegroom, and it was not till the king told him that the pope had pronounced in his favour, and that the instrument was safely deposited in his closet, that Lee consented to perform the ceremony. For his compliance the celebrant was made bishop of Chester, was afterwards translated to Lichfield and Coventry, and honoured with the presidentship of Wales.—This marriage of Harry, if such it can be called, for though the rites were performed, it could not be legal, being in defiance of both law and justice, and unauthorised by either church or state; this marriage may be considered the foundation stone of that church, which was afterwards established by law, and is now mainly supported by proscriptive tests and penal codes.—Burnet insinuates that the pope was influenced in his conduct, in this dispute about matrimonial rights, between Henry and Catharine, by his fears of the emperor, but there is not a shadow of pretence to bear him out; on the contrary, the testimony preserved, shews that Clement did not wish to meddle with the matter, but desired to see it decided without his interference; yet, when compelled to pronounce his judgment, no other motive appeared to influence him, than that of discharging his duty to God and his conscience, by doing justice to injured innocence, according to the canons of the church. The power of the emperor was not greater at Rome, when Henry went through the mock ceremony of marrying Anne Boleyn, than when she was living with him as his mistress, and he was seeking, by every disreputable means that could be contrived and put in practice by his corrupt agents, to obtain a favourable decision on his side; and it was only when his case became hopeless, that his pride was aroused, and his mercenary disposition set on fire. Then it was, and not till then, the monster threw off the mask of hypocrisy, banished all his scruples, and proclaimed himself head of a *new*, but not "a free" church. Till Henry assumed the supremacy of the church of England, as well as the state, the church might strictly be termed "free," as the ministers had immunities secured to them by Magna Charta, and her doctrine and discipline were not at the nod or caprice of a lecherous old man, a feeble child, or a cold-blooded lasci-

A REVIEW

OF

Fox's Book of Martyrs,

CRITICAL AND HISTORICAL.

No. 34. Printed and Published by W. E. Andrews, 3, Chapter-house-court, St. Paul's Churchyard, London. Price 3d.

EXPLANATION OF THE ENGRAVING.—*This cut represents Cranmer, Archbishop of Canterbury, urging the young King Edward VI. to sign the death warrant for burning Joan Bocher for heresy, which the young prince was at length compelled to do by the arch hypocrite, but with tears in his eyes.*

CONTINUATION OF THE REVIEW.

vious woman.—The church was then secured in her faith by the promises of God, in her morality by the exemplary lives of her most
eminent ministers, and the king, the nobles, the gentry, and people, all
bowed submission to her decrees, as emanating from the Spirit of Truth,
which was to be her guide, till the consummation of the world.—This
is indeed " a free" church, because she was not controlled by the will
of man, nor by any set of men, but by the omnipotent will of God, who
is the author of Justice, Virtue and Freedom.—Now, however, a new
church was to be formed, under the direction of one of the most consummate hypocrites, as we have shewn, and the most inexorable tyrant
that ever wore a crown, as we shall have to shew; and the creed of
this church was not to rest on the word of God, but on the enactments
of a lay parliament. So that as we shall see, by and by, the symbols
of faith were as variable as the wind, and were *changed* as often as it
suited the taste of the head of the church, and his wise counsellors.
Before, however, we enter on the bloody deeds of Henry, we will here
give an outline of the doctrine of supremacy, for adhering to which,

bishop Fisher and Sir Thomas More, two of the most virtuous and learned men of the age, and many other characters of great eminence and learning, suffered martyrdom, and the Catholics of the present day are debarred from exercising those civil immunities granted to the people of this country by the constitution.

THE SUPREMACY.

Burnet gives us in his Abridgment the following "ARGUMENTS FOR REJECTING THE POPE'S POWER," which the modern editors have extracted into their edition of the *Book of Martyrs*. He says,—" In England
" the foundations on which the papal authority was built, had been ex-
" amined with extraordinary care of late years; and several books were
" written on that subject. It was demonstrated that all the apostles
" were made equal in the powers that Christ gave them, and he often
" condemned their contests about superiority, but never declared in St.
" Peter's favour. St. Paul withstood him to his face, and reckoned
" himself not inferior to him. If the dignity of a person left any autho-
" rity with the city in which he sat, then Antioch must carry it as well
" as Rome; and Jerusalem, where Christ suffered, was to be preferred
" to all the world, for it was truly the mother-church. The other pri-
" vileges ascribed to St. Peter, were either only a precedence of order,
" or were occasioned by his fall, as that injunction. ' Feed my sheep,'
" it being a restoring him to the apostolical function. St. Peter had
" also a limited province, the circumcision, as St. Paul had the uncir-
" cumcision, of far greater extent; which shewed that Peter was not
" considered as the universal pastor.

" Several sees, as Ravenna, Milan, and Aquileia, pretended exemption
" from the papal authority. Many English bishops had asserted that
" the popes had no authority against the canons, and to that day no
" canon the pope made was binding till it was received; which shewed
" the pope's authority was not believed to be founded on a divine au-
" thority: and the contests which the kings of England had had with
" the popes concerning investitures, bishops doing homage, appeals to
" Rome, and the authority of papal bulls and provisions, shewed that
" the pope's power was believed to be subject to laws and custom, and
" so not derived from Christ and St. Peter; and as laws had given them
" some power, and princes had been forced in ignorant ages to submit
" to their usurpations, so they might, as they saw cause, change those
" laws, and resume their rights.

" The next point inquired into was, the authority that kings had in
" matters of religion and the church. In the New Testament, Christ
" was himself subject to the civil powers, and charged his disciples not
" to effect temporal dominion. They also wrote to the churches to be
" subject to the higher powers, and call them supreme, and charge every
" soul to be subject to them: so in scripture the king is called head
" and supreme, and every soul is said to be under him, which joined
" together makes up this conclusion, that he is the supreme head over
" all persons. In the primitive church, the bishops only made rules or
" canons, but pretended to no compulsive authority, but what came
" from the civil magistrate. Upon the whole matter, they concluded
" that the pope had no power in England, and that the king had an en-

" tire dominion over all his subjects, which extended even to the re-
" gulation of ecclesiastical matters.

" These questions being fully discussed in many disputes, and pub-
" lished in several books, all the bishops, abbots, and friars of England,
" Fisher only excepted, were so far satisfied with them, that they re-
" solved to comply with the changes the king was resolved to make."

Such is the account which Burnet gives, and it was certainly his interest, who held his prelacy by the king's, not by divine, authority, to
make the people believe what he told them, and unfortunately for the
cause of truth, they have too long given credit to his and such like assertions.—" The foundations on which the papal authority was built,"
we are told, " had been examined with extraordinary care of late years ;
" and several books were written on that subject."—But we ask, by
whom ? And *what* were the *titles* of these books ? The foundation of
the papal authority in England was never disputed till Henry had resolved on parting with his lawful wife Catharine, and the pope had determined not to consent to his iniquitous desires.—The supremacy of
the bishop of Rome, was a doctrine received with the Christian faith in
England, as it was in all other countries that embraced Christianity, and
it is still held by every Catholic nation and people in the world. There
might have been books written on the foundation of claims set up by
some of the popes, regarding the temporalities of the church, but these
claims on the one part, and objections to them on the other part, by no
means affected the *divine right* of the pope to preside over and guide
the church of God, as her visible head on earth. Burnet says, " it was
" demonstrated that all the apostles were *made equal* in the powers that
" Christ gave them, and he often condemned their contests about su-
" periority, but never declared in St. Peter's favour." This prelate of
the establishment did not want for brass, and it required some little
share of this metal to make such an assertion as this. In their ministerial functions, the apostles certainly were made equal, and so are all
Catholic bishops now in their respective dioceses, but Peter received
a charge from his Divine Master which no other apostle did, and consequently that *was* a declaration in his favour.—The charge to feed
Christ's lambs and sheep was given to Peter, and to Peter *only*, in the
presence of the other apostles—but all of them were empowered to
preach the word, to offer sacrifice, and to forgive sins. To Peter too,
and to Peter *alone*, were given the keys of the kingdom of Heaven, and
the promise that the church should be built on him as upon a rock.
(Matt. xvi. 17, 18, 19.) In the Protestant version of the bible, we find
St. Matthew, in the 10th chapter and 2d verse of his gospel, expressly
naming St. Peter as the FIRST apostle, and we also find in the scriptures that Peter was the *first* to confess his faith in Christ (Matt. xvi. 16.);
the *first* to whom Christ appeared after his resurrection (Luke, xxiv. 34.);
the *first* to preach the faith of Christ to the people (Acts, ii. 14.) ; the
first to convert the Jews (*Ibid.* 37) ; and the *first* to receive the Gentiles.
(*Ibid.* x. 17.) With what face then could a bishop, whose church is
said to be founded on scripture, make such an assertion that Christ
never declared in favour of Peter. Can any circumstances be more
clear and explicit than scripture on this question of pre-eminence in
favour of St. Peter ? As we before said, the Catholic bishops are equal

in power in their respective diocesses, but the successor of the first bishop of Rome (St. Peter) succeeded him in his superintendency or jurisdiction over the whole flock, for the purpose of preserving unity.

St. Paul, it is said, withstood him to his face, and reckoned himself not inferior to himself. St. Paul did not doubt St. Peter's right to the supremacy, though he might differ from him as to an *opinion* which Peter might have held. It is one thing to dissent from an opinion merely human, and another to reject a divine command. There is no law in the church to prevent an inferior from finding fault with a superior, provided it is done with due respect and deference, and this is one of the means by which the faith is preserved pure and entire, under the control of the Holy Spirit; for as all the clergy are human. and are therefore liable to fall individually; so, when a departure from truth, or an erroneous opinion is started, it becomes the duty of every man to detect the innovation, and caution the believers against it. It is also a proof that there is a pure system of liberty in the Catholic church, since the pope, though he is *head* of it, is obliged to govern according to the laws, and is not exempt from the censure of his brethren, any more than St. Peter was from the reproach of St. Paul. An instance of this occurred in the year 1331-2, when Pope John XXII. preached a doctrine from the pulpit in Avignon, then the residence of the popes, that was novel in the church. His doctrine was instantly and as openly denounced by an English Dominican, named Wales. The friar was imprisoned for his laudable courage and zeal, but a crowd of divines aided and supported him, and he was released, while the pope explained and retracted what he had advanced. It is said the holy father was written to by the then king of France in this laconic stile.—"Retract, or I will have you burned." St. Cyprian, St. Augustin, and St. Gregory did not consider the opposition of St. Paul, here alluded to, any prejudice to the authority of St. Peter, but, on the contrary, they gave entire submission to the see of Rome, as pre-eminent in dignity, and supreme over the whole flock.

Another objection started is, that "If the dignity of a person left " any authority with the city in which he sat, then Antioch must carry " it as well as Rome; and Jerusalem, where Christ suffered, was to be " preferred to all the world, for it was truly the mother church." To this we answer, that wherever St. Peter went, he still preserved his supremacy. At Jerusalem he presided, at the council held there, as related in the acts of the apostles, and pronounced the decision of the members, but he was not bishop of that city. St. James was the first bishop of Jerusalem. St. Peter established the see of Antioch, and appointed a successor, from whence he went to Rome, and there fixed the seat of supremacy, to which see it has been unalterably fixed to the present day. That this supremacy was to be centered in the Roman pontiff by divine power is clearly manifest, by the immutability of succession, which no other see, we believe, can boast. The sees established by all the other apostles, and even that of Antioch, have been dissevered in their succession; but Rome, the eternal city, notwithstanding the revolutions she has undergone in her temporal concerns and governments, has been the centre of unity of the church of Christ, and will so remain to the end of time; a glorious monument of the unerring word of God, who assured us that his church, founded on a Rock, should withstand every assault of the world and the devil; and here we find, as we have before observed, the supremacy of the see of Rome preserved in an uninterrupted succession for more than eighteen hundred years; a signal proof that a power more than human supports her.

It is also contended that St. Peter had a limited province, "the circumcision, as St. Paul had the uncircumcision, of a far greater extent; "which shewed that Peter was not considered as the *universal* pastor." In opposition to this statement, we shall produce a host of witnesses, who had better means of knowing whether St. Peter's mission was limited than Gilbert Burnet, the Protestant bishop of Sarum. It is really laughable to see the miserable shifts to which the impugners of the pope's supremacy are driven to prop up their cause; for, in one place, we see them contending that all the apostles were equal, though, as we have shewn from scripture, Christ gave more than one command, and promise to Peter *expressly*; and, in another, we have his commission to preach limited, though in conferring this power Christ spoke to them all in general terms. Besides, St. Peter had his commission given to him long before St. Paul was called to the ministry, and received the Gentiles in the person of the Centurion before the latter began to preach.

We have given in the first volume of this work the sentiments of St. Cyprian (p. 90), St. Basil (p. 169), and St. Gregory Nazianzen (p. 170), on the supremacy of the pope; we will here add a few other testimonies from the first ages, to shew that on this doctrine, as well as on all others believed by the Catholic church, there was no variation. To begin then with St. Leo. He calls Rome the head of the Christian world, and adds, that that name is properly hers by reason of the chair of St. Peter, and that Rome extends its authority further by the sacred rights of religion, than by those of temporal government.—*Serm. de Ratio. Apost. edit. Quenal.* p. 164.

St. Optatus says, that the first mark of the true church, is to communicate with the chair of St. Peter.—*Lib. 2. contra Parmen. edit. Dupin,* p. 91.

St. Prosper says the same as St. Leo.—*Lib. de Ingratis, ed. Fraisi. Novo,* p. 119.

St. Chrysostom writes to pope Innocent the first, begging him to annul all that had been done against him in a synod, where Theophilus, patriarch of Alexandria, presided; and to demand justice against his false accusers.—*Ep.* 1, *ad Inno. t.* 2, *con. Lab.* 1300.

Now as to the four first councils, and first as to that of Nice, it is evident that Osius, bishop of Cordova, and Vitus and Vincentius, priests of the church of Rome, presided over it, in the place and by the appointment of Sylvester pope, as Gelasius, who lived more than twelve hundred years ago, has left written.—*Synb. con. Uriæ. l.* 2, *cap.* 5.

Eusebius, l. 7, c. 30, tells us that Paul of Samosata, having been condemned by the second council of Antioch, he would not resign the episcopal palace to him who was chosen in his place, but the emperor Aurelian, though a Pagan, adjusted it to him, to whom the pope gave his communion.

Socrates the historian writes, that the holy canons forbid any thing to be decided in the church, without the consent of the pope.—*Lib.* 2, *c.* 8, *edit. Froben,* p. 296.

Sozomen relates, that St. Athanasius, being deposed by Eusebius of Nicomedia in the council of Antioch, appealed to Rome, and was by the pope reinstated ; the chief care of all things, says the historian, belonging to him by dignity of his chair.—*Lib.* 3, *c.* 8.

Theodoret maintains, that the mighty number of bishops who assembled at Rimini, no ways prejudiced the good cause, because the pope, whose advice, says he, ought in the first place to be taken, did not consent to what was transacted there.—*Lib.* 2, *c.* 22, *edit. Frob.* p. 462.

Evagrius assures us, that the fathers of the council of Ephesus, being on the point to judge Nestorius, said they were assembled in obedience to the canons, and pope Celestine's letter.—*Lib.* 1, *c.* 4, *edit. Froben,* p. 726.

Such a host of witnesses in favour of the supremacy of St. Peter, and his successors, the bishops of Rome, we think must stagger even Burnet himself, were he capable of resuming his prelacy and perusing our Review ; but lest there may be some of the present generation sceptically inclined, we will introduce two of the most celebrated characters of the Reformation, so called, to speak to the article impugned. These are the no less important personages than Luther and Henry. The former, in his letters to the pope before his condemnation, writes with all submission and acknowledgment of the right, power, and supreme authority of the see of Rome. In his letter to pope Leo X. dated on Trinity Sunday, 1518, he says, that he casts himself at his feet, that it belonged to him *alone* to condemn him or absolve him, that he abandoned both himself and his cause to the holy father, resolving to receive his decision as coming from *the mouth of Christ ;* and in another letter to the same pope, dated the 3rd of May, the year following, he acknowledges the church of Rome to be superior to all. Such were the sentiments of Luther before he threw off the spiritual obedience he acknowledged in the pope, and before that authority pronounced upon his conduct ; but when he found himself condemned, and required to retract his erroneous opinions, he then became furious, set up his own *ipse dixit* against the recorded testimony of ages, and in renouncing all rule of authority, save that of his own unbridled will, he gave loose to the flood-gates of the passions, by which he withdrew numbers to shake off the yoke which Christ had declared to be light, to put on the chains of despotism and ungovernable lust. It was this conduct on the part of Luther which called Henry forth to break a lance with him in the field of controversy ; and thus spoke the royal author, on the pope's authority, in his Defence of the Seven Sacraments, against Luther :—" I will " not wrong the bishop of Rome so much, as troublesomely, or care- " fully to dispute his right, as if it were a matter doubtful ; it is suffi- " cient for my present task, that the enemy is so much led by fury, " that he destroys his own credit, and makes clearly appear, that by " mere malice he is so blinded, that he neither sees, nor knows what " he says himself. For he cannot deny, but that all the faithful honour " and acknowledge the sacred Roman see for their mother and supreme, " nor does distance of place or dangers in the way hinder access there- " unto. For if those who come hither from the Indies tell us truth, " the Indians themselves (separated from us by such a vast distance, " both of land and sea) do submit to the see of Rome. If the bishop of

" Rome has got this large power, neither by command of God, nor the
" will of man, but by main force ; I would fain know of Luther, when
" the pope rushed into the possession of so great riches? for so vast a
" power, (especially if it begun in the memory of man) cannot have
" an obscure origin. But perhaps he will say, it is above one or two
" ages since; let him then point out the time by histories; otherwise,
" if it be so ancient that the beginning of so great a thing is quite for-
" got; let him know, that, by all laws, we are forbidden to think other-
" wise, than that thing had a lawful beginning, which so far surpasses
" the memory of man, that its origin cannot be known. It is certain,
" that by the unanimous consent of all nations, it is forbidden to change,
" or move the things which have been for a long time immoveable.—
" Truly, if any will look upon ancient monuments, or read the his-
" tories of former times, he may easily find, that since the conversion
" of the world, all churches in the Christian world have been obedient
" to the see of Rome. We find that, though the empire was translated
" to the Grecians, yet did they still own, and obey the supremacy of the
" church and see of Rome, except they were in any tribulent schism.
" When Luther so impudently asserts, and that against his former
" sentence,) ' That the pope has no kind of right over the Catholic church ;
" no, not so much as human ; but has by mere force tyrannically usurped
" it ; I cannot but admire, that he should expect his readers should be
" so easily induced to believe his words: or so blockish, as to think that
" a priest, without any weapon, or company to defend him, (as doubt-
" less he was, before he enjoyed that which Luther says he usurped)
" could ever expect or hope, without any right or title, to obtain so
" great a command over so many bishops, his fellows, in so many dif-
" ferent, and divers nations.
" How could he expect, I say, that any body would believe, (as I
" know not how he could desire they should,) that all nations, cities,
" nay kingdoms and provinces, should be so prodigal of their rights and
" liberties, as to acknowledge the superiority of a strange priest, to
" whom they should owe no subjection? But what signifies it to know
" the opinion of Luther in this case, when (through anger and malice)
" he himself is ignorant of his own opinion, or what he thinks? but he
" manifestly discovers the darkness of his understanding and knowledge,
" and the folly and blindness of his heart abandoned to a reprobate sense,
" in doing and saying things so inconsistent. How true is that saying
" of the apostle? ' Though I have prophecy, and understand all mys-
" teries, and all knowledge ; and though I have all faith, so as to re-
" move mountains, and have not charity, I am nothing.' Of which cha-
" rity Luther not only shews how void he is, by perishing himself
" through fury; but much more by endeavouring to draw all others
" with him into destruction, whilst he strives to dissuade them from
" their obedience to the chief bishop, whom, in a three-fold manner, he
" himself is bound to obey, viz. as a Christian, as a priest, and as a reli-
" gious brother; his disobedience also deserving to be punished in a tre-
" ble manner: he remembers not how much obedience is better than
" sacrifice: nor does he consider how it is ordained in *Deuteronomy*,
" ' That the man that will do presumptuously, and will not hearken
" unto the priest, (that stands to minister there before the Lord thy

" God,) or unto the judge, even that man shall die.' He considers not,
" I say, what cruel punishment he deserves, that will not obey the chief
" priest and supreme judge upon earth. For this poor brother, being
" cited to appear before the pope, with offers to pay his expenses, and
" promise of safe conduct; he refuses to go without a guard; troubling
" the whole church as much as he could, and exciting the whole body
" to rebel against the head; which to do, is as the sin of witchcraft;
" and in whom to acquiesce, is as the sin of idolatry. Seeing therefore
" that Luther, (moved by hatred) runs head-long on to destruction, and
" refuses to submit to the law of God, but desires to establish a law of
" his own; ' It behoves all Christians to beware, lest (as the apostle
" says) through the disobedience of one, many be made sinners;' but
" on the contrary, by hating and detesting his wickedness, we may sing
" with the prophet, ' I hated the wicked, and loved your law.' "

Having thus established beyond the power of contradiction the divine
right of supremacy in spiritual matters in the pope, we will now proceed to examine the next point which Burnet says was inquired into,
namely, " the authority that kings had in matters of religion and the
" church." He also states that " Christ was himself subject to the
" civil powers, and charged his disciples not to affect temporal domi-
" nion." Admitted; and such is the doctrine of the Catholic church at
this moment. The pope himself, when a subject of the Roman emperors, like his divine Master, was subject to the civil power, but he nevertheless exercised that spiritual authority which was committed to him
by that same Master, to rule and govern the kingdom He came on earth
to establish, which was to embrace every form of temporal government,
and every nation in every clime that chose to submit to the law preached
unto them. This law, as it related to the next world, made no distinction between the king and the peasant, the pontiff and the friar; all were
alike subject to its operations, and the ministers of this law were independent of the temporal governments in the exercise of their spiritual
functions. Their commission was received from God, and they were
amenable to God and his church only for the due performance of their
sacred duties. But let it not be understood that we are contending that
the clergy owed no obedience to the supreme temporal government under which they lived. As subjects of the state, whether monarchical
or democratical—an absolute or limited monarchy, or a republic—
they were bound to yield allegiance to the civil laws of that state, and
to inculcate the duty of obedience to their flocks. Thus, the allegiance
of the Catholic clergy and people is not divided, as is unjustly represented by that portion of the Established clergy which is opposed to
the claims of the Catholic laity of this kingdom to be admitted to those
civil immunities which unjust laws have wrested from them; but it
may be said to be more firmly grounded than that of other religious
denominations, because it springs from the essence of Truth, and is en-
grafted on the pillars of Justice. This question of the supremacy, we
see by the public papers, has been agitated in the House of Lords by the
bishop of Chester, (Dr. Blomfield), and it was some time ago objected
against the Catholics, by the bishop of Peterborough (Dr. Herbert
Marsh), that they could not be good subjects, because their *allegiance*
was divided. If this objection have any foundation, then were our Ca-

tholic ancestors but half subjects to their sovereigns; yet the page of history informs us that these ancestors were able, though the ages they lived in are described by modern editors as " *dark*," to discern the extent of the pope's supremacy, and to interpose their weight in favour of the rights of their kings, whenever an ambitious pontiff in the chair of Peter presumed to encroach upon them. We have many instances in the statute book of barriers to prevent the privileges of the English church from being invaded, but we need not insert them here.— The prelates uncandidly confound the *allegiance* Catholics owe and render to the sovereign power of the state, whether vested in a chief magistrate or a council, and the *obedience* they owe to the head of the Universal Church.—In the first case they give implicit fealty as subjects, in the second submission as children to the head of one family.—While they refuse to admit the right of the chief magistrate of the state to rule in the church of God, they at the same time deny any right on the part of the supreme head of that church, to interfere in the temporal affairs of independent states. Such was the allegiance and obedience rendered to the two supreme powers in Catholic times, when the martial prowess of England was renowned through the world, and her people the happiest in existence; and such is the allegiance and obedience which Catholics in these days give to monarchs and republics, nor can they give any other without flying in the face of the solemn injunctions of their God.

Burnet says the *king* is called *head* and *supreme* in scripture, and every soul is said to be under him, which, *joined together*, makes up this conclusion, that he is the *supreme head* over *all* persons. Who but must smile at the logic of this prelatic historian? In what part of scripture is the *king* called the "head and supreme?" When the Jews sent persons to tempt our blessed Saviour on the point of subjection to the Roman power, what was his answer?—"Render to Cæsar the things that "are Cæsar's, and to God the things that are God's." Or, in other words, Render to the temporal power, of whatever kind soever it may be, the duty of good subjects; and at the same time render to the Church, which I am about to establish on earth to be a light to all generations to lead them to heaven, that obedience which she may exact in my name. Thus SS. Peter and John, when they were desired by the synagogue to desist from preaching Christ crucified, refused to submit, observing they must obey God rather than men. So, when Henry and Elizabeth assumed the supremacy in spirituals as well as temporals, and commanded all to obey her dictates, the Catholics, following the example of the two apostles, refused to acknowledge the new spiritual supremacy, and many of them sealed the refusal with their blood, and all suffered penalties and proscriptions for thus following the divine injunctions of their God. In the Jewish theocracy the two authorities were separated, and when kings were appointed they were not allowed to interfere in the rites of religion, God having selected the high priest for that purpose. In the New Testament we see nothing about kings being "head and supreme;" and St. Paul, in his injunctions to the Romans, speaks not of the *emperor* as being supreme, but of the *power*, the thing itself, as coming from God. But if the scripture is so clear on this point, and conferred the *supremacy* on the king by *divine right*, how did it happen that Henry, when he coveted the title, applied to *Parliament* to confer that *honour* upon him? We know that Cranmer—the double-faced hypocritical villain Cranmer—composed a book to establish the divine right of kings; but Henry was not so ignorant of the constitution of the country as to ground his title on Cranmer's opinion; so far from it, he was sensible that unless he had the sanction of his Parliament, his claim would have the appearance of being illegal. By the power of Parliament then, and not by scripture, was the supremacy of the Church of England conferred on Henry the eighth, and by the same authority is it now held.

It is also contended, that "in the primitive church the bishops only " made rules or canons, but pretended to no compulsive authority but " what came from the civil magistrate;" and therefore, Burnet says, "up- " on the whole of the matter, they concluded that the pope had *no* power " in England, and that the king had an *entire dominion* over *all* his sub- " jects, which extended even to the regulation of *ecclesiastical* matters," This conclusion shews that the deciders paid as little regard to the principles of the civil constitution of England, as they did to the divine rights of the Church of God. Sir Thomas More, however, who refused to admit this power in the king, and was a true Catholic and sound lawyer, decided that this conclusion was illegal and unconstitutional. Our constitution knows of no "entire dominion" in the king " over all his subjects," nor of any *absolute supreme power* immediately under God, in *any sense whatsoever* independently of parliament. This made the venerable and learned More, who professed to have studied the subject as a lawyer with intense application for the last seven years of his life, say, " that a parliament can make a king and may depose him, and that " every parliament man may give his consent thereto, but that the sub- " ject cannot be bound so in the case of supremacy." *(See State Trials.)* Hence it is clear that Henry being dependent on his parliament, according to the principles of the constitution, he could not take upon himself his new title without being authorized by parliament; consequently it was a parliamentary grant and not a divine right.

We allow that the primitive bishops pretended to no compulsive authority, but what came from the civil magistrate; nor can the Catholic church ever claim such power, because it was never given to her; hence we ground our position, THAT PERSECUTION NEVER WAS A PRINCIPLE OF CATHOLIC FAITH OR DISCIPLINE. The church of England, however, in her 37th article, seems to have made *compulsive* authority a question of faith. It is laid down in that article, that power is given by God in the scriptures " to godly princes to " restrain with the civil sword the stubborn and evil doers;" and on this supposition did Harry and Elizabeth get laws passed making matter of conscience acts of high treason, and butchered their subjects without mercy for not conforming to their capricious creeds. It may not be amiss to relate here the means adopted by Henry to obtain an acknowledgement of his supreme headship in spiritual affairs. While the question of separation from Catharine was going on at Rome, Harry contrived to get the clergy into a premunire for admitting Wolsey's legatine power, though it was done by the king's privity, if not with his consent. By this step their persons became liable to imprison-

ment, and their estates to confiscation, so that he got them completely into his power; and as few of them were endued with the desire
of martyrdom, they basely and cowardly submitted to the monarch's
wishes, and agreed to allow him his demands, which were, that no constitution or ordinance should thenceforth be enacted, promulgated, or
put in execution by the clergy, unless the king's highness approved of
it. This took place in 1532. He next tried the council, where a debate was held, whether it were convenient for the king to assume to
himself the supremacy in ecclesiastical affairs? In opposition to this
question the following speech is put down in Lord Herbert's History: " Your highness is come to a point, which needs a strong,
" and firm resolution; it being, not only the most important in itself,
" that can be presented; but likewise of that consequence, that it will
" comprehend your kingdom and posterity. It is, whether in this
" business of your divorce, and second marriage, as well as in all other
" ecclesiastical affairs, in your dominions, you would make use of your
" own, or the pope's authority. For my own part, as an Englishman,
" and your highness's subject, I must wish all power in your highness.
" But when I consider the ancient practice of this kingdom, I cannot
" but think any innovation dangerous. For, if in every temporal estate,
" it be necessary to come to some supreme authority, whence all in-
" ferior magistracy should be derived; it seems much more necessary
" in religion, both as the body thereof seems more susceptible of a
" head, than any else; and, as that head again, must direct so many
" others. We should, therefore, above all things, labour to keep an
" unity in the parts thereof, as being the sacred bond, which knits and
" holds together, not its own alone, but all other government. But
" how much, sir, should we recede from the dignity thereof, if we (at
" once) retrenched this its chief and most eminent part? And who
" ever liked that body long, whose head was taken away? Certainly,
" sir, an authority received for many ages, ought not rashly to be re-
" jected. For is not the pope *communis pater*, in the Christian world,
" and arbiter of their differences? Does not he support the majesty of
" religion, and vindicate it from neglect? Does not the holding his autho-
" rity from God, keep men in awe, not of temporal alone, but eternal
" punishments; and therein extend his power beyond death itself?——
" And will it be secure, to lay aside those potent means of reducing
" people to their duty, and trust only to the sword of justice, and se-
" cular arms? Besides, who shall mitigate the rigour of laws in those
" cases, which may admit exception, if the pope be taken away?
" Who shall presume to give orders, or administer the sacraments of
" the church? Who shall be depositary of the oaths and leagues of
" princes? Or, fulminate against the perjured infractors of them?
" For my part (as affairs now stand) I find not, how, either a general
" peace amongst princes, or any equal moderation in humane affairs, can
" be well conserved without him. For, as his court is a kind of chancery
" to all other courts of justice in the Christian world; so if you take it
" away, you subvert that equity, and conscience, which should be the
" rule, and interpreter of all laws and constitutions whatsoever. I will
" conclude, that I wish your highness (as my king and sovereign) all
" true greatness and happiness; but think it not fit (in this case) that

" your subjects should either examine by what right ecclesiastical go-
" vernment is innovated; or enquire how far they are bound thereby;
" since, beside that it might cause division, and hazard the overthrow
" both of the one and the other authority; it would give that offence
" and scandal abroad, that foreign princes would both reprove and dis-
" allow all our proceedings in this kind, and upon occasion, be disposed
" easily to join against us.' "

Notwithstanding these excellent sentiments, which clearly shewed the
existence, utility, and necessity of a spiritual supremacy, to set bounds
to the ambition and violations of unjust sovereigns, Henry packed a
parliament in the year 1534, which passed an act setting forth, " That
" albeit, the king was supreme head of the church of England, and had
" been so recognized by the clergy of this realm in their convocation;
" yet, for more corroboration thereof, as also for extirpating all errors,
" heresies, and abuses of the same, it was enacted, that the king, his
" heirs and successors, kings of England, should be accepted and re-
" puted the supreme head on earth of the church of England, and have
" and enjoy, united and annexed to the imperial crown of this realm, as
" well the title and stile thereof, as all honours, dignities, pre-eminences,
" jurisdictions, privileges, authorities, immunities, profits and com-
" modities, to the said dignity of supreme head of the same church be-
" longing or appertaining.   And that our said sovereign lord, his heirs
" and successors, kings of this realm, shall have full power and autho-
" rity from time to time to visit and repress, redress, reform, order,
" correct, restrain, and amend all such errors, heresies, abuses, offences,
" contempts and enormities, whatsoever they be, which by any manner
" of spiritual authority or jurisdiction, ought or may lawfully be re-
" formed, repressed, ordered, redressed, corrected, restrained or amend-
" ed, most to the pleasure of Almighty God, the increase of virtue in
" Christ's religion, and the conservation of the peace, unity, and tran-
" quillity of the realm : any usage, custom, foreign laws, foreign prescrip-
" tion, or any thing or things to the contrary thereof notwithstanding."

Burnet would further persuade us that the clergy were unanimous in
acknowledging the right of the king to the supremacy, bishop Fisher
only excepted.—This is a brazen lie, and is contradicted by the records
of history.   Sir T. More suffered death for no other cause than denying
the supremacy of the king in matters of religion.   He, as we have before said, spent part of his time in studying the question, and there cannot be a doubt but that he examined the books published on both sides,
and particularly those in favour of Henry's claim, which Burnet represents to have had the powerful effect of converting " all the bishops,
abbots, and friars of England, Fisher only excepted," to the king's side.
Now what was the result of More's search?   On receiving sentence of
death, he thus addressed the court : " Well, seeing, that I am condemn-
" ed, God knows how justly, I will speak freely for the disburthening
" my conscience what I think of this law.   When I perceived it was
" the king's pleasure to sift out from whence the pope's authority was
" derived; I confess, I studied seven years together to find out the
" truth of it, and I could not meet with the works of any one doctor,
" approved by the church, that avouch a layman was or ever could be
" the head of the church."   And when the chancellor replied, would

you be esteemed wiser or to have a sincerer conscience than all the bishops, learned doctors, nobility and commons of the realm? Sir Thomas answered : "I am able to produce against one bishop, which " you can produce on your side, a hundred holy and Catholic bishops " for my opinion, and against one realm the custom of all Christendom."

Bishop Fisher held the same sentiments, as we find recorded in his Life by Dr. Bailey. After sentence of death had been passed upon him the prelate thus delivered himself to the judges :—" My lords, I am " here condemned before you of high treason, for denial of the king's " supremacy over the church of England ; but by what order of justice, " I leave to God, who is the searcher both of the king's majesty's con- " science and yours. Nevertheless, being found guilty (as it is termed) " I am, and must be, contented with all that God shall send ; to whose " will I wholly refer and submit myself. And now to tell you more " plainly my mind touching this matter of the king's supremacy, I think " indeed, and always have thought, and do now lastly affirm, that his " grace cannot justly claim any such supremacy over the church of God, " as he now taketh upon him ; neither hath it ever been seen or heard " of, that any temporal prince, before his days, hath presumed to that " dignity : wherefore if the king will now adventure himself in pro- " ceeding in this strange and unwonted case, no doubt but he shall " deeply incur the grievous displeasure of Almighty God, to the great " damage of his own soul, and of many others ; and to the utter ruin " of this realm, committed to his charge ; whereof will ensue some " sharp punishment at his hand : wherefore, I pray God, his grace may " remember himself in time, and hearken to good counsel, for the pre- " servation of himself and his realm, and the quietness of all Christen- " dom."

To shew how little reliance is to be placed on Burnet, and the total disregard he shewed for truth, when writing his History of the Reforma- tion, we will here insert some collections from Stow, of the sufferers for denying the supremacy of the king, beside the above mentioned illus- trious characters. The reader will then be able to judge whether " all " the bishops, abbots, and friars of England, Fisher only excepted, were " so far satisfied with them, that they resolved to comply with the " changes the king was resolved to make ;" and also of the bloody means that were put in execution to make them satisfied with these changes.

Sir William Peterson, priest, late commissary of Calais, and sir Wil- liam Richardson, priest of St. Mary's in Calais, were both there drawn, hanged, and quartered, in the market-place, for the supremacy. p. 579.

Dr. Wilson, and Dr. Samson, bishop of Chichester, were sent to the tower, for relieving certain prisoners who had denied to subscribe to the king's supremacy. And for the same offence Richard Farmer, grocer, of London, a rich and wealthy citizen, was committed to the Marshalsea, and after arraigned, and attainted in a *præmunire*, and lost all his goods ; his wife and children thrust out of doors. p. 580.

Robert Barns, D. D. Thomas Gerrard, parson of Honey-lane, and William Jerom, vicar of Stepney-heath, batchelors in divinity : also Edward Powel, Thomas Able, and Richard Fetherston, all three doctors, were drawn from the tower of London to West Smithfield. The three first were drawn to a stake, and there burnt : the other three were drawn to a gallows, and there hanged, beheaded, and quartered. The three first, as appears in their attainders, were executed for divers heresies : the last three for treason ; to wit, for denying the king's supremacy, and affirming his marriage with Catharine to be good. p. 581.

Thomas Empson, sometime a monk of Westminster, who had been prisoner in Newgate more than three years, was brought before the justices in Newgate ; and for that he would not ask the king pardon for denying his supremacy, nor be sworn thereto, his monk's cowl was plucked off his back, and his body reprieved, till the king was informed of his obstinacy. p. 591.

Dr. Forest, a friar observant, was apprehended, for that in secret he had declared to many, that the king was not supreme head of the church. Whereupon he was condemned ; and afterwards, upon a pair of new gallows, set up for that purpose in Smithfield, he was hanged by the middle and arm-pits, alive, and under the gallows was made a fire, wherewith he was burnt and consumed. p. 577.

Hugh Faringdon, abbot of Reading, and two priests named Rugg and Owen, were hanged, and quartered at Reading. The same day was Richard Whiting, abbot of Glastenbury, hanged and quartered on Torehill, adjoining to his monastery. John Thorn, and Roger James, monks, the one treasurer, the other under treasurer of Glastenbury church, were at the same time executed. Also, shortly after, John Beck, abbot of Colchester, was executed at Colchester : all for denying the king's supremacy. p. 577.

Six persons, and one led between two, were drawn to Tyburn ; to wit, Laurence Cook, prior of Doncaster, William Horn, a lay-brother of the Charter-house at London, Giles Horn, gentleman, Clement Philipp, gentleman of Calais, Edmond Bolhelm, priest, Darcy Jennings, Robert Jennings, Robert Bird : and all there hanged and quartered, as having been attainted by parliament, for denying the king's supremacy. p. 581.

Sir David Jenison, knight of Rhodes, was drawn through Southwark, to St. Thomas of Watterings, and there executed for the supremacy. ib.

German Gardiner, and Lark, parson of Chelsea, were executed at Tyburn, for denying the king's supremacy ; as likewise one Ashby. p.585.

It is a fact, indisputably proved, that Henry VIII. was the first king of England, that ever gave leave to bishops to exercise jurisdiction without being approved of at Rome, the first that ever stiled himself head of the church, and the first that ever made it treason to refuse that title.—This assumption surprised all Europe, and well might it do when this very same king had stood forth the champion of the pope's supremacy, as of divine right, against Luther, when that arch-heretic threw off the yoke of obedience.—Henry charged Luther with acting under the influence of anger, and malice, and hatred, and so it was with Henry himself.—His defence was written before he became enamoured of Anne Boleyn, and when his mind was impressed with the duties and obligations of a Christian sovereign ; but when his heart was filled with the flame of lust, and, like Luther, he found himself restrained and condemned by the lawful authority of the church ; then it was he gave loose to his passions, and in his rage to vex and mortify the holy father, who reproved him, with a view to bring him to a sense of duty, he resolved to destroy, as far as he was able, that supremacy which he had acknowledged and proved to be of divine origin, and involve his kingdom in all the horrors of schism and corruption.—Perfectly sensible that reason and argument would only retard and render his designs abortive, he employed the civil sword to establish his spiritual supremacy, and made PERSECUTION the basis of his new church. We have shewn the use he made of the knife and the halter, the fagot, to intimidate the clergy and learned into submission, it only remains for us to shew how the people were brought over to the views of the court. To grant spiritual supremacy to a lay prince was an idea so repugnant to the people, that the proposition was every where received with suspicion and wonder. To remove these feelings, Harry gave orders to have the word "Pope" erased out of every book used in the public worship of the church; every schoolmaster was ordered diligently to inculcate the new doctrine to his pupils; all clergymen, from the prelate to the curate, were directed to teach, every Sunday and holiday, that the king was true head of the church, and the pope's supremacy a mere usurpation; and to prevent the truth from being known, it was made HIGH TREASON for any one to PRINT or *publish* any work against the *spiritual* supremacy of this monarch!!! Thus, in the process of time, the people became immersed in error, and this state of darkness has continued to the present day; though, Heaven be praised, the mist is gradually dispersing, notwithstanding the efforts of designing and ignorant revilers, and the rays of Truth are beaming on this long benighted nation.

Having thus given an outline of the doctrine of Supremacy, we must now return to the subject of the divorce and introduce two more prominent characters in this momentous affair.

CRANMER AND ANNE BOLEYN.

Previous to the establishment of Henry's supremacy by act of Parliament, an act was passed, condemning all appeals to Rome, though the king had been for years appealing to that see, but in vain, to be released from his virtuous wife. This act, like the suppression of the pope's supremacy, had its origin from rage, vexation, and disappointment. The next circumstance of importance was the raising of Thomas Cranmer to the primacy of the English church, which is thus stated in the *Book of Martyrs:*—" Warham, archbishop of Canterbury, having " died the preceding year, was succeeded by Cranmer, who was then " in Germany, disputing in the king's cause with some of the emperor's " divines. The king resolved to advance him to that dignity, and sent " him word of it, that so he might make haste over: but a promotion " so far above his thoughts, had not its common effect on him; he " had a true and primitive sense of so great a charge; and instead of " aspiring to it, feared it; and, returning very slowly to England, " used all his endeavours to be excused from that advancement. Bulls " were sent for to Rome, in order to his consecration, which the " pope granted, and on the 30th of March, Cranmer was conse- " crated by the bishops of Lincoln, Exeter, and St. Asaph. The oath " of the pope was of hard digestion to him. He therefore made a " protestation, before he took it, that he conceived himself not bound " up by it in any thing that was contrary to his duty to God, to his " king, or to his country; and this he repeated when he took it."— The modern editors have made a little free here with Burnet, and left

out the conclusion of the last sentence, which is this : "so that if this
" *seemed too artificial* for a man of his *sincerity ;* yet he acted in
" it fairly, and above board." Such is the way this bishop Burnet
attempts to bolster up the *perjury* of his hero. But let us look a
little deeper into the conduct of this man of sincerity, this leader
in the work of reformation in England. It was in 1529 that Cranmer
put himself at the head of the party that favoured the divorce of
Catharine.—In the year following he wrote a book against the lawfulness of the queen's marriage, in which, he flattered the predominant
passion of the king, and became thereby a great favourite of the monarch. Burnet represents him, at this time, as devoted to Luther's
doctrine, and was considered as the most learned of those who favoured
it.—Miss Anne Boleyn, the same author states, had also received some
impressions of the same doctrine. Henry however was ignorant of these
dispositions and designs of the enemies of the Catholic faith, and the
better to deceive him, this arch-hypocrite continued to say mass and
conform to the Catholic worship, while, according to Burnet, he was a
Lutheran in his heart.—While the suit of the king was pending at
Rome, Cranmer was sent into Italy to manage the cause of Henry.
In the discharge of this duty he went to Rome, where he carried
on the work of dissimulation so well, that the pope made him his peniten-
tiary, which office he accepted, though he was a Lutheran in his
heart. From Rome he goes to Germany, to conduct the king's
case with his Protestant friends, and here, though he had voluntarily
sworn to observe perpetual chastity at his ordination as a priest, he privately married Osiander's niece, a brother reformer, and one of the
most profane and dissolute wretches of the age. Some authors say he
debauched her, and was then compelled to marry her. This circumstance
is not sufficiently authenticated to be given as fact, but the marriage itself is certain. Cranmer, as we have before stated, was expelled Jesus
college, Cambridge, for engaging in wedlock, contrary to the statutes
of the university, but his wife dying he was admitted into holy orders,
on which he solemnly engaged to lead a life of celibacy ; but with this
man of sincerity, solemn oaths were no more binding than the wind ;
nor did he stick at any profligate act of villany which was necessary to
further his ends, and serve the lustful passions of his master. It was
after Cranmer had engaged a second time in wedlock that the archbishopric of Canterbury was offered to him, which he accepted with apparent reluctance, in order to appear with better grace. But though
Cranmer and his reforming colleagues made a jest of the sacred canons
and their oaths, to gratify their brutal lusts, yet the new-elect bishop
was well aware that Harry had an utter aversion to *married* priests, and
therefore it was necessary to dissemble still. What then was he to do?
He had married a wife, he could not therefore desert her, nor could he,
poor fellow, do without her. In this perplexity a lucky device came
into his head, which however was very near ending tragically. Mr.
Mason, in his book of the Consecrations of English Bishops, says,
" Cranmer kept his wife secret for fear of the law, and that they re-
" ported she was carried up and down in a chest, and that at Gravesend
" the wrong end of the chest was set upwards," by which mistake the
good woman was in great danger of having her neck broke.
  Such was the man whom Henry nominated to the see of Canterbury.

A REVIEW

OF

Fox's Book of Martyrs,

CRITICAL AND HISTORICAL.

No. 35. Printed and Published by W. E. Andrews, 3, Chapter-house-court, St. Paul's Churchyard, London. **Price 3d.**

EXPLANATION OF THE ENGRAVING.—*The Execution of the Countess of Salisbury, daughter of George Plantagenet, brother to Edward IV. and mother to Cardinal Pole. Her shining qualifications caused her to be appointed governess to the Princess Mary, afterwards queen of England.—Reproving Henry VIII. for his irregular passions, she fell under his displeasure, and was condemned to be beheaded, without any trial, in the Tower. On the 27th of May 1541, Mr. Echard says, "This old lady, above 70 years of age, being brought to the scaffold, was commanded to lay her head on the block; but she positively refused, saying, So should traitors do, but I am none. Nor did it avail, that the executioner told her that it was customary; but turning her gray head every way, cried out, If you will have my head, get it as you can, so he was constrained to take it off barbarously.*—Hist. of Eng. vol. ii. p. 293.

CONTINUATION OF THE REVIEW.

The pope, who knew no error in him, but that of maintaining the invalidity of Henry's marriage, which, as the holy see had not then decided, he was at full liberty to do, granted him the necessary bulls, which Cranmer scrupled not to receive and acknowledge, though, according to his prelatic panegyrist, he disowned in his heart this very authority. We have seen him associating with the reformers in Germany, and approving of their new doctrines; we now see him, at the nomination of a Catholic king, for Henry had not yet renounced the pope's supremacy, and by the permission of the pope, submitting to the doctrine and discipline of the church of Rome, and consenting to take the highest dignity of that church in England, for the express purpose of preserving its privileges and seeing that its canons were duly enforced.—Previous to his consecration as archbishop of Canterbury, he had to take an oath of fidelity to the holy see; this, Burnet says, "was of hard digestion to him;" but Tom was never at a loss for expedients, until he had run his career, by meeting with that same terrible end which he had with cold-blooded malice prepared for so many others.—He who shammed unwillingness to accept the high station offered him—he, who had such " a *true* and *primitive* sense of so great a charge"—he, who, "instead of aspiring to it, feared it ;"—he could deliberately call his God to witness an act which he intended the world should think him *sincere* in performing, while inwardly and secretly, it is said, he protested against it. Was ever such a consummate act of perjury before committed ? Can we wonder that *perjury* is now become *a trade* in this Prostestant country—this land of bibles and immorality,—when we have such an example of premeditated false-swearing here set before them in the person of their first Protestant primate, who is extolled too as having a primitive sense of the high religious charge he was then entering upon.—One of the gross calumnies raised against the Catholics by the adherents to the blessed work of Reformation was, that they paid no regard to the sanctity of an oath, and that the pope could dispense with the obligations of an oath at his pleasure. Such an infamous charge, though often repeated, and believed by too many at this day, was never *proved* against the Catholics; but here we have Cranmer treating a solemn compact with his God, as a mere idle ceremony by no means binding, and absolving himself from its obligations even before he was invested with his high functions.

We have Cranmer now seated in the primate's chair of the English church, after having taken the oath of fidelity to the see of St. Peter, as supreme over the universal church of Christ. He had also as solemnly engaged to preserve the church of England in all her rights and privileges, such as he found them when he was installed archbishop of Canterbury, and as they had been secured by one of his predecessors, cardinal Langton, under Magna Charta.—Cranmer, however, was no sooner seated in his high office, than he began to play the sycophant, the hypocrite, and the tyrant. The pope, who had granted the necessary bulls to authorize Cranmer to act canonically as archbishop, could not be brought to consent to the divorce of Catharine, and Henry, who had taken upon himself to be supreme head of the church in England, was resolved upon a divorce; and he was further determined that there should be some *shew*, some *appearance* of *authority* for this separation from his lawful wife.—But then there was a great obstacle in the way, which was to discover in whom this power or authority was lodged, and who was to be the executive minister to put it in force.— To get over this difficulty, Cranmer abandons his promise of fidelity to the pope, and feigning himself another Nathan sent to reprove a second David, or a John Baptist censuring a Herod, he writes a serious letter, by virtue of his archiepiscopal authority, on his incestuous marriage with Catharine ; "a marriage," he said, "the world had long been scandalized with," and declared that for his part, he was determined to suffer no longer so great a scandal. He therefore concludes by requesting his majesty to empower him, the archbishop to *examine* and *pronounce* a final sentence on the question. Accordingly the king has an instrument drawn up, which he signs and seals, giving the primate authority to call a court, and put an end to the dispute between him and his faithful wife.—As this document is a novelty, in the annals of history, we will here give the words of it, for the amusement of the reader.—" Wherefore ye whom God and WE have ordained arch-" bishop of Canterbury, and primate of this our realm of England, to " whose office it has been, and is appertaining, by the sufferance of us " and our progenitors, as you write yourself most justly and truly, to " order, judge, and determine mere spiritual causes within this our " realm.——Therefore in your most humble wise, you apply unto us in " the said letters, to grant unto you our license, to proceed to the exa-" mination and final determination of the said cause, in exoneration of " your conscience towards God.—Wherefore we inclining to your hum-" ble petition, by these our letters, sealed with our seal, and signed " with our sign manual, do license you to proceed in the said cause, " and to the examination and final determination of the same."—Here is hypocrisy in perfection. When Cranmer wrote his letter, he knew that Catharine had been expelled the nuptial bed, and that a *private* marriage had already taken place between Anne Boleyn and Henry.— Then again, the king, who is the sinner, empowers Cranmer the re-prover, to sift and pronounce upon the case. The man by whom, next to God, Cranmer was raised to his office, according to Harry's laws, is to be judged by the creature he made; a very pretty judgment, a very impartial decision, by no means to be suspected, must of course be the result.—That the queen thought so, we may infer by the respect she paid to the farce about to be acted.

Cranmer was consecrated on the 30th of March, 1533, and on the 20th of May following, he opened a court at Dunstable, by the strength of the above instrument, consisting of bishops, divines and civilians. Here he summoned his royal ordainer, who answered by his proctor. He then summoned Catharine, who nobly scorned his summons and disowned his authority.—For this dignified conduct she was pronounced contumacious, and on the 23d of that same month, the archbishop pronounced sentence, that the marriage between Henry and Catharine was void from the beginning.—That such a sentence would follow, must have been anticipated by every man of common sense, but what can he think of the archbishop, who, though he denied in his heart the authority of the pope and the holy see, yet, in the sentence he pronounced, takes upon himself the title of legate of the holy see-apostolic ! ! !—Five days after he had separated Harry from his lawful wife, by a marriage that had received the sanction of the pope and all the learned men of that age; that had been defended as valid by the brightest and most learned men then living, Cranmer confirmed the private marriage of Anne Boleyn, though that marriage had been contracted before that of Catharine was declared null; a circumstance as irregular as unprecedented.—Thus then we see an affair which had occupied the court of Rome above seven years, decided by Cranmer in as many weeks, from the time he entered on his office. Tom soon found out the secret after he was elevated to the supremacy.—Let me alone, says he to Harry, I will find out the mode by which you shall get released from your old but excellent wife, and take an amorous young damsel to your bed;

and this too without *scruple* to your *tender conscience*, which, I know
has been goading you, most religious monarch, these seven long years.
But first make me archbishop of Canterbury, and you shall have every
thing to your wishes. So it turned out; for Cranmer consented to
every whim and cruelty the capricious and sanguinary-minded Harry
thought proper to indulge in.

Well, the decision of Cranmer was communicated to the king in a
letter from the former, who with the most exquisite hypocrisy, gravely
exhorted Harry to submit to the law of God, and to avoid those reproaches which he must have incurred by persisting in an incestuous
intercourse with his brother's widow.—But now another difficulty
started. It was asked, how could the king proceed to a new marriage
before the former one was annulled? Would the right of succession
be less doubtful, in the case of issue by Anne than by Catharine. To
silence these questions Cranmer soon adopted an expedient. He cited
another court at Lambeth on the 28th of May (excellent speed!) before
which the proctor of the king appeared, and declared officially that
Henry and Anne had been joined in wedlock, whereupon the pliant
archbishop *confirmed* the same by his *pastoral* and *judicial* authority, and
wo to those who had the temerity to call his decision in question.
Catharine received an order to assume no other title than that of princess dowager, to which order she refused to accede, nor would she
employ any one about her who did not address and acknowledge her as
queen. Her fate became the subject of commiseration with foreign
nations, and in England the popular feeling was in her favour.—Most
men, to be sure, had the prudence to be silent, but the women loudly
expressed their indignation at the treatment of their queen. To check
their boldness and inspire some awe, Henry committed the wife of the
viscount Rochford to the tower.—When Clement VII. learned what
Cranmer had been doing, and that Anne Boleyn was actually married
to the king, he hesitated no longer on the matter.—He formally annulled the sentence given by Cranmer as uncanonical and unauthorised,
and excommunicated Henry and Anne, unless they should separate by
a certain time, or shew cause why they claimed to be husband and
wife.

We must now bring Anne before our readers, and let our new archbishop retire for a time to the back ground.—Burnet and the Book of
Martyrs, say, "The convocation having thus judged in the matter, the
" ceremony of pronouncing the divorce judicially was now only want-
" ing. The *new queen* being pregnant, was a great evidence of her
" having preserved her chastity previously to her marriage. On Easter
" eve, she was declared queen." And in another place the account
says, "All people admired her conduct, who during so many years
" managed the spirit of so violent a king in such a manner, as neither
" to surfeit him with too many favours, nor to provoke him with too
" much rigour. They that loved the reformation, looked for better
" days *under her protection*; but many priests and friars, both in sermons
" and discourses, condemned the king's proceedings." Liars they say
have but short memories, and so it turns out with this bishop Burnet
and the modern editors of the Book of Martyrs; for here they confess
that many priests and friars openly condemned the proceedings of

Henry, whereas they told us but a few pages preceding, that "*all* the "bishops, abbots, and friars of England, Fisher only excepted," were' unanimously satisfied with Henry's proceedings. Again, how are we to reconcile this statement that Nancy's conduct was admired" during so *many years*" by the people, when the people are represented as taking part with her unfortunate but magnanimous rival, and she tried but *three* years with the king after her public marriage with him. If those "that *loved* the reformation, looked for better "days under her protection," they found themselves most egregiously mistaken, for Harry did not begin to be that sanguinary monarch he shewed himself, until he became acquainted with Miss Boleyn and Tom Cranmer, when he gave way to that insatiable lust and merciless cruelty which stain his character and cast a stigma on the human name. Even Burnet acknowledges that "it does not appear that cruelty was "natural to him. For in twenty-five years reign, none had suffered for "any crime against the state" except two individuals, while in the last ten years of his reign the scaffolds were reeking with blood, and the fagots constantly blazing. So that it is clear the merit here imputed to Anne Boleyn should be given to Catharine, with whom he lived happily and contented until he cast his eye on the wanton thus eulogized. But the most curious logic of these editors is the attempt they make to bolster up the chastity of this *Angel of the Reformation*, whose pregnancy *previous* to the divorce of Catharine is made a proof of her immaculate continency. What a system of deception have the people of England been subjected to since the days of that thing called the Reformation. It is a notorious fact to those who are acquainted with history, that Anne Boleyn was the kept mistress of Henry for some time, and that she would not have been married so hastily as she was, had she not proved in a family way *before* her marriage, which marriage took place previous to the former connubial contract the king had engaged in being declared void. Yet we are here told by men pretending to give a true knowledge of the principles of Christianity, that the very state of pregnancy of a woman *not* married, but afterwards married when the king had another wife, was "a great evidence of her having pre- "served her chastity previously to her marriage." This may be Protestant chastity—this may suit a Protestant bishop—but no Catholic, whether bishop or layman, will be found to whitewash such an open and barefaced state of incontinency and adultery.

Neither was her conduct, after she became queen, such as drew upon her the admiration of the people. For two years after her coronation historians take very little notice of her, only that she favoured the progress of Lutheranism, which pleased archbishop Cranmer, and was far from being agreeable to the king. One trait of her feeling we will here give in the words of Mr. Echard, a Protestant divine, from his History of England. Catharine died on the 5th of January, 1536, and "the "king," Mr. Echard says, "received the news of her death, not with- "out tears, and ordered her to be buried in the abbey-church of Peter- "borough. But queen Anne did not carry herself so decently as be- "came a happy rival, expressing too much joy, both in her behaviour "and habit. It was but a few months after that this flourishing queen "met with a fall more unfortunate and fatal than the other." This was in a violent death, which we shall relate by and by; but we must here apostrophize, to render a tribute due to virtue and misfortune, and relate the death of the noble-minded princess in the language of Dr. Lingard.

"During the three last years Catharine with a small establishment "had resided on one of the royal manors. In most points she submit-"ted without a murmur to the royal pleasure : but no promise, no in-"timidation could induce her to forego the title of queen, or to ac-"knowledge the invalidity of her marriage, or to accept the offer made "to her by her nephew, of a safe and honourable asylum either in Spain "or Flanders. It was not that she sought to gratify her pride, or to "secure her personal interests : but she still cherished a persuasion, "that her daughter Mary might at some future period be called to the "throne, and on that account refused to stoop to any concession which "might endanger, or weaken the right of the princess. In her retire-"ment she was harrassed with angry messages from the king : some-"times her servants were discharged for obeying her orders ; some-"times were sworn to follow the instructions which they should receive "from the court : Forest, her confessor, was imprisoned and condemned "for high treason : the act of succession was passed to defeat her claim : "and she believed that Fisher and More had lost their lives merely on "account of their attachment to her cause. Her bodily constitution "was gradually enfeebled by mental suffering : and feeling her health "decline, she repeated a request which had often been refused, that she "might see her daughter, once at least before her death. For Mary, "from the time of the divorce, had been separated from the company, "that she might not imbibe the principles, of her mother. But at the "age of twenty she could not be ignorant of the injuries which both "had suffered : and her resentment was daily strengthened by the jea-"lousy of a hostile queen, and the caprice of a despotic father. Henry "had the cruelty to refuse this last consolation to the unfortunate Ca-"tharine, who from her death-bed dictated a short letter to 'her most "dear lord, king, and husband.' She conjured him to think of his sal-"vation ; forgave him all the wrongs which he had done her ; recom-"mended their daughter Mary to his paternal protection ; and requested "that her three maids might be provided with suitable marriages, and "that her other servants might receive a year's wages. Two copies "were made by her direction, of which one was delivered to Henry, "the other to Eustachio Chapuys, the imperial ambassador, with a re-"quest that, if her husband should refuse, the emperor would reward "her servants. As he perused the letter, the stern heart of Henry was "softened : he shed a tear, and desired the ambassador to bear to her "a kind and consoling message. But she died before his arrival : and "was buried by the king's direction with becoming pomp in the abbey "church of Peterborough. The reputation which she had acquired on "the throne, did not suffer from her disgrace. Her affability and meek-"ness, her piety and charity, had been the theme of universal praise : "the fortitude with which she bore her wrongs, raised her still higher "in the estimation of the public."

Such is the account given by this eloquent writer of the last moments of this model of womankind, and even Burnet and the modern editors are compelled to acknowledge, that " she was exemplary, patient, and " charitable ;" and that " her virtues and her sufferings created an es- " teem for her in all ranks of people." This acknowledgment we con- sider a complete contradiction to their former statement, that all people admired the conduct of her rival, Anne Boleyn, whose personal manners and deportment were the very opposite of Catharine's. Anne had given birth to a princess eight months after her marriage, who was named Elizabeth, and afterwards became queen. In the same month that Ca- tharine died, she felt the pains of premature labour, and was delivered of a dead male child. This accident proved to Henry a bitter disap- pointment, as it was a second failure to his hopes of male issue : and in the moment of vexation he upbraided Anne, who retorted upon him that he had no one to blame but himself, and that her miscarriage had been owing to his fondness for her maid. This was Jane Seymour, who afterwards became queen, and the incident is thus related: When the news of Catharine's death reached the court, Henry, out of respect to her memory and virtues, ordered his servants to wear mourning on the day of her burial, while Anne decked herself out in the gayest of her apparel, and appeared in the highest spirits, saying that now she was indeed a queen, since she had no rival. But in this she found herself unluckily deceived, for in the midst of her joy, she accidentally dis- covered her servant Jane, before mentioned, sitting on the king's knee. Jane was the daughter of a knight of Wiltshire, remarkable for her beauty, and the sight of this familiarity awakened the flame of jealousy in Anne's mind, and produced premature labour. Thus the very cir- cumstance which she imagined was a completion of her triumph, by the dispensation of a just Providence, turned out to be her fall. By her levity and indiscretion, so contrary to the manners of the late queen, she had given occasion to the retailers of scandal to set up some ugly reports of her conduct, which coming to the ears of Henry, an unfa- vourable impression was made in him, which led to Anne's immediate disgrace and imprisonment. Before, however, we proceed in this im- portant and interesting affair, we will here give the account of it as we find it in the *Book of Martyrs.*

" The Popish party saw, with disappointment and concern, that the " queen was the great obstacle to their designs. *She grew not only in* " *the king's esteem, but in the love of the nation.* During the last nine " months of her life she bestowed above 14,000*l. in alms to the poor,* " *and seemed to delight in doing good.* Soon after Catharine's death, " Anne bore a dead son, which was *believed* to have made an unfavour- " able impression on the king's mind. It was also considered, that now " queen Catharine was dead, the *king might marry another,* and *regain* " *the friendship of the pope and the emperor,* and that the *issue by any* " *other marriage would never be questioned.* With these *reasons of state* " the king's affections joined ; for he was *now in love* (if so heartless a " monster was capable of feeling love) with Jane Seymour, whose dis- " position was tempered between the gravity of Catharine and the " gaiety of Anne. The latter used all possible arts to re-inflame his " dying affection ; but *he was weary of her,* and therefore *determined on* " *her destruction ;* to effect which he soon *found a pretence.* Lady Roch- " ford, wife to the brother of Anne, basely accused her husband of a

" criminal intercourse with his sister ; and Norris, Weston, and Brere-
" ton, the king's servants, with Smeton, a musician, were accused of
" the same crime.

" She was confined to her chamber, and the five persons before men-
" tioned were sent to the Tower, whither, the next day, she also was.
" carried. On the river some privy counsellors came to examine her,
" but she made deep protestations of her innocence ; and on landing at
" the Tower she fell on her knees and prayed God to assist her, protest-
" ing her innocence of the crimes laid to her charge. Those who were
" imprisoned on her account denied every thing, except Smeton, who,
" from hopes of favour and acquittal, confessed that he had been cri-
" minally connected with her ; but denied it when he was afterwards
" brought to execution.

" The queen was of a lively temper, and having resided long in the
" French court, had imbibed somewhat of the levities of that people.
" She was also free from pride, and hence, in her exterior, she might
" have condescended too much to her familiar servants.

" Every *court sycophant was now her enemy* ; and Cranmer formed *the*
" *only and honourable exception.* An order was therefore procured, *for-*
" *bidding him to come to court ;* yet he wrote the king a long letter upon
" this critical juncture, wherein he acknowledged, that .' *if* the things
" reported of the queen *were true*, it was the greatest affliction that ever
" befel the king, and therefore *exhorted him to bear it with patience and*
" *submission to the will of God ;* he confessed he never had a better opi-
" nion of any woman than of her ; and that, *next the king*, he *was more*
" *bound to her than to all persons living*, and therefore he begged the
" king's leave *to pray* that she *might be found innocent ;* he loved her
" not a little, because of the love which she seemed *to bear to God and*
" *his gospel ;* but if she was guilty, all that *loved the gospel* must HATE
" *her*, as having been the greatest slander possible to the gospel ; but
" he prayed the king not to entertain *any prejudice to the gospel on her*
" *account*, nor give the world to say, that *his love to that* was founded
" on *the influence she had with him.*' But the king was inexorable. The
" prisoners were put on their trial ; when Smeton pleaded guilty, as
" before ; the rest pleaded not guilty ; but all were condemned."

When we take into consideration the treatment of the Popish party,
as the Catholics are called by Burnet, we need not be surprised that
they felt concern, or that they looked upon Anne Boleyn as " the great
obstacle of their *designs*." Between the proclaiming of Anne as queen
and her fall, the nation had witnessed the violent death of two of the
greatest men of that age, and the execution of several religious men,
for denying the supremacy of the king, which he had assumed, the suppression of several religious houses, which were the friends and supporters of the poor, and all their lands and goods conferred upon the
king by an act of parliament, as were the first fruits and tenths, In
these acts of robbery and cruelty, Cranmer took an active part. The venerable bishop Fisher, who had been a counsellor to the king's father,
Henry VII. executor to the king's mother, and confidential adviser to
the king himself, was summoned before this base upstart and consummate hypocrite, in company with Cromwell, a butcher's son of Ipswich, but now in high favour with Henry, because he could pander to

his wishes, and a Lord Audley, who were appointed commissioners to take Fisher's answer concerning the oath of supremacy. The venerable bishop appeared according to summons, and had not Cranmer's conscience been seared with iron, he must have felt compunction and shame, on beholding a man gray in years, and clothed with the brightest and most heroic virtues, standing before him to speak to a question which he, his judge, had acknowledged under the solemnity of an oath. But Cranmer's heart was steeled against pity and virtue, and the appearance of the venerable confessor of the Catholic faith moved him not. When brought before the commissioners, he informed them that he had examined the oath in all its bearings, and that he could not take it with a safe conscience, unless they would give him leave to alter it in some particulars. To this request it was answered, that "the "king would not in any-wise permit that the oath should admit any ex- "ceptions or alterations whatsoever;" and, added Cranmer, "you must "answer directly, whether you will or will not subscribe." On this the bishop of Rochester promptly and nobly replied, "Then if you will "needs have me answer directly, my answer is, that forasmuch as my "own conscience cannot be satisfied, I absolutely refuse the oath."— Such a decision on the part of Dr. Fisher must have struck the pliant Cranmer to the soul, and no doubt did fire him with revenge. The bishop was instantly committed to the Tower, that is, upon the 26th of April in 1534. While the good prelate remained a prisoner in the tower, every art that cunning could devise was practised to gain him over to the oath, but he was inflexible. In the mean time a parliament was convened on the 23d of November, which though it lasted but fifteen days, was not idle in complying with the king's wishes. The bishop of Rochester's imprisonment, and that of all other men, that should refuse to take the oath of supremacy, was voted good and lawful, which authority was wanting before, and a statute was passed whereby the supremacy of the church of England was granted unto the king and his successors, as a title and stile to his imperial crown, with all its honours, &c. and with full power to repress, reform, correct, restrain, and amend all heresies, &c. Which act being passed was followed by another making it treason for any one, by word or deed, to deny the title of supremacy, as we have before noticed. After being held in confinement somewhat more than a year, he was at last compelled to take his trial like a common malefactor, the right being denied him to be tried by his peers. Several circumstances were deposed against him respecting the supremacy, but the only material evidence against him was a *private* conversation which he held with the solicitor-general, which officer was base enough to appear against him, but not without reproof from the aged and reverend prisoner, for treachery and breach of promise. On this testimony he was found guilty and condemned to suffer death, which sentence was executed on the 2nd of June, 1535, he being in the 77th year of his age. Of this great man the learned and indefatigable historian Dodd speaks thus in his Church History :—

"It happened in these days, what is observable upon most revolu- "tions; both persons and causes lay under a general misrepresentation, "nor was the strictest virtue able to defend itself against calumny.— "Bishop Fisher, a person of primitive behaviour, the oracle of learning,

" and whom Erasmus stiles the phœnix of the age ; a man universally
" applauded in every article of his life, excepting that point for which
" he died ; and yet even here he shewed such a contempt of all worldly
" advantages, that his greatest enemies, when passion did not transport
" them, were forced to acknowledge his sincerity. Yet notwithstand-
" ing the advantage of his character, to put a gloss upon the proceed-
" ings of the court, it was judged necessary to have him represented to
" the people as an obstinate, avaricious, lecherous old man, and a fit ob-
" ject of the king's wrath and indignation ; with which sort of calumnies,
" Bale, Ascham, and some other virulent writers have fouled their pens,
" whilst others of the party have generously removed the calumny.—
" However the people were so over-awed in their behaviour in his re-
" gard, that no one durst speak a word, or move a step in his behalf ;
" whereof there cannot be a greater instance, than the disrespect that
" was shewn to his body after he was beheaded ; no friend he had
" durst approach it ; it lay exposed naked upon the scaffold, from the
" time he suffered, till eight o'clock in the evening, when two watch-
" men hoisted it upon their halberts, and carried it into All-hallows
" Barking church-yard, where it was thrown naked into a hole, with-
" out either coffin, shroud, or any other ceremony becoming his dignity,
" or even that of a Christian. His head indeed was taken care of, and,
" as it is reported, first carried to Anne Boleyn, who being induced by an
" unnatural curiosity, to view that countenance which had so often been
" displeasing to her, and flirting her hand against his mouth with a
" kind of scorn, one of his teeth projecting, she struck her finger
" against it, which razed the skin, and afterwards became a charge-
" able wound, the scar whereof remained as long as she lived.—
" His head was afterwards placed upon London bridge, but within
" a fortnight, by order of council, was thrown into the Thames.—
" This was done to prevent superstition ; for the whole city crowded to
" to see it, upon a report that certain rays of light were observed to shine
" around it. It was also thought proper to remove it upon a political
" account ; for the clouds being now in a great measure dispersed which
" darkened the bishop's character, the people began to express them-
" selves with a great deal of freedom in his favour, and the exposition of
" his head only served to renew the memory of so worthy a prelate, and
" give occasion to many to exclaim against the proceedings of the court.
" He was a stout champion for the dignity of the sacerdotal order ; and
" though he would not suffer the laity to insult the clergy, upon ac-
" count of their misbehaviour, yet he was always one of the first that
" moved for a redress, in a canonical way, and was himself, by his life
" and conversation, the model of a true reformation." As a proof of
the very extraordinary learning and industry of this holy man, Dodd
sets down twenty-one works which he composed in Latin, which were
published in one folio volume, anno 1595, besides a History of the Divorce in MS. once in the possession of Dr. Philips, dean of Rochester,
who fearing it should be found upon him, and he by that means get into
trouble, committed it to the flames soon after bishop Fisher's death. It
is also said, that near a horse-load of manuscript works were burned after
he was condemned.

Of Sir Thomas More, who suffered in the following month, and who was upon the most intimate terms with bishop Fisher, we must be allowed to say something, as we passed his death over slightly in the preceding number. This great lawyer was trepanned in the same manner as the bishop, by Rich the solicitor-general, and Sir Thomas complained in court, that he had been drawn in by flattery and false friendship, and that his words had been strained and mis-reported. In our account of the supremacy, we stated that Sir Thomas More suffered death on no other account than that he would not consent to allow the king to be supreme head of the church, but we did not then state his reasons for this denial, which he grounded on a *political* as well as *a religious* principle. He told them that the oath imposed by the statute was new, and never heard of before, either in England or any other Christian country; that it was expressly against the law of the gospel, which had long conferred the spiritual supremacy upon St. Peter and his successor; that it was directly against several statute laws of England, still in force, and particularly against Magna Charta, whereby all the rights of the church, as usually practised, were constantly and expressly confirmed, among which obedience to the see of Rome, in all matters purely spiritual, was always understood; and that the statute was contrary to the king's coronation oath, which obliged him to maintain and defend the aforesaid privileges. This last objection reminds us of Cranmer's religious consideration of an oath, but to reverse an old saying, like man like master; Henry having got a primate to his own mind, and ready to do all his dirty work, Tom could dispense with Harry's oath as easily as he could with his own, and Harry had no conscientious scruples about it since the dispensation had all the *form* of law. Well, sir Thomas, as every one might have foreseen, and probably did foresee, was condemned to suffer the penalty of high treason, as his reverend and venerable friend had been a few weeks before him; and like Fisher he met his fate like a man, convinced of the uprightness of his conduct and the purity of his conscience. He had done his best to vindicate his own character, that himself and children might stand unblemished before posterity, and full of modesty and resignation, he submitted his neck to the block on the 6th day of July in the last named year, in the 52d year of his age. His head was set up on London bridge, where it remained fourteen days, when his daughter Margaret found means to convey it away. Of this great man Dodd, before quoted, gives the following character.

" I might dispense with myself for entering into a detail in giving the
" character of this worthy person, and content myself with saying, that
" he was the darling of the age, and a good abridgment of all those ex-
" cellences which can be thought to make a layman valuable. Any one
" of the good qualities, he was master of, was sufficient to have recom-
" mended him to posterity; he was an universal scholar, and though he
" lived at a time, and in a kingdom remarkable for learned men, yet he
" was without a rival, both in his way of thinking, and the manner he
" had in communicating himself to others. The gospel, the law, poetry,
" history, &c. were made familiar to him; I might have added his skill
" in politics, but this was the rock he split upon. It is true no one un-
" derstood the game better; but, when once he began to suspect foul

" play, he threw up his cards, and withdrew. ' Had his temper been
" mercenary and ambitious, he might have made his fortune to what de-
" gree he had pleased; but he was altogether above the consideration
" of money, his conscience was not flexible enough for this purpose.'—
" (*Collier's Ecclesiastical History*, vol. ii.) He had a strong genius, a
" soul impregnated with the best ideas of things, and so beautiful a way
" of expressing himself, that it was altogether peculiar to himself; he
" was capable of giving a relish to the most intricate points of law, the
" most abstracted notions of philosophy, and the sourest rules of morality.
" All the princes in Europe both valued and coveted him, excepting that
" one that enjoyed him; all the learned men in Europe were ambitious
" of corresponding with him. Both his writings and conversation were
" so well adapted for the general use of mankind, that he seemed formèd
" on purpose to please and instruct. He was witty upon the most se-
" rious matters, and all his satires were lessons of morality, and full of
" compassion. ' Some think he indulged his levity too far, and that his
" jests were somewhat unseasonable. But, on the other side, it may be
" said, the divertingness of some expressions might result from the for-
" titude and serenity of his mind; that his frequent contemplation of
" death had preserved him from the least surprize, and that the nearest
" prospect could not disconcert his humour, or make the least alteration
" upon him.'—*(Ibid.)* It is, indeed, reported of him, by way of abate-
" ment to his character, that he was no friend to the mendicant orders,
" and sometimes made himself merry with some of their ways and prac-
" tices. To which it may be replied, that his greatest admirers do not
" pretend to make him an angel, or exempt him from the common
" failings others are subject to; but, that, in the main, he was no
" enemy, either to the mendicants, or any other religious order, plainly
" appears from what he wrote in their defence, against Fish in a work
" called the *Supplication of Souls*. As for exposing abuses, provided he
" kept within bounds, he cannot suffer in his general character upon that
" account. And it may be farther said, in regard of his zeal, both for the
" church, and all the members that composed it, that, perhaps, no
" layman ever published more books in their defence, as his writings
" against Dr. Barnes, Joy, Tyndale, Fryth, but most especially against
" Luther, are an everlasting proof." The historian concludes with giving an account of the various compositions from the pen of this sound
lawyer and honest man, which comprised nineteen works in the English
language, verse and prose, and twenty-one in Latin.

We will leave the reader to decide, whether the persecution and death
of these most eminent and irreproachable men were likely to obtain the
favour of popular feeling. The insinuations therefore that Anne was
gaining on the love of the nation, was a gratuitous lie, which no one will
believe after what we have here stated on the authority of the most authentic writers. As to the prodigal bounty of this wanton to the poor,
and her delight in seeming to do good, who besides Burnet and the modern editors of Fox would have ventured such a brazen falsehood?—
Where did she get this sum of money? And *how* did she expend it?
Is it not notorious that her husband was employed during the last nine
months of her life in robbing the poor of their patrimony; and will

it be believed that this lady, whose life was one continued scene of wantonness and levity, was so intent on supplying the wants of the poor, while the king was increasing those wants.

We must now return to the account of Anne, which we have quoted from the *Book of Martyrs*. It is an abridgment of Burnet's *Abridgment*, and we perceive mutilated for the purpose of carrying on that system of deception which the people of England have been so long subjected to. For example, in the second paragraph, the queen is represented as protesting her innocence, and Smeton is made to charge her with guilt, and afterwards to retract the accusation at his execution. Now Burnet in his *Abridgment*, confesses that Anne's " cheerfulness was not always governed with *decency* and *discretion*;" that she " sometimes stood upon her vindication, and at other times she " *confessed* some indiscretions which she afterwards denied;" that " Smeton confessed lewdness with her;" that he " pleaded guilty on his " trial, and confessed that he had known the queen carnally three times;" and that " it *was said*, that he retracted all before he died; but of that " (he adds) *there is no certainty*." Let the reader now compare these admissions of Burnet, with the statement in the second paragraph of our quotation, and say if the modern editors, by their shameful suppressions have not been guilty of brazen-faced falsehoods. The fact is, her carriage was the very opposite of a virtuous and accomplished woman, as Catharine most undoubtedly was, and therefore she had it not in her power to command the affections of the king as Catharine had, even after he had deserted her to indulge in the pursuits of lewdness and debauchery. The designs and rumours about reasons of state and disappointment of party designs, regaining the friendship of the pope, and obtaining issue by another marriage, are only so many plausibilities, put forth to cover the shame and disgrace of this defiler of the king's bed.

We are next informed that, though, but a short time previous, this sweet lady was growing in the love of the nation, no sooner was she attainted of crime than every " court sycophant" became her enemy, except the redoubtable Cranmer, who is said to have adhered to her to the last. The contrary, however, was the case with our hero Tom, whose conduct towards his patroness Anne was marked with duplicity, heartlessness, ingratitude, and treachery, as we shall shew by and by. It is necessary here that we should examine the contents of the letter which our modern editors, on the authority of Burnet, says he wrote to the king. The exhortation of Cranmer to the king to bear his misfortune with patience, if the charges against his beloved friend Anne were true, is a piece with his hypocritical letter to Henry on his pretended incestuous marriage with Catharine, when these two rare characters, of English pope and deputy, conspired to remove the lawful wife to make room for the lady that had now been unfaithful to his royal holiness.— But the asking leave *to pray* for his unfortunate mistress is as curious a request as we ever heard of. What! could he not *pray* without permission from the king any more than *preach?* Then the cant about *the Gospel,* and the *love* which Anne seemed to bear to it and to God;—is any one silly enough to believe that Cranmer dared to use any such language to Henry who had so great a predilection for Catholic doctrine that he made Cranmer conform to it, say mass, and ordain priests ac-

ᐧcording to the Roman ritual for years, though he was, according to Burnet, a Protestant in his heart ?   Again, what are we to think of the archbishop's doctrine, that those who *loved* the gospel must HATE the *queen*,
!not the *crime* she had committed.   The charity of the Catholic church,
leads her to *condemn* the *offence* but *pity* the *offender;* here, however, it is
laid down that the *love* of the *gospel* inspires *hatred* to the *person* of the
ᐧwicked.   It is certainly not inconsistent with the avowed feelings of the
modern editors, who have given circulation to this false and unchari-
ᐧable production with the express view of exciting *hatred* and abhorrence
of the *professors* of Popery.   Next comes his hope that the *king* would
ᐧnot be *prejudiced* against the *gospel* on account of his *fickle wife.* Truly
ᐧthis is something for Cranmer to say. Did he imagine then that the
ᐧking founded his gospel notions on Anne's virtues ?   A precious founda-
ᐧtion, indeed ; but we will acquit Harry of being such a simpleton, for he
ᐧwas more rogue than fool, and was probably aware of the knavish qualities of the primate he had to deal with.

 Dr. Lingard gives a very different version of this affair.   This learned
ᐧhistorian says, Cranmer received an order, on the day after the arrest of
Anne, to repair to his palace at Lambeth, but with an express injunction,
ᐧthat he should not venture into the royal presence.   This order put the
ᐧpliant slave into a panic, and to smooth his way he wrote an ingenious
epistle to the king, in terms similar to those related.   Dr. Lingard's
ᐧauthority is *Burnet,* and he says the letter " certainly does credit to the
ᐧ" ingenuity of the archbishop in the perilous situation in which he
ᐧ" thought himself placed : but I am at a loss to discover in it any trace
ᐧ" of that high courage, and chivalrous justification of the queen's ho-
ᐧ" hour, which have drawn forth the praises of Burnet and his copiers."
Nor can any one else, whose eye is not clouded by prejudice and ignorance.   The alarm of the archbishop proved to be without foundation,
ᐧthough Harry had his reasons for infusing a little terror into him.
ᐧCranmer, though he had written his letter, had not dispatched it ere he
ᐧwas summoned to meet some commissioners in the star chamber,
ᐧwhere proofs of the queen's offence were laid before him, and he was
ᐧrequired to dissolve the marriage between Henry and Catharine.

 " It must have been," writes Dr. Lingard, " a most unwelcome and
" painful task. He had examined that marriage juridically ; had pro-
ᐧ" nounced it good and valid ; and had confirmed it byhis authority as me-
ᐧ" tropolitan and judge. But to hesitate might have cost him his head. He
" acceded to the proposal with all the zeal of a proselyte : and adopting
" as his own the objections to its validity with which he had been fur-
" nished, sent copies of them to both the king and thequeen, ' for the sal-
" vation of their souls,' and the due effect of law : with a summons to
ᐧ" each to appear in his court, and to shew cause why a sentence of
" divorce should not be pronounced.   Never perhaps was there a more
ᐧ" solemn mockery of the forms of justice, than in the pretended trial
ᐧ" of this extraordinary cause. By the king Dr. Sampson was ap-
ᐧ" pointed to act as his proctor : by the queen the Doctors Wotton and
" Barbour were invested with similar powers : the objections were
ᐧ" read : the proctor, on one part admitted them, those on the other
ᐧ" could not refute them : both joined in demanding judgment : and two
" days after the condemnation of the queen by the peers, Cranmer,

" ' having previously invoked the name of Christ, and having God alone
" before his eyes,' pronounced definitively that the marriage formerly
" contracted, solemnized and consummated between Henry and Anne
" Boleyn was and always had been null and void. The whole process
" was afterwards laid before the members of the convocation and the
" two houses of parliament. The former dared not to dissent from the
" decision of the metropolitan : the latter were willing that in such a
" case their ignorance should be guided by the learning of the clergy.
" By both the divorce was approved and confirmed. To Elizabeth, the
" infant daughter of Anne, the necessary consequence was that she,
" like 'her sister, the daughter of Catharine, should be reputed illegi-
" timate." (See the Record in Wilkins. Con. iii. 801.)

The same historian in a note observes, " Burnet, unacquainted with
" this instrument, informs us that the divorce was pronounced in con-
" sequence of an alleged pre-contract of marriage between Anne and
" Percy, afterwards earl of Northumberland : that the latter had so-
" lemnly denied the existence of such contract on the sacrament ; but
" that Anne, through hope of favour, was induced to confess it. That
" Percy denied it, is certain from his letter of the 13th of May; that
" Anne confessed it, is a mere conjecture of the historian, supported by
" no authority. It is most singular that the real nature of the objec-
" tion on which the divorce was founded, is not mentioned in the de-
" cree itself, nor in the acts of the convocation, nor in the act of parlia-
" ment, though it was certainly communicated both to the convocation
" and the parliament. If the reader turn to p. 118, 133, he will find
" that the king had formerly cohabited with Mary, the sister of Anne Bo-
" leyn : which cohabitation, according to the canon law, opposed the same
" impediment to his marriage with Anne, as had before existed to his mar-
" riage with Catharine. On this account he had procured a dispensation
" from pope Clement : but that dispensation, according to the doctrine
" which prevailed after his separation from the communion of Rome, was
" of no force : and hence I am inclined to believe that the real ground of the
" divorce pronounced by Cranmer, was Henry's previous cohabitation
" with Mary Boleyn : that this was admitted on both sides : and that in
" consequence the marriage with Anne, the sister of Mary, was judged
" invalid. Perhaps it may be thought a confirmation of this conjecture,
" that in the parliament, as if an alarm had been already created, Henry,
" at the petition and intercession of the lords and commons, assented
" that dispensations formerly granted by the pope should be esteemed
" valid, and all marriages made in consequence of such dispensations
" before November 3, 1534, should stand good in law, unless they were
" prohibited by the express words of scripture. St. 28 Hen. VIII. 16."

Let us pause here a moment, and look into the conduct of Cranmer
towards this unhappy woman.—We see him introduced into Harry's
favour, through the influence of the earl of Wiltshire, father to Anne
Boleyn ; we see him working zealously to place her on the throne of
England, and we find it stated by Burnet, that "they that loved the reformation, looked for better days under her protection ;" while Cranmer
is represented by the same historian as the head of the reforming party
in England; yet what do we here see ? Do we not behold the vile
and hoary ingrate, not only sacrificing the child of his friend and bene-

factor to please the whim of an inexorable tyrant, but even consenting to wound her tenderest feelings on the verge of death, by annulling that marriage which he had solemnly pronounced good and valid, and declaring the child she had brought forth, and which had been christened by him with all the pomp and splendour of religious and royal ceremony,—a bastard. This "courtly sycophant," who is described by Burnet and the modern editors, as forming "the only honourable exception" of attachment to Anne's cause, who is stated by the same authorities to have assured the king by letter, that next to him, "he was more bound to her than to all persons living;" this idol of the reformation, scrupled not to desert her the moment he found himself in jeopardy, and not only to desert, but even to stab her feelings by his base treatment, in officially tarnishing her character with infamy and her offspring with disgrace. Is there a human being impressed with the feelings of honour that can refrain from execrating the miscreant who could act so infamous and ungrateful a part? Yet this is the man who is put on a level, by Fox, and Burnet, and their copiers, with a Chrysostom, an Ambrose, and an Austin. It was well for him that he did not live till the infant Elizabeth, he thus bastardized came to the crown, as that virgin queen would most assuredly have given him a Roland for his Oliver, had he fallen in her way.

On the very day Cranmer pronounced his judgment, the companions of Anne, one of them her brother, were led to execution; and two days after Anne herself was taken to the fatal scaffold. In giving the relation of her trial and death, Burnet is scrupulously careful in screening Cranmer from any share in the transactions. His name is not once mentioned in the account, though he took so prominent a part, from his situation, in annulling the marriage. He gives us, however, more cant in a message said to have been sent by Anne to the king, in which she thanked him for all his favours, and particularly "for sending her to be " a saint in heaven." Her idea of sanctity must have been a little presumptuous we think, as it does not appear that she ever positively denied or acknowledged her guilt. That she prevaricated is admitted by her panegyrists, and this must be allowed but a hollow kind of holiness to entitle any one to the rank of a saint in heaven. The modern editors, we observe, have suppressed one circumstance connected with the death of this adultress from partiality, we presume to the character of Anne, and *hatred* to that of the *bloody* (as she is unjustly called) queen Mary. This princess, it will be recollected, was the daughter of Catharine, and was not allowed to see her own mother after her separation from Henry. Burnet says, that when Anne had intimation of her death, she among other things, " reflected on her carriage to lady Mary, to whom she had " been too severe a step mother; so she made one of her women sit " down, and she fell on her knees before her and charged her to go to " lady Mary, and in *that* posture, and in *her* name, to ask her forgive- " ness for all she had done against her." So, so; this candidate for a saintship in heaven; this protectoress of the reformation; this woman after Cranmer's own heart,—was *a cruel step mother* as well as *a faithless wife*. How creditable must this be to the reformation of which Anne and Cranmer are allowed to have been the chief props.

Thus, only four months after the death of Catharine fell her rival

A REVIEW

OF

For's Book of Martyrs,

CRITICAL AND HISTORICAL.

No. 36. Printed and Published by W. E. ANDREWS, 3, Chapter-house-court, St. Paul's Churchyard, London. **Price 3d.**

EXPLANATION OF THE ENGRAVING.—*Cranmer, though he had sworn at his ordination, to lead a life of celibacy, or single-blessedness, nevertheless took to himself a wife; but knowing Henry, his master, had a bitter antipathy to married clergymen, he, after he had been made archbishop of Canterbury, had a box made with air holes, in which Mrs. archbishop Cranmer used to be inclosed, whenever the primate removed from town to some one of his palaces. On landing her one time at Greenwich, the sailors not knowing the nature of the cargo, pitched her head downwards, by which the good woman was in danger of having her neck broke, while her good lord was in sad consternation lest he should be discovered.*

CONTINUATION OF THE REVIEW.

Anne Boleyn, as little regarded and respected by the people as Catharine was beloved and lamented. Even Henry, a remorseless barbarian, could not receive the news of his virtuous wife's death without emotions of grief and attachment; but the day on which Anne was executed he dressed himself in his gayest apparel, and the next day appeared as a bridegroom, by taking Jane Seymour for his wife. In closing our account of Anne Boleyn, for we have much more to say of Cranmer, it is worthy of observation; and is mentioned by Dr. Lingard in a note at the end of the fourth volume of his interesting History, that, if this queen was innocent, there was something very singular in the conduct of her daughter Elizabeth. "Mary," he says, "no sooner ascended the throne, than "she hastened to repeal the acts derogatory from the honour of her "mother. Elizabeth sate on it five-and-forty years; yet made no at-

" tempt to vindicate the memory of *her* mother. The proceedings were
" not reviewed; the act of attainder and divorce was not repealed. It
" seemed as if she had forgotten, or wished the world to forget, that
" there ever existed such a woman as Anne Boleyn."·

We must now revert back to the year 1533, the year Cranmer was
made archbishop of Canterbury. We find it stated th[.]. one Frith was
burned in this year for heresy, in which case Cranmer must have had a
hand in his death, he being the primate of England and one of the king's
council. Frith is described as being a young man *much famed for learn-*
ing, and was the *first* who wrote in England against the corporeal presence in the sacrament. This admission is not unworthy of notice.—
Christianity had been part and parcel of the law of the land about 900
years, and the belief in the real presence of the sacrament was part of
that system of Christianity, and had, in fact, been received with the
system by our pagan ancestors. Well, then, is it not somewhat singular that during this long space of years no one should become enlightened
with the truth in this country, though it abounded with learned men,
but this young man Frith? We are told, too, that his book falling into
the hands of Sir Thomas More, that learned scholar answered it. It
is further said that " Frith never saw the answer until he was put in
" prison; and then, though he was loaded with irons, and had no books
" allowed, he replied." Prodigious! This Frith must have been a
very clever man. But as he was not allowed to have any books, how
came he by Sir Thomas More's answer to him? And was he allowed
pen, ink, and paper, though denied books? This is rather inconsistent. Frith is stated to have followed the doctrine of Zuinglius, and
" in his reply he insisted much on the argument, that the Israelites did
" eat the same food, and drank of the same rock, and that rock was
" Christ; and since Christ was only mystically and by faith received by
" by them, he concluded that he was at the present time also received
" only by faith. He shewed that Christ's words, ' This is my body,'
" were accommodated to the Jewish phrase of calling the lamb the
" Lord's passover; and confirmed his opinion with many passages out
" of the fathers, in which the elements were called signs and figures of
" Christ's body; and they said, that upon consecration they did not
" cease to be bread and wine, but remained still in their own proper
" natures. He also shewed that the fathers were strangers to all the
" consequences of that opinion, as that a body could be in more places
" than one at the same time, or could be in a place in the manner of a
" spirit; yet he concluded, that if that opinion were held only as a
" speculation, it might be tolerated, but he condemned the adoration of
" the elements as gross idolatry."

This disciple must have been *learned* indeed to make these discoveries, but none but fools and enthusiasts, we think, can give credit
to his logic. How the plain words of Christ could be accomodated
to the Jewish phrase we cannot divine, but probably Frith had the same
being for a teacher that his master had. Zuinglius informs us that he
had great difficulty in obscuring the clearness of the expression of our
Saviour. This *is* my body; but in the midst of his difficulty the devil,
(whether *black* or *white* he could not tell) helped him out of it by assuring him that, in the language of scripture, " this *is* meaned this *sig-*

sises;" and upon this authority Zuinglius grounded his doctrine. With regard to the passages out of the fathers, we wish that these passages had been given, which we think would have been the case, if truth had been the object of Fox, or Burnet, or the modern editors. Of the fathers of the first five ages we have quoted passages from their works shewing that they believed the same as Catholics now and always did believe, and if Frith had discovered that the passages in the works of any of the fathers had been mistranslated or falsified by Catholic writers in defence of the doctrine of the real presence, why were they not pointed out. This would have been the way to defend the cause of truth; this would have confounded his antagonists, and shamed his persecutors. But such a course was not adopted, and the reason for it was, it could not be so, the fathers being clearly on the Catholic side.— Henry himself wrote in defence of the doctrine of transubstantiation against Luther, in which the royal author says, " the most holy fathers " seeing these things, took all possible care, and used their utmost en- " deavours, that the greatest faith imaginable should be had towards " this most propitiatory sacrament: and that it should be worshipped . " with the greatest honour possible. And for that cause, amongst many " other things, they, with great care, delivered us this also: ' That the " bread and wine do not remain in the Eucharist, but is truly changed " into the body and blood of Christ.' They taught mass to be a sacri- " fice, in which Christ himself is truly offered for the sins of a Christian " people: And so far as it was lawful for mortals, they adorned this im- " mortal mystery with venerable worship, and mystical rites: They " commanded the people to be present in adoration of it, whilst it is ce- " lebrated, for the procuring of their salvation. Finally, lest the laity, " by forbearing to receive the sacrament, should by little and little, omit " it for good and all; they have established an obligation that every " man shall receive at least once a year. By those things, and many of " the like nature, the holy fathers of the church, in several ages, have " demonstrated their care for the faith and veneration of this adorable " sacrament." The royal disputant is clearly opposed to Frith, and shews that so far from the fathers being strangers to the consequences of the opinion that a body could be in more places than one at the same time, they held it as a positive doctrine, that nothing was impossible to God, his body could be in as many places as he pleased, and who can dispute the fact without denying the omnipotence of God?

It is a piece of extreme modesty on the part of Frith to allow the toleration of the opinion if held only as a speculation, "but he condemned," we are told, " the adoration of the elements as gross idolatry." What then we are to suppose that if this enlightened reformer had been in possession of power, he would have served the believers in transubstantiation the same as they served him. But these words are put into this man's mouth, or rather they are foisted on him as part of his book.— Who are the men that adore the elements of bread and wine? Not Catholics. Indeed we know of no men so simple. It is a gross insinuation intended to impose on the credulous, and make them believe that Catholics in adoring the Host in the great and august sacrifice of the mass, give worship to the elements of bread and wine; whereas the homage is paid to God himself, which he commanded should be given, which the apostles gave to him, and every nation on the face of the earth on receiving the light of Christianity. It was left to the reformers of the sixteenth century to impugn the doctrine of the real presence, and deprive their blind followers of the most sublime sacrifice ever offered to the Creator of Mankind, as Luther and Zuinglius acknowledged in their works.

" For these *opinions*," the narration goes on, " Frith was seized in " May, 1533, and brought before Stokesley, Gardiner, and Longland." So, then, after all, Frith's discoveries were only *opinions*, grounded on the whim or caprice of the mind, and not the received doctrines delivered by Christ to the apostles. There was also an apprentice executed with him, one Hewett, on the same account. This Hewett, Stow writes, was a tailor, and we think it would have been better for him if he had minded his thimble and sleeve-board than dabble in theology, which he certainly could not be qualified to engage in. To come at the true circumstances of the death of these two men is a matter of great difficulty, we might say an impossibility at this day; we shall therefore content ourselves with observing that if Frith and Hewett confined their speculative opinions to themselves, and did not attempt to disturb the peace of the king, it was an act of injustice to punish them; but if they acted in defiance of the law, and attempted to beard the constituted authorities, surely those authorities were in duty bound to notice the transgression. We are persuaded that Frith and Hewett were notorious brawlers and disturbers of the peace, or they would not have been punished in the manner they were. We are neither attempting to palliate nor justify their deaths. We condemn *religious* persecution as much as any man, but it should be shewn that those who have suffered for their opinions or creed, have suffered *solely* and exclusively on that account, and not for creating sedition, tumult, or perhaps treason, as we shall shew to have been the case with some of the pretended martyrs in Mary's reign, and as we have shewn was the case with many that have already been noticed by us.

But why should the proceedings against Frith be thought to carry with them the spirit of persecution any more than the proceedings which occur in our days in the courts of justice, when religious fanaticism inspires some bewildered wight to create disturbance in the streets, or insult the ministers of religion? The public journals relate the trial of a man named Hale, in the month of March, 1825, for creating confusion and disturbing the service of the church in St. Clement's Danes, in the Strand. This man, who had been an industrious shoemaker, and realized a property, became fascinated with scripture interpretation, and conceived himself somebody of importance in Bible disputation. He got himself into trouble by spending his money in circulating handbills and pamphlets among the soldiers to dissuade them from fighting, which he maintained was contrary to the scripture. Now he is in prison for challenging the rector of a parish to public disputation in the church, having been tried and found guilty by a jury of his country, and sentenced to pay a fine, which being unable or unwilling to do, he is continued in imprisonment until he complies with his sentence. There can be no doubt that this man is impelled by what he considers a sense of duty; but it is evidently an erroneous impression, and therefore it is necessary, for the sake of peace and justice, that he should be restrained from playing his freaks. Such a proceeding can no more be fairly termed persecution, than the execution of a real malefactor; neither can we call the case of Frith an act of religious persecution, unless it can be clearly proved that he was burned solely and exclusively for believing in the opinions set forth. But admitting that he suffered for conscience sake, and that he was martyred for the truth, where was the great and heroic Cranmer, the chief promoter of the Reformation, that he did not attempt to save the life of Frith? He was then the primate of all England; he was fully convinced, we are informed, of the necessity of a Reformation; yet he coolly allowed poor Frith to be burned for opinions which he privately held himself, but openly taught the contrary. Verily, this Tom Cranmer was a villain of the blackest die.

The modern editors tell us, "this was the last instance of the cruelty of the clergy at that time;" and "gave the new preachers and their "followers some respite." They would have come much nearer the truth had they said, that *now* the bloody work commenced of hanging, bowelling, and quartering, for conscience sake. The king was now, by act of parliament, supreme head of the church, and was empowered to reform all *heresies* and *idolatries*; or rather what he and his satellites might term heresies and idolatries, as it suited their caprice or interest. The queen too, that is the chaste Anne Boleyn, for we are treating of a period anterior to her death, according to Burnet, "openly protected "the reformers; *she* took Latimer and Shaxton to be her chaplains, and "promoted them to the bishoprics of Worcester and Salisbury." Cranmer is represented as "well prepared for that work, to which the pro-"vidence of God now called him;"—and "Cromwell was his great and "constant friend." Thus then every thing was well arranged for the blessed work cut out by the reformers, and it is now our duty to point out what that work was. But first let us give the reader some account of the new character we have before us, and who made so conspicuous a figure in the transactions of the day, till he at last fell into the trap he had prepared for some of those who were opposed to his iniquitous deeds.

Thomas Cromwell was born at Putney, near London, his father being a blacksmith at that place. In the early part of his life he entered as a private soldier in the duke of Bourbon's army, and was at the pillage of Rome by that general, so that he was early initiated in the scenes of rapacity which afterwards followed in his own country. Returning home, he was taken into the service of cardinal Wolsey, by whom he was employed to manage the revenues of the dissolved monasteries, which the cardinal had designed for his projected new colleges. On the fall of his master, Cromwell rose out of his ashes, and became the favourite and confidant of Henry, who raised him to several places of honour and profit, and at last made him vicar-general to his royal popeship, a post never before heard of, and we believe never enjoyed by any other man. By degrees his honours swelled into titles. He was first created lord Cromwell, then made a knight of the garter, and afterwards earl of Essex. This last title was conferred upon him for being the chief projector of the match between Henry and Anne of Cleves, which afterwards turned to his downfall. Such was the man

who was made "vicar-general, and visitor of all the monasteries and
" churches in England, with a delegation of the king's supremacy to
" him; he was also empowered to give commissions subaltern to him-
" self; and all wills, where the estate was in value above 200l. were
" to be proved in his court. This was afterwards (Burnet says) en-
" larged: he was made the king's vicegerent in ecclesiastical matters;
" had the precedence of all persons except the royal family; and his
" authority was in all points the same as had been formerly exercised
" by the pope's legates."—Yet, be it observed, this Cromwell was all
along a layman.—In parliament this son of a blacksmith sat before the
archbishop of Canterbury, Cranmer, and he superseded him in the pre-
sidency of the convocation.—This degradation caused some murmurs
among the bishops, but farther mortifications were reserved for the men
who had basely deserted their duty and bowed to usurped power.—
They were exhorted, and meanly complied, to admit that they did not
derive their power from Christ, but were merely the delegates of the
crown. To such a degree of humiliation were these men reduced, who
but a short time before were looked upon as the instructors of the
people, the protectors of their rights, and the fathers of the poor.

DESTRUCTION OF THE MONASTERIES.

Before we proceed to detail the horrible sacrileges, and the Vandalic
outrages perpetrated by our Gospel reformers, under the cloak of Religion, in which savage and unjust proceedings Cranmer and Cromwell
acted so conspicuous a share, we shall put the reader in possession of
the origin and benefit of the Monastic orders, that a clear view may be
seen of the vast mischief that accrued to the literature, morality, freedom, and happiness of the country, by the destruction of these seats of
learning, virtue, and hospitality.—No order of men, we believe, have
been subjected to so much calumny, scurrility, and invective, as the
orders of Monachism in the Catholic church, and no order of men are
more entitled to the praises of the world for the good they have done
mankind.—The Monastic order is almost coeval with Christianity, and
existed in this island before the second conversion of its inhabitants by
St. Augustine, who was himself a monk. Dr. Milner, in his *History of
Winchester*, speaking of the monks of that cathedral, says, "It is certain
" there were many other monasteries at this period in Britain, as for
" example those of Bangor, Glassenbury, Abingdon, &c. Of the first
" mentioned monastery three abbots were famous, Pelagius, the here-
" tic, A. D. 400; Gildas, the writer, in 550; and Nennius, the historian,
" in 620." The monastic orders were also established in Ireland on
the preaching of Christianity there, the famous monastery on the isle of
Arran having been founded by St. Ailbee, who was a disciple of St.
Patrick, and as the light of truth spread through the country, monasteries were founded and endowed by the piety of the new converts.—
These institutions were governed by rules grounded on the purest principles of Charity and Piety, and every where shed a light of cheerfulness, virtue, and content, not only among the inmates of the cloister,
but among the different classes of villagers which sprung up around the
monastery; for it should be observed, that there was scarcely a town
or village in England that did not owe its origin to the foundation of

some monastery, the recluses in which were the instructors of the ignorant, the physicians of the sick, the comforters of the helpless, the supporters of the traveller, and the fathers of the poor. To give some idea of the extent to which the rules of hospitality were carried, it is recorded that there were sometimes no less than 500 travellers on horseback entertained at a time at Glassenbury abbey. Now as the monks were bound by their rules to provide all travellers, from the baron to the beggar, with all necessaries, some notion may be formed by this one fact of the vast public benefit that accrued from these institutions. But this is only a single advantage derived from these calumniated orders. To them we may consider ourselves indebted for those civil rights which form the fundamental pillars of the British Constitution, and which in its pure state is the most perfect system of rational Liberty ever devised by the human mind.

It has been fashionable, since the destruction of these religious orders, to represent the members of them as "lazy idle drones," and whether we look into a novel or romance, or glance at the stage, we shall see the monk pourtrayed as a monster of intemperance, gluttony, lewdness, and every species of villany that defiles the human heart. To set the reader right on these detestable practices to keep alive prejudices and foster ignorance we will here give the life of a monk, from Dr. Milner's *Winchester*, vol. ii. p. 116. The learned historian, speaking of the Benedictine order founded in that city, writes,—" The objects of this
" course of life may be learned from the rule of that saint; namely, to
" withdraw as much as possible from dangerous temptations, also to
" learn and practise the gospel lessons in their original strictness and
" perfection. Its primary and essential obligations were, to have all
" things in common with their brethren, no person being allowed to
" possess any property as his own; to observe perpetual chastity; and
" to live in obedience to their religious superiors. It will be supposed
" that prayer occupied a great part of their time. In the following ac-
" count, however, of the œconomy of a monastic life, it is to be observed
" that the spiritual exercises, called the canonical hours, were, with
" some variations as to the times of performing them, equally incum-
" bent on secular canons and the clergy in general, as on the monks.
" The time of the monks rising was different, according to the different
" seasons of the year, and the festivals that were solemnized; but the
" more common time appears to have been about the half hour after
" one in the morning, so as to be ready in the choir to begin the night
" office, called *Nocturnæ Vigiliæ*, by two. When these consisted of three
" nocturns, or were otherwise longer, the monks of course rose much
" earlier. In later ages, the whole of this office, and that of the Matu-
" tinæ Laudes, were performed together, and took up, in the singing
" of them, about two hours. There was now an interval of an hour,
" during which the monks were at liberty in some convents, (for this
" was far from being the case in all,) again to repose for a short time
" on their couches; but great numbers every where spent this time in
" private prayer. At five began the service called Prime; at the con-
" clusion of which the community went in procession to the chapter-
" house, to attend to the instructions and exhortations, which we have
" spoken of above. The chapter being finished, they proceeded again

" to the church, to assist at the early, or what was called the Capitular
" Mass. This being finished, there was a space of an hour, or an hour
" and a half, which was employed in manual labour or in study.   At
" eight they again met in the choir to perform the office called Terce,
" or the third hour, which was followed by the high mass; and that
" again by the Sext, or the office of the sixth hour.   These services
" lasted until near ten o'clock, at which time, in later ages, when it
" was not a fasting day, the community proceeded to the refectory to
" dine.   They returned after dinner processionally to the church, in
" order to finish their solemn grace.   There was now a vacant space of
" an hour or an hour and a half, during part of which, those who were
" fatigued were at liberty to take their repose, according to the custom
" in hot countries, which was called from the time of the day when it
" was taken, *The Meridian*.   Others employed this time in walking and
" conversing, except on those days when a general silence was enjoined.
" At one o'clock, None, or the ninth hour, was sung in the choir, as
" were Vespers at three.   At five they met in the refectory, to partake
" of a slender supper, consisting chiefly, both as to victuals and drink,
" of what was saved out of the meal at noon; except on fasting days,
" when nothing, or next to nothing, was allowed to be taken.   The in-
" termediate spaces were occupied with spiritual reading, or studying;
" or with manual labour, which frequently consisted in transcribing
" books.   After the evening refection, a spiritual conference or colla-
" tion was held, until the office called Complin began, which, with cer-
" tain other exercises of devotion, lasted until seven o'clock; when all
" retired to their respective dormitories, which were long galleries
" containing as many beds as could be ranged in them, separated from
" each other by thin boards or curtains.   On these the monks took
" their rest, without taking off any part of their clothes."   Let the reader
now say, whether the charge of *laziness*, so often applied to monkhood,
be or be not a false and foul imputation.

To this valuable body of men we are indebted for much of that ancient
literature we now possess, and indeed, had it not been for their industry and
are, the Bible itself might have been lost to the world.   To give some
light as to the extent and usefulness of the labours of these holy and humble men in transcribing books, before the art of printing was known, there
were in the library at Peterborough one thousand seven hundred MSS.
Leland and Stow tell us the library of the Grey Friars in London, built
by Sir Richard Whittington, was one hundred and twenty-nine feet long
and thirty-one feet broad, and well filled with books.   Ingulf says, that
when the library at Croyland was burned in 1091, seven hundred books
were lost by the fire.   In a word, each monastery had its library, and
the greatest care and labour were used to have them well furnished with
useful volumes.   The libraries of the greater monasteries were likewise the depositaries of the charter of liberties, the acts of parliament,
and other documents of moment.   The registers of kings and public
transactions were compiled and preserved in them.   It was in one of
these monasteries that Stephen Langton, the cardinal archbishop of
Canterbury, found a copy of the charter of liberties granted by Henry
the first, which he communicated to the barons, who were dissatisfied
with the faithless and tyrannical proceedings of king John, and by

means of this document and their own patriotic steadiness they wrung from the tyrant monarch the great bulwark of British freedom, Magna Charta.

Such is a brief outline of the religious orders which Cranmer and Cromwell sought to abolish, before they could introduce those novelties in religion which the former afterwards contrived to establish in this country. To prepare the way for this change and conspiracy against the liberties and happiness of the kingdom, the most malicious reports were set on foot, charging the monasteries with engrossing and monopolizing trade and manufactures; visitors were appointed by Cromwell, to sift and examine into the conduct of the religious of both sexes; and that this hitherto unheard of inquisition might not be disrelished by the people, plausible reasons were given out to smooth the most odious part of the business. Great pains were now taken to cause it to be believed that the most criminal abuses existed in these receptacles of rest for the traveller, and support for the infirm and the poor. Ignorance, sloth, lasciviousness, avarice, superstition, and frauds of all kind, were laid at the door of these institutions, and by daily lampoons and table talk, many people were brought to believe what but a short time before would have been thought incredible. But lest these oral calumnies should fail, the Press, which was now brought to some perfection, was put into requisition, and one Fish, a lawyer, published a most virulent book against all churchmen, in which he attacked the monks unsparingly, representing them as the cause of all the poverty in the nation, and to give a greater colour to his misrepresentations, he called the work *The Supplication of Beggars.*—Of this work Mr. Dodd says, "It is hard " to determine, whether the language or matter is more scandalous.— " He paints out all the bishops, deans, arch-deacons, priests, monks, " friars, &c. as a herd of lazy drones, that devour the king's lands; that " they are the occasion of all the taxes, of beggary at home, and want of " success abroad; that they excommunicate, absolve, &c. merely for " gain; that they debauch the wives, daughters and servants of the whole " kingdom; that they are thieves, highway-men, ravenous wolves and " cormorants; that he hopes the king will take it into consideration to " have them reduced, tied to a cart, whipped, turned adrift, and entirely " demolished, as enemies to his state and to all mankind. Had the devil " been employed in the work; he could not have made an apology more " suitable to the times; for though the book was levelled against religion " in general, and had the visible marks of iniquity stamped upon it, yet " such was the humour of king Henry's days, that when it was offered to " him by Anne Boleyn as an ingenious performance, it was read at court " with singular pleasure, and many hints taken from it in order to pro- " mote the cause in hand."

To such purposes was the press applied in its infancy; and to such ends it has been since employed, to keep the people of this country ignorant of the chief cause of the miseries they have endured, and now endure, and will continue to endure, until the vengeance of God shall have been satisfied for the crimes committed by the sham reformers against his divine commandments, and he shall once more deign to shower his blessings on the land which was once the seat of true religion and civil freedom.—When the invaluable art of printing (when

properly applied) was first invented, the clergy, though represented as
striving to keep the people in darkness, were its chief patrons and protectors.—Report says, the first printing office was in a chapel in Westminster abbey, and probably the first printers were monks.—From this
circumstance printing-offices are to this day called *chapels*, and *monk*
and *friar* are technical terms used for such parts of a page as are not
touched with ink or are blurred with too large a quantity of it.—We
have not heard that, previous to the event called the Reformation, but
which it has been justly observed, should rather be called a *Devastation*,
one single instance can be proved of the press being prostituted to the
service of falsehood, detraction, and calumny ; but no sooner did the
pretended reformers break with the Catholic church, than this instrument was put into requisition to vilify the most eminent characters
living, and spread forth the blackest lies that could be invented.   Even
Henry the eighth, before he assumed the supremacy of the church, had
recourse to the press in defence of the ancient faith, as we have before
shewn, and while he adhered to the unerring principles of truth, proved
how useful a discovery the art of printing was.   Of this advantage he
and his minions were so sensible, that when he departed from the
course of truth and justice, a law was passed which restricted every individual from applying the press in defence of those two attributes of
the Deity, while hirelings were employed to exercise it in the adverse
cause, and traduce every person who had the courage and honesty to
declare themselves in favour of the ancient laws and usages of England.
   Matters were thus prepared, and the visitors performed their parts
to the utmost satisfaction of their employers, by encouraging some
of the members of monasteries to impeach one another, and privately
setting lewd young men to tempt the nuns to impurity, that they might
purposely turn informers.   Speaking of the means used to blast the
reputation of these religious orders, Dr. Heylin, in his History of the
Reformation, observes, " Where these tricks were played, it may be
" feared that God was not in that terrible wind which threw down so
" many monasteries and religious houses in the reign of Henry VIII.
" The monks' offences were represented in such multiplying glasses, as
" made them seem both greater in number and more horrid in nature
" indeed than they were."   Exclusive of the charge of immorality, the
monks were represented, (as the Catholic priests of Ireland are now
by the Evangelicals and Bible Missionaries) as impostors, seducing
the people by false miracles, and strange operations performed by
images, crosses, relics, &c.   These calumnies and charges were laid
before parliament, and an act was passed for the dissolution of the
lesser houses of both sexes, as abandoned to sloth and immorality.
The parliament which passed this nefarious act had continued, by
successive prorogations, six years, and was the first we believe that
had ever sat so long a time in England.   The bill was introduced
and hurried through the two houses, though not without some opposition ; but opposition in those times, as well as in our own, have
but little weight in the scale of corruption.   The act having passed,
no time was lost in putting the same into effect, and how it was
done we think cannot be better described than in the following relation
by Sir Wm. Dugdale, in his celebrated History of Warwickshire

Speaking of the dissolution of a particular monastery of nuns, called Polesworth, he says,

"I find it left recorded by the commissioners, that were employed to take surrender of the monasteries in this shire, An. 29, Henry VIII. that after strict scrutiny, not only by the fame of the country, but by examination of several persons, they found these nuns virtuous and religious women, and of good conversation. Nevertheless it was not the strict and regular lives of these devout ladies, nor any thing that might be said in behalf of the monasteries, that could prevent their ruin then approaching. So great an aim had the king to make himself thereby glorious, and many others no less hopes to be enriched in a considerable manner. But to the end that such a change should not overwhelm those that might be active therein, in regard the people every where had no small esteem of these houses for their devout and daily exercises in prayer, alms-deeds, hospitality, and the like, whereby not only the souls of their deceased ancestors had much benefit, as was then thought, but themselves, the poor, as also strangers and pilgrims, constant advantage; there wanted not the most subtle contrivances to effect this stupendous work, that I think any age has beheld; whereof it will not be thought impertinent, I presume, to take here a short view.

" In order therefore to it, was that which cardinal Wolsey had done for the founding his colleges in Oxford and Ipswich, made a precedent; viz. the dissolving of above thirty religious houses, most very small ones, by the licence of the king, and pope Clement VII. And that it might be the better carried on, Mr. Thomas Cromwell, who had been an old servant to the cardinal, and not a little active in that, was the chief person pitched upon to assist therein. For I look upon this business as not originally designed by the king, but by some principal ambitious men of that age, who projected to themselves all worldly advantages imaginable, through that deluge of wealth which was like to flow amongst them by this hideous storm.

" First, therefore, having insinuated to the king matter of profit and honour, (viz. profit by so vast enlargement of his revenue, and honour in being able to maintain mighty armies to recover his right in France, as also to strengthen himself against the pope, whose supremacy he himself abolished, and make the firmer alliance with such princes as had done the like) did they procure Cranmer's advancement to the see of Canterbury, and more of the Protestant clergy to other bishopricks and high places; to the end that the rest should not be able in a full council to carry any thing against their design; sending out preachers to persuade the people to stand fast to the king, without fear of the pope's curse, or his dissolving their allegiance.

" Next, that it might be more plausibly carried on, care was taken so to represent the lives of monks, nuns, canons, &c. to the world, as that the less regret might be made at their ruin. To which purpose Thomas Cromwell, being constituted general visitor, employed sundry persons, who acted therein their parts accordingly: viz. Richard Layton, Thomas Leigh, and William Petre, doctors of law; Dr. John London, dean of Wallingford, and others; by which they were to enquire into the behaviour of the religious of both sexes: which commissioners, the better to manage their design, gave encouragement to the monks, not only to accuse their governors, but to inform against each other; compelling them also to produce the charters and evidences of their lands, as also their plate and money, and to give an inventory thereof. And hereunto they added certain injunctions from the king, containing most severe and strict rules; by means whereof, divers, being found obnoxious to their censure, were expelled; and many, discerning themselves not able to live free from some exception or advantage that might be taken against them, desired to leave their habit.

" Having, by these visitors, thus searched into their lives, (which, by a black book, containing a world of enormities, were represented in no small measure scandalous,) to the end that the people might be better satisfied with their proceedings, it was thought convenient to suggest, that the lesser houses, for want of good government, were chiefly guilty of these crimes that were laid to their charge; and so they did, as appears by the preamble to that act for their dissolution made in the twenty-seventh of Henry VIII; which parliament, (consisting in the most part of such members as were packed for the purpose through private interest, as is evident by divers original letters of that time, many of the nobility for the like respects also favouring the design) assented to the suppressing of all such houses as had been certified of less value than two hundred pounds per annum, and giving them, with their lands and revenues, to the king; yet so as not only the religious persons therein should be committed to the great and honourable monasteries of the realm, where they might be compelled to live religiously for the reformation of their lives, wherein thanks be to God, religion is well kept and observed, (they are the words of the act) but that the possessions belonging to such houses should be converted to better uses, to the pleasure of Almighty God, and the honour and profit of the realm.

" But how well the tenor thereof was pursued, we shall see; these specious pretences being made use of for no other purpose, than, by opening this gap, to make way for the total ruin of the greater houses, wherein it is by the said act acknowledged, that religion was so well observed. For no sooner were the monks, &c. turned out, and the houses demolished, (that being first thought requisite, lest some accidental change might conduce to their restitution) but care was taken to prefer such persons to the superiority in government upon any vacancy in those greater houses, as might be instrumental to their surrender, by tampering with the convent to that purpose; whose activeness was such, that within the space of two years several convents were wrought upon, and commissioners sent down to take them at their hands to the king's use;. of which number I find, that besides the before specified doctors of law, there were thirty-four commissioners.

" The truth is, that there was no omission of any endeavours that can well be imagined, to accomplish these surrenders; for so subtilly did the commissioners act their parts, as that, after earnest solicitation with the abbots, and finding them backward, they first tempted them with good pensions during life; whereby they found some forward enough to promote the work, as the abbot of Hales in Gloucestershire was, who had high commendation for it from the commissioners, as their letters to the visitor-general do manifest. So likewise had the abbot of Ramsey and the prior of Ely. Nay, some were so obsequious, that after they had wrought the surrender of their own houses, they were employed as commissioners to persuade others; as the prior of Gisborn in Yorkshire, for one. Neither were the courtiers inactive in driving on this work; as may be seen by the lord chancellor Audley's employing a special agent to treat with the abbot of Athelney, and to offer him a 100 marks per annum pension in case he would surrender; which the abbot refused, insisting upon a greater sum; and the personal endeavours he used with the abbot of S. Osithe in Essex, as by his letter to the visitor-general, wherein it is signified, that he had with great solicitation prevailed with the said abbot; but withal insinuating his desire, that his place of lord chancellor being very chargeable, the king might be moved for an addition of some more profitable offices unto him. Nay, I find that this great man, the lord chancellor, hunting eagerly after the abbey of Walden in Essex, (out of the ruins whereof afterwards that magnificent fabrick called by the name of Audley-Inn was built) as an argument to obtain it, did, besides the extenuation of its worth, allege, that he had in this world sustained great damage and infamy in serving the king, which the grant of that would recompense.

"Amongst the particular arguments which were made use of by those that were averse to surrender, I find that the abbot of Feversham alleged the antiquity of their monastery's foundation, viz. by king Stephen, whose body, with the bodies of the queen and prince, lay there interred, and for whom were used continual suffrages and commendations by prayers. Yet it would not avail; for they were resolved to effect what they had begun, by one means or other; in so much, that they procured the bishop of London to come to the nuns of Sion, with their confessor, to solicit them thereunto; who, after many persuasions, took it upon their consciences, that they ought to submit unto the king's pleasure therein, by God's law. But what could not be effected by such arguments and fair promises (which were not wanting or unfulfilled, as appears by the large pensions that some active monks and canons had in comparison of others, even to a fifth or sixth-fold proportion more than ordinary,) was by terror and severe dealing brought to pass. For under pretence of dilapidation in the buildings, or negligent administration of their offices, as also for breaking the king's injunctions, they deprived some abbots, and then put others that were more pliant in their rooms.

"From others they took their convent seals, to the end they might not, by making leases or sale of their jewels, raise money, either for supply of their present wants, or payment of their debts, and so be necessitated to surrender. Nay, to some, as in particular to the canons of Leicester, the commissioners threatened, that they would charge them with adultery and sodomy, unless they would submit. And Dr. London told the nuns of Godstow, that because he found them obstinate, he would dissolve the house by virtue of the king's commission, in spite of their teeth. And yet all was so managed that the king was solicited to accept of them; not being willing to have it thought they were by terror moved thereunto; and special notice was taken of such as gave out that their surrender was by compulsion.

"Which courses, (after so many, that through underhand corruption led the way) brought on others apace; as appears by their dates, which I have observed from the very instruments themselves; in so much that the rest stood amazed, not knowing which way to turn themselves. Some therefore thought fit to try whether money might save their houses from this dismal fate so near at hand; the abbot of Peterborough offering 25,000 marks to the king, and 300 pounds to the visitor-general. Others with great constancy refused to be thus accessary in violating the donations of their pious founders. But these, as they were not many, so did they taste of no little severity. For touching the abbot of Fountaines, in Yorkshire, I find, that being charged by the commissioners for taking into his private hands some jewels belonging to that monastery, which they called theft and sacrilege, they pronounced him perjured, and so deposing him extorted a private resignation. And it appears that the monks of the charter-house in the suburbs of London were committed to Newgate; where with hard and barbarous usage, five of them died, and five more lay at the point of death, as the commissioners signified; but withal alleged that the suppression of that house, being of so strict a rule, would occasion great scandal to their doings: for as much as it stood in the face of the world, infinite concourse coming from all parts to that populous city, and therefore desired it might be altered to some other use. And lastly, I find, that under the like pretence of robbing the church, wherewith the aforesaid abbot of Fountaines was charged, the abbot of Glastonbury with two of his monks being condemned to death, was drawn from Wells upon a hurdle, then hanged upon a hill called the Tor near Glastonbury, his head set upon the abbey gate, and his quarters disposed of to Wells, Bath, Ilchester, and Bridgewater. Nor did the abbots of Colchester and Reading fare much better, as they that will consult the story of that time may see. And for farther terror to the rest, some priors and other ecclesiastical persons, who spoke against the king's supremacy, a thing then somewhat uncouth, were condemned as traitors, and executed.

"And now, when all this was effected, to the end it might not be thought that these things were done with a high hand, the king having protested that he would suppress none without the consent of his parliament, (it being called April 28, 1539, to confirm these surrenders so made,) there wanted not plausible insinuations to both houses for drawing on their consent with all smoothness thereto; the nobility being promised large shares in the spoil, either by free gift from the king, easy purchases, or most advantageous exchanges, and many of the active gentry advancements to honours with increase of their estates; all which we see happened to them accordingly. And, the better to satisfy the vulgar, it was represented to them, that by this deluge of wealth the kingdom should be strengthened with an army of 40,000 men, and that for the future they should never be charged with subsidies, fifteenths, loans, or common aids. By which means, the parliament ratifying the abovesaid surrenders, the work became completed: for the more firm settling whereof, a sudden course was taken to pull down and destroy the buildings; as had been done before upon the dissolution of smaller houses, whereof I have touched. Next, to distribute a great proportion of their lands amongst the nobility and gentry, as had been projected; which was accordingly done; the visitor general having told the king, that the more that had interest in them, the more they would be irrevocable.

" And lest any domestic stirs, by reason of this great and strange alteration, should arise, rumours were spread abroad, that cardinal Pole laboured with divers princes to procure forces against this realm, and that an invasion was threatened; which seemed the more credible, because the truce concluded between the emperor and the French king was generally known, neither of them wanting a pretence to invade England. And this was also seconded by a sudden journey of the king unto the sea coasts; unto divers parts whereof he had sent sundry of the nobles and expert persons to visit the ports and places of danger, who failed not for their discharge upon all events to affirm the peril in each place to be so great, as one would have thought every place needed a fortification. Besides, he forthwith caused his navy to be in readiness, and muster to be taken over all the kingdom. All which preparations being made against a danger believed imminent, seemed so to excuse the suppression of the abbeys, as that the people, willing to save their own purses, began to suffer it easily; especially when they saw order taken for building such forts.

" But let us look a little upon the success: wherein I find that the visitor general, the grand actor of this tragical business, having contracted upon himself such an odium from the nobility, by reason of his low birth (though not long before made knight of the garter, earl of Essex, and lord high chancellor of England) as also from the Catholics, for having thus operated in the dissolution of abbeys, that (before the end of the abovesaid parliament wherein that was ratified, which he had with so much industry brought to pass) the king, not having any use of him, gave way to his enemies' accusations; whereupon, being arrested by the duke of Norfolk at the council table, when he least dreamt of it, and committed to the tower, he was condemned by the same parliament for heresy and treason, unheard, and little pitied; and on the 28th of July, viz. four days after the parliament was dissolved, had his head cut off on Tower-hill.

" And as for the fruit which the people reaped, after all their hopes built upon those specious pretences which I have mentioned, it was very little. For it is plain, that subsidies from the clergy and fifteenths of laymen's goods were soon after exacted: and that in Edward the VIth's time, the commons were constrained to supply the king's wants by a new invention, viz. sheep, cloaths, goods, debts, &c. for three years; which tax grew so heavy, that the year following they prayed the king for a mitigation thereof. Nor is it a little observable, that whilst the monasteries stood, there was no act for the relief of the poor, so amply did those houses give succour to them that were in want; whereas in the next age, viz. 39 Eliz. no less than eleven bills were brought into the house of commons for that purpose."

We might rest satisfied with this testimony in favour of the religious orders, and exposure of the black villanies of the devastators, but to render the cause of truth more firm, and prevent idle cavil, we will here add, a confirmation to the learned knight's statement, which is taken from Mr. Thomas Hearn's preliminary observations upon Mr. Brown Willis's View of the Mitred Abbeys.—This gentleman makes a solemn declaration of his being a sincere member of the church of England, and must therefore be deemed an unexceptionable witness. He writes thus:—" Popery (as I take it) signifies no more than the " errors of the church of Rome. Had he, (Henry VIII.) therefore, " put a stop to those errors, he had acted wisely, and very much to the " content of all truly good and religious men. But then this would not " have satisfied the ends of himself and his covetous and ambitious " agents. They all aimed at the revenues and riches of the religious " houses ; for which reason no arts or contrivances were to be passed " by, that might be of use in obtaining these ends. The most abomi- " nable crimes were to be charged upon the religious, and the charge " was to be managed with the utmost industry, boldness and dexterity. " This was a powerful argument to draw an odium upon them, and so " make them disrespected and ridiculed by the generality of mankind. " And yet, after all, the proofs were so insufficient, that from what I " have been able to gather, I have not found any direct one against even " any single monastery. The sins of one or two particular persons do " not make a Sodom. Neither are violent and forced confessions to be " esteemed as the true result of any one's thoughts. When therefore " even these artifices would not do, the last expedient was put in exe- " cution, and that was ejection by force ; and to make these innocent " sufferers the more content, pensions were settled upon many, and " such pensions were in some measure proportioned to their innocence. " Thus, by degrees, the religious houses and the estates belonging to " them being surrendered unto the king, he either sold or gave them to " the lay-nobility, and gentry, contrary to what he had at first pretend- " ed ; and so they have continued ever since, though not without visible " effects of God's vengeance and displeasure, there having been direful " anathemas and curses denounced by the founders upon such as should " presume to alienate the lands, or do any other voluntary injury to the " religious houses. I could myself produce instances of the strange " and unaccountable decay of some gentlemen in my own time, though " otherwise persons of very great piety and worth, who have been pos- " sessed of abbey-lands : but this would be invidious and offensive, and " therefore I shall only refer those that are desirous of having instances " laid before them, to shew the dismal consequences that have happened, " to Sir Henry Spelman's History of Sacrilege, published in 8vo. in the " year 1698.'

The reader has here before him an account of the vile artifices made use of by the visitors to blacken the fair fame of the religious orders, and bring about that destruction of ecclesiastical property which soon followed, and which was devoted to the most sacred purposes.—Let the bigots of the present day continue to circulate the venomous calumnies of Fox, and Burnet, and other lying writers, who, to palliate the infamy and scandal of these barbarous and gothic proceedings, in- vented the false charges of looseness and irregularity against the reli- gious orders ; thank God, the press is not now shackled as it was by the pretended evangelical disciples of liberty, at the very birth of their de- vastating Reformation, and the honest part of it will now perform its duty, and make known the real state of the case.—Opposed to the lies of Fox and Burnet, we have even the parliament of Henry declaring

A REVIEW

OF

Fox's Book of Martyrs,

CRITICAL AND HISTORICAL.

No. 37. Printed and Published by W. E. Andrews, 3, Chapter-house-court, St. Paul's Churchyard, London.   Price 3d.

EXPLANATION OF THE ENGRAVING.—*This cut represents a* PROTESTANT IN-QUISITION, *and the mode by which the Jesuits, and also the Gentry and other Catholics were tortured in the Tower of London. The Priests in particular were racked in order to extort confessions from them, and the names of those who had been present at mass and other religious ceremonies.*

CONTINUATION OF THE REVIEW.

that religion was well kept and observed in the greater houses, and Mr. Hearne, whom we have just quoted, states it as a positive fact, that not one direct proof was brought against any one single monastery, great or small, of the crimes laid to their charge.

· The modern editors of Fox, copying from his cousin-german Burnet, say, "The most horrible and disgusting crimes were found to be practised "in many of the houses; and vice and cruelty were more frequently the "inmates of these pretended *sanctuaries* than religion and piety. The "report (of the visitors) contained many abominable things, not fit to "be mentioned; some of these were printed, but the greatest part "*was lost.*" We have no doubt the report *did* contain many "abomi-nable things," but then these "abominable things" were mere *report,*— sheer slander and lies—invented for a cloak to conceal the *real* acts of vice and cruelty and injustice committed by the pretended reformers. If the monks and nuns were such dissolute and worse than beastly wretches, as represented by Burnet, why were they not punished for their abomi-

nable crimes, as an example to future members of religious orders, and
in vindication of the suppressing deeds of the visitors? But not one
criminal have we on record to support the base insinuations of Burnet
and Fox; not one single offender has Burnet and the modern editors
furnished to bear out their infamous charges—whilst history records the
slaughter of 59 persons, (among whom were a bishop, an ex-lord chancellor, six doctors of divinity, three abbots, several Carthusian, Benedictine, and Franciscan friars, and many secular clergymen) for opposing and denying the king's spiritual supremacy. Twenty were executed
for rising in defence of monastic lands. Nine for pretended plots
against the king, and sixty were *starved in prison,* chiefly Carthusian
and Franciscan friars, for denying the king's spiritual supremacy.
Cranmer all this time, observe, was archbishop of Canterbury.

In fact, it was this opposition to the assumed supremacy of the king
in spirituals, by the religious orders, that drew the vengeance of Henry
and the reformers upon their establishments. This we learn from the
modern editors and Burnet.—They say, "It was well known that the
" monks and friars, though they complied with the time (this is *false,*
" for if they had complied, they would in all probability have been un-
" molested), yet hated this new power of the king's; the people were
" also startled at it: (oh! then the people were sensible it was some-
" thing *new,* and something *alarming,* or why startle at it?) so one Dr.
" Leighton, who had been in Wolsey's service with Cromwell, propos-
" ed a general visitation of all the religious houses in England; and
" thought that nothing would reconcile the nation so much as to see
" some *good effect* from it." Certainly, the production of *good* was the
best way to reconcile the people to the measure; but, unfortunately for
the people of England, *no good whatever* has arisen to them from the
usurpation of the supremacy in spirituals by Henry.—The good, if such
it can be called, fell to the lot of the greedy and unprincipled courtiers,
and the evil to the share of the people. There can be no doubt that
abuses existed at the time we are speaking of, and that many of the
high dignitaries of the church were too well fed and too rich to do their
duty truly; for if this had not been the case, the bishops would not
have acknowledged the supremacy of Henry through fear of losing
their temporalities, with the exception of one only, namely Fisher,
bishop of Rochester.—But the *reforming* of *abuses,* and the *destruction*
of useful *institutions,* are two very distinct things, and the cry of reform
was merely a *pretence* to put in execution a diabolical *purpose.* The
stoutest opposers of the dissolution, as well as the divorce of Catharine, were the mendicant friars, whose holy poverty kept them independent in mind, and fearless of the threats of death. An example of
this heroic fortitude was shewn in the conduct of friars Peto and Elstow,
the former of whom boldly preached against the divorce in the presence
of Henry, and being attacked in the pulpit by one Dr. Curwin, chaplain
to the king, was as strenuously defended by Elstow, who challenged
Curwin before God and all equal judges, to prove him a false prophet
and a seducer.—This conduct of Elstow was in presence of the king
also, nor would he desist in his opposition to Curwin until the monarch
commanded him to be silent.—Not many days after the affair took
place, Peto and Elstow were ordered to make their appearance before

the lords of the council, and, in the conclusion were sent to prison.—Cromwell was present during their examination, and told Elstow that he ought, for his violent behaviour, to have been immediately tied up in a sack, and thrown into the Thames.—This observation caused Elstow to smile, and make the following noble reply :—"My lord, be
" pleased to frighten your court epicures with such menaces as these;
" men that have lost their courage in their palate, and whose minds
" are softened with pleasures and vanities. Such as are tied fast to the
" world, by indulging their senses, may very likely be moved with such
" kind of threats ; but as for us, they make little impression upon us.
" We esteem it both an honour and merit to suffer upon the occasion,
" and return thanks to the Almighty, who keeps us steady under the
" trial. As for your Thames, the road to heaven lies as near by water
" as by land, and it is indifferent to us, whether road we take." Here
we have a proof of the utility of voluntary poverty, inculcated by the
religious orders, which makes men fearless of death, and intent only on
seeing justice and religion flourish.

Before the dissolution of monasteries in England, twenty-seven abbots, sometimes twenty-nine, sat in the upper house of parliament; to prepare for the devastation, Henry created some close boroughs, whereby he got his creatures returned to ensure a majority, and thus the corruption of parliament was the interlude to the destruction of church property, and the robbery of the poor of their rights. The abbeys which enjoyed the privileges of being represented by their abbots in parliament were, St. Alban's; Glastenbury; St. Austin's at Canterbury; Westminster, the richest in all England; Winchester, founded by the first Christian king of the West Saxons; St. Edmund's Bury, founded by king Canute; Ely; Abingdon, founded by Cedwella and Ina, kings of the West Saxons; Reading, built by Henry I.; Thorney, in Cambridgeshire; Waltham, founded by earl Harold in 1062; St. Peter's in Gloucester, founded by Wulfere and Etheldred, kings of Mercia; Winchelcomb in Gloucestershire, founded by Offa and Kenulph, kings of Mercia also; Ramsey in Huntingdonshire, founded by Ailwyne, alderman of England, and earl of the East-Angles; Bardney, in Lincolnshire. This abbey was demolished by the Danes in 870, who slew three hundred monks, and was rebuilt by William the Conqueror. Crowland; St. Bennett's in Hulm, in Norfolk, founded about the year 800; Peterborough, begun by Peada, king of Mercia, in 665, and rebuilt by Adulf, chancellor to king Edgar; Battel, in Sussex, founded by William the Conqueror; Malmsbury in Wiltshire; Whitby, founded by king Oswy in 657; Selby in Yorkshire, begun by William the Conqueror; St. Mary's, at York, built in the reign of William Rufus; also Shrewsbury, Cirencester, Evesham, Tavistock, and Hide at Winchester. Besides these mitred abbeys, two priors had seats in the house of lords, namely, of Coventry, and of the knights of St. John of Jerusalem. According to the most exact calculation, at the suppression of the religious houses in England, the sum total of the revenues of the greater monasteries amounted to 104,919l. Of the lesser 29,702l. Of the head house of the knights hospitallers, or of Malta, in London, 2385l. Of twenty-eight other houses of that order, 3026l. The revenues of the clergy were laid at a fourth part of the revenues of the kingdom in the 27th of

Henry VIII, and Mr. Collier, in his Ecclesiastical History, says, that the revenues of the monks never did exceed a fifth part. With these revenues, the poor were not only provided for, churches built, and travellers hospitably entertained, but the church lands contributed to all public burdens, equally with the lands of the laity, while the leases granted by the monks were always on easy rents and small fines. Walsingham and Patrick say, that in 1379, every mitred abbot paid as much as an earl; and 6s. 8d. for every monk in his monastery. In 1289, a century previous, the abbot of St Edmund's-bury paid 666l. 13s. 4d. to the fifteenth granted that year, an enormous sum if reckoned according to the rate of money at this day. And when we take into consideration that this sum was paid by only *one* abbey, what an immense revenue must have been raised for the exigencies of the state by the contributions of these institutions throughout the kingdom. The people then were not teazed and harassed with the calls of the tax-gatherer or the distress warrant of the broker; nor were they subjected to the insults and tyranny of parish officers, if overwhelmed with pecuniary difficulties; they had only to apply to these mansions of charity, where they were sure to find succour in their distress and comfort to the wounded mind. If money was required it was lent without interest; if rest and sustenance, they were bestowed from brotherly love, not wrung from the fear of legal pains and penalties.

It has been fashionable, since what is called the era of the Reformation, to represent the clergy of Catholic times as ignorant, and the people superstitious, but these representations were no other than base devices to cover the deformity of that horrible fanaticism and worse than savage barbarism which marked the progress of the first pretended reformers' days. The libraries of the monasteries, as we have before stated, were filled with works of literature, and the destruction of these seats of learning and the sciences has been an irreparable loss to the country. Tyrrell, in his history of England, writes thus :—" From the " conversion of the Saxons most of the laws made in the Wittena Ge- " mote, or great Councils, were carefully preserved, and would have " been conveyed to us more entire, had it not been for the loss of so " many curious monuments of antiquity, at the suppression of Monas- " teries in the reign of Henry VIII."—How valuable would these records have been in our days as standards of reference for our statesmen, and models of legislation of which, God knows, we stand much in need, when we look at the verbosity of our present acts of parliament, and the shortness and perspicuity of the laws of our ancestors. Then the laws were made so plain that the meanest capacity could understand them; now they are couched in such terms as to bear various constructions, and in many instances it has been recorded in the public papers that one magistrate will define a law in a very different sense to what another will, and each act upon his own construction. Even the libraries of the two universities of Oxford and Cambridge were not spared in the Gothic rage displayed by the visitors and reformers of imputed monastic abuses. At Oxford there were two most noble public libraries, the one founded by Richard of Burg or Richard Aungerville, lord treasurer of England and bishop of Durham in the reign of Edward III. who spared no cost or pains, and he was a *bishop* be it remembered, to render this collection complete; the other was furnished with books by Thomas Cobham, bishop of Worcester in 1367, which were greatly augmented by the munificence of Henry IV. his sons, and by the addition of the library of Humphrey duke of Gloucester, filled with many curious manuscripts from foreign parts. Of the fate of this last library, Mr. Collier, in his Ecclesiastical History, says, "These books were many of them " plated with gold and silver, and curiously embossed. *This*, as far as " we can guess, *was the superstition* which destroyed them. Here ava- " rice had a very thin disguise, and the courtiers discovered of what " spirit they were to a very remarkable degree. . . . Merton college had " almost a cart load of manuscripts carried off and thrown away to the " most scandalous uses. . . . This was a strange inquisition upon sense " and reason, and showed that they intended to seize the superstitious " foundations, and *reform them to nothing*. The universities languished " in their studies the remainder of this reign, and were remarkable for " nothing, but some trifling performances in poetry and grammar."— The same author writes, " The books instead of being removed to royal li- " braries, to those of cathedrals, or the universities, were frequently thrown " into the grantees, as things of slender consideration. Now oftentimes " these men proved a very ill protection for learning and antiquity. — " Their avarice was sometimes so mean, and their ignorance so undis- " tinguishing, that when the covers were somewhat rich, and would " yield a little, they pulled them off, threw away the books, or turned " them to waste-paper. Thus many noble libraries were destroyed."— He further observes, that John Bale, sometime bishop of Ireland, " a " man remarkably averse to Popery and the monastic institution," gives this lamentable account of what he himself was an eye witness to. "I " know a merchant (who shall at this time be nameless) that bought " the contents of two noble libraries for forty shillings a piece; a shame " it is to be spoken. This stuff has been used instead of grey paper by " the space of more than these ten years. A prodigious example this " and to be abhorred of all men, who love their nation as they should " do. Yea, what may bring our realm to more shame, than to have it " noised abroad, that we are despisers of learning? I judge this to be " true, and utter it with heaviness, that neither the Britons under the " Romans and Saxons, nor yet the English people under the Danes and " Normans, had ever such damage of their learned monuments, as we " have seen in our time." (*John Bale's declaration on Leland's Journal*, an. 1549.) Fuller, too, has borne testimony to the devastating spirit of the reformers in those days. He breaks out into a passionate declama- tion on the occasion, and complains, " that all arts and sciences fell un- " der the common calamity. How many admirable manuscripts of the " fathers, schoolmen, and commentators were destroyed by these means? " What number of historians of all ages and countries? The holy scrip- " tures themselves, as much as the gospellers pretended to regard them, " underwent the fate of the rest. If a book had a cross upon it, it was " condemned for Popery; and those with lines and circles were inter- " preted the black arts, and destroyed for conjuring. And thus (he " adds) divinity was profaned, mathematics suffered for corresponding " with evil spirits, physic was maimed, and riot committed on the law " itself." We shall produce one testimony more. Chamberlain, in his

Present State of England, thus describes the havock committed by the Vandalic reformers, headed by Cranmer and Cromwell :—These men, " under pretence of rooting out Popery, superstition, and idolatry, ut- " terly destroyed these two noble libraries, and embezzled, sold, burnt, " or tore in pieces all those valuable books which those great patrons " of learning had been so diligent in procuring in every country of Eu- " rope. Nay, their fury was so successful as to the Aungervillian li- " brary, which was the oldest, largest, and choicest, that we have not " so much as a catalogue of the books left. Nor did they rest here. " They visited likewise the college libraries, and one may guess at the " work they made with them, by a letter still kept in the archives, where " one of them boasts, that New-College quadrangle was all covered " with the leaves of their torn books, &c. The university thought fit " to complain to the government of this barbarity and covetousness of " the visitors, but could not get any more by it than one single book, " given to the library by John Whethamstead, the learned abbot of St. " Alban's, wherein is contained part of Valerius Maximus, with the com- " mentaries of Dionysius de Burgo; and to this day there is no book " in the Bodleian library besides this and two more which are certainly " known to have belonged to either of the former libraries. Nay, and " the university itself, despairing ever to enjoy any other public library, " thought it adviseable to dispose of the very desks and shelves the " books stood on, in the year 1555." Enough is here related to make the cheek of a Protestant redden with shame, and cause him to forbear in future from charging the calumniated monks with ignorance and idleness.

The *Book of Martyrs* tells us that there were debates going on in the convocation concerning the different opinions which were found to be spreading in the kingdom, of which the lower house made a complaint to the upper house of no less than sixty-seven, in that early period of the king's supremacy. Of these opinions we shall have occasion to say something by and by; we must confine ourselves at present to the dis- solution of the monasteries. On this head the book says, " At *this time* " visitors were appointed to survey all the lesser monasteries: they were " to examine the state of their revenues and goods, and take inventories " of them, and to take their seals into their keeping; they were to try " how many of the religious would return to a secular course of life; " and these were to be sent to the archbishop of Canterbury, or the " lord chancellor, and an allowance was to be given them for their " journey; but those who intended to continue in that state were to be " removed to some of the great monasteries. A pension was also to be " assigned to the abbot or prior during life; and the visitors were par- " ticularly to examine what leases had been made during the last year. " Ten thousand of the religious were by this means driven to seek for " their livings, with forty shillings and a gown a man. Their goods " and plate were estimated at 100,000*l.* and the valued rents of their " houses was 32,000*l.*; but they were above ten times as much. The " churches and cloisters were in most places pulled down, and the ma- " terials sold."

Here then we have it admitted that Cranmer, the first Protestant primate of England, took a conspicuous part in the work of spoliation and robbery. It is also confessed that *ten thousand* of these innocent and useful class of men, were turned out of their peaceful habitations into the wide world, to seek a living wherever they could, with only forty shillings and a gown each man. The churches and cloisters in which many of them dwelled were pulled down and sold, and the proceeds went to enrich some base and hungry courtier, for his readiness to pander to the beastly vices of an unfeeling and depraved monarch. These doings, however, we are told, gave great discontent to the people, and who can wonder at it? So to remove this discontent, Burnet writes, that "Cromwell advised the king to *sell these lands* (belonging " to the monks) at very easy rates, to the *nobility* and *gentry*, and *to* " *oblige* them to keep up the wonted hospitality. This (he intimated) " would both be grateful to them, and would engage them *to assist the* " *crown in the maintenance of* THE CHANGES *that had been made,* " since *their own interests* would be *interwoven* with those of *their so-* " *vereign.*" Such was the advice of Cromwell, the blacksmith's son, and from this counsel we may date the division of England into parties, whereby the people have lost a great portion of their civil privileges, and a boroughmongering faction has been established in the room of the once free parliaments of the country. The degree of hospitality shewn by the new possessors of the lands of the hospitable monks, we may gather from Dr. Heylin, who in his *History of the Reformation,* speaking of the sacrilegious devastations carried on by Cranmer and the courtiers of Edward the sixth, writes, " But bad examples seldom end " where they first began. For the nobility and inferior gentry pos- " sessed of patronages, considering how much the lords and great men " of the court had improved their fortunes by the suppression of those " chantries, and other foundations which had been granted to the king, " conceived themselves in a capacity of doing the like, by taking into " their hands the yearly profits of those benefices, of which by law they " only were entrusted with the presentations. Of which abuse com- " plaint is made by bishop Latimer, in his printed sermons. In which " we find, ' That the gentry of that time invaded the profits of the " church; leaving the tithe only to the incumbent:' and ' That chan- " try-priests were put by them into several cures, to save their pen- " sions,' (p. 38); that 'many benefices were let out in fee-farms, (p. 71); " or given unto servants for keeping of hounds, hawks, and horses, and " for making of gardens,' (pp. 91, 114); and finally, ' That the poor " clergy, being kept to some sorry pittances, were forced to put them- " selves into gentlemen's houses, and there to serve as clerks of the " kitchen, surveyors, receivers,' &c. (p. 241). All which enormities " (though tending so apparently to the dishonour of God, the disservice " of the church, and the disgrace of religion) were generally connived " at by the lords and others, who only had the power to reform the " same, because they could not question those who had so miserably " invaded the church's patrimony, without condemning of themselves." That the interests of these receivers of stolen property were interwoven with the interests of their sovereign, or, in other words, that they considered it their interest to have a sovereign of the same disposition as themselves, is clear from the records of history. On the death of Edward, the faction attempted to set aside the right of Mary, a Catholic princess, in favour of Jane Grey, who had no claim whatever to the crown, and the same faction occasioned James the second, another Catholic sovereign, to abdicate the throne, because he sought to establish freedom of conscience for all.

Under such circumstances it is not surprising that the discontents of the people should increase, which was the case until at length they broke out into open rebellion. The account given by Burnet of this resistance on the part of the people is in part true, and in other parts false. The insurrection commenced in the North, where the people retained a strong feeling in favour of the ancient faith, and the clergy were removed from the influence of the court. Every succeeding innovation produced increased discontent. The people had looked with reverence from their childhood on the monastic establishments, from which they had experienced so much kindness and affection, and could not behold the ruin of these institutions without irritation and grief. To see the monks driven from their houses, and compelled in most instances to beg their bread; to behold the poor, who were formerly fed at the doors of the convents, now abandoned to despair and hunger; was more than mortal frame in those days could endure, and the people flew to arms, to demand a redress of their grievances. "They com-"plained chiefly," writes Dr. Lingard, "of the suppression of the mo-"nasteries, of the statutes of uses, of the introduction of such men as "Cromwell and Rich, and of the preferment in the church of the arch-"bishops of Canterbury and Dublin, and of the bishops of Rochester, "Salisbury and St. David's, whose chief aim was to subvert the church." Others of the insurgents required, the same writer says, "that hereti-"cal books should be suppressed, and that heretical bishops (alluding "probably to Cranmer and his party) and temporal men of their sect, "should either be punished according to law, or try their quarrel with "the pilgrims (the insurgents had taken the name of the pilgrims of "grace) by battle: that the statutes which abolished the papal autho-"rity, bastardized the princess Mary, suppressed the monasteries, and "gave to the king the tenths and first fruits of benefices, should be re-"pealed; that Cromwell, the vicar general, Audley, the lord chancel-"lor, and Rich, the attorney-general, should be punished *as subverters* "*of the law*, and maintainers of heresy: that Lee and Layton, the visi-"tors of the northern monasteries, should be prosecuted *for extortion*, "*peculation*, and other abominable acts: and that a parliament should "be shortly held at some convenient place, as Nottingham or York." These terms were rejected; but after some negociation an unlimited pardon was offered and accepted, with an understanding that the griev-ances complained of should be shortly discussed in a parliament to be holden at York; but with true Protestant magnanimity, the royal pope of England, as soon as he was freed from his apprehensions, did not think proper to keep his promise, and the parliament was never called. Two months after the pilgrims were again in arms, but were defeated in their measures, their leaders were taken and sent to London to be executed, and others were hung by scores at York, Hull, and Carlisle.

This was the only forcible opposition that Henry experienced in his designs upon the liberties of the church of England, which had been of so long standing, and were secured by the first clause in Magna

Charter. Of this insurrection, Mr. Collier thus speaks, " If resistance
" of the chief magistrate had been justifiable in any case, those who
" appeared in arms upon the dissolution of monasteries had a strong
" colour for their undertaking. For were not the old landmarks set
" aside, and the constitution newly modelled ? For do not the liberties
" and immunities of the church stand in the front of Magna Charta ?
" and are they not particularly secured in the first place ? Was not the
" king's coronation oath lamentably strained, when he signed the dis-
" solution act ? For had he not sworn to guard the property of his sub-
" jects ? to protect the religious ? and maintain them in the legal esta-
" blishment ? The ancient nobility were thrown out of the patronage
" of their monasteries, lost their corrodies, and the privilege of their
" ancestors' benefactions. The rents were raised, and the poor forgot-
" ten, as they complained, by the new proprietors. Besides, they were
" afraid their friends in another world might suffer by these alienations;
" and the dead fare worse for want of the prayers of the living. Grant-
" ing therefore the matter of fact, that the prosecutions were legal;
" which way are the abbots more to be blamed (who rose in the North)
" than the barons who took up arms in defence of liberty and property
" and appeared in the field against king John and Henry III. ? The
" abbeys, without question, had all the securities the civil magistrate
" could give them ; no estate could be better guarded by the laws.
" Magna Charta, as I observed, was made particularly in favour of these
" foundations, and confirmed at the beginning of every parliament for
" many succeeding reigns. These things considered, we must of ne-
" cessity either condemn the barons, or acquit the monks, and justify
" the Northern rebellion."

From these facts it may be discovered that Cranmer and his vile associates, though they could keep in favour with a brutal monarch, by
catering to his passions and dissembling their own views, were by no
means popular with the people of England. We have always contended
that the people generally are on the side of virtue and justice, and
though we have seen acts of injustice sanctioned by popular assemblies, yet they have always been done with a view (erroneous certainly)
of punishing those who were supposed to have been the betrayers of
their country, and the violaters of the laws of society. Till this period
England had been a truly free and happy country, and the office of
Judge was almost a sinecure. When the reformers meditated their designs on the church, they began by calumniating the clergy and hood-
winking the people; but, notwithstanding, when facts developed the
baseness of their conduct, the multitude we see became sensible of their
error, and called for the punishment of the betrayers of their country's
welfare. But power is sometimes, and we will say too frequently, an
overmatch for justice; and the complaints of the people are too often
disregarded, through the interests of courtiers. So it was in this case;
though Cranmer and Cromwell, and the rest of the corrupt gang, were
hated by the people, they nevertheless continued in office, and converted the once happy England into a great slaughter house. New
crimes were created, and new penalties enacted; men were put to death
without being arraigned or heard in their defence, or even without a
knowledge of their crimes, and the jails were filled to suffocation

with persons arrested on suspicion only. Hitherto the system of spoliation had been confined to the lesser monasteries, and it was supposed by some that the dangerous insurrection which had been quelled would have induced Henry to stay his hand and preserve the greater monasteries in their rights. This he had promised the nobility and gentry in the North, before they consented to lay down their arms. But the king having nothing now to apprehend from the insurgents, the seizure of the great monasteries was resolved upon, and the same means were resorted to as before to cheat the people. Rumours of an invasion by France were set afloat, and that as heavy taxes would be the natural consequence to meet the invaders, the seizure of the monasteries would be a better expedient, inasmuch as their revenues would defray all the expenses, and be a great easement to the people. These and such like specious pretences were found to be necessary now, because the charges of immorality could not be put forth, the character of the religious being established by the very act of parliament that dissolved the lesser convents. Therefore management and mystery must be resorted to, and how well they were practised the reader has seen in the account we quoted from Sir Wm. Dugdale. Suffice it to say, that, by stratagem and device, the commissioners, in about two years time, demolished the monuments of British, Saxon, and Norman glory, which for above one thousand years had given undeniable proofs of virtue and religion, and had been the fountains of learning and the arts.

To give an exact number of the religious houses thus demolished is a matter of difficulty. Mr. Camden states them at 645 in England and Wales; but a list taken out of the court of first fruits and tenths makes them 754. The annual revenue of these religious houses was computed at 135,522l. 18s. 10d. and the moveable goods were, it may be said, incalculable. To this list we have to add 90 colleges, 2374 chantries and free chapels, and 110 hospitals, which met with the same fate. Sir Robert Atkyns says, there were in England before the Reformation 45,009 churches and 55,000 chapels, from which we may judge of the piety of our ancestors in Catholic times, and the great share of employment that was given to the people by the erection of these temples to the worship of God, many of which were of the most beautiful structure and workmanship, and give a flat denial to the foul sneers so lavishingly thrown out, by the vain conceited Protestants of these days, of the darkness and ignorance of those ages. Of these the greater part were destroyed by the ruthless hands of the pretended reformers of religion, and time has nearly decayed the remainder. Though the abbey lands were granted to the king, to be applied to the benefit of the nation, but few of them went into the exchequer, the greater part being distributed amongst his favourites and partners in guilt. Thus a new race of upstarts sprung up to beard the ancient nobility of the king, and to this work of spoliation and sacrilege do many of the present noble families of this kingdom owe their origin and wealth. Of these we may name the families of Russell, Cavendish and Powlet. To give some idea of the manner in which these possessions of the church were disposed of, Stow relates, that he (Henry) made a grant to a gentlewoman of a religious house, for presenting him with a dish of puddings, which happened to please his palate; that he paid away

many a thousand a year belonging to the monasteries, and particularly
that Jesus' bells, belonging to a steeple not far from St. Paul's, London,
very remarkable both for their size and music, were lost at one throw
to Sir Miles Partridge. Many other of the ancient places of the divine
worship were turned into tippling houses, stables and dog kennels,
while others, as we have before observed, were left a heap of ruins,
which made Sir William Davenant complain of this havock in the following elegant lines :—

> " Who sees these dismal heaps, but will demand,
> " What barbarous invader sack'd the land ?
> " But when he hears no Goth, no Turk did bring
> " This desolation, but a Christian king—
> " When nothing but the name of zeal appears
> " 'Twixt our best actions, and the worst of theirs,
> " What does he think our sacrilege would spare,
> " Since these th' effects of our devotions are ?

Having described the manner in which the monastic institutions fell
by the hands of a barbarian king and his villanous courtiers, we will
conclude by drawing a hasty contrast between the situation of the
country, when these institutions flourished, and the present days of enlightened wisdom, as they are termed. But first it may not be amiss to
give a slight sketch of the *early* consequences of this work of destruction. The lure held out to the people to reconcile them to the project
of *a general dissolution* was, that by the king's taking the revenue of
these establishments into his own hands, he would be able to maintain
an army of 40,000 well trained soldiers, with skilful captains and commanders, without calling upon his subjects for subsidies, fifteenths,
loans, and other common aids. But no sooner did he get possession of
the lands and revenues of the monks, than he called upon the people
for subsidies and loans, and received them against the law.—The first
step taken, on the passing of the act of parliament to dissolve the
monasteries, was the appointment of a *Court of Augmentation*, to manage
the revenues accruing to the crown by the dissolution; and well did
the members of this court manage the business for their own interest,
as Fuller tells us, in his Church History, that "the officers of the court
" were many, their pensions great, crown profits thereby very small,
" and causes there defending few; so that it was not worth the while
" to keep up a mill to grind that grist where the toll would not quit
" cost."—But though this Protestant historian held this opinion, the
reformers were of another, for they continued to "keep up the mill"
during a space of 18 years, chiefly for the benefit of the clerks, &c.
and it was not stopped grinding the public till the first year of Mary I.
better known by the name of "bloody queen Mary," because she was
a Catholic princess, and governed her subjects according to the ancient
laws of the land.—While the courtiers were thus feeding their own
nest, every other order of men in every station of life, felt the heavy
weight of this calamitous event. Nobility and gentry, rich and poor,
young and old, clergy and laity, the ignorant and the learned, the living
and the dead, were alike sufferers, and experienced numerous miseries
flowing from it. In the same parliament that gave the king the great
and rich priory of St. John of Jerusalem (the last that was seized upon,
because the last that was left to seize) a subsidy from both laity and

clergy was demanded.—Sir Richard Baker says, in his *Chronicle,* "In
" his one and thirtieth year, a subsidy of two shillings in the pound of
" lands, and twelve of goods, with four fifteens, were granted to the
" king, towards his charges of making bulwarks. In his five and thir-
" tieth year, a subsidy was granted to be paid in three years, every
" Englishman being worth in goods twenty shillings and upwards to
" five pounds, to pay four pence of every pound ; and from five pounds
" to ten pounds, eight pence ; and from ten pounds to twenty pounds,
" twelve pence; from twenty pounds and upwards, of every pound two
" shillings : strangers, as well denizens as others, being inhabitants, to
" pay double. And for lands, every Englishman paid eight pence of
" the pound, from twenty shillings to five pounds, and from five pounds
" to ten pounds, sixteen pence, and from ten pounds to twenty pounds
" two shillings, and from twenty pounds and upwards, of every pound
" three shillings ; strangers double. The clergy six shillings in the
" pound of benefices, and every priest having no benefice, but an annual
" stipend, six shillings and eight pence yearly, during three years."
The same writer tells us that " In his six and thirtieth year, proclama-
" tion was made for the enhansing of gold to eight and forty shillings,
" and silver to four shillings the ounce ; also he caused to be coined
" base money, mingling it with brass, which was since that time called
" down the fifth year of Edward VI. and called in the second year of
" queen Elizabeth." Such were the consequences to the country immediately following the baneful measure ; we will now proceed to a
detail of the more remote results.

The spoils of the church and the lands of the monasteries were not
appropriated to the benefit of the people, but were distributed amongst
the favourites and panders of Henry, and subsequently, that is in the reign
of the boy-pope, his successor, Edward VI. amongst the hirelings of the
ruling factions which alternately governed the young monarch.—These
creatures were not selected for their attachment to the principles of the
constitution, and their love of rational freedom, though they had the
cry of "Liberty" constantly in their mouths ; but the possessions they
obtained were the recompense, from a bloody and merciless tyrant, for
the villanous services which they performed to gratify his insatiable lust
and brutal passions.—They were the dross of the nation, famed only for
their vices and villany, and thus they became the bane and scourge of
the unhappy people of England.—Conscious of the illegal tenure of
their property, and fearful that a knowledge of the truth might oblige
them to disgorge the property thus unjustly obtained, the possessors
thereof raised themselves into a party, the grand principle of which
was intolerance and fraud.—Thus, whenever, a disposition was shewn
to favour the Catholics of this country, false reports and unjust accusations were immediately circulated to inflame the minds of the ignorant,
and conspiracies were forged to alarm the timid.—The Gunpowder plot
in James the first's reign, and Oates's plot in Charles the second's, had
no other foundation than the intrigues of this party to keep alive the
embers of religious fanaticism, and thus prevent the public mind from
discerning the evils preying upon the country. The wishes of James
the second to establish liberty of conscience for all his subjects again
alarmed the party, and in the end, being a Catholic, he was driven from

the throne.—The reign of his successor William III. was one of war for the safety of the Protestant interest, and in support of it the national debt was commenced, the weight of which is now become insupportable.

We will now proceed to contrast the benefits derived to the country from the monasteries, with the miseries the people now endure from the want of them. In the first place, the convents both of men and women were schools of learning and piety, and were therefore of the greatest service to the education of children. In every monastic institution one or more persons were assigned for the purpose of teaching; and thus the children of the neighbourhood, both rich and poor, were taught grammar and music, without any charge to their parents, and in the nunneries, the female children were instructed in the useful branches of housewifery. Now, however, the case is altered. In those endowed schools, which bear the name of charity, interest must be used to get the children admitted, and though there are some supported by voluntary contributions, yet it can be considered in no other light than a tax which many pay from *fear* and others from ostentation.

In the second place, the monasteries were, in effect, great hospitals, where the poor were relieved and nursed in the time of distress and sickness; and they were likewise houses of entertainment for travellers of all ranks. From their revenues, they provided with a liberal hand for the wants of others, while their own diet was slender and frugal. Then we had no assessment upon parishes to relieve the indigent, now we have upwards of eight millions sterling levied upon the land and trade to supply the poor with but half a sufficiency, and indeed scarcely that. Then the poor fared sumptuously, the villagers were happy and cheerful, their hours were spent in paying homage to God, labouring for their families, and cracking the harmless joke before a plenteous board of meat and nut brown ale. Now the labourer is scarcely able to procure even bread for his family, and in most cases, he has to apply to the parish for relief; there he meets with the surly growl of the overseer, instead of the smiling welcome of the cowled monk, and is too often sent away with a refusal of assistance; instead of the plump and florid countenance of the rural swain, we see nothing but pallid and emaciated figures, pining in sorrow and care, or totally regardless of that noble feeling of independence which marked the peasantry of ancient days. Then the population were chiefly employed in agricultural pursuits, and the different branches of trade connected with the land, and the monks being the best landlords, a little colony was sure to spring up near to a monastery; now the people are congregated in large towns, and employed in great manufactories, whereby their morals are corrupted, and their health injured, while the profits of their labour go to enrich perhaps one individual, whose property is already immense, and applied probably only to his own individual gratification.

Thirdly, the nobility and gentry had, by means of the monasteries, a creditable mode of providing for their younger children and old servants. Now they are fastened upon the nation in the way of pensions, places, the half-pay list, and such like devices, by which they live out of the sweat of the poor, whereas in Catholic times they contributed to the comfort of the poor, by being their instructors, physicians and nurses.

Fourthly, the monasteries were of the greatest advantage to the commonwealth, inasmuch as they not only contributed to preserve the dignity of the crown, and the rights of the people,, but they had services reserved by their founders, which were of a military nature, but widely different from a standing army.   For example, the abbeys that held by knights' service, were bound to provide such a number of soldiers as their services required, and furnish them for the field at their own charge. Thus, when the country called, their men appeared at their musters, to attend the heirs of the founders, or such as had settled a knights' fee upon them.   Here then we had an army equipped at a moment's notice to support the honour of old England, and without a tittle of tax upon the people.   Now, however, we are compelled to employ recruiting officers and men at a heavy charge; individuals are bought or trepanned into the service; a large sum of money is annually wrung out of the sweat of the poor to maintain this army; and in the event of its being reduced, the officers are saddled upon the nation for life, so that one part of the people may be said to live upon the labour of the other; whereas in Catholic times, in the absence of debt, loans, pensions, sinecures, taxes, and tax-gatherers, every class of the community was usefully employed, and each contributed to the other's comfort.

When Henry VIII. came to the crown, he found his exchequer well filled.   The nation was without debt and the people content and happy. In this state he reigned over them near twenty years, when the passion of lust first turned him from the path of duty, and he became an inexorable tyrant. In this raging temper he was surrounded by men of the vilest qualities, who fanned the flame of his desires to an ungovernable fury, and by the most deceptive arts, led him to sanction the most disgraceful outrages, while they took care to profit by the villanies they projected.   But as the vengeance of God fell on the persecutors of the primitive Christians, so did his justice fall on the evil doers in the work of devastation we have just described.   Harry, who , as the head and supreme in these horrible sacrileges, demands the first notice, after living a voluptuous life, grew so corpulent and unwieldy that he was not able to go up stairs, or from one room to another, but was obliged to be hoisted up by an engine; his body too was filled with foul and nauseous humours, which caused such a stench as made it loathsome to attend upon him.   In his dying illness he affected some religious compunction, but no one gave credit to his actions, and he who had made so many men's wills void had his own totally disregarded by those who had been his greatest favourites.   He died unregretted, and his memory is only held in remembrance to execrate the bloody deeds which stain his life.   Dr. Heylin records that " he never spared woman in his lust, " nor man in his anger;" and Sir Walter Raleigh says of him, " That " if all the patterns of a merciless prince had been lost in the world, they " might have been found in this king."   Of his six wives the memory of one only is held in veneration by posterity; this is the unfortunate but magnanimous Catharine, whose cruel persecutions have been dearly paid for by the nation.   His second wife Anne Boleyn, who was instrumental in the sufferings of Catharine, was beheaded for incest with her own brother; the third, Jane Seymour, being in childbirth and in danger of death as well as the child, had her belly ripped up by order of the king to preserve the child; the fourth, Anne of Cleves, was cast off within two or three months; the fifth, Catharine Howard, was beheaded for adultery; and the sixth, Catharine Parr, was near sharing the same fate, but had the good fortune to escape and survive him.

We must now say a word or two on Cromwell, who was a principal actor in this tragedy of depredation and cruelty. This creature of crime and violence had risen so high in royal favour, that he seemed to engross all the power and influence of the court. He obtained a grant of thirty manors belonging to the suppressed monasteries, the title of earl of Essex was conferred upon him, and he was appointed to the office of lord chamberlain, in addition to his situation of vicar general and other trusts. In this sunshine of court patronage he conducted the business of the crown in parliament, and thought himself omnipotent. Indeed so little did he apprehend the fate that awaited him, that he actually committed the bishop of Chichester and Dr. Wilson to the Tower, on a charge of having *relieved* prisoners confined for refusing the oath of supremacy, and threatened with the royal displeasure the duke of Norfolk, and the bishops of Durham, Winchester and Bath, who were opposed to his views, when he suddenly found himself the object of the king's anger. Henry, it will be recollected, had taken a dislike to Anne of Cleves, his fourth wife, and he learned that Cromwell had been the prime negociator in this disagreeable match. Hence he contracted as violent a dislike to his favourite as he had entertained a strong partiality for him, and he was not slow in wreaking his vengeance. The butchering vicar-general seems not to have had the least suspicion of his fall, until he found himself, after he attended the house of lords in the morning, and the council board in the afternoon on the 10th of June, 1540, arrested and taken to the tower on a charge of high treason. As minister he was accused of receiving bribes and encroaching on the royal authority by issuing commissions, pardoning convicts and granting licences for the exportation of prohibited merchandize. As vicar-general he was charged with having betrayed his duty, by not only holding heretical opinions himself, but also by protecting heretical preachers. And to make him a traitor, he was accused of having expressed a resolution to fight against the king, if it were necessary, in support of his *religious* opinions. He was confronted with his accusers in presence of the commissioners, but was refused the benefit of a public trial before his peers. He was proceeded against by a bill of attainder, of which he had no reason, however, to complain, as he was the first to employ the iniquitous measure against others.—The modern editors of the Book of Martyrs, copying from Burnet, says, " Cromwell experienced the com-" mon fate of fallen ministers ; his pretended friends forsook him, and " his enemies pursued their revenge against him without opposition, ex-" cept from Cranmer, who, with *a rare fidelity*, dared to avow an attach-" ment to him, even at this time, and wrote a very earnest letter to the " king in his favour. But Henry was not easily turned from his pur-" pose, and being resolved on the ruin of Cromwell, was not to be dis-" suaded from his design."—Cranmer did, to be sure interpose in be-half of his friend and compeer in villany, but he took care to use such measured language, that the king could not take offence, for Tom was very careful to keep his own skin whole as long as he could.—His epistle rather enumerated the past services of Cromwell than defended his innocence, as the following extract will shew :—" A man," writes Cranmer, " that was so advanced by your majesty, whose surety was " only by your majesty, who loved your majesty no less than God, " (what blasphemy) who studied always to set forward whatsoever was " your majesty's will and pleasure, who cared for no man's displeasure " to serve your majesty, who was such a servant, in my judgment, in " wisdom, diligence, faithfulness, and experience, as no prince in this " realm ever had the like; who was so vigilant to preserve your ma-" jesty from all treasons, that few could be so secretly conceived but he " detected the same in the beginning; such a man, that if the noble " princes of memory, king John, Henry II. Richard II. had had such a " counsellor about them, I suppose they would never have been so " treacherously abandoned and overthrown, as those good princes were. " Who shall your grace trust hereafter, if you mistrust him? Alas! I " bewail and lament your grace's chance herein : I wot not whom your " grace may trust, &c." Such was the character given by Cranmer of his friend Cromwell; yet five days after this pattern of " rare fidelity," had thus addressed his majesty, this very Tom Cranmer, this Protest-ant archbishop of Canterbury, this prime reformer of the church of England, on the second and third readings of the bill of attainder, gave his vote in favour of it, thinking it safer to go with the stream than contend against the tide of Harry's will. Oh! blessed Tom Cranmer. In consequence of Tom's compliance the bill passed the lords without a dissentient voice; and probably with as little opposition through the commons. The bill was no sooner passed, than the prisoner was led out and beheaded on Tower-hill, a few days after he was arrested.

Thus fell the great favourite of Henry, whom he made use of to do his dirty work, and who was too ready, it cannot be denied, to perform the task set him. In the fall of this man there were three singular cir-cumstances attending his fate. Though appointed vicar general to the head of the church, with a power to reform all heresies, he was accused of heresy himself. Again, although he had, in his life-time, been the greatest destroyer of the church of all the innovators of that age, yet in his dying speech he declared himself a stanch Catholic. " I pray " you," says he, " that be here, to bear me record, I die in the Catho-" lic faith, not doubting in any article of my faith, no nor doubting in " any sacrament of the church. Many have slandered me, and reported " that I have been a hearer of such as have maintained evil opinions, " which is untrue; but I confess, that like as God, by his holy spirit, " doth instruct us in the truth, so the devil is ready to seduce us, and " I have been seduced : but bear me witness, I die in the faith of the " Catholic church." Next, he fell by a law of his own framing, the most odious and diabolical that could be devised, and intended to re-venge himself of those individuals who had the courage and honesty to oppose his infamous practices. We find in Dodd's account of the life of this monster in human shape, the following singular relation of his posterity :—" I meet with a pedigree of this family," writes this his-torian, " which makes the infamous Oliver Cromwell a branch of it, in " the following manner : Lord Cromwell, son to the earl of Essex, dy-" ing without issue male, a daughter of the family was married to one " Morgan Williams of Glamorganshire, whose son sir Richard Williams

A REVIEW

of

Fox's Book of Martyrs,

CRITICAL AND HISTORICAL.

No. 38. Printed and Published by W. E. ANDREWS, 3, Chapter-house-court; St. Paul's Churchyard, London. **Price 3d.**

EXPLANATION OF THE ENGRAVING.—*A representation of the execution of Mary, Queen of Scotland. This beautiful and accomplished Princess, after experiencing the greatest violence and brutality from the reforming Nobility and Preachers of Scotland, found herself necessitated to fly into England, and put herself under the protection of her cousin Elizabeth. On setting foot upon this once hospitable land, she was immediately cast into prison, and after a confinement of eighteen years was butchered by order of that tigress in human shape, the Virgin Queen Bess. Her only crime was that of being a Catholic. She was cruelly denied the consolations of religion in her last moments, and the earl of Kent insultingly told her, " Your life will be the death of our religion, as contrariwise your death will be the life thereof."*

CONTINUATION OF THE REVIEW.

" took the name of Cromwell, and settled in Huntingdonshire, from
" whom descended Sir Oliver Cromwell, knight of the Bath, in king
" James I.'s reign, who had a younger brother called Robert, father to
" Oliver the protector. Now if this pedigree may be depended upon,
" it is very remarkable how fatal the name has been both to church and
" state, both to Catholics and Protestants. About a hundred years after
" Thomas Cromwell had stripped the church of Rome of monastic lands,
" Oliver carried on the reformation, and stripped the church of England
" of the bishops' lands. Now to draw a parallel of their irreligious
" proceedings, there seems to be some resemblance both as to their
" motives and methods, and Catholics may be in hopes of being pitied

" under their oppression ; for altering the date of years, the same apo-
" logy will serve for both churches."

Such was the fate of Cromwell, who fell unpitied by his friends and
despised by the people ; nor was he the only example of God's vengeance on the cruel and remorseless destroyers of the pious monuments
and charitable institutions of their religious forefathers. The instances
of the resentment of Heaven at the injuries done to church property
and the rights of the poor were numerous and awful.—The monastic
institutions were chiefly designed to revive the piety of the primitive
Christians, and promote the great end of charity. We have seen how
well they performed that task, and the many benefits they conferred
upon those nations that fostered them, but especially on England, as
regarded religion, the sciences, and civil freedom.—The destruction of
these institutions was the death blow of England's liberties and happiness, but the perpetrators fell in the vortex of ruin they had prepared
for the church. The abbey lands, which were seized to gratify the
avarice and cupidity of courtiers, became the curse of the families who
alienated them from their lawful owners.—The effect of this curse was
so visible, that, within twenty years after the dissolution, more of the
nobility were attainted and died under the sword of justice, than suffered in that way from the conquest to the devastation, making a period
of 500 years.—To give the work an appearance of legality, the sanction
of parliament was obtained by corrupting the members, and see the
consequences which followed. Mr. Fuller in his Church History, c. vi.
writes, " If you examine the list of the barons in the parliament of the
" 27th of Henry VIII. you will find very few of them whose sons do at
" this day inherit their father's titles and estates ; and of these few,
" many to whom the king's favour hath restored what the rigorous law
" of attainder took, both dignity, lands and posterity. And doubtless
" the commons have drunk deeply of this cup of deadly wine ; but they
" being more numerous and less eminent, are not so obvious to obser-
" vation. However, it will not be amiss to insert the observation of a
" most worthy antiquarian Sir Henry Spelman, in the county where
" he was born, and best experienced ; who reporteth, that in Norfolk
" there were 100 houses of gentlemen, before the dissolution, possess-
" ed of fair estates, of whom so many as gained accession by abbey
" lands, are at this time extinct, or much impaired, bemoaning his own
" family, under the latter notion, as diminished by such an addition,"—
That Norfolk, our native county, was not alone marked with the finger
of God may be traced by history, for it will be found that every county
throughout England bore the same visible marks of God's signal displeasure of this work of sacrilege and spoliation.

DEBATES OF THE CONVOCATION.

Having shewn how the temporalities of the church fell a prey to the
avaricious designs of the panders of Henry, it is now time to take some
notice of the theological proceedings which took place among Henry's
divines, while the work of robbery and sacrilege was going on.—The
king, it will be observed, had caused himself to be acknowledged, by
the clergy and parliament, the supreme head of the church of England,
and consigned many of the most virtuous and learned men, such as

Fisher, More, Forest, and others, to the fagot and the block, for refusing to acknowledge this supremacy in him, so far as spirituals were concerned.—Having submitted to his supreme headship, the clergy, in convocation, obsequiously became the mere tools of the royal lay-pope.—A convocation, is an assembly of the clergy for consultation upon matters ecclesiastical, and in this country consisted of two distinct houses, like the parliament; the archbishops and bishops constituted the upper house, and the inferior clergy, represented by deputies, forming the lower house. Previous to the reformation, as it is called, this assembly was uninfluenced by royal power, as the church was secured in her privileges by Magna Charta, and in return was highly instrumental in securing to the people their privileges enjoyed under the same charter.—To bring the matter about, Henry had got all the clergy into a *premunire*, whereby they had forfeited all their temporal possessions to the king, and were in danger of being sent to prison at the king's pleasure. When the statutes of premunire were passed, a power was given to the sovereign to mitigate or suspend their operation, and hence it was customary for the king to grant letters of license or protection to particular individuals.—Wolsey held one of these patents under the great seal for fifteen years, during which no one ever accused him of violating the law.—When the cardinal was indicted for the offence, for some reason or other he neglected or refused to plead the royal permission, and suffered judgment to pass against him, and it was argued, on the ground of his conviction, that all the clergy were liable to the same penalty, because, by admitting his jurisdiction, they had become partners in his guilt. Accordingly, the attorney-general, to their consternation, was instructed to file an information against the whole in the court of king's bench. To get out of this predicament, into which they had fallen, the clergy of the province of Canterbury hastily assembled in convocation, and tendered to the king a present of one hundred thousand pounds in return for a full pardon. Henry, however, under the advice of Cromwell, through whose cunning the bishops and clergy had been caught in the snare, to their great grief and astonishment, refused the proposal, unless they at the same time consented to acknowledge him, the king, "to be the protector and *only* supreme head of the church and clergy of England."—Three days were consumed in useless consultation, and conferences were held with Cromwell and the royal commissioners.—In the course of the debates, bishop Fisher, who appeared to be almost the only individual of the clergy that had the courage to speak the sentiments of his mind, and oppose, as far as he was able, the irreligious innovation meditated by Henry, delivered his sentiments in the following terms:—"My lords, it is true, we are all
" under the king's lash, and stand in need of the king's good favour,
" and clemency; yet this argues not that we should therefore do that
" which will render us both ridiculous and contemptible to all the
" christian world, and hissed out from the society of God's holy Catholic
" church : for, what good will that be to us, to keep the possession of
" our houses, cloisters and convents, and to lose the society of the
" Christian world ; to preserve our goods, and lose our consciences ?
" Wherefore, my lords, I pray let us consider what we do, and what it
" is we are to grant ; the dangers and inconveniences that will ensue

" thereupon; or whether it lies in our power to grant what the king
" requireth at our hands, or whether the king be an apt person to re-
" ceive this; that so we may go groundedly to work, and not like men
" that had lost all honesty and wit together with their worldly fortune.
" As concerning the first point, viz. what the supremacy of the church
" is, which we are to give unto the king; it is to exercise the spiritual
" government of the church in chief; which, according to all that ever
" I have learned, both in the gospel and through the whole course of
" divinity, mainly consists in these two points.

" 1. In loosing and binding sinners; according to that which our
" Saviour said unto St. Peter, when he ordained him head of his church,
" viz. to thee will I give the keys of the kingdom of heaven. Now,
" my lords, can we say unto the king, *tibi*, to thee will I give the keys
" of the kingdom of heaven? If you say ay, where is your warrant? if
" you say no, then you have answered yourselves, that you cannot put
" such keys into his hands.

" Secondly, the supreme government of the church consists in feed-
" ing Christ's sheep and lambs; according unto that, when our Saviour
" performed that promise unto Peter, of making him his universal shep-
" herd, by such unlimited jurisdiction, feed my lambs; and not only
" so, but feed those that are the feeders of those lambs; feed my
" sheep: Now, my lords, can any of us say unto the king, *pasce oves?*

" God hath given unto his church, some to be apostles, some evange-
" lists, some pastors, some doctors; that they might edify the body of
" Christ: so that you must make the king one of these, before you can
" set him one over these; and, when you have made him one of these
" supreme heads of the church, he must be such a head as may be
" answerable to all the members of Christ's body: and it is not the
" few ministers of an island that must constitute a head over the uni-
" verse; or at least, by such example, we must allow as many heads
" over the church, as there are sovereign powers within Christ's do-
" minion; and then what will become of the supremacy; every mem-
" ber must have a head: *attendite vobis*, was not said to kings, but
" bishops.

" Secondly, let us consider the inconveniences that will arise upon
" this grant: we cannot grant this unto the king, but we must renounce
" our unity with the see of Rome; and, if there were no further matter
" in it than a renouncing of Clement VII. pope thereof, then the matter
" were not so great: but in this we do forsake the first four general
" councils, which none ever forsook; we renounce all canonical and
" ecclesiastical laws of the church of Christ; we renounce all other
" Christian princes; we renounce the unity of the Christian world; and
" so leap out of Peter's ship, to be drowned in the waves of all heresies,
" sects, schisms, and divisions.

" For the first and general council of Nice acknowledged Silvester's
" (the bishop of Rome) authority to be over them, by sending their
" decrees to be ratified by him.

" The council of Constantinople did acknowledge pope Damasus to be
" their chief, by admitting him to give sentence against the heretics
" Macedonius, Sabellinus, and Eunomius.

" The council of Ephesus acknowledged pope Celestine to be their

" chief judge, by admitting his condemnation upon the heretic Nestorius.

" The council of Chalcedon acknowledged pope Leo to be their chief
" head; and all general councils of the world ever acknowledged the
" pope of Rome (only) to be the supreme head of the church. And
" now shall we acknowledge another head? or one head to be in England,
" land, and another in Rome.

" Thirdly, we deny all canonical and ecclesiastical laws; which wholly
" do depend upon the authority of the apostolical see of Rome.

" Fourthly, we renounce the judgment of all other Christian princes,
" whether they be Protestants or Catholics, Jews or Gentiles; for, by
" this argument, Herod must have been head of the church of the Jews;
" Nero must have been head of the church of Christ; the emperor
" must be head of the Protestant countries in Germany, and the church
" of Christ must have had never a head till about three hundred years
" after Christ.

" Fifthly, the king's majesty is not susceptible of this donation:
" Ozias, for meddling with the priest's office, was resisted by Azarias,
" thrust out of the temple, and told that it belonged not to his office.
" Now if the priest spake truth in this, then is not the king to meddle
" in this business: if he spoke amiss, why did God plague the king
" with leprosy for this, and not the priest.

" King David, when the ark of God was in bringing home, did he
" place himself in the head of the priests order? did he so much as
" touch the ark, or execute any the least, properly belonging to the
" priestly function? or did he not rather go before, and abase himself
" amongst the people, and say that he would become yet more vile, so
" that God might be glorified.

" All good Christian emperors have evermore refused ecclesiastical
" authority; for, at the first general council of Nice, certain bills were
" privily brought unto Constantine, to be ordered by his authority; but
" he caused them to be burnt, saying, *Dominus vos constituit*, &c. God
" hath ordained you (priests), and hath given you power to be judges
" over us; and therefore, by right, in these things, we are to be judged
" by you; but you are not to be judged by me.

" Valentine, the good emperor, was required by the bishops to be
" present with them, to reform the heresy of the Arians; but he answered,
" swered, forasmuch as I am one of the members of the lay-people, it
" is not lawful for me to define such controversies; but let the priests,
" to whom God hath given charge thereof, assemble where they will
" in due order.

" Theodosius, writing to the council of Ephesus, saith, it is not lawful
" ful for him that is not of the holy order of bishops, to intermeddle
" with ecclesiastical matters: and now shall we cause our king to be
" head of the church, when all good kings have abhorred the very least
" thought thereof, and so many wicked kings have been plagued for
" so doing! Truly, my lords, I think they are his best friends that
" dissuade him from it; and he would be the worst enemy to himself,
" if he should obtain it.

" Lastly, if this thing be, farewell all unity with Christendom! For,
" as that holy and blessed martyr saint Cyprian saith, all unity depends
" upon that holy see, as upon the authority of St. Peter's successors;

" for, saith the same holy father, all heresies, sects, and schisms, have
" no other rise but this, that men will not be obedient to the chief
" bishop ; and now, for us to shake off our communion with that
" church, either we must grant the church of Rome to be the church
" of God, or, else a malignant church. If you answer, she is of God,
" and a church where Christ is truly taught, his sacraments rightly ad-
" ministered, &c. how can we forsake, how can we fly from such a
" church? certainly we ought to be with, and not to separate our-
" selves from such a one.

" If we answer, that the church of Rome is not of God, but a malig-
" nant church ; then it will follow, that we, the inhabitants of this land,
" have not as yet received the true faith of Christ ; seeing we have not
" received any other gospel, any other doctrine, any other sacraments,
" than what we have received from her, as most evidently appears by
" all the ecclesiastical histories : wherefore, if she be a malignant church,
" we have been deceived all this while ; and if to renounce the common
" father of Christendom, all the general councils, especially the first
" four, which none renounce, all the countries of Christendom, whether
" they be Catholic countries or Protestant, be to forsake the unity of the
" Christian world ; then is the granting of the supremacy of the church
" unto the king, a renouncing of this unity, a tearing of the seamless
" coat of Christ in sunder, a dividing of the mystical body of Christ
" his spouse, limb from limb ; and tail to tail, like Sampson's foxes, to
" set the field of Christ's holy church all on fire ; and this is it which
" we are about : wherefore let it be said unto you in time, and not too
" late, look you to that."—(*Bailey's Life of Fisher.*)

This profound and unanswerable speech had considerable effect upon
the whole convocation for a time, but, in the end, the king obtained the
consent of the assembly, through the artful persuasions of his emissaries, and the worldly-mindedness of some of the leading dignitaries.
In the mean time Cranmer, as we have before stated, got appointed to
the high dignity of archbishop of Canterbury and primate of all England. The link of unity formed by the divine Founder of the Church
being thus dissevered, the only means left to preserve a uniformity of
faith were acts of parliament and pains and penalties, but those were
found ineffectual almost as soon as the king assumed the character of pope.
Harry himself, with the exception of the supremacy, was rigidly attached
to the dogmas of the Catholic church, but, as he had no divine authority
to rule the consciences of men, he could not prevent others from exercising their visionary fancies in the way of religion making as well as himself, and hence the nation soon swarmed with religious tinkers, each batter-
ing the others' kettle until the people were distracted and almost mad-
dened with the discordant sounds. It is now time to give the account
of the modern editors of Fox of these proceedings, which we perceive
they have extracted from Burnet's Abridgement. They say, " The
" convocation sat at the same time, and was much employed. Latimer
" preached a Latin sermon before them ; he was the most celebrated
" preacher of that time ; the simplicity of his matter, and his zeal in
" expressing it, being preferred to more elaborate compositions. The
" convocation first confirmed the sentence of divorce between the king
" and queen Anne. Then the lower house made an address to the up-

" per house, complaining of sixty-seven opinions, which they found
" were very much spread in the kingdom. These were either the te-
" nets of the old Lollards, or of the new Reformers, or of the Anabap-
" tists; and many of them were only indiscreet expressions, which
" might have flowed from the heat and folly of some rash zealots, who
" had endeavoured to disgrace both the received doctrines and rites:
" They also complained of some bishops who were wanting in their
" duty to suppress such abuses. This was understood as a reflection on
" Cranmer, Shaxton, and Latimer, the first of whom it was thought was
" now declining, in consequence of the fall of queen Anne.

. " But all these projects failed, for Cranmer was now fully established
" in the king's favour; and Cromwell was sent to the convocation with
" a message from his majesty, that they should reform the rites and ce-
" remonies of the church according to the rules set down in scripture;
" which ought to be preferred to all glosses or decrees of popes.

. " There was one Alesse, a Scotchman, whom Cromwell entertained
" in his house, who being appointed to deliver his opinion, shewed that
" there was no sacrament instituted by Christ but baptism and the
" Lord's supper. Stokesly answered him in a long discourse upon the
" principles of the school divinity; upon which Cranmer took occasion
" to shew the vanity of that sort of learning, and the uncertainty of tra-
" dition: and that religion had been so corrupted in the latter ages,
" that there was no finding out the truth but by resting on the autho-
" rity of the scriptures. Fox, bishop of Hereford, seconded him, and
" told them that the world was now awake, and would be no longer
" imposed on by the niceties and dark terms of the schools; for the
" laity now did not only read the scriptures in the vulgar tongues, but
" searched the originals themselves; therefore they must not think to
" govern them as they had been governed in the times of ignorance.
" Among the bishops, Cranmer, Goodrick, Shaxton, Latimer, Fox,
" Hilsey, and Barlow, pressed the reformation; but Lee, archbishop of
" York, Stokesly, Tonstall, Gardiner, Longland, and several others,
" opposed it as much. The contest would have been much sharper,
" had not the king sent some articles to be considered of by them, when
" the following mixture of truth and error was agreed upon.

" 1. That the bishops and preachers ought to instruct the people ac-
" cording to the scriptures, the three creeds, and the four first general
" councils.

. " 2. That baptism was necessary to salvation, and that children ought
" to be baptized for the pardon of original sin, and obtaining the Holy
" Ghost.

. " 3. That penance was necessary to salvation, and that it consisted
" in confession, contrition, and amendment of life, with the external
" works of charity, to which a lively faith ought to be joined; and that
" confession to a priest was necessary where it might be had.

" 4. That in the eucharist, under the forms of bread and wine, the
" very flesh and blood of Christ was received.

" 5. That justification was the remission of sins, and a perfect reno-
" vation in Christ; and that not only outward good works, but inward
" holiness, was absolutely necessary. As for the outward ceremonies,

" the people were to be taught, 1. That it was meet to have images in
" churches, but they ought to avoid all such superstition as had been
" usual in times past, and not to worship the image, but only God. 2.
" That they were to honour the saints, but not to expect those things
" from them which God only gives. 3. That they might pray to them
" for their intercession, but all superstitious abuses were to cease ; and
" if the king should lessen the number of saint's days, they ought to
" obey him. 4. That the use of the ceremonies was good, and that
" they contained many mystical significations that tended to raise the
" mind towards God ; such were vestments in divine worship, holy wa-
" ter, holy bread, the carrying of candles, and palms and ashes, and
" creeping to the cross, and hallowing the font, with other exorcisms.
" 5. That it was good to pray for departed souls, and to have masses
" and exequies said for them ; but the scriptures having neither declared
" in what place they were, nor what torments they suffered, that was
" uncertain, and to be left to God ; therefore all the abuses of the pope's
" pardons, or saying masses in such and such places, or before such
" images, were to be put away. These articles were signed by Crom-
" well, the two archbishops, sixteen bishops, forty abbots and priors,
" and fifty of the lower house. The king afterwards added a preface,
" declaring the pains that he and the clergy had been at for the remov-
" ing the differences in religion which existed in the nation, and that
" he approved of these articles, and required all his subjects to accept
" them, and he would be thereby encouraged to take further pains in
" the like matters for the future.

" On the publication of these things, the favourers of the reforma-
" tion, though they did not approve of every particular, yet were well
" pleased to see things brought under examination ; and since some
" things were at this time changed, they did not doubt but more changes
" would follow ; they were glad that the scriptures and the ancient
" creeds were made the standards of the faith, without adding tradition.
" and that the nature of justification and the gospel-covenant was rightly
" stated ; that the immediate worship of images and saints was con-
" demned, and that purgatory was left uncertain : but the necessity of
" auricular confession, and the corporeal presence, the doing reverence
" to images, and praying to saints, were of hard digestion to them ;
" yet they rejoiced to see some grosser abuses removed, and a reforma-
" tion once set on foot. The Popish party, on the other hand, were
" sorry to see four sacraments passed over in silence, and the trade in
" masses for the dead put down. At the same time other things were
" in consultation, though not finished. Cranmer offered a paper to the
" king, exhorting him to proceed to further reformation, and that no-
" thing should be determined without clear proofs from scripture, the
" departing from which had been the occasion of all the errors that
" had been in the church. Many things were now acknowledged to be
" erroneous, for which some not long before had suffered death. He
" therefore proposed several points to be discussed, as, Whether there
" were a purgatory ? Whether departed saints ought to be invocated,
" or traditions to be believed ? Whether images ought to be considered
" only as representations of history ? and, Whether it was lawful for

" the clergy to marry ? He prayed the king not to give judgement in
" these points till he heard them well examined ; but all this was car-
" ried no further at that period."

We must now examine this account, which has a mixture of truth
with falsehood, and is calculated to disguise the former for the purpose
of leading the people into the latter. Why Latimer should be named as the
preacher, without giving the substance of the discourse, remains to be
explained, for the simplicity of his matter, and his zeal in expressing it,
conveys just nothing, unless we know what the matter consisted of.
However the first act of the convocation was to confirm the sentence
of divorce passed by Cranmer between Henry and Anne Boleyn. Here
then we have a specimen of the mean submission which this once
learned and spirited body of men paid to the mandates of a tyrant.
Cranmer and his associates were as pliant to the king's amours as ever
he could wish, and never was head of the church so well accommodated in his lewd and irreligious work as Henry found himself. The
clergy very civilly dissolved the marriage of Anne Boleyn, as they had
dissolved the previous marriage of Catharine with Henry, and the
parliament as kindly declared the issue of Anne, namely Elizabeth, illegitimate, as it had declared Catharine's daughter Mary to be the same.
But what shall we say of Cranmer's conduct in the case of Anne, to
whom of all persons living he was under the greatest obligations ? His
treatment of his benefactress was so barefacedly ungrateful, that even
his greatest panegyrist, Burnet, could not view without concern this
odious blot in the life of this most notorious dissembler and cold-blooded
villain. Well, this matter being settled to the king's wish, the lower
house, we are told, made complaint of the diversity of opinions which
were found to spread in the kingdom, and they further complained of
the negligence of some of the bishops, who were understood to be
Cranmer, and Shaxton, and Latimer. The former was raised to his high
situation by Henry, the two latter by the influence of Anne Boleyn.
So, then, as we have before observed, the acknowledgment of Henry
as supreme head of the *Church*, was followed by the introduction of innumerable heresies, and the perpetration of countless injustices and
murders. For more than a thousand years the people, by being locked
in the bonds of unity with the *whole* universe, by the profession of the
same faith, devoted themselves to the practice of every virtue, and were
careful to preserve their civil rights. Secure from the distraction of
silly fanatics, and grounded in the sure rule of Christianity, they devoted their time to the cultivation of the arts and sciences, and while
they raised magnificent temples to the worship of the living God, they
were not less tenacious of their country's honour, and by the prowess
of their deeds in arms, they became as renowned for their attachment
to religion, as for their valourous exploits. The laws of England were
founded on justice, and the people were then the freest of the free in all
Christendom. Every man could then sit and repose under the shade of
his own vine, and England was really then, what she is now nominally
considered, the envy of surrounding nations and the admiration of the
world. Now she is represented by Burnet, under the new pope, as the prey
of faction and the nursery of heresy and inquietude. Whatever might
have been the thoughts of Cranmer's opponents, Tom knew very well

how to keep in Harry's good graces. Burnet tells us that these three worthies, to secure their favour with Henry, protested to him "that "they meant to do *nothing* that might *displease the king*, whom they "acknowledged to be *their supreme head*, that they were resolved to "obey his laws, and they renounced the pope's authority with all his "laws." This compliable declaration the modern editors have sup-pressed, probably as reflecting no great credit upon the reforming heroes.

We must now look into the other proceedings of this shackled and corrupted assembly. One Alesse, a Scotchman, and a creature of Crom-well, we are told, was appointed to shew that there never were more than two sacraments of divine institution, though the whole Christian world from the first foundation of the Church believed there were seven. Who this Scotchman was we have no clue whatever, other than that he was a sojourner in Cromwell's house; but whether he was a learned divine or an ignorant fanatic we cannot learn, nor have we *one* argu-ment stated that he produced, supposing him to have-argued the case, on which to form a conclusion. Stokesley, the then bishop of London, it is said, answered this Scotchman in a long discourse upon the prin-ciples of the school divinity; upon which Cranmer took occasion to shew "the *vanity* of *that sort of learning* and the *uncertainty* of tradition; "and that religion had been so corrupted in the latter ages, that there "was no finding out the truth but by resting on *the authority of the* "*scriptures.*" Well said, Tom! but pray tell us on whom the authority of the scriptures rested. If religion had become so corrupted in the latter ages, as to render it difficult to discover the truth, what assurance have you that the scriptures were not corrupted by those who had so corrupted religion? When the reformers began to discover the truth they began at the same time to *corrupt the scriptures.* This is a noto-rious fact. The reformers in preaching the word of God, or rather in passing off their chimerical notions of divinity as articles of divine faith, corrupted and adulterated the original text of the bible, and imposed it upon their credulous hearers as the word of God. What blasphemy was not practised by these abandoned hypocrites, in addition to the work of sacrilege and robbery and bloodshed we have already detailed. For our part we look upon this account to be purely fictitious, the in-vention of Fox or Burnet's brain; for is it to be supposed that Cranmer, or any other of the bishops, who were Lutherans in their hearts, would dare openly to deny the divine origin of the seven sacraments, which Henry himself had defended against Luther, and held so steadfast that he would have shortened even his favourite archbishop Tom a head, if he had dared to impugn any one of them? But let us go a little fur-ther into this disputation. Fox, bishop of Hereford, we are informed, seconded Cranmer against Stokesley, "and told them that *the world* "*was now* AWAKE, and would no longer be imposed on by the nice- "ties and dark terms of the schools, for the *laity* now did not only read "the scriptures in the *vulgar tongues*, but *searched the originals them-* "*selves;* therefore they must not think to govern them as they had "been governed in the *times of ignorance.*" Ah! Gilbert Burnet, when you told this fine tale, you did not expect the people would really begin to see through the stratagems played off to lull them asleep. We do not believe that Fox was so lost to his character as to make such a statement as you have imputed to him, but allowing him to have made it, what does it amount to? Absurdity and falsehood! The world was said to be now wide awake; in which case it must be allowed to have slept a long time, since the Christian part of it had then existed 1500 years, with its eyes shut. But the concluding part of the statement is the most extraordinary. The laity are said not only to have read the translation of the scriptures, but even to have *searched the originals!* Is there any one credulous enough to believe this? The laity searching the *originals* of the sacred writings!! To be sure they must have been a very learned laity indeed; and we wonder much that, in this case, there was so great and Vandalic a destruction of the libraries of the monasteries and colleges which took place just at that time. And then as to the translations into the vulgar tongue, we believe at this period there was only one, namely Tyndal's, which was found to be filled with so many corruptions, and adulterated with such gross and scandalous opinions, that the king issued a proclamation, ordering all persons to deliver up their copies of this version, declaring that in respect to the *malignity* of the times it was better that the scriptures should be expounded by the *learned* than exposed to the misconstruction of the *vulgar.* Now this proceeding looks very much like the world being wide awake, and no longer inclined to be *imposed* upon, since it appears the reformers wished to *impose* upon them with their eyes open. To prevent this was the object of the king's proclamation, and he promised the people, that if it should afterwards appear that *erroneous* opinions were *forsaken,* and Tyndal's version destroyed, he would then provide them a new translation through the labours of learned, tried and Catholic divines. But what necessity could there be for all this attention on the part of his royal popeship, if *the people* were of themselves able to *search* the originals? The falsehood of the statement imputed to the bishop by Burnet is palpable. The suppression of Tyndal's bible, to be sure took place before the elevation of Cranmer to the primacy, and as Tom had witnessed the success of so powerful a weapon among the reformers in Germany, he took care, after he was raised to his high station, to recall to the recollection of the royal pope his promise to give a translation of the scriptures in the vulgar tongue, and his endeavours to procure one were seconded by petitions from the convocation and the recommendation of Cromwell. The king consented to this importunity, and two printers, named Grafton and Whitchurch, obtained the royal license to publish a folio edition of the bible.—" It " bore (says Dr. Lingard) the name of Thomas Matthewe, a fictitious " signature; and was made up of the version by Tyndal, and of another " by Coverdale, printed very lately, as it was thought, at Zurich. In- " junctions were now issued, that a bible of this edition should be placed " in every church at the joint expense of the incumbent and the parish- " ioners: and that any man might have the liberty of reading in it at " his pleasure, provided he did not disturb the preacher in his sermon, " nor the clergyman during the service. Soon afterwards this indul- " gence was extended from the church to private houses: but Henry " was at all times careful to admonish the readers, that, when they met " with difficult passages, they should consult persons more learned than

" themselves : and to remind them, that the liberty which they enjoyed,
" was not a right to which they possessed any claim, but a favour
" granted ' of the royal liberality and goodness.' " The recommendation and permission to print took place about 1534, the work was completed in 1537, and the indulgence to allow the bible in private houses
in 1539. We give these dates, as they will be found useful when we
come to detail the persecutions which followed, and which were sanctioned by Cranmer and his base compeers.

It is now time to examine the articles of faith which were sent by
the king to be considered by the convocation, and which, we are further told, though compounded of truth and error, were signed by Cromwell and Cranmer, and several of the dignified clergy. With regard
to the first, by adopting the three creeds and the first four general councils, they admitted the doctrines of the Catholic church, for Catholics
believe no more now than the fathers of the councils believed then.
Of baptism there is no difference in the belief, and with regard to penance we have the Catholic doctrine at once confirmed. We have confession to the priest taught as necessary to salvation, then we have contrition, and satisfaction by the external works of charity; all which are
considered as essentially necessary acts of the sacraments of penance.
As to the eucharist, or sacrament of the altar, the *real presence* is most
distinctly admitted, and, observe reader, Tom Cranmer, though he rejected this doctrine in his heart, yet he nevertheless subscribed to it,
and continued not only to say mass during Henry's lifetime, but consecrated priests to do the same. The eucharist is here said, as it is in the
present Church catechism, to be the very flesh and blood of Christ,
under the forms of bread and wine; Cranmer solemnly subscribes to
this doctrine which all Catholics hold, and shortly after he burns a poor
fellow and a fanatic old woman for not believing in this doctrine, as we
shall presently see : yet do Protestants at this day swear that such doctrine is damnable and idolatrous, to qualify themselves for office.

We have the system of venerating images retained also, though an
injunction is attached that the people ought to be taught to avoid superstition. And so they were taught, for there is not a Catholic that
will not deny that he renders any homage to the image he may pray
before, but that his adoration is directed to God and to God alone. The
custom of praying for the dead is also admitted, as well as saying
masses for the repose of their souls, which included the doctrine of
Purgatory; so that we have here nothing but Catholic doctrine, and the
reformers subscribing to such doctrine. It is true, Burnet and the
modern editors tell us that when these things were published the reformers did not approve "of every particular," yet they rejoiced to see
some grosser abuses removed, and a reformation *set on foot*. This was
some consolation to these dissembling and innovating spirits to be sure;
but if they did not approve of them why did the heads of the reforming
party sign them? Were these learned reformers ignorant of what was
most essential in the Reformation? or were they intimidated by the
overbearing temper of Henry? Principle was made to give way to policy, and though it is attempted to botch up Cranmer's reforming spirit
by the introduction of a paper which it is pretended he presented to the
king, exhorting him to proceed further in the work of reformation, yet

it is very well known Henry did not listen to Tom's suggestions, and the latter continued to profess Henry's creed with the most obsequious disposition. The points proposed for discussion had already been decided, and as to Cranmer's praying the king not to give judgment on them till he had heard them well examined, the act of the six articles which soon followed shewed how little influence Tom had over his master, and that Harry was resolved that Tom should obey him.

This assent of the convocation to Henry's book of "articles," which were presented to that assembly by Cromwell, was followed by the publication of a work called "The godly and pious institution of a Christian Man," subscribed by the archbishops, bishops, archdeacons, and certain doctors of canon and civil law, and pronounced by them to accord "in all things with the very true meaning of scripture." Dr. Lingard writes, "It explains in succession the creed, the seven sacra-
" ments, which it divides into three of a higher and four of a lower or-
" der, the ten commandments, the pater noster and ave Maria, justifi-
" cation and purgatory. It is chiefly remarkable for the earnestness
" with which it refuses salvation to all persons out of the pale of the
" Catholic church, denies the supremacy of the pontiff, and inculcates
" passive obedience to the king. It teaches that no cause whatever
" can authorize the subject to draw the sword against his prince : that
" sovereigns are accountable to God alone : and that the only remedy
" against oppression is to pray that God would change the heart of the
" despot, and induce him to make a right use of his power." Here then it is placed beyond contradiction that Cranmer, being a Lutheran in his heart, must have been one of the rankest dissemblers that ever bore human shape, seeing that he subscribed to a work which maintained the doctrine of the seven sacraments, purgatory and exclusive salvation, all which were according to the true meaning of scripture. Another of the blessed fruits of Henry's supremacy, as set forth in this book and subscribed by Cranmer and the clergy, was the doctrine of the *divine right of kings*, which till this period was never heard of in England. Sir Thomas More, who was a sound lawyer, laid it down as a fundamental principle of the British Constitution, that Parliament could make and unmake a king, though it could not alter a law of God. Thus then with the innovation of religion we may trace the invasion of the Constitution, and from the destruction of the monasteries we may lay all the evils which have afflicted this now unfortunate but once happy country for the last three centuries.

PERSECUTIONS FOR RELIGIOUS OPINIONS.

The reader is now in possession of the proceedings regarding religion which accompanied the work of spoliation and sacrilege in the destruction of monasteries and seizure of church property. While this work of impiety was going on, the reformers of Germany sent envoys over to Henry to bring the monarch into their views, but the obstinacy of Henry was insurmountable. This embassy was the work of Cranmer, who knowing well that if he dared to thwart his master his head would soon fly from off his shoulders, conceived that foreigners might take a liberty which he dared not do, and flattered himself that through their influence and learning the king might be won over. Several conferences were accordingly held, and Henry, with the aid of the bishop of Durham, was pleased to answer their arguments, which having done, he thanked them for the trouble they had taken, and sent them home. The pope, on the other hand, hearing of the scene of devastation that was going on in England, issued out a bull of excommunication against Henry, and threatened him with spiritual censures. Of this latter affair Burnet thus speaks;—" When these proceedings were known at Rome, the " pope immediately fulminated against the king all the thunders of his " spiritual store-house; absolved his subjects from their allegiance, and " his allies from their treaties with him; and exhorted all Christians to " make war against and extirpate him from the face of the earth. But " the age of crusades was past, and this display of impotent malice pro- " duced only contempt in the minds of the king and his advisers, who " steadily proceeded in the great work of reformation; and, the trans- " lation of the bible into English being now completed, it was printed, " and ordered to be read in all churches, with permission for every " person to read it, who might be so disposed.

" But, notwithstanding the king's disagreement with the pope on " many subjects, there was one point on which they were alike—they " were both intolerant furious bigots; and while the former was excom- " municated as an *heretic*, he was himself equally zealous in rooting out " *heresy*, and burning all who presumed to depart from the standard of " faith which he had established. Gardiner, bishop of Winchester, " strengthened this disposition of the king, and persuaded him, under " the pretext of a zeal for religion, to persecute the Sacramentarists, or " those who denied the corporeal presence in the sacrament."

This is Burnet's account, and we have here two remarkable circumstan- ces connected with the work of Reformation, which it will be well for the Protestant reader to notice. First, the steady progress of " the king and " HIS ADVISERS in the great work of reformation," exemplified in the circulation of the bible in the English language; and secondly, its accom- paniment of PERSECUTION, by burning those who dared to differ in opi- nion from the king and his advisers. Burnet would persuade us there was very little difference between the then-pope of Rome and the royal pope of England; both, he says, were intolerant furious bigots. Well, let it be so; still it must be confessed that the fury of the pope was given to the winds, while the rage of the English pope, unallayed by his advisers Cranmer, Cromwell, and the like, knew no bounds and saturated the earth with the blood of his victims. The crafty historian has placed Gardiner, bishop of Winchester, in front of the stage; but we shall see, by and by, even in his own words, that Cranmer was not an unconcerned spectator in these scenes of cruelty and slaughter. We have before shewn that Cranmer was no sooner in the primate's chair, than he was an actor in the burning of Frith and a poor tailor for denying the real presence. Of this fact we have the testimony of Cranmer himself, who gives the following account of the affair in a letter which he wrote to Master Hawkins:—" One Fryth which was in the Tower in pryson, was " appoynted by the kyng's grace to be examyned before me, my lorde of " London, my lorde of Wynchester, my lorde of Suffolke, my lorde Chan- " celloure, and my lorde of Wyltshire, whose opynion was so notably er- " roneouse, that we culd not dispatche hym: but was fayne to leve hym

" to the determynacion of his ordinarye, which is the bishop of London.
" His said opynion ys of such nature, that he thoughte it not necessary to
" be believed as an article of our faythe, that ther ys the very corporall
" presence of Christe within the oste and sacramente of the alter: and
" holdeth of this poynte most after the opynion of Oecolampadious.——
" And surely I myself sent for hym iii or iiii tymes to perswade hym
" to leve that his imaginacion; but for all that we culd do therein
" he woulde not apply to any counsaile: notwithstandyng he ys nowe
" at a fynall ende with all examinacions, for my lorde of London hathe
" gyven sentance, and delyvered hym to the secular power, where he
" looketh every day to go to a fyer. And ther ys condempned with
" hym one Andrewe a tayloure of London for the said selfsame opy-
" nion."—(_Archæol._ xvii. p. 81.)

Two years after the burning of Frith, that is, in 1535, a colony of
anabaptists came over to England from Germany, and were instantly apprehended; fourteen of them refusing to recant were consigned to the
flames. In 1538 another batch of them followed, and Cranmer was ordered by the king to call them before him (the archbishop) and three
other prelates, to admonish them of their errors, and deliver the contumacious over for punishment. Tom readily complied: four of the number abjured, and a man and woman suffered for their obstinacy at the
stake. The next sufferer was one of more than ordinary interest, and
we will here give the account as we find it in the _Book of Martyrs_, before we make any comment upon it.

" MARTYRDOM OF JOHN LAMBERT.—In consequence of this determi-
" nation, John Lambert, a teacher of languages in London, who had
" drawn up ten arguments against the tenets of Dr. Taylor, on the above
" subject, as delivered in a sermon at St. Peter's church, and presented
" them to the doctor, was brought before the _archbishop's_ court to de-
" fend his writings; and, having appealed to the king, the royal theolo-
" gian, who was proud of every occasion of displaying his talents and
" learning, resolved to hear him in person. He therefore issued a com-
" mission, ordering all his nobility and bishops to repair to London, to
" assist him against heretics. A day was appointed for the disputation,
" when a great number of persons of all ranks assembled to witness the
" proceedings, and Lambert was brought from his prison by a guard
" and placed directly opposite to the king. Henry being seated on his
" throne, and surrounded by the peers, bishops, and judges, regarded
" the prisoner with a stern countenance, and then commanded Day, bi-
" shop of Chichester, to state the occasion of the present assembly.
" The bishop made a long oration, stating that, although the king had
" abolished the papal authority in England, it was not to be supposed
" that he would allow heretics with impunity to disturb and trouble
" the church of which he was the head. He had therefore determined
" to punish all schismatics; and being willing to have the _advice_ of his
" _bishops_ and _counsellors_ on so great an occasion, had assembled to hear
" the present case.

" The oration being concluded, the king ordered Lambert to declare
" his opinion as to the sacrament of the Lord's supper, which he did,
" by denying it to be the body of Christ. The king then commanded
" CRANMER to refute his assertion, which the latter _attempted_: but

" was interrupted by Gardiner, who *vehemently interposed*, and, being
" *unable to bring argument to his aid*, sought by *abuse* and *virulence* to
" overpower his antagonist, who was *not allowed* to *answer* the *taunts*
" and *insults* of the bishop. Tonstal and Stokesly followed in the same
" course, and Lambert, beginning to answer them, was silenced by the
" king. The other bishops then each made a speech in confutation of
" one of Lambert's arguments, till the whole ten were answered, or ra-
" ther, railed against; for he was not permitted to defend them, however
" misrepresented.

" At last, when *the day was passed*, and *torches began to be lighted*, the
" king desiring to break up this pretended disputation, said to Lambert,
" ' What sayest thou now, after all these great labours which thou hast
" taken upon thee, and all the reasons of these learned men? Art thou
" not yet satisfied? Wilt thou live or die? What sayest thou? Thou
" hast yet free choice.' Lambert answered, ' I yield and submit my-
" self wholly unto the will of your majesty.' ' Then,' said the king,
" ' commit thyself unto the hands of God, and not unto mine.' Lam-
" bert replied, ' I commend my soul unto the hands of God, but my
" body I wholly yield and submit unto your clemency.' To which the
" king answered, ' If you do commit yourself unto my judgment, you
" must die, for I will not be a patron unto heretics; and, turning to
" Cromwell, he said, ' read the sentence of condemnation against him,'
" which he accordingly did.

" Upon the day appointed for this holy martyr to suffer, he was
" brought out of the prison at eight o'clock in the morning to the house
" of Cromwell, and carried into his inner chamber, where, it is said,
" Cromwell desired his forgiveness for what he had done. Lambert
" being at last admonished that the hour of his death was at hand, and
" being brought out of the chamber, into the hall, saluted the gentle-
" men present, and sat down to breakfast with them, shewing neither
" sadness nor fear. When breakfast was ended, he was carried straight
" to the place of execution at Smithfield.

" The manner of his death was dreadful; for after his legs were con-
" sumed and burned up to the stumps, and but a small fire was left un-
" der him, two of the inhuman monsters who stood on each side of him,
" pierced him with their halberts, and lifted him up as far as the chain
" would reach; while he, raising his half consumed *hands*, cried out
" unto the people in these words: ' None but Christ, none but Christ;'
" and so being let down again from their halberts, fell into the fire and
" there ended his life.

" The popish party greatly triumphed at this event, and endeavoured
" to improve it. They persuaded the king of the good effects it would
" have on his people, who would in this see his zeal for the faith; and
" they forgot not to magnify all that he had said, as if it had been ut-
" tered by an oracle, which proved him to be both ' Defender of the
" Faith and Supreme Head of the Church.' All this wrought so much
" on the king, that he resolved to call a parliament for the contradictory
" purposes of suppressing the still remaining monasteries, and extirpat-
" ing the ' new opinions.' "

We have given this long account of the death of Lambert, that the
re   may be able to judge for himself of the manner in which the rest

A REVIEW

OF

ﬀox's ﬁook of ﬀartyrs,

CRITICAL AND HISTORICAL.

No. 39. Printed and Published by W. E. Andrews, 3, Chapter-house-court, St. Paul's Churchyard, London.   Price 3d.

EXPLANATION OF THE ENGRAVING.—*This cut represents the visitors under Cromwell, the vicar general, pillaging the religious houses, and robbing them of that store which was appropriated to comfort the sick and entertain the traveller.*

CONTINUATION OF THE REVIEW.

of these pretended martyrdoms are detailed. We have no clue to learn from whence the account was obtained, and common sense dictates, that the tale is too highly coloured to be *true.* However there is one thing to be remembered, which is, that though great pains are taken to impress the reader that this execution of Lambert was the exclusive work of the Popish party, the chief actors in the drama were the prime movers of the reformation, Cromwell and Cranmer, and the *time* of performance *after* the king and his advisers had resolved to proceed steadily in the great work of the reformation, by translating the Bible into English, and granting permission for every person to read it. This fact must always be borne in mind. It is admitted that Lambert in the first instance was brought before "the *archbishop's* court, to defend his writings," and this archbishop was no other person than Tom Cranmer, a Lutheran in his heart, and who held the very opinions which Lambert himself held. Before this man's court was the unfortunate victim brought, and from the judgment of this court he appealed to the king himself. Of the proceedings before Henry we have a long and minute relation: indeed it is too minute to be correct; there is one circumstance however that must not be overlooked. Cranmer is ordered by the king to *refute* Lambert, which the base hypocrite, we are told, *attempted to do*, but, it should seem, *failed* in the attempt, as, it is said, he was interrupted by Gardiner, who took up the cudgels with vehemence and abuse. This attempt on the part of Burnet to screen the abject and slavish compliance of his hero, Cranmer, at the expense of another prelate, who, though culpable in acknowledging the supremacy of Henry, was still attached to the ancient faith, is only to be equalled by the infamy of Cranmer himself. What are we to think of the man who, holding such a high station as the primacy of England in spiritual affairs, would submit to be interrupted by one of his suffragans while in the performance of a duty imposed upon him by the king? Could he have the feelings of an upright mind? Must he not have been a most debased slave, or the most consummate hypocrite that ever breathed? But as we shall see, and have seen, the whole life of Cranmer, during the reign of Henry, was one continued act of dissimulation, and the practice and profession of religious rites and doctrines which he inwardly renounced and disbelieved. The hired cut-throat, the midnight assassin, the wretch who perjures himself for his daily bread, is a moral character compared with this hoary villain and sanctified murderer, who filled the primate's chair of England under Henry the first pope of the reformed church, and his successor Edward, the boyhead of the same church, though altered in faith and discipline. But to return to Lambert; he was not, Burnet says, allowed to answer the taunts and insults of Gardiner, but was even compelled to listen to further outrages on his own feelings from the other bishops, who had each a separate error to confute, and when Lambert made an effort to reply to them he was stopped by the king. Will any unprejudiced mind give credit to this story? Will it be believed that *ten* bishops were selected to convict *one* unhappy heretic of the same number of erroneous opinions he had imbibed, and this before the new pope to whom poor Lambert had appealed? The thing is incredible. To believe such a preposterous tale would betray a mind warped with the most bigotted prejudice, or devoid of the slightest pretensions to common sense.

The bishops having spent their breath in railing at the poor prisoner, and *torches* being about to be lighted, (had they no candles at that day?) Henry began to be a little weary, and wishing to break up the disputation, which, by the by, was all on one side, put some questions to Lambert, whose answers not being satisfactory, he ordered Cromwell to *read* the sentence of death against him, which was accordingly done. So then, we have one of Fox's blessed martyrs passing sentence of death upon another of these soldiers of the reformation. Pretty work this, it must be admitted. Well, the martyr Lambert is brought out of prison on the morning of his execution, and taken to the chamber of afterwards-martyr Cromwell, in order that the latter might ask of the former forgiveness for what he had done!!! What! Is it probable? Is it at all likely that the criminal should be paraded to the chamber of his judge on his way to execution, and that this judge, who was a principal

·performer in the work of desolation then going forward, and subsequently fell a victim to his crimes, should ask pardon for what he had done? But, not only was he permitted to pay this visit to Cromwell, he was also allowed to salute the gentlemen present in the hall, and then to SIT DOWN TO BREAKFAST WITH THEM, shewing neither sadness nor fear!!!! Well said, Gilbert Burnet! We defy Baron Munchausen to beat this specimen of the devil's art. One word more on poor Lambert. Could we believe the description of his death, we should blush for human nature; at least, we meant to say, we should blush for the honour of our country, because we are sorry to say, the cruelties practised by the reformers have equalled the sufferings detailed of Lambert, if nature were capable of sustaining what he is here stated to have undergone. But we do not believe it possible; the description is intended to excite a feeling of horror and abhorrence of the supposed cruelty of Popish executioners, but the tale is evidently overcharged, and palpably untrue. For example; it is said that *after* his legs were *consumed*, they were burned up to *the stumps;* and when the fire was nearly consumed under him, two monsters lifted him up with their halberts as far as the chain would allow them, and letting him fall into the almost expiring embers, the fire was not put out by the fall but his life was ended. But if the chain restricted the act of raising, would it not also prevent his falling—and would not the flames that consumed the poor victim's legs to ashes, stifle his breath, and release him from his torments? What prevented him from falling into the flames, while at their utmost height, if the chain permitted him, to fall into it when nearly extinguished? Oh! it is a bungling tale, calculated to impose on the unthinking and besotted fanatic; but cannot have any weight with the sensible and reflecting part of the community.

So much for the manner of Lambert's execution; with regard to the insinuation that his death was considered as *a triumph* by the Popish party, this is a trick of Burnet to cover the shame of his heroes, who basely truckled to Harry's inclinations, and flattered him in all his excessive vanities. The paragraph contradicts itself. It is said the Popish party did not forget to magnify what the king had said, and represented his words as an oracle, proving him to be both "Defender of the Faith and Supreme Head of the Church." Now, unluckily for Burnet's veracity, it so happened, that the Popish party not only denied this supremacy by word of mouth, but they exhibited a degree of fortitude which the reforming party did not possess; laying down their lives in support of their doctrines, and evincing by their courage and demeanour the purity of their lives and stability of their faith. Had the Popish party admitted the supremacy of the king in ecclesiastical matters, they would have renounced their faith, and consequently have ceased to have been of *that* party. The fact, however, is as we have stated it, the *reformers* were the flatterers. This is placed beyond a doubt by a letter which Cromwell wrote to Wyatt the ambassador in Germany. In this epistle, the vicar-general says, "The king's majesty presided at the dis-" putation, process, and judgment of a miserable heretic sacramentary, " who was burnt the 20th of November. It was wonderful to see how " princely, with how excellent gravity, and inestimable majesty his

" highness exercised there the very office of supreme head of the church
" of England: how benignly his grace essayed to convert the miserable
" man how strong and manifest reasons his highness alleged against
" him.　I wish the princes and potentates of christendom to have had a
" meet place to have seen it."　Collier, iii. 152.　After this testimony
who will credit Fox or Burnet?　Dr. Lingard notices the long stories
told by Godwin and Fox of this trial, which he considers unworthy of
credit.　The account states that Henry " regarded the prisoner with a
" stern countenance;" but this is contradicted by Cromwell's letter,
and as Cromwell was afterwards one of Fox's blessed martyrs, surely he
will not be charged with falsehood by the enemies of Popery.　Lambert
is also represented as " shewing neither sadness nor fear," when lead out
for death; but, according to Hall, who was present at his trial, he had
so little courage and as little ability, that he exhibited signs of great
terror on that occasion, and it is not too much to presume that he was
not more firm on one of greater moment.

THE ACT OF THE SIX ARTICLES.

We come now to another important transaction in this work of (as it
is called) Reformation.—The *Book of Martyrs* says, " All this," that is,
the flattery of the Popish party, which we have proved belongs to the
reformers, and the condemnation of Lambert; " all this wrought so
much on the king, that he resolved to call a parliament for the *contradictory* purposes of *suppressing* the still remaining monasteries, and *extirpating* the NEW OPINIONS."—Oh, oh! NEW OPINIONS!!　Then the
blessed work of Reformation was not grounded on *unchangeable* principles, but upon NEW OPINIONS; and these opinions were so often *renewed*
and have been so much *multiplied,* that it is really difficult nowadays
to know what men's *opinions* are with regard to *religion.*—The modern
editors say the parliament was called for the " contradictory" purposes
of suppression and extirpation; on looking into Burnet's Abridgment,
we find the words " contradictory" and " extirpation" have been introduced, by the way, we suppose, of improvement.—Burnet writes, that
the king " resolved to call a parliament, both for the suppression of the
monasteries and the new opinions."　By this mode of expression it
would seem that the bishop of Sarum, did not consider the two purposes for which the parliament was called " contradictory," though the
modern editors represent them as such.—But no matter; it is little to
our purpose whether they were contradictory or not, our object is to
shew the result and the conduct of the actors in the proceedings.—To
do this clearly we must borrow a little from Burnet, as we perceive
the modern editors have culled from this fabulous historian, and suppressed at their pleasure facts which will throw much light on the
subject, but which they did not wish should be elicited.

Burnet says, " upon Fox's death, Bonner was promoted to Hereford;
" and Stokesly dying not long after he was translated to London.
" Cromwell thought that he had raised a man that would be a faithful
" second to Cranmer in his designs of reformation, who indeed needed
" help; not only to balance the opposition made him by other bishops,
" but to lessen the prejudices he suffered by the weakness and indiscre-
" tion of his own party, who were generally rather clogs than helps to

" him. Great complaints were brought to the court of the rashness of
" the new preachers, who were flying at many things not yet abolished.
" Upon this, letters were writ to the bishops, to take care that as the
" people should be rightly instructed; so they should not be offended
" with too many novelties. Thus was Cranmer's interest so low, that
" he had none to depend on but Cromwell. There was not a queen
" now in the king's bosom to support them; and therefore Cromwell
" set himself to contrive how the king should be engaged in such an
" alliance with the princes of Germany, as might prevail with him,
" both in affection and interest, to carry on what he had thus begun."

From this account we may clearly perceive that the work so improperly termed a reformation, was nothing more nor less than the struggles of faction and interest, in which the people were the greatest sufferers, and the actors the most abandoned villains.—Cromwell it appears was at this time greater in influence at court than Tom Cranmer, who, we are told, needed help in his designs.—Again, the preachers of the new opinions are charged with rashness, and were rather clogs than helps in the godly work.—There was not a queen in the king's bosom to support the brace of diabolical villains, Cromwell and Cranmer, and therefore it was necessary to look out for one to further their ends.—After the death of poor Jane Seymour, who was ripped open, the king could not find a woman of sense and virtue willing to share his bed, so Cromwell looked out for one among the Protestants in Germany, and pitched upon Anne of Cleves.—He went to work, and got the lady's consent, and afterwards obtained Harry's, but it proved in the event his own ruin. While Cromwell and Cranmer were concerting these things between them, their interest with the king was declining, and the duke of Norfolk, an old opponent of the archbishop, was rising again in favour.—The Catholic sovereigns of Europe, by their negociations with each other, had excited some serious apprehension in the mind of Henry, and he therefore resolved on some project to convince the foreign powers that though he had renounced all subjection to the common father of Christendom, he was still determined to adhere to the ancient doctrine of the church. He therefore summoned a parliament to meet, which accordingly assembled at the call of the monarch. Before we proceed with the transactions of this body, we will give the modern editors' account, which we see is an abridgment of Burnet's Abridgment.—They say, "The parliament accordingly met on the 28th of
" April, 1538; and after long debates, passed what was called 'a bill
" of religion,' containing six articles, by which it was declared, that the
" elements of the sacrament were the real body and blood of Christ;
" that communion was necessary only in one kind; that priests ought
" not to marry; that vows of chastity ought to be observed; that pri-
" vate masses were lawful and useful; and that auricular confession
" was necessary. This act gave great satisfaction to the popish party,
" and induced them to consent more readily to the act for suppressing
" the monasteries, which immediately followed; by virtue of which,
" their total dissolution soon after took place. The king founded six
" new bishoprics from a small portion of their immense revenues, and
" lavished the remainder on his profligate courtiers and favourites."

Here then we have another admission that in the foundation of six

new bishoprics by the king, but a small portion of the immense revenues obtained by the suppression system, was appropriated to that
purpose, and the greater part was lavished on his profligate courtiers and favourites.   Now these courtiers and favourites were the
creatures of the prime villains Cranmer and Cromwell, as well as the
panders of the king, and we gather therefrom the precious materials
used to build the *new* church of England.   It is hinted that the six articles gave great satisfaction to the Popish party, and induced them to
consent more readily to the work of desolation and robbery ; now we
believe the Popish party had very little hand in the matter, for though
many actors in the drama might profess themselves Catholics, the
church itself we believe did not acknowledge them.   We admire the
easy manner in which this very interesting subject is glossed over by
the modern editors ; Burnet himself is more explicit, but he takes special care to screen the conduct of Cranmer in this affair.   Let us then
see how the case stands, and then the reader may decide for himself.—
We have before noticed that the renunciation of the pope's supremacy,
which being of divine right, is the link of unity in the Catholic church,
let in a flood of opinions which increased daily, and induced Henry, as
head of the church, to devise some method to preserve uniformity.   Accordingly on the meeting of this parliament, which took place on the
28th of April, 1539, a committee of *spiritual* lords was appointed to examine into this diversity of religious opinions.   This committee was
composed of the archbishops of Canterbury and York, the bishops of
Durham, Carlisle, Bath, Bangor, Salisbury, and Ely, and Cromwell the
lay vicar general.   On every question the members divided five against
four.   The prelates of York, Durham, Carlisle, Bath and Bangor being opposed to Cromwell, Cranmer, and the bishops of Salisbury and
Ely.   Eleven days were consumed in these divisions, and the head of
the new church grew impatient.   The duke of Norfolk, who had been
commissioned by the king to conduct the affairs of the crown in the
house of peers, observing the new pope's impatience, remarked that
there was nothing to be expected from the labours of the committee,
and proposed that six questions concerning certain points of doctrine
should be submitted to the house, which was accordingly done.   The
questions selected were the real presence, communion under one kind,
private masses, the celibacy of the priesthood, auricular confession, and
vows of chastity.   The bishops only took a part in the debate on the
first day, and on the second day the king-pope came down to the house
and took a share in the discussion.   Here was a trial for the two arch
deformers ; they had hitherto opposed with vehemence their prelatic
brethren, but to resist the king, to place themselves in opposition to the
new head of the church, in whom was centered the good things of this
world, and who could send them at almost an hour's notice to know
their fate in the next ; to resist such a mighty personage as this was
another matter ; it required more courage than either of them possessed and with meanness the most base and truckling did Cromwell
and hight Tom Cranmer, Burnett's famous hero of the reformation, gulp
down in the presence of the king all they had advanced before their
fellow-committee-men, and, excepting the bishop of Salisbury, acknowledged themselves vanquished by the superior reasoning and learning of

his popeship, as they said, but, as we believe, and as the reader will believe with us, by the terror of displeasing the inexorable tyrant. Though Cranmer and Cromwell could send poor Lambert to the stake, they had no inclination to follow him in defence of their opinions. Fox and Burnet both assert that Cranmer persisted in his opposition, but these mendacious writers are contradicted by the journals of the house and by the assertion of one of the lords who was present.—(*See Lingard*, note, vol. iv. p. 287, 4to. edit.)

Henry having thus far succeeded, was not a little proud of his victory, and sent a message to the lords congratulating them on their unanimity, and recommending the introduction of a bill to enforce conformity by pains and penalties. To comply with the royal recommendation, two separate committees were appointed to prepare a bill, and it is very singular that three of the prelates who were opposed to the measure at first, but became converts through royal influence, namely, the prelates of Canterbury (Tom Cranmer) Ely and St. David's, were selected to form one committee, and the bishops of York, Durham and Winchester, constituted the other. The two bills were submitted to the king by the lords, who chose that drawn up by the latter. The lord Chancellor then introduced it in the usual form to the house, through which it was passed, as also the commons, in a few days, and received the royal assent. As this is one of the most important acts of Henry's reign, we will here transcribe it at length for the satisfaction of the reader.

" The king's royal majesty, most prudently considering, that, by oc-
" casion of various opinions and judgments concerning some articles in
" religion, great discord and variance hath arisen, as well amongst the
" clergy of this realm, as amongst a great number of the vulgar people;
" and, being in a full hope and trust, that a full and perfect resolution
" of the said articles, would make a perfect concord and unity gene-
" rally amongst all his loving and obedient subjects; of his most excel-
" lent goodness not only commanded that the said articles should de-
" liberately and advisedly, by his archbishops, bishops, and other learned
" men of his clergy, be debated, argued, and reasoned, and their opi-
" nions therein to be understood, declared, and known; but also most
" graciously vouchsafed, in his own princely person, to come unto his
" high court of parliament and council, and there, like a wise prince of
" most high prudence, and no less learning, opened and declared many
" things, of the most high learning and great knowledge touching the
" said articles, matters, and questions, for an unity to be had in the
" same. Whereupon, after a great and long, deliberate and advised
" disputation and consultation, had and made concerning the said arti-
" cles, as well by the consent of the king's highness, as by the assent
" of the lords spiritual and temporal, and other learned men of the
" clergy, in their convocations, and by the consent of the commons in
" parliament assembled, it was, and is, finally resolved, accorded, and
" agreed, in manner and form following; that is to say,

" First, That in the most blessed sacrament of the altar, by the
" strength and efficacy of Christ's mighty word, (it being spoken by the
" priest) is present really, under the forms of bread and wine, the na-
" tural body and blood of our Saviour Jesus Christ, conceived of the
" Virgin Mary; and that, after the consecration, there remains no sub-

" stance of the bread or wine, nor any other substance but the substance
" of Christ, God and man.

" 2. That the communion in both kinds is not necessary (to salvation)
" by the law of God, to all persons ; and, that it is to be believed, and
" not doubted, but that in the flesh, under the form of bread, is the
" very blood, and with the blood, under the form of wine, is the very
" flesh, as well apart, as if they were both together.

" 3. That priests, after the order of priesthood received, may not
" marry, by the law of God.

" 4. That vows of chastity, widowhood, &c. are to be kept.

" 5. That it is meet and necessary that private masses be continued
" in the king's English church and congregation; as whereby good
" Christian people, ordering themselves accordingly, do receive both
" godly and goodly consolations and benefits, and it is agreeable also to
" God's law.

" 6. That auricular confession is expedient, and necessary to be re-
" tained, and continued, used, and frequented in the church of God.

" For the which most godly study, pain, and travel of his majesty,
" and determination and resolution of the premises, his humble and
" obedient subjects, the lords spiritual and temporal, and commons, in
" this present parliament assembled, not only render and give unto his
" highness their most high and hearty thanks, and think themselves
" most bound to pray for the long continuance of his grace's most royal
" estate and dignity ; but being also desirous that his most godly enter-
" prize may be well accomplished and brought to a full end and per-
" fection, and so established that the same might be to the honour of
" God, and after to the common quiet, unity, and concord, to be had
" in the whole body of this realm for ever, do most humbly beseech his
" royal majesty, that the resolution and determination above written of
" the said articles may be established, and perpetually perfected, by the
" authority of this present parliament.

" It is therefore ordained and enacted by the king our sovereign lord,
" and by the lords spiritual and temporal, and by the commons in this
" present parliament assembled, and by the authority of the same, that
" if any person or persons, within this realm of England, or in any other
" of the king's dominions, do by word, writing, printing, cyphering, or
" any otherwise, publish, teach, preach, say, affirm, declare, dispute,
" argue, or hold any opinion :

" First, That in the blessed sacrament of the altar, under the form
" of bread and wine, &c.————such persons are to suffer pains of death,
" as in cases of felony, without any benefit of the clergy, or privilege of
" church, or sanctuary; and shall forfeit all their lands and goods, as
" in cases of felony."

The passing of this act not only struck poor archbishop Tom with
terror, but all the rest of the tribe were in great alarm.   So little were
they inclined to become martyrs for their " NEW OPINIONS," and so desirous were they of keeping a whole skin, that it was deemed by them
most prudent to submit to the king's will, and, to insure their safety,
remain silent.   Latimer and Shaxton, bishops of Worcester and Salisbury, resigned their sees, and Cranmer found it necessary to be cautious
in his conduct to save his bacon.   It will be borne in mind that Tom,

before his promotion to the archiepiscopal dignity, had taken a niece of Osiander, the reformer, to be his wife, and that he used to transport her from place to place in *a box*, after his promotion to the primacy. By this woman he had several children, and though the matter was not made public, yet the secret was sufficiently known to induce many priests to follow Tom's example. The making it felony to cohabit with the sex, was a choaker to these lewd wretches, who already began to feel the rope round their necks, and to avoid its being drawn tight, many of them scampered out of the way and some others put aside their wives. Tom Cranmer had tried, previous to the passing of this tremendous law, to soften Harry's inflexible aversion to a married clergy, but the king was not to be moved, so the archbishop, on the passing of this act, not willing to lose his dignity, packed off his wife and children for Germany, and then following up his consummate baseness, wrote a crawling apology to Henry for his presumption in daring to differ from the monarch's will on this point.

Burnet tells us, " the poor reformers were now exposed to the rage " of their enemies, and had no comfort from any part of it, but one, that " they were not delivered up to the *cruelty of the ecclesiastical courts*, or " the trials *ex officio*, but were to be tried by juries; yet the benefit of " abjuration was a severity without precedent, and was a *forcing* mar- " tyrdom on them, since they were not to be the better for their apos- " tacy. It was some satisfaction to the *married* clergy (he adds), that " the incontinent priests were to be so severely punished; which Crom- " well put in, and the clergy knew not how they could decently oppose " it." Surely this act must have been devised by the archfiend, that it put the godly reformers into such a pickle. But why did they not follow the example of the two chiefs Cromwell and Cranmer, but especially the latter, who had been so long a Lutheran in his heart. Tom, when he saw no other resource, with his accustomed baseness, yielded to circumstances and subscribed to the doctrine of the six articles, though he disbelieved them. But what did that signify to him; it was the king's will, and therefore it was right he should obey the supreme head of the church, though he condemned inwardly the doctrine which the new lay pope promulgated. To preserve his life and his place this hero of the reformation so called could subscribe outwardly to what he inwardly rejected, thus setting the first example of mental reservation, which succeeding reformers fastened upon Catholics, though their church most strongly condemns such conduct. Though Cranmer denied infallibility to the pope, who could do him no harm, yet he was ready to allow Harry infallibility, because he had power over his life, and that Tom did not wish to part with by any premature means.

Connected with this measure, was an act of this parliament which few of the people of this country are acquainted with, but which every one of them should know, as it materially affects the principle of civil and religious liberty, and absolutely subverted the constitution. It was this : in the act which invested all the real and moveable property of the religious houses in the hands of the king, a clause was introduced which laid prostrate at the foot of the throne the liberties of the whole nation. It declared that the king's proclamations ought to have the effect of acts of parliament, and adjudged all transgressors of such proclamations to fine and imprisonment, and those who might endeavour to evade the punishment, by quitting the realm, incurred the guilt of high treason. Only think of this, reader.—The *ipse dixit* of a tyrant was made equal to the decrees of two deliberate assemblies, and in cases too involving the life and property of the people.—This scheme to obtain absolute power was the offspring of Cromwell, who was supported in it by that slave of despotism, Tom Cranmer.—The act was not carried through the two houses without considerable opposition, so repugnant was its enactments to every thing like British justice and liberty. But the nation was now distracted by two factions, and the crafty Cromwell succeeded in carrying this odious measure by the Machiavelian policy, *divide and conquer.*—It is a fruitful theme with Fox and Burnet, and other corrupt historians, to represent Gardiner, bishop of Winchester, as a merciless and tyrannical character; yet it is clear, even by the testimony of Fox himself, that Gardiner was averse to this unconstitutional measure, and opposed it even to Harry's face.—The wretch Cromwell had frequently inculcated this despotic doctrine before Henry, as we gather from a letter written by Gardiner. "The lord Cromwell," says he, "had once put in the king's head to take upon him to have his will and pleasure regarded for a law: and thereupon I was called for at Hampton Court. And as he was very stout, come on, my lord of Winchester, quoth he, answer the king here, but speak plainly and directly, and shrink not, man. Is not that, quoth he, that pleaseth the king, a law? Have ye not that in the civil laws, quod principi placuit, &c.? I stood still, and wondered in my mind to what conclusion this would tend. The king saw me musing, and with gentle earnestness said, answer him whether it be so or no. I would not answer the lord Cromwell, but delivered my speech to the king, and told him, that I had read of kings that had their will always received for law; but that the form of his reign to make the law his will was more sure and quiet: and by this form of government yet be established, quoth I, and it is agreeable with the nature of your people. If you begin a new manner of policy, how it frame, no man can tell. The king turned his back, and left the matter." *Fox,* ii, 65.

This attempt of Cromwell to establish an absolute despotism in this once free country, is only to be equalled by the conduct of Cranmer, the prime reformer, the hero of the reformation, and the idol of John Fox and Gilbert Burnet, who endeavoured to promulgate the idea of a *divine right* in kings to govern both in church and state, which notion he committed to paper, and Burnet has preserved in his Records.—The doctrine is unexampled, slavish, and disgraceful, as the reader will see by the following citation.—He (Cranmer) teaches, "that all Christian princes have committed unto them IMMEDIATELY OF GOD the whole care of all their subjects, as well concerning the administration of God's word, for the care of souls, as concerning the ministration of things political and civil governance: and in both these ministrations, they must have sundry ministers under them to supply that, which is appointed to their several offices; as for example, the lord chancellor, lord treasurer, lord great master, and the sheriffs for civil ministers; and the bishops, parsons, vicars and such other

" priests AS BE APPOINTED BY HIS HIGHNESS in the ministration of the
" word : as for example, the bishop of Canterbury, the bishop of Du-
" resme, the bishop of Winchester, the parson of Winwick, &c. All the
" said officers and ministers, as well of that sort as the other, must be
" appointed, assigned, and elected, and in every place, by the laws and
" orders of kings and princes, with diverse solemnities, WHICH BE NOT
" OF NECESSITY, but only for good order and seemly fashion ; for if such
" offices and ministrations were committed without such solemnity,
" they were, nevertheless, truly committed : and there is no more pro-
" mise of God, that grace is given in the committing of the ecclesiasti-
" cal office, than it is in the committing of the civil office."—It is the
fashion with Protestants to boast of the liberty produced by what they
call the Reformation ; but did the world ever before witness such doctrine of passive obedience and divine right as the arch-reformer Cranmer
here taught ? Did England ever witness a parliament in Catholic
times, that by its own act abrogated its own power, contrary to the
fundamental laws of the constitution, and center the sole power in the
crown ? Oh ! no : Catholics, imbibing the principles of true liberty
from the doctrines and canons of their church, knew not only *how to*
establish it, but likewise *how to* preserve it ; while Protestants despising the unerring rules of Divine Wisdom, and trusting to the vain
caprices of the human mind, have thrown away the substance of that
celestial blessing, without which life is valueless, to grasp at the
shadow.

FURTHER INSTANCES OF THE SLAVISHNESS OF CROMWELL AND CRANMER.

The submission of Cromwell and Cranmer to the act of the six articles, though the latter was, according to Burnet, a Lutheran in his
heart, was followed by another proceeding still more disgraceful and
infamous on the part of the latter. We have seen the fate of Anne
Boleyn and her relatives, who were accounted by this far-famed
historian the prop and pillar of the reforming party.—Jane Seymour,
who supplied her place, fell by the doctor's knife, being ripped open in
child-bed, to gratify the king's wish for a son, who was afterwards the
boy-pope Edward VI. Her fate, combined with that of her predecessor,
alarmed the sex, so that Harry could find no one willing to share part
of his bed, and it was while the king remained a widower, that the six
articles of religion were enacted, and the reformers put into such a
fright. Cromwell was not insensible of the ticklish situation in which
he stood, now that there were no more prizes to distribute from the
spoils of the church, and under these circumstances he turned his
eyes towards Germany, and sought among the Lutheran courts a
mistress for his capricious master.—At length he pitched upon
Anne of Cleves, whom Cromwell found willing to engage with
Harry, and he succeeded in gaining the king's consent to the marriage.
Cromwell and Cranmer both thought to forward the Reformation
scheme by this match, but, by a singular instance of the Divine hand,
it proved to be the downfall of the monastery destroyer. The marriage
contract had scarcely been concluded, than Harry conceived an utter
aversion for his new wife, and as suddenly became enamoured with
Catharine Howard. In consequence of this change in his desires, he

took a dislike towards Cromwell, considering this minister to be the cause of the hated match, and his being yoked for life, as he then thought, to a partner he detested. Harry resolved therefore to be revenged on Cromwell, who was soon after arrested, and, as we have before shewn, consigned to the executioner's hands. Previous, however, to his death, his partner in the work of reformation, Tom Cranmer, was called upon to perform a work, which even his panegyrist Burnet blushed at. Harry having disgraced his former favourite Cromwell, was resolved to be separated from his new wife, and accordingly he sent for Cranmer, who was ordered to summon the convocation, and prepare the business agreeably to the king's wishes. As Tom had readily performed such a job for his master before, it was not to be expected that he would be backward in complying with the second request, so he set to work, and though there was not the shadow of a pretext to disannul the marriage, it being legally and lawfully contracted, the king's whim must be gratified, and after only two day's sham ceremony of receiving depositions, and examining witnesses, the sentence of divorce between Henry and Anne of Cleves was pronounced on the 9th of July, 1540, by the compliable Tom Cranmer, in his capacity of primate of England. Burnet, as we have before observed, was ashamed of this act, and acknowledges that this was the greatest piece of compliance the king had from Cranmer and the clergy, for they all knew that there was nothing on which they could ground a sentence of divorce. Cranmer presided over the convocation, gave sentence, and afterwards carried the result to parliament, in which body Harry found as ready slaves to his will as he found among the clergy, so great a change was made in the dispositions of the nobility and gentry with the change of religion. An act was passed confirming the decision of the synod, and every person who should presume to believe or judge the marriage lawful, was subjected to the penalties of treason. Cromwell, the reader will observe, was at this time in disgrace and under arrest; and this situation of the once overbearing and haughty favourite is made an excuse by Burnet for the archbishop's obsequious conduct. This bishop historian represented his hero, Tom Cranmer, as a second Athanasius for his courage, and a second Cyril for his virtue; yet, in this case, he is obliged to admit that Tom's courage failed him, and how far his virtue came off without a stain we will leave the reader to conclude. Burnet says, that "overcome with *fear* (for " he knew it was contrived to send him quickly after Cromwell) he " (Cranmer) consented with the rest." Yes, yes; this pillar and underprop of the reformation, was too fond of life to lose it in defence of virtue and justice. The modern editors of the *Book of Martyrs*, speaking of this divorce, say, " The convocation unanimously dissolved the mar-" riage, and gave him (Henry) liberty to marry again; indeed it is " probable that if he had desired to have two or more wives at once, " the measure would have been sanctioned, so *base* and *servile* were the " *courtiers* and *priests* by whom this monstrous tyrant was surrounded." Say you so, most worthy instigators of hatred and abhorrence to the professors of Popery! But *who* were these *base* and *servile courtiers* and *priests?* Was not CRANMER at the *head* of the latter? Base and servile enough was Tom to the monstrous tyrant, who is *said to have res-*

eued this country from the tyranny of the pope. Anne, you know, most learned instigators of uncharitableness, was brought over from Germany by the *reforming party*, to be their prop in the bosom of the king; and yet this very party, base and servile to the king's wishes, no sooner found the king disliked her, than she was abandoned by them, without any ceremony. The clergy were base and servile to be sure; but they were not Catholics, strictly speaking, for they had forsaken and forsworn the head of the Catholic church, though some of them still adhered to her doctrines. But there were reforming clergy in the convocation, and as that body was unanimous in its consent, the "godly crew" were as base and servile as those represented to form the Popish party. This fact cannot be got over, and we agree with the editors, that Cranmer and his reforming brethren would have made as little scruple in granting Harry as many wives as the Koran allows to Mussulmen, had he required it, for we have a proof of the readiness of the reformers to gratify the beastly appetites of monarchs, in the license granted by Luther, Melancthon, Bucer, and other reforming divines, to the Landgrave of Hesse to have two wives at once.

So much for Cranmer and Anne of Cleves, who was expected to be as useful in the work of reformation as her namesake, but was abandoned without reserve when it was discovered she could not advance the cause. Her fate however was different from that of her predecessor, as she had the sense to submit without a murmur to the king's will, and retired to Richmond with a pension. The next wife selected by Henry was a *Protestant* lady too, namely, Catharine Howard, niece to the duke of Norfolk. She gained an ascendency in the king's affections which she maintained about a year, but as she was related to his grace of Norfolk, who had always been a stout opposer of Cranmer and Cromwell, and their party, a plot was formed which proved her downfall, and brought her to an untimely end. The modern editors say, on the testimony of Burnet, that the king was so delighted with the charms of Catharine Howard, his fifth wife, that he "even gave public thanks to God for the excellent choice he had made." The royal pope, however, was somewhat hasty in his conclusions, for the same historian states, that the very day after his public prayers, Cranmer appeared before his lay holiness, with an account of the infidelity of his most excellent wife. Harry was thunderstruck; he could not believe the tale; but Cranmer wrought on the unfortunate lady to make confession of her guilt, on which she admitted having been guilty of lewdness before her marriage, but denied that she had defiled the nuptial bed. The modern editors say "she was convicted *on the clearest evidence*," which does not appear to have been the case, at least so far as regarded her marriage. However, guilty or not, she was condemned and executed on the 14th of February, 1541, along with the lady Rochford, who was instrumental in bringing Anne Boleyn to the block. Burnet and the modern editors make a mystery of this circumstance, and consider it a Divine judgment on her baseness and falsehood to that *injured* queen;" we have no affection for this lady, as we consider them all tarred with the same stick, but we must deny that Anne Boleyn was "an *injured* queen," any more than Catharine Howard. Mrs. Anne was the concubine of Henry during the lifetime of his lawful wife, Catharine of Arragon, and was married to him after his mock divorce from that noble-minded princess. Kate Howard was a lewd hussey previous to her marriage with the king, which marriage, observe, was during the life of his lawful wife, Anne of Cleves.

Beside the lady Rochford, Dereham and Calpepper were put to death under suspicion of improper intimacy with Catharine, and the lord Howard, her father, his wife, four men and five women, were condemned in the penalties of misprision of treason, because they had not revealed the previous incontinency of the queen.—On the execution of this fifth wife of Henry, the first pope of England, Dr. Lingard has the following remarks:—" To attaint without trial was now become cus-" tomary : but to prosecute and punish for that which had not been " made a criminal offence by any law, was hitherto unprecedented. To " give, therefore, some countenance to these severities, it was enact-" ed in the very bill of attainder that every woman, about to be married " to the king or any of his successors, not being a maid, should disclose " her disgrace to him under the penalty of treason ; that all other per-" sons knowing the fact and not disclosing it, should be subject to the " lesser penalty of misprision of treason ; and that the queen, or wife " of the prince, who should move another person to commit adultery " with her, should suffer as a traitor."—Truly this is pretty work, and well worthy the event which gave rise to these scandalous and unholy doings, inimical alike to freedom of conscience, purity of morals, and personal liberty of the subject.

MORE MATTERS CONCERNING RELIGION.

Harry having thus rid himself of his fifth wife, began to turn his attention to the duties imposed upon him as head of the church.—The translation of the Bible into the vulgar tongue, had generated a race of teachers who propounded the most discordant and absurd doctrines.— The scriptures were taken to alehouses and taverns, discussions heated by the potent fumes of strong liquors were carried on, and generally ended in breaches of the peace. With a view to remedy these evils, a restraint was placed on reading the scriptures, Tindall's bible was condemned as " crafty, false, and untrue," but that the people might not be without spiritual food, his royal highness issued a code of doctrines and ceremonies, published under the title of "A necessary Doctrine and Education for any Christened Man ;" it was also distinguished as " the king's book," and being approved by both houses of the convocation, was considered the only authorized standard of English orthodoxy. On these labours of mending and devising new articles of faith, father Parsons has a very pleasant story in this *Three Conversions of England*, written in answer to Fox's *Acts and Monuments*, which has afforded us some amusement, and as it is equally applicable to the present times, as to those in which the learned author wrote, we will here insert it.

" A certain courtier at that day (some say it was sir Francis Byran) talking with a lady that was somewhat forward in the new gospel about this book of the king's then lately come forth, she seemed to mislike greatly the title thereof, to wit, *Articles devised by the King's Highness*, &c. saying, that it seemed not a fit title to authorize matters in religion, to ascribe them to a mortal king's device. Whereunto the courtier answered, truly (madam) I will tell you my conceit plainly: if we must needs have devices in religion, I would rather have them from a king than from a knave, as your devices are; I mean that knave friar Martin, who not yet twenty years agone was deviser of your new religion, and behaved himself so lewdly in answering his majesty with scorn and contempt, as I must needs call him a knave; though otherwise I do not hate altogether the profession of friars, as your ladyship knoweth.— Moreover (said he) it is not unknown neither to your ladyship nor us, that he devised these new tricks of religion, which you now so much esteem and reverence, nor for God, or devotion, or to do penance, but for ambition, and to revenge himself upon the Dominican friars, that had gotten for him the preaching the pope's bulls; as also to get himself the use of a wench, and that a nun also, which now he holdeth. And soon after him again three other married priests, his scholars, (to wit, Oecolampadius, Carlostadius, and Zuinglius), devised another religion of the Sacramentarians, against their said master. And since these again, we hear every day of fresh upstarts that would rather devise us new doctrines, and there is no end of devising and devisers.— And I would rather stick to the devising of a king, that have majesty in him, and a council to assist him, (especially such a king as ours is) then to a thousand of these companions put together.

" It is true (said the lady) when they are devices indeed of men, but when they bring scriptures with them to prove their sayings, then they are not men's devices, but God's eternal truth and word. And will you say so, madam, quoth he? And do you not remember what ado we had the last year about this time with certain Hollanders here in England, whom our bishops and doctors could not overcome by scriptures, notwithstanding they held most horrible heresies, which make my hair to stand upright to think of them, against the manhood and flesh of Christ our Saviour, and against the virginity of his blessed mother, and against the baptism of infants, and the like wicked blasphemies. I was myself present at the condemnation of fourteen of them in Paul's church on one day, and heard them dispute and allege scriptures so fast for their heresies, as I was amazed thereat; and after I saw some of these knaves burnt in Smithfield, and they went so merrily to their death, singing and chaunting scriptures, as I began to think with myself whether their device was not of some value or no; until afterwards, thinking better of the matter, I blessed myself from them, and so let them go.

" Oh (said the lady) but these were knaves indeed, that devised new doctrines of their own heads; and were very heretics, not worthy to be believed. But how shall I know (quoth the courtier) that your devices have not done the like, seeing these alleged scriptures no less than they; and did one thing more, which is, that they went to the fire and burned for their doctrine, when they might have lived, which your friar and his scholars before named have not hitherto done. And finally (madam) I say, as at the beginning I said, if we must needs follow devising, we courtiers had much rather follow a king than a friar in such a matter. For how many years (madam) have friars shorn their heads and no courtier hath ever followed them hitherto therein? But now his majesty having begun this last May (as you know) to poll his head, and commanded others to do the like, you cannot find any unshorn head in the court among us men, though you women be exempted. And so I conclude, that the device of a king is of more credit than the device of a friar. And with this the lady laughed; and so the conference was ended."

MARTYRDOMS OR PERSECUTIONS.

We have now forty-four pages of the modern book devoted to a relation of the martyrdoms and burnings of some of Fox's "godly" heroes, who, though holding notions the most wild, discordant, and ridiculous that can be imagined, are all classed as soldiers of Christ, though some of them denied his Godhead and others his existence. To enter into a minute detail of this mass of rodomontade and nonsense would sicken the reader, we shall therefore confine ourselves to some few particular cases. First on the list is an account of the "MARTYRDOM OF DR. ROBERT BARNES," which is followed by the "STORY OF THOMAS GARRETT," and of "WILLIAM JEROME." These effusions of a fanatic brain are ushered in with the following remarks. "The clergy now elated by the victory which they had gained, by the "death of Cromwell, persuaded the king to new severities against the "reformers; and three eminent preachers, Drs. Barnes, Gerard, and "Jerome, were picked out for sacrifices on this occasion." Here we have the clergy again charged with these acts of cruelty, and Tom Cranmer, observe, at the head of this clergy. But to the stories. The first hero, we are informed was educated at Louvain, in Brabant, and on coming to England he went to Cambridge, which he found steeped in the darkest ignorance; but with the assistance of one Parnel, his scholar, he not only promoted knowledge and truth, but he instructed the students in the classical languages, and soon caused learning to flourish in that university. Barnes was certainly a clever man, but not such a prodigy as he is here represented. The long account given of the proceedings between him and Wolsey is mere fiction; but if true, he must have been as base a villain as Tom Cranmer, for let it not be forgotten that he was the man who was consulted by Taylor in the case of Lambert, and disclosed the matter to Cranmer, and in consequence Cranmer had the poor Lambert summoned before his archiepiscopal court to answer for his presumption. Barnes was also a dependent of Cromwell's, and by his imprudence hastened that minister's fall. Gardiner of Winchester, as we have before said, was a stickler for the old doctrine, though through weakness he admitted the supremacy of the king. In a sermon preached by him at St. Paul's cross, he censured the extravagance of those preachers who inculcated doctrines opposite to the established creed. A fortnight after Barnes, who had imbibed Lutheran principles, boldly defended in the same pulpit the doctrines Gardiner had reprobated, and cast many scurrilous invectives against the bishop. Harry got a hearing of his conduct, and summoned the doctor before himself and a commission of divines, where the several points of controverted doctrine were discussed, and Barnes was prevailed upon to sign a recantation. He read his recantation before the audience, asked pardon of Gardiner, and immediately proceeded in a sermon to

A REVIEW

OF

Fox's Book of Martyrs,

CRITICAL AND HISTORICAL.

No. 40. Printed and Published by W. E. Andrews, 3, Chapter-house-court, St. Paul's Churchyard, London. Price 3d.

EXPLANATION OF THE ENGRAVING.—*When the Reformers obtained the power of the state, the Catholics were persecuted with the most horrid malignity. Besides having their property confiscated, they were chained together, as this cut represents, and marched to prison, where they were compelled to listen to the pulpit ravings of the new preachers against their will, and severely tortured for their constancy to the faith of their fathers.*

CONTINUATION OF THE REVIEW.

maintain the very doctrine he had but a few minutes before renounced. Such base and insulting conduct irritated the king, who committed him to the Tower with Garrett and Jerome, two fanatics of the same stamp, who had placed themselves in similar circumstances.

These men were tried for *heresy* and condemned, and we have a long account of their execution, but the editors forgot to relate, or have wilfully suppressed the fact, that with these three men were other three executed for denying the supremacy of the king, namely, Abel, Powel, and Featherstone. These six victims were coupled together, Catholic and Protestant, on the same hurdle, from the Tower to Smithfield, where the Catholics were hung and quartered as traitors, and the Protestants burned as heretics. Thus it appears the Catholics cannot with justice be blamed for the persecutions in this reign, especially after Henry was acknowledged head of the church, as they suffered in greater proportion than the Protestants. Fox reckons ten Protestants who suffered during the remainder of Henry's reign, and Dodd counts fourteen Catholics in the same period. It must be borne in mind too, that Cranmer, the hero of the thing called the Reformation, sat in the primate's chair during this work of blood and slaughter. In the account given by Fox of the Protestant martyrs, Barnes, Jerome, and Garrett, they are, of course, represented as the most perfect *lights* of the *new* gospel, and the most successful exposers of the supposed errors of the church of Rome. But there is a circumstance related of Barnes, so extravagantly presumptuous, that we must place it upon record. He is represented as making his profession of faith at the place of execution ; after which "a person " present asked him his opinion upon praying to saints. ' I believe,' " said he, ' they are in heaven with God, and that they are worthy of " all the honour that scripture willeth them to have. But I say, through- " out scripture we are not commanded to pray to any saints. There- " fore I neither can nor will preach to you that saints ought to be prayed " unto ; for then should I preach unto you a doctrine of my own head. " Notwithstanding, whether they pray for us or no, that I refer to God. " And *if* saints do pray for us, then *I* trust to pray for you within this " half hour, Mr. Sheriff, and for every Christian living in the faith of " Christ, and dying in the same as *a saint.* Wherefore, if the dead may " for the quick, I will surely pray for you." We have no stated authority for this precious narrative, but taking it for granted that such were the words of Dr. Barnes, it is clear that his opinions were new and contrary to the received doctrine of the Christian world. All England believed in the doctrine of praying to the saints, and that saints prayed for us, without an *if,* and it was the doctrine of the Catholic church from the time of the apostles. No nation whatever received the faith of Christ without receiving this dogma at the same time, and even here the martyr speaks as of an uncertainty, as he is made to introduce a convenient IF, by the way of evading a direct answer to the question. What reliance then is to be placed on Barnes's creed, when he himself is *doubtful* of its accuracy ? The martyrs of the primitive ages never doubted a single article of their faith, of which this of praying to the saints was one. The fathers who wrote in defence of the Catholic church, spoke positively of this doctrine as one of divine revelation, and they quote scripture in proof of it. But though the doctor-martyr was uncertain as to the veracity of his notions, he seems to have no doubt as to his fate in the other world ; this was as sure to him as if he had been before his judge and received the promised reward. But enough has been said of these sufferers, for such they were though they were enthusiasts.

We have now an account of the persecution of one Testwood, but so ridiculous a tale that we shall not notice it. Then follows the persecution of Anthony Pearson, and others equally as absurd, which the reader will admit when he has gone through the following relation, given of the proceedings of one of Pearson's companions :—" Marbeck " was five times examined, before the council ; the bishop of Winches- " ter ; one of the bishop's gentlemen ; the bishops of Salisbury, Here- " ford, and Ely ; Dr. Knight, and the bishop of Winchester's secretary.

" Throughout these examinations he defended the cause of truth with
" a spirit and boldness which confounded his accusers, but could not
" turn them from their cruel and bigotted purposes.

" Marbeck had begun a Concordance of the Bible in English, which
" was taken with his other papers, and laid before the council. The
" bishop of Winchester asked him if he understood Latin, and would
" scarcely believe that he did not; telling the other lords of the coun-
" cil, that it was probable his Concordance was a translation from the
" Latin, and asserting that 'if such a book should go forth in English,
" it would destroy the Latin tongue.' Marbeck was much pressed to
" disclose 'the secrets of his party,' and promised great rewards and
" preferment, if he would betray what he had heard of the opinions of
" Testwood, Pearson, and Haynes, on the mass, &c. He steadily re-
" fused all these offers, delaring that he knew nothing against them.

" On his fourth examination, he was told by the bishop of Salisbury
" that he must answer on oath, faithfully and truly, to such ques-
" tions as the commissioners should judge it necessary to put to him;
" which he promised to do, and was accordingly sworn. Then the bi-
" shop laid before him his three books of notes, demanding whose hand
" they were. He answered they were his own hand, and notes which
" he had gathered out of other men's works six years ago. ' For what
" cause,' said the bishop, 'didst thou gather them?'—'For no other
" cause, my lord, but to come to knowledge. For I being unlearned,
" and desirous to understand some part of scripture, thought by reading
" of learned men's works to come the sooner thereby : and where I
" found any place of scripture opened and expounded by them, that I
" noted, as ye see, with a letter of his name in the margin, that had set
" out the work.'—' So methinks,' said the bishop of Ely, who had one
" of the books of notes in his hand all the time of their sitting, ' thou
" hast read of all sorts of books, both good and bad, as seemeth by the
" notes.'—' So I have, my lord,' said Marbeck. ' And to what pur-
" pose ?' said the bishop of Salisbury. ' By my troth,' replied Mar-
" beck, ' for no other purpose but to see every man's mind.' Then the
" bishop of Salisbury drew out a *quire* of the Concordance, and laid it
" before the bishop of Hereford, who looking upon it awhile, lifted up
" his eyes to Dr. Oking, standing next him, and said, ' This man hath
" been better occupied than a great many of our priests.'

" Then said the bishop of Salisbury, ' Whose help hadst thou in set-
" ting forth this book ?'—Truly my lord,' replied Marbeck, 'no help at
" all.'—' How couldst thou,' said the bishop, 'invent such a book, or
" know what a Concordance meant, without an instructor ?'—' I will
" tell you my lord,' said the prisoner, what instructor I had to begin it.
" When Thomas Matthew's Bible came out in print, I was much desirous
" to have one of them ; and being a poor man, not able to buy one of
" them, determined with myself to borrow one amongst my friends, and
" to write it forth. And when I had written out the five books of
" Moses in fair great paper, and was entered into the book of Joshua,
" my friend Mr. Turner chanced to steal upon me unawares, and seeing
" me writing out the Bible, asked me what I meant thereby, And
" when I had told him the cause, 'Tush,' quoth he, ' thou goest about a
" vain and tedious labour. But this were a profitable work for thee, to
" set out a Concordance in English.' ' A Concordance,' said I , ' what

" is that ?' Then he told me it was a book to find out any word in the
" Bible by the letter, and that there was such an one in Latin already.
" Then I told him I had no learning to go about such a thing.
" ' Enough' quoth he, ' for that matter, for it requireth not so much
" learning as diligence.   And seeing thou art so industrious a man, and
" one that cannot be unoccupied, it were a good exercise for thee.
" And this my lord, is all the instruction that ever I had, before or after,
" 'of any man.'
        " ' And who is that Turner ?' asked the bishop of Salisbury.   ' Marry,'
" said Dr. May, 'an honest and learned man, and a bachelor of divinity,
" and some time a fellow in Magdalen college, in Oxford.'—' How
" couldst thou,' said the bishop of Salisbury, ' with this instruction,
" bring it to this order and form, as it is ?'—' I borrowed a Latin Con-
" cordance,' replied he, ' and began to practise, and at last, with great
" labour and diligence, brought it into this order, as your lordship doth
" see.'—' It is a great pity,' said the bishop of Ely, ' he had not the
" Latin tongue.'—' Yet I cannot believe,' said the bishop of Salisbury,
" ' that he hath done any more in this work than written it out after
" some other that is learned.
        " ' My lords,' said Marbeck, ' I shall beseech you all to pardon me
" what I shall say, and grant my request if it shall seem good unto
" you.'—' Say what thou wilt,' said the bishop.—' I do marvel greatly
" whereof I should be so much examined for this book, and whether I
" have committed any offence in doing it, or no.   If I have, then were
" I loth for any other to be molested or punished for my fault.   There-
" fore, to clear all men in this matter, this is my request, that ye will
" try me in the rest of the book that is undone.   Ye see that I am yet
" but at the letter L, beginning now at M, and take out what word ye
" will of that letter, and so in every letter following, and give me the
" word in a piece of paper, and set me in a place alone where it shall
" please you, with ink and paper, the English Bible, and the Latin Con-
" cordance ; and if I bring you not these words written in the same
" order and form, that the rest before is, then was it not I that did it,
" but some other."
        " ' By my truth, Marbeck,' cried the bishop of Ely, ' that is honestly
" spoken, and then shalt thou bring many out of suspicion.' This being
" agreed to by the commissioners, they bade Dr. Oking draw out such
" words as he thought best on a piece of paper, which he did ; and
" while the bishops were perusing them, Dr. Oking said to Marbeck,
" in a very friendly manner, ' Good Mr. Marbeck, make haste, for the
" sooner you have done, the sooner you shall be delivered.' And as the
" bishops were going away, the bishop of Hereford (who, as well as
" the bishop of Ely, had formerly known the prisoner, and was in se-
" cret his friend) took Marbeck a little aside, and informed him of a
" word which Dr. Oking had written false, and also, to comfort him,
" said, ' Fear not, there can no law condemn you for any thing that ye
" have done, for if you have written a thousand heresies, so long as
" they be not your sayings nor your opinions, the law cannot hurt you.'
" And so they all went with the bishop of Salisbury to dinner, taking
" Marbeck with them, who dined in the hall at the steward's board, and
" had wine and meat sent down from the bishop's table.
        " When dinner was done, the bishop of Salisbury came down into

" the hall, commanding ink and paper to be given to Marbeck, and the
" two books to one of his men to go with him ; at whose going he de-
" manded of the bishop, what time his lordship would appoint him to
" do it in. ' Against to-morrow this time,' replied the bishop, and so de-
" parted. Marbeck, now being in his prison chamber, fell to his business,
" and so applied himself, that by the next day, when the bishop sent
" for him again, he had written so much, in the same order and form
" he had done the rest before, as filled three sheets of paper and more,
" which, when he had delivered to the bishop, Dr. Oking standing by,
" he said, ' Well, Marbeck, thou hast put me out of all doubt. I assure
" thee,' said he, putting up the paper into his bosom, ' the king shall
" see this ere I be twenty-four hours older.' But he dissembled in every
" word, and did not shew it to the king ; but afterwards, the king be-
" ing informed of the concordance which Marbeck had written, said,
" that he was better occupied than those who persecuted him."

We have copied this long account that our readers may be able to
judge for themselves what stupid and gross nonsense, what palpable
falsehoods, and what improbable incidents, are coupled together to
amuse and deceive the wise children of the Reformation, the learned
disciples of bible-interpretation. Can any individual in his proper
senses be capable of believing this account of Marbeck's adventures ?
What ! a man who is unlearned, by his own confession, set about writing a Concordance of the Scriptures, and observe too, this concordance
was to supply the place of the bible. Marbeck could not read Latin,
but he meets with a copy of Matthew's bible in English, which pleases
him so much that he wishes for a copy, but being a *poor* man he could
not afford to *buy* one ; but mark, reader, though he could not find money to buy a *printed* bible, he could buy *paper* to copy it out, and spare
time for copying too, though it must have taken an immensity of time.
Well, with much labour this poor unlearned man gets through the five
books of Moses, and is beginning Joshua, when a friend pops in upon
him, and seeing what he was about, tells him he was *vainly* occupied,
and that a concordance in *English* would be a more PROFITABLE
work. Of the nature of this work Marbeck is completely ignorant, but
being told what it was, and that there was one in Latin already, he
makes another objection, namely, that he had no learning, and did not
understand Latin. This obstacle, however, is soon removed by telling
him that *learning* was not so much required as *diligence*. Let us here
observe, that we wonder much there has never appeared a concordance
to the scriptures from the hands of *an ignorant but diligent Protestant*
since the time of Marbeck, and we regret much that the MS. of our illiterate author has not been preserved, as it would form a curious relic
in one of our learned universities. The concordances now in use have
the name of some learned *divine* prefixed to the work by way of recommendation, as it has been generally supposed that learning and ability
were essential requisites in the performance of such a literary task ;
but it would appear from this tale that we have all along been in error,
and that it requires no more learning to compile a concordance than it
does to write a rhapsodical philippic against the supposed errors of
Popery.

But to return to the diligent and unlearned Marbeck. The only instruction he ever got, we are told, was from his friend Turner, who said that it required not so much learning as diligence, and that as he, Marbeck, was so industrious a soul that he could not remain idle, it were a good exercise for him. Now reader, what instruction do you call this? What information could Marbeck gain from Turner's words? Marbeck is ignorant of the construction of a concordance. He is ignorant of the Latin language—he had never heard of such a work—he was engaged in copying a bible—but all at once he quits his original intention, and engages in a work which he knows nothing about, and which would be of no use to him whatever, as it appears he could not get a bible, and without a bible a concordance is perfectly useless. Well might the bishop of Salisbury express his surprise that Marbeck was able to bring his manuscript into such form and order with such instruction as he said he had received. Well might the prelate be marvellous at hearing a man profess to be ignorant of the Latin language, and yet declaring that he obtained his knowledge from a book of that language? The whole relation is a mass of inconsistency and falsehood, but the more inconsistent and wonderful a tale, the better and readier it is gulped down by Protestant credulity. Where this circumstantial account was borrowed we are not informed. Burnet mentions Marbeck as a singing man, and gives some account of his great ingenuity in this work of the concordance, but he gives us no authority for his statement, any more than the modern editors, and surely, if it were not a work of fiction, such a circumstance might have been authenticated. Burnet admits that the work appeared to be the production of some learned man, and that it seemed incredible that Marbeck, who was known to be an illiterate man, was the author of it. Of the rest of the tale we need say no more, but it would appear that the persecutors of this learned illiterate singer were a little civil and hospitable to him, as they gave him plenty of wine and meat, and in the end he was let off scot free.

Pearson, Testwood, and Filmer, were not so fortunate, being condemned and led out to execution. From the account given by Fox of their last moments, we may suppose they were jolly old topers, as well as martyrs; for "being all three bound to the post," says Fox, " a young man of Filmer's acquaintance brought him a pot of drink, " asking, 'If he would drink?'—'Yea,' cried Filmer, 'I thank you; " and now, my brother,' continued he, 'I desire you, in the name of the " living Lord, to stand fast in the truth of the gospel of Jesus Christ, ", which you have received;' and so taking the pot into his hand, he " asked Pearson if he would drink—' Yea, brother Filmer,' replied he, " 'I pledge you in the Lord.' Then all three drank; and Filmer, re- " joicing in the Lord, said, 'Be merry, my brethren, and lift up your " hands unto God, for after this sharp breakfast I trust we shall have " a good dinner in the kingdom of Christ, our Lord and Redeemer.' At " which words Testwood, lifting up his hands and eyes to heaven, desired " the Lord above to receive his spirit, and Anthony Pearson joined in " the same prayer." These guzzling devotions and tippling pledges must have been truly edifying to the spectators; and no doubt have excited many a heavy and pious sigh from the readers of Fox, at the godly heroism of these Reformation martyrs, who practised good drinking to their last moments. One of these guzzling saints, we are told, on arrivng at the place of execution, "embraced the post in his arms and *kissing* " it, said, Now welcome my own *sweet wife;* for this day shalt thou " and I be *married* together in the love and peace of God." What are we to understand from this nonsense of the post and Pearson, for that was the sufferer's name, to be *married*, when they were both to be consumed? and then the *kissing* bout: was not this rank idolatry? The Catholic is charged with idolatry for kissing and venerating the Cross, the emblem of man's redemption, and surely the kissing a post must amount to the same offence : or is a Protestant martyr to have a greater *indulgence* for kissing than a Catholic sinner.

In concluding this account of the execution of these three tippling heroes, the editors say, "*Thus* they yielded up their souls to the Father " of Heaven, in the faith of his dear Son Jesus Christ, with such *humi-* " *lity* and *steadfastness,* that many who saw their patient suffering were " *convinced* that nothing but *real religion* could bestow so much con- " stancy and Christian courage." If this were the case, we wonder much that the conversions were not greater than they are said to have been; and it is still greater matter of astonishment that it was soon found necessary to frame cruel and bloody penal laws to prevent the people from relapsing into Popery. Notwithstanding the great exer- tions used to blind the people, and the horrid conspiracies entered into to alarm the timid with the supposed bloodthirstiness of the Papists, the Catholic religion has stood its ground in this country, and is now gaining in estimation among the people, while Protestantism has been shivered into a thousand different sects, and its advocates are sinking fast into the gulph of infidelity.

We are now treated with another martyrdom and history, namely of one Adam Damlip, who had been once a zealous Papist, but proceeding to Rome, he there found "such blasphemy of God, contempt of Christ's " true religion, looseness of life, and abundance of all abominations and " filthiness," that he soon discovered "the errors of Popery,' and gained "a perfect knowledge of the true religion;" at least so the story goes in Fox's Martyrology. Thus gifted with new light, "this " godly man, every morning at seven o'clock (how very minute is Fox " in his relations) preached very *learnedly* and *plainly* the *truth* of " the blessed sacrament of Christ's body and blood, inveighing against " all Papistry and confuting the same (but especially those two most " pernicious errors—transubstantiation, and the propitiatory sacrifice " of the Romish mass), by the *scriptures,* and from the ancient doc- " tors ;" but what this *truth* was we are not informed. Now we have clearly proved, in our first volume of this work, that the ancient fathers and doctors were decidedly in favour of these "two most pernicious errors," and that they brought *scripture* as well as tradition in *sup- port* of the doctrines of transubstantiation and the mass. It cannot be denied that these "two pernicious errors," as they are called, were coeval with Christianity, and were received with the Christian faith by the people of this country, and by them held at the very moment this Adam Damlip was inveighing against them, and that Tom Cranmer, the Protestant archbishop, had set his name to this belief; and are we to suppose that Adam was wiser than all the rest of the generation? To entertain such a notion would exhibit very little common sense; and, in truth, the people were actually frightened out of their senses, before they gave credit to such preposterous tales as Fox, and Burnet, and the lying crew of interested writers have told them. But though Master Adam rejected the real presence and the mass, we find he practised *confession*, for the story makes him meet the celebrated Concordance-maker Marbeck at this religious ceremony; so that here we have this Protestant martyr practising at least one Popish error. In another part of this precious tale, we find Adam was a bouser, as well as the three just mentioned, for he eat and drank as heartily as ever, the narrative says, when he was informed of his sentence as before. But the conclusion we think more extraordinary than any other part. Without any reason assigned, the prisoner is taken from London, after sentence, to *Calais*, and there, we are told, he was executed for *treason*, in receiving a trifling sum of money of cardinal Pole, a pardon having been granted him for his heretical opinions. Is this probable? Is it at all likely? We do not see him mentioned in Burnet, nor have we, as usual, any clue to ascertain the authenticity of the tale.

Next we have a long account, but from whence taken we know not, of the case of Anne Askew, who suffered for denying the real presence. Upwards of seven pages are devoted to this lady's examinations, which are pretended to be given from her own pen. We do not find that Burnet is very elaborate in his detail of her trial, and Dr. Lingard mentions a fact or two but little known to the generality of the people. This lady, who was married to one Kyme, but left her husband, and assumed her maiden name of Askew, that she might practice the work of an apostle more freely along with another female, who was afterwards burned by Tom Cranmer's order. This woman was evidently an enthusiast, like our modern Johanna Southcott, though she did not possess so much cunning as the latter, and lived in more violent times. She got it into her head that Christ was not present in the blessed Eucharist, though the fathers and all the world, from the time of the apostles, believed he was; and as it was against the act of the six articles, she was condemned to be burned for her contumacy, and suffered, after two recantations, in 1546. The council book mentions that June 19th, in that year, " both Kyme and his wife were called before the " lords; that the former was sent home to remain there till he was sent " for: and that the latter who refused him to be her husband without " alleging any honest allegation, for that she was very obstinate and " heady in reasoning matters of religion, wherein she shewed herself " to be of a naughty opinion, seeing no persuasion of good reason could " take place, was sent to Newgate to remain there to answer to law." *Harl*. MS. 256. fol. 224. Thus it is clear this martyr of Fox's was no other than a crazy madcap; yet is she represented as inspired with the spirit of wisdom, and more learned than all the bishops put together, even with Tom Cranmer at their head. But why is her death to be charged on the Catholics, when Cranmer, the renowned Cranmer, archbishop of Canterbury, and chief pillar of the Reformation, was consenting to this woman's death, although, being a Lutheran and a Reformer in his heart, he himself did not believe in the doctrine for rejecting which he consented to the death of this Anne Askew. Oh! let this never be forgotten. When the Protestant bigot is launching forth in the praises of this hero of that thing called the Reformation, let it be rung in his ears, that Cranmer, the vile, the truckling Cranmer, was assenting to the burnings and hangings of Protestant heretics and Catholic pretended traitors, and never crossed the will of the tyrant he served, whether it was to rob the church and poor of their property, the people of their rights, or the king's wives of their lives. The will of the tyrant was a law for Cranmer, who even preached in favour of despotism and passive obedience.

These burnings, we are told, " were so many triumphs to the Popish party," though the Catholics had no more hand in them than John Fox. The nation was at this time divided into two factions, and the Catholics were as much persecuted for denying the supremacy of the king, as the hot-headed reformers for denying the real presence in the blessed sacrament.—How unjust then is it to charge these executions to the account of the Catholics, when they were themselves the victims of party rage, and were despoiled of their property to gratify the avariciousness of profligate courtiers.—Harry, after the death of his fifth wife, who was sent out of the world by severing her head for adultery, married Catharine Parr, who was a widow, and a favourer of the reformers. Of course Cranmer and the queen rowed in the same boat, and it appears a plan was laid by their enemies to bring them both into disgrace.—Burnet says, " they persuaded the king that Cranmer was " the source of all the heresies in England; but Henry's esteem for " him was such, that no one would appear to give evidence against " him; they therefore desired that he might be committed to the Tower, " and then it would appear how many would inform against him."— Burnet then goes on to tell a story of the king's informing Cranmer of the designs against him, of Tom's fortitude and forbearance, and the king's suggesting a plan to entrap the rogues for daring to cast suspicion on the immaculate prelate and pander.—Of this state of parties Dr. Lingard writes thus:—" During these transac- " tions the court of Henry was divided by the secret intrigues of " the two religious parties, which continued to cherish an implacable " hatred against each other. The men of the old religion naturally " looked upon Cranmer as their most steady and most dangerous " enemy: and, though he was careful not to commit any open trans- " gression of the law, yet the encouragement which he gave to the " new preachers, and the clandestine correspondence which he main- " tained with the German reformers, would have proved his ruin, had " he not found a friend and advocate in his sovereign. Henry still " retained a grateful recollection of his former services, and felt no ap- " prehension of resistance or treason from a man, who *on all occasions,* " whatever were his real opinions or wishes, had moulded his conscience " in conformity to the royal will. When the prebendaries of Canter- " bury lodged an information against him, the king issued a commission " to examine, not the accused but the accusers; of whom some were " imprisoned; all were compelled to ask pardon of the archbishop. In " the house of commons sir John Gostwick, representative for Bedford- " shire, had the boldness to accuse him of heresy: but the king sent a " message to the ' varlet,' that if he did not acknowledge his fault, he

" should be made an example for the instruction of his fellows. On
" another occasion Henry had consented to the committal of the arch-
" bishop; but afterwards he revoked his permission, telling the council
" that Cranmer was as faithful a man towards him as ever was prelate
" in the realm, and one to whom he was many ways beholden: or, as
" another version has it, that he was the *only man* who had *loved his*
" *sovereign* so well, as never to have *opposed the royal plaasure*. In
" like manner Gardiner, from his acknowledged abilities and his credit
" with the king, was to the men of the new learning a constant object
" of suspicion and jealously. To ruin him in the royal estimation, it
" was pretended that he had communicated with the papal agents
" through the imperial ministers: and that, while he pretended to be
" zealously attached to the interests of the king, he had in reality made
" his peace with the pontiff. But it was in vain that the accusation
" was repeatedly urged, and that Gardiner's secretary was even tried,
" convicted, and executed, on a charge of having denied the supremacy:
" the caution of the bishop bade defiance to the wiles and malice of his
" enemies. Aware of the danger which threatened him, he stood con-
" stantly on his guard; and though he might prompt the zeal, and se-
" cond the efforts of those who wished well to the ancient faith, he
" made it a rule never to originate any religious measure, nor to give
" his opinion on religious subjects, without the express command of his
" sovereign. Then he was accustomed to speak his mind with bold-
" ness: but though he might sometimes offend the pride, still he pre-
" served the esteem of Henry, who, unmoved by the suggestions of his
" adversaries, continued to employ him in affairs of state, and to consult
" him on questions of religion. As often, indeed, as he was absent in
" embassies to foreign courts, Cranmer improved the favourable mo-
" ment to urge the king to a further reformation. He was heard with
" attention, he was even twice desired to form the necessary plan, to
" subjoin his reasons, and to submit them to the royal consideration:
" still, however, Henry paused to receive the opinion of Gardiner; and,
" swayed by his advice, rejected or suspended the execution of the mea-
" sures proposed by the metropolitan." Hence it is clear that what
was done by the two factions, was prompted by self-interest and passion,
while the good of the commonwealth was suffered to decay, as we shall
take occasion to shew.

The next story is the lucky escape of Catharine Parr from the trap
that was laid to shorten her life, and the death of the tyrant himself.
As we have noticed the judgments that befel this obdurate and beastly
head of the church of England in a former number, it is not necessary
to repeat them here. Suffice it to say, he died on the 27th of January,
1547, in the 56th year of his age, and the 38th of his reign, execrated
by thousands and regretted by none. The editors are obliged to confess that he was a monster in cruelty, and that " almost the last act of
" his life was one of barbarous ingratitude and monstrous tyranny;"
but then they basely attempt to screen the cruelties of this barbarian,
by insinuating that he was urged to these atrocious acts by the machinations of the pope and the clergy. Here reader is what they say,
which we see is copied from Burnet.—" The severities Henry used
" against many of his subjects, in matters of religion, made both sides

" write with great sharpness against him ; his temper was imperious
" and cruel; he was sudden and violent in his passions, and hesitated
" at nothing by which he could gratify either his lust or his revenge.
" This was much provoked by the sentence of the pope against him,
" by the virulent books cardinal Pole and others published, by the re-
" bellions that were raised in England by the Popish clergy, and the
" apprehensions he was in of the emperor's greatness, together with his
" knowledge of the fate of those princes against whom the popes had
" thundered in former times ; all which made him think it necessary
" to keep his people under the terror of a severe government; and by
" some public examples to secure the peace of the nation, and thereby
" to prevent a more profuse effusion of blood, which might have other-
" wise followed if he had been more gentle ; and it was no wonder, if
" after the pope deposed him, he proceeded to great severities against
" all who supported the papal authority." We may here see the malignity of Burnet, whose disregard for truth was only equalled by his
malicious insinuations against the Catholic clergy. Now it is well known
by those who have consulted history, that the pope did not proceed to
extremities until Henry had been guilty of the grossest violations of his
coronation oath, and had shed the blood of his innocent subjects and best
friends. Of the writings of cardinal Pole, it does not appear by the
catalogue of his works in Dodd, that he wrote more than one volume
folio in the lifetime of Henry, and surely it will not be contended, that
the subsequent writings of the cardinal were the cause of Henry's
cruelties.—The rebellions raised in England were occasioned not by the
clergy, but by the king himself in sanctioning measures, by which the
clergy were stripped of their possessions and the poor of their support
and rights. And if the modern editors agree with Gilbert Burnet, that
it was " necessary to keep his people under the terror of a severe govern-
" ment; and by some public examples to secure the peace of the na-
" tion, and thereby prevent a more profuse effusion of blood, which
" *might* otherwise have followed if he had been more *gentle* ;" why do
they make such a parade of the martyrs which they say suffered during
his reign ?—Burnet, after making these remarks, give a long list of Catholics who suffered in consequence of refusing to admit the king's
supremacy, but the modern editors have not been so candid as their
authority from whom they borrow. Instead of these real Catholic martyrs, they have introduced a number of pretended sufferers, occupy
fourteen pages of the veriest nonsense and absurdities ever submitted
to a credulous people.—As the greater part is evidently fictitious and
grossly inconsistent, we shall pass by these unauthorized details, and
conclude the eventful period of Henry's reign with Dr. Lingard's account of his character, and the consequences of the measures pursued
by him, during the course of his government of this realm.

" To form a just estimate of the character of Henry, we must distinguish between the young king, guided by the counsels of Wolsey,
and the monarch of more mature age, governing by his own judgment,
and with the aid of ministers selected and fashioned by himself. In
his youth the beauty of his person, the elegance of his manners, and
his adroitness in every martial and fashionable exercise, were calculated
to attract the admiration of his subjects. His court was gay and

splendid ; a succession of amusements seemed to absorb his attention :
yet his pleasures were not permitted to encroach on his more important duties : he assisted at the council, perused the dispatches, and
corresponded with his generals and ambassadors : nor did the minister,
trusted and powerful as he was, dare to act, till he had asked the
opinion, and taken the pleasure of his sovereign.   His natural abilities
had been improved by study : and his esteem for literature may be inferred from the learned education which he gave to his children, and
from the number of eminent scholars to whom he granted pensions in
foreign states, or on whom he conferred promotion in his own.   The
immense treasure which he inherited from his father, was perhaps a
misfortune; because it engendered habits of expense not to be supported from the ordinary revenue of the crown : and the soundness of
his politics may be doubted, which, under the pretence of supporting
the balance of power, repeatedly involved the nation in continental
hostilities.   Yet even these errors served to throw a lustre round the
English throne, and raised its possessor in the eyes of his own subjects
and of the different nations of Europe.   But as the king advanced in
age, his vices gradually developed themselves : after the death of Wolsey they were indulged without restraint.   He became as rapacious as
he was prodigal : as obstinate as he was capricious : as fickle in his
friendships, as he was merciless in his resentments.   Though liberal
of his confidence, he soon grew suspicious of those whom he had ever
trusted ; aud, as if he possessed no other right to the crown than that
which he derived from the very questionable claim of his father, he
viewed with an evil eye every remote descendant of the Plantagenets :
and eagerly embraced the slightest pretexts to remove those whom
his jealousy represented as future rivals to himself or his posterity.   In
pride and vanity he was perhaps without a parallel.   Inflated with the
praises of interested admirers, he despised the judgment of others ;
acted as if he deemed himself infallible in matters of policy and religion ; and seemed to look upon dissent from his opinion as equivalent
to a breach of allegiance,   In his estimation, to submit and to obey,
were the great, the paramount duties of subjects : and this persuasion
steeled his breast against remorse for the blood which he shed, and
led him to trample without scruple on the liberties of the nation.

" When he ascended the throne, there still existed a spirit of freedom,
which on more than one occasion defeated the arbitrary measures of
the court, though directed by an able minister, and supported by the
authority of the sovereign : but in the lapse of a few years that spirit
had fled, and before the death of Henry, the king of England had
grown into a despot, the people had shrunk into *a nation of slaves,*
The causes of this important change in the relations between the
sovereign and his subjects, may be found not so much in the abilities
or passions of the former, as in the *obsequiousness of his parliaments,*
the *assumption of the ecclesiastical supremacy,* and the *servility of the
two religious parties which divided the nation.*

" The house of peers no longer consisted of those powerful lords and
prelates, who in former periods had so often and so successfully resisted
the encroachments of the sovereign.   The reader has already witnessed
the successive steps, by which most of the great families of the preced-

.ing reigns had become extinct, and their immense possessions had been frittered away among the favourites and dependants of the court. The most opulent of the peers under Henry were poor in comparison with their predecessors : and by the operation of the statute against liveries, they had lost the accustomed means of arming their retainers in support of their quarrels. In general they were new men, indebted for their present honours and estates to the bounty of Henry or of his father : and the proudest among the rest, by witnessing the attainders and executions of others, had been taught to tremble for themselves, and to crouch in submission at the foot of a master, whose policy it was to depress the great, and punish their errors without mercy, while he selected his favourites from the lowest classes, heaping on them honours and riches, and confiding to them the exercise of his authority.

" By the separation of the realm from the see of Rome, the dependence of the spiritual had been rendered still more complete than that of the temporal peers. Their riches had been diminished, their immunities taken away : the support which they might have derived from the protection of the pontiff was gone : they were nothing more than the delegates of the king, exercising a precarious authority determinable at his pleasure. The ecclesiastical constitutions, which had so long formed part of the law of the land, now depended ou his *breath*, and were executed only by his *sufferance*. The convocation indeed continued to be summoned : but its legislative authority was no more. Its principal business was to grant money : yet even those grants now owed their force, not to the consent of the grantors, but to the approbation of the other two houses, and the assent of the crown.

" As for the third branch of the legislature, the commons of England, they had not yet acquired sufficient importance to oppose any effectual barrier to the power of the sovereign, yet care was taken that among them the leading members should be devoted to the crown, and that the speaker should be one holding office, or high in the confidence of the ministers. Freedom of debate was, indeed, granted : but with a qualification which in reality amounted to a refusal. It was only a *decent* freedom : and as the king reserved to himself the right of deciding what was or was not decent, he frequently put down the opponents of the court, by reprimanding the " varlets" in person, or by sending to them a threatening message.

" It is plain that from parliaments thus constituted, the crown had little to fear : and though Wolsey had sought to govern without their aid, Henry found them so obsequious to his will that he convoked them repeatedly, and was careful to have his most wanton and despotic measures sanctioned with their approbation. The parliament so often as it was opened or closed, by the king in person, offered a scene not unworthy of an oriental divan. The form indeed differed but little from our present usage. The king sate on his throne : on the right hand stood the chancellor, on the left the lord treasurer : whilst the peers were placed on their benches, and the commons stood at the bar. But the addresses made on these occasions by the chancellor or the speaker, usually lasted more than an hour; and their constant theme was the great character of the king. The orators, in their efforts to surpass each other, fed his vanity with the most hyperbolical praise. Cromwell was unable, he believed all men were unable, to describe the unutterable qualities of the royal mind, the sublime virtues of the royal heart. Rich told him that in wisdom he was equal to Solomon, in strength and courage to Sampson, in beauty and address to Absalom: and Audeley declared before his face, that God had anointed him with the oil of wisdom above his fellows, above the other kings of the earth, above all his predecessors; had given him a perfect knowledge of the scriptures, with which he had prostrated the Roman Goliath; a perfect knowledge of the art of war, by which he had gained the most brilliant victories at the same time in remote places; and a perfect knowledge of the art of government, by which he had for thirty years secured to his own realm the blessings of peace, while all the other nations of Europe suffered the calamities of war.

" During these harangues, as often as the words "most sacred majesty," were repeated, or as any emphatic expression was pronounced, the lords rose, and the whole assembly, in token of respect and assent, bowed profoundly to the demi-god on the throne. Henry himself affected to hear such fulsome adulation with indifference. His answer was invariably the same: that he laid no claim to superior excellence; but that, if he did possess it, he gave the glory to God, the author of all good gifts; it was, however, a pleasure to him to witness the affection of his subjects, and to learn that they were not insensible of the blessings which they enjoyed under his government.

" It is evident that the new dignity of head of the church, by transferring to the king that authority which had been hitherto exercised by the pontiff, must have considerably augmented the influence of the crown: but in addition, the arguments by which it was supported, tended to debase the spirit of the people, and to exalt the royal prerogative above law and equity. When the adversaries of the supremacy asked in what passage of the sacred writings the government of the church was given to a layman, its advocates boldly appealed to those texts which prescribe obedience to the established authorities. The king, they maintained, was the image of God upon earth: to disobey his commands was to disobey God himself: to limit his authority, when no limit was laid down, was an offence against the sovereign: and to make distinctions, when the scripture made none, was an impiety against God. It was indeed acknowledged that this supreme authority might be employed unreasonably and unjustly: but even then to resist was a crime; it became the duty of the sufferer to submit; and his only resource was to pray that the heart of his oppressor might be changed; his only consolation to reflect that the king himself would be summoned to answer for his conduct before a future and unerring tribunal. Henry became a sincere believer in a doctrine so flattering to his pride: and easily persuaded himself that he did no more than his duty in punishing with severity the least opposition to his will. To impress it on the minds of the people, it was perpetually inculcated from the pulpit: it was enforced in books of controversy, and instruction: it was promulgated with authority in the " Institution," and afterwards in the "Erudition of a Christian Man." From *that period* the doctrine of *passive obedience* formed a leading trait in the orthodox creed.

" The two great parties, into which religious disputes had separated the nation, contributed also to strengthen the despotic power of Henry. They were too jealous of each other, to watch, much less to resist, the encroachments of the crown. The great object of both was the same: to win the favour of the king, that they might crush the power of their adversaries: and with this view they flattered his vanity, submitted to his caprice, and became the obsequious slaves of his pleasure. Henry, on the other hand, whether it were through policy or accident, played them off against each other; sometimes appearing to lean to the old, sometimes to the new doctrines, alternately rising and depressing the hopes of each, but never suffering either party to obtain the complete ascendency over its opponent. Thus he kept them in a state of dependance on his will, and secured their concurrence to every measure, which his passion or caprice might suggest, without regard to reason or justice, or the fundamental laws of the land. Of the extraordinary enactments which followed, a few instances may suffice. The succession to the crown was repeatedly altered, and at length left to the king's private judgment or affection. The right was first taken from Mary, and given to Elizabeth; then transferred from Elizabeth to the king's issue by Jane Seymour or any future queen; next restored, on the failure of issue by prince Edward, to both Mary and Elizabeth; and lastly, failing issue by them, to any person or persons to whom it should please him to assure it in remainder by his last will. Treasons were multiplied by the most vexatious, and often, if ridicule could attach to so grave a matter, by the most ridiculous laws. It was once treason to dispute, it was afterwards treason to maintain, the validity of the marriage with Anne Boleyn, or the legitimacy of her daughter. It became treason to marry without the royal licence any of the king's children, whether legitimate or natural, or his paternal brothers or sisters, or their issue: or for any woman to marry the king himself, unless she were a maid, or had previously revealed to him her former incontinence. It was made treason to call the king a heretic or schismatic, openly to wish him harm, or to slander him, his wife, or his issue. This, the most henious of crimes in the eye of the law, was extended from deeds and assertions to the very *thoughts* of men. Its guilt was incurred by any person who should by words, writing, imprinting, or any other exterior act, directly or indirectly accept or take, judge or *believe*, that either of the royal marriages, that with Catharine, or that with Anne Boleyn, was valid, or who should protest that he was not bound to declare his opinion, or should refuse to swear that he would answer truly such questions as should be asked him on those dangerous subjects. It would be difficult to discover, under the most despotic governments, a law more cruel and absurd. The validity or invalidity of the two marriages was certainly matter of opinion, supported and opposed on each side by so many contradictory arguments, that men of the soundest judgment might reasonably be expected to differ from each other. Yet Henry, by this statute, was authorized to dive into the breast of every individual, to extort from him his secret sentiments upon oath, and to subject him to the penalty of treason, if those sentiments did not accord with the royal pleasure. The king was made in a great measure independent of parliament, by two statutes, one of which gave to his proelamations the force of laws, the other appointed a tribunal, consisting of nine privy counsellors, with power to punish all transgressors of such proclamations. The dreadful punishment of heresy was not confined to those who rejected the doctrines which had already been declared orthodox, but it was extended beforehand to all persons who should teach or maintain any [opinion contrary to such doctrines as the king might afterwards publish. If the criminal were a clergyman, he was to expiate his third offence at the stake ; if a layman, to forfeit his personal property, and be imprisoned for life. Thus was Henry invested, *by act of parliament*, with the high prerogative of *theological infallibility*, and an obligation was laid on all men, without exception, whether of the new or of the old learning, to model their religious opinions and religious practice by the *sole judgment* of their sovereign. By an ex post facto law, those who had taken the first oath against the papal authority, were reputed to have taken, and to be bound by, a second and more comprehensive oath, which was afterwards enacted, and which, perhaps, had it been tendered to them, they would have refused.

" But that which made the severity of these statutes the more terrible, was the manner in which criminal prosecutions were then conducted. The crown could hardly fail in convicting the prisoner, whatever were his guilt or his innocence. He was first interrogated in his cell, urged with the hope of pardon to make a confession, or artfully led by ensnaring questions into dangerous admissions. When the materials of the prosecution were completed, they were laid before the grand inquest : and, if the bill was found, the conviction of the accused might be pronounced certain : for in the trial which followed, the real question submitted to the decision of the petit jury was, which of the two were more worthy of credit, the prisoner who maintained his innocence, or the grand inquest which had pronounced his guilt. With this view the indictment, with a summary of the proofs on which it had been found, was read; and the accused, now perhaps for the first time acquainted with the nature of the evidence against him, was indulged with the liberty of speaking in his own defence. Still he could not insist on the production of his accusers that he might obtain the benefit of cross-examination; nor claim the aid of counsel to repel the taunts, and unravel the sophistry, which was too often employed at that period by the advocates for the crown. In this method of trial, every chance was in favour of the prosecution: and yet it was gladly exchanged for the expedient discovered by Cromwell, and afterwards employed against its author. Instead of a public trial, the minister introduced a bill of attainder into parliament, accompanied with such documents as he thought proper to submit. It was passed by the two houses with all convenient expedition ; and the unfortunate prisoner found himself condemned to the scaffold or the gallows, without the opportunity of opening his mouth in his own vindication.

" To proceed by attainder became the usual practice in the latter portion of the king's reign. It was more certain in the result, by depriving the accused of the few advantages which he possessed in the ordinary courts : it enabled the minister to gratify the royal suspicion or resentment without the danger of refutation, or of unpleasant disclosures : and it satisfied the minds of the people, who, unacquainted with

A REVIEW

OF

Fox's Book of Martyrs,

CRITICAL AND HISTORICAL.

No. 41. Printed and Published by W. E. Andrews, 3, Chapter-house-court, St. Paul's Churchyard, London. **Price 3d.**

EXPLANATION OF THE ENGRAVING.—*A young gentleman, a Catholic, having determined to leave England, in order that he might serve God according to his conscience, without being liable to the tortures which he saw inflicted on others, was arrested in one of the sea-ports, and being brought back to London, he was thrown into one of the cells in the Tower. Here he felt a victim to hunger, cold, and accumulated sufferings, and when the keepers afterwards stripped him, they dragged away pieces of his flesh, which, leaving his bones, adhered to his clothes.*

CONTINUATION OF THE REVIEW.

the real merits of the case, could not dispute the equity of a judgment given with the unanimous consent of the whole legislature.

"Thus it was that by the obsequiousness of the parliament, the assumption of the ecclesiastical supremacy, and the servility of religious factions, Henry acquired and exercised the most despotic sway over the lives, the fortunes, and the liberties of his subjects. Happily the forms of a free government were still suffered to exist: into these forms a spirit of resistance to arbitrary power gradually infused itself: the pretensions of the crown were opposed by the claims of the people: and the result of a long and arduous struggle was that constitution, which for more than a century has excited the envy and the admiration of Europe." With this account from the pen of one of the first writers of the day, we shall close our review of the transactions of the reformers during the portentous rule of the wife-killer and priest-slayer.—The reader will now be able to see the rueful consequences of submitting to the will of an arbitrary tyrant, and the direful effects which followed the investment of Henry with the supreme ecclesiastical authority of the church.—The people of England have been taught to look upon the rejection of the pope's supremacy as the dawn of the nation's liberties, whereas it is clear that this event led to the most arbitrary and unjust laws, and entailed upon the people the most deplorable miseries. Oh! England! what hast thou suffered since thou departed from the faith of the apostles, and separated thyself from the communion of the Christian world.

PERSECUTIONS IN SCOTLAND.

DURING THE FIFTEENTH AND PART OF THE SIXTEENTH CENTURY.

We are now going to reconnoitre the transactions in the Northern part of the island, where the "saints" were more violent than those who put some of them to death. PERSECUTION is a word familiar to every person in this country, but though every one knows its meaning, it is not every individual that is acquainted with history so as to know whether the term is correctly applied to the circumstance. To *persecute*, we are told by Dr. Johnson, is "to harass with penalties; to pursue with malignity—to pursue with repeated acts of vengeance or enmity;" and it will be seen, when the reader is put in possession of both sides the question, that the charge of persecution will apply with much more justice to the reforming party, who are represented as being persecuted, than to those who are described as persecuting.—We have, in the preceding remarks, been considering the progress of the Reformation so called under the protection of the government of the country, the head of that government having thrown off the submission exacted by the Divine Founder of true religion to his Church, and assumed the supremacy of that portion of it in England himself.—The case, however, was different in Scotland. There the Catholic religion was the religion of the state, as it was in England before Henry's usurpation, and the temporal authorities yielded the same obedience to the spiritual supremacy of the Church as the other Catholic sovereigns did.—The attempt therefore of the reformers to introduce their new-fangled notions into Scotland, and create confusion, was an *innovation* on the constituted authorities, and being such, it was natural that the attempt would be resisted. We are aware that the Catholic religion was introduced and established in the Roman empire, and in almost every place, in opposition to "the powers that be," and that persecution was practised to stop its progress, but without effect. But we must here observe, that the apostles, and their successors afterwards, in disseminating this holy faith, invariably abstained from mixing the affairs of this world with the kingdom they laboured to establish, which, they said, was *not* of this world, and that it did not interfere with the temporal concerns of the different states in existence, but was calculated for one form or constitution as well as any other, and indeed gave security to all, by inculcating the doctrine of obedience to the established forms of government. In no instance whatever do we read in history that the introduction of the Catholic or Christian religion produced disorder or destruction to the kingdoms or empires that received it. On the contrary, we see by the annals of our own country, that those monarchs who were the most celebrated for their attachment and devotion to the Catholic church, and who listened to the advice and admonitions of the most pious and sainted dignitaries of that church, were equally eminent for the establishment of just and wholesome laws, the protection they thus afforded to the lives and property of their subjects, and the consequent absence of all harsh and tyrannic measures, which only tend to brutalize and debase a people. To monarchs such as these do Englishmen owe all that is good and excellent in that civil constitution of which they make such a boast, though most of its privileges are frittered away since the period of the Reformation, so called, and to be eligible to enjoy the remainder, they basely and impiously swear the holy founders were DAMNABLE IDOLATERS ! ! !

It was not so, however, with the reformers; though they declaimed against the supposed errors of the Catholic church, with all the vehemence they were capable of, yet they found their cause made very little progress, until they instigated the ignorant and illiterate people to violence and rebellion, and thus sought by revolutionary means to subdue those in authority who were opposed to the wild notions they propagated, and grasped the civil sword to assist them in silencing the voice of truth and justice. In every country where the clamour of Protestantism was heard against the ruling powers, sedition, rebellion, and treason followed in its train; and where it was ushered in by the sanction of the civil magistrate, it was preceded by robbery, sacrilege, and murder.—We have seen by the transactions in Henry's reign the accuracy of the latter observation; it remains then to be shewn how far we are correct with regard to the former.—The reformers of Scotland imbibed the notions of John Calvin, who, in his commentaries on Daniel, says, "Princes forfeit their power when they oppose God in opposing "the Reformation; and it is better in such cases to spit in their faces "than to obey." Beza, Calvin's scholar, in his book, " Vindicæ, contra Tyrannos," says, "We must obey kings for God's sake, when they "obey God;" but otherwise, "as the vassal loses his fief or tenure, if he "commit felony, so does the king lose his right to the realm also." Such doctrines could not fail to produce turbulent and riotous disciples as the sequel will shew.

Fox, in the modern edition of the *Book of Martyrs*, commences his account of the Scottish persecutions, as *he* calls them, with the following prefatory observations :—" Having brought our account of the suf- " ferings and martyrdoms of the English reformers down to the death " of Henry the eighth, we shall now proceed to relate the *cruel persecu- " tions* of God's *faithful servants* in Scotland, to the same period; but " it will previously be necessary to give a short sketch of the progress " of the reformation in that country. The long alliance between Scot- " land and France, had rendered the two nations extremely attached to " each other; and Paris was the place where the learned of Scotland " had their education. Yet *early* in the *fifteenth* century, *learning was* " *more encouraged in Scotland*, and universities were founded in several

" *episcopal* sees. About the same time some of Wickliffe's followers
" began to show themselves in Scotland; and an *Englishman,* named
" Resby, was burnt in 1407 for teaching some opinions contrary to the
" pope's authority. Some years after that, Paul Craw, a *Bohemian,* who
" had been converted by Huss, was burnt for infusing the opinions of
" that martyr into some persons at St. Andrew's. About the end of the
" fifteenth century, Lollardy, as it was then called, spread itself into
" many parts of the diocess of Glasgow, for which several persons *of*
" *quality* were accused; but they answered the archbishop of that see
" with so much boldness and truth, that he *dismissed them,* having *ad-*
" *monished* them to content themselves with the *faith of the church,* and
" to beware of *new* doctrines. The *same* spirit of *ignorance, immorality,*
" *and superstition,* had over-run the church of Scotland that was so
" much complained of in other parts of Europe. The total neglect of
" the pastoral care, and the scandalous lives of the clergy, filled the
" people with such prejudices against them, that they were easily dis-
" posed to hearken to new preachers, among the most conspicuous of
" whom was Patrick Hamilton." Such is the statement we find in
this book, and it is of a piece with the other statements made in this
greatest mass of lies ever compiled in one work.—Early in the fifteenth
century, we are told, learning was more encouraged in Scotland than
before, that universities were founded by several bishops, and yet before the close of this same century the country is represented as over-
run with ignorance, immorality, and superstition!!! But mark, reader,
it does not appear from this account that any one was burned before
the year 1407, yet the Catholic religion had been the religion of Scotland upwards of nine hundred years. Can this be a persecuting religion?—The occasion of this burning, we are informed, was the introduction of some of Wickliffe's followers, and what sort of religionists these
Wickliffites were we have already shewn the reader in the preceding
pages. They have been shewn to be spoliators and rebels, and were
punished for their violations of the peace of society, rather than their religious notions. To represent such men as "God's servants" is rank blasphemy, and cannot be too strongly reprobated; but so it is with the interested opposers of Catholicism, that wherever they meet a man who is a
reviler of the Pope and the Catholic clergy, who is a clamourer against
the supposed errors and corruptions of the church of Rome, though, in
other respects he should be the vilest and most perfidious character,
yet will they represent him as the most immaculate of human beings,
and the chastisement he may receive for his outrages on the laws of
society as a persecution for his *religious* notions. Of Paul Craw we
have no authentic account; he is stated to have been converted by Huss,
but, from the life and conduct of this Huss, it should have been *cor-*
rupted. Then Lollardy spread itself in many parts of the diocess of
Glasgow, and several persons of quality, became infected with it, who,
on being accused before the archbishop, answered with so much boldness and *truth,* it is said, that they were only admonished " to content
" themselves with the faith of the church and to beware of *new* doc-
" trines." Well, as we are told to adhere to the faith *once* delivered to
the saints, whatever is *new* cannot be that faith *once* delivered, and
therefore the advice given must be acknowledged to have been good.

Next comes an account of "the spirit of ignorance, immorality, and superstition," which infected all parts of Europe, and at length contaminated Scotland. When we read this part of the account we fancied the editors were alluding to the present state of a certain church, in which we find a "total neglect of the pastoral care, and the scandalous lives of many of the clergy;" daily filling the people with disgust and indignation at such conduct, and causing them to run to conventicles to hearken to other preachers, We are ready to admit, nay we have frequently admitted, that there was a laxity in morals among many of the clergy at the close of the fifteenth century; for if this had not been the case, we should not have had such beastly and depraved characters as the chief of the reformers were, namely, Luther, Calvin, Beza, Zuinglius, Melancthon, Œcolampadius, and many others, whose immoral doctrine coupled with the impiety of their lives, soon covered that part of the world where their doctrines had taken root with the most horrible scenes of lewdness and wickedness. We have before given the admissions of the reformers of this state of things, it is not necessary, therefore, to repeat them here, but we will proceed to notice the pretended martyrs of this pretended persecution.

The first we see upon the list is Patrick Hamilton, the nephew of the earl of Arran, and by his mother's side the duke of Albany. This reformer is represented as having become acquainted with Luther and Melancthon, "and being convinced, from his own researches, of the "TRUTH OF THEIR DOCTRINES, he burned to impart the light "of the gospel to his own countrymen, and to shew them the errors and "corruptions of their own church." Before we proceed further, it may not be amiss to remind the reader of some of Luther's doctrines, that he may judge for himself what excellent use our reformers made of their researches, and how correct their convictions must have been. Here then are a few specimens of Luther's doctrines taken from his own works. "God's commandments are all equally impossible." (De Lib. Christ. t. ii. fol. 4.) "No sins can damn a man, but only unbelief." (De Captiv. Bab. t, ii. fol. 171.) "God is just, though by his own will he "lays us under the necessity of being damned; and though he damns "those that have not deserved it." (t. ii. fol. 434, 436.) "God works in "us both good and evil." (t. ii. fol. 44.) That the reader shudders at these horrible and blasphemous doctrines we feel convinced; but what are we to think of those men who, in the nineteenth century, have held forth the propagator of these diabolical notions as the paragon of Christian perfection, and his disciple Hamilton as "a godly martyr." Patrick, it is said, denied the doctrine of free will, which was taught by the apostles, and advocated the impious notion of justification by faith alone. Now, by this doctrine, a man was taught that though he committed the most heinous offence in the eyes of God, whether of murder, adultery, or any other immorality, he had only to believe himself a saint, and nothing could damn him. Such pestiferous notions were sufficient to set open the floodgates of vice, and it became the duty of every well-wisher to morality and good order to stop the current of devilism thus about to be spread over the kingdom. Hamilton was accordingly condemned as a heretic, and sentenced to the flames, which sentence was put into execution in the year 1527, under circumstances, the account says, of refined cruelty. We are not, as we have often said before, the advocate of these burnings, but, in the absence of authentic testimony, and taking into consideration the doctrines imbibed and preached by Patrick Hamilton, we think there can be but little doubt that he was condemned and suffered, not for his speculative opinions, but for the immorality and seditiousness of his doctrines. The *Book of Martyrs* says, " The views and doctrines of this *glorious martyr* were such as would " not fail to excite the highest admiration of every *real believer*; and " they were expressed with such brevity and clearness, and such pecu- " liar vigour and beauty (forming in themselves a complete summary " of the gospel) that they afforded instruction to all who sought to " know more of God." This is true sectarian cant. Why, if his views and doctrines were of such peculiar excellence;—why, we ask, were they not carefully preserved, for the edification and instruction of future generations? Catholics have carefully preserved the writings and testimonies of the fathers from the primitive age of Christianity: they have recourse to them as witnesses of the unity and impeccability of the Catholic faith; why then was not this complete summary of the gospel by Hamilton preserved by his disciples as a reference for every real believer? The fact is, Hamilton's views and doctrines would not bear a strict scrutiny, and we question whether they were ever put on paper. The account is a fabrication intended to excite prejudice against the Catholics and enthusiasm for the reformed, or rather deformed, doctrines.

The next martyr is one Henry Forest, described as *a young friar* of Lithgow. This disciple of the reformation is said to have fallen a victim for his faith by going . . . . . where do you suppose, reader? . . . . . by going to CONFESSION; and there SECRETLY disclosing his conscience, he told his confessor, " that he thought Hamilton to be a good " man, and wrongfully put to death, and that his doctrines were *true*, " and not heretical: upon which (the relation continues) the friar," whom Forest had caused to hear his confession, " came and related to " the bishop the confession which he had received. This was taken as " sufficient evidence against him; and he was accordingly declared to " be 'an heretic, equal in iniquity with Patrick Hamilton,' and sen- " tenced to suffer death." Here we have another most improbable story; for if Forest believed the doctrines of Hamilton to have been true, why did he follow the Popish custom of confession, which all the other reformers renounced with the doctrine of good works? This is a bungling tale. It smells rank of falsehood. Had he been what he is represented, he would not have chosen secresy for a disclosure of his conversion, but we may naturally suppose that he would have made an open profession of his faith, as the martyrs under the Roman heathen emperors did. Neither is it likely that his judges should rely only on the statement of his confessor, whose conduct, by the by, would have been reprobated in the strongest terms, as it is held one of the greatest sacrileges that can be committed, and there is no authenticated instance of such a disclosure having ever been made. Why should the proceedings against the young friar be more summary than against Hamilton?

Why had he not a trial; and why was he not called upon to abjure? It is, as we before said, a bungling tale, and enough has been said to shew its improbability.

We have now *two* martyrs, one named Norman Gourlay, and the other David Stratton. They both are said to have denied there being such a place as purgatory, and the former would have it, "that the "pope was not a bishop, but Antichrist, and had no jurisdiction in Scot-"land;" the latter contended, "that the passion of Christ was the only "expiation for sin, and that the tribulations of this world were the only "sufferings that the saints underwent." What rank and condition of life Gourlay moved in, we are not informed, but David we are told was a fisherman, and we suppose considered himself as well calculated to expound the mysteries of religion, fifteen hundred years after it had been established by the apostles, some of whom were fishermen, who were personally commissioned by Christ to teach his truths, and inspired by the Holy Ghost to fulfil their commission. Whether the martyrs Norman and David would have remained unmolested, if David had not proved refractory with his vicar, we cannot tell, but the story informs us, that the vicar asked David for his tithe-fish, and that Davy cast them out of the boat in so negligent a manner that some of them fell into the sea. Now this was very naughty of David, because the vicar did not appropriate the tithes wholly to his own use, as the parsons do now-a-days under a Protestant reformed establishment, but they divided the tithes among the poor, the sick, the widow, and the stranger, and it was therefore an ill-natured trick of Davy the fisherman to prevent the Catholic vicar from performing these charitable acts. Well, for his silly behaviour, he got accused of "having said that no tithes should be "paid;" and forthwith we find him and his companion Gourlay before the archbishop; but how Gourlay came into custody we have no information. In the end they were "condemned as obstinate heretics, and "sentenced to be burned upon the green side, between Leith and Edin-"burgh, with a view to strike terror into the surrounding country." How "the surrounding *country*" was to be terrified by this execution is not explained to such of the good people as may read this famous Book of Martyrs; however it is said they addressed the spectators, and continued to preach so long that the officers were under the necessity of stopping them. A moment's reflection we think is sufficient to shew the falsity of this relation. When we look at the state of letters in those times, and consider that literary knowledge was chiefly confined to the clergy, and persons destined for the orders of the church; when we take into consideration that printing was then scarcely known, and consequently that books were not so familiar with the working classes as they are now; is it probable, we ask, that a poor fisherman should be able to teach and discuss such knotty points as the mysteries of religion, or that he should know better what to believe than all the learned men in the world for fifteen hundred years before them? To entertain such an idea would be to proclaim a defect of common sense, yet is such trash sent forth in these "enlightened" days, as they are called, to excite a hatred against the greater part of the Christian world.

The next story of martyrdom is still more ridiculous, and we shall not do justice to it unless we give it as it is related.—The Book says,—

" Not long after the burning of Stratton and Gourlay, dean Thomas
" Forret was accused to the bishop of Dunkeld, as ' an heretic, and one
" that shewed the mysteries of the Scriptures to the vulgar people, in
" their own language, to make the clergy detestable in their sight.'

" The bishop of Dunkeld said to him, ' I love you well, and therefore
" I must give you my counsel, how you shall rule and guide yourself.
" My dear dean Thomas, I am informed that you preach the epistle or
" gospel every Sunday to your parishioners, and that you take not the
" cow, nor the uppermost cloth, from your parishoners, which is very
" prejudicial to the churchmen ; and, therefore, I would you took your
" cow, and your uppermost cloth, as other churchmen do, or else it is
" too much to preach every Sunday ; for, in so doing, you may make
" the people think that we should preach likewise. But it is enough
" for you, when you find any good epistle, or any good gospel, that
" setteth forth the liberty of the holy church, to preach that and let the
" rest be.'

" Forret answered, ' My lord, I think that none of my parishioners
" will complain, that I take not the cow, nor the uppermost cloth, but
" will gladly give me the same, together with any other thing that
" they have ; and I will give and communicate with them any thing
" that I have ; and so, my lord, we agree right well, and there is no
" discord among us. And where your lordship saith, ' it is too much to
" preach every Sunday,' indeed I think it is too little ; and also would
" wish that your lordship did the like.' ' Nay, nay, dean Thomas,'
" cried the bishop, ' let that be, for we are not ordained to preach.'

" Then said Forret, ' Where your lordship biddeth me preach when
" I find any good epistle, or a good gospel ; truly, my lord, I have read
" the New Testament and the Old, and all the epistles and gospels, and
" among them all I could never find an evil epistle, or an evil gospel ;
" but if your lordship will shew me the good epistle, and the good gos-
" pel, and the evil epistle, and the evil gospel, then I shall preach the
" good and omit the evil.'

" The bishop replied, ' *I thank God that I never knew what the Old and
" New Testament was* ; therefore, dean Thomas, I will know nothing but
" my portuise and pontifical.   Go your way, and let be all these fantasies,
" for if you persevere in these erroneous opinions, ye will repent when
" you may not mend it.'

" Forret said, ' I trust my cause is just in the presence of God ; and,
" therefore, I heed not much what may follow thereupon ;' and so he
" departed.

" A short time afterwards, he was summoned to appear before cardi-
" nal Beaton, archbishop of St. Andrew's ; and, after a short examina-
" tion, he was condemned to be burnt as a heretic. A similar sentence
" was pronounced, at the same time, on four other persons, named Kil-
" lor, Beverage, Simson, and Foster ; and they were all burnt togethe
" on the castle-hill at Edinburgh, February 28, 1538."

Having gone through this relation, we will now ask the reader if he
ever met with such a silly stupid tale before? Mercy upon us ! what
must be the state of that man's intellect, who could give credit to such
absurdity as this? We hear much of the superior excellence of Protestant intellectual capacity ; but can those who give credit to such bare-

faced falsehoods as we have detected in this *Book of Martyrs* be fit for any thing but to inhabit a bedlam? The recommendation of the bishop to the dean to take the cow and the uppermost cloth of the parishioners had been better omitted; because he reminds us too closely of the griping dispositions of the Protestant established clergy in Ireland to take the poor half-starved peasants' potato, and many is the time that the cow and sheep have been seized from the poor man, notwithstanding they were the support of his helpless family, to satiate the avarice of the unfeeling rector or his tithe-proctor. But at the time Fox is speaking of, the cow and the cloth did not come within the claims of the clergy, who, not having wives to maintain, as parsons have now-a-days, seldom or ever took the tithe or due to the full demand, but rather assisted the labourer in his difficulties than ruined him when in distress. Neither was it well contrived to hint at the backwardness of the bishop to preach, for we are again reminded that the state bishops in these days are as little prone to preaching as ever the bishop of Dunkeld could be. But when the bishop is made to say that they (bishops) " are not ordained " to preach;" when he is made to " thank God that he never knew " what the Old and New Testament was," the lie is so palpable, so openly barefaced, that we blush for the depravity of that mind that could be so base, so lost to shame, as to publish it. The bishop not to know what the Bible was!!! when to bishops of the Catholic church we are indebted for the preservation of that sacred volume. The bishop not to know what the Old and New Testament was, though he was compelled by the canons of his church to read certain portions of the scripture every day in his life, and could not celebrate mass without reading some parts of one or both. Oh! shame! where is the blush.

It is needless to enter into the details of all the persons selected as martyrs by John Fox; we will therefore be brief with the remainder. Forret and four others are said to have suffered on February 28, 1538, and we have then two more, named Russel and Kenedy, who were taken up the year following, viz. 1539, and executed. Kenedy is described as a youth 18 years of age, and being inclined to recant, felt himself suddenly refreshed by *divine inspiration*, and became a *new creature.*— They were examined, it is said, but we have no account of the examination; however, being declared heretics, " the *archbishop* (says the Book) pronounced the dreadful sentence of death, and they were immediately delivered over to the secular power." Here is another direct lie; for in no instance whatever do the clergy pronounce sentence of death on any criminal. They are forbidden to do so by the canons of the church, and it is an invariable rule at this day, borrowed from our Catholic ancestors, for the bishops to retire from the House of Lords in all cases where that tribunal has to pass sentence on a convicted peer.

The next martyr we shall notice is George Wishart, whose death led to many important events. Nine pages are devoted to the details of this man's proceedings, and contain the veriest cant and absurdity to be met with. Knox, the famous John Knox, who cut such a conspicuous figure in the pillagings, rebellions, and outrages committed in Scotland under pretence of religion, was, it appears, a disciple of George Wishart. The death of this man is, as usual, laid at the door of " the inveterate and

" persecuting prelate," Cardinal Beaton. To go through the silly sick-
ening detail would tire the reader; we shall, therefore, content ourselves with noticing the account of his execution, to shew the total disregard paid to probability and truth. After being made to address the
spectators, telling them to exhort their prelates to learn the word of
God, though we always thought the prelates were to instruct the people, the narrative goes on,—" He was then fastened to the stake, and
" the fagots being lighted, immediately set fire to the powder that was
" tied about him, and which blew into a flame and smoke. The go-
" vernor of the castle, who stood so near that he was singed with the
" flame, exhorted our martyr, in a few words, to be of good cheer, and
" to ask pardon of God for his offences. To which he replied, ' This
" flame occasions trouble to my body, indeed, but it hath no wise bro-
" ken my spirit. But he who now so proudly looks down upon me
" from yonder lofty place,' pointing to the cardinal, ' shall, ere long, be
" as ignominiously thrown down, as now he proudly lolls at his ease.'
" When he had said this, the executioner pulled the rope which was
" tied about his neck with great violence, so that he was soon strangled;
" and the fire getting strength, burnt with such rapidity that in less
" than an hour his body was totally consumed." Is there any one in
these days credulous enough to believe that the governor was so much
of a fool as to place himself so as to be singed with the flames that consumed the sufferer? We think not. Besides we are told that as soon
as Wishart was fastened to the stake, the fagots were lighted, which
set fire to some powder tied about him, which blew into a flame and
smoke. This flame and smoke must have rendered the criminal insensible, and it is, therefore, most unlikely that the governor should address a man stupified by the blowing up of gunpowder, or that the culprit should be able to return such an answer as is imputed to him. But
observe, reader; after blowing up the victim, and then recovering him
to reply to the governor, he is provided with a rope round his neck for
the executioner to strangle him, which he does, it is said, with great violence, and here ends the martyr's suffering. This bungling account of
his death is sufficient to satisfy every sensible mind that much, at least,
of the preceding part of the tale, is romance and fiction.

MURDER OF CARDINAL BEATON.

An account of this bloody deed follows the death of Wishart, who
was said to have predicted the Cardinal's untimely end. We know not
from whence Fox obtained the particulars of this event; we have examined Burnet and Heylin, but they differ widely from his narrative.—
If he copied from Buchanan, the character of this man, thus given by
Dr. Heylin, a Protestant writer and divine, in his *Cosmography*, will shew
that no reliance is to be placed on his testimony. "George Buchanan,
" an ingenious poet, but an unsound statesman; whose History and Dia-
" logue *De jure Regni*, have wrought more mischief in the world than
" all Machiavel's works." Dr. Stuart, another Protestant author, says
of him : " His zeal for the earl of Murray overturned altogether his
" allegiance as a subject, and his integrity as a man. His activity against
" Mary in the conferences in England, was a strain of *the most shame-
" less corruption*; and the virulence with which he endeavoured to de-

" fame her by his writings, was most audacious and criminal. They in-
" volve the complicated charge of ingratitude, rebellion, and *perjury*,"
(*Hist. of Scotland*, ii. 245.) So much for this writer Buchanan, who may
well be classed with Fox and the modern editors. But to the narrative.
Fox says the cardinal went to Finhaven to solemnize a marriage between the eldest son of the earl of Crawford, and his own natural daughter, Margaret, and that while there, " he received intelligence that an
" English squadron was upon the coast, and that consequently an inva-
" sion was to be feared. Upon this he immediately returned to St.
" Andrew's, and appointed a day for the nobility and gentry to meet,
" and consult what was proper to be done on this occasion." From
this statement it would seem that the cardinal was supreme in temporals, as well as in spirituals, or how could he summon the nobility to
attend upon him? As to the natural daughter, this is a gratuitous fabrication to cast a slur on the celibacy of the Catholic clergy, which
none of the reformed preachers had the gift to preserve. The appointment of a day of consultation we also deem a fiction; for though the
cardinal was, we believe, primate of the Scottish church, he was not the
regent of the kingdom, whose province was to guard and protect the
country against invasion. The fact is, the kingdom of Scotland was at
this time infected with the seditious doctrines of the Genevian reformers,
whose horrible cruelties and restless doings we have displayed in our review of the pretended Huguenot martyrs. James V. who reigned in
that kingdom, had been solicited by his uncle, Harry of England, to
throw off his spiritual obedience to the see of Rome, but refused, and
his premature death, leaving an infant daughter, the unfortunate Mary,
who was afterwards butchered by her cousin Elizabeth, then only a few
days old, threw the kingdom into a state of confusion, and it became the
prey of fanatical enthusiasm and faction. Such was the state of Scotland when the event took place of which we are treating. The manner in which the cardinal was put to death we shall give from the Book
of Martyrs. It says, " In the mean time Norman Lesley, eldest son of
" the earl of Rothes, who had been treated by the cardinal with injus-
" tice and contempt, formed *a design*, in conjunction with his uncle, John
" Lesley, who *hated* Beaton, and others who *were inflamed against him*
" on account of his persecution of the Protestants, the death of Wishart,
" and other causes, to *assassinate* the prelate, though he now resided in
" the castle of St. Andrew's, which he was fortifying at great expense,
" and had, in the opinion of that age, already rendered it almost impreg-
" nable. The cardinal's retinue was numerous, the town was at his devotion,
" and the neighbouring country full of his dependents. However, the
" conspirators, who were in number only sixteen, having concerted
" their plan, met together early in the morning, on Saturday the 29th
" of May. The first thing they did, was to seize the porter of the cas-
" tle, from whom they took the keys, and secured the gate. They then
" sent four of their party to watch the cardinal's chamber, that he might
" have no notice given him of what was doing; after which they went
" and called up the servants and attendants, to whom they were well
" known, and turned them out of the gate, to the number of fifty, as
" they did also upwards of an hundred workmen, who were employed
" in the fortifications and buildings of the castle; but the eldest son of

" the regent, (whom the cardinal kept with him, under pretence of su-
" perintending his education, but, in reality, as an hostage,) they kept
" for their own security.

" All this was done with so little noise, that the cardinal was not
" waked till they knocked at his chamber door; upon which he cried
" out, 'Who is there?' John Lesley answered, 'My name is Lesley.'
" 'Which Lesley?' inquired the cardinal; 'is it Norman?' It was
" answered, that he must open the door to those who were there; but
" instead of this, he barricadoed it in the best manner he could. How-
" ever, finding that they had brought fire in order to force their way,
" and they having, as it is said by some, made him a promise of his
" life, he opened the door. They immediately entered with their swords
" drawn, and John Lesley smote him twice or thrice, as did also Peter
" Carmichael; but James Melvil, (as Mr. Knox relates the affair) per-
" ceiving them to be in choler, said, 'This work, and *judgment of God,*
" although it be secret, ought to be done with greater gravity:' and
" presenting the point of his sword to the cardinal, said to him, 'Repent
" thee of thy wicked life, but especially of the shedding of the blood
" of that notable instrument of God, Mr. George Wishart, which albeit
" the flame of fire consumed before men, yet cries it for vengeance up-
" on thee; and we from God are sent to revenge it. For here, before
" my God, I protest, that neither the hatred of thy person, the love of
" thy riches, nor the fear of any trouble thou couldst have done to me
" in particular, moved or moveth me to strike thee; but only because
" thou hast been, and remainest, an obstinate enemy of Christ Jesus,
" and his holy gospel.' Having said this, he with his sword run the
" cardinal twice or thrice through the body; who only said, 'I am a
" priest! Fie! fie! all is gone!' and then expired, being about fifty-
" two years of age."

We have here the acknowledgment of Fox or his modern editors, that
a set of the " saints" were " *inflamed*" against the cardinal, and that
another *hated* him. But how different is this disposition to that which
is taught in the gospel of Christ, and which these pretended reformers
professed to follow. The rule laid down in the sacred volume by our
divine Lawgiver was, that we should love our enemies, return good for
evil, and pray for those that persecute us; but here, we are told, the
" new lights" entered into a murderous and secret design to assassinate an individual who had rendered himself obnoxious to them by his
zeal for the established order of things. We are not going to justify
the burnings of cardinal Beaton, because we are not sufficiently acquainted with the history of those transactions; but this much may be
said, that what he did was done under the sanction of the established
laws and usages of the country, and it cannot be proved, though it may
be asserted (falsely) that he was actuated by any other motive than a
sense of justice towards society, whose peace was endangered by the
wild and latitudinarian notions of the disciples of Calvin's school. The
executions under the cardinal must be attributed to the turbulence of
the times, and it would have been much better that the veil of oblivion
had been thrown over the deeds of those ages, than to have them placed
constantly before the eyes of the ignorant multitude for the express and
professed purpose of exciting the same passion, namely HATRED, against

the Catholics of the present day, that the bloody conspirators of the sixteenth century had imbibed against cardinal Beaton. How much more to the credit of these enlightened days would a contrary line of conduct have been ; and instead of exciting *hatred* against the professors of the most ancient faith of Christendom, a desire had been evinced to see justice done to all parties, and the spirit of Charity spread among dissentients on speculative doctrine. But since the Catholics have been so unceasingly and widely represented as cruelly inclined from the principles of their religion, it becomes the bounden duty of a press devoted to the cause of Truth, to let the public see both sides of the case, in order that a fair and just conclusion may be formed of the respective merits due to the party said to be persecutors, and the party said to be persecuted. It is with this feeling we have taken up our pen, and with no other view will we continue to exercise it, than that of enabling our readers to gather from our pages that knowledge of the history of the pretended Reformation so essential for them to know.

In the primitive ages of Christianity we observe nothing of the disposition shewn by the new reformers, who pretended to discover corruptions in the then established religion of all nations. On the contrary, we find the martyrs suffering persecution for righteousness sake, and confessing their faith in Christ with courage and fortitude, but at the same time with meekness and submission to their temporal rulers. Not' so, however, with the evangelical preachers of the new doctrines. They were *inflamed* with a diabolical hatred towards those whom they deemed their oppressors, and under the cloak of the most blasphemous pretences they committed murder and rebellion. We see it admitted by Fox, or the hatred-inspiring editors, that the work of assassination was committed in cold blood, on the part of one of the assassins, who affirmed that it was a judgment of God, and consequently that they looked upon themselves as the instruments of Divine vengeance, in seeking to satiate their malice. How far their judgment was correct we will leave Burnet to decide, who observes, " that scarce any of the conspirators died " an ordinary death ;" from which we may conclude that the vengeance of God followed them for the diabolical deed, and the blasphemous pretensions under which it was perpetrated.

There is another circumstance connected with this affair mentioned by Dr. Heylin, in his *History of the Presbyterians,* which is not generally known, and therefore deserving our notice. Speaking of the cardinal's death, this historian says, " In the relating of which *murder,* in Knox's " History, a note was given us in the margent of the first edition, " printed at London, in octavo, which points us to the *godly act* and *say-* " ing of James Melvin, for so the author calls this *most wicked deed.* " But that edition being stopped at the press by the queen's command, " the history never came out perfect till the year of our Lord 1644, " when the word *godly* was left out of the marginal note, for the avoid- " ing of that horrible scandal which had been thereby given to all sober " readers." Who indeed but must be scandalized and horrified at the conduct of men, who setting themselves up for the reformers of corruption and the preachers of true doctrine, held out *murder, secret cold-blooded assassination,* as a GODLY ACT ! ! !

The death of Cardinal Beaton was the signal for the work of *defor-*

mation in Scotland, which consequently had its rise in heartless revenge, shocking barbarity, religious mockery, and deliberate murder. The base then on which the thing called the Reformation was raised, was composed of materials containing the opposite qualities to those on which the Christian religion was founded. By the latter, man was taught, as we have before observed, to forgive an enemy, and to stifle in his heart the motions of anger; but we see the reformers, who pretended to act under the immediate impulse of the spirit of God, and to have been commissioned by him to reform his church, transported with rage, and inflamed with savage fury, breaking into the room of an old man, and there with fiend-like malice glutting their vengeance with the victim's blood. Nor did their fury cease with the death of their victim; for after the perpetration of the horrible deed, they exposed the mangled body of the cardinal over the walls of the castle, as a signal of their revolt against the constituted authorities of the country.

The latter and most important part of the affair has been suppressed by the modern editors, conceiving, we suppose, that but little credit would be added to their cause by a detail of the subsequent proceedings of these *godly actors* in the work of reforming Popery. We, however, have no such feelings, as we consider a full exposure of the deeds of the reforming heroes the best way to enable the reader to come to a right decision on their merits. Heylin says, " It was upon the 19th of " May (1547) that the murderers possessed themselves of that strong " place, into which many flocked from all parts of the realm, both to " contragulate the act and assist the actors; so that at last they cast " themselves into a congregation, and chose John Rough (who after- " terwards suffered death in England) to be one of their preachers; " John Knox, that *great incendiary* of the realm of Scotland, for another " of them. And thus they stood upon their guard till the coming of " one and twenty gallies and some land forces out of France, by whom " the castle was besieged, and so fiercely battered, that they were " forced to yield on the last of July, without obtaining any better con- " ditions than the hope of life."—*(Hist. of Pres.* l. iv. p. 123.) How they passed their time in the castle, while in a state of open rebellion against the regent, and after they had " cast themselves into a congre- " gation," we may learn from the account of Buchanan, a Presbyterian writer, and himself a zealous promoter of the reformation. He informs us, that " they made a very bad use of this respite, which this tempo- " rary accommodation procured them; and that notwithstanding the ad- " monitions of Knox, they spent the time in *whoredom* and *adultery*, and " all the vices of idleness."—*(Guthrie's Hist of Scot.* v. 397.) A precious edifying assembly to compose the first Presbyterian congregation or parish of Scotland, with John Knox at their head. It is not a little curious, too, that one of the conditions of the surrender of this pious knot of rebellious whoremongers and adulterers was, " that the government " should procure unto them a sufficient absolution from the pope; and " that themselves should give pledges for surrendering the castle, how " soon the absolution was brought from Rome, and delivered unto " them."—*(Ibid.* 306.) Thus these reforming saints could add hypocrisy to the list of their other crimes, but it is no wonder, for villains of a deeper dye never disgraced human nature than those who broached and carried on the reformation, as it is called, of Scotland. They may be equalled in this work of iniquity, but they never can be excelled.

PROGRESS OF THE REFORMATION IN SCOTLAND.

After recounting the execution of two other of the reformers, named Wallace and Mille, the modern editors conclude their account of the persecution in these words:—" The death of Walter Mille proved the " overthrow of popery in Scotland. The clergy were so sensible that " their affairs were falling into decay, that they, from that time, never " dared to proceed to a capital punishment, on account of religion : in- " somuch, that in the synod held in Edinburgh, in July this year, 1558, " some persons who had been impeached of heresy were only con- " demned, upon their non-appearance, to make a public recantation at " the market-cross of that city, on the 1st of September following, be- " ing St. Giles's day, the titular bishop of that place. It was usual, at " the feast of this saint, which now nearly approached, to carry his im- " age in procession through the town, and the queen-regent was to " honour the solemnity with her presence. But when the time was " come, the image was missing : it having been stolen from its station, " by some who were too wise to pray to it. This caused a halt to be " made, till another image was borrowed from the Grey-friars, with " which they set forward : and after the queen had accompanied them " a considerable way, she withdrew into the castle, where she was to " dine. But no sooner was she gone, than some persons, who had been " *purposely* appointed, tore the picture from off the shoulders of those " who carried it, threw it into the dirt, and totally destroyed it. This " gave such universal satisfaction to the people, that a general shout en- " sued, and *a riot continued in the street during some hours;* which was at " length suppressed by the vigilance of the magistrates.

" About the same time a great disturbance happened at Perth, the " circumstances attending which were as follow : a celebrated reformist " minister having preached to a numerous congregation, after sermon " was over, some *godly persons* remained in the church, when a priest " was so *imprudent* as to *open a case,* in which was curiously engraved " the *figures of many saints :* after which he made preparations for say- " ing mass. A young man observing this, said aloud, ' This is intolera- " ble ! As God plainly condemns, in scripture, idolatry, shall we stand " and see such an insult ?' The priest was so offended at this, that he " struck the youth a violent blow on the head, on which he broke one " of the figures in the case, when immediately *all the people fell on the* " *priest and destroyed every thing in the church that tended to idolatry.* " This being soon known abroad, the people assembled in large bodies, " and proceeded to the monasteries of the Grey and Black Friars, both " of which they stripped ; and then pulled down the house of the Car- " thusians ; so that in the space of two days nothing remained of those " noble buildings but the bare walls. The like kind of outrages were " committed in many other towns in the kingdom.

" At this time there were many persons who made it their business " *to solicit subscriptions in order to carry on the work of reformation, and* " *to abolish popery.* Among these were several of the nobility, particu- " larly the earl of Argyle, the lord James Stewart, the earl of Glencairn,

" &c. The endeavours of these *noble reformists* were attended with
" such success that they at length effected *a complete reformation in the*
" *kingdom*; though they met with many obstacles from their *inveterate*
" *enemies the papists.*"

Taking this account to be genuine, are the transactions therein detailed creditable to the cause of reform, and that reform said to be of a
religious nature? Did the apostles and their successors the bishops and
priests of the Catholic church act thus when they planted Christianity
in a Pagan country? Do we read of such exploits as are here unblushingly related when Paganism was subdued and Christianity established
in any part of the world through the labours of Catholic missionaries?
It stands acknowledged that the Catholics were violently attacked, that
sedition and outrage followed the sermon of a celebrated reformist minister, and that the work of destruction was commenced by some
" GODLY persons." What an admission! Could that religion, which it
is here admitted began with the destruction of noble buildings and "the
like outrages" throughout the kingdom, be grounded on the sublime
principles laid down in the gospel of Christ? It is impossible. But
the most curious part of the tale is that where we are told many persons
made it their business to SOLICIT SUBSCRIPTIONS in order to carry
on the work of reformation, and to abolish Popery!!! *Solicit subscriptions* truly! Ah! ah! had they confined themselves to *solicitations*, indeed, as the bible-mongers of the present day are forced to do, the *reformation*, as it is miscalled, would have made as little progress under
the hands of the early Scotch fanatics, as the abolition of Popery does
under the modern retailers of calumny against Catholicism. We have
historians, however, of greater credit than our hatred-exciting editors,
who give a very different colour to the transactions above quoted. The
solicitations are represented by them to have been *menacing demands*,
and the *subscriptions* no other than *forcible confiscations.* The " noble
reformists," were not endued with the gift of persuasion, nor were they
armed with the shield of Truth; they therefore combined to employ
brute force to aid the mad preachings of Knox and his associates, by
which they plunged their country into a state of anarchy and desolation,
which, after years of blood and misery, ended in the establishment of
Presbyterianism, but not in the total destruction of Catholicism. Its
seed was never extinct, and at this day it is flourishing in that part of
the island as well as in this.

After the perpetration of the above outrages, Dr. Heylin says, the
constituted authorities used much diligence to find out the principal
actors, but " the brethren kept themselves together in such companies,
" *singing psalms*, and *openly encouraging one another*, that no one durst
" lay hands upon them."—A very pious way, the reader will say, to
preach the gospel of Christ and true religion. It may be necessary here
to observe, that these rebellious proceedings were the offspring of a
connexion with John Calvin and the Genevian consistorians, who were
in open rebellion against their prince, and had excited a rebellion in
the kingdom of France; and the first fruit of them was a common
band or covenant, signed by the earls of Argyle, Glencairn, and Morton,
&c. in the name of themselves, their vassals, tenants, and defendants,
the tenure of which was to venture their lives to establish what they

A REVIEW

OF

Fox's Book of Martyrs,

CRITICAL AND HISTORICAL.

No. 42. Printed and Published by W. E. ANDREWS, 3, Chapter-house-court, St. Paul's Churchyard, London. **Price 3d.**

EXPLANATION OF THE ENGRAVING.—*In the parish of Chassenouilla, the French Huguenots apprehended a certain Catholic priest of the name of Ludovicus Fayard, who, from the testimony of men living in that place, was a man of the most virtuous and exemplary life. Having seized him, they immersed his feet so frequently and for such a length of time, in a cauldron of boiling oil, that his flesh was entirely boiled from his bones. Not satisfied with this cruel torture, they poured boiling oil into his mouth, and finding that he still existed, they afterwards dispatched him.*—THEATRUM CRUDELITATUM, 1594.

CONTINUATION OF THE REVIEW.

called " the most blessed word of God and his congregation." This beginning made; the work of confusion soon followed. We have seen the account from Fox of the outrages committed at Perth, but his story is not altogether correct. He attributes the commencement of the riot to the imprudence of a priest in attempting to say mass, and opening a curious case engraved with images, one of which he breaks about the head of a young man. This is mere fiction, introduced to screen the unprovoked assault, by casting the blame on the suffering party.—Dr. Heylin gives the following account of this affair :—After stating that Knox arrived at Perth on the 5th of May, 1559, he goes on, " In the " chief church whereof, he preached such a thundering sermon against " the *adoration of images*, and the advancing of them in places of God :

" public worship, as suddenly beat down all the images and religious
" houses within the precincts of that town. For presently after the
" end of.the sermon, when almost all the rest of the people were gone
" home to dinner, some few which remained in the church pulled down
" a glorious tabernacle which stood on the altar, broke it in pieces,
" and defaced the images which they found therein. Which being dis-
" patched, they did the like execution on all the rest in that church;
" and were so nimble at their work, that they had made a clear riddance
" of them, before the tenth man in the town was advertised of it. The
" news hereof causeth the rascal multitude (so my author calls them)
" to resort in great numbers to the church." He concludes by describing the destruction of the monasteries in nearly similar words as
Fox. The doctor then informs us, that Knox left Perth in company
with Argyle, &c. on his way to St. Andrew's, and that preaching at a
town called Craîle, his " exhortation so prevailed upon most of the
" hearers, that immediately they betook themselves to the pulling down
" of altars and images ; and finally, destroyed all monuments of super-
" stition and idolatry which they found in the town." The like proceedings took place at a place called Anstruther, from whence they
marched to St. Andrew's, " in the parish church whereof (continues
" the historian) Knox preached upon our Saviour's casting the buyers
" and sellers out of the temple, and with his wonted rhetoric so in-
" flamed the people, that they committed the like outrages there as
" before at Perth, destroying images, and pulling down the houses of
" the Black and Grey friars with the like dispatch." This last outrage
took place on the 11th of June, so that the evangelists made quick
work from the first preaching of Knox. The next scene of dilapidation
was the monastery of Scone, long famous for being the place where
the kings of Scotland were crowned ; the churches and monasteries of
Stirling and Linlithgow were next sacked and destroyed ; and Edinburgh shared the same fate. Dr. Heylin says, the queen retired from
the latter place to Dunbar in great fear, and the lord Seaton, then provost of the town, staid not long behind her. " But (he continues) he
" was scarce gone out of the city, when the rascal rabble fell on the
" religious houses, destroyed the convents of the Black and Greyfriars,
" with all the other monasteries about the town, and shared amongst
" them all the goods which they found in those houses : in which they
" made such quick dispatch, that they had finished that part of the re-
" formation, before the two lords and their attendants could come in to
" help them."

Such were the beginnings in Scotland of that change in religion which
is called the Reformation.—Our blessed Saviour, when he established
his church, laid down fixed rules for his ministers to follow ; and when
he was tempted by his enemies with regard to his loyalty and allegiance
to the Roman emperor, who then reigned in Judea, his answer was :
" Render unto Cæsar the things that belong to Cæsar ; and to God the
" things that belong to God."—In every case, as we have before remarked,
the apostles and their successors, on planting the Catholic faith in a
Pagan soil, invariably followed this maxim.—The religion they preached was to fit them for another world, by making them better members
of this.—The kingdom they came to establish was not of this world,

but a supernatural one, of which Christ was the head, and the Pope his visible vicegerent on earth. Hence every kingdom of the globe which received the light of faith acknowledged the spiritual supremacy of the pope, both monarchs, legislators, and people, while, at the same time, they were equally as tenacious of their own temporal rights and independence, nay more so than when they were heathens. At least such was the conduct of our English forefathers, and who has not heard of those Scottish heroes Bruce and Wallace, who were both stanch Catholics.—When the pretended reformers and disciples of evangelical liberty began to dogmatize, however, they preached up destruction and fury to the Catholic constituted authorities, which they cloaked under the hypocritical cant of rooting out idolatry and superstition, which cry is now set up by the Bible and School-mongers of the evangelical caste of the present day.—Forgetful of the commands of God, to go and *teach* all nations; or rather sensible that they had no claim to such divine commission, instead of persuasion and the power of miracles, they had recourse to physical force and the engines of death and destruction.—We see them here in open rebellion against their sovereign, carrying the work of desolation and pillage in their train, and fired with the most intolerant passions against every thing that savoured of Catholicism.—Dr. Heylin tells us, that at the outset of the violent proceedings of Knox and his party, the queen-regent issued a proclamation, in which she declared that her wish was to satisfy every man's conscience, and therefore she would call a parliament for establishing order. That in the mean time every man should be suffered to live at liberty, using their own consciences without trouble until further orders. She also charged the congregation with seeking more for the subversion of the crown then the benefit of religion.—This proclamation was answered by the congregationists, in which they denied any other intention than to banish idolatry (i. e. Catholicism) to advance true religion, and defend the *preachers* thereof; that they were ready to continue in all duty toward their sovereign, *provided* they might have the free exercise of their religion.—Here then we see the allegiance of these Protestant reformers made *conditional*, while the allegiance of the Catholic, under all circumstances, is *unconditional*, according to the laws and principles of the constitution under which they live. As to their love of liberty of conscience, about which so much noise has been made and clamour raised against the Catholic church, the reforming or rebel party soon gave an example of what was to be expected from the liberality of their principles.—Dr. Heylin says, that they wrote letters to the queen-regent herself, "whom they assured in the close, that if she would "make use of her authority for the abolishing of idolatry and super-"stitious abuses which agreed not with the word of God, she should "find them as obedient as any subjects within the realm. Which, in "plain truth, was neither more nor less than this, that if they might "not have their wills in the point of religion, she was to look for no "obedience from them in other matters: whereof they gave sufficient "proof by their staying in Edinburgh, her command to the contrary "notwithstanding; by pressing more than ever for a toleration, and "adding this over and above to their former demands, that such French "forces as remained in Scotland might be disbanded and sent back to

" their native country. In the first of which demands they were so un-
" reasonable, that when the queen offered them the exercise of their
" own religion upon condition that when she had occasion to make
" use of any of their churches for her own devotions, such exercise
" might be suspended, and the mass only used in that conjuncture; they
" would by no means yield unto it : and they refused to yield unto it
" for this reason only, because it would be in her power, by removing
" from one place to another, to leave them without any certain exercise
" of their religion, which in effect was utterly to overthrow it. And
" hereto they were pleased to add, that, as they could not hinder her
" from exercising any religion which she had a mind to (but this
" was more than they would stand to in their better fortunes), so could
" they not agree that the ministers of Christ should be silenced upon any
" occasion, and much less, that the true worship of God should give
" place to idolatry. A point to which they stood so stiffly, that when
" the queen regent had resettled her court at Edinburgh, she could
" neither prevail so far upon the magistrates of that city, as either to
" let her have the church of St. Giles to be appropriated only to the
" use of the mass, or that the mass might be said in it at such vacant
" times in which they made no use of it for themselves or their minis-
" ters." Thus it will be seen that on the very outset of the pretended
liberty-loving reformation, the most intolerant system of *persecution* was
commenced against the professors of the ancient faith of Christendom.

These proceedings of the " noble reformists" and evangelical tribe
were succeeded by other treasonable outrages. The lords of the congregation excited the whole kingdom, by a written instrument, to rise
in arms, and now the country was distracted with a civil war carried
on by religious fanaticism on one hand, and a struggle to preserve lawful authority on the other. One of the most successful engines used
by Protestants against the Catholics of this kingdom has been the supposed authority of the Pope TO DEPOSE KINGS. Of the two hundred and
odd bishops that have filled the chair of St. Peter, not half a dozen ever
laid claim to this power, and then not by the divine authority of the
church, which could not communicate such power to any of them, but
by the circumstances in which Christendom was then placed, the monarchs looking upon the pope as the common father of the faithful, and
often appealing to him to settle their differences; and it may be here
observed, that in no instance did the popes attempt to avail themselves
of this power, but in cases where the monarchs were the most immoral
and tyrannical of their class, hated by the nobles and detested by the
people. But not one of these obnoxious rulers lost his throne through
the interference of any of the popes, though many Catholic sovereigns
have felt the weight of the deposing power introduced by the very men
who raised the cry against the pope. As an instance, we must here
mention what took place at the period when the sham reformation was
set on foot in Scotland. We have noticed the excitement to rebellion
by the lords of the congregation; this was followed by a resolution,
Dr. Heylin says, to put in execution what had been long in deliberation,
that is to say, THE DEPOSING OF THE QUEEN-REGENT FROM THE PUBLIC
GOVERNMENT. " But first," writes the doctor, " they must consult their
" *ghostly fathers*, that *by their countenance and authority*, they might

" more certainly prevail upon all such persons as seemed unsatisfied in
" the point. Willock and Knox are chosen above all the rest to re-
" solve this doubt, if at the least any of them doubted of it, which may
" well be questioned. They were both factors for Geneva, and there-
" fore both obliged to advance her interest. Willock declares that
" albeit God had appointed magistrates only to be his lieutenants on
" earth, honouring them with his own title, and calling them gods;
" yet did he never so establish any, but that for just causes *they might*
" *be deprived.* Which having proved by *some examples out of holy scrip-*
" *ture,* he thereupon inferred, that since the queen-regent had denied
" her chief duty to the subjects of this realm, which was to preserve
" them from invasion of strangers, and to suffer the word of God to be
" freely preached : seeing also she was a *maintainer of superstition,* and
" despised the counsel of the nobility; he did think *they might justly*
" *deprive her from all regiment and authority over them.* Knox goes to
" work more cautiously, but comes home at last : For having first ap-
" proved whatsoever had been said by Willock, he adds this to it, that
" the iniquity of the queen regent ought not to withdraw their hearts
" from the obedience due to their sovereign ; nor did he wish that any
" such sentence against her should be pronounced, but that when she
" should change her course, and submit herself to good counsels, there
" should be place left unto her to regress to the same honours from
" which for just cause she ought to be deprived."—Such were the
opinions of the apostles of the reformation in Scotland, so lauded by the
modern editors of the *Book of Martyrs* ; but, we should be glad to learn,
whether they dare to avow the correctness of these opinions at this
day, on which the blessed reformation was founded If they did, we
think they would soon have the Attorney-general teaching them to
change their opinions.

Having shewn the pernicious tendency of their civil doctrines, we
must now give the reader some idea of the stability they attached to
their articles of faith. Hitherto no particular creed had been followed,
but on the death of Mary of England, and the accession of Elizabeth,
finding it necessary to secure the interests of the latter queen, the liturgy of the English church established by Elizabeth was the form of
worship adopted by the Scotch rebel reformers, by solemn subscription.
But when the king of France, Francis II. who was the husband of the
unfortunate Mary, died, and the reformers were no longer in fear of
the French, they then began to discover their affections for the Genevian discipline and creed, and their distaste to the form which they
before solemnly subscribed to. Dr. Heylin tells us that " Knox had
" before devised a new Book of Discipline, contrived for the most part
" after Calvin's platform, and a new form of Common-prayer was digest-
" ed also, more consonant to his infallible judgment than the English
" Liturgy. But hitherto they had both lain dormant, because they stood
" in need of such help from England, as could not be presumed on with
" so great a confidence, if they had openly declared any dissent or disaffec-
" tion to the public forms which were established in that church, Now
" their estate is so much bettered by the death of the king, the sad con-
" dition of their queen, and the assurances which they had from the
" court of England (from whence the earls of Morton and Glencairn

" were returned with comfort) that they resolve to perfect what they
" had begun ; to prosecute the desolation of religious houses, and the
" spoil of churches ; to introduce their new forms, and suspend the old.
" For compassing of which end they summoned a convention of the
" estates to be held in January.

" Now in this book of discipline (continues the doctor) they take
" upon them to *innovate in most things formerly observed and practised in the*
" *church of Christ*, and in *some things* which *themselves had settled*, as the
" *groundwork* of the reformation. They take upon them to discharge
" the accustomed fasts, and abrogate all the ancient festivals, not spar-
" ing those which did relate particularly unto Christ our Saviour, as
" his nativity, passion, resurrection, &c. They condemned the use of
" the cross in baptism, give way to the introduction of the new order
" of Geneva, for ministering the sacrament of the Lord's Supper, and
" commend sitting for the most proper and convenient gesture to be
" used at it. They require that all churches not being parochial should
" be forthwith *demolished*, declare all forms of God's public worship,
" which are not prescribed in his word, to be mere idolatry, and that
" none ought to administer the holy sacraments but such as are quali-
" fied for preaching. They appoint the catechism of Geneva to be
" taught in their schools, ordained three universities to be made and
" continued in that kingdom, with salaries proportioned to the profes-
" sors in all arts and sciences, and time assigned for being graduated
" in the same. They decree also in the same, that tythes should be no
" longer paid to the Romish clergy, but that they shall be taken up by
" deacons and treasurers, by them to be employed for maintainance of
" the poor, the ministers, and the said universities. They complained
" very sensibly of the tyranny of lay-patrons and impropriators in ex-
" acting their tithes, in which they are said to be more cruel and un-
" merciful than the popish priests; and therefore take upon them to
" determine as in point of law what commodities shall be titheable,
" what not; and declare also that all leases and alienations, which
" formerly had been made of tithes, should be utterly void."—Then
followed some regulations touching the ministry of the sacrament and
preaching, by which it was ordered that the ministers should be ELECTED
by the congregation.—The reader will here contrast the discipline set
forth in this book with the mode practised by the primitive Christians,
and followed by every nation that received the faith of Christ.—Dr.
Heylin says that they began with INNOVATION and even *changed* that
which they before considered the *groundwork* of their reformation.—
Under these circumstances it is impossible that the proceedings of these
rebel reformers could be guided by the influence of truth, because truth
is always *one* and *the same*, and will not bear *innovation* or *change*.—
The work then of these "noble reformists," as they are stiled by the
modern editors, must have been instigated by the powers of darkness,
under which it is clear they acted.

It is said by our divine Saviour, that the goodness of the tree shall be
known by its fruit, and common sense tells us it is only by following
this rule that we can come to a right conclusion on the respective merits of the reformation so called, and the principal actors therein. We
have seen them changing their creed as birds do their feathers, but they

clung with more pertinacity to the work of destruction. They solicited of the convention of estates, in the absence of the queen, for leave to demolish all the monuments of *superstition* and *idolatry*, by which they meant all cathedral churches, as well as monasteries and other religious houses, and before they could have the assent or dissent of the queen or her council, they proceeded to execute ecclesiastical censures, and arrogate to themselves the authority of nominating their own ministers over the heads of the old incumbents, and to hold their general assemblies. Emboldened by these unjustifiable acts, for they were neither authorized by law, or confirmed by the queen, nor sanctioned by the convention of estates, a petition is directed to the lords of the secret council from the *assemblies of the church*, in which their lordships are solicited to make quick work of it. " On the receipt of this petition," writes Dr. Heylin, "an order presently is made by the lords of the " council, for granting all which was desired; and had more been de- " sired, they had granted more: so formidable were the brethren grown " to the opposite party. Nor was it granted in words only which took " no effect, but execution caused to be done upon it; and warrants to " that purpose issued to the earls of Arran, Argyle, and Glencairn, " the lord James Stuart, &c. Whereupon followed *a pitiful devasta-* " *tion of churches and church-buildings in all parts of the realm;* no dif- " ference made, but all religious edifices of what sort soever, were ei- " ther terribly defaced, or utterly ruinated; the holy vessels, and what- " soever else could be turned into money, as lead, bells, timber, glass, " &c. were publicly exposed to sale; *the very sepulchres of the dead not* " *spared;* the registers of the church, and *the libraries thereunto belong-* " *ing, defaced and thrown into the fire.* Whatsoever had escaped the " former tumults, is now made subject to destruction; so much the " worse, because the violence and sacrilegious actings of these church- " robbers had now the countenance of law. And to this work of spoil " and rapine, men *of all ranks and orders* were observed to put their " helping hands; men of most note and quality being forward in it, *in* " *hope of getting to themselves the most part of the booty;* those of the " poorer sort, in hope of being gratified for their pains therein by their " lords and patrons. Both *sorts encouraged to it by the zealous madness* " *of some of their seditious preachers,* who frequently cried out, that the " places where idols had been worshipped, ought by the *law of God to* " be destroyed; that the sparing of them was the reserving of things " execrable; and that the commandment given to Israel for destroying " the places where the Canaanites did worship their false gods, *was a* " *just warrant to the people for doing the like.* By which encouragements " the madness of the people was transported beyond the bounds which " they had first prescribed unto it. In the beginning of the heats, they " designed only the destruction of religious houses, for fear the monks " and friars might otherwise be restored in time to their former dwell- " ings: But they proceeded to the demolishing of cathedral churches, " and ended in the ruin of parochial also; the chancels whereof were " sure to be levelled in all places, though the isles and bodies of them " might be spared in some."

Such was the deplorable effect of the reformation, as it is called, in Scotland; an effect much more destructive and disastrous to learning

and the sciences, than the devastating rapacity of the reformers in England, who by sticking to the order of episcopacy, preserved in some degree the beautiful cathedrals which adorned the kingdom, many of which are standing now, a sad testimony of the superiority of the dark ages of monkery and Catholicism, over the *enlightened* days of Bible-reading and sectarianism. The conduct of the unfortunate Mary in these days of tribulation and adversity, was that of a just and amiable sovereign, desirous of allaying the spirit of innovation by mild and gentle means, and granting the utmost liberty of conscience to those who had imbibed the noxious doctrines of Calvin and Knox. But these Christian feelings did not satisfy the boisterous reformers, who openly railed at the stipends proposed to be granted to their ministers, and exclaimed at the Catholic clergy being paid and encouraged in their idolatrous practices. John Knox, with daring impudence raved in the pulpit against his sovereign, a beautiful and defenceless woman, and even insulted her to her face at a conference she granted him. The modern editors of *Fox's Book of Martyrs* we have no doubt are all loyal men to the backbone, and would consent freely to the punishment of any of those individuals who lately sought a redress of the abuses known to exist in the civil administration of the country. They make a great noise about the tyranny of the Catholic church, and the cruelties of the inquisition; and they have lauded to the highest heavens the conduct of the authors of the Reformation, so called, in England and in Scotland; but they have most carefully concealed the blood-thirsty tyranny, the diabolical robberies and murders, the barbarous outrages, and the despotic temper of the miscreants who figured in that affair. It is but right however that the people should be informed of the proceedings which marked that epoch, and it is better late than never. We are therefore rejoiced that our loyal modern editors have imposed the task upon us; but that we may not be charged with dealing in assertions, without advancing proofs, we will here give the words of Dr. Heylin, from his History of the Presbyterians, from which we have before quoted. Thus writes this author:—" At Midsummer they held a
" general assembly, and there agreed upon the form of a petition to be
" presented to the queen in the name of the kirk; the substance of it
" was for abolishing the mass, and other superstitious rites of the Ro-
" mish religion; for inflicting some punishment against blasphemy,
" adultery, contempt of word, the profanation of sacraments, and other
" like vices condemned by the word of God, whereof the laws of the
" realm did not take any hold; for referring all actions of divorce to
" the church's judgment, or as the least to men of good knowledge and
" conversation; for excluding all popish churchmen from holding any
" place in council or session; and finally, for the increase and more as-
" sured payment of the ministers's stipends, but more particularly for
" appropriating the glebes and houses unto them *alone*. This was the
" sum of their desires, but couched in *such irreverent, coarse, and bitter
" expressions*, and those expressions justified with such animosities, that
" Lethington (the secretary of state) had much ado to prevail upon
" them for putting it into a more dutiful and civil language. All which
" the queen knew well enough, and therefore would afford them no bet-
" ter answer, but that she would do nothing to the prejudice of that·

" religion which she then professed; and that she hoped to have mass
" restored, before the end of the year, in all parts of the kingdom.
" Which being so said, or so reported, gave Knox occasion in his preach-
" ings before the gentry of Kyle and Galloway, (to which he was com-
" missioned by the said assembly) to forewarn some of them of the
" dangers which would shortly follow; and thereupon earnestly to ex-
" hort them to take such order that they might be obedient to autho-
" rity, and yet not suffer the enemies of God's truth to have the upper
" hand. And they, who understood his meaning at half a word, as-
" sembled themselves together on the 4th of September, at the town of
" Ayr, where they entered into a common bond, subscribed by the earl
" of Glencairn, the lords Boyd and Uchiltry, with one hundred and
" thirty more of note and quality, besides the provost and burgesses of
" the town of Ayr, which made forty more. The tenor of which bond
" was this that followeth.

" ' *We whose names are underwritten, do promise in the presence of God,*
" *and in the presence of his Son, our Lord Jesus Christ, that we and every*
" *one of us, shall and will maintain the preaching of his holy evangel, now*
" *of his mercy offered and granted to this realm; and also will maintain*
" *the ministers of the same against all persons, power and authority, that*
" *will oppose themselves to the doctrine proposed, and by us received. And*
" *farther, with the same solemnity we protest and promise that every one of*
" *us shall assist another, yea, and the whole body of the Protestants within*
" *this realm, in all lawful and just occasions; against all persons; so that*
" *whosoever shall hurt, molest, or trouble any of our bodies, shall be reputed*
" *enemies to the whole, except that the offender will be content to submit him-*
" *self to the government of the church now established amongst us. And*
" *this we do, as we desire to be accepted and favoured of the Lord Jesus,*
" *and accepted worthy of credit and honesty in the presence of the godly.*'

" And in pursuance of this bond, they seize upon some priests, and
" give notice to others, that they would not trouble themselves of com-
" plaining to the queen or counsel, but would execute the punishment
" appointed to idolaters in the law of God, as they saw occasion when-
" soever they should be apprehended. At which the queen was much
" offended; but there was no remedy. All she could do, was once
" again to send for Knox, and to desire him so to deal with the barons,
" and other gentlemen of the west, that they would not punish any man
" for the cause of religion, as they had resolved. To which he answer-
" ed with as little reverence as at other times, that if her majesty would
" punish malefactors according to the laws, he durst assure her, that
" she should find peace and quietness at the hand of those who profess-
" ed the Lord Jesus in that kingdom: that if she thought or had pur-
" pose to allude the laws, there were some who would not fail to let
" the Papists understand, that they should *not be suffered without*
" *punishment* to offend their God. Which said, he went about to prove
" in a long discourse, that *others* were by God intrusted with *the sword*
" *of justice*, besides kings and princes; which kings and princes, if they
" *failed in the right use of it*, and drew it not against offenders, they
" *must not look to find obedience from the rest of the subjects.*

" The same man (Knox) preaching afterwards at one of their general
" assemblies, made a distinction between the ordinance of God, and the

" persons placed by him in authority ; and then affirmed that men might
" lawfully and justly resist the persons, and not offend against the ordi-
" nance of God. He added as a corollary unto his discourse, that sub-
" jects were not bound to obey their princes, if they command unlawful
" things ; but that they might resist their princes, and that they were
" not bound to suffer. For which being questioned by secretary Lething-
" ton in the one, and desired to declare himself further in the other
" point ; he justified himself in both, affirming that he had long been
" of that opinion, and did so remain. A question hereupon arising
" about the punishment of kings, if they were idolaters ; it was honestly
" affirmed by Lethington, that there was no commandment given in that
" case to punish kings, and that the people had no power to be judges
" over them, but must leave them unto God alone, who would either
" punish them by death, imprisonment, war, or some other plagues.
" Against which Knox replied with his wonted confidence, that to affirm
" that the people, or a part of the people may not execute God's judg-
" ments against their king being an offender, the lord Lethington could
" have no other warrant, except his own imaginations, and the opinion
" of such as rather feared to displease their princes then offend their
" God. Against which when Lethington objected the authority of some
" eminent Protestants ; Knox answered, that they spake of Christians
" subject to tyrants and infidels, so dispersed, that they had no other
" force but only to cry unto God for their deliverance : that such indeed
" should hazard any further than those godly men willed them, he would
" not hastily be of counsel. But that his argument had another ground,
" and that he spake of a people assembled in one body of a common-
" wealth unto whom God had given *sufficient force*, not only *to resist*,
" but also *to suppress* all kind of open idolatry ; and such a people
" again he affirmed were bound to keep their land clean and unpollut-
" ed : that God required one thing of Abraham and his seed, when he
" and they were strangers in the land of Egypt, and that another thing
" was required of them when they were delivered from that bondage,
" and put into the actual possession of the land of Canaan."

We shall cite no further to shew the diabolical and dangerous doctrines introduced by the reformers into their new system of religion,
or more properly speaking irreligion. It is here clearly proved that
they were instigated, not by the principles of Charity and Truth, but
by the basest of passions, and hurried on by the spirit of intolerance,
cruelty, and slaughter. The doctrines advocated by Knox were of the
most revolutionary tendency, and grounded upon treachery and hypocrisy. We have here the very doctrines charged upon the Catholics
by their Protestant adversaries, which the former disclaim and deny as
forming any part of their civil and religious principles. How disgraceful, how dishonourable, how unjust then is that conduct, which attempts
to fasten upon a class of men crimes of the most abhorrent nature,
which they never practised but always condemned ; while these very
enormities were inculcated and acted upon by another set of men, who
are represented as the most perfect set of beings by the accusers of the
innocent.

But it is high time that we should have the testimony of credible
and unprejudiced witnesses to the character of the apostle and other

leaders of the Scotch reformation. Of John Knox, Dr. Stuart, in his History of Scotland, writes thus:—"The glory of God stimulated this " reformer to cruel devastations and outrages. Charity, moderation, " the love of peace, patience, and humanity, were not in the number of " his virtues. Papists as well as Popery were the objects of his detes- " tation; and though he had risen to eminence *by exclaiming again* t*the* " *persecution of priests, he was himself a* PERSECUTOR. His suspicions, that " the queen was determined to re-establish the popish religion, were " rooted and uniform; and upon the *most frivolous pretences,* he was stre- " nuous to break that chain of cordiality which ought to bind together " the prince and the people. He inveighed against her government, " and insulted her person with virulence and indecency. *It flattered* " *his pride to violate the duties of the subject, and to scatter sedition.* His " advices were pressed with heat, his admonitions were pronounced " with anger; and whether his theme was a topic of polity or of faith, " his knowledge appeared to be equally infallible. He wished to be " considered *as the organ of the divine will.* Contradiction inflamed " him with hostility, and his resentments took a deep and lasting foun- " dation. The pride of success, the spirit of adulation, the awe with " with which he struck the gaping and ignorant multitude, inspired " him with a superlative conception of his own merits. He mistook for " prophetic impulse the illusions of a heated fancy, and, with *an intem-* " *perate and giddy vanity,* he ventured at times *to penetrate into the* " *the future,* and to reveal *the mysteries of Providence.*"—(Vol. ii. p. 135.) Such were the qualities possessed by Knox, and we ask the sensible reader, of whatever religious denomination he may be, whether such a character as we have here described would be chosen by the divinity to work a reformation in the morals of the people, or establish a new system of faith, supposing the words of Christ to have failed, when he promised that the Spirit of Truth should abide with his Church, and guide her in all truth to the end of the world? Knox is here charged with being A PERSECUTOR, while he was exclaiming against the perse- cution of priests, and we charge the modern editors of Fox with the same hypocritical and unjust line of conduct; for they, while endea- vouring to raise the cry of persecution against the Catholics of the pre- sent day, are hostilely combined to persecute the accused, by debarring them from the exercise of their civil rights, for no other cause than following the dictates of conscience.

The next hero in the Scottish drama is George Buchanan, who was a man of undoubted literary talents, but of the most abandoned character. Dr. Stuart says of him, " while his genius and ability adorned the times " in which he lived, and must draw to him the admiration of the most " distant posterity; it is not to be forgotten, that his political conduct " was disgraceful to the greatest degree, and must excite its regrets " and provoke its indignation. His zeal for the earl of Murray over- " turned altogether his allegiance as a subject, and his integrity as " a man. His activity against Mary in the conferences in England, " was a strain of the most shameless corruption; and the virulence with " which he endeavoured to defame her, by his writings was most auda- " cious and criminal. They involve the complicated charge of ingrati- " tude, rebellion and perjury."—(*Hist. of Scot.* v. ii. p. 245.) This mis-

xsREVIEW OF FOX'S

creant, by his writings, contributed much to the poisoning of the public
mind, and inflaming the bad passions of the people against the old order
of things. He wrote a work entitled *The Detection of Mary's doings,*
whereof Dr. Stuart observes, " in the place of information and truth, he
" substitutes a boundless audacity of assertion, and the most pestilent
" rancour. An admirable but malicious eloquence, misrepresentations,
" and the vileness of calumny characterize his work : and it remains an
" illustrious monument of the wickedness of faction and the prostitu-
" tion of wit."—(*Ibid. p.* 415.) The Rev. Mr. Whitaker, another Protestant author, in his *Vindication of Mary,* says, Knox was " an original
" genius in lying," and he further writes, that " he (Knox) felt his mind
" impregnated with a peculiar portion of that spirit of falsehood, which
" is so largely possessed by the great father of lies, and which he so
" liberally communicates to some of his chosen children. And he ex-
" erted this spirit, with the grand views, which he uniformly pursued
" in both, that of abusing Mary, his patroness and benefactress; of
" branding her forehead with the hottest iron of infamy, which his un-
" derstanding could provide, and of breaking down all the fences and
" guards of truth, in the eagerness of his knavery against her. But
" Mary herself has told us a circumstance concerning him, that serves
" sufficiently to account for his flagitious conduct. Buchanan, she said,
" *is known to be a lewd man, and an Atheist.* He was one of those
" wretched men, therefore, who suffer their passions to beguile their
" understandings ; who plunge into scepticism to escape from sensibi-
" lity ; who destroy the tone of their minds, while they are blunting the
" force of their feelings; and at last become devoid equally of princi-
" ple and of shame, ready for any fabrication of falsehood, and capable
" of any operation in villainy."—(v. ii. p. 22.)

To these principal leaders in the work of devastation in Scotland we
must add the lord James Stuart, afterwards earl of Murray, and regent
of the kingdom, who, like the other actors, was an apostate from the
church of Rome. In fact he was originally an ecclesiastic under the name
of the prior of St Andrew's ; but says Mr. Whitaker, " when the Reform-
" ation broke out in all its wildness and strength, he put on the sancti-
" fied air of a Reformer, he wrapped himself up in the long cloak of
" puritanism, he attached all the popular leaders among the (reformed)
" clergy to him, and he prepared to make them his useful steps to the
" throne."—(*Vind.* vol. i. p. 22.) The reader must here be told that
this ambitious hypocrite was an illegitimate son of king James V. the
father of the unfortunate Mary, from which circumstance he conceived
the criminal project of dethroning his unprotected sister Mary, and taking
the sceptre into his own hands. To advance his aspiring object, Mr.
Whitaker continues,—" He had the address to make the most cunning
" and most ambitious of his contemporaries to be subservient to his cun-
" ning; to make them commit the enormities themselves which were
" necessary to his purposes; and even to dip their hands in murder,
" that he might enjoy the sovereignty. But he displayed an address
" still greater than this. Though he had not one principle of religion
" within him, though he had not one grain of honour in his soul, and
" though he was guilty of those more monstrous crimes, against which
" God has peculiarly denounced damnation; yet he was denominated

" A GOOD MAN by the reformers at the time, and he has been considered
" as an honest man, by numbers, to our own days." (*Ibid.* p. 24.)—
The colours in which Dr. Stuart has drawn his picture, are not more
favourable. " A selfish and insatiable ambition was his ruling appetite,
" and he pursued its dictates with an unshaken perseverance. His in-
" clination to aspire beyond the rank of a subject, was encouraged by
" the turbulence of his age; and his connections with Elizabeth over-
" turned in him altogether the virtuous restraints of allegiance and
" duty. He became an enemy to his sister, and his sovereign—his ob-
" ligations to her were excessive; his ingratitude was monstrous; and
" no language has any terms of reproach, that are sufficiently powerful
" to characterize his perfidiousness and cruelty to her. Uncommon
" pretensions to sanctity, and to the love of his country, with the per-
" petual affectation of acting under the impulse of honourable motives,
" concealed his purposes, and recommended him to popular favour.
" His manners were grave even to sadness; by a composed and severe
" deportment, and by ostentatious habits of devotion, he awakened and
" secured the admiration of his contemporaries. His house had a
" greater resemblance to a church, than a palace. A dark solemnity
" reigned within its walls; and his domestics were precise, pragmatical
" and mortified. The more zealous of the clergy were proud of resort-
" ing to him, and while he invited them to join with him in the exer-
" cises of religion, he paid a flattering respect to their expositions of
" scriptures, which he hypocritically considered as the sacred rule of
" his life.—To the interests of science and learning he was favourable,
" in an uncommon degree; and Buchanan, who had tasted his bounty,
" gives a varnish to his crimes. The glory of having achieved the re-
" formation afforded him a fame that was most seducing and brilliant.
" With a cold and prefidious heart, he conferred favours, without being
" generous, and received them, without being grateful. His enmity
" was implacable, his friendship dangerous, and his caresses, oftener
" than his anger, preceded the stroke of his resentment, The standard
" of his private interest directed all his actions, and was the measure
" by which he judged of those of other men. To the necessities of his
" ambition he was ready to sacrifice every duty and every virtue, and
" in the paroxysms of his selfishness, he feared not the commission of
" any crime or cruelty, however enormous or detestable.- To the great
" body of the Scottish nobles, whose consequence he had humbled, his
" death was a matter of stern indifference, or of secret joy; but to the
" common people, it was an object of sincere grief, and they lamented
" him long, under the appellation of the godly regent. Elizabeth be-
" wailed in him a strenuous partizan, and a chosen instrument, by which
" she might subvert the independency of Scotland; and Mary, tender
" and devout, wept over a brother, a heretic, and an enemy, whom a
" sudden and violent destiny had overtaken in his guilty career, with
" his full load of unrepented crimes"—(*Hist. of Scot.* v. ii. p. 52.)

Enough has been said of the character of these " noble reformists,"
as they are termed by the modern editors of Fox; it now remains for
us to show whether " a complete reformation in the kingdom" was
effected through their instrumentality, as the modern editors assert, or
whether the endeavours of the " noble reformists" were not followed

by an excess of immorality and the most direful calamities that could
afflict a nation. The testimonies we have adduced unequivocally prove
that the characters of the leading reformers were made up with the
unchristian dispositions of revenge, cruelty, ambition, revolt, hypocrisy, and every vice that disgraces the human heart; it is therefore not
to be expected that the followers of such leaders were to be found immaculate and undefiled in their actions. No, no; the consequences
that resulted from what is called the reformation were the very reverse
of what followed the planting of that faith and church which the reformers pretended *to reform*. When Catholicism was introduced by the
holy missionarie ssent from the pope of Rome for that purpose, the people were transformed from savage uncultivated heathens into orderly
and hospitable Christians. Learning and science were cultivated, churches
and monasteries were erected, hospitals were raised to support the sick
and infirm, the clergy were obliged to lead a life of celibacy and penance;
while pensioners and placemen, to suck the blood of the working classes,
were unknown. Such were the fruits of the establishment of Catholicism, or Popery, as the modern editors call it; alas! how altered is the
scene under the thing called the reformation. Duplicity, violence, ferocity, murder, fanaticism, became general in Scotland; the whole nation was impregnated with vice and iniquity, andthe very men who were
the cause of this general wickedness were compelled to bear witness
to their own work of infamy and guilt. In the year 1578, the commissioners of the kirk conceived that they had then a favourable opportunity to advance a new discipline, which had long been addling in their
noddles. To usher in their design they passed an act of the assembly,
the preamble of which set forth, that "the general assembly of the kirk
" finding *universal corruption* of the whole estates of the body of the
" realm, the great coldness and slackness in religion in the greatest
" part of the professors of the same, with the *daily increase* of all kind
" of fearful sins and enormities, as incests, adulteries, murders, (com-
" mitted in Edinburgh and Stirling,) cursed sacrilege, ungodly sedition
" and division within the bowels of the realm, with all manner of dis-
" ordered and ungodly living," they call for "such a polity and disci-
" pline in the kirk, as is craved by the word of God, &c." But with all
their endeavours to restore morality, it does not appear that they were
in any manner successful, which manifestly shews that the tree was not
good, since it yielded such bad fruit. In the year 1648, about seventy
years after, the general assembly of divines again complained that "ig-
" norance of God and of his Son Jesus Christ prevailed exceedingly in
" the land—that it were impossible to reckon up all the abominations
" that were in the land; and that the blaspheming of the name of God,
" swearing by the creatures, profanation of the Lord's day, uncleanness,
" excess, and rioting, vanity of apparel, lying and deceit, railing and
" cursing, arbitrary and uncontrolled oppression, and grinding of the
" faces of the poor by landlords and others in place and power, *were*
" *become ordinary and common sins.*"—(*An Acknowledgment of Sins.*)—
Nor was the kirk in a more flourishing state in 1778, than in the former
periods, for the divines of the associate synod of that year say, "It is
" surprising to think what gross ignorance of the meaning and autho-
" rity of the truths they profess to believe, prevails at present among

"many."—(*Warning*, p. 52.) "A general unbelief of revealed religion
" (prevails) among the higher orders of our countrymen, which hath by a
" necessary consequence, produced in vast numbers an absolute indiffer-
" ence as to what they believe, either concerning truth or duty, any fur-
" ther than it may comport with their worldly views."—(*Ibid.* p. 54.)
Then speaking of the country generally, they lament it is *now* "through
" the prevalence of infidelity, ignorance, luxury and venality, so much
" despoiled of all religion and feeling the want of it."—(*Ibid.* p. 64.)

Before we conclude our account of the transactions of the reformers
of Scotland, we feel it a duty to injured innocence to give a summary
view of the treatment which Mary, their beautiful, their accomplished
queen, experienced at their hands. She was the daughter and only legitimate child of James the fifth, whom she succeeded when in the
cradle, having her mother for queen-regent. She was promised in marriage to Edward the sixth of England, but through the power of the
Hamiltons was carried into France, where she married the dauphin, afterwards Francis the second of that kingdom. While residing in France,
the pretended reformation of Scotland commenced, and her royal husband dying, she was induced to leave that kingdom, and place herself
in person on the throne of Scotland. Finding herself an unprotected
woman, surrounded by nobles heated with faction and bent on rapine
and spoil, she married Henry lord Darnley, the eldest son of the earl of
Lennox. This marriage gave considerable umbrage to the reformed
party, and a conspiracy was entered into between the lords Morton,
Murray, and Bothwell to remove Darnley, and Bothwell was to obtain
possession of the queen's person by marriage. The plot was soon put into
execution, and Darnley was blown up by gunpowder whilst he lay sick
in his bed: the queen was seized by Bothwell and carried to Dunbar
castle. Here every art was used by Bothwell to induce the helpless and
indignant Mary to consent to a union with him but in vain, and he
had recourse at last to violence by an act of ravishment. The queen
wept and lamented over the degradation thus forced upon her, and
judging it wiser to conceal her misfortune than that the scandal should
go forth to the world; considering also the helplessness of her own situation, and the powerful confederacy raised against her, she at length consented to wed the cruel and haughty Bothwell. But the cup of sorrow
for this ill-fated princess was not yet filled. She had been attached to
the religion of her forefathers from her infancy, and neither force nor
intrigue could lessen her fidelity to God. She was unalterably fixed to
her religion, and this made her the devoted victim of the villany and
perfidy of the " noble reformists," as the modern editors call the leaders
in the diabolical concerns of Scotland. They openly accused the unhappy princess of being guilty of adultery with her ravisher, of murdering Darnley her husband, in order that she might indulge with her paramour, of having concerted a plan with him for her own seizure, for
her own ravishment, and for her own marriage, as if she, the queen of
the realm, could not have married the man she wished, without either
the seizure or the rape. But this is not all. Papers and letters were
FORGED by the reforming party to convict her of these horrible and
unnatural crimes, the villany of which attempt has been most ably detected and exposed by the Rev. Mr. Whitaker, in his *Vindication of*

Mary. To such a diabolical pitch did they carry this system of *forgery*, that the queen was constrained to give directions that no orders should be taken with regard to the lord Huntley, whose death they attempted by a forged warrant, except from her very LIPS. Who, with the feelings of nature in his breast, but must sigh over the misfortunes of a woman and a queen, lovely, mild, courageous, and refined; who, when looking on her portrait the day before her execution, now to be seen at the windows of almost every print shop in the metropolis, but must loath and execrate her persecutors, who, under the cloak of religion, offered to her the grossest insults and indignities? Nor was their revenge satiated even with her death, since they sought to tarnish her unblemished life by *forged* accusations.

Speaking of this base and cruel attempt to sully the character of this virtuous Catholic princess, Mr. Whitaker exclaims, "FORGERY, I blush " for the honour of Protestantism while I write, seems to have been " *peculiar to the Reformed.* I look in vain for one of these accursed out- " rages of imposition among the disciples of Popery."—(*Vind.* vol. ii. p. 2.) This author further says, " *the infamy of forgery* was not con- " fined to Scotland at this period. It extended equally to England."— Randolph, the agent of Elizabeth at the Scottish court, had recourse to the same disgraceful means of *forging* letters in the name of lord Lennox, to induce the scottish lords to draw their swords against their sovereign, by their regard for the reformed religion. " On the detection " of them (observes Mr. Whittaker) Randolph was justly reproached " with *the profligacy of his conduct.* Nothing but the peculiarity of his " situation, as an ambassador, could have screened him from the ven- " geance due to it. Even Elizabeth was very naturally considered as an " associate in the foul act of forgery with him. He acted, no doubt, " by her directions. The peculiar boldness of his proceedings shews " it. But, indeed, Elizabeth did not attempt to vindicate herself, " from the imputation. She never disowned either the violence " or the fradulence of her embassador. She did not even recall him. " She even justified him in form upon his return, as a man of integrity, " and as a friend to Scotland. And she thus made all his forgery her own. " She had long been habituated to the sight of forgery. She had seen " it displayed in its liveliest colours, at the conferences before her com- " missioners. She had made herself a party in that grand deed of " knavery, by assisting in the deception, and by uniting to prosecute " the purpose of it. But she afterwards went further in forgery. She " rose from the humility of an accomplice, to the dignity of a chief, in " the work. The vile arts, which she had seen practised by the Scots " against their queen, she practised with more confidence, and with " less success, against the Scots themselves. And she exercised them " equally against Mary afterwards; letters forged in the name of Mary " being sent to the houses of Papists, letters forged in the name of " Papists being pretendedly intercepted on their way to Mary, and even " forged letters from Mary, concerning Babington's conspiracy, being " pretended to be found in the wall of her prison. Elizabeth had pro- " bably been taught this highest act of flagitious policy, by that trio " of the most unprincipled politicians, which human impiety perhaps " ever generated all together; Murray, Morton, and Lethington. By

A REVIEW

𝕱𝖔𝖝'𝖘 𝕭𝖔𝖔𝖐 𝖔𝖋 𝕸𝖆𝖗𝖙𝖞𝖗𝖘,

CRITICAL AND HISTORICAL.

No. 43. Printed and Published by W. E. ANDREWS, 3, Chapter-house-court, St. Paul's Churchyard, London. **Price 3d.**

EXPLANATION OF THE ENGRAVING.—*At Ypres in Flanders, the Hugonots, after cutting off the heads of the Catholic priests who fell into their hands, with savage delight amused themselves with setting up the heads of their martyred victims as marks to play at bowls.*—Theatrum Crudelitatum Hæreticorum, Antwerp, 1592.

CONTINUATION OF THE REVIEW.

" them, probably, she had been initiated into those hellish mysteries of
" iniquity. And Lethington, no doubt, was the original initiator of
" them all."..." Such, such (continues the same author) were the persons
" that presumed to call themselves reformers, to tax the wickedness of
" Popery, and to be zealous for the purity of religion ! That great fer-
" ment indeed, which was sure to be excited in the body politic of
" Christendom by the necessary efforts for reformation, naturally threw
" out to the surface, a violent eruption of morbid matter on every side.
" But FORGERY appears to have been the peculiar disease of Protest-
" antism. Originally coming forth as a kind of leprosy, upon the brow
" of Presbyterianism in Scotland, it was conveyed by the intercourses
" of vice, to the profligate head of the church of England."

FORGERY, then, it is here declared by a Protestant divine, was the
peculiar disease of Protestantism. Before Cranmer and Knox commenced reformers in England and Scotland, this system of *fraud* and

villany, was *unknown* to the whole of Christendom, and the same authority that fixes it upon those who pretended to be inspired to reform religion says, that not one single act of this infamous kind can be proved against Catholics to this day.—What then are we to think of the conduct of men who could be guilty of such base actions?—From forging letters and documents to traduce the character of a Catholic queen and rob many eminent Catholics of their property and their lives, this work of deception has been carried on and multiplied in commercial transactions, until hundreds of Protestants within the last thirty years have ended their lives in this Protestant country for it at the gallows. Oh! God! how inscrutable are thy designs! how unsearchable thy ways! But forgery was not the only means by which the "*complete reformation*" in Scotland was brought about by the endeavours of the "*noble reformists*," as the modern editors stile the actors in this work of blood and desolation. PERSECUTION, for conscience sake, was a peculiar feature in its progress.—We have repeatedly said and shewn that Catholicism was established in every country that received it by the power of persuasion and conviction only. In no instance whatever was compulsion resorted to, but in many cases it was planted in opposition to the *civil sword*, numerous martyrs having sealed their testimony of the doctrines they preached by their blood. But such was not the case with our reforming gentry, for no sooner did they obtain possession of temporal power, than they exercised the most wanton and tyrannical authority over the consciences of men, in order to *force* all descriptions of people into a *blind* and *unlimited acceptance* of their new fangled *doctrines*, which were as variable as the wind, being changed at the caprice of those who held the reins of government.—In proof that PERSECUTION was part and parcel of the reformation in Scotland, we shall here take an extract from "*The National Covenant; or the Confession of Faith:* sub-
" scribed at first by the king's majesty, and his household, in the year
" 1580; thereafter by persons of all ranks in the year 1581," &c. subscribed again by all sorts of persons in the year 1590; approved by the general assembly 1638 and 1639; subscribed again by all ranks in the latter year; ratified by an act of parliament in 1640; and subscribed by king Charles II. at Spey in 1650, and Scoon in 1651.—The edition we take the extract from was printed at Edinburgh in the year 1815, by sir D. Hunter Blair and J. Bruce, printers to the king's most excellent majesty.—It says, " Likeas many acts of parliament, not only in
" general do abrogate, annul, and rescind all laws, statutes, acts, con-
" stitutions, canons civil or municipal, with all other ordinances, and
" practique penalties whatsoever, made in prejudice of the true religion,
" and professors thereof: or of the true kirk, discipline, jurisdiction,
" and freedom thereof; or in favours of idolatry and superstition, or of
" the papistical kirk: as act 3. act 31, parl. 1. act 23. parl. 11. act 114.
" parl. 12. of king James VI. That papistry and superstition may be
" utterly suppressed, according to the intention of the acts of parlia-
" ment, repeated in the 5th act, parl. 20. king James VI. And to that
" end they ordain all papists and priests to be punished with manifold
" civil and ecclesiastical pains, as adversaries to God's true religion,
" preached, and by law established, within this realm, act 24. parl. 11.
" king James VI.; as common enemies to all Christian government,

" act 18. ...). 16. king James VI.; as rebellers and gainstanders of our
" sovereign Lord's authority, act 47. parl. 3. king James VI.; and as
" idolaters, act 104. parl. 7. king James VI. But also in particular, by
" and attour the confession of faith, do abolish and condemn the pope's
" authority and jurisdiction out of this land, and ordains the maintainers
" thereof to be punished, act 2. parl. 1. act 51. parl. 3. act 106. parl.
" 7. act 114. parl. 12. king James VI. do condemn the pope's erroneous
" doctrine, or any other erroneous doctrine repugnant to any of the
" articles of the true and Christian religion, publicly preached, and by
" law established in this realm; and ordains the spreaders and makers
" of books or libels, or letters or writs of that nature to be punished,
" act 46. parl. 3. act 106. parl. 7. act 24. parl. 11. king James VI. do
" condemn all baptism conform to the pope's kirk, and the idolatry of
" the mass: and ordains all sayers, wilful hearers, and concealers of
" the mass, the maintainers and resetters of the priests, Jesuits,
" trafficking Papists, to be punished without any exception or restriction,
" act 5. parl. 1. act 120. parl. 12. act 164. parl. 13. act 193. parl. 14.
" act 1. parl. 19. act. 5. parl. 20. king James VI. do condemn all
" erroneous books and writs containing erroneous doctrine against the
" religion presently professed, or containing superstitious rites and
" ceremonies papistical, whereby the people are greatly abused, and
" ordains the home-bringers of them to be punished, act 25. parl. 11.
" king James VI. do condemn the monuments and dregs of bygone
" idolatry, as going to crosses, observing the festival days of saints, and
" such other superstitious and papistical rites, to the dishonour of God,
" contempt of true religion, and fostering of great error among the
" people; and ordains the users of them to be punished for the second
" fault, as idolaters, act. 104. parl. 7. king James VI."

It is not to be wondered that with such fiend-like laws as these, under which a person had no alternative but either to subscribe to this
Covenant or Confession of Faith, or perish by the sword, that the reformation made great progress, especially as the leaders in the work
were very zealous in enforcing obedience to those laws.—In the *Pres-
byteries' Trial*, p. 29, it is stated, that " at the beginning men only were
" admitted to subscribe the covenant; yea shortly after the more zeal-
" ous sisters obtained that favour; and others who were not seeking
" that courtesy, got it pressed upon them. At length, it came to chil-
" dren at school, to servants, young maids, and all sorts of persons,
" without exception. And those who could not write their own names
" into the covenant, behoved to do it by public notary; so that they
" would have none to be left out of God's covenant, and the covenant
" of grace, as they spoke."—Such was the detestable tyranny of these
pretended friends of evangelical liberty, whose freedom consisted in
forcing even *children* to subscribe their covenant, who could not even
read and understand what they thus subscribed, and not only were they
made to *subscribe*, but likewise to *swear* that this *new* form of religion
was God's undoubted truth grounded only upon his written word. Nor
was this all, for those who subscribed this covenant were made also to
protest and call *the searcher of all hearts* as a *witness*, that their minds
" and hearts did fully agree with their oath and subscription, and that

" they were not moved to it by any *worldly respect :*" whereas it was
notorious that the greatest part of those who thus swore and subscribed,
" were driven to obedience by ministerial armies, which consisted at
" the beginning of Highlanders, whom the old Protestants called
" Argyle-apostles, who, by their *sacking* and *burning* of some good
" houses, *converted* more to the covenant than the ministers had done."
(*Presby. Trial,* p. 29.)—These facts sufficiently display the atrocious
persecuting spirit of the reformers in a full light; it only remains to say,
that this cruel and bloodthirsty temper was fanned and exasperated by
the horrible and furious preachings of Knox and his associates, who, like
the devil, could quote scripture for every outrage and ruffianly deed
that was committed.—But none was more subject to their rancourous
rage than the unfortunate Mary, their amiable and Catholic queen.—
She was persecuted with the most diabolical vengeance that could inflame the passions of fanatical zealots, until she ended her miserable
days on the scaffold, by order of that tigress in human shape, the *virgin*
queen Bess.—This religious princess was even denied the consolations of her religion in her last moments, and was told by a reformed
divine at her execution, " your life would be the death of our religion,
" and your death will be the life of it."—When the executioner struck
off her head, he exclaimed, holding it up, " Long live queen Elizabeth,
" and so let the *enemies of the Gospel perish !*"—But enough of these
brutalities masked by religious hypocrisy.

We have now given a succinct account of the rise of the reformation,
as it is called, in Scotland, the practices by which it was carried on, the
consequences resulting from it, and the character of the men who
headed the deforming party. We shall now close this part of our labours with observing, that the testimony we have produced, from Protestant authorities be it remembered, does not accord with the unsupported assertions of the modern editors. They state that *subscriptions*
were solicited to carry on the work of the reformation ; but Dr. Heylin
shews it was carried on by sacrilege, violence, murder, and civil war ;
neither was the reformation so completely effected as the modern editors would have their readers believe. The despotic and intolerant
combination of fury and fanaticism called the Covenant, filled the kingdom with blood and desolation, and finally caused the overthrow of the
constitution in church and state, as well as the violent death of the sovereign, Charles the first. And are we in these days to have the rebellions, the devastations, the persecutions, and the wild enthusiasm of the
madbrained Covenanters held up as examples of praise and commendation? Surely the modern editors are like the Jews who crucified their
Saviour, not knowing what they did. Whether what we have here said
will open their eyes, and cause them to see their folly, not to say their
infamy, because we are willing to believe they are ignorant of the mischief they are doing, is more than we can say ; but we do flatter ourselves that the Protestant of liberal mind will see the motives which induced the pretended reformers of Scotland to shake off their obedience
to the church of Rome in their true light, and appreciate the merit or
infamy due to their actions.

PROGRESS OF THE REFORMATION IN ENGLAND,

IN THE REIGN OF EDWARD VI.

The modern editors commence this interesting period of the reformation with an account taken from Burnet of the qualities of the young king, who is represented as having "discovered very early a good dis-" position to religion and virtue, and a particular reverence for the " scriptures ; and was once greatly offended with a person, who, in or-" der to reach something hastily, laid a great Bible on the floor, and " stood upon it." This story may do for bible-readers, but we see very little probability that a person would make such use of a book, or that a child so young should take upon himself to chide his elder. We are next told that dissensions soon arose among the sixteen governors named in Harry's will to have the care of the young king's person, and that these dissensions were no more than what might have been expected. The lord Chancellor Wriothesley imagined that he would be placed, in virtue of his office, as head of the commission of sixteen, but by cunning and intrigue the earl of Hertford, afterwards duke of Somerset, the king's uncle, was declared governor of the king's person and protector of the kingdom. Thus he who had set so many wills and testaments aside to gratify his inordinate lust and ambition, had his own will disregarded and treated with as little ceremony as he had treated others. This appointment, we are next told, occasioned two parties to be formed, " the one headed by the protector, and the other by the chancellor: " the favourers of the reformation were of the former, and those that " opposed it of the latter." The consequences of this division in the government we shall see in the course of our review.

The first thing done, after the appointment of the protector, was the renewing of the commissions of the judges and other state officers, and among the rest the bishops, who came and took out commissions, by which they were *to hold their bishoprics only during the king's pleasure!!* Gentle reader! what do you think of these men, these pretended ministers of religion, who could thus submit to be the slaves, the obsequious tools of the faction in power? Cranmer, of whom we have had occasion to say so much, led the way in this work of degradation, and Burnet, another bishop of the established church, says, " this check upon the " bishops was judged *expedient* in case they should *oppose* the reforma-" tion;" that is, in case they should oppose the rapacity of the greedy courtiers, who were bent upon fleecing the church of what Harry had left. We are next told that " an accident soon occurred which made " way for great changes in the church. The curate and churchwardens " of St. Martin's in London, were brought before the council for re-" moving the crucifix, and other images, and putting some texts of " scripture on the walls of their church, in the places where they stood; " they answered, that in repairing their church they had removed the " images, which being rotten they did not renew them, but put the " words of scripture in their room : they had also removed others, " which they found had been abused to idolatry. Great pains were " taken by the Popish party to punish them severely, in order to strike " a terror into others; but Cranmer was for the removing of all images

" set up in churches, as being expressly contrary both to the second
" commandment, and the practice of the purest Christians for many
" ages: and though, in compliance with the gross abuses of Paganism,
" much of the pomp of their worship was very early brought into the
" Christian church, yet it was long before images were introduced. At
" first all images were condemned by the fathers; then they allowed
" the use, but condemned the worshipping of them; and afterwards, in
" the eighth and ninth centuries, the worshipping of them was, after a
" long contest, both in the East and West, at last generally received.
" Some, in particular, were believed to be more wonderfully endowed,
" and this was much improved by the cheats of the monks, who had
" enriched themselves by such means. And this abuse had now grown
" to such a height, that heathenism itself had not been guilty of greater
" absurdities towards its idols. Since all these abuses had risen out of
" the use of them, and the setting them up being contrary to the com-
" mand of God, and the nature of the Christian religion, which is sim-
" ple and spiritual, it seemed most reasonable to cure the disease in its
" root, and to clear the churches of images, that the people might be
" preserved from idolatry.

" These reasons prevailed so far, that the curate and churchwardens
" were dismissed with a reprimand; they were ordered to beware of
" such rashness for the future, and to provide a crucifix, and, till that
" could be had, were ordered to cause one to be painted on the wall.
" Upon this, Dr. Ridley, in a sermon preached before the king, inveighed
" against the superstition towards images and holy-water, and spread
" over the whole nation a general disposition to pull them down; which
" soon after commenced in Portsmouth.

" Upon this, Gardiner made great complaints; he said, the Luther-
" ans themselves went not so far, for he had seen images in their
" churches. He distinguished between image and idol, as if the one,
" which, he said, only was condemned, was the representation of a false
" God, and the other of the true; and he thought, that as words con-
" veyed by the ear begat devotion, so images, by the conveyance of
" the eye, might have the same effect on the mind. He also thought a
" virtue might be both in them and in holy-water, as well as there was
" in Christ's garments, Peter's shadow, or Elisha's staff: and there
" might be a virtue in holy-water, as well as in the water of baptism.
" To these arguments, which Gardiner wrote in several letters, the pro-
" tector answered, that the bishops had formerly argued much in an-
" other strain, namely, that because the scriptures were abused by the
" vulgar readers, therefore they were not to be trusted to them; and
" so made a pretended abuse the ground of taking away that which, by
" God's special appointment, was to be delivered to all Christians. This
" held much stronger against images forbidden by God. The brazen
" serpent set up by Moses, by God's own direction, was broken when
" abused to idolatry; for that was the greatest corruption of religion
" possible: but yet the protector acknowledged there was reason to
" complain of the forwardness of the people, who broke down images
" without authority: to prevent which, in future, orders were sent to
" the justices of the peace to look well to the peace and government of
" the nation."—(*Book of Martyrs,* pp. 349, 350.)

It is necessary to notice the assertions here made by Burnet, with a view to delude his readers on the doctrine of venerating and using images in churches, and to screen the sacrilegious rapine of the reformers, who pillaged the shrines and altars to glut their own avarice. Cranmer, it is admitted, took the lead in this matter, as we have proved him heading every other measure of iniquity and outrage. He is stated to have grounded his advice for removing all the images set up in churches, as being contrary both to the second commandment, and the practice of the purest ages of Christianity. That "all images were " condemned by the fathers, then the *use* of them was allowed, but the " *worshipping* of them was condemned." That abuses arose, and " had " now grown to such a height, that heathenism itself had not been " guilty of greater absurdities towards its idols." This is mere gratuitous assertion, unaccompanied by a single fact. The practice of using images is coeval with Christianity, and the worshipping or reverencing them was never condemned by the early fathers, but, on the contrary, the fathers wrote in defence of this doctrine. St. Gregory of Nyssa, who died late in the fourth century, and consequently lived in that age when Protestants admit the Christian church to have been pure, thus speaks to his audience, when celebrating the feast of the martyr Theodorus :—" When any one enters such a place as this, where the memory " of this just man and his relics are preserved, his mind is first struck " —while he views the structure and all its ornaments—with the gene- " ral magnificence that breaks upon him. The artist has here shewn " his skill in the figures of animals, and the airy sculpture of the stone; " while the painter's hand is most conspicuous in delineating the high " achievements of the martyr; his torments; the savage forms of his " executioners; their furious efforts; the burning furnace; and the " happy consummation of the laborious contest. The figure of Chris " is also beheld, looking down upon the scene. Thus, as in a book the " letters convey the history, so do the colours describe the conflict of " the martyr, and give the beauty of a flowery mead to the walls of our " temple. The picture, though silent, speaks, and gives instruction to " the beholder ; nor is the mosaic pavement, which we tread on, less " instructive."—(*Orat. de Theod. Martyr.* t. ii. p. 1011.)

The Book of Martyrs says, the worshipping of images was generally received in the eighth and ninth centuries, after a long contest. This is an allusion to the heresy of the Iconoclasts or image destroyers, which was opposed by all the prelates of the Catholic church, and, like all other heresies, when possessed of the civil sword, was supported by brute force and persecution. The founder of this sect was the emperor Leo III. sprung from a plebeian family in Isauria. He, like the reformers in our Edward's reign, sent forth an edict, ordering the images of our Saviour, and his virgin mother, and the saints, to be removed out of the churches under the severest penalties. This extraordinary declaration against the *universal* practice of the Catholic church excited murmurs and discontent at Constantinople, the seat of the empire. St. Germain, the patriarch of that see, tried by mild persuasion to disabuse the emperor of his error, and represented to him, that from the time of the apostles this relative honour had been paid to the images of Christ and his blessed mother. Leo was ignorant and obstinate, he commanded·

all the images and pictures to be collected and burned. The people resisted, and by an imperial order were massacred without mercy. St. Germain was driven into banishment, and a temporising priest, another Cranmer, was thrust into his place. This took place in the year 729. The holy pope Gregory III. on coming to the papal chair, wrote a long epistle to the emperor, exhorting him to desist from his unholy purposes, and among other things he tells him, " Our churches in their " rude state are but the work of the builders, a rough fabric of stone, " of wood, of brick, of lime, and mortar. But within they are adorned " with rich paintings; with historical representations of Jesus Christ " and his saints. On these the converted gentiles, the neophytes, and " children of the faithful gaze with no less profit than delight. In these " they behold the mysteries of our religion displayed before their eyes ; " by these they are animated to the practice of virtue, and silently " taught to raise their affections and hearts to God. But of these ex- " ternal helps to virtue and religious information you have deprived the " faithful, you have profanely stript the churches of their sacred orna- " ments, which so much contributed to edify, to instruct, and animate. " In doing this you have usurped a power which God has not given to " the sceptre. The empire and the priesthood have their respective " powers, differing from each other in their use and object. As it be- " longs not to the bishop to govern within the palace, and to distribute " civil dignities, so it does not belong to the emperor to command " within the church, or to assume a spiritual jurisdiction, which Christ " has left solely to the ministers of his altar. Let each one of us move " and remain within the sphere to which he is called, as the apostle ad- " monishes."—(*Reeve's Hist. of the Church*, vol. ii. p. 9.)

This emperor, however, continued the persecution whilst he lived, and his son Constantine Copronymus, when he mounted the throne, exceeded his father's barbarity, and extended the persecution through all the provinces. After a cruel reign of thirty-four years, Constantine was seized by death, and his son Leo followed his steps in harassing the church during the five years that he reigned. He was succeeded by his wife the empress Irene, who, being a Catholic, gave peace to the church, and by her desire a council was called by pope Adrian, which assembled at Nice, on the 24th of September, 787. It consisted of 377 bishops from Greece, Thrace, Natolia, the islands of the Archipelago, Sicily, and Italy. The prelates thus assembled were occupied in examining the fathers, the conduct of the Iconoclasts, and the objections made against the practice of venerating images. In the seventh session of the synod the bishops came to the following decision :—" After mature delibera- " tion and discussion, we solemnly declare, that holy pictures and images, " especially of Jesus Christ our Lord and Saviour, of his immaculate " Mother our Lady, of the angels and other saints, are to be set up in " churches as well as in other places, that at the sight of them the " faithful may remember what they represent; that they are to be ve- " nerated and honoured, not indeed with that supreme honour and " worship, which is called Latria, and belongs to God alone, but with " a relative and inferior honour, such as is paid to the cross, to the " gospel, and other holy things, by the use of incense or of burning " lights. For the honour paid to images passes to the architypes or

" things represented, and he who reveres the image, reveres the person
" it represents. Such has been the practice of our pious forefathers,
" such is the tradition of the Catholic church transmitted to us, this
" ecclesiastical tradition we closely hold conformably to the injunction
" given by St. Paul to the Thessalonians."—(2 *Thess.* c. ii. v. 14.) The
decree was published and received with loud acclamations by the people; Iconoclasm died away, and was heard of no more, till the reformers
of the sixteenth century thought fit to revive it with many other pernicious doctrines, that entailed misery upon the people where happiness
before reigned. To shew the concurrent belief of the Catholic church
in all ages on this ancient practice, we will here give the decree of the
council of Trent, which sat at the same period when the work of devastation was going forward in England, by comparing which with the
sentiments of Gregory III. and the council of Nice, the reader will see
that the doctrine of the Catholic church is invariable, and that what
was taught in the eighth century was grounded on the universal practice
of the church from the time of the apostles, as it was in the sixteenth
century, and is now at the present day. The council of Trent decreed,
" That images of Christ, of the blessed Virgin, and of other saints, are
" to be exposed and retained particularly in churches, and that due
" honour and veneration are to be shown them; not as believing that
" any divinity or virtue is in them, for which they should be honoured;
" or that any thing is to be asked of them, or any trust be placed in
" them, as the Gentiles once did in their idols: but because the honour
" given to pictures is referred to the prototypes, which they represent;
" so that through the images, which we kiss, and before which we
" uncover our heads, and kneel, we may learn to adore Christ, and to
" venerate his saints."—(*Sess.* xxv. *de Invocat. SS.* p. 289.) Having
thus clearly established the doctrinal part of the subject, we may now
proceed to examine the motives which induced the reformers of the
sixteenth century to adopt the violent measures of the Iconoclasts of the
eighth, or, as Burnet says, " to clear the churches of images, that the
" *people* might be PRESERVED from idolatry."

But though, as Burnet would make us believe, the advisers of the
youthful Edward were anxious to preserve the people from idolatry,
they were not so feelingly alive to preserve for them those civil privi-
vileges which had hitherto made them a free and happy nation. Of
this, however, we have not a word in the modern *Book of Martyrs*; it is
therefore necessary that we should supply the omission. The object of
the modern editors is to mislead the public mind, and excite *hatred*
against the Catholics and their religion; ours is to elucidate the truth,
and, by removing the veil of ignorance which has so long clouded the
Protestant mind, dissipate those groundless prejudices which interested
bigots have so long kept alive against the professors of the ancient faith
of the kingdom. While the chief reformers were hypocritically exclaiming against idolatry, or the use of images in churches, they were
worshipping and paying adoration to the mammon of iniquity, and contriving means how to aggrandize themselves both in titles and estates.
Though Harry's will was in some respects wholly disregarded, in others
it was made to sanction the schemes of ambition which the factious
leaders meditated. Set a beggar on horseback, and it is said he will

ride to the devil; the same we may say of the prominent characters who ruled under Edward VI. Of the sixteen individuals named as executors to the late king's will, it was remarked that they were men hitherto but little known, having no claim to high birth, but raised to their present rank by the partiality of Harry, and their readiness to pander to his vices. Of their moral character some estimate may be formed from the fact, that after having solemnly sworn to see the last will and testament of their late master scrupulously fulfilled, they almost immediately absolved themselves from the obligation of that oath, to comply with the ambitious projects of the protector Hertford. In another point of view, however, where their personal interests were concerned, they took care that nothing should be neglected that could help their own aggrandizement. In the body of Henry's will, there was a clause charging the executors with ratifying every gift, and performing every promise which he should have made before his death. Here was a sweeping charge, which it was resolved to turn to the best account. Dr. Lingard, in his History of England, says,—" What these " gifts and promises might be, must, it was presumed, be known to " Paget, Herbert, and Denny, who had stood high in the confidence, and " been constantly in the chamber of the dying monarch. These gen-" tlemen were therefore interrogated before their colleagues: and from " their depositions it was inferred, that the king had intended to give a " dukedom to Hertford, to create the earl of Essex, his queen's brother, " a marquess, to raise the viscount Lisle, and lord Wriothesley to the " higher rank of earls, and to confer the title of baron on sir Thomas " Seymour, sir Richard Rich, sir John St. Leger, sir William Willough-" by, sir Edward Sheffield, and sir Christoper Danby: and that, to enable " the new peers to support their respective titles, he had destined for " Hertford an estate in land of 800*l.* per annum, with a yearly pension " of 300*l.* from the first bishopric, which should become vacant, and the " incomes of a treasurership, a deanery, and six prebends, in different " Cathedrals: for each of the others a proportionate increase of yearly " income; and for the three deponents, Paget, Herbert, and Denny, " 400 pounds, 400 marks, and 200 pounds. Two out of the number, " St. Leger and Danby, had sufficient virtue to refuse the honours and " revenues which were allotted to them: Hertford was created duke of " Somerset, Essex marquess of Northampton, Lisle earl of Warwick, " Wriothesley earl of Southampton, and Seymour, Rich, Willoughby " and Sheffield, barons of the same name: and to all these, with the " exception of the two last, and to Cranmer, Paget, Herbert, and Denny, " and more than thirty other persons, were assigned in different pro-" portions manors and lordships out of the lands, which had belonged " to the dissolved monasteries, or still belonged to the existing bishop-" rics. But sir Thomas Seymour was not satisfied: as uncle of the king " he aspired to office no less than rank: and to appease his discontent " the new earl of Warwick resigned in his favour the patent of high " admiral, and was indemnified with that of great chamberlain, which " Somerset had exchanged for the dignities of lord high treasurer, and " earl marshal, forfeited by the attainder of the duke of Norfolk.—" These proceedings did not pass without severe animadversion. Why, " it was asked, were not the executors content with the authority which

" they derived from the will of their late master? Why did they re-
" ward themselves beforehand, instead of waiting till their young sove-
" reign should be of age, when he might recompense their services
" according to their respective merits?" Thus the reader will see that
though the crime of idolatry is represented as having touched the consciences of these menders of religion, they were not averse to the crimes
of self-aggrandizement, robbery, and sacrilege. We should have
added forgery too; for the same historian remarks, that though the
clause to the above effect appears in the body of the will, yet it is somewhat mysterious that it should be ordered, as the deponents testified,
to be inserted only when the king was on his death-bed, that is, about
January the 28th, and the will purports to be executed three weeks before, on the 30th of December.

We must now notice the funeral of Henry. The ceremony was performed with very great pomp, and while the body lay in state at
Whitehall, MASSES were said every day, so that it is as clear as the
sun at noon-day, that though Protestants are now compelled, in order
to qualify for civil office, to *swear* that the mass is idolatry, yet Cranmer,
and all the crew of reformers at the beginning of Edward's reign, as
well as the reign of the first pope of the English church, believed in and
followed the doctrine and practice of this great sacrifice. The king
himself, by his will left 600l. a year for masses to be said for the repose
of his soul, but this part of his will was soon violated and the money
appropriated to other purposes, as he had impiously deprived others of
the same religious benefit. Next followed the coronation of the young
king, the ceremony of which was much shortened, and an alteration was
made of so important a nature that we shall give the relation in Dr.
Lingard's words. "That the delicate health of the young king," says
the historian, "might not suffer from fatigue, the accustomed ceremony
" was considerably abridged: and, under respect for the laws and con-
" stitution of the realm, on important alteration was introduced into
" that part of the form, which had been devised by our Saxon ances-
" tors, to put the new sovereign in mind that he held his crown by the
" free choice of the nation. Hitherto it had been the custom for the
" archbishop, first to receive the king's oath to preserve the liberties of
" the realm, and then to ask the people if they were willing to accept
" him, and obey him as their liege lord. Now the order was inverted:
" and not only did the address to the people precede the oath of the
" king, but in that very address they were reminded, that he held his
" crown by descent, and that it was their duty to submit to his rule.—
" 'Sirs,' said the metropolitan, 'I here present king Edward, rightful
" and undoubted inheritor, by the laws of God and man, to the royal
" dignity and crown imperial of this realm, whose consecration, inunc-
" tion, and coronation, is appointed by all the nobles and peers of the
" land to be this day. Will ye serve at this time, and give your good
" wills and assents to the same consecration, inunction, and coronation,
" as by your duty of allegiance ye be bound to do?' When the accla-
" mations of the spectators had subsided, the young Edward took the
" accustomed oath, first on the sacrament, and then on the book of the
" gospels. He was next anointed, after the ancient form: the protector
" and the archbishop placed on his head successively three crowns,

" emblematic of the three kingdoms of England, France, and Ireland;
" and the lords and prelates first did homage two by two, and then in
" a body promised fealty on their knees. Instead of a sermon, Cranmer
" pronounced a short address to the new sovereign, telling him that the
" promises which he had just made, could not affect his right to sway
" the sceptre of his dominions. That right he, like his predecessors,
" had derived from God : whence it followed, that neither the bishop
" of Rome, nor any other bishop, could impose conditions on him at his
" coronation, nor pretend to deprive him of his crown on the plea that
" he had broken his coronation oath. Yet these solemn rites served to
" admonish him of his duties, which were, ' as God's vicegerent, and
" Christ's vicar, to see that God be. worshipped, and idolatry be de-
" stroyed; that the tyranny of the bishop of Rome be banished, and
" images be removed : to reward virtue, and revenge vice; to justify
" the innocent, and relieve the poor; to repress violence, and execute
" justice. Let him do this, and he would become a second Josias, whose
" fame would remain to the end of days.' The ceremony was concluded
" with a solemn high mass, sung by the archbishop."

Here we have Cranmer again upon the carpet. We see him not only
teaching the young king to look upon himself as holding the sceptre by
divine right, and authorized to *persecute* for *religious opinions*, but we also
see him celebrating that august sacrifice of the mass, which had been
offered up ever since the introduction of Christianity, but which was
soon after to be abolished, and by the instrumentality of this very
archbishop. Thus, then, to Cranmer, who is so much extolled by the
liberty-loving disciples of the reformation, we may lay the loss, in the
first instance, of those fundamental principles of civil freedom which
distinguishes the genuine constitution of our country, and the conduct
of our forefathers when Catholics, and the origin of those bitter grievances which the people have suffered from misrule and faction. Burnet,
who is the trumpeter of Cranmer, speaks of this deviation for the first
time from the form devised by our Saxon ancestors, as a matter of
common place, though he acknowledges the alteration to have been a
" remarkable" one. He says, " that formerly the king used to be pre-
" sented to the people at the corner of the scaffold, and they were
" asked, if they would have him to be their king? Which looked like
" a right of an election, rather than a ceremony of investing one that
" was already king. This was now changed, and *the people* were *desired*
" only to give assent and good will to his coronation, as by *duty of*
" *allegiance* they were bound to do." This is the language of a church-
of-England bishop, and one too who was raised to that dignity by William the Dutchman, who came over to this country to dethrone his
father-in-law, having married James the second's eldest daughter Mary,
and was placed on the English throne during the life time of James,
not, indeed, by divine right, but by the consent of the people, who in
Edward's reign, we are told by this bishop, had only to give their assent
to the *coronation* as by duty of allegiance they were bound to do. Such
was the regard which Cranmer, in the first instance, and Burnet, after
him, had for the rights and privileges of the people.

We must now return again to the modern *Book of Martyrs*, or rather
to *Burnet's Abridgement,* from which the editors have selected their ac-

count. In order to justify the work of desolation which followed the coronation of Edward the sixth, Burnet makes the following remarks on the Catholic doctrine of praying for the dead.   " The pomp of this en-" dowment (alluding to Henry's bequest for daily masses for his soul) " led people to examine into the *usefulness* of *soul-masses* and *obits*. " Christ appointed the *sacrament* for a commemoration of his death " among *the living*, but it was not *easy to conceive* how that was to be " applied to *departed souls*; and it was evidently a project for drawing " *the wealth of the world into their hands*. In the *primitive* church there " was *a commemoration of the dead*, or an *honourable remembrance* of " them made in the *daily offices*. But even this custom grew *into abuse*, " and some *inferred* from it, that departed souls, unless they were sig-" nally pure, passed through a purgation in the next life, before they " were admitted to heaven; of which St. Austin, *in whose time the opi-" nion began to be received*, says, that it was taken up *without any sure* " *ground in scripture*. But what was wanting in scripture-proof was " supplied by *visions*, *dreams*, and *tales*, till it was *generally received*. " King Henry had acted like one who did not much *believe it*, for he " had deprived innumerable souls of the masses that were said for them " in monasteries, by destroying those foundations. Yet he seems to " have intended, that if masses could avail the departed souls, he would, " himself be secure; and as he *gratified the priests* by this part of his " endowment, so he *pleased the people* by appointing sermons and *alms* " to be given on such days. Thus he died as he had lived, wavering be-" tween both persuasions." The modern editors have here cut off the pa-ragraph, which goes on thus, " And it occasioned no small debate, when " men sought to find out what his opinions were in the controverted " points of religion: for the *esteem* he was in, made both sides study " to justify themselves, by seeming to follow his sentiments; the one " party said, he was resolved never to alter religion, but only to cut off " some abuses, and intended to go no further than he had gone. They " did therefore vehemently press the others to innovate nothing, but to " keep things in the state in which he left them, till his son should " come of age. But the opposite party said, that he had resolved to go " a great way further, and particularly to turn the mass to a commu-" nion; and therefore religion being of such consequence to the salva-" tion of souls, it was necessary to make all the haste in reformation " that was fitting and decent."

This is Burnet's account to cover the shameful robberies that preced-ed and accompanied the famous or rather infamous reformation of which he was the historian.—Burnet was a bishop as well as a writer, but his sacred character did not prevent him from being as great a liar and falsifier as ever sat down to write for the purpose of deception.—We have proved in the first volume of this Review, from the testimony of the fathers, that Christ appointed the Eucharist to be *a sacrifice* as well as *a sacrament*; that there was a commemoration daily made in the mass for the dead as well as the living, in the primitive church; and that there was no difficulty among the faithful, in the pure ages of the church, nor is there any now, to conceive how the merits of Christ in the mass are applied to departed souls.—But it is insinuated that the project of *soul-masses* and *obits* or *anniversaries*, was evidently broached for the purpose of drawing the wealth of the world into their hands. This insinuation comes with a bad grace from a bishop of the established church, whose brethren draw a great deal of wealth by their vocation without doing much for it. Burnet forgot, or at least he did not wish his readers should know, the vast works of charity that were performed by the Catholic clergy through the revenues they derived from this custom of soul-masses; whereas, if we look to what has been done by the Protestant clergy since the change of religion, we shall find little for them to boast of.—It is notorious that all the beautiful churches, all the noble hospitals, the magnificent monasteries, the colleges and halls of the universities, the public schools, and, in fact, every public building of utility and ornament, were chiefly raised by the revenues of the church, aided by the donations of pious lay men and women. Not a farthing was contributed through compulsory means; the statute book in Catholic times does not contain one single clause imposing a tax upon the people to support those noble works of our forefathers, while it is notorious that numbers of the beautiful edifices were destroyed by the reformers, others were converted into profane uses, and even at this day the people, though taxed to the utmost to support a debt caused by a profligate and ruinous war, are compelled to pay an impost towards erecting new churches, the old ones having been suffered to fall into decay.—The doctrines of purgatory, Burnet says, began to be received about the time of St. Austin; this is a thumping lie, for St. Basil, long before St. Austin lived, maintained this doctrine, and Fox called him "the pillar of truth." (See Review, vol. i. p. 171.) But let St. Augustin speak for himself, and then let the reader decide whether he said, as this lying bishop asserts, "that it (the doctrine of purgatory) was taken up without any " sure ground in scripture." This great luminary of the Catholic church writes thus: " Before the most severe and last judgment, some " undergo temporal punishments in this life; some after death; and " others both now and then. But not all that suffer after death, are " condemned to eternal flames. What is not expiated in this life, to " some is remitted in the life to come, so that they may escape eternal " punishment." De Cevit. Dei. L. xxi. c. xiii. T. v. p. 1432.—"The " prayers of the church and of some good persons are heard in favour " of those Christians, who departed this life, not so bad as to be deemed " unworthy of mercy, nor so good as to be entitled to immediate happi " ness. So also, at the resurrection of the dead, there will some be " found, to whom mercy will be imparted, having gone through those " pains, to which the spirits of the dead are liable. Otherwise it would " not have been said of some with truth, that their sin shall not be for " given, neither in this world, nor in the world to come, (Matt. xii. 32.) " unless some sins were remitted in the next world." Ibid. c. xxiv. p. " 1446.—" It cannot be thought, that the souls of the dead are not re " lieved by the piety of the living, when the sacrifice of our Mediator is " offered for them, or alms are distributed in the church. They are " benefited, who so lived, as to have deserved such favours. For there " is a mode of life, not so perfect as not to require this assistance, nor " so bad as to be incapable of receiving aid.—The practice of the church " in recommending the souls of the departed, is not contrary to the de " claration of the apostle, which says: We must all appear before the

"*judgment-seat of Christ, that every one may receive the proper things of*
"*the body, according as he hath done, whether it be good or evil:* (2 Cor.
" v. 10.) For this merit each one, in his life, has acquired, to be aided
" by the good works of the living. But all are not aided : and why so ?
" Because all have not lived alike. When therefore the sacrifice of the
" altar or alms are offered for the dead ; in regard to those whose lives
" were very good, such offices may be deemed acts of thanksgiving ;
" acts of propitiation for the imperfect ; and though to the wicked they
" bring no aid, they may give some comfort to the living." *Enchirid.*
" *c. cx. T.* iii. p. 83.—" *Lord chastise me not in thy anger ; may I not be*
" numbered with those, to whom thou wilt say : *Go into eternal fire,*
" *which hath been prepared for the devil and his angels.* Cleanse me so
" in this life, make me such, that I may not stand in need of that puri-
" fying fire, designed for those who shall *be saved, yet so as by fire.*
" And why, but because, (as the apostle says) they have *built upon the*
" *foundation. wood, hay, and stubble ?* If they had built *gold and silver,*
" *and precious stones,* they would be secured from both fires ; not only
" from that in which the wicked shall be punished for ever, but like-
" wise from that fire which will purify those who shall be saved by
" fire. But because it is said, *he shall be saved,* that fire is thought
" lightly of ; though the suffering will be more grievous than any thing
" man can undergo in this life." *In Psal.* xxxvii. *T.* viii. p. 127.—" It
" cannot be doubted, that, by the prayers of the holy church, and by
" the salutary sacrifice, and by alms which are given for the repose of
" their souls, the dead are helped ; so that God may treat them more
" mercifully, than their sins deserved. This the whole church observes,
" which it received from the tradition of the fathers, to pray for those
" who died in the communion of the body and blood of Christ, when,
" in their turn, they are commemorated at the sacrifice, and it is then
" announced, that the sacrifice is offered for them." *De verbis Apostoli,*
" *Serm.* xxxii. *T.* x. p. 154.—" We read in the second book of Maccabees,
" (xii. 43.) that sacrifice was offered for the dead ; but though, in the
" old Testament, no such words had been found, the authority of the
" universal church must suffice, whose practice is incontrovertible. When
" the priest at the altar offers up prayers to God, he recommends in
" them the souls of the departed.—When the mind, sometimes, recol-
" lects, that the body of his friend has been deposited near the tomb of
" some martyr, he fails not, in prayer, to recommend the soul to that
" blessed saint ; not doubting, that succour may thence be derived.—
" Such suffrages must not be neglected, which the church performs in
" general words, that they may be benefited, who have no parents, nor
" children, nor relations, nor friends." *De cura pro Mortuis. c.* i, iv. *T.*
" p. 288—290.—The same sentiment is repeated through the whole
treatise, and we now leave it to the unbiassed Protestant to decide
whether there was any difficulty among Catholic fathers and divines
and people to conceive how the efficacy of the mass was applied to departed souls.

We must allow that Henry acted like one that did not believe it, by
his depriving so many souls of the benefit conferred by this Christian
and divine sacrifice ; but Harry was then blinded by his passions as
Burnet was by his interests ; but when Henry came to the last point,

and death was standing before him, he knew too well the value of this religious consolation to reject it at such an awful moment, though the Almighty so ordered that he should derive little or no advantage from it. In the passage we have added, and the modern editors suppressed, Burnet would persuade us that the monster in cruelty, Henry, was held *in esteem* by both parties. But where was the proof of this regard to the deceased tyrant when his last will was neglected almost as soon as the breath had left his body? One party said he resolved never to alter religion, and yet it is very well known that he *did* alter it. The other party contended that he had resolved " to go *a great way further, and particularly* to turn the *mass* into a *communion,*" and therefore " it was necessary to make all the haste in reformation that was fitting and decent."—Well said, Gilbert Burnet; but what authority have you for this statement? If Harry intended to have turned the mass into a communion, would he have left such a sum of money as he did by his last will, to have masses said for the repose of his soul? Come, Gilbert, get over this awkward predicament. No, no; it was not the people who began to be inquisitive into the *usefulness* of *soul-masses,* but the factious leaders in the work of reformation, who cast their longing eyes on the goods of the church, which had escaped the rapacity of the pre- ceding reign, and which they coveted the usefulness of for their own private gain. This it was that made them in such *haste* to commence the *change* in religion, which you, Gilbert Burnet, represent as being " of such consequence to the salvation of souls!"—Let us now have an account of their proceedings from the *Book of Martyrs.* It says, " The nation was in an ill condition for a war with such a mighty prince; "—labouring under great distractions at home; the people generally " crying out for a reformation, *despising the clergy,* and *loving the new* " *preachers.* The priests were, for the most part, very ignorant, and " scandalous in their lives; many of them had been monks, and those " who were to pay them the pensions which were reserved to them at " the destruction of the monasteries, till they should be provided, took " care to get them into some small benefice. The greatest part of the " parsonages were impropriated, for they belonged to the monasteries, " and the abbots had only granted the incumbents either the vicarage, " or some small donative, and left them the perquisites raised by masses " and other offices. At the suppression of those houses there was no " care taken to make provision for the incumbents; so that they were " in some measure compelled to continue in their idolatrous practices " for subsistence.

" Now these persons saw that a reformation of those abuses would " deprive them of their means of existence; and, therefore, they were " at first zealous against all changes; but the same principle made them " comply with every change which was made, rather than lose their " benefices. The clergy were encouraged in their opposition to the re- " formation by the protection they expected from Gardiner, Bonner, and " Tonstall, men of great reputation, and in power; and, above all, the " lady Mary, the next heir to the crown, openly declared against all " changes till the king should be of age.

" On the other hand, Cranmer resolved to proceed more vigourously: " the protector was firmly united to him, as were the young king's tu-

A REVIEW

OF

Fox's Book of Martyrs,

CRITICAL AND HISTORICAL.

No. 44. Printed and Published by W. E. Andrews, 3, Chapter-house-court, St. Paul's Churchyard, London. Price 3d.

EXPLANATION OF THE ENGRAVING.—*John Hieronymus, with several other Catholics, being led captive by the Hugonots to a place called Scagen in the northern part of Holland, they were subjected to the most horrid tortures. Some were bound, inverted vessels were placed over their naked bellies, in which living mice of a ferocious nature were confined; fires were enkindled over the vessels, by which the mice were excited to gnaw and perforate the bodies of the suffering victims with their teeth, and work themselves into them, by which unparalleled torments these innocent martyrs yielded up their souls to God.*

CONTINUATION OF THE REVIEW.

" tors, and Edward himself was as much engaged as could be expected
" from so young a person; for both his knowledge and zeal for true
" religion were above his age. Several of the bishops also declared for
" a reformation, but Ridley, bishop of Rochester, was the person on
" whom Cranmer most depended. Latimer remained with him at Lam-
" beth, and did great service by his sermons, which were very popular;
" but he would not return to his bishopric, choosing rather to serve the
" church in a more disengaged manner. Assisted by these persons,
" Cranmer resolved to proceed by degrees, and to give the reasons of
" every advance so fully, that he hoped, by the blessing of God, to con-
" vince the nation of the fitness of whatsoever should be done, and
" thereby prevent the dangerous opposition that might otherwise be
" apprehended."

We have here some more of Gilbert's thumpers, but before we proceed to examine them, we must notice a trifling liberty the modern editors have taken with their text. We have more than once informed the reader that this account of the "progress of the reformation," in the modern *Book of Martyrs*, is taken from Gilbert Burnet's "Abridgement of the History of the Reformation," &c. We have compared the above quotation with the original work now before us, and we find that Burnet thus speaks of Cranmer. "But on the other hand Cranmer, "WHOSE GREATEST WEAKNESS WAS HIS OVER-OBSEQUI- "OUSNESS TO KING HENRY, BEING NOW AT LIBERTY, "resolved to proceed more vigorously." Now, if the reader will turn to the last paragraph of the quotation, it will be seen that all the words we have put in capital letters have been omitted by the modern editors. So, then, these exciters of hatred against Popery were ashamed of the obsequiousness of their own dear Tom Cranmer, whose slavish compliance, under every circumstance, to the will of Henry, could not be passed over uncensured even by his greatest flatterer, Gilbert Burnet. Well, but Tom was *now at liberty* to set about the godly work of reformation, and it is time to see how he went to business. We are told that he "resolved to proceed by degrees," so that the nation might be convinced "of the fitness of whatsoever should be done." The first proceeding, we are informed, was an order for "a general visitation of all "the churches in England, which was divided into six precincts: and "two gentlemen, a civilian, a divine, and a register, were appointed "for each of these. But before they were sent out, a letter was writ- "ten to all the bishops, giving them notice of it, suspending their juris- "diction while it lasted, and requiring them to preach no where but in "their cathedrals, and that the other clergy should not preach but in "their own churches, without licence; by which it was intended to "restrain such as were not acceptable, to their own parishes, and to "grant the others licences to preach in any church of England. The "*greatest difficulty the reformers found,* was in the *want of able* and *pru-* "*dent men;* most of the reformed preachers being *too hot* and *indiscreet,* "and the few who were otherwise, were required in London and the "universities." Here we have more disclosures not very creditable to the performers in this scene of civil and religious innovation. The commissioners were appointed by the privy council, and consisted of laymen as well as divines. These commissioners, on their arrival in any diocess, assumed the spiritual authority over the bishop himself, who was not allowed to preach any where but in his own cathedral, and the other clergy were prohibited from preaching without *license.* The commissioners further summoned the bishops, the clergy, and householders before them, and not only compelled them to take the oaths of allegiance and supremacy, but also to answer such questions on oath as might be put to them. Here was a comfortable state of freedom for Englishmen to enjoy! But they had renounced the tyranny of the pope, and the slavery of the Catholic church, and therefore the despotic restrictions imposed upon them, being cloaked with the charm of evangelical liberty, the reformation of religion was hailed as a blessing. What a change was here worked for the downfall of England's liberties, and the happiness of Englishmen. Heretofore religion was held as of divine right and in the exercise of their spiritual functions the clergy had always been independent of the crown. Unfettered with the cares of wives and families; and enjoined, not only by the canons of the church, but by the laws of the kingdom, to follow the spiritual and corporal works of mercy, by visiting the sick, comforting the houseless, entertaining the stranger, and supporting the poor, their interests became identified with the privileges of the people, and they formed a barrier against the encroachments of the crown and the ambition of the nobles. Thus we see in the tenth century, king Edgar, while acting by the advice and counsels of an archbishop of Canterbury, St. Dunstan, governing his people like a father, and watching the administration of justice with a jealous eye. Falling into the foul sin of adultery, he was brought to a sense of his crime, and retraced his steps by making atonement for the scandal he had given to Religion and Morality. We are aware that the conduct of St. Dunstan has been censured as arrogant and insolent by many of our modern writers, who wrote for profit and not for truth; but did the courageous and noble-minded archbishop do more than Nathan, who reproved king David to his face for the offence he had committed? And would St. Dunstan have dared to reprove the king had he taken out a commission from Edgar, as the reforming bishops did under Edward the sixth?

Again, in the eleventh century, we see St. Anselm withstanding the innovations attempted by William Rufus, who, like his Norman father, governed the kingdom more by his own capricious and despotic will than by the laws and customs of the country, established and confirmed by the Saxon monarchs. No threats nor persuasions could induce the holy Anselm to relinquish his own rights, or sanction the violation of others. He preferred banishment and poverty to ease and riches in his see, and he outlived the tyrant by whom he was persecuted. But had Anselm been a man of the world, like Tom Cranmer; had he been encumbered with a wife and family, like our Protestant prelates; had he held his high possessions through the influence and will of the sovereign, would he have had the courage to withstand the power of the monarch, and brave the storms which gathered around him, in the rigid performance of his duty? Oh, no! the endearments of his wife, the cries of his children, the love of pleasure, and the fear of distress, would have crowded upon him, and he would probably have been as ready a slave to the whims of Rufus, as Tom Cranmer is acknowledged by Burnet to have been to the will of Henry, and as we shall shew him to have been to the will of the protector.

So, in the next century, we find St. Thomas à Becket resisting the encroachments meditated by Henry the second in the constitution of the country. St. Thomas was the first Englishman who rose to any considerable station under the Norman race of kings. He was well versed in the canon and civil law, was made lord chancellor, and afterwards archbishop of Canterbury. On being raised to the primate's chair, he resigned his civil office, considering the two offices to be incompatible with each other. Henry, like other ambitious sovereigns, meditated pretensions contrary to the established privileges of the constitution, and he required the assent of the archbishop. St. Thomas had taken an oath to preserve these privileges, and he refused to violate that oath and the constitution at the same time. This was the head and front of the archbishop's offence, and yet to this day his memory is maligned, and his patriotic firmness misrepresented. Even the great sir Walter Scott, in his last novel, those famous vehicles for calumny and abuse of the Catholic church, has spoken of the conduct of St. Thomas in the most injurious and unjustifiable terms. The archbishop is represented by the popular novelist, who, by-the-by, is a thorough-paced tory, as a proud and imperious prelate, which impression we suppose he borrowed from his countryman, Hume. The latter base and unprincipled writer, insinuates that St. Thomas à Becket was proud and ambitious, and covered his vicious inclinations with the cloak of sanctity and zeal for religion. Had St. Thomas not been a churchman, he would probably have been held in as high esteem as the most renowned of our statesmen since the reformation, but it was his misfortune, as the world will say, to be a Catholic prelate, and therefore, though his resistance to the will of Henry was purely conscientious, and he refrained from entering into any party strife, yet is he foully attacked by the infidel Hume, and the rage and violences of Henry, which ended in the archbishop's death, are extenuated. Had St. Thomas been a panderer and base violator of his oaths, like Cranmer; had he renounced the visible head of that divine religion, through whose influence we owe all that is valuable and venerable in our constitution; had he consented, like Cranmer, to become the mere tool and lieutenant of the king, exercising the functions of his office to cheat the people of their rights and customs, and enrich the hungry expectants that crowd a vicious court, out of the patrimony of the poor, we should have seen him extolled as one of the best benefactors of mankind, though he would have been, as Cranmer was, the disgrace of his sacred profession, and the curse of this once happy country. But St. Thomas was a disinterested and firm supporter of the laws and privileges of his country, and a Catholic prelate; it was not fit therefore that the Protestant people should be told the truth. Cranmer was a base truckler, a vicious sensualist, and a traitor to the constitution; but he was an instrument in bringing about that reformation which has led to all the evils the country has suffered, and will yet suffer—it is therefore necessary that the truth should here too be disguised;—thus the stout and good prelate is represented as ambitious and arrogant for doing his duty; while the corrupt and dissembling prelate, who basely betrayed his trust, is described as the paragon of excellence and perfection.

In the thirteenth century we have another example of the great advantages derived to civil freedom and the people's rights, by an independent and disinterested clergy. To whom does England owe so much, next to Alfred and Edward the confessor, as to cardinal Langton, archbishop of Canterbury, who advised and instructed the barons of England to curb the despotic conduct of an unprincipled king, and demand a restoration of the Saxon laws, which the Norman conqueror and his successors had abrogated? As might be expected, John, the reigning monarch, resisted this demand; but, encouraged by the counsels and example of the patriotic and inflexible primate, the barons persisted in their claims, and at length compelled the king to sign the great charter of English liberties, which was faithfully preserved till the bloody reign of Henry, the wife and priest slaughterer, when Cranmer and his associates in the work of reform, or rather of devastation, consented to its violation, by making the church the footstool of the state, and placing its ministers in subserviency to the will of the king and his courtiers.

Burnet has confessed that Cranmer was *over obsequious to the will of Henry,* nor was he less compliable to the will of the lord protector, after he was released from the control of the lustful and inexorable despot. On attaining the summit of power, Hertford allowed Cranmer to make some progress in what they called a reform, without the consent of parliament, and Cranmer, in return, assured the protector that he would find the episcopal order, who now held their sees during the pleasure of the crown, ready instruments to fulfil the wishes of their masters. Gardiner was the only bishop who stood out for episcopal rights, and he soon found himself in a prison. But what does Burnet say himself of the capabilities and character of the reformers? "The greatest diffi-"culty the reformers found was the want of *able* and *prudent men;* most "of the REFORMED PREACHERS being TOO HOT and INDIS-"CREET, and the *few* who were otherwise were required in London "and the universities. Therefore (he adds) they intended to make "those *as common as was possible,* and appointed them to preach as ITI-"NERANTS and VISITORS." The latter sentence of this quotation the wise editors of the modern *Book of Martyrs* have suppressed, thinking, we suppose, it reflected no great credit on the work they were extolling. But what, gentle reader, will you say of that reformation which was not performed by "able and prudent men," but was the work of "hot and indiscreet" preachers? Could a change of religion be good and true that had such hands to produce it? The Catholic religion was first founded by the apostles, who were inspired men, and renowned for their virtues, prudence, and invincible constancy. They selected others equally eminent for piety, integrity, and purity of conduct, to carry the faith delivered to them to other nations, and we find by the page of history, that kingdom after kingdom was subdued to the Catholic faith by holy, able, and prudent men, till in a word the whole world had been converted from Paganism and acknowledged the cross of Christ. We have it in the annals of our own country, that at the close of the sixth century, St. Gregory the great, who then filled the chair of St. Peter at Rome, sent a holy and prudent man, St. Augustin, to preach the Catholic faith to the Saxon inhabitants of Britain, and that, aided by other able and prudent men, the whole island in a short space of time became Catholic, and so continued through a series of nine hundred years, producing, during that period, the most just laws, the most valiant and wise kings, nobles, and legislators, the most pious and charitable prelates and priests, and the most learned and experienced scholars. And now we are unblushingly told, by the panegyrists of what is called " THE REFORMATION," that the change from Catholicism to Protestantism was the work of men who were wholly destitute of the qualities requisite to be a true servant of religion, being devoid of prudence and ability, and influenced by passion and indiscretion. From such a tree is it possible that good fruit could come? Need we wonder at the numerous evils that have sprung from this unhappy change from good to bad; from a system of perfect liberty and justice, to a chaos of licentiousness and oppression. The wonder is, that the people have remained so long under the reign of folly and delusion, but that wonder ceases when we reflect on the pains taken by interested and unprincipled writers to disguise and deface the truth, which however has been preserved by the care of learned and trusty scholars, and we rejoice to say is now making rapid progress among a people so long the dupes of designing men, an illustration of which we shall now proceed to give the reader.

Speaking of the progress of this hitherto unheard-of visitation, the editors of the modern Book of Martyrs say,—" The injunctions made " by Cromwell in the former reign, for instructing the people, for re- " moving images, and putting down all other customs abused to super- " stition; for reading the scriptures, saying the litany in English, for " frequent sermons and catechising, for the exemplary lives of the " clergy, their labours in visiting the sick, reconciling differences, and " exhorting the people to charity, &c. were now renewed; and all who " gave livings by simoniacal bargains, were declared to have forfeited " their right of patronage to the king. A great charge was also given " for the strict observation of the Lord's day, which was appointed to " be spent wholly in the service of God, it not being enough to hear " mass or matins in the morning, and spend the rest of the day in " drunkenness and quarrelling, as was commonly practised; but it " ought to be all employed, either in the duties of religion, or in acts " of charity. Direction was also given for the saying of prayers, in " which the king, as supreme head, the queen, and the king's sisters, " the protector and council, and all orders of persons in the kingdom, " were to be mentioned. Injunctions were also given for the bishops " to preach four times a year in all their dioceses, once in their cathe- " dral, and thrice in any other church, unless they had a good excuse " to the contrary: that their chaplains should preach often: and that " they should give orders to none, but to such as were duly qualified. " The visitors at length ended the visitation, and in London and every " part of England, the images, *for refusing to bow down to which many a* " *saint had been burnt*, were now committed to the flames." What we have here quoted is a *selection* from Burnet, with an *addition* of their own. The modern editors have shamefully violated the truth in stating that many a saint had been burned for refusing to bow down to images, as there is not a single burning on record for such an offence. We challenge the asserters to the proof, and we boldly defy them to produce one authenticated case of a saint, or even a sinner, having suffered for refusing to bow down to an image. What can we think of that cause which requires FALSEHOOD for its support? What are we to think of those men who can have recourse to such detestable practices to vilify and malign their neighbour's good name, and blind the unsuspecting reader? Having detected this *addition* to Burnet's tales, we shall now notice a *suppression* which the modern editors have been guilty of, on a very important subject. Among the directions given for praying, Burnet says, " they were also to PRAY FOR DEPARTED SOULS, that " at the last day, *we with them might rest both body and soul.*" This order too clearly proved that the reformers in Edward's day held, at first, the doctrine of purgatory and praying for the dead, which they afterwards abolished, when they had stripped the church of all the chantries, and violated the testamentary deeds of their ancestors, by appropriating the money left for masses for the repose of the souls of the testators to their own use. So clear a testimony of the Catholic doctrine, though recorded by Burnet, was too much for the modern editors, who profess to convey a true knowledge of Christianity to their readers, and therefore it was omitted. Thus the ignorant reader is confirmed in his ignorance, while they pretend to have the desire of enlightening him. The modern editors could not be ignorant themselves that this doctrine was not only *enjoined* but even *followed* by Cranmer and his associates at this time, for Collier, in his Ecclesiastical History, alluding to the death of the king of France, Francis I. on which occasion the injunction suppressed by the modern editors was observed by the too hot and indiscreet preachers, says, "on the 19th of June, a *dirge* was sung " for him, in all the churches of London. The choir of St. Paul's was " hung with mourning, and no other circumstance of state or solemnity " omitted. The archbishop of Canterbury, (CRANMER) with *eight* other " bishops, in their richest *pontifical* habits, sung A MASS ad requiem, " and a sermon was preached by Dr. Ridley, elect of Rochester." So, then, the reforming bishops, with Cranmer at their head, did not scruple to celebrate that august sacrifice which Protestants now swear is damnable idolatry, to qualify themselves for office under the crown of England. But it was necessary to keep up appearances for the present; therefore while these hypocrites were complying with the forms of the old religion, the preachers were ordered to inveigh against the doctrines of the Catholic church, in order to prepare the people for the change which the courtiers meditated. These proceedings did not pass, however, without opposition. Gardiner, bishop of Winchester, and some other of the prelates, stood so stoutly in the old belief, that neither threats nor persuasions could move them; and the princess Mary, afterwards queen, wrote to the protector, telling him that the changes made and about to be made, " were contrary to the honour due to her father's " memory, and that it was against their duty to the king to enter upon " such points, and endanger the public peace before he was of age." The protector wrote for answer, " that her father had died before he " could finish the *good things* he had intended concerning *religion;* and " had expressed his regret, both before himself and many others, that " he left things in so unsettled a state; and assured her, that nothing " should be done but what would turn to the glory of God, and the " king's honour." What hypocrisy and blasphemy! We shall soon see how far the glory of God and the honour of the king was respected by these base and iniquitous scourges of a once happy people.

The *Book of Martyrs* next proceeds to detail the new acts passed by the first and only parliament of Edward, but it does not furnish us with the origin of this parliament. The mode of selecting it was so dissimilar to the elections in the time of Catholicism, and was attended with such dire consequences to the nation at large that we shall give it in the words of Dr. Heylin, a Protestant divine, from his History of the Reformation. The doctor says, " And now it is high time to at- " tend the parliament, which took beginning on the fourth of Novem- " ber and was prorogued on the twenty-fourth of December following:

" In which the cards were so well packed by sir Ralph Sadler, that
" there was no need of any other shuffling till the end of the game,
" This very parliament, without any sensible alteration of the members
" of it, being continued by prorogation from session to session, until at
" last it ended by the death of the king. For a preparatory whereunto
" Richard lord Rich was made lord chancellor on the twenty-fourth of
" October; and sir John Baker chancellor of the court of first fruits
" and tenths, was nominated speaker for the house of commons. And
" that all things might be carried with as little opposition and noise as
" might be, it was thought fit that bishop Gardiner should be kept in
" prison till the end of the session; and that bishop Tonstal of Durham
" (a man of a most even and moderate spirit) should be made less in
" reputation, by being deprived of his place at the council table. And
" though the parliament consisted of such members as disagreed amongst
" themselves in respect of religion; yet they agreed well enough to-
" gether in one common principle, which was to serve the present time,
" and preserve themselves. For, though a great part of the nobility,
" and not a few of the chief gentry in the house of commons, were
" cordially affected to the church of Rome; yet were they willing to
" give way to all such acts and statutes as were made against it, out of
" a fear of losing such church lands as they were possessed of, if that
" religion should prevail and get up again. And for the rest, who
" either were to make, or improve their fortunes; there is no question
" to be made, but that they came resolved to further such a reforma-
" tion, as should most visibly conduce to the advancement of their se-
" veral ends. Which appears plainly by the strange mixture of the
" acts and results thereof; some tending simply to God's glory, and the
" good of the church; some to the present benefit and enriching of
" particular persons; and some again being devised of purpose to pre-
" pare a way for exposing the revenues of the church unto spoil and
" rapine." Look at this account, sensible reader, and then go back to
the time of John, when Langton and the barons stipulated for the nation's
freedom and rights. Alas! what a change. When the Catholic religion flourished, the parliaments were freely elected, and lasted only
during the session; so that parliaments were as frequent as they were
free. It was only in the preceding reign that parliaments were packed,
to carry the changes and inroads on the religion and constitution of the
country against the will of the people, and we here see how the system
of corruption was improved upon. Here we have an assemblage of men
influenced by the basest motives, and packed for the worst ends, legis-
lating for the church as well as the state, and forming new articles of
faith, at the whim of the moment.—Here we have it avowed that they
were actuated not with a love of country or of truth, but with the sordid view of enriching themselves by the spoil and rapine of the revenues
of the church, which had already suffered severely in the former reign.
—Here it is distinctly stated that the REFORMATION, as it is called, was
promoted by laymen under the fear that they would be obliged, in the
event of the old order of things being restored, to give up the ill-gotten
goods they were possessed of, which did not suit their worldly views.
Such then was the origin of that change of religion which took place in
this country in the sixteenth century, after having been Catholic nine

hundred years. Is it possible that the change could be good, springing as it did from such a source?

Of the acts passed by this parliament, some were of a civil nature, and others regarded matters of conscience.—The most material, however, were the act for placing the funds of the Chantries, Colleges, Free Chapels, and Hospitals, which had escaped the rapacity of the late king, at the disposal of the reigning monarch, that he might employ them in providing for the poor, increasing the salaries of the preachers, and endowing free schools for the diffusion of learning. All this however was no more than pretence; for the harpies of the court took especial care that very little of the spoil should be applied to public purposes. Dr. Heylin says there were then no less than ninety colleges, which being for the ends of education, why were they destroyed to make room for free schools? Of this we shall say more hereafter.—Another act was for the regulation of the election of bishops, by which the originators intended to weaken the episcopal authority, "by forcing " them," writes Dr. Heylin, " from their strong hold of divine institu- " tion, and making them no other than the king's ministers only, his " ecclesiastical *sheriffs* (as a man might say) to execute his will, and dis- " perse his mandates. And of this act (continues the doctor) such use " was made (though possible beyond the true intention of it) that the " bishops of those times were not in a capacity of conferring orders, " but as they were thereunto impowered by especial licence. The " tenor whereof (if Sanders be to be believed) was in these words fol- " lowing: viz. *the king to such a bishop, greeting, whereas all and all* " *manner of jurisdiction, as well ecclesiastical as civil, flows from the king* " *as from the supreme head of all the body, &c. We therefore give and* " *grant to thee full power and licence, to continue during our good pleasure,* " *for holding ordination within thy diocess of N. and for promoting fit per-* " *sons unto holy orders, even to that of the priesthood.* Which being look- " ed on by queen Mary, not only as a dangerous diminution of the epis- " copal power, but as an odious innovation in the church of Christ; she " caused this act to be repealed in the first year of her reign, leaving " the bishops to depend on their former claim, and to act all things " which belonged to their jurisdiction in their own names, and under " their own seals, as in former times. In which estate they have con- " tinued, without any legal interruption, from that time to this. But " in the first branch there was somewhat more than what appeared at " the first sight: for, though it seemed to aim at nothing but that the " bishops should depend wholly on the king for their preferment to " those great and eminent places; yet the true drift of the design was " to make deans and chapters useless for the time to come, and thereby " to prepare them for a dissolution."

But the most arbitrary and diabolical piece of tyranny remains yet to be recorded. This was the act legalizing SLAVERY in once free Eng- land, under the pretence of suppressing mendicity. This circumstance we must give in the words of Dr. Lingard. " The mendicants, who " had formerly obtained relief at the gates of the monasteries and con- " vents, now wandered in crowds through the country, and by their " numbers and importunities often extorted alms from the intimidated " passenger. To abate this nuisance a statute was enacted, which will

" call to the recollection of the reader the barbarous manners of our
" pagan forefathers. Whoever 'lived idly and loiteringly for the space
" of three days,' came under the description of a vagabond, and was
" liable to the following punishment. Two justices of the peace might
" order the letter V to be burnt on his breast, and adjudge him to serve
" the informer two years as his slave. His master was bound to pro-
" vide him with bread, water, and refuse meat ; might fix an iron ring
" round his neck, arm or leg, and was authorized to compel him to
" ' labour at any work, however vile it might be, by beating, chaining
" or otherwise.' If the slave absented himself a fortnight, the letter S
" was burnt on his cheek or forehead, and he became a slave for life ;
" and if he offended a second time in the like manner, his flight sub-
" jected him to the penalties of felony. Two years later this severe
" statute was repealed." Burnet attempts to soften the severity of this
infamous deed of the evangelical reformers, by insinuating that it was
" chiefly intended to operate against the vagrant monks who went about
" the country infusing into the people a dislike of the government,"
but Lingard, in a note on this law, says, " Similar penalties were enact-
" ed against clerks convict, who were no longer to make their purga-
" tion. Hence it has been inferred, I conceive erroneously, that the se-
" verity of the statute was chiefly directed against some of the monks
" who are supposed to have become beggars, and to have railed against
" the government. Clerks convict, are convicts claiming the right of
" clergy. Burnet, ii. 45. The young king in his Journal calls it ' an
" ' extreme law.' Edward's Journal in Burn. p. 5."
Of this law for *making slaves of Englishmen* it is impossible to speak
in measured language, or stifle those feelings of indignation which arise
at the very thought of such a measure. What would a Langton, what
would our Catholic ancestors have said or done, had such a tyrannous
and diabolical law been proposed to make slaves of them, in case they
felt the iron hand of poverty ? Well, thank Heaven, this law was the
fruit of Protestant legislation ; it was an offspring of the Reformation
which Englishmen are now taught to praise and admire, while a majority of them are steeped in misery, and numbers are made to supply
the place of beasts of burden. Talk of the tyranny of the pope, of the
slavery of Popery ! Alas ! who are greater slaves than the labourers
of England at this moment, who are not allowed to reap the profit of
their labour, but are compelled to give more than one-third of it to
support a race of idle and profligate tax-eaters.—In some measure the
present state of England is not unlike the state she was in under Edward
the sixth.—Schemes were entered into then to suppress mendicity,
which had been increased to a frightful degree by the rapacious spoliations of the court ; and schemes have been proposed in our days to reduce the population in consequence of the increase of pauperism arising
from the plundering of state cormorants.—Masters were authorized by
Edward's statute to cause the slave to perform any work, however vile,
by beating and chaining ; and in our own days men have been harness-
ed to carts to drag gravel, by order of overseers, and the whip is only
wanted to complete the parallel.
There is one other act of this parliament of Edward which we must
not overlook. It is that which legalized the marriages of the parsons,

and legitimated their children. By this law a heavy burden was entailed on the people, and the tithes which heretofore had gone to repair
churches and feed the poor, were not only given solely to the parsons,
but was found inadequate to maintain them, and millions have been
voted to support the poor clergy out of the public taxes. The church
and the poor were thrown upon the land and trade; the parsons'
sons and daughters are many of them fastened upon the taxes through
the sinecure and half-pay lists; and the bishops are not unmindful of
their families, as they take care to promote their sons and sons-in-law
to benefices in preference to others, though perhaps more able candidates, and thus the church property is made a kind of family patrimony
between the patrons and the prelates. Now this was not the case in
Catholic times; then the poor man's son stood as good a chance of a
parish or a mitre, if he possessed merit and abilities, as the son of the
most powerful nobleman, and the property of the church, as we have before observed, was expended in useful and charitable purposes. This is
one of the blessings of the Reformation, and to throw dust in the eyes
of the people, these parsons are ever and anon reviling the Catholic
church for not allowing *her* ministers to marry, contending that it is
contrary to the word of God, though the word is more in favour of
celibacy than otherwise. But what shall we say, after all the abuse
that has been lavished on Catholics, since the commencement of the
glorious work of reform, and especially after the passing of the parson-
marrying law, to the schemes lately proposed, and we believe actually
brought into parliament, to prevent THE POOR FROM MARRY-
ING!!! Not, reader, the poor clergymen, but the poor laymen and
women. And this infernal proposition originated too with a Protestant
parson. How glorious is the inconsistency, and how great the blessings of Protestantism!

Before we proceed further, we must recall the reader's attention to
the consequences which resulted from the act which granted possession
of chantries, colleges, &c. to the king. Of these establishments, besides the greater and lesser monasteries, which had been dissolved by
Harry, the number was computed to be about 2374, all endowed with
lands, pensions, and moveable goods to an immense value. "When
"the law passed," says Mr. Collier, "for their dissolution, the act pro-
"mised the estates of these foundations should be converted to *good*
"and *godly uses*, in erecting grammar schools, in further augmenting
"universities, and better provision for the poor and needy. But these
"lands being mostly shared *amongst the courtiers*, and others of *the rich*
"*laity*, the promise of the preamble was, in a great measure, impracti-
"cable."—Dr. Heylin is more diffuse in relating the rapacious and
scandalous proceedings of this reign, in his History of the Reformation.
—As many of the present aristocracy owe their estates and rank to the
spoliations and sacrileges of the courtiers of Henry and Edward, and as
the work of Dr. Heylin is little known at this time, and the transactions
he alludes to much less, from the base cupidity of our popular historians,
who wrote for *lucre* and not for *truth*, we will here give the doctor's
words, which, though long, will nevertheless be deemed important and
interesting.—He writes, "In the next place we must attend the king's
"commissioners, dispatched in the beginning of March into every shire

" throughout the realm, to take a survey of all colleges, free chapels,
" chanteries, and brotherhoods, within the compass of the statute or
" act of parliament. According to the return of whose commissions, it
" would be found no difficult matter to put a just estimate and value on
" so great a gift, or to know how to parcel out, proportion, and divide
" the spoil betwixt all such, who had before in hope devoured it. In
" the first place, as lying nearest, came in the free chapel of St. Stephen,
" originally founded in the palace at Westminster, and reckoned for the
" chapel royal of the court of England. The whole foundation con-
" sisted of no fewer than thirty-eight persons : viz. one dean, twelve
" canons, thirteen vicars, four clerks, six choristers ; besides a verger,
" and one that had the charge of the chapel. In place of whom a cer-
" tain number were appointed for officiating the daily service in the
" royal chapel, (gentlemen of the chapel they are commonly called)
" whose salaries, together with that of the choristers, and other servants
" of the same, amounts to a round yearly sum : and yet the king, if the
" lands belonging to that chapel had been together, and honestly laid
" unto the crown, had been a very rich gainer by it ; the yearly rents
" thereof being valued at 1085*l.* 10s. 5d. As for the chapel itself, to-
" gether with a cloister of curious workmanship, built by John Cham-
" bers, one of the king's physicians, and the master of the same, they
" are still standing as they were ; the chapel having been since fitted
" and employed for an house of commons in all times of parliament.

" At the same time also fell the college of St. Martin's, commonly
" called St. Martin's le Grand, situate in the city of London, not far
" from Aldersgate : first founded for a dean and secular canons, in the
" time of the conqueror, and afterwards privileged for a sanctuary ; the
" rights whereof it constantly enjoyed without interruption, till all pri-
" vilege of sanctuary was suppressed in this realm by king Henry the
" eighth. But the foundation itself being now found to be supersti-
" tious, it was surrendered into the hands of king Edward the sixth ;
" who after gave the same, together with the remaining liberties and
" precincts thereof, to the church of Westminster : and they, to make
" the best of the king's donation, appointed, by a chapter held the
" seventh of July, that the body of the choir and isles,
" should be leased out for fifty years, at the rent of five marks per
" annum, to one H. Keeble, of London ; excepting out of the said grant,
" the bells, lead, stone, timber, glass and iron, to be sold and disposed
" of for the sole use and benefit of the said dean and chapter. Which
" foul transaction being made, the church was totally pulled down, a
" tavern built in the east part of it : the rest of the site of the said
" church and college, together with the whole precinct thereof, being
" built upon with several tenements, and let out to strangers ; who
" very industriously affected to dwell therein (as the natural English
" since have done) in regard of the privileges of the place, exempted
" from the jurisdiction of the lord mayor and sheriffs of London, and
" governed by such officers amongst themselves as are appointed there-
" unto by the chapter of Westminster.

" But for this sacrilege the church of Westminster was called imme-
" diately in a manner to a sober reckoning : for the lord protector,
" thinking it altogether unnecessary that two cathedrals should be

" founded so near one another, and thinking that the church of West-
" minster (as being of a late foundation) might best be spared, had cast
" a longing eye upon the godly patrimony which remained unto it. And
" being then unfurnished of an house or palace proportionable unto his
" greatness, he doubted not to find room enough upon the dissolution
" and destruction of so large a fabrick, to raise a palace equal to his
" vast designs. Which coming to the ears of Benson, the last abbot
" and first dean of the church, he could bethink himself of no other
" means to preserve the whole, but by parting for the present with
" more than half the estate which belonged unto it. And thereupon a
" lease is made of seventeen manors and good farms, lying almost alto-
" gether in the county of Gloucester, for the term of ninety-nine years ;
" which they presented to the lord Thomas Seymour, to serve as an ad-
" dition to his manor of Sudley ; humbly beseeching him to stand their
" good lord and patron, and to preserve them in a fair esteem with the
" lord protector. Another present of almost as many manors and farms,
" lying in the counties of Gloucester, Worcester, and Hereford, was
" made for the like term to sir John Mason, a special confident of the
" duke's ; not for his own, but for the use of his great master ; which,
" after the duke's fall came to sir John Bourn, principal secretary of
" state in the time of queen Mary. And yet this would not serve the
" turn, till they had put into the scale their manor of Islip, conferred
" upon that church by king Edward the confessor ; to which no fewer
" than two hundred customary tenants owed their soil and service : and
" being one of the best wooded things in those parts of the realm, was
" to be granted also without impeachment of waste, as it was according-
" ly. By means whereof the deanery was preserved for the later times ;
" how it succeeded with the bishopric, we shall see hereafter. Thus
" Benson saved the deanery, but he lost himself ; for, calling to re-
" membrance that formerly he had been a means to surrender the abbey,
" and was now forced on the necessity of dilapidating the estate of the
" deanery, he fell into a great disquiet of mind, which brought him to
" his death within a few months after."

The doctor then goes on, " I had not singled these two (I mean St.
" Martin's and St. Stephen's) out of all the rest, but that they were the
" best, and richest in their several kinds, and that there was more de-
" pending on the story of them than on any others. But ' had examples
" seldom end where they first began.' For the nobility and inferior
" gentry, possessed of patronages, considering how much the lords and
" great men of the court had improved their fortunes by the suppres-
" sion of those chanteries and other foundations, which had been granted
" to the king, conceived themselves in a capacity of doing the like, by
" taking into their hands the yearly profits of those benefices, of which
" by law they only were entrusted with the presentations. Of which
" abuse complaint is made by bishop Latimer, in his printed sermons.
" In which we find, ' that the gentry at that time invaded the profits of
" the church, leaving the title only to the incumbent : and that chantery
" priests were put by them into several cures, to save their pensions ;
" pag. 38. that many benefices were laid out in free farms, (pag. 71.)
" or given unto servants, for keeping of hounds, hawks, and horses, and
" for making of gardens ; p. 91, 114.' And finally, ' that the poor

" clergy being kept to some sorry pittances, were forced to put them-
" selves into gentlemen's houses, and there to serve as clerks of the
" kitchen, surveyors, receivers, &c. p. 241.'   All which enormities
" (though tending so apparently to the dishonour of God, the disservice
" of the church, and the disgrace of religion) were generally connived
" at by the lords and others, who only had the power to reform the
" same; because they could not question those who had so miserably
" invaded the church's patrimony, without condemning of themselves."

Here let us pause a moment, and reflect upon the scenes thus described, and those which have passed since they occurred.   What apology can be offered for the outrages thus committed ?   Could Popery,
with all its imputed corruptions and oppressions, produce calamities
equal to what befel the country under the hands of the evangelical reformers ?   Burnet tells us the clergy were ignorant in the time of
Popery, but the sackings of the libraries of the public institutions, and
burnings of the valuable books found therein, proved the careful regard
in which learning was held by the calumniated Catholic clergy, and the
little value that was set upon it by the reformers.   See too the respect
shewn by the godly reformers for the clergy, by causing them to serve
the most menial offices in their families, to avoid the horrors of starvation.   Then again the appropriation of a portion of the tithes to lay purposes, many of the lords and gentry at this day deriving a part of their
income from the tithes thus diverted from their original purport.   All
these things considered, and many more that might be added, can any
reasonable being conceive that religion had any hand in this pretended
reformation, unless indeed to cloak the villanies of the devastators.—
Oh ! how deeply have the people had occasion to deplore this eventful
period.   Penalties upon penalties have been enacted to restrain their
comfort and abridge their liberties.   New offences have been heaped
upon each other in the statute book, till the most wary have reason to
fear they may become trespassers.   From the time of the separation of
this kingdom from the church of Rome, the laws have been multiplied
a hundred fold, and so numerous are they grown, and so complicated in
their bearings, that the wisest lawyer existing cannot digest them.—
Taxes have been imposed on the people till the country is brought
nearly to the brink of ruin, and, as in the time of Edward, while the rich
are rioting in luxury, the working classes are starving in the midst of
plenty.

Among other devices in the work of reform was the abolition of certain religious ceremonies, and the curtailment of the amusements of the
people.   Of these, the Book of Martyrs, follow Burnet, speaks thus:—
" Candlemas and Lent were now approaching, and the clergy and peo-
" ple were much divided with respect to the ceremonies usual at those
" times.   By some injunctions in Henry's reign, it had been declared
" that fasting in Lent was only binding by a positive law.   Wakes and
" Plough-Mondays were also suppressed, and hints were given that
" other customs, which were much abused, should be shortly done
" away.   The (Burnet says gross) rabble loved these things, as matters
" of diversion, and thought divine worship without them would be but
" a dull business.   But others looked on them as relics of heathenism,
" and thought they did not become the gravity and simplicity of the

" Christian religion." We doubt much that the customs thus alluded
to were abused, at least to any great extent. But allowing they were
abused, why not endeavour to *remove* the *abuse* and not *abolish* the *custom*.
Why deprive the people of their diversions, which had been of so long
standing, and afforded mirth and recreation to lighten labour and poverty?
The answer is obvious. The retaining the customs would have reminded
the people of the old religion, and of the sad changes which had been
made by the lamentable plans of the reformers, and therefore it was
deemed best to do away with the merriments, as well as with the more
solemn rites, which the Catholics had introduced to remind man of his
Maker, and cheer him in his pilgrimage through life. Next followed
a general order for the removal of all images out of the churches, and
stripping the sacred edifices of all unnecessary furniture. To this species of robbery bishop Hooper contributed largely by his doctrine.—
This reforming prelate was much displeased at the word *altar*, as well
as the situation of it. He therefore exerted himself to have all the altars removed, and a *table* to be placed in the middle of the chancel.—
Such a scheme was very serviceable to those who had cast their eyes
on the rich decorations which ornamented the Catholic cathedrals and
churches. The pretence was the superstitions and abuses occasioned by
the use of images, &c. but the real design was that of plunder. Notwithstanding the vast treasure obtained by the confiscation of the chantries, colleges, &c. the king's exchequer was in an empty condition,
and it was thought to replenish it by seizing the images, vestments,
jewels, crosses, and other costly utensils and ornaments of the church.
Commissioners were accordingly appointed to secure the delivery
of these spoils for the king's use. But, writes doctor Heylin,—" In
" all great fairs and markets there are some forestallers, who get the
" best pennyworth themselves, and suffer not the richest and most gain-
" ful commodities to be openly sold. And so it fared also in the pre-
" sent business, there being some who were as much before hand with
" the king's commissioners in embezzling the said plate, jewels, and
" other furnitures, as the commissioners did intend to be with the king,
" in keeping all or most part unto themselves. For when the commis-
" sioners came to execute their powers in their several circuits, they
" neither could discover all, or recover much of that which had been
" purloined; some things being utterly embezzled by persons not re-
" sponsible; in which case the king as well as the commissioners was
" to lose his right; but more concealed by persons not detectable, who
" had so cunningly carried the stealth, that there was no tracing of
" their footsteps. And some there were, who being known to have such
" goods in their possession, conceived themselves too great to be called
" in question; connived at willingly by those who were but their equals,
" and either were or meant to be offenders in the very same kind. So
" that although some profit was thereby raised to the king's exchequer,
" yet the far greatest part of the prey came to other hands: insomuch
" that many private men's parlours were hung with altar cloths, their
" tables and beds covered with copes, instead of carpets and coverlits;
" and many made carousing cups of the sacred chalices, as once Bel-
" shazzar celebrated his drunken feast in the sanctified vessel of the
" temple. It was a sorry house, and not worth the naming, which had

" not somewhat of this furniture in it, though it were only a fair large
" cushion made of a cope or altar cloth, to adorn their windows, or
" make their chairs appear to have somewhat in them of a *chair of state*.
" Yet how contemptible were these trappings in comparison of those
" vast sums of money, which were made of jewels, plate, and cloth of
" tissue, either conveyed beyond the seas, or sold at home, and good
" lands purchased with the money; nothing the more blessed to the
" posterity of them that bought them, for being purchased with the
" consecrated treasures of so many temples." Mr. Collier, speaking of
the same depredations, says, " This order for undressing churches was,
" it seems, represented to the king (as Burnet relates the fact) as an
" inoffensive expedient, and only calling for the superfluous plate, and
" other goods that lay in churches, more for pomp than for use. But
" those who called these things superfluous, and shewed so slender a
" regard for the honour of religion, were none of the best reformers.
" Had these people governed in the minority of Josiah, as they did in
" this of Edward VI, they would, in all likelihood, have retrenched the
" expense of the Mosaic institution, and served God at a more frugal
" rate. They would have disfurnished the temple of most of the gold
" plate, carried off the unnecessary magnificence, and left but little
" plunder for Nebuchadnezzar."

While these nefarious practices were going on among the factious lay
reformers, Cranmer and his apostate bishops were engaged in forming
a new liturgy, or office for the *new church about to be established by law*,
but now supported by the power and authority of the crown. Previous
however to this measure, Cranmer had published a catechism, " for the
" singular profit and instruction of children and young people," and it
is well deserving notice, indeed it is a thing not to be forgotten, that in
this very catechism, Cranmer comprises the prohibition of false gods
and of images under *one* commandment, as is the case with the Catholic catechism, and teaches that in the communion are received with the
bodily mouth THE BODY AND BLOOD OF CHRIST, inculcates,
in strong terms, the advantages of *confession* and *absolution*, and attributes the origin of ecclesiastical jurisdiction to Christ, in a manner
which seems to do away his former opinion on the same subject. Now,
however, the doctrine was to be *changed*, and some new method was to
be devised, with a view to consummate the separation of the kingdom
from the mother and mistress of all Christian churches. The *Book of
Martyrs* says, " The first step that was now taken was to make a new
" office for the communion, that is, the distribution of the sacrament,
" for the office of consecration was not at this time touched. In the
" exhortation, auricular confession to a priest is left free to be done or
" omitted, and all were required not to judge one another in that mat-
" ter. There was also a denunciation made, requiring impenitent sin-
" ners to withdraw. The bread was to be still of the same form as that
" formerly used. In the distribution it was said, ' The body of our
" Lord, &c. preserve thy body; and the blood of our Lord, &c. preserve
" thy soul.' This was printed, with a proclamation, requiring all to re-
" ceive it with such reverence and uniformity as might encourage the
" king to proceed further, and not to run to other things before the
" king gave direction, assuring the people of his earnest zeal to set forth

A REVIEW

OF

Fox's Book of Martyrs,

CRITICAL AND HISTORICAL.

No. 45. Printed and Published by W. E. Andrews, 3, Chapter-house-court, St. Paul's Churchyard, London. Price 3d.

EXPLANATION OF THE ENGRAVING.—*At the time the Hugonots took possession of the German province of Geldria, the soldiers forcibly entered a Carthusian monastery, vociferating* Gelt, Gelt, *signifying thereby that they wanted money. In the entrance three lay brothers, named Albert Winda, John Sittart, and Stephen Ruremundensis, were murdered; thence rushing into the temple, they attacked the venerable prior Joachin, when engaged in prayer, whom they grievously wounded, with others of the community, and left four monks dead on the spot.*

CONTINUATION OF THE REVIEW.

" godly orders; and therefore it was hoped they would wait for it: the
" books were sent all over England, and the clergy were appointed to
" administer the communion at the following Easter according to them."

We have now arrived at a most interesting period of the progress of
the *reformation*, as it is called, and we beg the reader's particular attention to it. It has been shewn that Cranmer in his Catechism admitted
the real presence of Christ in the blessed sacrament, as the law-estab-
lished Church Catechism now does, though the *law* compels all candidates
for civil and ecclesiastical office to *swear* that he is *not* present, and that
the doctrine is damnable, though the Church by *law* teaches it. Such
is the incongruity of the dabblers in error under the mask of truth.—
Well, we are told that the *first step* in this work of innovation was to

make *a new* office for the communion, which was only to affect the distribution of the sacrament, the office of the *consecration*, which is the essential part of the ceremony, remaining untouched. Still in the *distribution* of the sacrament, the words THE BODY and THE BLOOD of our Lord, which words imply the *real presence* of Christ, and had *always* been used by the Catholic church, as they *now* are, were retained, because it was found too glaring to abolish them precipitately, in consequence of the well-known doctrine of the Catholic church on that head, and the disposition of the people, who were accurately acquainted with the faith and discipline of their creed, notwithstanding the representations of Burnet and his followers that they were ignorant and demoralized. As an instance of this fact, the Catholic clergy were willing to abide by PUBLIC OPINION, but the reformers, who preached up evangelical liberty, would not consent to leave their cause to argument and persuasion, but were resolved to cram their *new* schemes and opinions down the people's throats by *main force*. So long as the reformers proceeded no farther than ceremony and discipline, the lukewarm adherents to the Catholic faith slumbered at their posts; but when it was found that there was a design to attack the Church both in doctrine and discipline, they began to arouse themselves from their apathy and published several books in defence of the old religion, and challenged the opposite party to try the cause by disputation. "But," says Collier, in his *Ecclesiastical History*, vol. ii. b. 4. p. 228, " the court, who, it is " thought, had something farther than religion in view, did not think it " advisable to venture the cause upon disputation, and rely wholly " upon arguments. They might be apprehensive, that, unless the dis- " agreement between Rome and England was carried on to a wider dis- " tance, the breach might possibly be closed, and that such an union " might prove unfriendly to their church estates. On the other hand, " they were not assured whether any farther alterations in doctrine and " worship would be well received. The minority of the prince was a " circumstance of disadvantage: and how far the people would be pas- " sive under a new face of things was not easy to conjecture. To guard " against the worst, it was thought fit to be furnished *with forces*, to " awe the opposite party and prevent them from giving disturbance. " And as an army was a seasonable provision, they wanted not a colour " to raise it. A marriage (as has been observed) was agreed, in the " late reign, between the young queen of Scotland and the present king; " but the Scots failed in their articles. The protector and council, " therefore, resolved to bring them to reason. For this purpose men " were levied, a fleet equipped, and the veteran troops of Boulogne and " Calais embarked for England. The protector likewise had several " regiments of Walloons and Germans in his pay: not that he had a " better opinion of their courage, but because he might believe them " more ready to execute any harsh service at home, if occasion required."

So, then, the preaching of the *new* doctrines was to be backed by an army, and that army too composed in part of FOREIGN TROOPS, of German mercenaries !!! What would the Catholic people of England have said to this gross violation of their constitutional rights and national honour and freedom? What can the liberal Protestant of the present day say in defence of his creed, which is here shewn to have been advanced, not by the power of miracles and the eloquence of reason, as the Catholic faith was planted in every part of the globe, but by the force of war, and the terror of bloodshed and rapine? By these unhallowed and unlawful means were the people terrified into a tacit acquiescence of the projected changes, and a commission was accordingly appointed in the year 1548, by the protector and council, consisting of certain bishops and divines, to draw up a *new* form of prayer or liturgy, a new ordinal, with a collection of articles, canons, and homilies, which were *intended* as a STANDARD, both for doctrine and discipline. But futile is the work of man in raising a standard to guide the conscience of his fellow-men, as we shall see in the progress of this pretended reformation of religion. The Catholic rests his faith on the hand of God, from whom it is derived, and, like Him, is immutable and indivisible. The Catholic can trace the finger of God sustaining his church through all the vicissitudes of earthly establishments, firm and erect like a citadel upon a rock, defying the waste of time or the assaults of adversaries; while the plans of the reformers to erect a standard of uniformity, were no sooner attempted than they were dispersed like sand before the wind, and scattered into thousands of discordant sects, each alike claiming the golden talisman of TRUTH, but all immersed in the slough of error. Of the articles of faith there were *forty-two* in number, and though pretended to have been drawn up under the influence of the Holy Ghost, yet under the popeship of queen Bess they were reduced to *thirty-nine*, and blasphemously imputed to the same divine oracle of Truth, though they are well known to have been the work of unprincipled men. As to the liturgy in English, it was a selection from the *Missal*, in which the collects, epistles, and gospels were preserved, and are the same as are now used by the Catholic church, which has not varied in her service, and even the essential part, relating to the great sacrifice of the mass, was not then omitted, though it has subsequently been erased. When this precious work was completed, it was some months before it obtained a legal establishment, and in the mean time many of the bishops and clergy continued to make use of the ancient liturgy in Latin. Others made use of it according to their own whims and pleasure. Some were for both forms, and some for neither. In a word, the flood-gates of discord were set open, and all was endless confusion. Collier says, that "some censured this provision of a common prayer, because it is said to have been composed by *one uniform consent*, and yet *four* of the bishops who were in the committee for drawing it up, *protested against the bill*. These were the bishops of Norwich, Hereford, Chichester, and Westminster." The latter bishopric was afterwards abolished by the king's letters patent. Here then we have a *lie set forth*, and this book too was specified in the act of parliament to have been carried on *with the aid of the Holy Ghost*.

Of this work Burnet thus speaks:—"It was now resolved to have a liturgy, which should bring the worship to a proper mean between the pomp of superstition and naked simplicity. It was resolved to change nothing merely in opposition to received practices, but rather (in imitation of what Christ did in the institution of the two sacraments of the gospel, that consisted of rites used among the Jews, but sanctified by him to higher purposes) to comply with what had been

" formerly in use, as much as was possible, thereby to gain the people.
" All the consecrations of water, salt, &c. in the church of Rome, being
" relics of heathenism, were laid aside. The absolutions on account of
" the merits of the blessed virgin and the saints, the sprinklings of
" water, fastings, and pilgrimages, with many other things; and the
" absolution given to dead bodies, were looked upon as gross impos-
" tures, tending to make the world think, that the priests had the keys
" of heaven in their hands, and could carry people thither on easier
" terms than the gospel prescribes. This induced the people to pur-
" chase their favour, especially when they were dying; so that, as their
" fears were then heightened, there was no other way left them, in the
" conclusion of an ill life, to die with any hopes of eternal happiness,
" but as they bargained with their priests; all this was now rejected."
Here we are told that it was resolved to *change nothing*, but to comply
with what had been *formerly in use*, as much as was possible, *thereby to
gain the people.* Out upon thee, hypocrite, thou must have known that
the way adopted by these reformers to gain the people, was by the force
of military coercion and penal laws. But what shall we say to the base
insinuation that the people were in those times induced to *purchase* the
favour of the priests; this we suppose is thrown in as a set-off to hide
the selfish disposition of the reformed clergy, of whom Burnet was one,
in seizing the tithes to themselves, and grinding the people as much as
they could, instead of gaining their favour. The priests were at that
time, as the Catholic clergy are now, and always have been, the fathers
of the people, and the supporters of the poor; they were the shepherds
of their flocks, and not the shearers of them, as the reformed clergy are.
But though it " was resolved to change nothing, merely in opposition
" to received practices, but rather to comply with what had been for-
" merly in use," it appears that the reformers were somewhat like the
old man in the fable, in trying to please every body they pleased nobody, for it must have been self-evident that the Catholics would not
be satisfied with the changes, moderate as they are represented to have
been, and as to the reformers themselves, Burnet says, "When the book
" came before the public, several things were censured: as particularly
" the frequent use of the cross, and anointing. The former was at first
" used as the badge of a crucified Saviour, but was much corrupted by
" the priests in after ages, so that it was at length believed to have a
" virtue for driving away evil spirits, and preserving one from dangers;
" and acquired a kind of sacramental character, entirely unfounded in
" scripture or reason; but the using it as a ceremony, expressing the
" believing in a crucified Saviour, could imply no superstition." This
representation may suit Mr. Gilbert Burnet, bishop of Sarum, and the
modern editors of the *Book of Martyrs,* but Catholics have better authority than this hireling historian, for retaining and using this glorious
and holy emblem of our redemption, wrought by a God-man. Why
were not the "after-ages" specified when the use of this badge was
first corrupted by the priests? Why not *name* the express time when
the belief was first introduced that the use of this badge drived evil
spirits from us, and preserved one from dangers? We have shewn, in
our first volume of this work, that Constantine the great obtained a
splendid victory over his enemy in arms under the banner of the Cross,

before he became a Christian, and which he was told in a vision would ensure him a triumph on adopting it. He afterwards embraced Christianity, and caused images of our Saviour, and representations of the Cross to be placed in the most conspicuous parts of Constantinople, viewing that sign as the defence and bulwark of his empire. But this was not the first time that the sign of the Cross was used by Christians, the custom being coeval with Christianity itself. Tertullian, who lived in the second century, writes, " Whenever we move : when we enter and go " out ; in dressing, and washing ; at table, when we retire to rest, " during conversation—we impress on our foreheads the sign of the " cross. Should you ask for the scripture authority for this and such- " like practices : I answer, there is none ; but there is tradition that au- " thorizes it, custom that confirms it, submission that observes it."— *De Corona Mil.* c. iii. iv. p. 289. Lactantius, a father of the Latin church, in the fourth century, says, " As Christ, whilst he lived amongst " men, put the devils to flight by his word, and restored those to their " senses whom these evil spirits had possessed ; so now his followers, " in the name of their master, and by the sign of his passion, exercise " the same dominion over them. The proof is easy. When the idola- " ters sacrifice to their gods, they cannot proceed, if, a Christian being " present, he sign his forehead with the cross ; nor can the diviner give " his responses. This has often been the cause of the persecutions we " have undergone. And, in like manner, when some masters were on " the point of sacrificing in the presence of their Christian servants, the " latter, by making the sign of the cross on the forehead, so frightened " away the gods, that nothing could be collected from the bowels of " the victims."—*Divin. Instit.* l. 4, c. xxvii. p. 325. St. Athanasius, of the Greek church, in the same century, says, " In the midst of the in- " cantations of the devils, only let the sign of the cross, which the gen- " tiles ridicule, be used ; let Christ be merely named : the devils will " be instantly put to flight ; the oracles be silent ; and all the arts of " magic reduced to nothing."—*De Incarnat.* t. i. p. 89. And St. John Chrysostom, of the same church and the same age, who for his profound learning and eloquence obtained the surname of *Chrysostom*, which signifies *Golden Mouth*, thus speaks of this ceremony :—" Let no one be " ashamed of these symbols of our salvation, of these signs. The pas- " sion of our Lord is the origin, is the fountain of that happiness, by " which we live, and are. With a joyous heart, as if it were a crown, " let us carry about with us the cross of Christ. For by it is consum- " mated whatever pertains to our salvation. When we are baptized, " the cross of Christ is there ; so also, when we partake of the most " holy food of the eucharist, and in every other sacred exercise. Where- " fore, let us, with earnestness, impress this cross on our houses and on " our walls, and our windows, on our foreheads also, and on our breasts. " It is the sign of our salvation, of our common liberty, of the meekness " and humility of our Lord. As often then as you sign yourself, pass " over in your mind the general concern of the cross, suppress all the " workings of anger and the other passions, and fortify your breast with " firmness. It should be made not only on the body, but with great " confidence on the mind. If it be done in this manner, not one of the " wicked spirits, when he sees the spear that inflicted the deadly wound,

" will dare to assail you."—*Homil.* iv. *in Matt.* c. xvi. t. vii. pp. 594, 595. We could produce many other fathers of this age in favour of the use of this sign of our redemption, but enough has been said to shew the spirit which induced the reformers to hate it, and Gilbert Burnet to become their apologist.

The modern editors, selecting from Burnet, go on to tell their readers, that " the Protestant religion now appeared almost *ruined* in Germany, " and *this* made the reformers *turn their eyes to England.* Calvin wrote " to the protector, and pressed him to go on to *a more complete refor-* " *mation,* and that *prayers for the dead,* the chrism, and *extreme unction,* " might *be laid aside.* He desired him to trust in God, and go on, and " wished there *were more preaching,* and in a *more lively way* than he " heard was then in England : but above all things he prayed him TO " SUPPRESS THAT IMPIETY AND PROFANITY that, as he heard " ABOUNDED IN THE NATION."—Oh Lord! what had the pious John Calvin, who had himself been branded in the shoulder for a most detestable crime, learned that *impiety* and *profanity* abounded in England ? And did he, most *apostolic* man, really exhort the *saintly* and *devout* reformer, Somerset, lord protector, to suppress that burning shame of the reformation, immorality of the grossest nature ? What a precious change to godliness and pure doctrine that must have been, which produced such a general scene of wickedness and dissoluteness of manners as overflowed those countries where the reformation, as it is improperly termed, took root.—But we need not wonder at such deplorable depravity, when we look at the character of the principal movers in those scenes.—Burnet tell us, but the modern editors thought proper to suppress this information, that " while these changes were under " consideration, there were great heats every where, and a great con- " tradiction among the pulpits ; some commending all the old customs, " and others inveighing as much against them : so the power of grant- " ing licences to preach, was taken from the bishops, and restrained " only to the king and the archbishops ; yet even that did not prove " an effectual restraint. So a proclamation was set out, restraining all " preaching, till the order, which was then in the hands of the bishops, " should be finished ; and instead of hearing sermons, all were required " to apply themselves to prayer, for a blessing on that which was then " a preparing, and to content themselves in the mean while with the " homilies." What a pretty description is this of the " Progress of the Reformation," under the evangelical apostles in the young pope Edward's time. Here we have a complete repetition of Babel-building confusion, till the *civil* power was exerted to obtain silence, and the teachers of— what shall we say ?—to say *religion,* would be to apply a wrong term —the teachers of corrupt doctrine and human notions were muzzled by a state proclamation.—But what else was to be expected from such a beginning ? Those who pretended to reform the supposed errors and abuses in the Catholic church, which, as we have shewn, was founded by a divine Architect, had no lawful commission to interfere in her regulations, and consequently not being invested with a divine commission, they had not the least power to restrain conscience or command obedience. Hence it followed that those who set up for *reformers* of the Church of Rome, were themselves taxed as infected with error by others who set up for reformers of the *new* Church of England and her liturgy; these latter reformers were in their turn beset by other reformers, and thus the work of reform has been going on among the children of the Reformation, so called, until faith has been frittered away and infidelity has taken its place. In the mean while, the Catholic church, securely seated on her imperishable foundation, has, by the aid of her missionaries, afforded all the succour in her power to those, who seek her help, and thousands have been rescued from the gulf of perdition, by entering the doors of her stately edifice and conforming to her divine precepts.

We must now notice another curious transaction of these reformers. —The modern editors, copying from Burnet, say, "Another act was "also passed respecting *fasting*, declaring, 'that though all days and "meats were in themselves alike, yet fasting, being a great help to "virtue, and to the subduing the body to the mind, it was enacted, "that Lent, and all Fridays and Saturdays, and ember-days, should be "*fish-days*, under *several penalties*, excepting the weak, or *those that had* "*the king's licence*.' Christ had told his disciples, that when he was "taken from them, they should fast: so in the primitive church they "fasted before Easter; but the same number of days was not observed "in all places; afterwards, other rules and days were established; but "St. Austin complained, that many in his time placed all their religion "in observing them. *Fast-days are turned to a mockery in the church of* "*Rome*, in which they dine on fish exquisitely drest, and drink wine." If fast-days be turned to a mockery in the church of Rome, we have here the avowal of the modern editors and Burnet that Christ commanded *his* disciples *to fast*; and yet the modern editors and their compeers in hatred to Popery, condemn fasting as a superstitious practice. How far it is a mockery in the church of Rome we will say no more, than, if the authors of this gross falsehood would but spend one week of Lent according to the discipline of the Catholic church, they would soon become convinced of the injustice they have done her, and acknowledge themselves to be what we tell them they are—brazen frontless liars. This act was abolished by queen Mary, but was renewed in the fifth year of Elizabeth, not however for the purpose of "subduing the body to the mind;" not because it was "a great help to virtue;" not because Christ had told his disciples that they should fast; but because it was deemed of *political* importance to provide for the increase of the navy.—It was therefore enacted by the parliament of her lady-popeship, that all Wednesdays, Fridays and Saturdays throughout the year, should be observed as *fast-days*, under a penalty of forty shillings for each offence, one third part of which was to go to the queen, one to the informer, and the other to the poor of the parish. This act we believe is still unrepealed, but not enforced.—But since it is allowed that *fasting* is not only of benefit to the mind, but a help to virtue, why are the Catholics the only class of religionists in England that follow this admitted apostolic practice? And why do Protestants revile and reproach them for it, when their own church, in her infancy, attempted to enforce the custom on them by civil pains and penalties. See again, too, that power was given to the king, as head of the new church, to dispense with the obligations of this law, yet Protestants object to a similar power being held by the pope and the prelates of the Catholic church. This is inconsistency with a vengeance! But it is like all the proceedings of the disciples of error, who have no other rules than their own visionary notions, which are drifted to and fro by every wind that blows from the different points of the compass.

We have seen that *foreign troops* were brought over by the lord protector to awe the people into an acquiescence of the changes then meditated in the religion of the country and of Christendom. It was now thought necessary to introduce *foreign doctors* in religion to reform what had already undergone reform.—Peter Martyr Vermilli, an Italian canon, Martin regular Bucer, a black friar, and Bernardin Ochin, a capuchin, were brought over by Cranmer to assist in that great work the latter and the protector had at heart.—As the tree is known by its fruit, we may as well give the reader some slight sketch of the character of these apostles in the Reformation.—They were all bound by the solemn vows of celibacy to lead a continent life, but they took upon themselves to dispense with these vows, and Peter brought over with him a woman, a nun, bound like himself to a life of chastity, whom he called his wife. Martin Bucer likewise broke through his solemn vows by a sacrilegious marriage : he was also chiefly instrumental in procuring the scandalous license which granted to the langrave of Hesse the privilege of having two living wives at once. He imposed upon Luther and others by shameful equivocations concerning the blessed sacrament, and was the first inventor of that contradictory system of a real presence of a thing really absent, that is, of receiving verily and indeed the body and blood of Christ in the sacrament, though they are not verily and indeed there. Bernard was not content with one wife, but wrote a book in defence of Polygamy, and at length proceeded so far as to deny the blessed Trinity.—Such were the auxiliaries introduced by Cranmer to complete the work of deformation which he had begun.

In the first liturgy, drawn up in the year 1548, which we have before spoken of, the consecration of the sacrifice of the Eucharist was retained, with the prayer, *With thy Holy Spirit vouchsafe to bless and sanctify these thy gifts and creatures of Bread and Wine, that they may be made unto us the Body and Blood of thy most dearly beloved Son, &c.*—This prayer was soon found to favour too much of the doctrine of transubstantiation, and therefore it was subsequently erased. The liturgy also retained something of prayer for the dead ; for at funerals, *they recommended the soul departed to God's mercy*, and, as Catholics now do, they *prayed that his sins might be pardoned*. This prayer savoured of the primitive doctrine of Purgatory, and reminded the people too much of the despoiled chantries, therefore it must now be banished from that liturgy that was said to have been compiled by the inspiration of the Holy Ghost. The sacrament of Confirmation was turned into a Catechism to renew baptismal vows, though the fathers, who received it from the apostles of Christ, say not one word of a Catechism—Here are a few examples.—St. Cyprian, who lived in the third century, and was a doctor of the Latin church, writes thus :—" It is moreover necessary, that he, who has been baptized, should be anointed, " in order that, having received the chrism, that is, the unction, he " may be the anointed of God, and possess the grace of Christ. Ep.

" lxx. p. 190.—'They who had believed in Samaria, (Acts vii.), had
" believed with a true faith; and were baptized in the one church by
" Philip, whom the apostles have sent. And therefore, because their
" baptism was legitimate, it was not to be repeated. That alone which
" was wanting, was supplied by Peter and John; that by prayer and the
" imposition of hands, they might receive the Holy Ghost. The same
" thing is now done by us, when they, who have been baptized in the
" church, are presented to the bishops, that by our prayer and the im-
" position of hands, they may receive the divine spirit, and be perfected
" by the seal of the Lord.'" Ep. lxxiii. p. 202.—St. Cyril of Jerusalem,
in the same age, says,—" To you, when you came out from the font,
" was given the chrism, which is the image of that with which Christ
" was anointed, that is, the Holy Spirit.—Take care, that you think it
" not mere ointment—with which the forehead and your bodily senses
" are symbolically anointed: the body, indeed, is anointed with that
" visible chrism, but the soul is sanctified by the Holy Spirit. Cat.
" Myst. iii. n. 1, 3, p. 289, 290.—As Christ, after his baptism and the
" coming of the divine spirit, went out to battle, and conquered the
" enemy; so you, after baptism and the mystical chrism, cloathed in
" the arms of the same spirit, are opposed to him and surmount his at-
" tacks." Ibid. p. 290.—St. Ambrose, likewise, at the same period,
says,—" Because thou hast received the spiritual seal, the spirit of wis-
" dom and understanding, the spirit of counsel and fortitude, the spirit
" of knowledge and piety, the spirit of holy fear; keep what thou hast
" received. God the Father has sealed thee; Christ the Lord has con-
" firmed thee, and has given the pledge of the spirit in thy heart, (2 Cor.
" i. 22.) as thou has learned from the apostle." De Initiand. c. vii. t.
iv. p. 349. And St. Jerom, the great and learned compiler of the
Bible, speaking to a schismatic, says, " You cannot be ignorant, that it
" is the practice in the church, to impose hands on those that have been
" baptized, and to invoke the Holy Spirit. Where, you ask, is it
" written? In the Acts of the Apostles: and although there were no
" authority of Scripture, the consent of the whole world on this point
" must be received as a law.—To this St. Jerom thus assents: I admit
" this to be the practice of the church, that when, in remote places,
" any have been baptized by the priests or deacons, the bishop goes to
" them, and having invoked the Holy Spirit, lays his hand on them."
Dial. adv. Lucif. t. i. p. 615.—Thus then it is manifest that Confirmation was deemed by the primitive fathers and Christians a sacrament of
divine institution, but it was considered by the reformers as too Papistical; and therefore must be altered.

Another alteration was in the sacrament of Extreme Unction. The
visitation of the sick was enjoined; but the use of the holy oil, though
spoken of by St. James in the New Testament, must be laid aside; under pretence that it was not heard of till the twelfth century.—To enable
our readers to decide this point, we will here lay before them, as we
have done on the ceremony of the Cross and the sacrament of Confirmation, the sentiments of some of the holy fathers, who all, observe, ground
their doctrine on the words of St. James and the practice of the apostles.
—It is stated in St. Mark, vi. 12, 13, that " going forth, they preached
" that men should do penance, and they cast out many devils, and ANOINTED

" WITH OIL many that were SICK and healed them."--To this practice of
the disciples of Christ, during his ministry on earth, St. James undoubtedly
refers, when he says, in his epistle, " Is any man rich among you ? Let
him bring in the priests of the church, &c."--Victor of Antioch, a priest of
that city, who flourished about the close of the fourth century, has left
us a commentary on St. Mark's gospel, in which he says, " St. Mark
" mentions (vi. 13.) that the anointing with oil was anciently used ;
" with whom St. James agrees when he says : Is any one sick among you ?
" &c. (v. 14.)   Oil relieves lassitude, and is the source of light and
" gladness ; the anointing with oil, therefore, denotes mercy from God,
" the cure of sickness, and the illumination of the heart."   Bibl. PP.
" Mar. T. iv. p. 381.   St. John Chrysostom speaks also in the same
terms.   He says, " To our parents we are indebted for the present life ;
" to the ministers of God for the life to come.   But they cannot ward
" off death from their children, nor even sickness ; while the latter, not
" unfrequently, save the soul labouring at the point of death, inflicting
" on some a lighter punishment ; and preventing others from being
" lost ; not by instruction only and admonition, but by the defence of
" prayer.   For they have obtained a power, not in baptism only, but of
" forgiving the sins which we afterwards commit.   Is any man sick
" among you ? says St. James ; Let him bring in the priests of the church,
" &c."   L. iii. de Sacerdot. c. 6. t. iv. p. 31.   Pope Innocent I. in reply to certain questions put to him by Decentius, an Italian bishop, remarks,--" You cite the words of St. James, Is any man sick among you ?
" Let him bring in the priests of the church, &c.   This passage, doubt-
" less, is to be understood of the sick among the faithful, who may be
" anointed with the holy chrism, which, when consecrated by the bishop,
" not only priests, but all Christians, may use in anointing themselves
" and others in cases of necessity.   It is idle to make any question about
" bishops, since the practice is allowed to priests.   For therefore are
" priests mentioned, on account of the many occupations in which
" bishops are engaged, which may hinder them from attending the sick.
" When the bishop can, or is inclined to attend, he may give his bless-
" ing, and anoint with that chrism, which it was his office to conse-
" crate."   Ep. ad Decent. Conc. Gen. t. ii, p. 1247, 1248.   St. Augustin too holds the same doctrine.   " As often," he says, " as sickness hap-
" pens, the sick man should receive the body and blood of Christ, and
" then anoint his body, in order to comply with the words of the apos-
" tle ; Is any man sick among you ? &c.   Consider, brethren, that he
" who, in his sickness, has recourse to the church, will deserve to ob-
" tain the restoration of his health, and the forgiveness of his sins."
Serm. ccxv. de Temp. t. x. p. 367.   We have thus established the
ancient tenure of this doctrine, and we think common sense will decide
that it is better to hold with a belief as old as Christianity itself, than
to renounce it on the authority of such worthless characters as the
prime movers of this new liturgy or bastard mass for the poor beguiled
and unhappy people of England.

It is now time for us to speak of the means used to establish this
form of prayer, as it was called, and to make it a standard of church
service for the people of England.   It was, as we have before stated,
first drawn up in the year 1548, and being put forth without any due

authority, gave rise to much confusion, some using it and some deriding it, which caused a proclamation to be issued in the king's name on the 24th of June, 1549, ordering that no one in future should, so much as in *private*, make use of any other liturgy, and that the mass in Latin should be laid aside. This was certainly a pretty stretch of power on the part of these evangelical liberty-men, to presume to dictate and regulate the *private* devotions of the people.—However this proclamation was found inefficient, and it was therefore followed by an *act of parliament*, called the *uniformity act*, which imposed severe penalties on those who had the temerity to refuse compliance with the orders of the new religion makers. Every clergyman not making use of it, in the church service, was, for the first offence, to suffer half a year's imprisonment, and forfeit half a year's profits of his benefice; for the second offence he was to be deprived *ipso facto* and lose all his spiritual emoluments; and for the third, to be imprisoned for life. Persons absenting themselves from church, or attempting to bring the new liturgy into contempt were also subjected to fine and imprisonment. Thus stood the common prayer of the new church of England as by law established, till it was revised and altered in the year 1552, just *three* years after its formation.—The reign of Mary rendered it nugatory, but her successor Elizabeth, on assuming the supreme headship of the church, had it revised and altered again in 1559. It was a *third* time altered under James I. in 1603; and a *fourth* time under Charles II. in 1662.—Several alterations were made at each of those times to please those who *dissented* from the established church, but equally hated Popery, and with a view to secure unity; but the more such uniformity was attempted the further were the meddlers from the mark, since each such successive age has proved more prolific in sectarianism than the preceding one.—There was an attempt made in 1669, the year after that era, termed "the glorious Revolution," from whence the bigotted favourists date the constitution of England to be essentially Protestant, though it is well known to have been the work of Catholic hands; but the attempt failed, and though there has been and is now much diversity of opinion on the contents of this book, and many divines are anxious that it should be *again revised*, yet they one and all swear before ordination, that it containeth in it nothing contrary to the word of God, that it may be lawfully used, and that they will use it, and none other. What consistent teachers to instruct and enlighten the most superiorly gifted people on the earth, as Protestant writers in modern times represent the English Protestants to be.

To secure a uniformity of doctrine and discipline, which had been so long preserved when the kingdom was Catholic, without the aid of penal laws, another notable scheme was devised by these reformers, which further disclosed the regard they entertained for the freedom of conscience and the liberty of the subject. The Church was now absorbed in the STATE, and the canon law established by the decrees of popes and councils who were invested by the DIVINE POWER to watch over the faith and morals of mankind, became nugatory through the abolition of the pope's supremacy. It was therefore thought necessary that some code of ecclesiastical laws should be forthwith formed that would answer the purposes intended. Such a scheme was in preparation dur, ing Henry's reign, but his death retarded the completion of the project, and it was left to Edward's wise counsellors to reduce the plan to practice. Accordingly a commission of thirty-two persons, one half of them ecclesiastics, and the other half laymen, were appointed by the king's letters patent, who were ordered to finish their work in three years. The wording of these new laws, however, was left to a sub-committee of eight persons, at the head of whom was TOM CRANMER, who had sided with every administration since his appointment to the see of Canterbury, and pandered to the vices both of Henry and the lord protector Somerset. The entire collection of these ecclesiastical constitutions was completed in 1552, and consisted of fifty-one titles, besides an appendix *De Regulis Juris*. It was called *Reformatio Legum Ecclesiasticorum*, but the king happening to die soon after, prevented its being confirmed either by parliament or the convocation. Of the tenor of these constitutions the reader will be able to decide when he has read the following account of them from the pen of Dr. Lingard. Speaking of the compilation, the learned historian says :—

" It commences with an exposition of the Catholic faith, and enacts
" the punishment of forfeiture, and death against those who deny the
" Christian religion. It then regulates the proceedings in cases of he-
" resy, the ceremony of abjuration, and the delivery of the obstinate
" heretic to the civil magistrate, that he may suffer death according to
" law. Blasphemy subjects the offender to the same penalty. The
" marriages of minors, without the consent of their parents or guardi-
" ans, and of all persons whomsoever, without the previous publication
" of banns, or the entire performance of the ceremony in the church
" according to the book of common prayer, are pronounced of no effect.
" The seducer of a single woman is compelled to marry her, or to en-
" dow her with one-third of his fortune: or, if he have no fortune, to
" charge himself with the maintenance of their illegitimate offspring,
" and to suffer some additional and arbitrary punishment. Adultery is
" visited with imprisonment or transportation for life. In addition, if
" the offender be the wife, she forfeits her jointure, and all the advan-
" tages she might have derived from her marriage : if the husband, he
" returns to the wife her dower, and adds to it one half of his own for-
" tune. But to a clergyman, in whom the enormity of the offence in-
" creases in proportion to the sanctity of his office, the penalty is more
" severe. He loses his benefice, and surrenders the whole of his estate,
" if he be married, to the unoffending party, for the support of her and
" her children ; if unmarried, to the bishop, that it may be devoted to
" purposes of charity.

" Divorces are allowed not only for adultery, but for cruelty, long
" absence, and incompatibility of temper ; and in all such cases the
" parties are permitted to marry again ; but where one deserts the
" other, this indulgence is confined to the innocent person ; the guilty
" is condemned to perpetual imprisonment. In cases of defamation,
" when from the destruction of papers or the absence of witnesses, the
" truth cannot be discovered, the accused is permitted to clear his cha-
" racter by his oath, provided he can produce a competent number of
" compurgators, who shall swear that they give full credit to his asser-
" tion. Commutation of penance for money is conceded on particular

" occasions : the right of devising property by will is refused to mar-
" ried women, slaves, children under fourteen years of age, heretics, li-
" bellers, females of loose character, usurers, and convicts sentenced to
" death, or perpetual banishment or imprisonment : and excommunica-
" tion is asserted to cut off the offender from the society of the faithful,
" the protection of God, and the expectation of future happiness ; and
" to consign him to everlasting punishment, and the tyranny of the
" devil."

We shall dismiss the minor transactions appertaining to religion detailed in the modern Book of Martyrs from Burnet's History, such as
the disputes concerning the real presence, which we proved to demonstration in the first volume of this work, from the testimony of the fathers of the first five ages, was of apostolical belief, and conclude the
theological part of the progress of the Reformation, with the following
remarks from Bossuet's *History of the Variations*, shewing how the hatred of the people was raised by degrees against the Catholic doctrine,
in which he furnishes a remarkable instance practised upon the young
king himself. The modern editors unblushingly avow that *their* motive
for profusely circulating this mass of lies, distortions, and misrepresentations, was to excite *hatred* and abhorrence against the (supposed)
crimes and corruptions of Popery and its professors. The reader will
here see that the *same* spirit that influenced the ancient reformers to
blacken and vilify the Catholic church and her institutions, now influ-
ences the modern exclusionists and admirers of Fox to follow the same
uncharitable practices. Treating on the changes made in the doctrine
of the blessed sacrament, the learned Bossuet says, " The cause of so
" irregular a proceeding, was the leading the people by motives of ha-
" tred, and not of reason. It was an easy matter to excite hatred against
" certain practices, whereof they concealed from the people the begin-
" ning and right use, especially when some abuses were interwoven
" with them : thus, it was easy to render priests odious who abused the
" mass for sordid gain : and hatred once inflamed against them, was by
" a thousand artifices insensibly turned against the mystery they cele-
" brated, and even, as hath appeared, against the real presence, the
" foundation of it.

" The same was done with respect to images, and a French letter,
" which Mr. Burnet gives us of Edward VI. to his uncle the protector,
" makes it palpable. To exercise this young prince's stile, his masters
" set him about collecting all the passages wherein God speaks against
" idols. ' In reading the holy scripture I was desirous,' said he, ' to
" note several places which forbid both *to adore and to make* any images,
" not only of strange gods, but also to form any thing ; thinking *to
" make it like to the majesty of God* the Creator.' In this credulous age
" he had simply believed what was told him, that Catholics made
" images, thinking ' they made them like to the majesty of God,' ' I
" am quite astonished,' proceeds he, ' (God himself and his Holy Spirit
" having so often forbidden it,) that so many people have dared to com-
" mit idolatry *by making and adoring images.*' He fixes the same hatred,
" as we see, on the *making*, as on the *adoring* them ; and, according to
" the notions that were given him, is in the right, since undoubtedly it
" is not lawful to *make* images with the thought of making something

" 'like to the majesty of the Creator.' ' For,' as this prince adds, 'God
" cannot be seen in things that are material, but will be seen in his own
" works.' This was a young child deluded by them. His hatred was
" stirred up against Pagan images, in which man pretends to represent
" the Deity: it was shewn him that God forbids to make such images:
" but they not having as yet taken it into their heads to say, that it is
" unlawful to make such as ours, or, unlawful to represent Jesus Christ
" and his saints, they took care to conceal from him that those of 'Ca-
" tholics were not of this nature. A youth of ten or twelve years old
" could not discover it of himself: to make images odious to him in
" general and confusedly was enough for their purpose. Those of the
" church, though of a different order and design, passed in the lump:
" dazzled with the plausible reasoning and authority of his masters,
" every thing was an idol to him; and the hatred he had conceived
" against idolatry was easily turned against the church.

" The people were not more cunning, and but too easy was it to animate
" them by the like artifices. After this, can the sudden progress of the
" reformation be taken for a visible miracle, the work of God's own
" hand? With what assurance could Mr. Burnet say it; he! who has
" so thoroughly discovered to us the deep causes of this lamentable suc-
" cess? A prince blinded with inordinate passion, and condemned by
" the pope, sets men at work to exaggerate particular facts, some odious
" proceedings and abuses which the church herself condemned. All
" pulpits ring with satires against ignorant and scandalous priests, they
" are brought on the stage, and made the subject of farce and comedy,
" insomuch that Mr. Burnet himself expresses his indignation at it.
" Under the authority of an infant king, and a protector violently ad-
" dicted to Zuinglianism, invective and satire are still carried to a higher
" pitch. The laity, that had long looked on their pastors with an evil eye,
" greedily swallowed down the poisonous novelty. The difficulties in
" the mystery of the eucharist are removed, and the senses, instead of
" being kept under subjection, are flattered. Priests are set free from
" the obligation of continency; monks from all their vows; the whole
" world from the yoke of confession, wholesome indeed for the correc-
" tion of vice, but burdensome to nature. A doctrine of greater liberty
" was preached up, ' and which,' as Mr. Burnet says, ' shewed a plain
" and simple way to the kingdom of heaven.' Laws so convenient met
" with but too ready a compliance. Of sixteen thousand ecclesiastics,
" who made up the body of the English clergy, we are assured by
" Mr. Burnet, that three parts renounced their celibacy in Edward's
" time, that is, in the space of five or six years; and good Protestants
" were made of these bad ecclesiastics, who thus renounced their vows.
" Thus were the clergy gained. As for the laity, the church revenues
" exposed to rapine became their prey. The vestry plate enriched the
" prince's exchequer: the shrine alone of St. Thomas of Canterbury,
" with the inestimable presents that had been sent to it from all parts,
" produced a royal treasure of immense sums of money. This was
" enough to degrade that holy martyr. He was attainted, that he might
" be pillaged, nor were the riches of his tomb the least of his crimes.
" In short, it was judged more expedient to plunder the churches,
" than, conformably to the intention of the founders, to apply their pa-

" trimony to its right use. Where is the wonder, if the nobility, the
" clergy, and the people were so easily gained upon? Is it not rather a
" visible miracle that there remained a spark in Israel, and that all other
" kingdoms did not follow the example of England, Denmark, Sweden,
" and Germany, which were *reformed* by the same means? Amidst all
" these *reformations*, the only one that visibly made no progress was
" that of *manners*."

DISCONTENTS OF THE PEOPLE.

We have seen the change made by the reformers in the doctrine and
discipline of the church; it is now time to see what effect this change
had upon the general condition of the people and the public credit of
the kingdom. Burnet, like all other writers who prostitute their
talents for lucre by lying and deception, would fain persuade us that
the reformation was pleasing to the people. He tells us, at the commencement of his account of this reign, that " the people generally were cry-
" ing out for a reformation, despising the clergy, and *loving the new*
" *preachers*." This disposition, however, it appears did not, if it ever existed, last long, for he was obliged to acknowledge, in a subsequent part
of his account, that the people grew discontented, and that rebellions
took place in Devonshire and others parts.—" About this time," he
writes, " a rebellion broke out in many parts of England, partly arising
" from a jealousy in the commons against the nobility and gentry, who
" finding more advantage by the trade of wool than by that of corn, gene-
" rally enclosed their grounds, and turned them to pasture, by which a
" great number of persons were thrown out of employment, and a general
" consternation was spread throughout the country. The other cause was
" the unquenched enmity of the Popish priests to the reformation, and their
" endeavours to revive in the minds of the blinded multitude their former
" errors." Here we have a base attempt to disguise the real state of the case,
by affixing part of the discontents to " the unquenched enmity of the Popish
priests," whereas it is incontrovertible that the commotions originated
in the cruel oppressions of the reformers towards the commonalty.—
Religion was undoubtedly mixed up with the grievances of the people,
but it ought not to surprise any one, that the people should bear an
affection towards a system of religion under which they had been so
happy, and a dislike towards that which had brought with it so many
ills, and rendered their situation so miserable and comfortless.—The disturbances arose out of the new order of things, by which mischievous inroads had been made in the constitution of the country, the currency was
depreciated, and a proportionate advance in all saleable commodities followed in consequence. The value of land rose with the value of its
produce, and the rents of farms had been doubled and in several instances trebled. Had the wages of the labourer kept pace with the advance of prices, little or no difference would have been occasioned. But
the demand for labour, in consequence of the land being in new hands,
was lessened, and the wages were reduced instead of being advanced.
This state of things we have in part witnessed within the last thirty
years, owing to the restrictions which were placed upon the bank of
England, whereby she was prevented from paying her notes in gold,

and, the country being thus deluged with paper money, the regular currency became depreciated, so that prices advanced to the injury of labour, and discontents succeeded as in the time of Edward.—In the Catholic times, particularly on the estates of the monks and clergy, considerable portions of the land were allotted to the common use of the labourers and poor inhabitants ; by which careful economy a great degree of comfort was afforded them, and pauperism was utterly unknown in England.　Now, however, the new landlords, after having robbed the clergy of their abbey lands, and the poor of their patrimony, conceived that these waste lands would add to their advantage, and wholly disregarding the wants of their indigent neighbours, began to inclose the commons, and thus cut off every hope of the poor for a subsistence.—Grazing too was found much more profitable than growing corn, and to such an extent was this new mode of farming carried, that it was stated in a proclamation issued by the king, that many villages, in which 100 or 200 people had lived, were now entirely destroyed ; that one shepherd now dwelt where industrious families dwelt before ; and that the realm is wasted by " bringing arable grounds into pasture, and letting houses, whole families, and copyholds, to fall down, decay, and be waste."—Under such a state of things it could not be expected that men would remain quiet, especially as we have seen that the projectors of the new liturgy so far anticipated resistance to their innovations, that they caused foreign mercenary troops to be brought into the country.　The people felt their own miseries, and they saw that the new holders of the land did not treat them with the same kindness as the former proprietors: it was natural therefore that they should couple their own grievances with the innovations of religion.—They found their own resources diminished, and were now compelled to listen to a dull cold inanimate form of worship instead of those soul-inspiring ceremonies they had been accustomed to from their very infancy.　Thus goaded nearly to madness, the people rose almost simultaneously in the counties of Surrey, Sussex, Kent, Wilts, Hampshire, Gloucester, Somerset, Berks, Warwick, Leicester, Worcester, Hertford, Essex, Suffolk, Norfolk, and Cornwall. —In Wiltshire, sir William Herbert put himself at the head of a body of troops, dispersed the insurgents, and executed martial law on the ringleaders.—In the other counties tranquillity was partially restored by the exertions of the resident gentry and the moderate among the yeomanry.—In Norfolk, Cornwall and Devon, the risings assumed the most alarming appearance, and threatened defiance to the government. In general, however, the insurgents acted without concert and without competent leaders ; still the issue would have been doubtful, had not the reformers availed themselves of the aid of FOREIGN TROOPS to cut down and massacre Englishmen contending for their rights.—Protestant reader, bear in mind, and never let it slip your memory, this great and important fact, that the reformation in religion in England, was crammed down the throats of the people by FOREIGN BAYONETS.

When the new liturgy was read the first time in the church of Samford Courteney, in Devonshire, on Whitsunday, the people compelled the clergyman the next day to restore the ancient service.　This act was the signal of a general insurrection, and in a few days the insurgents numbered ten　　　　　　　　　　by Humphrey Arundel, go-

A REVIEW

OF

Fox's Book of Martyrs,

CRITICAL AND HISTORICAL.

No. 46. Printed and Published by W. E. ANDREWS, 3, Chapter-house-court, St. Paul's Churchyard, London. **Price 3d.**

EXPLANATION OF THE ENGRAVING—*Father O'Hurle, O. S. F. the Catholic arch-bishop of Cashel, in Ireland, falling into the hands of Sir W. Drury, the sanguinary go-vernor of the province, in the year 1579, was first tortured by his legs being immersed in jackboots with quick-lime, according to Dr. Burke. The Theatrum Crudelitatum Hæreticorum from which we have taken this cut, says, the boots were filled with oil, and that his legs being placed over a large fire, the flesh was boiled off the bones. - This cruel torture was inflicted to force the archbishop to take the oath of supremacy, but being ineffectual, the holy martyr was executed at the gallows, having previously cited Drury to meet him at the tribunal of God within ten days, who accordingly died within that period amidst the most excruciating pain.*

CONTINUATION OF THE REVIEW.

vernor of St. Michael's Mount.—With the troops sent to oppose them were three preachers, named Gregory, Reynolds, and Coverdale, who received *a license from the king to declare the word of God to the people;* but these missionaries did not feel disposed to run the risk of martyr-dom, and the general not having confidence in their eloquence, entered into a negotiation with the malecontents.—The latter made fifteen de-mands, which they afterwards reduced to eight, requiring the restoration of the ancient service, the introduction of cardinal Pole into the council, and the re-establishment of two abbeys at least in every county.—Tom Cranmer composed a long reply to the former, and the king answered the latter by a proclamation, couched in no very gracious language.—

Arundel in the mean time attempted to take the city of Exeter, by laying siege to it, but without success, as he was bravely resisted by the inhabitants. After a siege of forty days, lord Gray arrived with a reinforcement of *German* horse and *Italian* arquebusiers, who drove the insurgents from the town, and eventually defeated them.—During the insurrection four thousand men are said to have perished in the field, or by the hand of the executioner.—During these disturbances martial law, we are told, was executed in every part of the kingdom. Sir Anthony Kyngstone, provost of the Western army, is stated by Speed and Hayward to have distinguished himself by the promptitude of his decisions, and the pleasantry with which he accompanied them.—Having dined with the mayor of Bodmin, writes Dr. Lingard, he asked him if the gallows were sufficiently strong? The mayor replied he thought so. "Then," said Kyngstone, "go up and try;" and hanged him without further ceremony. On another occasion, having received information against a miller, he proceeded to the mill, and not finding the master at home, ordered the servant to the gallows, bidding him be content, for it was the best service which he had ever rendered to his master.—The reader, we have no doubt, is disgusted with such pleasantry, and shudders at the callousness of the heart that could indulge in them, though acting in defence of the enlightened Protestant religion.—Let us then hear no more of Popish cruelties. The changes have been rung till the people are almost deafened with the barbarous deeds of Jefferies and Kirk, in Monmouth's rebellion against James II. who happened to be a Catholic prince, though in this case the Judge and Colonel were both Protestants.

In Norfolk the insurrection assumed a more formidable appearance. It commenced at Attleborough, on the 20th of June, 1549, according to Dr. Heylin, but the insurgents did not begin to appear in considerable numbers until the 6th of July following, when the people flocked from all the surrounding parishes to join them, and they were headed by one Kett, a tanner, of Wymondham, a town about six miles distant from Attleborough. "These men," writes Dr. Heylin, "pretended only
" against enclosures; and if religion was at all regarded by them, it was
" rather kept for a reserve, then suffered to appear in the front of
" the battle. But when their numbers were so vastly multiplied, as to
" amount to twenty thousand, nothing would serve them but the sup-
" pression of the gentry, the placing of new counsellors about the
" king, and somewhat also to be done in favour of the old religion.
" Concerning which they thus remonstrate to the king or the people
" rather; viz. first, That the free-born commonalty was oppressed by
" a small number of gentry, who glutted themselves with pleasure,
" whilst the poor commons wasted with daily labour did (like pack-
" horses,) live in extreme slavery. Secondly, That holy rites, estab-
" lished by antiquity, were abolished; new ones authorized, and a new
" form of religion obtruded, to the subjecting of their souls to those
" horrid pains, which no death could terminate. And therefore, thirdly,
" That it was necessary for them to go in person to the king, to place
" new counsellors about him during his minority, removing those who
" (ruling as they list) confounded things sacred and profane, and re-
" garded nothing but the enriching of themselves with the public trea-

" sure, that they might riot it amidst these public calamities." Such
are recorded as the complaints of the Norfolk malecontents at the origin
of the reformation, as it is called, and if we look at the present situation of the country, we shall see that it is not bettered in its condition.
—We have Jew loan jobbers, sinecurists and pensioners, half-pay
officers, and married parsons, glutting themselves with luxury, whilst
the poor commons are obliged to contribute more than a third of their
labour to support these idlers out of the taxes, and work like pack-
horses under the slavery of a criminal code a thousand times more
galling than the penances imposed upon them by the Catholic Clergy,
because these were voluntary, and of course performed with cheerfulness.

To the above demands no satisfactory answer was given, and the insurgents marched off for Norwich, where Kett planted his standard on
Moushold hill, which overlooked a great part of the city, and gave him
full command of it. Here, seated under a large oak, which he called
the *oak of reformation*, Kett kept his courts, and carried terror among
the neighbouring gentry and citizens of Norwich. The latter had allowed the marquess of Northampton to enter the city with one thousand English horse, and a body of ITALIANS under the command of
Malatesta, out of which the marquess was beaten by Kett, and returned
in disgrace to London.—The council then sent the earl of Warwick
with eight thousand men, two thousand being GERMAN horse, by whom
the insurgents were defeated, after a long and desperate struggle. More
than two thousand perished by the sword, Kett and nine others were
hanged, and the remainder were granted a general pardon.—Thus it
will be seen that the introduction of the *reformation*, as it is misnamed,
produced in its progress not only a change in religion, but a gross
violation of the principles of the constitution, the most impious sacrileges and spoliations, and a waste of human blood hitherto unparalleled
in the annals of the country, arising from the discontents of the people.
—England had been Catholic nine hundred years, and during that long
period but one insurrection occurred on the part of the people, namely
that under Wat Tyler, occasioned in part from the heavy taxation produced by a long war with France, and the seditious doctrines of ignorant preachers, instigated by Wickliffe and his adherents.—This rising,
however, was put down with a trivial loss of blood, compared with the
rivers that were spilled in the insurrections of Harry and Edward's
reigns, from the innovations then made on religion and the inroads on
the constitution.—The civil war between the houses of York and Lan-
easter, and the frequent appeals to arms by the Barons, had nothing of
the character of religion in them, nor did they spring from gross oppressions of the poor.—The people in those times were in the possession
of plenty and ease, but the *reformation* has taken from them those means
which secured them against want and contumely, and instead of the
profusion which abounded on the tables of the Catholic people of England, and the visible effects of good living displayed in their robust
countenances and hardy frames, we now see the hearty meal reduced to
the meagre mess of potatoes, and the people exhibiting the care-worn
visages of misery and the lank emaciated forms of want. And this
change in the time of Edward the sixth, when Tom Cranmer was archbishop of Canterbury, was effected by FOREIGN BAYONETS !!!

Connected with these scenes, we must notice the treatment of bishop Bonner, whose name is so familiar with the readers of the *Book of Martyrs*, where he is delineated a monster delighting in the blood of the innocent. Of this, however, we shall have to speak by and by.—Burnett has represented that the people were fond of the *new preachers*; the commotions we have recorded give the lie to this statement, and prove that nine-tenths of the nation were in favour of the creed of their fathers, and opposed to the mongrel doctrines invented by the reformers. The innovators, however, relied on the support of the crown, and resolved to get rid of some of the most obnoxious of their adversaries in the church who stood up for the old creed. Among these was bishop Bonner. He was summoned before the council, and ordered to perform the new service at St. Paul's; besides which he was commanded to preach at St. Paul's cross, and the heads of his sermon were selected for him.—One of these was to shew that " the rebels in Devonshire, Cornwall, and Norfolk, did not only deserve death as traitors, but accumulated to themselves eternal damnation, even to be in the burning fire of hell, with Lucifer, the father and first author of rebellion."—Mark! this was the doctrine of the reformers of the 16th century, who had rebelled against the lawful authority of the church, but would not admit of any resistance to their views under pain of damnation. At the day appointed, crowds of people assembled to hear the prelate, and Latimer and Hooper, the latter being afterwards made a bishop, were appointed to inform against him, if he did not comply with sufficient exactness. He was denounced by these reformers or spies to the council, who appointed a commission, of which Cranmer was at the head, before which Bonner appeared, and by his extensive knowledge in the canon law, and his dignified behaviour before his judges, he maintained his episcopal character, but was deprived of his bishopric, and committed to the Marshalsea prison, where he remained till the king's death.—Ridley, one of his judges, was appointed to the see of London, which Bonner filled, but under circumstances the most disgraceful. The bishopric of Westminster was dissolved, and Ridley accepted the lands and revenues, in exchange for the lands and revenues belonging to his own church. These, four days after, were given to three of the principal favourites at court, Rich, lord chancellor; Wentworth, lord chamberlain; and sir Thomas Darcy, vice chamberlain.

While these disastrous and afflicting matters were going on at home, the affairs of the kingdom were not less disgraceful and unfortunate abroad.—Boulogne as well as Calais had been for a long series of years in the hands of the English, and were looked upon as the most honourable appendage of the English crown.—The reformers, however, seemed to care as little for the honour of the nation, as for its constitutional rights.—The insurrections making so formidable an appearance, induced the king of France to declare war against England, while, we should have observed, this country was hostilely engaged also with Scotland.—In this state of things, Somerset, the lord protector, proposed to make peace with Scotland, to surrender Boulogne to Henry II. of France for *a sum of money*, and to enter into a treaty with that monarch *to support the Protestant interest in Germany* against the growing superiority of Charles the fifth. The majority of the council were opposed to this proposition, and pronounced the surrender of Boulogne a

measure calculated to bring odium on the king's government.—The French, however, were determined to obtain possession of it; they poured troops into the Boulognnois, and in less than three weeks they possessed themselves of the fortified outworks of Blackness, Ambleteuse, and Sellacques; the town itself prepared to sustain a regular siege.—Equally unfortunate were the English forces in Scotland, for after various disasters, nothing was left them of all their former acquisitions but the fort of Aymouth and the town of Roxburgh.—In the mean while, the government itself, as well as the country, was torn by factions and divisions, and a party was growing formidable in the ministry against the lord protector.—Boulogne had now sustained a twelvemonths' siege, but the internal troubles of the kingdom, occasioned by the rapacious robberies of courtiers and the impious presumption of the reformers of religion, had reduced it to a state of impotency, and it was now determined to crave the assistance of that monarch, who, but a year before, it was proposed to confederate against with the French king.—An ambassador was actually sent to the emperor Charles the fifth to demand succour of him, and request that he would take the town of Boulogne into keeping, till the youthful Edward could settle the differences between his own subjects. Charles would not listen to the request, unless the king would promise to restore the Catholic religion, which his councillors not being willing to accede to, Charles would have nothing to do with them. They then entered into a negociation with France, to bring about which they employed a *foreign* merchant, named Antonio Guidotti, through whose agency ambassadors were named, and conferences opened.—The French were sensible of their superiority, and accordingly dictated their own terms. The English talked big, but it was mere talk; their actions did not correspond with their words, for every day produced fresh secessions from their terms, and at last they agreed to surrender the town on the terms proposed by the French.—"The treaty," writes Dr. Lingard, "was
" prefaced by a long and fulsome panegyric of the two kings: Henry
" and Edward were the best of princes, the two great luminaries of the
" Christian world: personally they had no causes of enmity against
" each other: and as for the relics of that hostility which had divided
" their fathers, they were determined to suppress them for ever. With
" this view they had agreed, 1st, that there should be between the two
" crowns a peace, league, and union, which should last not only for
" their lives, but as long as time should endure: 2d, that Boulogne
" should be restored to the king of France, with the ordnance and
" stores which were found in it at the time of its capture: that in re-
" turn for the expense of keeping up the fortifications Henry should
" pay to Edward two hundred thousand crowns at the time of its deli-
" very, and two hundred thousand more within five months; on condi-
" tion that the English should previously surrender Dunglass and Lau-
" der to the queen of Scots, or, if Dunglass and Lauder were not in
" their possession, should raze to the ground the fortresses of Rox-
" burgh and Aymouth: 3d, that Scotland should be comprehended in
" this treaty, if the queen signified her acceptance of it within forty
" days; and that Edward should not hereafter make war upon her or
" her subjects, unless some new cause of offence were given: and last-

" ly, that all the rights, claims and pretensions of England against
" France and Scotland, or of France and Scotland against England,
" should be mutually reserved. Though Warwick had signed the in-
" structions to the ambassadors, he absented himself under pretence of
" sickness from the council on the day on which the treaty was con-
" firmed. By the public the conditions were considered a national dis-
" grace. The sum of two millions of crowns, which Francis had con-
" sented to give for the surrender of Boulogne at the expiration of eight
" years, had been cut down to one fifth: the right of enforcing the
" treaty of marriage between Edward and Mary of Scotland had been
" abandoned : and the perpetual pension, which Henry VIII. had ac-
" cepted in lieu of his claim to the crown of France, had been virtually
" surrendered. In fact the pretensions of the former kings of England
" were after this treaty suffered to sleep in silence by their successors.
" They contented themselves with the sole title of kings of France, a
" barren but invidious distinction, which after two centuries and a half
" has been wisely laid aside by the father of his present majesty."—
Such were the fruits, both foreign and domestic, produced by the departure of the nation from that system of religion which guiding all its
believers in the way of truth, and inculcating principles the most moral
and virtuous, filled our Catholic ancestors with the most noble and heroic actions, and rendered England the most happy and powerful kingdom on the earth.—Under the fifth Henry France was subdued, single
handed, to the crown of England; under the Protestant king Edward
the sixth her arms were sullied by cowardice and treachery, and her
honour stained by the bad faith of her rulers. Guidotti was rewarded,
according to Dr. Heylin, with knighthood, a present of one thousand
crowns, and an annual pension of as much to maintain his dignity, besides a pension of 250 crowns per annum for his son.

BURNING OF HERETICS.

Before we commence our remarks on this part of the "PROGRESS OF
THE REFORMATION," we will give the account of these burnings from
the modern *Book of Martyrs*.—We have compared it with Burnet's
Abridgement, and we find it is a still further abridgement, the most
material points regarding Cranmer being left out.—But to the story.—
The modern editors say,—" There were some Anabaptists at this time
" in England, who came from Germany. Of these there were two
" sorts; the first only objected to the baptizing of children, and to the
" manner of it, by sprinkling instead of dipping. The other held many
" opinions, anciently condemned as heresies : they had raised *a war* in
" Germany, and had set up *a new king* at Munster; but all these were
" called Anabaptists, from their opposition to infant baptism, though it
" was one of *the mildest opinions they held.* When they came to Eng-
" land, a commission was granted to some *bishops*, and others, *to search*
" *them out, and to proceed against them.* Several of these persons, on
" being *taken up* and brought before them, *abjured their errors*, some of
" which were, 'That there was not a trinity of persons; that Christ
" was not God, and took not flesh of the Virgin; and that a regenerate
" man could not sin."

" Joan Bocher, called Joan of Kent, one of their proselytes, persisted
" in her error, and denied that Christ took flesh of the substance of his
" mother; *she was intolerably vain of her notions*, and rejected with scorn
" all the *instruction* offered her: she was, *therefore*, condemned as *an*
" *obstinate heretic*, and delivered to the secular power. But it was with
" the most extreme relúctance that the king signed the warrant for her
" execution; he thought it was an instance of the same spirit of cruelty
" for which the reformers condemned the Papists; and notwithstand-
" ing all the arguments that were used with him, he was rather si-
" lenced than satisfied, and signed the warrant with tears in his eyes,
" saying to Cranmer, that since he resigned up himself to his judg-
" ment, if he sinned in it, it should lie at his door. This struck the
" archbishop; and both he and Ridley took great pains with her, and
" tried what reason, joined with gentleness, could do. But she grow-
" ing still more and more insolent, at last was burnt, and ended her
" life *very indecently*, breaking out often *in jeers* and *reproaches.*

" Some time after this, George van Parre, a Dutchman, was also con-
" demned and *burnt*, for *denying the divinity of Christ*, and saying, that the
" Father *only* was God. He had led *a very exemplary life*, both for fast-
" ing, devotion, and a good conversation, and suffered with extraordi-
" nary composure of mind. Against the other sort of Anabaptists no
" severities were used: but several books were written to *justify infant*
" *baptism;* and the practice of *the church*, so *clearly begun*, and so *uni-*
" *versally spread*, was thought *a good plea*, especially being grounded
" on such arguments in scripture as demonstrated at least its lawful-
" ness."

So, so; the reformers then could burn for *heresy* as well as Catholics;
and yet all the clamour, all the invective, all the brutal calumny raised
on this mode of punishment for religious error, has been levelled against
Catholics only.—The king, it seems, judged it an instance of cruelty for
which the reformers condemned the Papists, and objected to signing
the warrants; well, and how did the reformers reply to this objection?
This the modern editors have not told us, though Burnet mentions the
arguments used by Cranmer.—These men of veracity, who publish this
book for the purpose of conveying a knowledge of Christianity to their
readers, and exciting a hatred of Popery, *suppressed* the arguments of
Cranmer, for burning this crazy old woman, considering, we have no
doubt, that they would be thought to bear too hard upon the hoary old miscreant, who cared not who he sent to the stake, so that he escaped with a
whole skin. He was always ready to comply with the merciless edicts of a
beastly tyrant, and here he was urging a royal youth to an act of cruelty
against his inclination.—But let us see what he had to urge against the
" intolerably vain" heretic.—Burnet says that " Cranmer persuaded
" him, that he, being GOD's lieutenant, was *bound* in the first place *to*
" *punish* those offences committed against God: he also alleged the
" laws of Moses, for punishing blasphemy; and he thought the errors
" that struck immediately against the apostles' creed, *ought* to be *capi-*
" *tally* punished."—Dr. Heylin tells us, that she was convented before
archbishop Cranmer and his assistants in the church of St. Paul, and
that her crime was, " That she denied Christ to have taken flesh from
" the Virgin Mary, affirming (as the Valentinians did of old) that he

" only passed through her body, as water through the pipe of a conduit,
" without participating any thing of that body through which he pass-
" ed ;" and that when Cranmer " was upon the point of passing sentence
" upon her, for persisting obstinate in so gross an heresy, she most
" maliciously reproached him, for passing the like sentence of con-
"demnation on another woman, called Anne Askew, for denying the.
" carnal presence of Christ in the sacrament; telling him, that he con-
" demned the said Anne Askew not long before for a piece of bread,
" and was then ready to condemn her for a piece of flesh."—Dr. Lingard gives her answer to the archbishop in much more pungent terms
than Heylin does. This historian tells us she replied to Tom Cranmer
in these words. " It is a goodly matter to consider *your* ignorance. It
" was not long ago that you burned Anne Askew for a piece of bread;
" and yet you came yourselves soon after *to believe and profess the same*
" *doctrine for which you burned her;* and now, forsooth, you will needs
" burn me for a piece of flesh, and in the end will come to believe this
" also, *when you have* READ *the scriptures and* UNDERSTAND THEM."
We should like to have seen the reforming apostles of the Church of
England, when Joan threw this smart charge of inconsistency in their
face. Surely they must have looked very foolish at each other.—Burnet says " she was intolerably vain of her notions ;" it does not appear
that her judges were so vain of their notions, when they could condemn
a woman for a belief which they afterwards adopted themselves.—The
fact however was, Joan and Anne were both wild enthusiasts, while
their judges were cold and calculating reformists, veering with every
change of the tide at court; now believers in transubstantiation because Harry willed it so ; now rejecting it because it was more fashionable.; and had the wind blown the same notion that Joan was sentenced
to death for, there is no doubt but her judges would have fulfilled her
predictions. We are not surprsied that Burnet should think Mrs.
Joan " was intolerably vain of her notions" when she told her judges
that they were *ignorant*, not having *read the scriptures*, and therefore did
not understand them.—This is the same with all bible readers who build
upon their own superior knowledge of interpretation, and as the groundwork of the Reformation, so miscalled, was the allowing every one,
however illiterate, to interpret the mysterious word according to his
own fancy, who was to decide between the disputants ? What right
could Tom Cranmer, and Latimer, and the rest of her judges, have to
condemn Joan Bocher, or any other Joan or Judy among the whole
tribe of bible readers, for heresy, when they themselves had been guilty
of it, and had refused submission to the only unerring tribunal that had
legitimate cognizance of erroneous doctrines.—Only think, sensible
reader, of a man invested with the character of a judge, condemning a
poor silly woman under the authority of a tyrant, for having taken a
strange notion in her head on religious matters, and then embracing
and teaching the self-same doctrine which the unfortunate woman was
burned for. Then see this same man urging a youth (whose merciful
disposition made him shudder at the idea of sending a woman out of
the world while she remained in sin, lest her soul should be consigned
to everlasting torments) to sign the death warrant of his victim, and
quoting scripture to back his cruel request. Yet this unfeeling monster

—this hoary villain—this panderer to the vices of the basest men in power—is held up to this day, by bigotted and interested individuals, as a paragon of virtue, and a holy martyr to the Protestant religion, and believed to be so by hundreds of credulous and ignorant people!

We do not attempt to justify, but condemn, the putting heretics to death for mere speculative doctrine; but as Protestants have been guilty of burning for heresy, as well as ripping and hanging for truth, it may not be amiss to point out some shades of difference between them and Catholic states in the exercise of this civil prerogative, for there is no authority existing in the church to authorize the putting any one to death for an error of the mind. The Arians were the first to *persecute* for conscience sake, after the establishment of Christianity and the eradication of Paganism; the Iconoclasts the next; and we have it on record that St. Ambrose and St. Martin, two great luminaries of the Catholic church, refused to hold communion with a Spanish bishop, named Ithacius, even against the will of the emperor, because he sought to have certain Priscillian heretics put to death.—Heresy, we believe, was not made a capital punishment until those who broached it mingled with it doctrines that were dangerous to the peace and happiness of society, and threatened the subversion of all order. It consequently followed that kings and magistrates found themselves necessitated to adopt some strong measures to secure their own authority, and hence arose the statutes enacted to punish heresy with death.—In these cases the offender was taken before his ecclesiastical judges, who examined the doctrines he maintained, pointed out to him the erroneousness of his opinions, and if he continued obstinate, after due time was allowed him for reflection, he was pronounced contumacious and handed over to the secular power.

This was the mode of proceeding with Joan Bocher, but *who* were *her* judges, and *what* authority had *they* to pronounce her a heretic. In those cases where Catholics were concerned, it is to be observed that their decisions were made according to a rule believed to be unerring. They pronounced upon the authority of an undeviating system of faith, brought down from age to age, and followed universally throughout the world.—Here then it was antiquity and uniformity against novelty and disunion. Now this was not the case with Cranmer and Joan Bocher. —Her judges had departed themselves from the invariable rule; they had set up reason, fallible human reason, as their guide; they allowed private interpretation of the scriptures; and at the same time they passed laws to punish individuals who did not or would not think as they did; they have them arrested; they sit in judgment upon them; and with the utmost composure sentence them to death, though it does not appear that the error maintained in the least affected the safety of the state. Here then we have real sheer tyranny; because the judges in this case did not decide by legitimate authority, and were themselves infected with the same crime. They condemned the woman for exercising a right which they said she possessed, and was to use according to her own judgment, and punished her because she could not see as they pretended to see.—Thus we have shewn that there is a very great difference between Catholic divines pronouncing upon heresy, and the decisions of Protestants on that offence. The one decides according to

" men themselves, and by degrees a vilifying and contempt of their
" holy ministry? Nay, such a peccancy of humour began then mani-
" festly to break out; that it was preached at Paul's cross by one sir
" Steven (for so they commonly called such of the clergy as were un-
" der the degree of doctor,) the curate of St. Katherine Christ church,
" that it was fit the names of churches should be altered, and the names
" of the days in the week changed; that fish-days should be kept on
" any other days than on Fridays and Saturdays, and the Lent at any
" other time except only between Shrovetide and Easter. We are
" told also by John Stow, that he had seen the said sir Steven to leave
" the pulpit, and preach to the people out of an high elm, which stood
" in the midst of the churchyard; and that being done, to return into
" the church again, and leaving the high altar, to sing the Communion
" Service upon a tomb of the dead, with his face toward the North.
" Which is to be observed the rather, because sir Steven hath found so
" many followers in these latter times. For as some of the preciser
" sort have left the church to preach in woods and barns, &c. and in-
" stead of the names of the old days and months, can find no other title
" for them than the first, second, or third month of the year, and the
" first, second, or third day of the week, &c. so was it propounded not
" long since by some state-reformers, 'that the Lenten fast should be
" kept no longer between Shrovetide and Easter, but rather (by some
" act or ordinance to be made for that purpose,) betwixt Easter and
" Whitsuntide.' To such wild fancies do men grow, when once they
" break those bonds, and neglect those rules, which wise antiquity or-
" dained for the preservation of peace and order."

Wild as these fancies might be considered by the doctor, they were
followed by a general order for the taking down of altars, bearing date
the 24th of November, 1550, and subscribed by the duke of Somerset,
the archbishop of Canterbury, and others. For the advancement of this
work, John Hooper observed, in a sermon before the king, "that it
" would be very well, that it might please the *magistrate* to turn the
" *altars* into *tables*, according to the first institution of Christ; and
" thereby to take away the false persuasion of the people, which they
" have of *sacrifices* to be done upon *altars*. Because (said he) as long
" as altars remain, both the ignorant people, and the ignorant and evil
" persuaded priest, will dream always of *sacrifice*." Such was the recommendation of one of the chief and turbulent reformers, but though
his advice was followed to the destruction and pillaging of those necessary appendages to the temples of the living God, yet the adorable
sacrifice of the mass could not be wholly obliterated from the minds of
the people, and it is daily offered at this day in almost every part of
England. This change of *altars* into *tables* was the occasion of much
derision and satire. The differences of opinion among the reformers
might fairly be compared to the confused tongues among the Babel-
builders. The ministers who had to officiate were at a loss to know
where they were to stand at the table; whether at this end or that end,
or in the middle. Bishop Ridley called it an oyster board, and White,
of Lincoln, according to John Fox, in his original work, said, "that
" when their table was constituted, they could never be content in
" placing the same; now east, now north; now one way, now another;

" until it pleased God in his goodness to place it quite out of the church."
Dr. Heylin says, " The like did Weston, (the prolocutor of the convo-
" cation in the first of queen Mary) in a disputation held with Latimer;
" telling him with reproach and contempt enough, that the Protestants
" having turned their table, *were like a company of apes, that knew*
" *not which way to turn their tails;* looking one day east, and another
" day west; one this way, and another that way, as their fancies led
" them. Thus, finally, one Miles Hubbard, in a book called 'The
" Display of Protestants,' printed in 1556, p. 81, doth report the busi-
" ness, ' How long (say they) were they learning to set their tab es to
" minister the communion upon ? First they placed it aloft, where the
" high altar stood ; then must it be removed from the wall, that one
" might go between ; the ministers being in contention whether part to
" turn their faces, either toward the west, the north, or south ; some
" would stand westward, some northward, some southward.'" To
settle these diversities a rubrick was drawn up, and the north side
was pitched upon as the most proper place for the table. We have
before noticed the changes made in the liturgy, arising from the factious
and capricious whims of the leading reformers, who blasphemously
stated that every alteration was made under the influence of the Holy
Ghost, the Spirit of Truth.

Much has been said of late on the subject of EXCOMMUNICATION, and
it has been frequently brought as a heavy charge against the Catholic
Clergy of Ireland, to justify the exclusion of the Irish people from the
exercise of their civil rights. The power of excommunication, or
separating the unbeliever from the faithful, is clearly established in the
scriptures, and it is exercised by all sects, though we never hear any
complaint made against the use of this prerogative but only when applied to the Catholic church.—We have seen that the Anabaptists excommunicated Von Parris for Unitarianism, and we are now about to
shew that one of the greatest of the 16th-century reformers thought it
necessary to call for this ancient discipline of the church, the new
bishops of Edward's making, having some how or other lost, or were restrained in, the right of exercising it ; but were subsequently empowered
by *act of parliament*, to assume it.—The strifes amongst the reforming
divines, and the repeated changes and alterations made in the creed
and ceremonies of the new church, all tending to a relaxation of morals
and devotion, produced the most dismal consequences in the condition
of the people, whose habits were now marked by the grossest vices and
the most impure debaucheries. Latimer, who was appointed bishop of
Worcester, by Harry, but resigned his see rather than sign the six articles, in a sermon before the young head of the church, complained of
the luxury and vanity of the age, and of many called Gospellers, who
were concerned for nothing but abbey and chantry lands, and he thus,
according to Dr. Heylin, called for the restitution of the ancient discipline. " Lechery," says he, " is used in England, and such lechery as is
" used in no other part of the world ; and yet it is made a matter of
" sport, a matter of nothing, a laughing matter, a trifle not to be passed
" on, nor reformed. Well, I trust it will be amended one day, and I
" hope to see it mended as old as I am. And here I will make a suit
" to your highness, to restore unto the church the discipline of Christ,

"in excommunicating such as be notable offenders. Nor never devise
"any other way; for no man is able to devise any better than that God
"hath done with excommunication to put them from the congregation,
"till they be confounded. Therefore restore Christ's discipline for ex-
"communication; and that shall be a means both to pacify God's
"wrath and indignation, and also that less abomination shall be used
"then in times past hath been, or is at this day. I speak this of a
"conscience, and I mean to move it of a will to your grace, and your
"realm. Bring into the church of England the open discipline of ex-
"communication, that open sinners may be striken with all.'" He
also complained, Burnet says, that the king's debts were not paid; and
yet his officers grew vastly rich. What the Protestants understand by excommunication, and how the excommunicated are to be avoided, we may
gather from the 33d of the 42 of Edward's articles, and the 39 of Elizabeth's.—It says, "That person which, by open denunciation of the
"church, is rightly cut off from the unity of the church, and excom-
"municate, ought to be taken of the whole multitude of the faithful as a
"heathen and a publican, until he be openly reconciled by penance, and
"received into the church by a judge that hath authority thereunto."
And Roger's in his explanation of it tells us, "that the most severe and
"uttermost punishment that the visible church can inflict upon the
"wicked, is excommunication. Which is to put the wicked doer from
"the company of the faithful, to deliver him unto satan, and to de-
"nounce him a heathen and a publican. A man so cut off from the
"congregation, and excommunicated, is not to be eaten withal, nor to
"be received into a house."—Such is the punishment of excommunication by the church of England; let us then not hear it alleged any
more against the Catholics.

We have said enough to shew the progress that was made in the reformation so called, during the reign this boy pope. To the nation at
large the consequences were of the most afflicting nature.—While some
of the most unprincipled men were exalted at court, and enriched with
the spoils of the church, the people were reduced to the lowest state of
beggary and want, and the clergy of the new establishment were the
most ignorant and debased of their profession. Dr. Heylin, in summing
up the transactions of Edward's reign, says, "that such was the rapacity
"of the times, and the unfortunateness of his condition, that his mi-
"nority was abused to many acts of spoil, and rapine (even to an high
"degree of sacrilege) to the raising of some, and the enriching of others,
"without any manner of improvement to his own estate. For notwith-
"standing the great and most inestimable treasures, which must needs
"come by the spoil of so many shrines and images, the sale of all the
"lands belonging to chanteries, colleges, free chapels, &c. and the
"dilapidating of the patrimony of so many bishoprics, and cathedral
"churches; he was not only plunged in debt, but the crown lands were
"much diminished and impaired, since his coming to it. Besides
"which spoils, there were many other helps, and some great ones too,
"of keeping him from being both before-hand, and full of money, had
"they been used to his advantage. The lands of divers of the halls
"and companies in London were charged with annual pensions for the
"finding of such lights, obits, and chantry priests, as were founded

" by the donors of them : for the redeeming whereof they were con-
" strained to pay the sum of twenty thousand pounds to the use of the
" king, by an order from the council table ; not long before the pay-
" ment of the first money for the sale of Boulogne, anno 1550. And
" somewhat was also paid by the city to the king for the purchase of
" the borough of Southwark, which they bought of him the next year.
" But the main glut of treasure was that of the four hundred thousand
" crowns, amounting in our money to 133,338£. 13s. 4d. paid by the
" French king on the surrendry of the town and territory of Boulogne,
" before remembered. Of which vast sum (but small in reference to
" the loss of so great a strength) no less then four score thousand
" pounds was laid up in the Tower, the rest assigned to public uses for
" the peace and safety of the kingdom. Not to say any thing of that
" great yearly profit which came in from the Mint, after the inter-
" course settled betwixt him and the king of Sweden, and the decrying
" so much base money, had begun to set the same on work. Which
" great advantage notwithstanding. He is now found to be in debt to
" the bankers of Antwerp, and elsewhere, no less then 251,000£. of
" English money."

Such was the deplorable state of England, brought on by the reformers in religion.—By the same authority we learn too, that these
state cormorants, when they found the kingdom placed in such difficulties, adopted similar notable means to retrieve it from embarrassment
that we have seen put in practice in our time, when the cry of reform
became too loud to be passed unheaded.—The doctor tells us " they fell
" upon a course to lessen the expenses of his court and family, by sup-
" pressing the tables formerly appointed for young lords, the masters
" of the requests, serjeants at arms, &c. which though it saved some
" money, yet it brought in none. In the next place it was resolved to
" call such officers to a present and public reckoning, who either had
" embezzled any of the crown lands, or invested any of the king's mo-
" ney to their private use. On which course they were the more in-
" tent, because they did both serve the king, and content the people;
" but might be used by them as a scourge, for the whipping of those
" against whom they had any cause to quarrel. Amongst which I find
" the new lord Paget to have been fined six thousand pounds (as before
" was said) for divers offences of that nature, which were changed upon
" him. Beaumont, then master of the rolls, had purchased lands with
" the king's money, made longer leases of some other crown lands than
" he was authorised to do by his commission, and was otherwise guilty
" of much corrupt and fraudulent dealings : for expiating of which crimes
" he surrendered all his lands and goods to the king, and seems to have
" been well befriended that he sped no worse. The like offences proved
" against one Whaley, one of the king's receivers for the county of
" York ; for which he was punished with the loss of his offices, and
" adjudged to stand to any such fine, as by his majesty and the lords of
" his council should be set upon him. Which manner of proceeding,
" though it be for the most part pleasing to the common people, and
" profitable to the commonwealth, yet were it more unto the honour of
" a prince, to make choice of such officers whom he thinks not likely

" to offend; than to sacrifice them to the people, and his own displea-
" sures, having thus offended."

FATE OF THE PRINCIPAL ACTORS.

We have given a detail of the evil effects produced by the Reformation on the people, we shall now proceed to shew the fate of some of the
leading characters in the unholy transactions of this reign. The king
was the child of Jane Seymour, from whose body he was ripped, and
was of course the death of his mother, under his father's order. This
queen had two brothers, Edward and Thomas, who rose to great favour
under Henry, and to higher honours when their nephew came to the
throne. Edward was made lord protector, and Thomas had the post
of lord high admiral. The latter besides married Catherine Parr, the
queen dowager, and the former took for his wife one Anne Stanhope,
who is represented as a woman of an ambitious temper, and envious
that her husband's brother's wife should have been a queen. She knew
no will but her own, and she could not brook that she being the wife
of the lord protector, should give way to the wife of his younger brother, who claimed precedency of her as queen dowager. Dr. Heylin
tells us she thus said within herself, " Am I not wife to the protector,
" who is king in power though not in title, a duke in order and degree,
" lord treasurer, and earl marshal, and what else he pleased ; and one
" who hath ennobled his highest honours by his late great victory?
" And did not Henry marry Catharine Parr in his doting days, when he
" had brought himself to such a condition by his lusts and cruelty, that
" no lady who stood upon her honour would adventure on him? Do not
" all knees bow before me, and all tongues celebrate my praises, and
" all hands pay the tribute of obedience to me, and all eyes look upon
" me, as the first in state; through whose hands the principal officers
" in the court, and chief referments in the church, are observed to pass?
" Have I so long commanded him, who commands two kingdoms, and
" shall I now give place to her, who, in her former best estate was but
" Latimer's widow, and is now fain to cast herself for support and coun-
" tenance into the despised bed of a younger brother? If Mr. Admiral
" teach his wife no better manners, I am she that will; and will choose
" rather to remove them both, (whether out of the court, or out of the
" world, shall be no great matter) than be outshined in my own sphere,
" and trampled on within the verge of my jurisdiction."

With this disposition she went to work with her husband, and it was
not long before she contrived to fill his head with an implacable jealousy against his brother. The lord admiral was equally as ambitious
as the lord protector, and superior in abilities; he not only married a
queen, but he aspired to the hand of the king's sister Elizabeth, while
his dowager queen was alive. Dr. Lingard says, " his attentions to the
" princess were remarked ; and their familiarity was so undisguised,
" that it afforded employment to the propagators of scandal, and
" awakened the jealousy of his wife, by whom he was one day surprised
" with Elizabeth in his arms. But the queen in a short time died in
" child-birth; and her death happened so opportunely for his project,

A REVIEW

OF

Fox's Book of Martyrs,

CRITICAL AND HISTORICAL.

No. 47. Printed and Published by W. E. Andrews, 3, Chapter-house-court, St. Paul's Churchyard, London. Price 3d.

EXPLANATION OF THE ENGRAVING.—*When the destruction of the monasteries was meditated, the most infamous means were adopted to traduce and slander the monks and priests belonging to them. Having thus excited a prejudice against them among the unthinking part of the people, some of the religious were occasionally exposed to the gaze and mock of the populace in the pillory, and sometimes, as a torture, to make them conform to the new doctrines.*

CONTINUATION OF THE REVIEW.

" that by the malice of his enemies it was attributed to poison." He now redoubled his suit to the princess Elizabeth, began to intrigue with some of the discontented courtiers, and thus raised an excuse for his brother to have him arrested. This was accordingly done, he was committed to the tower, charges of high treason were preferred against him, a bill of attainder was brought into the house of lords, where his brother attended every stage of the bill, the third reading of which was agreed to without a division. In the commons it met with some opposition, but was eventually passed, and received the royal assent at the end of the session. Three days after the warrant for his execution was signed by the council, and, among other names, appear those of SEYMOUR and CRANMER, "both of whom," Dr. Lingard justly observes, "might, it was thought, have abstained from that ungracious

" office, the one on account of his relationship to the prisoner, the other
" because the canons prohibited to clergymen all participation in judg-
" ments of blood." Thus fell one of the uncles of the youthful pope
and king. He was a partaker in the spoils of the church and the poor,
and now received his reward for conniving at such unhallowed sacrileges. Dr. Heylin tells us, he had a grant of 100 marks annually, and
a convenient house out of the property of the dissolved order of St.
John of Jerusalem.—He was afterwards created Lord Seymour of
Sudley, having obtained possession of the manor and castle of Sudley
by the attainder of the rightful owner Lord Botteler, whose greatest
crime, Heylin says, was the being owner of so goodly a manor, which
the greedy courtiers had cast their eyes upon. The lord high admiral
obtained it with the title, but had scarcely got possession of it, when he
lost it with his head and the title, and it fell once more into the hands of
the crown, where it remained till queen Mary conferred it upon sir John
Bruges, who derived his pedigree from the ancient inheritors of the
estate.

The lord protector having removed his brother, the object of his
jealousy, but the prop of his house, now thought himself omnipotent,
and projected the erection of a magnificent palace, which should exalt
him in the eyes of the nation. To give the reader an idea of the veneration in which the reformers of religion held the temples of the living God
in these days, we will here give the account of the erection of this structure as told by Dr. Heylin.—" He had," writes the doctor, " been
" bought out of his purpose for building on the deanery and close of
" Westminster, and casts his eye upon a piece of ground in the Strand,
" on which stood three episcopal houses and one parish church ; the
" parish church dedicated to the Virgin Mary, the houses belonging to
" the bishops of Worcester, Lichfield, and Landaff. All these he takes
" into his hands, the owners not daring to oppose, and therefore will-
" ingly consenting to it. Having cleared the place, and projected the
" intended fabric, the workmen found that more materials would be
" wanting to go through with it than the demolished church and houses
" could afford unto them. He thereupon resolves for taking down the
" parish church of St. Margaret's in Westminster, and turning the
" parishioners for the celebrating of all divine offices into some part of
" the nave, or main body of the Abbey-church, which should be marked
" out for that purpose. But the workmen had no sooner advanced
" their scaffolds, when the parishioners gathered together in great
" multitudes with bows and arrows, staves and clubs, and other such
" offensive weapons ; which so terrified the workmen, that they ran
" away in great amazement, and never could be brought again upon
" that employment. In the next place he is informed of some super-
" fluous, or rather superstitious, buildings on the north side of St. Paul's ;
" that is to say, a goodly cloister, environing a goodly piece of ground,
" called Pardon-church-yard, with a chapel in the midst thereof, and
" beautified with a piece of most curious workmanship, called the dance
" of death, together with a fair charnel house, on the south side of the
" church, and a chapel thereunto belonging. This was conceived to
" be the safer undertaking, the bishop then standing on his good be-
" haviour, and the dean and chapter of that church (as of all the rest)

" being no better in a manner (by reason of the late act of parliament)
" than tenant at will of their great landlords. And upon this he sets
" his workmen on the tenth of April, takes it all down, converts the
" stone, timber, lead and iron, to the use of his intended palace, and
" leaves the bones of the dead bodies to be buried in the fields in un-
" hallowed ground. But all this not sufficing to complete the work,
" the steeple, and most parts of the church of St. John of Jerusalem,
" not far from Smithfield, most beautifully built not long before by
" Dockwray, a late prior thereof, was blown up with gunpowder, and
" all the stone thereof imployed to that purpose also. Such was the
" ground, and such were the materials of the duke's new palace, called
" Somerset-house; which either he lived not to finish, or else it must
" be very strange, that having pulled down two churches, two chapels,
" and three episcopal houses, (each of which may be probably supposed,
" to have had their oratories) to find materials for this fabric, there
" should be no room purposely erected for religious offices."

This sacrilegious destruction of so many sacred edifices was the prelude to the protector's fall. From this time he met with nothing but
disasters and disquietude. The death of his brother was looked upon
as a great blot in his character. While he was building his costly palace the exchequer was empty, and the people rose in rebellion. Next
followed the misfortunes in Scotland and the loss of Boulogne, which
fell into the hands of the French; all which circumstances conjoined
raised up a strong party against him in the cabinet, headed by Dudley
earl of Warwick, afterwards made duke of Northumberland, and the
lord protector found himself a prisoner in the Tower, under the accusation of high crimes and misdemeanours.

We must here notice some proceedings in the parliament which met
after the arrest of Somerset. An act was passed, the purport of which
was to make it felony for any persons to assemble to the number of
twelve or more for the purpose of abating the rents of farms or the
price of provisions, or of destroying houses or parks, or of asserting a
right to ways or commons, if they continued together one hour after
they had been warned to disperse by proclamation from a magistrate,
sheriff or bailiff; and raising the offence to high treason, when the object
of the meeting should be to alter the laws, or to kill or imprison any
member of the king's council. Another act was passed, subjecting
every individual, either clerk or layman, who should keep in his possession any book containing any portion of the ancient service of the
church, to a fine for the first and second offence, and to imprisonment
during the king's pleasure for the third. A proclamation had been
issued previous to the passing of this act, ordering all such books to be
delivered up, that they might be burned or destroyed. Thus it will be
seen that the era which is called the dawn of liberty was in fact the
birth of slavery in this formerly free and happy country; and that the
ejection of the pope's spiritual authority led to the tyranny of an olig-
archical faction far more oppressive than what had ever been felt
even under the most odious of the former sovereigns of the country.
From this period to the present day, laws have been passed infringing
on the rights of the people, and the six acts which were passed in 1819,
to counteract the proceedings of the reformers of that day remind us

strongly of the laws passed in Edward's parliament. It was never dreamed of by our Catholic legislators to make it high treason to kill or imprison a member of the king's council; and it was reserved for our own days to pass a law to banish a man for using words that may be construed into a tendency to bring the members of the king's council into contempt.

But we must leave this digression and return to Somerset. Though his behaviour was of the most haughty nature when in the plenitude of his power, in his fall he was as abject and crawling. He was told, if he hoped for pardon he must acknowledge his guilt. The condition, at which the noble mind would have spurned, was accepted with gratitude. He confessed his presumption on his knees, subscribed to the charges produced against him, and implored mercy. Life was promised him on condition that he should forfeit all his offices, his goods and chattels. A bill of pains and penalties was introduced, and, after some opposition, was passed and received the royal assent. In the mean time Somerset plucked up a little courage and remonstrated against the severity of his punishment; the council reprimanded him, and drew from him another and still more degrading submission. He was then pardoned and set at liberty, and his goods and lands were restored to him by the king's favour.

The downfall of Somerset was the prelude to the advancement and aggrandizement of his enemies. The earl of Warwick was now the greatest man at court, and highest in honours. He was preferred to the office of *Lord Great Master*, and lord high admiral; a sycophant of his, William lord St. John, was made earl of Wiltshire, and others of his creatures were placed in office or raised in title. But titles without estates were considered in those days, as in these, but empty honours. *Now*, when a poor peer is made, he is furnished with a pension out of the taxes of the labouring people; *then* they cast their eyes on the property of the church, out of which the poor, the sick, and the lame were supported. To shew how the poor were robbed in those days, and how some of the present noble families obtained their riches, we will give the following extract from Dr. Heylin's History of the Reformation.—
" Furnished with offices and honours," says the doctor, " it is to be pre-
" sumed, that they would find some way to provide themselves of suffi-
" cient means to maintain their dignities. The lord Wentworth, being
" a younger branch of the Wentworths of Yorkshire, had brought
" some estate with him to the court; though not enough to keep him
" up in equipage, with so great a title. The want whereof was supplied
" in part, by the office of lord chamberlain, now conferred upon him;
" but more by the goodly manors of Stebuneth (commonly called Step-
" ney) and Hackney, bestowed upon him by the king, in consideration
" of the good and faithful services before performed. For so it hap-
" pened, that the dean and chapter of St. Paul's laying at the mercy of
" the times, as before was said, conveyed over to the king the said two
" manors, on the twelfth day after Christmas now last past, with all
" the members and appurtenances thereunto belonging. Of which, the
" last named was valued at the yearly rent of 41*l*. 9*s*. 4*d*. The other
" at 140*l*. 8*s*. 11*d. ob*. And, being thus vested in the king, they were
" by letters patents, being dated the sixteenth of April then next follow-

" ing, (1550) transferred upon the said lord Wentworth. By means
" whereof he was possessed of a goodly territory, extending on the
" Thames from St. Katharine's, near the Tower of London, to the bor-
" ders of Essex, near Blackwall; from thence along the river Lea, to
" Stratford le Bow: and fetching a great compass on that side of the
" city, contains in all no fewer than six and twenty townships, streets,
" and hamlets; besides such rows of building, as have since been added
" in these latter times. The like provision was made by the new lord
" Paget, a Londoner by birth, but by good fortune mixed with merit,
" preferred by degrees, to one of the principal secretaries to the late
" king Henry; by whom he was employed in many embassies, and ne-
" gociations. Being thus raised, and able to set up for himself, he had
" his share in the division of the lands of chantry, free chapels, &c.
" and got into his hands the episcopal house belonging to the bishop
" of Exeter, by him enlarged and beautified, and called Paget's house;
" sold afterwards to Robert earl of Leicester: from whom it came to
" the late earls of Essex, and from them took the name of Essex house,
" by which it is now best known. But being a great house is not able
" to keep itself; he played his game so well, that he got into his pos-
" session the manor of Beaudesart (of which he was created baron) and
" many other fair estates in the county of Stafford, belonging partly to
" the bishop, and partly to the dean and chapter of Lichfield: neither of
" which was able to contend with so great a courtier, who held the see,
" and had the ear of the protector, and the king's to boot. What other
" course he took to improve his fortunes, we shall see hereafter, when
" we come to the last part of the tragedy of the duke of Somerset."

We will here remind the reader that the modern editors, on concluding the first book of Fox's work, make some " remarks on the Vengeance of God towards the persecutors of the Christians," in which they
shew that most of the persecuting Roman emperors met an untimely
end, as a punishment for their cruelty, and that the Jews, for their obstinacy and wickedness, were annihilated as a nation, and became the
scorn and reproach of every people on the earth. (See our first volume
of this work, p. 117, &c.) With equal force do these observations apply
to the principal actors in the dismal and destructive tragedy of *England's*
Reformation. Of the first promoter of the sacrilegious drama, Henry
VIII. we have before spoken. From the time he rejected the spiritual
authority of the pope, under which England was free in her domestic
affairs and renowned among the nations abroad, the kingdom became a
prey to faction and misery, and the life of Harry was one continued
scene of suspicion, caprice, cruelty, and injustice. He spared neither
woman in his lust nor man in his anger; his wives were sent to the
block with as little ceremony as cattle are sent to the slaughter-house;
his chief motive for seeking a divorce from his virtuous queen Catharine
was that he might have a male heir to succeed him, and secure the crown
of England to his family; but in this he was doomed to disappointment.
He had a son, it is true, but that son succeeded him when he was incapable of ruling himself, and was therefore a tool in the hands of the
most impious and unprincipled men that ever cursed an unfortunate
country. We have seen that this unhappy youth was constrained to
sign the death warrant of a fanatical old woman for *heresy* at the insti-

gation of Tom Cranmer, who afterwards met the same fate himself; we have seen the same Cranmer signing, in conjunction with the brother of the culprit, the sentence of death against an uncle of the king, who had to sign the death warrant himself, and we have now to shew the untimely fate of this unnatural brother himself, after having escaped for a short period, through the basest and most servile submission to the dictation of his enemies. Before, however, this act of the tragedy was performed, Dr. Heylin says there were several presages occurred in the year 1551, which were looked upon as prognosticating the concussions which afterwards happened in the court, which led to the fall of Somerset and several other noted performers, and ended in the death of the king. The first of these prognostics was a terrible earthquake which happened on the 25th of May at Croydon, and some villages adjoining in Surrey; another was the appearance of six dolphins in the Thames, three of which were taken at Queenborough, and three near Greenwich; but the most extraordinary and calamitous scourge was the breaking out of a disease called the *Sweating Sickness;* " appearing " first," writes Dr. Heylin, " at Shrewsbury on the 15th of April, and, " after spreading by degrees over all the kingdom, ending its progress " in the north, about the beginning of October. Described by a very " learned man to be a new, strange, and violent disease; wherewith if " any man were attacked, he died or escaped within nine hours, or ten " at most; if he slept (as most men desired to do) he died within six " hours; if he took cold, he died in three. It was observed to rage " chiefly amongst men of strongest constitution and years: few aged " men or women, or young children, being either subject to it, or dying " of it. Of which last sort, those of most eminent rank were two of " the sons of Charles Brandon; both dying at Cambridge, both dukes of " Suffolk, (as their father had been before,) but the youngest following " his dead brother so close at the heels, that he only out-lived him long " enough to enjoy that title. And that which was yet most strange of " all, no foreigner, which was then in England, (four hundred French " attending here, in the hottest of it, on that king's ambassadors) did " perish by it. The English being singled out, tainted, and dying of it " in all other countries, without any danger to the natives; called there- " fore, in most Latin writers, by the name of *Sudor Anglicus,* or *The* " *English Sweat.* First known amongst us in the beginning of the reign " of king Henry the seventh; and then beheld as a presage of that " troublesome and laborious reign which after followed : the king being " for the most part in continual action; and the subjects either sweating " out their blood or treasure. Not then so violent and extreme, as it " was at the present; such infinite multitudes being at this day swept " away by it, that there died eight hundred in one week in London " only." The singularity of this disease being confined exclusively to Englishmen, must carry conviction to the mind of every sensible reader that it was a mark of God's judgment on the nation, for the many impieties and abominable outrages which had been committed by the pretended reformers against his justice and religion.

While the nation was thus suffering by religious quarrels, fomented by imperious demagogues, and the awful visitations of God's anger, the court was thrown into confusion by a new quarrel between Somerset and Warwick. The former had recovered somewhat of his influence over the king, and aspired again to the office of protector, which it was, of course, the interest of the latter to prevent. Accordingly a renewal of the previous jealousies and dissensions between these two ambitious men and their partisans took place, and conspiracies and cabals became the order of the day. Each party beset the other with spies and informers, and both were deceived and inflamed by false friends and interested advisers. Warwick, however possessed the advantage over his adversary in the council, and to strengthen his interest a new promotion of titles and places was made in favour of his friends. He was himself created duke of Northumberland, the marquess of Dorset was made duke of Suffolk, the earl of Wiltshire marquess of Winchester, sir Wm. Herbert, baron of Cardiff and earl of Pembroke, and others had the honour of knighthood conferred upon them. These proceedings alarmed Somerset, and he began to suspect that some designs were in agitation against his person. These suspicions he soon found confirmed, for on the 16th of October, as he was going to court at Westminster, he was arrested with lord Gray and sent to the Tower. The day following his duchess and her favourites, Mr. and Mrs. Crane, sir Thomas Holcroft, sir Michael Stanhope, sir Thomas Arundel, sir Miles Partridge, with two others of the Seymours, and Hammond, and Newdigate, were committed to the same prison. Soon after they were followed by the lord Paget, the earl of Arundel, and lord Dacres of the north. Preparations were soon made for the trial of the prisoners, and we must not here forget the inscrutable designs of Divine Providence. The late lord protector, with unnatural cruelty, refused his unfortunate brother a trial by his peers, was present in the house of lords when the bill of attainder was in progress against him, and signed the order of council for his death. Now, when arraigned himself, among other charges, for attempting the life of Northumberland, under the act just passed, (see page 323) he found Northumberland, Northampton, and Pembroke, his known enemies, among his judges. Dr. Heylin observes, that these "being "parties to the charge, ought in all honesty and honour to have excused "themselves from sitting in judgment on him at the time of his trial." This is very true, but the same remark will apply to Somerset himself in his conduct towards his brother, and clearly shews that there was neither honesty nor honour in the transactions of those days. Another proof of this may be found in the mode of Seymour's trial. Although he was brought before his judges (twenty-seven peers, with the new marquess of Wiltshire as lord steward) yet he was not confronted with the witnesses: only their depositions were produced against him, which had been taken the day preceding the trial. His judges deliberated some time on their verdict, and at length pronounced him guilty of felony, for which he was sentenced to be hanged, but in consideration of his rank, the sentence was changed to that of beheading. As soon as the sentence was pronounced, this once proud and haughty courtier again fell on his knees, thanked the lords for their impartial conduct during the trial, though he had requested to have the witnesses confronted with him and was denied, asked pardon of Northumberland, Northampton, and Pembroke, whose lives he acknowledged he had sought to have taken, begged them to solicit the king for mercy in his behalf, and recommended his duchess and children to the pity of the young monarch, his nephew.

Six weeks after his condemnation, Somerset was led out to the scaffold on Tower-hill, on which his brother had suffered through his machinations, but three years before. The modern editors of the *Book of Martyrs* tell us that " Mr. Fox, the author of this work was present at the execution," and they favour their readers with his account of the execution. It is too long and tedious for us to give in full, but the following extract will give our readers some idea of Fox's love of truth and his proneness to romancing. In detailing the duke's speech, which he commences by avowing his innocence, Fox makes him say, " 'Moreover, " dearly beloved friends, there is yet somewhat that I must put you in " mind of, as touching Christian religion; which so long as I was in " authority, I always diligently set forth and furthered to my power. " Neither do I repent me of my doings, but rejoice therein, sith that now " the state of Christian religion cometh most near unto the form and " order of the primitive church. Which thing I esteem as a great " benefit given of God both unto you and me; most heartily exhorting " you all, that this, which is most purely set forth unto you, you will " with like thankfulness accept and embrace, and set out the same in " your living. Which thing if you do not, without doubt greater mis- " chief and calamity will follow.' When he had spoken these words, " there was suddenly a terrible noise heard; whereupon there came " a great fear upon all men. This noise was as it had been the noise of " some great storm or tempest, which to some seemed to be from above; " as if a great deal of gunpowder being inclosed in an armoury, and " having caught fire, had violently broken out. But unto some it " seemed as though it had been a great multitude of horsemen running " together or coming upon them. Such a noise then was in the ears " of all, although they saw nothing. Whereby it happened that all the " people being amazed without any evident cause, they ran away, some " into the ditches and puddles, and some into the houses thereabouts; " others fell down grovelling unto the ground, with their pollaxes and " halberds; and most of them cried out, 'Jesus save us! Jesus save " us!' Those who remained in their places, for fear knew not where " they were; and I myself, who was there among the rest, being also " afraid in this hurly burly, stood still amazed. It happened here, *as* " *the evangelist wrote of Christ*, when as the officers of the high priests " and pharisees, coming with weapons to take him, being astonished, " ran backwards and fell to the ground."

Fox then goes on to relate the remainder of the " meek and gentle" duke's speech, as he calls him, and would make it appear, if he could, that this destroyer of churches, this invader of the property of the poor, this despoiler of the livelihoods of learned men, this murderer of his own brother in cold blood, was an innocent sufferer for the cause of religion, and as pure and pious a martyr as those who suffered under the heathen persecutors. His regard for religion must have been truly great, when it was modelled and remodelled according to the interest and caprice of himself and those who acted under him. But what shall we say to the blasphemy and impiety of this eulogist of the reformation and recorder of lies, in comparing the accident which occurred at the death of this offender against God's laws, to the supernatural fear which struck the guards who were sent to apprehend the Saviour of Mankind!!!!!! Was ever any thing so outrageously impious! so shockingly disgusting! He represents the noise as terrible and somewhat miraculous upon his own view; let us now hear what another eye-witness, whose testimony is less tainted, say of this occurrence.

Stowe, in his *Chronicles*, thus relates the matter :—" Before eight of " the clock the duke was brought to the scaffold inclosed with the king's " guard, the sheriffs' officers, the warders of the Tower, and others " with halberds, the duke being ready to have been executed; suddenly " the people were driven into a great fear, few or none knowing the " cause; wherefore I think it good to write what I saw concerning " that matter. The people of a certain hamlet, which were warned to " be there by seven of the clock, to give their attendance on the lieu- " tenant, now came through the postern, and perceiving the duke to be " already on the scaffold, the foremost began to run, crying to their " fellows to follow fast after, which suddenness of these men, being wea- " poned with bills and halberts, thus running, caused the people which " first saw them to think some power had come to have rescued the " duke from execution, and therefore to cry ' away, away;' whereupon " the people ran some one way some another, many fell into the Tower " ditch, and they which tarried thought some pardon had been brought, " some said it thundered, some that a great rumbling was in the earth " under them, some that the ground moved; but there was no such " matter, more than the trampling of their feet, which made some " noise." Compare this plain statement, reader, with the fanatical blasphemy of Fox, and the true merits of the author of the *Book of Martyrs* will soon become manifest.

The confusion occasioned by this sudden movement had scarcely been allayed, when the duke was again interrupted in his speech by the appearance of sir Anthony Brown on horseback, which caused some of the populace to shout " A pardon, a pardon." The shout reached the scaffold, but the duke soon learned its inaccuracy, and the disappoint- ment called a hectic colour up in his cheeks; he however resumed his address, which having concluded, he laid his head on the block, and at one stroke it was severed from his body. Thus fell the second uncle of the young king Edward, and a great promoter of the deformation of religion and destroyer of the nation's happiness and riches, under the sign manual of his own nephew. Nor did the vengeance of his enemies forsake him here, but extended to his friends and children after his death.—This Seymour had two wives, and a son by each. Through the instigation of the second wife, she who plotted the death of his brother the lord admiral, he had procured an act of parliament to be passed in the 32d year of Henry, for entailing on the son by his second wife all his honours and estates. This act was now repealed, and the duchess and her son were divested of their property and he of his titles, so truly did the hand of God fall upon the guilty in these atro- cious deeds.

There was another brother of these Seymours, named *Henry*, who, though he has not made a conspicuous figure in history and was only a knight, yet being a partaker in the spoils of the church, the fatality of his family was such, that we should not do justice to the public were we to omit the account as we find it related in Heylin's History. Having given the pedigree of Edward the eldest, and Thomas the youngest, whose fate we have just recorded, the doctor writes, " As for sir Henry " Seymour, the second son of Sir John Seymour, he was not found to " be of so fine a metal as to make a courtier, and was therefore left " unto the life of a country gentleman; advanced by the power and " favour of his elder brother to the order of knighthood; and after- ." wards estated in the manors of Marvell and Twyford, in the county " of Southampton, dismembered in those broken times from the see of " Winchester. To each of these belonged a park, that of the first con- " taining no less than four miles, that of the last but two in compass; " the first being also honoured with a goodly mansion-house, belong- ." ing anciently to those bishops, and little inferior to the best of the " wealthy bishoprics. There goes a story, that the priest officiating at " the altar, in the church of Ouslebury (of which parish Marvell was a " part) after the mass had been abolished by the king's authority) was " violently dragged thence by this sir Henry, beaten, and most re- ". proachfully handled by him, his servants universally refusing to serve " him, as the instruments of his rage and fury; and that the poor priest " having after an opportunity to get into the church, did openly curse " the said sir Henry, and his posterity, with bell, book, and candle, ac- " cording to the use observed in the church of Rome; which, whether " it were so or not, or that the main foundation of this estate being laid " on sacrilege, could promise no long blessing to it; certain it is, that " his posterity are brought beneath the degree of poverty. For, hav- " ing three nephews by sir John Seymour, his only son; that is to say, " Edward, the eldest, Henry and Thomas, younger sons, besides seve- " ral daughters; there remains not to any of them one foot of land, or " so much as a penny of money to supply their necessities, but what " they have from the munificence of the Marquis of Hertford, or the " charity of other well disposed people, which have affection or relation " to them."

It is now time to notice the fate of the other individuals accused as the accomplices of the late protector Somerset. Four only were se- lected for capital punishment, namely, Partridge, Vane, Stanhope, and Arundel. The two first died under the gallows, the last on the scaf- fold.—Of these Partridge was the most despised, as he was the indivi- dual who won the beautiful ring of bells called Jesus' bells, at a cast of dice with king Harry, and caused them to be taken down and melted for his own advantage. Paget was never brought to trial, but made his submission, was degraded from the order of the garter, and paid a considerable fine. The earl of Arundel gained his liberty after an im- prisonment of twelve months, but then not till he had bound himself to pay annually to the king for six years the sum of one thousand pounds.

We shall now close our account of the punishments which fell on the guilty actors in this scene of devastation in Edward's reign, for some were allowed to fall in Mary's time, with the permature end of the young king himself. Warwick having dispatched his rival Seymour, now meditated the securing of the crown of England in his own family, and having procured a marriage between his fourth son lord Dudley and lady Jane Grey, the daughter of the duke of Suffolk, he persuaded the young king to make a will setting aside the right of his sisters Mary and Elizabeth, and conferring the sceptre on the said lady Jane and the heirs male of her body. This end was no sooner accomplished than the king began to increase in weakness, and his disease soon baffled the skill of his physicians. During his illness, Dr. Heylin says, he prepared himself for his end with the prayer subjoined and other meditations. We give it as a curious specimen of the plans devised by the reformers, as they called themselves, to instil prejudice into the youthful mind of the monarch, and to remind the reader how much the nation has gained by its being defended from *Papistry*, if we compare the present misery of the labouring classes and the happy state of plenty they enjoyed before the thing called the Reformation was known. Here then is the prayer, taken, as Dr. Heylin says, from his dying mouth.

" *Lord God deliver me out of this miserable and wretched life, and take me among the chosen. Howbeit, not my will, but thine be done. Lord, I commit my spirit to thee. O Lord, thou knowest, how happy it were for me to be with thee: yet for thy Chosen's sake, send me life and health, that I may truly serve thee. Oh, my Lord God! bless my people and save thine inheritance. O Lord God, save thy chosen people of England. Oh, Lord God! defend this realm from Papistry, and maintain thy true religion, that I and my people may praise thy holy name, for Jesus Christ his sake.*"

We must admire the devotion and ardour of the young pope in favour of " *true* religion," which, by the by, it was impossible for any one to discover amongst the reformers, as it was changed with the same facility as the camelion does the colour of his shin. The realm has been defended with as much zeal and vigour as penal laws and proscription could do, and yet it is now gaining ground to the dismay of the intolerants, while the system of Protestantism, if such it can be called, is in a rapid state of decay. The immense load of debt and its necessary attendant, taxation, supported by a base paper currency, have reduced the working classes to a state of pauperism, and the nation itself is on the verge of bankruptcy. The religion established by law in Edward's reign, and afterwards by his sister Elizabeth, has but few professors, many of its ministers being latitudinarians and freethinkers. It is only supported by test oaths and proscriptive laws, and should any sudden convulsion take place in the state, its dissolution will follow, But let us return to the pious king. Northumberland having obtained his consent to DEPOSE his two sisters, the young pope did not survive the deed many days, as death overtook him, after suffering much pain and torture, not without strong suspicions of being poisoned by Northumberland.— Thus fell the son of the first pope of the church of England, who was the victim of the most unprincipled men; of whom it may be said, he caused the death of his own mother on coming into the world, she being ripped open to give him birth; that he sent his two uncles to the scaffold under the royal warrant; and was himself snatched away by a violent death in the sixteenth year of his age. O God, how inscrutable are thy judgments! how unsearchable thy ways.

Here then we close our view of the fate of the principal characters in the dismal scenes of spoliation and sacrilege which accompanied the introduction of that change in the religion of the country which brought so many evils in its train. If the miserable and untimely death of the Roman persecutors of the primitive Christians were " manifestations of the great displeasure of the Almighty against the persecutors;" the same observation must be equally applicable to the violent ends which swept from this world the great destroyers of every thing truly religious, and the persecutors of those who stood stedfastly to the faith planted by the apostles, and for which, like the primitive Christians, they suffered martyrdom with the most heroic fortitude.—We have shewn in the preceding pages how the Protestant or Reformed religion was first broached in England under Henry, and propagated by the evil councillors of his son Edward. We have also shewn at the commencement of this volume how the Catholic religion was planted by the holy monk Augustin and his pious associates, and the blessings which attended the people on submitting to this divine system of faith and morals. The reader can now see the vast difference between the introduction of the Catholic religion and the destruction of it, with all its beneficent and useful institutions, by Cranmer, Cromwell, Seymour, and others.—We have laid bare who and what the men were who preached the pretended doctrines of reform; the means prescribed, and the effects produced; we will here add in corroboration the words of father Parsons, taken from the second part of his Three Conversions.—He writes, " As " for the men that first and principally broached these doctrines, they " were for the most part married friars and apostate priests, that living " in concupiscence of women, and other sensuality, desired to maintain " and continue the same by the liberty of this new gospel. The pro- " moters and favourers of these men were such especially of the laity " and clergy, as had more interest by the change for their own promo- " tion and advancement, than conscience, or persuasion of judgment, " for the truth of their religion; as would appear, if we should name " them one by one that then were of the council and chief authority. " The effects and spiritual fruits of this first change were (as you have " seen and heard) the most notorious vices of ambition, dissimulation, " hatred, deceit, tyranny, and subversion one of another; together with " division, dissension, garboils, and desolation of the realm; yea, plain " atheism, irreligion, and contempt of all religion that ever was known " to have risen up in any kingdom of the world within the compass of " so few years: and (that which is most remarkable) there followed " presently the overthrow of all the principal actors and authors of " these innovations by God's own wonderful hand; and this more in " these six years, than in sixty, or six score, or perhaps six hundred, " hath been seen to have fallen out in England in other times. And no " doubt but it is of singular consideration, that whereas true Christian " religion (but especially any change or reformation to the better part) " is admitted, there presently do ensue by usual consequence great ef- " fects of piety, devotion, charity, and virtuous life, if the reformation " be sincere, and come from God indeed; here on the contrary side the " providence of God did shew a notorious document to the whole world, " of the falsehood and wickedness of this new gospel, in that the first " professors and promoters thereof in our land, fell to more open wick- " edness in these five years, than in so many fifties before, as hath been " said."

REFORMATION IN IRELAND.

We are told, by the modern editors, that " *this* year," but no year is specified, " the reformation had gained more ground in Ireland than for-" merly. Henry VIII. had assumed to himself, by consent of the parliament " of that kingdom, the title of king of it : the former kings of England " having only been called lords of Ireland ; and though they were " obeyed within the English pale, yet the native Irish continued barbar-" ous and uncivilized, were governed entirely by the heads of their " names or tribes, and were obedient or rebellious, as they directed " them. The reformation was set on foot in the English pale, but made " small progress among the Irish. At length Bale was sent over to " labour among them. He was an eager writer, and a learned zealous " man. Goodacre was made primate of Armagh, and Bale was to be " bishop of Ossory. Two Irishmen were also promoted with them ; " who undertook to advance the reformation there. The archbishop " of Dublin intended to have ordained them by the old pontifical, and " all, except Bale, were willing it should be so, but he prevailed that it " should be done according to the new book of ordinations : he then " went into his diocese, but found all there in dark Popery, and before " he could make any progress the king's death put an end to his designs."

Such is the account given by the modern editors, and we must here observe that it is somewhat contradictory, inasmuch as it says that the reformation " had gained more ground," and a few sentences after, that it " made small progress," in Ireland. How these contradictions are to be reconciled we must leave to the advocates of Burnet and Fox. The duke of Wellington, who is an opposer of the rights of his Catholic countrymen, though his honours were won by their courage and fidelity, asserted in the house of lords, that the reformation was introduced into Ireland by the mouth of the cannon and the point of the bayonet, but this new mode of propagating the gospel our modern editors have suppressed. They tell us that Bale was sent over to labour among the Irish, who are described as being " barbarous and uncivilized ;" but they should also have stated that the lord protector, Somerset, sent over 600 horse, and 4,000 foot, to civilize this unfortunate people. And how did they proceed to enlighten the darkness of Popery ? Historians inform us, by those disgraceful practices which marked the " progress of the refor-mation," fraud and violence. Having succeeded in lulling the suspicions of the two most eminent chieftains, O'Moore and O'Connor, who surren-dered on the pledged faith of the English commander, they had no sooner arrived in England than they were cast into prison, their lands declared forfeited, and bestowed on the very men who had thus villanously vio-lated their plighted troth. Churches were despoiled of their sacred or-naments and exposed to sale, and the most fertile districts were laid waste by the ruthless hands of men who pretended to be the bearers of a religion that was to remove the Cimmerian darkness which had so long bound the Irish Papists. We are told that Bale was sent over to labour among the Irish ; that " he was an eager writer, and a learned " and zealous man ;" that he " was to be bishop of Ossory ; that the " archbishop of Dublin *intended* to have ordained him by the *old* pontifi-

" cal, but he prevailed upon the archbishop to have the ceremony per-
" formed according to the *new* book of ordination ;" that he went into
his diocess; that he " found all there in *dark* Popery;" and that " before
" he could make any progress, the king's death put an end to his de-
" signs." The only authority we have for this very pretty relation is
Gilbert Burnet, who produces no testimony to corroborate his statement.
We believe it to be a fabrication, and it seems to carry with it its own
confutation. Why not give us a few reasons which induced the archbishop to throw aside the ancient form and adopt the new ceremonial?
Why say that Bale *was* to be bishop, and then make him actually so ?
Why not *name* the two Irishmen, and the *sees* they were promoted to?
And how lucky it was that death should take away the king to save the
credit of Bale. The modern editors who have copied, or rather selected
their account of " the progress of the reformation," from Burnet, make
a little free, we see, with their authority, in order to suit their own purposes of deception. Burnet says, that Bale " was a busy writer, and
" a learned zealous man, *but did not write with that temper and* DECENCY
that became a divine." This latter part of his character the modern
editors have SUPPRESSED. Father Parsons, the able and learned detector
of Fox's lies, informs us that this John Bale, for we suppose there was
but one *learned* man of that name in those days, was an apostate friar,
and chief gospeller in the time of Henry and Edward, and that he
defended the *Jewish* custom of keeping Easter, in treating on a disputation between Colman, the Scottish bishop, and St. Wilfrid, the English
abbot, in a council held in Northumberland, in the year 664. Parson's
proves Bale guilty of misrepresentation, falsehood, and scurrility, and
quotes his own words to shew that he was a jester. " I have," says
Bale, " written jests and pastimes without any certain number."—
(Bal. cent. v. descript. Brit.) He is also represented by the same grave
authority, as taking an active part in the contention between the lord
protector, Somerset, and the lord high admiral, and their wives, before
noticed, in which dispute many other apostate friars, and among the rest
Hugh Latimer, were great sticklers. Latimer inveighed with much
bitterness, in his sermons, against the admiral, and, on the other side,
John Bale took the part of the admiral's wife, queen Catharine, whom he
set forth, in his book before quoted, as one of the miracles of womankind.
  So respectable a divine as John Bale must have performed wonders
in enlightening the darkness of Ireland, had Providence thought it wise
to prolong the life of the young pope.—But allowing this Bale to have
been what he is here represented by the modern editors, of what use
could his writings be to a people who could not *read*, and, if they could,
were not acquainted with the language of his writings ? In what way
could he, an Englishman, convert the Irish from their ancient faith, unless he had the gift of tongues, and was able to preach to them in their
native language ? And here we may be allowed to remark the inconsistency of these pretended reformers in regard to their propagating
the new invented forms and doctrines in Ireland. One of the charges
brought by them against the Catholic church was, that she kept the
people in ignorance by praying in a language which they did not understand, and consequently one of their first measures of *reform* was to
have the liturgy in the English language. For the natives of Jersey

and Guernsey a French translation was made; but it does not seem to have entered the heads of the reformers that the Irish required to have an edition in their own language.—If it were necessary that the English should have the benefit of a form of worship in their own tongue, had not the king's subjects in Ireland an equal right to the same benefit? —But strange to say, the very men who reproached the Catholic church with performing her service in a foreign language, issued a proclamation, by which the Irish were commanded to attend the English church service in a language they did not understand. The result was, that in Dublin, where the English language was somewhat familiar, Brown, the archbishop of Dublin, and four of his brethren, yielded submission to the order; but Dowdal, archbishop of Armagh, and the other prelates, stoutly resisted the decree, and the ancient service was retained, and has been preserved almost universally to this day. The modern editors say, "Goodacre was made *primate* of Armagh;" but this is another mistake or wilful misrepresentation of an historical fact. Dowdal, for his adherence to the faith of which he was appointed a guardian, was persecuted by the government, who took from him the *title* of *primate* of all Ireland, and transferred it not to his successor in the see of Armagh, but to his more servile brother the archbishop of Dublin. Dowdal was obliged to fly the realm, but recovered his see on the accession of Mary.

The sacrilegious and infamous robberies of the churches in Ireland, begun by the reformers in Edward's reign, met of course, a check by the succession of his sister Mary. She, however, was no sooner dead, and her place occupied by that *virgin* lady, who is called by the base writers, the "good queen Bess," though a more merciless tyrant never wielded a sceptre, than the work of devastation was again resumed, and carried to a pitch that was never exceeded by the Goths and Vandals in their inroads on Christian kingdoms. We will here give the testimony of Spencer, Sydney, Hooker, Davies, and Strafford, who lived in the time of the transactions described, and embraces a period of seventy years, commencing in the year 1560 to the year 1630. From these witnesses the reader will learn the gross abuses practised by the new established church, the utter neglect of duty by the bishops, and the utter want of persons to supply the churches or the appointment of illiterate incumbents of the most dissolute morals.

Leland writes, "The clergy, who refused to conform, abandoned " their cures. *No reformed ministers could be found to supply their places.* " The churches fell to ruins. *The people were left without any religious* " *worship or instruction.*—(Vol. ii. p. 174.)

" The prejudices conceived against the reformation, by the Irish na- " tives more especially, were still further increased by the conduct of " those who were commissioned to remove the objects and instruments " of popular superstition. *Under pretence of obeying the orders of state,* " *they seized all the most valuable furniture of the churches, which they* " *exposed to sale without decency or reserve.* The Irish annalists pathe- " tically describe the garrison of Athlone issuing forth, with a barbarous " and heathen fury, and pillaging the famous church of Clonmacnoise, " tearing away the most inoffensive ornaments, books, bells, plate, win- " dows, furniture of every kind, so as to leave the shrine of their fa-

" vourite saint, Kieran, a hideous monument of sacrilege."—(*Ibid.* 237.)

Spencer writes, "some of them, (the bishops,) whose dioceses are in re-
" mote parts, somewhat out of the world's eye, *doe not at all bestow the be-*
" *nefices, which are in their owne donation, upon any, but keep them in their*
" *owne hands, and set their owne servants and horse-boys to take up the tithes*
" *and fruites of them, with the which; some of them purchase great lands,*
" *and build faire castels upon the same.* Of which abuse if any question be
" moved, they have a very seemely colour and excuse, that they have no
" worthy ministers to bestow upon them, but keepe them so bestowed
" for any such sufficient person as any shall bring unto them."—(p. 140.)

" Whatever disorders you see in the church of England, yee may
" finde there, and many more. Namely, *grosse simony, greedy covetous-*
" *nesse, fleshly incontinency, carelesse sloath, and generally all disordered*
" *life in the common clergymen.* And besides all these, they have their
" particular enormityes; for all Irish priests, which now enjoy the
" church livings, *they are in a manner meere laymen,* saving that they
" have taken holy orders; but otherwise they doe goe and live like lay-
" men; follow all kinde of husbandry, and other worldly affaires, as
" other Irish men doe. *They neither read Scriptures, nor preach to the*
" *people, nor administer the communion; baptisme they doe; for they*
" *christen yet after the popish fashion; only they take the tithes and offer-*
" *ings, and gather what fruite else they may of their livings.*"—(p. 139.)

" It is great wonder to see the oddes which is between the zeale of
" popish priests, and the ministers of the gospell; for they spare not to
" come out of Spaine, from Rome, and from Remes, by long toyle and
" daungerous travayling hither; where they know perill of death away-
" teth them, and no reward or richesse is to be found, onely to draw
" the people unto the church of Rome; whereas some of our idle minis-
" ters, having a way for credite and estimation thereby opened unto
" them, and having the livings of the countrey offered unto them, with-
" out paines, and without perill, will neither for the same, nor any love
" of God, nor zeale of religion, or for all the good they may doe, by
" winning soules to God, bee drawne foorth from their warme neastes,
" to looke out into God's harvest, which is even ready for the sickle,
" and all the fields yellow long agoe."—(p. 254.)

Sydney writes thus:—" The first is, the churche is nowe so spoyled,
" as well by the ruine of the temples, as the discipacion and imbease-
" linge of the patrimonye, and most of all, for want of sufficient minis-
" ters; *as so deformed and over throwen a churche there is not, I am sure,*
" *in any region where Christ is professed;* and preposterous it seameth to
" me, to begin reformacion of the pollitique parte, and to neglect the
" religious."—(Vol. i. p. 109.)

" I was advertized of the perticuler estate of ech churche in the bi-
" shopricke of Meithe, (being the best inhabited countrie of all this
" realme,) by the honest, zealous, and learned bishop of the same, Mr.
" Hugh Brayde, a godlye minister of the gospell, and a good sarvaunt
" to your highnes, who went from churche to churche hym selfe, and
" found, that there are within his diocess 224 parrishe churches, *of*
" *which number one hundred and five are impropriated to sondrie possessions,*
" *nowe of your highnes,* and all leased out for yeares, or in fee farme,
" to severall farmers, and great gayne reaped out of theim above the

A REVIEW

OF

ꟻox's Book of Martyrs,

CRITICAL AND HISTORICAL.

No. 48.   Printed and Published by W. E. ANDREWS, 3, Chapter-house-court, St. Paul's Churchyard, London.   Price 3d.

EXPLANATION OF THE ENGRAVING—*Henry Percy, Earl of Northumberland, a man no less distinguished for his eminent virtues than his exalted birth, was thrown into prison a few years after his brother, Thomas Percy, had been beheaded, because he maintained the Catholic faith; but as there was no pretext for apprehending him publicly, he was most cruelly put to death in prison. Some of the heretics gave it out that he had destroyed himself, but the truth was afterwards discovered, and their falsehood and cruelty detected.—Theatrum Crudelitatum, &c.*

CONTINUATION OF THE REVIEW.

" rent, which your majestie receivethe; *no parson, or vicar, resident upon*
" *any of theim, and a very simple or sorrye curat,* for the most parte, ap-
" pointed to serve theim: amonge which number of curatts, *onely eigh-*
" *tene were founde able to speake English.*"—(p. 112.)
   " No one howse standinge for any of theim to dwell in. In maney
" places, the very walles of the churches doune; verie few chauncells
" covered, wyndowes and dores ruyned, or spoyled. There are 52 other
" parishe churches in the same dioces, who have viccars indued upon
" theim, better served and maynteined then the other, yet but badlye.
" There are 52 parishe churches more, residue of the first nomber of
" 224, which perteine to dyvers perticuler lords, and these though in
" better estate, then the rest commonlye are, yet farre from well. *If*

" this be the estate of the churche in the best peopled dyoces, and best go-
" verned countrie, of this your realme, (as in troth it is:) ensye it is for
" your majestie to conjecture, in what case the rest is, where little or
" no reformation, either of religion or manners, hath yet bene planted,
" and contynued amonge theim."—(Ibid. vol. i. p. 112.)

" Uppon the face of the earthe, where Christ is professed, there is
" not a churche in so miserable a case ; the miserye of whiche consist-
" ethe in thiese three particulars, the ruyne of the verie temples theim-
" selves; the want of good mynisters to serve in theim, when they shall
" be reedified; competent lyvinge for the ministers being wel chosen."
(Ibid.)

" And though the outrages in the civil government were great, yet
" nothing to be compared to the ecclesiastical state, for that was too
" far out of order, the temples all ruined, the parish churches for the most
" part without curates and pastors, no service said, no God honoured, nor
" Christ preached, nor sacraments ministered."—(Hooker, apud Hollin-
shed, vol. vi. p. 382.)

" There has been so little care taken, as that the greatest part of the
" churches within the pale be still in their ruins; so as the common peo-
" ple, (whereof many without doubt, would conform themselves,) have no
" place to resort to, where they may hear divine service."—(Davies, p. 240.)

" For the holding of two livings, and but two with cure, since you
" approve me in the substance, I will yield to you in the circumstance of
" time.   Indeed, my lord, I knew it was bad, very bad in Ireland ; but that
" it was so stark nought I did not believe, six benefits not able to find the
" minister cloths.   In six parishes scarce six to come to church."—(Strafford, vol. i. p. 254.)

" The best entrance to the cure, will be clearly to discover the state
" of the patient, which I find many ways distempered; an unlearned
" clergy, who have not so much as the outward form of churchmen to cover
" themselves with, nor their persons any ways reverenced or protected,
" the churches unbuilt, the parsonage and vicarage houses utterly
" ruined; the people untaught thorough the non-residency of the clergy,
" occasioned by the unlimited shameful numbers of spiritual promotions
" with cure of souls, which they hold by commendams; the rites and cere-
" monies of the church run over without all decency of habit, order, or gra-
" vity in the course of their service; the possessions of the church, to a
" great proportion, in lay hands; the bishops aliening their very principal
" houses and demesnes to their children, to strangers, farming out their ju-
" risdictions to mean and unworthy persons; the popish titulars exercising
" the whilst a foreign jurisdiction much greater than theirs."—(Ibid.
vol. i. p. 187.)

" There are seven or eight ministers in each diocess of good suffi-
" ciency; and, (which is no small cause of the continuance of the peo-
" ple in Popery still,) English, which have not the tongue of the peo-
" ple, nor can perform any divine offices, or converse with them; and which
" hold many of them two or three, four or more vicarages apiece; even the
" clerkships themselves are in like manner conferred upon the English,
" and sometimes two or three, or more upon one man, and ordinarily
" bought and sold or let to farm."—(Burnet's Life of Bedell, p. 46.)

" As scandalous livings naturally make scandalous ministers, the clergy

" of the established church were generally ignorant and unlearned, loose and
" irregular in their lives and conversations, negligent of their cures, and
" very careless of observing uniformity and decency in divine worship."—
(Carte, vol. i. p. 68.)

" Nor were the parochial churches in a better condition, than the cathe-
" dral. They had most of them in the country been destroyed in the
" troubles, or fallen down for want of covering; the livings were very
" small, and either kept in the bishops' hands by way of commendams
" and sequestrations, or else filled with ministers as scandalous as their
" income; so that *scarce any care was taken to catechise the children or*
" instruct others in the grounds of religion; and for years together, divine
" service had not been used in any parish church throughout Ulster, ex-
" cept in some city or principal towns."—(Ibid. vol. i. p. 17.)

" There were few churches to resort to; few teachers to exhort and
" instruct; fewer still who could be understood; and *almost all, at least*
" for the greater part of this reign, (Elizabeth's,) of scandalous insufficiency."
(Leland, vol. ii. p. 459.)

We are indebted to the researches of Mr. Carey, of Philadelphia, for
these extracts, which we have taken from his able and valuable work,
entitled, *Vindiciæ Hibernicæ; or, Ireland Vindicated,* in which he has
most feelingly and forcibly pourtrayed the horrible barbarities and outrages which marked the blood-stained progress of the Reformation in
Ireland.—Our blessed Saviour told his disciples that the tree would be
known by its fruits; pernicious then must that tree have been which
produced such fruits as are here described.—And yet we have men in
the nineteenth century—in an age that boasts of its learning and en-
lightenedness, extolling this work of devastation and slaughter as the
offspring of Heaven !!! Was ever such blasphemy and impiety before
known !

ACCESSION OF QUEEN MARY,

SUBVERSION OF RELIGION, AND PERSECUTIONS OF THE CHURCH OF ENG- LAND DURING HER REIGN.

This is the most interesting period of the work we are reviewing,
and we beg the serious attention of the reader to it.—Under the above
head the modern editors of Fox have introduced the following account
of the accession of Mary to the throne of her father and brother.—We
give the whole of it, that we may not be accused of partiality, as it
will be our duty to detect and expose the barefaced falsehoods and the
many misrepresentations of historical facts it contains.—The editors
say,—

" We now call the attention of the British Protestants to a period of their church
history that cannot fail to awaken in their hearts that love for their ancestors, which,
at present, we fear, lies dormant in too many. A long career of ease appears to
have obliterated from their minds the troubles of their generous forefathers, who,
for them, bled in every vein—for them, were consigned to the devouring flames in
every part of their country; preparing and establishing for their descendants, by
the sacrifice of themselves, political and religious liberty. And, while we behold,
with gratitude and admiration, the effects of their noble self-devotion, let us thence
learn to appreciate those blessings which, by the continued providence of God, we
have so long enjoyed; and let us be confirmed more and more in our determination
to resist every attempt, whether by open force or secret fraud, to deprive us and
our descendants of the privileges so dearly purchased.

" It has been asserted by the Roman Catholics, ' That all those who suffered death, during the reign of queen Mary, had been adjudged guilty of high treason, in consequence of their rising in defence of lady Jane Grey's title to the crown.' To disprove this, however, is no difficult matter, since every one, conversant in English history, must know, that those who are found guilty of high treason are to be hanged and quartered. But how can even a Papist affirm, that ever a man in England was *burned* for high-treason ? We admit, that some few suffered death in the ordinary way of process at common law, for their adherence to lady Jane ; but none of those were burned. Why, if traitors, were they taken before the bishops, who have no power to judge in criminal cases ? Even allowing the bishops to have had power to judge, yet their own bloody statute did not empower them to execute. The proceedings against the martyrs are still extant, and they are carried on directly according to the forms prescribed by their own statute. Not one of those who were burned in England, was ever accused of high-treason, much less were they tried at common law. And this should teach the reader to value a history of transactions in his own country, particularly as it relates to the sufferings of the blessed martyrs in defence of the religion he professes, in order that he may be able to remove the veil which falsehood has cast over the face of truth. Having said thus much, by way of introduction, we shall proceed with the Acts and Monuments of the British Martyrs.

' By the death of king Edward, the crown devolved, according to law, on his eldest sister Mary, who was within half a day's journey to the court, when she had notice given her by the earl of Arundel, of her brother's death, and of the patent for lady Jane's succession. Upon this she retired to Framlingham, in Suffolk, to be near the sea, that she might escape to Flanders, in case of necessity. Before she arrived there, she wrote, on the 9th of July, to the council, telling them, that ' she understood, that her brother was dead, by which she succeeded to the crown, but wondered that she heard not from them ; she well understood what consultations they had engaged in, but she would pardon all such as would return to their duty, and proclaim her title to the crown.'

" It was now found, that the king's death could be no longer kept a secret ; accordingly some of the privy council went to lady Jane, and acknowledged her as their queen. The news of the king's death afflicted her much, and her being raised to the throne, rather increased than lessened her trouble. She was a person of extraordinary abilities, acquirements, and virtues. She was mistress both of the Greek and Latin tongues, and delighted much in study. As she was not tainted with the levities which usually accompany her age and station, so she seemed to have attained to the practice of the highest fortitude ; for in those sudden turns of her condition, as she was not exalted with the prospect of a crown, so she was little cast down, when her palace was made her prison. The only passion she shewed, was that of the noblest kind, in the concern she expressed for her father and husband, who fell with her, and seemingly on her account ; though, in reality, Northumberland's ambition, and her father's weakness, ruined her.

" She rejected the crown, when it was first offered her ; she said, she knew that of right it belonged to the late king's sisters, and therefore could not with a good conscience assume it ; but she was told, that both the judges and privy counsellors had declared, that it fell to her according to law. This, joined with the importunities of her husband, her father, and father-in-law, made her submit.—Upon this, twenty-one privy-counsellors set their hands to a letter to Mary, telling her that queen Jane was now their sovereign, and that as the marriage between her father and mother had been declared null, so she could not succeed to the crown ; they therefore required her to lay down her pretensions, and to submit to the settlement now made ; and if she gave a ready obedience, promised her much favour. The day after this they proclaimed Jane.

" Northumberland's known enmity to the late duke of Somerset, and the suspicions of his being the author of Edward's untimely death, begot a great aversion in the people to him and his family, and disposed them to favour Mary ; who, in the meantime, was very active in raising forces to support her claim. To attach the Protestants to her cause, she promised not to make any change in the reformed worship, as established under her brother ; and on this assurance a large body of the men of Suffolk joined her standard.

" Northumberland was now perplexed between his wish to assume the command of an army raised to oppose Mary, and his fear of leaving London to the government of the council, of whose fidelity he entertained great doubts. He was, however, at length obliged to adopt the latter course, and before his departure from the metropolis, he adjured the members of the council, and all persons in authority, to be steadfast in their attachment to the cause of queen Jane, on whose success, he assured them, depended the continuance of the Protestant religion in England. They promised all he required, and he departed, encouraged by their protestations and apparent zeal.

"Mary's party in the mean time continued daily to augment. Hastings went over to her with 4000 men out of Buckinghamshire, and she was proclaimed queen in many places. At length the privy council began to see their danger, and to think how to avoid it; and besides fears for their personal safety, other motives operated with many of the members. To make their escape from the Tower, where they were detained, ostensibly to give dignity to the court of queen Jane, but really as prisoners, they pretended it was necessary to give an audience to the foreign ambassadors, who would not meet them in the Tower; and the earl of Pembroke's house was appointed for the audience.

"When they met there they resolved to declare for queen Mary, and rid themselves of Northumberland's yoke, which they knew they must bear, if he were victorious. They sent for the lord mayor and aldermen, and easily gained their concurrence; and Mary was proclaimed queen on the 19th of July. They then sent to the Tower, requiring the duke of Suffolk to quit the government of that place, and the lady Jane to lay down the title of queen. To this she submitted with much greatness of mind, and her father with abjectness.

"The council next sent orders to Northumberland to dismiss his forces, and to obey the queen. When Northumberland heard this, he disbanded his forces, went to the market-place at Cambridge, where he then was, and proclaimed Mary as queen. The earl of Arundel was sent to apprehend him, and when Northumberland was brought before him, he, in the most servile manner, fell at his feet to beg his favour. He, with three of his sons and sir Thomas Palmer, (his wicked tool in the destruction of the duke of Somerset) were all sent to the Tower.

"Every one now flocked to implore the queen's favour, and Ridley among the rest, but he was committed to the Tower; the queen being resolved to put Bonner again in the see of London. Some of the judges, and several noblemen, were also sent thither, among the rest the duke of Suffolk; who was, however, three days after, set at liberty. He was a weak man, could do little harm, and was consequently selected as the first person towards whom the queen should exert her clemency.

"Mary came to London on the 3d of August, and on the way was met by her sister, lady Elizabeth, with a thousand horse, whom she had raised to assist the queen. On arriving at the Tower, she liberated the Duke of Norfolk, the duchess of Somerset, and Gardiner; also the lord Courtney, son to the marquis of Exeter, who had been kept there ever since his father's attainder, and whom she now made earl of Devonshire.

"Thus was seated on the throne of England the lady Mary, who, to a disagreeable person and weak mind, united bigotry, superstition, and cruelty. She seems to have inherited more of her mother's than her father's qualities. Henry was impatient, rough, and ungovernable; but Catherine, while she assumed the character of a saint, harboured inexorable rancour and hatred against the Protestants. It was the same with her daughter Mary, as appears from a letter in her own handwriting, now in the British Museum. In this letter, which is addressed to bishop Gardiner, she declares her fixed intention of burning every Protestant; and there is an insinuation, that as soon as circumstances would permit, she would restore back to the church the lands that had been taken from the convents. This was the greatest instance of her weakness that she could shew: for in the first place the convents had been all demolished, except a few of their churches; and the rents were in the hands of the first nobility, who, rather than part with them, would have overturned the government both in church and state.

"Mary was crowned at Westminster in the usual form; but dreadful were the consequences that followed. The narrowness of spirit which always distinguishes a weak mind from one that has been enlarged by education, pervaded all the actions of this princess. Unacquainted with the constitution of the country, and a slave to superstition, she thought to domineer over the rights of private judgment, and trample on the privileges of mankind. The first exertion of her regal power was, to wreak her vengeance upon all those who had supported the title of lady Jane Grey.

"The first of these was the duke of Northumberland, who was beheaded on Tower-hill, and who, in consequence of his crimes, arising from ambition, died unpitied; nay, he was even taunted on the scaffold by the spectators, who knew in what manner he had acted to the good duke of Somerset.

"The other executions that followed were numerous indeed, but as they were all upon the statute of high treason, they cannot, with any degree of propriety, be applied to Protestants, or, as they were then called, *heretics*. The parliament was pliant enough to comply with all the queen's requests, and an act passed to establish the popish religion. This was what the queen waited for, and power being now put into her hands, she was determined to exercise it in the most arbitrary manner. She was destitute of human compassion, and without the least reluctance could tyrannize over the consciences of men.

"This leads us to the conclusion of the first year of her reign; and we consider it the more necessary to take notice of these transactions, although not, strictly speaking, *martyrdoms*, that our readers might be convinced of the great difference there is between dying for religion and for high treason. It is history alone that can teach them such things, and it is reflection only that can make history useful. We frequently read without reflection, and study without consideration; but the following portions of our history, in particular, will furnish ample materials for serious thought to our readers, and we entreat their attention to them."

This account is in part emitted from the pericraniums of the modern editors, and in other part selected from the *Abridgement of Burnet's History*.—The exordium is genuine, and a delectable specimen of Protestant veracity it is.—The attention of British Protestants is called to " a period of their *church* history that cannot fail to awaken in their " hearts that love for their ancestors, which at present (they say) we " fear, lies dormant in too many."—Yes, we believe it; the " devouring flames" so long fanned by lying historians begin to smoulder, and we are happy to say there is not an appearance that any efforts of bigotry will succeed in kindling the dying embers.—The modern editors talk of the sacrifices made by their ancestors in favour of political and religious liberty; but where are we to go for proofs of this spirit of patriotism? If we look into the pages of history, we see nothing but factious contentions and persecutions of the weaker by the stronger party. We see the Church-ascendancy party persecuting those who dissent from her; we see the Puritan-covenanters breathing nothing but fire and fury against Church of England-men; then the Independents succeeded and persecuted the Puritans; while the poor Papists were the victims of every faction.—If we examine the statute-book, we shall find that penal laws kept increasing in every succeeding reign; and as every penal law must be a restriction on the freedom of every one affected by it, the share of liberty now enjoyed by Englishmen is merely nominal, and therefore it is no wonder that they are so backward in listening to the warwhoop of hot-headed fanatics.—The sensible Protestant is not now to be deluded by the empty boastings of imaginary blessings under a Protestant system, which takes away more than one-third of the profits of the labourer to bestow upon a set of lazy and even rich sinecurists, pensioners, and half-pay officers, composed in a great measure of the sons of parsons and bastards of the nobility. He has now no relish for that system which upholds a rich and idle clergy in some measure without flocks, and careless whether those that remain secede to some neighbouring dissenting congregation. He is too well aware that the blessings which the Catholic labourer really enjoyed before the Reformation are never tasted by him, since he has to plod and toil every day to increase the luxuries of others, whereas the Catholic having only to labour for himself and his family, did not want to toil incessantly through the week, but had frequent days of rest, which were spent in devotion and mirthful recreation—Under these circumstances, when men in these days talk of privileges dearly purchased, and preserving them against force or fraud, they should have the decency to tell us what privileges are enjoyed, and likely to be wrested from them; where they are to be found, and by whom held.

The editors next tell us, "It has been asserted by the Roman Catho-"lics, 'That *all* those who suffered death, during the reign of queen "Mary, had been adjudged guilty of high treason, in consequence of "their rising in defence of lady Jane Grey's title to the crown," and they then proceed to prove the falsity of this assertion by some curious logic. But the statement is itself *false*, and therefore requires no refutation.— Why did they not *name* the Catholic who made the assertion? Because they could not.—Again they say, "Not *one* of those who were burned "in England was ever accused of high treason, much less were they "tried at common law."—Now this is another barefaced falsehood, for the most prominent character who suffered, and of whom we shall have to say much hereafter, namely, Tom Cranmer, was not only *accused* of high treason, but was actually *tried* and *condemned* for *that crime*, on the 14th of September, 1553, according to the testimony of Dr. Heylin. Ridley was sent to the Tower also on the same charge. So much for the accuracy of the modern editors.

Before we enter into the transactions of this short but interesting reign, we must notice another vile insinuation which the modern editors have cast on the memory of Mary's mother, the unfortunate but magnanimous Catharine.—Describing, or rather professing to describe, the qualities of Mary, these unfeeling bigots say, "She seems to have "inherited more of her mother's than her father's qualities. Henry "was impatient, rough, and ungovernable, (fine qualities for a Protest-"ant pope); but Catharine, while she assumed the character of a saint, "harboured inexorable rancour and hatred against the Protestants. It "was the same with her daughter Mary, as appears from a letter in "her own handwriting, now in the British Museum. In this letter, "which is addressed to bishop Gardiner, she declares *her fixed intention* "*of burning every Protestant*."—What unblushing asserters of falsehood! We might have supposed that the lies we have detected from the writings of Fox and Burnet would have contented these modern editors, without adding diabolical inventions of their own, which stand refuted by every historian of credit and respectability. But what can be expected from men, who, in their preface to this *Book of Lies*, thus speaks of our Review of it.—"But a few weeks," they say, "had elapsed from "our first publication, when the enemies of the Protestant religion, "alarmed at the sensation created by our work, set their usual engines "in motion, and announced a '*Review*' of what they are pleased to "term '*Fox's Book of Lies*.' Accordingly, in due time, this notable "performance made its appearance; and although it is, as might be ex-"pected, a mass of vulgar abuse, gross perversion, barefaced falsehoods, "and unsupported assertions, yet, such is the influence exercised by the "Popish priests over the deluded and ignorant creatures whom they "pretend to *teach*, that the publication still continues, and a sufficient "number are disposed of to defray the expenses, and to pay the wages

" of the miserable hack who puts together this farrago of trash, des-
" tined (as he *modestly* says) to *enlighten the Catholic world !*

" It may naturally be inquired, if this book be so utterly unworthy,
" how does it meet with purchasers? To this we reply, those who pur-
" chase it, are *compelled* to do so; it is a kind of *act of faith,* enjoined
" by the priests, and, of course, submitted to by their flocks, with the
" same willingness (though with *less pleasure*) as they would, had they
" the power, perform a real, Inquisitorial *Auto da Fé*, in which the
" editors of the Book of Martyrs should be consigned to the flames,
" amidst the savage yellings of the bigotted and infuriated multitude !
" That the sale of the ' *Review*' among these poor creatures-arises from
" a notion of its being necessary for the preservation of their souls
" from purgatory, and not from any possibility of amusement or in-
" struction to be derived from its perusal, is evident from the fact, that
" *three-fourths* of its ' *enlightened*' purchasers are not sufficiently skilful
" to *read* it; and of the remaining fourth, if ten persons were to come
" forward and swear that they had read this *erudite* performance through,
" we should certainly suspect that the *dispensing* power of his ' Holiness'
" had been exerted to relieve their *consciences* from the guilt of *perjury*.
" We have ourselves tried to wade through it, and are confident that it
" would be almost impossible to persevere through two pages, such is
" the soporific dulness of the matter, were it not that the attention is
" ever and anon aroused by a daring excursion beyond the bounds of
" truth, or, to speak in plain terms, *a shameless and outrageous falsehood !*
" Sincerely do we pity those, who can be imposed on by so gross an
" imposture; and we consider ourselves, and the cause we have
" espoused, doubly honoured by this attack; for while the abuse and
" impotent malignity levelled at our work, from such a quarter, is its
" highest eulogium, the countenance afforded to our adversary by the
" Papists, is the best proof of the veracity of our assertions as to the
" ignorance and besotted bigotry of the present, as well as former, pro-
" fessors of that belief. This is the *first* and *last* notice we shall ever
" take of this work, although we are *personally* abused in almost
" every one of its pages. The intolerant and malignant spirit display-
" ed throughout the whole, should be an additional inducement to Pro-
" testants to guard against the possibility of power being intrusted to
" such persons as the patrons of the *Review*."

We have here a specimen of the sectarian art of lying only to be equal-
ed by the gullibility of those who give credence to such montrous assertions. Are the editors and publishers—are the patronizers of such outrageous violations of common sense and decency—in sane mind? Or
are they not rather fit candidates for bedlam?—To charge us with
" *personally*" abusing *anonymous* scribblers is paying no great compliment to the sapiency of *their* readers; and to assert that *three-fourths*
of the *purchasers* of our Review cannot *read* it, and those who can *do
not*, though they continue to encourage it, is stretching even beyond
the capacity of Munchausen. But the priests *compel* them to purchase!
Do they, and for what? Merely for the sake we suppose of paying us
wages for rendering no service, since no one, according to their account, reads the Review. Admiral logicians! you have here shewn
your capacity at the trade of falsehood not to be surpassed by Fox him-

self, and from our hearts we PITY, most SINCERELY do we PITY those
poor deluded mortals, whose want of penetration and blind credulity
subject them to such gross and abominable impositions.

But we must return to the subject from which we have digressed.
The ill-fated Catharine, the modern editors say, "harboured inexorable
rancour and hatred against the Protestants!" Base libellers of a suffering queen and virtuous woman! where is your authority for this infamous accusation? Even Burnet stands to confront you in this falsehood, for he says "she was a devout and exemplary woman;" that
" she used to work with her own hands, and kept her women at work
with her;" that she practised severities and devotions, and gave alms
deeds; and that *all sorts* of people had a high esteem of her; and you
have acknowledged his testimony in the preceding pages of your work.
Catharine had too many misfortunes to afflict her, and was too helpless
in her situation to gratify the rancour you charge her with, had she
even entertained it; but this charge springs from the malice and rancour of your own hearts against Papists and Popery, which is manifest
in every line of your work.—Again, we ask you on what authority do
you state that there is a letter in the hand-writing of Mary, deposited
in the British Museum, in which she declares her fixed intention of
burning every Protestant? By whom was it deposited? Who vouches
for the hand-writing? To whose possession can it be traced before the
Museum obtained possession of it? These questions must be answered,
modern editors, before the sensible part of the community will believe
you; but this you will never do, because it is out of your power. Anticipating these awkward difficulties, you very wisely announce in your
preface that the only notice you will take of the detections of your base
falsehoods, is the rodomontade we have just quoted. But if Mary was
so firmly fixed in her cruel intentions towards Protestants, how came
Burnet to tell us that she declared in council, on the 22d of August,
1553, "that though she was fixed in her own religion, YET SHE
" WOULD NOT COMPEL OTHERS TO IT; but would leave that
" to the motions of God's spirit, and *the labours of good preachers.*" This
does not look like "a fixed intention of burning every Protestant."—
That Mary had "more of her mother's than her father's qualities" we
do not deny; but they were qualities the very opposite to those which
are imputed to her by the modern editors.—We know that Protestants
have been taught from their infancy to look upon this princess as a
woman of sanguinary disposition, and we never hear her name pronounced without the epithet of "bloody" prefixed to it; but we shall
shew that Protestant historians, who have soared above the vulgar prejudices of education, and having calmly considered the circumstances
of her reign, have done justice to her memory.—Collier, in his *Ecclesiastical History*, says, "It may be affirmed without panegyric, that the
" queen's private life was all along strait and unblemished. It must be
" said, that religion had the overbalance: the other world was upper-
" most with her, and she valued her conscience more than her crown...
" That she was not of a vindictive implacable spirit, may be inferred
" from her pardoning most of the great men in Northumberland's re-
" bellion." Vol. ii. b. 6. p. 400.—Camden in his introduction to the
Annals of Queen Elizabeth, writes, " A princess never to be sufficiently

" commended for her pious and religious demeanour, her commissera-
" tion towards the poor, and her magnificence and liberality towards
" the nobility and churchmen," p. 10.—Echard says, " She was a
" woman of a strict and severe life; who allowed herself few of those
" diversions belonging to courts : was constant at her devotions, &c...
" She much endeavoured to expiate and restore the sacrileges of the
" two last reigns." p. 327. Fuller, in his *Church History*, states, that
" she hated to equivocate in her own religion; and always was what
" she was, without dissembling her judgment or practice for fear or
" flattery...She had been a worthy princess, had as little cruelty been
" done under her, as was done by her." B. xiii. p. 42.—Baker, in his
Chronicle, says, " We shall not do her right, if we *deny her to be of a*
" *merciful disposition,* seeing often times she pitied the *person* where
" she shed the *blood*."—With these testimonies in her favour let the
reader decide between Mary and the base libellers of her character.—
We shall now proceed to detail some of the most prominent events in
her reign, which the modern editors have carefully and craftily suppressed, and when the reader has gone over our account, he will be
able to say whether Mary was " unacquainted with the constitution of
the country," or whether she was not one of the most constitutional
sovereigns that ever reigned over this once happy and Catholic country.

The reader has been already apprized of the design of Dudley duke
of Northumberland to set aside the two sisters of the young king Edward,
and get the wife of his son, lord Dudley, the lady Jane Grey, exalted to
the throne.—This young lady was daughter to the duke of Suffolk, who
was the son of Mary, sister to Henry VIII. by Charles Brandon, whom
she married on the death of her husband, Louis XII. king of France,
and who was afterwards created duke of Suffolk. The pretext for
transferring the crown from the rightful heir to that of a pretender was
that of religion, it being well known that Mary was rigidly attached to
the Catholic faith, and the chief reformers therefore saw that if she
came to the throne there was little chance for them to come off scot
free. Accordingly they worked upon the feelings of the young and
weakly sovereign, and prevailed upon him to sign an instrument whereby the crown was conferred upon lady Jane, contrary to the constitutional privileges of parliament, which was not consulted on the occasion. The young king did not live more than a fortnight after signing
this instrument, and every means were used to keep secret his death
till Northumberland had got his projects into proper training; but in
this they were frustrated, as the very night while the lords were sitting
in council, the princess Mary was informed of the event, as well as the
intentions of the conspirators.—She was then at Hoddesdon, in the
neighbourhood of London, and without losing a moment she mounted
her horse and rode with her household servants to Kenninghall in Norfolk.—On the 4th day after the king's death, the same was announced
to lady Jane, who was conveyed to the Tower in full state, and the next
day proclaimed queen. The people heard the proclamation with silence :
a vintner's boy had the hardihood to give his dissent, and the next day
he lost his ears for his folly. The morning following a letter from the
princess Mary was delivered to the council, in which she assumed the
style and dignity of the sovereign, reproached them with withholding

from her the intelligence of her brother's death, intimated that she was acquainted with their disloyal intentions to oppose her rights, and commanded them to proclaim her accession to the throne immediately. This letter was dated from Kenninghall, the 9th of July, 1553; but the document seemed to give the traitors no uneasiness; they looked upon themselves safe, as Mary was but a single and defenceless woman, but they reckoned without their host.—To this letter the lords in council returned an insulting answer, in which they upbraided her with illegitimacy, and called upon her to submit to their and her lawful sovereign, lady queen Jane, and abandon her false claim. This answer, the reader must bear in remembrance, was signed, in the first instance, by the hoary and lecherous old scoundrel, TOM CRANMER, and twenty other members of the council.

While these traitorous proceedings were concerting in the council, a different turn of affairs was going on abroad. The people knew nothing of lady Jane, but were not ignorant of the princess Mary and her rights. They hated Northumberland for his ambition, and there were strong suspicions that he had poisoned the young king to make way for his daughter-in-law, who eventually might be made to yield the crown to the aspiring duke. The very day on which they sent their insolent letter to Mary, intelligence reached the council, that she had been joined by some of the nobility, and that the gentry and people of the neighbouring counties of her residence were flocking round her standard. This put the conspirators into dreadful alarm, and Northumberland found himself sadly perplexed. He saw the necessity of making head against Mary, but how could he leave the capital, where his presence was necessary to secure the fidelity of his colleagues. They, on the other hand, wished to gain a point of safety in case of a reverse of fortune. Northumberland proposed that the duke of Suffolk should command the forces destined against Mary, while the secret partisans of that princess urged the propriety of Northumberland's taking the command upon himself, as the most proper of the two, in consequence of his great skill, valour and good fortune. Northumberland found himself constrained to consent, though reluctantly, and he took leave of his colleagues with a heavy heart. As he rode through the city at the head of his troops, he found the streets thronged with people, but heard no exclamations for success, on which he despondently remarked to sir John Gates, "The people crowd to look upon us; but not one says, God speed ye."

From the outset of these doings Northumberland suspected the fidelity of the citizens of London, and therefore before his departure he requested the assistance of the preachers, and exhorted them to appeal from the pulpit in favour of the reformed faith and lady Jane's cause. "By " no one," writes Dr. Lingard " was the task performed with greater " zeal than by Ridley, bishop of London, who, on the following Sunday, " preached at St. Paul's cross before the lord mayor, the aldermen, and " a numerous assemblage of the people. He maintained, that the daugh- " ters of Henry VIII. were, by the illegitimacy of their birth, excluded " from the succession. He contrasted the opposite characters of the " present competitors, the gentleness, the piety, the orthodoxy of the " one, with the haughtiness, the foreign connections, and the Popish " creed of the other. As a proof of Mary's bigotry, he narrated a chi-

" valrous but unsuccessful attempt, which he had made within the last
" year, to withdraw her from the errors of popery: and in conclusion,
" he conjured the audience, as they prized the pure light of the gospel,
" to support the cause of the lady Jane, and to oppose the claim of her
" idolatrous rival. But the torrent of his eloquence was poured in
" vain." As Ridley's attempt to make a convert of the princess Mary,
which he here alludes to in his sermon, is not without interest, we insert
it for the amusement of the reader, who will not fail to perceive the
superiority of Mary's mind over the apostate prelate. Ridley waited
on Mary, September 8, 1552, and was courteously received. After
dinner he offered to preach before her in the church. She begged
him to make the answer himself. He urged her again: she replied
that he might preach: but that neither she, nor any of her's, would
hear him. *Ridley*. "Madam, I trust you will not refuse God's word."
Mary. "I cannot tell what you call God's word. That is not God's
" word now which was God's word in my father's time." *Ridley*.
" God's word is all one in all times: but is better understood and
" practised in some ages than in others." *Mary*. "You durst not for
" your ears have preached that for God's word in my father's time,
" which you do now. As for your new books, thank God, I never
" read them, I never did, nor ever will do." Soon afterwards she
dismissed him with these words. "My lord, for your gentleness to
" come and see me, I thank you: but for your offer to preach before
" me, I thank you not." As he retired, he drank according to custom
with sir Thomas Wharton, the steward of her household; but suddenly his conscience smote him: "Surely," he exclaimed, "I have done
" wrong. I have drunk in that house in which God's word hath been
" refused. I ought, if I had done my duty, to have shaken the dust off
" my shoes for a testimony against this house."—(*Fox*, ii. 131.)

Northumberland, before his departure, requested and obtained a commission, signed and sealed by the lords of the council, at the head of
which was Cranmer, in which were certain instructions, and the marches
laid out and limited from one to another. Thus fortified, Northumberland set out for St. Edmund's Bury, where, instead of hearing of the
supplies that were to be sent him, he received letters from some of the
lords of the council, full of trouble and discomfort, which placed him between hope and despair. In the mean time the princess Mary was not
idle. She unexpectedly left Kenninghall for the castle of Framlingham
in Suffolk, a distance of forty miles which she rode without rest. Here,
in a few days, she found herself surrounded by more than thirty thousand men, all volunteers in her cause, who refused to receive pay, and
served to their immortal honour, through the sole motive of loyalty.
An attempt has been made by Fox and the modern editors to stain
Mary's character with having forfeited her word, but no proof whatever
is produced to substantiate the charge. The latter say, "To attach the
" Protestants to her cause, she promised not to make any alteration in
" the reformed worship, as established under her brother; and, on this
" assurance, a large body of men of Suffolk joined her standard." This
is another of the thousand lies to be found in this mass of falsehoods.
By the most unquestionable authority it appears that Mary made no
such promise. Dr. Heylin makes the earl of Arundel, in his speech to

the lords of the council, thus allude to this matter. "Yet how doth it " appear that the princess Mary intends any alteration in religion? Cer- " tainly, having been lately petitioned to on this point by the Suffolk " men, she gave them *a very hopeful answer.*"—Here then it is clear that there was no distinct promise made on the part of the queen, and therefore she could not be guilty of a breach of her word. Nay Fox himself, like all other liars, bears witness to the falsity of his own state- ment. "During the persecution," observes Dr. Lingard, in a note to Mary's reign, "these very persons presented to the queen's commis- " sioners a long petition in favour of their religion. It was certainly " the time for them to have urged the promise, if any had been given. " But they appear to have no knowledge of any such thing. They do " not make the remotest allusion to it. They speak, indeed, of their " services : but instead of attributing them to the promise of the queen, " they insinuate the contrary, by asserting that they supported her " claim, because their religion taught them to support the rightful heir." (*Fox*, iii. 578—583.)—Mr. Collier remarks, "If they engaged upon " condition, and articled with their sovereign, their caution went too " far. For either she had a right, or she had none : if she had none, " their correspondence was criminal ; if they believed she had a right, " they ought to have run the risk of her government, and served her " without terms, and rested the event with Providence." From all this testimony it is evident that Mary did not commit herself, but that she intended to leave all these matters to the wisdom and deliberation of parliament, as we shall hereafter shew.

This disposition of the people alarmed Northumberland and made him irresolute. The lords of the council too were by no means easy at the progress of Mary's cause. On the 18th of July, it was resolved to send for a body of mercenary slaves raised in Picardy, and to levy troops in the vicinity of the metropolis; but these measures were found too tardy, and, on the day following, Mary was proclaimed queen at St. Paul's cross, amidst the acclamations of the people, which drowned the voice of the herald. Thus ended the nine day's reign of the lady Jane Grey. The lords of the council now sent an order to Northumberland to disband his forces and acknowledge Mary for his sovereign, but the duke had already taken the only part which prudence suggested to save himself. He was at this time at Cambridge, and sending for the vice chancellor, he proceeded to the market-place, where with tears running down his cheeks he proclaimed Mary sovereign of England, and threw his cap into the air in token of joy.—The next morning the duke was arrested by the earl of Arundel, on a charge of high treason, together with several of his associates, and conducted to the Tower.— So incensed were the people at their disloyalty, that it required a strong guard to protect them from their vengeance. Bonfires, illuminations, and all the customary demonstrations of public joy took place, on the accession of Mary to the throne of her ancestors.—On her public en- trance into the metropolis, accompanied by her sister Elizabeth, their ears were stunned with the acclamations of the people, and when they entered the Tower, they found kneeling on the green, as state prisoners, the duchess of Somerset, (widow of the late lord protector) the duke of Norfolk, the son of the late marquis of Exeter, and Gardiner, the de-

prived bishop of Winchester. The prelate pronounced a congratulatory
address, and Mary was moved to tears.—She bade them rise, and having kissed them, she set them at liberty.—The same day she ordered
a distribution of eightpence to every poor householder in the city.—
Of the prisoners before mentioned, there were twenty-seven for trial;
namely, the dukes of *Suffolk* and Northumberland; the marquis of
Northampton; the earls of *Huntingdon* and Warwick; the lords *Robert*,
Henry, Ambrose and Guildford Dudley (sons of Northumberland); the
lady Jane Dudley (Grey, the pretended queen, and daughter of Suffolk);
the archbishop of Canterbury (old Cranmer); the bishops of *London*
(Ridley) and *Ely*; the lords *Ferrers, Clinton,* and *Cobham*; the judges
Montague and *Chomeley,* and the *chancellor of the augmentations;* sirs
Andrew Dudley, John Gates, Henry Gates, *Henry Palmer, John Cheke,*
John Yorke, and Thomas Palmer; and Dr. *Cocks,* When the list was
given to the queen, she struck out all the names in italics, and reduced
the number from twenty-seven to eleven, which act of mercy cannot
surely be construed into cruelty and vindictiveness of temper.—Of the
eleven thus left to be put upon their trial only seven were immediately
tried; these were the duke of Northumberland, the chief contriver of
the plot; the earl of Warwick, his son; the marquis of Northampton,
sir John Gates, sir Henry Gates, sir Andrew Dudley, and sir Thomas
Palmer, who had been Northumberland's principal counsellors and constant associates. Though urged to include the lady Jane Grey, who
had been her rival, Mary would not listen to the proposal, and even undertook her defence, contending that she was not an accomplice of
Northumberland, but merely a puppet in his hands. Neither was the
hoary old traitor Cranmer, who had been the instrument of divorcing
Mary's mother, had assisted to illegitamize the daughter, and afterwards
did all he could to deprive her of the crown, included among the seven;
an astonishing instance of the lenity of Mary's disposition, and how
much she acted on the charitable principles of that religion to which
she was stedfastly fixed, and for which she had already suffered persecution herself.

On the 18th of August, the three noblemen, Northumberland, Warwick and Northampton, were brought before their peers, and pleaded
guilty; the first petitioned that mercy might be extended to his children, and requested an able divine to prepare him for death; and that
he might be allowed to confer with two lords of the council on certain
secrets of state, which had come to his knowledge while he was prime
minister. 'To these requests Mary assented. The four commoners also
pleaded guilty, but only Northumberland, sir John Gates, and sir Henry
Palmer were ordered for execution. On the morning of their execution
they attended a solemn mass, and were afterwards led out to the scaffold.
The modern editors say that Northumberland died unpitied; nay, that
" he was even taunted on the scaffold by the spectators, who knew in
" what manner he had acted to the *good* duke of Somerset."—From
whom they borrowed this tale they do not tell us; we conjecture it is
an invention of their own.—Rapin, a Calvinist writer, speaks very
strongly of the unpopularity of the duke for his haughtiness and cruelty,
but we do not see any statement of his being taunted by the people at
his death. That he was generally disliked there can be no doubt, and

it is stated by Stow and Dr. Heylin, that when he and his fellow-sufferers were on the way to execution, some words arose between them, each laying the blame of their treason on the other; but afterwards they forgave each other and died in mutual charity.—That the modern editors have violated the truth we think is manifest, as all historians agree that Northumberland, previous to suffering, addressed the spectators in a long speech, which he would not have done had they been in the temper described.—After expatiating on the nature of his offence and acknowledging his guilt, he concluded by admonishing the people, "to stand to "the religion of their ancestors, rejecting that of later date, which *had* "*occasioned all the misery of the foregoing thirty years;* and that for "prevention for the future, if they desired to present their souls un- "spotted in the sight of God, and were truly affected to their country, "they should expel those trumpets of sedition, the preachers of the re- "formed religion: that for himself, whatever had otherwise been pre- "tended, he professed no other religion than that of his fathers, for "testimony whereof he appealed to his good friend and ghostly father "the lord bishop of Worcester: and finally, that being blinded with "ambition, he had been contented to make a wreck of his conscience "by temporising, for which he professed himself a sincere repentant, "and so acknowledged the justice of his death."—Thus fell the duke of Northumberland, another of the great actors in the tragedy of the Re- formation.—By Protestants his declaration as to religion is looked upon with suspicion; by Catholics his previous life is looked upon with de- testation. He was the eldest son of that Dudley, who, with Empson, pillaged and oppressed the people under Henry VII. for which crimes they suffered under Henry VIII. and here we have the son of the first offender, meeting an untimely end under Mary, the daughter of the last Henry, under strong suspicions of having poisoned the son of his greatest benefactor and sovereign. Heylin remarks, that though this duke had six sons, all of them living to be men, and all of them married, yet not one of them had lawful issue, as if, says the doctor, the curse of Jeco- niah had been laid upon them.

Sir John Gates and sir Henry Palmer both addressed the spectators before they were beheaded. The speech of the former, relating to bible- reading, which is now the favourite project of the silly fanatics of the day, we will here give from Stow, and recommend it to the careful perusal of those who are advocates for the indiscriminate circulation of the bible.—They will here see the use made of the sacred word in the early days of what is called the Reformation, and history points out to us that it has been equally abused down to our own days.—" My coming "here this day," said sir John, "is to die; whereof, I assure you all, I "am well worthy: for I have lived as viciously and wickedly as any "man hath done in the world. I was the greatest reader of scripture, "that might be, of a man of my degree; and a worse follower thereof "there was not living. For I did not read, to be edified thereby, nor "to seek the glory of God: but contrariwise, arrogantly to be sedi- "tious, and dispute thereof: and privately to interpret it, after my own "brain and affection. Wherefore, I exhort you all, to beware how, "and after what sort, you come to read God's holy word. For it is "not a trifle, or playing-game, to deal with God's holy mysteries.

" Stand not too muoh in your own conceits. For like as a bee of one
" flower gathers honey, and the spider poison of the same : even so you,
" unless you humbly submit yourselves to God, and charitably read the
" same to the intent to be edified thereby, it is to you as poison, and
" worse; and it were better to let it alone."

   The rest of the prisoners condemned were reprieved, and afterwards
pardoned, so that only three individuals suffered the loss of life for this
great conspiracy to deprive a princess of her throne. An act of clemency
unparalleled in the history of the world, and yet this is the queen only
known to Protestants as the " *bloody queen Mary*."—On the 3rd of November following, the lady Jane Grey, with her husband, the lord Guilford Dudley, his brother the lord Ambrose Dudley, and the pliable Tom
Cranmer, archbishop of Canterbury, were brought to trial at the Guildhall in London, on a charge of high treason, to which they all pleaded
guilty, and submitted themselves to the queen's mercy. Sentence was
passed upon them as a matter of course, but execution was stayed, and
in all probability, had not the lady Jane's father again engaged in an insurrection to dethrone Mary, and Cranmer not issued seditious papers,
neither of these prisoners would have been brought to execution. Stow
tells us the lady Jane had the liberty of the Tower, to walk in the queen's
garden and on the hill; and the lords Ambrose Dudley and Guilford
Dudley had the liberties of the ports where they were lodged. Does
this look like a cruel and bloody disposition?

   We must return again to the modern editors, who, though they copy
in a great measure from Burnet in this account of Mary's reign, have
taken care to *suppress* every circumstance that would tell against the
traitors or in favour of this libelled queen. They say, " every one now
" flocked to implore the queen's mercy, and *Ridley* among the rest, but
" he was committed to the Tower; the queen being resolved to put
" Bonner again into the see of London."—Burnet is more candid, for
he adds, after " he was sent to the Tower; *for she was both offended with*
" *him* FOR HIS SERMON, and resolved to put Bonner," &c. The words
in italics and small capitals, which bears materially on the case, inasmuch as they shew the *reason* why Ridley was committed, these instructors of Christian knowledge have wilfully suppressed. They have
also omitted in their relation of the " Accession of Mary," the treasonable act of Ridley's preaching against Mary's right to the throne, and
calling upon the people to rise in arms to oppose her, and support a pretender. Let us suppose that a Catholic bishop could have been found
disloyal enough to have preached against the right of his present majesty to the throne of these realms, and when he found his treasonable
practices abortive, throwing himself at the feet of the monarch to implore his favour : is any one so stupid as to imagine that he would obtain his request? Would not the modern editors be the loudest to call
for his punishment? Mary sent Ridley to the Tower certainly, and had
he received his deserts, he would have been immediately tried for his
treason and sent to the scaffold along with Northumberland and his two
associates. But Mary was lenient to the extreme, and to this clemency
of disposition she may attribute much of the inquietude she afterwards
suffered in her government, as we shall soon prove.

   We are next told, that Mary on her way to London " was met by her

A REVIEW

OF

Fox's Book of Martyrs,

CRITICAL AND HISTORICAL.

No. 49. Printed and Published by W. E. Andrews, 3, Chapter-house-court, St. Paul's Churchyard, London. Price 3d.

EXPLANATION OF THE ENGRAVING—*Among other species of torture inflicted by the Protestants on the Catholics, and especially on the Priests, was that of perforating the ears of their victims with burning hot irons.*

CONTINUATION OF THE REVIEW.

" sister, lady Elizabeth, with a thousand horse, whom *she had raised to*
" *assist the queen.*" This is stated on the authority of Burnet, but Dr.
Lingard gives a different version to Elizabeth's conduct. This able
writer says, " The lady Elizabeth had taken no part in this contest.—
" To a messenger, indeed, from Northumberland, who offered her a
" large sum of money, and a valuable grant of lands as the price of her
" voluntary renunciation of all right to the succession, she replied, that
" she had no right to renounce, as long as her elder sister was living.
" But, if she did not join the lady Jane, she did nothing in aid of the
" lady Mary. Under the excuse of a real or feigned indisposition, she
" confined herself to her chamber, that, whichever party proved vic-
" torious, she might claim the negative merit of non-resistance. Now,
" however, the contest was at an end : the new queen approached her
" capital, and Elizabeth deemed it prudent to court the favour of the
" conqueror. At the head of a hundred and fifty horse, she met her at
" Aldgate. They rode together in triumphal procession through the
" streets, which were lined with the different crafts in their gayest at-
" tire. Every eye was directed towards the royal sisters."—So much

for the veracity of Burnet and his copyists as regards the sister of Mary;
we must now point out another base falsehood, to injure the character
of the queen, the invention of the modern editors. Alluding to the
death of Northumberland, they say, " The other executions that fol-
" lowed were *numerous* indeed, but as they were all upon *the statute of*
" *high treason,* they cannot with any degree of propriety be applied to
" PROTESTANTS, or, as they were then called, *heretics.*" Of the persons
engaged in the conspiracy to prevent Mary from ascending the throne,
only the three before named were brought to execution on her gaining
the crown. All the others were either set at liberty or reprieved; no
more blood was shed during the first year of her reign, nor until a rebellion had been set on foot by the father of the late pretender, lady
Jane, and sir Thomas Wyat, which had nearly cost Mary her crown
and liberty too. But of this affair we shall have to treat more largely
as we proceed. The modern editors would have their readers believe
the whole reign of Mary was one of blood and cruelty, whereas there
were, as we have before said, only *three* executed in her first year, and
there is every reason to believe, if the reformers had not been guilty of
SEDITION and REBELLION, that no more would have suffered during her
whole reign.

PROOFS OF MARY'S TOLERANT DISPOSITION AND THE REST-LESS SEDITIOUS SPIRIT OF THE FANATICAL REFORMERS.

We agree with the modern editors, that there is a very great difference " between dying *for religion* and for *high treason.*" That " it
" is history alone that can teach them (their readers) such things, and
" it is reflection alone that can make history useful." But when we
speak of history, we mean a plain and honest narration of FACTS, not
a jumble of LIES and MISREPRESENTATIONS, such as these modern editors
have dressed up from Fox and Burnet: perverting circumstances to
mislead their readers, and suppressing others to prevent them from
coming to a clear conviction of the Truth. This is *not* history, and reflections on such productions only increase the mischief, by poisoning
instead of instructing the mind. The editors of this *Book of Martyrs*
say, " Mary was crowned at Westminster in the usual form; but *dread-*
" *ful were the consequences that followed.* The *narrowness of spirit* which
" always distinguishes *a weak mind* from one that has been *enlarged by*
" *education,* pervaded *all* the actions of this princess. *Unacquainted*
" with *the constitution* of the country, and a *slave to superstition,* she
" sought to *domineer* over the *rights of private judgment,* and *trample* on
" the *privileges of mankind.* The first exertion of her regal power was,
" to *wreak vengeance* upon ALL those who had supported the title of
" lady Jane Grey." And this, we suppose, these learned instructers of
their readers call *history.* This is the sort of stuff that is to teach them
the difference between dying for religion (read fanaticism) and high
treason. Bless us! how wonderfully wise must that generation be that
has to rely solely on this kind of information for reflection to become
useful members of society. We do not recollect meeting, even in this
production of lies, such a string of falsehoods in so small a compass.—
If Mary did wreak her vengeance on all those who supported lady Jane,
it must be admitted that her vengeance was soon satisfied, and partook

mose of mercy than of rancour. We have proved that of " all those" engaged in the support of lady Jane, only THREE suffered death, and even the father of the ci-devant queen was set at liberty. This is a kind of vengeance seldom practised by narrow minds, and could only arise from a heart filled with benevolence and compassion. That Mary possessed a noble mind, and was well educated, is incontestible, from the public proceedings in the early part of her reign, nor was she ignorant of the constitution of the country, as she governed only by constitutional measures, which we shall now proceed to shew.

Mary was proclaimed on the 19th of July, 1553; Northumberland was arrested on the 20th, and taken to the Tower on the 22d. On the 31st the queen made her entrance into London, and immediately after appointed her council, some of whom had been employed in offices of trust under her father, and had filled them faithfully. Of these Gardiner, bishop of Winchester, was made lord chancellor, on the 21st of September. On coming to the crown, Mary found herself in debt, from the policy of Northumberland, who had kept the officers of the state three years in arrear of their salaries; yet she issued two proclamations which drew upon her the applause and blessings of the whole people, with the exception of the rascally crew of evangelicals. " By the first," writes Dr. Lingard, " she restored a depreciated currency to its original " value; ordered a new coinage of sovereigns and half-sovereigns, an- " gels and half-angels, of fine gold; and of silver groats, half-groats, " and pennies of the standard purity; and charged the whole loss and " expense to the treasury. By the other she remitted to her people, in " gratitude for their attachment to her right, the subsidy of four shil- " lings in the pound on land, and two shillings and eight pence on goods, " which had been granted to the crown by the late parliament. At the " same time she introduced, within the palace, an innovation highly " gratifying to the younger branches of the nobility, though it forebode " little good to the reformed preachers. Under Edward, their fanati- " cism had given to the court a sombre and funereal appearance. That " they might exclude from it the pomps of the devil, they had strictly " forbidden all richness of apparel, and every fashionable amusement. " But Mary, who recollected with pleasure the splendid gaities of her " father's reign, appeared publicly in jewels and coloured silks: the " ladies, emancipated from restraint, copied her example: and the cour- " tiers, encouraged by the approbation of their sovereign, presumed to " dress with a splendour that became their rank in the state. A new " impulse was thus communicated to all classes of persons: and con- " siderable sums were expended by the citizens, in public and private de- " corations, preparatory to the coronation. That ceremony was performed " after the ancient rite, by Gardiner, bishop of Winchester: and was " concluded in the usual manner, with a magnificent banquet in West- " minster hall. The same day a general pardon was proclaimed, with " the exception, by name, of sixty individuals who had been committed " to prison, or confined to their own houses, by order of council, for " treasonable or seditious offences committed since the queen's acces- " sion." These proceedings by no means exhibit an ignorance of the principles of the constitution, nor do they display a narrowness of mind arising from a contracted education.

While these salutary proceedings were going on in the state, Mary was not unmindful of the affairs of the church. It must here be observed, that this princess was firmly attached to the faith of her forefathers, and that the Catholic church, to which she belonged, was always unconnected with the state in all ecclesiastical matters. By the first clause in Magna Charta, it was stipulated that the church should be free, and secured in all her rights and privileges. These rights and privileges were invaded and destroyed by Mary's father and brother, when they robbed and despoiled the church of that property which she held in trust for the benefit of the poor, the sick, the stranger, the widowed and the fatherless. When Mary ascended the throne she restored the church to her rights, and placed those bishops in their sees who had been illegally deposed from them, and expelled those who had been improperly thrust into others. In doing this she proceeded as cautiously as she could, in order to avoid any excitation to tumult and confusion by the discontented fanatical party, who saw all their hopes lost, while Mary was safely seated on the throne. But careful as she was, the seditious spirit of the evangelicals was too forward to be kept within the bounds of peace and good order. On the 13th of August, Dr. Bourn, the archdeacon of London, was grossly assaulted while preaching at St. Paul's cross, and a dagger was flung at his head. A riot was also occasioned by the celebration of mass in a church in the horse market. These seditious and disorderly outrages were occasioned by the inflammatory language of the reformed preachers from the pulpit, whose example is followed by the bigotted and intolerant preachers of the present day. These instigators to violence, clothed in the garb of ministers of peace, alarmed the passions of their hearers by inveighing against the Catholics and the church, which they stigmatized as idolatrous and tyrannical. Their turbulence occasioned the queen to forbid the preaching in public without a license, in which order she only followed the example of her two predecessors. She also issued a proclamation on the 18th of the same month, the tenor of which is thus given by Dr. Heylin :—

"The queen's highness well remembering what great inconvenience "and dangers have grown to this her realm in times past, through the di- "versities of opinions in questions of religion; and hearing also that now "of late, since the beginning of her most gracious reign, the same con- "tentions be again much revived, through certain false and untrue re- "ports, and rumours spread by some evil disposed persons, hath thought "good to give to understand to all her highness's most loving subjects "her most gracious pleasure in manner following.

"First, her majesty being presently, by the only goodness of God, "settled in her just possession of the imperial crown of this realm, and "other dominions thereunto belonging, cannot now hide that religion "which God and the world knoweth she hath ever professed from her "infancy hitherto. Which as her majesty is minded to observe and "maintain for herself by God's grace during her time, so doth her high- "ness much desire, and would be glad the same were of all her sub- "jects quietly and charitably entertained.

"And yet she doth signify unto all her majesty's loving subjects, "that of her most gracious disposition and clemency, her highness "mindeth not to compel any of her said subjects thereunto, until such

" time as further order by common assent may be taken therein: For-
" bidding, nevertheless, all her subjects of all degrees, at their perils, to
" move seditions, or stir unquietness in her people, by interpreting the
" laws of this realm after their brains and fancies, but quietly to continue
" for the time, till (as before said) further order may be taken; and
" therefore willeth, and straightly chargeth and commandeth, all her
" good and loving subjects, to live together in quiet sort, and Christian
" charity, leaving those new found devilish terms of Papist and heretic,
" and such like; and applying their whole care, study and travel to live
" in the fear of God, exercising their conversations in such charitable
" and godly doing, as their lives may indeed express the great hunger
" and thirst of God's glory, which by rash talk and words many have
" pretended: And in so doing they shall best please God, and live with-
" out danger of the laws, and maintain the tranquillity of the realm.—
" Whereof as her highness shall be most glad, so if any man shall rashly
" presume to make any assemblies of people, or at any public assem-
" blies, or otherwise, shall go about to stir the people to disorder or
" disquiet, she mindeth according to her duty, to see the same most se-
" verely reformed and punished according to her highness's laws.

" And furthermore, forasmuch as it is well known that sedition and
" false rumours have been nourished and maintained in this realm, by
" the subtility and malice of some evil disposed persons, which take
" upon them, without sufficient authority, to preach and interpret the
" word of God after their own brains in churches, and other places,
" both public and private, and also by playing of interludes, and print-
" ing of false fond books and ballads, rhymes, and other lewd trea-
" tises in the English tongue, containing doctrine in matters now in ques-
" tion, and controversies touching the high points and mysteries in
" Christian religion; which books, ballads, rhymes, and treatises, are
" chiefly by the printers and stationers set out to sale to her grace's
" subjects, of an evil zeal for lucre and covetousness of vile gain: Her
" highness, therefore, straightly chargeth and commandeth all and every
" of her said subjects, of whatever state, condition, or degree they be,
" that none of them presumeth from thenceforth to preach, or by way
" of reading in churches, or other public or private places, except in
" schools of the university, to interpret or preach any scriptures; or any
" manner of points of doctrine concerning religion. Neither also to
" print any book, matter, ballad, rhyme, interlude, process or treatise,
" nor to play any interlude, except they have her grace's special license
" in writing for the same, upon pain to incur her highness's indignation
" and displeasure."

We have quoted this document at length, because much of our defence of this basely calumniated princess will hinge upon it. We defy
the bitterest enemy of the Catholic religion to shew any thing like " a
narrowness of spirit," or a wish "to domineer over the rights of private
judgment," or a desire to "trample on the privileges of mankind," in this
proclamation of Mary, after the provocation she had received from the
listless and seditious spirit of the reformers. We see throughout the whole,
her anxiety was, that order and confidence should be restored between
the different factions; that party spirit and *false* teaching should cease;
that irritating language and epithets should be laid aside; that though

she openly and candidly declared her attachment to the Catholic faith, and her wish that all should think with her, yet, following the footsteps of her Saviour, she declared that she would not force the conscience of any individual, but leave the grace of God to work their conversion; but, at the same time, as the first magistrate of the realm, and the chief conservator of the peace of the kingdom, she apprized the people of her determination to punish severely those who should rashly disturb the peace and order of society, by exciting disturbances and violating the laws. Dr. Heylin admits that this proclamation commanded nothing contrary to the laws established, which might give trouble or offence to the reformed party. How unlike was the conduct of Elizabeth, her sister, who succeeded her on the throne. This lady has been extolled by bigots and hireling writers as the most illustrious and amiable of monarchs, and the most accomplished and virtuous of her sex; while her whole life was a continued scene of hypocrisy, debauchery, and cruelty. We have shewn her duplicity during the conspiracy to prevent her sister from ascending the throne; we shall now notice another instance of her deceitful conduct. As the reformed faction knew that Anne Boleyn, Elizabeth's mother, was the prop of their party in Harry's time, they now fixed their hopes on the daughter to oppose her sister Mary's intention. When the council were informed of these designs, they advised Mary to put Elizabeth under a temporary arrest, but she refused her consent to the measure, and endeavoured by persuasion and kind treatment to win Elizabeth over to the Catholic faith, and thus frustrate the expectations of the reformers. Bess made a shew of resistance at first, but when she learned that her repugnance was suspected not to arise from conscience, but from the intrigues of the factious, she threw herself on her knees before Mary, excused her obstinacy, and requested to be instructed in the Catholic faith, that she might see her errors, and embrace the faith of her fathers. From this time she accompanied her sister Mary to mass, opened a chapel in her own house, and outwardly demeaned herself as a Catholic. On coming to the throne she was crowned according to the Catholic ritual and took an oath to maintain the Catholic religion; yet, no sooner was she invested with the sceptre, than she resolved to abolish that religion which she had solemnly sworn to cherish and protect. And how did she proceed to accomplish her designs? Not in the benevolent and charitable footsteps of her sister Mary, so basely and unjustly termed "bloody," who did not enact a single new law nor create a single new offence to entrap her subjects into punishment; she did not, as Mary did, issue a proclamation, exhorting "all her good and loving subjects " to live together in quiet sort and Christian charity, leaving those de- " vilish terms of Papist and heretic, and such like; and applying their " whole care, study and travel to live in the fear of God, exercising their " conversation in such charitable and goodly doing;" no, no, this half-royal perjurer, this consummate hypocrite, this disgrace to her sex, who is known to few in this country, but as the "good queen Bess," the "virgin queen," the "illustrious Elizabeth," through the gross lies of the vilest press that ever cursed and hoodwinked a nation; this hyæna in human shape, regardless of the rights of her people, secured to them by the maxims of the constitution and the stipulations of the

Great Charter, resorted to the most compulsory and unconstitutional means to make the people forsake that faith which she had sworn to her sister Mary, who doubted her sincerity, she believed truly and conscientiously, and had given the same sacred pledge at her coronation to protect. Elizabeth ascended the throne on the 17th of November, 1558, and her first parliament was opened on the 25th of January following, at which the queen assisted in state by attending a solemn high mass, after which a sermon was delivered by a reformed preacher. In this parliament a bill was passed for suppressing the monasteries which Mary had re-established, and another was introduced for annexing the spiritual supremacy with the kingly authority. This bill met with much opposition, especially in the House of Lords, but it was finally carried by a court majority. By this act, Hume says, the crown was vested with the whole spiritual power, to be exercised WITHOUT THE CONCURRENCE OF HER PARLIAMENT, or even of the convocation; it might repress all HERESIES, might establish or repeal all canons; might alter every point of discipline; might ordain or abolish any religious rite or ceremony; and this at the mere whim or caprice of a lascivious and perfidious woman. If Mary was unacquainted with the constitution of the country, it is clear that Elizabeth and her myrmidons were totally disregardless of its principles, by rendering her independent of parliament, and making her an absolute despot. You tell us, modern editors of the *Book of Martyrs*, that Mary was "a slave to superstition;" that "she *thought* to domineer over the rights of private judgment, and trample on the privileges of mankind;" but pray shew us, ye stupid declaimers against the superstitions of Popery! ye brawlers against despotism and the dark ages! shew us, we say, the age or country when a pope or council usurped such an unlimited power as was here granted to an unprincipled woman, thus constituted head of the Church of England! You may talk of priestcraft, of tyranny, of domineering over the rights of private judgment, and trampling on the privileges of mankind, but you cannot produce such an instance of venal dependance and base slavish submission to spiritual and temporal thraldom, in the records of Catholic history, as this nation was reduced to by the corrupt parliament of the falsely called "*good* queen Bess."

This measure being carried, it was now determined by Elizabeth and her ministers, who were certainly some of the ablest, but the most wicked and diabolical, that ever directed the councils of England, to extirpate the Catholic faith out of the island, not by preaching and persuasion, but by the most sanguinary laws and proceedings that could be devised by merciless beings. It was made death to exercise the inalienable privilege of mankind, freedom of conscience, by attending or celebrating mass. Fines were imposed for absence from the new-fangled church worship, which Catholics could not attend without a violation of conscience. Thus it was Elizabeth, and not Mary, that *actually*, not in thought, domineered "over the rights of private judgment," and trampled upon "the privileges of mankind." We have before said that Mary invented no new laws or offences to punish her subjects, but Elizabeth added numberless penal statutes to the code of laws existing, all of which were infringements on the rights of conscience and the principles of the British constitution. It was not till her reign that persons were liable to punishment for what was called *constructive* treason! while it was made *high treason* to profess the same faith that was preached by the apostles of Christ, that was introduced into this island by one of their successors, the holy monk Augustin, and had continued to be professed by our forefathers for one thousand years. We will here restate our former words from the ORTHODOX JOURNAL for *December*, 1816, taken from an article in which we proved that ELIZABETH WAS AN ODIOUS PERSECUTOR OF CONSCIENCE. " In framing these merciless laws, the artful ministers had so interwoven religion and civil allegiance together, that an impeachment in either kind was equally serviceable to their purpose. The consequence was, no less than 200 persons suffered death in this reign only, many of them under circumstances of shocking barbarity, merely for exercising or embracing the Catholic faith; for their lives were offered them on condition of renouncing their religion, and conforming to the established church; an evident proof that the crime for which they were executed was not for conspiring against the state, but for refusing to submit to an arbitrary and unjust control over their minds. Beside these, many Catholics were doomed to pine in loathsome prisons, others were driven out of the kingdom to avoid the like confinement; and *the rack* is acknowledged by unimpeachable historians, to have been in constant use, to extort confession of treasons that were never thought of.—It is computed, that before the year 1538, which was anterior to the greatest heat of the persecutions, the number of persons who suffered death, banishment, imprisonment, or loss of estates, purely for their religion, amounted to about *twelve hundred!* Whilst Elizabeth was thus persecuting with cold-blooded cruelty her Catholic subjects in England, she was engaged in stirring up the Belgian Calvinists to revolt against the king of Spain; and encouraging the rebellion of Knox and his associates against the queen of Scotland, whom she looked upon as her rival for the sceptre; and enforcing the new doctrines of the Reformation in Ireland, by military slaughter and butchery, as well as extirminating penal statutes. To enter into a detail of the horrid atrocities committed on the people of Ireland by the agents of this queen and her wicked counsellors, would only disgust and tire the reader, but we cannot refrain from noticing a few facts, as they clearly demonstrate that religious persecution was not exclusively practised by Catholic governments. It is stated by the historians of that country, that thousands of the natives were swept off by the strict enforcement of the penal laws, whose only crime was the serving their Maker in the simplicity of their hearts, and presuming to exercise their own choice of the road to Heaven. The heat of persecution, and the disorder occasioned by civil disturbances prevented the obtaining a regular list of all the sufferers; but an account has been preserved of about two hundred Irish Catholics who underwent the punishment of death during this reign, solely for the profession of their religion. Of these six were prelates, namely, Patrick O'Kelly, bishop of Mayo; Dermot O'Hurle, archbishop of Cashel; Richard Creagh, archbishop of Armagh, and Edmund Magauran, his successor; Cornelius O'Duane, bishop of Down; and Edward O'Callagher, bishop of Derry. The two first of these are reported to have suffered the most excruciating tortures, previous to their execution, the former having his legs broken with hammers, and needles thrust under his nails; the other had his legs immersed in jack-boots filled with lime and water, until his flesh was burnt to the bone, in order to compel him to take the oath of supremacy.   It was a common thing to beat with stones the shorn heads of the clergy until their brains gushed out, and many were stretched on the rack, or pressed under weights.—The year before Elizabeth's death about 50 of the monks and clergy obtained permission of her majesty, to retire from Ireland to the Continent, and a vessel was appointed to convey them.   They embarked at Slattery, as they were ordered, but had not proceeded far on their voyage, when they were all thrown overboard and drowned.—The captain and officers of the ship were confined for a time, by order of the queen, to cover her from the disgrace attendant on such an atrocious deed, performed by her directions, and were afterwards rewarded with a grant of the lands belonging to the murdered individuals.   Nor was this benignant sovereign less kind to Protestant non-conformists than to Popish recusants.—By looking into Stow, Brandt, Limborch, Collier, Neale, and other Protestant historians, it will be found that in the year 1573, one Peter Burchet was examined, on the score of *heresy*; by Sands, Bishop of London, but he recanted his errors.   Two years afterwards, 27 heretics were at one time, 11 at another, and 5 at a third, condemned, most of them by the same Protestant prelate, for their erroneous doctrines.   Of these 20 were *whipped and banished*, others bore their faggots, and two of them, John Peterson, and Henry Tarwort, were *burnt to death* in Smithfield.—In 1583, John Lewis was burnt at Norwich, for denying the divinity of our Saviour; and Francis Kett, M. A. suffered the same kind of death at the same place, for similar opinions in 1589.   Two years afterwards, William Hackett, was *hanged* for heresy, in Cheapside.   Five others were also put to death in this reign, for being Brownists.   Most of the executions took place in consequence of Elizabeth's issuing an ecclesiastical commission, hitherto unparalleled for its arbitrary and extensive powers.—This commission consisted of forty-four members, twelve of whom only were clergymen, and the rest laymen; and any *three* were authorized to exercise the *whole* power of the commission.—' Their jurisdiction,' says Mr. Reeve, who takes his account from Hume and Neale, 'extended over the whole kingdom, and *over all orders of men*; their power was to visit and reform *all errors, heresies,* and *schisms,* to *regulate all opinions,* and to *punish* every *breach* of uniformity in the *public worship;* and THEIR POWER WAS SUBJECT TO NO CONTROL. They had directions to proceed in the execution of their office, not only by the legal methods of juries and witnesses, but by any other means they should judge fit; that is, by the rack, by tortures, and imprisonment.   The punishments they inflicted were arbitrary, and directed by no rule.   Their fines were so heavy as to bring total ruin upon those who had the misfortune to offend.   The very suspicion of being an offender was enough to make any man such in the eyes of those inquisitors, who in that case were authorized to administer an official oath, which *compelled* the suspected person to answer *all questions,* though tending to *criminate himself* or his dearest friends.   So cruel and so despotic were the powers which the supremacy was supposed in that age to confer upon the crown, and which Elizabeth exercised to their full extent.'"

These atrocious cruelties have been carefully concealed from the people of England by the bigotted adherents of the Reformation, as it is called, while the actions of the upright and honest Mary, whose heart was truly Catholic and English, have been blackened, vilified, and misrepresented. But the day is come when the veil of hypocrisy and falsehood shall be removed from the eyes of a blinded and misguided people, and they will then see the Truth in all her glorious attributes, and Mary's character will appear more brilliant than it has hitherto been disfigured. Let it always be borne in mind, that Mary did not begin to exercise coercive measures until the peace of her kingdom was broken by insurrection, and her life was menaced by the enthusiastic reformers. That she did not require them to embrace a faith of her own coining, but to return to that faith which had been the creed of the whole kingdom for one thousand years before, and was then the creed of the most illustrious and virtuous monarchs, statesmen, generals, and divines, in Christendom. Elizabeth, on the other hand, persecuted the professors of the old faith because they would not consent to relinquish doctrines which they knew were of *divine* authority, for opinions merely human and liable to change. She begun her persecutions without any provocation on their part, for while she was harassing the Catholics with tortures and confiscations, they were not only submissive to the laws of the state, but they actually took up arms in her defence, when the kingdom was threatened with invasion by a Catholic sovereign, the husband of Mary, and such as had property left were prodigal in their offers to equip men and fit out vessels for the defence of her throne and their country's independence. Such base ingratitude—such remorseless injustice—such unparalleled cruelty—was the base and tiger-hearted Elizabeth guilty of towards her loyal Catholic subjects, yet is she stiled the " *good queen Bess*," while her truly virtuous sister Mary, whose private life was unspotted and blameless, and who had to deal with a people heated by fanatical opinions and urged to insubordination by the most perfidious demagogues, is represented as the " *bloody* queen Mary," and her reign as one continued scene of persecutions, though two years had elapsed from her coming to the throne before any suffered on the score of religion. " Compare," we say, to repeat our own words in the ORTHODOX JOURN. for Nov. 1818, " this conduct of the *virgin* queen with the declaration of her *bloody* sister, before quoted, in which the latter assures her subjects, that, although she could not dissemble nor hide that religion which she had always professed, she did not intend to compel any of her subjects thereunto, but leave it to their own common consent ; exhorting them at the same time to lay aside all uncharitable terms towards each other, such as *Papist* and *heretic*, carrying themselves peaceably and in Christian charity with all. The *good* Bess, however, possessed no such merciful and laudable feeling.—*She* could *dissemble* her religion in the reign of her sister, and conspire with others to dethrone her. She could submit to be crowned according to the popish custom ; could *swear* to protect the church in all her rights and privileges, and almost instantly violate the obligation of her oath.—She could cause laws to be passed which intrenched upon the liberty of conscience, by making it *high treason* to exercise the right of it; she could hang, embowel alive, and quarter, innocent victims for *constructive* treason; she could encourage rebellion in states at perfect peace with her, under pretence of extending the light of *evangelical liberty*, but which was nothing less than irreligious intolerance and lawless despotism; witness the sanguinary massacres of the Catholics by the Huguenots of France; the pillaging and burning of churches and civil wars in that country, and in Germany and Flanders; the rebellions, murders, and sacrileges committed in Scotland, by Knox and his bloody associates; all which were connived at and aided by Elizabeth and her ministers.—Mary, on the contrary, as we have seen above, incited her people to charity; she repealed obnoxious laws, and contented herself with governing under those of her predecessors; she attempted not to force the consciences of the ignorant and deluded, nor would the blood of her subjects have been spilt, had they not proved ungrateful and rebellious to her mild and equitable admonitions. Were the Puritan revilers of Popery to conduct themselves against the present government of this country as Cranmer, Ridley, Latimer, and other rebels, behaved themselves towards their lawful sovereign Mary, they would certainly and justly experience a fate similar to that which some of their brethren met under the idol of their adoration, Elizabeth, for daring to profess a faith contrary to her commands.—Yet such is the perversion of our Puritan bigots, that this sweet lady, who is described by Protestant historians as revengeful, cruel, and vindictive in her disposition, is esteemed by them the *patroness* and *protectress* of *liberty of conscience* against *Popery* and *Slavery*; whilst, on the other hand, her sister Mary, who is described, by the same historians, to have possessed a merciful disposition, is condemned as a *bloody tyrant*, because she found it necessary to consign some of her turbulent subjects to the offended laws of the country!!!"

But we must return to the reign of Mary, and produce evidence to illustrate the cause which led to the execution of so many unhappy beings in the latter part of her sway, whilst she was influenced by every desire to augment the honour, the glory, and the happiness of her kingdom. The pope, on hearing of the accession of Mary, and forejudging the result, appointed cardinal Pole, an Englishman of royal descent, as legate to the queen, but the cardinal hesitated to accept the appointment until he had more satisfactory information as to the disposition of the people of England. It was evident that the queen wished the nation should be reconciled to the holy see, and the people return to the faith of their forefathers. In this disposition the queen met her first parliament on the 10th of October, when both peers and commoners, according to ancient usage, accompanied their sovereign to a solemn mass of the Holy Ghost. This religious ceremony is still followed in Catholic countries, both monarchical and republican, on the meeting of the legislative bodies. Gardiner, the lord chancellor, made a speech to the two houses, and the speaker, in his address to the throne, enlarged on the piety, the clemency, and other virtues of Mary, whose ears were greeted with the loudest demonstrations of loyalty and attachment. A bill was introduced of a comprehensive nature, intending to repeal at once all the acts that had been passed in the two last reigns, affecting either the marriage of the queen's mother, or the exercise of religion as it stood in the first year of the reign of her father. By the lords this bill met with no opposition, but it was objected to in the commons rather strongly; however, with some modifications, and a little manœuvering on the part of the ministry, the bill was divided into two and finally carried. The opposition to the measure for restoring the ancient form of worship was confined to the commons, and though the members in favour of the new doctrines appeared to be one-third of the house, yet after a debate of two days continuance, it was carried without a division. Thus fell by a vote in parliament that fabric raised by the hands of wicked and intriguing men, of whom Tom Cranmer was the head, though they had the blasphemy to assert that it arose by the inspiration of the Holy Ghost. The bill for confirming the marriage between Henry and Catharine, stated, writes Dr. Lingard, "that, after " the queen's father and mother had lived together in lawful matri- " mony for the space of twenty years, unfounded scruples and projects " of divorce had been suggested to the king by interested individuals, " who, to accomplish their design, procured in their favour the seals " of foreign universities by bribery, of the national universities by in- " trigues and threats; and that Thomas, then newly made archbishop " of Canterbury, most ungodlily, and against all rules of equity and " conscience, took upon himself to pronounce, in the absence of the " queen, a judgment of divorce, which was afterwards, on two occa- " sions, confirmed by parliament: but that, as the said marriage was " not prohibited by the law of God, it could not be dissolved by any " such authority; wherefore, it enacted that all statutes, confirmatory " of the divorce, should be repealed, and the marriage between Henry " and Catharine should be adjudged to stand with God's law, and " should be reputed of good effect and validity, to all intents and pur- " poses whatsoever. Against this bill, though it was equivalent to a " statute of bastardy in respect of Elizabeth, not a voice was raised in " either house of parliament."

The other bills passed by this parliament were indicative of the con- stitutional disposition of Mary and her regard for the welfare of the people. All contracts entered into by individuals during the usurpation of lady Jane were legalized; all treasons created since the reign of Ed- ward III. with the new felonies and cases of præmunire introduced by Henry VIII. were abolished; at the same time the act of Edward VI. against riotous assemblies was in part revived, and extended to such meetings as should have for their object to change, BY FORCE, the existing laws in matters of religion. To this last act the modern edi- tors and No-popery men cannot object, as there are laws now existing of the same tendency, to preserve the Church-of-England by law es- tablished from any attempts that may be contemplated of a similar strong nature. Bills restoring in blood those persons who had been iniquitously deprived of their hereditary rights were likewise passed, and one for attainting the chief authors and abettors of the late con- spiracy to exclude Mary from the throne; but its operation was limited to Tom Cranmer, lady Jane Dudley, her husband Guildford Dudley, and his brother Ambrose, who had, it must be observed, been before ar- raigned, and convicted on *their own confessions.* Mary had no intention, however, that they should suffer; what she hoped was, that while she kept the sentence suspended over their heads, she should secure the loyalty of their friends, and accordingly she gave orders that they should be treated with as much indulgence as their situation would allow.

The next object to which Mary turned her attention was that of a marriage, by which a successor in a direct line might be secured to the realm. During her brother's life, Mary voluntarily preferred a single life, and the breath of calumny has not dared to stain her continency; but she was no sooner seated on the throne, than she avowed her intention to marry.—The selection of her choice lay between the cardinal Pole and Courtney, the son of the countess of Exeter, who had been the individual companion of the queen.—The latter she had recently released from the Tower, where he had been unjustly imprisoned from his youth: both were descended from the house of York. The other competitor was the prince of Spain, son of the emperor Charles V.—Courtney, by his giddy and intemperate conduct, soon lost the affections of Mary; the cardinal, besides being an ecclesiastic, and therefore requiring a dispensation from his vows of celibacy, was deemed too old; the choice therefore fell on Philip. There were also many political motives which induced Mary to select the latter, which the French minister as strenuously endeavoured, but ineffectually, to counteract. The queen wisely judged that an union with a foreign prince would add to the security of her people, and it was manifest by the negociations that her happiness was centered in the happiness of her people and the honour of her country. In this resolution Mary experienced much opposition; the commons addressed her, requesting her to marry, but not to select her husband from a foreign family, but from some of the native nobility. The queen, however, was not to be moved, and secretly vowed to be the wife of Philip. And now may be said to commence the troubles that continued during the rest of the reign of this noble-minded but unfortunate sovereign.—The reformers were well aware that should Mary unite herself to Philip, who was a stanch Catholic prince, there was no chance for their new doctrines; they therefore began that system of sedition, cabal, insurrection, and treason, which marked their steps wherever the executive authority was opposed to their views.—Courtney, who owed so much to the queen, and had made him earl of Devonshire, was instigated to rebel against her, and prefer his suit to her sister Elizabeth. The latter was also worked upon, and while she became an object of suspicion to the friends of the Spanish match, she was the idol of those who opposed it. The greatest pains were taken to create dissension between the two sisters, and awaken jealousy on the part of the queen, but Mary would not listen to their representations, at least she shewed as much by her carriage towards Elizabeth; for though she kept her near her person till the dissolution of parliament, she treated her with the greatest kindness, and when she let her depart to one of her country seats, she made her a present of two sets of valuable pearls.

Gardiner, the lord chancellor and bishop of Winchester, had opposed the Spanish match and supported the claim of Courtney, but finding that Mary was resolute in rejecting the latter, whose conduct had been

lowed the advice of the conspirators nor the order of the queen: feigning indisposition, she removed to Ashridge, where she shut herself up in her chamber, ordered her servants to fortify the house, and calledup on her friends to arm in her defence. This statement is made by Dr. Lingard on the authority of Noailles the French ambassaor to the court of Mary, who took too great a part in the conspiracy, in the hope of frustrating the projected marriage, which could but be injurious to his master, the king of France.

Suffolk, in his way to his estates, called upon the inhabitants of the towns through which he passed to arm in defence of their liberties, which, he said, had been betrayed by the match to the Spaniards. He found, however, that the people did not think with him, and that his cause was hopeless; he abandonded it, therefore, and trusted himself to one of his tenants, who betrayed him, and in less than a fortnight from the commencement of his treasonable crusade, he found himself prisoner in the Tower. Courtney, through timidity and cowardice, seceded from the conspiracy; while Wyat, with a courage and address that gained him the applause of his enemies, drew the sword, and soon found himself at the head of fifteen hundred armed men, while others were ready to join his standard on notice being given. He was joined by 500 Londoners sent to oppose him, and began his march towards London, Wyat's force was now about fifteen thousand men, while the ministers were in a dreadful state of alarm and distrust. Mary alone appeared firm and undaunted.. She ordered her ministers to provide means of defence, and undertook herself to fix the wavering loyalty of the citizens. She desired the lord mayor to call an extraordinary meeting of the livery, and at three o'clock in the afternoon of Feb. 2, 1534, Mary, with the sceptre in her hand, accompanied by her ladies and officers of state, entered the Guildhall. She was received with becoming respect, and in a firm and dignified tone she complained of the disloyalty of the men of Kent, and expressed her conviction that her people, especially her good city of London, loved her two well to surrender her into the hands of rebels. "As for this marriage," she said, " ye shall understand that I " enterprized not the doing thereof, without the advice of all our privy " council: nor am I, I assure ye, so bent to my own will, or so affec- " tionate, that for my own pleasure I would choose where I lust, or " needs must have a husband. I have hitherto lived a maid; and doubt " not, but with God's grace I am able to live so still. Certainly, did I " think that this marrige were to the hurt of you, my subjects, or to " the impeachment of my royal estate, I would never consent thereunto. " And I promise you, on the word of a queen, that if it shall not appear " to the lords and commons in parliament, to be for the benefit of the " whole realm, I will never marry while I live. Wherefore stand fast " against these rebels, your enemies and mine; fear them not, for, I " assure ye, I fear them nothing at all: and I will leave with you my " lord Howard and my lord admiral, who will be assistant with the " mayor for your defence." With these words she took her departure, and we need not add, for base must have been the hearts of those who could not feel for such a sovereign, that the hall shook with acclamations of loyalty and transport. By the next morning more than twenty thousand men had enrolled themselves for the protection of the city.

A REVIEW

of

𝕱𝖔𝖝'𝖘 𝕭𝖔𝖔𝖐 𝖔𝖋 𝕸𝖆𝖗𝖙𝖞𝖗𝖘,

CRITICAL AND HISTORICAL.

No 50. Printed and Published by W. E. ANDREWS, 3, Chapter-house-court, St. Paul's Churchyard, London. **Price 3d.**

EXPLANATION OF THE ENGRAVING.—*One of the instruments of torture, called the Scavenger's daughter, employed in the Tower on Catholics in the sweet lady Elizabeth's reign, who is termed by Protestants "the good queen Bess." It was a broad iron hoop, consisting of two parts, fastened to each other by a hinge. The prisoner was made to kneel on the pavement, and to contract himself into as small a compass as he could. Then the executioner kneeling on his shoulders, and having introduced the hoop under his legs, compressed the victim close together, till he was able to fasten the extremities over the small of the back. The time allotted to this kind of torture was an hour and a half, during which time it commonly happened that from excess of compression the blood started from the nostrils; sometimes, it was believed, from the extremities of the hands and feet.—Thomas Cottam and Luke Kirbye, priests, suffered compression in the scavenger's daughter for more than an hour, on the 10th of Dec. 1580. Cottam bled profusely from the nose.—Dr. Lingard's History, Note U, vol. v. 4to.*

CONTINUATION OF THE REVIEW.

We must here add, that Fox allows that the queen spoke with so much ease in delivering this speech, that "she seemed to have perfectly "conned it with book."

. On that day Wyatt entered Southwark, but his followers had begun to forsake him, and his numbers were dwindled down to seven thousand men, who were hourly deserting. Upon his coming into Southwark, Stow says, "he made proclamation that no soldier should take any "thing, but that he should pay for it, and that his coming was to resist "the Spanish king. Notwithstanding forthwith divers of his company "being gentlemen (as they said) went to Winchester place, made

"havock of the bishop's goods (he being lord chancellor) not only
"of his victuals, whereof there was plenty, but whatsoever else, not
"leaving so much as one lock of a door, but the same was taken off and
"carried away, nor a book in his gallery uncut, or rent into pieces, so
"that men might have gone up to the knees in leaves of books cut out
"and thrown under feet." Such were the Vandalic proceedings of
these defenders of the new light and learning. Catholics are reproached
for their presumed ignorance and distaste of letters and the sciences,
while they have the mortification to know that many of the choicest
volumes of the classics, history, and the arts, the toil of the calumniated and abused monks before the art of printing was discovered,
were laid waste and destroyed by the ruthless hands of their savage
and unlettered accusers. After loitering two days in Southwark, "to
"no purpose at all," writes Dr. Heylin, "more than the sacking of
"Winchester house, and the defacing of the bishop's library there, un-
"less it were to leave a document to posterity, that God infatuates the
"counsels of those wretched men, who take up arms against their prin-
"ces," Wyatt marched to Kingston, and thence to Brentford towards
London, and soon after made his appearance at Hyde-park corner. Mary
then occupied the palace of St. James. The court was in the utmost
consternation; the ministers on their knees implored the queen to seek
her safety by retiring to the Tower. Mary, however, scorned the pusillanimity of her advisers, and announced her fixed determination to
continue at her post. A council of war was held, and it was determined
to place a strong force at Ludgate, and allow Wyatt to advance to this
post. In the mean time Wyatt, who seemed to be under a spirit of infatuation, wasted his time in the repair of a carriage of one of his pieces,
which had been dismounted by the breaking down of a wheel. This
delay prevented him from keeping his appointment with his associates
at Ludgate, which caused the chief of his advisers to abandon him in
despair. Among these was Poynet, the Protestant bishop of Winchester, who fled with all speed to the continent. Another of them, sir
George Harper, rode to St. James's and announced the approach of
Wyatt. At four in the morning of the 7th February, 1554, the drum
beat to arms, and in a few hours the royalists were in motion. Wyatt
reached Hyde park corner at nine, and though he found himself deserted
by many of his followers, he resolved to make a desperate effort, and
rushed forward to charge a body of cavalry, posted to intercept his progress. They opened and allowed a body of three or four hundred to
pass, and while they engaged the rear of the rebels, Wyatt, disregardless of the battle that raged behind him, passed hastily through Pic-
cadilly, and without noticing the palace of St. James's, hurried on through
the Strand to Ludgate, where he found himself hemmed in on both
sides, and constrained to yield himself prisoner, after making a stout
resistance with forty of his followers. Wyatt was taken first to St.
James's, and then conveyed to the Tower, where he was rejoined by
the chief of the surviving conspirators.

Burnet says, "The Popish authors studied to cast the blame of this
"on the reformed preachers; but did not name any one of them that was
"in it; so it appears that what some later writers have said of Poynet's
"having been in it is false; otherwise his name had certainly been put

"in the number of those that were attainted for it." This attempt of
the bishop of Sarum to screen the reformed preachers from *rebellious
practices* is congenial to his character. Sir John Dalrymple, in his
Memoirs, says, "I have never tried Burnet's facts by the test of dates
"and original papers without finding them wrong." Who the Popish
authors were, Burnet does not name; we however can produce Protestant authorities to substantiate the fact that some of the reformed
preachers *did* take an active part in this conspiracy. Dr. Heylin, says,
"It cannot be denied but that the restitution of the reformed religion
"was the matter principally aimed at in this rebellion, though nothing
"but the match with Spain appeared in the outside of it. Which
"appears plainly by a book writ by Christopher Goodman (associated
"with John Knox, for setting up presbytery and rebellion in the kirk of
"Scotland) in which he takes upon him to shew *how far superior magis-
"trates ought to be obeyed.* For having filled almost every chapter of
"it with railing speeches against the queen, and stirring up the people
"to rebel against her, he falleth amongst the rest upon this expression;
"viz. 'Wyatt did but his duty, and it was but the duty of all others
"that profess the gospel, to have risen with him for maintenance of
"the same. His cause was just, and they were all traitors that took
"not part with him. O noble Wyatt, thou art now with God, and those
"worthy men that died in that happy enterprise.' But this book was
"written at Geneva, where Calvin reigned; to whom no pamphlet
"could be more agreeable, than such as did reproach this queen; whom
"in his Comment upon Amos, he entituleth by the name of Proserpine,
"and saith, that she exceeded in her cruelties all the devils in hell.
"Much more it is to be admired, that Dr. John Poynet, the late bishop
"of Winchester, should be of counsel in the plot, or put himself into
"their camp, and attend them unto the place where the carriage brake.
"Where when he could not work on Wyatt to desist from that unpro-
"fitable labour in remounting the canon, he counselled Vanham, Bret
"and others, to shift for themselves, took leave of his more secret
"friends, told them that he would pray for their good success, and so
"departed and took ship for Germany, where he after died."

Thus, then, it stands confessed by a Protestant historian, that the
reformers sought to re-establish their religion by the power of the
sword, and not by the force of reason, while the queen herself had,
during this period, abstained from any harsh or severe measures towards
her enemies. When the former conspiracy was subdued, she would
not allow more than *three* persons to be put to death, an instance of
lenity unparalleled in the history of any age, and a damning refutation
of the base statement made by the modern editors of Fox, that "the
"first exertion of her regal power was to *wreak vengeance* upon ALL
"those who had supported the title of lady Jane Grey." Mary was
proclaimed in July, 1553, consequently seven months of her reign had
passed over since the first attempt to deprive her of the crown, and only
three traitors had suffered for it. Others who had incurred the guilt of
treason in that plot had been sentenced to death, but were respited through
the clemency of Mary. Of these were Tom Cranmer, lady Jane Grey,
and her husband, the lord Dudley. While Mary is represented by the
modern editors of this *Book of Martyrs* as trampling on the privileges

of mankind, other and more correct historians state, that she was reproved by the emperor and some of her own counsellors for her too
great love of mercy. They argued, that impunity would encourage the
factious to a repetition of their treasonable practices, and that if they
chose to brave the authority of their sovereign and the laws, it ought
to be at the peril of their lives. The queen herself began to feel the
truth of these maxims; she considered her former lenity as the cause of
the insurrection just suppressed, from which she had narrowly escaped
with her life, and in the moment of irritation and while she was agitated
with her late escape from danger, she was induced to sign a warrant for the execution of Guildford Dudley and his wife at the expiration of three days.   Much opprobrium has been cast by Protestant
writers on this order for executing so young an offender as the lady
Jane Grey, and she is looked upon as a martyr for the Protestant religion.   Had she been termed a martyr to her father's treasonable ambition, the truth would not have been outraged; for had the duke of
Suffolk remained faithful to his promise, after having been pardoned
his first traitorous designs towards this good but maligned queen, his
daughter might have followed her religion and died a natural death, as
well as her husband, so little inclined was Mary to shed their blood.
But the guilt of the duke her father brought on the punishment of his
daughter, the lady Jane, which his ambition had first caused her to
incur.   The sentence, as we before observed, had been put off above
half a year, and it was not until the duke of Suffolk, with his brothers,
the lords Thomas and Leonard Grey, had endeavoured to raise the
counties of Warwick and Leicester for the purpose of dethroning Mary
herself, that she consented to the lady Jane's death, to prevent any
further pretext for turbulent and fanatic spirits to rise against their
lawful sovereign, and disturb the peace of the community.   No part
of the late conspiracy was imputed to the lady Jane, but she stood
legally convicted, and was under sentence of death for assuming roy-
alty at king Edward's death.   The order for her execution being intimated to her, she received it with much composure, and said, she had
deserved it for usurping a crown which belonged to another; but at the
same time she related the little share she had in that transaction, and
the constraint put on her by her family; that it was no easy matter for
a person so young as she was to withstand the authority of a father and
a husband, and of so many of the nobility; and it would be her peculiar
fate to be justly condemned, and yet die innocent.   On the 12th of
Feb. after her husband had been beheaded on Tower hill, she was led
out to a scaffold which had been erected on the green within the Tower,
where, after a few words to the spectators, she laid her head on the
block, and it was severed from her body at one stroke of the executioner.—We agree with Dr. Lingard, that " it would perhaps have been
" to the honour of Mary if she had overlooked the provocation, and re-
" fused to visit on the daughter the guilt of the father.   Her youth
" ought to have pleaded most powerfully in her favour; and, if it were
" feared that she would again be set up by the factious as a competitor
" with her sovereign, the danger might certainly have been removed by
" some expedient less cruel than the infliction of death."   Still we must
observe that Mary could not act without her counsellors, and probably

could they have foretold the handle that would have been made of their decision to blacken and defame the religion of Christ, they would have decided differently. One thing is certain, namely, that the death of this lady did not proceed from religious bigotry and intolerance on the part of Mary and her advisers, as the people of England have been so long led to believe by the intolerant haters of Popery. Even Burnet admits that it was rather reason of State than private resentment that instigated the queen to consent to the execution.

The trial of the Duke of Suffolk soon followed the execution of his daughter. He was found guilty, condemned and executed. Burnet says " He was the less pitied, because by his means his daughter was " brought to her untimely end." Dr. Lingard likewise observes, " that " his ingratitude to the queen, his disregard or his daughter's safety, " and his meanness in seeking to purchase forgiveness by the accusa- " tion of others, had sharpened public indignation against him." He was followed by his brother, the lord Thomas Grey. Wm. Thomas, esq. stabbed himself in prison, but died on the scaffold. To these three fol- lowed sir Thomas Wyatt, whose weak and wavering conduct in prison brought discredit upon him. Croft, another of the principal conspirators, obtained his pardon, and sir Nicholas Throgmorton pleaded his own cause with such success, that he obtained a verdict in his favour from the jury. About fifty of the common men were hanged in the different parts of the metropolis : half a dozen suffered in Kent, and four hun- dred of the remainder were marched up to the palace with halters round their necks, where Mary appeared at the balcony, pronounced their par- don herself, and desired them to go home in peace. " These execu- " tions," writes Dr. Lingard, " have induced some writers to charge " Mary with unnecessary cruelty ; perhaps those who compare her with " her contemporaries in similar circumstances, will hesitate to subscribe " to that opinion. If, on this occasion, sixty of the insurgents were sa- " crificed to her justice or resentment, we shall find in the history of the " next reign that, after a rebellion of a less formidable aspect, some " hundreds of victims were required to appease the offended majesty of " Elizabeth." This learned historian, in a note, farther remarks, " If we " look at the conduct of the government after the rebellions of 1715 " and 1745, we shall not find that the praise of superior lenity is due to " more modern times ;" or, he might have added, to Protestant rulers.

We noticed, page 397, that the princess Elizabeth was not an uncon- cerned spectator in this conspiracy against her queen and sister, as well as Courteney, the earl of Devonshire. The latter was committed to the Tower, and three members of the council were ordered to repair to Ashbridge to conduct Elizabeth to court. The modern editors, we see, have devoted nearly seventeen pages of their work to relate the " miracu- " lous preservation of the lady Elizabeth from extreme calamity and " danger in the time of queen Mary, her sister," as detailed, we believe, by John Fox himself, and worthy it is of that celebrated inventor of lies. It is not to be expected that we can enter into a complete refutation of this farrago of cant and fiction ; suffice it to say, that the extreme cala- mity and danger of lady Elizabeth lay in her being a suspected traitoress, and being ill or pretending to be ill at the time these messengers were sent to bring her up to town, She received them in bed, complaining of severe illness ; but two physicians attesting that she was able to travel, she was reluctantly obliged to accompany her trusty guides to London by short stages, not however, as a prisoner, but in state, in a litter, attended by two hundred gentlemen. What dreadful calamity and danger this lady traitor must have been in from her sister, queen Mary! She appeared unwell, and it was reported that she had been poisoned, but a week restored her to health, and she demanded an audience of her sister. Mary returned for answer, that she must first establish her innocence. The council was in possession of a considerable mass of presumptive evidence against Elizabeth ; the duke of Suffolk and Wyatt declared against her and Courteney, and though both declared their innocence, a warrant was made out for the committal of Elizabeth, who received the intelligence with terror, and stamped and swore with fury. She was however compelled to submit, and took possession of her cell, under the fear that she would soon share the fate of her mother. From this state of " extreme calamity and danger" she was saved by the man who is represented by the unprincipled bigots of the day as thirsting for her blood. Gardiner, while he acknowledged that Elizabeth and Courteney had been privy to the designs of the rebels, and deserved punishment for their treason, yet contended they had not implicated themselves by any overt act, and therefore could not be convicted legally. His enemies seized the opportunity to ruin Gardiner with the queen, but Mary listened to the reasoning of her chancellor, found he was correct in his exposition of the law, and the next day Elizabeth was released from the Tower. Does this shew a narrowness of spirit, or an ignorance of the constitution, which the modern editors accuse this injured queen of ? Courteney was sent to Fotheringay castle, there to remain in custody.

Wyatt's rebellion occasioned a delay of the intended marriage between Mary and Philip, for a few weeks, but the restless spirit of the fanatical reformers was still active in shewing itself. Three days before the execution of Wyatt, namely, on the 8th of April, " being then Sunday," says Stow, " a cat, with her head shorn, and the likeness of a vestment cast " over her, with her fore feet tied together, and a round piece of paper " like a singing cake betwixt them, was hanged on a gallows in Cheap, " near to the cross in the parish of St. Matthew, which cat being taken " down was carried to the bishop of London, and he caused the same to be " shewed at Paul's cross by the preacher, Dr. Pendleton." On the 10th of June following, the same historian says, " Dr. Pendleton preached at " Paul's cross, at whom a gun was shot, the pellet whereof went very near " him, and lit on the church wall. But the shooter could not be found." This daring attempt at assassination by the evangelical religionists, was followed by a proclamation, forbidding the shooting of handguns and the bearing of weapons. These outrageous proceedings arose not only from the intended marriage with the prince, but likewise from the desire the queen had always expressed that the people should return to the ancient faith and join the bosom of the universal church, under which their ancestors had enjoyed so much glory and happiness. In order to prepare the way for this wished-for event, the queen, about the 15th of March, in this year, issued out a commission, by which all the MARRIED clergy were deprived of their benefices, being unqualified to possess them. This inability was founded on the *constant practice* of the western church, on the *unanimous authority of the canons,* and the *solemn engagement* made by every ecclesiastic at his ordination: likewise on the 4th of Henry VIIIth's six articles, which the parliament had passed into a law, and a late statute of Mary's parliament, which recalled all religious matters to their condition at that prince's death, had ratified. So that Mary, instead of being "*unacquainted* with the *constitution of the country,*" as the modern editors shamelessly assert, did nothing but in the most constitutional manner; for this injunction was as legal and parliamentary as it was just and canonical. In consequence of these orders, Holgate, archbishop of York, and the bishops of St. David's, Chester, and Bristol, who had been regulars, and, besides the promise made at their ordination, had broken the solemn vows made on entering a religious state, and those of Gloucester and Hereford, who were of the secular clergy, were deprived. Scory and Barlow, bishops of Chicester and Bath, who were in the same predicament, fled the kingdom. As much calumny and misrepresentation have been resorted to by the advocates of Protestantism and the enemies of Catholicism to extol the character of the early reformers, so called, and brand the opposers of religious innovations and defenders of truth and unity with cruelty and love of blood, we deem it our duty to give the reader some account of the chief of these deposed bishops, from the testimony, observe, of PROTESTANT historians.

Holgate, archbishop of York, not only made use of the indulgent doctrine, which, in Edward's reign, allowed the clergy to marry, but extended the licence to take another man's wife.—(*Collier's Eccles. Hist.* vol. ii. b. 5, p. 349.)

Robert Farrar, was first, chaplain to Cranmer; and then, by the protector Seymour's favour, promoted to the bishopric of St. David's; but, on that nobleman's fall, fifty-six articles were exhibited against him, for which he was confined during the remainder of Edward's reign, and now degraded.—(*Ath. Oxon.* p. 679.)

John Bird, bishop of Chester, was a Carmelite friar, and for his obsequiousness to the court measures at the dissolution of the monasteries, and a remarkable sermon in support of the lay supremacy, was promoted to a see in Ireland; from whence he was translated to Bangor, and in 1541 to Chester. He went all the lengths of Henry's and Edward's reigns, and made use of the indulgence which the latter allowed of taking a wife. Being deprived of his bishopric, he lived privately at Chester till his death, in 1556.—(*Bale,* cent. ii. No. 41—*Pitts, de Illust.—Ang. Script.—Godwin, de Præsul. Ang.*)

Paul Bush, bishop of Bristol, was an Augustine friar, and had been chaplain to Henry VIII. who promoted him to that see, for his compliance with the court measures. But though he betrayed the same passive disposition during Edward's reign, and took a wife, he was never known either to preach or write against the ancient religion.— He readily gave up his bishopric at the queen's command, and parted from his wife, and lived privately in Bristol till his death, in 1558.— (*Godwin de Præsul. Ang.—Ath. Oxon.*)

William Barlow, bishop of Bath and Wells, was a Canon Regular, and very active both in promoting the dissolution of religious houses in Henry's reign, and forwarding the various innovations of Edward's

Being deprived of his bishopric on account of marriage, he fled to Germany.—(*Godwin de Præsul. Ang.*—*Ath. Oxon.* vol. i. p. 156.)

Such were some of the chief performers in the work of doctrinal novelty and ministerial rapacity; with what discernment their places were supplied, so far as firmness and interest of principle were concerned, the event verified. On the queen's death, when her successor, after swearing to protect the Catholic religion, thought proper to restore the new form of public worship, only Kitchin, bishop of Llandaff, who, Pro-'teus like, had put on all the forms of religion in the three last reigns, could be induced, of that venerable bench, to submit to the change.— Neither loss of wealth and dignity, nor the hardships of imprisonment or deportation, shook their constancy to the true faith; and Dr. Heath, archbishop of York and lord Chancellor, having succeeded Holgate in the one and Gardiner in the other, made a discourse, at the opening of the first parliament of Elizabeth, on that lady's assuming the *spiritual* supremacy of the kingdom, which, for clearness and solidity, may vie with any of the pleadings of Tully or Demosthenes.

These proceedings alarmed the already discontented and turbulent leaders of evangelism, who; to their outrages already mentioned, and finding they were not likely to succeed by open force and rebellion, had recourse to stratagem and artifice, thinking thus to befool the people, and work them into hatred against Mary's government. This device we shall give in Dr. Heylin's words. " A young maid," writes the doctor, " called Elizabeth Crofts, about the age of eighteen years, was tutored " to counterfeit certain speeches in the wall of a house not far from " Aldersgate, where she was heard of many, but seen of none; and that " her voice might be conceived to have somewhat in it more than or-" dinary, a strange whistle was devised for her, out of which her words " proceeded in such a tone as seemed to have nothing mortal in it.— " And thereupon it was affirmed by some of the people (great multi-" tudes whereof resorted daily to the place) that it was an angel, or at " least a voice from heaven; by others, it could be nothing but the Holy " Ghost; but generally she passed by the name of the *Spirit in the Wall.* " For the interpreting of whose words there wanted not some of the " confederates, who mingled themselves by turns amongst the rest of " the people, and taking on them to expound what the spirit said, de-" livered many dangerous and seditious words against the queen, her " marriage with the prince of Spain, the mass, confession, and the like. " The practice was first set on foot on the 14th of March, which was " within ten days after the publishing of the articles, and for a while it " went on fortunately enough, according to the purpose of the chief " contrivers. But the abuse being searched into, and the plot discovered, " the wench was ordered to stand upon the scaffold near St. Paul's cross, " on the 15th of July, there to abide during the time of the sermon, and " that being done, to make a public declaration of that lewd imposture. " Let not the Papists be from henceforth charged with Elizabeth Bar-" ton, whom they called the *Holy Maid of Kent;* since now the Zuinglian " gospellers, (for I cannot but consider this a plot of theirs) have raised " up their Elizabeth Crofts, whom they called the *Spirit in the Wall,* to " draw aside the people from their due allegiance." Another of the inconsistencies of these pretended reformers was, the interpretation of

" should depart this life without lawful issue, that then the heir surviv-
" ing of this marriage, though female only, should succeed in all the
" kingdoms of Spain, together with all the dominions and estates of Italy
" thereunto belonging."

These conditions must appear to every unprejudiced mind by far
more advantageous to the realm of England than to the crown of
Spain. In fact, every advantage was on the side of this country. Had
there been issue between the parties, the territories of England would
have been considerably extended, and, as it was, she obtained the most
powerful alliances by the match. But Philip was a Catholic, and it
was not in the nature of the disciples of the new doctrines, as we shall
soon shew, to be satisfied with the *political* advantages of the country,
when their *fanatical* notions on *religion* were likely to be superseded by
a return to sound sense and an unerring rule of faith. Gardiner explained the articles to the lord mayor and aldermen, in an eloquent discourse, in which he pointed out the many valuable benefits to be anticipated from such an union with the heir apparent, for Philip was only
prince of Spain at the time of the treaty, to so many rich and powerful
territories. The public announcement of the match, however, was far
from satisfying the opponents of the measure, whose restless and unprincipled disposition began to display itself by the practice of the most
abominable artifices. They circulated the most incredible stories; the
private character of Philip was loaded with the basest imputations that
could disgrace the lowest of mankind, much more a prince; it was given
out at one time that an army of Spaniards and imperialists were coming
to take absolute possession of the kingdom; at another, that Edward
was still alive; that the queen had broken her promise to the Suffolk-
men not to alter the religion settled in Edward's time; that the marriage would be but an introduction to a second vassalage to the popes
of Rome; and that Mary had therefore forfeited her right to the crown.
By these and such like reports, the leading conspirators against the
queen and the realm had prepared the ignorant and fanatical people
for rebellion, and it was agreed that the duke of Suffolk, who still had the
ambition of seeing his daughter replaced on the throne, should arm his
tenants in Warwickshire; that Courtney, should raise the discontented
in Devonshire, under the assurance of marrying the lady Elizabeth; and
sir Thomas Wyat was to put himself at the head of the malecontents in
Kent. The conduct of the duke of Suffolk in this business was most
base and ungrateful. Though implicated with Northumberland in the
first conspiracy against Mary's claim, instead of suffering with him, he
was allowed to retire to his own house, after a detention of three days
in the Tower; his duchess was received at court with a distinction
which excited the jealousy of Elizabeth; the forfeiture of his property
and honours had been preserved to him by the clemency of Mary; and
he had given to her the most solemn assurances of his approbation
of her marriage. Such was the vile ungenerous conduct of this preci-
sian in religion, this disciple of Puritanism and treason. The lady Elizabeth, too, was not an unconcerned observer of this conspiracy. A letter to her from Wyat, recommending her removal from the vicinity of
the metropolis to Dunnington castle, was intercepted by the council,
and Mary sent an order for her to return to court; but she neither fol-

tholic church was brought about. The incidents attending this most
important event are so truly interesting to Englishmen, that we shall
give them in the words of Dr. Lingard, not being willing to trust our
pen with the narration. "In consequence of a royal message," writes
the learned historian, "the lords and commons repaired to the court:
" and, after a few words from the chancellor, Pole, in a long harangue,
" returned them thanks for the act which they had passed in his favour,
" exhorted them to repeal, in like manner, all the statutes enacted in
" derogation of the papal authority; and assured them of every facility
" on his part to effect the re-union of the church of England with that
" of Rome. The chancellor, having first taken the orders of the king
" and queen, replied, that the two houses would deliberate apart, and
" signify their determination on the following morning.

. " The motion for the re-union was carried almost by acclamation.
" In the lords every voice was raised in its favour: in the commons,
" out of three hundred members, two only demurred, and these desisted
" from their opposition the next day. It was determined to present a
" petition in the name of both houses to the king and queen, stating,
" that they looked back with sorrow and regret on the defection of the
" realm from the communion of the apostolic see: that they were ready
" to repeal, as far as in them lay, every statute which had either caused
" or supported that defection: and that they hoped, through the me-
" diation of their majesties, to be absolved from all ecclesiastical cen-
" sures, and to be received into the bosom of the universal church.

" On the following day, the feast of St. Andrew, the queen took her
" seat on the throne. The king was placed on her left hand, the legate,
" but at greater distance, on her right. The chancellor read the peti-
" tion to their majesties: they spoke to the cardinal: and he, after a
" speech of some duration, absolved all those present, and the whole
" nation, and the do   nions thereof, from all heresy and schism, and all
" judgments, censures, and penalties for that cause incurred: and re-
" stored them to the communion of the holy church in the name of the
" Father, Son, and Holy Ghost. Amen, resounded from every part of
" the hall: and the members, rising from their knees, followed the king
" and queen into the chapel, where Te Deum was chaunted in thanks-
" giving for the event. The next Sunday the legate, at the invitation
" of the citizens, made his public entry into the metropolis; and Gar-
" diner preached at St. Paul's cross the celebrated sermon in which he
" lamented in bitter terms his conduct under Henry VIII.; and exhorted
" all, who had fallen through his means, or in his company, to rise with
" him and seek the unity of the Catholic church.

" To proceed with this work, the two houses and the convocation
" simultaneously presented separate petitions to the throne. That from
" the lords and commons, requested their majesties to obtain from the
" legate, all those dispensations and indulgences, which the innovations
" made during the schism had rendered necessary, and particularly such
" as might secure the property of the church to the present possessors
" without scruple of conscience, or impeachment from the ecclesiastical
" courts. The other, from the clergy, stated their resignation of all
" right to those possessions of which the church had been deprived;
" and their readiness to acquiesce in every arrangement to be made by

" the legate. His decree was soon afterwards published : 1. That all
" cathedral churches, hospitals, and schools founded during the schism,
" should be preserved ; 2. That all persons, who had contracted mar-
" riage within the prohibited degrees without dispensation, should re-
" main married ; 3. That all judicial processes made before the ordi-
" naries, or an appeal before delegates, should be held valid ; and 4.
" That the possessors of church property should not, either now or
" hereafter, be molested, under pretence of any canons of councils, de-
" crees of popes, or censures of the church ; for which purpose, in vir-
" tue of the authority vested in him, he took from all spiritual courts
" and judges the cognizance of these matters, and pronounced, before-
" hand, all such processes and judgments invalid and of no effect.

" In the mean time a joint committee of lords and commons had been
" actively employed in framing a most important and comprehensive
" bill, which deserves the attention of the reader, from the accuracy
" with which it distinguishes between the civil and ecclesiastical juris-
" dictions, and the care with which it guards against any encroachment
" on the part of the latter. It first repeals several statutes by name,
" and then, in general, all clauses, sentences, and articles in every other
" act of parliament made since the 20th of Henry VIII. against the
" supreme authority of the pope's holiness or see apostolic. It next
" recites the two petitions, and the dispensation of the legate ; and
" enacts, that every article in that dispensation should be reputed good
" and effectual in law, and may be alleged and pleaded in all courts
" spiritual and temporal. It then proceeds to state that, though the
" legate hath by his decree taken away all matter of impeachment,
" trouble, or danger to the holders of church property ; yet, because
" the title of lands and hereditaments in this realm is grounded on the
" laws and customs of the same, and to be tried and judged in no other
" courts than those of their majesties : it is therefore enacted, by au-
" thority of parliament, that all such possessors of church property
" shall hold the same in manner and form as they would have done, had
" this act never been made ; and, that any person who shall molest such
" possessors by process out of any ecclesiastical court, either within or
" without the realm, shall incur the penalty of praemunire. Next it
" provides, that all papal bulls, dispensations, and privileges, not con-
" taining matter prejudicial to the royal authority, or to the laws of the
" realm, may be put in execution, used, and alleged in all courts what-
" soever : and concludes by declaring, that nothing in this act shall be
" explained to impair any authority or prerogative belonging to the
" crown, in the 90th year of Henry VIII, that the pope shall have and
" enjoy, without diminution or enlargement, the same authority and
" jurisdiction, which he might then have lawfully exercised ; and that
" the jurisdiction of the bishops shall be restored to that state, in which
" it existed at the same period. In the lords, the bill was read thrice
" in two days ; in the commons, it was passed after a sharp debate on
" the third reading. Thus was re-established, in England, the whole
" system of religious polity, which had prevailed for so many centuries
" before Henry VIII."

The same writer observes, in a note on the 20th of Henry VIIIth,
" Most readers have very confused and incorrect notions of the juris-

" diction, which the pontiff, in virtue of his supremacy, claimed to ex-
" ercise within the realm. From this act, and the statutes which it
" repeals, it follows, that that jurisdiction was comprised under the
" following heads : 1. He was acknowledged as chief bishop of the
" Christian church, with authority to reform and redress heresies, er-
" rors, and abuses within the same. 2. To him belonged the institu-
" tion or confirmation of bishops elect. 3. He could grant to clergy-
" men licences of non-residence, and permission to hold more than one
" benefice, with cure of souls. 4. He dispensed in the canonical impe-
" diments of matrimony ; and 5. He received appeals from the spiritual
" courts."

We cannot pass over this memorable event, without taking a slight
review of some of the causes which seem to have prepared the nation
for so speedy and universal a revolution ; one of which seems to have
been the shortness of time, not more than twenty years, since England
had renounced the religion to which she had now returned, and which
had been her faith for above nine centuries. Another was probably, so
far as the great body of the people were concerned, the deplorable state
of misery and starvation to which the poor had been reduced by the
dissolution of monasteries and religious houses, which it was hoped, no
doubt, would be removed by the re-establishment of those receptacles
of virtue and charity.—To these facts we shall add the authority of
witnesses who, in this case, being Protestants, must be above all exception ; one of them assigns very natural reasons for the little satisfaction which sensible and well disposed minds could find in such novelties ; and the other sets forth, in a very impartial light, some arguments, " which," as he expresses himself, " may prevail on men of
" much reason and more piety," to entertain a favourable opinion of
the religion which the nation now embraced.

The first acknowledges, " that the licentious and dissolute life of
" many of the professors of the gospel, and which was but too visible
" in some of the more eminent among them ; the open blemishes of
" some of the clergy, who promoted the reformation, contributed to
" alienate the people, to raise a general aversion, and to make the na-
" tion entertain as advantageous a notion of the religion they had quit-
" ted, as their prejudices had been strong against it : and to look upon
" all the innovations that had been made as so many inlets into all man-
" ner of vice and wickedness."—Bishop Burnet's History of the Reformation. vol. iii. p. 217.

" The members of the Roman Catholic communion," says the other
author, " whose authority I have pleaded, may say, that their religion
" was that of their forefathers, and had the actual possession of men's
" minds before the opposite opinions had even a name ; and having
" continued in it through such a length of time, it would be objected
" to them with an ill grace, that this was the effect of invention or de-
" sign ; because it was not likely that all ages should have the same
" purposes, or that the same doctrine should serve the different ends
" of several ages. This prescription, moreover, rests on these grounds;
" that truth is more ancient than falsehood ; and that God would not,
" for so many ages, have forsaken his church, and left her in error.
" To this antiquity of doctrine is annexed an uninterrupted succession of

" their bishops from the apostles, and particularly of their superior bi-
" shop from St. Peter, whose personal prerogatives were so great, and
" the advantageous manner in which many eminent prelates of other sees
" have expressed themselves with regard to the church of Rome. This
" prerogative includes the advantages of monarchy, and the constant
" benefits which are derived from that form of government. Nor does
" the multitude and variety of people, who are of that persuasion, their
" apparent consent with elder ages, and their agreement with one an-
" other, form a less presumption in their favour. The same conclu-
" sion (he says) must be inferred from the differences which have arisen
" amongst their adversaries, and from the casualties which have hap-
" pened to many of them : from the oblique and sinister proceedings
" of some who have left their commission ; from the appellation of he-
" retic and schismatic, which they fix on all who dissent from them." To
these negative arguments he adds those of a more positive kind ; viz.
" the beauty and splendour of the church of Rome, her solemn service,
" the stateliness and magnificence of her hierarchy, and the name of
" Catholic, which she claims as her own due, and to concern no other
" sect of Christianity. It has been their happiness to be instrumental
" to the conversion of many nations. The world is witness to the piety
" and austerity of their religious orders ; to the single life of their
" priests and bishops ; the severity of their fasts and observances ; to
" the great reputation of many of their bishops for faith and sanctity,
" and the known holiness of some of those persons, whose institutes
" the religious orders follow."—*Dr. Jeremy Taylor on the Liberty of
Prophecying.*

The renouncement of the supremacy of the see of Rome was the first
breach of this nation with the Catholic church, and the acknowledgment of it was the first step of a return to the ancient faith. We are
aware that there is much difficulty to satisfy the Protestant reader of
the expediency and much more the necessity of such a measure ; however, we will here quote the authority of a learned Protestant writer on
the subject, and leave it to his own common sense to decide the point.
" It is well known," says *Grotius,* speaking of himself, in his last reply
to *Rivet,* written a short time before his death, " that I have always
" wished to see Christians re-united in the same body ; and I once
" thought this conjunction might be begun by an union of Protestants
" among themselves. I have since perceived that this is impossible,
" not only because the Calvinists are averse to all such agreements ;
" but because Protestants are not associated under any one form of go-
" vernment, and therefore cannot be united in one body, but must ne-
" cessarily be separated into other new sects and divisions. I, there-
" fore, and many others with me, plainly see that this concord of Pro-
" testants can never be effected, unless they are united to the Roman
" see, without which no common church goverment can take place :
" for which reason I wish that the separation, which has been made,
" and the causes of it, may cease. Now, amongst these, the canonical
" primacy of the bishop of Rome cannot, as Melancthon himself con-
" fesses, be placed ; for he judges that very primacy necessary, in order
" to maintain and preserve unity." If this testimony is not sufficient
to convince the reader of the necessity of having a supreme head to

preserve unity in the body, let him consult Dr. Field's preface to his Book on the Church. Dr. Hammond, in his Treatise on Heresy, §13. No. 2, 3, and his Comment. on 1 Tim. iii. 15. Dr. Jackson on the Creed, b. 2, chap. iv, p. 165, and Dr. Fenne; who all seem to extort from their readers the same concession in this article of the Catholic faith, which St. Paul drew from Agrippa with respect to the Christian religion in general, *Thou persuadest me almost to be a Christian.* Acts, xxvi. 28.

The reconciliation was concluded by a general pardon for offences against the queen, and among other prisoners discharged were, according to Stow, the late archbishop of York, sir John Rogers, sir James a Crofts, sir Nicholas Throgmorton, sir Nicholas Arnold, sir Edward Warner, sir George Harper, sir William Sentlow, sir Andrew Dudley, and sir Gavin Carew, knights. These prisoners were set at liberty on the 18th of January, 1555, and it clearly shews that Mary did not then seek " to domineer over the rights of private judgment, and trample on the liberties of mankind." No, no, modern editors of *Fox's Book of Martyrs,* it was not Mary that sought to play the tyrant, but the pretended martyrs of John Fox, and their confederates at home and abroad, who, by their plottings and preachings, sapped the basis of social order and civil liberty, and compelled the Catholic sovereigns of Europe to resort to harsh measures to preserve the rights and privileges of mankind. We have seen that Poynet, bishop of Winchester, fled to the continent, after engaging in Wyatt's rebellion. Others of the reforming party betook themselves likewise to flight, some to Frankfort, and some to Geneva, where they practised their treasons under hand. Of these were Whittingham, Goodman, Soory, Wood, Knox, John Fox, Jewel, Horn, Sands, and Grindal, and they had not long been at the first mentioned place, before they began to wrangle about the book of Common Prayer, and other matters, as well as to hatch up treason.—" When " Whittingham, and divers others of a more violent humour" says the author of, The Survey of the pretended Holy Discipline " came first " to Frankfort, they fell presently into a very special liking of the " Geneva discipline, as finding it to contain such rules and prac- " tices as did greatly concur with their own dispositions, viz. that if " bishops and princes refused to admit of the gospel, they might be used " by their subjects as the bishop of Geneva was used, that is, DE- " POSED. And that every particular minister with assistants, ac- " cording to the platform of that discipline, was himself a bishop, and " had as great an authority within his own parish as any bishop in the " world, might lawfully challenge, even to the excommunication of the " best, as well princes as peasants, &c. Howbeit, many there were, as " Dr. Cox, Dr. Horn, Mr. Jewel, with sundry others, who perceiving " the tricks of that discipline, did utterly dislike it." (p. 45, 46.) So in the History of the Troubles at Frankfort, p. 44, 45, we find Knox making use of the following language towards this country. " Oh, " England! England! if thou wilt obstinately return into Egypt, that " is, if thou contract marriage, confederacy, or league with such princes " as do maintain and advance idolatry, such as the emperor, who is not " less an enemy to Christ than was Nero; if for the pleasure and friend- " ship, I say, of such princes, thou return to thine old abominations be-

"fore used under Papistry, then, assuredly, O England, thou shalt be "plagued and brought to desolation by the means of those whose favour "thou seekest, and by whom thou art procured to fall from Christ, and "serve antichrist." For these and such like treasonable sentiments against the emperor, his son Philip and queen Mary, Knox was compelled to fly from Frankfort, and was followed by some of his party.— These turbulent spirits were in correspondence with their co-mates in England. It may here be proper to remark, that the reformers or gospellers were themselves the asserters of the right of the civil power to punish evil doers, and Calvin set the example by burning Servetus.—It must not be forgotten too, that Cranmer was consenting to the death of Lambert and Anne Askew, under Henry the eighth, and urged the young prince Edward to sign the death warrant of Joan Bocher and Von Paris for HERESY. Nay, in a code of ecclesiastical discipline compiled by Cranmer, for the government of the reformed church of England, it was ordained that individuals accused of holding heretical opinions should be arraigned before the spiritual courts; should be excommunicated on conviction; and after a respite of sixteen days should, if they continued obstinate, be delivered to the civil magistrate, to SUFFER THE PUNISHMENT PROVIDED BY THE LAW. This code was levelled against the professors of the ANCIENT FAITH, for, by this new code, the doctrines of transubstantiation and supremacy, and the denial of justification by faith only, were made heresy, and, of course, would have subjected every Catholic to the punishment of death. The demise of Edward VI. put an end to this scheme of Cranmer to wreak his vengeance on the believers of that faith which he had repeatedly sworn to teach, when it was his interest, and basely violated his solemn pledges when he could do it with safety to his neck. But only think, reader, of the consistency of those writers who clamour so loudly against the persecuting spirit of the Catholics, when the page of genuine history proves that the gospellers were as sanguinary towards Catholics as ever Catholics could be towards them. Besides the Catholics did not invent their religion, but received it from the apostles and their successors, which religion, the scripture says, is unchangeable and immutable. Whereas the religion, if such it can be called, of Cranmer and the gospellers, was of human invention, ever varying and unsettled; yet did he propose a code to burn those who should constantly adhere to the ONE invariable faith professed in England for nine hundred years before him, but, in a short time, he and his associates fell into the trap he had contrived for others.

With whom the persecution originated in Mary's reign is, according to Dr. Lingard, a matter of uncertainty. Gardiner and Bonner have both been charged with cruelty, and as being the instigators of these lamentable proceedings; but this learned writer has ably rescued the character of Gardiner from being of a mercenary disposition, and though it must be admitted that Bonner, from his situation, was compelled to pronounce a decree of heresy against a great number of the gospellers, yet it does not appear that he was a persecutor from choice, or went in search of victims, as the Protestants did, and were encouraged to do so, by rewards in the time of Elizabeth; the "glorious" queen Bess, who was a more merciless tyrant than her father Henry. All that is known

for certainty is, that the question of severe measures to reduce the restless spirit of the new preachers, was frequently debated in council *after*
the queen's marriage, but she was not apprized of their final resolution
before the beginning of November, when she returned the following
answer in writing:—" Touching the punishment of heretics, we thinketh
" it ought to be done *without rashness,* not leaving in the mean time to
" do justice to such as, by learning, would seem to deceive the simple:
" and the rest so to be used, that the people well perceive them not to
" be condemned without just occasion : by which they shall both under-
" stand the truth, and beware not to do the like. And especially within
" London, I would wish none to be burnt without some of the council's
" presence, and both there and every where good sermons at the same
time." This we have on the authority of Collier, and certainly here is
nothing of a spirit indicating a desire " to domineer over the rights of
" private judgment, and trample on the privileges of mankind," which the
modern editors charge this queen with harbouring. While these discussions were going on in the council, an act was brought into parliament
to revive the statutes which had formerly been enacted to suppress the
doctrines of the Lollards. Every voice was in its favour, and in the
course of four days it had passed the two houses. Here then was no shew
of ignorance, nor any desire to violate the constitution of the country;
on the contrary, the proceedings were perfectly constitutional and regular. The passing of this act alarmed the reformed preachers, many
of whom were at the time in custody. They composed and forwarded
petitions, including a confession of their faith, to the king and queen and
to parliament, and in which they made professions of loyalty. But while
the preachers in prison professed submission to the laws, those who
were at large acted with intemperance and outrage. On the 31st of
December, one Ross, a celebrated preacher, openly prayed for the death
of the queen. He was surprised in the fact, and taken to prison with
some of his disciples. Parliament immediately passed a law making it
treason to pray for the queen's death ; while lying John Fox eulogizes
these traitors as honest citizens, and bishop Hooper considered them
as suffering saints.

We have seen in our own days the dreadful evils arising from heated
imaginations and the want of sterling religious principles to guide the
opinions of political theorists. The horrors and dreadful outrages arising
from the French revolution are fresh in every one's memory ; nor can
the modern editors of Fox be ignorant of the penal statutes that have
been passed within the last forty years to stop the progress of philosophical and unbelieving sophistry. Have not the British parliament
made new laws of treason and sedition, and have not numerous individuals been punished with death and banishment under them ? We have
had gagging bills, power of imprisonment bills ; sun-set and sun-rise
bills for Ireland, under which the poor peasant may be transported
without trial by Jury, for being out of his house a quarter of an hour,
and a distance of a quarter of a mile, before sun-rise or after sun-set.—
We have had individuals tried and imprisoned for years for writings and
publications tending to bring the Christian religion into contempt. We
have had all these things done by our Protestant government, and in
our own times, and are Catholics to be insulted by exaggerated tales of

A REVIEW
OF
Fox's Book of Martyrs,
CRITICAL AND HISTORICAL.

No 51. | Printed and Published by W. E. Andrews, 3, Chapter-house-court, St. Paul's Churchyard, London. | Price 3d.

EXPLANATION OF THE ENGRAVING.—*Anna Boleyn causing the head of bishop Fisher to be brought to her, when she struck it passionately, and wounded her hand in so doing, the scar of which remained to the end of her life, which was terminated on the scaffold.*—See Dr. Bayley's Life of Bishop Fisher.

CONTINUATION OF THE REVIEW.

cruelty said to have been done three hundred years ago? The alleged motive of these modern proceedings was the preservation of " social order and holy religion;" the same motives were alleged by Mary's counsellors. The latter contended that rigid justice was absolutely necessary to overawe that fanatical mob, and to quell the spirit of sedition.

Mary's counsellors, it must be observed, did not make *new* laws, nor forge *new* crimes, to punish her refractory subjects, as was the case with her father and brother, whose example was followed by her sister Elizabeth These usurpers of the *spiritual* authority coined *creeds* as well as *crimes*, from mere caprice, and punished men, not for doing *wrong*, but for believing and adhering to that faith which was the *right* one. Mary's advisers contented themselves with reviving the ancient statutes of the land, which we will explain hereafter. The religion which the nation had again embraced was the religion of their ancestors, and of the whole world. It had been introduced nine hundred years by the force of persuasion and miracles, and was nurtured by the blood of the saints. Under it the most wholesome and equitable laws had been enacted to secure the rights and properties of every class of the community, both ecclesiastical and civil, and at no time was England more powerful and happy than when she submitted to the spiritual supremacy of the Head of the Catholic Church, and preserved the people from religious feuds and fanaticism. Until the time of Wickliffe no penal law was passed concerning religious opinions, nor would there even after his doctrine began to spread, had they not been the cause of rebellion and bloodshed. We have, in the preceding part of this work shewn the evil results of the Wickliffite heresy, but these results are carefully kept from the people by interested or prejudiced writers, who represent the professors of truth as cruel and sanguinary for attempting to stop the progress of error and delusion, and the disciples of error as the champions of truth. It was only on the 15th of December, 1825, (our birth-day, and St Eusebius's day) that a London paper put forth an article which was headed, "*Penal Laws against Protestants, or Specimens of ancient Catholic Legislation.*" The Acts passed at the period alluded to might as well be alleged to have been passed against the modern philosopers of France as against Protestants, for there was not a Protestant in existence at the time the Acts were made, as Wickliffe held the doctrine of the Mass, which Protestants deny, and swear that it is damnable idolatry. Consequently Wickliffe was not a Protestant, though he and his disciples were condemned for preaching heterodoxy.

But allowing that Wickliffe was a Protestant, and "the true author of the Reformation," the Protestantism which he preached would no more be tolerated by our present Protestant government than it was by the government of the Plantagenets and Tudors. Most of our readers are acquainted with the insurrection of Wat Tyler and Jack Cade, but they are not so well acquainted with the cause of their rebellion. It arose chiefly from the pernicious notions imbibed by the people through the means of ignorant preachers, who went about the country dogmatizing against the clergy and their possessions, and instigating the people to dispossess them of their benefices. All men of letters were objects of hatred with these precursors of the Reformation, and it was found necessary to repress their tumultuous conduct by the strong arm of the law. On this occasion, an act was passed in the fifth year of Richard II. cap. i.—which says, "Forasmuch as it is openly known, that there be " divers *evil* persons within the realm, going from county to county, " and from town to town, in certain habits under *dissimilation of great* " *holiness*, and without the licence of our holy father the pope, or other " *sufficient authority*, preaching daily, not only in churches and church- " yards, but also in markets, fairs, and other open places, where a great " congregation is, divers sermons, containing *heresies* and *notorious* " *errors*, to the great emblemishing of the Christian faith, and *destruc-* " *tion of the laws*, and of the estate of the holy church ; to the great peril " of the souls of the people, and of all the realm of England, &c.— " which preachers cited or summoned before the ordinaries of the places, " there to answer of that whereof they be impeached, will not obey to " their summons and commandments ; nor care not for their monitions, " nor the censures of the holy church, but expressly despise them : and

"moreover, by their subtil and ingenious words to draw the people to
"hear their sermons, and do maintain them in their errors by strong
"hand; and by great routs, &c.—Enjoin, that persons indicted and ac-
"cused of such heresy, should be committed to the ordinaries, and
"openly tried, and being convict, should abjure and do penance, or suffer
"imprisonment, &c."

We take this extract on Protestant authority, and we should be glad
to know what objection can be made to the tenour of this Act, which
will not apply to the penal statutes passed by Protestant parliaments;
unless, indeed, it should be contended that people may act with impunity against Catholic rulers, but must be obedient in all things when
Protestants are set over them.—This law was not intended against men
of godliness, but against "evil persons," who affected great holiness,
and harangued the people without authority, insinuating heresies amongst
the ignorant; which, according to Dr. Johnson, means, "an opinion
of private men different from that of the Catholic and orthodox Church,"
and consequently were, as the Act sets forth, "notorious errors," dis-
figuring the truth and menacing "destruction to the laws."—And is
there a man of common sense, in this enlightened age, to be found condemning this statute of our Catholic forefathers, when the very same
proceedings would be punished at this day, in this Protestant country,
were the modern editors or any other stanch Protestants to tread in the
footsteps of Wickliffe's disciples. Yes, in the United States of America
would these precursors of the Reformation meet with a little wholesome castigation, though there is no state religion in that republic, if
any of them were to act with open force as the Wickliffites were known
to do, though this important fact is studiously suppressed by those writers who arraign the conduct of the Catholics in what they call the
"dark ages."—Does not this very law specify that these new pretenders to holiness and truth, after drawing the people into error by subtle,
that is sly, artful, cunning words, instigated them to maintain "their
errors by strong hand and by great routs," which is manifestly contrary
to the spirit of the Catholic religion, as that religion was spread, in
every case, by the very opposite means of force and commotion, and
when it was persecuted, those who professed it surrendered their lives
rather than be guilty of the least violence to dishonour their faith.

But before we proceed farther in our remarks, we must give from
the same authority two extracts from the 2d of Henry IV, who forcibly
deposed the former sovereign, but found it necessary to guard against
the evil doings of the precursors of the Reformation.—The writer of
the article says, this act of the last named monarch "more particularly
defines the persons here spoken to be."—It says, "A new sect of the
"faith, of the sacraments of the church, and of the authority of the
"same damnably thinking, and against the law of God and of the church,
"usurping the offices of preaching, and who do perversely and maliciously
"in divers places within the said realm, under the colour of dissembled
"holiness, preach and teach these days, openly and privily, divers new
"doctrines, and wicked, heretical and erroneous opinions, contrary to the
"same faith and blessed determinations of the holy church; and of such
"sect and wicked doctrine and opinions, they make unlawful conventicles
"and confederacies, they hold and exercise schools, they do make and

" write books, they do wickedly instruct and inform people, and so much
" as they may excite and stir them to SEDITION and INSURRECTION," &c.
—And " Ordains that persons convicted of such offences, and who shall
" refuse duly to abjure the same; or who, after abjuration, shall be pro-
" nounced, do fall into relapse, so that according to the holy canons he
" ought to be left to the secular court.— After due process the mayor,
" sheriff or sheriffs, &c. of the place where the offence shall be com-
" mitted, shall, after sentence, receive them before the people in an
" high place do to be burnt; that such punishment may strike fear into
" the minds of others, whereby no such heretical doctrine, nor their authors
" and fautors in the said realm against the Catholic faith, Christian law,
" and determination of the holy church, which God prohibit, be sustain-
" ed or in any wise suffered."

From these extracts we find the same crimes of sedition and insurrection made the groundwork of the punishment, and the same cause named
as producing these crimes, namely, hypocrisy in affecting piety, and
perversity and malice in spreading their errors.   The doctrines and opinions are denominated wicked, and the conventicles unlawful; now had
not our ancestors, though they were Catholics, as much right to guard
against wicked errors as our Protestant government?   We have had several acts passed within the last twenty years to prevent the holding of
unlawful and seditious assemblies; and why should not Catholic parliaments be allowed to protect the peace and safety of the realm at the
close of the 14th and beginning of the 15th centuries, against similar
disturbers of the common weal, as Protestant parliaments in the 19th
century?   If the Protestant reader would divest himself of that prejudice imbibed by his education, and look to the two cases, with religion
substracted from the first, he would find that had not our Catholic ancestors taken the precautions which they did to resist and destroy the
pernicious subtilties and seditious practices of the Wickliffites, more
generally known by the name of Lollards, the Protestants would not
now have had any privileges to be alarmed for, lest the Catholics should
regain the ascendency and take away these rights from them.   A circumstance which, if attempted in our time, we would oppose with all
the energy of our mind.

We have shewn, to demonstration, that the two statutes of Richard II.
and Henry IV. were not directed to invade the right of conscience, but
to repress the exercise of force to benight and hold the mind in error,
and prevent those dire calamities which naturally follow a state of insubordination and licentiousness among the people.   Although punishment
was enacted in the case of obstinacy and depravity, yet it does not follow that mild means were not resorted to, for the prevention of crime;
and in fact no endeavour was left untried to bring the mistaken disciples of the new doctrines and wicked practices to a sense of their
duty.   That prevention and not punishment was the object of the
rulers of those days is unanswerably proved by the few executions
that occurred under these two acts, which have been so much reprobated by Protestant writers, during the reign of the Catholic sovereigns, till the rule of that merciless bloody tyrant, Henry VIII. who
became the first Protestant Head of the Church of England.— Wickliffe himself died a natural death, the mischievous effects of his doc-

trines not appearing till after he had passed into the grave; of his followers not more than twenty-two suffered under the laws above, which were found necessary to be enacted, during the long space of 113 years, even according to John Fox himself, who includes in this number sir John Oldcastle, a notorious traitor. Nor did Mary's advisers recommend the renewal of these laws, to glut their vengeance with the blood of the misguided and turbulent victims of delusion, but with a view to intimidate and restrain those tumultuous ebullitions which the seditious writings and preachings of the gospellers were fanning to a flame.—We have before shewn that the queen received the greatest provocations to resort to harsh measures which she forbore with a lenity hitherto unparalleled, and never yet followed. To this period not one had been punished for an offence touching religion. Those who suffered were convicted traitors, and but one, namely, the lady Jane Grey, was an object of pity with the people. This merciful forbearance, however, instead of gaining on the affections of the infatuated disciples of the gospellers only tended to embolden them in their outrageous conduct; but what was evidently the feeling of charity, inspired by true religion, was mistaken for the effect of fear. Fresh provocations were given, and it was at length resolved to try what coercion would do to heal the disorders which now raged with so much excess. But this determination was not come to without opposition from some of the council. Cardinal Pole, who, as legate of the pope, represented the head of the Catholic church, was strenuous for mild measures. Dr. Heylin says, the cardinal " was clearly of opinion, that they should rest themselves "contented with the restitution of their own religion; that the said " statutes should be held forth as a terror only, but that no open perse-"cution should be raised upon them; following therein, as he affirmed, " the counsel sent unto the queen by Charles the emperor, at her first " coming to the crown, by whom she was advised to create no trouble " unto any man for matter of conscience." Dr. Lingard also bears testi-mony to the clemency of the legate's disposition. " In a confidential "letter to the cardinal of Augsburgh," writes that historian, " he has " unfolded to us his own sentiments without reserve. He will not, he " says, deny that there may be men, so addicted to the most pernicious " errors themselves, and so apt to seduce others, that they may justly be " put to death, for the same purpose as we amputate a limb to preserve " the whole body. But this is an extreme case: and, even when it happens, " every gentler remedy should be applied before such punishment is " inflicted. In general lenity is to be preferred to severity: and the " bishops should remember that they are fathers as well as judges, and " ought to shew the tenderness of parents, even when they are com-" pelled to punish. This has always been his opinion: it was that of " his colleagues, who presided with him at the council of Trent, and " also of the prelates who composed that assembly." The lord chan-cellor Gardiner, is said by Dr. Heylin to have differed from the legate, and to have contended for the enforcing of the statutes on the principal supporters of the heretics, whether they were of the ecclesiastical hier-archy or the lay nobility; and bishop Bonner is represented by the same authority as furious in favour of persecution, which he justified, the doctor says, by precedent from the evangelists or gospellers themselves.

——" Have I not seen (saith he) that the heretics themselves have broke
" the ice, in putting one of their own number (I think they called him
" by name of Servetus) to a cruel death? Could it be thought no
" crime in them, to take that more severe course against one of their
" brethren, for holding any contrary doctrine from that which they had
" publicly agreed amongst them? And can they be so silly, or so par-
" tial rather, as to reckon it for a crime in us, if we proceed against
" them with the like severity, and punish them by the most extreme
" rigour of their own example?"—Cranmer too, be it observed, and
never forgotten, was an advocate for persecution even of Protestants,
or such as are now called so. he having laboured with Ridley to instil
into the youthful mind of Edward, " that as Moses ordered blasphemers
" to be put to death, so it was the duty of a Christian prince, and more
" so of one, who bore the title of *defender of the faith*, to eradicate the
" cockle from the field of God's church, to cut out the gangrene that
" it might not spread to the sounder parts." (*Rym.* xv. 182.)—Elizabeth, also, that darling the pope and foundress of the established church,
she who is hailed with the title of " Virgin queen," and " glorious Bess,"
while her sister Mary is denominated the " bloody" queen—this sweet
lady could issue out her commissions for *burning heretics*, in one of which,
to sir Nicolas Bacon, she says, " they have been justly declared heretics,
" and, therefore as corrupt members to be cut off from the rest of the
" flock of Christ, lest they should corrupt others, professing the true
" Christian faith. . . . We, therefore, according to regal function, and
" office, minding the execution of justice in this behalf, require you to
" award and make out our writ of execution," &c. (*Rym.* xv. 740.)—
From these facts it is clear that both parties seem to have been agreed
in the right of the *secular* power to put heretics to death, and as we have
proved that the legate, cardinal Pole, as well as others, were opposed to
severe measures, it is not too much to expect of the Protestant reader,
that he will acquit the Catholic *church* of holding persecuting doctrines,
which she really does not admit, when persecution has been practised to
a much greater degree and with less shew of justice by Protestants
than by Catholics. Because the latter adhere to *one* only *divine* faith,
whereas the former admit the right of every individual to chose his own
individual opinion, and then punish him for so doing ! ! !

The council having decided on strong measures, on the 22d of January, 1555, the chancellor called before him the chief of the prisoners,
put them in mind of the tendency of the statutes revived in the last parliament, and admonished them to avoid the punishment that would succeed a spirit of contumacy. A few days after the court was opened, at
which Gardiner presided, and thirteen bishops were present, with a
number of lords and knights. The presence of the latter plainly shews
that the court was not exclusively ecclesiastic. Six prisoners were
called before them; of these, Hooper, the deprived bishop of Gloucester; Rogers, a prebendary of St. Paul's; Saunders, rector of Allhallows
in London; and Taylor, rector of Hadley, in *Suffolk*, according to Dr.
Lingard's testimony, but of *Hertford*, if we are to credit Heylin, refused to subscribe to the Catholic doctrine. One of the others feigned
a recantation; and the sixth petitioned for time, which was granted. A
delay of twenty-four hours was allowed the first four; and on their

second refusal they were excommunicated. The excommunication was followed by the delivery of the prisoners to the civil power. Here we will just observe, that the proceedings do not appear to have been conducted with haste and severity. Although we disapprove of the mixing up religious questions with political crimes, still justice ought to be done to the persecutors as well as to the persecuted, and such was the nature of the doctrines taught by the gospellers that it was next to an impossibility to separate the two subjects in the case of these offenders. Rogers was the first of the four that was executed, and he was burned in Smithfield on the 4th of February. Gardiner from this time declined all further attendance, and his place was occupied by Bonner. This latter prelate, on the 9th of the same month, accompanied by the lord mayor and sheriffs and several members of the council, excommunicated six other prisoners, and turned them over to the civil power. On the day following, however, a circumstance occurred which should never be forgotten, in justice to the parties, but which is wilfully suppressed by those who are led by their prejudices to calumniate and vilify the Catholic church.—A Spanish friar, named Alphonso di Castro, and confessor to king Philip, was ordered to preach before the court, and to the astonishment of his hearers, but to his own immortal honour, condemned the harsh proceedings just adopted in the most pointed and severe manner. He pronounced them to be in direct opposition not only to the text, but to the spirit of the gospel: it was not by severity, he said, but by mildness, that men were to be brought into the fold of Christ; and it was the duty of the bishops not to seek the death, but to instruct the ignorance of their misguided brethren. "Men were at a loss," says Dr. Lingard, " to ac-
" count for this discourse, whether it were the spontaneous effort of the
" friar, or had been suggested to him by the policy of Philip, or by the
" humanity of the cardinal, or by the repugnance of the bishops. It
" made, however, a deep impression: the execution of the prisoners
" was suspended: the question was again debated in the council; and
" five weeks elapsed before the advocates of severity could obtain per-
" mission to rekindle the fires of Smithfield." Nor would they in all probability have been rekindled, had not the turbulent spirit of the gospellers provoked the court to resume harsh measures.—That Mary had no desire to "domineer over the right of private judgment and trample, on the privileges of mankind," as the modern editors of Fox unjustly accuse her, she about this time released Courteney, the earl of Devonshire, from confinement, a ndhe with Elizabeth repaired to Hampton-court, to enjoy the festivities of Easter with the queen. The bishops too were very reluctant to take upon themselves the odious task of calling the prisoners before them, and it was not till Bonner had received a reprimand, through the instigation of the new marquis of Winchester, who, in the former reign, was a pious gospeller, but had now become the most furious persecutor, that the fires were again lighted. And they were made to blaze more freely from the riotous proceedings of the fanatical imbibers of evangelism.

In the month of March a new conspiracy was detected, which had been organized in the counties of Norfolk, Suffolk, and Cambridge. On Easter Sunday, Stowe says, a priest, some time a monk of Ely and

also of Bicester, named William Branch, *alias* Flower, wounded another priest with a knife, as he was administering the sacrament to the people in St. Margaret's church at Westminster: for which deed the said William Flower, on the 24th of April, had his right hand cut off, and for opinions in matters of religion was burned in St. Margaret's church-yard. Dr. Heylin likewise says, "Though Wyatt's party was so far sup-
"pressed as not to shew itself visibly in open action, yet such as for-
"merly had declared for it, or wished well unto it, had many secret
"writings against the queen, every day growing more and more in
"dislike of her government, by reason of so many butcheries as were
"continually committed under her authority. Upon which ground,
"as they had formerly instructed Elizabeth Crofts to act the spirit in
"the wall, so afterwards they trained up one William Constable, *alias*
"Featherstone, to take upon himself the name of king Edward, whom
"he was said to resemble both in age and personage. And this they
"did in imitation of the like practice used in the time of king Henry
"VI. by Richard Plantagenet, duke of York, who when he had a mind
"to claim his title to the crown, in regard of his descent by the house
"of Mortimer, from Lionel of Antwerp, duke of Clarence, he caused
"one Jack Cade (a fellow altogether as obscure as this) to take upon
"himself the name of Mortimer, that he might see how well the peo-
"ple stood affected unto his pretensions, by the discovery which might
"be made thereof on this false alarm. And though this Featherstone
"had been taken and publicly whipped for it in May last past, and
"thereupon banished into the north, where he had been born, yet the
"confederates resolved to try their fortune with him in a second adven-
"ture. The design was to raise the people under colour of king Ed-
"ward being alive, and at the same time to rob the exchequer, wherein
"they knew, by some intelligence or other, that 50,000*l.* in good Spa-
"nish money had been lodged." To these provocations may be added
the licentious spirit of the preachers of the new opinions, who heaped
upon the queen, the prelates, her council, and her religion, every op-
probrious and indecent epithet that the fury of man, or the malice of
hell, could device. Tracts filled with the most abominable and treasonable matter were industriously sent over by the exiles in Germany,
and as sedulously circulated through the kingdom by the disaffected at
home. During this period, the queen was led to believe, from appearances, that she was pregnant, and preparations were made for her ac-
couchement. Prayers were offered for her safe delivery, but it afterwards turned out that her situation was occasioned by bodily disease.
This disappointment was the occasion of great rejoicings by her enemies, who indulged themselves in sarcasms, epigrams, and lampoons.
Under such circumstances it cannot be a subject of wonder that the
the fires of Smithfield and elsewhere were rekindled; our astonishment
is only excited that so great a degree of forbearance was manifested,
which we conceive must be taken by every unbiassed mind as a proof of
the great clemency of Mary's disposition.

Exasperated and goaded by the seditious spirit of the new lights,
Mary's council unfortunately resolved on an endeavour to strike terror
into the deluded, and accordingly Ridley and Latimer were ordered to
be burned. These leaders of the new opinions and instigators to fana

ticism suffered on the 16th of October, 1555. Cranmer was next called forth. He had seen his two friends led to execution from the window of his cell, and the sight made him relent ; but he recovered himself, and wrote a long letter to the queen in defence of his doctrine, which, at Mary's request, was answered by cardinal Pole. News was now received from Rome, that Cranmer had been formally condemned by the pope, Paul IV. in a private consistory, and the usual sentence pronounced. Cranmer was again alarmed ; he had no inclination to meet death. To save his life, he therefore recanted and openly condemned his errors. In no less than *seven* instruments, gentle reader, did this over be-praised martyr of the Protestant sect or sects abjure the opinions he had taught, and approve of the faith which he had opposed. But all would not now do. He had been long a convicted traitor, though his life had been spared. He was now a condemned heretic, and as such looked upon as an enemy to God and man. We must give it as our opinion that it would have been better to have spared his life, that he might have sincerely repented of his errors; but as we did not live in those turbulent times, we are not competent to decide whether the excitements given were not sufficient to justify the putting this hoary traitor to death. But we here again repeat, and it cannot be too often impressed upon the mind of the Protestant reader, that heresy, especially when accompanied with sedition and rebellion, as was the case with the Wickliffites and the Protestant gospellers in Mary's reign, was always looked upon as a heinous crime against the *state*, as well as a grievous sin against Almighty God. That, in consequence, the legislature of this country enacted the civil penalties, although the bishops as the judges of doctrine were called upon to examine those who were suspected of it. Thus, then, those who suffered were punished by the statutes of the *realm*, and not by the canons of the *church* ; therefore it is both cruel and unjust to charge Catholics, as Catholics, with the severities of Mary's reign, which were caused by motives of policy arising out of the commotions and treasons of the guilty parties who suffered. As well might Catholic nations lay the late massacre at Manchester, or the number of the executions in the last 30 years, at the door of the Protestant church of England, as the modern editors, or any other bigotted writers, to impute the burnings in Mary's reign to the principles of the Catholic church. Even in the case of Cranmer, the holy father Paul, who was as jealous of his prerogatives as any pontiff that that ever filled the papal throne, in his decree of Cranmer's condemnation, directed to Philip and Mary, only requires them " to deal with him, after he is delivered up to the *secular* court, as THE LAW directs," without conveying the slightest intimation of any corporeal punishment.—Cranmer was judged a fit criminal for THE LAW to take its course, and he was ordered for execution. The writ for this purpose expressly says, that the criminal being condemned for heresy and degraded ; as the CHURCH *neither had*, nor OUGHT to proceed any farther in the affair, he was delivered over to the king and queen, *according to the laws and customs of the* REALM *provided in such cases*, and condemned to be burned, in detestation of his guilt, and for *a warning* to other Christians. On the 31st of March Cranmer was led out to execution,

where he recalled, to the astonishment of the people, all his former recantations, which he said had been wrung from him by the hope of
life. His sufferings were short, as the flames rapidly ascended over his
head, and he expired in a few moments. Fox has a story about his
heart remaining unconsumed after his body was reduced to ashes, but
there is no authority produced to bear out his assertion. If such had
been the case, what had become of it, after such a miraculous preservation? Were there not one disciple to secure the false heart of this
falsest of traitors and bishops, and hand it down for the admiration of
Protestant devotees and bigots. We shall enter more at large into the
circumstances which preceded Cranmer's death in our next volume.

Two hundred and seventy persons are stated by Fox to have suffered
the same punishment during Mary's reign, but this account is exaggerated, and many deductions are to be made for those who died as felons,
and traitors; also for such as were found to be *alive* after the publication of Fox's Calendar; and likewise those who would have been sent
to the fire by Cranmer himself, had he been in power. Of the last there
was a very great number, which father Parsons has pointed out in his
Examination of Fox's Calendar, and we intend to republish in our third
volume. Of the former were W. Flower, who stabbed the priest at the
altar at St. Margaret's; W. Gardiner, who was executed at Lisbon, for
attempting to assassinate the cardinal prince Henry while officiating at
the altar; and the three famous Guernsey women, whom Parsons proves,
to have been prostitutes and guilty of theft. One of them was the mother of the pretended infant martyr, concerning whom such violent
outcries have been raised, and representations made, which are now to
be seen at the shop windows of respectable booksellers in Paternoster-
row. Of those who were found living after the first edition of Fox's
work came out, Anthony Wood, the Oxford historian, relates, that one,
Grimwood was actually present in a church, when the clergyman was
describing, on the authority of Fox's Acts and Monuments, the circumstances of his (Grimwood's) supposed miserable and preternatural death,
" his bowels, by the judgment of God, falling out of his body in consequence." Grimwood, however, finding his bowels still in his body,
brought an action against the clergyman, for we suppose Fox was out
of his reach, for defamation. As we before said, we shall give a full
detail of Fox's Calendar, which will form the third volume of this work,
and will afford the reader a fund of information not generally known, in
consequence of the scarceness of Parson's excellent work, but will be
found highly interesting at this moment, as furnishing a true history of
those individuals who have been so long looked upon as Protestant
saints by the deluded people of England.

That the persecution was not general, but chiefly confined to the
metropolis and its vicinity, the usual seat of restless demagogues and
discontented incendiaries, is strikingly clear by the few that suffered in
the different parts of the kingdom. Not one was put to death in the
diocess of Canterbury, after cardinal Pole was appointed to that see.
Only one in that of York, of which Dr. Heath was archbishop, and
very few in the four Welch diocesses. One in each of those of Wells,
Exeter, Peterborough, and Lincoln; two in that of Ely; three in each

of those of Bristol and Salisbury; and none in those of Oxford, Gloucester, Worcester, and Hereford, according to the testimony of Dr. Heylin.

While these scenes of death were going on, to strike awe among the infatuated gospellers, Mary was not unmindful of the wants of the church, and accordingly she directed the attention of her ministers to the condition of the poor clergy.—On the opening of her parliament, after assuring the lay possessors of church property, that they had nothing to apprehend, she restored the property of the church then in the hands of the crown, and called upon the commons' house for a subsidy. It was the first that she had ever asked of her subjects, so frugal had she been in her wants. It was proposed to grant two-fifteenths, with a subsidy of four shillings in the pound; but Mary, by a message, declined the two-fifteenths, and was content with a subsidy of less amount than what was originally proposed.—The editors of Fox may term this a "narrowness of spirit," but it is such an one as the people would be glad to see followed by the present Ministers, who, being stanch Protestants, have certainly not exhibited a narrowness of spirit in raising loans, granting pensions, and imposing taxes, by which the people are reduced to a state of poverty and misery, not much unlike the days of Edward VI. when the monasteries were destroyed, the tithes appropriated solely to the parson, and the poor left to shift for themselves, as well as they could.—By the bill introduced and passed, Mary gave up the tenths and first fruits, &c. vested in the crown by the 30th of Henry VIII. producing a yearly revenue of 60,000l. for the augmentation of small livings, the support of preachers, and the furnishing of exhibitions to scholars in the universities.—Here was a nobleness of spirit which it would be well if Protestant sovereigns were to imitate, as their people would feel the less weight of the state clergy than they do now-a-days. But the delirium into which the people had then been worked would not allow them to appreciate Mary's good intentions towards them. The death of the lord chancellor Gardiner emboldened the gospellers to renew their machinations against the government; secret meetings were now held, infamous libels on their majesties were scattered about the streets, and even in the precincts of the palace; and a new conspiracy was formed, which had for its object to depose Mary and place her sister Elizabeth on the throne.—Taking this state of things into consideration, is it, we again ask, any matter for astonishment that severe measures were pursued against the gospellers and their preachers?—Elizabeth was again proved to have been concerned in this traitorous design and again pardoned.—A fresh conspiracy was attempted, and a disposition was shewn by Elizabeth to fly into France, fearing she might be at length detected and punished. Troubles now succeeded on troubles, and Mary began to droop in health and spirits. The absence of her husband Philip on the continent, the unquenched fanaticism of the people, the death of her able and honest minister Gardiner, but, above all, the loss of Calais, which had been so long an appendage to the crown of England, preyed on her mind and shook constitution naturally delicate.—Like the Catholic sovereigns who preceded her, she had the honour of England at heart, and consequently felt the loss of so important a fortress as Calais most poignantly.—Still she met her parliament, she saw the spirit of the nation roused, but she could not rally her own fortitude. On her death bed she told her attendants that if her breast was opened, the word "Calais" would be found engraven on her heart. The reign of Mary was now about to close. Exhausted both in mind and body, for the exiles in Geneva continued to increase the number and virulence of their libels against her, she was removed from Hampton court to St. James's, when she was found to be attacked with a fever which had proved fatal to thousands of her subjects. Under this disease she languished for three months, but never recovered sufficiently to leave her apartment.

" During this long confinement," writes Dr. Lingard, " Mary edified " all around her by her cheerfulness, her piety, and her resignation to " the will of Providence. Her chief solicitude was for the stability of that " church which she had restored; and her suspicions of Elizabeth's " insincerity prompted her to require from her sister an avowal of her " real sentiments. In return Elizabeth complained of Mary's incredu- " lity. She was a true and conscientious believer in the Catholic creed ; " nor could she do more now than she had repeatedly done before, " which was to confirm her assertion with her oath. To the duke of " Feria, who had come on a visit to the queen from her husband, " the princess made the same declaration : and so convinced was that " nobleman of her sincerity, that he not only removed the doubts of " Mary, but assured Philip that the succession of Elizabeth would " cause no alteration in the worship now established by law." In a note to this passage, the historian adds on the authority, of the duchess of Feria, that Elizabeth " prayed God that the earth might open and " swallow her alive, if she were not a true Roman Catholic." Before her death, which happened on the 17th of November, 1558, she sent one of her maids of honour, Jane Dormer, afterwards duchess of Feria, to deliver to the princess Elizabeth the jewels in her custody, and to make three requests from her : namely, that she would be good to her servants, would repay the money which had been lent on the privy seals, and would support the Catholic religion. Mass was said on the morning of her death in her chamber, and she expired a few minutes before its conclusion. Cardinal Pole survived her only twenty-four hours.

We have dwelt long on the reign of this unfortunate queen, but not longer than was necessary to vindicate her injured character. Though short in duration, the lies and calumnies that have been forged and heaped upon the memory of Mary, and through her cast upon the Catholics and their religion, have been gross and innumerable, and demanded a full refutation. In accomplishing this task we are happy in having the assistance of a Protestant writer, Mr. Brewer, who, though not generally known, has most ably defended this virtuous but ill-fated princess, and we think it but justice to the author and our readers to give his letter or rather " Hints respecting the real Character of Mary Queen of England," from the Universal Magazine, vol. IX, 1808, p. 396. He says,—

" The motives for partiality and causes for detraction among historians of every nation, but particularly England, where convulsions in religion and politics have been perpetually occurring, and where party has raged with proverbial illiberality at almost every period, would appear too obvious to admit the possibility of implicit reliance in even the cursory reader, did not experience assure us that not only the interested but dispassionate are hourly the dupes of the vilest calumny or most egregious adulation.

"The increasing candour of the latter eras of literature has nobly endeavoured, in many instances, to remove that meretricious veil from the face of historic truth, with which venality had shaded her instructive features. The spirit of 'Historic Doubts,' (by Lord Orford) has stimulated an inquiry into the genuine failings and pretensions of the unfortunate Scottish beauty, whose head not even a diadem could preserve from the block and scaffold; but still the English sovereign of the same name, though of more splendid fortunes, remains the victim of declamatory detestation and merciless tyranny. The examination of this reign, by some scholar at once inquisitive and unprejudiced, I hold a desideratum in English literature; and should feel particular pleasure if this remonstrance, through the medium of your impartial publication, call forth a pen adequate to the task, wielded by a hand which knows no enthusiasm, except such as a love of veracity inoxiously engenders.

"Should a writer generously step forward, he will not droop for want of materials. At the very outset he will perceive the evident possibility of misrepresentation respecting this reign, when he finds that its historians have been men of an opposite (though confessedly of a more correct and desirable) religious persuasion. Taking natural probability for his guide, he will maintain the reasonableness of supposing that a writer whose aim was the gratification of popular credulity, would rather concentrate his invective on one defenceless head, than venture on the attack of a numerous and well-lettered party, whose descendants, if themselves had sunk to the peaceful bourne where content is no more, would be found ready to retort the abuse to the vexation, if not discomfiture, of the assailant.

"Thus will he be tempted to transfer from queen Mary to her advisers a portion of that outcry which party first set up, and which credulity echoes to the discredit of philanthropy, good sense, and the mild tenets of the Christian doctrine.

"When Mary came to the crown she found the state in the most perilous condition, (as far as regarded individual conduct) that possibly could exist for a zealot in any particular mode of faith. Her father, in the plenitude of his caprice, and at the suggestion of his avarice, had thrown off the papal power and commenced champion of the new cause. Not contented with the wealth, he rioted in the blood of the overthrown Papists. The scene is too melancholy to admit an enumeration of the victims. Fire, fagot, and the halter were administered with an unsparing hand! As a sample, suffice it to observe, that at one massacre, More, Fisher, and eleven monks, were beheaded for denying the king's supremacy!

"Edward VI. from the simple circumstance of his adolescence occurring while his august father was in a Protestant mood, received an education from persons directed to instruct him in the reformed religion. During his short reign, accordingly, the foot was still kept on the neck of the Roman Catholic party; and they remained disgraced, in penury, and danger. No scaffolds were built for the express purpose of decapitating the noble Papists, nor gibbets erected for the death of the meaner sort, but an act was passed of the most horrible and oppressive cruelty. The poor wandering monks and ejected friars were, at this time, supported by the private alms of those who did not dare openly to entertain them. To drive them from the miserable corners in which they hovered, it was enacted, that if any person should loiter for three days together without offering himself for hire as a labourer, he should be adjudged as a slave for two years to the first informer, and should be marked on the breast with the letter V, for vagabond. The mark to be made with a hot iron.

"Whether Protestant or Papist, man is still subject to the passions of human nature; and revenge, of all passions the most terrific, and in history the most frequent, even Christianity, under its more favourable modification, is unable to suppress. Perhaps, therefore, a candid and benignant Protestant, now that all violent dissension between the two parties has long since ceased, will scarcely feel surprise at the severity with which those of the ejected persuasion conducted themselves, on a sudden and nearly unexpected restoration to power. Be that as it may, humanity had already blushed for the triumphant Protestants; a blush of a still deeper dye must assuredly glow on her cheek while beholding the unlimited vengeance which their opponents inflicted, when the dangerous talisman of power reversed the tumultuous scene, and recalled the friars from manual labour, or the mortification of the prescribed brand, to their stalls, their mass-books, and all the scattered parade of their glittering rituals. But in the detestable operations which now took place, why is the torch ever placed by the historian in one hand? Is it likely that a single female should possess more rancour than all the heads of a disjointed church, inflamed with personal pique, impoverished by expulsion from their benefices, and inflated by a bigotry of the most decisive nature? Our historians, in this instance, have studied, like the tragic poet, to bring one person forward in the drama, in order to exhibit all the tremendous beauties of contrast. In strict conformity to the pernicious system of dressing up their characters like puppets, either strikingly attractive or utterly deformed, the dramatic recorders who assume the name of historians, studiously decorate the sixth Edward with those clement qualities which they describe his sister as wanting; and freely place all the ignominy of that unprecedented act, the branding of the ejected friars, to the account of his advisers. In this latter procedure they are unquestionably correct. Few persons feed on subjects of religious ascendancy with the acuteness of those who, by their 'sacred calling,' look on church power as the highest object of mundane interest; and therefore to his advisers less as freely attribute all the asperity of the hostile edicts which passed in the short reign of this juvenile sovereign. But, admitting the justice of this appropriation, why shall we deny Mary the same indulgence? Edward was surrounded by churchmen, and, as they advised, he acted; his successor stood in the same predicament, and acted in the same way. If it be objected, that difference of years enabled queen Mary to conduct the government with greater judgment and decision, it may be answered, that her feminine education (for she had not in any view the advantages in this weighty respect of Elizabeth) reduced her nearly to the level of her youthful brother. From infancy to maturity churchmen were her

guides and preceptors; and nearly every action of her life proves that
she had learned to sacrifice her opinions habitually to those of her guardians.

"Our historians have an ungracious custom of illustrating the characters of their dramatis personæ by comparison. Mary they invidiously
place by the side of Elizabeth; and while they lavish panegyric on the
brow of the 'Virgin Queen,' they solicit the reader's abhorrence of
her unhappy foil—not by argument, but by the epithets of "bloodthirsty Mary!' and 'sanguinary tyrant!' The management of the state
this misguided princess appears to have left to the ecclesiastics. The
management of her family, the bishops likewise imperiously solicited;
but in this solitary instance Mary was inflexible; and as I think an examination of her conduct in this particular essential to the right understanding of her character, permit me, from authentic documents, though
testimonies too much neglected by our historical writers, to develop it.

"In regard to Elizabeth, it will be recollected that Mary did not
stand in a situation pointedly dissimilar to that in which Elizabeth herself was afterwards placed with Mary Queen of Scots. As it appears to
me, the conduct of the two sisters in this predicament would, if related
with impartiality, redound by comparison (to adopt the historical fashion)
to the high honour of the elder.

"The behaviour of Elizabeth (though some minute circumstances
may admit of controversy) is too well known to need in this place any
resemblance of a prolix detail. Mary's chief offence, except precedence
in personal beauty, was her right of heirship to the crown, for which
Elizabeth hated and feared her. Mary threw herself on her kinswoman's
protection, and was imprisoned, with circumstances of severity incredible, if not authenticated. A rumour of conspiracy was spread, and she
was put to death.

"Elizabeth was also heir to the crown, and was accused by Sir Thomas Wyat of a conspiracy against her sister's government. Thus, even
in respect to political motives, was Mary as strongly tempted to rid herself of the danger of a rival caballer, as was afterwards the 'Virgin
queen.' But Mary as a woman had much stronger temptations than as
a sovereign. The earl of Devonshire, a young nobleman of the most
engaging qualification, had won the heart of Mary in earliest youth. He
was a particularly suitable match. He was an Englishman, and nearly
allied to the crown. But the first ardent wish of the queen was defeated, and that by her sister, for the earl attached himself to the princess:
the queen was slighted, and Elizabeth triumphed.

"The ancient quarrel between their mothers, likewise, must be supposed not quite forgotten in the breast of the ruling party, especially
when the great share Anna Boleyn took in the Reformation is duly considered: yet these two circumstances conjoined were insufficient to provoke her to that foul crime which Elizabeth taught the world, on a future occasion, how to commit without a blush. It is true the rivalry of
Elizabeth caused the queen to look with coolness on her; and therefore
the princess retired to her house of Ashbridge, in Hertfordshire, but the
style in which she there resided may be gathered from the parade with
which she entered London, when summoned thither on account of the
accusation of Sir Thomas Wyat. "Between four and five of the clock

at night,' says a MS. quoted in Nichols' Progresses, ' my lady Elizabeth's grace came to London, through Smithfielde, untoo Westminster,
with a hundred velvet cotts after her grace. And her grace rode in a
charytt open on both sides; and her grace had, ryding after her, a hundred in cotts of fine redde, gardyd with velvett,' &c. With this pomp
was the person conducted to London, who was accused of conspiring,
against her sister's life—Surely a sanguinary tyrant should be made of
' sterner stuff.'

  " As so much publicity of grandeur was allowed to the princess on
her entry, it is but just to conclude that she could not satisfactorily exonerate herself from the heavy charge preferred against her, when more
strenuous measures were resorted to. This supposition is strengthened
by the deliberation with which the circumstances were investigated, as
she remained a fortnight at court before she was ordered to the tower.
While in confinement, under the suspicion of treasonable practices,
though at first she was attended only by the lieutenant's servants, yet,
suddenly, an order came for her table to be served by a part of her own
establishment, viz. two yeomen of her chamber, one of her robes, two
of her pantry and ewry, one of her buttery, one of her cellar, another of
her larder, and two of her kitchen. By all but the prejudiced it must be
admitted probable, that the first indignity offered the princess was by command of the privy council, at whose head was bishop Gardiner ; and that
on her applying to the queen for a more respectful attendance, her wish
was immediately granted. It is certain that Mary received letters from
her at this juncture, as one is quoted by Camden in his Elizabeth.

  " When Wyat, at the place of execution, made confessions favourable
to the character of Elizabeth, she was released from the tower, and conveyed to Woodstock, where she was lodged in a chamber ' curiously
carved, and painted blue sprinkled with gold.' We can scarcely avoid
supposing that her confinement here was not the most dreary imaginable, since, when queen, she was particularly attached to this palace as
a residence, and Bedingfield her ' jailor,' whom history represents in all
the terrific colours of the hired assassin, with a scowling brow, a curled
lip, and a hand ever grasping a dagger, which points to a poisoned bowl
—this horrible janitor she visited during her progress in 1578, and was
in the habit of receiving frequently at court ! ! To common sense I propose these queries :—Is it likely that a female, possessed of sovereign
power, would fondly revisit the prison in which she had often slept under
the horrible dread of assassination ? And could human lenity so far
conquer the natural suggestions of repugnance, as to allow the possibility of a voluntary and convivial intercourse with the wretch from
whose poinard she had escaped by chance, little short of miracles ?—
The prison-room, iron-bars, assassin, bowl of hemlock, &c. were the of-
spring of Fox's poetical imagination. From Fox, Holinshed transcribes ;
and Holinshed succeeding historians refer to as an authority ! Such is
the basis of historical assertion ! !

  " But the part of queen Elizabeth's story rendered most dramatic by
the legend-bearers is the circumstance of her being removed from a
prison to a throne. Here is a contrast in perfection. A frightful ex-
cavated recess: on the one hand, with bolts and bars rusted by noxious
vapours : on the other, a crown, the dazzling rays of diamonds, the ho-

A REVIEW

OF

Fox's Book of Martyrs,

CRITICAL AND HISTORICAL.

No. 52. Printed and Published by W. E. Andrews, 3, Chapter-house-court, St. Paul's Churchyard, London. **Price 3d.**

EXPLANATION OF THE ENGRAVING.—*Father Garnett, a Jesuit, who, though he had used his best endeavours to prevent the Powder Plot, yet was sentenced to be hung, drawn and quartered as a traitor.—On his way to execution, he was placed on the hurdle with his head out of it, to beat against the stones, in order to deprive him of his senses, and render him incapable to address the people.*

CONTINUATION OF THE REVIEW.

mage of the world, the possession of absolute power. In the back-ground (a striking figure !) behold ' blood-thirsty Mary !' In dreadful secresy she sharpens the knife intended to pierce, in the dark solitude of a dungeon, the bosom of her enchained sister!—The vizor would be highly attractive, says the fable, if it had brains ; and this story would be extremely interesting, if it were true.

" The prison from which Elizabeth was moved, on the death of her sister, was, it may be recollected, the palace of Hatfield. Here she had a retinue and establishment befitting her exalted rank. An extract from a curious MS. chronicle describes one of her entertainments as ' a great and rich maskinge, wher the pageants were marvellously furnished. There were thar twelve ministrels, anticly disguised, with forty six, or more, gentlemen and ladies, many of them knights or nobles ; and there was a devise of a castell of cloth of gold, &c. At night the cuppboard in the hall was of twelve stages, mainlie furnished, with garnish of gold and silver vessyl, and a banket of seventie dishes, &c. The next day the play of Holophernes was performed,

"Not only were the personal expenses of the princess unlimited, and her liberty entire, but she was allowed to maintain a sort of court at Hatfield, and possessed a palace in town. Strype tells us, that, on such a day, 'the lady Elizabeth came riding from her house at Hatfield to London, *attended with a great companie of lords, and noblemen and gentlemen,* unto her place called Somerset place, beyond Strand bridge to do her duty to the queen.' In another part he says, 'that ⬛⬛⬛⬛the lady Elizabeth's grace took her horse, and rode to her pa⬛⬛⬛⬛ne, with many lords, knights, ladies, and gentlemen, and a good⬛⬛ company of horse, (i. e. attendants).'

"Her visits to court were far from infrequent, and her entertainment there, now that she preserved herself from all suspicion of political intrigue, was friendly and magnificent. In one of her visits she went by water in the queen's barge, which was richly hung with garlands of artificial flowers, and covered with a canopy of the most costly description. Six boats attended the procession, filled with her highness's retinue, habited in russet-damask, and blue embroidered sattin, spangled with silver. On Christmas eve, the great hall of the palace was illuminated with a thousand lamps, curiously disposed. The princess supped at the same table in the hall with the king and queen, next to the cloth of state. On the 29th day of December, she sat with their majesties, at a grand spectacle of justing, &c.

"From these brief quotations, the nature of Mary's severity towards her sister must fully appear; and the drama of history be proved deficient in all but poetical justice. Would the woman, who treated an offensive sister with so much real generosity, have beheaded Mary queen of Scots?

"The invidious comparison between the sister-queens, suggested by most historians, and admired by many readers, surely, in this particular, defeats its own purpose. On a strict and fair parallel, Mary would be found deficient in two instances, which unhappily rendered nearly useless that natural integrity of heart, which, from her demeanour towards Elizabeth, I must believe she possessed:—She was inferior in strength of mind, and in those qualifications which are the result of instruction. It is well known that the Papists of this distant age were not fond of disseminating learning among the laity; and the priests from whom Mary received her education had a particular and obvious interest in preserving her in such a state of mental deficiency, as would render her a more obedient instrument of their wishes, should she ever attain supremacy in the state. On every occasion Mary's want of expanded views and extensive information may readily be detected. In no one instance did she ever exhibit proofs even of natural shrewdness, or untutored political ability. Is it not then equitable to place her acquiescence in religious cruelty which marked her reign rather to her want of independence of sentiment than to such a constitutional barbarity as would entitle her to the appellation of a sanguinary tyrant? When we view the extreme forbearance with which she acted in regard to Elizabeth, so truly offensive in so many particulars, we must be bigots, though in an opposite direction to Mary, if we persist in thinking otherwise, spirit may be inferred from her prudence, most of the great public.

"If (intent on preserving the stigma which historians have affixed to the name of this unfortunate princess) it is contended that Elizabeth was saved from destruction, purely by the interference of Philip, Mary's husband, I reply, that in no instance, on valid authority, can this be proved the case; but even admitting the possibility of such a presumption being correct, it must assuredly strengthen the grounds on which I affirm that scarcely any act of Mary's reign was the result of her personal inclination. Since, if she spared her most offensive foe, whether we look on the enmity as religious or otherwise, at the solicitation of a man who had not individual power to command, certainly, without determined to be impartial or unjust, we must suppose that she was equally undeterminate on all other subjects to which her assent was necessary.

"But Sir Thomas Wyat's conspiracy (a rare opportunity for ridding herself of her rival, if such a purpose had occupied her mind) occurred before her marriage. From this peril therefore, of course, Elizabeth was not preserved by her brother-in-law. Philip was likewise absent in Spain for a considerable period, and a sanguinary tyrant would scarcely have failed to profit by his absence. A thousand hands only waited for her signal to stretch Elizabeth a corpse on the floor of that Hertfordshire palace, which, by favour of a poetical license, our historians are pleased to term a dungeon.

"Should any writer undertake the history of this reign, with the generous wish of eliciting truth, he will find more MS. chronicles to assist his labour than would the narrator of any other remote period of our history; and I repeat that, from Mary's conduct in regard to Elizabeth, accurately investigated, he will be able to exhibit her personal character in a light quite different from that in which it has usually been placed."

The liberal sentiments thus expressed by this Protestant writer does equal credit to his head and heart. He has most triumphantly vindicated Mary's character from the charge of *blood-thirstiness*, so cruelly and unjustly lavished on her by bigotted and unprincipled writers. We must however differ from the opinion he has formed of Mary's education, which we think did not restrict her mental faculties, nor did she display any deficiency in the exercise of her intellectual capacities, more than the constitutional sovereign does to the capricious tyrant. Mary followed the principles of justice according to the rule of her ancestors; Elizabeth knew no other system than that of expediency and her own despotic will. Mary's letters to her brother Edward, the lords of the council, her discourse with Ridley, and other documents preserved by Dodd, in this Church History, by no means betray a want of political or theological ability.

Desirous to place on record the most exceptionable testimony in favour of this slandered princess, we shall produce four other Protestant historians as witnesses on her side. Collier writes thus:—"It may be affirmed, without panegyric, that the queen's private life was all along strict and unblemished. It must be said, that religion had the over-balance: the other world was uppermost with her; and she valued her conscience above her crown......That she was not of a vindictive implacable spirit, may be inferred from her pardoning most of the great men in Northumberland's rebellion." (*Eccl. Hist.* vol. ii. b. 6. p. 406.) Camden says, "A princess never sufficiently to be commended of all men, for her pious and religious demeanour, her commiseration towards the poor, and her magnificence and liberality towards the nobility and churchmen." (*Intr. to the Annals of Q. Eliz.* p. 10.) Echard testifies, "She was a woman of a strict and severe life; who allowed herself few of those diversions belonging to courts: was constant at her devotions, &c..... She much endeavoured to expiate, and restore the sacrileges of the last reigns." (*Hist. of Eng.* p. 327.) And Fuller states, that " she hated to equivocate in her own religion; and always was what she was, without dissembling her judgment, or practice, for fear or flattery....She had been a worthy princess, had as little cruelty been done under, as was done by her." (*Ch. Hist.* b. viii. p. 42.)

We shall close this vindication of the memory of a calumniated and ill-treated virtuous princess with Dr. Lingard's vivid delineation of Mary's character;—" The foulest blot (he says) on the character of this queen is her long and cruel persecution of the reformers. The sufferings of the victims naturally beget an antipathy to the woman, by whose authority they were inflicted. It is, however, but fair to recollect what I have already noticed, that the extirpation of erroneous doctrine was inculcated as a duty by the leaders of every religious party. Mary only practised what *they* taught. It was her misfortune, rather than her fault, that she was not more enlightened than the wisest of her contemporaries.

" With this exception, she has been ranked by the more moderate of the reformed writers among the best, though not the greatest of our princes. They have borne honourable testimony to her virtues; have allotted to her the praise of piety and clemency, of compassion for the poor, and liberality to the distressed; and have recorded her solicitude to restore to opulence the families that had been unjustly deprived of their possessions by her father and brother, and to provide for the wants of the parochial clergy who had been reduced to penury by the spoliations of the last government. It is acknowledged that her moral character was beyond reproof. It extorted respect from all even the most virulent of her enemies. The ladies of her household copied the conduct of their mistress, and the decency of Mary's court was often mentioned with applause by those, who lamented the dissoluteness which prevailed in that of her successor.

" The queen was thought by some to have inherited the obstinacy of her father: but there was this difference, that before she formed her decisions, she sought for advice and information, and made it an invariable rule to prefer right to expediency. One of the outlaws, who had obtained his pardon, hoped to ingratiate himself with Mary by devising a plan to render her independent of parliament. He submitted it to the inspection of the Spanish ambassador, by whom it was recommended to her consideration. Sending for Gardiner, she bade him peruse it, and then abjured him, as he should answer at the judgment seat of God, to speak his real sentiments. 'Madam,' replied the prelate, ' it is a pity that so virtuous a lady should be surrounded by such sycophants. The book is naught: it is filled with things too horrible to be thought of.' She thanked him, and threw the paper into the fire.....

" It had been the custom of her predecessors to devote the summer months to 'progresses' through different counties. But these journeys produced considerable injury and inconvenience to the farmers, who were not only compelled to furnish provisions to the purveyors at inadequate prices, but were withdrawn from the labours of the harvest to aid with their horses and waggons in the frequent removals of the court, and of the multitude which accompanied it. Mary, through consideration for the interests and comforts of the husbandmen, denied herself this pleasure; and generally confined her excursions to Croydon, a manor belonging to the church of Canterbury. There it formed her chief amusement to walk out in the company of her maids, without any distinction of dress, and in this disguise to visit the houses of the neigbouring poor. She inquired into their circumstances, relieved their wants, spoke in their favour to her officers, and often, when the family was numerous, apprenticed, at her own expense, such of the children as appeared of promising dispositions.....

" Though her parliaments were convoked for temporary purposes, they made several salutary enactments, respecting the offence of treason, the office of sheriff, the powers of magistrates, the relief of the poor, and the practice of the courts of law. The merit of these may probably be due to her council; but of her own solicitude for the equal administration of justice, we have a convincing proof. It had long been complained that in suits, to which the crown was a party, the subject, whatever were his right, had no probability of a favourable decision, on account of the superior advantages claimed and enjoyed by the counsel for the sovereign. When Mary appointed Morgan chief justice of the court of common pleas, she took the opportunity to express her disapprobation of this grievance. ' I charge you, sir,' said she, ' to minister the law and justice indifferently, without respect of person ; and, notwithstanding the old error among you, which will not admit any witness to speak, or other matter to be heard in favour of the adversary, the crown being a party, it is my pleasure, that whatever can be brought in favour of the subject, may be admitted and heard. You are to sit there, not as advocates for me, but as indifferent judges between me and my people.'.....

" Mary may also claim the merit of having supported the commercial interests of the country against the pretensions of a company of foreign merchants, which had existed for centuries in London, under the different denominations of Easterlings, merchants of the Hanse towns, and merchants of the Steelyard. By their readiness to advance loans of money on sudden emergencies, they had purchased the most valuable privileges from several of our monarchs. They formed a corporation, governed by its own laws : whatever duties were exacted from others, they paid no more than one per cent. on their merchandize : they were at the same time buyers and sellers, brokers and carriers : they imported jewels and bullion, cloth of gold and silver, tapestry and wrought silk, arms, naval stores, and household furniture : and exported wool and woollen cloths, skins, lead and tin, cheese and beer, and Mediterranean wines. Their privileges and wealth, gave them a superiority over all other merchants, which excluded competi-

tion, and enabled them to raise or depress the prices almost at pleasure. In the last reign the public feeling against them had been
manifested by frequent acts of violence, and several petitions had been
presented to the council, complaining of the injuries suffered by the
English merchants. After a long investigation it was declared, that
the company had violated, and consequently had forfeited its charter:
but by dint of remonstrances, of presents, and of foreign intercession,
it obtained, in the course of a few weeks, a royal licence to resume
the traffic under the former regulations. In Mary's first parliament,
a new blow was aimed at its privileges: and it was enacted in the
bill of tonnage and poundage, that the Easterlings should pay the
same duties as other foreign merchants. The queen, indeed, was induced to suspend, for awhile, the operation of the statute; but she
soon discerned the true interests of her subjects, revoked the privi-
ledges of the company, and refused to listen to the arguments adduced,
or the intercession made in its favour. Elizabeth followed the policy
of her predecessor: the steelyard was at length shut up; and the
Hanse towns, after a long and expensive suit, yielded to necessity, and
abandoned the contest."

v. The modern editors of Fox charge Mary with being "unacquainted
with the *constitution of the country*," and that "she sought to *domineer
over* the rights of *private judgment* and *trample* on the *privileges of mankind*." The above facts, however, prove most incontestibly that Mary
was not only a constitutional queen, but that she was careful of the
privileges of her subjects, and anxious that justice should be meeted
out to them. Had these editors applied the charge to their darling
Bess, they would not have swerved from the truth. This lady has
been lauded to the skies as a pattern to all sovereigns, though there
never was a more merciless tyrant on the throne of England, not even
excepting her father Henry. We have given her character from the
pen of the last named historian, in the first volume, page 147, and we
recommend its perusal here, that the unprejudiced Protestant may
see how much he has hitherto been deceived in the conduct of Elizabeth, and be enabled to draw a fair contrast between the qualities of
the two sisters. We will say nothing of Elizabeth's birth, but let her
be judged by her actions after she came to the crown.—In the first
place she committed perjury, by swearing to protect the Catholic religion, and immediately after destroying it.—If she preferred the new
doctrines, why not openly avow her sentiments, as her sister did in favour of the old faith, and not call Heaven to witness what she did not
intend to perform! She destroyed most of the ancient nobility of the
kingdom by the most unjust and iniquitous ways, and raised up a race
of titled upstarts, governed by the worst vices.—She persecuted and
displaced the old clergy, who were men of learning, and thrust in their
places the refuse and scum of the ecclesiastical order, as well as idle
tradesmen, who thought they should get more by thumping a cushion
than mending a kettle. She sold licences, pardons, dispensations, &c.
and put military law into execution on trivial occasions. In a word,
authentic history proves that Elizabeth was a sovereign disregardless
of the honour of her crown, or the lives and property of her subjects;

yet, being the founder of the Church established by law, she is cried up
by those interested in its loaves and fishes, and others out of hatred to
the ancient faith, as a glorious queen, and the honour of her country.

The modern editors, after giving near 360 pages of the sufferings
of martyrs, as they are dubbed, conclude their tenth book with some
remarks on "the severe punishment of God upon the persecutors of
his people, and such as have been blasphemers, &c." which are not
worth criticising. We shall, therefore, dismiss this book with one observation.—If national calamities are to be considered a mark of God's
judgment on the wicked, the broils and civil wars, the execution of a
king, the exilement of his son for years, the foundation of debts,
taxes, poor-rates, pauperism, and every evil that can impoverish and
enslave a people—all which may be traced in the page of history, as
progressively befalling this country, since the period of the Reformation so called, and are now nearly arrived at a crisis, threatening the
most dreadful results—England has most assuredly experienced God's
wrath, for abandoning the religion he came on earth to establish with
his blood, and which was the creed of the country for more than nine
hundred years.

BOOK XI.

THE eleventh Book of this work is headed—"A general Account of
the Attempts made by the Papists to overturn the Protestant Government of England, from the Accession of Queen Elizabeth to the Reign
of George II."—It commences with "The Spanish Armada," of which
we shall only say, that if this was an attempt by the Papists to overturn Elizabeth's government, the Catholics of England were not parties
to it, as it is acknowledged by all authorities worthy of credit, that
they took the most conspicuous part, and were principally successful, in
destroying this Spanish Armada.—One fact we think quite sufficient to
establish this statement, and that is, that the lord high admiral who
commanded the English fleet was a Catholic. As to the instruments
of torture, the modern editors had better look at home, as we shall, in
our next volume display barbarities practised, on Catholics, in Elizabeth's reign, which none but monsters of cruelty could enforce.

THE GUNPOWDER PLOT.

The next subject is the "Horrid Conspiracy by the Papists for the
destruction of James I. the Royal Family, and both Houses of Parliament; commonly known by the name of the Gun-powder Plot." Had
the modern editors termed it a horrid conspiracy on the part of Protestant statesmen, for the destruction of the Catholics of England, they
would have come much nearer the truth.—The father of James I. was
actually blown up with gunpowder at his house at Kirk-a-field, near
Edinburgh, as he lay sick in his bed, by Protestant conspirators; but it
was not intended to serve James in like manner. This plot was a
sham one, to answer political purposes, contrived by Cecil, the secretary of state, and the hypocritical celebration of it with the mockery of
a religious ceremony, was jocosely called by James himself, Cecil's Ho-

liday. That there were a few desperate Catholics engaged in it we do not deny; but it should be also known that to a Catholic lord is attributed the discovery of it.—It is admitted by all men of learning and sound understanding, at this day, that the plot was a *forgery* palmed upon the people to inspire them with hatred against the Catholics, and conceal the designs which the then ministry entertained, and afterwards put into execution, of harassing, robbing, and persecuting the remnant of the Catholic aristocracy who had escaped the fangs of Elizabeth's satellites. The author of "*The Political Catechism*," printed in 1658, the Hon. Peter Talbot, an ingenious writer, says, that Cecil was not so secret in his intrigues, but that some of his own domestics became acquainted with them, and, in consequence, a friend of one of them, a Catholic, named Buck, was advised, two months before the disclosure of the plot, to be upon his guard, as great mischief was in the forge against the Catholics.

We shall content ourselves, on this subject, with giving the following acute remarks on the *Gunpowder Plot* by Dr. Milner, which we extract from the seventh of his unanswerable *Letters to a Prebendary*. "I have mentioned," writes the venerable author, "some of the reasons there are for supposing that Cecil, earl of Salisbury, was as deep in this plot, as his father, lord Burleigh, is proved to have been in that of Babington.—(*Politician's Catechism*.) Certain it is, that these reasons have had equal weight with many intelligent Protestants, as with Catholics. One of them calls it, ' a neat device of the secretary;'—(*Osborne's Hist. Memoirs of James* I.)—another says, that he ' engaged some Papists in this desperate plot, in order to divert the king from making any advances towards Popery, to which he seemed inclinable, in the minister's opinion.'—(*The author of the Political Grammar*.) James himself was so sensible of the advantages which his minister reaped from this plot, that he used afterwards to call the 5th of November, Cecil's Holiday. Finally, a third Protestant writer assures us, ' that this design was first hammered in the forge of Cecil, who intended to have produced it in the time of Elizabeth;.....that, by his secret emissaries, he enticed some hot-headed men, who, ignorant whence the design first came, heartily engaged in it.'—(*Short View of Eng. Hist. by Bev. Higgons*.)— Thus much seems certain, that the famous letter delivered by an unknown messenger to Lord Monteagle, never was written by a real conspirator, whose life was concerned in the issue of the plot. Such a character would not unnecessarily, and with infinite risk to his cause and his life, have given his friend a written notice not to attend parliament, at a time when he could not know whether parliament would or would not be further prorogued, and whether a hundred accidents might not otherwise prevent Monteagle from being present at it. He would not have given such advice ten days before parliament could possibly meet, when the previous notice of a few hours, or even minutes, would have answered the supposed purpose as effectually in his friend's regard, and ensured his own safety. In a word, he would not have explained the nature of the horrid scheme, in those significant terms which occur in the letter, to a person who is supposed not to have been sufficiently tried to be admitted into the band of conspirators. But if, on the other hand, we suppose the letter to have been written and sent by Cecil in order to draw that young lord into the punishment, if not into the guilt of the conspiracy, and that, in case he had not made it known, other Catholic peers, in succession, would have received similar letters, a certain space of time was evidently necessary for this purpose, and still more so for devising the means of breaking the matter to James himself, so as to give himself the credit of first discovering the mystery.

"Secondly, The secretary's delaying for the space of five days to communicate a business of that importance to his master, and his purposely deferring to have the cellars under the parliament-house examined previously to the very day of opening the session, prove that he had the management of the plot in his hands, and that he delayed the disclosure of it in order to have time for throwing his net over a greater number of persons, and those of higher quality than were yet engaged in it.*

"Thirdly, The character and history of Francis Tresham, esq. one of the conspirators, leads us to suspect that he was to the earl of Salisbury in this plot, what Maud and Polley had been to his father, lord Burleigh and Walsingham, in a former plot, almost twenty years before. Tresham was of a restless and intriguing disposition, and had been concerned in the conspiracy of the earl of Essex. He was well acquainted with Cecil, and is known to have had some communications with him concerning the affairs of the Catholics. At the disclosure of the plot, he never attempted to fly, presuming, no doubt, that he was sufficiently protected at court; but, on the contrary, he offered his services to apprehend the conspirators. (*Baker's Chron.*) Being, however, seized upon and committed to the Tower, he met with a sudden death in the course of a very few days, and before any trial or examination had taken place. On this occasion a report was spread abroad, that he was carried off by a strangury, which is not a disorder that takes a sudden turn; whereas the physician who attended him pronounced that he died of poison.†—(*Wood, Athen. Oxon.*)

"Lastly, The fraudulent art and consummate hypocrisy with which it is now evident that Cecil acted in disclosing this plot, confirms the idea that he had the management of it from the beginning. It is proved then from this secretary's own papers, that he had known of a conspiracy amongst the Papists, of some kind or other, three months before the letter was brought to him by Monteagle, Oct. 26. (*Relation of the Discovery, Archæol,* vol. xii. p. 203.) It is proved by his own confidential letter to the ambassador at the court of Spain, written immediately after the breaking out of the plot, (Nov. 9, 1605. *Winwood's Memorials,* vol. ii. p. 170.) that he was acquainted with the whole diabolical malice of it, viz. that it was intended to blow up the parliament with gunpowder. Accordingly, as soon as he had received the letter, he communicated it for his own security to the lord chamberlain Suffolk, whose office it was to attend to the security of the parliament-house when the king was to go thither: and these two ministers conversed together about the different apartments adjoining to it, and particularly about

---

"* See a Relation of the discovery of the Gunpowder, &c. preserved in the Paper Office, and corrected in the hand writing of Cecil, earl of Salisbury.—(*Archæol.* vol. xii. p. 204.)
"† Tresham was upon such terms with Cecil that he had access to him at all hours, not only of the day, but also of the night.—(*Politician's Catechism,* p. 94.) Goodman, bishop Gloucester, quoted by Foulis, in his Popish Treasons, expressly says that Tresham wrote of the letter to Monteagle. If so, it cannot be questioned who dictated it."

the great vault under it. (*Winwood's Memorials*.) They agreed, however, (that is to say, the prime minister thought it best) that the search in it should not be made before the session of parliament, which was not to take place for ten days, in order, as he confesses, that ‘ the plot might run to full ripeness ;’ (*Relation of the Discovery*) and to see whether any other ‘ nobleman would receive a similar advertisement,’ (*Ibid.*) that is, to allow him time to send fresh letters to persons of that rank (whom most of all he wished to entangle) if he found it expedient ; finally, to attack the king on his weak side, by making him pass for the Solomon of Great Britain, and to work up the nation to a paroxysm of fury against the Papists, by the apparently imminent danger to which all that was illustrious in it would appear to have been exposed. Having in his custody a letter of this importance to the nation and the king's person, he nevertheless declined giving James any information of it, by writing or messenger, where he was, at Royston, during five whole days, that is to say, during half the time that he was to run before the winding up of the catastrophe ; because he wished to deliver it in person, in order to guide both the king and the plot to his intended ends. On the last day of October, (*Relation of the Discovery*) the king being then at Whitehall, he presents the letter privately ; no one but himself and the earl of Suffolk being present. We are told that neither of them delivered any opinion of his own concerning its contents, attending to hear ‘ his majesty's conceit ;’ and there is no doubt that Cecil then addressed to him that fulsome and ridiculous compliment, which he afterwards committed to writing as his genuine sentiments concerning him, viz. that ‘ his majesty was endued with the most admirable guifts of piercing conceit, and a solide judgement that was ever heard, of in any age ; but accompanied also with a kind of divine power in judging of the nature and consequence of such advertisements.’ (*Ibid.* p. 205.) Such a bait was too well seasoned for James's appetite, not to be swallowed by him. Accordingly, at the opening of parliament a few days afterwards, the king declared himself to have been supernaturally assisted in detecting the plot, (*King's Speech, Nov. 9, Journal of Lords*,) by interpreting the letter in a different manner from any other learned man, however well qualified, would have done. (*Relation, &c.*) His artful minister, still more to indulge his vanity, and afford him greater matter of subsequent triumph, affected to ridicule the whole business, telling him, that ‘ the letter must be written either by a fool or a madman, because of those words in it, *the danger is past as soon as you have burnt this letter* ; for if the danger were so soon past, what need of any warning.’ (*Echard's History of England. Baker's Chronicle.*) The king, notwithstanding, persisted in interpreting the letter as every other man, without his majesty's inspiration, would have done, namely, he said there was a mine stored with gunpowder under the parliament-house ; and accordingly, he ordered it to be searched for. Cecil however makes him insensibly fall into the measure which he had previously concerted with the lord chamberlain, to defer the examination until the very eve of the parliament's meeting. Accordingly, in the evening of that day, the chamberlain surveys the parliament-house and the vault under it, and finds every thing just as he expected. He sees the heap of faggots under which the powder was collected, and he meets with Guy Fawkes, who had been engaged to fire it. The moment, however, was not yet come for disclosing the catastrophe of the drama with suitable effect. Hence it was pretended that this visit into the vaults below was made for the purpose of looking for some furniture belonging to the king, (*Archæol.* vol. xii. p. 206,) and though the lord chamberlain, as Cecil himself tells us, (*Ibid.* p. 207,) 'observed the commodity of the place for devilish purposes,' and suspected Fawkes, on hearing he was the servant of Percy, he neither gave any orders then for examining the former, nor for detaining the latter. (*Ibid.*) At length, near the solemn hour of midnight, sir Thomas Knevet, a popular justice of peace, is sent with his attendants to secure that wretch, and to uncover the barrels of powder, by which means the news of the discoveries would reach the members of parliament in the morning just as they were preparing to attend it. Thus Cecil gained his second point, that of rousing the nation to a degree of consternation and horror, proportionable to the supposed nearness of its approach to the brink of destruction, and of making its escape appear the effect of a particular providence, and absolutely miraculous. Accordingly the people were taught to believe, that as nothing less than inspiration had enabled the king rightly to interpret Monteagle's letter; so nothing short of a miracle (*Archæol.* vol. xii. p. 196) had enabled ministry to find thirty-six barrels of gunpowder lying on the ground, and only covered over with faggots, a few hours before they were to have been fired; whereas, we have seen, that they knew of gunpowder being lodged in the very cellar where it was found, at least ten days before, and that they agreed together not to look for it till this very time, that is, till the very day of the parliament's meeting."

FIRE OF LONDON AND POPISH PLOT.

We are next treated with an "Account of the Horrid Plot concerted by the Papists for destroying the City of London by Fire, in the year 1666." Of this event we shall say no more than what we have said in our first volume of this Review, page 23, to which we refer our readers. Next follows the "Life and Death of sir Edmundbury Godfrey, with an Account of the Popish and Meal Tub Plots." The death of sir Edmundbury Godfrey is still involved in mystery, but not the odium, which remains to this day fixed upon the Catholics by bigots, though a slight reflection will satisfy any reasonable man, that the Catholics were the last persons in the world, so far as regarded their own interest, to commit such a crime. Of the Popish or Oates's Plot, no one but the most blind and bloated entertain any doubt of the flagitious perjuries that were committed by the villain Oates and his colleagues to swear away the lives of innocent Catholics. We have published a Narrative of this Plot, to which we refer our readers for a full development of that disgraceful event. The modern editors say, that Oates "made the most solemn appeal to heaven, on his trial for perjury, and the strongest protestations of the veracity of his testimony." This may be, for the man who could swear away the lives of innocent persons, would not scruple to swear himself honest, to save himself from punishment. But, observe, reader, he was found guilty on the evidence of SIXTY persons, nine of them Protestants. The Meal tub Plot is too contemptible to call for a single remark,

It has been well observed that the time of the Stuarts was an age of forgery, plots, perjury, and imposture, practised for the purpose, and but too successfully, of exciting public feeling against the Catholics and their religion. Some of these were of the most preposterous nature, and wholly discreditable, yet were they believed by the poor deluded people, who were now become as mad as March hares, having been bitten with the *poperyphobia*.

MODERN PROTESTANT MARTYRS.

To the martyrs of John Fox, we have now a list of traitors graced with that title. The first is Stephen College, called the *Protestant Joiner*, who was a furious partizan in Oates's Plot, and was convicted of high treason, for which he was executed. Of this man the modern editors say,—" thus died Mr. College, whose blood, as he himself desired it might, *sufficiently spoke* the justice of his cause, and who seemed in his speech, to have some *prophetic* intimations, that his blood would not be the last which must be shed to satisfy *the cravings of tyranny and Papistry*." Now, reader, this man's Judge, Jury, and witnesses were all *Protestants*, observe, and the Continuator of *Baker's Chronicle* says,— " Dugdale, Turberville and others, swore many dangerous and treasonable words against him, which such an indiscreet hot man was likely enough to speak, though without any thought of putting them in practice. College was upon a negative; so that he could only defend himself by invalidating the credit of the witnesses. The famous Titus Oates engaged now openly with his brethren, Dugdale and Turberville ; and the positive contradictions upon oath that passed between ese men at this trial, lessened very much the credit of the plot they had before sworn to. Oates attested solemnly, that Dugdale and Turberville, had both denied to him that they knew any thing against College, with some other things to weaken their testimony; while the others in return protested on their oaths, that every thing he testified so confidently was utterly false ; so that they fell out in the open court in a very indecent manner. This made good diversion for those who disbelieved the plot; but it was very shocking to considerate persons to see what wretches these were whose testimony had taken away so many lives, and thrown the nation into such a dangerous combustion."

Lord William Russell is next on the list, as deep a traitor and as intolerant a religionist as could be found in those days. When lord Stafford was found guilty, on the perjuries of Oates, and sentenced *to be hanged*, the king commuted his punishment to beheading, in consequence of his rank. This lord William Russel denied the power of the king to alter the sentence, and actually carried up an address from the Commons to that effect. A very charitable saint, truly, but a fit associate for the modern editors. Then comes Algernon Sidney, another traitor of the deepest hue ; and amongst the rest Alderman Cornish, who was sheriff when lord Stafford was executed, and strove hard to have him hanged like a common person. Monmouth's rebellion is also introduced, and the barbarities of Jefferies, a *Protestant* Judge, and Kirk, a *Protestant* Colonel, are laid to the charge of the Catholics. This is an act of barefaced injustice, too glaring to require comment, and none but the most prejudiced would make the charge.

IRISH MASSACRE.

We are also presented with the "Rise and Progress of the Protestant Religion in Ireland; with an Account of the barbarous Massacre of 1641."—The reader is already in possession of the cruelties, the robberies, the murders, and other horrible crimes which marked the blood-stained progress of the Reformation, as it is called, in Ireland. Of the massacre in 1641, on which so much has been said and written, and on which the bigots are never tired of ringing the changes, we shall be more explicit, and give to the reader authentic facts on which he may form a correct conclusion.—The modern editors say, "The design of this horrid conspiracy was, that a general insurrection should take place at the same time throughout the kingdom; and that all the Protestants, without exception, should be murdered. The day fixed for this horrible massacre was the 23d of October, 1641, the feast of Ignatius Loyola, founder of the Jesuits, and the chief conspirators in the principal parts of the kingdom made the necessary preparations for the intended conflict."—Now, unfortunately for the veracity of the modern editors, the feast of Ignatius Loyola is celebrated by the Catholic church on the 31st of July, and therefore the Jesuits may stand excused of intending to honour their founder with a general massacre. They further say, "The day preceding that appointed for carrying this horrid design into execution was now arrived, when, happily for the metropolis of the kingdom, the conspiracy was discovered by one Owen O'Connelly, an Irishman, for which most signal service the English parliament voted him 500*l.* and a pension of 200*l.* during life."—Fortunately for the cause of truth, we have before us Mr. Carey's admirable work, called *Vindiciæ Hiberniæ*, in which he gives us the examination of this Owen O'Connally, and a greater Munchausen tale never was told. This able writer proves, on the authority of Temple, that "notwithstanding the pretended generality of the plot, the lords justices, by public proclamation, on the 29th of October, declared that the insurrection was confined to the mere old Irish of the province of Ulster and others who adhered to them." This strong fact proves the inaccuracy of the statement as to the general extent of the conspiracy, and the plot "that all the Protestants, without exception, should be murdered."—This writer also observes, "That the original views of the insurgents did not comprehend a general massacre, or even single murders, we have further testimony, clear and decisive, derived even from Temple, as well as Warner and Leland, which, independent of all other proof, would be sufficient to settle this question for ever, and utterly overwhelm O'Connally's perjured legend. Moreover, if there had been a plot for a general insurrection, and such a massacre as O'Connally swore to, there would have been evidence produced from some of the conspirators: but notwithstanding the lord justices had recourse to the execrable aid of the rack, and put Mac-Mahon and others to the torture, there is not, in the examinations of the former, a single word to corroborate the sanguinary part of O'Connally's deposition. The examinations of the rest were never published. There is not to be found in Temple, Borlace, Carte, Warner, Leland, Clarendon, nor as far as I have seen, in Rushworth, the examination of a single person engaged in a con-

spiracy which was said to have extended throughout the whole kingdom, except those of Mac-Mahon and lord Macguire ! ! ! ! !   That of the
latter was not taken till March, 1642.

The modern editors follow up their description of a general massacre,
which we have shewn to be false, with a detail of particulars unsupported by authority, purporting to shew that the bloody work was not
of one day, but that the Protestants fell victims to the fury of the Irish
in all parts of the kingdom, day after day. They, however, take care
to suppress the cruel acts of tyranny which drove the unfortunate people to deeds which every feeling heart must deplore, and wish for humanity sake they were buried in oblivion. To exculpate the Catholics of
Ireland from the charges brought against them, we shall here enter
into some of the grievances inflicted on them before they resorted to
this act of desperation. At the beginning of Charles's reign, the Irish
experienced a degree of lenity and toleration to which they had been
strangers, since the era of "evangelical liberty;" but the clamours of
the Puritan party compelled this prince to recall his indulgent deputy,
lord Falkland, and entrust the administration of the kingdom to two
lords justices, namely, viscount Ely and the earl of Cork. Of these
two Protestant statesmen, Leland, the Irish historian, says, "They,
without waiting for the king's instructions, fell at once with great severity
on the recusants, and *soon extended the most rigorous execution of the
penal laws to every part of the kingdom.*" These merciless deputies were
succeeded by the earl of Strafford, then lord Wentworth, who took upon
him the charge of government in 1633, and held it until a short period
of his death, which happened by decapitation on the 12th of May, 1641.
The transactions of this governor are thus spoken of by Mr. W. Parnell,
in his *Historical Apology for the Irish Catholics.* "Another material
cause of the rebellion, (says Mr. P.) which had no connection with
religion, was lord Strafford's resumption of the plan *for confiscating the
province of Connaught.* The unfortunate landed proprietors had already
twice purchased their titles from *the crown,* yet Strafford did not hesitate to outrage every feeling of humanity, and every rule of justice, by
subverting them a *third time.* This transaction may not perhaps
be the most infamous that ever occurred, but certainly the most infamous act of oppression that was ever perpetrated by *a plea of law,* under
the *sanction of juries.* It is uncomfortable to dwell on so abominable
an outrage, it is sufficient to observe, that it was in *part carried by silence,* by fining the sheriffs, imprisoning jurors, and fining them to the
amount of 4000l. each, by the terrors of the Star-chamber, and the presence of the lord deputy." Another cause, in which religion was concerned, was the perfidy of the Protestant governors, in cajoling the
Irish Parliament to grant subsidies to the king, and after obtaining the
money, withholding from the people the promised benefits stipulated in
return. It must here be observed that the Irish parliament consisted
mostly of Catholic noblemen and gentlemen, and as the refractory disposition of the Protestant parliament of England prevented the king
from succeeding in gaining the necessary supplies from the Puritan
members, he had recourse to his Irish Catholic subjects, and the readiness with which they complied with his demands, will be best related
by the insertion of the following letter from the privy counsellors, mem-

bers of the Irish house of commons, to secretary Windebank, in 1639, taken from lord Strafford's State Letters, vol. ii, fol. 397 :—

"Sir,—The happy resolution, this day taken in the commons house of parliament, and the observable circumstances which occurred therein to our view, who have the honour to serve his majesty as his privy council here; and who, as members of the house of commons, were present, and co operating in that resolution, have rendered to us such inward joy and contentment, in the apprehension of the entire affections and great loyalty of this people, abundantly testified thereby, as we esteem it our duties to hasten the glad advertisement thereof to his sacred majesty.

"After the proposal of such acts of grace and advantage to the subject, as we conceived most fit to lead, in order to the propounding of the subsidies, six subsidies were demanded for his majesty: whereupon divers members of the house spake thereunto; some of the *natives* declaring that, as six were granted the last parliament towards enabling the king to pay the debts contracted for the occasions of his crown, and for the better settlement of the revenues: so, at this time, six or more, are fit to be given; it being apparent, that the peace and safety of the kingdom are become so nearly concerned.

"Some also of the natives shewing divers precedents in ancient times, and, among these, some whereby the king, by a mandate from himself alone, without a parliament, caused monies and goods to be taken in Ireland, from merchants and others, towards defraying the charges of his expeditions against the Scots, for the defence of his kingdom; and those having enlarged themselves in that point, mentioned the abundant piety and clemency of his majesty, in being so indulgent to his subjects, as to decline that example of his progenitors, and to require aid of his subjects in a parliamentary way; some of them said, that his majesty should have a fee simple of subsidies in their estates on like occasions, for the honour of his person, and safety of his kingdoms: it was fit to be done, though it were leaving themselves nothing besides hose and doublet. Some of them with much earnestness, after forward expressions of readiness towards advancing the business, concluded, that, as his majesty is the best of kings, so this people should strive to be ranked among the best of subjects.

"Thus, every of them seeming, in a manner, to contend one with another, who should shew most affection and forwardness to comply with his majesty's occasions, and all of them expressing, even with passion, how much they abhor and detest the Scotch covenanters, and how readily every man's hand ought to be laid to his sword, to assist the king in reducing of them by force to the obedience and loyalty subjects; they desired that themselves and others of this nation might have the honour to be employed in this expedition, and declared, with very great demonstration of cheerful affections, that their *hearts* contained *mines of subsidies* for his majesty; that twenty subsidies, if their abilities were equal with their desires, were too little to be given to so sacred a majesty, from whose princely clemency, by the ministration of the lords lieutenant, so many and so gracious favours are continually derived unto them.

"— In the end, considering the present condition of the kingdom, and how unable they are, without too much pressure to them to advance more at this time, they humbly besought that, by the lords lieutenant's interposition to his majesty, four subsidies might be accepted from them at this time; yet with declaration made by them, with as much demonstration of loyalty as ever nation or people, expressed towards a king, that, if more than these four should be requisite, and the occasions of the war continue, they will be ready to grant more, and to lay down their persons, lives and estates, at his majesty's feet, to further his royal design for correction of the disordered factions in Scotland, and reducing them to a right understanding of themselves, and for the defence and safety of his majesty's kingdoms and people. And they earnestly desired us, of the council then present, that immediately after the rising of the house, we would represent this from the house to the lord lieutenant; which they did with general acclamations and signs of joy and contentment, even to the throwing up of their hats, and lifting up their hands.

"The question being then put, for the granting of four subsidies, with such a declaration to be made besides the act of subsidies, it was unanimously assented to by the whole house; their being found therein not one negative voice: which we mention for the glory of his majesty, that hath so good and loyal subjects, and for the honour and government of this nation.

"And because no words are able fully to set forth the cheerfulness, wherewith this people did, in this particular, manifest their sense of his majesty's occasions, their desire to further his majesty's royal intentions, and their entire affections to the honour of his person ; and all with most lively expressions of duty and loyalty towards him ; we of his council could have wished, if it had been possible, that his majesty had been in his own person an eye witness of this day's carriage, which we humbly conceive would have been of far more value in his royal estimation than twenty subsidies.

These demonstrations of sincere loyalty were accompanied with a remonstrance of real grievances, among which *the persecutions* they had suffered on account of *their religion* were not the least ; and they solicited the enactment of certain laws, for the security of toleration, property, and justice. The king accepted the grants, and promised that these laws should be assented to ; but the Puritan faction, alarmed at the unshaken fidelity of the Catholics to the throne, by the basest and most treacherous arts, contrived to render the designs of the monarch abortive, and to foment what they called a Popish rebellion. At the head of this detestable party were the two lord-chief-justices, Borlase and Parsons, who succeeded lord Strafford, and *revived the persecutions* against the Catholics with unrelenting cruelty, disseminating, at the same time, throughout the kingdom, the different petitions presented by their faction to the English parliament, and calling for the *extirpation of the Popish religion* and the lives and estates of the professors thereof. The intolerant and disgraceful terms of the Scottish covenant, entered into by the Puritans of that country, and afterwards assented to by their brethren, in England, we have given in preceding pages : to alarm the Irish people, as to the designs of the covenanters, it is stated in Carte's Life of the Duke of Ormond, that " a letter was intercepted coming from Scotland to one Freeman of Antrim, giving an account that a covenanting army was ready to come for Ireland, under the command of general Lesley, to *extirpate* the Roman Catholics of Ulster, and leave the Scots *sole* possessors of that province ; and that to this end, a resolution had been taken in their private meetings and councils, to lay heavy fines upon such as would not appear at their kirks, for the first and second Sunday ; and on failure of the third, TO HANG *without mercy, all such as were obstinate* AT THEIR OWN DOORS. This notion, (adds Mr. Carte) as appears from a multitude of depositions taken before Dr. H. Jones, and other commissioners, prevailed universally among the rebels, and was chiefly insisted upon by them as one of the principal reasonings of their taking arms."—Enough has been said to prove, that so far from the Irish people living in a state of peace previous to their rising, they were smarting under the basest persecutions, and every engine was set to work by their merciless enemies to infuriate their minds, and urge them to deeds of vengeance: Thus instigated and alarmed for the safety of their lives as well as their consciences, some few of the Catholics in the north did take themselves to arms, and committed violences, at all times to be deplored, but not to the extent asserted by the modern editors.

Notwithstanding the unqualified assertion, that the insurrection was general, and that nothing less was intended than cutting the throats of all the English Protestants throughout the whole kingdom, it is a fact, incontestibly proved by unimpeachable testimony, that the rising was at first confined to the province of Ulster, and that few or no English

Protestants were destroyed at its commencement, or during its continuance. It is a farther truth, that upon intelligence being received of the commotion, the greater part of the Catholic nobility and gentry proffered their services to quell the insurrection, yet their offer was not only rejected, but they were themselves soon obliged to stand upon their own defence against the cruel villanies of the two Puritan chief-justices, one of whom, Parsons, had declared at a public entertainment, that "*within a twelvemonth, no Catholic should be seen in Ireland.*"

That we may not be accused of dealing in vague assertions, in refuting the vile falsehoods advanced by the modern editors, we shall confine ourselves to authenticated documents, which are the best tests in favour of a legitimate cause. In the first place, however, let the reader bear in mind, that for a considerable time previous to the actual rising of the Irish people, which is stated to have happened on the 23d of October, 1641, the Puritan leaders in the English parliament, those stanch stragglers for liberty of conscience, had been at variance with the king, principally on account of the lenity shewn to his Catholic subjects, and they had, by the most infamous intrigues, perverted the public mind, inflaming it to a degree of phrensy at the supposed bloody principles of Popery, notwithstanding they were constantly assailing the monarch with remonstrances to induce him to spill the blood of innocent Catholics. During these contentions with the sovereign, the Parliamentarians were fully sensible of the faithful and steady loyalty of the Irish Catholics to Charles, although a Protestant, and therefore they were determined to have their revenge. Instigated by this diabolical spirit, the faction kept up a correspondence with the Puritan justices, Parson and Borlase, who, accordingly, by their own authority, commanded many things contrary to the express direction of the king, for the double purpose of exasperating the Irish Catholics, and driving them to resistance.—"The favourite object, both of the Irish government and English parliament," says Leland, " was *the utter extermination of all the Catholic inhabitants of Ireland.* Their estates were already marked out, and allotted to the conquerors; so that they and their posterity were consigned to inevitable ruin." And well did these mercenaries play their parts. The Irish parliament having sent deputies over to England to obtain the consent of the king to some bills which had been passed by the two houses for the removal of grievances, his majesty expressly commanded the lords-justices by letter " to suffer that parliament to sit until his majesty should think fit to determine the same;" but, in order to prevent these bills from passing into laws, the lords-justices caused that parliament to be adjourned for three months, against the declared wish of its members, and that too but a few days before the arrival of the deputies from England with the royal assent; nor would they permit proclamation to be made, although urgently solicited so to do, of the gracious intentions of the sovereign to remove every subject of complaint. On the contrary, they were determined to drive the Catholics, who were looked upon already as rebels, by the most cruel measures, into a state of insurrection.—Accordingly, we find in Carte's Collection of Letters the following order from these lords-justices and the privy council to the earl of Ormonde, then lieutenant-general of the army, dated at the castle of Dublin, 22d

of February, 1641 :—"It is resolved, that it is fit that his lordship do
endeavour with his majesty's said forces to wound, *kill and destroy*, by
all the ways and means he may, all the said rebels, (meaning the CA-
THOLICS) and their adherents and relievers, and *burn, spoil, waste, consume, destroy* and *demolish*, all the *places towns, and houses,* where the
said rebels are, *or have been* relieved and harboured, and all the *corne
and hay* there, and KILL and DESTROY ALL THE MEN *there inhabiting,*
ABLE TO BEAR ARMS."

: On the 3d of March following, as we find from the same Collection,
the said lords-justices issued further orders to the earl of Ormonde,
directing him to march with 3000 foot and 500 horse " to such places
between the Boyne and the sea as his lordship should think fit; and
burn and destroy the rebels of the pale, WITHOUT EXCEPTION OF ANY. That
those, *who should offer to come in,* should in no other manner be taken
in than *as* PRISONERS *taken by the power and strength of his majesty's army.*
That, if any of them came to the army, it should be the SOLDIERS *that
seized on them, before they had access to his lordship; and that they should
be denied access to his person.* That *no difference* should be made between
the noblemen that were rebels and other rebels."—How these orders
were executed may be gathered from Dr. Nalson, a Protestant divine,
who, in his Historical Collection, assures us, that " the severities of the
provost-marshals, and the barbarism of the SOLDIERS to the *Irish,* were
such, that he heard a relation of his own, who was a captain in that service, relate that *no manner of compassion* or *discrimination* was shewed
either to *age* or *sex,* but that the *little children* were promiscuously sufferers with the guilty; and that, if any, who had some grains of compassion, reprehended the soldiers for this *unchristian inhumanity,* they
would scornfully reply, ' *Why nits will be lice!*' and so would dispatch
them."

- Goaded by these and numberless other acts of perfidiousness and
barbarity, can any one think it surprising that some of the Irish people
were in the end roused to commit reprisals on their inhuman persecutors? Is it not rather a matter of surprise that they bore the nefarious
practices of their despotic rulers with such patience and forbearance?
Would Protestants have been so quiet under Catholic governors? Did
the German Lutherans, or the French Calvinists, display such patient
suffering under Charles V. and the Bourbons, as the Irish Catholics
under Puritan intolerance? Have we not seen the Protestants repeatedly in arms against Mary, and every artifice used to stir up sedition,
while she was sedulously devising, and earnestly desirous that *all* her
subjects should be governed *by law* and *justice,* and secured in their property and comforts? Had, in fact, the Puritans in Scotland and England a twentieth part of the grievances to complain of against Charles
and his ministers, which the Irish Catholics had against them? See
what Dr. Warner, who was by no means desirous of favouring the
Irish, says of the rebellion :—" The arbitrary power exercised by these
lords-justices; their illegal exertion of it by bringing people to *the rack*
to draw *confessions* from them; their sending out so many parties from
Dublin and the other garrisons *to destroy the rebels,* in which expeditions care was seldom taken to discriminate, and men, women, and
children, were promiscuously slain; but, above all, the *martial-law,*

executed by sir Charles Coote, and *the burning of the pale for seventeen miles in length*, and *twenty-five in breadth*, by the earl of Ormonde. *These* measures not only exasperated the rebels, and *induced* them to commit the like or greater cruelties, but they terrified the nobility and gentry out of all thoughts of submission, and convinced them that there was no room to hope for pardon ; *nor no means of safety left them but in the sword.*[1] Thus the Irish people found themselves *compelled* to arm ; and yet this rising is called by the modern editors and English historians an unnatural and odious insurrection, while the rebellion of the English and Scotch covenanters, fomented by imaginary discontent and religious delusion, is still looked upon as a meritorious struggle for civil and religious freedom ! ! !

We have thus established, on the clearest evidence, the fact, that this Irish massacre, as it is called, was originated by Protestants, whose cruelties and extortions urged the Catholics to deeds of retaliation. It is now time to return to the modern editors, They proceed in a strain of unblushing impudence, and a total disregard of truth, to detail a variety of instances of imputed murders and acts of barbarity, through which it is impossible to follow them, as they take care to suppress both dates and authorities to prevent us from probing their veracity. It is true, they occasionally give the name of a place to throw dust in the eyes of *their* readers. We will here give the following for examples:—

" At the town of Lissenskeath they hanged above 100 Scottish Protestants, shewing them no more mercy than they did the English...

" Upwards of 1000 men, women, and children, were driven, in different companies, to Portendown bridge, which was broken in the middle, and there compelled to throw themselves into the water ; and such as attempted to reach the shore were knocked on the head.

" In the same part of the country, at least 4000 persons were drowned in different places. The inhuman Papists, after first stripping them, drove them like beasts to the spot fixed for their destruction ; and if any, through fatigue, or natural infirmities, were slack in their pace, they pricked them with their swords and pikes ; and to strike a farther terror on the multitude, they murdered some by the way. Many of these poor creatures, when thrown into the water, endeavoured to save themselves by swimming to the shore ; but their merciless persecutors prevented their endeavours taking effect, by shooting them in the water.

" In *one place* 140 English, after being driven for many miles stark naked, and in the most severe weather, were all murdered on the same spot, some being hanged, others burnt, some shot, and many of them buried alive ; and so cruel were their tormentors, that they would not suffer them *to pray* before they robbed them of their miserable existence....

" In Kilkenny all the Protestants, without exception, were put to death ; and some of them in so cruel a manner, as, perhaps, was never before thought of. They beat an Englishwoman with such savage barbarity, that she had scarce a whole bone left ; after which they threw her into a ditch ; but not satisfied with this, they took her child, a girl about six years of age, and after ripping up its belly, threw it to its mother, there to languish till it perished. They forced one to go to mass, after which they ripped open his body, and in that manner left him. They sawed another asunder, cut the throat of his wife, and after having dashed out the brains of their child, an infant, threw it to the swine, who greedily devoured it.

" After committing these and many other horrid cruelties, they took the heads of seven Protestants, and among them that of a pious minister, all which they fixed at the market cross. They put a gag into the minister's mouth, then slit his cheeks to his ears, and laying a leaf of a Bible before it, bid him preach, for his mouth was wide enough. They did several other things by way of derision, and expressed the greatest satisfaction at having thus murdered and exposed the unhappy Protestants. It is impossible to conceive the pleasure these monsters took in exercising their cruelty ; and to increase the misery of those who fell into their hands, while they were butchering them, they would cry, " Your soul to the devil !"..

" In Munster they put to death several ministers in the most shocking manner. One, in particular, they stripped stark naked, and driving him before them, pricked him with swords and pikes till he fell down, and expired."..

These examples we think sufficient to shew the want of truth in the relations of these modern pretenders to the " knowledge of the genuine principles of Christianity," which abhor lying as an emanation from the evil spirit; but to put the question beyond dispute, we shall cite authorities that will clearly prove the accounts to be totally void of foundation. Were credit to be given to the wholesale massacres of the modern editors, we must believe that the Catholics were the minority of the population, instead of being the vast majority of it. We admit the tales are well detailed to excite the prejudices of the ignorant, but the time is nearly gone by, when such unsubstantiated stories could obtain credence, and by giving a few unimpeachable facts of an opposite tendency we hope to accelerate the dispersion of those clouds of falsehood which have too long shaded the page of English history. It has been sensibly observed, by a very acute writer, that there have been no bounds to the exaggerations of our historians as to the number of Protestants said to have been massacred by the Irish in this rebellion. Sir John Temple says, that 150,000 Protestants were massacred in cold blood in the first two months of it. Sir William Petty coolly calculates 30,000 British killed, out of war, in the first year. Lord Clarendon laments, that in the first two or three days of it, 40, or 50,000 of them were destroyed. Rapin and Echard both concur in stating the number of Protestants actually murdered at 45 or 50,000, and the Continuator of Baker's Chronicle reckons them at 200,000. The discrepancy of this testimony is sufficient to shake its credit; for is it to be supposed that men possessing a sincere regard for truth could differ so widely on so important an event? However, we shall proceed with our evidence, and then leave the reader to decide upon the respective merits due to both. The insurrection and massacre is stated to have taken place on the 23rd of October, 1641 ; now lord Clarendon says, in his *History of the Affairs of Ireland*, p. 329, " About the *beginning of November*, 1641, the English and *Scotch* forces in Carrickfergus, murthered, in *one night*, ALL the inhabitants of the island Gee (commonly called Mac Gee), to the number of above 3,000 men, women, and children, ALL INNOCENT PERSONS, in a time when *none of the Catholics* of that country were in arms or rebellion. Note, that *this* was the FIRST massacre committed in Ireland of either side." The same historian records his testimony of the Irish suffering without retaliation in Munster. " In Decy's county, the neighbouring English garrisons of the county of Cork, after burning and pillaging all that county, murthered above 300 persons, men, women, and children, *before any rebellion began in Munster*, and led 100 labourers prisoners to Caperquine, where being tried, by couples were cast into the river and made sport to see them drowned. Observe, that this county is not charged with any murthers to be committed on Protestants."—(*Ibid.* p. 369.)

To this testimony we shall add the following extract from Carte's *Life of the Duke of Ormond* :—" Sir W. Petty computes the British (including therein both English and Scotch) to be, before the rebellion, in proportion to the Irish (in Ireland) as two to eleven; at which rate, there were about *two hundred and twenty thousand* in the *whole* kingdom. Now it is certain that the *great body* of the *English* was settled in *Munster* and *Leinster*, where *very few* murders were committed; and that in *Ulster*, which was the dismal scene of the massacre, there were above one hundred thousand Scots, who, before the general plantation of it, had settled in great numbers in the county of Down and Antrim, and new shoals of them had come over upon the plantation of six escheated counties, and they were so very powerful therein, that the Irish, either out of fear of their numbers, or from some other political reason, spared those of that nation (making proclamation, on pain of death, that no Scotchman should be molested in body, goods, or lands, &c.) It cannot, therefore be presumed, that there were, at most, above twenty-thousand English souls of all ages and sexes in Ulster at this time; and of these, as appears by the lords-justices' letter, March 4th, 1641-2, there were *several thousands got safe to Dublin*, &c. besides six thousand women and children, whom captain Mervyn saved in Fermanagh; and others that got safe to Derry, Colerain, Carrickfergus, &c."

This latter evidence is directly at variance with the statements of the modern editors, and by far more entitled to credit. The accounts then of the hanging of 100 Scottish Protestants at Lissenskeath, the drowning of 1000 of both sexes and all ages at Portendown, the destruction of 4000 in different *nameless* places, the putting all the Protestants to death, without exception, at Kilkenny, and the murder of several ministers in Munster, must now be given to the winds, since sir W. Petty states that but few, *very few* murders were committed in the two provinces of Munster and Leinster, and the Scotch were exempted from death by proclamation!!! Oh! Truth! how are thy beauties disfigured; thy divine attributes abused! Instead of a *general* massacre of all the Protestants, not one hundredth part of the number stated to have been slain in cold-blood met with an untimely fate, and those who did suffer must lay their deaths at the door of Protestant persecutors, who, by their merciless and unhuman conduct towards the unhappy natives of the country, drove them to a state of madness and desperation, after having borne the persecutions of these monsters in cruelty with unexampled forbearance and patience.

So far from the Irish Catholics conspiring the destruction of the Protestants, the plan was laid by the latter to exterminate all the Catholics of that unhappy country. This statement may appear incredible; it is nevertheless as true as it is horrible. Clarendon, Carte, Warner, Leland, and a host of other writers, concur in proving that the predominant Protestant party in England and Ireland meditated, for a long time, the execrable and diabolical project of an utter destruction of the Catholics and colonising the country with Protestant settlers. The following testimony, will shew the infernal spirit which actuated the Protestant party in those days.

Leland writes, " The favourite object of the Irish governors, and the English parliament, was the *utter* EXTERMINATION *of all the Catholic inhabitants of Ireland!* Their estates were already marked out and allotted to their conquerors ; so that they and their posterity were consigned to inevitable ruin."—(iii. 192.)

Warner says, " It is evident from their (the lords justices) last letter to the lieutenant, that they hoped for *an* EXTIRPATION *not of the mere Irish only, but of all the English families that were Roman Catholics.*—(176.)

Clarendon states, " The parliament party, who had heaped so many reproaches and calumnies upon the king, for his clemency to the Irish, who had grounded their own authority and strength upon such foundations as were inconsistent with any toleration of the Roman Catholic religion, and even *with any humanity to the Irish nation,* and more especially to those of the old native extraction, *the whole race whereof they had upon the matter sworn to* EXTIRPATE, &c. &c."—(i. 115.)

Carte says,—" If it be more needful to dispose of places out of hand, and that it may stand with his majesty's pleasure to fill some of them with Irish that are Protestants, and *that have not been for the* EXTIRPATION *of the Papist natives,* it will much satisfy both, and cannot justly be excepted against."—(iii. 226.)

" Mr. Brent landed lately here, and hath brought with him such letters as have somewhat changed the face of this government from what it was, when the parliament pamphlets were received as oracles, their commands obeyed as laws, and EXTIRPATION *preached for Gospel.*"— (*Idem.* 170).

" Though *extirpation both of nation and religion* be not named, yet I conceive *it is contrived almost in every proposition;* and the consideration thereof confirms me in a full belief of the malicious practices of the Cootes and Ormsbyes, in the county of Roscommon."—(*Idem.* 311.)

" *The term of* EXTIRPATION *is worn out here,* and the intention not acknowledged to me by the prime authors therein, with whom I have been plain after my blunt way."—(*Idem.* 155.).

" The reason of their (the justices) advice is founded upon *their darling scheme of an* EXTIRPATION *of the old English proprietors, and a general plantation of the whole kingdom with a new colony;* for this is the meaning of what they allege, to shew it to be ' unsafe for his majesty, and destructive to the kingdom, to grant the petitioners' request; as being altogether inconsistent with *the means of raising a considerable revenue for his crown, of settling religion and civility in the kingdom;* and of establishing a firm and lasting peace, to the honour of his majesty, the safety of his royal posterity, and the comfort of all his faithful subject." —(*Idem.* i. 391.)

" These difficulties and considerations were of little weight with the lords justices ; who, having got a thin house of commons to their mind, of persons devoted to their interests and measures, resolved to improve the opportunity offered, and to get such acts passed, as might distress the king, *exasperate the bulk of the nation, spread the rebellion, and so promote their darling scheme of* EXTINGUISHING *the old proprietors, and making a new plantation of the kingdom.*"—(*Idem.* 330.)

" Such considerations as these were not agreeable to the views of the lords-justices, *who had set their hearts on the* EXTIRPATION, *not only of the mere Irish, but likewise of all the old English families that were Roman Catholics,* and the making of a new plantation all over the kingdom, in which they could not fail to have a principal share ; so all their reasonings, upon all occasions, were calculated and intended to promote that their favourite schemes."—(*Idem*, 493.)

" These measures *served their own scheme of an* EXTIRPATION, by racking those gentlemen, whose treatment could not fail of deterring every body from venturing themselves into their power for the future."—(*Idem*, 301.)

" These propositions certainly came from some of *that party of men which first formed the design of an* EXTIRPATION *of the Roman Catholics, and, by publishing that design, made the rebellion so general as it proved at last.* They all breathed the same spirit ; and *though* EX-TIRPATION *both of nation and religion was not expressly mentioned,* yet it seemed to be contrived effectually in all the propositions. They appeared so monstrous and unreasonable, that it was thought they could proceed from nothing but an high degree of madness or malice."—(*Idem*, 502.)

" There is too much reason to think, that, as the lords justices really wished the rebellion to spread, and more gentlemen of estates to be involved in it, that THE FORFEITURES MIGHT BE THE GREATER, *and a general plantation be carried on by a new set of English Protestants, all over the kingdom,* TO THE RUIN AND EXPULSION OF ALL THE OLD ENGLISH AND NATIVES THAT WERE ROMAN CATHOLICS ; so, to promote what they wished, they gave out speeches upon occasions, insinuating such a design, and that *in a short time there would not be a Roman Catholic left in the kingdom.* It is no small confirmation of this notion, that the earl of Ormonde, in his letters of January 27th, and February 25th, 1641-2, to sir W. St. Leger, imputes the general revolt of the nation, then far advanced, to the publishing of such a design ; and when a person of his great modesty and temper, the most averse in his nature to speak his sentiments of what he could not but condemn in others, and who, when obliged to do so, does it always in the gentlest expressions, is drawn to express such an opinion, the case must be very notorious. I do not find that the copies of these letters are preserved : but the original of sir W. St. Leger's, in answer to them, sufficiently shows it to be his lordship's opinion ; for, after acknowledging the receipt of these two letters, he useth these words, *The undue promulgation of that severe determination, to* EXTIRPATE *the Irish and Papacy out of this kingdom, your lordship rightly apprehends to be too unseasonably published.*"—(*Idem.* i. 263.)

We have here produced evidence sufficient to convince every candid mind that the spirit of Protestantism has been the origin of those evils that have afflicted Ireland for these last three hundred years, and made the people of that country the most miserable of human beings. To a system of misrule and proscription, and not to the pretended arts and intrigues of the Catholic priesthood, are the Irish indebted for the sufferings they have endured, and now endure. The sword and cannon, the knife and gibbett, plunder and destruction, were the means used to introduce the Protestant religion into Ireland. Penal Laws and Proscription have been continued by every ruling faction to maintain its existence in that country ; but neither force nor fraud has succeeded in subduing the invincible constancy of the Irish People to the faith planted by St. Patrick in their green isle. Let us hope, then, that after so long a trial of un-

shaken constancy, their reward is near at hand, and that they are soon
to receive, what they have always been ready to grant to others, equal
civil rights and perfect freedom of conscience.

REBELLIONS AND CONSPIRACIES OF THE PAPISTS, FROM
THE REVOLUTION TO THE REIGN OF GEORGE II.

Hard is the case of the poor Papists, who, it seems, are doomed, by
these modern editors, not only to father their own sins, but such as may
be imputed to them by any bigot, and those, too, that are actually committed by Protestants. These sagacious writers say, " It is now our
task to relate another of those horrible plots which will for ever disgrace the name of POPERY, and render it obnoxious to every one who is
not blinded by the *specious* statements of its supporters—we mean the
ASSASSINATION PLOT, formed for the destruction of that truly great and
good monarch, William III." Now is it not a little singular that the
greatest part of Christians are so blind that they prefer this obnoxious
name to the more modern one of Protestantism? But are Papists the
only plotters? Did not Protestants conspire against their king, James
II? and is it lawful on the part of Protestants to dethrone their sovereign,
and unlawful on the part of Catholics only? William assisted to drive
his father-in-law from his throne, and James could not be blamed for
seeking to regain it. But the scheme was to ASSASSINATE William, and,
if we are to believe the modern editors, " it was first projected by the
French king, and furthered by the Popish emissaries in England." And
they further tell us, that the principal persons in England concerned in
the plot for assassinating the king were the following:—the earl of
Aylesbury; lord Montgomery, son to the marquis of Powis; sir John
Fenwick; sir William Parkins; sir John Friend; captain Charnock;
captain Porter; and Mr. Goodman." As we are desirous of bringing this volume to a close, we must be brief in our notice. Well,
then, the majority of these individuals were, we believe, Protestants.
Of the plot we have our suspicions that it was not a real one. Of the
conspirators tried and executed, three of them, namely, Charnock, King,
and Keyes, acknowledged their guilt, but endeavoured to palliate it.
We quote from the Continuator of Baker. Friend denied his knowledge
of the assassination, but Parkins admitted something of a design against
William, though he was not to act in it. He was *absolved*, at the place of
execution, by three nonjuring clergymen, be it remembered, and they
were Protestant ministers. Rockwood, Lowick, and Cranburn, were
also tried, condemned, and executed. The latter professed himself a
Protestant, the other two were Catholics. Sir John Fenwick was
tried and acquitted, there being only one witness produced; a bill of
attainder, however, was passed against him, and he was beheaded. He
was a Protestant, and denied any guilt,

The modern editors, in concluding their account of this plot, say,
" Thus was this horrid conspiracy happily frustrated, and the authors of
it brought to that condign punishment which their infamy merited.
The king's life was the security of his subjects, who heartily rejoiced, as
they had reason to do, in being THEREBY PRESERVED FROM THE MISERIES
OF POPERY AND ARBITRARY GOVERNMENT." We shall say nothing in de-

fence of the conspirators; but content ourselves with protesting against the insinuation that the Catholics, as a body, had any thing to do with it. That William's subjects had occasion to rejoice we have our doubts, and as to their posterity, let the present miseries endured by the people of England bear testimony whether the miseries of Popery could be more afflicting than what are now borne by the nation? When James, a Catholic, filled the throne, there was not a shilling of debt contracted; but he was a Papist, as Catholics were opprobriously termed, and therefore *must* be a tyrant. Well the leaders got rid of him, and introduced William, a Dutchman. He soon began to engage in wars, which could not be supported without money; and money could not be safely raised without *borrowing*. The money was accordingly borrowed; a bank was established to manage the money system, and thus was laid the foundation of all the misery, degradation, and poverty, so heavily felt by all classes at this moment, excepting those who live by the system. At the death of William, the nation was in debt about 14,000,000*l.* sterling; at this time it is increased to an enormous sum—upwards EIGHT HUNDRED MILLIONS, while the imposts on the people, in taxes, church and poor rates, &c. amount to sixty millions annually. Blessed effects of excluding the miseries of Popery and arbitrary government. Of the laws that have been passed since the reign of William it is impossible to give even an outline; suffice it to say, they have been so multiplied, that lawyers are not able to become conversant with the whole code. More have been passed within the last reign to restrict the liberty of the subject, than were ever passed by all the Catholic kings of England, previous to the Reformation, for all purposes; and men are now liable to be sent to confinement for displeasing a watchman of the night. Oh! sweet Liberty! how preferable to the miseries of Popery and arbitrary government!!! William commenced the debt to preserve the imaginary balance of Europe and Protestant ascendency; at the end of one hundred and thirty years, England is so crippled by the accumulation of that debt, that she is now unable to man a ship, or raise a regiment, to resent any insult that may be offered; her manunfacturers are starving, because they cannot compete with foreign nations in the articles of trade; and many of those who live on the taxes have fled to France, there to spend the sweat and labour of the people of England, because there they have no taxes to pay, and provisions are less than one-half the price than in this blessed Protestant country. Oh! the charming effects of being " preserved from the miseries of Popery and arbitrary government."

The next plot mentioned is called ATTERBURY's, who was a bishop of the Church of England, namely of the see of Rochester; we may therefore hope the sensible reader will exonerate the Catholics generally from being implicated in it.

PERSECUTIONS IN THE SOUTH OF FRANCE IN 1814 AND 1820.

Our limits are narrowed, and we must be brief. The modern editors have bestowed eighteen pages on these pretended persecutions, and they have served up some of the most detestable tales ever invented to gull the veracious appetites of the prejudiced.—The whole is a mass of improbabilities, contradictions, and falsehoods.—Some of the punishments said to have been inflicted on the female part of the Protestants are grossly indelicate and wholly unworthy of credit. However there are two or three facts stated that are deserving a slight notice.—The Catholics are said to have been furnished with 1000 muskets and 10,000 cartouches by the ENGLISH (Protestants) off Marseilles. The French Catholic soldiers are represented as devils incarnate in cruelty, while the Austrian troops (CATHOLICS too) overflowed with the milk of human kindness.—The king of France issued a decree in favour of the poor Protestants which was not attended to, and the persecution was put down by *the interference of the British Government!!!* They begin their relation with the arrival of Louis XVIII. at Paris in 1814, which they say was known at Nismes on the 13th of April, 1814, and was received by the Protestants with every demonstration of joy, but they were met by the Catholics with bigotry and intolerance, who succeeded in procuring an address to the king, in which they stated "that there ought to be in France but one God, one King, and one Faith." We do not know how many Gods or Kings the Protestants would have, but we think *one* is sufficient to worship and one to rule a nation—as to the number of faiths, there can be only *one* that is TRUE, and therefore the fewer the better, but let no *force* be made to reduce them. That the Catholics were not intolerant at that period we have the testimony of a Rev. Isaac Cobbin, who published a pamphlet against the Catholics and the pretended Persecution, in the month of November, 1815, but he was compelled to acknowledge, that "the CATHOLICS THEMSELVES FIRST OPENED THEIR ARMS TO THIS PROSCRIBED PEOPLE, (the French Protestants) and exclaimed ' *Let us embrace—we are now to participate in the same rights—your calamities, and the abuses of the country, are terminated together—Vive la Liberte.*" Now this does not look like the spirit of persecution, and is directly opposed to the relation of the modern editors. By the charter of the French, granted on the restoration of Louis XVIII. in 1814, all Frenchmen were made eligible to civil office—the free exercise of religious worship was granted—Protestant Ministers were paid by the Catholic Government, and allowed about twenty pounds a year more than the Catholic rectors, and where there were 500 Protestants a church was built and kept in repair for them at the expense of the Government, nor were the Protestants there, as Catholics are here, called upon to pay tithes to the Clergy of the established Church. Here then is nothing of the spirit of Persecution. Let us now see what the modern editors say on the subject of the interference of the British Government.

"To the credit of England, the reports of these cruel persecutions carried on against our Protestant brethren in France, produced such a sensation on the part of Government as determined them *to interfere;* and now the persecutors of the Protestants made this spontaneous act of humanity and religion the pretext for charging the sufferers with a treasonable correspondence with England ; but in this state of their proceedings, to their great dismay a letter appeared, sent some time before to England by the duke of Wellington, stating ' that much information existed on the event of the south.'

" The ministers of the three denominations in London, anxious not to be misled, requested one of their brethren to visit the scenes of persecution, and examine with impartiality the nature and extent of the evils they were desirous to relieve. The Rev. Clement Perrot undertook this difficult task, and fulfilled their wishes with a zeal, prudence, and devotedness, above all praise. His return furnished abundant and incontestible proof of a shameful persecution, materials for an appeal to the British parliament, and a printed report which was circulated through the continent, and which first conveyed correct information to the inhabitants of France.

" *Foreign interference was now found eminently useful;* and the declarations of tolerance which it elicited from the French government, as well as the more cautious march of the Catholic persecutors, operated as decisive and involuntary acknowledgments of the importance of that interference which some persons at first censured and despised; but though the stern voice of public opinion in England and elsewhere produced a reluctant suspension of massacre and pillage, the murderers and plunderers were still left unpunished, and even caressed and rewarded for their crimes ; and whilst Protestants in France suffered the most cruel and degrading pains and penalties for alleged trifling crimes, *Catholics,* covered with blood, and guilty of numerous and horrid murders, were acquitted."

' So, then, FOREIGN INTERFERENCE is very useful and beneficial in the case of *Protestants ;* but why then not let the Catholics make the *same* application in their case to the House of Bourbon ? What is sauce for the goose must be sauce for the gander, most sagacious editors. However, the fact is, the British government did *not* interfere, and though this busy Perrot, and the secretaries to a London society for protecting religious liberty, made application to the duke of Wellington at Paris, the noble duke contradicted the charge made against the French government, and denied that there was any persecution of the French Protestants. His grace was corroborated by the French Protestant minister, M. Maron, who published a letter which gave the lie to all the reports spread against the Catholics as persecutors. These documents with others may be seen in our *Orthodox Journal* for December, 1815, and January, 1816.—We have there shewn that the affair at Nismes, which, by the by, took place in 1815, and not 1814, was a political squabble between the Bonapartists and the Bourbonists ; the first being Protestants, and the latter Catholics. The former were assailants when Bonaparte was in power, and a few of the Catholics of the lowest class retaliated when the Bourbons were reseated on the throne. We were favoured with an authenticated document, by the late Rev. Peter Gandolphy, taken and attested at Lyons, in December 1815, and we think we cannot do better than lay it before the reader, in order that he may see what a trivial POLITICAL affair has been magnified into a terible RELIGIOUS persecution, by these unprincipled and shameless modern editors :—

" Religion was no otherwise concerned in the disputes of the inhabitants of Nismes, than inasmuch as it served to distinguish the political principles of the Protestants and Catholics ; the former having almost universally professed themselves Bonapartists, whilst the latter generally embraced the cause of the Bourbons. In such cases animosity usually runs high, and reaction or revenge is almost always the consequence of the return of the proscribed party to power. On the restoration of the Bourbons in 1814, the Protestants at Nismes openly expressed their dissatisfaction at the event, and designated it to the Catholics, as the signal for a second St. Bartholomew's day. At the return, therefore, of Bonaparte from Elba, they all took a most active and decided part in his cause; and in the fury of their politics violently assailed the Catholics, plundering their houses, destroying their property, and ill-treating their persons. With many others, one Tartalion of Nismes became a great sufferer, whilst serving in the army of the Duke of Angouleme.— On the disbanding of that small royal army, this individual at his return to Nismes found his property plundered, his house destroyed, his wife and children forced to conceal themselves in the woods, deriving a substance from the commonest herbs and berries, and was himself compelled to subsist in the same manner. When the Bourbons returned, however, in the summer of 1815, and the Bonapartists became again proscribed, this man, half naked, and with an unshorn beard that gave him all the appearance of a savage, issued from his retreat, and, armed with a ca-rabine, entered the city of Nismes ; and, in open day, posting himself in one of the streets, deliberately and repeatedly discharged his piece at those whom he con-ceived had been active in the destruction of his property. As others took up arms, blood was soon shed on both sides ; the Catholics, however, prevailed, being the most numerous ; and they concluded the affair by forcibly shutting up the conven-ticles of the Protestants. In the mean time General Lagard received orders from the duke of Angouleme to exert himself in protecting the Protestants ; and whilst endeavouring to disperse a body of the royalists assembled before the doors of one of the Protestant churches, he was wounded by a pistol shot fired by one of the Ca-tholic party, whom he had struck with his sabre. The duke on this, observing the determined opposition made to the king's mandates, himself marched with cannon and the national guard of Montpelier, and re-opened those Protestant conventicles which had been shut up. Tartallon was also seised and committed to prison. The total number of the sufferers on the side of the Bonapartists was thirty-three ; in which only one was of respectable condition in life. He was a merchant, had failed, and without satisfying his creditors, had afterwards realised a considerable fortune. He was shot in his cabriolet, and is supposed to have lost his life more on account of this private affair, than any other of a more public nature. Another Bourbonist of the name of Pointu took the same revenge at Avignon, as Tartallon at Nismes, and is now in prison, waiting the sentence of the law ; but at the latter place only three or four lives were lost. It is acknowledged by the very Protest-ants that none but the lowest of the populace were concerned in these affairs of Nismes and Avignon, and that the Catholic clergy, as well as the civil authorities, exerted themselves in protecting the Protestants, and bringing the royalist offend-ers to punishment. Such, however, has been the rebellious spirit of the Protestants in that part of France, and so determined their opposition to the Bourbons, that the government has been under the necessity of disarming them, and arms to the number of 26,000 have been collected ; whilst it is supposed that as many more re-main undiscovered. Their designs were evidently hostile to the reigning family, which they reproach with bigotry and superstition, because more friendly to the established religion than the family of Bonaparte. The Jacobins of France, as well as some Protestants of England have equally endeavoured to extract some-thing useful to themselves from the disturbances as Nismes. But in France the plot has completely failed, and the affair is scarcely ever mentioned. All is now quiet at Nismes, as well as in every other part of France."

Concluding their account, such as it is, of the pretended persecution of the French Protestants, and with it the work itself, they say, "With respect to the conduct of the Protestants, these highly outraged citizens, pushed to extremities by their persecutors, felt at length that they had only to choose the manner in which they were to perish. THEY UNANIMOUSLY DETERMINED THAT THEY WOULD DIE FIGHTING FOR THEIR OWN DEFENCE. This firm attitude apprized their butchers that they could no longer murder with impuni-ty. *Every thing was immediately changed.*" Oh! Oh! Oh! here was a change!!! So then these blessed Christian people did not like to die like the primitive martyrs, who endured persecution for conscience sake, according to the precepts of their Divine Master, who suffered without resistance to set them an example : but they must die like TRAITORS, if their persecutors acted under the authority of the Government, which the modern editors have been labouring to shew. What would be said by Protestants if such an avowal was made by Catholics ? But enough has been said, and this one fact is sufficient to prove that the SPIRIT OF PROTESTANTISM is NOT the SPIRIT of the GOSPEL.

END OF THE SECOND VOLUME.

Printed by W. E. Andrews, 3, Chapterhouse court, St. Paul's, London.